HITLER *A Life*

HITLER
A Life

PETER LONGERICH

Translated by Jeremy Noakes and Lesley Sharpe

OXFORD
UNIVERSITY PRESS

OXFORD

UNIVERSITY PRESS

Great Clarendon Street, Oxford, OX2 6DP,
United Kingdom

Oxford University Press is a department of the University of Oxford.
It furthers the University's objective of excellence in research, scholarship,
and education by publishing worldwide. Oxford is a registered trade mark of
Oxford University Press in the UK and in certain other countries

© Peter Longerich 2019

The moral rights of the author have been asserted

First published as Hitler: Biographie
by Siedler Verlag © Peter Longerich, 2015

Impression: 1

Published in the United States of America by Oxford University Press
198 Madison Avenue, New York, NY 10016, United States of America

British Library Cataloguing in Publication Data

Data available

Library of Congress Control Number: 2018962563

ISBN 978–0–19–879609–1

Printed and bound in Great Britain by
Clays Ltd, Elcograf S.p.A.

Links to third party websites are provided by Oxford in good faith and
for information only. Oxford disclaims any responsibility for the materials
contained in any third party website referenced in this work.

Acknowledgements

I should like to express my thanks to everyone who helped me write and publish this biography. It could not have been written without the support of the staff of the various archives and libraries I consulted. I am very grateful to them all, and in particular, once again, to the staff at the Institute for Contemporary History in Munich for their tireless efforts.

In the early stages of this book I had the opportunity to discuss its subject's personality with a group of psychoanalysts in Hamburg and a circle of psychotherapists and psychoanalysts in Munich. I am grateful for the help I received from Sabine Brückner-Jungjohann, Christiane Adam, Gundula Fromm, Ulrich Knocke, Rüdiger Kurz, Astrid Rutezki, Dirk Sieveking and Gudrun Brockhaus, Falk Stakelbeck, Heidi Spanl, and Corinna Werntz.

My sincere thanks go to Thomas Rathnow and Jens Dehning of Siedler Press and to all their colleagues at Siedler, and also to Daniel Bussenius and Jonas Wegerer for their work in editing the text.

Munich, October 2015

Contents

IV. CONSOLIDATION

V. SMOKESCREEN

VI. TRIUMPH

VII. DOWNFALL

Abbreviations

(A)	Abendausgabe (evening edition)
AA	Auswärtiges Amt (Foreign Office)
ADAP	*Akten zur deutschen auswärtigen Politik*
AHA	Allgemeines Heeresamt
(B)	Berlin edition
BAB	Bundesarchiv, Abt. Berlin
BAF	Bundesarchiv, Abt. Freiburg
BAK	Bundesarchiv, Abt. Koblenz
BDC	Berlin Document Center
BDM	Bund Deutscher Mädel
BHStA	Bayrisches Hauptstaatsarchiv
BK	*Bayerischer Kurier*
BMP	Bayerische Mittelpartei
BT	*Berliner Tageblatt*
BVG	Berliner Verkehrsbetriebe
BVP	Bayerische Volkspartei
ČSR	Tschechoslowakische Republik (Československ. republika)
DAF	Deutsche Arbeitsfront
DAP	Deutsche Arbeiterpartei
DAZ	*Deutsche Allgemeine Zeitung*
DBFP	*Documents on British Foreign Policy*
DDP	Deutsche Demokratische Partei
DNB	Deutsches Nachrichtenbüro
DNVP	Deutschnationale Volkspartei
Domarus	Hitler, Adolf, *Reden und Proklamationen 1932–1945*, ed. Max Domarus
DSP	Deutschsozialistische Partei
DStP	Deutsche Staatspartei
DVFP	Deutschvölkische Freiheitspartei
FRUS	*Foreign Relations of the United States*

FZ	*Frankfurter Zeitung*
Gestapo	Geheime Staatspolizei (Secret State Police)
Goebbels TB	*The Diaries of Joseph Goebbels*
GPU	Vereinigte staatliche politische Verwaltung (Gossudarstwennoje Polititscheskoje Uprawlenije)
Gruppenkdo.	Gruppenkommando
GVG	Grossdeutsche Volksgemeinschaft
GWU	*Geschichte in Wissenschaft und Unterricht*
HJ	Hitlerjugend (Hitler Youth)
HL	Heeresleitung
HSSPF	Höherer SS- und Polizeiführer
IfZ	Institut für Zeitgeschichte, Munich
IMT	*International Military Tribunal*
Inf.Rgt.	Infanterieregiment
JK	*Hitler. Sämtliche Aufzeichnungen 1905–1924*, ed. Eberhard Jäckel and Axel Kuhn
KAM	Kriegsarchiv München
KdF	Kraft durch Freude
Kp.	Kompanie
KPD	Kommunistische Partei Deutschlands
KPdSU	Kommunistische Partei der Sowjetunion
KTB	Kriegstagebuch (war diary)
KTB OKW	*Kriegstagebuch des Oberkommandos der Wehrmacht (Wehrmachtführungsstab)*
KTB Seekriegsleitung	*Das Kriegstagebuch der Seekriegsleitung*
k.u.k.	kaiserlich und königlich
KZ	Konzentrationslager
LA Berlin	Landesarchiv Berlin
LHA	Landeshauptarchiv Linz
LT	*Linzer Tagespost*
(M)	Midday edition; in the case of *VB*, Munich edition
MB	*Münchener Beobachter*
MGM	*Militärgeschichtliche Mitteilungen*
MK	Hitler, Adolf, *Mein Kampf*
MNN	*Münchner Neueste Nachrichten*
Ms.	Manuskript
MSPD	Mehrheitssozialdemokratische Partei Deutschlands
(N)	Norddeutsche Ausgabe (North-German edition)

NARA	US National Archives and Records Administration, Washington
NL	Nachlass (private papers)
NS	nationalsozialistisch/Nationalsozialismus
NSBO	Nationalsozialistische Betriebszellenorganisation
NSDAP	Nationalsozialistische Deutsche Arbeiterpartei
NSDStB	Nationalsozialistischer Deutscher Studentenbund
NSFB	Nationalsozialistische Freiheitsbewegung
NSKK	Nationalsozialistisches Kraftfahrkorps
NSV	Nationalsozialistische Volkswohlfahrt
NZZ	*Neue Zürcher Zeitung*
OA	Oberabschnitt
OA Moskau	Osobyi Archive, Moskow
OB	Oberbefehlshaber (commander-in-chief)
OBdH	Oberbefehlshaber des Heeres (c-in-c of the army)
OKM	Oberkommando der Marine (navy high command)
OKW	Oberkommando der Wehrmacht (armed forces high command)
ÖStA	Österreichisches Staatsarchiv
PA	NS-Presseanweisungen der Vorkriegszeit
PAA	Politisches Archiv des Auswärtigen Amtes, Berlin
PolDir.	Polizeidirektion
PrGS	Preussische Gesetzsammlung
(R)	Reichsausgabe
RAD	Reichsarbeitsdienst
RDI	Reichsverband der Deutschen Industrie
RFM	Reichsfinanzministerium
RFSS	Reichsführer-SS
RGBl.	Reichsgesetzblatt
RIB	Reserve-Infanterie-Brigade
RIR	Reserve-Infanterie-Regiment
RM	Reichsmark
RMBliV	Reichsministerialblatt für die innere Verwaltung
RMI	Reichsministerium des Innern
RPL	Reichspropagandaleitung
RSA	Hitler, Adolf, Reden, Schriften, Anordnungen
RSHA	Reichssicherheitshauptamt
RVE	Reichsvereinigung Eisen

SA	Sturmabteilung
SAM	Staatsarchiv München
SD	Sicherheitsdienst
Sopade	Sozialdemokratische Partei Deutschlands im Exil
Sopade	*Deutschland-Berichte der Sozialdemokratischen Partei Deutschlands Sopade 1934–1940*
SPD	Sozialdemokratische Partei Deutschlands
SprkAkte	Spruchkammerakte
SS	Schutzstaffel
StA Riga	Staatsarchiv, Riga
StAnw.	Staatsanwaltschaft
StJb	*Statistisches Jahrbuch für das Deutsche Reich*
TB	Tagebuch (diary)
TP	Tagesparole
TWC	*Trials of War Criminals before the Nuernberg Military Tribunals*
UF	*Ursachen und Folgen. Vom deutschen Zusammenbruch 1918 und 1945 bis zur staatlichen Neuordnung Deutschlands in der Gegenwart*, ed. Herbert Michaelis and Ernst Schraepler
USPD	Unabhängige Sozialdemokratische Partei Deutschlands
UWW	*Unser Wille und Weg*
VB	*Völkischer Beobachter*
VEJ	*Die Verfolgung und Ermordung der europäischen Juden durch das nationalsozialistische Deutschland 1933–1945*
VfZ	*Vierteljahrshefte für Zeitgeschichte*
VK	*Völkischer Kurier*
VZ	*Vossische Zeitung*
YV	Yad Vashem
ZStL	Zentrale Stelle Lugwigsburg
1. M.	Erstes Morgenblatt (first morning edition)
2. M.	Zweites Morgenblatt (second morning edition)

Introduction

Arguably no individual in modern history has managed to accumulate such immense power in such a relatively short space of time as Adolf Hitler; no-one else has abused power so extravagantly and finally clung on to it so tenaciously, to the point where his regime collapsed totally, with the loss of millions of lives. Hitler is thus an extreme example of how personal power can be acquired and monstrously abused – a phenomenon that bursts the confines of a conventional historical biography. In Hitler's case even the interpretative model frequently employed by historians of exploring the interaction of structural factors and individual personality is inadequate. For we are dealing with a figure who did not exercise power within the framework of established constitutional politics or the generally accepted rules of a political system, but instead dismantled this framework and created new structures of power to suit himself. These structures were indissolubly linked to him personally, and indeed in general his dictatorship represented an extraordinary example of personalized power. The regime's 'structures' are inconceivable without Hitler and Hitler is nothing without his offices.

Yet at the same time this dictatorship cannot be reduced to Hitler as an individual or explained in anything like adequate terms by his biography. We must instead adopt a much broader view that takes in the history of the period as a whole: for example, the phenomenon of National Socialism, its causes and roots in German history, and the relationship between Hitler and 'the Germans', to name but a few factors. While any interpretation that dwells too much on Hitler himself risks falling into 'Hitlerism' and begins to read like an apologia, any comprehensive examination of the historical circumstances and conditions runs the opposite danger of losing sight of Hitler as an agent and presenting him as a mere puppet of external forces, a blank screen on which contemporary movements are projected. That would result in Hitler, of all people, being marginalized as a figure of historical importance and his personal responsibility within this historical process being obscured.

The main challenge of a Hitler biography is thus to explain how such an extreme concentration of power in the hands of a single individual could arise from the interplay of external circumstances and the actions of that individual. On the one hand, it must present the forces that acted upon Hitler and, on the other, those that were set in motion by him.

Contrary to a widely-held view, our present-day knowledge of National Socialism is by no means complete or even close to being complete. Historical research into National Socialism has developed many specialized branches and is constantly bringing new knowledge to light on a very wide range of aspects of the movement and the regime. One thing becomes clear from looking at a cross-section of these studies, namely that Hitler was actively involved in the most disparate areas of politics to a much greater extent than has hitherto been generally assumed. He himself created the conditions in which this could happen, by bringing about the step-by-step fragmentation of the traditional state apparatus of power into its component parts, ensuring that no new and transparent power structures developed, and instead giving far-reaching tasks to individuals who were personally answerable to him. This consistently personalized leadership style gave him the opportunity to intervene largely at will in the most diverse areas, and, as the scholarship of the last two decades in particular has demonstrated, he made liberal use of these opportunities. However, as the structures of power in Hitler's regime were diffuse, there is no consolidated and comprehensive collection of sources relating to Hitler's exercise of that power; it is the mosaic produced by the numerous studies of specific areas that reveals Hitler's decision-making as wide-ranging and frequently informal. It is becoming increasingly evident that in a whole series of key political areas he really did hold the reins and involve himself (though with varying degrees of intensity at different times and in different spheres) in matters of detail, on top of dealing with the business of day-to-day politics. This will become clear not only in the realm of foreign policy, but also in particular with regard to the persecution of the Jews and the Nazi state's eugenic policies, constitutional issues, rearmament (along with efforts to balance its economic impact), Church and cultural policy, propaganda, and a complex set of issues connected with managing the Party. During the war new areas were added: the military command of the Wehrmacht and its supplies and equipment, as well as matters of importance to the home front such as food supplies and female labour.

In the course of time Hitler created for himself immense scope for his own activity and indeed in some areas of politics he was virtually autonomous. He was capable of deciding on war or peace, he established the foundations of the European continent's 'new order' as he saw fit, and he made arbitrary decisions about genocide and other programmes of mass murder on the basis of 'racial' factors. Yet although this freedom of action Hitler enjoyed was probably unique in modern European history, it nevertheless arose from historical preconditions and was certainly not limitless.

The most important of these preconditions was the emergence of an extreme right-wing mass movement as a reaction to defeat in war, revolution, and the Versailles Treaty, and to the world economic crisis and the failure of democracy to tackle this crisis. Additional potent factors present in German society and in particular among the elites – nationalism, authoritarianism, racism, militarism, revisionist attitudes in foreign policy, and imperialism – could be exploited by this mass movement, once it had come to power. And not least among the historical factors that smoothed the way for Hitler was the fact that countervailing forces, in the first instance inside Germany itself and then later within the European context, were incapable of putting up adequate resistance, did not exist at all, or failed. Thus Hitler really was in a position, first in Germany in 1933/34 and then in Europe during 1938–41, to create tabula rasa and to realize many of his plans in the power vacuum that had come about through the destruction of established orders.

Hitler acted not simply as a 'catalyser' or 'medium' for historical processes that existed independently of him.[1] Rather, he shaped these in a very distinct and highly individual manner by channelling, reinforcing, and concentrating existing forces and energies, while mobilizing dormant but potential ones, and by exploiting ruthlessly the weakness or passivity of his opponents and deliberately destroying them. Although in the process he took account of tactical considerations, his political priorities were unambiguous: from the beginning of his career the notion of an empire ['Reich'] ordered on racial lines was central. For two and a half decades he never wavered from this. With regard to the external borders and the structure of this empire, however, and to the time-scale and means to achieve this aim he proved extraordinarily flexible. Hitler's political strategy can no more be explained by positing a 'programme' or a 'phased plan' (which was a central element in the interpretation advanced by the 'intentionalist' school of historians[2]) than it can by the notion of some kind of unbridled opportunism.[3] The challenge is rather to account for this special blend in Hitler of obsession with a utopian goal combined at times with unscrupulous pragmatism; the latter propensity could amount almost to a reversal of ends and means. The figure who emerges is not so much a political strategist or ideologue as above all a ruthless, hands-on politician. I argue in this biography that critical turning points in Hitler's policies cannot be seen as the result of external constraints and structural determinants but were the product of decisions he forced through in the face of resistance and significant retarding factors.

Yet Hitler could not always have his way. This is true, first of all, of his core domestic policy, namely the attempt to produce a population that was completely bound by solidarity and geared to war. It is also true of his efforts to make his 'racial policies' popular with the population at large and of his radical anti-Church policies. Again, during the war he was unsuccessful in reconciling the conflicting aims of his occupation policy and his alliance policy in a single strategy that could fully mobilize the resources of the territory he controlled to support the war he was waging.

What then were the foundations of this dictator's extraordinarily extensive powers? The idea that Hitler's regime was primarily based on charisma and thus derived above all from the enthusiastic assent to his policies on the part of a large majority of the German nation, who credited him with superhuman abilities, is most definitely inadequate. For any attempt to interpret him as expressing the longings and hopes of 'the Germans' comes up against the fact that, before National Socialism came on the scene, German society was split into various camps and even the Nazi state was able only to a very limited extent to build bridges between them. The Nazi 'national community', united in solidarity behind Hitler, turns out more than anything to be an invention of contemporary propaganda. Hitler's 'charisma' is not primarily the result of the masses believing him to possess extraordinary abilities (let alone of his actually having any), but rather, in an age of mass media, bureaucracy, and social control, is more than anything the product of a sophisticated use of technical means to exert power.

This approach has two consequences for the analysis I am offering: First, by contrast with the 'structural' analysis put forward by Ian Kershaw in his Hitler biography, this study does not explain Hitler as a phenomenon primarily on the basis of social forces and the complex of factors that determined the Nazi system of power.[4] My contention is that we have to abandon once and for all the image of a man who, overshadowed by his own charisma, allegedly became increasingly estranged from reality, let things take their course, and to a great extent withdrew from actual politics. This is the view of Hitler as an, in many respects, 'weak dictator', as Hans Mommsen pithily summed up this thesis.[5] Instead I emphasize Hitler's autonomous role as an active politician. Secondly, I examine critically the claim often made that 'the Germans' largely welcomed Hitler's policies and identified with their dictator as a person. The result is a more nuanced picture: Throughout his dictatorship there was both active support from broad sections of the population and a significant undercurrent of discontent and reserve. The fact that Hitler's regime nevertheless functioned more or less without a hitch was above all the result (and this factor is frequently underplayed) of the various means of coercion available to a dictatorship. In addition to institutionalized repression there was the Party's local surveillance of 'national comrades', as well as Nazi control of the 'public sphere'.

Over and above the specifics of their lives, biographies of politicians who direct and control complex systems of power provide insight into the distinguishing features of power structures and decision-making processes, in particular when, as in this case, these structures and processes were created in large measure by the protagonist himself. In addition, as a result of his presence in a variety of political spheres Hitler was repeatedly able to reconfigure complex and problematic situations to suit his purposes by 'dropping a bombshell'. What is more, the history of the Nazi dictatorship as told from the perspective of the man who stood at the pinnacle of this structure provides insights into the connections between the individual political spheres in the so-called Third Reich and creates an opportunity to combine the specialized discourses developed by historians in their particular fields in an overview linked by a single, overarching chronology. Thus a biography of Hitler also produces a history of his regime.

Joachim Fest's dictum that Hitler was basically a 'non-person'[6] is typical of the prevalent disinclination of historians to encounter Hitler on a 'human' level. By contrast, this biography assumes that, in common with everyone, Hitler had a personality, that this personality demonstrates certain constants, developments, and discontinuities that can be described and analysed, and that this analysis of his personality can be productive in explaining his political career. This personal element not only played a significant role in some important political decisions, but it contributed fundamentally to his political outlook as a whole. Thus the behaviour and attitudes of a dictator in possession of absolute power were necessarily and fatefully influenced by his deeply rooted tendency to develop megalomaniacal plans and projects, by his inability to accept humiliations and defeats, and by the resulting reflex to react to his fear of obstacles and opposition by a strategy of annihilation. Whenever Hitler's use of this absolute power is being discussed, these personality factors must be given due weight, though not to the extent of reducing his decision-making and policies to them alone. Hitler's psyche, his emotions, his physical being, his life-style, his interactions with others and so on – such aspects cannot replace analysis of complex historical material, but nor can they be treated in a voyeuristic manner in a special chapter called 'Hitler, the private man'. Rather, the challenge is to view them as integral to this person and, where fruitful, to make them part of the biography.[7]

By writing his autobiographical work *Mein Kampf* [My Struggle], Hitler, supported by the Nazi propaganda machine, later contributed significantly to the creation and manipulation of his own history. Whereas he described his pre-1914 years as a time when he taught himself the things that laid the foundation for his political career, this version was frequently reinterpreted after the Second World War as the history of a failure, who in the narrow provincial world of Linz, in the slums of Vienna, and in the cafés of Munich internalized the resentments that he was then able to act out in his later life. Yet this interpretation too reads purpose and linearity into Hitler's development when there is in fact no evidence for these. Hitler's extraordinary later career – and this is my focus in this book – cannot be explained by the first three decades of his life. It is therefore important to resist later reinterpretations and exaggerations. Only then do we see clearly that what we are dealing with is no more or less than the history of a nobody.

Prologue
A Nobody

A genius. That was how Hitler saw himself and how he wanted others to see him. Though unrecognized at first, he had, the story went, followed the path predestined for him, thanks to his exceptional abilities, his strength of will, and his determination. Hitler invested a considerable amount of effort in creating this perception of himself. It was at the core of the image that he and his supporters spent a lifetime burnishing. Bound up with this image-making was his attempt to obscure his family background and to portray his childhood and youth as a preparation for his later role as politician and 'Führer'. He had good grounds for doing so, for when separated out from this subsequent 'narrative' and confined to the (relatively sparse) facts that can count as assured, Hitler's early life presents a very different picture. While providing insights into the development of the young Hitler's personality, these facts also show that his first thirty years gave no inkling of his future career.[1]

Hitler's ancestors came from the Waldviertel, a poor agricultural and forested region in the north-west of Lower Austria. In 1837 Hitler's father, Alois Schicklgruber, was born in the village of Strones near Dollersheim, the illegitimate son of Maria Anna Schicklgruber. Whether by chance or not, shortly after the Anschluss in 1938 both of these places were completely depopulated and destroyed when a large Wehrmacht training area was created.[2] It is not clear whether Alois was the son of a miller, Johann Georg Hiedler, whom Anna Schicklgruber married in 1842 and who died in 1857, or the offspring of a relationship with his younger brother, a peasant, Johann Nepomuk Hiedler. In any case, shortly before the early death of his mother in 1847, Johann Nepomuk took the boy to live with him in the village of Spital and, in 1876, with the aid of three witnesses and in a procedure of very dubious legality, had his elder brother posthumously declared to be the boy's father.[3] In future Alois used the name Hitler, a variation of 'Hiedler' that was common in the district. The dubious legality of this procedure (which was seemingly necessary so that Johann Nepomuk, who finally died in 1888, could make Alois his heir) has led to repeated speculation about the true identity of Alois's father. In 1932, for example, a rumour surfaced, exploited by Hitler's opponents,[4] that Alois was the son of a Jew and so there was no way that his son, Adolf, could (according to his own criteria) claim to be a 'pure Aryan'. However, despite the persistence of this rumour, it has no basis in fact.[5] Nevertheless, it is understandable that, in view of this and other scandalous rumours that kept emerging, Hitler had no interest in discussing his family background, particularly since Johann Nepomuk was also the grandfather of Hitler's mother, Klara Pölzl. Given the doubts about who his grandfather was, Hitler's great-grandfather on his mother's side may also have been his grandfather on his father's side.

This uncertainty about Hitler's family history was not, in fact, untypical among the rural working class of this period and it continued into the next generation. To begin with, Alois Hitler concentrated on his career. Originally trained as a shoemaker, he managed to secure a post in the Austrian customs service and so acquired the status of a civil servant. In view of his poor educational qualifications this represented a significant career achievement. His first posting was to Braunau am Inn on the German–Austrian border in 1871.[6]

Alois Hitler was married three times and before that had already fathered an illegitimate child. His first marriage, to a woman fourteen years older than him, failed because she discovered his affair with a young servant girl. Alois lived with her and they had an illegitimate child (also called Alois), who was born in 1882. After the death of his wife they married and had another child, a daughter, Angela. The following year his wife became very ill and Alois employed Klara, his niece twice removed, to help out. She had already worked in his household as a maid and, even before his wife died, he had fathered a child with her. They married in January 1885, a papal dispensation being required because they were related. In 1885 Gustav, their first child arrived, followed by Ida a year later, and Otto the year after that. In the winter of 1887/88 they lost all three children, Otto dying shortly after birth, while Gustav and Ida succumbed to diphtheria. However, in 1888 Klara once again became pregnant and on 20 April 1889 her fourth child was born and given the name Adolf.

In 1892, the family – Klara, Adolf and his two half siblings – moved to Passau, to which Alois Hitler had been reassigned. In 1894 Edmund was born[7] and Klara and the children stayed in Passau, while Alois spent his last year of service in 1894/5 in Linz. On receiving his pension Alois moved back to the country, buying a farm in Hafeld near Lambach for his retirement.[8] However, he soon sold it and, after a brief stay in Lambach, in 1898 moved with his family to a small house in Leonding near Linz.[9] By this time, the family had undergone further changes. In 1896 a daughter, Paula, was born; in the same year, fourteen-year-old, Alois (junior) had left home after a major quarrel with his father and been disinherited.[10] In 1900, their son, Edmund, died of measles.[11]

During the nineteenth century, marriage between relatives, illegitimate children, a lack of clarity over fatherhood, large numbers of births, and the frequent deaths of children were all characteristic of the lives of the rural working class. Alois Hitler succeeded in climbing out of this social class but, as far as his family life was concerned, continued to be part of it. Although he had achieved a relatively high status as a civil servant, his mind-set did not adjust to the 'orderly', petty bourgeois norms of his time and, significantly, on his retirement, he once more sought a rural milieu. It appears that his life was determined by this tension, a tension that Alois was able to overcome through his strong, even brutal, self-confidence. In most of the few surviving photographs he is shown in uniform. To his subordinates he was evidently a pedantic and strict superior who was not very approachable. After his retirement in the village environment of Lambach and Leonding, in which Adolf Hitler grew up, his father's position as a former civil servant gave him a superior status. To the villagers he appeared lively and sociable.[12] However, this cheerfulness was mainly evident outside the house; at home he was an undisputed paterfamilias with distinctly despotic qualities, who frequently beat his children.[13] In contrast to Klara, who was a regular churchgoer, he was anticlerical, a committed Liberal.

In 1903 Alois senior suddenly collapsed and died while drinking his morning glass of wine in the local pub. Reminiscences of him proved very varied. In an obituary in the *Linzer Tagespost* he was described as a 'thoroughly progressively-minded man' and, as such, a good friend of free schools, a reference to the fact that he supported Liberal efforts to reform the school system.[14] He was described as 'always good-humoured, marked indeed by a positively youthful cheerfulness', a 'keen singer'.[15] Years later, the local peasant, Josef Mayrhofer, who was appointed Adolf Hitler's guardian, painted a totally different picture. Alois had been a 'grumpy, taciturn old man', 'a hard-line Liberal and like all Liberals of that period a staunch German Nationalist, a Pan-German, yet, surprisingly, still loyal to the Emperor'.[16]

Adolf Hitler himself later maintained that his relationship with his father was the key to the development of his personality. Yet a glance at his family history suggests that his relationship with his mother may well have been more significant. In Hitler's family death was very present: Adolf lost a total of four siblings, three before his own birth and then, aged eleven, his brother Edmund. Three years later, his father died and, finally, his mother, when he was seventeen.

The fact that his mother had lost her first three children before Adolf's birth and – everything points to this – had little emotional support from her husband, must have had a strong impact on her behaviour towards Adolf. We do not know how she responded to her fourth child. It is conceivable that she came across as an unfeeling mother, who after her painful losses was afraid to invest too much emotion in a child who might not survive. He would then have experienced her as cool, lacking in feeling, distant, an experience that would explain Hitler's own emotional underdevelopment, and also his tendency to try to assert his superiority over others and to seek refuge in megalomaniacal ideas of his own greatness. Or, on the other hand, his mother may have thoroughly spoiled her fourth child, placed all her hopes in the boy, and sought in him a substitute for the lack of a warm rela-tionship with her husband. Being brought up as a mother's boy, as a little prince, and a domestic tyrant would be an equally satisfactory explanation for why Hitler, even in his early years, became convinced he was someone special and how, in the course of his development, his ability to form nor-mal human relationships was severely damaged. This would explain the conflict with his father, whose very existence Adolf must have seen as a threat to his special role in the family. It would also mean that his relation-ship with his mother was more one of dependence than of a son's love for his mother. A combination of the 'dead' and the spoiling mother is also pos-sible: Klara Hitler may, because of her losses, have treated her son during his first years with a lack of emotion and then, later on, have attempted to com-pensate for her neglect by showing excessive concern for him.[17]

The memoirs of Hitler's boyhood friend, August Kubizek, and his own recollections indicate that the spoiling mother is the more likely scenario. However, even without knowing the details of this mother–son relationship, it is possible (and that is what matters here) to find plausible arguments for attributing Hitler's evident lack of feeling in his dealings with others, his marked egocentricity, his flight into a fantasy world focused on himself, in short, his narcissistic personality, to his family background.

Adolf Hitler himself emphasized his relationship with Alois, which he described as a classic father–son conflict. In *Mein Kampf* he maintains that, whereas as a ten-year-old he had hoped to go to university and so wanted to attend the humanist Gymnasium [grammar school], after he had finished primary school in 1900[18] his father had sent him to the Realschule [vocational school] in order to prepare him for a subordinate career in the civil service. He had massively rebelled against this. At the age of twelve he had again clashed with his father over his decision to become an artist. Thus his poor school results allegedly resulted from his determination to get his way with his father.[19]

His results in the Realschule were indeed modest. He had to repeat his first year and in 1923 his class teacher, Huemer, reminisced that Hitler was 'definitely talented' (albeit 'one-sidedly'), but not particularly hard-working, and in addition, unbalanced, 'contrary, high-handed, self-opinionated, and irascible'.[20] In 1904, evidently as a result of another poor report, Adolf switched to the Realschule in Steyr, approximately forty kilometres away, where he stayed in lodgings. Hitler loathed the place, an attitude he retained for the rest of his life.[21] In 1905 he once again failed to pass his exams and, thereupon, left school for good.[22] An illness, which Hitler subsequently, and no doubt with much exaggeration, described as a 'serious lung complaint', seems to have made it easier to get his mother to accept that his school career had finally come to an end.[23]

Linz

It was in Linz that Hitler received his first political impressions. They can be roughly reconstructed from the few statements he himself made in *Mein Kampf* and from the limited reminiscences of contemporaries. These must be set in the context of the political currents determining the political history of the city during the first decade of the twentieth century. From all this it is clear that Hitler's early political views were geared to the political–social milieu within which his family was situated.

At the start of the century, Linz, the capital of Upper Austria, was marked by artisan traditions, expanding industry, and a lively cultural scene. Between

1900 and 1907 the population increased from almost 59,000 to nearly 68,000.[24] Politically, as in the rest of Austria, three political camps had emerged: the Christian Socials, the German Nationalists, and the Social Democrats.[25] Against the background of the political mobilization of the masses, all three were competing with one another to take over from the previously dominant Liberals. In Linz, during the course of the 1890s, the German Nationalists had succeeded in winning this competition. Large sections of the population who were not tied to the Catholic Church had exchanged their liberal political ideals for nationalist ones. This was also true of Alois Hitler, whom Hitler's guardian, Mayrhofer, had described as 'Liberal' [i.e. anti-clerical], 'German Nationalist', and 'Pan-German', but also as 'loyal to the Emperor'.[26]

Within the Austro-Hungarian empire the German Nationalists [Deutschfreiheitliche] demanded the leadership role for the German Austrians within this multi-ethnic state and emphasized their links with the Germans in Bismarck's Reich. The majority were loyal to the Habsburg monarchy, but distinguished themselves from the Liberals and the Christian Socials in German Austria through their commitment to their 'German' identity. Their stance also had an anticlerical slant, for many German Nationalists suspected the Catholic Church of trying to strengthen the Slav elements within the empire. The Slavs (in Upper Austria and Linz this meant mainly the Czechs) were seen as the real threat, as their growing self-confidence and demand for equal treatment threatened the Germans' leadership role. This was being played out, in particular, through the so-called 'language dispute', which came to a head in the years after 1897. These political views found expression through the German People's Party [Deutsche Volkspartei], the dominant political force in Linz and Upper Austria.[27] Its main newspaper was the *Linzer Tagespost*, already referred to, a daily subscribed to by Hitler's father and which Hitler himself stated he had 'read from his earliest youth'. It was not of course by chance that the paper printed an obituary of his father.[28]

From the 1890s onwards, the German Nationalists in Linz not only succeeded in winning votes in elections but also in establishing a well-integrated German Nationalist milieu. The gymnastics clubs, very much in the tradition of the 'Father of Gymnastics', Friedrich Ludwig Jahn,★ saw themselves

★ Translators' note: Friedrich Ludwig (Father) Jahn (1778–1852) established a nationalist gymnastic movement in 1811 to encourage and prepare young men to resist French occupation. Banned during the period of Reaction, the movement was revived in the 1860s as part of the campaign for German unification and over the following century became widespread throughout the German-speaking world.

as 'centres for fostering German national consciousness and patriotic-mind-edness'[29] and were sympathetic to the German Nationalists.[30] The same was true of the General German Language Society [Allgemeiner Deutscher Sprachverein], which opposed the 'foreign infiltration' of the German language, and of the German School Association [Deutscher Schulverein], and the Association for the Defence of the Eastern Marches [Schutzverein Ostmark]. The latter, like other 'defence associations' with local branches in Linz, advocated strengthening the German element in the border provinces of Austria that were allegedly being threatened by alien 'ethnic groups'. Year after year, and with increasing enthusiasm, big festivals were staged, for example at the summer solstice, or to celebrate some jubilee, at which 'German' or, as the various announcements put it, 'Germanic' or 'ethnic German' [völkisch] customs and consciousness were cultivated and invoked.[31] Thus, in reporting the 'Yule Festival' of the Jahn Gymnastics Club, the Linzer Tagespost considered it an 'exceptionally gratifying sign of the times' that 'ethnic German festivals, which are calculated to rekindle national feelings and sensibilities, are being attended, in particular by the upper classes of our city, with such enthusiasm and in such numbers'.[32] Moreover, the German Nationalist associations were subsidized by the local council and, during the years after 1900, Linz often hosted supra-regional festivals of German Nationalist associations.[33]

The struggle against the allegedly increasing influence of the Czechs in Upper Austria, against 'Slavisization', was a standard topic in Linz. It was a classic case of a problem that was created by being discussed, a 'minority problem without a minority'.[34] In 1900 there were hardly more than 3,500 Czech speakers in Upper Austria. By 1910 that number had reduced to 2,000, a little more than 0.2 per cent of the population. Around half of this minority lived in Linz.[35] Nevertheless, from 1898 onwards, the German Nationalists used their presence in the Landtag [regional parliament] to keep pressing for German to be made the sole official language and language of instruction in Upper Austria. This provided a welcome opportunity to campaign in parliament and in the public sphere against the alleged threat of foreign influence. In 1909 this demand, which, given the small number of Czechs in Upper Austria, was a piece of pure demagogy, was finally met, as it was in the monarchy's other German 'crown lands', by the passage of a provincial law.[36] The Linzer Tagespost reported regularly on German–Czech disputes, most of which occurred in Bohemia or Vienna. However, alleged manifestations of Czech nationalism in Upper Austria

were kept under suspicious review and dubbed Czech 'presumption' or
'cheek'.[37] When, in 1903, a celebration was going to be held in a church to
mark fifty years of services in the Czech language, the Linz city council
passed a unanimous resolution condemning this 'Czech nationalist demonstration', urging local businesses in future only to employ 'German assistants
and apprentices'. The regional parliament also discussed the matter at
length.[38] In 1904, a concert by the Czech violinist, Jan Kubelik, was prevented by riots; the world-famous musician had to flee the city down side
streets. This was in response to demonstrations by Czech nationalists in
Budweis and Prague and was reported with satisfaction by the *Tagespost*.[39]

The Pan-Germans should also be included in the German Nationalist
camp, viewed in a broader sense. They too believed in intimate national solidarity between the Austrian Germans and the Germans 'in the Reich'.
However, in contrast to the majority of the German Nationalists, who
aimed at acquiring dominance within the Habsburg empire, the Pan-
German supporters of Georg von Schönerer wished to follow the opposite
path. They wanted to dissolve the empire, with the unambiguously Slav
parts being given their independence and the German parts uniting with
the Reich. In addition, they were committed to a racial form of anti-
Semitism and a marked anti-clericalism. After the turn of the century this
developed into the 'Away from Rome' movement, a mass conversion to
Protestantism, which was seen as the Germans' national religion.[40] However,
in Linz the Pan-Germans were only a marginal group. Indeed, during the
first decade of the new century, the years when Hitler was exposed to his
first political impressions, the leaders of the German Nationalists distanced
themselves from the Pan-Germans, forming an alliance with the Liberals,
whom they could largely dominate. It was only after this constellation had
suffered a heavy defeat in the Reichstag [imperial parliament] elections of
1911 that the Pan-Germans were integrated more closely into the German
Nationalist camp.

The new political constellation after the turn of the century prompted
the German Nationalists to refrain from the use of anti-Semitic slogans in
the public sphere in order not to damage their relationship with the Liberals.
They did, however, introduce the so-called Aryan clause, excluding Jews
from membership, into the constitutions of all the associations of which, by
1900, they had acquired leadership from the Liberals.[41] Nevertheless, they
did not want to make too much of their hostility to the Jews; the 'threat
from the Czechs' was a much more successful slogan.[42] It appears, therefore,

entirely plausible when Hitler writes in *Mein Kampf* that his father was far from being anti-Semitic, not least because of his 'cosmopolitan views, which, despite his pronounced nationalist sentiments, not only remained intact but also rubbed off on me'. During his school days – there were a number of Jewish boys in the Linz Realschule – he himself had seen no reason to challenge this attitude. It was only when he was around fourteen or fifteen (he writes) that he, partly through political conversations, had come across the word 'Jew', which had engendered 'a slight distaste', 'an unpleasant feeling'.[43] In fact, there is no evidence that anti-Semitism played a dominant role in the Realschule in Linz that Hitler attended between 1900 and 1904.[44]

Against the background of the 'nationalities dispute', with which the city was so preoccupied and in which the German Nationalists were so heavily engaged, the confrontation with the 'Slavs' played a much more important role in the life of the school. But in Hitler's school, as elsewhere, this conflict was largely fought against an imaginary opponent. For, contrary to Hitler's later statements that, growing up during the 'struggle on the frontier for German language, culture, and mentality', he had taken part in fights with Czech schoolmates,[45] in fact there were hardly any Czech-speaking pupils in the school; in 1903 there were precisely two. However, although Hitler's encounters with Czech schoolmates were a fantasy, they indicate that his life-long contempt for Czechs was rooted in the anti-Czech climate of his favourite city of Linz.

The Realschule in Linz was undoubtedly a hotbed of German Nationalism. Two of Hitler's teachers were active representatives of this movement: Leopold Poetsch, who taught him geography between 1901 and 1904 and history from 1900 to 1904, and Edward Huemer, Hitler's German and French teacher during this period. Poetsch was a local councillor for the German People's Party, and active in the Südmark Defence Association. He undertook an extensive programme of lectures dealing above all with the importance of the Teutons, a very positive assessment of Prussia, the cultural superiority of Germans, and the need for closer ties between the two empires. These were all favourite topics from which conclusions can be drawn about the content of his teaching. Like his colleague, Huemer, however, Poetsch was loyal to the Austrian state and its monarchy.[46] Hitler praised Poetsch warmly in *Mein Kampf* as someone who had been very successful in appealing to his pupils' 'sense of national honour'. In a letter from 1929 he called him a 'teacher, to whom I owe a huge amount, indeed the person who to some extent prepared the foundations for the path that

I have subsequently followed'.[47] However, significantly, as an Austrian civil servant, Poetsch did not want to be held accountable by his prominent pupil for the latter's radical views and, therefore, in future, distanced himself from him,[48] whereas Huemer became an enthusiastic Hitler supporter.[49]

In fact, Hitler then conceded in *Mein Kampf* that, while his becoming a 'young revolutionary' and an embittered opponent of the Austrian monarchy had been influenced by Poetsch's teaching, this had probably not been his teacher's intention, at least not to that extent.[50] This statement, like other remarks in *Mein Kampf*, is quite revealing about the political situation at the Realschule in Linz. Hitler wrote that, in line with the dominant trend in the school, in a very short time he had become a fanatical German Nationalist. Collections for the 'Südmark and the Schulverein' had been held in the school; they had worn cornflowers, the symbol of the Pan-Germans and the German Nationalists. In addition, he and his schoolmates had made no bones about their 'Greater German' views: by displaying the colours black-red-gold, using the 'Heil greeting', and by singing 'Deutschland, Deutschland über alles' to the tune of the Kaiser Hymn. These were all actions the school authorities disapproved of.[51] Moreover, the extreme German Nationalist atmosphere of the Realschule in Linz evidently provided fertile soil for more radical examples of 'Greater German' ideology. The pupils apparently enjoyed provoking their teachers with slogans that were frowned on by the imperial authorities, with the excuse that they were only carrying the nationalism that was being preached to them to its logical conclusion.[52] However, such demonstrations of loyalty to the 'Greater German' cause were not expressions of radical opposition. Rather, they should be seen as expressions of the conventional German Nationalist views that dominated those sections of the middle and lower-middle classes who were not religiously inclined at the beginning of the twentieth century.

In 1905, after leaving school, Hitler returned from Steyr, which he hated, to Linz, where his mother had moved in June of that year.[53] From now onwards, his mother, his younger sister Paula, and his aunt Johanna, who was living with them, spent their lives looking after him in their two-room flat. Reviewing this period, Hitler described it in *Mein Kampf* as 'the happiest days of my life'.[54] During this time, Hitler does not appear to have had any concrete plans for his further education. He had vague dreams of becoming a great artist and so he spent most of his time drawing, painting, and reading; he briefly took piano lessons,[55] and in the evenings went to the opera or to concerts.

In 1905, he met August Kubizek at the opera. Kubizek, nine months older than Hitler, worked in his father's upholstery business, shared Hitler's enthusiasm for opera, and was himself a talented pianist. This friend of his youth has provided extensive memoirs of the next two years that Hitler spent in Linz and of the following period when they were together in Vienna. However, the reliability of these memoirs is highly dubious. Kubizek, who remained for the rest of his life an admirer of Hitler, produced an initial version of his memoirs during the Second World War at the behest of the Nazi Party Chancellery, and then expanded them considerably in 1953 incorporating, among other things, excerpts from *Mein Kampf*.

Part II of the original manuscript concerning their period together in Vienna has survived.[56] The fragment shows very clearly how Kubizek doctored the book version of his memoirs, which appeared in the 1950s and is the most important source for Hitler's youth. Whereas in the original text Kubizek tried to portray Hitler's eccentricity, of which he left the reader in no doubt, as clear proof of his genius, in the book version he dealt with it as a purely private matter and from the perspective of a curious but distant observer. In particular, he significantly revised the passages concerning Hitler's anti-Semitism. Whereas in the original manuscript hatred of the Jews was treated as something quite normal, in the book it appears as if it was a strange obsession of Hitler's. As a former intimate of Hitler, Kubizek had been interned by the Americans and, as a former civil servant, at the beginning of the 1950s he was anxious to rehabilitate himself. He therefore tried to avoid being identified in any way with Hitler. According to the rather innocent message of the book, it was possible to be friendly with Hitler on a purely private basis without sharing his peculiar inclinations or views, let alone recognizing them as harbingers of a later catastrophe. The book, however, shows quite clearly that such a private friendship with Hitler was an illusion, an illusion that Kubizek was still holding on to forty years later.

It is remarkable that, in describing the personal qualities of his young friend in his book, Kubizek sticks to the line already taken in the original manuscript.[57] He describes the young Hitler as slight and pale, always very simply but correctly dressed; he was well-behaved and, above all, very articulate.[58] It is clear from Kubizek's account that Hitler dominated this relationship. He decided what the friends were going to do, in the process high-handedly controlling Kubizek's very limited free time. When the two were together, Hitler liked making long-winded speeches about music, art, architecture, or politics and Kubizek, who considered himself 'basically a quiet and contemplative person', impressed by so much knowledge and eloquence, had simply to listen. According to Kubizek, Hitler had no other friends and did not allow Kubizek to make friends with anybody else.[59]

Kubizek records that, during the four years of this 'friendship', Hitler showed no interest in members of the opposite sex – with one, admittedly very strange, exception. Kubizek mentions a girl named Stefanie, the daughter of a comfortably off widow of a civil servant, with whom Hitler was infatuated, without even once summoning up the courage to speak to her. Hitler told Kubizek that he was deeply in love with Stefanie and he spent much of his time making plans for his future life with his ideal woman. In his fantasies Hitler dreamed that he would become a successful artist, marry his beloved, and live with her in a marvellous villa, which he had already designed down to the last detail.[60] Kubizek counted himself lucky to have been told of Hitler's love for Stefanie, for 'nothing binds a friendship so closely as a shared secret'.[61] When Hitler fell ill for a lengthy period and later, when he was living in Vienna, Kubizek was obliged to go in place of his friend and stand at a particular spot in the town in order to watch out for Stefanie and then report on his observations.[62]

Apart from Stefanie, according to Kubizek Hitler was moved by another passion that they shared – the music of Richard Wagner. The friends went to numerous performances of the master at the Linz Landestheater, and their enthusiasm helped them to overlook the inadequacies of provincial productions.[63] Wagner's mythical opera world appealed to Hitler's enthusiasm for the German heroic sagas. In this connection Kubizek mentions Gustav Schwab's popular edition of the sagas of the classical world as Hitler's favourite book; his friend had been completely absorbed in it.[64] This was at the root of Wagner's 'appeal' for him. Kubizek believed that through Hitler's intensive study of Wagner's work and biography it was as if he were trying to incorporate him as 'part of his own being'.[65]

It is clear from Kubizek's memoirs that Hitler spent most of his time immersed in a fantasy world. When Kubizek first visited his friend in the little room he had in his mother's flat, he thought he had 'entered an architect's office'; the whole room was covered with architectural plans and drawings. For apart from heroic sagas and his passion for Wagner, at this time Hitler was preoccupied with comprehensive plans for the reconstruction of the whole of the city of Linz and its surroundings. But he also wrote poems, drew, and painted, and acquired a strong interest in politics and various contemporary developments.[66] Kubizek describes the young Hitler as almost entirely focused on himself and his fantasy projects, which he pursued with monomaniacal energy. According to his friend, Hitler's personality was marked by something 'fixed, obdurate, inflexible, stubborn, obsessive, which showed itself to the outside world in the form of an uncanny degree of seriousness'. This was 'the basis on which all his other characteristics developed'.[67] Kubizek illustrates this trait with the following story: At Hitler's request, the two of them bought a joint lottery ticket and Hitler, absolutely convinced that they would win the main prize, encouraged Kubizek to join him in planning their future lives. They looked for and found a suitable flat, went into all the details of its furnishing, aiming to use it as the centre for a group of cultivated friends, and made plans to go on educational trips together. The household was to be run by a distinguished lady of advanced years, so that, as Kubizek summed up Hitler's thinking, 'no expectations or intentions can arise that might be detrimental to our artistic calling'. Then, when, contrary to Hitler's clear expectations, they failed to win the main prize, he was naturally hugely disappointed.[68]

Vienna

In the spring of 1906 Hitler went on his first trip to Vienna. During his stay of several weeks, he spent most of his time visiting the architectural sights of the city. He went to the city theatre and the Court Opera, where he attended performances of 'Tristan' and the 'Flying Dutchman', both produced by the current director of the Opera, Gustav Mahler.[69] This Vienna trip made a deep impression on Hitler, reinforcing his desire to become an artist in the metropolis.[70]

More than a year later, in September 1907, he took a decisive step in that direction. He set off for Vienna in order to study at the Academy of Fine Art. He found lodgings in the Mariahilf quarter, at Stumpergasse 31, where he rented a room from a seamstress from Bohemia, Maria Zakreys.[71] Hitler cleared the first hurdle for study at the Academy, admission to a drawing examination lasting several hours, by presenting a set of drawings he had brought with him. But, like three-quarters of the examinees, he completely failed the actual examination. The assessment of the clearly conservative professors read: 'Few heads'. The examiners had evidently disapproved of the fact that Hitler's talent was too one-sidedly focused on drawing buildings and his ability to depict the human figure was seriously underdeveloped. Hitler had no real interest in people.[72] This rejection came 'like a terrible bolt from the blue' for Hitler, who, according to his own recollection of the incident as described in *Mein Kampf*, was entirely convinced of his own talent. But in *Mein Kampf* he reinterpreted the experience as an opportunity that was to determine his future life. For the rector of the institution had referred to his undoubted architectural talent. 'In a few days', he continued, 'I myself knew that some day I would become an architect'. Although he lacked the requisite school leaving certificate, he was determined to meet the challenge: 'I wanted to become an architect.'[73] In fact, however, he was to apply once again to the Academy's *painting* class.[74]

But first he returned to Linz. In January 1907, Klara Hitler had had to undergo an operation for breast cancer and her condition worsened in the autumn of 1907. Hitler took over looking after his mother, who, after an agonizing final stage of her cancer, died on 21 December.[75] The Jewish general practitioner, Eduard Bloch, who treated Klara Hitler – given the state of medical expertise at the time, she was a hopeless case – made an attempt to reduce her pain. In 1941 Bloch, by then living in exile in New York, published a piece in a journal in which he described the powerful emotional impact which the sickness and death of his mother had had on the young Adolf Hitler, but also the devoted care he had given her. 'In the whole of my practice I have never seen anyone so prostrate with grief as Adolf Hitler.' Hitler was very grateful for the selfless efforts of the doctor (who, moreover, had charged only a small fee), as is indicated by two postcards Hitler sent Bloch from Vienna. When, thirty years later, after the Anschluss with Austria, he returned to Linz in triumph, he is said to have made friendly enquiries after Bloch. During the following period Bloch enjoyed a special status in Linz, until he finally succeeded in emigrating in 1940.[76] Like other Jewish doctors, he had been forced to close his practice, but he was left in peace by the local Nazis and the Gestapo.

Hitler and his younger sister, Paula, most probably divided the cash left by their mother between them. In 1905, after the sale of the Leonding farm, this had amounted to 5,500 Kronen. But some of this was undoubtedly needed to defray part of his mother's living expenses, and also the costs of her medical treatment and burial. Hitler may have received 1,000 Kronen, a sum that would more or less cover a year's living expenses. Furthermore, he and his sister successfully applied for an orphans' pension, which provided them with a monthly income of 50 Kronen until the age of 24 and which they shared between them. However, the precondition was that they were both unprovided for. This applied to Hitler for as long he continued his education, or at least gave the impression in Linz that he was doing so.[77]

After he had disposed of his mother's effects, in February 1908 Hitler returned to Vienna, where he once again took up lodgings in Stumpergasse 31. A former neighbour of his mother's from her days in Linz had arranged an interview for him, via a Vienna friend of hers, with Alfred Roller, the famous set designer of the Vienna Opera, whose work Hitler admired. But, in the end, the shy young man lacked the courage to take up the opportunity, as he told Roller on meeting him decades later.[78]

A short time after Hitler's arrival in the capital his friend Kubizek, whom he had persuaded to study music at the Vienna Conservatoire, followed him there. He had even succeeded in persuading his friend's parents to agree to this.[79] For details of the following months that Hitler and Kubizek spent together in Vienna we have, in addition to Kubizek's book, the original, much shorter, text he prepared for the Party Chancellery prior to 1945.

In his book Kubizek recalled how Hitler had waited for him impatiently at the station: 'In his dark, good quality overcoat, dark hat, and with his walking stick with an ivory handle, he appeared almost elegant. He was obviously pleased to see me, greeted me warmly and, as was then the custom, kissed me lightly on the cheek'.[80] Evidently in order to prevent speculation about his friendship, Kubizek had slightly altered the original text, which read: 'My friend...greeted me with joyous enthusiasm with a kiss and then took me straight to his lodgings.' Kubizek then goes on to describe in his book how they both succeeded in persuading Hitler's landlady to exchange his room for the sitting room, which the two of them now shared. Kubizek was accepted by the Vienna Conservatoire and borrowed a piano, which he managed with some difficulty to fit into the small room.[81]

In the meantime, Hitler continued with what he had enjoyed doing in Linz: reading a fair amount, drawing, and developing his architectural plans. Soon he started preparing comprehensive plans for the remodelling of the Austrian capital. In fact, it is evident that Hitler's architectural knowledge and preferences were very strongly influenced by Vienna models, in particular the prestige architecture of the Ringstrasse.[82] According to Kubizek, Hitler also attempted to write a play and an opera,[83] both of which were based in the world of Germanic heroes, but without success. Kubizek reports that, during this period, Hitler concocted all sorts of fantastic projects, particularly after his mental balance had been upset by the death of his

mother and his rejection by the Academy. He tortured himself with recrim-
inations, which, however, could suddenly turn into tirades aimed at the
'whole of humanity', who 'did not understand him, did not respect him and
by whom he felt persecuted and cheated'.[84]

Kubizek claimed that Hitler had delayed telling him about his rejection
by the Academy, saying that he had not informed his mother because of her
illness.[85] However, he had in fact told his mother's landlady in Linz in
February 1908,[86] and it is clear from Kubizek's original text that the latter
knew about it before arriving in Vienna. Thus, the idea that Hitler made a
secret of his rejection by the Academy is a piece of fiction by Kubizek from
the 1950s designed to explain Hitler's eccentric traits as a response to a
major disappointment.

In fact, Hitler used his stay in Vienna in order to prepare for a further
attempt to get into the Academy in autumn 1908, at least that is how he is
likely to have viewed it. Kubizek's report reflects the contradictory impressions that the capital city, Vienna, made on the two young men from the
provinces. On the one hand, they enjoyed the privilege of living in one of
the most brilliant cultural metropolises in Europe. The two friends visited
the Vienna theatre and the musical venues, particularly the Court Opera,
and Kubizek noted 'their undivided love and enthusiasm for the music
dramas of Richard Wagner'. For Hitler a Wagner opera was not simply a visit
to a cultural event, but 'the opportunity of being transported into that extraordinary state which Wagner's music produced in him, that trance, that
drifting into a mystical dream-world which he needed in order to cope
with the enormous tension of his turbulent nature'. In Vienna it was possible to see almost all of Wagner's operas; Hitler had certainly seen his
favourite opera, 'Lohengrin', at least ten times.[87]

On the other hand, it was only too obvious that all this prestige architecture and high culture was in striking contrast to the reality of life for most
people in the city. The stark social differences and the misery of the masses
– the two young men were living on the borderline of poverty – the movements of social protest that were emerging among the working class and
also among the lower-middle class, who were fearing social decline, were all
too apparent. Moreover, in a multi-ethnic city like Vienna the monarchy's
nationality conflicts were omnipresent.[88] In three places in the book
Kubizek claims that Hitler was anti-Semitic: Hitler disliked going to the
Mensa [student cafeteria] because it was also frequented by Jews; he was
annoyed by an encounter with a begging Jewish peddler; and he had signed

both of them up as members of the 'Anti-Semitic League' [Antisemitenbund], although this association did not in fact exist in Austria before the First World War. In the original manuscript this last reference and the one about the peddler do not occur, whereas Hitler's anger about the Jewish visitors to the Mensa receives much more space, and there is also a lengthy section about Hitler's negative opinion of Jewish visitors to the opera, which does not appear in the book. However, Kubizek notes in both versions of his memoirs that, despite his anti-Semitic views, Hitler defended Mahler's Wagner productions, which at the time were subject to anti-Semitic attacks.[89]

Kubizek was convinced that, during their time together in Vienna, despite being 18–19 years old, Hitler had not had a relationship with a girl or a woman. Although members of the opposite sex often showed interest in his friend, he had ignored them and, what is more, had refused to allow Kubizek to have a love affair. In general, Hitler had been decidedly hostile to women.[90] Yet, despite his prudishness and rejection of sex, and, according to Kubizek, this included homosexuality, at the same time Hitler was fascinated by sexual topics. In the course of long nocturnal conversations he had expatiated on the 'flame of life' and, accompanied by Kubizek, had paid an extensive visit to a Vienna red-light district.[91]

In the summer of 1908, at the end of term, Kubizek went back to Linz, assuming that he would once again be sharing accommodation with Hitler in the Stumpergasse when he returned to Vienna in the autumn. His friend wrote him a few letters during the summer, but when Kubizek returned to Vienna in November Hitler had moved out without leaving an address.[92]

In the meantime, Hitler had moved to lodgings in Felberstrasse 22, near the Westbahnhof railway station and had failed in his second attempt to gain admission to the Academy of Fine Art, this time without even being short-listed for the examination.[93] It is plausible to assume that this final blow to his future study plans hit Hitler much harder than his initial rejection. Then he had been able to maintain the illusion that he could correct the flaws in his work by practice; but now it was clear that, in the eyes of the Academy professors, he was simply not suited to be an artist.

According to Kubizek, Hitler had already been unstable and irascible when he was living in Linz;[94] he had suffered periodically from depression and spent whole days and nights wandering the streets.[95] It is clear from Kubizek's report that Hitler regarded his friend above all as a patient audience and admirer to whom he could outline all his grandiose pipe dreams.

He evidently exploited the relationship one-sidedly to his own advantage, protecting it jealously against outside interference; he did not even bother to seek out other friends. His infatuation for Stefanie had only served as the key to a dream world in which the young woman merely functioned as an accessory to a career as a successful artist. Hitler only acquired an interest in other people when he could fit them into his fantasy world – even if Kubizek, who could never escape from the spell of this 'friendship', continued to maintain, decades later, that Hitler had been a good and true friend, who had always been considerate towards him, respecting his feelings and needs.[96]

Hitler's grand ideas about his future invariably envisaged his playing roles in which he would be admired and celebrated. The almost manic efforts which Hitler put into his plans to reconstruct first Linz and then Vienna – his later places of residence, Munich and Berlin, would also be subjected to his mania for reconstruction – demonstrate an extreme determination completely to reshape his immediate surroundings in accordance with his ideas. But all this, the eccentric plans and roles, was not just playing around; it formed the actual content of his life. At the turn of the century, Hitler was admittedly by no means alone in his flight from reality, his conviction that he was basically an unrecognized genius and must now pursue his own path as an artist, a future that was preordained by his exceptional talent. Youthful escapism as a reaction to a society that set strict limits for young people was a favourite trope of contemporary literature: 'the artist's life' versus the complacent world of the bourgeoisie. Above all, his favourite composer, Wagner, evidently provided him with the appropriate role model for the unrecognized genius.[97]

Kubizek perfectly summed up Hitler's tendency to compensate for the deficiencies of his private life by creating a huge 'public self': 'He made up for the complete insignificance of his own life by making categorical statements on all public issues. His desire to alter the status quo thereby acquired a sense of direction and a goal.' What is also clear from Kubizek's report, however, is that Hitler had become so caught up in his fantasies that he could no longer tolerate disappointments, the simple confrontation with reality. The only thing that helped Hitler in such situations was to indulge in monologues for hours at a time, to which Kubizek had patiently listened and during which Hitler was once again able to revive his vulnerable dream world and in an even more grandiose fashion.

However, the rejection of his second application to the Academy of Fine Art had damaged his self-image to such an extent and was so intolerable that this time his only way out was to do something drastic. He did not mention this at all in *Mein Kampf*; instead, he tried to create the impression that, after the death of his mother, he was preparing to be trained as an architect, which, as we know, was untrue. In fact, he had tried once more to be admitted to the Academy's painting class.[98] Now he not only broke off all contact with Kubizek but also with his relatives, presumably because he was ashamed of his failure.[99] Moreover, he wished to conceal from his sister the fact that, after his plan to study had proved abortive, he was no longer entitled to draw half the orphans' pension they had been granted jointly. His second rejection produced an even more intensive flight into megalomaniacal plans, which were so monomaniacal that Hitler could no longer envisage any alternative form of education or future career. As a result, he experienced a rapid decline in his social status. He lived in the Felberstrasse until August 1909 and then moved for a few weeks to Sechshauserstrasse 58. Although, in the summer of 1908, he had secured a loan of 924 Kronen from his aunt,[100] a year later these not inconsiderable financial reserves had been used up and he could no longer afford a room or a regular place to sleep. At any rate, no address for him can be found; his tracks were lost in the metropolis; he may have spent the night in the open or in a café.[101] Hitler himself provided an extensive description of his miserable existence in Vienna during this period in *Mein Kampf*, but stayed silent about the details of his life at this time.[102] This remained the case throughout his life, although occasionally he referred to casual labour 'on building sites' or claimed to have studied art history or related subjects.[103]

We do, however, have a detailed report that provides some information about Hitler's life between autumn 1909 and the summer of 1910. It comes from Reinhold Hanisch and appeared in 1939 (two years after Hanisch's death) in the American journal *New Republic*; the publication was based on Hanisch's own written account of his encounter with Hitler, which is also available as a document in the NSDAP-Hauptarchiv.[104] Hanisch was a rather dubious figure. In the early 1930s he made his living from the sale of forged Hitler 'originals', and by providing journalists hostile to Hitler with revelations about the man who in the meantime had become a prominent figure. Nevertheless, his report appears entirely plausible. His descriptions of Hitler's lifestyle tally in many respects with Kubizek's memoirs and in some cases can be verified from other sources.

In 1909 Hanisch was living as a city tramp in Vienna. According to his account, during the autumn of that year he had encountered Hitler in the

Meidlinger hostel for the homeless in the next bed. Down at heel, hungry, and without any money, Hitler joined up with Hanisch and the two of them got through the next fortnight together. In the evenings they attempted to get beds in the various hostels; during the day, they tried to find casual work. In the process it became clear that Hitler was either too weak or too inept for most of the work on offer. Hanisch persuaded Hitler, who had evidently mentioned attending an art academy, to enter a business partnership. Hitler would paint picture postcards, which Hanisch would then sell. The project proved successful and soon the two of them had enough money for a permanent base: the men's hostel in the Brigittenau district, in which Hitler was to stay between February 1910 and May 1913. This men's hostel was a superior form of charitable institution and, by contemporary standards, a model of its kind. It was intended, in the first instance, for single workers on a low income, who were able to stay there for lengthy periods, being well and cheaply looked after. There were no mass dormitories, but instead individual cubicles; the sanitary facilities were adequate and there was a reading room.[105]

This is where Hitler sat during the day painting his postcards, which were copies of pictures of famous Viennese buildings and intended for tourists. They were produced as a cheap series, but soon Hitler quarrelled with Hanisch, who kept demanding more pictures. Hanisch reported that Hitler's productivity suffered because he preferred to read the newspapers and have discussions with the other visitors to the reading room. According to Hanisch, Hitler's anger was mainly directed at the Catholic Church and the Jesuits. He spoke very approvingly of the Pan-German leader, Georg von Schönerer, and of Karl Hermann Wolf, the dominant figure among the German Radicals, but also of the mayor of Vienna, Karl Lueger.

According to Hanisch's memoirs, Hitler discussed the issue of anti-Semitism at length, generally criticizing anti-Semitic positions; indeed, apparently he made positive comments about the Jews. Hanisch reported that there were Jews among Hitler's closest acquaintances at the hostel and with one of them Hitler had a close relationship. This man has been verified through the files of the registration office: Josef Neumann, born in 1878, a copper polisher, of the Mosaic religion. Neumann and another Jewish peddler (his name is also in the files) now began selling Hitler's pictures, leading to a quarrel with Hanisch.[106] Hanisch even maintains that, after receiving a substantial sum for a big order, Hitler disappeared from the hostel with Neumann and went to stay in a hotel for a week. There is in fact evidence that in June 1910 Hitler deregistered from the hostel for ten days. It is not clear what he did with Neumann during this period; he told Hanisch they had been sightseeing.[107]

Shortly afterwards, the quarrel with Hanisch escalated: A postcard seller accused Hanisch of stealing a picture painted by Hitler. Hitler was interviewed by the police – the report has survived – and confirmed the accusation. Hanisch, who had registered with the police under a false name, was kept in custody for seven days.[108] After the break with Hanisch – Neumann left Vienna in July 1910 – Hitler now sold his pictures himself, in particular to two Jewish picture-framers, Jacob Altenberg and Samuel Morgenstern.[109]

While Hanisch's report can be verified in part through official documents, other sources are much more dubious.[110] Indeed, there is hardly any reliable information about Hitler's life for the period 1910 to 1913. One thing, however, is clear from the official documents: When his Aunt Johanna died in 1911 it emerged that Hitler had received payments from her, in particular the loan in 1908 of 924 Kronen. Hitler was now compelled to admit in a declaration to the district court in Vienna-Leopoldstadt that he was not an art student without an income, but easily in a position to support himself; the orphans' pension was thus assigned solely to his sister, Paula. This admission that he had been deceiving his sister for years, which also involved admitting that his plan to study had failed, was probably the reason why, having already broken off contact in 1908, he continued to avoid her. He only saw Paula again at the beginning of the 1920s, after he had begun his political career and could regard himself as a success. He seems to have had occasional contact with his half-sister, Angela.[111]

There is a further report from a fellow occupant of the men's hostel covering 1913. It was by Karl Honisch and written in 1939 at the request of the Nazi Party archive. Honisch, born in Moravia in 1891 and a clerk by profession, was evidently anxious in 1939 to write a harmless report that would not conflict with the official Hitler story. It is clear from Honisch's account that Hitler had basically maintained his customary way of life. He spent a large part of his time in the reading room working on his pictures. Honisch describes him as someone of 'slight build, with hollow cheeks and a shock of dark hair flopping over his forehead, wearing a shabby suit'. He had noticed Hitler's 'invariably steady, extremely regular way of life'. He had been subject to mood swings: on most occasions he was friendly and relaxed, but from time to time he had been withdrawn and been something of a dreamer; sometimes he had been irascible. According to Honisch, Hitler had

had a fixed plan to go to Munich to attend the Academy of Art. He took an active part in the political discussions that frequently occurred in the reading room among his regular circle of 'intellectuals', becoming particularly engaged when 'the Reds' or the 'Jesuits' were being attacked.[112]

That poses the question: What were Hitler's political views during his time in Vienna? His assertion in *Mein Kampf* that, during his Vienna years, he had become a strong supporter of Schönerer and his Pan-Germans is entirely plausible. Given the strongly German Nationalist milieu in Linz in which he had grown up, he may well have already been attracted by the more radical Pan-Germans.[113] In her dissertation on Hitler's image of Austria, written in the 1960s, Eleonore Kandl systematically collated Hitler's comments on the old Austrian empire contained in *Mein Kampf*, his Table Talk and other sources, carefully comparing them with relevant articles in the Vienna press during the years he spent in the capital. The result is clear: on every essential point Hitler had adopted Pan-German propaganda to an amazing extent, even using the same terminology. This involved in particular:

- the conviction that the Habsburg monarchy was in its death throes, as the political elite, with its 'feeble' politics bent on compromise, was not in a position to maintain the dominance of German-speakers over the multi-ethnic mishmash;[114]
- accusations that the Habsburg monarchy had repeatedly betrayed the interests of the German nation and had encouraged the 'Slavisization' of the empire;[115]
- references to the threat of 'Slavisization' and the allegedly fateful role of the Church in this process;[116]
- his rejection of Social Democracy as a force that was nationally unreliable;[117]
- the enumeration of fatal mistakes made by the monarchy and the government that had served to 'weaken' the German-speakers;[118]
- his furious tirades against parliamentary democracy;[119]
- his demand for a close alliance with Germany because of their common 'blood';[120]
- complaints about the ethnic mixing in the Austrian army;[121]
- his criticism of the 'Jewified' press in the Austrian capital;[122]
- his deep distrust of Vienna, indeed his hatred of this 'racial Babylon', and of 'all this ethnic mishmash' in the capital as the embodiment of 'racial disgrace'.[123]

The extent of agreement between the two is so great that Hitler must have totally absorbed these polemics during his stay in Vienna.

However, when Hitler arrived in Vienna in 1908 the Pan-Germans had long passed the high point of their political influence. While during the 1880s and 1890s Schönerer's political ideas had been seriously considered as a possible option for the reorganization of the Habsburg Empire, his movement was now regarded as merely a political sect. In the election of 1907 his group of twenty-one deputies was reduced to three, albeit very vociferous ones; he himself was not elected. His aggressive behaviour and extreme politics had turned him into a caricature, although Hitler would have observed the cult his supporters still made of him.[124] He praised Schönerer's assessment of the situation in the Habsburg monarchy in *Mein Kampf*, supporting Schönerer's main demand for the Anschluss of German Austria with the German Reich, but strongly criticizing him as a politician. Schönerer had lacked clear ideas about the 'importance of the social problem', had allowed himself to become involved in parliamentary politics, and had carried on a completely pointless struggle against the Church.[125]

Hitler noted in *Mein Kampf* that, having originally been a keen Schönerer supporter, in the course of his stay in Vienna he had more and more come to admire its mayor, Karl Lueger, and his policies.[126] While he was at odds with Lueger's Christian Social ideology, Hitler considered him a political genius on account of his pragmatism and realism and indeed 'the greatest German mayor of all time'. He had had 'a rare knowledge of people' and had developed 'an exceptionally clever relationship with the Catholic Church'.[127] Lueger, who held the office of mayor between 1907 and 1910, had, through major local government projects, not only contributed to turning this city of two million people into a viable, modern metropolis, but had also established an extremely popular autocratic regime. This regime was based not least on consistently applied anti-Semitic demagoguery, in which 'the Jews' were made responsible for simply anything and everything.[128]

Hitler's two political models, Lueger and Schönerer, both used crude political rhetoric. It would, therefore, seem logical to describe them as his anti-Semitic mentors. However, in *Mein Kampf* he adopted another approach, portraying his development into a radical anti-Semite as the result of personal experiences and as his 'most difficult transformation', lasting more than two years and a phase of 'bitter internal struggle'.[129] Although this reappraisal had been initiated by his admiration for Lueger and his Christian

Social Party, Hitler made it absolutely clear that Christian-motivated anti-Semitism of this kind was a 'pseudo anti-Semitism' and, as it was not based on 'racial theory', had not grasped the core of the problem.[130] Describing how he came to rethink the issue, he wrote that his first experience was when he took offence at the appearance of orthodox Jews on the streets of Vienna: their foreignness, their strangeness led him to conclude that the Jews were a separate people. He had then looked into the question of Zionism, but had soon realized that the debates between Zionist Jews and liberal Jews were phony disagreements that only diverted attention from the real sense of solidarity that existed among Jews.

He had been disgusted by their (alleged) dirtiness – physical, but above all moral: 'was there any form of filth or shamelessness, above all in cultural life, that did not involve at least one Jew?'[131] In particular, he deplored the disastrous role played by Jews in the press, art, literature, and the theatre; he also blamed them for organizing prostitution and the white slave trade. Finally, he claimed to have got to the heart of the problem when he noticed that the whole of the Social Democratic leadership was in the hands of Jews. All these 'insights' produced an apocalyptic vision: 'If the Jew with his Marxist creed' proved victorious over the other nations of the world 'his crown' would be 'the dance of death of the human race'.[132]

This putative 'conversion' to anti-Semitism as the result of his own observations, reading, and reflexion is, however, contradicted by the reports of the witnesses, quoted above, which show that Hitler was certainly not a keen anti-Semite and describe various personal relationships he had with Jews. How can this contradiction be resolved?

When dealing with the question of Hitler's political views during his Vienna years, it is essential to ignore the hugely influential self-image Hitler cultivated in *Mein Kampf.* This was of someone predestined for an exceptional career, systematically working out his own ideology, and preparing for his extraordinary future role through a kind of course of personal study. Nothing could be more misleading. In fact, at the time, Hitler was a nobody struggling to survive day by day, who from time to time sounded off about politics, coping with his frustrations by believing that the Vienna that was treating him so badly was the capital of an empire that was doomed to destruction. His apathy and inability to liberate himself from his situation on the margins of society are remarkable when compared with the energy he unleashed from 1919 onwards. As we shall see, it was only in the particular post-war situation and in the context of revolution and counter-revolution in Bavaria, in other words very largely as a result of external circumstances, that Hitler was effectively catapulted into a political career.

Thus to pose the question of whether or not Hitler acquired his radical anti-Semitism in Vienna, or rather how far his Vienna years laid the foundations for his further 'career' as an anti-Semite is to approach the problem from the wrong angle. Anti-Semitism basically represents a distorted awareness of social reality; it provides pseudo-explanations for complex phenomena. Anti-Semitism must always be seen and interpreted within the context of the prevailing political and social ideas; its 'arguments' are, depending on the context, almost completely interchangeable. As a supporter of Schönerer's ideology, Hitler considered that he was confronted with a veritable phalanx of enemies: the monarchy, the state apparatus, the nobility, parliament, the Catholic Church, Slavs, Jews, as well as the Marxist workers' movement. All, in his view, formed a fateful coalition, whose efforts were bent on humiliating the German-speakers in the Habsburg empire. Seen in this light, his anti-Semitism referred to one enemy among a number of 'antis'. In a city in which anti-Semitism was a fixture of everyday life and formed the basis of the popular city government, and with his anti-Semitism 'bracketed' by many other enemies, Hitler was in no way remarkable. What was really radical about his ideology at the time was not his anti-Semitism but his rejection of the current political order, based as it was on numerous imagined enemies.

Apart from the ever-present anti-Semitism, during his stay in the Austrian capital Hitler is likely to have come into contact with all sorts of ethnic and racist ideas via Pan-German journalism. Notions such as that of a superior Nordic race, the racial inferiority of Jews, 'Negroes', and Asiatics, and ideas of racial breeding and of the need to maintain racial purity to prevent degeneracy were fairly widespread in Vienna, particularly during the pre-war years. But the notion that, during his Vienna years, he had already had one or more ideological 'mentors' from the racist-esoteric scene cannot be proved any more than can the thesis, put forward in the first instance by Hitler himself, that he had distilled a fully-formed world view from the existing concoction of ethnic nationalist (völkisch) and anti-Semitic ideas.[133]

Munich

In May 1913 Hitler turned his back on Vienna. Together with a certain Rudolf Häusler, an acquaintance from the men's hostel in Meldemannstrasse, he moved to Munich, where he basically resumed his old life-style. During the first months, he tried to live as best he could from his paintings. Apart from that, he pursued his various 'studies', without apparently having tried to acquire any formal education or regular work. During this period, apart from Häusler, with whom he shared lodgings for a time at Schleissheimer Strasse 43, a boarding house belonging to a widow, Anna Popp, he does not appear to have had any close acquaintances, let alone friends, and was considered by those who knew him to be very much a loner.[134]

Anton Joachimsthaler has collected various documents from which it is clear that Hitler wandered through the centre of Munich selling his pictures, mainly water colours of historical buildings, in bars or to shops. He evidently tried to play the sympathy card: his customers saw in this rather shabby young man an impecunious student or an unemployed artist. Some even placed orders with him.[135] As far as officialdom was concerned, he called himself an artist. In later years he repeatedly claimed that he had maintained his interest in politics during his Munich years, not so much by attending meetings as by intensive reading. He had allegedly concentrated in particular on 'Marxism' and anti-Semitism, thereby providing 'positively granite foundations' for his political views.[136] There are good reasons for regarding this account of his 'personal study' as a further addition to the legend that Hitler was constructing around himself; at any rate, there is no evidence that he ever became politically engaged.[137]

What prompted Hitler to move to Munich? There were probably several reasons for this decision.

On reaching 24 years of age he could claim his inheritance from his father, and the sum of 700 Kronen, on which he could easily live for a year, enabled him to move. His dislike of Vienna after five 'years of suffering' was obvious, whereas Munich as a 'city of culture' offered him the opportunity of continuing his bohemian existence in new surroundings. The pre-war years in Munich, he wrote in *Mein Kampf*, were 'the happiest and by far the most contented of my life', not least because he had felt Munich to be a 'German city', to which he had been bound by 'heartfelt love'.[138] Because he had felt so happy on the banks of the Isar, in *Mein Kampf* he put back the start of his stay by a year and claimed that he had already moved to Munich in 1912.

In his Table Talk in October 1941 Hitler gave a further reason for his move: he had thought of attending an architectural academy in Germany, for which an advanced school certificate was not required, as was the case in Austria. But then, once in Munich, he had decided to do three more years of 'practical training' before applying to become a draughtsman at the leading construction firm of Heilmann & Littmann. Evidently, he had planned to use this position as a springboard for a future career as an architect.[139]

In addition, he had a further, very practical motive for quitting Austria. In 1909, at the age of twenty, Hitler should have registered with the army recruitment authorities and then a year later been called up. This he had failed to do, nor had he done so subsequently. To move abroad without having registered for military service was a serious offence. Moreover, it was exacerbated by the fact that, on leaving Vienna, he had not given Munich as his future place of residence, thereby indicating that he wanted to cover his tracks from the Austrian authorities. From August 1913 onwards, Hitler was being sought by the Linz police for 'avoiding call-up', and in January 1914 he was located, thanks to the cooperation of the Munich police and brought before the Austrian Consulate-General in Munich. His excuse that he had registered as a potential conscript in 1910 in Vienna and had had no intention of avoiding military service was accepted, as it was impossible to disprove it in Munich. He was permitted to undergo his medical in Salzburg on 5 February 1914, where he was declared 'unfit for military service'.[140] Six months later, the First World War broke out.

World war

The response to Germany's declaration of war in the summer of 1914 within Germany itself was mixed: on the one hand, enthusiastic approval, on the other open discontent and protest, and in between, much nervousness, apprehension, and anxiety. The 'August experience', that spontaneous wave of nationalist enthusiasm that had allegedly united the nation (an idea that played such a large role in the press reports of the time and in the memories of nationalistic Germans) is a very one-sided portrayal of the national mood of the time and one subsequently spread by the authorities.

In fact, it was only certain sections of the Munich population who greeted the threat of war at the end of July 1914 with patriotic enthusiasm.[141] When Germany mobilized and declared war on Russia on the evening of 1 August, there was a spontaneous demonstration in the city centre; a few thousand people surged to the Wittelsbach palace and paid homage to the king. The following day a crowd assembled at 12 o'clock, when there was a changing of the guard in front of the palace, in order to express their patriotism, among other things by singing patriotic songs. There is a photograph of the scene, taken by Hitler's subsequent personal photographer, Heinrich Hoffmann, in which Hitler can be identified, albeit not wholly reliably, being swept up in the enthusiasm. However, Hoffmann's photograph is not so much a document of the actual popular mood as part of a patriotic propaganda campaign: the photographer pressed the button just at the point when the crowd, which filled only part of the Odeonsplatz, was being filmed by a film camera at the edge of the square and when it was expressing its enthusiasm in a particularly visible way.[142]

The outbreak of war jolted Hitler out of his apathy. For him, he wrote in *Mein Kampf*, 'those hours seemed like a release from the most painful feelings of my youth'.[143] In the confusion of the first phase of mobilization he succeeded in being taken on as a volunteer by the 2nd Infantry Regiment. The fact that he was an Austrian citizen and therefore not really eligible to serve in the Bavarian army was ignored; his only recently having been declared unfit for service was also evidently deemed irrelevant. On 16 August, he joined the regiment and on 1 September was assigned to the recently formed 16th Reserve Infantry Regiment.[144]

In the army, Hitler for the first time in his life found himself subject to a regime of rules, accepted as a member of a group (albeit in the role of an outsider), and acquiring a purpose in life. In one of his Table Talks in October 1941 he described the almost five years he spent in the army as the 'only time' in his life when he had 'no worries'.[145] From his point of view, as a soldier he had for the first time the chance of carrying out a concrete and purposeful task that matched his high-flown fantasies: he was absolutely convinced that the war would produce a victorious 'Greater Germany'.

Contrary to the long-standing legend, the 16th Reserve Infantry Regiment was not a regiment of volunteers; only 30 per cent of the soldiers who joined in 1914 did so voluntarily. The majority of the members of the regiment consisted of 'Ersatz-Reservists', in other words men who had hitherto been excused national service.[146] The social composition of the regiment was similar to that of the Bavarian population as a whole.[147] On 10 October, after being inspected by King Ludwig III of Bavaria, the regiment moved into Lechfeld camp where it underwent a ten-day course of fairly intensive training that almost exhausted a large number of its members. The first five days at Lechfeld, Hitler wrote to his former landlady, Frau

Popp, 'were the most taxing of my life'.[148] On 21 October, the regiment was transferred to the western front; according to Hitler, during their journey through the Reich, the troop trains were enthusiastically greeted by the population.[149] On 24 October, the infantrymen arrived in Lille, from where, after a few days, they were marched to the front.[150]

On 29 October, the regiment had its first experience of combat. As part of the so-called First Battle of Flanders, which had begun on 20 October, an attack group was created from the German 6th Army, with the aim of supporting the offensive of the 4th Army further north, along the Channel coast. The 6th Bavarian Reserve Division including Hitler's regiment, which was commonly called the List regiment after the name of its first commander, formed part of this attack group. On the morning of 29 October, the regiment had the task of taking the village of Gheluvelt, held by troops of the British IV Corps. The inexperienced, inadequately trained, and poorly equipped soldiers from Bavaria – for example, they had not received any helmets, but wore territorial army caps – found themselves confronted by well-trained units made up of professional soldiers, although during the three-day engagement the latter made numerous tactical errors.[151] Moreover, the List regiment not only had to fight the British; numerous losses were caused by friendly fire because the members of the List regiment were thought to be British on account of their unusual head gear.[152]

Hitler's own account and the reports of other members of the regiment provide a striking picture of the fearful chaos of this 'baptism of fire'. The attack took place on broken ground with numerous obstacles: hedges, fences, and ditches held up the advance, while farmsteads, copses, and spinneys provided the enemy with sufficient cover to mount ambushes. Governed no doubt by a mixture of fear and desperate courage, the inexperienced troops, who had not yet felt the effects of artillery and machine-gun fire, pressed forwards; the attack then broke up into a series of uncoordinated bands, who were continually pushed to go on by their officers and NCOs. Three months later, using his unique orthography, Hitler described this experience in a detailed letter to a Munich acquaintance, a lawyer, Ernst Hepp,[153] as if it had only just happened. Even by February 1915 Hitler had evidently still not got over his experiences during the previous autumn.

'We creep along the ground until we reach the edge of the forest. Shells scream and whistle overhead, tree trunks and branches are flying all around us. Then once again shells crash into the edge of the wood sending up clouds of stones, earth and sand, uprooting the biggest trees and suffocating everything in a yellow–grey stinking mist.... Then, our major arrives. He goes on ahead. I jump up and run as fast as I can over meadows and turnip fields, over ditches, climb over wire and hedges and then, in front of me, I hear shouts: "In here, everybody, in here." I see a long trench in front of me; a moment later I jump in, as do a large number of others, in front of me, behind me, to the left and right. Beside me there are Würt[t]embergers, under me dead and wounded Britons.' After their own artillery had begun targeting the British lines, the attack continued: 'We advance rapidly across the fields and, after, in some cases bloody, hand-to-hand combat, we kick the chaps out of their trenches one after the other. Many put their hands up. Those who don't surrender are killed. We clear them out trench by trench.' But finally the attack stalled until the battalion commander intervened: 'The major quickly reviews the situation and orders us to prepare to attack to the right and left of the road. We have no more officers left and hardly any NCOs. So those of us who are a bit plucky go back to get reinforcements. When I return a second time with a troop of Würt[t]embergers who had become separated from their units the major is lying on the ground with his chest split open and surrounded by a pile of bodies. Now there is one officer left, his adjutant. We are boiling with rage. Everybody shouts: "Lieutenant, take the lead and let's attack!" So, on we go through the forest to the left; we can't get through on the road. Four times we press forward and each time have to go back again; from my whole lot there is only one left apart from me, and in the end he too falls. A bullet has torn off the whole of the right arm of my coat, but miraculously I am unharmed and OK. Finally at two o'clock we make a fifth attempt and this time we manage to take the edge of the forest and the farmstead.'[154]

In *Mein Kampf* Hitler describes how the attacking soldiers had sung 'Deutschland, Deutschland über alles', and how this had spread from company to company.[155] His own report of the battle, composed much closer to the events, does not contain this incident and nor do the other contemporary reports of this attack. Evidently Hitler took the liberty of borrowing from the numerous post–war descriptions of the patriotic courage of those 'volunteer regiments' who, based near Langemarck (a good ten kilometres north of Gheluvelt), had been cut down by British machine guns while singing 'Deutschland, Deutschland über alles'.[156]

After three days of bitter fighting the regiment finally succeeded in taking the village, but they did not secure the real goal of the offensive, namely the capture of the city of Ypres. Around 75 per cent of the reserve regiment had been killed or wounded. Among the dead was its commander, Julius List.[157] The offensive became bogged down in trench warfare and little changed in this respect during the following four years.[158] To begin with, however, after a short break for rest and recuperation, in November the regiment was integrated into the front running through Flanders, initially near Messines,[159] then a few days later, near Wytschaete,[160] where it took part in more heavy fighting, and then again near Messines.[161]

After the war had come to a halt, the soldiers directly on the front line inevitably had to dig themselves in using a system of trenches and dugouts. With the onset of winter, fighting on this part of the front gradually died down, even though casualties still occurred through artillery salvos, enemy snipers, and occasional British reconnaissance sorties.[162]

During the winter it was above all the unpleasant conditions in the trenches that made the soldiers' lives a misery. 'As a result of the endless rain (we don't have any winter), the proximity to the sea and the low-lying land, the meadows and fields are like bottomless marshes, while the roads are covered with mud a foot deep. And our trenches run through this bog', Hitler wrote to Munich.[163] The soldiers often stood up to their knees in water, trenches had to be abandoned because they had been transformed into streams. Maintaining even a minimum of hygiene under these conditions was impossible.[164]

On 3 November, Hitler was promoted to the rank of corporal and, on 9 November, assigned to the staff of the regiment as a runner.[165] In this capacity his job was primarily to take messages from regimental headquarters several kilometres behind the front line to the forward battalion headquarters or to neighbouring regiments, but generally not to the front line itself.[166] In the event that their own positions were under heavy attack this was a dangerous job; most of the time, however, there was relative peace on the front line and the advantages of being a runner predominated. Unlike his regimental comrades, Hitler did not have to spend days and nights in the bog and dirt of the trenches; most of his time was passed on standby in the (forward) headquarters of the regiment or in the relatively secure regimental headquarters further in the rear, where he had fairly comfortable sleeping quarters, and one can assume that his constant proximity to staff officers would have provided certain privileges. In quiet periods he could read, draw, and paint; he even kept a little dog called Foxl. While around a quarter of the soldiers of the List regiment, which was continually being replenished, were killed, none of the eight members of Hitler's group of runners, who were with him from 1915 onwards, were killed during their military service.[167] Hitler did everything he could to hang on to his posting.[168]

According to Fritz Wiedemann, who was the regimental adjutant at the time, Hitler was considered particularly reliable. Thus, along with two or three other comrades, he was used as little as possible for conveying routine messages, and kept back for especially difficult assignments. From a military standpoint, however, Hitler had not cut 'a particularly impressive figure': his bearing was sloppy, his head 'usually tilted towards his left shoulder'. His responses were 'anything but soldierly and brief'; he did not have 'what it takes to be in command of others', but nor had he sought promotion. After the Second World War, Max Amann, Hitler's sergeant-major and later head of the German press, stated that Hitler had been 'quite appalled' when offered promotion. Amann described Hitler as 'obedient, zealous in the performance of his duties, and modest'.[169]

On 15 November 1914, Hitler was accompanying the new regimental commander, Philipp Engelhardt, to the front, when the latter unexpectedly came under fire. Together with another soldier – according to another account, there were four of them – Hitler placed himself in front of the officer to protect him and urged him to take cover.[170] When, at the beginning of December, sixty Iron Crosses Second Class were given out to members of the regiment, among those honoured were the runners who had saved the regimental commander a fortnight earlier.[171] Hitler wrote to Joseph Popp, a Munich acquaintance: 'It was the happiest day of my life'.[172]

On 12 March 1915 the regiment took part in a costly German counter-offensive near Neuve Chapelle,[173] subsequently taking up new positions in front of the village of Fromelles.[174] The regiment was holding a section of the front just over 2,300 metres in length; six companies took it in turns to man the front line, with six remaining in reserve, of which three were quartered in the rear.[175] Most of the time in the forward section was spent in the routine of trench warfare with relatively little combat; the soldiers were occupied, above all, with expanding trenches and fortifications, as well as the struggle to keep water from leaking into the trenches and dealing with vermin. However, there were a number of major engagements. In May 1915 the British breached the line of the 16th Reserve Regiment, which suffered heavy casualties in retaking the position on the following day.[176] In July they managed to thwart a British-Australian attack.[177]

In September 1916 the regiment was relieved and, at the beginning of October, deployed to the Battle of the Somme, which had been raging since July as the British ambitiously tried to wear down the German forces in a 'battle of attrition'. On 5 October, the regimental runners' dugout, which was approximately two kilometres behind the front line, was hit by artillery fire. Hitler suffered a wound to the leg and was sent to hospital in Beelitz.[178] He remained there for eight weeks and, while recuperating, used the opportunity to visit nearby Berlin, where, among things, he visited the National Gallery.

At the beginning of November Hitler travelled to Munich in order to join a replacement unit, the 2nd Infantry Regiment. Reflecting on his visits to Beelitz, Berlin, and Munich, Hitler noted in *Mein Kampf* that he had become aware of a powerful mood of defeatism: 'irritation, discontent, and grumbling', cowardice, and 'skiving'. And, he went on, the offices of the home army were packed with Jews; the war economy was in the hands of the Jews.[179] Anti-Semitism was in fact increasing during the second half of the war; there was widespread talk of alleged Jewish 'skivers' and 'war profiteers'. It would, however, be simplistic to assume that this atmosphere reinforced Hitler's anti-Semitism. It is, indeed, remarkable that we do not have any documentary evidence of Hitler's anti-Semitism for the period of the First World War.[180]

To prevent his being transferred to another regiment Hitler wrote to Wiedemann, who responded by requesting his transfer to the staff of the 16th Reserve Regiment and, at the beginning of March 1917, Hitler rejoined the regiment, which was now based near La Bassée.[181] In April the regiment was driven out of its positions by a Canadian attack,[182] but a few weeks later, after a short pause for rest and recuperation, it was in action once again in the Battle of Arras.[183] The following months were largely spent resting behind the lines,[184] interrupted by short and bloody engagements in the second half of July, when for two weeks the regiment lay under constant enemy fire, losing 800 men. No longer capable of fighting, it was withdrawn from the front line, but parts of it became involved in the major British offensive that began on 31 July.[185]

At the beginning of August the exhausted regiment was transferred to the front in Alsace. Here, in the middle of September 1917, Hitler received the Military Service Cross Third Class[186] and, at the end of the month, was permitted to go on leave, which he spent in Berlin with the parents of a comrade.[187] In the meantime, his regiment had been transferred to the

Champagne region. In March and April 1918 it was once more involved in costly engagements, this time in support of Germany's spring offensive, the last major attempt by the German Army to defeat the Western Allies. In April alone the regiment lost almost half of its soldiers through death, wounds, and disease. After the German offensive came to a halt at the beginning of June, the regiment was pulled out of the front line, but was transferred after only a fortnight to the Marne front and, during the second half of July, became involved in the Battle of the Marne, the last attempt of the German Army to reach Paris. At the end of July, the regiment was withdrawn from this section of the front as well.[188] At the beginning of August, Hitler was awarded the Iron Cross First Class, an extremely rare distinction for someone who was not an officer. It was justified on the grounds that Hitler had carried an important message to the front under heavy enemy fire, although it was probably in recognition of his overall performance.[189] He was put forward by Wiedemann's successor, the regimental adjutant, Lieutenant Hugo Gutmann. As Gutmann was a Jew, in later years Hitler slandered him as a 'coward'.[190]

It seems difficult to deny that Hitler was a conscientious and, when it mattered, courageous soldier, even if many accounts by former comrades and superiors are contradictory or seem to have been influenced by the Nazi Party.[191] What is crucial, however, is the fact that as a runner he had a special role, which meant that his 'war experiences' were markedly different from those of the majority of German soldiers. Unlike millions of others, he did not have to spend years putting up with living in trenches, which in winter filled up with mud and water, where illnesses such as dysentery and typhus were rampant, and where soldiers were plagued with lice and rats and in summer with huge numbers of flies.

In *Mein Kampf* Hitler is quite frank about his anxieties and inner conflicts during the first phase of the war: the 'romance of the battlefield' was soon replaced by 'horror', the initial exuberant joy was 'stifled by mortal fear'. Like everybody else, he too had had to cope with 'the struggle between the instinct for self-preservation and the admonitions of duty'. He describes in striking images how always when 'death was on the hunt' 'a vague something' inside him had tried to revolt, tried 'to represent itself to my weak body as reason', an inner voice, which he had nevertheless been able to identify as nothing but cowardice. It was only after lengthy inner struggle, 'a strong tugging and warning', he wrote, that he was able to overcome these temptations. But 'the more this voice urged me to take heed, the louder and the more insistently it tempted me, the tougher was my resistance, until finally, after a long inner struggle my sense of duty triumphed.' 'Already in winter 1915/16', in other words after more than a year's experience of war, this inner struggle had ended: 'At last my will was undisputed master.'[192]

Even though this passage is clearly shaped by Hitler's desire to project himself as a 'man of will', it nevertheless reveals something about the inner conflicts he was going through at the time: he was not totally unaffected by the horrors of war. The extreme stress he felt during the first months also left its mark on his letters. In January 1915 he wrote that he was hoping that the attack would soon be launched: 'otherwise, one's nerves are liable to go to pieces'. A fortnight later he confessed to being 'very stressed'; 'in the end' heavy artillery fire 'ruins the strongest nerves'.[193] Two and a half decades later he had evidently completely rationalized this experience, using it to provide a justification, based on his life experience, for his ideological maxims. In September 1941, in one of his Table Talks, he declared that, in view of the massive suffering and death on the battlefields of the First World War, he had become aware that 'life is a continuous cruel struggle, serving in the final analysis to maintain the species'.[194] Both of these statements – his comments in Mein Kampf and the remarks in the Table Talk – show how concerned Hitler was after the event to master the shock of his wartime experience and to use his success in overcoming those anxieties to form part of his self-image.

In the memoirs of his former comrades and superiors Hitler remains a colourless figure, accepted by the group, but a somewhat eccentric loner. During the trips he made with his comrades to the nearby city of Lille, he usually kept to himself and avoided the usual pleasures available behind the front line such as alcohol binges or amorous adventures.[195] In fact, it seems that throughout the war years he had no relationship of any kind with a woman.[196] And, when conversation among his comrades turned to 'Topic No. 1', he brushed it aside, according to Brandmayer, saying he did not have a girlfriend and 'I'll never get round to having one'.[197]

His sergeant-major, Amann, recalled that Hitler was the only one of the men under him who never received a parcel from home: 'He didn't have anyone; he was modest and undemanding. But he was a bit odd.' When, on one occasion, there was a surplus in the canteen funds, he had offered Hitler, as the 'poorest man', a small sum of money. But he had rejected the gift.[198]

Despite spending years living together with a relatively small and unchanging group of soldiers and NCOs, Hitler did not to try to establish closer contacts or become friends with his comrades. After the end of the war he evidently did not feel the need to maintain personal contacts or cultivate 'war comradeship' with his fellow soldiers. He kept his distance from Amann, whom he employed in the Nazi Party from 1921 onwards, and the same was true of Wiedemann, who became his adjutant in 1933. It is true that after 1933 he was generous in providing jobs or sums of money for any former comrades who turned to him with a request for support; he received them when they visited him and, in 1940, even allowed one of them, Fritz Schmidt, to accompany him on a tour of their old battlefields in Flanders. However, these were the condescending gestures of a powerful patron and had nothing to do with friendship.[199] Significantly, when speaking of his wartime experiences in later years Hitler referred to only one relationship that had affected him emotionally, the one with his dog, Foxl, to which he had become closely attached and which he allowed to sleep with him.[200]

Politics do not seem to have played a significant part in his conversations with his comrades. However, Hitler became annoyed when anyone cast doubt on a German victory and invariably allowed himself to be provoked by such talk.[201] One of the other regimental runners, who published his war memoirs in 1932, recalled that Hitler had criticized the munitions workers' strike of January 1918 (a mass protest against the war organized by the Left) and, in particular, attacked the leadership of the Social Democrats. However, Hitler's wartime comrade, Brandmayer, made no mention of endless anti-Semitic tirades, which were to figure so prominently in Hitler's standard repertoire in later years when the question of the 'betrayal' of the front by the homeland came up for discussion.[202] Thus, although he writes in another section of his book that Hitler was 'the only one of us... who recognized what has now become a certainty, namely that the war [was] started by Freemasons and Jews', Hitler does not seem to have bothered his comrades with this 'insight'.[203]

As far as his political comments at the time were concerned, Hitler expressed himself in *Mein Kampf* in remarkably general terms. He wrote that although, in principle, he had not wanted 'to have anything to do with politics', he had been unable to avoid defining his attitude towards 'certain phenomena that affected the nation as a whole, but most of all us soldiers'. In other words, even he himself did not claim to have tried to inform his comrades at the time about his purported insights concerning the Jews.[204]

In a letter he wrote at the beginning of February 1915 to an acquaintance, Ernst Hepp, a Munich lawyer, Hitler remarked that he and his comrades were hoping after the war to find the homeland cleansed 'from foreign influence'; they were fighting at the front against an 'international world of enemies' and wanted 'our internal internationalism to be eliminated as well'.[205] This comment exactly reflected the extreme hostility to foreigners and aggressive nationalism that dominated Germany after the outbreak of war; his criticism of 'internal internationalism' no doubt referred to the Social Democrats.

The fact that, even within the army, Hitler remained an outsider and through his role as a runner managed to secure a special position for himself outside the routine of trench warfare[206] is a key to his personality. His time in the army is the only period in his life in which, as a thoroughly unorganized person, someone who enjoyed sleeping in, a daydreamer and loner, he was compelled to conform to an organization with fixed rules, structures, and roles; and yet he succeeded relatively quickly in evading these demands as far as he possibly could. He very wisely omitted to mention his role as runner in Mein Kampf. In praising the 'iron front of grey helmets', which he had joined out of a sense of duty and without complaint, he did so in order to provide as little detail as possible about his four years of military service.[207] And, in fact, when, in the early 1930s, it looked as though Hitler might be about to take over power in Germany, a number of former comrades emerged to accuse him of having led a privileged and less dangerous life in comparison with that of the normal front-line soldier.[208]

In the last week of August 1918 Hitler was sent to Nuremberg on a short course for couriers, while his regiment had to face further major and costly defensive engagements.[209] Shortly afterwards, Hitler was given a second two and a half weeks' leave, which he once again spent in Berlin. He does not mention this stay in Mein Kampf, giving the impression that he had spent the whole summer involved in the defensive battles in Flanders. In fact, he only returned to his unit at the end of September.[210]

A few days later, on 3 October, a newly-formed German government, which, for the first time, was responsible to parliament, approached the American president, Woodrow Wilson, with the request for an armistice. This was in response to the 'advice', in effect an ultimatum, from General Ludendorff, who had reached the conclusion that Germany was in immediate danger of losing the war. The request for an armistice – in effect an admission of defeat – came as a complete surprise to the German population and the army, and must have shocked Hitler, who had always been confident of victory. Later, in Mein Kampf, he blamed the defeat on the 'poison in the home front', which had increasingly affected the troops.[211] According to his later interpretation of events, the disaster had been planned by a coalition of Socialists and Jews. However, it is highly doubtful that he was already thinking along these lines in the autumn of 1918.

Two weeks after his return – in the meantime, the regiment had been transferred to Ypres, in other words the section of the front where it had begun the war four years earlier – Hitler, together with other members of the regimental staff, were caught up in a British gas attack, from which he suffered an eye injury and temporary damage to his sight (according to Hitler, temporary blindness). From 21 October onwards, he was hospitalized in Pasewalk in the Prussian province of Pomerania; while he was there, revolution broke out and the war came to an end.[212]

With a good deal of self-pity and exaggerated emotion Hitler described in *Mein Kampf* the moment when news reached him in hospital of the fall of the Kaiser's Reich and the conclusion of the armistice, which sealed Germany's defeat. According to his account, he was sunk in the deepest despair, had wept for the first time since the death of his mother, and had felt a deep shame, which had had an immediate physical effect. 'While everything began to go black again before my eyes, stumbling, I groped my way back to the dormitory, threw myself on my bunk and buried my burning head in the blankets and pillows.' The more he tried 'to take in this terrible event, the more the shame, indignation and disgrace were branded on my brow'. We do not know what Hitler really thought in Pasewalk. The quotations are evidence from 1924, in which Hitler was trying subsequently to convey to readers how defeat had affected him at the time. But these quotations also have much to say about him.

This picture of a man who was almost thirty years old, throwing himself onto his bed and burying his face in the pillows, wanting to hide because he could not face reality, suggests someone who is reverting to childish behaviour in the face of a situation with which he simply cannot cope. The proof of Hitler's assertion that his shame was so great that he lost his sight can no longer be tested; it can, however, be read as a metaphor for his refusal to face facts. Shattered by news of the defeat, he responded to this 'disgrace' and 'humiliation' as an individual who was isolated, in despair, and unable to explain or process these alarming developments.

In November 1918 millions of German soldiers had to get used to the fact that the years of bloody struggle had been for nothing. But for the majority this was a collective experience and not primarily a personal catastrophe.

For most soldiers German defeat meant at the same time the longed-for end to mass slaughter, their return to their families and civilian jobs, and the beginning of a new stage in their lives. Hitler, however, a loner and a loser, could not share the shock of defeat with others and this was primarily the result of his psychological make-up rather than the objective circumstances, nor did he have another life to which he could return. On the contrary: while the outbreak of war in 1914 had given him the chance to get his aimless life back on track, now, after four years of military service, this prospect had been suddenly removed.

According to Hitler's description of his state of mind at the time, during the following days his depression had turned into fury and hatred – hatred of the forces he blamed for the defeat, primarily the 'leaders of Marxism' and 'the Jews'. And, while still in Pasewalk, he claimed he had reached a decision that was to give his life a completely new direction: 'I decided to become a politician'.[213]

This 'decision' is undoubtedly part of the subsequent self-image that Hitler was creating. Everything points to the fact that, after his release from Pasewalk, far from laying the foundations for a political career, he was simply swept along in the stream of millions of returning soldiers, waiting to see how things would develop after the defeat. It took several months before he emerged from this state of passivity and lethargy, and he only began to become politically active in the summer of 1919 following the initiative and under the auspices of the Reichswehr [German army]. The Pasewalk epiphany – the 'recognition' that 'Jewish Marxism' was responsible for the fatherland's misery – and the resultant decision to 'become a politician' was an attempt by Hitler to conceal his uncertain behaviour during the immediate post-war period. His account is nevertheless highly significant because, if we read between the lines, Hitler is actually describing quite frankly how he succeeded in overcoming his deep shame about the defeat, which had initially plunged him into a state of helplessness. He refused to undertake a sober analysis of the causes of the catastrophe; he was not prepared to admit weaknesses and failure, but instead tried to explain the revolutionary events as the result of a gigantic manipulation. This stoked his anger and his desire for revenge, thereby providing him with the destructive energy necessary to punish those whom he blamed for the deepest humiliation of his life and to overcome his shame.

PART I

The Public Self

I

Back in Munich

Politicization

Following his release from Pasewalk hospital, Hitler arrived in Munich on 21 November 1918. As the 16th Reserve Infantry Regiment, to which he had belonged during the previous four years, was still on its way back from the western front, he was assigned to the 7th Company of the 1st Replacement Battalion of the 2nd Infantry Regiment.[1]

On 4 November 1918, a sailors' uprising in the naval base of Kiel sparked off a revolution in Germany; five days later, the Reich government in Berlin was taken over by a Council of People's Representatives, composed of members of the two Socialist parties. Meanwhile, on 7 November the revolution had triumphed in Munich. The uprising under Kurt Eisner, the leader of the Munich branch of the Independent Social Democratic Party of Germany [USPD], had quickly forced King Ludwig III to flee from his palace, enabling Eisner, who had met with no resistance, to proclaim Bavaria, the second largest German state, a 'free state'. The war-weariness felt by broad sections of the population and the widespread discontent with the monarchical regime had resulted in major political change. On the following day, 8 November, a 'National Council', made up of representatives of peasants' and soldiers' councils, the parliamentary groups of the SPD and the Bavarian Peasant League, as well as three Liberal deputies, took over the government and declared Eisner Prime Minister.[2] Soldiers' councils were established in the city's barracks with the 2nd Infantry Regiment council dominated by moderate Social Democrats.[3]

At the beginning of December, Hitler was assigned to guard duties with the main task of guarding prisoners of war in the Traunstein prisoner-of-war camp, approximately 100 kilometres east of Munich. Surviving reports on conditions in the camp indicate that the discipline of the troops there was deteriorating fast, of which Hitler must have been fully aware.[4] At the beginning of February, the camp was closed. Hitler had presumably already returned to Munich in January,[5] where he was assigned to the regiment's demobilization battalion.[6] His demobilization was thus only a matter of time.[7]

He had, however, been chosen as his company's soldiers' council representative, a fact that he understandably kept quiet about throughout his life.[8] The role of these representatives – they were not really soldiers' councillors – was primarily to facilitate the supply of soldiers for farm work.[9] A special department of the Munich soldiers' council did try to use the representatives to influence soldiers, although it is difficult to estimate the effect of these efforts and there is no evidence for Hitler's involvement.[10] There is, however, no doubt that the Munich troops were under strong left-wing revolutionary influence at this time. On Sunday 16 February, for example, the off-duty soldiers of the demobilization battalion were ordered by the battalion to take part, along with the whole of the Munich garrison, in a demonstration of the revolutionary workers' council to demand the establishment of a Räterepublik (republic based on the councils).[11] However, in the state elections of 12 January Eisner's left-wing Independent Social Democratic Party of Germany suffered a crushing defeat, winning only three seats, whereas the moderate Majority Social Democrats [MSPD] won 61 and the Catholic Bavarian People's Party [BVP] 66 seats, each representing about a third of the electorate. Eisner, therefore, decided to resign.

A series of events then occurred which prevented a return to stability. On 21 February, Eisner was assassinated on his way to the opening of parliament by Lieutenant Arco auf Valley, an anti-democrat and anti-Semite. This led to a second revolution in Munich: the MSPD, USPD, Communist Party [KPD], and the Bavarian Peasant League established a Central Council of the Bavarian Republic and martial law was invoked in the city.[12] Eisner's funeral procession on 26 February turned into a powerful demonstration of the Left; 100,000 people are alleged to have taken part, among them *possibly* Adolf Hitler. A film and a photograph have survived, both of which show a soldier who could be Hitler, and in fact twenty-five men of Hitler's battalion and six barracks representatives had been ordered to take part in the procession.[13]

On 17 March, the MSPD, USPD, and Peasants' League formed a new government under the Majority Social Democrat, Johannes Hoffmann, which obtained a parliamentary majority. This led to a split in the Central Council, with the radical majority aiming to set up a Räterepublik.[14] The barracks councils of the 1st and 2nd Infantry Regiments supported this initiative.[15] On 7 April, a Revolutionary Central Council, made up of various council and party representatives, proclaimed a Räterepublik heavily dominated by the USPD.[16] On 13 April, the government, which had fled to Bamberg, failed in its attempt to crush the revolutionary regime with the aid of troops stationed in Munich. This led to the establishment of a new communist Räterepublik,[17] which the following day won the support of the soldiers' representatives of the Munich garrison. A new election of representatives was held on 15 April in which Hitler was re-elected by the 2nd Company. He was now a Replacement Battalion councillor. This, however, does not prove that Hitler was a supporter of the council movement during the first months of 1919, any more than do other examples of Hitler's activity during this period. The fact that he was elected twice by his comrades suggests above all that he wanted to remain in the disintegrating army for as long as possible; as an elected representative he could not so easily be demobilized. In this situation he was obliged to follow the orders of the soldiers' council and, on certain occasions, to act as the representative of his company, although we cannot know what his own political attitude was.[18] This also applies to the brief phase of the communist Räterepublik. Presumably, he behaved much like the other soldiers of his unit, namely waiting to see which way the wind would blow, neither actively supporting the communist regime nor outwardly opposing it.

His own account in *Mein Kampf*, in which he claims to have actively opposed the communist regime and to have escaped arrest on 27 April only by threatening to shoot, is implausible.[19] For there is evidence that, at the time, Hitler did not simply see the MSPD as 'November criminals'. When, at an NSDAP meeting in July 1921, he was defending his fellow Party member, Hermann Esser, against the serious accusation of being a spy, Hitler dismissed it by saying: 'We've all been Social Democrats at one time or another'.[20] Also, various statements in his Table Talk from the years 1941/42 make it clear that, with hindsight, he did not see the role of the MSPD during the revolutionary period in entirely negative terms.[21] However, such comments reflected a view of Social Democracy as an anti-revolutionary force, as a force for order that in the spring of 1919 had opposed further left-wing radicalization. For, united in the aim of bringing the revolutionary experiment in Bavaria to an end as quickly as possible, both the Reich government and the government in Bavaria had been led by Majority Social Democrats.

The rapid radicalization of the political situation, leading to the establishment of a communist regime, was supported by only a relatively small minority of the population in Munich. The Reich government declared a state of emergency for Bavaria and, at the beginning of May, had the state capital occupied by a large force of troops; hundreds of citizens, accused of supporting the Räterepublik, were murdered.[22] The soldiers of the Munich garrison did not take part in the conflict and were disarmed in their barracks by the invading Reich government troops. According to the orders of the new military authorities, those soldiers who had been resident in Munich before the war, were to be demobilized.[23] For Hitler, who had no prospects in civilian life, this would have represented a personal catastrophe. But, once again, he found a way out. Within a week after the end of the Räterepublik he was nominated as a member of a three-man investigation team to look into the behaviour of members of the regiment during the recent events. Had he been using his role as a council representative openly to support the Räterepublik he would not have been picked for this job. As it was, by proving a keen 'investigator' he could now refute any accusations that he had compromised himself politically during the Räterepublik. During his appointment to the investigation commission, on 10 May 1919, he was assigned to the 'Detached Company' and so, for the time being, remained in the army.[24] Hitler's former superior on the regimental staff, Sergeant-Major Amann, was very surprised when, on his release from the army, he found himself confronted by Hitler in his new role.[25] The commission was investigating, in particular, the former barrack councillor, August Klumpf, who in fact had been an opponent of the councils' regime; the investigation concluded with his complete rehabilitation.[26] In another case there is evidence that Hitler was a witness in the court martial of the former chairman of the battalion council of the Demobilisation Battalion, Georg Dufter; he was found not guilty.[27]

Munich after the crushing of the revolution

Remarkably, conservative Bavaria had been the scene of a socialist revolution that had quickly become radicalized. Now, after the crushing of the councils' regime, there followed a massive political counter-revolution.

On 11 May 1919, Major-General von Möhl, who had used his troops to crush the Munich Räterepublik at the beginning of the month, established Reichswehr Headquarters 4, and, initially with the aid of a state of siege and martial law, took over full authority in Bavaria. Since the government, which had retreated to Bamberg, and the parliament did not return until August, Möhl dominated the political scene in the Bavarian capital for several months. This resulted in a military regime that completely destroyed the radical Left, largely marginalized the MSPD, and decisively encouraged all right-wing, 'counter-revolutionary forces' including the radical ethnic nationalists (Völkische). Public agencies, especially the military and police apparatus, were subjected to a systematic purge and a comprehensive 'security apparatus' was constructed. The Reichswehr headquarters established its own 'information', that is, intelligence department, whose task was to oversee political life in Bavaria and to influence it in the interests of the counter-revolution. This department in turn worked closely with the press and legal department in the city military headquarters under the control of the later Minister of Justice, Christian Roth, as well as with the new police chief, Ernst Poehner. Poehner had an exceptionally loyal assistant in the shape of the head of the police's political department and future Nazi Reich Interior minister, Wilhelm Frick. The newly created state police [Landespolizei] provided a force that had been militarily trained and was particularly geared to the suppression of disturbances and uprisings. In addition, in May 1919, not least through the initiative of Reichswehr captain, Ernst Roehm, home guard units [Einwohnerwehren] were established, a largely middle-class citizens' militia, which, within the space of a few months had a membership of over 200,000. Under right-wing conservative leadership it was considered a reliable guarantee against further revolutionary attempts.[28]

Thus, the army provided the context for political life during the following months. It was dominated above all by an apparently hysterical fear of revolution, seen as liable to produce a Bolshevik reign of terror; by a resultant excessive desire for security and order at all costs; by a wave of anti-Semitism, as a number of leading representatives of the revolution were Jews; and by frustration with the unexpectedly harsh conditions of the peace treaty revealed on 7 May 1919, which produced defiant nationalist protests. The model form of parliamentary democracy introduced in the Reich in autumn 1918 in the expectation of a mild peace treaty had now been discredited, particularly among bourgeois, nationalist circles.

The heated debate that dominated German domestic politics until the acceptance of the peace conditions by the Reichstag on 23 June 1919 and the campaign against the 'November criminals' and the 'fulfillment politicians' hardened attitudes towards any left-wing or liberal politics, especially in Munich.

Hostility to socialism, fear of disorder, anti-Semitism, and nationalism were all key attitudes the dominant right-wing conservative circles in Munich shared with the extreme rightist völkisch element in the city. The latter's radical activities were not new, indeed they pre-dated the war, but, under the post-revolutionary military regime, groups that in the past had been considered marginal sects now acquired political importance.[29] This produced the fertile soil that made Munich the 'birthplace' of National Socialism. And, it was only in this febrile atmosphere that, as we shall see, Hitler was to become politically engaged.

A dense network of extreme right-wing organizations emerged under the protection of the army and police, with a central role played by the Thule Society. It had been established in the summer of 1918 as a lodge-type association by an already existing anti-Semitic secret society, the Germanenorden. Disguised as a society 'for Research into German history and the Promotion of German Ways', it provided the Germanenorden with a public platform and recruitment centre. The founder of the Thule Society and the dominant figure in it was Adam Alfred Rudolf Glauer, who called himself Rudolf von Sebottendorf. Under the leadership of this adventurer the Thule Society established itself during the Räterepublik as the clandestine fulcrum of the counter-revolution. In particular, it assisted in the formation of the Free Corps★ Epp and Oberland and placed its headquarters in the prestigious Hotel Vier Jahreszeiten at the disposal of other extreme right-wing groups. When the counter-revolutionary troops marched into Munich in May, the Thule Society, along with other extreme right groups, tried to start its own uprising. A number of its leading activists were shot by supporters of the Räterepublik and from then onwards were regarded as martyrs of the 'red terror'. After the capture of the city the Thule Society continued to remain in the background, at the heart of the völkisch-extreme right milieu and linking it closely

---

★ Translators' note: Free Corps were paramilitary units recruited by the Reich government from volunteers in order to suppress revolution, not unlike the Black and Tans in Ireland during the same years.

with the right-wing conservative establishment. This elitist, doctrinaire racist society had approximately 250 members.[30] However, its newspaper, the *Münchener Beobachter*, bought by the society in August 1918, was the main mouthpiece of the völkisch movement in post-war Munich.

The Deutsch-völkische Schutz- und Trutzbund [German League for Protection and Defiance] was also of vital importance for Munich's extreme right-wing scene during 1919. This organization, with its headquarters in Hamburg, had been founded in February 1919 by the extreme nationalist and imperialist Pan-German League as a platform for an anti-Semitic campaign aiming for the broadest possible impact.[31] It had a nation-wide organization, was centrally controlled, and flooded Germany with hitherto unprecedented amounts of extreme anti-Semitic propaganda.[32] In the summer of 1919, Munich acquired one of its most active local branches, with, in November 1919, 1,500 and, in the summer of the following year, 4,000 members;[33] it met in the rooms of the Thule Society. One of its leading figures was Dietrich Eckart, a dynamic figure within the völkisch intelligentsia, who provided it with pamphlet material and offered close cooperation with his – admittedly only moderately effective – Deutsche Bürgervereinigung [German Citizens' Association], which, in turn, was supported by Sebottendorf's *Münchener Beobachter*.[34] Eckart acted as a speaker for the Schutz- und Trutzbund, as did the civil engineer, Gottfried Feder, one of the leading figures in the Munich völkisch movement, whose slogan 'breaking interest slavery' was adopted by the Schutz- und Trutzbund.[35] The publishers, Julius Friedrich Lehmann and Ernst Boepple, as well as the journalists, Erich Kühn and Marc (really Max) Sesselmann, also joined the Munich branch.

Lehmann, who, like Sesselmann, was also a member of the Thule, had a prominent role in the Munich branch of the Pan German League, maintaining the link between this organization, which was now operating more in the background, and the Schutz- und Trutzbund's activities.[36] The Munich branch of the Bayerische Mittelpartei [Bavarian Middle Party], which represented the conservative German Nationalist People's Party (DNVP) in Bavaria, had close personal links with the Schutz- und Trutzbund. While in its December 1918 programme the party had included a clause clearly rejecting German Jewry, in the second half of 1919 it significantly hardened its anti-Semitic stance. It was now demanding nothing less than the exclusion of German Jews from the 'direction of all our political, economic, and cultural affairs'.[37]

In the second half of 1919 the völkisch–extreme right-wing movement in Munich launched an anti-Jewish campaign that resulted in anti-Semitism developing into a dominant political force in the city and the surrounding area. Elsewhere in the Reich the Schutz- und Trutzbund and many other extreme right-wing groups were also active,[38] but in Munich the 'anti-Semitic wave' (as people quickly called it) that had been unleashed, had a devastating effect. Apart from the high level of engagement on the part of the Munich right-wing extremists, this resulted from the fact that, during spring and summer 1919, the de facto military regime not only tolerated this agitation but actively encouraged it, for example through a systematic policy of expelling 'Eastern Jews'.[39] Also, the extensive suppression of the Left allowed anti-Semitism to spread almost unhindered.

Thus, during these months, anti-Semitic agitation, particularly in Munich, was ubiquitous: Jews were accused of being war profiteers and black marketeers, and of having avoided front-line service during the war; fear of the immigration of eastern Jews was stoked; there were attacks on the 'Jewification' of German culture and so on. However, out of this confusion of resentments emerged a particularly potent stereotype as the core idea stoking anti-Jewish feeling: the assertion that the revolution that had just been suppressed had been above all a 'Jewish' affair. Was it not the case that numerous leaders of the Soviet and Hungarian revolutions were Jews? And did not Eisner and a number of prominent revolutionaries in Bavaria such as Ernst Toller, Erich Mühsam, Gustav Landauer, or Eugen Leviné have Jewish, in some cases eastern Jewish, roots? Although the Jewish revolutionaries had long since given up their Jewish identity, and the majority of revolutionaries were not Jews, just as the majority of Munich Jews had not been revolutionaries, such objections had little effect. The fear on the part of large sections of the population of a recurrence of revolution could be exploited with the slogan 'Jewish Bolshevism'. A slogan had been found that appealed to the masses, including many in the political centre, ground and could be linked to all the other anti-Jewish prejudices and attitudes that were so rife in the Bavarian capital at that time.[40]

'Take the Jews into protective custody and then there'll be peace at home!' was the message that the Schutz- und Trutzbund regularly published in the *Münchener Beobachter* from spring 1919 onwards, and which continued:

Jews agitate in favour of Spartakism[†]
Jews whip up the people in the streets
Jews push themselves to the top everywhere
Jews prevent Germans from reaching an understanding with one another

Therefore:

Away with the Jewish profiteers and troublemakers
Germany for the Germans! Let that be the watchword in our struggle for
liberation.

Hitler's indoctrination by the Reichswehr

This massive anti-Semitic campaign and general shift to the Right provides
the background to the Reichswehr Information Department's plan of using
political and ideological indoctrination in order to immunize the soldiers of
the Munich garrison against socialist and other 'dangerous' ideas. In June 1919
the department began holding courses at Munich University. Research has
shown that Hitler, who had so far managed to avoid demobilization, took part
only in the third course, which lasted from 10 to 19 July.[41] Before the start of
the course he had been assigned to the 'winding-up unit', which was demo-
bilizing his old regiment.[42] The courses were organized by Captain Karl Mayr,
the very active head of the propaganda section within the Information
Department, who at this time was a hard line anti-Semite and important supporter of the extreme Right. During the final phase of the Räterepublik he
had played a significant role in the coordination of the military activities of
the Thule[43] and, among other things, was close to Dietrich Eckart.[44]

This indoctrination took the form of lectures and seminars, which
involved discussion and coaching in public speaking. The seminars were led
by the writer, Count Carl von Bothmer, who worked for 'Heimatdienst
Bayern', a propaganda organization established immediately after the crushing

---

† Translators' note: The Spartakist League was a group of left-wing Socialists opposed to the
decision of the majority of the SPD to participate in the First World War and committed to a
proletarian revolution. In 1916 it acquired the title 'Spartakus League' (Spartakistenbund) from
the title of its newsletters, the *Spartakusbriefe*. On 1 January 1919 it was subsumed into the new
German Communist Party (KPD). Shortly afterwards it began an uprising in Berlin against the
Socialist government, which was quickly crushed by right-wing Free Corps, who murdered its
leaders Rosa Luxemburg and Karl Liebknecht.

of the Räterepublik, with a largely 'anti-Bolshevist' agenda.[45] Bothmer was on the extreme Right, had known Eckart for a long time and often published articles in the latter's paper, *Auf gut deutsch*.[46] According to the surviving course programme he was involved in giving two lectures: about the SPD's Erfurt programme of 1891 and about 'the connexion between domestic and foreign policy'. Other lecturers spoke on various topics concerning economics and social policy.[47] Course III did not follow this programme exactly; for example, it is evident that Gottfried Feder stood in with a lecture on the 'breaking of interest slavery'.[48] Yet even if it is not possible to know the exact content of the third course, it is clear from the overall pattern of the lectures given in the various courses that the indoctrination was composed primarily of anti-Bolshevism, rejection of 'war guilt', the encouragement of confidence in future economic developments, and a good dose of nationalism.[49] Although the topic was not specifically referred to in the programme, anti-Semitism must also have played a vital role, at least under the surface. Mayr, Bothmer, and Feder were all anti-Semites, and the Munich Reichswehr garrison saw the growth of anti-Semitism in the barracks during the summer as a positive sign, while officially disapproving of its more extreme manifestations.[50]

In August 1919, Hitler, who had apparently stood out as a particularly enthusiastic participant on the course,[51] was selected by Mayr's department as a propaganda speaker.[52] In Lechfeld camp near Augsburg a so-called enlightenment commando made up of two dozen soldiers was deployed to politically indoctrinate soldiers returning from prisoner-of-war camps in order to inoculate them against revolutionary tendencies. For the Munich Reichswehr commanders believed the situation in the camp was explosive. The head of the section responsible for recruiting soldiers to serve in the post-war Reichswehr was reporting that he had obtained a very 'unfavourable impression' of the mood in the camp: the soil there had been 'already contaminated with Bolsheism [sic!] and Spartakism'.[53]

It is clear from the available reports of the indoctrination, which in fact was directed not at returning soldiers but at soldiers on guard duty,[54] that, apart from the commanding officer of the commando, it was above all Hitler who had distinguished himself with a series of lectures and contributions in the discussion. In general, his talent as a 'born popular speaker' was emphasized, and his lively and easily understood lectures had had a positive impact on the soldiers. According to the report, Hitler had talked about 'Peace Conditions and Reconstruction' and 'Social and Economic Slogans'. However, his performance led to a discussion among the organizers as to whether it was tactically advisable for him to be so overtly anti-Semitic in his statements, if they were to avoid the accusation of 'anti-Jewish rabble-rousing'. The commander of the guard unit responsible for the lectures then felt obliged to issue an order requiring the exercise of more caution on this issue and 'as far as possible to avoid too overt references to this race that is foreign to the German people'. However, in his report to his superiors the same officer emphasized his agreement with the content of such tirades; it was thus merely a question of whether Hitler's overtly anti-Semitic language was *opportune*.[55] In fact, the 'enlightenment' of the troops, in the form in which it had taken place in Lechfeld, was discontinued, as it was judged by the Reichswehr and indeed by Mayr himself to have been ineffective.[56]

The Reichswehr's view of anti-Semitism as an essential component of their 'enlightenment programme' is particularly evident from a letter that, at Mayr's instigation, Hitler wrote after the conclusion of the course to a participant, Adolf Gemlich, who had requested further clarification of the 'Jewish question'. Hitler replied in detail and in his letter of 16 September compared various forms of hostility to the Jews. He advised against anti-Semitism as a 'purely emotional phenomenon'. Rather, 'anti-Semitism as a political movement' must be determined by 'the recognition of facts'. Hitler then spent the following pages outlining some of these 'facts'. Jewry was 'definitely a race and not a religious community' and, what is more, a race that had preserved its characteristics through 'thousands of years of inbreeding', so that now living 'among us' was a 'non-German, foreign race' that differed markedly from the Germans and yet possessed the same rights. Jewish ideas and actions, Hitler continued, were determined solely by the desire for material possessions; Jewish power, therefore, is 'the power of money, which in the form of interest effortlessly and endlessly accumulates in their hands and burdens the nations with that dangerous yoke....Everything that prompts humanity to strive for higher things, whether religion, socialism, or democracy', was for 'the Jew' merely a 'means to the end of satisfying his desire for money and power'. From this Hitler concluded: 'His activities will infect the nations with racial tuberculosis'. His central message was contained in the following paragraph: 'Emotional anti-Semitism' will 'find its ultimate expression in the form of progroms' (Hitler did in fact spell the word wrongly); 'rational anti-Semitism, on the other hand, must [lead] to the planned legal combatting and removal of Jewish privileges', in other words to 'legislation for foreigners' aimed at the Jews. The final goal of this 'rational anti-Semitism' must, however, 'irrevocably be the removal of the Jews altogether'. However, the current government was incapable of carrying out such steps, indeed rather was compelled 'to seek support from those who have exploited and are continuing to exploit the new situation in Germany and who, for this reason, were the driving forces of the revolution, the Jews'.

In order to confer authority on the position adopted by Hitler, Mayr enclosed an accompanying letter in which he declared that he basically agreed with the views of his speaker. There was only one point, Mayr made clear, on which his views differed from those of Hitler: in his opinion the 'interest problem' was not, as Hitler, basing his views on his indoctrination lecturer, Feder, had written, the result of Jewish machinations, but rather essentially the consequence of a 'healthy instinct for acquisition'. It was thus only necessary to combat its 'excesses', which were of course caused by Jews. However, by indicating this difference in view, Mayr was in effect underlining his agreement with Hitler on the other central points.[57] Thus, this first anti-Semitic statement by Hitler that we possess should not be read simply as documenting the anti-Jewish attitude that he was developing during these months. In the first instance, it represents an official statement by the Munich Reichswehr's Information Department, outlining the stance it was adopting towards anti-Semitism. The letter, therefore, throws light on what kind of indoctrination Hitler had been receiving during this period.

The arguments that Hitler used in this letter were not at all original but are expressed in very similar terms in contemporary anti-Semitic literature.[58] Thus with his distinction between 'P(r)ogrom' and 'rational anti-Semitism' Hitler had adopted a trope that was current during these weeks and months. The concept of a pogrom, which before the war had almost solely referred to violent attacks on Jews in Eastern Europe, now, in 1919, was increasingly also being used as a synonym for a radical 'solution' to the 'Jewish question' in Germany.[59] In August the well-known Leipzig anti-Semite Heinrich Pudor had published an article in the pamphlet series *Deutscher Volksrat* in which he maintained that the state had missed the opportunity to limit the alleged dominance of the Jews by legal means; in view of this situation, there could be 'no objection to pogroms if they fulfilled their purpose'.[60] In the *Münchener Beobachter* of 29 October 1919 there appeared an article signed 'Hartmut', which rejected the 'solution of the Jewish question' through pogroms and instead demanded that Jews be stripped of their civil rights. Thus, with his comments in the so-called

Gemlich letter Hitler was very much au fait with the discussions going on within the anti-Semitic movement.

Thus, Hitler's growing interest in politics and the initial shaping of his ideology took place within the context of the crushing of the revolution and his indoctrination by the Reichswehr. There is no reliable contemporary evidence that Hitler had been politicized at an earlier stage: no written statements of his, no memoirs of comrades, no references in the army files. His efforts in *Mein Kampf* to date his gradual politicization from 1916 and to declare the revolution to have been the key event is part of an obvious attempt at creating a self-image. More than that, Hitler's politicization in spring 1919 was not the result of his own initiative (in the sense of: 'I decided to become a politician'), but rather occurred through a job involving political topics which he was given by the Reichswehr as part of its attempt to prevent its soldiers from participating in revolution. He had proved himself in the eyes of his superiors through his work in the counter-revolutionary investigation commission and had become involved in Mayr's propaganda activities: it was through him that Hitler received a real political education.[61]

The role of propagandist and agitator in turn offered Hitler the only opportunity of maintaining his status as a soldier. That is what he had been trying to achieve for months. For what other opportunities did he have? As far as his family was concerned, he only had relatives with whom he had broken off contact. He had no educational qualifications and the thirty-year-old lacked the financial means and the school leaving certificate that would enable him to embark on the course of study to which he had aspired in the past. Was he going to have to resume selling his painted post-cards and water colours round about the Munich Frauenkirche?

Moreover, the counter-revolutionary programme that Mayr had tried to drum into the soldiers – anti-socialism, nationalism, anti-Semitism – was entirely compatible with the basic convictions Hitler had acquired in the course of his youth. As we have seen, he came from a 'German Nationalist' milieu in old Austria and since his school days had developed increasingly strong 'Pan-German' sympathies. For him it was obvious that the Austrian Germans should join a powerful German Reich. Now, after the collapse both of the Habsburg Monarchy and of the 'little German' Kaiserreich, these ideas seemed to be about to be fulfilled; it looked as if the greater German solution, the national unity of all those with a German heritage and of German origin, was now on the table as a serious option. It offered new perspectives for Germany's severely damaged national consciousness.

Indeed, on 12 February 1919 a large majority of the German national assembly voted in favour of such a union, as had the Austrian parliament in Vienna. But it was blocked by the victorious Allies.

Hitler had been wary of the socialist workers' movement, not least because of his lower middle-class background, and in the anti-revolutionary wave that swept through Munich in spring 1919 he did not find it difficult to move from wariness to hostility and hatred. He was bound to agree with the legend successfully peddled by the old military elite that the German army had been defeated through 'a stab in the back' from the home front.[62]

Above all, however, anti-Semitism, which spread like wildfire during the summer of 1919, provided Hitler with both a convincing explanation for the catastrophic conditions as well as a handbook for the future. Hitler was one of those who eagerly grasped the idea that the revolution had been above all the work of Jews and it was now necessary to eradicate 'Jewish Bolshevism'. Moreover, as the Gemlich letter shows, for him the notion 'Jew' represented the unscrupulous and amoral greed of finance capital and so anti-Semitism (and not the socialism of the Left) was the key to removing this exploitative system. The stereotype 'Jewish capitalism' would also offer him an explanation in the future for the ruthless policy of the Western Allies, who, in the process of implementing their tough peace conditions, evidently wanted to 'destroy' Germany. This was in fact a very widespread view in post-war Germany.[63]

While during his time in Vienna Hitler had, as we have seen, considered anti-Semitism one among a number of 'antis', one factor among others that appeared to explain the impending collapse of the Habsburg empire (at that time the decisive issue in his Pan-German world view), now the whole situation had radically changed. In the shape of the dual threat posed by 'Jewish Bolshevism' and 'Jewish capitalism' Hitler felt confronted with a set of dangers that threatened not only the existing social order and the German people but the whole of the civilized world. From his distorted perspective it represented an apocalyptic threat. Thus, anti-Semitism moved from the margins to the centre of his world view. The image of the enemy that he worked out in the course of these months also enabled him to overcome the deep shame that he had felt in Pasewalk and to master the uncertainty of the months that followed. The defeat, which initially had seemed to him completely incomprehensible and undeserved, and the rapid political radicalization prompted by the revolution, in which he too had been swept up, all this could now be seen as the result of a manipulation that had been a long time in the planning.

2

Joining the Party

After his return from Lechfeld Camp, Hitler, who was still with the 'demobilization unit' of the 2nd Infantry Regiment, carried out a number of small tasks for Mayr.[1] However, as the Reichswehr had abandoned the idea of indoctrination courses such as those held in Lechfeld, Hitler was on the look-out for a new job in his role as a propagandist. He found one quite quickly after Mayr spotted the small German Workers Party (DAP) among the fifty or so political groups that had established themselves in Munich and the surrounding area.[2]

The story is well-known; it has been told a thousand times. On 12 September 1919, on an assignment from the Reichswehr's Intelligence Section, Hitler attended a meeting of the German Workers' Party in the Sterneckerbräu, a pub near the Isartor, where slightly more than forty people had assembled to listen to speeches by Gottfried Feder and a Professor Baumann.[3] During the subsequent discussion Hitler drew attention to himself with a forceful contribution and was then invited by the chairman of the local branch, Anton Drexler, to become a member. After careful consideration Hitler agreed to do so and, thanks to his rhetorical gift, soon became the party's main attraction. Under his dominant influence it rapidly expanded, consolidating its organization, until he formally took over the party leadership.[4] The story represents the core of the 'party legend', invented by Hitler, outlined at length in *Mein Kampf*, referred to again and again in hundreds of his speeches, and continually repeated after 1945.[5]

The legend can, however, be disproved with relative ease. For a start, during the 1930s, Drexler, the chairman in 1919, understandably objected to Hitler's claim that he joined the party as member No. 7. The only thing that is certain is that Hitler was one of the first 200 or so members who had joined the party by the end of 1919.[6] But much more important is the fact that the success of the DAP, later NSDAP, in Munich was not, as Hitler later maintained, the result of his 'decision' to join it.

As we have seen, at the time when Hitler came across the DAP, an extreme right-wing and völkisch milieu, composed of a network of organizations with close links to the Munich establishment, already existed. The DAP was a well-established component of this milieu; in 1919 there were already a number of key figures in the extreme right-wing and völkisch scene who were active in the party and, before the end of the year, in other words before Hitler had become a major player, the young party had received support from various quarters. The aim was to establish, and provide continuing support for, a political party within the extreme right-wing movement that would focus its appeal specifically on the working class, in order to immunize it against socialist ideas.

The DAP and the extreme right-wing scene in Munich

The initiative had been taken, at the end of 1918, by Anton Drexler,[7] a locksmith in a workshop of the Bavarian railways, and Karl Harrer,[8] a sports journalist on the *München-Augsburger Abendzeitung*. They founded a 'Workers' Political Circle' in which a handful of members – most of them railway workers like Drexler – discussed the political situation produced by the defeat and revolution. They were primarily concerned with the question of how to produce a counterweight to the dominant socialists, whom they blamed for the outcome of the war, and focused on trying somehow to introduce a social component into nationalism and anti-Semitism.

At the beginning of 1919, the 'Workers' Political Circle' gave birth to the German Workers' Party [Deutsche Arbeiterpartei]. Under Harrer's leadership it had around two dozen members, most of them railwaymen, who were loyal to the established order and strongly nationalist. This move was evidently influenced by the Thule Society, of which both Harrer and Drexler were members. At any rate, in a book published in 1933 and quickly withdrawn by the regime, Sebottendorf claimed to have been responsible, together with Harrer and Drexler, for establishing, on 18 January 1919 in the premises of the Thule Society, a 'national socialist workers' association'.[9] It was necessary for the DAP formally to operate as an 'association' [Verein] in order to satisfy the terms of the Law of Associations. In the 1930s Drexler recalled that the party had met in the premises of the Thule Society.[10] Membership meetings were held, and in addition the 'Workers' Circle', which initially formed the de facto leadership, met separately to discuss above all the causes of the defeat and the revolution.[11] Drexler, who also wrote for the *Münchener Beobachter*, the mouthpiece of the Thule Society, and was highly praised by Eckart in his paper, *Auf gut Deutsch*,[12] published a forty-page political pamphlet, claiming that the existing socialist movement was 'simply the vehicle…for dominating the whole world through Jewish money and the Jewish press'.[13]

According to Hitler, he encountered the DAP as part of an intelligence assignment and then 'decided' to join. What is certain is that he attended a party meeting on 12 September 1919 and a few days later – in response to Drexler's prompting – joined the DAP. The circumstances were, however, probably somewhat different from what he later maintained. For everything points to the fact that Mayr, the propaganda chief of the Reichswehr's Information Department, placed his star speaker, Hitler, at the disposal of the DAP, in order to increase the party's influence within the extreme right-wing milieu, which he was actively supporting.[14] Thus Hitler had not been given an intelligence assignment but rather a purely propaganda role within the range of tasks that he performed for Mayr until March 1920, when he left the Reichswehr. From October 1919 onwards, he was employed by Mayr as an assistant to the education officer of the 41st Rifle Regiment, where he looked after the regimental library and so had the opportunity of perusing right-wing propaganda material, with which the Reichswehr was well supplied.[15] In addition, during January and February 1920, Hitler also gave lectures to members of the Reichswehr[16] and wrote a number of articles at Mayr's request.[17]

Moreover, Hitler did not attend the DAP meeting alone; he was accompanied by Sergeant-Major Alois Grillmeier, who, like Hitler, had been a member of the Investigation Commission into Bolshevik Activities and who also joined the DAP,[18] and by six other of Mayr's former propagandists.[19] Mayr had himself been expected to attend the meeting, as is noted on the attendance list;[20] on 12 November, he did indeed turn up to a DAP meeting.[21] And Mayr did more: he assigned a second propagandist to the DAP in the shape of Hermann Esser, a former NCO and editorial assistant in Mayr's press department, who soon assumed a prominent role in the party, becoming one of its leading speakers, along with Hitler, Drexler, and Feder.[22] Moreover, by introducing Captain Ernst Röhm to the DAP, Mayr provided it with an important contact. For Röhm was adjutant to the commander of the 21st Infantry Brigade, Colonel von Epp,[23] and himself heavily involved in the Reichswehr's support for the Einwohnerwehren. According to Röhm, he had already got to know Hitler before the latter had joined the DAP at Mayr's instigation. They had met at an event at the *Eiserne Faust* [Iron Fist], a right-wing officers' club. Hitler later recalled that he had already met Röhm in spring 1919. The first evidence we have of Röhm attending a meeting of the DAP is from October, shortly after which he joined the party. He was to become one of Hitler's keenest supporters.[24]

The DAP and Hitler also had a direct line to the city commandant's office, which played an important role in the re-establishment of 'law and order' after the crushing of the Räterepublik. The city commandant of Munich, Major Konstantin Hierl, was an early mentor of the DAP and went on to become the head of the Reich Labour Service during the Third Reich. In July 1920 Hitler sent him a detailed description of the party's organization, which reads like an official report.[25] Thus, at the beginning of Hitler's political career, the DAP enjoyed the support of three important military institutions, which during these months were heavily involved in reorganizing political life in Munich: the Information Department [Mayr], the City Commandant's Office [Hierl], and the staff of the Reichswehr unit stationed in Munich (21st Infantry Brigade/Röhm).

Other members of the Reichswehr also helped the DAP to get started. Thus, in the autumn of 1919, Captain Eduard Dietl was already a member of the DAP. And, although he left it again in 1920 – officers were in principle not permitted to be members of political parties – he remained sympathetic. When Dietl, by then a Colonel-General of the Wehrmacht, was killed in an air crash in 1944, Hitler commented at his memorial service that he, Dietl, had been the first Reichswehr officer to give him the opportunity to speak to his company and that Dietl had subsequently declared his absolute loyalty to him. In 1923 Dietl was to prove this by, on the instructions of the Reichswehr, helping to train the SA and then, finally, on the occasion of the so-called Hitler putsch of 8 November, declaring his support for the putschists.[26] Vice-Sergeant-Major Rudolf Schüssler can be shown to have taken part in a meeting of the DAP on 16 October 1919 at which Hitler spoke; he joined the party at the end of 1919, becoming party secretary at the beginning of 1920. He is believed to have dealt with party business in his barracks.[27] Among the other early members of the DAP whom Hitler recruited from the Reichswehr was Karl Tiefenböck,[28] a former member of the group of runners from the 16th Reserve Infantry Regiment. And another old acquaintance whom Hitler won over to the DAP was Joseph Popp, his pre-war landlord.[29]

In addition, within the DAP Hitler met several important figures involved in extreme right-wing journalism. Among them was Dietrich Eckart, a modestly successful völkisch poet, dramatist, and journalist, who has already been referred to. Eckart's best-known work was a translation, or rather a freely rendered version, of Ibsen's *Peer Gynt*, which was regularly performed on the German stage. During the war, he had become politicized: he published a series of pamphlets in which he complained that negative reviews by Jews were responsible for his lack of success and that Jews were to blame for everything.[30] In 1915 he established the Hoheneichen-Verlag publishing company and, in December 1918, the anti-socialist and anti-Semitic weekly, *Auf gut deutsch*, in which, among others, Feder and Bothmer published articles.[31] Eckart was involved in the DAP before Hitler arrived, among other things as a speaker.[32] He was not a member but acted as an influential sponsor. He had a sound reputation in conservative circles, enabling him to collect considerable donations for the party.[33] He also supported it out of his own resources.[34] Among the authors writing for *Auf gut deutsch* and published by the Hoheneichen-Verlag was Alfred Rosenberg, a young Baltic German who had emigrated from Reval (Tallin) to Munich in December 1918. Rosenberg, who was also recorded as a 'guest' of the Thule Society,[35] introduced several members of the Baltic German emigré scene to the DAP. He got to know Hitler through Eckart.[36]

In March 1920, Julius Friedrich Lehmann, head of the Lehmann publishing house and referred to previously, joined the now renamed NSDAP. Apart from publishing learned medical works, he was also responsible for a series of eugenic, anti-Semitic and nationalist books and pamphlets. Through his leading role in the Pan-German League and the Deutsch-völkische Schutz- und Trutzbund Lehmann ensured that the NSDAP secured support from these organizations as well.[37] The extent to which the völkisch scene formed a dense network is demonstrated by the Deutscher Volksverlag press, which Lehmann founded in April 1919. Run by Ernst Boepple, another early member of the DAP,[38] who was simultaneously a member of the Schutz- und Trutzbund, it was responsible for publishing Drexler's pamphlet as well as the early works of Alfred Rosenberg and Eckart's *Peer Gynt* translation. Another example is Wilhelm Gutberlet, a member of the Thule Society and a partner in another völkisch publishing firm, the Eher Verlag, who was one of those who attended the DAP meeting of 12 September at which Hitler appeared for the first time and, in October 1920, gave his shares in the firm to the DAP.[39]

In October and November 1919 Erich Kühn, the editor of the Pan-German League's journal *Deutschlands Erneuerung* [Germany's Renewal], spoke at meetings of the DAP.[40] In return, Hitler, who in the meantime had become moderately well-known, defended the League against the accusation of having been responsible for the war: 'it wasn't Pan-Germans; it was Pan-Jews'.[41] Three and a half months later, Privy Councillor Heinrich Class, the influential chairman of the Pan-German League, who was based in Berlin, sent the DAP 3,000 Reich marks [RM]. Significantly, the money was received via Captain Mayr. In other words, the captain was still keeping a protective eye on the party. Soon afterwards, Class donated another 1,000 RM to finance a propaganda trip by Hitler round Austria.[42] Also, right from the start, the DAP received a helping hand from the Deutsch-völkische Schutz- und Trutzbund.[43] Apart from Lehmann, this was true above all of Paul Tafel, an engineer with idiosyncratic ideas about a new economic order, who had already become a member of the DAP in 1919,[44] and of Ferdinand Wiegand, the Munich district manager of a Hamburg firm, who for a few months in 1920 even became the DAP's first secretary.[45]

In addition, Gottfried Feder, who has been frequently referred to, played a key role as a link man in the völkisch scene in Munich. An early member of the DAP[46] and founder of his own modestly successful organization, the Combat League for Breaking Interest Slavery, Feder was a valued speaker for the extreme Right. Apart from giving speeches for his own organiza-tion,[47] the DAP,[48] and the Reichswehr – Hitler had heard him speak at Mayr's indoctrination course – Feder was also on the bill at the first public meeting of the Munich Schutz- und Trutzbund on 1 December 1919.[49] Marc Sesselmann was equally well connected. Born in 1898, a member of the Thule Society and the early DAP,[50] he was active in the Schutzbund and also involved in founding the Deutschsozialistische Partei (DSP) in Munich.[51] In May 1919, Sesselmann, along with Thule members Hans Georg Müller and Friedrich Wieser, took over the editorship of the *Münchener Beobachter*, retaining it until March 1920;[52] its national edition had been renamed the *Völkischer Beobachter* in August 1919. In the autumn of 1919 and at the beginning of 1920 he and Hitler spoke at various engage-ments organized by the DAP and the Schutzbund.[53]

Sesselmann, who was active in the DAP and the DSP, was not the only member of the dense völkisch–anti-Semitic network in Munich who joined more than one political party. At the end of 1918, Alfred Brunner, a mechanical engineer from Düsseldorf, proposed founding a German Socialist Party [*Deutschsozialistische Partei* = DSP],[54] and his idea was taken up by the Thule Society. At Christmas 1918, the Society launched the party with a programme drafted by Brunner (although he was not mentioned by name). Alongside its initiative in founding the DAP, Thule supported the establishment of a local branch of the DSP in Munich,[55] which, mainly thanks to the efforts of Müller and Sesselmann,[56] took place in May 1919. In the autumn of 1919, a German Socialist Working Group [*Deutschsozialistische Arbeitsgemeinschaft*] was also established in Munich.[57] In November, another important DSP local branch was founded, this time in Nuremberg, which was recruited largely from members of the Schutz- und Trutzbund. The party was officially established at Reich level in April 1920. Its programme was more or less identical with that of the DAP: the main difference was that the DSP followed a parliamentary strategy, albeit initially without success. In the election to the first Reichstag on 6 June 1920 it received only 7,186 votes (0.03 per cent).

On 16 October 1919, at the DAP's first public meeting, the main speaker was not Hitler but the Pan-German journalist, Erich Kühn.[58] However, Hitler, a new member, intervened in the discussion with a lengthy anti-Semitic diatribe and, from November onwards, spoke at further DAP meetings in Munich beer halls, often with other speakers from the party (Feder, Drexler, and others), to audiences of 300–400 people.[59] On 10 December 1919 and then again on 23 January 1920 he was the main speaker.[60]

Before the DAP took the stage in front of a wider public, Hitler succeeded in getting rid of the party leader, Harrer. Hitler maintained later that Harrer had wanted to hang on to the idea of the party as a kind of political study group, thereby blocking Hitler's more ambitious plans. However, this account is implausible.[61] In fact, at the end of 1919, Harrer was sounding out the possibility of cooperation with the *Deutschnationale Volkspartei* [German National People's Party (DNVP)] in Berlin. This was the most important right-wing Conservative party in Germany, which was trying to bring together all the right-wing conservative and völkisch forces in the Reich; however, it did not yet have a state-wide organization in Bavaria. It was only in March 1920 that it managed to establish a permanent link with the (Bavarian) *Mittelpartei*. In December 1919, the secretary of the DNVP,

Hans-Erdmann von Lindener-Wildau, met Harrer during a trip to Bavaria and they both concluded that politically they were largely in agreement. Harrer gave assurances that the DAP would not put up its own list of candidates in future elections provided that the DNVP included a 'white-collar employee' in its list.[62] This conversation totally contradicts the image of Harrer as a cautious person merely interested in being a member of a political sect that Hitler later tried to convey.[63] Almost certainly Hitler's engagement in a public conflict with the party chairman was primarily because he was determined to maintain the independence of the DAP and, unlike Harrer, was unwilling to cooperate with a powerful partner. His determination not to be forced into a right-wing 'united front' was to be a leitmotif of Hitler's future policy.

At the beginning of December 1919, Hitler pushed through new rules of procedure for the party, according to which an already existing six-man committee, which contained Drexler, Harrer, two secretaries, and two treasurers, but not Hitler, should take over the actual running of the party. According to a commentary on the rules, composed by Hitler, the aim of the change was to exclude any 'paternalistic form of control' by a 'superior or co-existing authority', by which was meant Harrer's original 'Workers' Political Circle'.[64] Under pressure, Harrer resigned as party chairman at the beginning of January 1920 and disappeared from the political stage. He was succeeded by Drexler.[65]

The DAP was able to acquire much larger audiences after February 1920 not, as Hitler insisted on maintaining,[66] because Harrer was no longer blocking the way, but as a result of close cooperation with the Schutz- und Trutzbund or, to put it more accurately, through its patronage. For the DAP was only able significantly to increase its audiences within the context of the anti-Semitic mass meetings organized by the Bund at the beginning of 1920. The first mass public meeting organized by the Schutz- und Trutzbund took place on 7 January 1920 in the Kindl-Keller beer hall in Munich. Kurt Kerlen, the secretary of the North Bavarian Schutz- und Trutzbund, was the main speaker before an audience of 7,000; Feder, Sesselmann, and Hitler were among those who spoke in the discussion. Hitler made a strong anti-Semitic statement. While a general ban on public meetings in Munich was imposed from 12 January to 9 February, the Bund continued its agitation in membership meetings and then went public again with two mass meetings on 19 and 21 February 1920. This exceptionally successful series of mass meetings represents the breakthrough for anti-Semitism as a mass movement in Munich.[67] The seed that the Schutz- und Trutzbund had sown in the second half of 1919 with its massive anti-Semitic agitation had now germinated and the Nazis would by and large be the ones to harvest its fruits.

It was in the heated atmosphere of these February days that the DAP took the plunge and held its first meeting in front of a large audience.[68] Around 2,000 people turned up at the Hofbräuhaus beer cellar on 24 February. The main attraction was a speech by the well-known völkisch speaker and doctor, Johann Dingfelder.[69] After his speech Hitler read out and explained the new party programme he had produced together with Drexler[70] and which the already excited audience now confirmed point by point through acclamation. Moreover, at this meeting the DAP was renamed the Nationalsozialistische Deutsche Arbeiterpartei [National Socialist German Workers' Party: NSDAP]. From now onwards, 24 February 1920 was regarded as the official date of the Party's foundation.

The programme reflected contemporary völkisch demands.[71] The Party was committed to the 'union of all Germans' in a 'Greater Germany'; it demanded the suspension of the peace treaties signed in Versailles and St Germain; and it demanded colonies. Jews should be excluded from German citizenship since they were not 'of German blood' and so were not 'national comrades'. A close reading of the programme shows that a considerable number of demands were clearly anti-Semitic, even if, taken literally, some of them were aimed only at 'non-Germans'. As 'guests' in the Reich they were to be subject to 'aliens' legislation' and were not permitted to hold any public office; if there was insufficient food they were to be deported. Moreover, all non-Germans who had entered the Reich since the start of the war were to be forced to leave, a demand that was aimed at the so-called 'Eastern Jews'. As a matter of principle, only Germans could become journalists and publishers. The economic demands also had anti-Semitic implications, indeed they can only be understood in the context of völkisch polemics against allegedly 'Jewish capitalism' and 'Jewish war profiteers'. The Party demanded the 'abolition of income not earned by work', the 'breaking of interest slavery' and the 'confiscation of all war profits'. It demanded profit sharing in all large enterprises, the 'communalization of large department stores' and their lease at a cheap rate to small traders, the abolition of 'speculation in land', the death penalty for 'common criminals, usurers, profiteers etc.'. There followed general statements of social policy such as the demand for an improvement in provision for old age, for the expansion of the 'whole education system' and the 'improvement of public health'. A specific commitment was made to 'positive Christianity', including a polemic against the 'Jewish materialist spirit'.[72]

Thus, at the time of its first mass meeting, the NSDAP was operating as part of a wider völkisch network. Indeed, in spring 1920, together with fourteen other extreme right-wing groups in Munich, it formed a German-Völkisch Working Group, which included, among others, the Pan-German League, the Thule Society, the German Socialists, the Deutschnationale Handlungsgehilfenverband [a white-collar trade union], and the Deutschvölkische Schutz- und Trutzbund.[73]

The Kapp putsch and the Emergence of Bavaria as a 'Cell of Order'

On 13 March 1920, a group of right-wing conservative politicians and army officers attempted a putsch or coup against the constitutional government in Berlin. They were aided by Free Corps units, whose existence was being threatened by Allied demands for a reduction in the German armed forces. The two main organizers of the putsch, who had won the support of the former Quartermaster General of the old imperial army, Erich Ludendorff, were Wolfgang Kapp, the director of the East Prussian Landschaft, a public corporation providing credit to the landed nobility, and Walther Freiherr von Lüttwitz, the former commander of the Reichswehr units in Berlin, who had just been relieved of his command. The putsch collapsed after only a few days as a result of a general strike in Berlin during which civil servants refused to obey the new 'government' under its self-appointed 'Reich Chancellor' Kapp, while the conservative establishment, although sympathizing with the coup, for tactical reasons remained aloof from it. The putsch did, however, lead to a change of government and (one of the key demands of the plotters) a general election.[74]

On 16 March, Eckart, a long-time supporter of Kapp,[75] acting under instructions from Mayr, who was also a political ally of Kapp,[76] flew to Berlin in order to make contact with the right-wing putschists. He was accompanied by Hitler and they both travelled in a plane supplied by the Reichswehr. (The pilot was Lieutenant Robert Ritter von Greim, whom twenty-five years later Hitler was to appoint as his last commander-in-chief of the Luftwaffe.) However, by this time the affair was hopeless and, on

18 March, the two emissaries returned to Munich without having achieved anything.[77]

Although the Kapp putsch had failed at Reich level, in Bavaria it resulted in a further shift to the right: The commanders of the Einwohnerwehren [home guard], the police president of Munich, Ernst Poehner, and the provincial governor of Upper Bavaria, Gustav von Kahr, pressured the commander of the Reichswehr units stationed in Bavaria, Arnold von Mohl, to declare a state of emergency, allegedly in order to prevent the putsch from reaching Bavaria. The Social Democrat Prime Minister, Johannes Hoffmann, then resigned, making way for a new cabinet under the right-wing Conservative, von Kahr. His government was subsequently confirmed in office in the state elections of June 1920.[78]

Kahr took a strongly anti-Semitic, anti-Socialist and anti-Reich government line and the political radicalization that had gripped Bavaria in 1918/1919, intensified. Under Kahr Bavaria became a 'cell of order' [Ordnungszelle], in other words the nucleus of a new 'regime of order' directed against the Left and against democratic ideas, and intended to 'restore to health' the whole Reich. Through the close cooperation of the army, the police, the administration, and the judiciary, and protected by the continuing state of emergency, Bavaria became a secure base and assembly point for right-wing extremists and anti-Republican elements. Thus, after the failure of the Kapp putsch, Ludendorff, in particular, the most important figure in the anti-Republican–völkisch scene, moved from Berlin to Munich, taking a whole crowd of assistants and supporters with him. From his new base he attempted to spin a web of contacts among nationalist forces in Austria, Hungary, and elsewhere, in order to establish a 'White International' with the aim of overthrowing the post-war order created by the Allies and radically reshaping the map of Europe. Finally, with the aid of his new allies and the Russian emigrés in Munich, he planned to overthrow the Bolshevik regime in Russia.[79] Captain Hermann Ehrhardt, the commander of Naval Brigade II, the core unit involved in the Kapp putsch, and his staff set up the headquarters of the Organisation Consul in Munich. This was a secret organization, which, among other things, planned the assassination of leading democratic politicians and, despite the existence of a warrant for Ehrhardt's arrest, was under the protection of Munich police headquarters. Thus, the völkisch–right-wing extremist scene in Munich was greatly strengthened, receiving even more support from state agencies and right-wing conservative organizations than hitherto. Not only that: right-wing establishment conservatives and right-wing extremists moved much closer together. The reduction of politics to a friend–enemy mindset, the permanent threat of violence against political opponents, and the militarization of politics, all of which were being practised in the Ordnungszelle, contributed greatly to this development.[80]

The Kahr government received significant support from the Bavarian Order Bloc,[81] which was established after the Kapp putsch as the 'union of all patriotically-minded German elements on the basis of the idea of the Reich as a federal state and of a Christian-German-völkisch world view'.[82] The Bloc operated as an umbrella organization for roughly forty organizations, including the Pan-German League, the Bayerische Heimat- und Königsbund, the Bund Bayern und Reich, and the NSDAP. The Order Bloc sought to win over the public with mass meetings, leaflets, and pamphlets and, from summer 1920 onwards, was chaired by Paul Tafel, an early supporter of the DAP.

However, the most important basis for the Kahr regime was probably provided by the 'self-defence' organizations, which had been established throughout the Reich during the revolutionary period and which, in the case of Bavaria, were represented by the very tightly organized Einwohnerwehren, now with some 300,000 members. They served not only as an instrument for maintaining order, but also as a military reserve in the event of war. This meant that they were bound to raise suspicions among the Allies. When, in March 1920, the Allies demanded the disbanding of the self-defence organizations within four weeks, the Reich government initially adopted delaying tactics, but then agreed to their abolition. Kahr, however, was determined to oppose this. The conflict between the Bavarian government, the Reich government, and the Entente lasted a whole year until finally, in June 1921, the Allies issued an ultimatum forcing Bavaria to disband the paramilitary organizations. This represented a major defeat for Kahr, from which radical forces such as the NSDAP, demanding a hard line on the matter, were to profit. Hitler described the disarming as 'self-emasculation' and equated it to the 'start of the Jewish dictatorship'.[83]

This example shows that the political atmosphere in Kahr's cell of order provided the NSDAP with excellent opportunities to progress. Apart from their receiving crucial support from various quarters – we shall look at this in detail – the fact that Kahr's policies were addressing precisely the same issues on which Hitler and the NSDAP were concentrating proved exceptionally advantageous for the Party: much of what the Party was demanding seemed to be being legitimized by the Bavarian government's own policies, but with the NSDAP pursuing them more systematically.

Propaganda for the NSDAP

Between the 'founding meeting' of the NSDAP in February 1920 and the end of the year Hitler spoke at over sixty meetings, most of them in Munich; he was the Party speaker who was most in demand. In September and October he was involved in an election campaign in Austria; apart from that, he spoke a dozen times outside the state capital.[84]

The topics that Hitler addressed in these speeches, usually in front of several hundred, occasionally a crowd of several thousand people,[85] were always the same: usually he began with a comparison between Germany's pre-war position and the current unenviable one, which he described as dramatically as possible; he dealt in detail with the origins of the war (for which he blamed the Allies), with the defeat and the revolution, with the injustice of the Versailles Treaty and the government's helplessness when faced with the humiliations imposed by the victors. The blame for all of this lay primarily with the Jews. Inspired by Feder's criticism of 'finance capital', Hitler attacked 'international Jewish big capital',[86] which was directing the Allied war policies, and the Jewish 'black marketeers' and 'profiteers',[87] who were mainly responsible for the economic distress and, moreover, were dividing the fatherland and dragging it ever deeper into the abyss.[88]

During these speeches, Hitler kept emphasizing the unbridgeable differences that existed between Germany and the western powers, dominated as they were by 'the Jews'. France was the 'hereditary enemy',[89] but at this time Britain too was for him an 'absolute opponent'.[90] 'It's Britain that's mainly to blame for wars,' he exclaimed in June 1920.[91] This assessment prompted the notion of seeking close cooperation with Russia, but a Russia that had been liberated from 'Jewish Bolshevism'. This idea appeared in several of Hitler's speeches in the summer of 1920, for example in a speech in Rosenheim in July: 'Our salvation will never come from the West. We must seek contact with nationalist, anti-Semitic Russia, but not with the Soviets.'[92] This theme came up in his speeches until spring 1922. It was due not least to the influence of the Baltic German emigrés (of whom there were a considerable number in Munich) associated with Alfred Rosenberg and Max Erwin von Scheubner-Richter, a subject to which we shall return.[93]

In addition to 'international Jewish big capital', from spring 1920 onwards, Hitler increasingly emphasized[94] the 'Jewish' character of Russian 'Bolshevism',[95] at the same time positing the German and international labour movements as instruments of a Jewish conspiracy.[96] Indeed, these tropes gave him the great leitmotif that increasingly shaped his speeches from summer 1920 onwards: the 'Jewish question' as the key to understanding Germany's international situation and its domestic and economic plight.[97] It is clear that, in developing his by now multifaceted anti-Semitic world view, he had borrowed ideas from his mentor Eckart, an 'educated' anti-Semite.[98] Thus, on 13 August 1920, in a three-hour speech in the Hofbräuhaus, Hitler was ready to present his anti-Semitic prejudices as an apparently coherent 'theory', one that was dotted with numerous historical 'facts' and extensive observations on politics, economics, and culture. Jews, according to Hitler, did not generally have a positive attitude to work, had been weakened by centuries of incest, and lacked 'inner spiritual experience'. For these three reasons they were incapable of 'building a state' and, instead, corrupted the existing state structure. To ward off this threat, anti-Semitism, together with Socialism and 'nationalism', formed 'the core elements of our programme'.[99]

But what was this anti-Semitism going to involve? In his speeches he repeatedly rejected pogroms and 'emotional anti-Semitism'.[100] Instead, 'we are imbued with the ruthless determination to get to the root of the evil and exterminate it root and branch'; for this to happen 'we must be willing to use every means, even if we have to be in league with the devil'.[101] Again and again such tirades concluded with the demand for the 'removal of the Jews from our nation'.[102] His watchword was: 'Out with the Jews'.[103] At an international meeting of National Socialists in Salzburg he compared Jews with germs, which were responsible for 'racial tuberculosis' and so must be fought like the causes of an epidemic. 'Jewish activities will never cease and will go on poisoning our nation until the pathogen, the Jew, has been removed from our midst'.[104] A few weeks later, in a speech in Rosenheim he worked himself up into a frenzy of anti-Semitic hatred: 'Jews are the brutal representatives of unearned income', the 'parasites of our economic life', the 'ferment of the moral decomposition of our nation', in short, the 'Jewish swindlers must get out of our nation'.[105]

According to the notes and reports of his speeches, they were very warmly received by the majority of the audiences, being met with enthusiastic outbursts and huge applause. There is no doubt that the effect of his speeches was based on this dialogue with the public, with Hitler often working himself up into tirades lasting several hours; indeed, speeches of two or three hours were not unusual. To achieve an adequate appreciation of the effect of his rhetorical talent one has to imagine the hothouse atmosphere in his meetings; simply reading the notes and reports is not sufficient.

The historian, Karl Alexander von Müller, who in 1919 may have been the first person to become aware of Hitler's rhetorical gifts, described a meeting in the Löwenbräukeller four years later as follows: 'Neither during the war nor during the revolution had I experienced on entering such a scorching breath of hypnotic mass excitement'. People were waiting in tense anticipation and then at last the speaker arrived. 'Everybody jumped up from their seats shouting "Heil" and through the shouting crowds and the streaming flags came the one they were waiting for with his entourage, striding quickly to the podium, with his right arm raised stiffly. He passed by quite close to me and I saw that this was a different person from the one whom I had encountered from time to time in private houses: his gaunt, pale features contorted as if by inward rage, cold flames darting from his protruding eyes, which seemed to be searching out enemies to be conquered. Did the crowd give him this mysterious power? Did it flow from him to them?'[106]

Writing about one of his visits to an early Nazi Party meeting, the writer, Carl Zuckmayer reported: 'Once I managed to get a seat so close to the podium that I saw the spit spurting out of his mouth. For people like us the man was a howling dervish. But he knew how to rouse and carry away those crowds squashed together under a cloud of tobacco smoke and sausage smells: not through arguments, which during a rabble-rousing speech can never be checked, but through the fanaticism of his performance, the shouting and screaming, combined with his petty bourgeois convictions; above all, however, through the drumming force of repetition in a particular, infectious rhythm.' He succeeded, according to Zuckmayer, 'in putting people into a trance like a primitive tribe's medicine man'.[107]

Recalling Hitler's early rhetorical performances, his former sergeant-major, Max Amann, wrote: 'The man screamed, he behaved in a way that I've never seen before. But everyone said: "He really means what he's saying." The sweat ran off him, he was soaking wet, it was incredible and that was what made his reputation...'[108] It was this eccentric style, his almost pitiable quality, his awkwardness, his obvious lack of training, and at the same time his intensity and ecstatic quality, all of these evidently conveyed to his public an impression of uniqueness and authenticity.

But Hitler was not simply a good speaker, who, as a 'man of the people', could instinctively hit the right note. Rather, his success must also have derived from factors that lay deep in his personality. We have already explored the fact that Hitler experienced the major upheaval of the immediate post-war period – military defeat, revolution, virtual civil war, and the substantial collapse of the economy – as a personal catastrophe. Unlike the majority of his contemporaries, who consigned these events to the abstract sphere of 'politics' and were able to maintain their own private life, in fact could shield themselves from the crisis as far as possible, Hitler lacked this private retreat. While many of his audience, even under the miserable post-war conditions, were able to fall in love, get married, have children, and lead a family life with its ups and downs, enjoy celebrations, and mourn their dead, Hitler felt the defeat and the challenge of the revolution with every nerve in his body as a deep inner wound and personal humiliation. But he was not prepared to confront the real reasons for this catastrophe. He could not admit that the defeat and the subsequent political chaos were self-inflicted, were the result of military weakness or of the illusions under which Germany had been living until the end of the war and which then were so abruptly shattered. He could only come to terms with them if he could regard them as the result of intrigue. And he now believed he could name those behind the scenes who were responsible: the Jews, who had used Socialism for their own ends. As part of this refusal to recognize reality Hitler developed a glorious view of the future; this concealed the miserable reality. He had a utopian vision of a national revival on a grand scale, enabling him to escape the lethargy and depression that had afflicted him in Pasewalk.

This mixture of hurt, blind fury, and a megalomaniacal refusal to accept reality – the expression of his psychological disposition – was evidently essential to his impact as a speaker. Here was someone who was openly displaying to the astonished public how he was struggling to come to terms with his shock at the prevailing conditions. He began hesitantly, with awkward gestures, searching for words. But then he got going, using crude accusations to provide simple explanations, and finally giving hope to his listeners by opening up the prospects of a glorious future. But he gripped his audience above all through the effort that he was clearly putting into it – grimaces, exaggerated gestures, uninhibited bellowing and screaming, interrupted by interludes of sarcasm and irony, the whole performance producing vast amounts of sweat, running down his face, sticking to his hair, and soaking his clothing.

Hitler had already impressed his friend Kubizek with his endless monologues, with his flight into an imagined world he had talked himself into believing in and which protected him from having to face his emotional inadequacies in dealing with other people. He must have felt the opportunity of speaking for hours on end to mass audiences with which he could establish direct contact, stirring them to enthusiastic applause and deep emotion, to be real compensation for his lack of feeling and inner emptiness. At the same time, this process of transformation that was taking place in front of everybody, the fact that an obviously inhibited person was succeeding, through a close bond with his audience, in rising to an ecstasy of emotion, was what made his speeches so fascinating. For in the intoxication of speaking and thanks to the ecstatic response of his audience, Hitler was reconfiguring reality in his own mind, and this process was an experience many listeners took with them from his speeches.

Because of his success as the most important party speaker Hitler soon acquired the role of the DAP's head of propaganda, a task he accorded the highest priority in the domestic political struggle. What was vital, he wrote in 1921, was to organize 'protest after protest, in beer halls and in the streets'. They must 'inspire a passionate wave of defiance, fury, and bitter anger...in our nation'. 'We want to pour hatred, burning hatred into the souls of millions of our national comrades...'[109] Hitler assumed that well-thought-out and cleverly delivered propaganda could have an almost unlimited impact. This very much reflected current opinion. In his influential book, *The Psychology of the Masses* (1895), published in German translation in 1908, Gustave Le Bon had effectively outlined how the weak-willed masses could be easily seduced. A similar line was taken in a pamphlet by the Munich neurologist, Julius R. Rossbach, with the title *The Soul of the Masses: Psychological Observations on the Creation of Popular (Mass) Movements (Revolutions)*, which he published in 1919 and which was extensively reviewed by Marc Sesselmann in the *Münchener Beobachter*. Rossbach frequently referred to Le Bon and so the similarity of the views held by Hitler and Le Bon, which has long been remarked upon, may be attributable to this pamphlet.[110] It appears entirely plausible that Hitler became acquainted with these ideas in the course of his training to become a propagandist during 1919.[111]

Hitler himself wrote in *Mein Kampf* about the effectiveness of the Christian Social and Social Democratic propaganda in pre-war Austria[112] and, above all, about Allied wartime propaganda, from which he had 'learnt a huge amount'.[113] The propaganda maxims that Hitler developed in this connection reveal his total contempt for the audience he was addressing. Propaganda must 'always speak to the masses. Its intellectual level must be adapted to the least intelligent among those it is addressed to. Thus, the larger the masses it is trying to reach, the lower its purely intellectual level will have to be.'[114] In addition to his view of the primitive nature of the masses, he stressed the importance of repetition: 'The masses' receptive ability is only very limited, their intelligence is small, but their memory is very short. As a result of these facts, all effective propaganda must be limited to a few points and use these as slogans until the very last member of the public understands what you want him to understand by your slogan.'[115] Propaganda was all about emotion. 'The people in their overwhelming majority are so feminine by nature and attitude that their thoughts and actions are determined far less by sober reasoning than by emotion and feeling. And this sentiment is not complicated but very simple and all of a piece.'[116]

Propaganda, according to Hitler, must get the masses moving and prepare the ground for 'the organization', indeed it must 'run far in advance of the organization and provide it with the human material to be worked on'.[117] As early as 1921, he had written that it was necessary 'to go from house to house in order to build up the organization that will bind together the hundreds of thousands of committed people and so fulfill the deep longings and hopes of the best of our nation'.[118] But he was, he wrote in *Mein Kampf*, 'an enemy of organizing too rapidly and too pedantically'.[119] In any case, it was important to make a clear distinction between the two tasks. 'Propaganda primes the general public to accept a particular idea and makes it ripe for the victory of this idea, while the organization secures victory by constantly welding those supporters who appear willing and able to carry on the fight for victory into an organic and effective fighting force.'[120]

Hitler noted down this principle in 1925, but he appears to have already been following it right from the start of his political career when he was acting as chief propagandist of the NSDAP. At the beginning of 1921, he had declined an invitation to join a new committee of the Party leadership, a three-man crisis 'Action Committee', which had been confirmed at the membership meeting of the Munich branch in January 1921 on Drexler's initiative.[121] Influencing his decision to reject this offer was not only his conviction that in the early phase of the Party's development propaganda should have priority over organization, but also and above all his awareness that his talents lay in the field of propaganda, while the essential preconditions for his taking on the Party leadership were lacking.[122] If he had accepted the chairmanship, he would have had to fit into an already existing structure, take on responsibility, be accountable, regularly take decisions, and in general adopt an orderly life, establish stable personal relations with leading Party figures based on mutual trust, and, not least, listen to others and possibly have to deal with their arguments. But it was impossible for him to reconcile all this with his unstable, restless personality, and irregular way of life. By contrast, producing wonderful visions in mass meetings, announcing apodictic eternal truths in newspaper articles, or addressing the clique of his closest colleagues in endless monologues about everything under the sun – that was the way in which Hitler could cope with his obvious personal flaws.[123]

The influential German Nationalist journalist, Max Maurenbrecher, wrote a leading article in the *Deutsche Zeitung* on 10 November 1923 as a kind of obituary for the failed putschist, Hitler. In it he remarked that he had had a long conversation with him in May 1921. At that time, Hitler had declared that he was not the 'leader and statesman', who could rescue the fatherland, but the 'agitator'.[124] In April 1920, Hitler had announced; 'We need a dictator who is a genius if we are going to rise again'.[125] In May he demanded that 'we must acquire a powerful and authoritative government that can ruthlessly clear out the pigsty'.[126] He complained in January 1921 that there were no men capable of taking on Bismarck's legacy.[127] He expressed the hope that 'one day an iron man will come along, who may have dirty boots but a pure conscience and a steely grip, who will silence these darlings of society and get the nation to act'.[128] With all these statements he was articulating the yearning for leadership widespread on the right. But he was a long way off putting himself forward as the leader.

3

Hitler becomes Party Leader

The NSDAP was able to build up its organization under the protection of the authoritarian regime in Bavaria. The number of new members increased between January and the end of 1920 from around 200 to over 2,100.[1] The first local branch outside Munich was founded in Rosenheim in April 1920.[2] By the end of the year it had been followed by Stuttgart, Dortmund, Starnberg, Tegernsee, Landsberg, and Landshut.[3] The Party's growth was based among other things on the fact that, during the course of 1920, it succeeded in largely taking over the Schutz- und Trutzbund's mass anti-Semitic agitation. It benefited from virtually the whole of the latter's Munich local branch leadership also being members of the NSDAP. Elsewhere too, new NSDAP local branches often emerged out of branches of the Schutzbund.[4] Hitler, however, who initially wanted to concentrate activity in Munich, advised caution in the creation of new branches, a policy that the Party duly followed.[5]

In March 1920, Hitler, who had delayed this for as long as possible, was finally discharged from the army. In Mayr's service he had learnt lessons vital for his future political career: to perceive the world in terms of friends and enemies, how to get his way in the face of opposition from his own colleagues, the basic principles of agitation and propaganda, how to secure and cultivate sponsors, and other things besides. Hitler's departure did not affect the army's support for the NSDAP. In June 1920 Mayr paid for 3,000 propaganda pamphlets, published by Lehmann and delivered to the NSDAP[6] and, after his own discharge from the Reichswehr in July 1920, continued to provide active support.[7] Thus, in September he told his mentor, Wolfgang Kapp, leader of the failed putsch, who had since been living in exile in Sweden: 'The national workers party must provide the basis for the strong assault force for which we are hoping. It's true that the programme is a bit crude and may also be inadequate.... Since July last year I have been doing my best to encourage the movement. I have mobilized some very effective young people. A certain Herr Hitler, for example, is a dynamic figure, a first class popular speaker.' As the next step Mayr wanted to get hold of the *Münchener Beobachter*, but he needed another 45,000 Marks: 'Could you possibly, Herr Privy Councillor, provide me with a source of funds?'[8] The Bavarian Army district command also had a benevolent regard for the Party. In December it reported to Berlin that the 'series of meetings held by the National Socialist Workers Party is having a very positive patriotic effect.'[9]

Hitler had been working to take over the *Münchener Beobachter* since the summer. The project had been discussed in the meetings of the NSDAP committee since July and increasingly since November 1920.[10] In December he saw that the chance to act had arrived: during the night of 16/17 December he warned important friends of the Party that there was a threat of the paper falling into the hands of separatists, and during the following days the money was raised for its purchase. Eckart was able to get General von Epp to put up 60,000 RM of Reichswehr funds (for which Eckart acted as guarantor) and Hitler persuaded an Augsburg entrepreneur, Gottfried Grandel, to come up with another 56,000 RM. The shares in the newspaper were formally transferred to Drexler.[11]

Hitler also sought financial support for the newspaper, which was never profitable, in Berlin. Backed with a letter of recommendation from police president, Pöhner, declaring that he had 'had lengthy conversations with Herr Hitler and become convinced that he is an exceptionally clever and energetic supporter of our cause', Hitler travelled to meet Heinrich Class, the chairman of the Pan-German League, who had previously helped him out. This meeting may have been the result of Mayr's September letter because Class had not gained an especially positive impression of Hitler from previous encounters.[12] After the meeting Class, who was prepared in principle to seek financial support for the *Völkischer Beobachter* because he wanted to acquire a base in Munich, contacted Otto Gertung, chairman of the engineering firm MAN, who initially responded that he would examine the matter in a positive light.[13] Following a second visit to Class that Hitler made in spring 1921, the former enquired of Tafel whether it was true, as he had been informed, that Hitler was unsettling civil servants and, above all, students with his 'socialist' propaganda.[14] Class remained uncertain.

The Munich police headquarters under its president, Pöhner, and the head of its political department, Wilhelm Frick, had no such qualms. At

Hitler's trial in 1924 Frick stated that he and Pöhner had been supporting the DAP right from the start, as they were convinced 'that this was the movement that would be able to win support from the workers, who had been infected by Marxism, and win them back to the nationalist cause. For this reason we held a protective hand over the National Socialist Party and Herr Hitler.'[15] In particular, the approval of political posters, which was required under the state of emergency, was dealt with in a generous fashion. Kahr had 'quietly tolerated' this policy, he claimed. Hitler subsequently thanked Frick and Pöhner warmly for their support in *Mein Kampf*.[16]

Thus, the NSDAP continued its propaganda during 1921, supported and protected in various ways by the right-wing conservative establishment. On 3 February 1921, Hitler spoke for the first time at a meeting in the Circus Krone in front of 6,000 people, ranting for two and a half hours against the Versailles Treaty.[17] With this quickly arranged meeting Hitler had pre-empted a major demonstration planned by the right-wing organizations against the impending agreement by the Reich government to pay a sum of 226 billion gold marks in reparations that had been finally agreed at the Paris Conference. As in the previous year, when he had used the hot-house anti-Semitic atmosphere created by the Schutz- und Trutzbund for the NSDAP's first big meeting in the Hofbräuhaus, now, once again pushing himself into the limelight at just the right moment, he exploited the excitement generated by his political rivals. However, his rivals had their revenge: when Hitler tried to generate support for the NSDAP at the protest demonstration arranged by the patriotic organizations on the Odeonsplatz on 6 February the organizers sabotaged his speech.[18] On 6 and again on 15 March, with Hitler as speaker, the NSDAP succeeded in filling the huge Circus Krone. As usual, he fulminated against 'new humiliations for the German nation' and the 'disgrace of the Versailles treaty'.[19] During the course of 1921, he gave a total of over sixty speeches.[20]

But who came to these meetings? In contrast to the Party's title it was not so much the workers who joined but rather members of the lower middle class. In July Hitler reluctantly admitted this in a letter to Major Hierl, the city commandant of Munich and a Party sympathizer. In response to the latter's enquiry he remarked: 'Your concern that our meetings are not attended by enough people from the industrial working class is only partially correct. We recognize the difficulty of winning over to us workers who, in some cases, have been members of organizations for decades. The precondition for this was to begin by holding mass meetings in order to have a propaganda method with which to attract the masses. For workers, as down-to-earth people, will always only respect a movement which presents itself in a way that demands respect. But, to ensure the peaceful running of our meetings we were obliged to appeal to a certain middle class, whose attitudes and feelings we knew were nationalist and some of whom, because of the current miserable state of our parties, are politically homeless. As a result of this our meetings have inevitably been somewhat mixed.'[21]

Hitler's entourage

It was not only the NSDAP's propaganda that was aggressive. Responding to the violent style of politics that had emerged during the post-war era, the Nazis set about organizing their own 'protection troop'. The Munich police first became aware in September 1920 that the Nazis had acquired a protection squad. From the end of 1920 this squad called itself the 'Gymnastic and Sports Section'.[22]

In the course of this development a group of dubious characters attached themselves to Hitler to take care of his personal protection and used physical violence against his political opponents. The most prominent of these personal bodyguards was Ulrich Graf, born in 1878, and employed in the municipal abattoir. He claimed to have got to know Hitler as early as 1919 and joined the NSDAP at the beginning of 1921. Among his work colleagues he recruited 'eight tough, reliable men' to act as Hitler's 'security service' and himself took on the role, as he later recorded, of 'permanent escort...responsible for the Führer's personal security'.[23] Apart from Graf, there was also Christian Weber, born in 1883, a groom by trade and, during the post-war period, registered in the Munich trade directory as a horse dealer. According to his own statement, he had supported the Party since February 1920 and his main role had been as Hitler's 'muscle'. Weber was notorious for his involvement in a number of violent incidents: before the 1923 putsch he had had 152 court appearances.[24] Emil Maurice, born in 1897, a watchmaker's assistant, acted as Hitler's chauffeur from 1921 onwards.[25] Gradually, an informal circle within the NSDAP began to form around Hitler, the Party's most important propagandist. For example, in addition to Graf, Weber, and Maurice, and Hitler's earliest supporters, Anton Drexler, Dietrich Eckart, Alfred Rosenberg, and Hermann Esser, Rudolf Hess joined the group. During the war he had been a Lieutenant in the air force; he was a member of the Thule Society and had been actively involved in the conspiracy against the Räterepublik. He joined the NSDAP in July 1920 and, as he proudly wrote in a letter to his parents, in the late summer he established the Party's first link with Ludendorff. This contact must have led to a meeting between Hitler and the former Quartermaster General in spring 1921.[26]

Hess was also part of a delegation of Nazis which, headed by Hitler, was received by Kahr for an exchange of views on 14 May 1921. Following this meeting, in an effusive letter to Kahr Hess described Hitler as a man who combined 'a rare sense of what the people are feeling, political instinct, and tremendous will power'.[27] Hess was registered as a student at the University and was a kind of private pupil of the former general and honorary professor, Karl Haushofer; at the same time, he was organizing a Nazi student group.[28]

Alfred Rosenberg established contacts with a number of Baltic German emigrés who supported the Party. Probably his most important contact was Max Scheubner-Richter, who was born in 1884 in Riga. During the war, he had been engaged in military and political activities (among other things for the German eastern High Command's press office) and then in the recruitment of German Free Corps in the Baltic and their campaign against Soviet Russian forces; subsequently, he had taken part in the Kapp putsch and, after its failure, had transferred his activities to Munich. There, in 1920, Scheubner-Richter established the 'Wirtschaftliche Aufbau-Vereinigung' (Association for Economic Development), which worked secretly to coordinate the interests of Baltic German and White Russian emigrés with the plans of German right-wing extremists for eastern Europe and for this purpose ran a newspaper agency.

Scheubner-Richter became Ludendorff's eastern Europe expert and close confidant; he joined the NSDAP in November 1920 and, alongside Hess, formed the link between the Party and the former Quartermaster General. He was also important for the Party as a link-man to the circles of monarchist Russian emigrés; it may also have profited from his contacts to industry. Moreover, like Rosenberg, he was a member of the Riga student fraternity, Rubonia, with a branch in Munich, to which other Baltic Germans belonged such as Otto von Kursell, who worked as an illustrator for Nazi publications, and Arno Schickedanz. Both knew Scheubner-Richter from their Riga days and now worked for his Aufbau Association.[29] The group round Rosenberg and Scheubner-Richter considered themselves pioneers in the struggle for a German strategy of using the Baltic as a springboard for an aggressive policy towards the young Soviet Union. They greatly influenced Hitler, in particular with their notion that the Bolshevik revolution was entirely in Jewish hands and must, therefore, be defeated in order to open the door to the East.

The seizure of power in the Party

In summer 1921 Hitler swapped the role of chief propagandist for that of Party leader. This happened at the high point of a crisis, which had broken out concerning a proposed fusion of the NSDAP with its 'sister', the German Socialist Party. Attempts to combine the two parties can be traced back to August 1920, when Hitler and Drexler met with representatives of the DSP in Salzburg and agreed a demarcation of respective 'spheres of authority'; according to this, the NSDAP was supposed to restrict itself to operating in southern Germany.[30] However, at the beginning of 1921, the NSDAP leadership told the Austrian Nazis, who had been planning a union of the various national socialist parties, of their reservations about the DSP. In a letter signed by Drexler, but, on the basis of its language almost certainly written by Hitler, they claimed that the DSP was wasting its energies by establishing far too many, ultimately useless, local branches, was sticking to its commitment to the parliamentary system, and failing to recognize the possibilities of mass propaganda such as was being carried out by the NSDAP.[31] Drexler, however, appeared to be not unsympathetic to this union. In March, at a meeting with representatives of the DSP in Zeitz in Thuringia, and presumably acting on the authority of the majority of the NSDAP leadership, he reached provisional agreement for an amalgamation of the two parties. However, the subsequent negotiations to clinch the deal, held in Munich in April, were blocked by Hitler, who melodramatically threatened to resign if it went through.[32]

Only a few months later, the Munich NSDAP leadership renewed its initiative while Hitler was away on a lengthy stay in Berlin during June and July, where among other things he visited Class, in order to tap him for funds for the *Völkischer Beobachter*.[33] They established contact with Otto Dickel, an Augsburg schoolmaster, who had founded yet another völkisch group, the *Deutsche Werkgemeinschaft*.[34] After a successful speech by Dickel in Munich, on 10 July, they met with him and the Nuremberg DSP in

Augsburg to explore the possibility of closer cooperation. Hitler, arriving straight from Berlin, turned up at the meeting unexpectedly trying to block the impending cooperation. However, despite his abrupt departure during the negotiations, he was unable to prevent the Munich delegation from agreeing to Dickel's suggestion for loose cooperation in future. On the following day, Hitler announced that he was in fact resigning from the NSDAP.[35]

Hitler was afraid that cooperation with the DSP would mean the NSDAP giving up its programme and its identity as a 'revolutionary-nationalist' movement hostile to any form parliamentary activity, and that Dickel would take overall control, with the main focus of action shifting to Augsburg.[36] This was a particularly sensitive point, as Hitler was strongly in favour of concentrating the Party's activities in the Munich local branch, in other words the area over which he, as the leading propagandist and celebrated speaker, exercised total control. In short, he considered the identity of the NSDAP, which he had been largely responsible for constructing, to be in danger. Whereas hitherto, as the Party's main agitator and policy maker, he had been able to do what he liked, he now feared being bound by an alien structure that he had had no say in shaping. He rebelled against this on the principle of 'all or nothing', deciding, more or less overnight, to alter his previous role in the Party. However, he did not simply seek the post of chairman, for in doing so he would have been simply integrating himself in a different form into structures that he did not control; instead, he went for unlimited, total leadership.[37]

His threat to abandon his work for the Party was thus not the result of carefully prepared tactical calculation, not merely the pretext or the occasion for what was actually a long-held ambition to secure a dictatorial form of leadership of the Party, but instead a spontaneous reaction that reflected his unstable character, prone as it was to fits of rage and intuitive 'decisions'. For the cooperation with Dickel, which had been agreed behind his back and initiated against his objections, represented for him an intolerable loss of face; he was in danger of suffering a defeat that would destroy his self-image as the 'drummer' for the nationalist cause, admired by his supporters, that he had devoted most of the previous two years to creating. After threatening to resign in the spring he now had to go through with it if he was not to lose credibility. In order to prevent such potential defeats from happening in the future he had to demand a dictatorial form of leadership for himself. From his point of view this was not a triumphal take-over of power in the

Party, but rather a difficult decision that had been forced on him by outside circumstances. Significantly, in *Mein Kampf* Hitler dismisses the dramatic disagreements of summer 1921 in a few sentences. He does not mention his resignation, but writes, in accordance with his dogmatic separation of propaganda and organization, that the time had come when, 'after the slow visible success of propaganda, the organization [had to be] adapted and adjusted' to it.[38] Also, the summer crisis played no role in the 'Party legend' that he was to repeat in hundreds of speeches in the future.

After Hitler's threat the Party leadership gave in. Drexler, who involved Eckart as mediator, sought to conciliate Hitler, who, however, imposed conditions on his return to the Party. He demanded the summoning of an extraordinary general meeting at which the following points were to be on the agenda: the resignation and re-election of the Party committee, which was required to elect him 'No. I. Chairman with dictatorial powers', so that he could immediately set up a three-man 'Action Committee' to carry out a 'ruthless purge of the Party'. Secondly, Hitler demanded the 'establishment of the irrevocable principle that the headquarters is and always will be in Munich'. The Party programme and the Party's name should not be altered for an initial period of six years. There was to be no cooperation with the DSP; such groups would have to 'join' the Party. Negotiations with such groups would require his prior personal approval.[39] The committee yielded to Hitler. It declared its willingness 'in view of your tremendous knowledge, your services to the movement marked by rare self-sacrifice and carried out in an honorary capacity, your remarkable rhetorical talent' to grant Hitler 'dictatorial powers'.[40]

However, Hitler's internal Party opponents did not remain inactive. They succeeded in excluding Hermann Esser, one of Hitler's closest associates, from the Party and an anonymous pamphlet appeared in which Hitler was accused of having 'brought disunity and division into our ranks at the behest of dubious men acting behind the scenes'.[41] Drexler informed the police that a leaflet announcing a membership meeting on 26 July had not been authorized by the Party leadership, but had been issued by opponents of the Party in Hitler's and Esser's camp who were no longer members of the NSDAP. Drexler explained that there were 'two factions in the Party, which are strongly opposed to one another', namely 'the Hitler one, which wants to achieve the Party's goals in a revolutionary way, possibly using terror, violence and other means', and the 'Drexler line', which wished to 'achieve [its aims] in a legal (sic!), parliamentary way'. Later, Schüssler, the Party manager, appeared seeking authorization for a poster, which contained an invitation on behalf of the Party leadership to a membership meeting on 29 July. Schüssler remarked on Hitler's opaque sources of finance and made negative comments about his 'protection squad'.[42]

However, in the end the two rival factions managed to reach an accommodation. The membership meeting called by Hitler's opposition group for 26 July was now used to prepare for what became a demonstration of Party unity three days later.[43] At this meeting in the Hofbräuhaus on 29 July, Hitler was able to push through all his demands in front of 554 members of the Party. He had been correct in acting on the assumption that the vast majority of Party members regarded him as the leading figure in the NSDAP and as indispensable, above all because of his impact in the public arena. He had never striven to become Party chairman, indeed had even declined it in the past; but now, Hitler informed the meeting, he no longer felt able to resist the request of his loyal friend, Drexler.[44] The new Party statutes, carried with only one vote against, consolidated the central role of the Party leader, who in future was no longer answerable to the Party committee but only to the membership meeting. Finally, Hitler was elected Party chairman and Drexler, as Hitler had proposed, elected honorary president for life.[45]

Esser was welcomed back into the Party and made propaganda chief. Schüssler lost his position as Party manager and was replaced by Hitler's former sergeant-major, Max Amann. Christian Weber was given a post in the Party headquarters to support Amann in running the organization.[46] A new larger Party headquarters was established in a former pub in the Corneliusstrasse; it replaced the room in the Sterneckerbräu pub which had been rented in 1920.[47] Eckart, who had warned Hitler's critics in the *Völkischer Beobachter* that no one could 'serve a cause in a more selfless, devoted, and honest way than Hitler' but also in no 'more decisive and vigilant'[48] a way, was appointed editor of the *Völkischer Beobachter*; Rosenberg became his deputy.[49] Its financing, however, remained uncertain. In accordance with his maxim of concentrating on Munich, in July Hitler had refused a request by the Pan-Germans to extend the activities of the NSDAP into north Germany; as a result Class did not pursue further contact.[50]

Hitler's seizure of power within the Party coincided with a significant development in Bavarian politics. The dissolution of the Einwohnerwehren at the behest of the Allies had heralded the demise of the Kahr government, for they had been its main basis of support and, with this defeat, the govern-ment suffered a serious loss of prestige. Kahr's attempts, immediately after the dissolution of the Einwohnerwehren, to try to create a substitute organization led by the governor of the Upper Palatinate and head of the Einwohnerwehr state office, Medical Councillor Otto Pittinger, proved only partially suc-cessful. For a number of paramilitary leagues declined to join the so-called Pittinger Organization or only did so with reservations. They included Bund Oberland, which had emerged from the Free Corps Oberland, the Reichsflagge, and the Verband der Vaterländischen Bezirksvereine Münchens [League of Munich Patriotic District Associations], which former Einwohnerwehr members had joined.[51]

Against this background of the increasing fragmentation of the paramili-tary organizations in Bavaria, the Munich Reichswehr command began to show growing interest in the NSDAP's Gymnastic and Sports section, the Party's relatively small protection squad. It appeared suited to producing cadres for a new paramilitary league; assistance for this was to be provided by the illegal Organisation Consul led by Captain Ehrhardt. In August 1921, immediately after his seizure of power within the Party, Hitler made an agreement with Ehrhardt to proceed along these lines. As a result, Hitler and the NSDAP were now actively involved in creating a military reserve in Bavaria, giving the Party considerably more influence. It is highly probable that NSDAP member Ernst Röhm, the Reichswehr officer responsible for arming the paramilitary leagues, played an important role in arranging this agreement. Indeed, one can go a step further and wonder whether Hitler's success in acquiring a dictatorial position within the Party in summer 1921 was assisted by the Reichswehr, which needed a Party chairman who would support its use of the Party for paramilitary purposes. In view of the lack of sources this must remain speculation. What is certain, however, is that the inclusion in the illegal rearmament programme of what would soon acquire the name Sturmabteilung (SA), which in November 1921 had a member-ship of around 300,[52] represented a further increase in the Reichswehr's support for the Party, but also a greater dependence on the military. The creation of his own paramilitary league, however, enabled Hitler to establish links with other paramilitary organizations, namely those that were opposed to Pittinger's semi-state run umbrella organization, which came into the open in July 1922, now calling itself 'Bayern und Reich'. The constellation that was to lead to the Hitler putsch in November 1923 was already begin-ning to form.[53]

Heading for conflict with the
Bavarian government

On 26 August 1921, Matthias Erzberger, who had signed the armistice on 11 November 1918 and, as a result, had become a target of criticism for the whole of the Right, was murdered. This act of violence and the subsequent refusal of Kahr's government to apply the national state of emergency that had been declared by Reich President Ebert in the state of Bavaria (where a state of emergency had already been in operation for years), raised the temperature of what was already a tense political atmosphere in Munich still further.[54] In addition, the population was becoming discontented about the growing inflation, which, in summer 1921 and not for the first time, led to protests against rising prices.[55] Hitler immediately tried to portray the protests as the result of a 'Jewish swindle' and generally to pour oil onto the flames; Jewish 'crooks' and 'profiteers' were to blame for the 'people's starvation'.[56]

Kahr, who had failed to get his way in his conflict with the Reich, resigned in September as prime minister together with his whole cabinet; the government was taken over by the moderate conservative, Count Lerchenfeld, with a cabinet made up of members of the Bavarian People's Party (BVP), the German Democratic Party (DDP), and the Bavarian Peasant League. The NSDAP could no longer rely on the political support of the government as it had done under Kahr: the Bavarian Middle Party (the Bavarian branch of the DNVP) had left the government; a critic of the NSDAP, the former state secretary, Xaver Schweyer, had become interior minister; the police president, Poehner, had resigned; and the Justice Ministry had been taken over by Lerchenfeld himself.[57] As a result, Hitler decided to engage in a confrontation with Lerchenfeld; he sensed the opportunity of playing a leading role in the extreme right-wing movement, which was now acting increasingly independently, and began subjecting Lerchenfeld to a series of vicious attacks.[58] When he also mounted a number of provocations with the aim of drawing attention to himself, the police and judiciary did not stand idly by.

On 14 September Hitler and his supporters attempted to break up a meeting of the Bavarian Peasant League, which the NSDAP regarded as a 'separatist' organization. In the course of the disorder provoked by the NSDAP in the Löwenbräukeller, the chairman of the Peasant League, Otto Ballerstedt and another representative of the League were injured and the police closed the meeting.[59] On the following day, the police banned the *Völkischer Beobachter* for two weeks and, a week later, while in the Party's headquarters, Hitler was taken into custody for a short time and his flat searched.[60] After further disorder, unauthorized demonstrations, and violent clashes between Nazis and the police during October 1921, Hitler was ordered to attend police headquarters. He was accused of causing massive public disorder and, in the event of a repetition, threatened with deportation.[61] Hitler, of course, claimed to have had nothing to do with these events and declared his willingness to do his utmost to prevent such things from happening in the future. In fact, on the following day, he did warn the SA at a meeting to exercise more discipline: 'we mustn't ruin things with the police'. But he obviously made this declaration in order to reassure the security forces.[62] However, just over a week later, there was a further incident: on 4 November his SA beat up hecklers at a meeting in the Hofbräuhaus where he was speaking, an event that Hitler described in suitably dramatic terms as the SA's 'baptism of fire'.[63]

In November the Munich police produced a list of the numerous occasions on which, during the previous months, it had banned Nazi leaflets and posters.[64] In January 1922 a Munich court sentenced Hitler to three months imprisonment for the attack on Ballerstedt and, during the summer, he spent five weeks in Munich-Stadelheim prison. Hitler never forgave his opponent for the humiliation of his imprisonment; on 30 June 1934, Ballerstedt was murdered near Dachau concentration camp. More than twenty years after his dispute with the leader of the Peasant League Hitler was still maintaining that he had been 'his biggest opponent' and had deployed a 'diabolical sophistry'.[65] Unlike his stay in Landsberg prison in 1924, Hitler seldom referred to his Munich prison sentence in later years.

After he had been sentenced, Interior Minister Schweyer contemplated Hitler's deportation, but, following vigorous protests from the moderate Right, it did not happen.[66] Hitler was not going to let the opportunity slip and, on 12 April, took two pages of the *Völkischer Beobachter* to respond to the plan to deport him. He wrote that he felt himself to be a German citizen, although 'according to the letter of the current Jewish law [I am] in fact a "foreigner"'. This was because of 'my blood link to our nation', 'my clan link to Bavaria' (his birthplace, Braunau, belonged to Bavaria until 1816), as well as 'above all the service that I performed for nearly six years in that grey uniform, which in the old days was honoured as the king's uniform and seemed to me at any rate the noblest uniform a citizen can wear'. Hitler maintained that the case against him had only been brought to create an opportunity to deport him and went on to attack Lerchenfeld, whom in future he referred to ironically as 'Herr Count'.

Only two weeks after Hitler's sentence for his attack on Ballerstedt, the NSDAP held a general membership meeting in Munich from 29 to 31 January 1922, attended by around 1,500 people in the Hofbräuhaus. Hitler greeted delegations from, among other places, Hanover, Leipzig, Halle, Zwickau, Stuttgart, Mannheim, and Nuremberg as well as from a number of Bavarian local branches.[67] According to figures that he announced at the meeting, at this point the Party had '35 well-organized local branches'.[68] In fact there were fewer than twenty active ones. The numbers had stagnated following Hitler's take-over of the Party in July 1921, reflecting Hitler's basic principle of concentrating on building up the Party in Munich.[69] This was in fact where most of the members were registered. The number of members had doubled during the course of 1921 from 2,000 to 4,000.[70]

In an article published in the *Völkischer Beobachter* to coincide with the Party meeting Hitler regaled his readers once again with his favourite topic, the history of the Party, although it was only three years old. His contribution contained a reckoning with his internal Party opponents during the summer crisis in which he once again emphasized the importance of Munich as 'the bastion of the national socialist movement', as the 'model...school, but also granite base'. He expressed the hope that one or two of those who had come to the meeting would see beyond the 'grumbling, complaining, slandering, and back-biting' and be convinced that the headquarters had 'carried out a terrific amount of work, which should give us in Munich the right to carry on and direct the organization of our movement'.[71]

The meeting itself was exceptionally peaceful. After the conclusion of the usual formalities, Hitler was once again elected chairman with Oskar Körner his deputy. Together with the two secretaries and treasurers, they formed the Party's 'main committee'.[72]

Looking for donors in Berlin and Munich

In December 1921 Hitler had another meeting in Berlin with Class, the chairman of the Pan-German League, the secretary, Leopold von Vietinghoff-Scheel, and with the executive chairman of the Vereinigte Vaterländische

Verbände [Union of Patriotic Leagues], Fritz Geisler.[73] They met in the exclusive National Club of 1919, which was associated with the DNVP. A few months later, on 29 May and 5 June 1922, Hitler was permitted to speak there in front of a large audience. These occasions were largely the result of invitations from Class, who was once again acting as Hitler's mentor in the hope of establishing a base in Munich and subordinating him to Berlin. He even paid his travel expenses.[74]

During 1922–23, an important role in securing Party donations was played by a Berlin pharmacist, Dr Emil Gansser. A friend of Eckart's and a Party supporter, Gansser would invite potential donors to a confidential meeting at which they were addressed by Hitler.[75] In his speech of 29 May Hitler emphasized that, while there was a certain amount of agreement with the right-wing parties about 'the nationalist aim of liberating Germany', when it came to winning over the workers they were totally incapable of 'competing' with the 'Marxist parties'. He insisted: 'We can only win power and revive Germany on a completely new social and political foundation, not in parliament and on a democratic basis, but only through the violent assertion of our healthy national energies and by bringing together and preparing our youth for this task'. A nationalist dictatorship must then reorganize Germany's political, economic and social constitution, excluding the fateful influence of Jews, Freemasons, and political Catholicism. In contrast to the other right-wing parties, he claimed the NSDAP was free from their influence.[76] His second speech, which took a similar line to the first, was attended by the influential industrialist, Ernst von Borsig, who subsequently arranged a meeting with Hitler designed to provide him with the financial means to expand his party into north Germany. Given his commitment to concentrating on Munich and Bavaria, Hitler's response was no doubt ambivalent. Borsig was supported in his efforts by Karl Burhenne, the administrator of the Siemens social fund, who had already been introduced to Hitler by Gansser in March 1922. Burhenne also had a meeting with Hitler and, after the meeting, Gansser strongly recommended further support for Hitler.[77] Borsig and Burhenne then tried to drum up donations for Hitler among Berlin industrialists, evidently to little effect.[78] However, in summer 1922, Class appears to have transferred 150,000 RM to the NSDAP.[79]

His speeches in the National Club had also opened the doors of the Bavarian Industrialists' Association to Hitler, a contact that was arranged through Hermann Aust, the managing director of a Munich company, who had attended them. Subsequently, Hitler had two meetings with representatives of the association and gave a speech to a large audience at the Munich Merchants' Club. Aust declared at Hitler's trial in 1924 that he had transferred several donations from businessmen to Hitler.[80]

On 12 October Hitler was once again in Berlin, as is clear from Nazi records that state he had talks with 'north German nationalist circles', in particular with the Vereinigte Vaterländische Verbände, the Stahlhelm [Steel Helmet] veterans' organization, the Deutsche Handlungsgehilfenverband [a white-collar union] and the Deutschbund.[81] A few days after his stay, he penned a memorandum on the 'Expansion of the National Socialist Workers' Party', which was obviously intended for potential donors. It stated that the main aim of the NSDAP was 'the annihilation and extermination of the Marxist world view' to be achieved through an 'incomparable, brilliantly organized propaganda and indoctrination machine' and through an 'organization marked by the most ruthless force and the most brutal determination' (i.e. the SA). In other words, Hitler was once again adopting his distinction in principle between 'propaganda' and 'organization'. Spelled out in concrete terms, he wanted to turn the *Völkischer Beobachter* into a daily paper, improve the equipment of and partly motorize the SA, and acquire a new headquarters. In total, he worked out, he needed the sum of 53,240,000 RM (equivalent to 95,000 pre-war Marks).[82]

We do not know whether or from whom Hitler received such a substantial sum; in practice, however, his wishes were largely fulfilled. In autumn 1922 the Party acquired three vehicles, a motor car – an open-topped, four-seater touring car, a Selve – for Hitler's personal use, as well as two lorries (provided by a Reichswehr cover organization under Röhm's control) for transporting Party members.[83] From February 1923 onwards the *Völkischer Beobachter* appeared as a daily. During the summer of 1923, the Party headquarters moved into rooms belonging to the *Völkischer Beobachter* in Schellingstrasse 39/41 and, shortly afterwards, Hitler was already inspecting Schellingstrasse 50. The Party did not, however, open its new headquarters here until 1925, on account of the ban on the Party following the failed putsch of November 1923.[84]

Even after his take-over of power in the Party and receiving increasing support from the upper classes, Hitler's personal circumstances remained demonstratively modest. He lived in a furnished room in Thierschstrasse and most of the time wore shabby suits.[85] His irregular, bohemian life style, his frequent and lengthy visits to cafés, where he surrounded himself with strikingly mixed company – his entourage – aroused the mistrust of both

internal and external opponents. What was Hitler living off? they were asking, now that he had been discharged from the Reichswehr. He was being
called the 'King of Munich', an image that Hitler 'did not particularly want
to go into'.[86] His opaque financial circumstances had already become an
issue during the 1921 summer crisis.[87] He declared that he did not receive
any fees for his speeches for the Party, but was supported 'in a modest way'
by Party members; apart from that, he lived off his income as an 'author'.
That can really only refer to his regular articles in the *Völkischer Beobachter*,
for which he presumably received payment. In addition, he may have
received fees for occasional speeches unconnected with the NSDAP.[88] It is
plausible that he personally received money from one or more Party donors
(who hoped thereby to acquire influence), but this cannot be proved.

4

The March to the Hitler Putsch

In summer 1922 the conflict between Bavaria and the Reich broke out again with renewed bitterness. The murder of Reich Foreign Minister, Walther Rathenau by members of the Organization Consul, on 24 June 1922, prompted the Reich to pass a 'Law for the Protection of the Republic', which seriously impinged on the responsibilities of the federal states. The Bavarian government responded by replacing the Reich law with a state decree, whereupon the Reich President demanded the withdrawal of the decree. When Prime Minister Lerchenfeld subsequently worked out a compromise with the Reich and, in August, finally withdrew the decree, he found himself confronted with a broad front of right-wing groups accusing him of having sacrificed Bavarian interests. Anti-Prussian and anti-socialist sentiments were being exploited once again.[1] During the following months Hitler was able to profit from these bitter conflicts.

The agitation against the Reich government and Lerchenfeld's policy came to a head on 16 August with a major demonstration of the right-wing leagues on the Königsplatz in Munich. The NSDAP took part in this event as a distinct formation, with Hitler, the second speaker, receiving warm applause from the crowd.[2]

Another major demonstration, arranged for only a few days later, was banned by the police because of rumours about a putsch. In fact, Pittinger, who was trying to unite the most important paramilitary leagues under the umbrella of his organization Bayern und Reich, wanted to use this opportunity to proclaim Kahr dictator. However, Georg Heim, the Bavarian peasant leader, as well as a number of Reichswehr officers who were in the know, refused to join in prompting Pittinger to approach Hitler. In the event, relatively few demonstrators came to the Königsplatz (most of them

were Nazis) and the police cleared the square, forcing Pittinger to cancel
the operation.³ Finally, instead of the demonstration taking place on the
Königsplatz, around 5,000 demonstrators made their way to the Kindlkeller,
where Hitler found he had no alternative but to follow police instructions
and order his followers peacefully to disperse. The evening had turned into
a fiasco for Hitler. One thing had become clear: the more the NSDAP
became involved in the complicated relationship between government,
army, and paramilitary leagues, the greater the danger of being used by
others for their own purposes.⁴ Hitler interpreted the botched 'Pittinger
putsch' as confirmation of his previous policy of maintaining the NSDAP's
independence at all costs.

These highly fraught political confrontations were taking place against
the background of an increasingly precarious economic situation brought
about by the rapid devaluation of the currency. For during the summer of
1922 the steady deterioration in the value of the Mark that had been going
on since the war turned into hyperinflation. A memorandum from the
Bavarian state government to the Reich Chancellor from September 1922
stated: 'The wave of price increases that is currently sweeping through the
country, which in size and extent far exceeds all previous ones, has created
a situation that poses a threat to the economy, to the state, and to society in
equal measure.'⁵

In October 1922, Hitler accepted an invitation from the Schutz- und
Trutzbund for his Party to attend the German Day in Coburg, a gathering
of völkisch supporters from all over the Reich. It was the first time that
Hitler had mobilized his Party supporters in any numbers for an event outside Munich. It is claimed that 800 SA men travelled on 14 October to the
town in Upper Franconia in northern Bavaria. Despite a police ban, they
marched through the town in tight formation with flags flying and a band
playing. The provocation had the desired effect. There were numerous fights
with socialist counter-demonstrators, culminating in a street battle. By the
end, the SA had provided an exemplary demonstration of how to conquer
the streets.⁶ A few days later, Hitler achieved another triumph, this time in
Middle Franconia. On 20 October, the members of the Nuremberg branch
of the Deutsche Werkgemeinschaft (mainly previous supporters of the DSP)
were ceremoniously received into the NSDAP. At the beginning of the
month, after a row with Otto Dickel, the founder and leader of the
Werkgemeinschaft, the branch leader, Julius Streicher, who was a school
teacher and rabid anti-Semite, had agreed to throw in his lot with Hitler.

The fact that the Munich Party was prepared to take on his newspaper, the *Deutscher Volkswille*, and pay off its debts, which were in his name, provided an additional incentive. By the end of 1922, the march through Coburg and Streicher's joining the NSDAP with his supporters had significantly increased the Party's support in Middle and Upper Franconia.[7]

In total, by the end of 1922, 8,000 people had joined the Party since its foundation, of whom half had joined during the second half of 1922, although, in view of the high degree of fluctuation, the actual number of members was probably significantly lower.[8] Moreover, the number of local branches had markedly increased. Their number rose from 17 at the beginning of 1922 to 46 by the end of the summer and, finally, to 100 at the end of the year. This also shows that the NSDAP's expansion occurred mostly during the last months of 1922.[9] The main focus of the Party organization continued to be Bavaria, where its presence could no longer be ignored. Whereas the NSDAP was banned in Prussia in November 1922, the political situation in Bavaria moved in the Party's favour. Lerchenfeld was replaced as prime minister in November, and his successor, Eugen von Knilling, who was a right-wing conservative, once more tried to link the extreme right-wing forces more closely to the government. Knilling's attitude to the NSDAP was ambivalent. He tried to limit its extremism, but believed the Party's potential could be utilized for a nationalist initiative coming from Bavaria. Thus, in November, only a few days after Knilling's arrival in office, the NSDAP was included in the re-founded Vereinigte Vaterländische Verbände, a relatively broad umbrella organization, containing both civilian and paramilitary, moderate and radical right-wing groups. Apart from the Nazis, it included Pittinger's Bayern und Reich, the Bayerische Ordnungsblock, the Wehrverband Reichsflagge, the Verband der Vaterländischen Bezirksvereine Münchens as well as the Pan-German League and the Schutz- und Trutzbund.[10]

At the same time, the Party demonstrated that it was quite capable of acting on its own. In November 1922, rumours were circulating that Hitler was planning a putsch, rumours that increased during January.[11] They seemed to be entirely justified by the NSDAP's aggressive behaviour, for, before the end of the year, the SA engaged for a second time in a massive operation outside Munich. In December 1922 a large group of SA men turned up in Göppingen in Württemberg and engaged in a bloody confrontation with socialist opponents.[12] Moreover, on 13 December, the NSDAP organized ten mass meetings running in parallel in Munich, with the slogan 'Jews and Marxists: the True Gravediggers of the German Nation and the German

Reich'.[13] A few days later Hitler held an SA parade in the Munich Hofbräuhaus. In front of an audience of – the police estimated – 2,800, Hitler, referring to the violent events in Göppingen, demanded that the SA show 'loyalty unto death and beyond, as the Führer himself also pledges loyalty unto death'.[14]

From 'drummer' to 'Führer'

The growth in support for the NSDAP in autumn 1922 marks the point at which the image and self-image of Hitler as 'Führer' began to develop within the Party. During the post-war period, the call for a 'Führer' was common within the German Right, but not only the Right. In politics, literature, journalism, the humanities, the youth movement, and also within the Protestant Church there was a widespread longing for an exceptional personality, the 'one', to appear and lead the nation out of its humiliation and back to honour and national glory. This call from multiple voices was religiously, or rather pseudo-religiously, charged to a high degree. For many this anticipated hero could only be one sent by God. The longing for a national saviour figure was so ubiquitous and so intense that, for many, the numerous prophecies of a messianic redeemer had almost become a certainty.[15]

Such expressions of anticipation of a 'Führer' can also be shown to have been present in the milieu within which Hitler gradually emerged as 'Führer' between 1919 and 1923. In September 1919, in other words at the moment when Hitler first attended a DAP meeting, Scheubner-Richter's newsletter, *Aufbau*, published a poem by Emanuel Geibel ('German Laments from the Year 1844'),[16] which contains the following lines:

> We need a man, a scion of the Nibelungs,
> To take control of our madly galloping age
> With iron fists and thighs.

In December 1919, Dietrich Eckart, Hitler's mentor in the DAP, published a poem 'Patience', in which the last verse reads:

> He waits silently, the hero to whom we look;
> Only now and then the sword clinks in his scabbard,
> Then all around, with dreadful groans and howls
> That progeny of hell, the Huns.

He waits in silence, his eyes fixed on one object:
The countless crimes others have committed against us –
Already a bright dawn seems to be breaking
…
Patience! Patience![17]

During 1922, Hitler was usually referred to as Adolf Hitler or 'Pg. (Party comrade) Hitler' in the announcements of his speeches in the *Völkischer Beobachter*. From spring 1922 onwards, however, increasingly the term 'our leader Pg. Adolf Hitler' is used. When, at the end of October 1922, the Italian Fascists secured Mussolini's take-over of power with their 'March on Rome' this boosted the NSDAP's prestige among right-wing groups and in particular Hitler's role as political leader. 'What a group of courageous men managed to do in Italy' announced Esser in a speech on 3 November in the Löwenbräukeller, 'we can do in Bavaria as well. We too have Italy's Mussolini. He's called Adolf Hitler'.[18] On 6 December, the *Völkischer Beobachter* wrote about a meeting which had taken place a few days before: 'Wherever Hitler went the cheering went on and on; it was for the man who through his boundless enthusiasm, determination to reach his goals, and uncompromising energy embodies what today millions long for, hope for, and indeed foresee.'[19]

At the same time Rudolf Hess gave a boost to the Hitler cult in his own particular way. At the end of 1922, he won a competition organized by the University of Munich for an essay with the title 'What kind of a man will restore Germany to greatness?' Hess's prize-winning essay[20] did not name names, but it is clear to whom he is attributing the exceptional abilities he describes. He argued that the 'German dictator' – as far as he was concerned there could be no other title for the future leader – had 'first to reawaken and train up' national consciousness. And he continued: 'Profound knowledge in all areas of the life of the state and of history, and the ability to learn lessons from it, belief in the righteousness of his cause and in final victory, and immense will power will enable him to give thrilling speeches and win the applause of the masses. In order to save the nation he will not shrink from using the weapons of his opponents – demagogy, slogans, street demonstrations. Where all authority has vanished, popularity is the only source of authority. Mussolini has demonstrated that. The deeper the dictator is rooted in the broad mass of the people, the better he will know how to handle them psychologically.... He himself has nothing to do with the masses; he, like every great man, is entirely himself. Through strength of personality he radiates a certain something, a compelling quality that draws more and more people to him.' Finally, he quoted from a poem by Eckart, published in December 1919:

> Storm, storm, storm,
> Rings the bell from tower to tower,
> Rings for the men, the old ones and young ones,
> Awakens the sleepers from their beds,
> Rings the serving girls down the narrow staircases,
> Rings the mothers away from their cribs.
> It must boom and peal through the air,
> Rush, rush in the thunder of revenge,
> Ringing the dead from their tombs.
> Germany awake![21]

Hess's essay shows that heroic myths and effusive redemption poetry were the ingredients that in undiluted form shaped the image of the future 'Führer' in the eyes of those close to him.

As the Party grew in numbers and prestige, Hitler managed to secure more sources of finance.[22] This was vital because, apart from anything else, in 1923 the Reichswehr began increasingly to concentrate on transferring the payments previously made to the NSDAP to the SA.[23]

Gansser continued to play an extremely important role in negotiating donations to the NSDAP. In summer 1923, in particular, he secured a loan of 60,000 Swiss francs from Richard Franck, a malt coffee manufacturer, which were used to support the *Völkischer Beobachter*.[24] On Hitler's instructions, Amann deposited jewellery in a bank as security. It probably came from Helene Bechstein, who together with her husband Erwin, the piano manufacturer, had already been introduced to Hitler by Eckart in 1920; the couple regularly made contributions to the Party.[25] Between April and December 1923, on at least six occasions, Gansser spent lengthy periods in Switzerland, where he secured large donations from sympathizers in Swiss francs, which were much sought after during the hyperinflation. Hitler himself is alleged to have returned from one trip to Switzerland during 1923 with 33,000 francs. Hitler's chauffeur, Julius Schreck, stated after the Munich putsch that his boss had often been paid in Swiss currency.[26] Gertrud von Seidlitz, a doctor's widow who joined the NSDAP in 1921 and shortly afterwards got to know Hitler personally, assisted the Party by securing currency from Finland.[27] Heinrich Becker, a Swabian underwear manufacturer from Geislingen, was another donor.[28]

Figure 1. Dietrich Eckart's poem 'Storm' became the inspiration for an early
NSDAP anthem. In 1922 Hans Gansser, the brother of the successful fundraiser
Emil Gansser, set the poem to music and dedicated it to Adolf Hitler. First
performed in 1923 at the first Party Rally, the song later lost its pre-eminence
because it was too difficult to sing.
Source: SZ Photo/Süddeutsche Zeitung Photo

Kurt Lüdecke, a 32 year-old adventurer, globetrotter, and businessman,
came into contact with Hitler in summer 1922. He possessed foreign
exchange in various denominations, some of which he clearly placed at the
disposal of the NSDAP. However, his main role in the Party was to arrange
foreign contacts. He claimed to have met Mussolini during 1922, even
before the March on Rome, in order to inform him about the NSDAP.[29]
In 1923 he went on another foreign trip, this time to Budapest and Italy,
where he once more visited Mussolini, who had come to power in the
meantime. However, according to Lüdecke, the 'Duce' showed no interest
in his report on the impending conflicts between Munich and Berlin,[30]
and Lüdecke's independent actions soon alienated the Party leadership. At
the beginning of 1923, following a tip-off from Hitler, the police began
investigating Lüdecke on the grounds of espionage.[31] He was arrested and

held on remand for two months. After his release he continued to work for the Party, but in future Hitler and the Party leadership regarded him with suspicion.[32]

Ernst Hanfstängl, a partner in an important fine art publishing house, joined the NSDAP in 1922 following his return to Munich in 1919 after a ten-year stay in the United States. Hitler was a frequent guest in his flat in the bohemian district of Schwabing and, especially during these visits, Hanfstängl was able to provide him with important introductions to the Munich upper-middle class.[33] In 1923 Hanfstängl gave Hitler an interest-free loan of 1,000 dollars that he had acquired from sales in America; during the hyperinflation this represented a serious amount of money and contributed a great deal towards ensuring that, from February 1923 onwards, the *Völkischer Beobachter* could appear as a daily paper. However, Hanfstängl recalled that it proved very difficult to secure the repayment of the loan.[34]

The rise of the Party ensured that, by the end of 1922, Hitler had gained increased access to Munich high society. He associated with the Hanfstängls, with the Bechsteins, who, during their visits to Munich, stayed in the Hotel Vier Jahreszeiten, and with the Görings (the famous World War fighter ace had moved to Munich at the beginning of 1923). Despite their being impressed by him, many stories were told in these circles about Hitler's lack of social graces, his poor table manners, his unsuitable clothing, his uncivilized behaviour, his impossible taste, and his gauche manner, all of which betrayed his lower-middle-class origins. However, it was precisely this enigmatic aura he conveyed that made him such a social hit. But Hitler's behaviour changed; among other things, his growing success was reflected in his choice of ever more luxurious motorcars. In February 1923 he exchanged the Selve, which had been seriously damaged in an accident, for a larger six-seat car, also a Selve, and in September he treated himself to a shiny red Benz, also a six-seater.[35]

However, Hitler continued to dress in a style that was, by contemporary standards, eccentric, an eccentricity summed up by the fact that he always carried a riding crop. In 1936 the writer, Friedrich Percyval Reck-Malleczewen, recalling a private visit by Hitler to a cultured family in Munich in 1920, noted that with his 'riding boots, riding crop, Alsatian dog and floppy hat' he had appeared on the scene like a 'cowboy' wanting to take over the conversation and preach 'like a military chaplain'.[36] The historian, Karl Alexander von Müller, also reported how, when arriving at a soirée at the Hanfstängls, in the hall Hitler 'had put down his riding crop, taken off his trench coat and leather hat, and lastly unbuckled a belt with a revolver attached, and then hung them all on a clothes peg. It looked weird and reminiscent of Karl May'.* While at this point Hitler had already had some public success, according to Müller 'there was still something gauche about him and one had the unpleasant feeling that he felt that himself and resented the fact that people noticed it'.[37] In his anecdotal memoirs even Hanfstängl cannot help repeatedly commenting with a certain smugness on the contrast between his own cultivated milieu and the shabbily dressed petty bourgeois, Hitler, with his philistine behaviour and lack of education.[38] It is no longer possible to check the truth of these anecdotes, but they clearly show that the members of the Munich upper-middle class, who sought to associate with or support Hitler, were also concerned to emphasize their social superiority to this 'phenomenon'.

Around 1922, Hitler's intimate circle was joined by Heinrich Hoffmann, the owner of a Munich photographic studio in Schellingstrasse 50. Hoffmann had been a member of the Party since 1920. The fact that it took two years for him to become closely acquainted with the Party leader was probably for professional reasons: at the start of his career Hitler refused to be photographed. Hoffmann made some attempts to overcome this taboo and gradually, through invitations, lengthy discussions about the artistic interests they had in common and so forth, he managed to win Hitler's trust. In fact, in September 1923, he was permitted to publish the first studio photograph authorized by Hitler and taken only a few days after a press photographer had succeeded in snatching a photo of Hitler at the German Day in Nuremberg. From now onwards, Hoffmann became Hitler's official and exclusive photographer, possessing a monopoly of the pictures authorized by Hitler, and in the process becoming a rich man.[39]

Hitler's initial refusal to allow himself to be photographed was not, as has been often imagined, one of his clever propaganda ideas to create an aura of mystery around him; the advantages of such a strategy of concealment would undoubtedly have been outweighed by its disadvantages. A more plausible explanation would be that he wanted to remain incognito outside Bavaria in order to avoid the police – on occasions there were arrest warrants out for him – and the attentions of his political opponents.[40] Hitler's unwillingness to be photographed and his policy, from autumn 1923

---

* Translators' note: Karl May (1842–1912) was a popular author, known mainly for his Wild West stories, of which Hitler was a fan.

onwards, of controlling published pictures of himself through Hoffmann also point to Hitler's fears that the self-image he had created of a heroic political fighter could be damaged or revealed as a farce by other photographs. For the rest of his life he was haunted by the fear of being made to look ridiculous by unsuitable photographs.[41] Now that he could no longer avoid public interest in how he looked, he ensured that pictures of him were widely distributed in a series of standard poses: holding himself stiffly with a determined, indeed grim facial expression. In later years, Hoffmann and Hitler expanded the repertoire, but this does not alter the basic fact that, with Hoffmann's help, Hitler was himself largely responsible for devising and controlling the image we have of him to this day.

Under Hitler's leadership the rapidly expanding NSDAP remained remarkably unstructured; it developed into a real Führer party, in which Hitler assigned tasks to confidants on an ad hoc basis. He did not have a deputy who could really represent him; there was no executive committee meeting regularly that might have been able to control Hitler; the Party bureaucracy under Amann was intentionally kept weak and had no means of contesting Hitler's claim to absolute power. Hitler was the unchallenged chief propagandist, was in charge of the most important local branch, Munich, and prevented the emergence of any strong Party organization outside Munich from which competition might have arisen. In 1922/23 his informal circle included Amann (Party manager), Rosenberg (editor of the *Völkischer Beobachter* and link man to the Baltic Germans), Esser (propagandist), Scheubner-Richter (link man to Ludendorff), Hanfstängl and Lüdecke with their social contacts, the 'bodyguards' Graf, Weber, and Maurice, although the last two increasingly took on organizational tasks, the two early mentors, Feder and Eckart, and Hoffmann as court photographer. Significantly they did not meet in formal sessions, but mainly in cafés, in Café Heck,[42] and later in Café Neumayr near the Viktualienmarkt,[43] or in Hitler's favourite restaurant, the Ostaria Bavaria in Schellingstrasse.

Membership of this group depended on Hitler's favour, and acquiring and maintaining it required the willing subordination of the person concerned to the Party leader. Anyone who lost Hitler's confidence, such as Eckart and Lüdecke, soon found themselves consigned to the political wilderness. The former had to give up the editorship of the *Völkischer Beobachter* in 1923, presumably because he was not efficient enough. When Hitler's former mentor returned to Munich in October 1923 after six months' absence – he was lying low in Berchtesgaden because of a Reich arrest warrant – he found that he was completely isolated within the NSDAP and that Hitler no longer consulted him.[44] The deep 'friendship' that Hitler, in later years, repeatedly claimed existed between the two men[45] did not last.

The SA represented an important exception to this informal structure. It was organized hierarchically along military lines. Its position within the Nazi movement depended not so much on the personal connections of its leaders with Hitler, but rather it was heavily dependent on its links to the Reichswehr and the other paramilitary leagues. Apart from that, as an armed force it represented a power factor sui generis, which was to become clear during the turbulent year of 1923.

1923: The crisis year

On 11 January 1923 Belgian and French troops marched into the Ruhr in response to arrears in German reparation payments. The Berlin government replied with a declaration of passive resistance and the growing number of confrontations between the Ruhr population and Belgian and French troops during the following weeks and months produced another serious political crisis. The general outcry of national anger provided further food for Nazi agitation. At the same time, Hitler was fully aware that the new situation also contained risks. For as a result of the NSDAP becoming incorporated into a broad nationalist front – in November 1922 it had already joined the Vereinigung der Vaterländischen Verbände – the Party and, in particular, its leader threatened to lose their distinctiveness. From Hitler's point of view, it was vital for the NSDAP to retain its independence so that he could maintain the role that, over the previous three years, he had established for himself on the Munich political stage. He found a way out by ensuring that the NSDAP did not, like other right-wing groups, direct its agitation against the hated French but instead, in the first instance, against those 'November criminals in Berlin', as he put it in a Nazi meeting, who were to blame for Germany's humiliation. In this way he hoped the NSDAP could use the crisis to sharpen its image. Consequently, he declined to attend a protest meeting intended to unite all the right-wing organizations in a common struggle.[46]

Instead of that, he concentrated on a series of spectacular events with which the NSDAP tried to distinguish itself from the numerous 'nationalist' protest rallies. They began at the end of January with the NSDAP's first 'Reich Party Rally'. Originally, the Bavarian government had wanted to limit its scope. In his negotiations with the police chief Hitler began by issuing wild threats: 'The government could shoot them down; he would be in the front row. They could shoot him too, but the one thing he would say was: the first shot would unleash a blood bath and they would see what would happen then: within two hours of the first shot being fired the government would've fallen.'[47] Two days later, his approach to the police chief was much more restrained; he was humble and in despair. According to his interlocutor, he 'requested on bended knees that no more difficulties be created for him. As a result of the constant changes of decision, his supporters and guests were almost going wild and if the programme were changed it was inevitable that there would be serious and unavoidable repercussions'.[48] Thus, while acting as supplicant, Hitler was simultaneously making a veiled threat. Finally, prompted by Röhm, the Reichswehr intervened with the Bavarian government and, despite the state of emergency that had been declared in the meantime, secured the removal of the various conditions that had been imposed.[49] On the evening of 27 January, Hitler made brief appearances at twelve meetings in Munich beer halls[50] and, the following day, there was a parade of 6,000 SA men on the Marsfeld, where Hitler 'dedicated flags'.[51] Afterwards, the actual meeting of Party delegates took place with 300 chairmen of local branches, followed by a general membership meeting at which Hitler was unanimously confirmed as Party chairman.[52]

Röhm used the difficulties associated with the Party rally to break with Pittinger's Bayern und Reich, blaming its leader for the restrictions imposed by the government.[53] Shortly after this, he founded the Arbeitsgemeinschaft der vaterländischen Kampfverbände [Working Group of Patriot Combat Leagues], to which, apart from the SA, Röhm's own paramilitary league, the Reichsflagge, as well as Bund Oberland, the Vaterländische Vereine Münchens [Patriotic Clubs of Munich], and the Kampfbund Niederbayern [Combat League of Lower Bavaria] all belonged. The Arbeitsgemeinschaft had its own military high command; its members received military training from and were supplied with weapons by the Reichswehr. In setting it up Röhm had brought together the radical völkisch leagues with the clear aim of opposing the moderate conservative Bund Bayern und Reich.[54] At the same time, Röhm did what he could to protect the NSDAP against unwelcome attentions from the police.[55]

In addition, at the beginning of 1923, the retired Captain Hermann Göring, a highly decorated fighter pilot and former commander of the famous Richthofen squadron, was appointed the new commander of the SA. Göring, who had some private means through his Swedish wife, Carin, and enjoyed a high reputation in nationalist and military circles, interpreted his new role primarily as a representational one. However, many simple Party members took offence at the exaggerated and pompous way in which he performed it.[56] His villa in Obermenzing became a meeting place for the political Right, and Hitler was often to be found there with his entourage. According to Carin Göring's official biographer, writing in 1934, it was here that, surrounded by the rustic decor of the large basement room, 'after the serious discussions... they spent relaxed and enjoyable times together'.[57] Under Göring's leadership the SA increasingly changed from being a Party strong arm squad to becoming a paramilitary league, with its own high command and military structure, independent of the Party's local branches. In other words, the military wing – Röhm and Göring – were gaining the upper hand within the NSDAP.[58]

On 26 February 1923, Ludendorff called a meeting of the leaders of the important paramilitary leagues in Berlin and demanded their support for the existing government in the event of war. However, they were unwilling to allow their men to be incorporated into the Reichswehr as reservists, insisting that they should only be attached to the army as separate units. Hitler, who also claimed to have been in Berlin at the time, maintained at his 1924 trial that he had been willing to put his men at Ludendorff's disposal.[59] According to Hitler, in the course of these negotiations there had been a lengthy discussion with the army chief, General Hans von Seeckt, whom he had urged to take military action against the Ruhr occupation – without success.[60]

Shortly afterwards, Röhm's Arbeitsgemeinschaft began a campaign of provocation against the Bavarian government by holding big military parades and similar events. On 1 May 1923, the labour movement's traditional annual day of celebration and also the fourth anniversary of the crushing of the Munich Räterepublik, the Arbeitsgemeinschaft decided to mount a challenge. Together with the Vereinigte Vaterländische Verbände, it sent an ultimatum to Prime Minister von Knilling demanding that the planned demonstration by the SPD and the trade unions be banned. When the government refused, the Arbeitsgemeinschaft assembled thousands of their men in Munich, some of whom had acquired weapons from

Reichswehr stores, despite the fact they were only supposed to receive them in the event of war. However, when the police and the army made it clear that they were not going to back down in the face of the threat, the men returned their weapons and departed. This represented a major loss of prestige for the Arbeitsgemeinschaft and not least for Hitler, whose dependence on the Reichswehr had been clearly exposed.[61] That evening at the Circus Krone Hitler celebrated the 'alliance of defence and defiance' represented by the leagues united in the Arbeitsgemeinschaft, although in fact the Vereinigte Vaterländische Verbände had pulled out at the last minute. But he could not conceal the fact that he had suffered a major defeat.[62]

Hitler's behaviour had in fact offered the Bavarian judicial authorities the opportunity of starting proceedings against him and revoking the suspension of his three-month prison sentence, of which he had served over a third the previous year. Hitler, however, sent the prosecuting authorities a memorandum in which he threatened to expose the secret cooperation between the Reichswehr and the paramilitary leagues in the event of his being charged. In response, the Bavarian minister of justice decided to postpone the case and it was never proceeded with.[63]

During the following months, the general crisis worsened. In addition to the nationalist mood stoked by the Ruhr invasion, the hyperinflation, which had been developing since the previous year, induced a sense of deep depression. Large sections of the middle class found their savings being wiped out and unemployment rose dramatically. The number of those in Munich receiving welfare benefits went up from 40,000 at the start of the year to 140,000 at the end.[64] The widespread hatred of the 'November criminals' was given a further boost not only by the entry of the Social Democrats into the new Reich government formed by Gustav Stresemann in August, but also by the growing cooperation between the SPD governments in Thuringia and Saxony and the Communist Party (KPD); in both states communist ministers joined the government.[65]

In September the SA, Bund Oberland and the Reichsflagge established the Deutscher Kampfbund [German Combat League] at a ceremonial 'German Day' in Nuremberg. This alliance had come about largely through the efforts of Ludendorff, who was to exert considerable influence on the Kampfbund as an eminence grise.[66] His confidant, Hermann Kriebel, took over the military leadership, while Ludendorff's 'political' advisor 'on the East', Scheubner-Richter, ran the organization. On 27 September, a day after the end of passive resistance in the Ruhr, which produced a further

wave of nationalist anger,[67] Röhm succeeded in securing the political leadership of the Kampfbund for Hitler and now left the Reichswehr, in order
to devote himself full time to the Kampfbund. In fact, it was the military, not
Hitler the politician, who were in future to make the decisions about the
Kampfbund. Meanwhile, concerned about the situation, the Bavarian government now declared a state of emergency, appointing the former prime
minister, Kahr, General State Commissioner, in other words, temporary
dictator.[68]

Kahr now tried, on the one hand, to organize a 'coming together of all
patriotic forces', and, on the other, to introduce concrete economic measures in order to alleviate the impact of the crisis on the masses.[69] He fixed
bread and beer prices, while attempting to force farmers to make larger
deliveries and to reduce the profits of entrepreneurs.[70] Moreover, as in 1920,
he initiated measures to deport eastern Jews, this time with the excuse of
combatting 'profiteers' and 'racketeers'. By 1 November 1923, around thirty
people had been deported from Munich alone, evidently with the aim of
taking the wind out of the sails of the radical anti-Semites and their agitation.[71] Kahr was barely in office when he imposed a ban on all the meetings
the NSDAP had planned for 27 September and demanded a declaration of
loyalty from the Kampfbund. Hitler responded with the statement that the
attitude of the Kampfbund to the General State Commissioner would
depend on the attitude that he adopted 'towards the major questions of our
time'.[72]

The appointment of a strong man with populist policies led to a decline
in support for the Kampfbund. At the beginning of October, the Reichsflagge
declared for Kahr, prompting Röhm to organize the most radical elements
in a new league, the Reichskriegsflagge. Since the Reich government had
responded to the new Bavarian state of emergency by declaring a Reich-
wide state of emergency, the Reichswehr commander in Bavaria, Otto
Hermann von Lossow, was placed in a dilemma. When he refused to obey
an order from the Reichswehr minister to ban the *Völkischer Beobachter* for
an article insulting the Reich Chancellor, he was dismissed. However, the
Bavarian government immediately reappointed him as Bavarian state commander, assigning him command of the Reichswehr division stationed in
Bavaria.[73]

This conflict provided the background to the development of a vicious
rivalry in Bavaria between the conservative Right and the forces of the radical
Right, with the so-called Triumvirate of von Kahr, von Lossow, and Hans

von Seisser, the chief of the state police, on the one side, and Ludendorff, Hitler, and Röhm on the other. They were both totally committed to bringing down the Reich government, but differed over the means of doing so. The Kampfbund wanted to set up a dictatorship in Munich under Ludendorff and Hitler, crush the socialist governments in central Germany, and then stage a 'March on Berlin' in order to seize power in the Reich. Kahr, on the other hand, while wanting to see the Reich government in Berlin replaced by a 'Directorate' with dictatorial powers, aimed to achieve this in the form of a cold coup by working together with right-wing circles in north Germany and the Reichswehr. The aim was to put pressure on the Reich President, who would then use his special powers under Article 48 of the Constitution to establish some form of dictatorship.[74] In the context of these general preparations for a coup, the Kampfbund was now in danger of simply being used by the Triumvirate. But Hitler was determined to retain his freedom of action; for him retreat was out of the question.

Tension was increased by the fact that the Reichswehr forces stationed in Bavaria and the right-wing leagues in northern Bavaria, supported by the military, were making preparations to mobilize. The state police, which had been reinforced by members of the right-wing leagues, including the Kampfbund and SA, was organizing a 'border defence force' under Captain Erhardt, who was still being sought under a Reich arrest warrant. While the pretext was defence against the left-wing governments in Thuringia and Saxony, the aim of the leagues was to use this force for an impending 'operation' in the north. The Kampfbund and the SA were both taking part in this mobilization.[75] The Reichswehr's plans were altogether more ambitious, as von Lossow explained to the leagues' leaders at a meeting on 24 October. The plan was to reinforce the Reichswehr units stationed in Bavaria with members of the leagues with the main aim of establishing a 'nationalist dictatorship' in Berlin.[76] The representatives who were present concurred, although in many cases with the proviso that their members should not be directly integrated into the Reichswehr but retain their independence. Thereupon the Reichswehr began preparing to expand the single division stationed in Bavaria into three divisions. Since the Nazis were not present at this meeting,[77] they had not issued any statement concerning their participation. However, at the end of October, the Reichswehr began rapidly training the SA in its barracks and, according to Hitler's statements at his 1924 trial, this was with the intention of embarking on a 'military campaign in the north'.[78]

During the following days, there was a series of discussions and soundings between the rival parties, though they had the effect, if anything, of intensifying the differences between their respective objectives. Hitler's most important interlocutors were Lossow and Seisser. On 24 October, when Lossow was meeting the leagues, Hitler subjected Seisser to a four-hour monologue about his aims,[79] and then, the following day, this time accompanied by Friedrich Weber, the leader of Bund Oberland, once more arranged to meet Seisser, this time together with Lossow. Now he demanded that the planned Reich Directorate should be composed of himself, Ludendorff, Seisser, and Lossow, which Seisser and Lossow both rejected in view of Ludendorff's status.[80] According to Lossow's statement at the 1924 trial, during this period he had been subjected to a positive 'wave' of visits from Hitler, during which the latter had kept making the same arguments in favour of his plans and had been completely impervious to the objections raised against them.[81] On 25 October, Seisser and Lossow also arranged a meeting between Hitler, Ludendorff, and the industrialist Friedrich Minoux, who had been identified as a potential member of the Directorate; but they were unable to reach agreement on how to alter the political situation in Berlin.[82]

Lossow's impressions of his meetings with Hitler, which he repeated in the 1924 trial, seem typical of the latter's way of carrying on a conversation and its supposedly grandiose effects. 'Hitler's well-known thrilling and suggestive rhetoric initially had a big effect on me ... but the more I listened to Hitler ... the less impressed I became. I noticed that his long speeches almost always made the same points. ... In general, during such conversations, Hitler is the only one who is allowed to speak. It's difficult to raise objections and they have no effect.' Lossow then referred to a statement by Hitler, according to which the latter claimed that, during one of their conversations, Lossow had been 'very depressed'. Lossow made it clear that his mood had been provoked less by the general political situation and much more by Hitler's endless talking: 'May I be permitted to point out that a different conclusion could be drawn, namely that, having been obliged to listen to these remarks on numerous occasions, General Lossow's patience was more or less exhausted and that, while he did not wish to tell Herr Hitler: "Please, I've had enough!", he did want to indicate that by his demeanour.'[83] It is typical of Hitler that he interpreted Lossow's manner, which indicated that Hitler's endless talking had worn him out, as dejection, which he then tried to overcome with another torrent of words. Hitler was unable to recognize that he was misinterpreting the situation, but instead exerted all his efforts to try to achieve his increasingly unrealistic goals.

The Putsch: Hitler takes on the role of 'Führer'

The tide of events during the crisis-ridden year of 1923 gradually removed Hitler's qualms about taking on the role of 'Führer'.

The NSDAP only became a mass movement in 1923: between January and November around 47,000 new members joined the Party so that, on the eve of the putsch, there were over 55,000 names (including an unknown number of those who had left) on the membership list.[84] A fragment of the list, containing around 4,800 members who joined between September and November, provides a more detailed picture. More than three-quarters of the new members came from south Germany, although by then the Party was no longer concentrated in Munich itself; only 10 per cent were resident in the Bavarian capital. Analysis shows that the organization benefited above all from expanding into the countryside, particularly in Bavaria. More than half of the new members came from rural districts. Craftsmen, white-collar employees, civil servants, the self-employed, and farmers (over 10 per cent) made up the bulk of the membership and so the Party's profile remained middle-class.[85]

From April 1923 onwards, 'our Führer', became the standard title when Hitler was being referred to in press announcements.[86] The fact that he now became universally known as 'Führer' within the Party was evidently largely due to the homage paid to Hitler by Eckart, Rosenberg, and Göring in the *Völkischer Beobachter* on the occasion of his birthday on 20 April. It is unclear from Hitler's public statements whether he yet envisaged playing this role outside the Party. Thus, while in his speeches during the first half of 1923 there are repeated calls for 'strong leaders',[87] on the other hand, in his speech in the Circus Krone on 4 May, for example, he was still evading the issue: 'What Germany needs for its salvation is a dictatorship of nationalist willpower and nationalist determination. That poses the question: Does a suitable person exist? Our task is not to seek this person. He will either be sent by heaven or he won't be. Our task is to create the sword that this person will need when he arrives. Our task is to give the dictator a nation that is ready for him.'[88]

In July his ambition was already becoming more obvious: 'As leader of the National Socialist Party I see my task as being to take over responsibility.'[89]

From August onwards, he repeatedly demanded the establishment of a dictatorship, an objective that, as the crisis intensified, became widespread within
the whole of the Right.[90] In an interview with the *Daily Mail* on 2 October,
he drew a significant parallel with Mussolini: 'If a German Mussolini is given
to Germany, he said, people would fall down on their knees and worship him
more than Mussolini has ever been worshipped.'[91]

Gradually, however, he felt himself being pushed by his own supporters
into taking on the role of dictator. On 14 October, at a Nazi meeting in
Nuremberg, he strongly criticized Kahr, for 'a true statesman, a real dictator
does not depend on anyone; the nation depends on him; he gives it fresh
heart and then leads it along the path that he has defined as the right one'.
And there were models: 'three great Germans' – Luther, Frederick the Great,
and Wagner – who were great 'because they led a truly heroic life in defiance of everybody else'. Simply because 'they relied exclusively on their
great insights all three became pioneers and thus national heroes'. That,
Hitler made clear to his supporters at the end of his speech, was what he too
was seeking to do: 'to go on fighting and not to lose sight of the goal I have
set myself of being a pioneer of the great German freedom movement that
will bring us unity within and without, not relying on anyone else but only
on my immense resolve and with it and through it either gaining victory or
going down to defeat'.[92] His ambition to become 'Führer', 'dictator', and
therefore 'hero' must have become clear to his audience. His supporters too
had considerable ambitions. If one reads the *Völkischer Beobachter* during this
period, it becomes clear what hopes he had inspired in the meantime. For
example, on 1 November, it declared: 'Then, the black swastika flag will be
unfurled over the heads of the cowards and this moribund regime, and,
under Hitler's leadership, will lead us on to victory.'[93] These quotations show
that, by the autumn of 1923, Hitler had arrived at the point where he was
ready to declare himself 'Führer' and take on the role of 'hero'. In the end,
if he was not to make a fool of himself, he had no choice but to meet the
high expectations of his followers by carrying out the 'act' of liberation, his
'heroic deed'.

However, while psyching himself up to take on his grand role, Hitler
completely overlooked the fact that, by the end of October, the chances of
carrying out a successful putsch were rapidly disappearing. The Reich government had decided to depose the socialist-communist governments in
Thuringia and Saxony and ordered Reichswehr troops to intervene.[94] This
removed the pretext for the mobilization on the Bavarian border. Moreover,

by establishing the Rentenbank in October, the Reich government had introduced an important measure for combatting inflation and then, by creating a new currency, had taken a decisive step towards stabilizing the economy.

The paramilitary leagues in the Kampfbund began to doubt whether Kahr really wanted to launch a coup. On 1 November, there was a further meeting between Seisser, Hitler, and Weber at the latter's house. Hitler renewed a previous promise not to undertake any action against the Reichswehr and the state police, but at the same time made it clear that he was coming under considerable pressure from his own people and could not afford to wait much longer.[95] Seisser, however, having taken soundings in Berlin on 3 November, discovered that the army chief, General von Seeckt, had definitely decided not to move against the Reich government. This effectively scuppered the Triumvirate's plans for a coup.[96] At a meeting of the leagues on 6 November Kahr urgently warned them not take the 'abnormal' path towards establishing a dictatorship.[97] However, the members of the Kampfbund were afraid that they were in danger of missing the opportunity for a putsch. 'The Kampfbund people', Hitler told the prosecutors after his putsch, 'had been pressing for action; they couldn't wait any longer; they had been promised that something was going to happen for so long and had been in training for so long, that now they wanted to see some real action. Otherwise, there was a danger that suddenly some group or other (not the Nazis, as Hitler explicitly emphasized!) would act on their own (for example, grab a few dozen Jews and string them up!). That had to be prevented from happening.' Apart from that, the money had run out, people were discontented, and there was a danger that the Kampfbund would fall apart.[98]

Too weak to act without the Reichswehr, state police, and the Bavarian government, let alone against them, Hitler and the Kampfbund leadership decided to seize the initiative themselves and drag the hesitant Triumvirate with them. The Triumvirate had announced a mass meeting in the Bürgerbräukeller for 8 November and this appeared to provide the opportunity to act. According to Hitler's own account, he made the decision on the evening of 6 November in a discussion with two other Nazis, whose names he later refused to reveal; they were probably Scheubner-Richter and Theodor von der Pfordten. The decisive Kampfbund meetings took place on 7 November.[99]

On the evening of 8 November, Hitler surrounded the beer hall with his Kampfbund units and, adopting a martial pose, made a dramatic entry. At the head of a small group of close associates, including Hanfstängl, Amann, and Hess, he marched into the packed hall, waving a pistol, and interrupted Kahr's speech. Describing the scene a few months later to the Munich People's Court, he commented: 'It's obvious that one can't go in waving a palm leaf'. He held his pistol to the head of an officer who approached him. In the meantime, storm troopers put a guard on the entrance and set up a heavy machine gun aimed at the audience.

Hitler now got up onto a chair and, unable to make himself heard, fired a shot into the ceiling. He made a short speech in which he announced that the 'nationalist revolution' had broken out and the Munich and Berlin governments had been deposed. He then ordered Kahr, Lossow, and Seisser to follow him into an adjacent room. There, waving his pistol around, he explained to them that they were going to establish a new government in Bavaria under former police chief Pöhner, while Kahr was to be state governor. Bavaria, continued Hitler, was to be the jumping off point for the takeover of power in the Reich; a government would then be established under his leadership, with Ludendorff in charge of the army and Seisser the police.[100] Finally, Hitler is supposed to have said: 'I know that you gentlemen will find it difficult, but we must take this step; we shall have to make it easier for you gentlemen to make the break. Each one of us must take up the position to which he is assigned; if he doesn't then he'll have no right to exist. You must fight with me, triumph with me, or die with me. If it all goes wrong I have four bullets in my pistol, three for my collaborators and the last one for myself.'

Hitler then returned to the hall and gave a second speech announcing the composition of the new Bavarian and Reich governments.[101] Shortly afterwards, Ludendorff entered the Bürgerbräukeller and he and Hitler now tried to put moral pressure on the Triumvirate. Finally, the three declared their agreement with the coup, returning to the hall to proclaim their 'unity'. Then, in brief speeches, Kahr, Lossow, Seisser, and Pöhner all announced they had agreed to participate in the coup d'état.

Meanwhile, the putschists had been trying to occupy government buildings and army barracks in the city, although in most cases meeting resistance and failing to achieve their objectives.[102] When Hitler left the Bürgerbräukeller late in the evening in order to find out why they had failed to occupy the pioneer corps barracks, Kahr, Lossow, and Seisser seized the opportunity to leave the beer hall and immediately began taking steps to crush the putsch.[103] In the meantime, Prime Minister von Knilling, various Bavarian ministers, and the Munich police chief, who were present in the hall, had been taken hostage by the putschists and were kept prisoner throughout the following day.[104] During the night, various armed groups had also taken captive a number of mainly upper-middle-class Jews and taken them off to the Bürgerbräukeller.[105] The next morning, following Göring's orders, storm troopers forced their way into the town hall and took hostage the deputy mayor and seven city councillors belonging to the KPD, SPD, and USPD; all were freed the following day.[106] In addition, the putschists 'confiscated' a large quantity of paper money from two printers, in order to pay the troops. Legally, this was clearly theft.[107]

As became clear during the night, the Reichswehr and the paramilitary state police remained loyal to the existing government, which meant that the putsch was doomed to fail.[108] During the morning, the putschists assembled in the Bürgerbräukeller decided to make a final attempt to turn the tide: they began a demonstration march aiming to go through the centre of the city towards the military district headquarters, which Röhm had occupied with his Reichskriegsflagge. Shortly before reaching the building, at the Feldherrnhalle, the roughly 2,000 putschists came up against a barricade manned by the state police. Suddenly a few shots rang out – those responsible were never identified – leading to an exchange of fire during which four policemen, thirteen putschists, and a bystander were killed; two further putschists were killed as a result of an exchange of fire at the military district headquarters. Among the dead were Scheubner-Richter, who, marching arm in arm with Hitler, had pulled the latter to the ground as he fell. Hitler escaped in the fleeing crowd with a dislocated shoulder. Göring, who was also able to escape, had a bullet wound. Streicher, Frick, Pöhner, Amann, and Röhm were all arrested at the Feldherrnhalle; Ludendorff, who had marched towards the police cordon oblivious to the shooting, was also arrested.[109]

Hitler succeeded in making his way to Hanfstängl's house in Uffing on the Staffelsee, where he was found by the police two days later in a desperate and depressed state and taken into custody. In Hanfstängl's house Hitler composed a 'political testament', appointing Rosenberg Party chairman and making Amann his deputy.[110]

5

The Trial and the Period
of the Ban

On 13 December 1923, Hans Ehard, the public prosecutor who was conducting the prosecution of the putschists, travelled to Landsberg prison in order, as he put it in his report, 'to attempt to interrogate Hitler'.[1] However, Hitler, now a prisoner on remand, declined to make any statement; he was not, Ehard recorded, going to 'be tricked into giving himself away'. Instead, he promised to produce a political memorandum explaining his actions in detail.[2] Hitler even refused to say anything about his youth and personal development because he was not going to allow himself to be 'interrogated like a criminal'; he did not want a 'court report' to be produced, which might later be 'used against him'. Ehard also learnt that Hitler declined to provide the prison doctor with any information about his previous life on the grounds that 'he was healthy and that they should forget about all that nonsense'. He had broken off an almost fourteen-day hunger strike at the end of November.[3]

It is clear from these statements that Hitler was afraid that the prosecution investigations and the impending trial would show him up. Not only would the weak points in his Führer biography, which he had hitherto been careful to conceal, be disclosed (his stay in the Viennese men's hostel, his flight to Munich to avoid military service in Austria, his dubious role during the Räterepublik, his unrealistic plans for a professional future),[4] but a careful analysis of the pre-history of the putsch would inevitably reveal how foolhardy his decision to launch it had been. For Hitler had not simply been driven to act by his supporters. In fact, unwilling to admit he had misjudged the political situation, he had taken the bull by the horns so as not to appear to his followers (and himself) as a failure. He did not want to be seen as a muddle head whose life so far had been a dead end, and it was precisely his fear of such a blow to his self-esteem that gave him the impetus to challenge Ehard. Hitler benefited greatly from the fact that the Triumvirate had been thoroughly compromised by their own plans for a coup d'état in autumn 1923. He dropped dark hints to Ehard that, during the trial, he would call 'numerous witnesses' who had not been members of the Kampfbund and then they would see 'whether "certain gentlemen", when confronted by these witnesses in the courtroom, would actually have the courage to perjure themselves'.

Faced with Hitler's torrent of words, Ehard gave up the attempt to take a statement; instead, he asked for the typewriter to be removed and had a five-hour conversation during which Hitler refused to allow him to take notes. As far as his general mood was concerned, he told Ehard that, after the 'collapse of his enterprise,... [he had been] initially quite apathetic, then he had raged and now he had got his "Schopenhauer" and so had regained his philosophical serenity; he had also regained his energy and would now fight like a "wild cat" to save his skin and "act ruthlessly to discredit his opponents".'

Hitler strongly denied that he had committed treason, as the current constitutional order was, after all, based on the revolution of November 1918. He would also provide proof at his trial that the existing constitution had been repeatedly contravened in recent times: for example, by the overthrow of the Hoffmann government after the Kapp putsch, for which the Reichswehr was responsible, and by the appointment of the General State Commissar [Kahr], which had only happened because the public had been misled about the political situation at the time. His 'high treason' of 8 November had also been 'sanctioned and legalized by Kahr, Lossow, and Seisser, who were the legal representatives of the state'. He would prove that the three 'had not simply feigned acceptance of the proposals he had made in the Bürgerbräukeller, but seriously intended implementing the agreement that had been reached' and that 'afterwards they had only been persuaded to change their minds and break their word as a result of persuasion, and partly compulsion, from outside'. In fact, Kahr, Lossow, and Seisser had not only participated for several hours on the 8 November, but 'for months had been preparing with him everything that was agreed in the Bürgerbräukeller on the evening of 8.11.23'. They had discussed the '"march on Berlin" to be launched from Bavaria down to fine detail and had been in total agreement. Basically, he, Kahr, Lossow, and Seisser had had identical aims'. Hitler then indicated that during the trial he was going to raise the whole question of the 'secret mobilization', in other words the collaboration between the Reichswehr and the paramilitary leagues.

Essentially, Hitler had been explaining to Ehard the strategy that he was going to adopt for his defence in the coming trial, which began in Munich on 26 February 1924, and in which, apart from him and Ludendorff, there were eight other defendants. He had made it clear that he was prepared to mount a counter-offensive against the Bavarian state and was assuming that his threat of 'revelations' would persuade the prosecution and the court to be lenient with him. And that is indeed precisely what happened. Hitler agreed to let the issue of the Reichswehr's secret mobilization be dealt with in a session closed to the public, and refrained from touching on the question during his hours-long speeches in the public sessions.[5] The defence also did not attempt to compromise the government or cause problems for it by calling 'numerous witnesses', as Hitler had threatened to do. In return, the government dealt with the matter under its own jurisdiction instead of referring it to the Reich Supreme Court in Leipzig, which was officially responsible for cases of high treason. The prosecution refrained from trying the various serious crimes committed during the putsch – homicides, kidnapping, and robbery – separately, restricting itself to the charge of high treason. The judge permitted Hitler to use the court as a stage for his propaganda and, at the end, imposed a lenient sentence allowing for a generous term of suspension, and did not deport him to Austria. It is hardly conceivable that this leniency was not the result of a deal between the various parties involved in the case.

With his counter-offensive Hitler also avoided being personally exposed during the trial. Thanks to the avoidance of a full public investigation of the pre-history of the putsch, he could blame its failure mainly on intrigues that were outside his responsibility. In the court he portrayed his attempt to involve the Triumvirate in his putsch on 8 November (an enterprise that, in view of the general political situation at the end of October/beginning of November, was doomed to fail) as the heroic deed of a credulous man, who had relied on promises that had been made to him. Thus, after a relatively brief depressive phase, he had restored the overblown self-image he had developed on the eve of the putsch and of which now, in the course of the trial, he had become utterly convinced. He saw his actions as having ennobled him as a heroic leader, who had disregarded all petty considerations. He persuaded himself and his public that the collapse of the putsch merely revealed the failure of his opponents and indeed provided the proof of his qualities as a national leader.

The court gave Hitler the opportunity, right from the start of proceedings, to take the stage with a three and a half hour speech.[6] He began with an account of his miserable years in Vienna: 'I arrived in Vienna as a citizen of the world and left it as an absolute anti-Semite, as a deadly enemy of the whole Marxist world view.'[7] He continued with his time in Munich, his military service and the post-war period, with his speech increasingly turning into a general attack on Marxism and the 'November criminals'. The final section was devoted to an exhaustive account of the 1923 crisis and its culmination in the autumn. In the process he made one thing clear: 'During this whole period, Lossow, Kahr, and Seisser had exactly the same aim as us, namely to get rid of the Reich government with its current international and parliamentary world view and replace it with a nationalist, absolutely anti-parliamentary national government, a Directorate. If some people subsequently try and make out that they wanted that too, but that it ought to have been achieved not through force but instead through pressure, pressure through force, but not by using force; that they wanted a coup but not like a normal coup as it has been historically understood hitherto, but rather as they understood it, then I can only regret that we weren't informed at the time about this special Lossow idea of a coup.' In other words: 'If our whole operation was high treason then Messrs Lossow, Seisser, and Kahr have committed high treason along with us, for throughout all those months we didn't discuss with them anything other than that for which we are now sitting in the dock.'[8]

With this introductory speech Hitler had taken the first step towards dominating the future court proceedings, particularly since none of the other defendants showed any desire to challenge his leading role in this case of high treason. Apart from his stress on the complicity of Kahr, Lossow, and Seisser, during the trial Hitler emphasized an additional theme: the wavering and hesitation of his former conservative allies had forced him to act; he alone had shown the necessary decisiveness, while the members of the Triumvirate, a bunch of losers, were now not even prepared to stand up for what they had done. In the closed sessions Hitler repeatedly used his right to cross-examine witnesses to an excessive extent. On several occasions his torrent of words prompted the chairman to call him – gently, it must be said – to order.[9]

Hitler tried, for example, to drive Kahr into a corner. Together with his defence counsel and supported by Ludendorff, he interrogated him in the manner of an inquisitor as to how much he had known about the mobilization of the Bavarian army, the provision of ammunition, and its financing with Bavarian funds.[10] And why had he thought that Friedrich Minoux, who had been envisaged as a member of the Directorate, was entitled 'to put pressure on the Reich president and on the cabinet that was not legitimated by the Constitution'? Kahr ought to answer the question as to whether his actions had not 'very seriously damaged the constitutional foundations of the Reich, in other words, basically, what Kahr is accusing us of having done'.[11] When Lossow reminded him that he had broken the promise that he had given to Seisser on 8 November not to use force, Hitler responded that he did not have a guilty conscience, since 'the only one of us two who has broken his word [is] the Herr Lieutenant-General', a reference to the events of 1 May 1923.[12] Hitler also took the liberty of referring to the 'high treason committed by the gentlemen, Lossow, Kahr, and Seisser', the very ones who had provided him with the instrument with which to launch his putsch.[13]

The judge repeatedly permitted Hitler to digress from his cross-examination of witnesses into making extensive political statements. He did not object to Hitler continually referring to 'November criminals' during the course of the trial, or to one of the defendants insulting the eagle in the national flag by calling it a 'vulture'.[14] He tolerated Hitler making several derogatory comments about the Social Democrat Reich President, Friedrich Ebert.[15] When Lossow mentioned the fact that, on the evening of 8 November, Nazis had aimed their guns at him when he had briefly looked out of the window, Judge Neithardt tried to excuse this by remarking: 'I can imagine that they did it out of high spirits in order to give the gentlemen a fright.'[16] The reporter of the *Bayerischer Kurier*, a paper close to the Catholic Bavarian People's Party, noted that the courtroom seemed to be being increasingly 'transformed into a political meeting' in which 'applause and heckling' were tolerated.[17]

During the trial, Hitler repeatedly mentioned his personal political ambitions; they were not exactly modest. While he referred to Ludendorff as the '*military* leader of the future Germany' and said the general was to be the 'leader of the great future reckoning', he insisted, 'I am going to be the *political* leader of this young Germany. Since it was I who founded this youthful völkisch movement, it's obvious that everybody in Germany who supports this youthful völkisch trend sees me as their leader. For I started it four years ago with a huge propaganda campaign and, during these past four years, I have created a great wave, which has now become a power factor even in the case of elections.'[18] However, as far as he himself was concerned, he had 'no interest in acquiring a ministerial post. I consider it unworthy of a great man to go seeking after titles'; that was the wrong way to 'make . . . a name for yourself in world history. . . . Thousands of people can become ministers. I resolved to be the destroyer of Marxism. That is my task. . . . It wasn't from modesty that I wanted at that time to be the drummer, for that is the highest there is. The rest is insignificant.'[19] The roles of 'drummer' and 'Führer' now merged in his mind. He wanted to be seen as historically unique, as someone who was far above the usual norms of conventional politics. This also meant that his decision to lead his supporters into a putsch, while completely ignoring the reality of the political situation, could appear entirely justified.

It was not surprising that, after twenty-four days of court proceedings, Hitler's final statement was another speech lasting several hours, during which he gloried in his sense of superiority.[20] The accused adopted the role of an accuser. Among other things, he declared: 'The broad masses will not recover their belief and confidence in the dignity of the law until the day when a prosecutor can stand up in court and say: I accuse Ebert, Scheidemann, and comrades of treason and high treason committed in 1918 . . .'[21] At the end, as the final judge in his case, he called on the 'Goddess of history': 'for, gentlemen, it is not you who will pronounce the final verdict upon us, it will be the goddess of the court of the last judgment, who will rise up from our graves and from your graves as "history". And, when we stand before her, I already know what her verdict will be. She won't ask us: Have you committed high treason? In her eyes the Quartermaster-General of the World War and his officers will count as Germans who wanted the best, as Germans who wanted to fight for their fatherland. You may pronounce us "guilty" a thousand times, but the goddess who presides over the eternal court of history will smile and tear up the charge of the public prosecutor, and smile and tear up the judgment of the court, for she will acquit us.'[22] Hitler had become so detached from the reality of the court proceedings that the inevitable verdict of guilty appeared tolerable. He had finally overcome the insecurity and shame which he had initially experienced as a result of the failure of the putsch.

On 1 April, sentence was pronounced: Hitler, like Weber, Kriebel, and Pöhner, was sentenced to five years' 'fortress imprisonment'; five other accused received shorter prison sentences; Ludendorff was acquitted. Since, as a result of Hitler's new sentence, the suspension of his 1922 sentence was no longer valid, no part of his sentence should have been suspended. But, ignoring the specific legal regulations concerned, the court decreed that his sentence (along with those of Pöhner, Weber, and Kriebel) should be suspended after only six months. The court rejected his deportation to Austria on the grounds of his military service, again ignoring the specific regulations of the Law for the Protection of the Republic, which laid down that foreigners convicted of high treason were without exception to be deported.[23]

Except in the extreme right-wing press, the sentence was strongly criticized: the *Bayerischer Kurier* wrote of a 'judicial catastrophe', the *Kölnische Volkszeitung* of a 'Munich scandal', the *Berliner Tageblatt* of 'judicial bankruptcy', and the *Münchener Post* claimed this represented the 'death of Bavarian justice'.[24]

The Nazi movement without its 'Führer'

Hitler returned to Landsberg, where he and the other Nazis who had been sentenced to 'fortress imprisonment' were exempted from the normal prison regime and enjoyed more comfortable conditions. (Because he had been elected to the Bavarian parliament or Landtag, one prisoner, Gregor Strasser, was released after a short time, while Pöhner did not need to start his sentence until January 1925.) The prisoners were permitted to spend five hours a day outside, doing sports or walking; they were able to visit each other in their spacious and comparatively comfortable rooms (they could hardly be called cells). Significantly, there was a large swastika flag hanging in the common room, which was removed only when senior officials came to inspect; the prison guards evidently had no objection to it. Hitler had two 'secretaries' at his personal disposal in the shape of Hermann Fobke, a law student, and Emil Maurice, to assist him with his correspondence and other writing activities.[25] The prison authorities reported that, among the extremely large number of visitors Hitler received (350 between April and October 1924, 150 in the first month alone),[26] were: 'people seeking favours or jobs, creditors, friends, and some who were simply curious'; in addition, there were lawyers, businessmen who wanted to use his name, and publishers seeking to sign him up him as an author.[27]

In retrospect, Hitler described his time in prison as a phase that, above all, gave him time to reflect on his policies and his programme; moreover, in Landsberg he gained in 'self-confidence, optimism, and faith'.[28] While the trial had confirmed him in his self-image as a 'Führer' of national importance, in his Landsberg cell he became convinced that he was one of those rare personalities in world history in whom 'the politician is combined with the political theorist capable of producing a programme' ['Programmatiker']. The fact that, once again, as in October 1923, he referred in this context to the, in his eyes, great visionaries, Frederick the Great, Luther, and Wagner, indicates that, in the meantime, his self-image had reached Olympian proportions.[29] But Hitler was not alone in his views.

On the occasion of his thirty-fifth birthday, his supporters arranged a 'demonstration of homage' in the Bürgerbräukeller attended by 3,000 people. A resolution was passed demanding the 'immediate release' of Hitler and his comrades and the lifting of the ban on the Party and the *Völkischer Beobachter*.[30] The extreme right-wing press also celebrated Hitler as a hero. In *The People's Book of Hitler* Georg Schott wrote a comprehensive account of Hitler 'the man', 'the politician', and the 'liberator'.[31] His personal photographer, Hoffmann, published a book of photographs with the title *Germany's Awakening in Words and Pictures*, in which he celebrated Hitler as the 'strongest political personality in the nationalist movement and as the leader of the völkisch-German freedom movement'.[32] To cite another example from the plethora of such expressions of adulation: following a visit to Hitler, Rudolf Jung, a Sudeten German Nazi, compared him in a newspaper article in January 1924 with Jesus.[33]

The perception of Hitler as a martyr and as the future leader of the extreme Right was given a further boost by the fact that, during his imprisonment, the NSDAP disintegrated into several competing groups. Hitler kept largely aloof from these divisions and so was able to retain his aura as somebody above mundane politics; indeed, he was able to view the conflicts and the damage to his potential rivals with a certain amount of satisfaction, safe in the knowledge that, after his release, he would be able to intervene to sort things out and revive the movement under his leadership.

After the putsch, the NSDAP, the Kampfbund, Reichskriegsflagge, and Bund Oberland were all banned and their property confiscated, including the *Völkischer Beobachter* and its printing presses.[34] Shortly before his arrest, Hitler had tasked Rosenberg with leading the banned party during his absence. On 1 January 1924, Rosenberg, together with Hans Jacob, the last deputy chairman of the NSDAP, founded the Grossdeutsche Volksge-meinschaft [Greater German National Community, GVG] as a successor organization.[35] However, by the summer, Esser and Streicher had succeeded in taking over this party from Rosenberg, who was unpopular with the mem-bership.[36] Moreover, on 6 January, the Völkisch Bloc was founded in Bamberg as an umbrella organization covering former supporters of the NSDAP as well as other right-wing groups such as Oberland, Reichskriegsflagge, and Jungdeutscher Orden. This organization also operated outside Bavaria under the name Völkisch-Sozialer-Bloc [VSB].[37] At the end of February, the Völkisch Bloc and the GVG agreed on a joint list of candidates for the approaching Bavarian Landtag elections.[38] The Völkisch Bloc rapidly expanded into Thuringia, where it competed in the Landtag elections of 10 February under the name Vereinigte Völkische Liste, winning 9.3 per cent of the vote. This enabled it to exercise some influence on the newly elected right-wing government in Thuringia by providing it with parliamentary support. At the beginning of 1924, the VSB also took part in elections elsewhere, such as in the Rhineland and Hesse.[39]

However, it quickly became clear that the vacuum created by the ban on the NSDAP could not be filled simply by the GVG and the new-right wing umbrella organization, the VSB. They soon began to face competition from the Deutsch-völkische Freiheitspartei [German-Völkisch Freedom Party, DVFP], which was founded mainly by extreme right-wing former mem-bers of the conservative DNVP, and was already established in north Germany in autumn 1922. In March 1923 Hitler had been obliged to con-cede dominance in north Germany to this new party.[40] But now the DVFP began to try to expand into south Germany as well.[41] During negotiations, first in Salzburg in January and then on 24 February 1924 in Munich, the DVFP managed, despite Rosenberg's dogged resistance, to insist on closer cooperation with the GVG. According to the agreement of 24 February, the two parties would retain their separate organizations at local level, but com-mon structures would be created at regional level, unless one of the parties was clearly dominant.[42] Hitler only accepted the agreement with the pro-viso that it should be limited to a period of six months.[43] The main result of this agreement was to confirm the dominance of the DVFP in north Germany. On 25 February, the day before the start of his trial in Munich, Ludendorff had appointed the chairman of the DVFP, Albrecht von Graefe, to be his representative in north Germany. At the same time, the agreement gave the DVFP enough scope to compete with the GVG in south Germany.[44]

Despite Hitler's objections – he had always rejected the NSDAP's participation in elections – the Völkisch Bloc (the alliance of extreme right-wing forces in Bavaria) took part in the Bavarian Landtag elections on 6 April 1924, winning 17.1 per cent of the vote. In Munich itself, with the election taking place only a few days after Hitler had been sentenced, they even won almost 35 per cent.[45] Their twenty-three deputies included the Landtag librarian Rudolf Buttmann, the Landshut pharmacist Gregor Strasser, the former Munich police chief Ernst Pöhner, the founder of the DAP Anton Drexler, and Julius Streicher (as the representative of the Grossdeutsche Volksgemeinschaft). However, as a result of disagreements within the parliamentary group and losses to other parties, the group was soon reduced to 17.[46] In the Reichstag election of 4 May 1924 the combined völkisch list won 6.5 per cent of the vote and thirty-two seats, of which only ten were held by members of the banned NSDAP, the remainder by members of the DVFP.[47] In Munich the combined list still gained 28.5 per cent. However, this election result did not mean that by 1924 Hitler had already succeeded in winning over a quarter of the Munich population to be solid Nazi supporters, for, at the next Reichstag election in December 1924, support for the völkisch list in the Bavarian capital was reduced to 9.1 per cent.[48] Thus, the elections of April and May should rather be seen as protests against the Bavarian government, whose radical and vociferous anti-Berlin policy had clearly come to grief during autumn 1923.

Meanwhile, Ludendorff was trying to assert his authority as the dominant figure within the extreme Right. In May, during two visits to Hitler in Landsberg, he tried to gain Hitler's support for uniting the DVFP and the supporters of the banned NSDAP in a new Nationalsozialistische Freiheitspartei [National Socialist Freedom Party]. Hitler reluctantly agreed, but among other things, insisted that the headquarters of the new party should be in Munich. Before the details could be agreed, at a conference in Berlin Ludendorff persuaded the Reichstag deputies of both parties to unite under the name Nationalsozialistische Freiheitspartei (which was dominated by the DVFP), announcing in a press release, which Hitler had not approved, that the latter was in support of a unified party.[49]

Opposition to the merger now grew among the Nazis in north Germany. On 25 May, leading Nazis in Hamburg committed themselves to recreating an independent Nazi Party and opposed parliamentary cooperation with the DVFP. They sent a four-man delegation to Landsberg, which discussed the situation with Hitler on 26 and 27 May.[50] He explained that he was against participation in elections, that the agreement of 24 February had taken him by surprise, and his only option had been to limit it to six months. However, cooperation with the DVFP should be restricted to the parliamentary group. Within this alliance the NSDAP must assert its claim to the leadership and insist on the headquarters being in Munich.[51] As a result, on 3 June, a conference of north German Nazi Party functionaries decided to create their own leadership in the form of a three-man directorate with dictatorial powers.[52]

Finally, on 7 July, Hitler officially announced in the press that he was withdrawing from politics. He requested that Party comrades should cease their visits to Landsberg, explaining that he needed more time to work on a 'substantial book'.[53] In fact, the main reason for this public declaration of neutrality was probably his expectation of being released early, on 1 October, which had been envisaged in his sentence.[54]

Two days later, both the GVG and the Nationalsozialistische Freiheitspartei responded to this development. The GVG decided to establish a new directorate under Streicher as first and Esser as second chairman. They considered a union with the DVFP as 'impossible at the present time', but sought 'reasonable cooperation as far as possible' at local level if there were local branches of both parties in the same place.[55] The Freiheitspartei issued a press release according to which Hitler had requested Ludendorff and Graefe to take over the leadership of the whole movement in his place. After his release Hitler would then 'rejoin them as the third member', a formula which implied a challenge to his claim to sole leadership.[56] Until this time, the press release continued, Gregor Strasser would act as his deputy in the 'Reich leadership'.[57] However, in response to their immediate enquiry, Hitler informed the north German Nazis that he had not appointed Strasser; this had been done by Ludendorff, although he had nothing against him. In any case, he was determined after his release to take on the leadership once again.[58] However, the north German group of Nazis refused to merge with the DVFP and rejected any involvement in parliament. Its three-man directorate believed they were keeping Hitler's seat warm for him or, as Adalbert Volck, a member of the directorate, wrote to Fobke, Hitler's secretary: 'Our programme has two words: Adolf Hitler.'[59]

Meanwhile, the re-establishment of the SA was making considerable progress, a development that Hitler regarded with mixed feelings. On 1 April, the day on which sentence had been pronounced, Hitler sent Röhm a handwritten note appointing him military leader of the Kampfbund.[60]

Appointed deputy leader of the SA by Göring, Röhm was able to secure his de facto leadership of the SA at a meeting of SA leaders from all over Germany and Austria held in Salzburg on 17 and 18 May.[61]

Röhm immediately initiated a national reorganization of the SA. Alongside this, however, he also attempted to construct an autonomous, Reich-wide Nazi paramilitary organization with the title 'Frontbann'. It was intended to include other leagues apart from the SA and to be organized along hierarchical, quasi-military lines. When Röhm visited Hitler in Landsberg he was told that these plans were not viable, but was not put off.[62] Established in August 1924, the Frontbann soon contained 30,000 members, with Ludendorff formally assuming the 'overall leadership'. However, in September the Bavarian government ordered the Frontbann headquarters to be searched and some of its leaders arrested; in the end, however, legal proceedings were halted by an amnesty. Hitler's entourage blamed Röhm and his Frontbann activities for the postponement of Hitler's release, after the public prosecutor intervened to stop it; it had been scheduled for October.[63] In the meantime, there was no sign of the various groups competing to replace the NSDAP coming together; a meeting of eighty Nazis in Weimar on 20 July ended without agreement.[64]

Hitler continued to adopt a neutral position in public, but made his reservations clear in comments to close associates: Ludendorff had 'a bee in his bonnet about mergers', 'Esser is a rake', 'I'll draw a veil over Streicher', Strasser had become so high profile that he was not going to make him second chairman after his release as he had intended. As far as he was concerned, the question of a merger with the DFVP was over and done with.[65] Volck, the representative of the north Germans, took the same line when he wrote in a letter to Fobke that they did not recognize Strasser as their representative, as he had not been appointed by Hitler. But 'H overestimates his strength; despite the chaos, he thinks he'll easily be able to sort things out.' If Hitler was still thinking of Bavaria as the 'base', he was under a misapprehension: 'It's only from the north that a real völkisch storm can be unleashed.' Volck's main concern was that, while Hitler was in prison, a rival group could emerge within the movement and become involved in parliamentary affairs. Did Hitler know, for example, that election posters were being put up with his portrait on them? For Volck this was 'a slap in the face for H'.[66] Hitler appears to have immediately responded to this criticism, for he issued a statement, published in the *Völkischer Kurier*, objecting to the misuse of his name in the Völkisch-Sozialer-Bloc's election campaign.[67]

Meanwhile, on 26 July, the Reichstag passed a resolution lifting bans on political parties; all the states affected by this decision obeyed, albeit Prussia and Bavaria only after a delay of several months. Nazis throughout the Reich must undoubtedly have taken courage from this resolution.[68] At a second conference in Weimar from 15 to 17 August 1924 a merger of the NSDAP and the DVFP under the name Nationalsozialistische Freiheitsbewegung [National Socialist Freedom Movement, NSFB] was finally agreed 'under the Reich leadership of Ludendorff, Hitler, and von Graefe'.[69]

However, the north German group of former Nazis under Volck and Ludolf Haase, a Göttingen medical student, kept their distance. Confused by Hitler sending a greetings telegram to the Weimar meeting, they now enquired about his attitude to the new combined organization and how he envisaged the Party's future activities. Fobke once more gave an evasive answer: Hitler rejected a complete merger and a 'parliamentarization of the movement'. However, he was not totally opposed to 'cooperation with Graefe and the Gen. [Ludendorff] in a single organization', and whether he would establish an anti-parliamentary movement, like the old NSDAP, or 'order a withdrawal from parliament' he 'could not yet say'. However, as 'there was now a group of [völkisch] Reichstag deputies', he wanted 'to use it as an instrument'. Apart from that, as a matter of principle, he was not prepared publicly to support any of the existing groups. He still believed that he would be released on 1 October and then be able 'first of all to sort out Bavaria'. The north Germans should 'keep going' for the time being.

They were by no means satisfied with this reply.[70] At a meeting in Harburg on 7 September the north Germans distanced themselves from the Reich leadership of the NSFB, who were giving the false impression that they were acting on Hitler's authority. They rejected any form of participation in elections and reemphasized that their three-man directorate regarded itself as simply 'keeping warm' Hitler's position as leader until he regained his freedom of action.[71] Hitler, who was still expecting soon to be released, responded to a further pressing letter from Volck by indicating that he could only summon all those involved to meet him after this had happened. In any case, he was not prepared to accept a Reich leadership (a kind of 'soldiers' council type arrangement') under any circumstances; it would be simply a question of 'who would support him as the sole leader'.[72] During the following weeks, Hitler continued to refuse to recognize a merged organization.[73] His silence left the north German Nazis floundering. Volck, who was clearly at a loss, told a meeting in Uelzen at the beginning of

November that they would try to 'act in his spirit'; it was assumed that he would advocate a boycott of the Reichstag election that had been called for December.[74]

On 19 October, after much debate, the GVG decided to join the NSFB. A dispute broke out, however, because the Bavarian state organization of the NSFB, established a week later largely on the initiative of the Völkisch-Sozialer-Bloc, refused to accept the leaders of the GVG, Esser and Streicher, as members of the new organization. Thereupon, at the beginning of November, the GVG decided at a 'Reich party conference' to retain its independence after all.[75] In the meantime, on 30 October, the NSFB had held its first mass meeting at the Bürgerbräukeller and, under the chairmanship of Anton Drexler, Gregor Strasser subjected Esser and Streicher to a vicious attack.[76]

In the light of these petty squabbles, it is clear that nobody was in a position to step into Hitler's shoes and unite the Nazis, neither Ludendorff nor Strasser, nor any of those in Hitler's old entourage such as Rosenberg or Streicher. Instead, the former party, having disintegrated into a number of feuding groups made a catastrophic impression. In the Reichstag election of 7 December 1924 the NSFB won only 3 per cent of the vote; among the fourteen deputies elected there were only three former Nazis. The result was a reflection of the fact that the Republic was beginning to stabilize both politically and economically, but also undoubtedly a consequence of the deep divisions within the Nazi movement that had become apparent during 1924. Hitler, at any rate, did not hide the fact that he was not unhappy with the result.[77]

Mein Kampf

The 'substantial book', which, according to his 'assistant', Fobke, Hitler began during his imprisonment, has been interpreted by historians primarily as a programme; thus Mein Kampf is seen as evidence of Hitler's early aims, which he then, during the 1930s and 1940s, endeavoured more or less systematically – and that remains in dispute – to put into practice.[78] However, his decision to write a book was in the first instance clearly prompted by his need to explain the defeat of 9 November and to underpin his projection of himself as the leader of the extreme Right.

While during his trial he had presented himself as the leader of the extreme Right, possessing superhuman abilities, now, in the process of writing *Mein Kampf*, he managed to invent a background story that made sense of his lack of youthful success. In the 'mundaneness of everyday life', he wrote in *Mein Kampf*, often 'important people' appear 'unimportant'; it is only when confronted with exceptional challenges, by which Hitler primarily meant war, that 'someone ordinary and unprepossessing' emerges as 'a genius'. In the case of these special individuals the 'hammer blow of fate' that fells most people 'suddenly lands on steel', and now, 'to the astonishment of the onlookers, the core that has hitherto been hidden' becomes visible. It is not difficult to see that he is referring here to 9 November, during which his heroic genius became apparent for the first time. Hitler emphasized, however, that the individual's 'genius' 'did not suddenly appear at this moment'; in the case of 'truly creative people' it was naturally inborn.[79] In his lean Vienna years he had laid the foundations for his career as a leader of genius, and Schopenhauer, Houston Stewart Chamberlain, and Wagner always provided him with the models for this self-image. He also borrowed from Wagner and Chamberlain the anti-Semitic line according to which true genius must succeed in defeating the Jews, the 'destroyers of genius'.

The failure of his artistic ambitions to be a painter or architect thus became a *magnificent* failure. Hitler now claimed to have transferred basic elements of the heroic artist–genius to his new role as 'Führer'; in this way he could still fulfil his alleged destiny to be an exceptional individual, albeit in another sphere. For he believed that, as an artist, he was bringing valuable abilities into politics: the strength of will and resolution with which he was following the path set out for him by 'destiny'; a particularly marked intuition, in other words his sensitivity to the psychological weaknesses of other people, but also to the depths of the 'soul of the masses'; the emotion he could generate in order to release the emotions of the masses. He already saw himself as the superman, predestined to be a genius in his role as 'Führer' and certain of success.[80]

When it came to his decision to write a political polemic, a mixture of autobiography and programme, his supporters would undoubtedly have preferred him to continue with the strategy pursued at his trial, namely of portraying himself as the victim of a political intrigue, who nevertheless was going to carry on the fight. Originally, in fact, the book was going to end with the 1923 putsch,[81] but, surprisingly, there is no mention of 9 November and its immediate pre-history. Hitler's ability to avoid these topics is tied up with the history of its publication. While in prison he postponed publication because of the danger of his imminent release being delayed, which was still theoretically possible.[82] During the months after his release, he continued work on the manuscript, but, after being banned from speaking in March 1925, decided to include the particularly sensitive parts in a second volume. In May 1925, he finished work on the first volume, which appeared in the same year.[83]

The first volume mainly contains an extremely self-aggrandizing autobiography of Hitler up until his early years in the DAP/NSDAP, interspersed with chapters containing general reflections on the 'World War', 'War Propaganda', 'Revolution', the 'Causes of the Collapse', and 'Nation and Race'. The claim contained in the subtitle, 'A Reckoning', is hardly realized, as his account ends in 1920.

The second volume, *The National Socialist Movement*, written between August 1925 and November 1926 and published at the end of 1926, continues the autobiography and the history of the Party in a rather haphazard way. The chronological account finally peters out and is replaced by (often indirect) references to and comments on all kinds of topics, including current affairs.[84] The structure of this volume shows very clearly that Hitler had abandoned his plan to continue his full-scale autobiographical account of the nobody who, while making great sacrifices, set out to save the fatherland, taking it stage by stage up to the decisive point of November 1923. Nor was he able to turn his extensive reflections into a coherent manifesto. It is, therefore, difficult to distil anything like a political programme from his long-winded and confused observations. At the end of the volume he took up his autobiography once again, describing the crisis of 1923 up until the end of passive resistance in the Ruhr in September 1923. He did not want to continue with the story: 'I do not wish to because I do not see any future benefits from it and, above all, because it is pointless to reopen wounds that are only just healing.'[85] However, Hitler's decision not to seek a further 'reckoning' with the right-wing establishment in Bavaria was definitely not influenced merely by such tactical considerations; the most decisive factor must have been his personal difficulty in coping with his defeat. He was simply not prepared to accept that he had miscalculated in November 1923. Instead, he attempted to obscure it with grandiose visions of his 'mission'. During his trial, he had portrayed himself as the victim of an intrigue and, at the same time, tried to shed this victim role through his behaviour during the proceedings, in which he portrayed himself as the leader of 'young Germany', whose heroic deed, in historical perspective, must appear entirely justified. He maintained this line during the coming years, a reinterpretation that, after 1933, culminated in the annual ceremony associated with 8/9 November, in which he created a kind of resurrection myth of the 'dead heroes'. The overarching message was: 'The deed was not in vain!'

By *not* dealing with November 1923 in *Mein Kampf*, Hitler failed to give the work a clear focus. For it was supposedly intended to be a piece of confessional writing, whose plausibility depended essentially on being rooted in the autobiographical basis of the 'programme' that was being put forward. And yet the author had nothing to say about what had been hitherto the high point of his career or about its provisional failure. This fact and his lack of ability to give his ideas a systematic focus and his tendency to engage in monologues produced a conglomeration of flattering autobiography and political tirades that was hard to unravel. The result was confused and unreadable.

The second volume of *Mein Kampf* was largely written in the seclusion of Berchtesgaden.[86] In it Hitler, for the moment a failed politician, adopted the role of a political visionary with a programme containing a set of ideas of world historical importance. In doing so, he was once again escaping into his typical overblown fantasies and megalomaniacal dreams, now designed to help him come to terms with the shame of November 1923. The contrast between the down-to-earth Hitler, who in 1925 was busy trying to rebuild the split NSDAP, and the theoretician [Programmatiker] speculating in world historical dimensions could hardly have been greater.

His 'programme', although it can be elicited only by careful analysis of the second volume, was a repetition and expansion of the ideas that he had already been putting forward before 1923. In addition to his notorious virulent anti-Semitism and his identification of Jews with Bolsheviks/ Marxists, he now introduced another important theme, 'the question of space'. During his imprisonment, Hitler had become interested in 'geopolitics', the study of the dependence of politics on geographical space. This was probably under the influence of his fellow-prisoner, Rudolf Hess, whose academic supervisor, Professor Karl Hofer, was an exponent of the theory.[87] By combining these ideas with his anti-Semitism and racism, Hitler developed the thesis of the eternal struggle between nations for 'living space', in which superior racial qualities would triumph. In this 'world view' the Jews played the role of a 'counter-race' that was diametrically opposed to the superior 'Aryan race' and trying to undermine the 'Aryans' attempt to 'gain space'. As parasites, they must, therefore, be removed from the Aryans' 'national body'. That had to be the prerequisite for any kind of revisionist foreign policy.

He did not make clear how in practice he envisaged the 'removal' of the Jews. However, a few passages reveal violent fantasies. Thus, for example, he wrote: 'we shall only succeed in persuading our masses to become nationalists if, in addition to a positive struggle for the soul of our people, their international poisoners are exterminated'.[88] Elsewhere, he complained about the 'Marxist' workers' leaders' behaviour during the World War, noting: 'If at the start and during the course of the war twelve or fifteen thousand of these Hebrew corrupters of the people had been held under poison gas, as was the case with hundreds of thousands of the best of our German workers from all walks of life on the battlefield, then the sacrifice of millions of those killed at the front would not have been in vain.'[89] Although the mention of poison gas leaps off the page, such threats and fantasies do not mean that he already had a plan for the systematic murder of European Jews.

What emerges clearly from *Mein Kampf* is that the main goal of a future Nazi foreign policy was to be the conquest of living space in eastern Europe. Hitler relied on ideas that before and during the war were being put forward by the Pan-Germans. They were modelled on the 'great Eastern solution', which Ludendorff, among others, had planned in 1918 following the advance of German troops into the Ukraine. Up until spring 1922, Hitler had been open to the idea of an alliance with a Russia liberated from 'Jewish Bolshevist' rule; he even thought a combined expansion by the two powers was feasible. In a speech in October 1922 he maintained that had Germany made an alliance with Russia against Britain before the war, it would have 'created the opportunity for an unlimited eastwards expansion'.[90] However, as the Soviet regime consolidated its position during 1922/23 he changed his view. He now began to contemplate the idea of an alliance with Italy and Great Britain, transforming his previous notion of securing 'the East' for German settlers *with the aid of* Russia into its opposite: this goal was now to be achieved by *destroying* the Soviet Union.

The basic issues determining Hitler's views on the relationship with Italy were the question of the South Tyrol and his old dream of an Anschluss with Austria. Hitler had initially not been prepared to accept Italy's annexation of the South Tyrol;[91] the 1920 NSDAP programme demanded the 'unification of all Germans...in a greater Germany'. No exceptions were envisaged. However, Hitler altered this position at the end of 1922. No sooner had the Fascists seized power in November 1922 than Hitler claimed that it was essential that 'Germany [should] clearly and decisively abandon the Germans of South Tyrol'. The giving up of the South Tyrol was the precondition for Italy's agreement to the Anschluss of Austria with the Reich.[92] However, since this demand was unacceptable to the majority of nationalist Germans and supporters of a 'greater Germany' who wanted to integrate Austria *including* the South Tyrol into the Reich, Hitler did not make any further public statements on this issue. At the end of 1922, he told Eduard Scharrer, co-owner of the *Münchener Neueste Nachrichten* and a Nazi sympathizer, in confidence, that for the time being they should play down the South Tyrol issue; it might be possible to solve it later 'through a form of compensation'.[93]

As far as the western powers were concerned, in the light of the 1923 Ruhr crisis, Hitler began to bank on a clash developing between British and French interests. He was working on the assumption that, given its traditional foreign policy principles, Britain would not stand idly by and watch France finally gaining hegemony on the continent. At the end of 1922, he was already contemplating Anglo-German cooperation against France and Russia as well as the idea of 'colonizing the East'. In December he told Scharrer they should try for 'the destruction of Russia with the aid of England. Russia had enough land for German settlers and provided big opportunities for German industry; England would then not get in our way when we come to deal with France'.[94] But Hitler did not publicly demand an alliance with Britain nor did he develop the idea of conquering 'soil' in Russia any further. In 1924, when he was already in prison, he published an article in which he simply criticized pre-war German foreign policy as hopelessly indecisive. There had been two alternatives: '...they should have either decided to conquer farmland, dispensing with overseas trade, colonies, and excessive industrialization, in which case the German government should have recognized that this could only be achieved in alliance with Britain against Russia; or, if they wanted sea power and overseas trade, this would only be possible in alliance with Russia against England'. But, at the time, they had been unable to decide between the two alternatives. Hitler does not let on that at this point he was already leaning towards an alliance with Britain.[95]

During his imprisonment Hitler had the opportunity for a more thorough consideration of this whole set of issues. In particular, he began to combine the 'space question' in a systematic way with the 'race question'. Already in the first volume of *Mein Kampf*, which had been largely written in Landsberg, he had developed the idea of an alliance with Britain, in order 'with our backs covered' to be able to launch 'the new German drive to the East' in the direction of Russia. However, once again he expressed these ideas within a critique of pre-1914 German policy.[96] It was only after his release and with his obsessive urge to communicate curbed by a speaking ban, that he wrote down the basic ideas of a future foreign policy unequivocally in the second volume of *Mein Kampf*. He returned to his ideas about pre-war German foreign policy, now openly advocating alliances with Britain and Italy[97] and stated that abandonment of the South Tyrol was the precondition for the improvement of relations with Italy.[98] He then devoted a lengthy section – typical of his linking of foreign policy issues with his racial obsessions – to the question of whether the influence of international Jewry would prevent these alliances; his response was a lengthy emotional declaration, culminating in the claim that in the end the 'evil enemy of humanity' would be overcome.[99]

The next chapter – 'Eastern Orientation or Eastern Policy' – focused on the core of his ideology: 'We shall stop the endless German drive to the South and West and direct our gaze towards the lands in the East. At long last we shall bring to an end the colonial and commercial policy of the pre-War period and shift to the territorial policy of the future.... Neither western nor eastern orientation should be the future goal of our foreign policy but an eastern policy in the sense of acquiring the necessary soil for our German people.'[100] The 'destruction of the Soviet Union' would, however, not only result in the acquisition of 'soil' but also a further vital goal would have been achieved. Since he saw in 'Russian Bolshevism...the attempt by the Jews during the twentieth century to secure world domination', the 'end of Jewish hegemony in Russia' would simultaneously destroy the basis of these plans for world domination, whose next target was, in his opinion, definitely Germany.[101]

In this way he was able to combine his imperialist and racist goals. Radical anti-Semitic aims were the link between his future domestic and foreign policy objectives. The violent 'removal' of the Jews from Germany was now supplemented by a war of conquest, which was intended to put an end to 'Jewish rule in Russia'. However, on the publication of the second volume in 1926, such far-reaching views must have appeared completely unreal and utopian.

In the second volume Hitler also develops another element in his ideology for the first time in a systematic manner: his views on 'racial hygiene' [i.e. eugenics]. During his imprisonment he had evidently studied the relevant literature and adopted central demands of 'racial hygiene', which in Germany (but not only there) was, at the time, considered a science. This was noted with considerable satisfaction in a journal article published in 1931 by its leading proponent, the Munich professor, Fritz Lenz.[102] Basically, it involved subjecting the population to eugenic assessment, with the hope of identifying the 'racially valuable' elements, on the one hand, and the 'inferior' and 'hereditarily diseased' elements, on the other. The aim was then to 'improve the racial value' of the German nation by introducing measures to encourage the former to reproduce and to prevent the latter from doing so. Hitler now confirmed that in a future völkisch state this would be taken care of: 'the demand that defective people should be prevented from begetting defective offspring is a totally rational demand and its systematic implementation represents a most humane act.'[103] This formulation was chosen with care and implied that 'inferiors' should be compulsorily sterilized, as was indeed the aim of radical exponents of racial hygiene at the time. Hitler continued: 'The prevention of the ability and opportunity to procreate on the part of physically degenerate and mentally sick people, over a period of only six hundred years, would not only free mankind from an immeasurable misfortune, but would lead to a recovery which appears scarcely conceivable today.'[104] Professor Lenz was delighted: 'Hitler is the first politician, possessing considerable influence, who has recognized that racial hygiene is a crucial political task and is prepared actively to support it.'

PART II

Creating a Public Image

6

A Fresh Start

On 20 December 1924 Hitler was released from custody; after the Supreme State Court of Bavaria had rejected an objection from the Attorney General, he was let off the remainder of his sentence.

In the first few weeks after his release Hitler kept a distinctly low profile as far as his political future and the issue of the re-founding and leadership of the NSDAP were concerned; he was reluctant to be drawn into the disputes among the various factions and instead wanted to preserve his special role as 'leader' of the 'movement' as a whole.[1] He was quick to get to work behind the scenes, however. With the help of Pöhner he was given an appointment with the Bavarian prime minister, Heinrich Held (BVP), on the day after his release; on the following day they met again. During these talks Hitler promised not to attempt any further putsch and distanced himself from Ludendorff. This clearly made a favourable impression, for Held, as a Catholic politician, objected to Ludendorff's repeated anti-clerical attacks. Hitler also gained Held's consent for his fellow prisoners to be released.[2] On 23 December Hitler was a guest for the first time at the home of the publisher Hugo Bruckmann, whose wife Elsa, a fervent supporter of Hitler's, had visited him in prison. By inviting him to her salon on numerous occasions, she was to provide him with the opportunity of meeting members of Munich high society. Hitler used these invitations to attract attention by delivering endless monologues – a crass violation of the unwritten rules of the salon![3]

The new year brought renewed infighting in the völkisch camp. On 17 January, at a conference in Berlin, three leading representatives of the NSFB, the Reichstag deputies Reinhold Wulle, Wilhelm Hennig, and Albrecht von Graefe, strongly objected to Hitler as the new leader. According to Wulle, Hitler was in danger of giving in to Ultramontanism; his meeting with Held was the first indication that he was moving in that direction. His leadership style, it was stressed, relied too much on emotional appeal and he lacked well thought out policies; Hitler was being influenced by 'immature young blabbermouths'.[4] Immediately after the conference Graefe, along with Wulle, Ernst Graf zu Reventlow, and Theodor Fritsch (who had already all played a leading role in the NS Freedom Party) founded a German-Völkisch Freedom Movement (DVFB) and began to put pressure on the NSFB members to decide between this new party and the Munich National Socialists.[5] In the light of Held's agreement to lift the ban on the NSDAP, Hitler told his supporters in the north that he had no intention of 'doing deals' with the Freedom Party, but would use Bavaria as a base from which to rebuild the Nazi Party in the Reich as a whole.[6] On 12 February Ludendorff smoothed the way for this project by dissolving the leadership of the NSFB, in other words the troika he had formed with Graefe and Strasser. He did, however, wish to continue as 'patron' of the various völkisch organizations.[7]

In the middle of February the bans affecting the NSDAP and the *Völkischer Beobachter*, which had already been lifted in the other German states, were lifted in Bavaria too.[8] The GVG responded by calling on all 'Hitler's loyal supporters' to join it.[9] At a gathering in Hamm on 22 February numerous functionaries from western and northern Germany, which during Hitler's detention had developed into a main focus of Nazi activities, affirmed to Hitler their 'steadfast loyalty and allegiance'.[10] On 26 February, Hitler used the first issue of the *Völkischer Beobachter* since the ban was lifted to address the Party comrades.[11] He claimed the leadership of the Party for himself, emphasizing that he opposed any attempt 'to drag religious controversies into the Party', thereby distinguishing it from other völkisch organizations. In the same issue Hitler proclaimed that Party comrades could 'now feel themselves brothers again in a great fighting community'. His call on readers to 'honour' Ludendorff, the 'immortal leader of the heroic German armies'[12] was a blatant political obituary; Hitler was in fact determined to exclude Ludendorff from the 'movement'.[13]

A suitable opportunity arose very soon after. Friedrich Ebert's death on 28 February 1925 triggered an unexpected election for the office of Reich President. Hitler pushed Ludendorff as National Socialist candidate for the office, even though – or precisely because – he reckoned Ludendorff had no chance of winning.[14] His appeal for support for Ludendorff in the 19 March issue of the *Völkischer Beobachter* appeared only five days after he had declared in an article in the same paper that the result of the election was completely irrelevant to the nation's fate.[15] Ludendorff's prospects faded altogether when the DVFP decided to support Karl Jarres, the right-wing parties' candidate. In the first round of voting on 29 March Ludendorff won only 1.1 per cent of the votes, significantly less than extreme Right candidates in the December 1924 election. In the second round the parties of the Right exchanged Jarres for a new candidate, sponsoring Field-Marshal Paul von Hindenburg. Hitler now used the *Völkischer Beobachter* to call for him to be elected, while the abandoned Ludendorff pulled out of the race.[16] In the second round on 26 April Hindenburg was victorious over Wilhelm Marx, the candidate of the parties supporting the Weimar constitution. For Ludendorff this meant a considerable loss of prestige and he never recovered politically. In addition, primarily through the influence of his second wife, Mathilde von Kemnitz, he adopted some decidedly strange, cultish ideas and thus finally lost any kind of role as a figurehead of the Right, standing above the grubby world of everyday politics, and so ceased to pose a threat to Hitler's absolute claim to lead. Ludendorff's lacklustre candidacy marked the beginning of the end of the German-Völkisch Freedom Movement.

In the *Völkischer Beobachter* of 26 February Hitler had also published 'Basic Guidelines for the Reestablishment of the National Socialist German Workers' Party'. He stated clearly that the new party would adopt 'in its principles and programme the guidelines of the old Nat. Soc. G. W. P. that was dissolved on 9 November 1923', while the 'Reestablishment of the SA...' would take place 'on the same lines that applied up to February 1923'. Armed groups or organizations were, he said, to be excluded from the SA, the purpose of which was 'as before February 1923 to make our young people physically tough, to train them in discipline and devotion to the great common ideal, and in service to the movement by keeping order and spreading the word'. He was thus rejecting plans to use the SA as a paramilitary organization, in other words the organizational model that the army had introduced into the Party in the spring of 1923: Hitler was no longer prepared to accept such a restriction on the scope of his power as leader.[17] These different perspectives led quickly to a rupture with Röhm, who wished to incorporate the SA in the Frontbann, which he had been building up in the meantime, with the aim of creating a 'National Socialist paramilitary movement'. This movement would exist independently of the NSDAP and have only a loose association with the 'Adolf Hitler idea'. Since Hitler insisted on the SA being integrated into the NSDAP, Röhm rejected the leadership of the SA when it was offered to him and withdrew from political life.[18]

In the new NSDAP Esser took over propaganda; Philipp Bouhler, who before the ban had been the second Party secretary and after that secretary of the GVG, now had the same function in the NSDAP; Amann remained as director of the Party's publishing company, Eher, and Franz Xaver Schwarz, who had been treasurer of the GVG, became the Party's Reich Treasurer.

On 27 February 1925 Hitler made a speech at the first big Party occasion since the lifting of the ban; it was, of course, held at the Bürgerbräukeller, where Hitler had last appeared on 8 November 1923. Ludendorff, Strasser, and Röhm were not present and even Rosenberg chose to stay away, as the whole business risked taking on too much of a 'theatrical quality' for his liking.[19] Before an audience of 3,000 Hitler began with a detailed exposition of the reasons that had originally led to the founding of the DAP. After some lengthy anti-Semitic tirades he stated that the aim of the NSDAP remained clear: 'To fight against the satanic power that plunged Germany into this misery; to fight against Marxism and the intellectual carriers of this world-wide plague and epidemic, the Jews; to fight, but not "tentatively" in a bourgeois fashion so that it does not hurt too much.' Finally, he came to the central point of the speech. He did not intend, he said, to take up a position in favour of one side or the other in the quarrels within the Party: 'Gentlemen, from now onwards let me be responsible for representing the interests of the movement!' And addressing his critics he added, not without some malice: 'You had ten months in which to "look after" the interests of the movement.' Now he was leader of the movement and 'nobody is going to tell me how to do it'. He would soon call together a provisional membership meeting and there hold elections for the leadership of the Party. Until then all criticism, particularly of him personally, should be put aside. After a year he intended, he said, to appear before the Party comrades and give an account of himself. There followed the great reconciliation scene, in which, amid thunderous applause from the audience, Esser, Streicher, and Artur Dinter from the GVG, as well as Buttmann, Feder, and Frick from the Völkisch Block, all shook hands on the podium and swore an oath of loyalty to Hitler.

After the re-founding of the NSDAP the GVG was dissolved and its members joined the newly formed NSDAP local branches. Most members of the Völkisch Block, which was also dissolved, followed suit, even though its leaders had not advised them to, but had merely said they were free to do so.[20] The same thing happened with the Munich branch of the NSFB, though elsewhere it remained in existence as an independent party and continued to compete with the NSDAP outside Bavaria in particular. Its gradual decline continued until 1932.[21]

Yet even the NSDAP soon suffered a setback. On 9 March 1925, after making only a few speeches in Nuremberg and Munich,[22] Hitler was banned by the Munich police headquarters from making any more public appearances. The reason given was that in his speech at the re-founding of the Party on 27 February 1925 Hitler had attempted 'in an unmistakable manner to incite the masses to acts of violence or to prepare them to commit such acts'.[23] Other states joined in the ban, such as Baden in April and Prussia in September.[24] The NSDAP was thus deprived of its most important propaganda tool; Hitler was obliged in future to confine himself to closed members' meetings.

The situation was made more complicated by the fact that in May 1925 Anton Drexler, a co-founder and former honorary chairman of the NSDAP, founded the National-Sozialer Volksbund [National-Social People's League] in Munich along with a number of city councillors and state assembly deputies from the Völkisch Block. This grouping kept going until 1927. Although its members regarded themselves as supporters of Hitler, his close circle of Party associates – Hermann Esser was considered the most objectionable – put them off joining the NSDAP and they quarrelled irreconcilably with it.[25]

Creation of the Führer Party

This time Hitler was determined to establish the NSDAP across the whole Reich. Apart from anything else, he was compelled to take this step by the fact that numerous local Nazi branches existed outside Bavaria and his völkisch competitors were extremely active. However, the centrality of Munich as the Party's base had, in his view, to be preserved, for his name was closely linked with the city.

Gregor Strasser was the man Hitler entrusted with the task of establishing the NSDAP in the north of Germany. In February Strasser organized a regional conference of Nazi functionaries in Hamm and in March a similar one in Harburg.[26] He then appointed a number of men who had emerged as leaders in their regions as Gauleiters: Heinrich Haake for Cologne, Hinrich Lohse for Schleswig-Holstein, Franz Pfeffer von Salomon for Westphalia, Bernhard Rust for Hanover, Josef Klant for Hamburg, and Axel Ripke for Rhineland North. Hitler formally confirmed these appointments in March.[27] As a rule Gauleiters also sought the approval of their regional organizations.[28] In this way the Party headquarters accepted the power relations in the regions[29] and tolerated changes. When, for example, in the middle of 1925 Haake, the Gauleiter of Cologne, invited Robert Ley to succeed him, Hitler recognized Ley as the new Gauleiter[30] and in August 1925, when Axel Ripke was replaced at a meeting of Gauleiters by Karl Kaufmann, Party headquarters knew nothing about it until five months later, when Kaufmann asked for confirmation in Munich.[31]

The Party was thus not structured in a rigidly hierarchical and centralized manner, but rather activists recruited members at a regional level and organized them, while accepting the authority of the Munich HQ, which in turn recognized them as 'Gauleiters'. Only in Bavaria (which up until 1926 was not split into Gaus) were the local branches directly subordinated to the Munich HQ. Hitler kept out of staffing disputes as far as possible. In October 1925 Amann told a party comrade from Hanover: 'Herr Hitler's view today is clearer than it has ever been that the most effective fighter in the National Socialist movement is the man who can assert himself as leader on the basis of his own efforts. If you yourself say that you have the confidence of virtually all the members in Hanover, why do you not simply take over the leadership of the local branch?'[32] The Party leadership, which had at first been housed in the offices of the *Völkischer Beobachter* and in June 1925 moved to Schellingstrasse 50,[33] the business premises of Hitler's personal photographer Heinrich Hoffmann, did, however, gradually centralize the issuing of membership documents.[34]

In the summer Hitler set off on quite a long speaking tour that took him to Saxony, Württemberg, and several places in Bavaria.[35] In his speeches he stressed repeatedly that the Party's headquarters must remain in Munich,[36] for 'leaving Munich would spell the end of the Party'. For him and for the movement, he said, the city was 'hallowed ground'.[37] By founding the National Socialist German Workers' Association on 21 August 1925 the NSDAP registered officially as an association, which was the precondition for its being a legal entity. In the clause inserted for this very purpose it was stated that the 'association's programme' was the 'basic programme of the National Socialist German Workers' Party as issued on 24 February 1920 in

Munich; it was 'immutable' and would 'be terminated only through its ful-filment'. This clause also established that for the time being the national leadership would be linked to that of the Munich branch.[38] This absolute insistence on Munich was Hitler's response to the increasing influence of the Party organization in north-west Germany and its growing criticism of the Party's leadership style. The Munich HQ's structures were hard to dis-cern from the outside, which suited Hitler very well when asserting his claim to absolute power. The dictatorial power he wished to continue to wield was bound up with the Munich location, with the structures of the Party HQ that he dominated, and with the myth of the November putsch, an important source for his claim to absolute power.

The DAP/NSDAP up to 1923 was very much the product of the Bavarian 'counter-revolution' and the desire to overturn the existing democratic order was central to its approach. In view of its basic orientation towards action and its militant character the Führer principle appeared as the appro-priate organizational model. Now that the Republic had stabilized, the pros-pects of mounting a coup were zero, and the Party had to face the question of whether it would not be better to refocus its efforts on participating in regular elections; it had to produce concrete economic and social policies. The 1920 'programme' had been largely non-committal about these mat-ters. And if the NSDAP aimed to be successful in the industrial centres and densely populated regions of north-west Germany, it had in particular to clarify what the word 'socialist' in the Party's name actually meant. The main concern of the group of branches that began to form in the north and west was to make the programme more concrete by tackling these issues.

On 20 August Gregor Strasser travelled to Elberfeld, where the Gau lead-ership of Rhineland North was located, and came to an agreement in prin-ciple with Kaufmann and Joseph Goebbels, who had joined the Party the previous year, to form a 'western bloc' in the Party, an idea that had already been aired at the February conference in Hamm.[39] This would be a means of providing a counterweight to what Goebbels noted as the 'total balls-up' at HQ and the 'big wig old fossils' in Munich; Hitler, they said, was sur-rounded by the wrong people and 'Hermann Esser will be the death of him'.[40] This perception was reinforced in the weeks that followed. Esser, it was said, had absolute power in the Party administration and was the real cause of the slow-down in the growth of the NSDAP, while Hitler, who was busy writing the second volume of *Mein Kampf*, was letting things slide. To halt this development, on 10 September 1925 the Gauleiters from the north-west, spurred on by Strasser, set up a working group in Hagen to better coordinate their efforts. Strasser (who for personal reasons could not in the end attend the Hagen meeting) took over as chair with Goebbels as secretary. They also agreed to issue a fortnightly newsletter with the title *Nationalsozialistische Briefe* [National Socialist Letters], which Goebbels was responsible for editing.[41] Although motivated to lay greater emphasis on the 'socialist' character of the NSDAP, the majority of the gathering opposed attempting anything that might be viewed as a rebellion against Munich, let alone as opposition to Hitler.[42] They simply opposed participation in elections, demanding that the Party leadership issue a clear statement on the matter.[43] At the end of September Strasser had a meeting with Goebbels in Elberfeld,[44] to agree on 'statutes' for the working group, through which they hoped to achieve uniformity in the organization and promote the exchange of information.[45]

At the end of October Hitler was planning to travel to the Ruhr area with the aim of establishing contact with representatives of the working group. Then he cancelled at short notice, on the grounds that he would be on Prussian soil, where since the end of September he had been banned from speaking in public, and so feared he might be arrested. It is possible that he was trying to avoid pinning himself down on content. Hitler preferred to engage with the North German oppositional group on his own territory.[46]

The first official meeting of the working group took place on 22 November 1925 in Hanover. High on the agenda was the task of developing their own draft programme for the NSDAP, one that in particular would contain concrete social policies (even though in August Hitler had declared the 1920 programme to be 'immutable'). Strasser expounded some initial thoughts on the matter to representatives of eleven Gaus[47] and by December they had been developed into a written version.[48] In it Strasser envisaged an authoritarian constitution, with a President elected for a seven-year term and equipped with extensive powers, and a 'Reich Chamber of Estates', an economy based in part on private capital, in part on state control, in part on cooperatives, and in part on corporatist organizations. The 1914 borders would be re-established and Austria annexed, including the South Tyrol and the Sudetenland, which had been separate since 1918. Strasser's draft programme fell into the hands of Gottfried Feder, who by this time had made himself the Party's chief economic ideologue; as Strasser informed Goebbels, Feder was 'furious that it had been disseminated without Hitler's or his knowledge' and intended 'to prime Hitler'.[49] On 24 January the working group had another meeting in Hanover to discuss the programme.[50] Feder arrived uninvited to represent Party HQ. According to Goebbels, 'an interminable, confused debate' then followed,[51] and in the end a programme committee was set up under Strasser to produce a final version of the draft. In addition, the working group decided that royal houses should not be given compensation for their expropriation during the revolution. This issue was high on the national political agenda as the result of an initiative, originating with the KPD and finally co-sponsored by the SPD, to make it the subject of a referendum.[52] Feder had heard enough to let Hitler know that the Party's inner cohesion was threatened.[53]

The decision on the NSDAP's programme was scheduled to be taken at a leaders' conference that Hitler called for Sunday 14 February 1926 in Bamberg. Some sixty Party functionaries attended at his invitation. There Hitler pushed through a decision that determined the Party's direction: in a speech lasting several hours he swept aside all the basic concerns raised by the working group. He expressed support, among other things, for the alliance with Italy and thus rejected any attempt to reverse the annexation of the South Tyrol. He also spoke out sharply against any cooperation with Russia, of the kind contemplated by Goebbels,[54] for this would be 'national suicide'. What was needed was rather 'a focus on and colonization of the East'.[55] That was precisely the line he had taken in the as yet unpublished second volume of *Mein Kampf*. Hitler went on to express views that were as shocking as they were depressing for the North German functionaries. While the working group had expressed support for the planned referendum opposing the settlement being offered to royal houses, Hitler took the opposing view: 'The law must remain the law. Even for princes. Don't cause an upset over private property! Ghastly!', as Goebbels noted with horror. He was also disappointed that Hitler did not want to open up discussion again about the matter of the programme: 'The programme is OK. It will do. Feder nods. Ley nods. Streicher nods. Esser nods. "It grieves me deeply to see you in that company!!!"'* After a brief discussion Strasser spoke up: 'Hesitating, trembling, clumsy.' It was a total defeat: '. . . Oh God, we're just no match for those swine down there!'[56]

Through his performance at Bamberg Hitler had once and for all gained acceptance for the principle of the NSDAP as a Führer Party. The Party's

---

* Translators' note: Quotation from the first part of Goethe's *Faust*.

political line was not linked to a precise programme but rather to an abstract 'idea' that only the 'Führer' himself could interpret in an authoritative manner.[57] In the months following he set about shaping the Party organization in accordance with this principle and in the process to put his various rivals firmly in their places.

After the Bamberg defeat Strasser and his supporters gave up the struggle for a time. Strasser was forced to promise Hitler that he would ask the members of the working group to return all copies of the draft programme.[58]

At the same time Hitler, now triumphant, was conciliatory over other matters. He stood by as in March the Greater Ruhr Gau was created without prior permission from the Party leadership; he also accepted the fact that Goebbels, Pfeffer, and Kaufmann had taken on the leadership of this new unit as a team, which hardly exemplified the Führer principle.[59] At the beginning of April he even invited them all to Munich and courted the delegates from West Germany with all means at his disposal.[60] Goebbels returned the favour on the evening of 8 April, when he made a speech at the Hackerbräukeller presenting the 'social question' as the key problem the NSDAP needed to resolve, while at the same time rejecting the demand for 'socialism'.[61] Hitler, who was present, was extremely pleased with this, whereas Kaufmann and Pfeffer were openly critical of Goebbels's speech.[62]

The following morning on a visit to the Party offices the three guests had to put up with Hitler subjecting them to a 'whole mish-mash of accusations'. However, after this philippic he shook hands with them in a gesture of reconciliation. In the afternoon he lectured them for three hours on foreign policy and economic matters, which led to a sharp exchange of views. Goebbels was not convinced by all of Hitler's arguments, but set aside his reservations because he was so impressed by the Party leader as a personality: 'I bow before a greater man, a political genius!' The three ambassadors from the Ruhr were, according to Goebbels, given 'decisive confirmation' of their position in the Party and Kaufmann and Pfeffer returned to Wuppertal. Goebbels, however, spent several more days with Hitler, who gave him the impression of having 'taken him to his heart like no other'. Goebbels's verdict on the visit was clear: 'Adolf Hitler, I love you because you are both great and unassuming at the same time. That is what is called genius.'[63] Hitler responded to criticism of the Party leadership, in so far as he moved Esser out of Party HQ in April and a few months later transferred Esser's brief, namely propaganda, to Strasser.[64] For his part, Goebbels revised his views on foreign policy with regard to the Soviet Union and the South Tyrol.[65]

In May Hitler called a general meeting of the Party membership in Munich. In his report he made it clear that he did not ascribe any particular political significance to this meeting, which was a legal requirement for associations. The meeting passed off in a remarkably low-key manner. As expected, Hitler was, by unanimous acclamation, confirmed as Party chairman; the question whether there was any other candidate met with laughter among those present.[66] Hitler used the opportunity to expatiate once again on the history of the NSDAP, while vigorously defending the decision to participate in elections. His central point, however, was an attack on the Left: It was, he said, the 'Nazi movement's mission . . . to oppose this red torrent, which one day will turn into a violent and brutal force, with a national one that is no less ideologically charged and no less determined to use brute force. . . . One of the two will succumb and the other will triumph'. Goebbels, who had made a special journey from Elberfeld, was gratified that the Party leader had praised him by name several times.[67]

The general meeting decided in particular to amend the statutes, as a result of which Hitler's power within the Party was strengthened still further: Whereas up to that point the Party chairman had been at the head of a committee elected by the membership, made up, in addition to him, of a second chairman, a first and second secretary, and a first and second treasurer, now the membership had the right to elect only the chairman, one of the treasurers (up to then it had been Schwarz), and one of the two secretaries (until then it had been Hermann Schneider). The deputy positions disappeared, in particular that of Hitler's deputy, which up to then had been filled by Amann. The demise of the original committee also removed the possibility that did still formally exist of using it to call extraordinary general meetings and thus provide a platform for any opposition within the Party to the chairman. The elected members of the committee were now joined by six chairmen of special 'committees' (for propaganda, finance, youth, the SA, complaints and disputes, and organization), all of whom were appointed by Hitler, and by a chief secretary (Bouhler's role was enhanced by this) also appointed by the Party chairman. It was also Hitler's prerogative to appoint Gauleiters. It was typical of Hitler's leadership style that in his words of introduction at the meeting he said nothing at all about these important changes to the structure of the Party organization; no discussion was scheduled, in any case.

Thus the Party leader made it increasingly difficult for any internal opposition to organize. Even the trio leading the Greater Ruhr Gau were left stranded after Goebbels's demonstrative show of friendship with the Party leader.[68] In the middle of June Hitler travelled to western Germany in order to settle the disagreements at the Gau conference in Kaufmann's favour with Kaufmann then taking over as Gauleiter.[69] Meanwhile Hitler was already planning more wide-ranging personnel changes: he proposed to Goebbels that he should move to Munich as 'General Secretary of the movement', while also weighing up whether to make him Gauleiter of Berlin.[70]

In July 1925, however, before these plans could come to fruition, the Party held its first Party rally since 1923; Hitler chose Weimar as its location, for it was there that in August 1924 the NSDAP and the DVFP had joined to form the National Socialist Freedom Movement – a move he had disapproved of. It was also a place where he was not banned from speaking. In Weimar the Party leadership established a ritual that was to guide all subsequent Party Rallies. Hitler gave the lead and set the tone in an article in the *Völkischer Beobachter*, stressing that this was not the place to give vent to 'personal quarrels' or to attempt to 'clarify confused and vague ideas'.[71] It was no accident that only two days before, on 1 July, he had banned working groups such as the unwelcome one involving the north-western Gauleiters; since the NSDAP was itself one 'big working group', there was 'no justification for individual Gaus to join together'.[72] No, he said, they should work to make the Party Rally 'a great demonstration of the youthful vigour of our movement'.[73] Hence Hitler ruled that instead of discussing matters raised in plenary sessions they should be referred to special panels holding their own sessions. There such matters as electoral issues, press affairs, propaganda and organization, as well as, for example, social topics, were debated vigorously, though no votes were taken. The chairmen he appointed for the special panels had, as Hitler instructed, the freedom and authority to deal with the matters raised as they saw fit, but he himself reserved the right to decide finally whether they would be taken further or not.[74] In the face of this careful stage-management, the attempts made by several NSDAP politicians to secure a resolution against participation in elections did not get off the ground. Instead, Hitler insisted on his view that the matter of elections should be treated purely tactically and that the Party should therefore not allow itself to be drawn into 'positive' cooperation with other parties.[75]

The Party Rally, attended according to the police by between 7,000 and 8,000 people and according to the *Völkischer Beobachter* by 10,000,[76] opened

early in the morning with a speech by Hitler to more than 3,000 members
of the SA in the National Theatre. He also used the occasion to hand over
the 'Blood Flag' to Joseph Berchtold, the Reich leader of the 'Schutzstaffel'
(Protection Squad) or SS, which had been set up the previous year with the
special task of guaranteeing the safety of the 'Führer' when he appeared in
public and hence saw itself as something of an elite unit. The Blood Flag, as
Hitler put it, was the 'assault flag of 9 November 1923, consecrated with the
blood of a comrade who fell as a martyr to the vision' of National Socialism.
After that special standards were distributed to the individual SA groups,
who then had to take the following oath: 'I swear to you, Adolf Hitler, that
I will be faithful to our flag to the last drop of my blood.'[77] The actual delegates' conference began at 10 a.m. with addresses by Dinter, Feder, and
Schwarz. From 12 noon onwards the chairmen of the special panels, some
of which had met the previous day, gave their reports. Then, as the climax
of the rally Hitler gave a keynote address in which he invoked the 'spirit
through which the Reich to come is embodied in us, in which the union of
nationalism and socialism is realized in an idealized form.' This speech was
far removed from the political issues of the day. 'Deep and mystical. Almost
like a gospel', was how Goebbels, who was in the audience, described it.[78]
There followed a march through Weimar that culminated in a demonstration on the market square and led to some serious rioting.[79] Munich HQ
considered the event a total success.

Hitler now attempted to use preferential treatment and promotion to
build closer ties with the main representatives of the 'north-west German'
opposition. First of all he invited Goebbels straight after the Party conference to his house on the Obersalzberg, where, accompanied by Hess, Rust,
Strasser, and others they went sightseeing in the area. During these days
Hitler managed, through hours of monologues, to impress Goebbels so
much that the latter considered him the 'self-evidently creative instrument
of divine fate'. Hitler had quite obviously recognized Goebbels's weak spot,
his intensely narcissistic personality causing him to respond with positive
rapture to Hitler's attentions.[80] The first results of Hitler's tactics were soon
evident: in August Goebbels and Strasser conducted a controversial correspondence about their relationship, and Goebbels believed it necessary to
defend himself in the *Nationalsozialistische Briefe* over his changed attitude to
the question of socialism: it was, he claimed, no 'Damascene conversion'
to be solidly behind the 'Führer', who was after all 'an instrument of that
divine will that shapes history'.[81] In September, on the other hand, Hitler

made Strasser NSDAP propaganda chief,[82] and at the beginning of October Strasser announced in the *Nationalsozialistische Briefe* that the working group had been dissolved.[83] At the end of October 1926 Goebbels was rewarded by being made boss of a new Gau, which Hitler created for this occasion from the two existing Gaus of Berlin and Brandenburg.[84] He also appointed the retired Captain von Pfeffer in November to be the new head of the SA.

Hitler envisaged the future role of the SA as being purely to support the Party: as he impressed on Pfeffer in SA Order No. 1, the NSDAP did not need 'a couple of hundred bold conspirators, but rather hundreds of thousands of fanatical fighters for our world view', who would appear in huge massed ranks and prepare the way for the NSDAP by 'conquering the streets'.[85] Hitler had already set the ball rolling by issuing a new set of statutes limiting the SA's tasks essentially to 'keeping order', 'protecting meetings', and distributing propaganda material.[86] It should specifically not develop once more into a paramilitary force, for the existing paramilitary organizations had in his view no concrete 'political purpose of their own' and it was out of the question to provide men with 'paramilitary' training for 'today's state' by means of private associations.[87] Thus in February 1927 Hitler went as far as to forbid National Socialists categorically to join paramilitary organizations, a measure that caused something of stir because it affected quite a number of Party members.[88] The motive for Hitler's rejection of paramilitary organizations was his fear that, as in 1923, they might extend their influence into his Party. At the same time, the NSDAP was interested in the men who belonged to these organizations, with their resolutely nationalist and militaristic mindset. The long-term aim was therefore to distance the Party from the standard model of the paramilitary organization and its hierarchy, while at the same time recruiting its members and convincing them of the NSDAP's entitlement to political leadership.[89]

By the end of 1926 Hitler had carefully dismantled the core of the group that had put itself forward as the advocate of a 'programmatic course' for the NSDAP; in pushing through the new Party statutes he had structured the Party in such a way that its leaders were completely subordinate to him and could not turn into a body that might call him to account. The Party Rally was there essentially to applaud what had already been decided, the Party programme was 'immutable', and he was the only one who could interpret it. By re-establishing a central leadership for the SA, he had ensured that no new alien body controlled by military men would emerge within the NSDAP; he had distanced it from the milieu in which paramilitary organizations flourished, while also creating in the SS a second paramilitary organization that was specifically committed to him personally. Less than two years after the founding of the Party there appeared to be no one who could challenge his position as its absolute leader.

The Führer personality

By establishing a weak organizational structure for the NSDAP, Hitler had created an environment almost perfectly adjusted to his singular personality.[90] The lack of formalized decision-making procedures permitted him to keep out of internal Party conflicts as far as possible, to place himself in authority over those in conflict, and to be the final court of appeal in deciding these disagreements. This lack of procedures enabled him to pursue a political strategy that was frequently ambivalent and multi-layered in order to avoid confrontation with opposing Party comrades, and to settle disputes about the programme through spontaneous, 'lone' decisions. Reluctant to commit himself, he was thus able to sidestep the need to turn the programme into concrete proposals and instead to focus on nebulous 'visionary' goals. Unpredictability was a carefully calculated element in his politics. 'Personal' access was another, as we have seen in the case of Goebbels. In this context 'personal' should not be understood as denoting either friendliness or commitment; what is crucial is rather the fact that, on the one hand, Hitler surrounded himself with people who never doubted his claim to be the 'Führer' and, on the other, was capable of neutralizing political disagreements by dispensing carefully calibrated doses of coolness or friendliness. When it suited him he could make himself inaccessible even to prominent Party comrades. In the Party complaints were heard about the Munich 'clique' that shielded him from the outside world[91] and, it was assumed, had a negative influence on him.[92] By contrast, anyone who was permitted to bask in the sunshine of his attention often repaid him with special devotion, particularly because it was well-known that Hitler as a rule kept aloof from people. The entourage that had again assembled around Hitler since 1925 in Munich was therefore a mixed bunch of ambitious political operators, willing helpers, and patient listeners; they included in particular his 'private secretary' Rudolf Hess, his factotum and later adjutant Julius Schaub, his personal photographer Heinrich Hoffmann, and his driver Julius Schreck. There was no discussion in this group, whether confidentially or in the wider circle. Instead Hitler preferred to come to his own conclusions about problems by pouring forth an endless torrent of words.[93]

These idiosyncrasies had the intended effect on his entourage. The fact that he was distant from everyday events in the Party, and never discussed anything as an equal, but rained down interminable monologues on his 'interlocutor', seemed to his supporters to be evidence of his extraordinary Führer quality. The fact that his day was normally unstructured, he avoided systematic and disciplined work as much as possible, and had the tendency to surprise those around him with 'lone-wolf' decisions were features his retinue interpreted as marks of his 'genius'. The fact that he ignored day-to-day politics in favour of megalomaniacal fantasies confirmed to his followers that he was a 'visionary'. His rigid adherence to decisions once made, which was in reality motivated by the fear of losing face and diminishing his aura as 'Führer', was interpreted by Party members as clarity of purpose and consistency. The fact that he was capable of expressing his individual phobias in terms that turned them into vivid, collective anxieties, and at the same time of presenting his audience with violent scenarios in which these threats were destroyed, was interpreted by his devotees as just one more exceptional gift.

In his demeanour, too, Hitler attempted to live up to his role as leader of a radical party of the New Right. Not least to distinguish himself from the stereotypical dignitary, frequently seen in the upper echelons of the political Right, who cultivated the style of Wilhelmine Germany, he continued to appear in a light-coloured trench coat and fedora and with a riding crop, which in the eyes of contemporaries amounted to dressing down. He enjoyed turning his engagements outside Munich into long automobile tours – from 1925 onwards he drove around in a large and showy Mercedes – frequently in the company of members of his entourage. When he was in Munich he was to be found almost every afternoon spending long periods at Café Heck or in the palace gardens café opposite.[94]

Hitler was extremely conscious of his outward appearance, constantly fearful of committing a solecism by making what he saw as an inappropriate impression.[95] In long sessions with his personal photographer, Heinrich Hoffmann, he worked out a repertoire of poses for portraits that would present him to the public. In the majority of these pictures, which were then often circulated as postcards, he appears with an intentionally determined expression in mostly rigid and commanding poses, now in a suit and affecting to be a serious politician, now in the uniform of an SA member as a comrade ready for battle, with the intense expressiveness and expansive gestures of the orator or as a relaxed countryman in his Lederhosen.[96] Group portraits with Party comrades show him in an unchanging pose with an inscrutable expression, hands clasped in front of his stomach. Not only in photos but also in the majority of his public appearances his gestures made a rehearsed and stereotypical impression, for example, his practice of always greeting Party comrades with a firm, manly handshake and 'penetrating' look; the way in which on official occasions he presented himself as a lover of children; even his fits of rage at Party events.[97] As we shall see, his appearances as an orator were pre-planned from the first moment to the last and increasingly took on the form of a ritual.

Just as Hitler hoped to create an impenetrable impression as a politician, so the financing of his lifestyle remained impenetrable too. At first he lived in ostentatiously modest circumstances in two small furnished rooms in Thierschstrasse in Munich. Even at this stage he spent a large part of his leisure time on the Obersalzberg above Berchtesgaden. He had had frequent stays there since the spring of 1923, either alone or with Party comrades. In 1925 he had written sections of the second volume of *Mein Kampf* there in the 'seclusion of the mountains'. On these visits he would at first stay in various boarding houses, but in 1928 he made use of an opportunity that was opening up to rent the Wachenfeld house on the north-eastern slope of the Obersalzberg. Hitler brought his half-sister Angela from Vienna to keep house for him in his new refuge.[98] He kept the fact that he had a holiday home hidden from the tax authorities, however, claiming he had rented the house as a home for his sister and that he was seldom there and then only as a guest.[99]

In 1929, before the NSDAP's breakthrough as a mass movement, he gave up his two rooms and moved into a luxurious apartment on Prinzregentenplatz in Munich. His patron Bruckmann stood surety for the rent with the landlord. Hitler took the Reicherts, from whom he was renting in Thierschstrasse, with him as caretakers to the new flat, where along with a servant and his wife they occupied the spacious servants' quarters.

Hitler told the tax office[100] that he lived from his income as an author, mainly (in some tax years exclusively) from royalties from the sales of *Mein Kampf*: in 1925 these had been almost 9,500 copies, in 1926 almost 7,000, in 1927 a little more than 5,600, in 1928 a little more than 3,000, and in 1929 more than 7,600 copies. His whole taxable income accordingly amounted in 1925 to 19,843 RM and was less than that in the following years: in 1926 it was 15,903 RM, in 1928 as little as 11,818 RM. His outgoings far exceeded his income, however. In the second half of the 1920s he spent 300 RM each month on his private secretary, 200 for an additional assistant, and 200 for his driver. On top of that were sums of 800 RM per year for social security payments, as well as car insurance and taxes of about 2,000 RM per year, plus travel costs and the cost of a loan. If the upkeep of the little house in Berchtesgaden (from 1928 onwards) and a large flat in Munich including staff (from 1929 onwards) are taken into consideration, it is hardly surprising that by his own admission he was predominantly running a deficit.[101] In 1926 Hitler declared his outgoings to the tax office as being 31,209 RM, while his income was 15,903. As he explained to the tax authorities, he was financing the deficit by means of a loan. In 1927 the deficit amounted to 1,958 Reich marks, for which he gave the same explanation. In 1928 and 1929 his declared income exceeded his outgoings. In 1929, in addition, he had, on the evidence of these documents, repaid his bank debts, which is hardly believable on the basis of the sums given. The only explanation can be that he received additional income and/or donations that the tax office was unaware of.

Hitler's staging of his public persona as the 'Führer' who was above it all extended to every aspect of life, including his relationships with women. He had already had difficulties with such relationships, but from now on his role as 'Führer' gave him the opportunity to confer deeper meaning on his awkwardness. Although it was part of the bohemian lifestyle that Hitler consciously adopted at this time to be seen frequently in the company of young women (and he clearly had nothing against them being taken for his lovers) a wife, as he repeatedly impressed on those around him, was something that he, as a popular party leader, could not afford; Germany was his 'bride'.[102] If we look more closely at his relationships with these female companions, there is some justification for the view that, contrary to rumour, these were in fact harmless associations. Just as he had no interest in friendships, so he was indifferent to love affairs. This supposition of course takes us into the realms of speculation, but the signs all point in the same direction.

Eugenie Haug, two years younger than Hitler, a Party member since 1920 and the sister of Hans Haug, Hitler's first driver, was frequently seen with him in 1922/23. Although it was rumoured at the time that they were 'engaged', there is no foundation for such a claim.[103] In 1925 Adelheid Klein, who, aged twenty-two, joined the re-founded NSDAP with great enthusiasm and began work as an editorial assistant with the *Völkischer Beobachter*, got to know Hitler, who frequently invited her to the theatre or to a café. She too came soon to be regarded as his lover, but if her memoirs are to be believed the relationship did not go beyond the exchange of a few kisses. After about a year Hitler discontinued it.[104]

Around this time Hitler met Maria Reiter, then sixteen, from Berchtesgaden, and they were friendly for several months; in the middle of 1927 he broke it off. A series of letters he wrote to her has survived in which, on the one hand, he uses harmlessly romantic words such as 'my sweet girl' and, on the other, gives her good advice in a fatherly tone. There is nothing to suggest that the friendship turned into a sexual relationship. During the war Hitler himself in his evening monologues recalled 'Miezel', whom, like the other women he met during those years, he had been unable to marry because of his political career. There were, he said, 'several opportunities' but he 'did not take' them: 'I made myself draw back.'[105]

Maria July,[106] the daughter of a publican whose pub on Gärtnerplatz Hitler frequented, knew him as a schoolgirl in 1922. In 1927 she joined the NSDAP; the following year she accompanied Hitler, his sister Angela, and Angela's daughter Geli on two visits to Berlin. In Hitler's circle she was known as the 'little princess', an allusion to a role she had played at a Fasching party.

Hitler's relationships with these young women follow a particular pattern: he liked to have their company and enjoyed being seen with them. In his estimation, the combination of the mature, busy, famous man and the unspoilt 'girl' ensured that his image as 'Führer' was enhanced by his also being seen as 'successful with women' and that at the same time he could go on enjoying admiration and have a grateful audience even during his leisure hours. Hitler showered these young women with compliments, gazed at them romantically, and possibly exchanged affectionate words with them, but that seems to be as far as these relationships went. After a time he let them slide, presumably at the point when he could no longer avoid the question of whether his intentions were serious.

They clearly never ended in a quarrel: in later years, after he had become Reich Chancellor and Eva Braun was regarded as his girlfriend, Hitler maintained what might be called diplomatic relations with various women: Jenny Haug, Adelheid Klein (now Schultze), Maria Reiter, Maria July, and Sigrit von Laffert (whom Hitler met in 1932 when she was sixteen and invited to his home on occasions, although always in company with others),[107] were members of the exclusive group of about a hundred people that regularly received personal gifts through Hitler's adjutancy.[108] In addition, there are various indications of continuing correspondence.[109]

Geli Raubal, his niece, was to assume a much greater significance in Hitler's life. This young woman, who travelled to Berlin in 1927 with Hitler and Maria July, had finished her school leaving examinations in Linz a short time before and had moved to Munich, where she first of all registered as a medical student but then took singing lessons instead. She began a romantic relationship with Hitler's driver Maurice, but when Hitler discovered the relationship he dismissed Maurice and demanded that Geli put off the planned wedding until she should come of age in June 1929. As a result of pressure from Hitler, Geli finally broke off the engagement in the summer of 1928, after which she seems to have had a number of other relationships.[110] When in 1929 Hitler rented his large apartment on Prinzregentenplatz, Geli moved in too and was registered as the tenant of the couple who were his caretakers and lived in the servants' quarters.

Vivacious, fun-loving, and headstrong, Geli was Hitler's constant companion in the years 1929 to 1931. He went shopping with her,[111] took her to the theatre[112] and to the usual social occasions held by Party comrades, and she accompanied him when he was invited privately to people's homes.[113] She appeared with him at political demonstrations[114] and at the Party Rally in August 1929,[115] and frequently accompanied him to Berlin, where she was introduced to Party comrades.[116] In July 1930 she attended the Passion Play at Oberammergau with Hitler and Goebbels.[117] In the Party she was soon treated as Hitler's lover, and in fact there were rumours of a triangular relationship involving Hitler, Maurice, and Geli.[118]

Geli Raubal fitted Hitler's preference for somewhat naïve and childlike women. The fact that they were related allowed him, in spite of the speculation, to make her part of his household, while at the same time removing the issue of a shared future, which he wished to avoid. Taking the pattern of his previous relationships as a yardstick, we can be fairly confident that in this one too 'Uncle Adolf', as Geli called him, did not engage in any sexual intimacy. What mattered to him was to have a companion and audience close to hand, someone who admired him and who looked presentable in public. In addition, he liked to appear as the generous uncle dispensing treats. His opposition to the marriage with Maurice suggests that he also intended to safeguard Geli's virtue. He evidently watched over her as though she were his personal possession.

As far as we know, Hitler had no sexual contacts with women either before or during the First World War or in his early Munich years. There are grounds to suppose that, after his release from detention, by which time he was thirty-five, this was still the case. In view of Hitler's personality, it seems altogether plausible that his life was asexual: any intimate relationship would simply have been incompatible with his arrested emotional development with regard to other people and with his self-perception as a public figure through and through with an extraordinary historic mission. But whatever the nature of his relationships with members of the opposite sex as individuals may have been, for him as leader of the 'movement' and future 'saviour' of Germany, women were simply insignificant.

7

Hitler as a Public Speaker

For the time being, however, Hitler's impact was restricted to the Party. Because of the ban on his speaking in public, imposed in 1925, he was mainly forced to seek an outlet for his oratorical skills in closed meetings for Party members. In other words, he was speaking to audiences that were already largely on his side. The dominant motive behind these appearances was not to win people over but to reinforce the ties binding the Party leader and his followers, and he regarded such occasions as an important method of gaining acceptance in the NSDAP for his claim to be the absolute leader. It is hardly surprising that these addresses were ideologically charged to a high degree and marked by an aggressive attitude towards the opponents of National Socialism.

These speeches were not particularly frequent: in 1925 Hitler made thirty-eight speeches, fifty-two in 1926. This reticence was due not only to the fact that he had to spare his voice, but to his careful management of his public appearances. They were regarded as a mark of distinction for the local branches in question, which were obliged to drum up as many Party comrades as possible and to comply with particular requirements. Thus, for example, Hitler wanted his speeches to be taken down in shorthand as he spoke, so that he would be prepared in case of any later legal challenges.[1] Over time a clear routine, in fact an established ritual, developed for 'Hitler Meetings': first, the expectant audience was put in the right mood; then Hitler would walk solemnly into the hall to the cheers of his supporters, accompanied by a group of local Party dignitaries; then came the official welcome, followed by the speech itself, which lasted several hours and grew in intensity through the careful calibration of his rhetoric; finally there was tumultuous cheering by Hitler's supporters, which, as a kind of communal oath of loyalty, ended in a final, united 'Sieg Heil'.

The fact that for two years Hitler made speeches almost exclusively to Party members had a lasting effect on his development as an orator. Interjections, disturbances, or altercations with opponents, of the kind that were altogether normal up to 1923 (even if the SA had often suppressed them with brute force), were now impossible. Hitler was speaking to firm supporters, who awaited his appearance with enthusiasm and wished to have their essential beliefs confirmed. These people belonged to a small, fanatical community of the faithful, a marginal group of extremists within the growing stability of the Weimar Republic. By contrast with the mass rallies of 1923, dominated by febrile expectations of an imminent and final showdown with the hated democratic system, Hitler now did not need to motivate the undecided or those on the margins. Instead, his supporters expected to be given a long-term view, a vision of a Nazi Germany. Hence his speeches did not engage with everyday politics and focused instead on 'fundamentals'. He was, after all speaking to the 'chosen few', who were already capable of understanding the 'truths' he proclaimed. From the point of view of his supporters, the speaking ban imposed on him in any case only went to show how desperate a Republic must be that was driven to repressive measures to prevent Hitler from reaching the broad mass of people with his message − an interpretation that served to reinforce the connection between him and his audience.[2]

When addressing his supporters, Hitler's speeches were always strongly anti-Semitic. In short, the Jews were responsible for all the country's fundamental problems and disasters.[3] For him they were the masters of international capital[4] as well as the puppeteers who controlled 'Marxist' parties and had been behind the 1918 revolution.[5] By means of this two-pronged attack they now had almost total control over Germany and had penetrated deep into the nation: 'Our blood is being poisoned and bastardized. We are tolerating those who create our social problems and incite our nation. As Germans we must be racially aware and anti-Semitic.'[6] If the Nazis were to form the government they would 'make ruthless use of the power given to us legally by the sacred numerical majority to exterminate the Jews by means of this wholly legal power'.[7] He even went as far as to suggest that in 'fighting the Jews' they were doing Christ's work: in a report on a speech from the end of 1926 we read: 'For thousands of years Christ's teaching has formed the basis for the fight against the Jews as the enemy of the human race. What Christ began but was unable to finish, he (Hitler) would complete.'[8]

In his speeches Hitler declared the 'removal' of the Jews to be the precondition for a national resurgence. This could be achieved, however, only if the division of Germany into a 'nationalist' middle-class camp and a 'socialist' proletarian camp could also be overcome.[9] The reconciliation of the middle classes and the proletariat, the second major subject of Hitler's addresses in this period, was possible only through a synthesis of nationalism and socialism, for which he claimed the NSDAP was striving. Yet the National 'Socialism' advanced by Hitler had absolutely nothing to do with taking the means of production into public ownership, as demanded by the Socialist movement. This alleged synthesis of the two terms amounted rather to the complete abandonment of classic socialist aims in favour of a militant nationalism with its roots in a racially defined notion of the nation [Volkstum]. Hitler constantly came out with new formulations but they all made one thing clear: National Socialism was nothing more or less than völkisch (ethnic) nationalism. 'The nationalist and the socialist need to understand each other. If socialism is love for one's nation, then socialism is the highest form of nationalism. But then nationalism is the highest form of socialism.'[10] Another variant was: 'To be nationalist is identical with being socialist.... There is no kind of socialism that does not find its liveliest expression in ardent admiration for and love of one's nation [Volkstum] and in the unconditional devotion to this nation that alone sustains the fatherland and thus at the same time the promise of the future social wellbeing of its children. There is no idea of the nation that is not one and the same as living together with one's children, sound in mind and body.'[11] It would take an extraordinary effort to achieve a synthesis of nationalism and socialism and that was the third great subject of these speeches: the German nation had to realize that its entire existence was dependent on three factors. It had to acknowledge the importance of race (or 'blood', as he frequently expressed it), recognize the significance of leader figures, and accept the need for struggle. 'The value of race', 'the value of personality', and 'the idea of struggle' were, he claimed, 'the pillars' of the Nazi movement, which alone was called to restore power and glory to Germany. These three notions formed a trio of national virtues that recurred in a variety of forms in Hitler's speeches to his supporters.[12]

He adopted a somewhat different tone when he had the opportunity to escape the confines of Party events. This happened on various occasions in 1926/27, when the audience was made up of invited middle-class guests drawn mainly from business. In these speeches Hitler did not affect to be speaking as a 'simple man of the people' to the broad masses, but rather attempted to impress his audience by appearing to offer insights into his very individual style of 'leading the masses' or spoke with pretended candour about his foreign policy goals. He adopted a predominantly condescending, indeed contemptuous, tone in speaking of the 'masses' he promised to lead towards these goals; anti-Semitism was not mentioned.

He made the first of these speeches on 28 February 1926 to about 400 members of the famous Hamburg National Club, a right-wing conservative association of prosperous residents of the Hanseatic city. Hitler portrayed himself on this occasion as a ruthless demagogue who, by using nationalist agitation and making a strong 'socially-orientated' impression, would suc- ceed in turning the masses away from 'Marxist' parties. The nation, Hitler began, had not recovered from defeat and revolution and was still deeply divided: in addition to those who were indifferent to politics, there was a majority of people who were 'international' in outlook (or seriously lacking as far as their attitude to their own nation was concerned), namely the Social Democrats, communists, middle-class pacifists, and sections of the [Catholic] Centre Party and of the so-called parties of the Right. They faced a bloc of Germans who were unambiguously 'nationalist' in outlook. Hitler reduced the future political battle to 'a simple formula: The problem of the resurgence of Germany is the problem of how to eliminate Marxist ideol- ogy in Germany. If this ideology is not eradicated, Germany will never rise again, any more than you can restore someone to health without curing him of tuberculosis.' That goal had to be achieved 'by all possible means' and it could be achieved only with help from 'the masses'. But how were the masses to be won over? First of all, by means of greater openness in address- ing social matters, which, as he hastened to reassure his listeners, did not necessarily mean paying higher wages, but rather increasing national pro- duction, which benefited everyone. Secondly, however, the masses, who were 'feminine' and thus easily manipulated, 'blind and stupid', indeed 'primitive in outlook', had to be 'offered a political creed, an immutable programme, an unshakable political faith'. The middle-class parties were incapable of doing this. He, however, regarded it as his 'mission'.[13]

Before invited audiences at five subsequent events he pressed on with this attempt to woo business. On 18 June 1926 in Essen he spoke to about fifty or sixty 'business leaders' specifically 'in support of private property' and promised to protect 'the market economy ... as the most effective and only feasible economic system'.[14] In December he addressed 500 invited 'business leaders' in Königswinter on 'German economic and social policy'[15] and about 200 invited guests a few days later in Essen, where he spoke relatively openly about his foreign policies. The speech, which lasted almost three hours, had the characteristic title 'New Paths to Power'. He assured his business-orientated audience that his basic aim was 'to acquire more territory that would open up new markets to German commerce'.[16] In April 1927 he was in Essen again, speaking once more to an audience of businessmen on the topic of 'The Führer and the Masses', in which he expounded the 'view that any leader of the masses who aims to be successful must emerge from the masses and engage in daily dispute with the leaders of the masses'.[17] On 5 December 1927 he was already making his fourth speech to a 'circle of invited Rhineland-Westphalian business men' in Essen, this time more than 600 of them. Once again Hitler shared some of his foreign policy ideas, although he was much more circumspect than he had been a year previously, when he had outlined an imperialist programme. This time he took a pragmatic line: any agreement with France was fundamentally out of the question and preference should be given to an alliance with Great Britain and Italy.[18]

The speaking ban is lifted

In May 1926 the speaking ban was lifted in Oldenburg, in January 1927 in Saxony, and finally in March in Bavaria and Hamburg. During the following months most of the states removed restrictions until they remained in place only in Prussia and Anhalt until the autumn of 1928.[19]

Hitler soon discovered, however, that it was not easy to pick up the threads of past successes. After completing his first engagement before a general audience in Bavaria on 6 March 1927 in Vilsbiburg (the Bavarian government had insisted on his first appearance being outside Munich)[20] he gave a speech three days later in the Circus Krone building in Munich. The hall was only half full.[21] At subsequent events in the massive auditorium the NSDAP managed to attract nowhere near the numbers that Hitler had attracted between 1921 and 1923. This negative trend continued for the whole of 1927 and, according to official reports, was repeated in the Bavarian provinces; indeed the numbers attending Hitler's meetings here actually shrank.[22] At the Party Rally, which in this year was being held in Nuremberg, the number of participants similarly fell below expectations.[23] Hitler had to get used to the idea that his eccentric, politically provocative style appealed to few people at a time when the Weimar Republic was experiencing a period of political and economic stability. In January 1928 at the general membership meeting of the NSDAP's Schwabing branch Hitler felt it necessary to emphasize that his most recent meetings in central Germany had been 'jam packed', claiming that 'soon Munich too will be back to what it was before 1923'.[24]

At first the basic tenor of his speeches was unchanged. As before, he stressed the restoration of the nation's power through the 'removal' of the Jews, the union of 'nationalism' and 'socialism', and the need to recognize the national core virtues of race, leadership by a 'Führer', and preparedness to fight. Now, however, another element was added that had been largely absent from earlier speeches, namely the problem that Hitler still rather tentatively skirted round by referring to the 'disproportion' of 'soil' and 'nation'. In volume two of *Mein Kampf*, which had appeared at the end of 1926, Hitler had argued that the German national rebirth the NSDAP was striving for should not be understood as an end in itself or as the construction of a more just social order, but as the precondition for the 'superior' German nation to fulfil the task for which it was destined by the laws of history. Thus, what was required was 'a political strategy for the East, namely the acquisition of the land needed for our German nation'.[25] That meant nothing more nor less than rearmament and a war of conquest. The fact that the territory he had in view was mainly on Soviet soil could be inferred only indirectly from Hitler's speeches: he repeatedly stressed that in relation to the size of population 'Russia' had an area eighteen times bigger than the German Reich and that this massive size was the result of a historical development that could most certainly be challenged.[26] In the main he merely hinted at his ideas, using ponderous formulations as he explored the various theoretical possibilities of alleviating the problem he kept emphasizing of the 'disproportion' between 'soil' and 'nation'.[27]

Thus, from the spring of 1927 onwards, Hitler regularly used speeches to develop the core elements of his ideology, albeit expressed in a convoluted way. Whenever he presented the central concepts of his political programme – hostility to the Jews, National Socialism, race, the Führer principle, struggle, the conquest of 'soil' – in speeches lasting several hours, he indulged in long digressions, historical musings, polemical interludes, using insinuations and indirect references. In addition, at the big, central Party Rallies, where from 1929 onwards he was again speaking to more than 10,000 people, many in his audience could only pick up fragments of what he said. When from the end of the 1920s the NSDAP introduced microphones and loudspeakers, audibility was still limited in part because of technical difficulties.[28]

For anyone who was not already familiar with the ideological core of Hitler's thought – through having read *Mein Kampf*, for example – the inner logic of this elaborate structure of ideas and its implications were not necessarily easy to grasp. But that was not really the point: the effect of his speeches derived rather from how they were staged. Before the putsch Hitler had carried his audience along because his despair appeared so evident and he seemed to present to his listeners a way out of it. After the bans on his speaking had been lifted in 1927/28, he applied himself to perfecting his public appearances.

One element in this was the fact that he did not show himself too often. He could speak only every three days, if only on account of the strain on his vocal chords, or at least that was the line taken by the Party's Reich propaganda headquarters.[29] In 1927 Hitler appeared at only sixty-two events, in 1928, an election year, it was seventy-eight, and in 1929 it was only thirty-nine; the overwhelming majority of these speeches each year were made in Bavaria.[30] The Party branches had positively to compete for him and convince the propaganda HQ that they were capable of creating the required ambience. Most of these requests were turned down.[31] The procedure was fairly elaborate. First of all, the local branch had to fill in a questionnaire describing the proposed venue and providing detailed information on the size of the branch, the probable composition of the audience, and recent propaganda efforts. If an appearance by the Party leader was then approved by the Munich HQ, the local group received the compulsory 'Guidelines for Hitler meetings' produced by his private office, which had meanwhile been set up in Munich.[32] In them every last detail of the local branch's duties was set out. They document not only how organized and precisely calculated the Führer propaganda already was at the end of the 1920s, but they also reveal Hitler's anxiety about being caused embarrassment by the incompetence of Party comrades in the provinces; all risks and imponderables that might have a negative impact on his public appearance had as far as possible to be eliminated.

The guidelines prescribed that the meeting be kept secret for as long as possible and that problems, even if they arose at the last minute, should be immediately reported to Munich. Hitler thus had the option of pulling out at the last moment. This he did, for example during the campaign for the elections to the Mecklenburg–Schwerin state assembly in May 1927, when he had all the speeches he had scheduled cancelled at short notice, possibly because the election campaign was poorly organized.[33]

Generally speaking, for 'Hitler meetings' there was an entrance charge of one Reich mark. Half of the sum raised was to be sent to Party HQ. If the demand was great enough, the price could rise to three marks. In the Weimar Republic it was unusual for a political party to charge entry to its propaganda events, but it was a method of ensuring that the audience consisted mainly of supporters.[34] The posters made it explicit from the outset that Jews were forbidden to attend.

If all preparations were complete and the hall was full, the great moment approached: the 'Führer's' arrival. Hitler always came late, which was not only the result of his notorious unpunctuality but part of the calculated drama of the occasion. With swastika flags leading the way he would walk through the hall in a solemn procession with local Party functionaries following, with a band playing military music and the audience cheering. In the hall itself there was an 'absolute ban on smoking', again required by the guidelines because of the 'heavy demands on Adolf Hitler's voice'. Hitler never spoke from behind a lectern but rather stood on an empty stage so that all of his body language was visible to the audience. A small table always had to be positioned to his left for his notes, which contained headings that Hitler generally kept to fairly closely.[35]

As an introduction he usually offered his audience a historical event they could relate to and which he used to conjure up a collective historical memory or a shared experience. It might be the Wars of Liberation against Napoleon or the founding of the Reich, but most often he chose the World War. As he proceeded certain key terms functioned as an expression of 'community', and during the speech the majority of the audience could identify themselves as members of it. Usually these terms were 'race', 'blood', 'leadership'. Other key words aroused a sense of being under threat – Jewry, Marxism, the Allies' policies that limited Germany's freedom, lack of space, the inner degeneration of the German nation – while others provoked the audience's aggression ('annihilation' of Marxists and Jews, 'struggle', conquest of 'soil'). The conclusion was always a vision of triumph: the nation, united under National Socialism, would in the end overcome all enemies.

An address of this kind normally lasted several hours.[36] Hitler usually began hesitantly, giving an impression of uncertainty; then he would become

increasingly fluent and emotionally charged, until finally he reached his
rhetorical climax, straining his voice to its limits and gesticulating wildly.
The effort made him lose litres of fluids,[37] which is why the guidelines specifically asked for an 'unopened bottle of Fachingen mineral water at room
temperature and a glass' to be on the small table, with additional bottles to
hand. On very hot days ice was to be available for Hitler to cool his hands.
So that he retained future control of the spoken text of his speech, 'two reliable stenographers' had to make a transcript of it and to send it immediately
to Party HQ in Munich. In addition, six men, 'known to be honourable and
if possible elderly', had to sit on the podium behind Hitler in order 'if necessary to give evidence about the content of the speech'. At the start of the
meeting the chairman should strongly emphasize that, in view of the 'witnesses' and the stenographers, 'attempts to falsify' the proceedings were
pointless.

The next stipulations clearly sprang from the fear that Party comrades in
the provinces might try to steal the show and detract from the star turn. The
chairman was instructed to be 'very brief' when opening the meeting and,
as Hitler's speech spoke 'for itself', to desist from appreciative closing
remarks. The meeting should end simply with a 'Hail Germany' (but not
'Hail Hitler'). Songs were also to be dispensed with. Should members of the
audience start to sing the Deutschland anthem or any other song, the chairman was to interrupt it with a 'Hail Germany' after one verse, 'as experience
shows that the majority of those present do not know the words of the
other verses'. As Hitler 'needed absolute peace and quiet' after his exertions,
the local branch had 'to accept the fact that after the meeting he could not
spend any time with them' but would withdraw to his hotel, where the
organizers had to arrange a room with a bathroom.[38]

Yet these carefully honed techniques and the enthusiastic reception he
was regularly given on such occasions could not disguise the fact that Hitler
was regarded as the 'Führer' only on the extreme right of the political spectrum. The Party was relatively well organized and made a comparatively
united impression. It had in fact established itself as the dominant force
within the extreme Right. But it could not find a way out of this political
subculture and had only very moderate success in elections during these
years. Its vote never exceeded 5 per cent and the results were mostly distinctly poorer than that.[39]

8

A New Direction

From 19 to 21 August 1927 the Party held its third Party Rally in Nuremberg.[1] According to police records a total of 15,000 to 20,000 people took part, including some 9,000 uniformed members of the SA, SS, and Hitler Youth.[2] Although the NSDAP had gathered together about twice as many supporters for this quasi-military review as the previous year, over all the Party was stagnating. On top of this, various internal conflicts came to light at the rally and this situation was hard to reconcile with the image of a Führer party.

For one thing, although the disputes with the 'working group' had been dealt with in 1926, there were still major differences between Hitler and supporters of a 'socialist' path. While he had divided its most important advocates from one another, they were nevertheless to return repeatedly to their basic concern. Since 1926 they had also developed an intellectual and journalistic base in the Kampf publishing house belonging to the Strasser brothers.[3] The representatives of the so-called left of the Party exploited the fact that Hitler often used 'anti-capitalist' rhetoric to keep on citing him as their authority. But in using such arguments Hitler was not interested in a restructuring of the German economy along socialist lines; rather his polemics against 'international' and 'Jewish' capital were designed to support the demand that Germany be 'liberated' from the bonds of the Versailles Treaty and the Jews 'removed' from Germany.[4] By contrast with the left wing of his Party he had no interest in fleshing out Points 11 to 17 in the Party programme as an 'anti-capitalist' programme of economic reform.[5] When, at the beginning of 1927, Gregor Strasser and Alfred Rosenberg had a public disagreement about whether the 'socialist' or the 'nationalist' element in National Socialism should predominate[6] (to emphasize the former element, Strasser wanted to hold on to the term 'National Socialism'), Hitler attempted to terminate the discussion by using one of his well-known rhetorical tricks. Both terms, he said, had fused into an indissoluble unity with new content: 'Socialism is becoming Nationalism and Nationalism Socialism.'[7]

For another thing, conflicts were developing over the future role of the SA: whereas Hitler saw its function as being above all to protect and support the Party's activities, the SA leadership, with its collection of former World War officers, continued to favour the idea of a paramilitary outfit that should take its place prominently among the various other paramilitary organizations. The fact that the SA's rank and file was left-leaning made the situation more difficult. This conflict first came out into the open in Munich itself in the spring of 1927. Although Hitler placed all his authority behind his attempt to explain his 'legal' path to the renegade SA men, he could not prevent a large number of the 'activists' in the Munich SA from splitting off from the movement; nor could he prevent more heavy criticism being voiced at the beginning of 1928 among the remaining SA members that the Party leadership was not moving in a sufficiently 'revolutionary' direction.[8]

The fact that the NSDAP simply could not manage to break out of its marginal position on the far right and appeal to the masses made these conflicts more bitter and led to constant friction that was frequently tactical or purely personal. There was some point to Hitler's warning at the Party Rally about 'the local branches holding too many members' meetings', as they were just a 'source of conflict, petty jealousies and intemperate outbursts, and a waste of energy.'[9] Changes were therefore necessary.

After the 1927 Party Rally the NSDAP gradually shifted its public image away from being first and foremost a 'workers' party' and increased its efforts to target other sections of the population, in particular the urban lower middle classes and the rural population. This refocusing of Party propaganda did not follow on from any particular 'decision' taken by the Party leader but had a number of causes. It was the logical outcome of the failure of the 'socialist' wing of the Party to rewrite the Party programme along the lines it favoured. It was also an acknowledgement of practical experience gained by the Party organization: the fact that the Party resonated more with the middle classes than with the workers had in the end to be taken into account. And it now better fitted Hitler's own ideas, for he had vehemently opposed the use of overly 'socialist' slogans and instead had already sought support for his Party among middle-class business people. An opportunity to introduce this new emphasis came early in 1928, when Gregor Strasser, the main advocate of orienting the Party towards the working classes, moved from being the head of Reich propaganda to being head of the Party organiza-tion. Although Hitler was formally in charge of propaganda, Heinrich Himmler, until now Strasser's deputy, in effect took over this role. He was simultaneously the Party's designated agriculture expert and strongly sup-ported the inclusion of rural areas in the Party's propaganda efforts.[10]

In concentrating propaganda on the rural population the Party was also responding to an increasingly evident crisis developing in agriculture. In 1927/28, as a result of the global agrarian crisis, the price of agricultural products collapsed, while production costs rose. Farmers gave vent to their frustration by means of a nationwide protest movement. There were dem-onstrations and mass meetings, violence was used to prevent compulsory evictions and auctions, and taxes were withheld. In Schleswig-Holstein in particular a hard-line opposition formed, the so-called Landvolkbewegung, which became so radical that it openly rejected 'the State' and even carried out bomb attacks on tax offices. In the final analysis, however, this move-ment, which spread as far as Lower Saxony and the Oldenburg area, was heterogeneous; its political aims and tactics remained confused, while many country people were deterred by the terrorist excesses. At the same time, in Protestant areas in particular, the protests shook people's confidence in the established agricultural associations and in the DNVP, the conservative party representing the political interests of agriculture. The NSDAP now had the opportunity of deploying its propaganda to attract a new source of support.[11]

In December 1927, as the Landvolkbewegung was just getting organized, Hitler made his first speech at a major Party event that was specifically geared to agriculture. His audience was made up primarily of members of the Schleswig-Holstein Farmers' Association, the Movement for Small Peasants [Kleinbauernbewegung], and the Farmers League [Landbund]. They had come to Hamburg specially since the Prussian ban on his speak-ing in public, which was still in force, prevented him from speaking in Schleswig-Holstein. Even in this speech, however, Hitler quickly managed to marginalize the topical issues of agricultural policy – heavy taxation, pricing policies, import restrictions, the indebtedness of many farms – turning to more fundamental matters. The Germans, he assured his audience, had always been a 'peasant people with all the health that comes from an exist-ence rooted in the soil', whereas the impact of modern city life was 'gradu-ally' having a 'debilitating and degenerative' effect. What was needed was a 'vigorous, active, outward-facing territorial policy, in other words a clear political goal that can hold for centuries', 'making the territory fit the size of the nation's population'. Population growth, adequate space for it, and the 'worth of a nation' that was manifest 'first and foremost in the worth of our race and in our blood' were the factors that were decisive for the future.[12] In order to allay suspicion that the NSDAP was contemplating a land reform, in April 1928 Hitler even took the step of committing himself to a particular gloss on a fundamental point in the Party programme that he himself had declared to be 'immutable'. He announced that, although Point 17 contained a demand for 'the expropriation without compensation of land for public use', such a law only envisaged the expropriation of land that 'had been acquired unlawfully or was not being administered in a manner that respected the common good'. This measure, he added pointedly, was directed first and foremost 'against Jewish companies involved in land speculation'.[13] In addition, by campaigning among rural artisans, the NSDAP in North Germany succeeded in establishing a foothold in the local artisans' associations and in putting pressure on the leaders of the Northwest German Artisans' League.[14]

Students were another group that the Party leadership increasingly began to focus on. A National Socialist German Students' League (NSDStB) had been founded in February 1926, although to begin with it was unable to build on the Party's successes with Munich students before 1923. Unlike in the immediate post-war years, during the period when the Republic was stabilizing, the student body was no longer under the influence of former combatants and those who had been growing up during the war years, who were eager to take a chance on a possible counter-revolution. Now it consisted of young men and women who were studying in order to lay the foundations for a professional career.[15] Up to now Hitler had said virtually nothing on student matters. In January 1927 he had published an article in the *Nationalsozialistische Hochschulbriefe* [National Socialist University Newsletters], the organ of the NSDStB,[16] and on 21 November 1927 he held the first large-scale demonstration for students. At a meeting of the NSDStB in Munich he made a speech to an audience of between 2,000 and 2,500. He offered them his standard repertoire, taking trouble at the same time to cater for the needs of an audience that was more highly educated than was the norm by giving numerous historical examples and quotations and speaking in more inflated language than usual. So, for example, he expounded the idea that politics was 'history in the making, because every political event in the moment it happens becomes the history of a nation'.[17]

In 1928 the Party leader also began to modify his position with regard to paramilitary organizations. Up to this point he had fundamentally questioned the existence and political function of paramilitary organizations, forbidden NSDAP supporters to be members of such organizations, and recommended to their members that in order to avoid further difficulties they should quite simply acknowledge his political leadership.[18] He now adopted a more conciliatory tone and smoothed the way for a limited amount of cooperation with the paramilitary organizations. From May 1928 onwards the rank and file of the Party was instructed to avoid making any verbal attacks on them.[19]

This gradual change of propaganda focus revealed itself in Hitler's speeches through two topics in particular. First, Hitler altered the importance he placed on anti-Semitism: anti-Jewish comments, allusions, and sideswipes were still evident in his public utterances and recognizable in particular to Party supporters,[20] and he continued to indulge in long-winded anti-Jewish tirades and accusations;[21] but, crucially, anti-Semitism no longer functioned as a central leitmotiv of the Party programme. In particular, Hitler avoided making statements about the fate in store for the Jews in a Nazi Germany. He now appeared to have given up his idea of realizing his vision of a Germany united under the Nazis through the 'removal' of the Jews. His retreat from this demand was indicated in February 1928 when he announced to a packed meeting in the main hall of the Hofbräuhaus that the matter could be resolved if the Jews were 'shown clearly who's boss; if they behave themselves they can stay; if not, then out they go!'[22] While on this occasion the expulsion of the Jews was made to depend on their good behaviour, Hitler was later to drop this threat altogether. Thus he was adapting to the type of anti-Semitism prevalent during those years in right-wing conservative circles. Although the DNVP and the Stahlhelm, which soon became his preferred alliance partners, had also gone about excluding their Jewish members in the mid-1920s,[23] their anti-Semitism was shaped more by a social code, a kind of universally accepted habitus expressed more through the rejection of all things 'Jewish' and less through specific attacks couched in radical language. Excluding the Jews from German citizenship, as the NSDAP programme demanded, was not, as yet, a measure that would have met with broad agreement in these right-wing conservative circles. Hitler knew that his radical anti-Semitism, the vision of a nation without Jews, did not represent a particularly attractive propaganda slogan by which to win support from the conservative right, let alone the lower middle classes. At the same time, a certain amount of anti-Jewish polemic did the Party no harm in these circles, for anti-Semitic stereotypes, prejudices, and resentments were too deep-rooted in German society for that.[24]

Secondly, Hitler now began to make another important ideological theme a leitmotiv of his speeches: the acquisition of 'Lebensraum' (living space) as the goal of Nazi policy.[25] The fact that this increase in living space made another war necessary and that in fact permanent 'struggle' in general was fundamental to National Socialism emerged clearly from these speeches. Although Hitler did not state openly that the conquest of living space in eastern Europe was to be primarily at the expense of the Soviet Union, anyone who wanted to have more detail had only to take to heart the second volume of *Mein Kampf*. Hitler did not need to fear that his demand that German borders be forcibly revised would put off his potential right-wing conservative allies and their supporters, whom he wished to win over to the NSDAP. On the political right there was a consensus about wanting to see Germany as a great power, and war was by no means excluded as a means towards that political end. Hitler could certainly lay claim to originality with his concept of living space, for unlike the political right he was not demanding the restoration of Germany's 1914 borders. Instead he was aiming for a position of power, based on geopolitics and secured by a network of alliances, that would safeguard the German Reich of the future from dropping back into the hopeless 'centre position' that was widely blamed for defeat in the World War.

Positioning after the 1928 elections

Elections for the Reichstag and various state parliaments were set for 20 May 1928. In preparation, Hitler made an election speech in Munich in the middle of April that, contrary to his usual practice, had less of a 'visionary' quality and instead was concerned with concrete political issues. He strongly criticized Gustav Stresemann's foreign policy since the Ruhr conflict of 1923, violently attacking the minister personally. The *Völkischer Beobachter* turned this speech into a special issue with the significant title of 'Down with Stresemann'.[26] Given this background, it was hardly a coincidence that the following week the Nazis disrupted an election rally Stresemann was holding in Munich, an occurrence Hitler referred to maliciously a few days later in an election speech in the city: he personally had 'immensely regretted that the

affair had come to this'. Then for several hours he attacked Stresemann's foreign policy in a speech that the *Völkischer Beobachter* published once again in
a special issue entitled 'Intellect and Dr Stresemann'.[27]

Yet Hitler's sarcastic and furious assaults on Stresemann could not disguise the fact that in this election campaign he was increasingly being put
on the defensive and in particular with regard to his own foreign policy
programme. This was because Stresemann made criticism of Mussolini's
policy of 'Italianizing' the South Tyrol one of the main themes of the election, and the other parties, not wanting to lag behind, also declared their
solidarity with the German-speaking minority south of the Brenner. As
Hitler had always advocated accepting the annexation of the South Tyrol in
the interests of forging an alliance with Italy, he found himself wrong-footed
by the focus on this issue. He was unprepared to argue for his position on
the South Tyrol in the election campaign, for it made sense only in the context of his ideas about foreign policy alliances. In addition, shortly before
election day the SPD in Munich produced a poster that, under the heading
'Adolf Hitler Unmasked', claimed that Hitler was being supported financially by Mussolini.[28] In the final stages of the campaign he thus found
himself in the extremely uncomfortable position of having to defend himself against the charge of being nationally unreliable and he attempted to do
just that in a furious speech the night before the election.[29]

The elections brought gains above all for the SPD and the KPD, while
the nationalist parties suffered heavy losses. The increased support for splinter parties from 7 per cent to 13 per cent showed clearly the beginnings of
an erosion of the conservative and liberal camps. Yet the NSDAP could
benefit only slightly from this, and with only 2.6 per cent of the vote it had
done badly. In the state parliament elections held at the same time the Party
achieved 6.1 per cent of the vote in Bavaria, 1.8 per cent in Prussia and
Württemberg, 2.1 per cent in Anhalt, but 7.5 per cent in Oldenburg.[30] On
election night Hitler was still hailing the results as a success when addressing
Party comrades in the Bürgerbräukeller: It could now be taken for granted
'that from now on there is and will be only one *völkisch* movement, the
National Socialist German Workers' Party'. Above all, however, 'the watchword is: The election battle has finished and the fight goes on!' Their goal
was 'to be in four years' time where Marxism is now, and for Marxism to fall
to where we are now'.[31]

That was merely rhetoric. On the contrary, the election results had confirmed that so far the NSDAP, in spite of its efforts, had made no inroads at

all into the working-class vote. On the other hand, gains had been made in a whole series of rural areas and these gains lent weight to those in the Party who saw the middle classes as having the most potential NSDAP voters. It was not only in its Bavarian heartlands that the Party's share of the vote was clearly higher than the national average (6.2 per cent in Upper Bavaria and Swabia, 3.5 per cent in Lower Bavaria) but also in a series of predominantly Protestant, rural areas (3.7 per cent in Thuringia, 4.0 per cent in Schleswig-Holstein, 5.2 per cent in Weser-Ems, 4.4 per cent in Hanover-South-Brunswick, 3.6 per cent in Hesse-Nassau, 5.7 per cent in the Palatinate, and 4.4 per cent in Chemnitz-Zwickau).

Hitler now attempted to extend these gains. On 14 October he spoke to some 15,000 people at a large NSDAP rally on the Holstein heath. Four days later he was in Oldenburg, another centre of the agricultural protest movement, speaking to 2,000–3,000 people. When in March 1929 in Wörden in Dithmarschen [Schleswig-Holstein] two SA men were killed during violent clashes with communists, the Party turned the funeral into a propaganda event, with Hitler delivering the eulogy. The victims, Hitler said with emotion, had died as 'martyrs' for the 'fatherland'. This personal engagement on the part of the Party leader resulted in an immediate increase in support for the NSDAP in the whole of the Dithmarschen area,[32] a stronghold of the Landvolk movement. Having infiltrated it extensively during the winter of 1928/29, the NSDAP was now making gains everywhere in Schleswig-Holstein from that movement's efforts to mobilize support among the rural population which had been badly hit by the crisis. People turned to the Party in droves.[33]

Yet one matter went on troubling Hitler after the elections, namely whether his position on the South Tyrol question, which he had not successfully communicated to the voters, had been an important factor in the poor election result. Only three days after the Party's disappointing performance, he spoke at great length to a meeting of the NSDAP in Munich attended by some 3,000 people, defending himself against the accusation of having 'betrayed' the South Tyrolians. By advertising the meeting under the title of 'Adolf Hitler Unmasked' he was taking to its absurd limit the accusation the SPD had levelled against him in the final phase of the election campaign. Yet he was also revealing how much the attack had hit home, so much so that he made the elementary tactical mistake of making his Party comrades focus on this subject again, whereas it would have been much simpler to draw a veil over it.[34]

If that were not enough, Hitler also wanted to clarify his foreign policy once again in a lengthy memorandum of principle. He therefore retreated over the summer to Berchtesgaden to write that 'second book' that was never to be published in his lifetime. During this period he was hardly ever seen in public.

The manuscript of 239 pages contained a condensed version of his foreign policy goals that did not differ essentially from what he had set out in *Mein Kampf*.[35] In the introduction he expanded on the meaning of 'struggle for existence' [Lebenskampf] and 'living space' [Lebensraum] as determining factors in the history of nations. Then he went into detail on the possible combinations of alliances for Germany. Russia, he wrote in his summing up, could never, even under a non-communist regime, be considered as a possible ally. The obvious allies were rather Great Britain and Italy, and he expatiated on relations with Italy in the last and longest chapter, which made up almost a quarter of the manuscript and in which he once again set out in detail his argument concerning the South Tyrol. These discussions certainly constitute the real heart of the manuscript, while the earlier chapters are geared to his efforts to present his thoughts on the South Tyrol as the logical outcome of a comprehensive programme. In his view the only future foreign policy option for Germany was to decide 'to adopt a clear and far-sighted politics geared to living space. In doing so it will turn away from all experiments in global industry and the politics of global trade, and will concentrate all its resources on giving our nation a direction for the future, by securing sufficient living space for the next hundred years'.[36] He made no bones about the fact that this 'great geopolitical goal' lay in the east,[37] while the obvious implication was that it could be achieved only by means of a war of conquest. The book naturally also contained a lengthy passage about 'Jewish dominance'; any 'victory of Jewry' would be, he wrote, an 'accursed crime against humanity', and the Nazi movement had 'taken up the struggle' against it.[38] It was most probably precisely these unambiguous statements about his goals in foreign and racial policy, which he usually avoided in his speeches, that in the following months made him judge it inopportune to publish this text.[39]

One new aspect of his thinking was his estimation of the United States, which in *Mein Kampf* he had not yet recognized as a vital factor in world politics. He now realized that it was a growing economic power but regarded it therefore primarily as a challenge because it was in essence a 'Nordic-Germanic' state. Under German leadership there might admittedly be scope 'in the distant future perhaps for a new union of nations, which, consisting of nation states with high ethnic value, might oppose any threatened world domination by the American Union'. This, however, was obviously a task that stretched beyond his own lifetime.[40]

In the middle of July Hitler interrupted his stay in Berchtesgaden in order to present the most important results of his foreign policy deliberations to a closed meeting for members of the NSDAP in Berlin (in Prussia he was still banned from speaking in public). Hitler summed up his aims in two points: 'The first is to gain freedom and the second is to gain territory, so that we never again get into the same position that the World War and even the pre-war period put us in.' He explained the possible implications as he had outlined them in his manuscript. He spoke against any alliance with Russia and in favour of one with Italy, even if that meant giving up any claim to the South Tyrol. This, he was sure, was a price worth paying, for 'the day will come when France and Italy will face each other as mortal enemies'. For Great Britain, on the other hand, any further war with Germany was 'even more senseless, as the enemy of the future will be North America'. What was going through Hitler's mind (and this sentence makes it clear once again) was less the vision of a decisive struggle between Germany and the United States for world domination but rather the expectation that increasing rivalry between Britain and the United States would offer Germany the chance to move closer to Britain and take over the leading role on the continent.[41]

He returned to this idea in February 1929 in an article for the Party's *Illustrierter Beobachter*: the 'great conflict to come' between the United States and Great Britain, as he wrote here, could 'bring our people freedom too ... if our political leaders do not indulge in the historical folly of wanting to remain neutral, and if they also do not fall victim to our old German tradition of choosing if at all possible the weakest and most backward state as an ally' (alluding to Russia). What was needed, in other words, was a shrewd and long-term strategy to exploit the emerging competition between the United States and Great Britain.[42] During the following months he was frequently to set out his position regarding the South Tyrol, the starting point for his sweeping thoughts on foreign policy, both in speeches and in writing.[43] In addition, in May 1929, he brought an action for libel in the Munich magistrates court against those who had started the rumour that he had been in the pay of Mussolini.

Since November 1928 the *Illustrierter Beobachter* had been offering Hitler the opportunity under the heading 'This week in Politics' of making statements in extended leading articles about topical matters (something that in the main he expressly refused to do in his speeches).[44] Adopting the worldly-wise tone of a writer who was familiar with how to deal confidently with complex political and historical events, at times adding explanatory or sarcastic comments, he used these articles principally as a polemical running commentary on the foreign policy pursued by Stresemann, whose efforts to secure a peaceful revision of the Versailles Treaty were defamed by the entire political right as 'fulfilment policy'. Thus, for example, he informed his readers, in positively statesmanlike cadences and imbued with the conviction that he was imparting irrefutable insights into political and historical truths, that 'I have therefore regarded Italy as the most suitable ally for Germany, because even pursuing its interests in the most level-headed way must at some stage bring it to the point of decisive conflict with France'. And: 'I have rejected any thought of an agreement with France as absurd. I have become more and more convinced of this from year to year.'[45] He presented Stresemann, on the other hand, as an inexperienced dilettante, and, alluding to his doctoral dissertation,[46] derided him as a 'born bottled-beer salesman'[47] and, in addition, as a tool of 'Jewry'*: 'But Gustav Stresemann is only in charge of German foreign policy because the Jews know for certain that they need not fear any resurgence of Germany under this intelligent leadership.'[48] At the end of January 1929 he went so far as to express his 'fervent wish' with regard to the German Foreign Minister: 'May Heaven grant him long life so that this man, who today is shielded by the Constitutional Court for the Protection of the Republic, receives that sentence from a Constitutional Court for the protection of the honour and life of the German nation that history has hitherto been used to imposing for deeds of this enormity.'[49]

Hitler's public call for Stresemann's execution (and earnest hope that this outcome would not be frustrated by his arch-enemy's death from natural causes) makes one thing clear: There was no other politician in the Weimar 'system', nor any 'Marxist' or figure with a Jewish background who annoyed Hitler to the same extent. Stresemann's policy of a peaceful revision of the Treaty of Versailles in the context of a system of European security seemed

---

* Translators' note: Stresemann's father had run a small business making and distributing bottled Berlin *Weiss* beer and Stresemann had written his doctoral dissertation on the Berlin bottled beer industry.

to reduce the premises of Hitler's foreign policy – an alliance with Italy and Great Britain against the 'mortal enemy' France and the conquest of living space in the East – to absurdity. Stresemann had been particularly instrumental in stabilizing the Republic in 1923 and had thus cut the ground from under Hitler's putsch. In Hitler's eyes he represented the loss of face he had suffered in the 1928 election campaign as a result of his slogans concerning the South Tyrol. All these insults could be blotted out only through the physical annihilation of his hated opponent. When at the beginning of October 1929 Stresemann died suddenly of natural causes Hitler used the *Illustrierter Beobachter* to taunt him one last time. The 'generation ruling today', he wrote, which would soon be labelled the generation 'that cast away and surrendered all the sovereign rights of our nation', had indubitably found in 'Gustav' its perfect representative; in short, he was 'the epitome of our times'.[50]

When, more than three months after their electoral defeat, the NSDAP set about discussing their future strategy at a leaders' conference, it was not, however, foreign policy that was prominent, but rather another source of conflict that Hitler was determined at all costs to sort out. With the 'Dinter case' in mind, those assembled focused on the issue of the attitude the NSDAP should adopt towards the Christian Churches.

The former Gauleiter of Thuringia, Artur Dinter, was attempting, in the tradition of the 'völkisch movement', to get the Party to adopt an anti-Church policy and to found a German–völkisch religion. This had already led Hitler, who vigorously opposed the NSDAP's involvement in religious matters,[51] to remove Dinter from his post as Gauleiter at the end of September 1927, officially citing 'work overload'; but Dinter was not to be silenced. On 25 July 1928,[52] Hitler felt he had to write again to Dinter:

> As leader of the National Socialist movement and as someone who possesses a blind faith that one day he will be among those who make history, I regard your activities, in so far as they relate to your reforming purposes, as damaging to the National Socialist movement.... At a time when perhaps a matter of a few years will be decisive for the very life and future of our nation, the National Socialist movement, in which I can see the only real force opposing the annihilation threatening us, will be weakened internally if it involves itself with religious problems.... The fate of our nation, at least in so far as it is a racial issue, will be decided faster than it would take to complete a religious reformation. Either our nation will be pulled back as quickly as possible from the downfall that threatens it, racially in particular, or it will degenerate.

Hitler went on to insist that this was an existential matter – for him person-ally and thus also for Germany's destiny: 'I am 39 years old, Dr Dinter, so that, unless fate decrees otherwise, I have at best just 20 years remaining to me when I will still have the energy and resolve demanded by such an immense task. During these 20 years it may well be that a new political movement can be victorious in the struggle for political power.' That length of time was, on the other hand, much too short for a religious reformation.[53]

In his reply of 19 August Dinter asked to be allowed to address the next general members' meeting, which took place in parallel with the leaders' conference.[54] He also included a request to that members' meeting that a Party senate should be formed as the supreme NSDAP ruling body. This was a direct attack on the position of the supreme Party leader and at the leaders' conference at the end of August Hitler dismissed it out of hand.[55]

Hitler sent Dinter a reply via Hess saying there was no opportunity to address the general meeting but that he should present the issue at the next leaders' conference.[56] When Dinter rejected this,[57] Hitler, again through Hess, sent him an 'official command' to be in Munich on 1 September. Dinter, however, was unwilling to fall in with this suggestion.[58] After further fruitless correspondence,[59] Hitler finally withdrew from Dinter the author-ity to represent Party interests in the Thuringian state parliament[60] and on 11 October excluded him from the Party.[61]

At the three-day leaders' conference held in Munich in late August/early September 1928 in place of the Party Rally, which had been called off for financial reasons,[62] Hitler addressed not only the inadequacies of the Party organization but also expressly opposed any comment on religious matters as damaging to the Party: 'The issue of Catholic or Protestant is as irrelevant to a National Socialist as are the issues of monarchy or republic, middle class or working class, Prussian or Bavarian. His central concerns are state and nation. Religion is the least of a nationalist's concerns. At any rate, founders of religions have no place whatever in our movement.'[63]

The most important outcome of the leaders' conference was, however, the matching of the boundaries of twenty-two Party Gaus to the Reichstag con-stituencies, a reform prepared in essence by Strasser, who since the beginning of the year had been head of the Reich Party administration.[64] From now on the only 'Greater Gau' was Bavaria. Consisting of eight Gaus, this unit was con-trolled by Hitler alone. In addition, Party Gaus were set up beyond the Reich borders, in Austria, the Saarland, and in Danzig (Gdansk). This significant

organizational improvement with an eye to the next elections complemented
the orientation of Party propaganda towards middle-class voters.[65]

In addition, in September an Association of National Socialist Lawyers
was created[66] as the first step towards organizing a middle-class membership
around 'professional status'. In April 1929 the NS Teachers' Association was
founded, followed in August 1929 by the NS German Doctors' Association,
and in November 1929 by the NS Pupils' Association, which recruited
members almost exclusively from grammar schools.[67] On 1 October 1929,
a few weeks after the leaders' conference, the NSDAP issued membership
number 100,000. The actual total of members was lower, as numbers that
became vacant could not be reallocated;[68] when in February 1929 Hitler
claimed the movement had 115,000 members he was presumably using this
method and not the actual headcount.[69]

'The lesser of two evils': Rapprochement with the right-wing Conservatives

At the state parliament elections in Saxony on 12 May 1929 the NSDAP
achieved 5 per cent of the vote, in Mecklenburg-Schwerin on 23 June they
reached 4 per cent, and in the same month in Coburg they even became the
majority party on the city council.[70] By now they were concentrating their
efforts on gaining middle-class votes, and their propaganda had become largely
purged of 'socialist demands', thus resembling that of the right-wing conservative camp. The obvious next move, therefore, was to make overtures to these
groups and offer themselves as political allies against Weimar democracy, with
the ultimate aim of assuming the leadership as soon as possible in this marriage
of convenience and taking as many voters as possible away from the right-wing
conservative and moderate middle-class sections of the electorate.

In the summer of 1929, after some argument, Hitler managed to get
agreement for the first time on this policy of approaching the Conservatives.
The elections to the Saxon state parliament on 12 May 1929 had led to a
stalemate between a centre-right bloc and the parties of the left, and at first
it was impossible to see how a government could be formed. Then, in July
1929, Hellmuth von Mücke, who belonged to the 'left wing' of the Party,
floated with the SPD and KPD the possibility of support from the NSDAP
for a left-wing government. The workers' parties refused the offer and made
Mücke's approach public, in spite of his request for confidentiality. Hitler

distanced himself from Mücke, who in fact declared that he had taken his initiative with the agreement of the Party leader (a matter that can no longer be verified) and left the NSDAP. If 'fate gives us the role of either being neutral and thus being useful to the Marxists or of acting and facilitating a government of nationalists, even if they are weak and hollow bourgeois nationalists', Hitler now declared in the *Völkischer Beobachter*, 'we must in spite of everything renounce neutrality and choose the lesser of two evils'.[71] This was a clear decision on the Party's direction. Although a coalition with bourgeois parties of the kind Hitler advocated did not come about at this stage, as early as July 1929 the Nazis in Saxony were to help put a bourgeois government in power and tolerate it in parliament.[72]

The gradual approach of the NSDAP to the right-wing conservative camp, however, took place primarily through a joint initiative for a plebiscite. Since the autumn of 1928, the veterans' organization, the Stahlhelm, had been pursuing a plan to use a plebiscite to change the constitution, transferring power from parliament to the Reich President, and thus to transform Weimar democracy into an authoritarian state.[73] In its search for support the Stahlhelm turned to the NSDAP, where the project divided opinion; Goebbels, for example, feared that Hitler would go too far in making concessions to the Stahlhelm,[74] and made a critical statement in his Berlin paper *Der Angriff* about 'reactionaries'.[75] Hitler responded to the initiative in April 1929 in a lengthy letter to the national leadership of the veterans' organization: The changes to the constitution sought by the Stahlhelm were, he wrote, 'irrelevant' as far as the realization of a 'German resurgence' was concerned. For simply redistributing powers in the context of the Weimar constitution made no difference to the essential nature of 'our "western-style" democracy'. 'A man who has been chosen by Providence . . . to be the Führer, will in any case never allow his actions to be prescribed or confined by the ridiculous limits on powers imposed by a constitution, if acting in accordance with the constitution must bring his nation to ruin.' And what, he asked more as a tactical objection, would the Stahlhelm do if a 'Marxist' President were to come to power? Besides, plebiscites must arise from issues of internal national conflict of a kind that 'might literally split the nation in two', such as the restoration of the monarchy, the continuation of war reparations, or the acknowledgement of war guilt.[76] For all these reasons the NSDAP would not be involved.

The right-wing conservatives were, however, already trying to initiate another plebiscite, this time opposing the Young Plan, which had been accepted by the Reich government on 21 June. Although this Plan made certain concessions to Germany in respect of reparation payments, its opponents argued that it preserved German payments and so set them in stone. And this time Hitler agreed. On 9 July he supported a call from the Reich Committee for German Plebiscites that had the backing of, amongst others, the DNVP chairman and media tycoon Alfred Hugenberg, Franz Seldte, the national leader of the Stahlhelm, as well as Privy Councillor Class of the Pan-Germans. It was in other words a campaign platform of the combined parties of the right and had a national network at its disposal.[77]

Writing to Party comrades in the *Völkischer Beobachter* on 25 July 1929, Hitler made it clear that his participation arose 'from a desire to achieve a tactical subordinate goal on a broad basis', which did not affect the Party's 'ultimate goal'.[78] On the same day he ordered Party functionaries[79] not to be drawn into joint activities by 'partner organizations' without express permission from the leadership.[80] The article was paving the way for the Party Rally, which this year took place once again. Hitler's opponents in the Party were also positioning themselves.

On 28 July Otto Strasser published '14 Theses on the German Revolution' in the newspapers of Kampf publishing house. In its essentials, this manifesto drew heavily on the 1920 Party programme and thus presented an alternative model to Hitler's approach to the conservatives. At the fourth Party Rally at the beginning of August 1929 in Nuremberg Hitler found himself having, on the one hand, to defend the fact that he had made approaches to the right-wing conservatives and, on the other, to make clear to Party comrades that he was not prepared to be co-opted by the 'reactionaries'. This dual strategy determined the character of the Rally, whose respectability was to be emphasized in this particular year by a number of prominent honorary guests. Winifred Wagner attended as did the leading industrialist Emil Kirdorf, who for some time had been sympathetic to the NSDAP. In addition, Theodor Duesterberg, the second Reich chairman of the Stahlhelm was there, demonstrating the controversial policy of alignment with the Conservatives, also Count von der Golz, the leader of the Union of Völkisch Associations. Some 30,000–40,000 Party supporters had made the journey, around double the number that had attended two years before.

On 1 August, a Thursday, the nineteen panel meetings of the Rally began. Hitler had issued the instruction 'to ensure that, in spite of the grand setting for these Rallies and the freedom to discuss, they do not degenerate into general chaos. Experience shows that nothing ever came of endless discussions.'[81] The atmosphere that prevailed during the panel meetings was characterized by Goebbels in a lapidary and telling manner: 'Everyone in agreement because nobody dared say anything.'[82] Yet contrary to Hitler's intentions controversial views could not be suppressed altogether. At the section for members of the Reich and state parliaments, Rudolf Rehm, the deputy Gauleiter of Brandenburg and one of Strasser's circle, moved that the Party should pronounce a general ban on coalitions at Reich and state level. This was a direct attack on Hitler's approach to the parties of the right. Hitler put a stop to this initiative, citing as a reason that this move would be 'the equivalent of forbidding a nation state ever to make alliances'. The panel then declared that it had no authority to make a decision about this matter.[83]

The actual delegates' conference, with some 1,200–1,500 participants, met in three big sessions from Friday to Sunday. Hitler exploited his wide-ranging opening remarks, read out by Gauleiter Adolf Wagner, to make pointed attacks on the 'bourgeois parties' in addition to 'Marxists' and 'Jews': they 'do not wish to achieve any fundamental separation of the Germans from Marxism.... Our bourgeoisie has in general abandoned the völkisch approach with its focus on and commitment to the issue of blood.' The bourgeois parties were thus turning into 'defenders of the poisoning of the nation, and in fact were downright advocates of the racial violation of their own nation'. This vehement attack was Hitler's demonstrative attempt to answer criticism from the Party and he spoke twice more on the last day of meetings.[84] For several days the city was dominated by the presence of the NSDAP: the city centre was decorated with swastikas; Nazi uniforms and cries of 'Heil' were everywhere. By mounting a firework display in the evening and a concert in the stadium, the Party also used the conference programme to make its mark.[85]

On the Saturday 18,000 uniformed Nazis marched through the city. On the Sunday a 'commemoration of the fallen' took place outside the hall of honour on the Luitpoldhain, followed by the presentation of standards and flags to the SA and SS units.[86] More than 25,000 Nazis were said to have taken part in the march afterwards through the city. On the periphery of the Party Rally there were numerous clashes with members of the Reichsbanner† and with communists. An exchange of gunfire in the inner city left a female

---

† Translators' note: The Reichsbanner Black-Red-Gold was a paramilitary organization established in 1924 to defend parliamentary democracy against right-wing and communist paramilitaries. It was mainly composed of members of the SPD.

NSDAP member dead and another shooting incident caused the deaths of two further Party supporters. These acts of violence were quite useful to the NSDAP, as they provided confirmation that the Party was fighting in the front line against 'Marxism'.[87]

The National Socialist parade in Nuremberg emphasized the fact that, compared with the last such event two years previously, the NSDAP had grown considerably in strength. Even so, this was still a small party on the edge of the extreme right. The subsequent months would have to demonstrate whether Hitler's new direction – the plan to use an alliance with the right-wing conservative parties to lure away some of their core voters, above all among the urban middle classes and the rural population – would be successful.

9

Conquering the Masses

In spite of his vehement criticism of the 'bourgeois' parties, after the 1929 Party Rally Hitler continued to join in the campaign against the Young Plan. Up to September 1929 the Reich Committee for the German Plebiscite was working on a draft plebiscite that would ban the Reich government from accepting further financial burdens or commitments arising from the Treaty of Versailles. Instead, it was to make a solemn declaration retracting Germany's acknowledgement of responsibility for the war, as set down in the treaty, and to annul any obligations deriving from that acknowledgement. Furthermore, members of the government or any of its agents who concluded any agreements at variance with these provisions would be punished as traitors. In the concluding phase of discussions this final stipulation led to disagreement, with Hitler, who favoured a more aggressive form of words, unable to get his way.[1]

In the end the plebiscite took place in the second half of October. During this period the sponsors had to gather the signatures of 10 per cent of all those entitled to vote as a precondition for the actual referendum. The campaign propaganda was carried out by the participating organizations – the DNVP, the Stahlhelm, and the NSDAP – by Hugenberg's press group, and by the Reich Committee, which produced large quantities of propaganda material and, importantly, raised donations that were shared among the participating organizations.[2]

On 25 October, Hitler himself, accompanied by Hugenberg, spoke at a large rally of the Bavarian State Committee for the German Plebiscite at the Circus Krone.[3] He also defended the initiative in his weekly column in the *Illustrierter Beobachter*, accusing the government, among other things, of rigging the procedural arrangements.[4] Looking back, he claimed that this move had at least led to the political forces in favour of the treaty measures showing their true colours.[5] In using these arguments the Party leader was manifestly responding to critics from his own ranks. For the 'Party Left' around the Strasser brothers viewed the behaviour of the DNVP as dishonest, given their earlier 'fulfilment policy', and Goebbels, the Gauleiter of Berlin, believed the NSDAP had been taken in by its partners in the Reich Committee.[6] He did not want to take his criticism too far, however, because Hitler was still dangling in front of him the promise made in May 1929 that Goebbels should take over as head of Reich propaganda and so had him on a short lead.[7] Even the Strasser brothers finally fell in with Hitler's strategy and tried from inside the anti–Young campaign to emphasize the 'nationalist revolutionary' direction of the NSDAP, in contrast to the 'reactionary' Stahlhelm and 'capitalist' DNVP.[8]

Ostensibly, the Party gained very little from the considerable propaganda effort occasioned by the campaign against the Young Plan. The Hugenberg press gave the Nazis comparatively little space in the campaign, and it appears that the Party's membership of the Reich Committee did little to improve its chances of receiving donations from industry.[9] But in Hitler's view one result outweighed everything: through the plebiscite the NSDAP had built bridges to the right-wing conservative camp and gained potential allies. At the same time, by repeatedly distancing himself from his new 'partners' and in fact even permitting himself furious and insulting tirades against them, he ensured that the NSDAP was not simply absorbed into a united front of the right but retained its own profile.

When at the end of October the opponents of the Young Plan had narrowly achieved the 10 per cent of signatures they needed and, as expected, parliament refused to agree to their request, the government scheduled the referendum for the last shopping Sunday before Christmas. In spite of another intensive propaganda effort on the part of the Reich Committee, the referendum was heavily defeated, with only 13.8 per cent of votes in favour.[10] The initiators nevertheless agreed to maintain the Reich Committee for the time being and possibly use it as a platform for further joint initiatives.

Hitler continued to defend his actions, stressing that at least the referendum had 'stirred up public opinion in Germany in such a way that the government parties are now feeling very uncomfortable today'.[11] What ensued seemed to prove him right: the growth of the NSDAP into a mass movement began precisely at the time of the Young Plan campaign. Whereas the Party had never managed to gain more than 5 per cent of the votes in the 1929 elections up to that point, in the autumn it achieved significant electoral successes: 7 per cent in the state parliament elections in Baden on 27 October; 8.1 per cent in Lübeck on 10 November; 5.8 per cent a week later in the local elections in Prussia. In the elections taking place simultaneously for the assemblies in the Prussian provinces the Party made above-average gains in Brandenburg, Hanover, Hesse, Saxony, and Schleswig-Holstein, with results between 5.6 per cent and 10.3 per cent.[12] The NSDAP's propaganda machine was already in high gear as a result of the anti-Young Plan campaign, and the Party succeeded in focusing it immediately on the electoral battles, thereby securing a significant advantage over the DNVP, whose potential for mobilizing support was nowhere near as great.

The electoral gains made by the NSDAP were possible only because the entire spectrum of predominantly middle-class parties was in the meantime in deep trouble.

Many of the 'middle-class bloc' coalitions formed in the mid-1920s at local and regional level were breaking apart, and the project of expanding the DNVP into a large nationalist-conservative party at national level was threatening to collapse under the weight of overwhelming conflicts of interest and the absence of compelling nationalistic slogans. In the 1928 Reichstag elections it had lost already almost a third of its voters, while the liberal parties' share of the vote had also shrunk drastically: that of the centre Right German People's Party (DVP) from 13.9 per cent in the Reichstag elections of 1920 to 8.7 per cent; that of the centre Left German Democratic Party (DDP) from 8.3 per cent to 4.9 per cent. At the end of the 1920s the numerous new parties, regional parties, and parties representing very narrow economic interests also found themselves in very choppy waters.

This crisis afflicting bourgeois parties was in essence caused by the fact that in the later 1920s both the conservative and the liberal milieus lost their integrative power. Neither was able, to the extent it had been in Imperial Germany, to hold people's loyalty through a dense network of clubs and of associations representing economic interests. Large sections of the Protestant middle classes and also of the Catholic middle classes, in so far as they were not anchored in the Centre Party, were searching for new political allegiances.[13] The momentum behind the NSDAP was now so evident that Strasser was already preparing his senior staff in the Party's national organization to assume power in the Reich. In September 1929 he established a second branch of the organization (Organization II), led by the former Munich city commandant Konstantin Hierl, to make plans for the period following the appointment of a Nazi government. As head of the first branch of the Reich organization (Organization I), meanwhile, he retained actual control over the Party apparatus, which was to be significantly expanded during the following years.[14]

Just when the NSDAP had got its propaganda machine into high gear and was enlarging its central organization, a major economic slump began. On 25 October 1929 the New York stock exchange crashed. The American banks withdrew short-term loans from their main creditor, Germany, and in so doing hit an economy that was already heading towards recession. It was very quickly evident that the established parties were incapable of working together effectively to contain the crisis.[15] The NSDAP was able to profit from the situation, as was shown by the hugely improved result it achieved in the Thuringian state elections on 8 December 1929: 11.3 per cent of the votes as compared with only 3.5 per cent in the 1927 elections. Against vehement opposition from the Left of the Party,[16] Hitler insisted that the NSDAP should help form the state government along with the DNVP and DVP. He went in person to Weimar to take charge of the coalition negotiations and secured the Interior Ministry and Education Ministry for the Party. A further success he could chalk up was that Wilhelm Frick, whom the DVP had at first rejected because of his part in the Munich putsch, was put in charge of both ministries. Hitler himself attributed the fact that the DVP dropped their objections principally to a speech he made during his stay in Weimar to a gathering of middle ranking industrialists.[17] After tolerating a bourgeois government in Saxony he was now able to consolidate his policy of alignment with the right-wing conservatives in Thuringia.[18]

Praised by Hitler as 'the fiercest National Socialist fighter',[19] Frick immediately adopted a consistently racist policy in education and cultural matters and began to 'purge' the civil service. In doing so he was acting in accordance with Hitler's aims in joining the coalition, which included the creation of a chair of 'Racial Studies' at the University of Jena. It was taken up by the 'racial scientist' Hans Günther and was regarded by Hitler as the 'starting point for an…intellectual revolution' that he compared with the Reformation.[20] From now onwards Frick repeatedly tried to see how far he could implement Nazi policies in the context of the existing democratic state constitution.[21] On the strength of an 'enabling law' he aimed to exclude the state parliament from the legislative process, although because of his concerns about constitutional legitimacy he had the decrees issued under the enabling law confirmed retrospectively by the state parliament. Frick brought the local police forces under state control, excluding many politically undesirable members. He removed democratically inclined civil servants from the administration and as education minister introduced prayers in schools that were full of bombastic völkisch language. With a range of measures he attempted to 'purify' cultural life, banishing the influence of 'alien races' and any elements of 'negro culture'.[22] By appointing the architect Paul Schultze-Naumburg as head of the Combined Art Schools in Weimar he chose someone with a racially based view of art. Amongst other things Schultze-Naumburg mounted a campaign against 'degenerate art' in the state. His home, close to the ruined castle of Saaleck, became the meeting place for a circle of völkisch intellectuals that Hitler himself deigned to join on two occasions.[23]

The Nazis exploited their participation in government to establish important priorities in their propaganda campaign, emphasizing their aggressive opposition to democracy and modernist culture and thereby providing a foretaste of the so-called Third Reich. They did not succeed, however, in hollowing out the state of Thuringia from the inside and conquering it. In the end, Frick went too far with his radical policies and came to grief on 1 April 1931 through a perfectly normal parliamentary procedure: a motion of no confidence put by the SPD and KPD found support among the DVP, which had long grown tired of the NSDAP's continuous attacks.[24] Thus the first Nazi experiment in government in a German state ended in failure.

Yet, in the meantime, throughout Germany Hitler and the NSDAP had become a factor the established parties had to reckon with. He was now intervening more and more frequently in public discourse,[25] and doing so with increasing self-confidence and in the manner of the towering 'Führer', who stood above the banalities of everyday politics. For example, in June 1930 he intervened in the electoral battle for the Saxon parliament with the surprising declaration 'that he did not care to make an election speech', and thus preferred 'not to comment on the conditions in Saxony'.[26] As the Nazis 'encompassed all social classes in the nation he could not, unlike individual interest groups, work with propaganda slogans and promises'. National Socialism was rather built on a 'basic principle': 'The fate of the individual is determined by the fate of the nation as a whole.'[27] What he actually had to offer revolved mainly around the all too familiar slogans and topics: the 'value of personality', to which the Nazis, by contrast with democrats, accorded supreme significance; the 'blood value' of the German nation, the racial composition of which made it superior to every other nation;

'struggle, without which nothing comes into being in the world and nothing is preserved'.[28] Anti-Semitism was a further integral part of these speeches, even if Hitler basically avoided any detailed statements about his aims regarding the Jews living in Germany. If ever he did give more away, he did not go beyond what was already in the 1920 Party programme. 'A National Socialist will never tolerate an alien – and that is what the Jew is – having a position in public life', Hitler said in November 1929. 'He will never ask, "Is he up to the job?" No, my world view tells me that I must keep the national body free from alien blood.'[29]

In virtually every speech Hitler emphasized 'lack of space'; this had become the norm from 1928 onwards: 'A healthy nation always seeks to extend its space.'[30] Thus, if the 'balance of numbers and space' is crucial, then National Socialism must clearly respond 'that every nation has the right to take the territory it needs and can cultivate and manage.'[31] Emigration, limiting the number of births or increasing exports did not provide the answer,[32] as he explained in an article in the *Illustrierter Beobachter* of 15 February, for what was important was 'the creation of a living space for our nation, not only to provide enough food for our present population but to allow it to grow.... To that end we need for the foreseeable future in Europe to look for allies whose interests are least in conflict with Germany's and most with France's.' Italy was the most obvious choice.[33] As usual, he was unwilling to be more specific, although he informed Robert Wagner, the Gauleiter of Baden, in November 1929 that he had 'the acquisition of territory in Central Europe in mind', for this would be 'much more important than territory overseas for the political power of the German Reich'. In the final analysis this was a commitment to war rather than to the acquisition of colonies. The latter were not to be dismissed but it was necessary to be 'vigilant in case striving for colonies diverted the German nation, possibly intentionally, from more important matters'.[34] All in all, although Hitler varied the tone of his statements, he did not alter their content. Mixing vague pronouncements with allegedly universally accepted ones had proved a successful formula in elections and neither he nor his public was much concerned about the specifics.

Upheavals in the Reich and the Party

In March 1930 the Reich government under the Social Democrat Hermann Müller and formed from the Centre Party, SPD, DDP, and DVP collapsed, after finding it impossible to reach agreement on the issue of the future financing of unemployment insurance. The background to this disagreement was the dramatic rise during the winter in the numbers of unemployed. In January the total reached 3.2 million, the highest figure to date, and as spring approached no real recovery was on the horizon.[35] The world economic crisis had a devastating effect on Germany. In this situation President Hindenburg appointed the Centre Party's leader, Heinrich Brüning, as Müller's successor. Hindenburg explicitly instructed Brüning not to try in the first instance to form a new coalition, but instead, given that he had no majority in parliament, to rely on the Reich President's extraordinary powers under Article 48 of the Weimar constitution. Hindenburg's aim was to use this arrangement to keep the SPD, the strongest party, perpetually out of government, to marginalize parliament, and to transform the Weimar democracy into an authoritarian regime.[36]

When the SPD's parliamentary group moved a vote of no confidence in this new government, made up exclusively of members of bourgeois parties, the DNVP in the Reichstag found itself in a key position: If it voted for the motion supported by SPD, KPD, and NSDAP, new elections would be necessary. In a long discussion with Hugenberg, the party chairman, on 31 March Hitler tried to convince him to do this, gambling on his own party's success in new elections.[37] In the end, however, the DNVP voted against the motion of no confidence.[38] Hitler took the DNVP's stance as an excuse to stop participating in the Reich Young Plan committee, as the DNVP had 'expressed confidence in the parties guilty of accepting the Young Plan'.[39] Although he told Hugenberg he was prepared to wait for fourteen days before making this step public (the DNVP leader having assured him he would topple the Brüning cabinet by then), to Hitler's annoyance it became known prematurely, as the result of an indiscretion that appeared in the *National Socialist*, the Strasser brothers' paper.[40] A few days later, the DNVP once again rescued Brüning's government: on 12 and 14 April the majority of the party, in spite of Hugenberg's opposition, voted for the budget thereby preventing the dissolution of the Reichstag.[41] Goebbels noted that Hitler, who had come to Berlin specially, was 'seething with rage at the DNVP'. He had 'let his illusions run away with him'.[42]

The fact that the secret of Hitler's departure from the Reich Young Plan committee was given away by a Strasser publication in the spring of 1930 was not down to chance. For just as the NSDAP was getting ready to profit from the emerging widespread economic and political crisis in the elections, which were now about to be brought forward, the conflict that had long been smouldering between Hitler and the Strasser brothers came to a head in public. Hitler benefited from the fact that in 1926 he had succeeded in playing off individual members of the so-called left wing of the Party against each other. This was particularly true of Goebbels and the Strassers. The Gauleiter of Berlin had for some time been annoyed that in the Kampf-Verlag Gregor and Otto Strasser had at their disposal an active publishing house in the Reich capital that was not under his control. He was also offended that Otto in particular, who along with a series of like-minded comrades was steering the Kampf-Verlag in a 'national-revolutionary' direction, presented himself openly as his rival within the Party.[43] Otto Strasser above all criticized Hitler's tendency to be drawn into parliamentary alliances or arrangements with right-wing conservatives, as had happened with the formation of the government in Thuringia in 1929.[44]

From the beginning of 1929, Goebbels had been pursuing the idea of expanding his newspaper *Der Angriff*, which appeared twice a week, into a daily, not least in order to win the newspaper battle with the Strassers. In January 1930, however, he found that the Strassers were also planning their own daily. Although, when approached, Hitler took Goebbels's side, from 1 March onwards, to the latter's dismay, the *Nationaler Sozialist* began appearing as a daily in Berlin and Hitler lacked the resolve to take effective action against the Strasser brothers,[45] trying to avoid committing himself in the conflict. At all costs he wanted to avoid an open rupture with the Strassers as it might lead to the 'left wing' breaking away. Thus he was prepared to turn a blind eye to the independent line they were taking in their publishing operation. Goebbels was forced to shelve his ambitious newspaper plans and was as a result very annoyed, but Hitler could live with that. By repeatedly holding out to Goebbels the prospect of his own daily newspaper and of taking over as head of Reich propaganda, he could keep the ambitious Gauleiter on side. By deliberately avoiding settling the quarrel between the Strassers and Goebbels, he ensured that these former allies did not combine to form any internal opposition to him.

However, in the spring of 1930 Hitler gave instructions not to support a strike called by the unions in the Saxon metal industry, whereas Otto Strasser and the Kampf-Verlag came out on the side of the strikers.[46] It was only now that his authority was being plainly challenged that Hitler decided to nail his colours to the mast. At the NSDAP leaders' conference on 26 and 27 April in Munich he openly criticized the two brothers, the Kampf-Verlag, the 'drawing-room Bolsheviks', and other undesirable groups in the Party. At the same time he finally announced that Goebbels had been appointed as the NSDAP's head of Reich propaganda.[47] Shortly after, when on a visit to Berlin at the beginning of May, Hitler banned the sale of the *Nationaler Sozialist*.[48] Gregor Strasser felt in the end compelled to agree to sell his share of the paper to Amann and announce that its final edition would appear on 20 May.[49] Yet in spite of this agreement, the *Nationaler Sozialist* continued to appear after this date. Although Hitler again made very negative remarks to the deeply disappointed Goebbels about Otto Strasser, no action followed.[50] On 21 and 22 May Hitler had long discussions with Otto Strasser, in Berlin, and these gave the latter the final impetus he needed to leave the Party.

After quitting the Party at the beginning of July he went on to publish a detailed account of these discussions, effectively a public denunciation of Hitler, who made no attempt to challenge his account.[51] According to Strasser, Hitler had at first offered to buy the Kampf-Verlag from him and his brother. He, Otto, had refused and, according to his altogether credible version of events, had succeeded during the ensuing argument, which stretched over two days, in goading Hitler to come out with a clear statement opposing socialist policies: demands for socialist policies for large-scale industries or for their nationalization, or even for workers to be given a larger share in the profits or management of businesses were, Hitler had said, frankly nonsensical.

Although this clarification of their differences made his split with Otto Strasser inevitable, Hitler at first wanted to wait for the Saxon parliamentary elections on 22 June.[52] Elections had become necessary because the NSDAP had terminated its toleration of the state government after the coalition of bourgeois parties had voted for the Young Plan in the federal council (Reichsrat). On 22 June 1930 the NSDAP gained 14.4 per cent of the votes, a clear success. The NSDAP at first tolerated the new bourgeois 'ministry of experts', but in the end brought it down after a few weeks in conjunction with the parties of the left.[53]

Meanwhile, to Goebbels's annoyance,[54] Hitler's conflict with the 'left wing' of the Party had led only to his excluding a few insignificant rebels from the Berlin Gau.[55] Gregor Strasser decided against his brother and for Hitler and, at the end of June, finally stepped down as head of the Kampf publishing house and editor of the *Nationaler Sozialist*.[56] On 1 July the paper printed a rallying call with the headline 'Socialists quit the N.S.D.A.P.' in which Otto Strasser and those loyal to him broke with the Party,[57] whereupon

Hitler declared that the Kampf-Verlag publications were to be treated from then on as 'hostile'.[58] Without the support of his brother, however, Otto Strasser's efforts to develop a national *socialist* alternative under the banner of 'Revolutionary Socialists' were destined to pose little threat to Hitler.

Hitler now came up with the idea of none other than Gregor Strasser, who in the NSDAP had always opposed compromise with the bourgeois parties, taking up the post of Minister of the Interior in the Saxon government. Presumably Hitler intended this tactical move to bind the head of the Reich Party organization more closely to the Party, while compromising him in the eyes of his supporters. This venture collapsed, however, when the bourgeois parties opposed it, and in future Saxony was no longer to provide the venue for further internal conflicts over Hitler's policy of trying to work with them. For, in the end, the former Saxon government remained in office, tolerated by the Social Democrats, an arrangement that held until 1933.[59]

The 1930 Reichstag elections

On 18 July the Reich President dissolved the Reichstag. Chancellor Brüning had intended to rescue his Reich budget proposal, after parliament had rejected it, with recourse to an emergency decree issued by President Hindenburg, but parliament had also defeated this, leaving Hindenburg no option under the Constitution but to dissolve the Reichstag.[60] In view of the deepening economic crisis and the considerable electoral successes of the NSDAP in recent months, fresh elections were risky. The Reich President and Chancellor, who took the decision, and the leaders of the parties that had provoked it through their inability to compromise with Brüning accepted the consequences with their eyes open, namely to maintain a parliament that was incapable of producing a majority and thus to turn the use of Article 48 into a permanent state of affairs. The decision to hold fresh elections in such circumstances thus set a course in which Weimar democracy moved towards becoming an authoritarian regime – precisely the goal that the President and his Chancellor, as well as right-wing conservative interest groups influencing them, were aiming for.

On 19 July Hitler held a meeting to discuss the line to be taken in the election campaign and the selection of candidates.[61] On this occasion he took those present, among them Epp, Frick, Goebbels, Göring, Hierl,

Rosenberg, and Strasser, to the future Party headquarters, the Palais Barlow on Königsplatz, which Hitler had ordered the Party to purchase in May. Goebbels considered the building, which was still being renovated, 'pompous and spacious',[62] a mixed response that he shared with others. Faced with such criticism Hitler felt obliged in February 1931, before its grand opening, to print a detailed justification of its purchase in the *Völkischer Beobachter*: 'The National Socialist movement is a power political phenomenon and cannot be compared with our ridiculous main-stream parties, with their focus on the economy and parliament', he wrote. 'The object of its struggle and exertions is so immeasurably great that its overwhelming significance must be evident to everyone, even in its external appearance.'[63] Given his limited emotional range, Hitler was incapable of experiencing personal satisfaction and contentment through success achieved. If he wished to give expression to his political achievements he could do so only through triumphal gestures and overpowering symbols.

At the end of July, the campaign strategy and candidates were finalized at a Gauleiters' conference. In an address Hitler told them that 'from the start they had to go on the fiercest and most ruthless offensive against the combined forces of the Young parties'. Goebbels was officially put in charge of managing the election campaign,[64] although this undertaking had its limitations, as the Party's propaganda apparatus was anything but unified, but instead highly dependent on regional and local initiatives.[65] What Goebbels could manage to arrange was that the entire campaign would be fought, as Hitler wished, under the banner 'Fight the Young parties'. The Party's propaganda directed against the ruling parties of the SPD, Centre, DVP, and DDP, which had voted for the new schedule for reparations in March, harked back to the anti-Young Plan campaign of the previous year, although this had been controversial within the Party. Hitler may also have regarded this as a retrospective justification for his strategy.

Posters, marches, and mass events were set in motion.[66] For the last four weeks alone before the election on 14 September Reich propaganda headquarters was planning 34,000 rallies.[67] Naturally, the speeches the Party leader was scheduled to make were regarded as especially important. He made twenty appearances between 3 August and 13 September in towns and cities all over Germany, where before audiences of thousands and sometimes tens of thousands[68] he tore into the 'Young parties' for having 'accepted the revolution . . . accepted subjugation, the lot of them'. How could anyone give them credence, if monarchist parties 'acknowledge the Republic', bourgeois parties make pacts with 'Marxists', Christian parties 'give a leg up to the Jews', socialist parties 'march hand in hand with international finance and deliver a whole nation into its power'? 'At moments of crisis', Hitler impressed on his audiences, nations should look 'always to dictatorship and never to democracy', for 'the highest concentration [of power and energy; P. L.] is always to be found in the superior individual'.[69] The democratic parties, on the other hand, had 'sinned for years. For years they have focused their policies on the most petty interests and for years they have appealed only to particular groups, and now they no longer have a German nation but tenants, landlords, clerks, workers, employers, civil servants, and so on. The nation is fragmented and today we have reached a low point.'[70] There then followed, in a manner typical of these speeches, the rhetorical turning point, the vision of national unity under the leadership of National Socialism: 'A German nation must again emerge from the confusion of interest groups.'[71] That was also, he proclaimed on 12 September in Breslau, the foundation for true socialism, and there is no doubt that this remark was a sideswipe at his critics inside the Party. 'The sham of party politics cannot give rise to a German nation. Nationalism is the only option. If this nationalism means the dedication of each individual to the whole then it has in fact become the most noble form of socialism.'[72] Although his other standard topics, such as diatribes against the Jews and on the Germans' lack of space, came up in these speeches, they took second place to the election slogan. In fact, Hitler, who was presenting himself above all as an aggressive demagogue and polemicist against the 'system', touched on the demand for 'living space', which was after all part of his core ideology, only three times during the entire election campaign.[73]

In the press there was much speculation that big business had made this expensive campaign possible, yet this assumption was incorrect. In fact it is likely that for the most part the Party financed the organization and propaganda itself.[74] For the NSDAP took up a strongly 'anti-capitalist' stance in the election, in spite of the fact that the 'Party's 'left wing' had recently split off, and this tended rather to arouse mistrust within business.[75] Thus the journal of the employers' association carried a critical appraisal of the Nazi economic programme, and the Reich Federation of Industry called on its members to support only parties that scrupulously abided by the constitution and rejected all 'collectivist experiments', comments that referred to the NSDAP.[76]

The election campaign had just begun when the Berlin SA decided to flex its muscles. The conflict arose from the demand made by the SA leadership to be included on the NSDAP's electoral list. Pfeffer, the SA leader, had already been rebuffed over this matter on 1 August, but this did not prevent Walther Stennes, leader of the SA in Eastern Germany, from demanding three seats from Goebbels, the Gauleiter of Berlin, for his area of command a few days later. Failing that, Stennes had, according to Goebbels, threatened a 'palace revolution'. Hitler, however, was not prepared to agree and described Stennes's move, as Goebbels learnt from Pfeffer, as 'mutiny' and 'conspiracy'.[77]

At the end of the month the SA launched an open revolt. Stennes issued an ultimatum demanding seats, finance, and more independence for the SA[78] and decided to speak in person to the Party boss in Munich. Hitler, however, refused to see him. In response, the SA leaders under Stennes resigned their posts and decided that the SA would withdraw support for the Party until their demand for at least two seats was met. Stennes and his SA men took part in a rally at the sports stadium on 29 August, at which Goebbels dismissed reports about disunity in the NSDAP as mere rumour, and Stennes also made a declaration of loyalty in *Der Angriff*.[79] The following day, however, an SA squad stormed the Party offices and engaged in a brawl with the SS guards posted there; the latter called the police, who brought the situation under control.

Alerted by Goebbels, Hitler arrived in Berlin on 31 August. In the evening Hitler and Goebbels toured the SA pubs where, according to Goebbels, Hitler was greeted everywhere 'with enthusiasm'. And yet, they could clearly sense a 'subdued atmosphere' everywhere they went, and the animated exchange of views with SA leaders in Goebbels's apartment failed to resolve matters. Stennes, who joined the group during the discussion, talked for hours with Hitler without achieving any concrete results.[80] On 1 September, the following day, however, Hitler finally arrived at a decision. He demoted Pfeffer, took over himself as head of the SA, and at the same time granted increased financial support to the SA to be paid for by the Party and its members.[81] The rebellious SA leaders accepted this proposal and the same evening a demonstrative reconciliation took place at the premises of the Veterans' Association. The Berlin police report recorded that Hitler made a long speech calling for loyalty from the SA, in the process 'raising his already over-strained voice until he was shouting almost hysterically'. He 'waved aside' the ensuing shouts of 'Heil', 'because, his hands folded and as though immersed in prayer, Hitler was still hearing the echo of his own words'. Stennes spoke after Goebbels, and according to the same report was

applauded as the victor in the dispute he had initiated.[82] A final confrontation with Stennes had, however, simply been postponed.

Breakthrough

In the 14 September elections the NSDAP greatly increased its share of the
vote from 2.6 per cent to 18.3 per cent. Its total number of seats therefore
rose from 12 to 107, making it after the SPD the second biggest party in the
Reichstag. In spite of the 14.4 per cent the Party had already gained in
Saxony's elections in June, the scale of its success surprised supporters as
much as opponents. The Party had succeeded in triggering the greatest
migration of voters in the history of parliamentary government in Germany.
It was now at Reich level a political force that could not be ignored.

In the early 1990s a team working with the psephologist Jürgen W. Falter
produced the hitherto most complete analysis of this movement of voters.
According to their calculations 24 per cent of NSDAP voters were voting
for the first time, 22 per cent were former DNVP voters, 18 per cent came
from the liberal camp, and at least 14 per cent from the Social Democrats.
To put it another way, by comparison with 1928 the DNVP lost 31 per cent
of its voters to the NSDAP, among the non-voters it was 14 per cent, among
liberal voters it was 26 per cent, and among SPD voters it was 10 per cent.
Analysis of these changes of allegiance indicates that the most important
movements of voters were from the conservative and liberal parties to the
NSDAP.[83] These parties suffered correspondingly large losses. The right-
wing conservative DNVP's share of the vote dropped from 14.2 per cent to
7 per cent, the right-wing liberal DVP's from 8.7 per cent to 4.7 per cent.
Only the left liberal DDP, renamed from that summer the German State
Party (DStP), escaped with relatively little damage, securing 3.8 per cent as
against 4.7 per cent in 1928. The SPD achieved only 24.5 per cent as against
29.8 per cent, while on the other hand the KPD managed to increase its
share from 10.3 per cent to 13.1 per cent and the Catholic parties, namely
the Centre and the Bavarian BVP, maintained their support with 14.8 per
cent (as against 15.2 per cent in 1928). The remaining parties (splinter groups
from the DNVP and a miscellany of groupings representing regional, agricultural, and small business interests) together gained an almost unchanged
share at 13.8 per cent. At the next elections these splinter parties would
prove to be one of the essential reservoirs of voters for the NSDAP.

The psephologists in Falter's team also brought to light a series of trends that were to become typical of the NSDAP's electoral successes in the years to come. Men voted NSDAP significantly more than women, and even more striking were confessional differences. The probability that a Protestant would vote NSDAP was twice as high in 1930 as for a Catholic. Catholic voters were remarkably resistant to the temptations of National Socialism.[84] Admittedly, at most only half of German Catholics (in 1930 making up about a third of the total population) still had strong ties to the Catholic Church and thus an overwhelmingly negative attitude to the Party. Those Catholics who had no strong Church ties were much more open to the Nazi movement.[85] A quarter of Nazi voters came from the working class and 40 per cent from the middle class (the population as a whole was made up roughly of the same proportions). In particular, members of the 'old middle classes' – small independent retailers, artisans, and farmers – were more likely to support the NSDAP, whereas white collar workers and civil servants developed no greater liking for the NSDAP than was the average for the population as a whole.[86] As far as the working class was concerned, the Party most likely appealed above all to craft apprentices, agricultural workers, workers in small businesses and in the service sector, and less to industrial workers, who continued to form the bedrock of the parties of the Left. Leaving aside these refinements, this analysis demonstrates that the NSDAP was the only party in Germany that was attractive to people from all social classes, and to both Protestants and Catholics. To that extent it really was a people's party.

As far as the Party's core areas in the regions were concerned, in 1930 it was above all the constituencies in the more rural and predominantly Protestant provinces, as well as the smaller, independent states in northern Germany that produced a disproportionately large vote (over 20 per cent) for the NSDAP: East Prussia, Pomerania, Hanover, Schleswig-Holstein (where the Party's 27 per cent was its best result), Brunswick, and Oldenburg. The Party was equally successful in Protestant Lower Silesia (although, significantly, not in Catholic Upper Silesia, where it achieved only 9.5 per cent) and in other predominantly Protestant regions such as the Bavarian Palatinate, the Prussian province of Hesse-Nassau, the Prussian district of Merseburg, and the Saxon constituency of Chemnitz-Zwickau. The Party's performance was also above average in Franconia, although not in Catholic Lower Franconia.

The question of what political motives influenced these voters is harder to answer. First of all, the link to the economic crisis that began in 1929/30 is undeniable. Here the mass of voters turning to the NSDAP must be seen less as the direct consequence of economic misery than as a reaction to the absence of any active measures to tackle the crisis on the part of the government and to the praxis of the presidential system: the government was no longer firmly anchored in parliament and it marched into the crisis without attempting to include broad sections of the electorate in its policies. The inevitable results were a loss of confidence in the political system and a widespread collapse of social cohesion. A crucial factor in this is that the massive support for the NSDAP was mainly drawn from sections of the population that, as a result of the erosion of the liberal and conservative milieus in the 1920s, had already lost their connection with particular parties and their social world and were in search of a new political direction. The hostility of the conservative DNVP towards democracy and the scepticism with which it was regarded by the nationalist liberal DVP made it easier for their supporters to make the transition from a moderate right-wing stance to an extreme right-wing one. Fundamental beliefs such as nationalism, militarism, hatred of socialism, and anti-Semitism, which were shared by all parties of the Right, acted in this process of radicalization as a bridge to the extreme Right camp. A further factor was that, by contrast with other extreme Right groups, the NSDAP was able to make a broad offer to the masses flocking to it. That was true ideologically as well as organizationally. The NSDAP was not only a political party but in the shape of the SA and SS it had its own paramilitary organizations, while its numerous specialized affiliated groups offered alternatives to the organizations and associations representing particular interests that were losing significance in this crisis period. As the 1930s began, the Party was creating a dense network of organizations and a high level of local activity, such that it was taking over the functions of the traditional German clubs and associations and was able to build up structures that absorbed and retained many 'refugee' voters from the former liberal and conservative milieus. If one attempted to explain the mass movement of voters to the NSDAP in terms of the social history of politics, one might speak of a change of milieu affecting above all the middle classes.

In this extreme right-wing Nazi milieu that developed rapidly and extensively in the early 1930s the idea of subordination to a commanding leader ('Führer') figure was widespread. Indeed, it was probably essential to the cohesiveness of the whole, not only because so many adherents looked obsessively for authority figures, hoping for 'redemption' through a saviour, but above all because the 'Führer' with his 'vision' had to hold things together in spite of irresolvable contradictions. Hitler was now confronted with the complicated task of living up to the high expectations of his supporters, while avoiding being completely imprisoned by this role. What he needed to achieve was rather the maximum scope for political action.

The first event immediately after the great electoral successes, however, was a high-profile trial heard before the Supreme Court in Leipzig that promised to shed light on the future stance of the NSDAP. Three army officers stationed at Ulm had attempted to form a Nazi cell within the army and were now accused of high treason. To clarify the NSDAP's attitude towards the Republic and its constitution, the court had summoned leading Nazis as witnesses.

Hitler, who after all had already been convicted of treason himself, had been brought in as a witness by the defence attorney, the Nazi Hans Frank, to convince the court that the NSDAP aimed to acquire power only by 'legal' means. When he was called, Hitler at first spoke at length, as he usually did, on the subject of the founding and early development of the Party, as though he was making one of his popular speeches. In particular, he tried to persuade the court that in the attempted putsch of November 1923 he had been in a dilemma and did his best to portray himself with hindsight as the victim of a complex power struggle. He explained that he had not been responsible for the move to build up the SA into a fighting force, but rather it had been 'initiated by official agencies'. In the final analysis, he said, the conflict in the autumn of 1923 was about 'whether it [would be] a struggle under the Bavarian flag against the Reich government or under the banner of Greater Germany'. In this dilemma he had been 'forced into deciding to fight for Greater Germany'. In 1925, however, he had realized 'that the transitional period of 1923 had come to a complete end and that the movement had to be brought back to its original fundamental purposes'. He had done everything possible, he claimed, to demilitarize the SA. In the course of his testimony Hitler grew increasingly fired up, so that in the end the chair of the judges, Alexander Baumgarten, pointed out that he was 'beginning to give a propaganda speech' and should calm down. When asked to comment on 'revolutionary' tendencies in the present NSDAP, Hitler distanced himself from Otto Strasser and his associates and explained that Strasser had recently left the Party.

The chairman confronted Hitler with various quotations from the *Nationalsozialistische Briefe* that expressed support for a Nazi revolution.

Below them was a statement attributed to Hitler: 'Adolf Hitler leaves us in no doubt as to the ferocity of the battle when he says: "In this struggle heads will roll in the sand, whether ours or others'. So let's make sure it's the others'.'" Hitler insisted that the author had surely 'been referring to the great intellectual revolution we find ourselves in today. But I can assure you that if our movement is victorious in its lawful struggle, there will be a German State Court, November 1918 will be avenged, and heads will roll.' The National Socialist movement, Hitler continued, 'will seek to achieve its aim in this state by constitutional means. The constitution prescribes only the methods but not the goal. We shall seek to take the constitutional path by gaining decisive majorities in legislative bodies, in order, as soon as we succeed in this, to pour the state into the mould shaped by our ideas.'[87]

Soundings

The trial attracted attention because, after his electoral success, Hitler found himself at a stroke in a key political position. He now began to test the waters to see whether and under what conditions it might be possible to participate in the government. The best chance would be to form part of a Reich government led by the Centre Party. For Hitler two things were at stake: the Centre Party not only provided the Reich Chancellor, now backed by the President, but also shared in the government of Prussia, by far the largest state, under the Social Democrat prime minister, Otto Braun. Hitler, therefore, aimed to achieve a comprehensive deal with the Centre, involving both the Reich and the Prussian governments. On a visit to Berlin in September he spelt out his demands to Goebbels: Foreign Office, Reich Interior Ministry, and Reich Defence Ministry for Rosenberg, Frick, and von Epp and, in addition, the Centre had to abandon the coalition government in Prussia. If this were to happen, Goebbels noted, he would 'provisionally gain power in Prussia', which suggests that, in the event of cooperation between the NSDAP and the Centre Party, Hitler may have raised the prospect of his becoming Minister of the Interior (or even Prime Minister?) of Prussia.[88]

On 29 September Hitler held a two-hour meeting with the former Chancellor and Hamburg shipping magnate Wilhelm Cuno in the Hotel Esplanade in Berlin. Among those present were Göring, retired Rear Admiral Magnus von Levetzow, who played an important role in the right-wing conservative scene as the former Kaiser's go-between in the Reich and who had arranged the meeting, and retired General Rüdiger von der Goltz, the leader of the United Fatherland Associations. This group of ultra-conservative politicians wanted to find out if the NSDAP would support Cuno's candidacy for the office of Reich President in the elections due in 1932. Hitler delivered a lengthy monologue setting out his foreign policy goals, in particular: 'An end to Stresemann's policy of rapprochement with France', and instead rapprochement with Italy and 'via Italy with England'. He wished also to adopt a hostile stance 'to France's satrap Poland with the aim of regaining the Corridor and Upper Silesia'. As the status quo of 1914 could not be restored at the moment, he said, the immediate political aim should be the 'restoration of the eastern border'. Young Plan payments should cease, as France would not respond militarily. With regard to Hitler's ideas on domestic policy Levetzow noted: 'The most radical break with the present democratic system.' He noted also that Hitler had said emphatically: 'No measures to be taken against Jewish people as such but an end to Jewish dominance in the state.' As far as support for his candidacy for the office of Reich President was concerned, however, Cuno was no further forward. The following day Göring signalled to Levetzow that the NSDAP could see itself presenting Cuno for that office; it was, he said, more probable, however, that Brüning would offer the National Socialists two ministerial posts, to which they would respond by demanding the Reich Interior Ministry, the Defence Ministry, and the office of Prussian Prime Minister (there was no more mention of the Foreign Office). For his part, Cuno wondered if it would not be better to support Hitler as candidate for the Reich Presidency instead of making himself dependent on Hitler.[89] Although in the ensuing months Levetzow, Göring, and Cuno continued to pursue the idea of a Cuno candidacy for the highest office, the following year the plan was dropped, above all, evidently, because soundings among the other right-wing parties did not progress. On the evening of 29 September, in other words on the same day he had met with Cuno, Hitler was a guest at Göring's home, where Göring introduced him to Frau von Dirksen, who had an influential salon in Berlin, as well as to the head of Deutsche Bank, Emil Georg von Stauss, a DVP Reichstag deputy. Thus Hitler was now considered socially acceptable in Berlin.[90]

On 5 October Hitler, accompanied by Frick and Strasser, discussed with Chancellor Brüning the general situation after the election. To ensure the meeting was confidential it was held in the apartment of Gottfried Treviranus, minister without portfolio in Brüning's cabinet. According to his own account, Brüning expounded to the Nazi delegation the core elements of his future policy: The economic crisis should be used to get rid of reparations; the precondition for this would be an international disarmament agreement. Brüning emphasized that the NSDAP's fierce opposition to his foreign policy would chime in well with his plans and suggested that he would reach detailed agreement with the NSDAP on the form this opposition would take. In other words, by colluding behind the scenes, the NSDAP would form an integral part of his government's policy. Hitler's response was at first reserved, even 'shy' and 'hesitant', as Brüning recalled it, but then it quickly rose to a crescendo, a two-hour tirade in which there was one main theme, namely the annihilation of all enemies of National Socialism. That meant the SPD and KPD at home, followed by France and the Soviet Union. Hitler did not even engage with Brüning's remarks but merely declared himself prepared to have three ministers in the latter's government, but without committing himself to any future course of action. Brüning ignored this request and instead offered the NSDAP the prospect of forming coalitions with the Centre Party in those state parliaments where they had a combined majority.[91] After the talks Hitler told Goebbels he was convinced that he had 'hugely impressed' Brüning.[92] For his part, Goebbels hoped that the break-up of the coalition in Prussia would mean 'my hour' would come.[93]

As Brüning would not countenance a coalition with the NSDAP and there was no possibility of a grand coalition because of Hindenburg's refusal to accept SPD members in the cabinet, the Reich Chancellor continued in government propped up by the President's emergency decrees. He had, however, to ensure that his government retained a majority in parliament, in other words that the Reichstag would not use its constitutional veto against the President's emergency decrees. In the end the Social Democrats were prepared to accept this, on the one hand so that Brüning would not become totally dependent on the parties of the Right, and, on the other hand, so that its coalition with the Centre would hold in Prussia. In October Brüning even succeeded in gaining the Social Democrats' consent to a law on amortization of debt and in recessing parliament until the beginning of December.[94] In the course of 1931 the Social Democrats agreed further generous parliamentary recesses, thus giving the government some cover. For example, in March 1931, in particular, the Reichstag was sent on a Reich 'summer recess' that lasted until October.[95]

Meanwhile, Brüning was handling the NSDAP with care. In October the cabinet refused the demand made by Joseph Wirth, the Interior Minister, for police funds for the state of Brunswick, where since September the Interior Minister had been a member of the NSDAP, to be curtailed. In December Brüning declared himself in favour of Nazis no longer being banned, as they had been up to this point, from the armed services and of Party members no longer being excluded from the volunteer border service.[96]

German business was also affected by the NSDAP's startling electoral success. Interest in the Party grew, as did donations, even if the amount of support was still comparatively modest. Big industrial concerns and other economically significant groups directed their funds primarily towards the bourgeois parties of the Right, namely the DVP and the DNVP, whereas the NSDAP still covered its costs first and foremost by means of membership dues, donations, and other monies contributed by its own members.[97] From the point of view of business the NSDAP was not an ideal representative of its interests, as the Party showed no willingness to adopt the standpoint of business in its public pronouncements. On the contrary, the NSDAP even introduced a wide range of rabble-rousing 'anti-capitalist' motions in the new Reichstag, among them the nationalization of the major banks, a ban on bond trading, and a capping of interest rates.[98] In addition, in autumn 1930 the Party supported the Berlin metal workers' strike.[99] Hitler's refusal to support the Saxon metal workers' strike a few months previously had provoked Otto Strasser to leave the Party, and Hitler's comments were ambiguous: in the *Illustrierter Beobachter* he expressed sympathy for the workers' standpoint, but also warned against any escalation of the strike.[100] This ambivalence was typical of his statements on economic matters. He wished neither to alienate the business world nor to fan the flames of the Party's social demagoguery, but neither did he want to turn his back publicly on the workers.

The selection of Gottfried Feder to represent the NSDAP's views in the budget debate in December 1930 makes clear once again that, in spite of the departure of the 'socialists' surrounding Otto Strasser, the NSDAP was not prepared to abandon its populist 'anti-capitalist' stance. This became apparent also when in December the Party twice voted in favour of KPD motions to raise significantly the state and social security payments to the unemployed. At the same time, articles appeared in the *Völkischer Beobachter* also emphasizing the NSDAP's 'left-wing' stance.[101]

When, however, on 1 December 1930, Hitler took the opportunity of again addressing leading business figures at the renowned Hamburg National

Club (an invitation he owed to his dealings with Cuno in September), his audience was hoping to hear the very opposite, namely that Hitler distanced himself from the 'anti-capitalist' views of his Party. Hitler began with a depressing description of economic developments since the end of the war before arriving at the central argument of his speech: 'Political power cannot be regained by economic means, but only through struggle. The nation's vital strength must be utilized to preserve the state. The economy and business can exist only when protected by a strong state.' It was, he said, 'madness for Germany to starve when on its borders indolent nations leave vast territories unused. If we want these territories we can get them only through the law of might is right.' That was certainly a very clear signal of his intention to take territory from other nations by force. The preconditions for this, however, were, he said, national reconciliation at home, which only the NSDAP could bring about, and the abandonment of 'internationalism', of 'democratic rule', and of 'pacifism'. For as far as foreign policy was concerned, the world could not 'be won through ideas of reconciliation, but rather the watchwords are: Seek, find, and fight to gain what is ours by right.' The speech ended with a storm of applause from those present.[102] Hitler's argument about the primacy of politics had allowed him to avoid making any concrete economic statements.

While Göring was working to dispel any misgivings on the part of industry about the NSDAP's 'socialist' direction, Hitler went on extending his contacts in the business world, although he was far from making any kind of 'breakthrough' there. At the home of the coal magnate Emil Kirdorf, presumably at the end of November 1930, Hitler met a number of Ruhr industrialists, among them Ernst Poensgen, the head of United Steel. The only account of this meeting comes from Poensgen, who claims he approached Hitler candidly and stressed that industry supported Brüning.[103] In January 1931, at Göring's home and in the presence of Fritz Thyssen, another heavy industrialist sympathetic to the NSDAP, Hitler had a meeting with Hjalmar Schacht, who had resigned in March 1930 as head of the Reich Bank in protest at the acceptance of the Young Plan and, though formerly a liberal, was moving increasingly to the right. Schacht gained a positive impression of Hitler, although in public he remained reserved.[104] Otto Wagener, who since January 1931 had been in charge of the economics department in the Brown House, reports in his memoirs that there were further contacts with business in the early months of 1931, among them with Emil von Stauss, the head of Deutsche Bank.[105]

From Hitler's point of view, however, these contacts with business in the aftermath of his big electoral success were in danger of becoming obsolete, when demands were again being heard within the Party for its economic statements to contain more details. Goebbels had already argued for more concrete statements in his paper, *Der Angriff*, at the end of September. In October he followed this up. The 1920 Party programme, which had referred in general terms to 'profit-sharing in large firms' and 'agricultural reform', was, he wrote, only the 'bare bones' and needed urgently to be fleshed out. Leading Party comrades (and not, for example the leader in isolation) should clarify the evident problems through discussion.[106] That sounded suspiciously like a repeat of the discussion of the programme that Strasser, Goebbels, and others had attempted to bring about in 1925/26. Goebbels's initiative may have been prompted by the fact that, from the end of 1929 onwards, preparatory work had been under way on the Party's economic policy from which Goebbels had been excluded.[107]

Hitler disliked collective deliberations as much as he did precise programme statements and ultimately regarded his Party's economic statements primarily from a tactical point of view. From this standpoint it seemed to him of overriding importance not to alienate those business and industrial circles that had begun to support the Party or at least to show some interest in it. For that reason in January 1931 he set up the aforementioned economics department under Otto Wagener, up to this point SA chief of staff, so that in competition with other Party offices it would generate an economic plan free from demands for overly 'socialist' experiments.[108]

What was meant by that was demonstrated, for example, by a consultation on 16 and 17 February 1931. When Wagener brought up the issue of a minimum wage Hitler criticized it as the 'intellectual justification for communism' and then in a lengthy exposition developed principles for the 'calculation of wages based on the value of a person's contribution to the community'. The notes that compose the minutes of the meeting contain the following statements by Hitler: 'Healthy people for the national community's struggle only from healthy parents'; 'people unequal in value'; 'Having many children must not be a disadvantage'; single people were on principle to receive 'very limited' remuneration.[109] Hitler in other words exploited a discussion about 'equitable' wages to expand on his views on biology and the nation. Later in the proceedings he spoke out against 'collectivism' in business and put the case instead for free enterprise: 'A guy who makes a lot of money, even if he is ruthless, is always starting up new things, taking risks etc.

Not harmful!' In connection with this Hitler mentioned Thyssen, his old acquaintance Bechstein, and Ford as models. When the issue of unemployment was broached Hitler immediately steered discussion onto familiar territory: 'Overpopulation. Shortage of land.' The problem cried out for a solution: 'If our space is not expanded, we are exposed militarily to any attack. Situation increasingly critical without expansion.' 'Health' will in any case be restored only if a ratio of '70% to 30%' is created between those working in agriculture and those in industry.[110] These economic meetings conducted by the Party leaders under Hitler's chairmanship were continued during the following months. Unlike Wagener, Gregor Strasser, Hierl, Rosenberg, Pfeffer, and Feder, Goebbels, significantly, was still being excluded.[111]

In March 1931 Hierl presented a paper he had written with Wagener in which a private enterprise economy was proposed under the 'state's overarching control of the economy through planning'. Goebbels was positively horrified ('No trace of socialism left') and wrote a fiercely critical appraisal,[112] but concerns were also voiced by big business, which got hold of the unpublished memorandum.[113] A pamphlet published in 1931 and written by Hans Reupke, who worked for the Reich Association of German Industry and was a secret sympathizer of the NSDAP, was designed to dispel these doubts. In it Reupke the insider explained that all earlier proposals from the NSDAP that pointed to the nationalization of businesses had in the meantime become obsolete.[114] In Goebbels's view the work was a 'bare-faced betrayal of socialism',[115] but after the Völkischer Beobachter carried a negative review[116] and a few days later Hitler distanced himself from Reupke in a conversation with Goebbels, the latter was reassured.[117]

This patent confusion about the NSDAP's future economic plans appears to have been systematically created by Hitler himself. For in these debates the Party leader was concerned above all with one thing: He wanted at all costs to prevent 'anti-capitalist' slogans of the kind repeatedly used by Goebbels and others from blocking his access to big business and the big banks. Whatever his economic experts advised was kept under wraps. In November 1931 Hitler ordered Wagener's department to set up an 'Economic Council' chaired by Gottfried Feder. Its task was to vet official Party statements on economic policy before publication.[118] When in April 1932 the council blocked the publication of economic articles even by Wagener himself, he used this as an excuse to resign his office. In the meantime his position had in any case become precarious as a result of the arrival of Hitler's new economic adviser Wilhelm Keppler. The attempt to pin the Party leader down to specific economic objectives had failed; the Economic Council had completed the task for which it was created and after little more than a year it was dissolved.[119]

Hitler's policy of legality on trial

In addition to the arguments concerning the Party's economic statements, after the September Reichstag elections it was above all the clashes between the Party and the SA that were building up to a final confrontation. At first Hitler attempted to bring this source of conflict under control by an idiosyncratic staffing decision.

The future relationship between the SA and the Party organization was the subject of a leaders' meeting that Hitler held in Munich on 30 November 1930. He responded to the confident demands of the SA leaders for more influence in the movement as a whole by the surprise introduction of Ernst Röhm as the future SA chief, leaving it open for the time being whether he intended to appoint the retired captain as supreme leader of the SA or as its chief of staff. In Hitler's view Röhm had the advantage of having spent the previous few years as a military instructor in Bolivia and thus of not being involved in the conflicts among the various Party cliques. This coup was not unproblematic, however. He had after all broken with Röhm in 1925 after they had found it impossible to reach agreement about the incorporation of the Frontbann, the organization set up in place of the banned SA, into the NSDAP, and Röhm had not relinquished his idea of the primacy of the 'soldier' over the 'politician', as was revealed in the autobiography, *Geschichte eines Hochverräters* [History of a Traitor], that he published in 1928. The issue of the future role of the SA, whether as a predominantly independent paramilitary organization or as quasi-military aid for the Party, was therefore completely unclear. In November 1930, however, Hitler's main concern was to promote a man who enjoyed authority inside the SA leadership corps, whose members like Röhm were mostly former officers. Apart from this, Röhm had proved his worth before the November putsch in 1923 at the interface of the army and paramilitary organizations and thus seemed the right man to impress on the Reich Defence Ministry the 'defence' importance of the SA and thus to engender an overall positive attitude to the NSDAP within the Defence Ministry.[120] At the beginning of January 1931, however, only a few weeks after Röhm had taken up his post, Hitler felt obliged to comment on discussions in the Party and the SA prompted by Röhm's widely known homosexuality. Without addressing the accusations in detail Hitler spoke out against 'attacks on the private life' of individual SA leaders. After all, the SA was 'not a moral institution for the education of the daughters of the nobility but an association of rough fighters'.[121]

As far as Hitler was concerned there were other conflicts connected with the SA that he took more seriously. In February and March he had cause to warn the SA several times about acts of excessive violence. In doing so he gave the impression that the violence was being introduced into the SA from outside. In the *Völkischer Beobachter* on 18 February, for example, he aimed to warn SA members 'against provocateurs . . . , who are sent into our ranks and try every means of forcing the SA into the role of aggressor, in order to provide the present regime with legitimate reasons for persecuting our movement'.[122] He took a similar line in a speech on 7 March 1931 at an SA rally in Munich, saying he would not let spies and provocateurs goad him into 'marching the SA into the machine guns'.[123] When at the end of March the Reich President issued an emergency decree restricting the right to demonstrate and the propaganda of political parties, the SA was being particularly targeted and this fuelled discontent in the organization with the 'lawful' route to power advocated by the Party leadership. In Berlin Goebbels was already worried that the undiminished activism of Stennes and his fellow SA leaders might lead to the Party being banned.[124] In the *Völkischer Beobachter* Hitler issued another warning that members of the SA must keep 'strictly to the path of legality'.[125]

Hitler brought Party leaders together in Weimar on 1 April, the day on which the first Nazi minister, Wilhelm Frick, was removed from office by the Thuringian state parliament. Although Stennes was fired at that meeting, as SA boss in East Germany he had not been idle. He had gone onto the counterattack and had ordered the SA to occupy the Party offices in Berlin and the editorial office of *Der Angriff*. The front page of the 1 April edition of *Der Angriff* carried a large-format declaration by Stennes.[126]

During the night of 1/2 April Hitler returned to Munich with Goebbels to put down the 'putsch' from there.[127] The *Völkischer Beobachter* published a decree from Hitler empowering Goebbels, as he had done in 1926, 'once more to carry out and complete a thorough purging of the movement'.[128] Goebbels made use of the special powers invested in him to exclude the 'traitors' from the Party. From 4 April *Der Angriff* was back under his complete control: He made the headline of that number 'Mutineers' faction destroyed' and next to it printed a call from Hitler to the Party comrades. The same day Hitler published a 'Final Reckoning with the Rebels' in the *Völkischer Beobachter* in which he gathered together various accusations against Stennes from a wide range of sources. Amongst other topics he defended the acquisition and extension of the Brown House in Munich, a move that Stennes had inveighed against. He would 'ensure that a memorial will be set to our comrades in the struggle today that will be seen in the decades, indeed in the centuries, to come!' He emphasized once again the Party's 'strict legality' and thundered that he would not let anyone 'make him an oath-breaker, least of all retired Police Captain Stennes'.[129] Once again he announced there would be a 'thorough purging of the Party of all unreliable elements'[130] and on 8 April in the same publication he claimed he would 'neither slumber nor sleep until this poison is utterly and completely eradicated from our movement'.[131] Absolute 'loyalty' was the leitmotiv of two speeches he made during the following days to the SA,[132] and on 21 April he decreed that, as a further consequence of the Stennes affair, a 'General Inspectorate' would be created within SA headquarters to support 'the development of the SA and SS in accordance with one set of agreed guidelines through personal contact and inspection'.[133]

Goebbels, who had just about stood loyally by Hitler, took the opportunity to make another attempt to influence policy. Following a leaders' conference in Munich at the end of April, at which propaganda and organizational issues were discussed, he pressed Hitler in private to make the Party 'more Prussian, more active and more socialist'. According to Goebbels's account Hitler had 'tactical misgivings' but agreed with his propaganda chief that he should devote 'more attention to the matter of socialism'. Goebbels was not satisfied, however,[134] and during the following weeks made critical comments on the Party leader in his diaries.[135] Meanwhile in May another conflict was brewing, for a public statement Goebbels had issued some years previously was threatening to land Hitler in considerable difficulties.[136]

In the so-called Stennes trial in Berlin members of the notorious SA-Sturm 33 were accused of attempted murder. The joint plaintiff (the lawyer Hans Litten was representing four workers injured by the SA in the attack) was now claiming that the SA's assaults were part of a strategy and that those responsible were the leaders of the SA and the Party. Stennes had been head of the SA in East Germany at the time of the incidents, although he had since been removed from his post. He and Hitler were summoned as witnesses.

Stennes adopted a surprisingly loyal stance towards the leaders of his former party and testified that in his day the NSDAP had stuck strictly to
legality. Then Hitler was forced to undergo a cross-examination lasting several hours by Litten, who was very well briefed. Litten was not satisfied with
the diffuse explanations Hitler used to reaffirm his 'lawful' course of action
but rather presented him with a passage from Goebbels's pamphlet *Der
Nazi-Sozi* that stated that the Nazis wanted 'revolution': 'Then we shall
boot out parliament and establish the state on the strength of German
fists and German grit!'[137] Litten's cross-examination visibly unsettled
Hitler. He could not remember, he said, whether he had been aware of
Goebbels's publication when he was appointed as Reich head of propaganda. Furthermore, it had not been 'officially sanctioned'. Goebbels was in
any case obliged to 'stick to the guidelines I give him as Party leader' and it
was well known that he insisted on the Party taking a lawful path. Litten
finally asked Hitler the provocative question whether he had 'promised
Reich Chancellor Brüning to dissolve the SA if the Party should join the
government'. Hitler challenged this accusation and became very worked up.
The suggestion that he would 'dissolve the SA in order to join a government would be tantamount to offering to commit suicide himself or for the
Party to commit suicide'.[138] That evening, when they were sitting together
in the Kaiserhof, Goebbels remembered that he had cut the dubious passage
out of the second, updated edition,[139] thus removing any risk that he could
be called as a prosecution witness against Hitler's claims to be pursuing a
lawful course.

This episode demonstrates how very precarious this course was and how
little Hitler told those closest to him about his 'true' intentions.

In the spotlight

It was evident that there was extreme and irreconcilable tension between
Hitler's ostensible pursuit of 'lawful' tactics in his policy of rapprochement
with the moderate Right and the SA's activism and demands for a more
'socialist' Party profile. Hitler coped with this internal Party conflict by not
permitting any more opposition in the NSDAP to him as 'Führer' and by
instead ensuring that potential opponents wore each other out. Thus
Goebbels, who had strong reservations about Hitler's path, the Strasser
brothers, and also the 'revolutionary' elements within the SA could not, as

we have seen, come together to create a united front, but rather spent most of their time fighting each other. A central component of this style of leadership was a policy of extreme personalization, through which Hitler could nip in the bud any internal Party structures that might limit his power to define what was good for the Party. To avoid the emergence of leadership by committee, he adopted a system in which he allocated tasks in the Party leadership to particular trusted people, both individually and in specific combinations, while simultaneously ensuring that an atmosphere of rivalry, indeed of suspicion, was dominant among them. Six men in particular were significant in this regard: Gregor Strasser as head of the Reich Party organization; Wilhelm Frick as leader of the Party in the Reichstag and figurehead in the NSDAP's first coalition government in Thuringia; Ernst Röhm as SA chief of staff; Hermann Göring as the go-between with German nationalist, arch-conservative, and business circles in Berlin; Alfred Rosenberg as the Party's chief ideologue and editor-in-chief of the Party organ, the *Völkischer Beobachter*, and Joseph Goebbels as Gauleiter in the capital and Reich propaganda chief. As Hitler continued to make all essential decisions himself, while communicating them only hesitantly and in careful stages, those around him were, as described, kept in a state of permanent anxiety and bewilderment about what aims and strategies the Party leader was actually pursuing. The situation was only made more difficult by the fact that these 'solo decisions' could turn out to be bafflingly flexible, while Hitler was being simultaneously inflexible in other matters.

Yet Hitler's unique position in the Party, his stance as one who tried to keep out of internal Party wranglings and arguments about policy, reserving for himself the function of ultimate arbiter, his remoteness, his unpredictability, and his air of being a 'visionary', in short his position as 'charismatic leader', were first and foremost important to the NSDAP's active members, the diehard Nazis. Now that the Party was turning into a mass movement, however, the majority of its supporters consisted of protest voters who were not already under Hitler's 'spell'. The NSDAP's election propaganda was aimed primarily at this audience and supported above all by unrestrained agitation against the Weimar 'system' and by wide-ranging promises directed at the various different groups of voters rather than by propaganda focusing on Hitler personally as a 'saviour' figure. In other words, Hitler had to perform a balancing act between the role of the charismatic Party leader who stood above the action and the demands being placed on him as a politician who had to gain power by one means or another on behalf of a rapidly growing movement, before it was destroyed by its own inner contradictions.

These demands placed on Hitler's so carefully created public persona also had an impact on his life as a private individual, in so far as one can speak of such a thing. For from his standpoint, as we have seen, no area of his life was truly 'private'. Now that he considered himself to be on the way to becoming a 'statesman', he modified his circumstances to correspond to how he imagined his new role. He adopted a grander lifestyle, habitually staying in first-class hotels, and made his home in the luxurious nine-room Munich flat he had moved into in 1929 and which he shared with Geli Raubal. As early as 1923 his connection with the Bechsteins had brought him into the exclusive Wagner circle in Bayreuth, where he was a guest at the Wagners' home and had a particularly close relationship with Winifred Wagner, who was widowed in 1930 and as head of the Wagner Festival continued to maintain his idol's musical legacy.[140] He now no longer found himself periodically short of money. As he became better known, sales of *Mein Kampf* increased, and the income he declared to the tax office increased threefold from 1929 to 1930 to 48,000 RM, rising further in the following years.[141] Hitler was now in a position to give himself bohemian airs, but also live in comfort. The same was true of his relationships with women.

As already described, in the 1920s Hitler cultivated acquaintanceships with young, still rather childlike, girls who looked up to him and admired him. Since 1927 his niece Geli Raubal had been his constant companion. Although at first the rumour that his niece was also his lover boosted his self-presentation as a genius who came from nowhere, it was likely to be a positive hindrance to his planned elevation to the highest offices of state. Marriage, however, or even a deep and lasting relationship that could offer him some respite from politics was something he could not imagine. Then, in the summer of 1931, a new situation arose.

On one of his visits to Berlin Goebbels introduced Hitler to Magda Quandt, a confident, educated, and cultivated woman of 29, who had been living an independent life since her divorce from the industrialist Herbert Quandt. To Goebbels Hitler expressed the view that Magda was 'fabulous', as Goebbels noted, and he enjoyed the hospitality she offered him and his entourage. They had been invited to lunch but Hitler stayed on into the evening at her comfortable home on Reichkanzlerplatz in Berlin-Charlottenburg and the next day he was there again with his whole entourage. Goebbels, who had evidently not told Hitler that he and Magda had been having a relationship for several months,[142] became jealous when he heard about these meetings and Hitler's attentions: 'Magda has been behaving in a rather unladylike way with the boss. I'm very upset about it. She's not quite a lady.' Goebbels clearly blamed Magda for the situation: 'I don't mind the boss enjoying a bit of affection and charm, though. He gets so little of it.' The ensuing quarrel with Magda was so violent that for a while at the end of August the relationship was in the balance.[143]

At the beginning of September, while Goebbels was away on a trip, Hitler again visited Magda. Goebbels's impression was that he had simply 'invited himself for a meal'. 'Agonizing jealousy' kept Goebbels awake that night and he decided that Magda had to tell Hitler 'how things stand between us'.[144] Even so, the same situation occurred a few days later, when Goebbels was again away. A phone call to Magda late one evening interrupted a conversation she was having with Hitler. Back in Berlin, he learnt more details about that evening's conversation. After it Magda declared to Hitler that she wanted to marry Goebbels, at which Hitler was 'devastated'. 'But he's standing by me, and Magda is too.' Goebbels's conclusion was: 'Hitler is resigned. He's so lonely. He has no luck with women. He's too soft. Women don't like that. They have to feel a man is a master over them.'[145] When he discussed the matter with Hitler on a visit to Munich two days later, Hitler was 'very sweet to me. A friend and a brother. I'm the lucky winner, he says. He loves Magda, but he's happy to see me happy. "An intelligent and beautiful woman. She will not get in your way but will further your career." He clasped both my hands with tears in his eyes. All the best! . . . We're to marry right away.' They pledged for the future: 'All three of us will be good to each other. He intends to be our most loyal friend.'[146]

These speedy wedding plans may well have taken Goebbels somewhat by surprise, for up to this point he and Magda had agreed not to marry until after the 'seizure of power'. During his absence, Magda and Hitler seem to have come to an arrangement. The engagement took place at the end of October and it was Hitler who enabled Goebbels to give Magda an expensive engagement present, an exquisite sports car financed by the manufacturer being given free advertising in the *Völkischer Beobachter* on Hitler's instructions.[147] The wedding took place less than two months later. Hitler was of course the best man.

The suggestion that Hitler's interest in Magda Quandt caused him to push for the marriage to Goebbels is supported not only by Goebbels's own diaries but also by a second account, which, although there are one or two

discrepancies in the time sequence, nevertheless concurs fully with what
Goebbels reports. It comes from Otto Wagener, at that time Hitler's close
confidant, who writes that Hitler became aware of Magda but was disappointed to discover she was in a relationship with Goebbels. In discussion
with Wagener Hitler then developed the idea of creating a close and confidential friendship with Magda because in his work she could 'act as the female
opposite pole to my one-sided male instincts'. Hitler hinted that he considered
it an advantage for Magda to be married. Wagener soon had an opportunity
of presenting this idea to Magda. Hitler, he told her, simply needed someone
who could bring him back to earth from his grandiose schemes and 'show
him everyday life', someone who would go with him to the theatre, the opera
or to concerts and spend some time talking to him afterwards. In short, he
needed a woman who would 'make him human'. According to Wagener,
Magda had understood this line of argument at once and had declared for her
part that in such a situation she would have to be married. The next step was
for Wagener to suggest that she and Goebbels marry soon. After reflecting on
this for a time both said they were happy to do so.[148]

The arrangement agreed by Hitler, Magda Quandt, and Goebbels can
certainly be described as a triangular relationship. For Hitler it had great
advantages, as it fitted in with his self-perception as a public figure without
a significant 'private' life. He could enjoy a close relationship with a woman
he admired without entering into an actual commitment. In addition, he
had found a woman with whom he could engage in conversation, one
whose social skills and good taste would be useful to him, and who could
fit into the role of First Lady of the National Socialist movement. Magda
was to become accustomed to visiting Hitler without her husband, receiving him at home on her own, travelling with him or, in later years, spending
a few days, occasionally with her children, on the Obersalzberg. As Magda
was married, the relationship acquired a veneer of respectability and boundaries were established that Hitler was only too ready to accept, having
excluded the possibility of marriage for himself and having, as we may safely
assume, no interest in a sexual relationship. Hitler became not only a close
friend of the Goebbelses but was treated as a member of the family, which
grew quickly during the following years. For his part, he regarded the
Goebbels children, who were all given names beginning with the letter H,
as his special favourites. Thus Hitler was able to experience some kind of
family life without any ties or obligations, and that was exactly how he
wanted it. For Goebbels and Magda too this extensive opening up of their

married life to Hitler brought rewards: Goebbels could hope through Magda to exercise undreamt of influence on Hitler, whom he idolized, and the ambitious Magda had the opportunity to take pride of place close to the man she admired hugely and whom she regarded as Germany's rising star.

This arrangement, made in mid-September 1931 with Magda Quandt, necessarily had an effect on Hitler's relationship with Geli. We know too little about the emotional aspect of this relationship even to speculate. It seems evident, however, that after forming a relationship after his own fashion with Magda he reconsidered the role Geli had played in his life thus far. It is possible that Hitler's changed attitude to Geli expressed itself through increased strictness and a desire to control her life more completely. This change may account for a quarrel he had with her at this time, after he forbade her, although she was now 23 years old, to go to Vienna for an extended period without her mother to continue her training as a singer. Geli refused to comply.[149] The argument was not resolved by the time Hitler left the apartment on Prinzregentenplatz on the morning of 18 September. The following morning Geli Raubal was found shot dead in the apartment. The shot had been fired from his pistol a few hours after his departure. It was generally assumed she had committed suicide. 'I daren't search for motives', was Goebbels's comment in his diary.[150] Three days after her burial Hitler visited her grave in the Central Cemetery in Vienna.[151] Early in 1932 he had the sculptor Ferdinand Liebermann make a bust of Geli and when it was delivered in February he was, according to Goebbels, 'very upset'.[152]

IO

Strategies

Chancellor Brüning's main political objective was to end reparations. A satisfactory outcome to the Geneva disarmament conference planned for 1932 would, he hoped, help him achieve this. Settling the disarmament issue would, he calculated, prompt the United States to cancel repayment of the outstanding debts owed by its allies, which in turn would incline the latter to mitigate the demands they were making on Germany. To emphasize the urgency of the situation, even before the start of negotiations, Brüning sought to demonstrate the absolute insolvency of the Reich, even if this meant exacerbating the financial and economic crisis. The increase in support for the Nazis as a result of the deteriorating situation did not conflict with this plan but rather was to serve as proof of Germany's desperate state and prompt the western powers to come round.

In the summer of 1931 the crisis in the Reich reached a temporary peak. The Second Emergency Decree for the Protection of the Economy and Finances of 5 June 1931 brought in massive welfare cuts, reductions in wages and salaries for public sector employees, and a crisis tax, all of which caused a serious deterioration in the relationship between Brüning and the DVP (which was represented in the government) as well as with the SPD (which continued not to oppose him in parliament). Along with the Emergency Decree the government published an appeal regarding reparations designed to demonstrate the desperate situation in the Reich. It appeared on the day Brüning arrived at Chequers, the British prime minister's country residence, for several days of talks with the British government. The unintended consequence was a massive collapse in the creditworthiness of the Reich. Brüning's tactics seemed to be working, however, when on 30 June the American President Herbert Hoover proposed a temporary international moratorium on debt repayments, limited to one year. This covered not only German war reparations but also war debts among the allies themselves.

After international negotiations, the moratorium came into force at the beginning of July. In spite of this, the crisis in Germany deepened. The collapse of the textile firm, *Nordwolle*, put pressure on its bank, the *Darmstädter und Nationalbank*. The bank's closure on 13 July 1931 started a run on other banks. The government declared two bank holidays and intervened massively in the money markets but failed to stabilize the situation as it had hoped. Foreign banks called in their debts and more German banks, businesses, states, and local authorities got into financial difficulties. Although the seasonally-adjusted number of unemployed dropped from 4.9 million in January to 4 million in July 1931, more than 1.2 million people more were unemployed than in the July of the previous year. Social provision was overstretched and could not prevent mass unemployment turning into mass poverty. In addition, the Bank of England's abandonment of the gold standard in September 1931 caused a massive devaluation of the pound and a dramatic reduction in German foreign trade.[1]

'Nationalist Opposition'?

In the light of these events Hitler began to weigh up his options for getting into power. First of all, he continued to pursue his policy of rapprochement with right-wing conservative groups for which a new plebiscite organized by the veterans' organization Stahlhelm provided an opportunity. In April 1931 it gained the signatures of 10 per cent of the eligible voters required for a plebiscite calling for the dissolution of the Prussian parliament with the aim of destabilizing Brüning's government. For the Reich government led by the Centre Party politician, Brüning, was dependent on toleration by the SPD, while the SPD prime minister of Prussia, Otto Braun, relied on the Centre as his most important coalition partner. The advocates of the plebiscite calculated that bringing forward the elections in Prussia would produce a fundamental change in the position of the majority parties, thereby undermining the coalition between the Centre and the SPD. After the Prussian parliament rejected the referendum, the vote on the plebiscite was set for 9 August 1931; in addition to the NSDAP,[2] the DVP, DNVP, and the KPD all supported the plan.[3] The project came to grief over the turnout. Barely 40 per cent of the electorate, although overwhelmingly supporters of the measure, went to the polls, rather than the 50 per cent required.

Hitler now turned his attention elsewhere. When he met Goebbels on 23 August in the Hotel Kaiserhof in Berlin he announced he was in the capital 'to undermine Brüning's position through a hundred meetings'.[4] On the evening of the following day he made a start. At a soirée at Göring's house he met Schacht and leading representatives of arch-conservative political opinion in Germany. Leopold von Kleist, the Prussian royal house's pleni-potentiary, was there; also Rüdiger von der Goltz, the chairman of the United Fatherland Associations, and Magnus von Levetzow, another trusted agent of the ex-Kaiser. The discussion of what common policies they might adopt lasted until 4 a.m. in the morning.[5] A week later, on 30 August, in Kreuth in Upper Bavaria, Hitler met the DNVP leader, Hugenberg, to con-sider how to approach the imminent elections for Reich President.[6] They decided to mount a major demonstration of the 'nationalist opposition' (which essentially consisted of the DNVP, Stahlhelm, and NSDAP) in October and in subsequent meetings between Frick and Strasser acting on behalf of the NSDAP and representatives of the Stahlhelm and the DNVP it was agreed to put up Otto von Below, a former First World War general, a leading member of the United Fatherland Associations and a member of the Reich Committee which had organized the Young Plan plebiscite, as their joint candidate for the office of Reich President.[7] Following the plan that Hitler had pursued with conservative circles the previous year to sup-port Cuno for the highest office of state, this was now his second attempt to strengthen the alliance with this political camp by supporting the candidacy of a conservative politician.

Yet only a few days later Hitler made it clear to his most important political ally, Hugenberg, that he was by no means set on forming an alliance with the DNVP. On 7 September 1931 in a letter to Hugenberg he complained bitterly about the Stahlhelm and the DNVP. When working with the NSDAP in the governments of Thuringia and Brunswick both, he claimed, had proved disloyal; any alliance between the NSDAP and 'bourgeois organ-izations', Hitler suspected, seemed designed to end 'in our being squeezed into submission in a malicious and deceitful manner'. As far as the situation in Brunswick was concerned (the DNVP prime minister, in view of the disastrous financial position, wished to make savings by cutting the post of a Nazi minister who had resigned), Hitler gave Hugenberg an ultima-tum: If by 15 September another Nazi minister had not been appointed, on 16 September he would regard 'the National Socialist Party as having quit the nationalist opposition' and would make this public.[8] Hugenberg gave way and on 15 September Dietrich Klagges, a Nazi, became a new minister in the Brunswick state government.[9]

In the meantime Brüning's government was in crisis. In the autumn of 1931 the Reich Foreign Minister Julius Curtius (DVP) resigned after a plan he had supported for a customs union with Austria failed, and Brüning found himself facing a demand from Hindenburg to give his cabinet a decisively right-wing reshuffle. Hitler came to Berlin in order to engage in talks with various people about the possibility of joining the government. This was only a few days before the planned demonstration of the 'nationalist opposition' to be held in Bad Harzburg that was to focus on the demand for the Reich and Prussian governments to resign. On 3 October he first met Major General Kurt von Schleicher, in charge of the ministerial office in the Defence Ministry, who, as an important figure working behind the scenes in 1929/30, had helped to organize the transition to a presidential style of government and was now sounding out the possibilities of extending the base of the Brüning government in a right-wing direction. Afterwards Hitler reported on the meeting to Goebbels, saying he had responded negatively to Schleicher's pointed questions about whether the NSDAP would tolerate Brüning's government in parliament, but had on the other hand declared himself prepared either to enter the government – on condition there were fresh elections – or to take over government with the NSDAP acting on its own.[10] Goebbels's notes continue: 'We shall give up Prussia for now, if we can secure a decisive position of power in the Reich…Marxism in Prussia can be put down by a state commissar.' The so-called nationalist opposition would be left empty-handed, for Hugenberg would not get anywhere with Hindenburg. Instead, as Goebbels's notes tell us, a political deal was taking shape: the NSDAP would take over the government in the Reich, while accepting in return a Reich Commissar in Prussia appointed by the Reich President.

A different solution was, however, found to the government crisis. On 7 October Brüning resigned so that Hindenburg could give him the task of forming a new cabinet. This was done by 9 October. The DVP was no longer part of the government, Brüning took over the Foreign Ministry, and Reich Defence Minister, General Wilhelm Groener, became acting Interior Minister in place of the Centre Party politician, Joseph Wirth. Three further ministries were reshuffled. Over all, the result was that Brüning's government had acquired a more conservative profile, although with the departure of the DVP and that party's links to big business it had lost some of its support from industry.[11]

On 10 October, only hours before Hitler set off for Bad Harzburg, Brüning requested a meeting with him. The Reich Chancellor noted that, although at the meeting Hitler's 'increased self-confidence' had been noticeable, what he said about foreign policy had been confused and on economic and finance policy he had been totally vague. As the precondition for continuing to move the government's course more 'towards the right' Brüning demanded that Hitler should declare his position with regard to the re-election of the Reich President, which Hitler refused to do.[12] The same day Hitler, accompanied this time by Göring, was received by President Hindenburg, a meeting that was brought about by the head of Deutsche Bank, Emil von Stauss,[13] although it suited Brüning too, for the latter was hoping to weaken Hitler's position in the run-up to the imminent demonstration by the Right. For Hitler, however, Hindenburg's invitation was also very convenient precisely because of the Harzburg event.[14] He had delivered 'an hour-long lecture', he reported afterwards to Levetzow, seeking to use 'military analogies' so as to avoid overtaxing the Reich President; he had, he said, evaded Hindenburg's question about which parties he might possibly form a cabinet with. Although Hindenburg put out some positive signals after the meeting, in private he expressed reservations about Hitler as an individual.[15] The reception, which was reported by the press,[16] nevertheless signified a certain rise in status for the NSDAP. Before then the Reich President had always refused to have any direct talks with its leader.[17]

Meanwhile, delegations from the NSDAP, the Stahlhelm, the DNVP, the Pan-German League, and the Reichslandbund, numerous representatives of the old Prussian conservative ruling classes, and also leading figures from German business had all gathered in Bad Harzburg. This small town in the state of Brunswick had been chosen because the NSDAP was part of the government there and thus there was no ban on uniforms, as in Prussia.[18] Hitler's right-wing conservative colleagues were keen to make a powerful show of combined strength with the aim of putting the government under pressure, indeed to topple it and replace it with a Conservative–National Socialist government. Hitler was once again determined to present himself in Harzburg first and foremost as the confident leader of the 'nationalist opposition', whose freedom of action could not be restricted by anyone and who could treat even his political allies more or less as he liked, and this was indeed how he behaved.

Hitler and his companions, Goebbels and Göring, did not arrive in Bad Harzburg until 2 a.m. in the morning – too late to confer with his 'partners' about the following day, as he had originally agreed to do. This was part of Hitler's strategy not to be drawn into binding commitments in Harzburg, an approach that led to his behaving in a curt and abrasive manner through-out the event. What is more, he grew more and more convinced that the others were wanting to get the better of him. He told Goebbels he was 'furious that people want to elbow us aside'. The following morning he did not attend the joint meeting of NSDAP and DNVP parliamentary deputies, but instead used a meeting of the National Socialist parliamentary party to read out a declaration he had worked out with Goebbels that was consider-ably more sharply worded than the agreed joint communiqué of the 'nationalist opposition'.[19] He stayed away from the joint lunch and after-wards at the parade of the various organizations he left the site after the SA had marched past him. He did not bother with the Stahlhelm's march-past. During an hour-long discussion Hugenberg was only just able to prevent Hitler from leaving early.

During the addresses to the assembled company Hitler, in Goebbels's view, was 'not on good form' because he was so furious. Hugenberg had spoken before him and after him came the head of the Stahlhelm, Franz Seldte, and his deputy, Theodor Duesterberg, Eberhard Count von Kalckreuth, Hjalmar Schacht, the former president of the Reichsbank, a surprise guest who sharply attacked the government's financial policy, and after him Count von der Goltz.[20] Then finally the limited common ground was covered in the aforementioned communiqué, which called for the Brüning and Braun governments to resign and for fresh elections in the Reich and in Prussia. After the event the Nazis claimed that in Harzburg the leadership of the 'nationalist' camp had passed to them. The *Völkischer Beobachter* of 14 October reported that the 'rally of intellectual forces in Harzburg was concentrated round Hitler as its epicentre'.[21] The announce-ment of the candidacy of General von Below for Reich President, which had been planned to follow Harzburg, was quietly dropped.[22]

On 13 October 1931, a few days after the Harzburg rally, the Reichstag reconvened after a recess of more than six months to debate a government statement by the old/new chancellor, Brüning. In an extraordinarily long letter, published on 16 October in the *Völkischer Beobachter*, Hitler took issue with his speech. Amongst other things, he took up Brüning's comment that during the previous weeks he had tried without success to draw the parties into government; Hitler retorted that as far as the NSDAP was concerned he had been unaware of such a step.[23] The same day Brüning's government survived by a slim margin a motion of no confidence from the DNVP and NSDAP. This had been the first objective of the Harzburg Front and Hitler had invested great hopes in it. The tiny group of Business Party members decided at the last moment to support Brüning, having previously been in contact with Hugenberg and Hitler. The Reichstag adjourned again, this time until February of the following year.[24] Hitler's two-pronged strategy had turned out to be a total failure, for the 'nationalist opposition' not only appeared disunited, but had not achieved its central objective, the overthrow of the government. At the same time, Hitler's alternative approach, seeking a rapprochement with Brüning and Hindenburg, had not led to any tangible results either.[25]

The next day Hitler, accompanied by Goebbels and his girlfriend Magda Quandt, went to the city of Brunswick, where on 18 October a parade of 100,000 members of the SA, SS, and Hitler Youth lasting six hours was held. It was the largest Nazi demonstration before they came to power. At the rally afterwards Hitler almost implored the SA men present: 'Hold your nerve! Hold together! Don't waver one metre from the goal!' This demonstration of strength was designed to blot out the recent parliamentary defeat and the tactical flirtation with the parties of the right that had preceded it.[26]

Hitler was, nevertheless, dependent on their cooperation. In November he succeeded in penetrating the highest conservative circles. At a small gathering in the Berlin salon of Baroness Marie Tiele-Winckler, he met 'Empress' Hermine, the second wife of Kaiser Wilhelm II. Others there included Leopold von Kleist, the Prussian royal house's plenipotentiary, Göring, and Levetzow. Yet again Hitler delivered a long and almost uninterrupted monologue with the intention of leaving a lasting impression on the distinguished guests. With regard to being a possible candidate for the office of Reich President he said, according to Levetzow's account, that he 'would consider it beneath his dignity to accept a position and a title that had been created by a criminal revolution. In his eyes there was only one "Imperial Regent".' On the other hand, he became enraged when he was reminded of 9 November: He intended to 'outlaw all November criminals when the Nazis come to power'. He wanted them to be 'publicly garrotted...'[27]

At the end of November 1931 both the NSDAP and Brüning found themselves in an extremely embarrassing position. The so-called Boxheim documents, plans prepared by leading members of the Hesse NSDAP for a violent take-over of power, fell into the hands of the police. Just at this point, however, the Reich Chancellor was promoting negotiations between the

Centre Party and the NSDAP for a coalition in Hesse, which, following the results of the state elections of 15 November, would have enjoyed a majority in parliament. This would be a way, so Brüning thought, of creating the basis for close cooperation with the NSDAP at Reich level. He was gambling above all on securing the support of the NSDAP for an extension of the term of office or the re-election of Hindenburg as Reich President, when the latter's period of office came to an end in the spring of 1932.[28] This was a position he could hardly maintain after the discovery of the Boxheim documents.

For his part, Hitler brusquely dismissed all speculation, particularly by the German Nationalist press, about his alleged involvement in negotiations with the Centre Party to enter the cabinet. In the 1 December issue of the *Völkischer Beobachter*, he asserted that such reports were 'pure invention'. At the same time he used the denial to take a sideswipe at the German Nationalists, who intended through their allegedly misleading reports to 'discredit... the National Socialist movement above all in the eyes of German Nationalist voters'. He said nothing in public about the Boxheim documents. (Behind the scenes the Party leadership distanced themselves from them.)[29] Instead he changed tactics and once again aimed his attacks at his potential political allies, whose 'intrigues' were 'no more suited to reinforcing the "Harzburg Front"' than to challenging the existing system'. That could in any case be achieved not by 'the German Nationalist Party or its press... but only by National Socialism'.[30] He renewed the claim to leadership vis-à-vis the Stahlhelm that he had asserted at Bad Harzburg. In December 1931 he used a letter published in the press to explain once again in detail his autocratic bearing in Harzburg, peppering it with polemics directed at the veterans' organization; a correspondence ensued that reached a crescendo of mutual reproaches.[31]

The dynamics of the crisis

In fact Hitler escaped lightly from what was at the time a political fiasco but proved to be only the provisional end of the 'nationalist opposition'. The deepening economic and political crisis of the Weimar Republic set developments in train that opened up other opportunities to seize power.

In the winter of 1931/32 the economic crisis in Germany was reaching its climax. In 1932 industrial production dropped to 60 per cent of what it had been in 1928. In January 1932 the number of registered unemployed rose to over six million (almost 1.2 million more than in January 1931) but in reality at least 1.5 million more people were out of work. Only a minority of those registered as unemployed could claim unemployment benefit, which was constantly being cut as a result of the financial burden. Most of the unemployed had to live on meagre local authority welfare benefits. Those in work were faced with higher contributions to social security funds, wage cuts, and frequent short-time working, critical losses that were not compensated for by falling prices. Millions of people sank into poverty. The consequences were malnourishment, indeed starvation, and the associated illnesses. Homelessness became a mass phenomenon, while criminality arising from the immediate pressures of poverty increased, as did the suicide rate.

From Brüning's point of view the deepening economic crisis did in fact improve the prospects of getting rid of reparations once and for all and beyond that of bringing down the whole system of the Versailles Treaty. Any vigorous policies aimed at tackling the crisis would have defeated this purpose, which in Brüning's estimation was now within reach. Instead, it was important, as he thought, to stick to a strict policy of deflation, at least for a few months longer, not least to make the German economy 'leaner and fitter' by reducing state expenditure, cutting wages, and lowering prices. This strategy had no appeal to the impoverished masses. In place of a government that was looking ever more helpless, they turned in increasing numbers to radical parties such as the KPD and in particular to the NSDAP. The political system looked as if it would soon be totally blocked, something the chancellor sought to avoid by incorporating the NSDAP in his political strategy. This seemed particularly necessary in the light of two major events: in spring 1932 President Hindenburg's first period of office was coming to an end and at the same time there were forthcoming elections in Prussia and most of the other states, in which NSDAP landslides were indicated. In this case the question would arise in Prussia in particular of whether and to what extent the NSDAP should participate in government or would make it possible for other parties to form a government by agreeing to tolerate them.

Thus, at the beginning of 1932 Hitler found himself in an extremely advantageous position. During the course of the year he was to exploit these favourable circumstances to establish himself once and for all as the most important figure on the national political stage. Spoken of more and more often as the 'coming man', he now began in earnest to prepare to take over the responsibility of government and to counteract his image as an unrestrained demagogue. In addition to giving a series of interviews to leading foreign newspapers, in which he tried to calm fears about the rise of a radical right movement in Germany,[32] during the winter of 1931/32 Hitler made particular efforts to improve his links with industry. His purpose was to dispel fears about the NSDAP's 'socialist' plans and to bring in donations.

On 26 January Hitler made a speech lasting over two hours to a full house of some 650 guests at the Düsseldorf Industry Club. As always when speaking to a business audience, he presented himself as a moderate. He avoided any mention of the 'Jewish question' and did not demand the conquest of 'living space' in the east. Instead of focusing on the political issues of the day, he gave a kind of lecture, peppered with economic concepts, on the relations between the nation, politics, and the economy, although without giving any systematic presentation of his economic policy. In his view this was unnecessary, given that he consistently stressed the primacy of a 'nationalist' policy. To this end, he first developed his usual line of argument regarding 'the value of the nation', 'the value of the individual', and 'the principle of struggle and achievement' – values, he claimed, that were irreconcilably in conflict with equality and the principle of the majority, the bases of democracy, but which were recognized in the business world. Thus Hitler was attesting to his belief in private property, one expressly derived from the principles of his 'world view'. His audiences were also pleased to hear him declare his intention of 'eradicating Marxism root and branch in Germany'. The decisive precondition for national resurgence was, he said, that Germany again became 'a player in the political power game', regardless of whether that happened by a strengthening of the export market, a renewal of the home market, or a solution to the 'issue of space'. Whereas in other circumstances he rejected the first two options in favour of solving the 'issue of space' by force, here all three were put forward with apparently equal emphasis.[33]

Hitler made his Düsseldorf speech at a time when industry was taking decidedly more interest in him as a person and in the NSDAP. Thus, for example, one day after the speech, on 27 January, Hitler was a guest at Fritz Thyssen's Villa Landsberg along with Göring and Röhm, where he met Ernst Poensgen and Albert Vögler, the leading board members of United Steel.[34] At the end of February the steel magnate Friedrich Flick visited the

Party leader in the Hotel Kaiserhof in Berlin, although the discussion appears not to have led to any concrete conclusion. This was not so in the case of Paul Reusch, the influential chairman of the board of the mining concern Gutehoffnungshütte. On 19 March 1932 Hitler came to a reciprocal agreement with him regarding the 24 April elections to the Bavarian parliament: Hitler agreed that his Party would cease to hurl scurrilous abuse at the BVP, while Reusch, who had considerable business interests in southern Germany and was banking on a coalition of BVP and NSDAP in Bavaria, promised that the newspapers he controlled, the *Münchner Neueste Nachrichten* and the *Fränkischer Kurier*, would desist from making personal attacks on Hitler and other Nazi bosses.[35]

Also at this time the former president of the Reichsbank, Hjalmar Schacht, secured Hitler's agreement for the establishment of a 'bureau' to ensure ongoing contacts between business and National Socialism. This project had the support of industrialists such as Reusch, Vögler, Thyssen, Fritz Springorum, and Gustav Krupp von Bohlen und Halbach.[36] Through his plan for a 'bureau', Schacht came into contact with a working group made up of owners of small to medium-sized businesses that the chemicals manufacturer, Wilhelm Keppler (since 1932 Hitler's personal adviser on economic matters), had established with other entrepreneurs he knew personally.[37] Hitler seems to have made a more positive impression in this milieu of small and medium-sized businesses than among big industrialists. The Nazis' participation in the Thüringian government in 1930/31 had come about to a great extent through the involvement of locally-based small and medium-sized firms. As with Keppler, a number of small and medium-sized businessmen were trying to position themselves for when the NSDAP, as expected, came to power. Among them were Albert Pietzsch, the owner of a chemicals factory in Munich and from 1936 onwards head of the Reich Chamber of Commerce, Paul Pleiger, the owner of a small machine factory in Witten, Hans Kehrl, a textiles manufacturer (both he and Pleiger were to assume leading roles in the war economy in the Third Reich), and Fritz Kiehn, a maker of cigarette papers from Trossingen in Württemberg, who after 1933 became President of the Württemberg Chamber of Commerce and built up a small business empire.[38]

In spite of Schacht's efforts, by the end of 1932 heavy industry had in fact given only a relatively modest amount of direct financial support to the NSDAP. There is evidence of payments by individual businessmen and associations, but they represented only a fraction of the total donations to political parties made by industry during this period. They were in the main a form of insurance for the future rather than a sign that industry wanted to see the Nazis come to power, for company boards preferred the parties traditionally well-disposed to industry, the DVP and DNVP. All the same, Hitler used the closer contacts that were gradually developing to position himself consistently in opposition to the 'anti-capitalist' wing of the NSDAP, cutting the latter down to size in order to gain favour with influential figures in the business world as a partner in any future right-wing coalition. This is the real significance of these contacts. But to begin with Hitler tested a further strategy for turning the growing support for the NSDAP into concrete power.

Going it alone

At the beginning of December 1931 Brüning had responded to the discovery of the Boxheim documents by taking a more critical line with regard to the NSDAP. On the occasion of the signing of the Fourth Emergency Decree he delivered an address on the radio casting serious doubt on Hitler's declarations that the NSDAP was pursuing the path of 'legality'. The fact that the new decree also contained a general ban on uniforms and insignia (although this did not come into force immediately) was intended as a warning to the NSDAP.[39] Brüning wished to try to secure NSDAP support for an extension of the Reich President's term of office, for which, as it would require a change to the constitution, a two-thirds majority was needed. A reminder of the Chancellor's powers could, from his point of view, be very useful.

During an audience with the Reich President on 11 December Göring agreed that the Party would 'welcome re-election or an extension for the Reich President'.[40] On 5 January Hindenburg gave Brüning the task of beginning talks that would lead to his term of office being extended.[41] After this there were four days of talks with Hitler; on 7 and 9 January Brüning and Hitler talked directly and the rest of the time through intermediaries (Groener, Schleicher, and the President's state secretary, Otto Meissner).[42] As an opening gambit on 7 January Brüning (according to his own recollection) declared that for Hitler the opportunity had arrived to 'be the first' to promote 'the re-election of the Reich President' (by parliament) and thus to 'assume political leadership'.[43] That was a clear offer: If the NSDAP were to support Hindenburg, Hitler's path to the office of Chancellor would be unimpeded.[44]

Meanwhile, however, Hitler had been pursuing another approach. On 11 January the indications were becoming more numerous that Hitler and Hugenberg (with whom Brüning was engaged in parallel negotiations) would not agree to parliament extending the President's term of office. In a letter to the Chancellor Hitler now voiced 'constitutional concerns' about these proposals and published it in the *Völkischer Beobachter*. The plan was for Brüning to be left as the man who had attempted to pressurize the head of state into a breach of the constitution.[45] Hitler's attempt to drive a wedge between Hindenburg and Brüning failed, however, for the President was not yet prepared to abandon Brüning. The leaders of the NSDAP felt they had suffered an embarrassing defeat,[46] although his abortive attempt to extend the President's term of office also led to a significant loss of prestige on the part of the Chancellor, who contemplated resignation.[47]

Thus a further election for Reich President was now unavoidable. Hitler hesitated to put himself forward as a candidate. In an interview at the beginning of December for the British mass circulation newspaper *Sunday Graphic* he had dismissed rumours to that effect as nonsense.[48] Although the situation had changed fundamentally, he could not be moved to change his mind, not even by Goebbels, who made several attempts,[49] and not even after a 'Hindenburg Committee' was formed in Berlin at the end of January to re-elect the serving President. Hitler wanted to let Hindenburg go first in announcing his candidacy and wait for signs of support to come from the republican parties, in particular the Social Democrats.[50] On 15 February, as expected, Hindenburg announced he would stand for re-election. The fact that in the meantime the Centre Party and the SPD had publicly come out in support of him gave Hitler an excuse to announce that he rejected Hindenburg's candidacy.[51] It was not until a week after this, on 22 February, that Hitler, when on a visit to Berlin 'at last', as Goebbels noted, gave him permission to announce that he too would run. Goebbels did just that the very same evening at an event at the Sportpalast. On the same day the Stahlhelm and the DNVP put up their own candidate, namely Theodor Duesterberg, the second national chairman of the Stahlhelm, thereby demonstrating that the 'Harzburg Front' was incapable of taking concerted political action.[52]

A few days later the coalition government in Brunswick, which included members of the NSDAP, removed a not insignificant obstacle to Hitler's candidacy. On 25 February it appointed Hitler as a Brunswick government official, thereby making him a German citizen. Before then the Party leader had not even been eligible to assume public office.[53]

The election campaign, which began on 27 February, was conducted by the NSDAP propaganda HQ above all through 'posters and speeches'.[54] The prominent message of the campaign was that the election was a 'decisive struggle' between the Weimar 'system' and National Socialism. As the 'Leader of a young Germany' Hitler was to impress the public as a contrast to Hindenburg, the old man who was finding no way out of the crisis. This was the first time that the NSDAP had geared its entire propaganda to the 'Führer'.[55] Between 27 February and 11 March Hitler made speeches in thirteen different places,[56] turning the fact that Hindenburg's candidacy was supported by the Social Democrats, of all people, into the crux of his argument. He therefore spoke at length about November 1918 and attempted to convince his audience that the intervening 'thirteen years' (he kept on repeating this catchphrase) had brought nothing but suffering and had led to a series of bad decisions and failures that had inevitably produced the present political and economic crisis, with its temporary measures and emergency decrees. In line with the campaign strategy he frequently referred to his adversary as an 'old man' who, though he was revered for his service to the fatherland, was now no more than a puppet of the Social Democrats and Republicans: 'Venerable old man, you must stand aside so that we can destroy those who are standing behind you.'[57] He was 'immensely proud', Hitler boasted, 'to have forced the SPD to kneel now before the Field-Marshal in less than thirteen years.'[58] Unlike Hindenburg, he, Hitler, was the dynamic leader of a movement that embodied a new, young Germany and would heal the rifts in society by creating a national community.[59] Carried away by his self-image as saviour of the nation, he turned repeatedly to the notion of what might have happened if he had been born ten or fifteen years earlier and 'had already had my political education by 1915'. If that had been the case, he continued in his grandiose attack on his two targets, he might have succeeded as early as 1918 in forcing the Social Democrats to accept the authority of Field-Marshal Hindenburg: 'Germany would not have lost the war and there would have been no revolution. We would not have had this endless sequence of madness, anxieties, and misery.'[60]

On election day, 13 March, however, the NSDAP gained only 11.3 million votes (30.2 per cent), whereas more than 18.6 million Germans (49.6 per cent) voted for the current office-holder, Hindenburg, who thus just missed achieving the absolute majority required. As the Stahlhelm and DNVP now withdrew their candidate, Duesterberg, who had managed to win two and a half million votes (6.8 per cent), and also declared in favour of Hindenburg, the latter's victory in the obligatory second round of voting was more or less assured. In a telephone conversation with Goebbels on the evening of 13 March Hitler appeared surprised and disappointed about the result but also determined to continue the battle into the second round.[61] This obvious determination also characterized the calls to action he addressed on 13 March to Party comrades.[62] His decision to continue to the next round was not prompted by any calculation that he could still defeat Hindenburg, but rather by the hope of mobilizing voters for the imminent parliamentary elections in Prussia and other states.[63] At a Party leaders' conference on 19 March in Munich Goebbels was evidently obliged to put up with a fair amount of criticism of his propaganda campaign in the previous few weeks.[64] Yet Hitler appealed to the Party leaders to continue the fight in spite of everything. The NSDAP, he said, could bear anything except 'immobility or giving up the struggle'. They had 'to fight to their last breath'.[65]

After an Easter truce established by emergency degree, the second round of the election campaign began on 3 April and lasted only a week. In view of the short time available, and in order to increase the impact of the Party leader's public appearances, Hitler used an aircraft for his speaking tour and so was able to reach a mass audience in at least three or four cities each day, although he had only between fifteen and thirty minutes per stop and so was forced to restrict himself to short addresses consisting in essence of a denunciation of the 'system' and the vision of a nation united under his leadership. In these speeches he hardly even mentioned the imminent election for the presidency for he was already focused on the electoral battles to come after it. These short speeches exuding confidence in victory were to become typical of his oratorical style in 1932.

Nazi propaganda trumpeted the 'flight around Germany' as a kind of victory parade. The huge crowds that Hitler was mobilizing day after day in cities throughout the Reich were an expression, it was claimed, of his extraordinary popularity, while the use of a plane was designed to reinforce Hitler's 'modern' image, in particular in his contest with the 'elderly' Hindenburg.[66] The fact that first of all he had had to overcome his fear of flying, as Hans Baur, his pilot at the time (later his chief pilot), reports, was another story. Hitler had all too vivid memories of his first flight from

Munich to Berlin in a superannuated military aircraft in 1920. Since then he had tried to avoid aeroplanes.[67]

Once again the NSDAP's election campaign was disrupted by the SA. On the evening before the first round of voting rumours of a Nazi putsch had started to circulate in the wake of large-scale SA 'manoeuvres' in the Berlin area.[68] A few days later, on 17 March, the police carried out searches of Nazi premises throughout Prussia, and there were hints of an impending ban on Nazi organizations.[69] Hitler's protests about the 'merry-go-round of arrests and confiscations cooked up in the old familiar ways' had no effect.[70] In addition, Röhm's homosexuality put increasing strain on the Party. On 6 March 1932, in the middle of the election campaign, the *Welt am Montag* had published a private letter of Röhm's, openly admitting his homosexuality.[71] Hitler immediately instructed Goebbels by telephone that he was to declare any more accusations of that kind against Röhm to be 'a pack of lies'.[72] When the accusations continued Hitler gave an assurance of his confidence in Röhm, defending him against 'the most filthy and vile harassment'.[73]

Hindenburg was able to win the second round on 10 April with a decisive 53 per cent of the votes. The NSDAP had increased its share of the vote by more than two million and achieved 36.7 per cent of the total vote, while Thälmann, the KPD candidate, gained a little over 10 per cent. Although on the evening of election day Hitler celebrated the result as a 'victory' and made efforts to direct the energies of his supporters to the regional parliamentary elections scheduled for 24 April,[74] in the final analysis the campaign as such, with its emphasis on Hitler as the hope of the nation, had been a massive failure. The slogan 'Hitler' was far from convincing to the majority of German voters. Although Goebbels's strategy of reducing the campaign's focus to Hitler himself was, as stated above, controversial in the Party, he, as the architect of the campaign, tried after 1933 to declare that strategy retrospectively to have been the winning formula that led to the Party gaining power, presenting the 1932 election as part of a success story that was beyond challenge and culminated in the enthusiasm for the 'Führer' shown in the so-called Third Reich. But looked at objectively, the attempt to sweep the NSDAP to power on a wave of enthusiasm for Hitler had been a failure.[75]

That Hitler's appearances were cheered by hundreds of thousands of people could also not disguise the fact that his strategy hitherto of ignoring the political issues of the day and his tendency to be vague about his immediate and medium-term goals were becoming less and less effective the closer he got to power. His standard argument (that National Socialism had first to win power and unite the nation, before the immediate problems could be solved) could only go so far in convincing the voters. His opponents even came to the conclusion that he had no political programme at all. At the beginning of April Hitler thus felt obliged to publish a twelve-point declaration entitled 'My Programme', although in essence it contained only the general slogans he had been putting out for years. Thus, as before, he claimed he would 'draw together the socialist and nationalist elements in our nation into a new German national community' (Point 1), which must be 'imbued with real national life and animated by a truly national will' (Point 2). He demanded authoritarian government (Point 3), postulated that the nation must be 'systematically toughened in order to overcome life's adversities' (Point 4), and asserted in Point 5 that he firmly intended always to tell the truth. He became more specific about how he would treat his opponents when he wrote that he considered the 'defeat and extirpation of political, economic, cultural and intellectual Marxism to be absolutely necessary in the interests of the survival of the whole German nation' (Point 6). There is no mention at all of the 'Jewish question' or of living space. In Point 7 he made the by now universal demand for the 'promotion of a healthy peasantry' and in Point 8 for a strengthening of small and medium-sized enterprises [Mittelstand]. As far as his economic ideas were concerned, in Point 9 he went so far as to say that 'in a truly healthy nation the citizen does not exist for the sake of business and the economy, and business does not exist for the sake of capital, but rather capital should serve business and business and the economy should serve the nation.' On social policy he commented that 'caring for and protecting those who work is in reality caring for and protecting the nation, the people' (Point 10). He acknowledged that in modern society women were moving into new activities, but clearly stated that 'the ultimate goal of a truly organic and logical development' must 'always be the creation of families' (Point 11). Finally, the state's role was to 'embody in itself and its laws all ideas of acting in good faith, law and morality that it in turn demands of its citizens' (Point 12).[76] 'My Programme' was not a programme at all but rather a collection of statements of general principle and empty slogans.

By contrast, the difficulties posed by the Republic Hitler was aiming to topple were very concrete for him as Party leader and for his team. The raids conducted by the Prussian police on 17 March on various SA offices had uncovered incriminating evidence. Groener, the Reich Minister of the Interior, had previously had misgivings as Minister of Defence about imposing a nationwide ban on the SA 'for defence reasons' [i.e. its potential as an Army reserve], and these misgivings were shared by large sections of the officer corps.[77] Under pressure from state interior ministers, however, he set aside his doubts. Brüning and Groener exerted the necessary pressure on a reluctant Hindenburg until on 13 April, a few days after the second round of Presidential elections, the latter signed an emergency decree imposing the ban. The police occupied SA and SS premises and dissolved these organizations. The Nazis were tipped off about this move, however, and prepared to continue the SA and SS in a clandestine form.[78] But, as is clear from his call to the SA and SS of 13 April, Hitler found it rather difficult to explain to his supporters the logic of his continued 'lawful' course.[79]

Even though the ban on the SA was not unexpected, it nevertheless proved a hindrance to the NSDAP's campaign for the forthcoming state parliament elections. During the two weeks remaining before election day Hitler again travelled the country by air. Between 16 and 23 April he spoke at a total of twenty-six events, from Miesbach to Flensburg, from Trier to Allenstein. He concentrated in these short addresses on biting criticisms of the 'prevailing system' and its representatives. 'They have demolished Germany in the most terrible moment of its existence and shattered it into fifty parties, groups and associations!' he declared on 22 April in Frankfurt an der Oder. 'They have ruined the economy and plunged the peasantry into poverty; they have 6 million unemployed on their consciences and caused the inflation.'[80] The trope introduced during the Presidential election of the 'thirteen years' during which people had experienced failed, indeed destructive, policies, again became a leitmotiv. The '13 million' NSDAP voters who, he claimed, had made the NSDAP the 'biggest political organization that Germany has ever known' were also a usable rhetorical resource. They were no prelude to a 'fragmentation' of the nation, as his opponents claimed, but rather 'the first great rallying' on the road to national unity.[81]

The NSDAP achieved outstanding success in the elections to the Prussian state parliament on 24 April 1932. It increased its share of the vote sensationally from 1.8 per cent (1928) to 36.3 per cent and was now the strongest party in the largest German state. Because of the poor performance of the DNVP, however, the 'nationalist opposition' did not have a majority in the Prussian parliament; in order to achieve this, the NSDAP needed the support of the Centre Party. Until a new government was formed the Social Democrat prime minister Braun and his government, made up of SPD, Centre, and left liberal Deutsche Staatspartei ministers, remained in office. In Bavaria, Württemberg, and Hamburg the NSDAP achieved comparable results but had the same problem: it could not form a government. Only in Anhalt could the NSDAP create a parliamentary majority with the help of other right-wing parties. Thus the impressive results achieved by the Party did not bring about decisive political change in the states. This was the background to Goebbels's resigned comment in his diary: 'We must get power, or victories will kill us off.'[82]

An approach to the Centre Party?

The Presidential election and the state elections in Prussia and the other states had shown that the NSDAP could not come to power on its own. After the collapse of the 'Harzburg Front', the strategy of going it alone had now also failed. The NSDAP leadership now looked to an approach to the Centre Party as offering the most likely route to success. In the weeks that followed, the Nazis concentrated on this third variant. 'Without the Centre we can't do anything anywhere. Neither in Prussia, nor in the Reich', Goebbels noted on 27 April. The same day he heard from the Berlin SA chief Wolf-Heinrich Count Helldorff that General von Schleicher was willing to 'shift his position': 'Under pressure from him the Centre is expected to fall into line. Changes in the Reich too. Centre to be willing to tolerate in Prussia.' Armed with this information from Goebbels, on the following day Hitler paid Schleicher a visit. From Helldorff Goebbels learned that 'agreement had been reached' at the meeting,[83] but the next day Hitler said he wanted to keep the Centre 'dangling' for a while. Schleicher's initiative had been prompted by Hindenburg, who for his part envisioned a hard Right solution for both the Reich and Prussia that would ideally involve the Centre Party, the DNVP, and the NSDAP.[84]

Schleicher, who had opposed the SA ban so as to avoid barring the way to a possible coalition with the NSDAP in Prussia, had indicated to Brüning before the Prussian parliament elections that his days as Chancellor were numbered.[85] For although Hindenburg had won the Presidential election, he had done so only because Social Democrats and Catholics had voted for him, whereas in Hitler he had had a serious opponent from the 'nationalist' camp. Brüning had not succeeded in uniting the right-wing parties in support of an authoritarian regime, as Hindenburg had expected him to do; instead, his survival in parliament depended on the continuing support of the SPD. Thus for Hindenburg the Chancellor was expendable.

At this point Brüning intended to intervene in Prussia if the coalition talks with the NSDAP in the largest German state should break down. In the first week of May the Chancellor ordered the state secretaries in the Reich Interior and Justice Ministries to prepare an emergency decree placing the Prussian police and the judicial system under the control of the Reich.[86] These plans were, however, thwarted by Schleicher, who was now openly seeking to bring Brüning down. During the night of 2/3 May he visited Brüning (at the time Hitler and the Goebbelses were on a motoring tour for several days between Berlin and Berchtesgaden) and suggested he should make way for the right-wing government that had been discussed with the leaders of the NSDAP. When Brüning replied that he intended to remain in office as Chancellor and Foreign Minister until his policy of bringing about a revision of the Versailles Treaty was sure of success, Schleicher made it clear that he would no longer support him.[87]

Hitler, now in Berchtesgaden with Goebbels and his wife, observed events unfolding. The news from Berlin, as Goebbels records it in his diary, was 'that the generals are still digging... Brüning and Groener will have to go.' On 5 May Hermann Warmbold, the Economics Minister in Brüning's cabinet, resigned after he was unable to win support for his plans to stimulate economic growth in opposition to Brüning's policy of retrenchment. 'Schleicher has let the bomb go off', noted Goebbels on the minister's resignation, hinting that this move was part of Schleicher's intrigue to dismantle the government. Optimistically he added: 'Brüning and Groener are wobbling.'[88] Hitler set off for Berlin where on 7 May, accompanied by Röhm and Helldorff, who acted as his intermediaries with Schleicher, he met state secretary Meissner, Hindenburg's son and adjutant, Oskar, and Schleicher himself. 'Brüning is going to fall this week', gloated Goebbels afterwards. 'The old man will withdraw his support. Schleicher is pressing for it.... Then there'll be a Presidential cabinet. Reichstag dissolved. The laws hemming us in will go. We'll have freedom to agitate and we'll produce our *tour de force*.'[89] Later that day the Party leaders assembled in Berlin agreed by telephone with Schleicher to accelerate Brüning's fall, thereby allowing him no opportunity of putting the issue to a vote of confidence in the Reichstag.[90] Goebbels's diary entries reveal the role played by the NSDAP in Schleicher's plotting. The Party was to tolerate the new government in parliament and in return received a promise that the ban on the SA would be lifted and fresh elections held. These concessions would inevitably lead to a new out-break of SA terrorism and, given the NSDAP's recent electoral successes in the various states, would inevitably make it the strongest parliamentary party in the Reichstag.

Originally the decisive talks between Hitler and Hindenburg were planned for 11 May. Brüning, however, told the President's office that they would be seen as the first step in a government reshuffle, thereby reducing his effectiveness as Foreign Minister just when he was about to go into the crucial negotiations aimed at finally removing Germany's war reparations. He thus managed to have this date (and the talks Hindenburg was planning to have with the other party leaders) put back. The end of the month was now scheduled as the time when the parties, from the Centre to the National Socialists, would look for ways of working together in order to form a gov-ernment in Prussia. Under those circumstances Brüning declared himself ready to accept a reshuffle of the Reich government as well.[91]

After this the President went to his Neudeck estate for more than two weeks. One day later Groener resigned as Defence Minister, ostensibly as the direct consequence of a poor performance in the Reichstag on 10 May but in reality as a result of the overwhelming pressure exerted on him in particular by Schleicher and the generals, whose superior he was. Hindenburg too was clearly distancing himself from his Defence Minister.[92] Groener had defended the ban on the SA during these weeks against all protests and his departure meant that an important obstacle to closer cooperation between the right-wing conservatives and the Nazis had been removed.

As Brüning's fall was imminent, Hitler at first saw no more reason to continue with the project of an alliance with the Centre. Speaking to the NSDAP parliamentary party in the Prussian parliament on 19 May he clearly distanced himself from such coalition plans, saying that they had not 'struggled for thirteen years in order to continue the politics of today's Germany in some coalition or other'.[93] During this time Goebbels learnt more details about Schleicher's plot to topple Brüning from Werner von Alvensleben, a close friend of Schleicher.[94] Alvensleben already had a list of ministers that Schleicher had agreed with Hitler: 'Chancellor von Papen, Foreign Minister Neurath.'[95]

Schleicher's candidate for Chancellor, Franz von Papen, was a Centre Party deputy in the Prussian parliament and chair of the editorial board of the party newspaper, *Germania*. Although he was not well known to the general public he certainly enjoyed some influence in the party. His arch-conservative cast of mind, his aristocratic background, and appropriate career to match it (Papen had been a diplomat and officer in Imperial Germany), were likely, Schleicher assumed, to make him acceptable to Hindenburg. The fact that Papen was a Centre Party deputy in the Prussian parliament again opened up prospects of a comprehensive arrangement with the Nazis: Dissolution of the Reichstag and fresh elections, and at the same time the formation of a coalition government with the Centre in Prussia.[96] Hindenburg responded as Schleicher wished; during these days he informed his 'still Chancellor' Brüning through his state secretary Meissner that he intended to create a government that would strengthen the right of the political spectrum. He was considering, he said, a situation where the National Socialists would tolerate the new Reich cabinet in exchange for being given a share in government in Prussia.[97]

In Prussia, however, obstacles remained. Although after discussions with the Centre[98] the NSDAP had managed to secure agreement that at the opening session of the Prussian parliament on 25 May the NSDAP deputy Hanns Kerrl would be elected as President of the House, the coalition negotiations between the two parties were not progressing.[99] Hitler set off for the state of Oldenburg on an election tour, as state parliament elections were taking place there on 29 May.[100] At the end of May he let Goebbels, whom he met on the journey, know that 'things are looking bad for Brüning. On Sunday he'll learn his fate from Hindenburg.'[101] Hitler was showing once again that he was extremely well informed. Brüning's position vis-à-vis Hindenburg had finally become untenable when representatives of the Reichslandbund and the DNVP made an emphatic appeal to the Reich President to prevent Brüning's government from forcing the auctioning off of bankrupt estates in eastern Germany that could no longer be bailed out and turning them over to be settled by peasants. The slogan 'Agrarian Bolshevism' was flying around.[102] On Sunday 29 May the Reich President summoned Brüning and informed him 'very coldly', as the latter recorded, that he was not minded to issue any more emergency decrees for his government; Brüning responded as expected, by offering his and his cabinet's resignation, which the President immediately accepted.[103]

The same day the NSDAP won an absolute majority in the Oldenburg election.[104] On 30 May Hitler had already reached agreement with Hindenburg in Berlin that he would support or tolerate the new cabinet, if the following conditions were met: dissolution of the Reichstag and fresh elections, a lifting of the ban on the SA, and access for the Party to the radio network. Hindenburg accepted these conditions.[105] The following day Papen confirmed to Hitler that he also agreed[106] and Hindenburg charged Papen with forming a government.

I I

On the Threshold of Power

Papen's government, the so-called cabinet of the barons, was made up predominantly of arch-conservative ministers from the nobility. Significantly, in the public mind they were associated with (and not without a certain polemical undertone) the exclusive Berlin Herrenklub [Gentlemen's Club], to which Papen himself and at least two other cabinet ministers did actually belong.[1]

The new government was to a great extent isolated in parliament and could only count on support from the small German Nationalist Party (DNVP). The Centre Party refused to cooperate with its own Chancellor because of his blatant intrigues against Brüning. In response, on 31 May, one day before he was appointed Chancellor, Papen left the party. Thus the foundation for the government as originally envisaged by Schleicher was removed. From the NSDAP's point of view, the fact that Papen had broken with the Centre Party reduced their interest in supporting the Chancellor, because the anticipated comprehensive arrangement in the Reich and in Prussia, for which the Centre Party was required, would now be much harder to achieve. Up until the last moment Schleicher had acted on the assumption that the Centre would finally come to terms with Papen and support him in parliament.[2] Now hopes were focused on the Nazis and Hindenburg and Papen upheld the concessions already made, namely the lifting of the ban on the SA and fresh elections.[3]

During the week after Brüning's fall, Hitler had speaking commitments in the election campaign in Mecklenburg-Schwerin, where elections to the state parliament were held on 5 June. The NSDAP hoped that the anticipated gains would strengthen its hand in the negotiations taking place in Berlin. Hitler made no secret of this in his campaign speeches. 'The battle in the states', he stated on 3 June at an election meeting, 'is nothing less than a preliminary skirmish before the major confrontation coming in the Reich, and that will not be a matter of simply taking over purely formal power but of the reorganization of the German nation.'[4] The same day Hitler again had a meeting with Schleicher, who told him that the other side was sticking to what it had agreed.[5] The next day the President, in accordance with the cabinet's wishes, signed the decree dissolving parliament and set 31 July 1932 as the latest possible date for fresh elections.[6]

Four days later, on 8 June, the NSDAP began negotiations with the Centre Party and Papen over the formation of a new government in Prussia that would include the DNVP. The NSDAP demanded the posts of prime minister and minister of the interior and also the support of the Centre Party in the Reichstag for Papen's government, for it insisted that, even after the changes in the majority situation in Prussia and the fall of Brüning, the formation of the governments in Prussia and in the Reich were still closely interlinked. However, while the Centre might have agreed to these demands in order to prop up a Chancellor from their own party, now that a renegade from their party had become Chancellor there was no reason for them to agree. They had no wish to shore up Papen's government. The reverse was the case: the Centre wanted instead to bring about a coalition of all parties of the Right, including the NSDAP. Hitler had entirely reckoned with the Centre Party's refusal to accept the NSDAP demands in the negotiations over Prussia. Goebbels's diaries clearly show that the NSDAP was intentionally making demands it knew the Centre Party could not accept. Hitler shared Goebbels's view that the Nazis could only get into government in Prussia if 'we get total power'. All their efforts were therefore now focused on winning the elections and then acquiring the Chancellorship.[7]

The NSDAP leaders already had a solution in view for Prussia that Schleicher had suggested the previous autumn, namely the appointment by the Reich government of a State Commissar on the strength of Article 48 of the Weimar Constitution. On the evening of 4 June Goebbels had made notes of a telephone conversation between Hitler and Schleicher: 'The Prussian matter still undecided. Commissar or Prime Minister to come from us.'[8] The failure of the negotiations over the formation of a government in Prussia made this solution, which was designed to force the Centre Party out of the power game, the preferred option, especially as the lifting of the ban on the SA on 16 June removed the last possible inducement for the NSDAP to tolerate Papen in the Reichstag. The Party's storm troopers were now fully prepared for the election campaign.

Hitler was now determined under all circumstances to reject a role in the Prussian government unless the Party simultaneously went into government in the Reich.

Election battle and Prussian coup

In the summer of 1932 the NSDAP began the election campaign with the firm expectation of soon holding power. Gregor Strasser was to use this critical phase to expand his position within the Party as the head of its Reich organization. He persuaded Hitler to return the sections of the Reich Headquarters that had been separated off in 1929 as Reich Headquarters II under the control of Hierl to his, Strasser's, authority. Hierl was given other responsibilities.[9] In addition, Strasser used another directive from Hitler to strengthen greatly his authority to determine the Party programme. It ruled that all NSDAP motions in the Reichstag, the state parliaments, and local government that 'concern matters of principle, including economic matters or that by the nature of their content represent an important statement by the Party or will attract particular attention in the public sphere' should be sent to the head of the Party's Reich Organization for expert scrutiny before they were submitted.[10] There were now also two Reich Inspectors (Paul Schulz and Robert Ley), one responsible for the north and the other for the south of the Reich, who were intended to increase the influence of the Party HQ in the Gaus.[11] Both men were considered confidants of Strasser.

The latter's continuing efforts to centralize, bureaucratize, and create a hierarchy for the NSDAP (on 17 August he was to introduce a further level of control into the Party structure by appointing 'state [Land] inspectors')[12] was inevitably going to clash sooner or later with Hitler's claim to be an absolute 'Führer'. For his position as 'Führer' of the Party rested in essence on a very personal, indeed personalistic, style of leadership that put him in a position to intervene at any time at any level of the Party structure, whereas a Party apparatus with something like a general staff and established areas of responsibility of the kind Strasser was about to create would inevitably conflict with this in the longer term. At a conference of Gauleiters held in Munich at the end of June 1932 Goebbels gained the impression that by means of 'organizational changes' Strasser had 'got his hands on the Party', was aiming to become 'General Secretary', and wished to make Hitler 'Honorary President'.[13]

Strasser's increased importance became evident above all through the decisive impact he had on the content of the Party's electoral campaign. On 10 May he had made a speech in the Reichstag advocating a consistently 'anti-capitalist' line and demanding increased state benefits for the millions of people who because of the crisis had lost all their money or were facing imminent poverty.[14] In view of the strict austerity pursued by Papen's government this line seemed an appropriate starting point from which to launch a popular political alternative to the policies of the 'barons'. When on 14 June Strasser as official representative of the Party gave a talk on the radio he therefore advocated above all state intervention to support the crisis-ridden economy and reduce unemployment. Strasser also had 600,000 copies of his pamphlet 'The NSDAP's Emergency Economic Programme'distributed via the Party organization.[15] In it he put forward the same ideas. All this undercut Hitler's policy of creating good relations with business. The working group formed around Hitler's economic adviser Keppler had begun its work, and on 20 June a dozen men from the business world, including Hjalmar Schacht, the Cologne banker Kurt von Schröder, and the chairman of United Steel, Albert Vögler, had a meeting with the Party leader in the Hotel Kaiserhof at which Hitler tried hard to present his party's economic line as 'not doctrinaire'.[16] Yet in the light of the NSDAP's 'anti-capitalist' election propaganda such efforts were more or less fruitless. The majority of business leaders saw their interests well represented in Papen's cabinet.

In the election campaign the Reich propaganda machine particularly stressed the Party's distance from the current government and the equal importance it attached to its fight against the KPD, and against the 'system' and its parties, principally the SPD and the Centre Party.[17] The Party organization was instructed to use every means possible to reach people: mass rallies, loudspeaker vans, films, gramophone records, flags and banners, leaflets, the election newspaper Der Flammenwerfer [The Flamethrower], pamphlets, posters,[18] not forgetting 'individual propaganda', which meant talking in person to individuals.[19]

The main attraction of the campaign was, however, once more Hitler's tour by air of the whole of Germany, the third he had undertaken and celebrated in the Party's press as the 'Freedom Flight'.[20] Between 15 and 30 July he made appearances in fifty places, from Tilsit in East Prussia via Silesia, from where he embarked on a circular tour that took him through Central, North, and West Germany down to the South-West until he arrived for the final rally on 30 July in Munich.[21] On this journey Hitler presented the election as the 'turning point in the fate of a nation'[22] and continually conjured up the vision of a strong Reich united by the NSDAP. Admittedly, he could no longer avoid descending to the level of the political issues of the day. For on 19 July the Centre Party newspaper, *Germania*, published details of the negotiations that Papen had conducted with the NSDAP in June about a governing coalition in Prussia and the toleration of his government in the Reichstag. Hints about deals between Papen and the Nazis that had already appeared in the left-wing press were thereby confirmed, with the result that the Social Democrats geared up to describe Papen's government as holding the ladder for the Nazis.[23] As Hitler's main line of campaigning had been to claim that the 'cabinet of the barons' with its callous policy of austerity was hostile to the nation and socially destructive, he found himself with some explaining to do. He defended himself by saying that through the 'dissemination of falsehoods' an attempt was being made to pin the blame on the Nazis 'for what has been happening for the last six weeks under Papen's government'.[24]

An enduring theme in his campaign speeches was the by now familiar litany of the '13 years' of the Weimar Republic, with which he contrasted the '13 million' NSDAP voters as the advance guard of the nation unified. He became more specific whenever he engaged with statements by politicians in opposing parties, criticized the Papen government's foreign policy, and repeatedly pilloried the 'fragmentation' of the political landscape into more than thirty parties which he, as he announced candidly, was minded 'to sweep out of Germany'.[25] He consistently kept quiet, however, about his longer-term aims if he should come to power. He wasted no words at all on the main theme of his party's campaign, namely Strasser's work-creation programme. It was evident that there were yawning gaps in the Party leader's propaganda that Strasser was increasingly filling with his announcements about pragmatic policies to combat the crisis. One thing was clear, however: Hitler's unsparing criticism of Papen's government ruled out any resumption of a policy of toleration of this cabinet.

On 8 July Hitler went to Berlin for another meeting with Schleicher. The next day Goebbels heard from Schleicher's close friend Werner von Alvensleben that Schleicher and Hitler were in the process of preparing to move jointly against Papen, who, as Goebbels noted, would have to 'fall' along with his cabinet.[26] Thus Schleicher had made another U turn, breaking with Papen, whom he had previously 'invented' as Reich Chancellor, after only a few weeks, following the latter's almost complete political isolation.

In this situation Papen's government now resorted to Schleicher's scheme of using a commissar to solve the Prussian problem.[27] Amongst other things such a move freed Papen from the now impossible task of getting the Centre Party to make a deal with the NSDAP in Prussia in order to persuade the NSDAP to tolerate his government in the Reich. By taking over Prussia, the largest German state, and its apparatus of power – control of the police, judicial system, and local administration – Papen believed he finally possessed the resources to compel the NSDAP to be more cooperative in supporting his policies in the Reich.

The 'Bloody Sunday' in Altona gave him the excuse he was looking for to appoint a commissar. On 17 July this violent clash between police, Nazis, and communists in Altona claimed the lives of eighteen people.[28] It was the high water mark for a wave of acts of violence that had swept across the entire country following the lifting of the ban on the SA.[29] Regardless of the fact that he had revoked the ban himself, Papen now argued that the Prussian government was no longer capable of guaranteeing security in its own state and on 20 July introduced an emergency decree signed by Hindenburg[30] on the strength of which he appointed himself Reich Commissar for Prussia and Franz Bracht, the Oberbürgermeister of Essen, as Prussian Minister of the Interior. The existing Social Democrat ministers were dismissed.[31]

The NSDAP leaders had been informed at the latest by 9 July about the concrete preparations for the so-called Prussian coup. On 21 July Goebbels noted that 'everything is going according to plan'; a 'list of requests' had been put together for Bracht, as well as a 'list of the people in Prussia who have to go'.[32] This indication of an understanding between the NSDAP leadership and the government regarding the Prussian issue makes it clear that from Papen's point of view the Prussian coup was a preliminary offering to the NSDAP that he hoped would bring him greater support for his government – a miscalculation, as soon became evident.

Triumph and humiliation

In the Reichstag elections of 31 July the Nazis gained 230 seats with 37.4 per cent of the votes. They thus became the strongest party in the Reichstag. At the same time the DNVP and the smaller right-wing splinter parties were so decimated that it was impossible to create a right-wing majority. The

DNVP emerged with 6.2 per cent (it had gained 7 per cent in 1930) and all the others combined reached only 2 per cent rather than the previous 13.8 per cent of the votes. The liberal parties' losses were dramatic. The DVP secured only 1.2 per cent, the German State Party (DStP) only 1 per cent of the votes, whereas in 1930 they had managed 4.7 per cent and 3.8 per cent respectively. The Catholic parties, the Centre Party and the BVP, increased their combined result from 14.8 per cent to 16.2 per cent. In the left-wing camp there was a shift; whereas the Social Democrats dropped from 24.5 per cent to 21.6 per cent, the communists increased their share of the vote from 13.1 per cent to 14.5 per cent.

According to the analysis carried out by the psephologist Jürgen Falter and his team, referred to in Chapter 9, 'Conquering the Masses', this time 12 per cent of the NSDAP voters were previous non-voters, 6 per cent had previously voted DNVP, 8 per cent had voted for the two liberal parties, the DStP and the DVP, 10 per cent had previously voted SPD, and no fewer than 18 per cent came from all the others, which lost almost half of their voters to the NSDAP; the numerous splinter parties had turned out to be half-way houses in the migration of conservative and liberal voters to the far right.[33] As in the case of the first great electoral victory of 1930, NSDAP voters were disproportionately male and Protestant, were relatively often members of the traditional Mittelstand (craftsmen, shopkeepers, and farmers), and tended to live in the countryside rather than the city. Over all, the NSDAP had once again succeeded in reaching large numbers of voters from all social classes and sections of the population.[34]

On election night Hitler was in Munich. Goebbels, while visiting him there, noticed he appeared uncertain as to what to do next: 'Hitler is pondering. Big decisions coming. Legal path? With the Centre? Nauseating!'[35] Papen soon made another attempt to come to terms with the NSDAP,[36] but instead Hitler approached Schleicher and, at the beginning of August, discussed with him in Berlin the best way to secure the chancellorship.[37] Hitler had first tried to gain power through a nationalist front of right-wing conservatives. Then he had tried going it alone, but without success, falling back temporarily on a compromise deal with the Centre Party. Then, when Papen had taken over from Brüning and this solution was no longer viable, he had been drawn into an apparent toleration of Papen's government. Now, after resounding success at the polls, he was toying with the idea of a further permutation, namely to become chancellor himself; however, lacking a parliamentary majority he could do this only through the powers of the President, and for this he needed Schleicher's support. 'In a week's time it'll all start happening', Goebbels noted confidently about the discussion. 'The boss will be Reich Chancellor and Prime Minister of Prussia. Strasser Reich and Prussian Minister of the Interior. Goebbels Prussian Minister of Culture and Reich Education Minister. Darré Agriculture in both Reich and Prussia, Frick State Secretary in the Reich Chancellery. Göring Air. Justice will be ours.' According to Goebbels's notes an 'enabling law' was planned; should the Reichstag reject this, 'it will be sent home. Hindenburg wants to die with a nationalist cabinet. We'll never give up power again. They'll have to carry us out as corpses.'[38]

In fact, Hitler seems to have made more modest demands with regard to personnel. At any rate Schleicher announced in cabinet that the Party leader had merely asked for the chancellorship for himself and the Interior Ministry for Strasser, with Göring possibly also having to have a role. Thus most of the ministers in the old government would have remained in post, thereby making the new government more palatable to the German Nationalists and possibly other right-wing deputies.[39]

Before Hitler could take over the Chancellery, however, he had to get over a further crucial hurdle. When on 11 August the NSDAP leadership met in Prien on the Chiemsee it was clear to everyone that Hindenburg was continuing to reject Hitler's appointment as Chancellor. The consensus round the table was to go on negotiating with the Centre Party in order to put Papen and Schleicher under pressure to act.[40] The fact that the Nazis were drawing attention to themselves at this time through acts of terror and threatening gestures had evidently reinforced Hindenburg's rejection of the Party. On 1 August, immediately after the election, the SA and SS had ramped up their terrorism to a level not yet seen. In East Prussia and Upper Silesia in particular a series of bomb attacks and assassination attempts had occurred, causing many injuries and even some deaths.[41] Papen's government intervened quickly and decisively. On 9 August it passed a set of measures to tackle political terrorism, in particular through heavier penalties (including the threat of the death penalty for repeat offenders) and through the creation of special courts. Where necessary, the Reich President instituted these measures by using emergency decrees.[42] A few hours later the wave of terror reached its climax: during the night of 9/10 August in Potempa in Silesia a small band of Nazis murdered a communist in the most brutal fashion.[43] In addition, the SA was carrying out extensive 'manoeuvres' in the Berlin area in order to put the government under increased pressure.[44]

Figure 2. Hitler's setback on 13 August 1932 prompted John Heartfield to represent him satirically as Kaiser Wilhelm II, who had boldly promised the Germans, 'I shall lead you to a glorious era!' Instead of the inscription 'Pour le mérite', the order of merit pinned to his chest below the crossed swords bears the words 'Pour le profit'.
Source: © The Heartfield Community of Heirs / DACS 2018. Image kindly provided by Akron Art Museum

The immediate political consequences of the Reichstag election reached a conclusion on 13 August. Hitler spoke first to Schleicher and then to Papen, who both tried to persuade him to become Vice-Chancellor, but he declined the offer.[45] It was renewed during his subsequent interview with the Reich President but he turned it down again. Instead, he demanded of Hindenburg the office of Chancellor. The President responded by declaring that he could not 'be responsible before God, his conscience, and the Fatherland' for transferring the entire power of government to a party that was 'so intolerant towards those with a different point of view'. In addition, he admonished Hitler to conduct his opposition in a 'chivalrous' manner and stated in no uncertain terms that he intended to intervene 'with the utmost severity' against SA members who committed further acts of terrorism.

The entire meeting lasted only about twenty minutes, and when he returned Hitler reported that he had been well and truly 'lured into a trap'.[46] This fear turned into certainty later that day when the official communiqué from the meeting arrived presenting Hitler's demand to be made Chancellor as a demand that he be 'put in charge of the Reich government and that complete power in the state be transferred' to him. Hitler felt obliged to issue his own account of the meeting.[47]

The impression that he as leader of the most important political party in Germany, and as one who was now presumably within striking distance of 'seizing power', had been publicly shown up by Hindenburg wounded Hitler deeply. Naturally he could not admit that he might have misjudged the situation and thus brought the humiliating defeat upon himself; the fault lay with the others, who had laid a 'trap' for him. In the weeks and months that followed he was to return constantly in speeches to 13 August. Of course, he spoke of his 'decision' not to participate in a coalition government rather than of a rejection. Thus his humiliation was turned into a courageous resolve. But the fact is that he felt that 13 August (along with 9 November 1918 and 9 November 1923) was one of the greatest defeats of his life and it dogged him to the end, though it was always bound up with the idea that he had very quickly succeeded in freeing himself from this undeserved situation and triumphing over his adversaries. His narcissism permitted him to remember the humiliation he had suffered only if he was able simultaneously to acquit himself of all responsibility for it and instead conjure up a vision of his own greatness and history of success. Nazi supporters also felt Hitler's blunt rejection by Hindenburg as a depressing setback, which also inevitably encouraged doubts about the Party leader's 'lawful' strategy. The SA in particular had believed the takeover of power was imminent and so was hard to keep in check.[48] On 17 August Röhm felt obliged to use the *Völkischer Beobachter* to issue an appeal to the SA and SS for a 'pause in hostilities'.[49]

To put pressure on the government the Party leadership once again sought a parliamentary solution to the conflict in Prussia. Negotiations with the Centre Party were resumed, the Nazis demanding the post of Prime Minister (putting Hitler forward) as well as the Ministries of the Interior, Culture, and Finance. At this point Brüning, still a highly influential figure in the Centre Party, intervened in the negotiations, ensuring that further talks regarding a black–brown alliance took place from the end of the month onwards at Reich level.[50]

An alignment of the NSDAP with the Centre in the Reich appeared even more desirable as the wave of Nazi terror and the Papen government's counter-measures were leading to open confrontation between the government and the Nazis. The Potempa murderers were quickly apprehended and convicted on 22 August by the newly established special court in Beuthen: five death sentences were pronounced. The same day Hitler declared his solidarity with the perpetrators and the next day issued a proclamation ferociously castigating Papen's government: 'Herr von Papen has thus inscribed his name in the history of Germany with the blood of nationalist fighters.'[51] Although the sentences were not carried out, the wave of terror had negative repercussions. For Schleicher now began to move away from the project of a Presidential cabinet led by the Nazis.[52]

On 25 August Goebbels, Frick, and Strasser visited Hitler on the Obersalzberg. According to Goebbel's jottings, Strasser reported a conversation he had just had with Brüning in Tübingen, to the effect that the Centre Party wanted a 'long marriage' and for the Leipzig Oberbürgermeister, Carl Friedrich Goerdeler, to become Prime Minister of Prussia. Strasser said he had strongly supported this 'Centre Party solution'. Hitler and he, Goebbels, had on the other hand spoken up for the 'continued pursuit of a Presidential cabinet'. After lengthy discussions there was agreement on the three possible options: '1. Presidential 2. Coalition 3. Opposition. To be worked on in that order.'[53]

At the end of August the actual negotiations began in Berlin between the Centre and the NSDAP with both parties making them public in a joint declaration.[54] On 29 August Hitler also arrived in Berlin for talks with Brüning and then with Papen and Schleicher. As far as Brüning was concerned, Goebbels was told that he was 'prepared to do anything', whereas Papen and Schleicher held out the usual 'vague promises'. There was, he reports, a danger that the Reichstag, which had only just been elected, would be immediately dissolved.[55] Yet the incipient cooperation between the Centre and the Nazis produced its first concrete results. At the constitutive meeting of the Reichstag on 30 August Göring was elected its President with the support of the Centre votes, while the Centre Party deputy Thomas Esser was elected as one of three Vice-Presidents. The new President recalled parliament for 12 September.

The same day Papen, accompanied by Schleicher and his Interior Minister, Wilhelm Freiherr von Gayl, discussed matters with Hindenburg at his Neudeck estate. As Papen hoped, Hindenburg provided him with authority to dissolve the Reichstag in order, just as the Nazis feared, to torpedo the coalition negotiations between the NSDAP and the Centre Party. In addition, Hindenburg accepted Papen's proposal that fresh elections might be delayed beyond the constitutionally established interval of sixty days, as a state of emergency had clearly developed that could not be tackled simply by repeated visits to the polling booth.[56]

The NSDAP leadership was already at work on a countermove. On 31 August Hitler discussed with a small group consisting of Goebbels, Göring, and Röhm a plan to remove the Reich President from power. They had discovered Article 43 of the constitution, which allowed for the possibility of a referendum to remove the Reich President if it was supported by a two-thirds majority in the Reichstag.[57] Further negotiations with the Centre Party, at which Hitler asked for support for this plan, were held on 8 and 10 September in Göring's residence as Reichstag President. The Centre Party representatives, however, asked for time to consider.[58] Brüning, however, threatened to leave the party, causing the Centre to reject this option.[59] As far as the question of who should become Chancellor was concerned, the Centre conceded that anyone might be a contender who was acceptable to the Reich President.[60] The NSDAP and the Centre nevertheless agreed on the outline of a bill concerning the appointment of a deputy for the Reich President, according to which the President of the Reich Supreme Court rather than the Reich Chancellor should deputize for the Reich President if the latter should be unable to fulfil the demands of his office. This manoeuvre was designed to prevent Papen from acquiring a key political position in the event of Hindenburg, now eighty-five, becoming seriously ill. A law to that effect altering the constitution was, in fact, passed by the Reichstag in December 1932.[61]

At the Reichstag session of 12 September the KPD surprised everyone by proposing a motion of no confidence in Papen; the NSDAP and the Centre quickly agreed to support it. The result was 512 votes to 42 in favour.[62] Admittedly, the vote took place only because the President of the House, Hermann Göring, quite simply ignored the red folder containing the order to dissolve parliament that Papen had placed on his desk during the session.[63] Constitutionally, however, this made no difference to the fact that the Reichstag was dissolved. Fresh elections were set for 6 November.

November elections

On 13 September Hitler gave the NSDAP Reichstag deputies the slogan for the coming election: 'Vote no to Papen and Reaction'. The election campaign was built around that.[64]

By contrast with the June/July campaign of 1932, Nazi propaganda focused not on the 'parties of the system' but rather on Papen and his 'reactionary' backers, in other words the DNVP in particular.[65] One target attacked fiercely by the NSDAP was the emergency decree Papen issued on 4 September in an attempt to get unemployment under control through measures favourable to business, such as tax breaks and lowering the basic wage for new employees. Much as this course of action was welcomed by industry, it was vigorously opposed by the NSDAP. Yet unlike in the July election campaign, which had been strongly influenced by Strasser's anti-capitalist demands, such social and economic policy arguments did not constitute the main thrust of the campaign.[66]

After Strasser's early summer programme of immediate economic measures drew heavy criticism from industry, Hitler had agreed to the request from Schacht, now one of his most important go-betweens with business circles, that it should be binned. In addition, on 17 September Hitler made changes to the Party's economics department (Wagener's former sphere of activity) by making Feder responsible in future for 'economic matters involving the state' and Walter Funk, an economic journalist sympathetic to business, who had joined the Party in 1931, for dealing with the sensitive issues involved with the 'private sector'. This was designed to ensure that the leaders of the Party's organization would in future refrain from any fundamental criticism of 'capitalism'.[67]

As far as possible, concrete issues were to be kept out of the NSDAP's campaign, which was personalized to a high degree. The Party leader himself was contrasted with 'reaction' and presented as 'our last hope', as a poster slogan put it.[68] The election campaign was in other words dominated by Führer propaganda.

On 6 October Hitler launched the election campaign at a Party propaganda conference in Munich by issuing a warning directed at the 'Reich President's palace' that either his party would be given 'power or it would not be given power, in which case they will be defeated by the power of this movement'.[69] He was, in other words, determined to reverse the deep humiliation and loss of prestige that he had suffered on 13 August by launching a second attempt to convince the President of his claim to the Chancellorship. After this Hitler completed his fourth 'flight around Germany' and was able to make almost fifty speeches between 11 October and 5 November throughout the Reich. He gave prominence in each to a detailed justification of his 'decision' of 13 August not to enter government under another Chancellor. He had refused, he said, to be made responsible for failed policies. The long sections devoted to explaining this decision reveal how exercised he was by the public humiliation of 13 August and how he dealt with it. For the decisive factor had not, as he was now claiming, been his refusal to go into government, but rather Hindenburg's refusal to offer him the Chancellorship, which had been Hitler's aim as the clear victor in the 31 July election. He then went on to make detailed criticisms of Papen's economic policies, which only treated the symptoms while ignoring the political causes of the economic crisis, such as Germany's lack of political power and the German nation's fragmentation following defeat and revolution.[70]

The central document in Hitler's election campaign was, however, an 'open letter' in which he responded to a programmatic speech that Papen made on 12 October 1932 to the Bavarian Industrial Association in Munich. Hitler published his reply on 21 October in the *Völkischer Beobachter* and in the form of a pamphlet.[71] Around sixty manuscript pages long, the text refuted Papen's speech and contained an unsparing criticism of his economic, domestic, and foreign policies in which Hitler plainly expressed his belief that Papen was completely unable to understand the fundamentals of the political situation. Two and a half weeks before the elections he could not have distanced himself more clearly from the serving Chancellor.

The document contains a number of 'programmatic' statements by Hitler that indicate how he thought the current crisis could be solved, though without descending to the nitty gritty of day-to-day politics. Thus he argued that the 'ultimate causes' of the present economic crisis in Germany could not be grasped 'through a purely economic analysis'. Rather, the origin of the crisis lay in the 'imbalance between, on the one hand, the numerical size of the German nation, its significance in terms of the abilities inherent in its blood, its consequent need for cultural expression and a certain general standard of living and, on the other hand, the area currently allocated to the Reich as living space for the German nation'. This line of argument is only too familiar from his public statements from 1925 onwards. Yet he was not willing to be explicit in the document about the only solution he saw to the problem, namely that of correcting the 'imbalance' between population size and living space by means of a war.

Meanwhile in Berlin in the run-up to the elections a conflict was brewing that put the NSDAP in a difficult position. The Berlin city transport services were on strike and the NSDAP, which in the meantime had established its own employees' association in the form of the National Socialist Factory Cell Organization, joined with the KPD in supporting the strike action. On 3 November public transport in the Reich capital was largely at a standstill. As the two sides in the dispute were unable to reach agreement, the state arbitrator declared the outcome of arbitration to be binding and the unions called on their members to return to work. The KPD and the NSDAP, however, united to oppose this decision. The strike action escalated until there were violent clashes and several people died in shootings.[72] Hitler publicly defended the strike, referring to the workers' low pay,[73] but on 7 November the dispute had to be abandoned. This was yet another embarrassing defeat for the NSDAP. The strike had been unsuccessful and by cooperating with the communists the Party had damaged itself in the eyes of many potential voters.

This was an important reason why the NSDAP dropped more than four percentage points in the Reichstag elections of 6 November, securing only 33.1 per cent of the votes. The general perception was that the Party had already peaked. The chief gains were made by the KPD, which increased its vote by 2.6 per cent to 16.9 per cent over all, but the DNVP also gained 2.4 per cent. After the 'Harzburg Front' had collapsed in the elections for Reich President, Hitler had failed to bring about either an alliance with Papen or with the Centre Party, and finally Hindenburg had refused to countenance the idea of Hitler as Chancellor ruling through Presidential decree; it was, therefore, hard to see how Hitler could possibly realize his leadership ambitions in German politics. Given the political impasse he and his party now found themselves in, the strategy of concentrating Party propaganda predominantly on him as an individual had backfired and damaged the NSDAP and its 'Führer', as the November election result had clearly demonstrated.

In spite of this defeat Hitler remained defiant and confident of victory. In the *Völkischer Beobachter* he proclaimed: 'Single-minded continuation of the struggle until these partly open and partly secret opponents of a real resurrection of our nation are brought low! No compromises of any kind and no suggestion of any kind of deal with these elements.'[74]

When, after the elections, Papen began talks with the party leaders, he therefore got nowhere with Hitler, who responded to the conciliatory tone of his written invitation with a detailed letter setting out a series of manifestly unrealistic conditions for such talks. Hitler made it blatantly obvious that he was not prepared to be drawn into Papen's political strategy but was sticking to his demand to become Chancellor with a cabinet governing through Presidential decree.[75] Papen's efforts thus came to nothing and the cabinet offered the President its resignation on 17 November. Hindenburg accepted it, while asking the government to remain in office for the time being.[76]

Hitler hurried to Berlin to meet Hindenburg on 19 November,[77] again demanding the office of Chancellor and also the President's support on the basis of Article 48. Once appointed Chancellor, he said, he would conduct talks with the parties on forming a government and obtain from parliament an 'enabling act' to make the government independent of emergency decrees from the President. After the NSDAP's losses, Hitler could not have been seriously expecting Hindenburg suddenly to support his demand to be Chancellor, given that Hindenburg had dismissed the idea on 13 August. The fact that Hitler nevertheless made the demand may well have been due to his calculation that in spite of his party's losses he still had the upper hand. For it was clear that Papen's government was unsustainable without some kind of support from the NSDAP and that Hindenburg would be forced sooner or later to find another solution. With the next government crisis on the horizon, Hitler persisted in demanding the office of Chancellor. Had he relinquished this demand he would have been renouncing his own claim to political leadership at home and then the humiliation of 13 August would have been complete. Hindenburg, however, merely offered him and the NSDAP a number of ministerial posts in what was fundamentally a 'non-party' government. If, however, Hitler wished to be Chancellor, the President said, he would first have to demonstrate, on the basis of exploratory talks with the parties, that he had a parliamentary majority.[78] At a further meeting on 21 November both Hindenburg and Hitler stuck to their positions, Hitler having delivered beforehand to the President a written version of his own stance.[79] For his part, Hindenburg set a series of conditions that would have to be met if Hitler were to form any majority government. He was to be left in no doubt that, if appointed Chancellor, Hindenburg would give him relatively little freedom of action.[80] During the course of these negotiations Hitler referred repeatedly to the fact that by going into government he was gambling with the future of his 'movement', thereby revealing his altogether justified fear that if he as 'Führer' made a tactical error the current dissatisfaction in the Party could cause it to collapse.[81]

Both meetings were followed by further correspondence between Hitler and Hindenburg's state secretary Meissner,[82] in which Hitler made it clear that under the conditions laid down by the President it was impossible to secure a parliamentary majority and repeated his suggestion of an 'enabling law'.[83] We can infer from Goebbels's diary that Göring meanwhile had contacted the Centre Party and discovered that there was 'no objection to Hitler as Chancellor'. On the other hand, Hugenberg, representing the DNVP, was prepared to negotiate only with Hitler personally, which the latter refused to do. Now 'the Presidential solution was the only one worth considering'. This diary entry shows that Hitler had absolutely no interest in serious discussions to achieve a parliamentary majority. Goebbels's view that Hindenburg's offer was a trap to 'exclude Hitler from power, make it his own fault, and thus destroy him' sums up the attitude at the Kaiserhof.[84]

Thus on 23 November Hitler pronounced the task the President had given him of negotiating a solution to be impossible.[85] The NSDAP leadership now decided to make the whole correspondence public and Göring did so at a press conference on 24 November, saying that the Nazis would as a result 'neither support nor tolerate any cabinet whatsoever. They would bring down any cabinet in the very same way they had brought down Papen's cabinet. The German nation could be saved only by Hitler.'[86] Among the material published was the following passage from a letter from Meissner to Hitler, which could not be clearer: The President did not believe he could

> justify to the German nation giving his prerogatives as President to the leader of a party that had continually emphasized its exclusive claims and that had taken up a predominantly negative position with regard to him personally as well as with regard to the political and economic measures he considered necessary. Under these circumstances the Reich President inevitably fears that any cabinet under your leadership ruling by Presidential decree would develop into a party dictatorship with all the consequences that would ensue as regards an escalation of the conflicts in the German nation. He could not be true to his oath or his conscience if he had been responsible for bringing about such a situation.[87]

On 23 November Hitler once again met Schleicher, who reported back to the cabinet on 25 November. Hitler was unwilling in any circumstances to join the government, even if Papen were not the Chancellor, and would not allow any other Nazi, whether as a minister or as 'an observer or go-between', to be part of a cabinet of which he was not the leader. He wished to have no connection with the Reich government at all.[88] In spite of this, Schleicher entertained hopes of the Nazi parliamentary party tolerating the government, although one led by another Chancellor.

Hitler then convened a meeting of leading Party comrades in Weimar for 29 November.[89] Goebbels commented on the deliberations: 'Schleicher can't bring it off. Wants us to tolerate it. Conditions for and against.' The situation was discussed at length with Göring, Strasser, and Frick: 'Strasser wants to take part. Otherwise it will be a disaster. Hitler strongly against him. Sticks to his guns. Bravo! Göring and I back him up to the hilt. Strasser gives in. Hitler has the right view of the situation.'[90] On 30 December Hitler decided to respond to an invitation from Meissner to come to Berlin to discuss the situation with the Reich President with a polite 'No'.[91] Instead, Schleicher was asked to send a 'negotiator' to Weimar.

The next day Schleicher's close friend Lieutenant Colonel Eugen Ott arrived in Weimar. Goebbels learned from Hitler about the deliberations that followed: 'Reichstag adjourned until January. In exchange amnesty, the streets clear [for the SA] and the right to self-defence. Otherwise we go on fighting. Total chaos in Berlin. Our seed corn is ripening.'[92] The next day, on 1 December, Hitler spoke for several hours to Ott, telling him that Schleicher should not take the office of Chancellor himself so as not to harm the army. However, Goebbels noted that Ott had received a telephone message from Berlin that for Schleicher there was 'no going back': 'He's asking us to tolerate him.'[93]

In response to Schleicher's request for the Chancellorship, however, Hindenburg saw no prospect of a government led by him surviving if it were dependent on toleration. Instead, he preferred once again to give Papen the task of forming a new government.[94] But in fact Schleicher had already begun taking steps to succeed Papen. On 2 December he had his colleague Ott, just back from Weimar, present to the cabinet the results of a 'war games' exercise carried out by the Defence Ministry. In essence they boiled down to the fact that, in the event of a serious domestic or foreign crisis, the Reich's and federal states' security forces would be incapable of maintaining law and order in the face of the Nazis and communists. The study gave the clearest indication possible that the armed forces were no longer prepared to support Papen's policies, if necessary by introducing martial law. This presentation reinforced the cabinet's already existing inclination to appoint Schleicher Chancellor.[95] The President appointed him the very same day.

Crisis in the Party

Hitler's uncompromising demands had not brought him one step closer to becoming Chancellor. Instead, the Party was facing new problems. At a meeting of Party leaders on 5 December at the Kaiserhof to discuss what attitude to take towards the new government, Frick and Strasser revealed they had spoken to Schleicher, who intended to dissolve parliament 'if we won't tolerate [his government]'.[96] In the meantime the NSDAP saw fresh elections as a serious threat to the existence of the Party, for in the local elections in Thuringia on 4 December it had suffered serious losses in comparison with the previous Reichstag elections.[97] The Nazi leadership responded by formulating conditions under which they would agree to an adjournment of parliament: 'Amnesty, social improvements, the right of self-defence and to demonstrate.' At the following meeting of the parliamentary party Hitler, according to Goebbels, 'strongly rejected compromises'. 'Strasser becomes stony-faced. Deputies are unanimous about us maintaining consistent course. If possible, no dissolution before Christmas.'[98]

When in 1934 Goebbels published extracts from his diary under the title *Vom Kaiserhof zur Reichskanzlei* [From the Kaiserhof to the Reich Chancellery] he inserted a passage that revealed that the previous evening Schleicher had offered Strasser the post of Vice-Chancellor. Strasser, Goebbels wrote, had not only agreed but had informed Schleicher that at the next elections he would run for election with a 'Strasser list' of candidates, which according to Goebbels represented 'the worst kind of treachery towards the Führer and the Party'. Closer comparison of the published book with the original diary shows that Goebbels made numerous other alterations to make Strasser appear to be Hitler's malevolent opponent who had planned his 'treachery' over a long period. Goebbels's tampering with his own diary laid the foundation for a long-lasting legend, namely the idea that at the beginning of December 1932 Schleicher had attempted to use the offer of the Vice-Chancellorship to split the NSDAP with the aim of getting rid of the sclerotic party system and of governing with the support of a 'cross-front' made up of trades unions, employees' associations, and 'left-wing' Nazis. In fact this idea of bypassing the chaotic situation in domestic politics had been frequently mooted in Schleicher's entourage, but in the concrete political situation that prevailed at the start of his Chancellorship he was preoccupied first and foremost with reaching agreement with the NSDAP over the modalities of their tolerating his government.[99]

Whereas Strasser was prepared to compromise and indeed recommended that the NSDAP join the government (in which case he would in fact have been the main candidate for Vice-Chancellor) Hitler set out more stringent conditions for any agreement with the Chancellor. When parliament next met, from 6 to 9 December, a possible arrangement between the NSDAP and the government was already emerging. With the votes of the NSDAP parliament passed resolutions fully in line with the demands the Party leadership had put to Schleicher. An amnesty law was passed and important welfare cuts that had been contained in Papen's emergency measures of 4 September were reversed.[100] In December stringent measures introduced during the previous months to control domestic political terrorism were relaxed, in accordance with the Nazis' demands for the 'right of self-defence' and 'freedom to demonstrate'. Amongst other things the special courts set up in August were suspended.[101] Parliament was then adjourned until the middle of January. Schleicher assured his government on 7 December 'that the National Socialists have decided to opt for toleration'.[102] During this time Hitler, who had been staying in Berlin for the parliamentary session, was seen at various evening parties looking relaxed. There was no sign of any crisis in the NSDAP.[103]

This changed on 8 December, when Strasser suddenly decided to inform Hitler by letter that he was relinquishing all Party offices. Among the explanations Strasser gave for this move was the fact that Hitler was undermining Strasser's reform of the Party organization. Above all, however, he warned that Hitler's political strategy, which aimed to create 'chaos... and present this as the Party's moment of destiny', was neglecting the Party's real task, namely 'to create a large and broad front of working people and bring them into a reformed state.'[104] The letter came as a bombshell to the Party leadership. Around midday Hitler heard that Strasser had explained his motives in detail to the Party's regional inspectors, at least to those who were in Berlin. One of those present recalled that Strasser had criticized Hitler's policy of staking everything on being appointed Chancellor as a failure. Hitler therefore invited the same group of people, a total of seven top NSDAP functionaries, to the Kaiserhof in order to refute Strasser's argument point by point.[105] In the middle of the night Hitler, alarmed by newspaper reports about a serious crisis in the NSDAP, called an emergency meeting at the Kaiserhof attended among others by Goebbels, Röhm, and Himmler. From Hitler's perspective, the crisis seemed to threaten to split the Party. Goebbels quotes him as saying, 'If the Party falls apart I'll end it all in three minutes.'[106]

At the meeting Hitler decided to dismantle the Party apparatus created by Strasser. He took personal charge of the Party administration, appointing Robert Ley as his 'chief of staff'.[107] During the following days he disbanded several departments within the extensive bureaucracy, carried out additional changes, and finally established under Rudolf Hess a 'Political Central

Committee'. Supported by three subcommittees, it was to be responsible for promoting and monitoring the work of the Party's elected representatives both at federal state and local level, for supervising the Nazi press, and for dealing with economic issues.[108] Hitler explained the reorganization of the Party headquarters in a two-part memorandum that he sent out to the NSDAP department heads and Gauleiters in December. It contained clear criticism of the principles on which Strasser had restructured the Party during the summer, emphasizing the need in future for 'as clear as possible a separation between the structures of the movement's administration and those of its political leadership.'[109]

Yet on 9 December, the day after Strasser's resignation, Hitler's primary concern was to prevent the crisis from escalating into a Party revolt. He therefore spoke in Göring's official residence first to the Gauleiters and Party inspectors and then to the NSDAP Reichstag deputies. Goebbels's impression was that his words had a devastating impact: 'They were all howling with rage and pain. A really great success for Hitler. At the end a spontaneous demonstration of loyalty. They all shake Hitler's hand. Strasser is isolated. A dead man!'[110] Goebbels's satisfaction may have been boosted by the fact that Strasser's departure meant he was rid of the rival who had achieved greater success with the key issues on which he had focused in the 1932 summer election campaign than Hitler and Goebbels with their Führer propaganda in the autumn.

In the days following Hitler spoke at a series of meetings for NSDAP functionaries in Breslau, various cities in Central Germany, and in Hamburg. The overarching message he attempted to convey was confidence in victory and internal unity and he mentioned the conflict with Strasser only in passing as a crisis that had already been resolved. In a speech to the NSDAP deputies in the Prussian state parliament on 16 December he also concentrated on criticizing Schleicher's government and made only ironic and fleeting reference to 'hopes entertained in certain circles of splitting the NSDAP'.[111]

Towards a Hitler–Papen government

During the early days of 1933 the Party was concentrating all its efforts on the elections due to take place on 15 January in the small state of Lippe. Between 5 and 14 January Hitler spoke at sixteen different events, while other leading Party figures were keen to follow his example.[112] Hitler made Grevenburg Castle, an old moated castle owned by Baron Adolf von Oeynhausen, the headquarters of his Lippe campaign; from there he could easily reach all his speaking engagements.[113]

On 4 January, en route to the Lippe campaign, Hitler had a confidential meeting with ex-Chancellor Papen arranged by the Cologne banker Kurt von Schröder at his house. Hitler was accompanied by Hess, Keppler, and Himmler, but he and Papen had their discussion without them. Schröder noted that there had been talk of a coalition of right-wing conservatives and Nazis, with Hitler laying claim to the Chancellorship for himself. In view of the composition of parliament such a solution would still be dependent on Presidential powers. It was decided to continue the discussions.[114] A few days later Hitler revealed further details to Goebbels during a night-time journey to Berlin. Papen was 'dead set against Schleicher'. He wanted to 'topple' him and 'remove him entirely', and had the 'old man's ear' in this. An 'arrangement' had been prepared in which the Nazis would be granted either the Chancellorship or 'power ministries', in other words Defence and Interior. The diary entry makes clear that Hitler had not made the Chancellorship a condition for continuing discussions. And Goebbels learnt something else: Schleicher had no order from the President entitling him to dissolve parliament and so did not have carte blanche to prevent a parliamentary defeat.[115]

This strictly confidential meeting was, however, made public as the result of an indiscretion and prompted wild speculation in the press. As a result, Papen decided to go on the offensive. At a meeting with Schleicher he evidently created the impression that Hitler had demanded the Defence and Interior Ministries for himself – in a government with Schleicher as Chancellor.[116] As Hindenburg would never give Hitler the Ministry of Defence (a conclusion Schleicher passed on to his cabinet), the assumption was that Hitler could not really be interested in entering the government.[117] A few days later, on the other hand, at an audience with Hindenburg Papen declared that during the talks Hitler had relaxed his demand for a Chancellorship supported by Presidential powers and was now in fact prepared to join a government under conservative leadership. Hindenburg received Papen's report in a positive spirit, authorizing him to continue working behind the scenes on a conservative–National Socialist coalition.[118] Meanwhile Schleicher's government was still losing ground. On 11 January the Reichslandbund presented their grievances about the cabinet's agricultural

policy to the President and Chancellor and the same evening issued a declaration of war on the government.[119] In the meantime Schleicher was trying
to gain support from another quarter; in mid-January the leadership of the
NSDAP put about the rumour that Strasser, who was presumed to have had
a meeting with Hindenburg on 6 January, might join Schleicher's cabinet as
Vice=Chancellor.[120] At the cabinet meeting on 16 January Schleicher did in
fact speculate that it might be necessary for the government to create 'a
broad basis, perhaps ranging from Strasser to the Centre Party'. Strasser, he
said, would 'gladly' join the cabinet, although it was doubtful whether he
'would bring many supporters with him'.[121]

One day before this, on 15 January, the NSDAP had gained 39.5 per cent
of the votes in the Lippe elections, less than in the record-breaking July
election, but considerably more than in the Reichstag election in November.
Party propaganda declared the result an overwhelming victory, dispelling
any idea of the Party's having ground to a standstill.[122] Hitler immediately
set about putting an end once and for all to his association with Strasser. At
a Gauleiters' meeting he had summoned for 16 January he at first left it to
Ley to present 'the case'. There was a lively exchange of views, after which
all the Gauleiters supported Hitler, who did not appear in the hall until after
this discussion had taken place. He then made a three-hour speech dealing
with Party principles, which, as Gauleiter Rudolf Jordan recorded, turned
the event into a 'something like a profession of faith'.[123] Their confidence
boosted by the Lippe elections, the NSDAP leaders continued the exploratory talks with Papen. On 18 January there was a meeting at the villa of the
urbane wine and spirits wholesaler Joachim von Ribbentrop. This time
Hitler was accompanied by Röhm and Himmler. Hitler again demanded to
be made Chancellor and when Papen raised objections he refused to continue discussions. Papen, however, arranged a further meeting with Hitler
for 22 January at Ribbentrop's villa, taking with him Hindenburg's son,
Oskar, and his state secretary Meissner.[124] On this occasion Papen indicated
that he would be prepared to settle for the post of Vice-Chancellor.[125]

The following day Papen reported back to Hindenburg, but the President
was still unwilling to accept Hitler as Chancellor.[126] Schleicher too was
unsuccessful in getting what he wanted. That morning, apprised of the
meeting between Papen and Hitler, he had asked Hindenburg for an
undated dissolution order for the Reichstag in order to prevent any no confidence vote that might arise when parliament convened a few days later. In
addition, he wished to delay the fresh elections that were due beyond the

time frame of sixty days laid down in the constitution – a move that the President had consented to already under Papen's government. In the meantime, however, Schleicher, who had taken up office promising to bring the Nazis on board, had blocked his own path to finding an extra-constitutional solution to the crisis by 'proving' by means of the 'war games' exercise worked out with von Ott that in a civil war situation the army would not be capable of resisting the forces of the radical Left and Right. It was therefore only logical for Hindenburg to refuse his request and tell him simply to reconsider dissolving parliament.[127]

Meanwhile the negotiations between the Nazis and Papen had reached a decisive stage. On 24 January Frick and Göring again had a meeting with Papen at Ribbentrop's villa, where there was a discussion about whether a Hitler/Papen cabinet could attract support from a wider circle of conservatives.[128] The 'Harzburg Front' was therefore to be revived. To that end offers were made in the days following to Hugenberg and Seldte. Whereas the leader of the Stahlhelm was ready to talk, the negotiations with Hugenberg proved more difficult. On 27 January a meeting took place between, on the one side, Hugenberg and the chair of the DNVP Reichstag parliamentary party, Otto Schmidt-Hannover, and, on the other Hitler, Göring, and Frick, at which Hitler demanded the Prussian and the Reich Interior Ministries for the NSDAP. When Hugenberg objected and indeed demanded numerous appointments for his party, Hitler terminated the discussions and threatened to leave for Munich.[129] Papen, however, who met afterwards with Ribbentrop and heard from him about Hitler's furious reaction, indicated to the Nazis that he attached no great importance to Hugenberg's uncooperative attitude. He himself was now fully behind Hitler as Chancellor and would do his very best to get the President to agree to it.[130]

Around midday on 28 January Schleicher, who was looking for support, once again had an interview with the President. When Hindenburg once and for all refused to grant him the crucial instrument, namely the dissolution order, Schleicher, who that morning had agreed on this course of action with his cabinet, offered his government's resignation, which the President accepted.[131] Hindenburg then officially gave Papen the task of conducting talks leading to the creation of a new cabinet. Papen, however, had been notified that same morning by the President of Schleicher's imminent resignation and at around 11 a.m. had told Ribbentrop that after a lengthy discussion with Hindenburg he considered it possible that Hitler might be made Chancellor. Ribbentrop and Göring passed on this message to Hitler at the Kaiserhof.

Both tried to dissuade Hitler from making any new demand, namely the post of Reich Commissar for Prussia. In the end Hitler declared himself prepared to reconsider the matter and to meet Papen the following day.[132]

On the afternoon of 28 January Papen succeeded in overcoming Hugenberg's resistance to the appointment of National Socialists to the two Interior ministries. In addition, he managed to persuade the majority of members of the old government to remain in office under a Hitler/Papen government.[133] The same evening representatives of the Centre Party and the BVP contacted Hitler and declared themselves prepared to participate in a majority cabinet led by him, but met with no response.[134] When Papen called on Hindenburg once again in the late evening[135] the latter now in fact indicated that he would not stand in the way of Hitler becoming Chancellor, provided appropriate safeguards were built in. These included the continuation in office of the majority of serving ministers, among whom Hindenburg was particularly keen to see the Foreign Minister, Konstantin von Neurath, remain. He also insisted on Papen's agreement to serve as Vice-Chancellor and the appointment of Werner von Blomberg, commander of the East Prussian defence district and military adviser to the German disarmament delegation in Geneva, as Defence Minister.[136]

On 29 January there were further negotiations between Hitler, Göring, and Papen at which Hitler got agreement to Frick becoming Reich Minister of the Interior and Göring Prussian Minister of the Interior, while in return accepting Hindenburg's demand that Papen be appointed Vice-Chancellor and Reich Commissar in Prussia. In addition, Hitler now for the first time demanded the dissolution of parliament and fresh elections, stipulating also that the new Reichstag should provide him with an enabling act. He regarded both these demands as crucial if he was later to circumvent the safeguards that Papen and Hindenburg had built into the composition of the government.[137] At a round of talks in the afternoon Papen sought to gain the support of the Stahlhelm and the DNVP by offering Seldte the Ministry of Labour and Hugenberg the Ministries of Economics and Agriculture in the Reich and in Prussia in a Hitler-led cabinet. Papen kept quiet about Hitler's demand for fresh elections.[138] Whereas Seldte and Hugenberg were inclined to agree to this proposal, Duesterberg, the number two national Stahlhelm leader, and a series of prominent German nationalist politicians strongly opposed these coalition plans and tried to influence Hugenberg and Papen to bring about a Presidential cabinet under Papen that would govern, as it were, dictatorially.[139]

Then, all of a sudden, rumours began circulating in Berlin that Hindenburg in fact intended to appoint a Presidential government under Papen – and that the army leadership was planning to prevent this by force. This false information, the source of which cannot be established, accelerated the formation of the government. The Defence Minister designate, Blomberg, was met at Anhalter Station by Oskar von Hindenburg, who brought him to the Presidential office, where he was to be sworn in by Hindenburg as the new Defence Minister, even before the cabinet was officially appointed.[140] Hindenburg's son arrived just ahead of another officer who was supposed to bring Blomberg to Schleicher so that he could be persuaded not to accept the appointment. President Hindenburg, who demonstrated by this move his particular confidence in the 'unpolitical' General Blomberg, did not at this point know of the existence of special contacts between Hitler and Blomberg's staff in Königsberg.[141]

On the evening of 29 January Papen presented Hindenburg with the list of cabinet members he had negotiated and agreed that they would be sworn in the next morning. In doing so he had complied with the President's wishes in two respects. The latter could believe that the new government was beholden to him personally, as his go-between Papen and not the future Reich Chancellor had concluded the negotiations,[142] and he could see that the Nazi members of the government were 'framed' by conservative politicians and experts. Four politically unaligned ministers from Schleicher's government were to be in the cabinet: Neurath (Foreign Office), Count Lutz Schwerin von Krosigk (Finance), Paul von Eltz-Rübenach (Post and Transport), and Günther Gereke as Reich Commissar for Work Creation. Hugenberg was to be 'Super Minister' for Economics and Agriculture, Blomberg Minister of Defence, Seldte Minister of Labour, Papen as Deputy Reich Chancellor (a title that was supposed to emphasize his significance as Vice-Chancellor) and Reich Commissar for Prussia. The Nazis were represented only by the Chancellor, the future Minister of the Interior, Frick, and by Göring as Reich Minister without portfolio and Reich Commissar for Aviation. The simultaneously agreed appointment of the Nazis Göring and Bernhard Rust as Reich Commissars in Prussia responsible for the Ministry of the Interior (Göring) and the Ministry of Education (Rust) respectively was to be balanced by the fact that the other Reich Commissars in Prussia were on the conservative wing (in addition to Papen there was Hugenberg for Economics and Agriculture, Johannes Popitz for Finance, and Heinrich Hölscher as acting state secretary in the Justice Ministry).[143] In addition,

Papen hoped to persuade the President to assume the post of 'State President in Prussia', which would have completed the 'framing' of the Nazis.[144] This 'framing' notion proved to be illusory, however. Instead, in the next few weeks the Nazis exploited precisely the arrangements created for Prussia as a lever by which to free themselves from this 'framing', in fact using the Prussian police, now in Göring's hands, as their instrument. Within a very short time Hitler, Göring, and Frick proved able to coordinate their actions and thus lay the foundations for the dictatorship. They could do this because, thanks to Papen's Prussian coup of 20 July 1932, the old balance of power between the Reich and the largest German state, which had been controlled by democratic forces and in previous years had acted as a crucial barrier to the ultimate destruction of the Weimar Republic, had ceased to exist.

On 29 January the Reich Minister of Justice had not yet been appointed. Papen thus gave Hindenburg the impression that this ministry was being reserved for the Centre Party, which would most likely also participate in the government. Thus, on the evening of 29 January, Hindenburg gave his approval to a government that he assumed would sooner or later be able to command a majority in the Reichstag.[145]

On the morning of 30 January a meeting took place at Papen's house at which Duesterberg and Schmidt-Hannover expressed serious reservations about the appointment of Hitler as Chancellor. A little later Hitler and Göring arrived. Hitler succeeded in allaying Duesterberg's fears by assuring him that he deeply regretted the attacks the Nazi press had made on him personally (some months previously it had come to light that some of Duesterberg's ancestors had been Jewish).[146] The designated cabinet members then went to the nearby Reich Chancellery. Immediately before they were sworn in there was a final row when Hugenberg found out that Papen had told Hitler he could have fresh elections. Hugenberg refused to agree to this demand, whereas Hitler absolutely insisted on it. After a heated debate, which almost caused the negotiations to collapse, Hitler gave Hugenberg his word of honour that after the elections he would not alter the composition of the government. Under great pressure, for it was already 15 minutes past the time agreed for them to meet the President, Hugenberg finally gave way.[147] The new government was sworn in at 11.30 a.m.

Anyone examining the way in which the Hitler/Papen government came into being is struck by the extraordinary skill and low cunning of Papen. A reckless gambler, Papen had done much to undermine the reputation of his successor, Schleicher, with the President and had secured his assignment of negotiating a government by at first keeping quiet to Hindenburg about Hitler's demand for the Chancellorship, while creating in Hitler the impression that Hindenburg approved of him as Chancellor. He pulled off the feat of convincing the President that he, Hindenburg, had the final say on the formation of the government while simultaneously making it appear that Hitler's government was searching for a parliamentary majority. He managed to bring Hugenberg and Hitler together by making Hugenberg believe that he would become a sort of economic dictator, while on the other hand granting the Nazis the Reich and Prussian Ministries of the Interior, and making Hindenburg believe that he, Papen, as Vice-Chancellor and Reich Commissar for Prussia, could prevent the Nazis from taking control of the Prussian police. Finally, he delayed telling Hugenberg of Hitler's crucial demand for fresh elections, forcing him to concede them at the very last moment. For all his negotiating acrobatics, however, he had created an extremely fragile edifice dependent on conflicting and unfulfillable commitments. It could not survive.

On the Nazi side, Ribbentrop and Göring had performed important roles as mediators, while Hitler had taken more of a patient and passive role as the candidate Papen was wooing, until, having seen through Papen's deceptive and risky negotiating strategy, he exploited it gradually to introduce three crucial demands that in the end would give him the upper hand in the new government. At first he had left the question of his claim to the Chancellorship open, then demanding it all the more insistently and finally succeeding. He had demanded the Interior ministries and then managed to get fresh elections. To achieve all this he had several times put at serious risk the whole project of a government that included the NSDAP through his abrupt and unbending attitude. Yet what his negotiating partners may have construed as an unrestrained, irrational, even hysterical side to his character can also be interpreted as calculated unpredictability, which he used to put his opponents under pressure to act, knowing full well that they had no alternative.

Since 1929 Hitler had tried various strategies on his path to power, sometimes using them in parallel, sometimes trying one and then the other: cooperation with the Right, agreements with the Centre Party, working with the President, or the NSDAP pressing forward on its own, whether taking a constitutional path (as in the case of the Presidential elections) or by recourse to 'revolutionary tactics', in spite of the Party's official policy of 'legality'. In the end he came to power through a combination of these strategies. He revived the Harzburg Front, but within the framework of

Presidential government, and he created the impression that he wished to include the Centre Party in the government. At the same time, he gave the impatient 'revolutionary' elements in the Party some prospect of a 'show-down' with their political opponents (the SA had offered a foretaste of this with its wave of terror in the summer of 1932) and exploited these elements as an unmistakable threat always in the background. Finally, contrary to all agreements and safeguards he was successfully to secure a monopoly of power for the Party.

Hitler was neither swept into the Chancellor's office by a mass movement nor hoisted into the saddle by a conservative clique that aimed to use him as a means to an end. While both elements are essential to any explanation of the particular constellation leading to Hitler's becoming Chancellor, any-one wishing to get to the bottom of how this arrangement would inevitably lead to dictatorship must factor in Hitler's actions as an individual. He exploited the room for manoeuvre he enjoyed in late 1932 and early 1933, precisely after his party had *lost some of its electoral support*, to create an arrangement that (a) satisfied the conservatives, (b) still allowed him the possibility of a 'seizure of power' by the NSDAP, and (c) as a result, provided a safety valve for the pent-up dissatisfaction in the Party.

Hitler's persistent demand at the end of 1932 to be made Chancellor governing through Presidential decree only appeared to be leading to a dead-end from which he was rescued by Papen. In fact through his unwavering refusal to join a government supported by Presidential decree merely as a minister or to be made to commit himself to a course of tol-erating a conservative government, he put pressure on his conservative opponents, thereby involving Papen in the process. For within the Presidential regime Hindenburg and his advisers had in the meantime exhausted all pos-sible political options and were faced with the question of whether they should suspend the constitution and set up a military dictatorship. As they could not bring themselves to take this step, however, they had no choice but to give the office of Chancellor to the leader of the strongest party, Hitler, a man who in the final stages of negotiation exploited his position without scruple, consistently stepped up his demands, and thus made the safeguards that had originally been planned ineffective. Thus at the end of January 1933 Hitler had with considerable political skill created the crucial base from which a change of Chancellor could be turned into a compre-hensive take-over of power.

PART III

Establishing the Regime

12

'The Seizure of Power'

When Hitler was appointed Chancellor on 30 January 1933 the Weimar Republic had already ceased to function as an effective democracy. Under the authoritarian Presidential regime parliament and the political parties had been marginalized in the political process, the democratic 'bulwark' of Prussia had been destroyed by Papen, and, for some years, the state and the judiciary had been encouraging right-wing extremism. Nevertheless, at the turn of the year 1932/33, the NSDAP still had no more than one-third of the electorate behind it and it was by no means a matter of course that the whole of the state apparatus, as well as the wide range of very varied social organizations would simply yield to the Nazis' drive for power. Significantly, the majority of political observers did not regard the new government as the start of a change of regime, but rather reckoned with another brief government that would soon be exhausted by the major problems confronting it.[1] Thus the establishment of a dictatorship was not the inevitable result of Hitler's becoming Chancellor. On the contrary, the transformation of the Presidential government of Hitler/Papen/Hugenberg into a Hitler dictatorship was a complicated process, lasting eighteen months and requiring a considerable amount of direction and great political skill.

Hitler was able to establish his dictatorship only because he had an army of millions of active supporters behind him bent on taking over power. However, this support was heterogeneous, with very diverse goals. The SA, nearly 500,000 strong, wanted first of all to take revenge on their political opponents; these so-called 'brown shirts', however, also assumed that under the new regime they would be rewarded for all their efforts and sacrifices during the 'time of struggle' and would be looked after in some way. The Party functionaries (the NSDAP had around 850,000 members at the beginning of 1933) were after jobs in the state apparatus; those small retailers organized in the Kampfbund für den gewerblichen Mittelstand [Combat

League for Small Business] wanted to put an end to department stores; the members of the National Socialist Factory Cell Organization (NSBO) demanded workers' participation in business; industrialists who supported the Nazis demanded an end to trade union representation on company boards; and journalists, doctors, teachers, and the like who were members of the Party's professional associations wanted to dominate their various professional bodies. Thus, this very diverse movement wanted to bring every organization in the state and society under its control, and the Party membership's ambition to take over power provided the real dynamic behind the measures adopted by Hitler and the Party leadership.

While Hitler and the Party leadership needed to keep these various, and to some extent contradictory, claims in view, to satisfy them, and in some cases to reconcile them, they had at the same time to make sure that these diverse ambitions did not undermine the alliance with the conservatives or damage the economy. Thus, it was vital to acquire power in stages, so as to allow the Nazis to concentrate on one goal, or a limited number of goals, at a time. Basically, this process took place in two stages. In the first, which lasted until the summer of 1933, political power was concentrated in the hands of the largely Nazi-controlled government. In the second, which came to an end in the late summer of 1934, the decisive moves were the action taken against the SA on 30 June 1934 and the take-over of the office of Reich President. These enabled Hitler permanently to exclude the conservatives from influence in the government, to eliminate opposition within the Party, and to establish a dictatorship without any constitutional limitations.

This chapter is concerned with the first phase, the period between January and the summer of 1933, in other words those months covering what is generally known as the 'seizure of power'. In this analysis we are following the model of a 'seizure of power' in stages set out by Karl Dietrich Bracher over fifty years ago in his ground-breaking book, which is still essential reading.[2] This model, however, shows clearly that the process was by no means automatic; Hitler intervened decisively at every stage and to a considerable extent controlled and steered the course of events.

Stage 1: Neutralizing the political Left

The first meeting of the new cabinet took place on the afternoon of 30 January. The following day, the Reichstag was supposed to be reconvening after a two-month break and Hitler pointed out that they would need the support of the Centre Party to secure a postponement, unless they were to ban the KPD and secure a majority that way. Unlike Hugenberg, Hitler did not want to go down that path as he feared serious domestic unrest and a possible general strike. So it would be best if parliament were dissolved, thereby providing the government with the opportunity to establish a majority through a new election.[3] Thus, Hitler was demanding that his coalition partners immediately fulfil the important promise they had made to him just before his government took office.

On the evening of 30 January, the Nazis celebrated their triumph in Berlin with a torchlight procession lasting several hours through the government quarter. In Wilhelmstrasse Hindenburg received the ovations of the marching columns, which, in accordance with his wishes, included the Stahlhelm. However, the cheering was, above all, for Hitler, who appeared on a balcony in the Reich Chancellery. Goebbels immediately took advantage of his new powers by providing a running commentary on the radio.[4]

As Hitler had hoped, a meeting arranged for the next day with senior members of the Centre Party failed to reach agreement on the question of postponement. The Centre Party negotiators were understandably unwilling to agree to a suspension of parliament for a year without receiving guarantees of their influence on the government in the meantime. Hitler immediately used these reservations as an excuse to break off negotiations.[5] At the next cabinet meeting, which took place on the same day, his conservative coalition partners were only too happy to agree with Hitler that future negotiations with the Centre were pointless and so they should call new elections.[6] Hitler had initially kept the post of Minister of Justice vacant, leaving open the option of filling it with a member of the Centre Party. This reinforced the conservatives' concern that he could after all arrange a coalition with the Centre Party behind their backs. For the time being, this option was now blocked and, on the following day, the conservative, Franz Gürtner, who had been Reich Minister of Justice under Schleicher, was appointed to the post. Finally, at the cabinet meeting of 31 January, Hitler noted that the cabinet were all agreed that these should be the last elections: a 'return to the parliamentary system was to be avoided at all costs'.[7] Hitler aimed to secure a majority for the Nazis mainly because he wanted to free himself from his reliance on the President's authority to issue emergency decrees and so from his dependence on the right-wing conservatives.

On 1 February Hindenburg signed the decree to dissolve the Reichstag 'after', as Hitler made clear to him, 'it has proved impossible to secure a working majority', and he called new elections for 5 March.[8] Up until then, the cabinet was able to govern by using the President's right to issue decrees.

On the same day, Hitler put to the cabinet an 'Appeal to the German People', which he read out on the radio late that evening. He began with his usual narrative about the last – in the meantime – '14 years' in which the country had presented 'a picture of heartbreaking disunity'. Now, at the height of the crisis, 'the Communist method of madness [is trying], as a last resort, to poison and subvert a damaged and shattered nation'. Everything was at stake: 'Starting with the family, and including all notions of honour and loyalty, nation and fatherland, even the eternal foundations of our morals and our faith.' Thus, Hitler continued with feeling, 'our venerable World War leader' had appealed 'to us men, who are members of the nation-alist parties and associations, to fight under him once again, as we did at the front, but now, united in loyalty, for the salvation of the Reich at home'. Employing a hollow and clichéd set of values, he referred to 'Christianity as the basis of the whole of our morality', the 'family as the nucleus of our nation and our state', the consciousness of 'ethnic and political unity', 'respect for our great past', 'pride in our old traditions' as the basis for the 'education of German youth'. Hitler intended to improve the catastrophic economic situation by 'reorganizing the national economy' with the help of two great 'four-year-plans', which would secure the peasants' livelihoods and start to get to grips with unemployment. 'Compulsory labour service' and 'settlement policy' were among the 'main pillars' of this programme. As far as foreign policy was concerned, the Chancellor contented himself with the comment that the government saw 'its most important mission as the preservation of our nation's right to live and, as a result, the regaining of its freedom'; he expressly committed himself to maintaining international limits on armaments. Hitler concluded by appealing to the Almighty to bless the work of the new government.[9]

On 2 February, the new Chancellor introduced himself to the Reichsrat [Reich Federal Council] and asked the state governments for support. The SPD and the Centre Party still had a majority in the Council, for Hamburg, Bavaria, Baden, and Württemberg were still not yet in Nazi hands, and in Prussia, thanks to a ruling by the Prussian Supreme Court of 25 October 1932, the constitutional and SPD-dominated Braun government was still able to perform certain functions, in spite of the appointment of the Reich

Commissar the previous July.[10] These included the representation of Prussia in the Reichsrat and Hitler inevitably regarded it as an affront that the Social Democrat civil servant, Arnold Brecht, in his reply to Hitler's address warned him to obey the constitution and demanded the restoration of constitutional conditions in Prussia.[11] Hitler was now more than ever determined to get rid of the opposition bloc in Germany's biggest state, made up of the SPD and Centre Party. When the NSDAP parliamentary group's motion to dissolve the Prussian parliament was defeated, he secured a Reich presidential decree 'to restore orderly government in Prussia',[12] transferring all responsibilities from Prime Minister Braun to Reich Commissar Papen. Braun appealed against this breach of the Reich and Prussian constitutions and contravention of the Prussian supreme court's judgment, but the issue was delayed until March and, finally, following Braun's emigration, became redundant.[13] Thanks to his new powers, Papen was able to dissolve the Prussian parliament on 6 February.[14] Already on the previous day the acting government had dissolved all the Prussian provincial parliaments, district councils, city and town councils and called new elections for 12 March. This measure was aimed at getting control of the Prussian State Council, the Prussian second chamber.

On 3 February, the cabinet issued a decree 'for the protection of the German people', intended to facilitate the banning of meetings and newspapers during the coming general election. Hitler had rejected the original draft, which had gone even further, containing heavy penalties for strikes in 'plants essential to life', because it would have involved a public acknowledgement that the government feared a general strike. However, this fear was unfounded. Although, on 30 January, the KPD had called on the SPD and the trade unions for a joint general strike, the lack of preparations, the deep divisions within the labour movement, and the hopelessness of such a move – the regime controlled all the instruments of state power as well as the paramilitary SA and SS – prevented common action.[15]

On 3 February, the Defence Minister, General Werner von Blomberg, invited Hitler to meet the senior Reichswehr commanders for the first time. They met in the house of the Chief of the General Staff, General Kurt Freiherr von Hammerstein-Equord, where the new Chancellor expounded the basic ideas of his foreign and defence policy to the assembled company. After an introduction about the importance of 'race', Hitler quickly got to the main point: the current unemployment could be dealt with in only two ways: through an increase in exports or 'a major settlement programme, for which the precondition is an expansion of the German people's living space.... This would be my proposal'. In fifty to sixty years' time they would then be dealing with a 'completely new and healthy state'. 'This is why it is our task to seize political power, ruthlessly suppress every subversive opinion, and improve the nation's morale.' Once 'Marxism' had been eliminated, the army would 'have first-class recruits as a result of the educative work of my movement and it will be guaranteed that recruits will retain their high morale and nationalist spirit even after they have been discharged'. This is why he was aiming to acquire 'total political power. I have set a deadline of 6–8 years to destroy Marxism completely.[16] Then the army will be capable of pursuing an active foreign policy and the goal of extending the German people's living space will be achieved with force of arms. The objective will probably be the East.' Since it was 'possible to Germanize only land' and not people, in the course of the conquest they would have 'ruthlessly to expel several million people'. However, they needed to act with 'the greatest possible speed' so that, in the meantime, France did not intervene and ally itself with the Soviet Union. Hitler concluded with an appeal to the generals 'to fight along with me for the great goal, to understand me, and to support me, not with weapons, but morally. I have forged my own weapon for the internal struggle; the army is there only to deal with foreign conflicts. You will never find another man who is so committed to fighting with all his strength for his aim of saving Germany as I am. And if people say to me: "Achieving this aim depends on you!" Fine, then let us use my life.'[17]

In his speech Hitler had revealed not only his long-term plans for conquest and Germanization, but above all the basis for a close cooperation between the Reichswehr and his regime. In fact the aim of making the Reichswehr ready for war in six to eight years was entirely compatible with the military's own rearmament plans.[18]

With his announcement that his movement would deliver the army first-class recruits and maintain the morale of the reservists even after their discharge, Hitler was recognizing the Reichswehr's claim to dominance in the sphere of military policy, with the implication that in future the SA would be restricted to auxiliary functions. At the same time, it confirmed an agreement that he had made with Blomberg in the cabinet meeting on 30 January that, in contrast to its role under Papen and Schleicher, the army would, as a matter of principle, no longer be used to support the government in domestic politics and instead concentrate entirely on its role as a future instrument of war.[19]

A few days later, the close cooperation between Hitler and Blomberg was given practical expression. At the cabinet meeting on 8 February Hitler emphasized that 'the next five years must be devoted to the remilitarization of the German people'; every publicly supported measure to create work should be judged on whether it was necessary for this purpose.[20] However, at this point, as he openly admitted to his cabinet, Hitler was in any case not prepared to authorize a major programme of pump-priming the economy – for electoral reasons. Issuing more credit was liable to meet with opposition from his conservative coalition partners.[21]

Thus, contrary to Hitler's bombastic announcement of 1 February, the new government confined itself to using the money provided by the Schleicher government for work creation, which had been financed with credit. This occurred the following day at a cabinet committee presided over by Hitler with 140 million RM to distribute. They decided to provide 50 million RM for the Reichswehr and 10 million RM for aviation. Defence Minister Blomberg explained that the Reichswehr had launched 'a large rearmament programme spread over several years'; he was referring to the so-called Second Rearmament Programme, which had been agreed in 1932 in anticipation of the lifting of the Versailles Treaty's restrictions on armaments, and was intended to start on 1 April 1933.[22] Blomberg asked Hitler directly to approve the finance for the whole programme, which was costed at around 500 million RM. Hitler agreed that rearmament would require 'millions of Reich Marks' and was 'absolutely' decisive for the future of Germany. 'All other tasks must be subordinate to the task of rearmament.' The cabinet also approved the statement by the Reich Commissioner for Aviation that he had agreed a three-year 'minimum programme' with the Defence Ministry costing 127 million RM.[23]

After only a few days, therefore, it was apparent that Hitler's determination to rearm Germany, was matched by a military leadership that was about to ignore the military restrictions of the Versailles Treaty. It was true that the Second Rearmament Programme, with its planned expansion of the 100,000-strong professional army by 43,000 professional soldiers over five years and the training of 85,000 short service volunteers per year, was relatively modest. However, already on 1 April 1933, as the first stage, 14,000 professional soldiers were to be recruited in contravention of the provisions of Versailles. It was impossible to keep this secret over the long term. In other words, the military were determined to overcome the Versailles armament restrictions – either within the context of an international disarmament agreement or through independent action by Germany – and Hitler was only too ready to adopt these concrete rearmament measures himself.[24] From the point of view of the generals his 'take-over of power' could not have come at a better time.

Now it was a matter of making sure these plans could be realized. The NSDAP totally dominated the campaign for the Reichstag election of 5 March.[25] The Party concentrated its campaign entirely on Hitler; 'Hitler is going to rebuild' was the slogan, which once again aimed at arousing vague emotions – trust and hope – while dispensing with concrete political aims. At the cabinet meeting on 8 February Hitler had recommended that 'election propaganda should, if possible, avoid all detailed statements about a Reich economic programme. The Reich government must win 18–19 million votes. An economic programme that could win the approval of such a huge electorate simply does not exist'.[26] The second theme of the NSDAP campaign was the struggle with the left-wing parties. On 8 February, Hitler bluntly told a group of leading journalists: 'In ten years' time Marxism will not exist in Germany'.[27]

On 10 February, for the first time since his appointment as Chancellor, Hitler spoke at a mass meeting in the Berlin Sportpalast. The speech, introduced by the head of the Party's propaganda Joseph Goebbels, to create the appropriate 'mood', was broadcast by all radio stations and designed to project the energy with which the new government intended to solve the crisis and unite the nation. After '14 years' of decline they must 'completely rebuild the German nation'. 'That', as Hitler taunted his political opponents, 'is our programme!' He was not, however, going to provide any further details. Instead, he reached the high point of his rhetoric, an 'appeal' to his audience: '... Germans, give us four years and then assess us and judge us. Germans, give us four years and I swear that, just as we, and just as I, have taken on this office, I shall then leave it.' Hitler finished with a kind of confession of faith in the German people, which in its cadences and formulation was intended to be reminiscent of the Lord's Prayer:

> For I must believe in my nation. I must hold on to my conviction that this nation will rise again. I must keep loving this nation and am utterly convinced that the hour will come when those who hate us today will be standing behind us and will join us in welcoming the new German Reich we have created together with effort, struggle, and hardship, a Reich that is great, honourable, powerful, glorious, and just. Amen.[28]

During the following days and weeks there were more mass meetings, modelled on the Sportpalast one, in Stuttgart, Dortmund, and Cologne, introduced by Goebbels in the guise of a 'reporter'. Radio had already been used for government propaganda under Papen, but the broadcasting of election meetings was new. Some states that were not yet in Nazi hands raised objections to this breach of radio's party political neutrality. On 8 February the cabinet had agreed the following arrangement: Hitler would be given privileged access to radio only in his capacity as head of the government, not as a party leader; Goebbels's introductions should not exceed ten minutes, a limit which Goebbels did not, of course, abide by.[29]

At this point, the regime took tough action against the Left. On 1 February, Göring had already issued a general ban on KPD meetings in Prussia, which the other Nazi-controlled states (Brunswick, Thuringia, Mecklenburg, Oldenburg, and Anhalt) then also introduced; the communist press could not appear regularly as a result of numerous bans, so that the party's election campaign soon came to a halt. Karl Liebknecht House, the KPD's Berlin headquarters, was repeatedly searched and, on 23 February, shut down altogether. In response, after 7 February, the party began adopting illegal methods of operating, but worked on the assumption that there would not be a ban before the election. In the second half of February, the SPD's campaign was also significantly restricted by bans on meetings and newspapers and the large-scale disturbance of its meetings by Nazi mobs.[30] The two workers' parties, which had been engaged in a bitter struggle since 1918/19, had no means of countering these attacks: they did not have the resources for an armed uprising and they were not geared for a general strike or even for continuing political work underground. On the contrary, the SPD tried to keep its struggle against the government within legal bounds for as long as possible.

However, the repression did not affect the Left only. On 15 February, Hitler used a big meeting in Stuttgart to mount strong attacks on the Centre Party, which in Württemberg formed the majority of the government. However, political opponents interrupted the broadcast of the meeting by cutting the main cable. The cabinet regarded this action as 'sabotage' and a 'major blow against the authority of the Reich government'.[31] Hitler's Stuttgart attacks on the Centre marked the start of a Reich-wide campaign against the Catholic party, which in the light of the 'Stuttgart act of sabotage' increased in intensity and in some cases became violent. Centre Party meetings and newspapers were banned; civil servants who were party members

were, like Social Democrats, suspended or dismissed;[32] a torchlight procession of Centre Party supporters, following a meeting with Brüning in
Kaiserslautern, suffered an armed attack. Following a subsequent complaint
by the chairman of the Centre Party in the Rhineland to the Reich President
and the Vice-Chancellor about the continuing 'terror', Hitler felt compelled
to intervene.[33] A major offensive against the Centre Party *at this point* did
not suit his intentions. Thus, acting on his authority as Party leader, he
ordered a stop to the attacks by Nazi activists with the statement: 'The
enemy that must be crushed on 5 March is Marxism! All our propaganda
and thus the whole of the campaign must concentrate on that!'[34]

And that is exactly what happened during the remaining two weeks
before the election. It now became apparent how Papen's 1932 Prussian
coup played into the hands of the NSDAP. Göring, who had taken over the
Prussian Ministry of the Interior in an acting capacity, systematically purged
the top ranks of the Prussian administration and police of democratic officials.[35] On 17 February, he instructed the police to provide the 'nationalist
leagues', the SA, SS, and Stahlhelm, and the propaganda of the government
parties with wholehearted support. By contrast, they should proceed against
the agitation of 'organizations hostile to the state' with all means at their
disposal and, if necessary, 'make ruthless use of their weapons'.[36] On 22
February, he ordered the creation of (armed) auxiliary police units from
members of the SA, SS, and Stahlhelm. Simply by putting on an arm band,
members of paramilitary leagues became enforcers of state policy.[37]

On 27 February, the cabinet agreed a decree that not only increased the
penalties for espionage, but was above all directed against 'activities amounting to high treason', including resistance to the police and military, as well
as calls for general and mass strikes. The Justice Minister Gürtner's desire to
publish the decree before election day shows that the new government was
hurriedly creating a new weapon that would enable it to crush any opposition effectively and conclusively.[38]

Meanwhile, Hitler had been continuing his election campaign with mass
meetings that were broadcast on the radio.[39] On 20 February, he was able to
fill the NSDAP's election campaign coffers; at Göring's official residence in
Berlin he addressed two dozen leading industrialists whom he promised
that 'Marxism' would be 'finished' either in the coming elections, 'or there
will be a fight fought with other weapons'. In the end, he ensured that the
guests agreed to put up a total of three million RM, which the NSDAP
urgently needed to finance its election campaign.[40]

Stage 2: The removal of basic rights

During the night of 27/28 February, the Reichstag was set on fire. To this day the background to this event has remained obscure and may well remain so. The Nazis' claim that the fire was started by the KPD as a signal for an uprising can be dismissed; it proved impossible to provide any decisive proof. On the contrary, the Reich Supreme Court was obliged to acquit the accused communist functionaries and it was to become clear that the communists were totally unprepared for an uprising.[41] The second explanation, according to which the 24-year-old Dutch worker, Marinus van der Lubbe was solely responsible for the fire, has dominated research for a long time. Its main flaw is that it is difficult to see how a single individual could set fire to and destroy such a large building. The third explanation, which blames the fire on a Nazi plot, possibly organized by the President of the Reichstag, Hermann Göring, is plausible given the systematic persecution that followed, but cannot be adequately proved.

The debate between the supporters of the Nazi plot idea and those claiming a single individual was responsible has been shaped by two important alternative theories about the functioning of the Nazi state: on the one hand, the assumption that the seizure of power was carefully planned, and on the other that the Party leadership had largely improvised its take-over.[42] However, these alternative explanatory models do not necessarily contribute much to answering the question: who started the fire? In fact, this question is basically of secondary importance for the history of the seizure of power and Hitler's role in the process. What is decisive is the fact that, as early as that night, he used the situation to introduce extensive emergency powers, thereby removing legal restrictions on the persecution of his political opponents and establishing arbitrary rule.

Hitler was spending the evening of 27 February with Goebbels when he received the telephone call informing him of the Reichstag fire. They both quickly set off for the parliament, where Göring and Papen were already waiting for them. They soon agreed that the communists must have been responsible. After an initial consultation with Papen, Hitler met Goebbels, who, in the meantime, had mobilized the Gau headquarters, in the Kaiserhof. It is clear from Goebbels's diary that they were not exactly concerned about a communist uprising: 'Everyone's delighted. That's all we needed. Now we're really in the clear.'[43] Hitler and Goebbels drove from the Kaiserhof to the editorial offices of the *Völkischer Beobachter*, where Hitler personally took over redesigning the next issue.[44]

The impression given by Goebbels of a very calculating and determined Hitler, coolly using the situation for his own ends, is reinforced by the measures he took the following day. At the cabinet meeting on the morning of 28 February 1933 Hitler announced that 'a ruthless confrontation with the KPD was now urgently necessary', the 'right psychological moment' had arrived, and the fight against the communists must 'not be made dependent on legal considerations'. Göring stated that 'a single individual could not possibly have carried out the arson attack'.[45] A second cabinet meeting, which took place in the afternoon, agreed the Decree for the Protection of People and State, thereafter often termed the Reichstag Fire Decree.[46] Suspending 'until further notice' the basic rights of the Weimar constitution, it imposed restrictions on personal freedom, free speech, and freedom of association, and authorized interference with postal communications, house searches, confiscations, and limitations on property rights. In addition, the decree authorized the Reich government to take over power in the individual states, on a temporary basis, in the event that the measures taken by the states proved inadequate 'to restore law and order'. In effect, the government was usurping the Reich President's constitutional right of intervention; the federal structure of the Weimar Republic, the careful balance between the Reich and the federal states, was history. Moreover, the death penalty was introduced for a whole series of offences, to enable the regime ruthlessly to crush resistance.[47] The state of emergency created by the decree was to remain in force throughout the Third Reich. Hitler's regime was based from start to finish on depriving the nation of its basic rights.

That very night thousands of KPD functionaries were arrested in Prussia, using comprehensive lists prepared under the Papen and Schleicher governments in case of a communist uprising; the other states soon followed suit. On 3 March, the police achieved an important coup by arresting the party's chairman, Ernst Thälmann. The party machine was systematically destroyed just at the point when it was preparing to go underground.[48] Göring also had the whole of the SPD press in Prussia banned for a period of fourteen days and renewed the ban several times until 10 May, when the party's newspapers were confiscated. It was only outside Prussia that a few papers could continue to be published until the beginning of March.[49] Philipp Scheidemann, Wilhelm Dittmann, and Arthur Crispien, all members of the SPD central committee, had fled to Austria before the Reichstag fire; at the beginning of March, the former Prussian prime minister Otto Braun and the former Berlin police president, Albert Grzesinski, went abroad too.[50] The Reichstag Fire Decree also gave the government the pretext for arresting unpopular intellectuals, for example, Carl von Ossietsky, Erich Mühsam, Ludwig Renn, Egon Kisch, and the lawyer Hans Litten, who had caused Hitler so much embarrassment in a Berlin courtroom in 1931.[51]

After issuing the emergency decree, Hitler returned to the election campaign, speaking on 1 March in Breslau, the following day in the Berlin Sportpalast, and on 3 March in Hamburg.[52] Finally, on 4 March – government propaganda declared the Saturday before the election to be the 'Day of National Awakening' – Hitler made an appeal to the electors from Königsberg, the capital of East Prussia. His speech was not only broadcast on the radio but was also carried over loud speakers, installed in public squares throughout the Reich. In Berlin alone Party formations were involved in twenty-four public demonstrations in various parts of the city. Hitler used his appearance above all as a massive denunciation of the 'November criminals' and, as usual, refrained from making any concrete statements about his government's future policies. According to Hitler, when asked by his opponents about his 'programme', there could be 'only one reply: "the opposite of yours"'.[53] At the end, in a solemn conclusion, his audience in Königsberg, but also the masses all over the Reich listening to the loudspeakers, began singing the 'Netherlands Prayer of Thanksgiving', consciously taking up a tradition from pre-war Germany, when it was played on important occasions.[54] The transmission ended with the pealing of the Königsberg church bells.

On election day, the new government was already in a position to dominate the streets throughout the Reich. Swastikas and black-white-and-red flags were ubiquitous; the coalition parties' posters were prominent everywhere, while those of the opposition parties were banned. The streets were patrolled by the SA and the police, armed with rifles.[55] In the end, the NSDAP managed to win 43.9 per cent of the vote. Together with their coalition partners, the DNVP, who had adapted themselves to the new era by fighting the election under the name Kampffront Schwarz-Weiss-Rot [Combat Front Black-White-Red (the colours of the pre-1919 Reich)], they had an overall majority of 51.9 per cent. This meant that the NSDAP had managed to increase its hitherto highest vote of July 1932 by 6.5 per cent (compared with its vote in November 1932, by 10.8 per cent). The biggest losses were suffered by the KPD (4.6 per cent) and SPD (2.1 per cent). In view of the massive obstacles placed in the way of the left-wing parties and the numerous advantages gained by the NSDAP since 30 January, the result was worse than expected by Hitler and the Party leadership. The NSDAP was still dependent on its coalition partner.

Stage 3: 'Cold revolution'

Hitler was certainly exaggerating when he claimed in the cabinet meeting of 7 March that the election result was a 'revolution'.[56] But what followed – a mixture of illegal actions by the Party rank and file and quasi-legal measures by the government – did indeed, within a few weeks, revolutionize Germany's political system.[57] Goebbels described this process accurately as a 'cold revolution':[58] through a series of actions resembling a coup d'état the government destroyed the constitutional order, concentrating power in its own hands.

To begin with, it set about 'coordinating'★ the states not yet controlled by the National Socialists. With the Reichstag Fire Decree the Reich government had expressly given itself the authority 'temporarily' to take over 'the powers of the highest authorities in a state' in order to 'restore law and order'. Hamburg, which was ruled by a coalition of DVP, DSt.P, and SPD, was the first casualty of this clause.[59] The Social Democrat members of the senate had already resigned on 3 March, in order to avoid giving the Reich a pretext to intervene in Hamburg's affairs. The following day, the first or senior mayor, who was a member of the Deutsche Staatspartei, also resigned. This prompted the local National Socialists to demand the post of police chief and, when the senate refused, on 5 March – election day – the Reich Interior Minister, Frick, simply stepped in and appointed an SA leader as acting police chief. In February, with the aim of conciliating the bourgeois parties, the Hamburg Nazis had already proposed – naturally with Hitler's approval[60] – a non-Party figure and leading business man, Carl Vincent Krogmann, as first mayor. This proved successful: on 8 March, a new senate was formed under Krogmann's leadership, including the bourgeois parties. During the following days, similar developments occurred in the other states: on 6 March in Bremen and Lübeck, on 7 March in Hesse, on 8 March in Schaumburg-Lippe, Baden, Württemberg, and Saxony. Only Bavaria was

---

★ Translators' note: The Nazi term is *Gleichschaltung*, borrowed from electrical engineering, where it means to switch to the same current. In the Third Reich it meant bringing into line, i.e. enforced conformity. 'Coordination' has become the generally accepted translation.

not yet subject to Nazi rule; but, on the evening of 8 March, Hitler and his closest advisors decided to put an end to this state of affairs.[61]

In Munich 'coordination' ran as smoothly as in the other states. The reassurances that the leader of the Bavarian People's Party, Fritz Schäffer, had received from Hindenburg on 17 February, and prime minister Heinrich Held had received from Hitler on 1 March,[62] that the Reich would not intervene in Bavaria proved completely worthless. As had been agreed in Berlin the previous evening, on 9 March an NSDAP delegation, led by SA chief Röhm and Gauleiter Adolf Wagner, demanded from prime minister Held that a member of the delegation, Ritter von Epp, be immediately appointed general state commissar. The large numbers of SA marching around the city provided a suitably threatening backdrop to their demand. The Bavarian government refused to agree; but that evening Frick transferred the powers of the state government to Epp on the grounds that 'the maintenance of law and order in Bavaria is currently no longer being guaranteed'.[63] That same evening Held complained both to Hitler and to Hindenburg. The Reich President instructed his state secretary to find out from Hitler what was going on, and then accepted his explanation that the situation could not be dealt with in any other way.[64] Epp now took over power without more ado and, after a few days, Held was forced to go. This was the same Held who, eight years before, had made Hitler promise that his party would abide strictly by the law.[65]

At the beginning of March, in moves often directly linked to the 'seizure of power' in the states, the Nazis also took over the administration in numerous towns and cities. Typically, the SA occupied the town hall, drove out, and in some cases mistreated, the councillors, and hoisted a swastika on the roof. The local government elections, called by the new government for 12 March, were immediately followed by another wave of take-overs in numerous towns and villages in which the Nazis had hitherto been unable to make an impact.[66]

Immediately after their election victory of 5 March, the Nazis also increased their anti-Jewish attacks, directed above all against lawyers and businesses, throughout the Reich.[67] But, department stores, one-price shops, co-op stores, in other words businesses (whether they were Jewish or not) which the Party had attacked for years as unfair competition for 'German' retailers, were also targeted by activists. Party supporters, above all Storm Troopers and members of the National Socialist small business association, demonstrated in front of the shops, prevented customers from entering, and stuck notices or scrawled slogans on the shop windows. This often led to disturbances. On 9 March, SA formations marched to the Berlin stock exchange to try – unsuccessfully – to force the resignation of the 'Jewish' board.[68] While some leading National Socialists (for example Göring, with his announcement of 10 March that he refused to accept that 'the police should be a protection force for Jewish department stores'[69]) encouraged such attacks, Hitler, conscious of the need to consider his conservative coalition partners and the economic situation, was obliged to calm things down. On 10 March, he issued a statement forbidding 'individual actions' and he used a radio broadcast on the 'National Day of Mourning' to underline this ban and to demand 'the strictest and blindest [sic!] discipline'.[70] As a result, with a few exceptions, the attacks decreased.

The government responded differently to the attacks on Jewish lawyers. In this case, official statements actually encouraged the occupation of court buildings and the expulsion of Jewish judges, prosecutors, and attorneys. These attacks were not simply an expression of radical anti-Semitism; rather, they represented an early trial of strength with the state apparatus, for they challenged the rule of law, preparing the way for legal interventions in the judiciary and civil service.[71]

During this period, Hitler sought to demonstrate his solidarity with conservative Germany. On 10 March he ordered that all public buildings should fly the black–white–red flag to mark the National Day of Mourning.[72] This was very much in accordance with the views of Hindenburg, who on the following, day sent a flag decree to the Reich Chancellery,[73] which Hitler then announced in his radio broadcast of 12 March: 'until the final decision concerning the Reich colours has been taken, the black–white–red flag and the swastika are to hang side by side', as this would link 'the proud history of the German Reich with the powerful rebirth of the German nation'. However, Hindenburg had also instructed that the Reichswehr was to use only the black–white–red flag, thereby demonstrating that he continued to regard the army as being above party. Hitler also announced a decree from Reich Interior Minister Frick that to 'celebrate the victory of the nationalist revolution' all public buildings should be decorated with flags in the new form for three days.[74] This gesture was a foretaste of the ceremonies envisaged for the opening of the new Reichstag session on 21 March in Potsdam and intended to seal the alliance between Nazis and conservatives.

The elections and the coordination of the federal states had shifted the balance of power in the cabinet in Hitler's favour. He was now in a position to appoint a further Nazi minister. On 11 March the cabinet agreed to establish a Reich Ministry for Popular Enlightenment and Propaganda, and, on 15 March, having returned from a short trip to Munich, where three days previously he had celebrated the final 'conquest' of the city and laid a wreath for 'the fallen' at the Feldherrnhalle,[75] Hitler was able to congratulate Joseph Goebbels on his appointment as his youngest minister. Originally he had promised him a Ministry of Culture with comprehensive powers, but now Goebbels had to content himself with the fact that the main focus of his work would be state propaganda.[76]

Hitler supported the establishment of the new ministry by getting the cabinet to give him special powers to transfer a considerable number of responsibilities from other government departments to the new ministry.[77] By July, it had acquired its basic structure. The responsibility for radio, hitherto divided between the Postal Ministry, the Interior Ministry, and the states, was assigned to Goebbels and, despite stalling by the states, all regional transmitters now became 'Reich transmitters'.[78] Goebbels took over responsibility for theatres from the Education Ministry (although Göring retained significant power over the Prussian theatres),[79] and for fine art and other cultural and media responsibilities from the Interior Ministry.[80] Also, despite opposition from the Foreign Ministry, he was able to establish his own foreign department.[81]

Among other personnel changes that strengthened the Nazi element in the government were Hitler's replacement on 17 March of Hans Luther as president of the Reichsbank with Hjalmar Schacht, and the appointment at the end of March of Konstantin Hierl as state secretary in the Reich Ministry of Labour and head of the state Labour Service (despite opposition from Labour Minister, Seldte). Fritz Reinhardt, the head of the NSDAP's 'Speakers' School', was made state secretary in the Reich Finance Ministry at the beginning of April.[82]

On 21 March, on the occasion of the opening of the Reichstag, the alliance between Nazis and conservatives, between the 'nationalist revolution' and Prussian tradition, was to be celebrated with pomp and ceremony in Potsdam.[83] On 2 March, at Papen's suggestion, the cabinet had decided on the Garrison Church as the venue for the occasion, a choice full of symbolism. It contained the tombs of two Prussian kings, Fredrick William I and Frederick II [the Great], and up until the end of the First World War enemy flags and banners captured by the Prussian army were kept there. After a few pious qualms, the Reich President had agreed, but secured himself the main role in the ceremony, which was now clearly designed to resemble the opening of the first ever Reichstag by Kaiser William I.[84]

Potsdam Day is often described as the Nazis' first great propaganda success, for they succeeded in shamelessly and hypocritically appropriating Prussian traditions so revered by Germans. Looked at more closely, the occasion has rather the appearance of a demonstration of conservative Germany. With Potsdam a sea of black-white-red flags and hundreds of thousands there primarily to cheer the Reich President, the Nazis were in danger of being downgraded to mere assistants in the restoration of the monarchy.[85] Moreover, Hitler's lack of control of the event was rubbed in by the friendly invitation from the representative of the Catholic Church in Potsdam to attend the service inaugurating the event and thereby demonstrate his oft-expressed 'belief in God and Christianity'.[86] This prompted Hitler and Goebbels, the day before it started, to try to put a stop to all this. Instead of attending the church service, they decided to make a demonstrative visit to the graves of members of the SA buried in the Luise cemetery in Berlin. They justified their absence by claiming that leaders and supporters of the NSDAP had been accused of being 'apostates' by representatives of the Church and excluded from the sacraments, a claim that was immediately rejected as an inaccurate generalization.[87]

Hitler and Goebbels arrived on time for the start of the state ceremony at 12 noon. The Reichstag deputies from the Nazi and bourgeois parties were all assembled in the church; the Social Democrats had declined to participate. Apart from the deputies, the church, which could hold around 2,000 people, was mainly filled with representatives of 'nationalist' Germany, including many wearing the colourful uniforms of the old army. After a few words, the Reich President called on Hitler to speak. Hitler praised the recent election result as the expression of a 'marriage . . . between the symbols of the greatness of the olden days and the vigour of youth'. The handshake between Hindenburg in his field-marshal's uniform and Hitler in his civilian tailcoat represented the high point of the ceremony.

After laying wreaths on the tombs of the Prussian kings in the crypt, Hindenburg took the salute at a parade of Reichswehr, police, and the 'nationalist leagues' (SA, SS, Hitler Youth, and Stahlhelm) lasting several hours, while Hitler and his cabinet were obliged to watch the march past from the second row. The photograph of Hitler taking his leave of Hindenburg with a reverential bow, as carried in the media – Goebbels's first major coup as Propaganda Minister – became the iconic image of the day. It was intended to symbolize the alliance between the Nazis and the conservative elites. However, two days later, Hitler rejected the restoration of the monarchy, towards which the conservatives had clearly been moving; he declared that, given the misery of the masses, the government considered the issue 'inappropriate for discussion at the present time'.[88]

Immediately after the Potsdam ceremony the government ministers agreed further emergency powers. An emergency decree imposed severe penalties for 'malicious attacks' on the government (even the death penalty in particularly serious cases). Special courts were set up, intended to ensure the rapid sentencing of offences against both this decree and the Reichstag Fire Decree.[89]

Two days later, the Enabling Law was on the Reichstag's agenda. This law, which the cabinet had been discussing for several weeks, envisaged the Reich government being able to pass laws without the participation of parliament, and the Chancellor rather than the Reich President being responsible for the final approval of laws.[90] The government was also expressly authorized to issue legislation contrary to the constitution, provided it did not affect the Reichstag and the Reichsrat as institutions or the 'rights of the Reich President'. With this fine distinction between the two legislatures and the Presidency – the office of Reich President, including the method of election and the position of deputy, was no longer guaranteed – the first step was being taken towards an unconstitutional settlement of the succession to the Reich Presidency in the event of Hindenburg's death. The law was intended to last for four years, but would become invalid 'if the present Reich government is replaced by another'. In other words, it was the Hitler/Hugenberg coalition government that was being 'enabled'; in the event of the government being replaced, the Reich President could insist on the Enabling Law being suspended. He could achieve this through his right to appoint the Chancellor and the ministers. Thus, in principle, the Enabling Law had a built-in guarantee against an unbridled extension of Hitler's power at the expense of his conservative partners.[91] However, it freed him from any kind of parliamentary control. For although, since the recent elections, the government had a majority, he had no intention of subjecting himself to the day-to-day tedium of parliamentary majority government and having to take account of the particular interests of conservative deputies on each issue as it arose. Thanks to his majority, the Chancellor was also no longer dependent on the Reich President's power to issue emergency decrees. As a result, Hindenburg's authority, on which the conservatives had based their efforts 'to contain' Hitler, was inevitably weakened.

However, the law had not yet been passed. To achieve the requisite two-thirds majority, a change in the procedural rules decreed that those communist deputies who were in prison, had fled, or gone underground should be regarded as non-existent, with the result that the quorum required for the chamber to take decisions was reduced.[92] Nevertheless, the support of the Centre Party was still required for the law to pass. To secure this, on 20 and 21 March Hitler made oral promises to the chairman of the Centre, Ludwig Kaas, which he reiterated in the government declaration to the Reichstag on 23 March. They included a guarantee to maintain the federal states in their present form and – with qualifications – for all 'those elements positively disposed towards the state' a guarantee of the rights of the religious confessions, of the civil service, and of the Reich President.[93]

At the Reichstag session on 23 March, which because of the fire was held in the Kroll Opera House, Hitler appeared not in a suit but in his brown Party uniform. At the start of his speech, he expatiated once more on the 'decline' that the German people had allegedly suffered during the previous fourteen years, going on to put forward a 'programme for the reconstruction of nation and Reich'. This proposed law was designed to serve the goal of furthering the 'welfare of our local authorities and states', by allowing the government to achieve, 'from now onwards and for ever after, a consistency of political goals throughout the Reich and the states'. The Reich government wanted to put a stop to the 'total devaluation of the legislative bodies' as a result of frequent elections, with 'the aim of ensuring that, once the nation's will has been expressed, it will produce uniform results throughout the Reich and the states'.

Hitler announced that 'with the political decontamination of our public life . . . [would come] a thorough moral purging of the national body' and praised the two Christian confessions as 'the most important factors for the maintenance of our nation'. Then he moved to conciliate the Centre Party and to calm fears that the National Socialists intended to attack the Churches. As requested by the Centre Party, Hitler conceded that the 'judges are irremovable', at the same time issuing an unambiguous warning that they must 'demonstrate flexibility in adjusting their verdicts to the benefit of society'. His economic policy announcements remained vague. He talked about 'the encouragement of private initiative' and the 'recognition of private property' as well as of the simplification and reduction of the burden of taxation. They were going to 'rescue the German peasantry', 'integrate the army of unemployed in the production process', and protect the self-employed.

In the foreign policy section of his speech Hitler emphasized the government's willingness to disarm and to seek peace and friendly relations. The
Reich government aimed to do everything possible 'to bring the four great
powers, England, France, Italy, and Germany', closer together and was also
willing to establish 'friendly and mutually beneficial relations' with the
Soviet Union (the persecution of communists was a purely domestic matter
for the Reich). However, any attempt to divide nations into victors and van-
quished would remove any basis for an 'understanding'. Finally, Hitler gave
the commitments agreed with the Centre Party, while stating that the government 'insisted' on the law being passed. As far as its application was concerned, while 'the number of cases... would be limited', the cabinet would
regard 'rejection' as a 'declaration of resistance'.[94]

Despite the intimidating atmosphere in the hall (which was decorated
with swastikas and dominated by SA men), the SPD leader, Otto Wels, while
welcoming in his response the foreign policy section of the government
statement, nevertheless announced that the SPD opposed the draft bill, and
concluded by declaring his commitment to basic human rights and justice,
to freedom, and to socialism. Hitler then embarked on an apparently spontaneous 'settling of accounts' with Wels, although in fact it was well prepared, as he had already seen a copy of Wels's speech. Accompanied by
thunderous applause from the Nazi deputies, Hitler brusquely rejected
Wels's positive response to the regime's foreign policy plans. Indicating his
contempt for democratic procedures and legality, he made it clear that the
Reichstag deputies were simply being requested 'to agree to something that
we could have done anyway'. He, Hitler, would not 'make the mistake of
simply irritating opponents instead of either destroying or reconciling
them'. He did not want the SPD to vote for the law: 'Germany must become
free, but not thanks to you!'[95]

Ludwig Kaas of the Centre Party and the representatives of the BVP,
the Staatspartei, and the Christlich-Sozialer Volksdienst [Christian Social
People's Service] then declared their groups' support for the Enabling Law.
When the final vote was taken, there were 94 SPD votes against; the remainder of their total of 120 deputies had either emigrated, were in protective
custody, or had excused themselves for reasons of personal security. The
overwhelming majority of 444 deputies voted for the law.

The mass arrests of political opponents had begun immediately after the
Reichstag fire and increased significantly after the election of 5 March. In
addition, from the beginning of March, the SA imprisoned thousands of

people, mainly supporters of the left-wing parties, in cellars and provisional camps, of which there were several hundred scattered throughout the Reich, where they were held for months and often tortured.[96] Moreover, since the Reichstag Fire Decree, the police had been able arbitrarily to impose 'protective custody' on presumed opponents of the regime, without reference to any breach of an existing law, for an indeterminate period, outside judicial control, and without access to legal assistance.[97] This extraordinary power in the hands of the security apparatus was to remain the basis of the regime's system of terror until the end of the Third Reich.

By April 1933, around 50,000 people had been taken into protective custody, albeit many of them only temporarily.[98] In spring 1933, some seventy state camps were established to accommodate these prisoners, including in workhouses and similar institutions for 'asocials', as well as around thirty special sections in prisons and remand prisons.[99] From March onwards, the following camps established along these lines included: Dachau, Oranienburg (near Berlin), Sonnenburg (near Küstrin), Heuberg (Württemberg), Hohnstein (Saxony), and Osthofen (near Worms). In spring 1933 the foundations of the later system of concentration camps were being laid.

Stage 4: Exclusion and coordination

Through the Enabling Law, Hitler had, by the end of March, done much of what was needed to give him a monopoly of power. He rounded off this stage with the elimination of the trade unions and the SPD and the dissolution of the bourgeois parties. But before that happened the NSDAP wished to present itself on 1 May as a party representing the whole nation. Thus, in April, the Party leadership was confronted with the need to control three contradictory developments. The activism of the Party rank and file must not be allowed to flag; the violence must not, however, be permitted to get out of hand; the anti-capitalist ambitions of the Party's rank and file, which had emerged during March, would have to be directed into safe channels. For there had been numerous cases of 'interference in business', particularly at the beginning of March, and they were no longer confined to 'Jewish' businesses, but were affecting banks, chambers of commerce, and firms of all descriptions, and, despite bans, kept recurring. They were causing growing concern to conservative politicians and leading business figures and had prompted numerous complaints to the government. The Party leadership needed to put an end to these excesses once and for all.[100] Moreover, during March and April there were complaints about the harassment of foreign diplomats and assaults on and the arbitrary imprisonment of foreigners, above all by members of the SA.[101]

A way out of this situation was provided by a revival of anti-Jewish initiatives, but this time authorized and controlled from 'above'. The NSDAP had been aiming to reduce the economic influence of Jews for a long time and, since the end of the 1920s, boycotts of Jewish businesses had been routine for many local branches.[102] Many Party activists considered it obvious that the 'seizure of power' should lead to an increase in such actions. By combining the continuing attacks on Jewish businesses with the ongoing harassment of Jewish lawyers in a joint campaign tolerated by the government, Hitler could present himself as a politician responding to the anti-Semitic demands of the Party activists, while controlling their aggression. In this way the Nazi leadership hoped to create a 'mood' conducive to the introduction of anti-Semitic legislation, while at the same time silencing the growing foreign criticism of the new regime's arbitrary measures. The German Jews were to be used as hostages in order to put a stop to international 'atrocity propaganda' (soon termed 'Jewish atrocity propaganda' by the NSDAP).

At the end of March, Hitler and Goebbels, who had been summoned to Berchtesgaden to discuss the matter, decided on a boycott of German Jews.[103] A 'Central Committee for the Rejection of Jewish Atrocity and Boycott Propaganda' was set up, chaired by the Franconian Gauleiter and notorious anti-Semite, Julius Streicher.[104] On 28 March, it announced a boycott, expressly authorized by Hitler and the cabinet,[105] starting on 1 April.[106] To keep matters under control and in order to take account of the concerns of conservatives about potential damage to German exports, on the evening of 31 March, Goebbels announced that the boycott would be 'suspended' from the evening of the first day, a Saturday, until the following Wednesday, and only revived if the 'foreign atrocity propaganda' continued.[107]

The official boycott turned out to be very similar to the 'wild', that is, unauthorized, actions carried out by Party activists in March: SA and Hitler Youth stood outside stores that had been marked as Jewish and tried to stop customers from entering. Soon crowds of people formed in the shopping districts and most shops closed during the course of the day. There were a number of brave people who deliberately shopped in Jewish shops, but the majority of the population behaved as the regime expected: they avoided the shops.[108] That evening, as planned, the boycott was suspended, with the Committee declaring it a success, as the hostile 'atrocity propaganda' had largely ceased.[109] In fact, the regime had managed to persuade a number of Jewish organizations and individuals to call for an end to foreign boycotts of German goods.

The Party activists, however, continued with their campaign against Jewish lawyers and the judicial authorities responded by transferring or suspending Jewish judges and prosecutors and introducing quotas for Jewish attorneys.[110] At this point, as anticipated, the regime intervened, in effect legalizing these measures. The Law for the Re-establishment of a Professional Civil Service of 7 April decreed that those public servants 'who are not of Aryan descent' were to be retired. Following an intervention by Hindenburg, civil servants who had been in post before 1 August 1914, who had fought at the front, or whose fathers or sons had been killed in the war were exempted from this regulation.[111] During the following months around half of the 5,000 Jewish civil servants lost their jobs.[112] The Law concerning the Admission of Attorneys, also issued on 7 April, banned attorneys 'not of Aryan descent' from practising, with the same exemptions as contained in the Professional Civil Service Law.[113] During the following months, similar bans were introduced for other state-approved professions, such as patent lawyers and tax advisers. The Law against the Overcrowding of German Schools and Colleges issued on 25 April limited the number of Jewish pupils and students,[114] while Jewish doctors and dentists were excluded from the health insurance system.[115] More ambitious plans to prevent Jewish doctors from practising at all were initially blocked by Hitler, who told the Cabinet that 'at the moment' such measures were 'not yet necessary',[116] clear proof of the extent to which the Chancellor controlled policy detail during these weeks.

The Professional Civil Service Law broke with the principle of the legal equality of Jews throughout the German Reich for the first time since its foundation in 1871. In the past, Hitler's conservative coalition partners had always rejected the idea of revising Jewish emancipation, so their acceptance of this step represented an important moral victory for the National Socialists over their 'partners'. But that was not the only point. For the Professional Civil Service Law not only brought about the dismissal of Jewish civil servants, but also paved the way for a large scale 'purge' of the civil service, thereby effectively removing the privileged status of German officials with their 'traditional rights and responsibilities' and contributing to a disciplining of the state apparatus. Approximately 2 per cent of the civil service was affected by the provisions of the law, which included dismissal on political grounds, but also demotion and premature retirement.[117]

At the end of March, a Reich law transferred the right to legislate in the federal states from parliaments to governments, while the number of each party's deputies in the state parliaments was adjusted in accordance with the results of the Reichstag election of 5 March (with the communist vote being ignored); the local councils were also reorganized on the basis of the 5 March election.[118] Under the Second Law for the Co-ordination of the Federal States of 7 April Reich Governors (Reichsstatthalter) were appointed to the states with the power of appointing the state governments.[119] This meant that the hitherto lauded autonomy of the states had been finally removed. The first Reich governor to be appointed by Interior Minister Frick on 10 April was Ritter von Epp in Bavaria. In the meantime, Epp had created a provisional Bavarian government composed of Nazis and his rapid appointment suggests that Hitler wanted to prevent Bavaria from becoming too strong a power base for the Party; Epp was not a member of the local Party clique. In the other states the Gauleiters were appointed Reich Governors; they now exercised control over the state governments in the name of the Reich government, assuming they had not already become prime minister of their state. This meant that those states in which the NSDAP could never have achieved a majority were now also firmly in the hands of the Party. Hitler's conservative coalition partners, on the other hand, had been left empty-handed with nothing to say in all these federal states, each of which had sub-stantial administrations carrying out important functions.[120]

In Prussia Hitler took over the responsibilities of governor himself, which meant that Papen's post as 'Reich Commissar' in Prussia had ceased to exist and so another element in the 'taming concept' had proved useless. On 11 April, Hitler appointed Göring (and not Papen) prime minister of Prussia (after Göring had indicated that he was going to get the Prussian parliament to elect him prime minister). Göring kept the office of Prussian interior minister and, on 25 April, Hitler also transferred to him the responsibilities of Reich governor. With the appointment of the acting Nazi Reich Commissars, Hanns Kerrl as Prussian Minister of Justice and Bernhard Rust as Prussian Minister of Culture, Göring had created in Prussia another power base that was firmly in National Socialist hands. Significantly, he had no intention of appointing Reich Commissar Hugenberg to the Prussian ministries of Agriculture and Economics.[121]

In April the Nazis also had considerable success in coordinating associations. Initially, this involved primarily economic associations. Among the extremely woolly economic ideas held by various Nazis before 1933, the notion of a 'corporatist state' [Ständestaat] had been particularly prominent. The idea was that in a future Third Reich the individual 'professions/occupations' [Stände] would to a large extent regulate their own affairs in professional organizations, thereby bridging the conflicts of interest between capital and labour, regulating the markets, and preventing domination by large industrial firms.[122]

During the first months after the take-over of power, the representatives of the self-employed within the NSDAP, organized in the Combat League for the Commercial Middle Class, set about trying to realize this idea.[123] At the beginning of May, commerce and the artisanal trades were formed into separate 'Reich groups' and Adrian von Renteln, the leader of the Combat League, took over the leadership of the new artisanal trades' organization.[124] The representatives of the self-employed saw it as an initial victory when the cabinet introduced a special tax for department stores and chain stores, banned department stores and chain stores from having artisan shops such as hairdressers, and forbade the opening of new chain stores.[125]

To begin with, the Reich Association of German Industry's (RDI) response was guarded. On 24 March, under massive pressure from Fritz Thyssen, it declared its support for the government. However, in a memorandum, released simultaneously, it made clear its intention of sticking to its basic policy of economic liberalism.[126] On 1 April, the day of the Jewish boycott, Otto Wagener turned up at the RDI's offices demanding changes to its board. Wagener was the former head of the NSDAP's economic department and, after the seizure of power, had established his own section, dealing with economic policy, within the Party's Berlin liaison office.[127] He insisted that the general manager, Ludwig Kastl, was unacceptable on political grounds, that several Jewish members should leave, and that a number of people should be appointed whom the NSDAP could rely on to 'coordinate' the RDI's activities with government policy. All attempts by the industrialists to get access to Hitler to persuade him to withdraw these demands proved unsuccessful. Meanwhile, on 24 April, in an attempt to maintain his influence, Hugenberg appointed Wagener and Alfred Moeller, a DNVP supporter, Reich Commissars for the RDI and for the economy generally (apart from agriculture). The RDI acceded to Wagener's demands, reorganized its board in accordance with the Führer principle and finally, on 22 May, dissolved itself. Then, just over a month later, it amalgamated with the Association of German Employers' Organizations to form the

Reichsstand der Deutschen Industrie. The new name paid lip service to the ständisch [corporatist] line of the Nazi economic reformers; but the fact that the old chairman of the RDI, Krupp, was also chairman of the new organization indicated the continuity that existed between the two organizations.[128]

In the agricultural sphere Hugenberg had initially concentrated on raising prices through higher tariffs and by intervening in food production, and also on protecting agriculture with state subsidies and the prevention of foreclosures. These measures represented the most important points on the cabinet's agenda since the start of the year;[129] they were pushed through by Hugenberg, in some cases against Hitler's wishes, who often made detailed comments at meetings on agricultural issues.[130] Moreover, on 5 April, the Chancellor defended this policy in a speech to the German Agricultural Council, the umbrella organization of the Chambers of Agriculture, despite the fact that it was against the interests of consumers and creditors, and threatened the export-oriented manufacturing industries. According to Hitler, it was the peasants who secured 'the nation's future'.[131]

Figure 3. The executive committee of the Berlin Police used the force's ninth indoor games on 17 March 1933 to put on a show of loyalty to the new regime. This photo shows the 'Friedrich Karl' division of the Prussian state police, rifles raised, in a swastika formation. The Nazi emblem was displayed throughout the Berlin Sportpalast.
Source: Scherl/Süddeutsche Zeitung Photo

However, in the meantime, Richard Walther Darré, the leader of the Nazi Party's agricultural department, had begun coordinating all the agricultural organizations one after the other, thereby undermining Hugenberg's position as Agriculture Minister.[132] In contrast to Hugenberg's policy of concentrating on protecting agrarian economic interests, Darré's policy was dominated by the ideology of 'blood and soil', which aimed at subordinating the agrarian economy as an 'estate' [Stand] to an 'ethnic political' conception, and transforming the whole agricultural sector into a compulsory cartel. In May 1933, despite the opposition of Hugenberg as acting Prussian Agriculture Minister, he succeeded in pushing through an 'hereditary farm law' for Prussia, subjecting farms to permanent entailment, preventing their division or sale, and tying the hereditary farmer's family to that particular piece of land. This provided the model for later entailment legislation applying to the Reich as a whole.[133] With his appointment as Reich Minister of Food at the end of June, Darré was finally able to get the better of Hugenberg, who had become increasingly isolated in the cabinet as a result of his one-sided agricultural policies and for other reasons that will be dealt with later.[134]

Apart from coordinating the leading economic associations, the Nazis placed great emphasis on gaining control of every kind of club and association. To start with, the workers' associations were crippled by the elimination of the SPD and KPD and then later formally closed down. The numerous and locally diverse artisan associations[135] were also subjected to this process, as were sports and youth clubs. The sports clubs were reorganized by SA leader Hans von Tschammer und Osten, who was appointed Reich Sports Commissar on 28 April and finally, on 19 July, Reich Sports Leader.[136] The Hitler Youth leader, Baldur von Schirach, took control of the Reich Committee of German Youth Associations, which represented some five to six million young people. On 5 April 1933, he ordered a Hitler Youth squad to occupy its offices and took over the management. On 17 June, Hitler appointed Schirach Youth Leader of the German Reich and, through this new office, authorized him to supervise all work relating to young people. On the day of his appointment, Schirach ordered the closure of the Grossdeutscher Jugendbund [Greater German Youth Association], to which most members of the bündisch youth movement were affiliated.[†] As a result of the integration of numerous youth organizations and the huge increase

† Translators' note: 'Bündisch' refers to the youth movement that developed among middle-class Germans in the early twentieth century with a particular form of organization ('Bund'), stressing its separation from adult society and bourgeois values, and a Romantic mindset.

in new members, both boys and girls, between the beginning of 1933 and the end of 1934 the membership of the Hitler Youth (HJ) went up from around 108,000 to 3.5 million. Around half of young Germans aged between 10 and 18 were now in Nazi organizations as 'cubs' (Pimpfe), young lasses (Jungmädel), Hitler Boys (Hitlerjungen), or 'lasses' (Mädel).[137]

In the end, every form of club and association, whether it was the volunteer fire brigades, stamp collectors, rabbit breeders, or choral societies, was caught up in this process of 'coordination'; every single association was forced to submit to the Nazis' demand for total control. In these associations millions of Germans came together in order to follow the most diverse economic, cultural, and social pursuits and to organize their spare time in their own way. The regime was determined to prevent any possibility of such associations providing a future forum for criticism or opposition; opportunities for the formation of public opinion outside the parameters established by the regime and the Party were to be blocked right from the start. The associations were obliged to subordinate themselves to Nazi-dominated umbrella organizations, to alter their statutes in order to replace a committee structure with the Führer principle, to ensure that people who were objectionable in the eyes of the local Party were excluded, that Nazis were appointed to leading positions, and finally to introduce the so-called 'Aryan clause' banning Jews from membership.[138] In many cases the associations were only too happy to adapt to the new circumstances and hurried to conform, whereas in others the process took until the following year or even longer to complete. Many middle-class associations appear to have been hesitant in responding to the demands of the new order and to have only superficially conformed to Nazi requirements, with the old life of the association continuing broadly unchanged. Thus, in reality, it was impossible for the Party to establish total control over every club, society, or association.[139]

The coordination of associations and interventions in business occurred alongside massive Nazi attacks on the DNVP and the Stahlhelm. In cabinet too Hitler's tone, which had initially been conciliatory, became increasingly authoritarian and uncompromising, and he sought to avoid lengthy discussion of technical issues.[140] Both within and outside the government, the Nazis increasingly turned against the bourgeois-nationalist milieu they considered 'reactionary'.

From the beginning of April, a growing number of complaints reached DNVP headquarters about attacks by members of the NSDAP on the

DNVP and its organizations. Hugenberg frequently complained about the attacks to Hitler and the Reich President, but almost invariably to no effect.[141] His performance as a multiple minister was also subjected to ferocious criticism in the Nazi press. On 20 April, Hitler's birthday, he published a newspaper article, pointing out that the use of the Enabling Law depended on the continuing existence of the coalition and complaining about 'unauthorized personnel changes in economic organizations and public bodies'. This, together with a similar complaint from Reich Bank president, Schacht, did in fact lead to an order from Hitler to the Party organization, issued via its Berlin liaison staff, to refrain in future from unauthorized interference in business.[142] This, however, did not affect the continuing attacks on the members and organizations of the DNVP.[143]

During February and March, there had also already been repeated attacks by SA men on members of the Stahlhelm. At the end of March, the Brunswick interior minister had even banned the local Stahlhelm on the grounds that the organization was being infiltrated by former members of the [largely socialist] Reichsbanner.[144] In view of the growing pressure, by the beginning of April, the leader of the Stahlhelm, Franz Seldte, had already decided to subordinate himself to Hitler and abandon his organization's independence. On 28 April, he finally dismissed his deputy, Theodor Duesterberg (who was being criticized by the Nazis for his doubts about the formation of the Hitler government and because his wife was Jewish), and the following day declared that he was subordinating himself and the Stahlhelm to Hitler.[145]

The process of coordination was in full swing on 20 April, Hitler's 44th birthday, which was celebrated as though it were a public holiday. Many private houses as well as public buildings had put up flags and were decorated with flowers. Throughout the Reich, church services, marches, and torchlight processions were held to mark the day. Radio programmes were entirely geared to the event. 'The whole German nation is celebrating Adolf Hitler's birthday in a dignified and simple way', reported the *Völkischer Beobachter*,[146] and the non-Nazi press joined in the praise almost without reservation.[147] In numerous places Hitler had been made an honorary citizen and streets had been named after him; a regular kitsch industry had sprung up, offering a broad range of devotional items dedicated to Hitler.[148] However, this picture of a nation united behind the 'Führer' was dramatically contradicted by the numerous conflicts that characterized the domestic political situation in spring 1933. The orgy of celebration around Hitler's birthday tells us much more about the propaganda apparatus that was being constructed, which had fastened on the Hitler cult as a central element, than it does about ordinary people's real attitude to their new 'people's chancellor'.

Hitler himself had left for the Obersalzberg on 12 April, where he spent Easter, and, on 16 April, received a visit from Joseph and Magda Goebbels. Whereas Goebbels left for Berlin the following day, Hitler changed his plans and stayed on at the Obersalzberg, where Magda kept him company. On 19 April, he was granted honorary citizenship of the Free State of Bavaria at a ceremony in the Munich town hall, which he described as recompense for his imprisonment in 1924. He celebrated his actual birthday privately on the Tegernsee.[149]

Less than three months after the take-over of the Chancellorship, the Nazis were in a position to shape Germany's public image in accordance with their wishes. They owed this opportunity to their coordination of the political institutions and of associational life, as well as of the media and cultural life. The attempt to take control in this sphere also had begun immediately after the seizure of power, but rather in the slipstream of the other major 'actions'. To begin with, radio was placed in the service of the regime and the left-wing press eliminated through bans; but, after spring 1933, the Catholic, bourgeois, and non-Nazi right-wing press came increasingly under pressure from the regime. It moved against uncooperative newspapers by issuing threats, intervening directly to change the composition of editorial boards, and through bans.[150] During February 1933, and then even more vigorously after the election of 5 March, Nazi activists caused considerable upheaval. This was true above all of self-proclaimed cultural guardians, organized in Rosenberg's Combat League for German Culture. In their attempt to 'purge' art, literature, theatre, and intellectual life of everything that was considered 'modern', 'left-wing', or 'Jewish', they caused disturbances in or prevented concerts, for example, by the world-famous [Jewish] conductors, Bruno Walter and Otto Klemperer; they also occupied educational institutions, theatres, and opera houses in order to force through personnel changes.[151]

In fact, Hitler positively encouraged such actions. On 15 February, he announced at an election rally in Stuttgart that it would be 'our task to cauterize these manifestations of decadence in literature, in the theatre, in schools, and in the press, in short in the whole of our cultural life, and to remove the poison that has flowed into our lives during the past fourteen years'. And, in the government announcement introducing the Enabling Law, he had promised 'a thorough moral purge of the national body', which would cover 'the whole of the education system, theatre, film, literature, press, radio'.[152]

At the beginning of April, in response to complaints from Germany's star conductor, Wilhelm Furtwängler, about attacks on his Jewish colleagues, Goebbels tried to create the impression that artists 'who are really talented' would be allowed to appear in public under the new regime.[153] In fact, however, the new rulers used the recent Professional Civil Service Law to confirm officially dismissals that had already been enforced by the mob. In addition to numerous conductors and general music directors, as well as directors of art galleries, by the autumn of 1933 seventy-five theatre direct-ors had been dismissed. The remaining forty-seven were under strict obser-vation by the new cultural establishment,[154] who also, in April, subordinated all those involved in the theatre to the German Theatre Employees' Cooperative.[155] All these measures had a negative impact on theatre reper-toires: works by Jewish authors, or by those who were politically undesir-able, were removed from the German stage. The result was that almost the whole of modern drama, hitherto making up some 40 per cent of the rep-ertoire, disappeared. It was replaced by 'nationalist' and 'völkisch' plays.[156]

In the middle of February, the acting Prussian Minister of Culture, Bernhard Rust, intervened in the Prussian Academy of Arts by forcing the novelist Heinrich Mann to step down from the chairmanship of the German literature section. From the middle of March onwards, increasing numbers of 'Republican' or 'non-Aryan' writers were obliged to leave the Academy and were replaced by loyal Nazis.[157] Finally, on 7 June, the Nazi poet, Hanns Johst, took over as chairman of the Academy.[158] The German section of the International PEN Club was coordinated at the end of April; the Association of German Bookshop Owners submitted to the regime in May; and the various writers' associations were integrated into the Reich Association for German Writers, which had been re-founded in June.[159]

Lists of official bans issued by the Prussian Culture Ministry now appeared in the book trade's paper, the *Börsenblatt des deutschen Buchhandels*; the Gestapo and self-appointed culture guardians issued other blacklists.[160] From April onwards, 'eyesore exhibitions' were organized in a number of German towns, attacking every style of modern art as 'corrupting' or 'decadent', using examples from public galleries. Although there were a number of Nazis who defended Expressionism against attacks by Rosenberg and his supporters, claiming that it was 'German' art worthy of encouragement, Hitler officially condemned these trends at the Party rally in September 1933.[161]

In many places the Nazis celebrated their recently acquired control over cultural life in a barbaric ritual: the public burning of books. During March and April, such 'actions' were more an offshoot of the general terror attacks on cultural institutions organized mainly by the SA. However, from the beginning of April, the Deutsche Studentenschaft, the umbrella organization for all the student representative bodies at German universities, which had been under Nazi control since 1931, began to take the matter systematically in hand. The Studentenschaft responded to its official recognition by a law of 22 April (which, significantly, excluded Jews from membership)[162] by launching an 'action' against 'un-German' ideas. From mid-April onwards, its members started a four-week operation, sorting out 'smutty and trashy literature' from public libraries, private lending libraries, and bookshops. The high point of this 'purge' was the public burning of books that took place on 10 May in numerous German cities. Propaganda Minister, Joseph Goebbels, could not resist presiding over the main event in the Opera Square in Berlin, where, with the flames leaping up in the background, he announced that 'the age of exaggerated Jewish intellectualism' was over.[163] Among the authors whose works were being burnt on that evening (and during the coming months)[164] were Karl Marx, Leon Trotsky, Heinrich Mann, Erich Kästner, Sigmund Freud, Emil Ludwig, Theodor Wolff, Erich Maria Remarque, Alfred Kerr, Kurt Tucholsky, and Carl von Ossietsky.[165] Mann, Tucholsky, Remarque, and Wolff, like many other left-wing or Jewish intellectuals, had by this time already left the country. The public condemnation of artists and the coordination of cultural institutions did not fail to make an impact. Many of those involved in the arts, who had hitherto kept their distance from Nazism, now declared their support for the regime.

During April and May 1933, Nazi students at various universities also demanded the dismissal of Jewish academics and those who were politically unacceptable, even organizing disturbances and boycotts against them.[166] At the same time, the autonomy of university institutions came under growing pressure from the state. From April onwards, the culture ministries of the states demanded new elections for rectors and university committees.[167] Whereas the vast majority of the conservative professors were either uneasy about or hostile towards the ending of university independence, a number saw it as a promising departure. In his inaugural address on 27 May 1933, the new rector of Freiburg University, the internationally respected philosopher

Martin Heidegger, for example, contrasted conventional, allegedly merely superficial, 'academic freedom' with the positive future integration of students in the 'national community', the nation, as well as 'the intellectual mission' they had been given by the 'German nation'.[168] A few months later, universities lost the right to elect their rectors altogether; in future, they were appointed by the ministries and senates were reduced to mere consultative bodies for the rectors.[169]

As in the cultural field, many employees in the universities fell victim to the Professional Civil Service Law. By autumn 1934 614 university academics had been dismissed; by the end of the dictatorship it was one in five (1,145), 80 per cent of whom were Jewish or married to 'non-Aryans'.[170] The extensive 'purge' of German cultural and intellectual life resulted in an irretrievable loss of talent. During the Third Reich, more than 10,000 intellectuals turned their backs on Germany: around 2,000 academics, 2,500 from the world of journalism, 4,000 from the theatre, and 2,000 from the film world, a substantial number of whom were Jews.[171]

Stage 5: Labour market and rearmament

By the beginning of May, the new regime had become secure enough to move against another major organization, the trade unions, although by now they did not present much of an obstacle to the Nazis' drive for absolute power. Since February, they had been increasingly distancing themselves from their traditional ally, the Social Democrats, and endeavouring instead to appear as loyal organizations purely concerned with looking after the social and economic interests of their members. The Free [formerly Social Democratic] Trade Unions won a clear majority in the works council elections in March and April. This prompted the regime to postpone further works council elections for six months – de facto to stop them altogether – and to ensure that workers' representatives who had already been elected and were regarded as 'politically or economically hostile' (that is, members of the Free Trade Unions), were replaced by members of the National Socialist Factory Cell Organization. Tough dismissal procedures for employees suspected of being 'hostile to the state' soon ensured that employers were able to assert their authority.[172]

As compensation for these drastic measures, the regime declared 1 May to be a public holiday. Since the end of the nineteenth century, in many countries 1 May had been celebrated by socialist parties and trades unions as the 'The Day of the Struggle of the Working Class'. However, the labour movement had not managed to secure 1 May as a paid public holiday in the Weimar Constitution of 1919, and so this move represented a remarkable gesture by the new government of 'national concentration' towards the working class, most of whom had not hitherto voted for the NSDAP.[173] The celebrations, which were organized at the last minute, the Cabinet having only made their decision on 7 April, were planned to be suitably grand and elaborate.[174] On the morning of 1 May, Goebbels and Reich President Hindenburg spoke at a large youth rally in the Lustgarten in Berlin. Following Hindenburg's speech, Hitler stepped up to the podium and asked the young people to give three cheers for the President.[175] In the afternoon, according to official figures, 1.5 million people assembled on the Tempelhofer Feld, among them delegations of workers from all over the Reich. The rally was broadcast so that everyone in the Reich could listen to Hitler's emotional declaration that the 'symbol of class struggle, of eternal conflict and discord' was being transformed into being 'once again a symbol of the nation's great coming together and revival'.[176]

The General German Trade Union Federation had expressly welcomed the designation of 1 May as a celebration of 'national labour', asking its members to take part in the festivities; the trade union offices put up black-white-red flags on the day.[177] The trade unionists were unaware that, on 7 April, Hitler had decided forcibly to coordinate their organizations straight after the 1 May celebrations.[178] On 2 May, SA and NSBO squads occupied the trade union offices, confiscated trade union property, and arrested numerous functionaries.[179]

On 12 May, the trade unions were replaced by a Nazi organization, the German Labour Front (DAF), under the leadership of Dr Robert Ley, the chief of staff of the NSDAP's political organization. At the DAF's founding congress Hitler claimed to be someone who, from his own experience as a building worker and as an ordinary soldier, understood the lives of workers and of ordinary people.[180] But, in fact, the regime was mainly concerned about preventing the DAF from becoming a kind of substitute trade union. Right from the start, the DAF was intended to be an organization for 'all productive Germans'; in other words, it was not intended to represent workers' interests but rather to unite employees and employers. On 19 May, the Labour Ministry blocked the DAF's attempt to take responsibility for future wage agreements by appointing 'Trustees of Labour', whose job was to impose compulsory wage agreements.[181] The DAF now concentrated primarily on 'supervising' [Betreuung] and disciplining employees and, using the resources of the trade unions, it constructed its own services operation.

The Trustees of Labour acted in the interests of the regime by imposing wage freezes at the low levels prevalent during the economic crisis.[182] It was only possible for employees to increase their wages by working longer hours, although many plants were on short time. At the same time, the prices of consumer goods were going up, particularly as a result of the state's agricultural policies, which were aimed primarily at improving the profits of the agrarian sector. Although the Hitler government continued Brüning's price controls, in July 1933 it decided to transfer the powers of the Reich Prices Commissioner, who had been appointed to control prices (the post had not been filled since December 1932), to (of all people!) the Minister of Agriculture, with the result that there was effectively no prospect of a reduction in food prices.[183]

As far as the grave unemployment situation was concerned – in March 1933 there were almost six million people without jobs[184] – the new government focused less on directly financed work programmes and more on trying to kickstart the economy through tax breaks. Although, in February, it distributed the funds for work creation left over from Schleicher's government to various individual programmes, it did not launch any new initiatives. Hitler liked to project an image of being keen on technology and looking towards the future and, on 11 February, at the opening of the Berlin motor show, he announced the first stage of an elaborate programme designed to encourage motor transport, which the cabinet soon put into effect.[185] On 7 April all new vehicles were freed from motor vehicle tax, a measure which, together with other tax breaks,[186] stimulated the already growing motor industry. In the second quarter of 1933, one and half times as many four-wheeled motor vehicles were produced as in the same quarter of the previous year and the revival of the motor industry had a positive and rapid effect on the supply industry. In fact, however, the recovery in the motor industry, as in other key industries,[187] had already begun at the end of 1932, in other words before Hitler's appointment. Thus, the significance of Hitler's support for the motor industry was exaggerated, thereby increasing his prestige.[188]

In March Hitler took the first steps towards launching a comprehensive road-building programme. At the end of the month he met Willy Hof, the managing director of Hafraba, which since the mid-1920s had been preparing the construction of a motorway from the north German Hanseatic cities to Basel, via Frankfurt am Main.[189] When, at the beginning of April, Hof had the opportunity of putting his plans for the first section of the planned road to Hitler, the 'Führer' responded enthusiastically, making many concrete suggestions, and encouraging Hof to 'start planning the whole network straightaway and to go full steam ahead... with this terrific idea'. In the middle of May, therefore, at a meeting with Hitler, attended also by transport experts, Hof presented a plan for a Reich-wide motorway network. On this occasion, Hitler spoke at length in favour of privileging the construction of motorways over the existing road network. The number of motor vehicles in Germany, currently around 600,000,[190] must be increased to between three and five million. 'The development of motor traffic was also necessary for social reasons, while strategic factors were also important'. According to Hitler, 'for military reasons the new roads must be built of reinforced concrete', in order to limit the impact of enemy bombs. When the head of the road traffic department in the Transport Ministry, Ernst Brandenburg, pointed out that implementing the plans for repairs to the existing road network would have an immediate impact on unemployment, while the new roads would first have to go through the planning stage, Hitler rejected these objections, making further 'fundamental' statements.[191] Finally, in June, the cabinet agreed to the Law concerning the Establishment of a Reich Autobahn Concern, and, on 30 June, Hitler appointed Fritz Todt, an engineer, to be General Inspector for German Roads. Todt was an old Nazi, who in December 1932 had sent Nazi headquarters a detailed memorandum on road construction.[192]

The effect of the autobahn programme on the labour market was in fact initially limited; the necessary planning had not been done, and work on the first section began only in September. At this point, Hitler estimated that 300,000–350,000 workers would be required to construct the autobahns; in fact, during 1934 an average of only 54,000 each month were employed on autobahn construction. Thus its contribution to the reduction of unemployment was relatively insignificant.[193] Its military significance, which Hitler had emphasized, was also limited. The autobahn network was not designed in accordance with strategic priorities; instead, up until the end of the Third Reich, the extensive railway network remained the backbone of military transport. The measures taken to support car production were also of secondary strategic importance, above all because a range of cars of very different types was built. Looked at from a long-term perspective, the expansion of civilian car ownership was the prerequisite for an increased number of mobile divisions, but in 1933 such considerations were overshadowed by other priorities. 'Social' and propaganda factors were much more decisive for Hitler's support of a large-scale programme of motorization. In his regime, owning one's own car was intended to be a standard part of middle-class life and, as a gigantic construction programme, the autobahn network was to symbolize the new regime's efficiency and modernity.

At the end of April, the government abolished the Reich Commissariat for Work Creation established by Schleicher and transferred its powers to the Reich Labour Ministry. Reich Commissar Gereke represented the policy of employment programmes financed by credit, which Hitler's conservative partners, in particular, considered suspect. At the end of March, he was arrested on the pretext of embezzlement.[194] Yet, Seldte's Labour Ministry sympathized with the idea of a large-scale programme for combatting unemployment,[195] such as had been demanded by Gregor Strasser from the summer of 1932 onwards. This view was shared by the Finance Ministry, but regarded with scepticism by super minister Hugenberg.[196]

Hitler showed little interest in all the various concrete plans that were being discussed within the government from April onwards. In his view additional employment should be achieved through a combination of directly financed programmes and tax breaks. On 29 May, accompanied by Reich Bank President Schacht, Transport Minister Julius Dorpmüller, high-ranking civil servants, and senior Nazi Party officials, he sought the support of leading industrialists for this programme. Significantly, in addressing this audience, Hitler initially spoke of impending German rearmament and the risk of a preventive war, which during the early years would require massive rearmament. Hitler placed the measures envisaged for work creation in this context of the revival of Germany as a European power. This would involve a focus on two points in particular: first, on the renewal of private housing. Since the First World War, many houses had not been maintained and renovated, and this would now be rectified through the provision of subsidies. This represented a remarkable change of political emphasis in the direction of the lower-middle class; in the summer of 1932 the NSDAP had considered the construction of 'workers' flats' as the most urgent task of work creation.[197] Secondly, the construction of motorways: Hitler outlined in detail the advantages of a road network that was designed exclusively for the use of modern motor vehicles, emphasizing in particular its 'strategic' importance.[198]

Two days later, the government agreed the so-called 'Reinhardt programme', named after the new state secretary in the Finance Ministry, Fritz Reinhardt, who had revised the Labour Minister's proposals to produce a two-pronged programme. Apart from further funds for direct work creation measures, it now included tax breaks, which industry preferred.[199] The programme envisaged providing credit of up to one billion Reich Marks for the carrying out of repairs to buildings, the construction of housing estates, as well as improvements to infrastructure; furthermore, exemption from tax for money spent on job creation and replacements, but also the provision of marriage loans in order to remove women who had hitherto been employed from the labour market.[200] On 21 September, there followed a Second Law for the Reduction of Unemployment,[201] with additional money for the autobahn programme as well as for substantial work creation measures by the railways and Post Office. Between 1933 and 1935, a total of 4.7 billion RM was provided for work creation measures; over 1.5 billion of this money was spent in 1933, of which only a little more than 10 per cent came from programmes initiated by the Hitler government.[202]

In addition, the regime drove forward rearmament as never before. The new Reich Bank president, Schacht, provided the financial instruments with which such a programme could be financed in secret. On 4 April, the government had already decided no longer to include the funds earmarked for the rearmament of the Wehrmacht in the Reich budget and so to exclude it from the usual budgetary controls. The budget plans no longer included purchases and investments, only running costs.[203]

Three days later Schacht announced a moratorium on Reich debt.[204] The withdrawal from the international payments system, which was actually triggered on 30 June, was intended to enable the Reich government to delay repaying overseas debt until export surpluses had been achieved.[205] This moratorium coincided with a second fundamental decision in which Schacht again played a central role. To finance German rearmament he declared himself willing to provide the gigantic sum of 35 billion RM, spread over a period of eight years, as credit.[206] For the purposes of comparison: in previous years the total defence budget had been only 600–700 million RM per year.[207] Schacht exemplifies the extent to which the rearmament programme being pushed through by Hitler had the support of a broad consensus among the conservative elites. When Hitler came to power the Reichswehr and German diplomats (the Foreign Ministry's role will be dealt with in the next chapter) assumed that the armaments limitations imposed by the Versailles Treaty would soon be ignored; industry saw in rearmament new business opportunities; and the conservative bourgeoisie greeted the return of 'defence sovereignty' as the basic precondition for the restoration of German greatness.[208]

Stage 6: The end of the political parties and development of policy towards the Churches

These measures initiating a gigantic rearmament programme provided the real background to Hitler's so-called 'peace speech' to the Reichstag on 17 May. In the next chapter we shall look at the content of his speech in the context of his foreign policy; the point to be made here is that Hitler was once again using the parliamentary deputies elected on 5 March as extras. And, in fact, the Reichstag approved Hitler's government statement unanimously, with the votes of the Centre Party, the German State Party, and those members of the SPD who were still in Germany and not under arrest.[209] To achieve this, Hitler had personally approached Brüning the previous day to assure him of his willingness to discuss changes to those emergency decrees which limited civil rights.[210] Thinly disguised threats by Interior Minister Frick to murder imprisoned Social Democrats contributed to persuading the majority of the forty-eight remaining SPD deputies, at a meeting of their parliamentary group, to support the government statement.[211]

Two weeks later, Brüning reminded Hitler to keep the promise he had made. Brüning reports in his memoirs that Hitler denied that any politicians had been mistreated, to which Brüning responded that he should 'come at once with me to the Hedwig Hospital and see for himself the barbaric wounds inflicted on harmless people who simply held different political views'. Hitler did not reply, instructing Frick to negotiate with Brüning. However, these negotiations were continually 'postponed from one day to the next'.[212]

Hitler concluded that in future he would be better off doing without any further 'involvement' by other parties. Thus, their formal abolition in July 1933 represented the last stage in the seizure of power. The first victim of this policy was the SPD, which had stuck systematically to its policy of legality and had to accept its organization being gradually and comprehensively shut down.[213] With the elimination of the trades unions at the beginning of May, it was clear that the end of the SPD was only a matter of time. Thus, on 4 May, the SPD's executive committee decided that all full-time officials should go abroad; during the following days, this step was taken by, among others, Otto Wels, Friedrich Stampfer, and Erich Ollenhauer. On 10 May, the whole of the party's assets were confiscated on the grounds of alleged embezzlement.[214] The behaviour of the Reichstag group in the 17 May session led to bitter disagreements, contributing to the committee finally splitting into those who remained in the Reich and the group who fled into exile in Prague.[215] In view of this desperate situation, the official ban on the party by the Interior Ministry on 22 June 1933 simply confirmed what *de facto* had already happened – the SPD had ceased to exist.[216]

On 14 July 1933, a new expatriation law provided the regime with the grounds for removing their citizenship and property from all those who 'through their behaviour have damaged German interests by failing in their duty of loyalty to the Reich and the nation'. On 23 August, the Reich Interior Ministry announced the names of thirty-five prominent opponents of Nazism who had fled abroad and now were to come under the law; among them were the left-wing politicians Rudolf Breitscheid, Albert Grzesinsky, Philipp Scheidemann, Otto Wels, and Bernhard Weiss, as well as the authors Georg Bernhard, Lion Feuchtwanger, Alfred Kerr, Heinrich Mann, and Kurt Tucholsky. Further cases were to follow and by 1939 the law had affected more than 39,000 emigrés.[217]

Unlike the SPD, the DNVP, now operating as the German Nationalist Front, had a key position in spring 1933. For the Hitler government was basically still a coalition government of NSDAP and DNVP, and the latter's cabinet member, the Economics and Agriculture Minister, Hugenberg, represented the interests of influential circles in industry and agriculture; it would be risky to force him out of the government. Moreover, Hugenberg could rely on considerable support from the Reich President, who still had the power to appoint and dismiss Chancellor and ministers. The Enabling Law, which made Hitler independent of parliament and President, applied after all to the 'present government'; thus, in the event of the coalition breaking up, it was theoretically possible for this 'enabling power' to be jeopardized. It would be followed by a power struggle between conservatives and Nazis, which at this juncture Hitler had to avoid at all costs. In fact, he managed to exclude Hugenberg and the DNVP without provoking this power struggle and was assisted in this by the clumsy and indecisive behaviour of his coalition partner and now opponent.[218]

Hugenberg responded to increasing Nazi attacks during the spring by appointing his deputy, Friedrich von Winterfeld, to take over the leadership of the DNVP, and concentrating entirely on his work as a multi-minister. Despite this, he was unable to avoid being isolated in the Reich cabinet and in the Prussian government (Göring refused to upgrade his status from act-ing to permanent minister).[219] At the end of May, there were the first bans on DNVP meetings; members of the 'combat squads', the paramilitary wing of the party, were arrested and the organization itself subjected, for the time being, to local bans. Prominent members of the DNVP joined the NSDAP. In his address to the Reich and Gau leaders of the NSDAP meeting in Berlin on 14 June Hitler announced that the 'law of the nationalist revolu-tion had not yet lapsed'[220] and this was clearly intended as a threat to the DNVP. A week later the 'combat squads' were subjected to a Reich-wide ban.[221]

In the meantime, Hugenberg had submitted a memorandum to the World Economic Conference in London, in which he proposed that, in order to improve Germany's ability to pay its debts, it should be given col-onies and territory for settlement in the East.[222] This ran counter to the Foreign Ministry's position and that of Hitler himself, since they were seek-ing to calm the international situation in line with the Chancellor's govern-ment statement of 17 May. On 21 June, Hitler stressed to Hugenberg his desire 'to maintain the pact of 30 January'.[223] Encouraged by this, two days later, at a cabinet meeting on 23 June, Hugenberg decided to risk a trial of strength. He complained about Foreign Minister Neurath, who had dis-tanced himself from Hugenberg's London memorandum, and demanded the recall of the deputy head of the German delegation, Hans Posse, on the grounds that unbridgeable differences had emerged between them. However, Hitler politely informed Hugenberg that he supported Neurath; to recall Posse would be a sign of weakness and so was out of the question. The cab-inet agreed with Hitler.[224]

After this defeat Hugenberg was put hopelessly on the defensive, particu-larly as his attempts to seek support from the President met with no response.[225] He now decided to resign, but without informing the other DNVP leaders and in a way that did not involve a break-up of the coalition, but appeared simply as a personal decision. In doing it this way, he was fail-ing to deploy the only means of pressure he still possessed. Had he linked his resignation with the DNVP quitting the government (he was the only member of the party in the cabinet), then, at least theoretically, further use of the Enabling Law, crucial for the government's position, would have been at risk. However, this assumes that the non-party ministers and, above all, the President would have had the determination to resist the NSDAP's drive to monopolize power and, by June 1933, this was certainly not the case. On 24 June, Hugenberg informed only his closest party colleagues about his plans and, on 26 June, composed a resignation letter that he submitted to Hindenburg in person. In it he asserted his conviction that the 'basis on which the cabinet was formed on 30 January no longer exists and will no longer exist'.[226]

Despite clearly outlining his assessment of the situation, Hugenberg was a long way from advising the President to act on the basis of this assessment. Hugenberg himself was not contemplating a break-up of the coalition; he wanted to move the DNVP into a position of 'benevolent neutrality'[227] towards the new state, a kind of reserve position, from which, at a later stage, they might once again take part in the government. But, by acting in the way he did, Hugenberg prevented those elements within the DNVP who did not want to leave the field without a struggle from rousing themselves and joining forces. On 26 June, under pressure from Nazi threats and behind Hugenberg's back, the party's central committee decided to dissolve the DNVP. Thus, Hitler had found it easy to get rid of his coalition partner.[228]

Unlike Hugenberg, Hitler was aware of the DNVP's decision to dissolve itself when he received his minister for a final meeting on 27 June.[229] In view of the anticipated disappearance of the DNVP, Hitler was concerned above all to retain Hugenberg in the cabinet (albeit without all his posts), in order to avoid creating the impression of a bitter and definitive rift with the German Nationalists. In the course of the conversation, Hugenberg, who was still insisting on his resignation, introduced a new scenario: he could imagine returning to the cabinet in a few months' time when Hitler, in the impending conflict with 'the left-wing elements who were present in his party ... [would] require the help of my friends'. Hitler immediately interpreted this offer as a significant attempt to restrict his claim to power. He told Hugenberg that the latter's proposal was 'one of those suggestions with a counter-revolutionary tendency' that were current in German Nationalist circles, who were hoping 'they would get into power when he and his government had failed'. Hitler feared the continuation of a conservative power base with strong support in the civil service, the military, among big land-owners, and in industry. According to Hugenberg, the conversation became 'very lively' and was carried on while they were 'standing up and moving around'. The Chancellor urged Hugenberg to remain in the cabinet, but no longer as a coalition partner, merely as a departmental minister; the DNVP had to be wound up. If he went, the DNVP would inevitably end up becoming an opposition party and 'there would be a struggle'. 'Thousands of civil servants', Hitler threatened, 'who belong to your party, will then lose their jobs – I can't prevent that because my lot will demand it and – many people, through your fault, will suffer, and a ruthless struggle will begin all along the line'. This struggle, and Hitler was now addressing Hugenberg, the 'media mogul', would also occur 'in press and film' and 'within three days it will have been settled, and not in your favour'.

However, these threats were not necessary to achieve the dissolution of the DNVP, since the party had already indicated to Hitler its willingness to do so. Hitler's violent reaction is explicable more from the fact that Hugenberg's suggestion that he and his friends were waiting in the background, ready if necessary 'to support' him, seemed to Hitler to challenge his dominance.

Hugenberg wanted Hitler to take responsibility for banning the DNVP, with all the consequences that would flow from the break, and had prepared a resignation statement for the press.[230] However, the DNVP's executive, anxious to avoid any disagreement with the Chancellor, had decided, on the evening of 27 June, to dissolve the party.[231] There was now only one thing left for Hugenberg to do. He informed Hindenburg of the content of his conversation with Hitler, including the threats, and requested that he, as the 'patron of the whole of the nationalist movement in Germany' should guarantee the 'safety of those who hitherto have been under my leadership'. He also gave, as a reason for his resignation, his position 'as a Protestant Christian', a clear hint to Hindenburg of the threats to German Protestantism posed by Nazi Church policy. Only a few days earlier, the Prussian government had appointed a state commissar for the Protestant Church, a development we shall examine in more detail.[232] In fact, it may well be that Hugenberg's intervention with Hindenburg contributed towards preventing the campaign of vengeance that Hitler had threatened in the event of the former's departure from the cabinet. In any event, on 29 June Hitler agreed with Hindenburg on a reshuffle of the cabinet and on sorting out the situation in the Protestant Church. This meeting appears to have established a kind of modus vivendi between Nazism and Protestant conservatives.

The dissolution of the DNVP was followed by that of the State Party on 28 June, of the Christlich-Sozialer Volksdienst on 2 July, of the German

People's Party and the Bavarian People's Party on 4 July, and the Centre Party on 5 July. The dissolution of the Catholic parties was closely linked to the conclusion of a Concordat between the Reich government and the Vatican, which will be dealt with later. During the last phase of negotiations in June, the Nazis had applied considerable pressure on Catholic organizations in order to achieve their goal of a depoliticized Catholic Church.[233]

Alongside the enforced dissolution of the DNVP, the regime set about removing the organizational independence of its third partner in the revived Harzburg Front of 30 January, the Stahlhelm. Having 'subordinated' himself to Hitler on 26 April, on 21 June Seldte agreed to the transfer of the younger Stahlhelm members (18–35 year olds) to the SA. In future the Stahlhelm leadership would be in charge only of the older members, the 'core Stahlhelm'. The integration into the SA took place on 26 June, together with the admission of the German Nationalist Scharnhorst Youth into the Hitler Youth.[234] Shortly afterwards, at the beginning of July, Hitler announced to a meeting of leaders of the SA, SS, and Stahlhelm in Bad Reichenhall that the core Stahlhelm would now also join the SA. By the end of October, the amalgamation had been completed, although the Stahlhelm continued to exist. In March 1934 it was renamed the League of National Socialist Front Line Fighters (Stahlhelm).[235]

As has already been indicated, it was no accident that, alongside the dissolution of the Catholic parties and the DNVP (which was the embodiment of Prussian Protestantism), Hitler had also set about sorting out the regime's relationship with the two Churches. As far as the Catholic Church was concerned, the main aim was to prevent the relatively well-organized Catholic population from becoming opposed to the new government. The conclusion of a Concordat with the Vatican appeared to be the right way to avoid this danger. At the same time, Hitler aimed to achieve a comprehensive reform of the Protestant Church in order to create a counter-weight to the Catholic bloc.

Hitler had already offered the Churches a guarantee of their legal rights in the government declaration linked to the Enabling Law, referring to a 'sincere co-operation between Church and State'.[236] The Catholic bishops had responded to this signal and, on 28 March, in a joint declaration, had withdrawn their hitherto resolute opposition to Nazism.[237] The first meeting between Hitler and representatives of the Catholic Church took place at the end of April; Hitler had already made contact with Rome via Papen. At this meeting Hitler had expressed the view that without Christianity 'neither a personal life nor a state could achieve stability', but he had become convinced that the Churches 'in recent centuries had not summoned up the strength or determination to overcome the enemies of the state and of Christianity'. Nevertheless, he would 'not permit any other form of religion'. He referred in this connection to Rosenberg's 'Myth', which he rejected. He said he wanted to retain the confessional schools ('Soldiers who have faith are the most valuable ones') and did not wish to restrict the Catholic associations.[238]

During this meeting, Hitler declared that, as a Catholic, he could 'not find his way round the Protestant Church and its structures'. This was due not least to the division of the Protestant Church into twenty-eight state Churches, which were only loosely held together by the League of Protestant Churches. Hitler aimed to get rid of this lack of transparency; he wanted to establish a unified Reich Church and to 'coordinate' it with the aid of the 'German Christians', the Nazi 'faith movement' within Protestantism. This fitted in with the regime's aim of achieving 'national unity'; but it also chimed with a variety of long-held aspirations among Protestants, whose leaders, not least under Nazi pressure, now adopted the idea of a 'Reich Church'.[239] At the end of April, Hitler pushed ahead with his scheme by appointing as his representative for Protestant Church questions someone whom he could trust in the shape of the Königsberg military district chaplain, Ludwig Müller. He intended Müller to become the first 'Reich bishop' of a unified Protestant Church.[240] However, at the end of May, the representatives of the state Churches appointed not Müller but Friedrich von Bodelschwingh as the first Reich bishop. Hitler refused to receive Bodelschwingh,[241] and the 'German Christians' began a campaign against the Reich bishop that soon led to his resignation. On 24 June, the Prussian ministry appointed a commissioner for the Protestant state Churches in Prussia, who immediately began a purge of the Churches' leadership.[242] On 28 June, with the help of the SA, Müller took over the headquarters building of the League of Protestant Churches (which the state Churches had combined to form in 1922), claiming to be the leader of German Protestantism.[243]

On the same day, Hitler was forced by a courageous Berlin clergyman to comment on the situation in the Protestant Church. After a speech to the German Newspaper Publishers' Association, on leaving the building Hitler was accosted by Erich Backhaus, a Berlin vicar and opponent of the German Christians. He appealed to him: 'Herr Reich Chancellor, please save our Church! Preserve it from division and violation.' Hitler engaged in a twenty-minute conversation with Backhaus, conducted in a serious manner. He denied having anything to do with 'Church matters', but, as Backhaus persisted, admitted that he had been 'affronted' by Bodelschwingh's appointment as Reich bishop. 'He was getting increasingly fed up' with Church matters, he said, and had no intention, as Backhaus claimed, of making Müller Reich bishop; in fact, he would oppose such an appointment.[244]

When Hitler met Hindenburg the following day at his Neudeck estate, the President expressed his concern about developments in the Protestant Church. Hitler, who was seeking Hindenburg's approval of the cabinet reshuffle following Hugenberg's departure and wanted to avoid any disagreement with the President, made sympathetic noises. Hindenberg then recorded the content of the conversation in a letter that he released to the German press on 1 July. In the letter he committed the further development of Protestant Church policy to his Chancellor's statesmanlike vision.[245] Hitler immediately responded to the President's admonition by taking the bull by the horns. Prior to the publication of the letter, he instructed Frick to press the Church to produce, under Müller's direction and in the shortest possible time, a uniform 'German Protestant Church Constitution' and to organize Reich-wide Church elections in order to legitimize the new unified Church. The promise then to withdraw the Church commissioner provided an incentive.[246]

The new Church constitution was published on 11 July and the Church commissioner was in fact withdrawn. Three days later, Hitler made the personal decision to issue a Reich law ordering Church elections for 23 July.[247] The day before, Hitler commented on the issue at stake in a broadcast. He said that, as with the Concordat with the Vatican, which had been agreed on 8 July, they 'could achieve an equally clear arrangement with the Protestant Church'. However, the precondition for this was that 'the numerous Protestant Churches would, if at all possible, be replaced by a single Reich Church'.[248] As expected, the German Christians managed to secure a large majority in the elections, not least thanks to the support of the whole Party machine. They at once began a comprehensive purge of the Church organization, introducing the 'Aryan clause'. Thus, the Protestant Church had been finally subjected to Nazi coordination. In September, the first German Protestant National Synod, meeting in Wittenberg, appointed Hitler's candidate, Müller, Reich bishop.[249]

By summer 1933, the concentration of power in the hands of the government, now largely controlled by the Nazis, was complete; the cabinet had

removed all vital countervailing forces and freedoms, which, in a democratic state operating under the rule of law, prevent a government from
misusing its power. It had achieved this by suspending civil rights and emas-
culating the constitutional institutions with their independent powers, by
eliminating the political parties, by coordinating associations and social
organizations, by neutralizing an independent press, by excluding critical
voices from cultural life, and by significantly undermining the moral authority of the Churches.

This process depended on a sophisticated technique of acquiring power
in stages, which enabled the Party and the regime to concentrate all their
energy on a limited number of opponents at any given time. The famous
quote from Martin Niemöller, the founder of the Confessing Church, who
disappeared into a concentration camp in 1937, sums up the effects of this
method very well: 'When the Nazis came for the Communists, I stayed
silent because I wasn't a Communist. When they came for the Social
Democrats I stayed silent because I wasn't a Social Democrat. When they
came for the trades unionists I stayed silent because I wasn't a trade unionist.
When they came for me there was no one left to protest.'[250] In the course
of the various stages the Nazi leadership developed a method that very cun-
ningly combined the violence of the activists with legal, in most cases
pseudo-legal, measures. The cunning consisted in calibrating the amount of
force used in order to secure particular goals, without letting the violence
get out of control or directing it permanently against other groups apart
from the Left, and also in giving the state measures provoked by the use of
violence an appearance of legality. For it was vital that the use of force was
controlled and the formal framework of the 'rule of law' preserved in order
to retain the alliance with the conservatives.

Hitler played the central role in the complicated direction of this process,
which depended on a close synchronization of the Party activists and the
regime. He defined the opponents who were to be fought; he spurred on
the Party activists and then called them to order; he took the initiative in
setting in motion the measures necessary for the next stage of the conquest
of power; he shielded the whole process from conservative opposition. He
canalized and refereed the rivalries and power struggles between the individual Party functionaries. Usurping parts of the state machine at central
and regional level, they combined the state responsibilities they had acquired
with their Party functions, thereby acquiring their own power bases. The
idea that the seizure of power happened more or less automatically, with

Hitler playing only a largely passive role, limiting himself to authorizing and legitimizing the actions of others, fails to recognize his skill as an active politician.[251] Hitler naturally utilized the many initiatives and suggestions of those who 'worked towards' him, but he was the one who directed the numerous actions of his supporters towards particular goals, coordinating them so that they served his aims.

Evolution rather than revolution

After almost six months of constant political activity devoted to taking over power, Hitler decided the time had come to put the brakes on the Party activists. He was primarily concerned about the response of the conservative establishment. Following the dissolution of the bourgeois parties, the government reshuffle, and the turbulence caused by the restructuring of the Protestant Church, Hitler wanted to prevent Party supporters from further alienating the middle classes.

Thus, on 6 June, a day after the dissolution of the Centre Party, Hitler told a meeting of Reich Governors in Berlin that the conquest of power was over: 'The revolution is not a permanent condition; it must not be allowed to continue indefinitely. The river of revolution that has broken free must be diverted into the secure bed of evolution.' He made the Reich Governors responsible for ensuring that 'no organization or Party agency claims governmental authority, dismisses people, or appoints people'. All this was the sole responsibility of the Reich government, and in the case of economic matters, the Reich Minister of Economics. The Party had 'now become the state'.[252] Six days later Hitler also demanded restraint from the Gauleiters, the state leaders of the NSBO, and the newly-appointed Reich Trustees of Labour. As far as intervention in business was concerned, they should 'move forwards step by step without radically smashing up what already exists, thereby jeopardizing the basis of our own existence'.[253]

With these clear statements Hitler was inaugurating a new economic policy for his government, amounting to a break with all 'corporatist' [ständisch] and 'revolutionary' experiments.[254] To achieve this, in mid-July 1933, he and the new Reich Economics Minister, Kurt Schmitt, agreed informally that the corporatist structure would be replaced by, as the new magic formula put it, an 'organic' economic structure.[255] In practice, this meant that in future entrepreneurs would be free from arbitrary Nazi interventions, the 'anti-capitalist agitation' of the small business activists within the Party would be stopped, wages would be kept at a relatively low level with the aid of the Trustees of Labour, public works projects would be scaled down, and economic recovery would instead be encouraged by tax breaks and other business incentives. Instead of corporatist employee organizations, compulsory associations, subordinate to the Economics Ministry, were introduced for the various sectors of the economy. A General Economic Council was established, whose members came largely from the financial sector and heavy industry.[256] However, this remained a purely symbolic act, since the Council never played any role. Schmitt ensured the implementation of these decisions in the state sector by explicitly referring to the Chancellor's authorization. Hitler sacked his old associate, Wagener, who had been acting as Reich Commissar for the Economy since May 1933 and was making no secret of his wish to become Economics Minister. He also subordinated all Nazi Party economic policy agencies to his economic advisor, Keppler, whom he appointed the Reich Chancellor's Representative for Economic Affairs.[257]

The new economic policy represented a basic compromise underpinning the Third Reich. Six months after the 'seizure of power' with its various upheavals Hitler had reached a deal with German business, according to which their authority within their enterprises was increased in return for an agreement to submit to overall direction by the state.[258] The introduction of a few measures against department stores represented more of a symbolic gesture to the small business section within the Party, responding to the main focus of their agitation.[259] The idea of permanently subjecting department stores to special taxes – a March law was a first legal step in that direction – was dropped and there was no more talk of banning them, as demanded by the Combat League of Small Business.[260] Instead, on 7 August, Hitler ordered Ley to dissolve the Combat League and, albeit reluctantly, even agreed to grant financial support for department stores.[261]

There was, however, one economic sector where the NSDAP's ständisch ideologues succeeded in getting their way.[262] In the spring of 1933, Darré, the head of the NSDAP's agrarian political machine, had succeeded in coordinating all the various agricultural organizations. After taking over from Hugenberg as Reich and Prussian Minister of Agriculture at the end of June, he acquired the title of Reich Peasant Leader and set about establishing the 'Reich Food Estate'. This compulsory organization included not only all agricultural enterprises, but fisheries, agricultural trade, and the food industry. The Reich Food Estate regulated the whole agricultural sector through a special market organization fixing prices and production quotas.[263] In September 1933, Darré also introduced a Reich Hereditary Farm Law, turning 700,000 farms into 'hereditary farms', which could not be sold, mortgaged, or divided. As mentioned above, he had already introduced such a law in Prussia. According to the preface to the law, it was intended to secure the food supply, prevent further agricultural indebtedness, and be a means of preserving the 'peasantry' as 'the German nation's blood spring'. In fact, however, its impact proved to be double-edged, as the children who were not entitled to inherit left the land, and farms could not be adequately modernized because of a lack of credit.[264]

Hitler's banning of unauthorized actions carried out by the SA and other 'revolutionary' Nazis culminated in a number of laws agreed at the cabinet meeting on 14 July, the last before the summer break; on the one hand, they served to stabilize the regime, and, on the other, set the course for future policy. The 'sorting out' of the parties, which had been achieved a few days earlier through massive political pressure, was now legalized by the Law against the Creation of New Political Parties, which stated that in future 'the National Socialist German Workers Party [will be] the sole political party' in Germany. In the meantime, on 7 July, all Social Democratic seats in the legislatures of the Reich, the states, and local government had been withdrawn.[265] The relationship with the Churches was placed on a new basis through the Concordat with the Catholic Church and the Law concerning the Constitution of the Protestant Church. The so-called Law on Plebiscites was designed to transform the democratic right to a plebiscite contained in the Weimar Constitution into an instrument of the regime, as the government was now entitled to ask the people 'whether they approved of a measure proposed by the government or not'.[266] The Law concerning the Revocation of Naturalization and the Deprivation of German Citizenship was aimed in the first instance at 'Eastern Jews' who had been naturalized since 1918, and at émigrés.[267] In addition, there were laws that marked turning points in racial and population policy: apart from the Law for the Recreation of a German Peasantry,[268] above all, the Law for the Prevention of Hereditarily Diseased Offspring. The latter introduced the compulsory sterilization of men and women, when specially created Genetic Health Courts diagnosed a hereditary illness that would lead to any offspring suffering serious mental or physical handicaps. However, the list of such illnesses was drawn up according to such vague criteria ('congenital feeble-mindedness', 'serious alcoholism') that in the majority of cases decisions were made not on medical grounds, but on the basis of social discrimination.[269] The law caused controversy in the cabinet, with Vice-Chancellor Papen opposing it. Hitler, who had already proposed a policy of systematic birth control in *Mein Kampf*, responded by arguing that the measure was 'morally irrefutable' on the basis that 'people suffering from a hereditary disease reproduce in considerable numbers, whereas, on the other hand, millions of healthy children [remain] unborn'.[270] Thus, at this early stage, he had taken a hard line on a key issue of Nazi racial policy.

The cabinet meeting on 14 July saw the culmination of the legislative work of Hitler's cabinet and, with this series of laws, the process of concentrating power in the hands of the NSDAP was, for the time being, concluded. After the government had ceased to be a coalition, cabinet meetings had lost their point as far as Hitler was concerned; now he could secure laws by simply getting the agreement of the most important ministers concerned via the head of the Reich Chancellery. Thus the start of the 1933 summer holidays marked a turning point in Hitler's relationship with the government as a collective body. After forty-one meetings up until the summer break, between then and the end of the year the government met only twelve times and, during the whole of the following year, the cabinet had only eighteen meetings. After that it met only sporadically.[271]

Summer break

Despite Hitler's warning to the SA and his reining in of the Party's 'economic experts', with their unwelcome experiments, one reason why the Party avoided open divisions for the time being was because he demonstratively called a temporary halt to politics. Instead of mass meetings, violent incidents, and coordination slogans, the public sphere was now dominated by the joys of summer. Hitler spent the last week of July, in other words the days immediately following the Protestant Church elections, at the Wagner festival in Bayreuth. Newspaper photos show him wearing a tailcoat rather than a Party uniform or in the posh double-breasted suit he had worn – acting the statesman – during recent months. In the relaxed atmosphere of the festival he found time, among other things, to concern himself with the Goebbelses' marital problems. Following a domestic row, the Propaganda Minister had arrived on his own. Hitler promptly had Magda flown in from Berlin, invited them both for the evening, and reconciled them.[272]

After that, he went to the Obersalzberg where, apart from a few short trips, he remained until the start of the Party rally at the beginning of September. However, during the dictator's 'vacation' political decision-making by no means came to a halt. During this period, his refuge in Upper Bavaria became a kind of provisional power centre.[273] Thus, on 5 August, he used the seclusion to give a three-hour speech revealing some of his more important objectives to a meeting of Reichsleiters and Gauleiters. He mentioned the plan for a Party senate, which was to be composed of the 'oldest, most reliable, and loyal Party comrades'; his statements about Church policy were, however, more significant. For two weeks after the German Christians' victory in the Church elections, he had come to the conclusion that his precipitate intervention in internal Church affairs – which had been prompted ultimately by the complaint made by the Reich President at the end of June – together with the coordination of the Protestant Church, had, viewed in the longer term, contributed towards maintaining, even strengthening, the institution. Given Hitler's fundamentally anti-Christian views, this was the opposite of his intention. It was only natural, therefore, that he should tell the Reichsleiters and Gauleiters leaders that the Party was neutral in Church matters.[274] In fact, it is clear from the brief note that Goebbels made of this speech that Hitler regarded this 'neutrality' as the first stage in the elimination of Christianity: 'A hard line against the Churches', he notes. 'We shall become a church ourselves.'[275] It had become clear to those present that the German Christians, with their attempt to achieve a nationalist–religious amalgamation of Nazism and Protestantism, could no longer count on the NSDAP's or Hitler's support. The consequences of this change in religious policy were to become apparent during the autumn.[276]

Apart from Goebbels, other leading politicians came for a tête-à-tête with Hitler. Magda also arrived – two days before her husband; she stayed a week longer than him.[277] In his conversation with Goebbels on 24 August, Hitler advocated, among other things, the complete abolition of the federal states; all Gauleiters should become Reich Governors. Hitler also returned to the topic of a Party senate, which was intended to guarantee the 'regime's stability'.[278] The succession to the 85-year-old Hindenburg was another topic for discussion. Only five months earlier, when talking to Goebbels in March, Hitler had been uncertain about it. He had wondered whether the Prussian prince, August-Wilhelm, known as Prince Auwi, might not be a possibility, if only to prevent Göring from becoming Chancellor. So, at that point, he had not thought of combining the two offices.[279] But now, in conversation with Goebbels, Hitler showed that he was determined to take over as Reich President straight after Hindenburg's death; this would then be subsequently legitimized through a plebiscite. His change of mind demonstrates the extent to which his self-confidence had grown during the past months.[280]

13

First Steps in Foreign Policy

In the summer of 1933 Hitler declared that the 'National Socialist revolution' had come to an end, thereby concluding six months of intensive engagement in domestic policy. He could also look back on a series of foreign policy initiatives through which he had gone a long way towards turning the Foreign Ministry into a tool of his policy.

At the start of his Chancellorship, Hitler had remained largely passive as far as foreign policy was concerned. That was not simply because the individual stages of the seizure of power required his full attention. It was also because, in appointing the government, Hindenburg had been careful to make sure that the posts of Foreign and Defence Minister were occupied by people of whom he approved.[1]

At the beginning of April, Foreign Minister Neurath had outlined to the cabinet the basic principles of a future foreign policy, emphasizing continuity with the policies of previous governments. The main aim, according to Neurath, was the revision of the Treaty of Versailles, a goal that required the 'application of all our efforts'. In view of the progress that had been achieved hitherto – the ending of reparations and the withdrawal of the French from the Rhineland – now the focus must be on two issues: the achievement of military parity for Germany (in other words, rearmament) and territorial revision. As far as rearmament was concerned, there was no prospect 'of regaining military parity with other nations...for a long time to come'. In the current disarmament negotiations they must 'for tactical reasons concentrate in the first instance on trying to get the other nations to disarm'. Neurath urged caution. Foreign countries were suspicious of German attempts to rearm; military intervention was not inconceivable. Foreign conflicts should be avoided as they were not up to coping with military engagements. Even frontier revision could be tackled only when Germany was once more 'militarily, politically, and financially stronger'. The most important task was 'revision of the eastern border' and this would require 'a total solution', including Danzig. By contrast, there was no point in raising the issue of Alsace and Lorraine. As far as colonies were concerned, they would, 'for the time being, have to restrict themselves to propaganda'; and Anschluss with Austria was, for the moment, not on the cards because of Italy's hostility. In the case of bilateral relations, they would need to seek good relations with Britain and also with Italy. An understanding with France, however, was 'more or less out of the question for the foreseeable future'. An 'understanding with Poland', Neurath added with remarkable bluntness, 'is neither possible nor desirable'. 'Defence against Poland' was, however, 'only possible if Russia's support has been secured' and at the moment it was unclear whether they could rely on the indispensable 'backing of Russia against Poland'. As far as the League of Nations was concerned, although they were dissatisfied with its performance, 'a German withdrawal [was] out of the question'.[2]

Although this programme was dictated by Realpolitik and caution, Neurath's statements clearly show that the Foreign Ministry's long-term goal was the restoration of Germany's great power status in Europe. His aim of revising the eastern border, Anschluss with Austria, and regaining colonies represented a minimal consensus for the conservative elites at this point. However, examined more closely, their foreign policy aims included other goals that were widely supported: hegemony in the Baltic states and the extension of German influence in 'Mitteleuropa', in other words the states that had emerged from the collapse of the Habsburg monarchy.[3] This was only partly compatible with Hitler's long-term foreign policy ideas, focusing above all on the conquest of 'living space' in eastern Europe; but such differences did not emerge to begin with, for they were all agreed on the intermediate aim of overturning the post-war order and establishing German hegemony in central Europe. This provided sufficient common ground with which to bridge their fundamental differences regarding long-term goals. However, it soon became apparent that, during the first stage of this agreed revisionist foreign policy, Hitler was setting a very different course from that of his diplomats.

Within a period of a little over a year Hitler would succeed in more or less turning Neurath's revisionist programme on its head. He withdrew from international armaments controls and engaged in massive rearmament, without allowing himself to be put off by the negative responses from abroad; he permitted, indeed even specifically welcomed, a freeze in

German–Soviet relations. In fact, dispensing with the supposedly necessary 'backing from the Soviet Union', he made a non-aggression pact with Poland in January 1934, turning it into Germany's most important partner, and thereby completely downgrading the revision of the eastern border. He withdrew Germany from the League of Nations in October 1933 and tried to achieve Anschluss with Austria through a violent coup d'état, thereby risking a serious breach in relations with Italy. He pushed through these policies against opposition from the conservative and nationalist diplomats in the Foreign Ministry, in some cases by dispensing with their services.

However, Hitler's first spectacular foreign policy move occurred in a very different sphere, one closely linked to the domestic situation in Germany.

Recognition and demarcation: the Concordat

Since Hitler's government statement on 23 March on the occasion of the Enabling Law, extending an olive branch to the Christian confessions, relations between Nazism and the Churches had to some extent relaxed. While actively involved in the unification of the Protestant Churches to form a Reich Church, Hitler also sought a dialogue with Catholicism. As we have seen, after the Catholic Church had withdrawn its previous opposition to Nazism on 28 March, Hitler met with its representatives in April. He was concerned above all to achieve a Concordat with the Vatican, hoping that such an agreement would produce a modus vivendi with the Catholic Church, enabling him to eliminate political Catholicism from Germany once and for all.

There is evidence that Vice-Chancellor von Papen, the Centre Party dissident, had been pursuing the idea of a Concordat since early April 1933. In the middle of April, during Easter, he began talks with the cardinal secretary of state, Eugenio Pacelli. Papen succeeded in securing the chairman of the Centre Party, the priest Ludwig Kaas, as an advisor, and, after Papen's departure from Rome, Kaas continued the negotiations by correspondence.[4] What was at issue above all was whether the Church could tolerate a general ban on Catholic clergy taking part in politics. Hitler had several times insisted on this demand to Papen and had made it a prerequisite for the conclusion of the agreement.[5]

At a second round of talks, which began in Rome on 30 June and in which the German participants were Papen, Kaas, and Archbishop Conrad

Gröber, agreement was reached on a text that was approved by the Pope and which Papen forwarded to Hitler on 3 July. He in turn sent it to the Interior Ministry, which requested numerous alterations. A senior Ministry official then flew to Rome in a special aircraft in order to carry on last-minute negotiations, a clear disavowal of the Vice-Chancellor and head of the delegation. Among other things, the Germans managed to tighten further the ban on priests taking part in politics.[6]

The Concordat was initialled on 8 July. In the agreement the state guaranteed the freedom of religious expression and continued to grant parishes the status of public corporations. Basically, the Concordat guaranteed the Church's existence and granted it a number of privileges. Among other things, it was guaranteed the right to continue imposing Church taxes; the seal of the confessional was recognized; the continuation of Catholic university faculties was confirmed; the teaching of religion as a subject within the official school curriculum in state schools was conceded; and the maintenance of Catholic schools was guaranteed, including the establishment of new ones. In return, the bishops, on appointment, were obliged to swear a special oath of loyalty to the German Reich. On Sundays there were to be prayers for the 'welfare of the German Reich and people'. The withdrawal of the Church from political life, on which Hitler had placed such emphasis, was expressed in particular by the provision that Catholic associations were to be restricted to purely religious, cultural, and charitable activities; anything beyond that was de facto subject to official approval. Moreover, the Vatican agreed not only to ban priests from being members of political parties but also from acting in any way for them.[7]

The conclusion of the Concordat had been brought about under considerable pressure from the regime. A big gathering of the Catholic Kolping Associations,* scheduled for 8–11 June in Munich, had to be cancelled because of major Nazi disturbances.[8] From 25 June onwards, almost 2,000 deputies and councillors of the Bavarian People's Party (BVP), the Bavarian version of the Centre Party, were arrested, among them 200 priests.[9] Elsewhere in the Reich members of the Centre Party lost their jobs in the civil service or were arrested. On 23 June, Papen spoke out against the Centre Party's continued existence and, on 28 June, Goebbels publicly demanded the party's dissolution.[10] During the last phase of the negotiations,

---

* Translators' note: Catholic workers' ('journeymen's') associations named after their founder, the Catholic priest, Adolf Kolping (1813–65).

Figure 4. The Concordat of July 1933 seemed to have established a mutually satisfactory relationship between the regime and the Catholic Church. Hence at a Catholic youth rally at the Berlin Neukölln stadium on 20 August 1933 Church dignitaries, who included Erich Klausener, seen on the far left, of the Catholic Action organization, duly paid homage to the new state. Less than a year later Klausener was murdered by the regime.
Source: bpk / Harry Wagner

on 1 July, the political police of the federal states closed the offices of a number of Catholic organizations on the grounds that these 'confessional aides of the Centre Party' had 'taken part in activities hostile to the state'.[11]

On 4 July the BVP and on 5 July the Centre Party announced their voluntary dissolution, in other words just at the moment when the Concordat negotiations were entering their critical final phase. On 3 July, Papen had already informed Foreign Minister Neurath that, during the final meeting of the negotiators, in other words with Kaas present, it had become clear that 'it was accepted and approved that, with the conclusion of the Concordat, the Centre Party will dissolve itself'.[12] Thus, the renunciation of 'political Catholicism' can be seen as part of the overall arrangement between the Catholic Church and the Nazi state. It cleared the way for the guarantee of the existence of the Catholic Church and its network of (unpolitical) organizations and institutions. By promising to ban priests from taking any part in political parties, the Vatican had effectively abandoned the Centre Party. Kaas's involvement in the negotiations suggests that the regime had been seeking such an overall solution from the very beginning.[13] Given the political situation, it would have been impossible to sustain the Centre Party and the BVP, but what was decisive was that, as a result of the Concordat, the dissolution of the Catholic parties was part of an overall arrangement with the new regime. On the same day as the initialling took place, Hitler suspended the bans on the non-political Catholic organizations and the other anti-Catholic measures, in other words he made a show of removing the pressure.[14]

At the cabinet meeting of 14 July already referred to, Hitler described the Concordat as a great success, as it had created a 'sphere of trust', which, 'in view of the pressing struggle against international Jewry, would be particularly important'. The willingness of the Catholic Church to get the bishops to swear allegiance to the German state was an 'unqualified recognition of the present regime'. But, even more important was the fact that the Catholic Church was withdrawing from associational and party political life and closing down the Christian trades unions. The dissolution of the Centre Party would be finally confirmed only when the Vatican instructed its priests to withdraw from party politics.[15]

The solemn signing of the Concordat by Pacelli and Papen occurred in Rome on 20 July in the Vatican; it was ratified by the Reich government on 10 September 1933.

Rearmament and détente: flexibility towards the western powers

Despite the importance of the Concordat for the regime's international reputation, there was another issue at the heart of German foreign policy in 1933: securing German rearmament against pressure from the western powers.

In mid-December 1932, after a short break of three months, the German delegation had returned to the Disarmament Conference in Geneva along with delegates from sixty-four other countries. The other participants had in principle accepted Germany's demand for equal treatment, while simultaneously recognizing French security concerns. With the clear aim of torpedoing the conference, Foreign Minister Neurath and Defence Minister Blomberg bluntly rejected proposals for armaments controls put forward by the British and French delegations. They wished to put the blame for the failure on the western powers, thereby enabling Germany to escape from the Versailles armaments restrictions and launch a general programme of rearmament.[16] Hitler, on the other hand, saw the danger that, given her actual armaments position, if Germany absented herself from international attempts to control armaments, she would become hopelessly isolated and be exposed to the risk of a possible preventive war. For the time being, therefore, he advocated limited German rearmament within the framework of international security – initially without success, however.[17] Neurath circumvented Hitler's intention of giving way to British pressure and of sending a member of the cabinet to the next round of negotiations in Geneva,[18] and also the attempt in March by the head of the German delegation at Geneva, Rudolf Nadolny, to seek Hitler's backing for the continuation of the conference.

During the following weeks, Hitler became convinced that Neurath's attempt to put the blame for the failure of the conference on the French was too risky. But his own plan of initially moderate rearmament secured by international agreement could also not easily be realized. For, at the end of April, the German delegation at Geneva was to a large extent isolated, since its very assertive demands for immediate German equality were only too obviously designed to wreck the conference.[19] On 12 May, there was a further setback when an expert committee at the conference decided that the paramilitary units, in other words the SA, SS, and Stahlhelm, should be counted towards the size of Germany's army.[20] Hitler responded by going onto the offensive. He told the cabinet the same day that he had come to the conclusion 'that the sole purpose of the Disarmament Conference was either to destroy the German armed forces or to put the blame on Germany for its failure'. Thus, the time had come to make a government statement pointing out the 'dire consequences of a failure of the Disarmament Conference', in effect to threaten Germany's withdrawal from the League of Nations.[21]

He did this in a 'peace speech' to the Reichstag on 17 May. The 'employment of force of any kind in Europe' would inevitably 'increase the threat to the balance of power... [resulting in] new wars, new insecurity, more economic distress,' he told the deputies. He warned of 'a Europe sinking into communist chaos' that would 'produce a crisis of unforeseeable dimensions and incalculable length'. It was 'the most earnest wish of Germany's national government to prevent such strife through honest and active participation', and to achieve this they were willing to make concessions, namely to Poland and France. For they no longer believed, as was the case in the previous century, in the idea of 'Germanizing' people, of 'being able to turn Poles and Frenchmen into Germans'. The key point in his statement on the disarmament question was the German claim for equal treatment. Having fulfilled the disarmament terms of the Versailles Treaty, they had 'an entirely justified moral claim on the other powers to fulfil their commitments that derive from the Versailles Treaty', in other words they should themselves disarm. He rejected the demand that the SA should be included in Germany's army figures with the comment that it had only 'domestic political functions'. Germany 'would be totally prepared to abolish its entire military establishment and destroy the few remaining weapons left to it, provided its neighbours would do the same in an equally radical fashion'. However, so long as this was not the case, Germany must demand that 'a transformation of our present defensive arrangements (i.e. the Reichswehr P.L.), which we did not choose but were imposed upon us from abroad, must coincide step by step with the actual disarmament carried out by other countries'. Hitler then proposed a 'transitional period' of five years, during which Germany should be allowed 'to establish its own national security in the expectation that, after this period, it will then actually have achieved equality with the other states'. This meant that he was departing from the demand for *immediate* equality that the German delegation in Geneva had been putting forward hitherto. Germany was even 'prepared to dispense with offensive weapons altogether, provided that, within a certain time frame, the nations who had rearmed were prepared to destroy their offensive weapons, and that their further use was banned by an international convention' – always provided that there was agreement on the principle of equality of treatment for Germany. Any other attempt to 'rape Germany by simply using a coercive majority, contrary to the clear meaning of the treaties', could 'only be intended to remove us from the conference'. Germany would then, albeit with a heavy heart, draw the only possible conclusions: 'as a nation that is being constantly defamed, we would find it difficult to continue to belong to the League of Nations'.[22]

After his speech, Hitler ordered Neurath to instruct the Geneva delegation that the British draft, the so-called 'MacDonald Plan', according to which, after a transitional period of five years, the military strength of Germany, France, Italy, and Poland would all be the same, could be regarded as a 'possible basis for the proposed convention';[23] and, on 8 June, the conference did indeed agree to accept the British plan as the basis for the convention.[24]

In clearly indicating his readiness for an understanding with France, Hitler was at odds with his Foreign Minister, Neurath, who, as he had told the cabinet on 2 April, considered that an understanding with France was impossible, and indeed not even desirable.[25] Contrary to this view, Hitler had told the French ambassador, André François-Poncet, at their first meeting only a day later, that he had 'no aims' in the West, whereas 'the alteration of the impossible eastern border' was and would remain 'a major issue for German foreign policy'.[26] This attempt to win the confidence of the ambassador by revealing his aims in the East was also a significant departure from the Foreign Ministry's policy that the revision of the eastern border should not be raised with the French until it was the right moment to do so.[27] Significantly, there was no representative of the Foreign Ministry at Hitler's meeting with the ambassador. During the following weeks, Hitler put out a number of feelers for an understanding. In a speech at the Niederwald Memorial on 27 August he made a similar comment about the renunciation of French territory,[28] and, on 15 September, he informed François-Poncet that 'for us the Alsace-Lorraine question simply doesn't exist'.[29] His offers to France revealed a remarkable flexibility in his foreign policy; before 1933 he had always regarded Germany's western neighbour as 'the hereditary enemy', whom he hoped sooner or later to marginalize by provoking a conflict between it and Italy.

In fact, since the spring, the French Prime Minister, Edouard Daladier, had been wondering how he could establish direct contact with Hitler, and had put out feelers to Germany.[30] Early in September, Ribbentrop arranged for a French journalist, Fernand de Brinon, to visit Berlin; he was considered to be Daladier's foreign policy advisor and had many German contacts. In Berlin he had a number of conversations with high-ranking German officials, finally meeting Hitler in Berchtesgaden on 9 September. During the conversation, at which Ribbentrop and Blomberg were also present, the idea of a meeting with Daladier was discussed at which a public statement would be made about a German–French rapprochement.[31] These contacts were continued during the following weeks.[32]

During the spring and early summer of 1933, Hitler also tried to overcome Germany's isolation with regard to the Versailles Treaty through an approach to Italy via Mussolini. In March 1933, the Duce had put forward the idea of a four-power pact: Germany, France, Great Britain, and Italy should take on the leadership role in Europe, solving the current problems through negotiation with each other. However, in the course of talks lasting several months, Mussolini's original intentions were completely watered down above all by the French government. His idea that, in the event of a failure of the Geneva negotiations, the four powers should take responsibility for sorting out the revision of the peace treaties and the granting of permission for staged German rearmament was removed from the treaty, so that it became merely a politically toothless agreement of the four parties to consult one another. It was signed on 15 July but never ratified.[33]

Neurath considered the treaty 'completely worthless', indeed actually damaging, as it contained particular formulations that could potentially burden future German policy with undesirable commitments.[34] But Hitler wanted to sign it and eventually got his way. For him the prestige that Germany gained by being received into the exclusive group of leading European powers was the decisive factor, even if, in practice, there was little chance of achieving anything within this arrangement. Above all, he hoped that by supporting Mussolini's project he was taking the first step towards achieving an alliance with Italy.[35]

Ideology and activism: the Austrian question and the Soviet problem

According to the fundamental ideas on foreign policy that he outlined in March, Neurath had also wanted to postpone the issue of Anschluss with Austria, a stance that threatened to neutralize the activism of the NSDAP, organized as it was on the basis of a 'Greater Germany'.[36]

The Austrian Federal Chancellor, Engelbert Dollfuss, had utilized a parliamentary crisis in March 1933 to override the legislature completely, and since then had been effectively ruling as a dictator, supported by his Christian Social Party and the paramilitary Heimwehr [Home Guard]. When the Austrian Nazis demanded new parliamentary elections, he cancelled the impending local government elections and emasculated the Constitutional Court. On 19 June, Dollfuss issued a ban on the Austrian NSDAP. The Austrian Nazis' response to these measures became increasingly violent: street attacks, assassination attempts, explosions, attacks on political opponents and Jews became commonplace. From mid-March onwards, these disturbances were accompanied by a major propaganda campaign waged by the German government, and broadcast to Austria via radio, and by pamphlets dropped from aeroplanes.[37] In addition, an 'Austrian Legion', formed in Bavaria and made up of Nazi refugees, caused numerous frontier provocations.

Both the Nazi leadership in the Reich and the Austrian Nazis believed that the 'coordination' measures carried out in the Reich that spring could be simply extended to Austria. Hitler wanted to bring down the Dollfuss government through a combination of pressure from within and without, and replace it with a government influenced by, and later dominated by, Nazis. He thought that a second 'seizure of power' would enable the Austrian question to be solved through coordination, thereby obviating the need to raise the political and constitutional questions involved in an Anschluss, which was in any case impossible at that time because of Italian opposition. In April, he was already intervening in Austro–German relations in order to weaken Dollfuss's position. Thus, he decided to break off negotiations over the Austro–German customs treaty, which were in their final stage, because he was unwilling to reach an agreement with Dollfuss.[38]

He told the cabinet on 26 May that they must not fall into the 'pre-war trap' of making an alliance with the 'official rulers' of Austria; the fateful role played by the Habsburgs in suppressing the German Austrians was now being taken on by 'Viennese half-Jews' and 'Legitimists' (i.e. the supporters of the Austrian monarchy). He had remained faithful to the hostility towards the Austrian state he had developed during his stay in Vienna. At the same meeting Hitler announced the introduction of a visa for trips to Austria, costing 1,000 RM, which was introduced a few days later. Hitler thought this significant blow to Austrian tourism would lead to the collapse of the Dollfuss government.[39]

Dollfuss turned for help above all to Fascist Italy and to France and Britain. At the beginning of August, under strong international pressure, Hitler ordered the Austrian Nazis to cease their activities.[40] This showed that Hitler's attempt to crush Austria through economic pressure and organized disturbances had failed. The NSDAP in Austria had to pull back; the disputes had alienated the western powers (which Hitler had wanted to avoid) as well as damaging the relationship with Italy, in other words the country with which Hitler had hoped to develop a close alliance.

Relations with the Soviet Union were also determined more by the Party's ideology and its activism than by diplomacy. Following the creation of the new government, Foreign Minister Neurath had initially attempted to stabilize the relationship with the Soviet Union. In February he won over Hitler, who, in his government statement à propos the Enabling Law, committed the government to a 'positive policy towards the Soviet Union'; the large-scale persecution of the communists was, he said, a purely domestic matter.[41] Thus, the secret military collaboration, begun during the Weimar Republic, continued; in February 1933 a credit agreement was reached; and, at the beginning of May, the extension of the 1926 German–Soviet treaty of neutrality (the Berlin Treaty) was ratified with Hitler's express approval.[42] Only a few days earlier, receiving the Soviet ambassador, Hitler had stressed that nothing should be allowed to alter the 'friendly relations' between the two countries.[43] Strains continued, however, not so much as a result of the suppression of the Communist Party, but more because of Nazi violence against Soviet citizens and institutions in Germany.[44]

This openly anti-Soviet atmosphere continued throughout the summer and neither the Party leadership nor the government did anything to prevent it. On the contrary, Hitler gradually responded to the activists' ideologically motivated hostility. When the Reichstag Fire trial opened in September, Hitler personally ordered that the Soviet press should be barred.[45] The Soviets responded to the affront by imposing a temporary freeze on official press relations between the two states. During the summer, military relations ceased altogether and trade went into a sharp decline.[46] When, during the cabinet meeting of 26 September, state secretary Wilhelm von Bülow suggested taking initial steps to improve relations with the Soviet Union, Hitler strongly objected, making it clear that 'restoration of the German-Russian relationship' was 'impossible'; future relations between the two countries would be marked by a 'fierce antagonism'. They must have no illusions about the fact 'that the Russians have always deceived us and would one day leave us in the lurch'.[47]

Thus, within a few months of taking over the Chancellorship, Hitler had intervened in the foreign policy of the Reich with far-reaching consequences. He had substantially determined the final form of the Concordat, not least through exercising significant pressure on the Catholic Church in Germany, thereby achieving an important foreign policy success and boosting his prestige. He had tried to put an end to the Dollfuss regime through a combination of pressure from outside and within, causing considerable damage to German foreign policy in the process. He had produced a dramatic alteration in relations with the Soviet Union. In contrast to the

Foreign Ministry, he had sought exchanges with French contacts, signalling his willingness to abandon the idea of a revision of the western border. Up until September 1933, he was not actually working to torpedo the Geneva Conference, but kept this option open by threatening in his 'peace speech' of 17 May to break off negotiations and leave the League of Nations.

In this way Hitler indicated that he intended to abandon the Foreign Ministry's cautious, tentative, and long-term revisionist policy. Complete freedom from armament restrictions as the prerequisite for power politics, anti-communism, and the idea of a greater German Reich (which required the alliance with Italy) were the goals that determined his first foreign policy moves rather than rigidly sticking to the idea of restoring the frontiers of 1914. The Concordat and the attempted rapprochement with France, in particular, clearly show that, from the start, Hitler demonstrated a remarkable tactical flexibility, which the Foreign Ministry, with its commitment to continuity, failed to understand. As the months went by, he became more and more confident in striking out on his own, when it came to differences of opinion with the Foreign Ministry until, by the summer of 1933, he had seized the initiative in foreign policy. In this way, he managed to stymie the Reich President's original intention of retaining control of foreign policy with the help of 'his' foreign minister.

14

'Führer' and 'People'

In mid-July Hitler had reduced the tempo of the Nazi conquest of power and introduced a kind of summer break in domestic policy. But, from the beginning of September, he once again became actively and visibly engaged in politics. However, during the following months, coordination measures reinforced by violence were replaced by propaganda campaigns and major events, underlining his central role as 'Führer'. The image of a nation united behind Hitler was designed not least to underpin his next foreign policy moves: in October the Geneva disarmament negotiations were restarted.

On 1 September, the NSDAP held a Party Rally for the first time since 1929. Whereas in the 1920s controversial issues were at least debated, now it was all about demonstrating the strength of the Nazi movement and the complete unanimity between members and 'Führer'. To this end Hitler spent five days as the focus of parades, marches, and displays of adulation attended by tens of thousands of his devoted followers. His various appearances created a standard set of ceremonies that was hardly altered during the five Party Rallies that followed until 1938. It began with his speech at the reception in Nuremberg town hall on the evening before the Rally, followed by his proclamation opening the event, which was always read by Gauleiter Adolf Wagner. At the Party's cultural session he projected himself as a connoisseur of art and an expert in cultural policy, and to the various Party sections (political leaders, women's organization, Hitler Youth, SA, SS, and Labour Service) as the supreme leader of every Party unit. The introduction in 1933 of the dedication of flags ceremony at the SA and SS parade was a particular high point. This involved his touching the new SA and SS flags and standards with the 'blood flag', which had been carried at the march to the Feldherrnhalle in November 1923. From 1934 onwards, these Party parades were supplemented by military demonstrations by the Wehrmacht, giving Hitler the opportunity to pose as commander-in-chief.

In his speech to the diplomatic corps he presented himself as a statesman, while his speech at the final congress brought the Rally to a conclusion. The Party Rally provided the opportunity to display the variety of roles Hitler attached to the office of 'Führer'.

On 13 September, only a week after the end of the Party Rally, Hitler presented himself in the role of the caring 'Führer', who was close to his people. At the opening of the Winterhilfswerk [Winter Aid Programme, WHW] he celebrated the new institution as an expression of 'solidarity, which [is] eternally in our blood' and as embodying a 'national community', which represented 'something really vital'.[1] The Winter Aid Programme was designed to supplement the state welfare system through a whole series of measures that the individual citizen could hardly escape (street collections, lotteries, donations from wages, and various services). In the winter of 1933, more than 358 million RM was collected. From now onwards, the regime portrayed the annual increases in the sums collected for the WHW as important evidence of the growing support for the regime. In fact, these figures merely indicated the regime's growing skill at extracting larger and larger contributions through various forms of pressure.[2] The Winter Aid Programme was carried out by the Nationalsozialistische Volkswohlfahrt [NS-Welfare Organization, NSV], which had been founded in Gau Berlin in 1931 mainly to provide welfare services for Party members. After 1933, the NSV radically changed its role. Following an order from Hitler dated 3 May 1933, it developed into the main Party organization responsible 'for all matters concerning the people's welfare'. Under its new leader, Erich Hilgenfeldt, it spread throughout the Reich, becoming the second largest mass organization after the German Labour Front (DAF).[3] It acquired a complex structure modelled on the Party organization, reaching down to local branch level with separate sections for welfare, youth care, health, propaganda, and indoctrination. By the end of 1933, it had acquired a membership of 112,000, which increased to more than 3.7 million by the end of 1934.[4]

The main aim of the NSV was the 'improvement of the people's welfare'. The focus was not on supporting individuals through welfare and charitable activities, but entirely on strengthening the 'national community', in other words essentially on supporting 'hereditarily healthy' and socially efficient families. To this end, the NSV provided a primarily ideologically determined framework for care and support, in addition to the state welfare benefits; it did not regard caring for 'inferiors' and 'the weak' as part of its responsibilities. Far from being an organization designed to support the needy, the NSV was a political and ideologically charged mass movement concerned with fundamentally improving the fitness of the 'national body'.[5] Following its official recognition in summer 1933 as the leading organization within the charitable welfare sector, the NSV gradually took control of all the other organizations operating in the welfare field; it increasingly claimed the state subsidies, on which the whole charitable welfare system depended, for itself. This affected above all the extensive Church welfare organizations, which continued to exist until 1945. The other charitable welfare associations were dissolved, coordinated or lost their privileged status.[6]

The Party Rally and the establishment of the Winter Aid Programme marked the start of a whole series of major events and propaganda initiatives that aimed to produce a good 'mood' in the German population and to cement the relationship between 'Führer' and 'people'. Thus, on 23 September, Hitler broke the ground to initiate the construction of the first phase of the Frankfurt–Heidelberg autobahn, celebrated by Nazi propaganda as a great national achievement.[7] The building of the autobahns, the biggest Nazi construction project, provided its most senior master builder with the opportunity to demonstrate the effectiveness of his regime and his determination to create employment through regular ground breaking ceremonies, section openings, and the like. At the same time, the particular aesthetic of the 'Führer's roads', with their stone-clad bridges, functional buildings adapted to regional styles, and the sweeping panorama of stretches of road hugging the landscape, enabled the construction of this road system to be portrayed as a major cultural achievement.[8]

At the end of September came the new 'Harvest Festival Day'. Hitler opened the celebrations with a reception in the Reich Chancellery for peasant delegations from all over the Reich, who were served a stew for lunch. This was Hitler's personal contribution towards launching a broader propaganda campaign. In future, all citizens were expected to dispense with the normal Sunday roast in favour of a stew, giving the money saved to the Winter Aid Programme. Party members ensured that this was carried out by stationing themselves on Sundays in the vestibules of blocks of flats sniffing for the smell of roast meat and, if necessary, demanding that 'one pot Sunday' should be observed. The Party was literally spying on people's cooking pots. As far as Hitler was concerned, having to eat a stew on Sundays did not represent a sacrifice; it was what he normally ate. After the reception, Hitler, together with members of his government, went to the Bückeberg near Hamelin, where the main celebrations of the Harvest Festival took place. Half a million people had assembled on a festival ground on the side of a hill.[9] Hitler then confidently announced in his speech that the event was 'the greatest demonstration...of this kind that has ever been held on earth'.[10]

A few weeks later, on 26 November, and this time without Hitler's personal involvement, the DAF's new leisure organization was launched in Berlin, and given the title Kraft durch Freude [Strength through Joy, KdF]; Ley, Goebbels, and Hess gave the ceremonial addresses.[11] The KdF took over not only the organization of leisure activities and holidays (including the planning of a huge seaside resort on the island of Rügen and the construction of its own fleet of cruise ships), but also got involved in welfare at work. For example, it demanded improvements in work facilities and organized 'factory performance competitions' to raise standards. Like the Party, its organization was Reich-wide and went down to local branch level.[12]

Thus, the Nazis attempted to provide a form of compensation for the wage freeze and the reduction in workers' rights and privileges (or their freezing at the low crisis levels).[13] From 1 May to the 'Harvest Festival', 'working people' were the focus of large-scale celebrations and propaganda campaigns, and the ambition to create a 'national community' was expressed through the establishment of uniformly structured, mass organizations led by Nazis. All these organizations – the Hitler Youth with the League of German Girls, the National Socialist Welfare Organization, the German Labour Front, and KdF, but also other organizations such as the NS Frauenschaft [NS Women's Organization] or the NS Kraftfahrkorps [NS Motor Corps], which unified the various automobile associations – provided the Party with a variety of ways of ensuring a varied and intensive 'supervision'★ of the 'national comrades', offering a wide range of activities and providing armies of full-time functionaries and volunteer helpers with new tasks. During the first year of the regime these big Nazi organizations were to a large extent taking over the functions of the great variety of clubs and associations that had existed in the Weimar Republic, but had been divided by social, political, and confessional differences. Now, people were offered the opportunity to pursue their professional/

★ Translators' note: Betreuung was the word often used by the Nazis to describe their relationship with the German people. It means 'being responsible for', but in Nazi terminology had a more than usually authoritarian flavour, hence 'supervision'.

specialist interests, leisure activities, hobbies, and other interests within uniform official organizations.

These Nazi organizations owed their rapid expansion in part to the fact that, faced with a huge increase in membership after the seizure of power, the NSDAP imposed a ban on new members on 1 May; by then, membership had grown from over 800,000 at the beginning of 1933 to around 2.5 million.[14] Now those who wanted to secure their own future by demonstrating their loyalty to the new state could do so only in one of these mass organizations. The sheer variety of what was on offer indicates that the Nazis were aiming to achieve a total organization of German society. Every sphere of life was to be covered by at least one organization; people were to be integrated into a hierarchical command structure, which, following the example of the Party, went from the local level up to a Reich leadership. This total penetration and structuring of society was the logical counterpart to the Führer principle.

At the same time, Hitler's regime, and indeed the 'Führer' himself, had taken decisive steps towards the final and complete coordination of the whole of cultural life and the media. This was a process that, in contrast to the conquest of power phase during the first six months, took place, at least overtly, with relatively little fuss. After Hitler had initially concentrated on supporting his propaganda minister, Goebbels, in turning the regional broadcasting authorities into 'Reich radio stations', in the second half of 1933 he moved to extend and complete control over the press. To begin with, the regime had used newspaper bans and the intimidation of critical journalists, but now it established a proper system of press control. On 1 July 1933, the Propaganda Ministry took over the Berlin Press Conference, hitherto an institution organized by the journalists themselves, using it in future to issue the press with binding instructions. These 'oral press directives' were then confirmed by written instructions to the whole of the press; the news agencies were also coordinated. In addition, in August Goebbels persuaded Hitler to agree to an Editors' Law. Issued at the beginning of October, it secured the 'transformation of the press into a public institution and its legal and intellectual integration into the state'. The profession of 'editor' was now a 'public office'. Hitler could also give direct instructions to the press through the 'Reich government's press chief', the former economic journalist, Walther Funk, whom he had imposed on Goebbels as state secretary and who was directly subordinate to the Führer.[15]

In summer 1933, after extensive discussions with Goebbels,[16] Hitler also approved the latter's idea of creating, in addition to the Propaganda Ministry with its variety of control mechanisms, an additional supervisory agency. This was the Reich Chamber of Culture, established in September 1933 and ceremonially opened in Hitler's presence in November.[17] The establishment of the Chamber of Culture, another mammoth organization taken over by Goebbels, was designed to bring together the members of the professions supervised by the Propaganda Ministry in separate 'chambers' for film, literature, press, radio, theatre, music, and fine art. Membership of a chamber was a prerequisite for exercising a profession and the chambers were authorized to regulate the economic relations in their particular sphere.[18] However, Hitler also left significant cultural responsibilities in the hands of the Prussian Prime Minister, Göring, Reichsleiter Rosenberg, and the Reich Education Minister, Bernhard Rust. Thus Nazi coordination did not exclude the possibility of several potentates intervening in cultural life. Indeed, Hitler frequently used the competition among these politicians involved in the cultural field to exercise influence and assert his authority. In addition, his 'cultural speeches' at the Party Rallies served to assert his claim to preeminence in cultural affairs. In 1933 he used this opportunity to claim that all cultural activity was 'racially determined', announce 'a new Aryan cultural renaissance', and mount an abusive attack on the whole of modern art.[19] On 15 October, he presented himself in Munich as Germany's leading artistic Maecenas, celebrating German Art Day and laying the foundation stone for the House of German Art. This was designed by his favourite architect, Paul Ludwig Troost, who had supervised the alterations to the Brown House and whose furniture designs he admired. It was to replace the Glass Palace, which had burnt down in 1931, as the exhibition hall for German contemporary art.[20] This new building, whose location Hitler determined was to be on the southern edge of the Englischer Garten, represented in several respects a programme in itself. Architecturally, with its massive Neoclassicism, it set the standards for future architecture in the Third Reich. Above all, however, it was intended to be the visual expression of Hitler's aim of making Munich 'for all time the centre of a new form of artistic creation and artistic life'.[21]

During these months, Hitler was heavily preoccupied with buildings and plans for new buildings intended to demonstrate Nazism's claim to power, its efficiency and dynamism; he used sketches and ideas he had been developing since the 1920s.[22] In addition to the autobahns, this involved the

construction of show-piece buildings in Munich, Berlin, and Nuremberg.
When Hitler laid the foundation stone for the House of German Art, planning was already far advanced for turning the neo-classical Königsplatz into
a major Nazi forum, composed of a new 'Führer building', an equally massive administrative building, and two 'Ceremonial Temples' on the eastern
side of the square to honour the dead of the Munich putsch of 1923. The
simultaneous transformation of the Königsplatz itself increased the monumental effect of the new Führer building, for it was covered with large
granite flagstones to within a few metres of the new buildings, so that it
could be used it as a parade ground. The integration of the new building
complex on the 'old' Königsplatz into the surrounding area underlined the
new political system's claim to power, while at the same time symbolizing a
link between the new regime and 'classical' Munich, the artistic city of the
nineteenth century. Munich, as the 'Capital of the Movement' (as the city
was officially known from 1935 onwards), was, in Hitler's view, necessary as
a counterweight to the state's power centre in the Reich capital.

Hitler had already criticized Berlin's public buildings as extraordinarily
inadequate in *Mein Kampf*.[23] On 19 September 1933, during a meeting with
representatives of the Reich railways and the city of Berlin to discuss a north–
south railway line through the city, Hitler told them that Berlin was basically
an 'arbitrary agglomeration' of buildings, just a 'series of shops and blocks of
flats'; the city must be 'architecturally and culturally improved to such an
extent that it can compete with all the world's capitals'.[24] After he had repeatedly indicated to the city fathers his great interest in practical aspects of the
city's development,[25] on 29 March 1934 a plan that he had initiated for a
north–south axis through Berlin was discussed at a meeting in the Reich
Chancellery with representatives of the city and the Reich railways. Hitler had
very precise proposals for how the axis should be built and made many decisions concerning future monumental buildings.[26] The meetings were continued on 5 July 1934, with Hitler once more leading the discussion.[27]

The granting in 1931 of the 1936 Olympic Games to Berlin proved a stroke
of luck for Hitler's craze for building. He took personal charge of the project
and, right from the start, ensured that the whole Games took on a much more
representative character than originally envisaged by the last Weimar governments. Immediately after viewing the building site on 5 October 1933, and at
two further meetings on 10 October and 14 December in the Reich
Chancellery, he decided not to stick to the original plan to transform the
already existing 'German Stadium' and instead to replace it with a much larger

new building by the architect Werner March. Moreover, in front of the stadium he also wanted a large parade ground big enough for half a million people. The later so-called Maifeld, together with other buildings, was integrated into a sports complex that was given the name 'Reich Sports Field'. Hitler also intervened in the planning process for the first major post-January 1933 construction in Berlin, the extension to the Reichsbank begun in 1934 (in which the German Foreign Ministry has been housed since 1999), backing Heinrich Wolff's design, which was then implemented.[28]

Nuremberg was the third city in which, early on, Hitler wished the Nazis' claim to power to be immortalized through architecture. At a meeting in Bayreuth on 22 July 1933 he promised representatives of the city that the Reich Party Rallies would always be held in Nuremberg and agreed with them a 'radical alteration to the Luitpoldhain' on the basis of a sketch that he provided.[29] Hitler's continuing involvement in the planning can be documented for the following months; he produced ideas, expressed wishes, approved plans.[30] The increasingly gigantomaniacal plans for a parade ground that could contain hundreds of thousands of people were realized from 1935 onwards.

It is remarkable how single-mindedly Hitler set about consolidating his position as 'Führer' given that, in the summer of 1933, he had only just concluded a series of campaigns against his opponents and political rivals. This was the point of his constant presentation of himself, as already described; he secured even more tight control over this by closing any remaining gaps in his command of the media. While Hitler presented himself as the benevolent supporter of culture and its authoritative mentor, and also as the greatest and most liberal promoter of buildings, to workers and peasants he was the 'people's chancellor', showing the way towards the creation of the much invoked 'national community'. This underpinning and furnishing of his position as 'Führer' through propaganda, culture, and (with the help of newly-created large-scale organizations such as the DAF and the NSV) social policy should be borne in mind when we come to consider Hitler's further 'successes' in foreign and domestic policy.

A 'Führer' without a private life

The comprehensive creation of a Führer aura resulted in Hitler's inner distance from his immediate entourage increasing still further. Personal friendships and close human ties were, as far as he was concerned, incompatible with his position as 'Führer'. In any case, being emotionally distant from people was part of his character. According to Albert Speer, in retrospect, he had become a cold, friendless dictator.[31]

In getting to know Eva Braun in 1932, an employee in Hoffmann's photographic studio, he had once again found a much younger woman who was soon being regarded as his girlfriend.[32] During his first years as Chancellor, however, his relationship with her was limited to occasional meetings; she visited him in his Munich flat or on the Obersalzberg. Hitler defended her when her presence on the speakers' podium at the 1934 Party Rally led to gossip. He banned his half-sister, Angela Raubal, whom he blamed for the gossip among the women of his entourage, from the Berghof, where she had hitherto presided. Eva Braun now increasingly took on the role of his lady companion at his Berchtesgaden residence; after its renovation in 1936 she moved into a small flat with direct access to his private quarters. Apart from that, Hitler was careful to keep her away from Berlin and avoided attending official occasions with her; at most, she was permitted to take part as a member of his wider entourage.

Given the lack of evidence, one can only speculate about the relationship between the dictator and this woman. From what we know, Eva Braun, who was twenty-three years younger than him, was not an advisor, muse, or inspiration, nor did he give any indication of needing to develop a private life with her away from politics. There were differing opinions among his close circle as to whether or not it was an intimate relationship. The previous history of his relationships with young girls and women would suggest not. The gossip about the 'Führer' having a secret lover at least spared him from speculation among his immediate circle about any personal reasons for his not having a woman in his official life. This appears to have been Eva Braun's function.

This was particularly the case, given that Joseph and Magda Goebbels continued to provide Hitler with a kind of substitute family. He often appeared in the evening – he liked to surprise them – in their official Berlin flat or at the weekend at his propaganda minister's summer residence on Schwanenwerder, an island in the Wannsee; here the Goebbelses had a guest house built for Hitler in the hope that he would treat it as home. During these visits, Hitler appeared relaxed, happy to chat, and played with the children. Goebbels was not only a permanent guest at Hitler's lunch table, but also regularly attended Hitler's evening film shows in his private cinema in the Reich Chancellery. The family often spent their holidays on the Obersalzberg, with Hitler's 'invitations' sometimes being more like commands. Magda also frequently travelled to Berchtesgaden on her own or saw Hitler in Berlin. When, for example, she gave birth to her second child, Hilde, in April 1934, and her husband visited her two days later, he noted laconically in his diary: 'Clinic: Führer just arrived.'[33] Although Goebbels may sometimes have found Hitler's presence in his family life a burden, in his view this was outweighed by its advantages: Hitler provided him with special bonuses and preferential treatment from the Party's publishing house, the Eher Verlag. All this enabled the Goebbels family to enjoy an exclusive life style. Above all, however, he hoped that the privileged relationship he and his wife had with the 'Führer' would increase his prestige and political influence. Hitler encouraged this notion in his numerous conversations with Goebbels, in which he conveyed the impression that he was putting his trust in him, without in fact allowing Goebbels to influence his key policy areas.[34]

Hitler had a relatively close relationship with Albert Speer, who also established a base on the Obersalzberg and, with his wife Margarete, soon became a member of the so-called Berghof society.[35] Speer was sixteen years younger than Hitler and, after Troost's death, became his favourite architect; they shared a common interest in architecture, town planning, and architectural history. Hitler made a habit of summoning Speer, dropping in on him in his studios in Berchtesgaden or Berlin, viewing his latest plans and discussing building projects with him. It seems that in his many meetings with Speer he had someone with whom he was on the same wavelength to an unusual degree. Being together with Speer diverted, relaxed, and energized him. Hitler evidently saw in Speer his alter ego, someone who was able to have the career as an eminent architect that had been closed to him, someone with whom he could share the architectural fantasies which had preoccupied him since his youth. There are many similarities with his relationship with his adolescent friend Kubizek; but while Kubizek had simply patiently listened to him, Speer could realize Hitler's megalomaniacal fantasies, or at least present him with plans and models based on his sketches. Thus, for Hitler Speer was his most important link to what he considered his true calling as artist and architect. While Hitler praised Speer as a 'brilliant architect'[36] and told his entourage that he was a 'soulmate',[37] in retrospect Speer hesitated to call this relationship a friendship. He had rarely met anybody in his life 'who so seldom revealed his feelings and, when he did so, immediately suppressed them'.[38] Speer never clearly described his own feelings. He mainly saw in Hitler 'my catalyst', who infused him with exceptional energy and enabled him to have a dazzling career, or, in Speer's own words 'an enhanced identity'.[39]

The Brandts were also welcome guests on the Obersalzberg, moving into a flat close to the Berghof. Anni Brandt, née Rehborn, a German swimming champion, was a famous sportswoman and had known Hitler before the take-over of power. In 1933 she was a guest on the Obersalzberg with her fiancé, a young doctor, Karl Brandt, and in March 1934 Hitler attended their wedding. Shortly afterwards, he appointed Brandt his 'personal physician', whose task was to provide him with emergency medical assistance in the event of accidents or assassination attempts during his numerous trips. In addition, he gave advice on medical matters. During the war, this position of special trust led to Brandt receiving special assignments with serious consequences.[40]

Among the other members of the Obersalzberg circle were Reich Youth Leader Baldur von Schirach and his wife Henriette, like the Speers and the Brandts members of the younger generation, as well as Henriette's father the 'Reich Photo Journalist', Heinrich Hoffmann with his second wife. Hoffmann was regarded as the entertainer and joker of the group; he was a heavy drinker, although Hitler, who was teetotal, overlooked this. Hitler valued Hoffmann above all as a connoisseur of art, whose taste coincided with his own and whose advice he valued. As Eva Braun's former employer, Hoffmann also discreetly arranged the renting of a flat, later the purchase of a house, in Munich for her.[41] In 1935, Unity Mitford, a young Englishwoman living in Munich, joined the circle. Mitford, a fanatical Nazi, whose sister, Diana, married the British Fascist leader, Oswald Mosley, in 1936, remained a member of Hitler's intimate circle until 1939.[42] In despair when Britain declared war on Germany, she attempted suicide, which she survived albeit severely wounded. In the end her family brought her home.

Unlike in Berlin, where the distinction between the two was more clear-cut, in Hitler's refuge on the Obersalzberg private guests mixed with his personal entourage. The most important of the latter was Martin Bormann, who, apart from his role as chief of staff in the office of the 'Führer's' Deputy, increasingly dealt with Hitler's personal affairs. Thus, on the Obersalzberg, where he had his own house built, he operated as a kind of major domo and head of construction. In addition, there were Hitler's personal adjutants, Wilhelm Brückner and Julius Schaub (in later years also the various military adjutants), and his secretaries.

The situation at the Berghof clearly demonstrates that, even after 1933, Hitler showed no inclination to create a private sphere separate from his official position. On the contrary, the people around him were linked to him in such a way that it is impossible to discern any kind of privacy. Hitler's perception of himself as above all a public figure left no room for that. A private Hitler outside his public role simply did not exist.

15

Breaking out of the International System

The series of major events and propaganda campaigns that had begun with the Reich Party Rally in September was intended, amongst other things, to impress international public opinion. A divided nation, despairing and impoverished, appeared overnight to have been united by a charismatic 'Führer' and to be determined to restore its national honour. That was the picture propaganda was trying to get across, by displaying Hitler in all his various roles.

In autumn 1933, it was the role of statesman that was most in demand, for in October in Geneva the Disarmament Conference, adjourned in June, began a new round of talks. In foreign policy terms this was a critical moment. Foreign Minister Neurath was still trying to cause the conference to fail. On 13 September, he told a cabinet meeting that after a 'total collapse of the Disarmament Conference and after the final settlement of the Saar question' it would also be time to leave the League of Nations.[1] However, to begin with, they wanted to demonstrate their peaceful intentions; thus, at Neurath's suggestion, Hitler sent Goebbels to Geneva so that, at the opening session of the League of Nations on 22 September, he could play the part of a sensible politician for a change.[2] The appearance of the internationally notorious Nazi fanatic was not in fact particularly successful. On 24 September, Neurath reported to the Foreign Ministry from Geneva that at the forthcoming Disarmament Conference there would be opposition from both the French and the British to the acquisition by the Reichswehr of the 'defensive weapons' that had hitherto been banned 'and that negotiations would presumably break down over this point'.[3]

However, Hitler, who had already threatened to leave the Conference and the League of Nations in his May speech, was still trying to save the

Disarmament Conference. When, on his return from Geneva, Neurath reported to Hitler, the latter stated that, instead of 'delaying or breaking off negotiations', it was definitely desirable 'to secure a disarmament agreement, even if it does not contain all that we want'.[4]

A few days later he had changed his mind. On 4 October, he and Defence Minister Blomberg concurred that Germany should withdraw from the Disarmament Conference and leave the League of Nations. Bernhard von Bülow, the state secretary in the Foreign Ministry, was only brought into the discussions at a later stage and then merely informed of the decision; Foreign Minister Neurath was evidently not consulted at all. The decision was prompted by news of a new British initiative, the so-called Simon Plan, according to which Germany should be granted equality of treatment in armaments only after a probationary period lasting several years. Hitler feared that the Conference might impose this compromise solution on Germany, which would have the effect of postponing German rearmament for years. The only way of 'preventing such a development' would be for Germany to leave the Conference and the League of Nations and to insist that she would negotiate about disarmament only on the basis of equality of treatment for all European nations.[5] On 13 October, Hitler informed the cabinet about the new policy: Germany would withdraw from all international bodies that denied her equality, and that applied specifically to the League of Nations. He said he would announce this decision along with a declaration of peace, and have it confirmed by a plebiscite in the form of new Reichstag elections.[6] The following day, the ministers accepted the plans.[7]

The idea of having his policies confirmed by such a 'plebiscite' was not new. Hitler had already discussed it with Goebbels in July after the issuing of the new Plebiscite Law. As yet there had been no reason for such a plebiscite,[8] but now one was provided on 14 October, when the British Foreign Secretary, Sir John Simon, put forward his new disarmament proposals. Foreign Minister Neurath informed the President of the Disarmament Conference that the German Reich would take no further part in the negotiations, since it was evident that they were not planning general disarmament but merely a continuation of discrimination against German armaments.[9] On the same day, Hitler made a government statement concerning both this decision and Germany's departure from the League of Nations; he also announced in a radio broadcast that the German people would be given the opportunity in the form of new elections to the Reichstag and a plebiscite not only to approve his government's policy, but to 'solemnly commit themselves to it'.[10] He gave detailed reasons for these decisions in a further broadcast on the evening of 14 October. The speech contained an olive branch to France: After the Saar territory had returned to the Reich, as far as Germany was concerned, there would be 'no more territorial differences' between the two countries and 'only a madman' could still 'believe in the possibility of war between the two states'.[11] At a cabinet meeting on 17 October, Hitler noted that the 'critical moment has probably passed'.[12]

For Germany, leaving the League of Nations represented a radical change of direction in foreign policy and began a turbulent period in relations between the European states. The idea of maintaining long-term peace in Europe through a system of collective security, was therefore fatally weakened. A new phase was beginning, with Germany embarking on independent initiatives and surprise coups. International stability became precarious: in future 'security' was to be maintained through bilateral relationships, rearmament, and military deterrence. Massive German rearmament killed off the idea of general European disarmament and an armaments race began in which Germany was able to get on equal terms with the other states and in part overtake them. Yet, almost inevitably, this would trigger an international competition in armaments and so in a few years' time Germany would lose its advantage. Thus, the time frame for a successful German policy of aggression was limited.

However, Hitler's decision to risk a breach with the League of Nations and Germany's departure from the disarmament process in autumn 1933 were not simply the result of his assessment of the international situation. The plan of having this step confirmed by the German people through a plebiscite fitted in perfectly with the policy of an active 'leadership of the people', which the regime had embarked upon in September with its series of major events and propaganda campaigns. By taking this dramatic step in October 1933, Hitler demonstrated his clear-sighted awareness of how extremely effective coordinating foreign policy coups with domestic politics could be. By unilaterally abrogating Germany's armaments restrictions, he could link the plebiscite campaign, which was intended to demonstrate the nation's support for his regime, to the causes of 'freedom to rearm for defence' and 'restoration of equality for Germany'. Then, with the aid of the subsequent propaganda campaign, he could demonstrate to foreign powers the German Reich's self-confidence, thereby establishing a strong position for the bilateral negotiations to come.

Plebiscites as a tool of government

On 22 October, Hitler began the 'election campaign' with two speeches outside the Hall of Liberation in Kelheim; on 24 October, he spoke in the Sportpalast in Berlin, and, during the following days, there were speeches in Hanover, Cologne, Stuttgart, and Frankfurt, in November in Weimar, Essen, Breslau, Elbing, and Kiel.[13] The campaign tour was interrupted by the commemoration of the 1923 Munich putsch. On the evening of 8 November, Hitler gave the memorial address in the Bürgerbräukeller, where he felt obliged to defend the unsuccessful coup. He was determined to prevent the impression arising that he had suffered a defeat on that occasion. 'On that evening, here in this hall, and on the following day, the nation heard the voice of our young movement; we opened the eyes of the whole of the German people, and we nurtured in the movement in its infancy the heroism which it later needed.' Above all, the putsch enabled him later on to maintain the facade of a 'legal' movement. 'If we hadn't acted then, I could never have founded a revolutionary movement, built it up and maintained it, and still been able to remain legal. People would have rightly said: You're just like the others; you talk a lot, but like the others you're never going to act. But that day, that decision, enabled me to get through nine years against all the odds.'[14] By openly admitting the pseudo-legality of his tactics in the 'time of struggle', he was signalling to the old Party members that his rejection of a continuation of the revolution four months previously might not have been set in stone. The following day, he took part in a commemoration march from the Bürgerbräukeller to the Feldherrnhalle, made another speech there, and then unveiled a bronze memorial plaque.

A gathering of the 'old fighters' in the Bürgerbräukeller, a commemoration march, and a memorial ceremony (in later years switched to the Königsplatz) were from now onwards all included in the annual calendar of Nazi rituals. The martyr cult, which was created around the 'fallen' of the putsch, and in which the motif of the 'resurrection' of these dead heroes clearly played a part, was intended to demonstrate every year to all that the sacrifices of 1923 had not been in vain. The new ceremony concluded on the evening of 9 November with the recruits of the SS Leibstandarte, Hitler's bodyguard, taking their oath of loyalty outside the Feldherrnhalle. The square became hallowed ground, where young SS men took the oath to Hitler in person, swearing that they would sacrifice their lives for him as the sixteen Hitler supporters had done in November 1923. In this way the death cult had come full circle. The victims of 1923 had been elevated to the status of being the core element of an indissoluble bond of loyalty between Hitler's supporters and their 'Führer'. Hitler played a significant part in determining the form of this ritual and never missed it until it was abandoned in 1944. He had found a way of reinterpreting his complete miscalculation of the political situation in autumn 1923 and his actions at the time, which in reality had been dictated by fear of personal disgrace, and fabricating them into a national mythology.

After the Munich ceremonies Hitler hurried to Berlin for the high point of the election campaign, where on 10 November, with Goebbels acting as his warm-up, he spoke to workers in the Dynamo Hall of the Siemens works.[15]

Once again, Hitler portrayed himself as a man of the people: 'In my youth I was a worker just like you and through hard work and studying and – I can say this as well – by going hungry, I managed slowly to work my way up.' He wanted 'once again to provide the German people with work and bread', but could 'only do it when there was peace and quiet'. He was not 'crazy enough…to want a war'. After all, he had been in the war. 'But – and I'm certain of this – none of those people who are now attacking Germany and slandering the German people has heard a single bullet whistle past them.'[16]

On election day, 12 November, those citizens entitled to vote had a single choice on their ballot paper: the NSDAP list, which also included Papen and Hugenberg, although they were not members of the Party. Their inclusion shows how careful Hitler was being not to break with the original idea of a coalition government. The ballot paper also included the following question: 'Do you, German man, and you, German woman, agree with this policy of your Reich government, and are you prepared to declare that it expresses your own will and solemnly to commit yourself to it?' Numerous cases of fraud during the voting procedure have been documented: ballot papers were marked or numbered beforehand; in many polling stations there were no polling booths; locally known members of the opposition were barred from voting; ballot papers were subsequently altered; and, throughout the Reich, the Party organization was careful to ensure that even those who were undecided went to the polls; invalid votes, which often contained protests, were not counted.[17]

The official result of the plebiscite broke all records with 95.1 per cent of the votes in favour. In fact, 89.9 per cent of those entitled to vote had voted 'yes'. However, the ballot paper had not contained the option of a 'no' vote. The vote for the NSDAP Reichstag list was given as 92.1 per cent.[18]

Hitler had linked withdrawal from the Geneva Disarmament Conference with the decision to establish a 300,000-strong army. This superseded the Reichswehr's existing plans. In response, during November and December 1933, the Defence Ministry introduced the decisive measures required to accelerate rearmament and restructure the army.[19]

Basically, since Hitler's take-over of power, the following measures had been taken in the rearmament field. On 1 April 1933, the Reichswehr had begun implementing the second rearmament plan, which had been agreed in 1932 and envisaged, within five years, increasing the 100,000-man army by 40,000 long-service soldiers, and providing short-term training for 85,000 volunteers annually.[20] It was intended that, after their training, these volunteers would be integrated into the SA,[21] to enable an army of twenty-one divisions to be formed in the event of war. In addition, it was envisaged that, during spring and summer 1933, the Reichswehr[22] would train a total of 90,000 men for frontier defence duties, a task which in practice only the SA could carry out. Moreover, in July 1933, Hitler ordered the SA to train 250,000 of their men so 'that in the event of war they can be placed at the disposal of the Reichswehr'.[23]

Now these plans were abandoned and the 100,000-strong army with its seven infantry divisions was to be replaced by a peace-time army with twenty-one divisions and 300,000 men (representing half the size of the French army), which in wartime could be expanded to a total of sixty-three divisions. The majority of troops would initially serve for one year; the intention was to introduce conscription from 1 October. It was to provide the basis for recruitment, replacing the old idea of taking a large number of half-trained men from the SA. At the decisive meeting in the Defence Ministry on 20/21 December 1933, Blomberg announced that Hitler agreed with him that 'apart from pre-military training, the Wehrmacht [was to be] in charge of everything'. This removal of the SA from the Reichswehr's rearmament plans was a logical consequence of, on the one hand, a professionalization of the army, which now no longer needed to conceal its training, and, on the other, the determination of the Party leadership, Hitler in particular, to prevent as far as possible the restless Party army from increasing its power in the new state.[24]

To avoid the impression that Germany was about to embark on a major rearmament programme, a few days after quitting the League of Nations,

and in the middle of the election campaign, Hitler put forward a new disarmament proposal. At the end of 1933, Germany would have been relatively helpless in the face of sanctions or pressure from the western powers;
thus, it was only logical that Hitler sought limited and controlled German
rearmament within the framework of bilateral agreements (or at least to
give the impression that that was his intention). To try to achieve this he put
out feelers in various directions.

He took a first step on 24 October by proposing to the British ambassador a convention with an eight-year term, which envisaged freezing the
armaments of France, Poland, and Czechoslovakia, while Germany would
be permitted to increase its army up to 300,000 men on the basis of one-
year conscription, but would dispense with heavy weapons.[25]

On 16 November, Hitler renewed his contacts with France. This was four
days after the plebiscite, and with his position strengthened by the 'people's'
apparently enthusiastic support. Accompanied by Ribbentrop and Blomberg,
he once again met the French journalist and intimate of Daladier, de Brinon,
whom he had already met in September and whose link with Ribbentrop
was still intact. They decided to publish Hitler's statements in the form of a
newspaper interview. This first interview that Hitler gave to a French newspaper was published on 22 November in *Le Matin* and reprinted in the
Völkischer Beobachter on 23 November. He reiterated at length his wish for
an understanding and for peace. 'People insult me when they continue to
say that I want war' he declared angrily. Once the Saar issue had been
resolved there were no further insoluble problems in the German–French
relationship: 'Alsace–Lorraine is not a matter of dispute.' The controversial
armaments question could be solved through a bilateral agreement with
France. But these grandiose statements were too transparent to produce a
change in French public opinion.[26]

Overcoming isolation?

By contrast, there was a significant change in Germany's policy towards
eastern Europe. As already mentioned, at the end of September, Hitler had
declared in the cabinet that relations with the Soviet Union would in future
be marked by a 'sharp antagonism'. In August 1933, the former head of
the delegation to the Disarmament Conference, Nadolny, was appointed
German ambassador in Moscow. At the end of 1933, assuming that he was

expressing the official view, Nadolny prepared a comprehensive scheme for improving German–Soviet relations; however, by January 1934, he had been forced to toe Hitler's line.[27]

In spring 1933, Hitler had already put out friendly feelers to Poland.[28] On 15 November, he received the Polish ambassador, Josef Lipski; this was only three days after the Reichstag election, and before the meeting with de Brinon. According to the official statement, in future both states intended to deal with matters affecting the two countries 'through direct negotiations', avoiding 'any use of force'.[29] The communiqué made it clear that both states were aiming to negotiate a non-aggression pact. The Foreign Ministry was sceptical, since a formal non-aggression pact could be seen as Germany renouncing a revision of the eastern border.[30] Thus, Hitler agreed that the planned pact should take the form of a joint statement[31] and the negotiations with the Polish side were conducted on that basis. After a final meeting between Hitler and the Polish ambassador[32] the negotiations finally led to the German–Polish statement of 26 January 1934. The agreement was to last ten years and basically involved a joint renunciation of the use of force. Moreover, the text clearly indicated the intention of engaging in closer cooperation in the future.[33]

Throughout the Weimar period German foreign policy had focused on a revision of the eastern border; Poland had been regarded as hostile and the aim had been to join with the Soviet Union in forcing her into submission. With the so-called German–Polish Non-Aggression Pact of 26 January Hitler was pursuing a very different policy. In the short and medium term he intended this move to break through Germany's diplomatic isolation, provide apparent proof of his peaceful intentions, and significantly undermine France's anti-German alliance policy. In the longer term he had another objective: Poland could play an important role as a base and junior partner for a policy of acquiring living space in eastern Europe.[34]

The friendly signals that Hitler sent to the Soviet Union in January and February 1934 (for example his deportation of the Bulgarian communists, Georgi Dimitroff, Wassil Taneff, and Blagoi Popoff, who were still in custody despite having been found not guilty in the Reichstag Fire trial[35]) were simply intended to disguise his unambiguously anti-Soviet policy. In April, Neurath rejected a proposal by Moscow for a German–Soviet guarantee for the Baltic States.[36] When the German ambassador in Moscow visited Berlin at the end of May, Hitler told him bluntly that he did not want to have anything to do with the Soviets.[37]

The German–Polish rapprochement inevitably led to a further cooling of relations with France. Germany provided more precise details of its disarmament proposals in a memorandum submitted to France on 18 December, but the new conservative government under Prime Minister Gaston Doumergue, with Louis Barthou as Foreign Minister, was unimpressed.[38] In March 1934, Hitler sent his foreign policy advisor, Ribbentrop, to France; however, in his conversation with Barthou Ribbentrop encountered open distrust of German policy.[39] Further attempts by Ribbentrop to negotiate at Hitler's behest[40] were prevented when France broke off the contacts on 17 April on the grounds that Germany was rearming unilaterally. Negotiations could restart only if Germany rejoined the League of Nations.[41]

France now began a diplomatic offensive, which soon drove Germany into almost complete isolation. In the first place, Foreign Minister Barthou, together with the Soviet Union, pursued an eastern pact which, by including the Soviet Union, Poland, Finland, the Baltic states, and Germany, was intended to fix the existing borders in eastern Europe in the same way that the Locarno Pact of 1925 had fixed Germany's western border. This eastern pact, which preoccupied Germany a great deal during summer 1934, ultimately failed, but the Soviet Union moved much closer to France. In September 1934, not least under pressure from the French government, the Soviet Union joined the League of Nations and, in May 1935, Barthou's successor, Pierre Laval, even made a pact for mutual military assistance with the Soviet Union. In addition, Germany's Austrian policy was an important factor in bringing France and Italy closer.[42]

At the end of 1933, Hitler had initially continued his cautious Austrian policy, aiming to limit the damage caused by his attempt at coordination in the spring.[43] During a visit to Rome in November 1933, Göring, who was increasingly being used by Hitler for special diplomatic missions, told Mussolini that at the moment Hitler had no intention of threatening Austrian independence. The union of Austria and Germany was absolutely unavoidable, but should only occur in agreement with Italy. Hitler used the visit of Fulvio Suvich, Italian Under Secretary of State, to Berlin in December to demand Dollfuss's removal from power, but in vain.[44] Meanwhile, Dollfuss increasingly sought protection from Italy. To this end, he crushed the Austrian Social Democratic Party in February 1934 and set about establishing an authoritarian regime, an Austrian version of fascism. Inevitably, he then found himself becoming diplomatically dependent on Italy.[45] Although Hitler emphasized his change of course with regard to Austria,[46] he could not prevent Dollfuss from signing the Roman Protocols with the Hungarian prime minister, Gyula Gömbös, and Mussolini on 17 March. This was a consultative agreement attached to a series of economic arrangements; it underpinned Austrian independence under Italian protection and rebuffed German ambitions in south-east Europe.[47]

Gömbös, representing a state that, like Germany, was seeking a revision of the post-war international order, had been the first head of government to visit Hitler in Berlin in June 1933. However, the Nazis' only too obvious ambitions vis-à-vis Austria had damaged German–Hungarian relations. In 1934 Germany's only success was in managing to sign a series of trade treaties with south-east European states.[48]

The signing in summer 1933 of the Concordat was Hitler's first diplomatic success. Yet, although he had managed during the rest of 1933 and the beginning of 1934 to push through his own foreign policy ideas against opposition from the Foreign Ministry, the results were of dubious value. In the first place, unlike his chief diplomat, he had not banked on the collapse of the Geneva Disarmament Conference, but instead had spectacularly seized the initiative and taken the risk of leaving the Conference and the League of Nations. However, after the French government broke off negotiations in spring 1934, his assumption that he would be able to secure future German rearmament through bilateral agreements had, for the time being, been proved wrong. As a result, Germany found itself relatively unprotected in the 'risk zone' right at the start of its major rearmament programme. Secondly, Hitler had been successful in seeking a rapprochement with Poland in order to break out of isolation, but in doing so had put at risk the Foreign Ministry's main priority, namely revision of the eastern frontier. The Non-Aggression Pact with Poland had also had the result of pushing the Soviet Union towards the western powers and damaging Germany's relations with France. Indeed, both powers were eventually prompted by German policy to make a military pact. Thirdly, it became clear that Hitler's attempt to pacify Austria had failed to rectify the damage that he had caused by his aggressive coordination policy in spring 1933; instead, he had strengthened the Dollfuss regime and caused it to align itself with Italy. Above all, the Austrian question had caused significant damage to Germany's relationship with Italy, the key partner he had hoped to win over.

16

Becoming Sole Dictator

Hitler's increasing influence on foreign policy before spring 1934 resulted, above all, in the Third Reich becoming more and more diplomatically isolated while, at the same time, serious problems were emerging in domestic politics. The series of propaganda campaigns and major events with which the regime had swamped Germany during its first year in order to demonstrate to the outside world how united the nation was proved less and less capable during its second year of disguising the very real problems that existed.

To start with, there was the problem of the SA. After Hitler's refusal in July 1933 to continue the Nazi 'revolution', the conflict between the Party leadership and the SA, which had run through the Party's history since 1923, continued. Initially, Röhm pursued a strategy of expanding the membership from 500,000 men at the beginning of 1933 to over four and a half million in mid-1934; this was achieved by admitting new members and integrating other coordinated paramilitary organizations. Röhm believed that the sheer weight of this mass organization would guarantee his SA a powerful position in the Nazi state.[1] During the months after the seizure of power, he had tried to secure a decisive influence over the state administration, particularly in Bavaria, by appointing SA special commissioners. However, by the autumn of 1933, this attempt had clearly failed. The SA auxiliary police had been dismissed,[2] and the SA had not managed to maintain its role in supplying concentration camp guards.[3] In addition, Röhm had attempted to transform the SA into a popular militia and, initially, during 1933, had in fact succeeded in integrating it into the Reichswehr's rearmament plans. However, during the autumn of 1933, it became apparent, as has been described above, that Hitler and the Reichswehr leadership were moving towards adopting another model for the Reichswehr's development. The Reichswehr was to become a conscript army, with the SA responsible only for pre-military training and for maintaining the military effectiveness of reservists.[4]

At the same time, Hitler cautiously, and without seeking a confrontation with Röhm, set about limiting the role of the SA elsewhere. At the end of 1933, he began to extend his control over the whole of the Nazi movement, and to 'integrate' the entire Party organization into the state apparatus, with the aim of further strengthening his own position.

On 21 April 1933, Hitler had already appointed Hess, who, since December 1932 had been head of the Political Commission of the NSDAP, to be his deputy for Party affairs, giving him authority 'to take decisions in my name in all matters involving the Party headquarters';[5] on 1 September 1933, he gave him the title 'Deputy Führer'.[6] After this initial regulation of internal Party matters, on 1 December 1933, the Law for securing the Unity of Party and State was enacted, which stated that the NSDAP was the 'bearer of the concept of the German state and is indissolubly linked to the state'. The Party was made an 'official body under public law', which represented a promotion from its previous status as a 'registered association', but still subordinated it to state law. However, the members were subjected to a special Party judicial system, which in theory was entitled to order 'arrest and detention'. In practice, however, it never came to what would have been a breach in the state's monopoly of the penal code; instead, there were disciplinary measures such as expulsion from the Party.[7] Moreover, Hitler used this law to appoint two more Nazi ministers: Rudolf Hess, the 'Führer's' Deputy, and Ernst Röhm, the chief of staff of the SA, became ministers without portfolio. All these measures had the effect of integrating the Party into the state rather than, as many Party functionaries had been anticipating,[8] enabling the Party to dictate to the state. During this period, Goebbels repeatedly recorded this as being Hitler's intention.[9] However, the 'Führer' deliberately left open the question of how he was going to regulate the relationship between Party and state over the longer term.

The appointment of Röhm as a Reich minister was also intended as compensation for the decline in his real power. However, he did not accept this basic presupposition behind his promotion; instead, he responded to his appointment by announcing that the SA was now integrated through 'my person into the state apparatus' and 'later developments will determine' 'what spheres of operation' may be acquired in the future.[10] In fact, he stepped up his attempt to turn the SA into an entirely independent organization, by trying to create a kind of state within the state. He set up a separate SA press office; he maintained foreign contacts,[11] for which he even established a special 'ministerial office'; he attempted to influence higher education policy; and there were even signs of the emergence of an 'SA legal code' with its own norms.[12]

Röhm had good reason to do what he could to offer his people hope for the future. For the SA was an exceptionally heterogeneous mass body and, as a result of having expanded through integrating a range of different organizations, had a very unstable structure; discontent and lack of discipline were rife. Most of the 'old fighters', who had often suffered a loss of social status as a result of the economic crisis, still had few prospects of employment and now saw themselves being cheated out of a reward for their years of commitment to and sacrifices for the Party. At the same time, the masses of new members were having to face the fact that, despite their support for the movement, their position had not improved overnight. The SA men's frustration was being expressed in numerous excesses and acts of violence, which, since all their political enemies had been crushed, were often directed at the general population.[13] At the turn of the year 1933/34, Röhm once again publicly asserted his old claim for the primacy of the soldier over the politician and confidently demanded the completion of the National Socialist revolution; his aim was, in part at least, to provide an outlet for this pent-up frustration.[14]

Hitler responded by once more proclaiming the end of the revolution and the preeminence of the Party. All the greetings telegrams he sent on 31 December to Röhm, Hess, Göring, Goebbels, and other Party bigwigs referred to 'the end of the year of National Socialist revolution'.[15] He was equally unequivocal when he spoke to the SA leadership, assembled in the Reich Chancellery on 22 January 1934, of the 'increasingly strong position of the Party as the commanding representative and guarantor of the new political order in Germany'.[16] And, at the same time, Hess was warning the organization in a newspaper article not to 'go its own way'.[17] Hitler's appointment of Alfred Rosenberg, on 24 January, to be responsible for 'supervising the entire intellectual and ideological indoctrination and education of the NSDAP' can be seen as not only strengthening the dogmatic-völkisch elements in the NSDAP, but also as an additional means of tightening up the whole of the Party's operations.[18]

Church policy

Apart from the conflict with the SA, the disputes within the Protestant Church were reaching a climax in the autumn and winter of 1933. It was becoming clear that Hitler's unwillingness to give further support to the German Christians (that was the implication of his declaration of neutrality on the Church question, made to the Gauleiters on 5 August 1933) in the longer term was undermining their dominant position within the Church.

On 6 September 1933, the General Synod of the Protestant Church of the Old Prussian Union, dominated by the German Christians, issued a Church law according to which, in future, all clergy and Church officials had to prove that they were of 'Aryan descent'.[19] This immediately prompted Martin Niemöller and Dietrich Bonhoeffer to set up a Pastors' Emergency League. This became the core of an opposition movement within the Church to resist the German Christians' ruthless use of their majorities within Church bodies to introduce Nazi ideology into the Church. Hitler's ambivalent attitude to the Protestant Church had enabled such an internal opposition to emerge, and in fact it suited him. For although he had wanted a unified Protestant Church in order to use it as a counterweight to Catholicism, he regarded both Churches in the longer term as ideological competitors. Thus, it was entirely in his interest for them to be weakened by internal splits. The Emergency League, of which, in January 1934, more than a third of pastors were members,[20] kept stressing its basic loyalty to the Hitler regime. Thus, in a telegram sent to 'our Führer' on 15 October, on the occasion of Germany's departure from the League of Nations, it pledged its 'loyalty and prayerful solicitude'.[21]

On 13 November, the German Christians organized a major event in the Sportpalast. There was a scandal when one of the speakers, the Gau chief of the Berlin German Christians, Reinhold Krause, publicly expounded völkisch religious principles. Also, the audience of 20,000 passed a resolution in which, among other things, they distanced themselves from the 'Old Testament and its Jewish morality', demanding a 'militant and truly völkisch Church', which alone would 'reflect the National Socialist state's claim to total domination'.[22] The Pastors' Emergency League then sent an ultimatum to Bishop Müller demanding that he publicly distance himself from this gross abandonment of the core principles of Christian belief. There was the threat of a split in the Church. Müller responded by stripping Krause of all his Church functions,[23] suspending the Church's 'Aryan clause', and reshuffling the Reich Church's governing body, with German Christians in future being banned by Church law from membership of it.[24] At the end of November, Hitler informed Müller in the course of a private conversation that he had no intention of intervening in the Church conflict, announcing this publicly in the *Völkischer Beobachter*.[25] On 8 December, Goebbels noted in his diary that Hitler had 'seen through . . . the unctuous parsons and Reich Bishop Müller'. Krause was 'the most decent of them'. He 'at least [had made] no bones about his contempt for the Jewish swindle of the Old Testament'.[26]

On 20 December, off his own bat, Müller ordered the integration of the Evangelisches Jugendwerk [Protestant Youth Organization] into the Hitler Youth. It was the umbrella organization for the Protestant Church's youth work with a membership of around 700,000. Müller, however, was wrong in his assumption that this would win back Hitler's trust. For, annoyed by the situation in the Protestant Church, for which he himself bore much of the responsibility, Hitler was not even prepared to send the letter of appreciation that Müller had requested.

On 25 January, with the aim of clarifying the whole situation, Hitler, accompanied by Frick, Göring, Hess, and the head of the Interior Ministry's religious affairs department, Rudolf Buttmann, received a delegation from the Protestant Church composed of German Christians and their opponents. Reich Bishop Müller was present, as was Pastor Niemöller.[27] At the meeting Göring, who had used the Gestapo to spy on the Church opposition,[28] began by reading out the report of a recording of a telephone conversation Niemöller had had that morning. Niemöller had discovered that, as a result of an intervention by the Church opposition, the Reich President had suddenly summoned his Reich Chancellor on the morning of the 25th. Niemöller had then said on the telephone that Hitler was being given the 'last rites' before the meeting with the Church representatives. With this revelation Hitler was able to dominate proceedings right from the start. He took Niemöller to task in front of his colleagues and made further accusations against his visitors during the course of the meeting, forcing them continually to justify themselves. Finally, he ended by appealing to them to cooperate, effectively demanding that the Church representatives should subordinate themselves to his regime.

Hitler's annoyance at Niemöller's contemptuous remark was definitely not simply tactically motivated in order to dominate the meeting. It arose from his deeply rooted fear of being humiliated or shamed in front of others, a fear he characteristically tried to overcome by means of a massive attack on Niemöller. Niemöller was now on the list of enemies Hitler intended to destroy. The fact that, a few years later, Hitler had Niemöller incarcerated in a concentration camp as his personal prisoner until the end of his regime was almost certainly largely the result of his disrespectful comment on 25 January, for which Hitler could not forgive him.

Göring's dossier and Hitler's appeal to the 'patriotic sense of responsibility' of the Church leaders finally persuaded them after the meeting to issue a declaration of loyalty both to Hitler's regime and to the Reich Bishop.[29] The conflict in the Protestant Church was, however, by no means settled.

Party and state

Hitler used his government statement on 30 January 1934, the first anniversary of the seizure of power, above all to settle scores with various regime opponents and other unreliable 'elements'. However, he did not mention the SA; his criticisms were aimed at a very different target. First, he silenced those who had hoped that his regime would bring about the restoration of the monarchy. The issue of the final constitution of the German Reich was 'not up for discussion at the present time'. He saw himself as merely the 'nation's representative, in charge of implementing the reforms that will eventually enable it to reach a conclusive decision about the German Reich's final constitutional form'.[30] Hitler's statement had an immediate effect: four days later, the Reich Interior Minister banned all monarchist associations.[31]

Then, in his speech, Hitler went on to tackle in a highly sarcastic and disdainful manner 'the numerous enemies', who had attacked the regime during the past year. Among them were the 'depraved émigrés', 'some of them communist ideologists', whom they would soon sort out. By the end of 1933, 37,000 Jews and between 16,000 and 19,000 other people – the estimates vary – had emigrated, mainly for political reasons. The majority were communists but there were also around 3,500 trade unionists and Social Democrats, as well as pacifists, liberals, conservatives, and Christians.[32] Hitler also attacked members of our 'bourgeois intelligentsia', who rejected 'everything that is healthy', embracing and encouraging 'everything that is sick'. A few days earlier in a lengthy interview with the Nazi poet, Hanns Johst, he had violently attacked 'un-political' people.[33] Relying on the result of the November 1933 'election', Hitler claimed that all these opponents 'did not even amount to 2.5 million people'. They could not be 'considered an opposition, for they are a chaotic conglomeration of views and opinions, completely incapable of pursuing a positive common goal, able only to agree on opposition to the current state'. However, more dangerous than these opponents were 'those political migrant birds, who always appear when it's harvest time', 'who are great at jumping on the bandwagon', 'parasites', who had to be removed from the state and the Party.

Thus, according to Hitler, apart from the communists who had survived the persecution of the first year of the regime, there was a diffuse agglomeration of opponents, people standing on the sidelines, and opportunists; they did not pose an existential threat to the regime, but obstructed the development of the Nazi state. He did not mention the fact that there were millions of other people – for example, Social Democrats or Christians of both confessions – who did not support his regime for other reasons. Despite his attempts to ridicule, belittle, and marginalize this combination of opponents and 'grumblers', his strained rhetoric betrayed considerable uncertainty. The first anniversary of the seizure of power was by no means a brilliant victory celebration.

In his speech Hitler specifically defended the regime's policy of taking action against those whose 'birth, as a result of hereditary predispositions', had 'from the outset had a negative impact on völkisch life', and announced that, after its 'first assault' on this phenomenon – the previous summer's Sterilization Law – his government was intending 'to adopt truly revolutionary measures'. In this context, he strongly criticized the Churches for their objection to such interventions: 'It's not the Churches who have to feed the armies of these unfortunates; it's the nation that has to do it.'

Following this speech, the Reichstag adopted the Law concerning the Reconstruction of the Reich, which, among other things, abolished the state parliaments, enabled the Reich government to issue new constitutional law without the need for Reichstag approval, and subordinated the Reich Governors, most of whom were Gauleiters, to the Reich Interior Ministry when performing their state functions.[34] This meant that Hitler had succeeded to a large extent in 'integrating' the regional Party agencies into the state apparatus. A few days later, on 2 February, he made this crystal clear by telling a meeting of Gauleiters that the Party's 'vital main task' was 'to select people, who, on the one hand, had the capacity, and, on the other, were willing to implement the government's measures with blind obedience'.[35]

At the end of February, Hitler's position as absolute leader of the Party was demonstrated in a large-scale symbolic act. On 25 February, Rudolf Hess presided over a ceremony, which was broadcast, in which leaders in the Party's political organization, and leaders of its ancillary organizations at all levels were assembled throughout the Reich to swear personal allegiance to

Hitler; according to the *Völkischer Beobachter*, it was the greatest oath-taking ceremony in history. On the previous evening, Hitler had given his usual speech in the Munich Hofbräuhaus to commemorate the official founding of the NSDAP fourteen years before, and once again defined the Party's future function:'The movement's task is to win over Germans to strengthen the power of this state'.[36]

The subordination of the Reich Governors to the Reich Interior Ministry raised the fundamental question as to whether the Reich Governors were also subordinate to the other Reich departmental ministers. On 22 March, Hitler explained his basic approach in a speech to the Reich Governors in Berlin in which he clarified their 'political task': it was not the job of the Reich Governors to represent 'the states vis-à-vis the Reich , but the Reich vis-à-vis the states'.[37] In June 1934, he made his position absolutely clear in a written order. The Reich Party leaders were, in principle, subordinate to the ministries; however, in matters of 'special political importance', he would himself decide on disputes between the Governors and ministers. He would also decide whether a matter was 'of special political importance'. This instance shows how skillfully Hitler exploited the rivalry between the state apparatus and the Party in order to enhance his position as the final arbiter.[38]

The strengthening of the Reich government in Berlin also served gradually to undermine the Prussian government; this was the only way of preventing a rival government from emerging under Göring. In September 1933, Göring had attempted to raise his status as Prime Minister of Prussia by creating a Prussian State Council; significantly, Hitler had not attended the inauguration. Now Göring was forced to agree to the amalgamation of the Prussian ministries with their Reich counterparts. Thus, in February the Prussian Ministry of Justice was combined with the Reich Justice Ministry; and, on 1 May 1934, Hitler appointed the Prussian Culture Minister, Bernhard Rust, to be Reich Minister of Science, Education, and Further Education, thereby transferring his previous Prussian responsibilities to the Reich. At the same time, he appointed Reich Interior Minister Frick to be Prussian Interior Minister; by November 1934 both ministries had been amalgamated. However, as Prime Minister, Göring continued to be responsible for the Prussian state police, while, even after Himmler had taken over the Gestapo in April 1934, he continued to claim the formal status of 'chief' of the Prussian secret police. As compensation for his loss of power in Prussia Göring was put in charge of a new central Reich body, the Reich Forestry

Office. Finally, during 1934–35, the personal union of the Reich and Prussian Ministries of Agriculture (Darré) and of Economics (Schacht) was brought to an end with the amalgamation of each of these two sets of ministries.[39]

More and more 'grumblers and whingers'

Hitler's commitment in October 1933 to establish a 300,000-strong army on the basis of conscription for one year, and the measures taken by the Reichswehr during the following two months to put that commitment into effect represented a definite decision against the model of an SA militia, as envisaged by Röhm. Nevertheless, on 1 February, Röhm presented the Defence Minister with a memorandum in which he described the future role of the Reichswehr as a training school for the SA. Blomberg responded by informing a meeting of military commanders that the attempt to achieve an agreement with Röhm had failed and Hitler must now decide between them.[40] At the same time, an increasing number of incidents was occurring between members of the Reichswehr and the SA.[41]

On 2 February, Hitler told the Gauleiters that 'those who maintained that the revolution was not over' were 'fools'[42] and, on 21 February, he informed a British visitor, Anthony Eden, that he did not approve of an armed SA. However, on 28 February he went further: he summoned the leadership of the SA and the Reichswehr and spelled out to them the basic outlines of the future military arrangements. He argued that a militia, such as that envisaged by Röhm, was unsuitable as the basis for a new German army. The nation's future armed force would be the Reichswehr, to be established on the basis of general conscription. The 'nationalist revolution', as he made absolutely clear, was over. Immediately after the meeting, Röhm and Blomberg signed an agreement containing the guidelines for future cooperation between the SA and Reichswehr, which involved the subordination of the Party troops to the generals. Röhm had to recognize their sole responsibility for 'preparing the defence of the Reich'; the SA was left with the pre-military training of young people, the training of those eligible for military service who had not been drafted into the Reichswehr, and a number of other auxiliary services.[43]

Röhm pretended to accept Hitler's decision, but at the same time made it very obvious that he was claiming a greater role for his SA within the state. Thus, in a number of widely reported speeches he called the SA the embodiment of the National Socialist revolution, for example in an address to the diplomatic corps on 18 April, which he had published as a pamphlet.[44] Moreover, in spring 1934, the SA organized major field exercises and parades,[45] and established armed units in the shape of so-called 'staff guards', about which Defence Minister Blomberg submitted a written complaint to Hitler at the beginning of March.[46] On 20 April, on the occasion of Hitler's 45th birthday, Röhm issued an order of the day, which could be read as an enthusiastic declaration of loyalty to the 'Führer'. However, it contained a distinctly provocative sentence: 'for us political soldiers of the National Socialist revolution' Hitler 'embodies Germany'.[47] A few days earlier, Hitler had been sailing through Norwegian waters on the battleship 'Deutschland', discussing his military plans with Blomberg, Admiral Erich Raeder, and other high-ranking Reichswehr officers.[48]

In the meantime, the domestic opponents of the SA had been mobilizing. The Nazi Party bosses in the individual states tried to form a counterweight to the growing ambitions of the SA by supporting the SS. They began handing over to Himmler control over their political police departments; indeed, with his take-over of the Prussian Gestapo on 20 April 1934, he had finally become head of a Reich-wide secret police.[49] The political police and the Nazi Party's security service (SD) were collecting material to use against the SA; the same was true of the Reichswehr, at the latest from April 1934 onwards; and, from May 1934, Göring, the SS, and the military appear to have been passing information about the SA to Hitler. Röhm responded by giving instructions in May for evidence to be collected concerning 'hostile actions' against the SA.[50]

This complex power struggle in spring 1934 was occurring at the same time as a serious crisis of confidence was emerging between the regime and the German people, resulting above all from significant socio-economic failures. This provides the background to the escalation in the conflict over the SA during the spring and early summer of 1934.[51] The main danger did not arise from the issue on which the regime had been concentrating its efforts since 1933: unemployment. The number of those registered as unemployed had reduced from six million in January 1933 to under 2.8 million in March 1934 and declined further depending on the season. Of the 3.2 million who were no longer recorded in the statistics over a million were employed in various work creation projects.[52] However, an important reason for the reduction in the unemployment statistics was that they were being rigged; the regime defined the term 'unemployed' in such a way that certain groups of employees no longer appeared in the unemployment insurance statistics.[53] Hitler proclaimed the 'second battle of work' with the start of the construction of the Munich–Salzburg autobahn on 21 March 1934,[54] and the regime highlighted this topic in its socio-political propaganda during the following weeks with some success.[55] However, any further positive economic developments had for a long time been under threat from another quarter altogether.

For during 1933–34 German exports had been in continual decline.[56] There were various reasons for this. The world economic crisis had led to protectionist trade restrictions, in which Germany had also been involved. Germany's unilateral debt moratorium in summer 1933 had provoked counter-measures abroad that had further damaged German exports. After the pound and dollar devaluations in autumn 1931 and spring 1933, the Mark became relatively overvalued; however, Schacht and Hitler rejected a devaluation of the Mark because of Germany's large foreign debt and for fear of inflation.[57] The incipient rearmament programme guaranteed the domestic market, diverting attention from attempts to increase exports. The international movement to boycott German goods, a reaction to the regime's arbitrary and oppressive behaviour and, in particular, the persecution of the Jews, also had a negative impact. At the same time, Germany was heavily dependent on raw material and food imports. As a result, by the beginning of 1934, the Reichsbank's foreign exchange reserves had been reduced to almost zero. Germans travelling abroad were subjected to drastic foreign currency restrictions.[58]

While the shortage of foreign exchange prompted renewed fears of inflation, the population was also upset by actual price increases for foodstuffs[59] and by shortages.[60] The hopes that millions had invested in the promise of a favourable policy for self-employed artisans and retailers were being disappointed;[61] peasants felt under pressure from the strict regulations imposed by the Reich Food Estate. Those who had been previously unemployed and had now found employment compared their present situation with that before the crisis and concluded that they had been better off in 1928. The idea that the reduction in unemployment resulted in millions of grateful workers turning to the regime is an exaggeration often found in the literature; there is little evidence for it. On the other hand, there were several developments that can account for the continuing discontent in factories. First, there was the removal of the workers' rights contained in the Weimar social constitution: works' councils had been replaced by 'Councils of Trust', which only had the right of consultation. Secondly, the Law for the Ordering of National Labour of 20 January 1934 had shifted the balance of power within factories decisively in favour of the employer, to whom the employees, as his 'retinue', now owed a duty of loyalty. The results of the elections to the 'Councils of Trust' in spring 1934 were so poor that the regime did not publish them. In addition to the economic problems, there was the continuing conflict within the Protestant Church, which also involved Hitler's prestige, as he had strongly supported the 'unification project'. But, above all, people were alienated by the loutishness of the SA and the high-handed behaviour of the local Party bigwigs. There was little left of the euphoria inspired by a new beginning that the regime had had some success in creating during the previous year.[62]

Typically, the regime responded not by addressing the causes of the crisis but by using every means possible to silence opponents and those allegedly responsible for encouraging 'negativity'. After Hitler had used his speech on 1 May for a renewed attack on 'critics' in general, on 3 May the Nazi Party's Reich propaganda headquarters launched a 'comprehensive propaganda campaign involving meetings', 'which will focus, in particular, on whingers and critics, rumour-mongers and losers, saboteurs and agitators, who still think they can damage National Socialism's constructive work'. The campaign was intended through 'a barrage of meetings, demonstrations, and events to mobilize the people against this plague'. Deploying the 'old methods of the time of struggle, the meetings [must] mobilize everybody right down to the last village, up the tempo every week, make ever tougher demands on people, putting in the shade all previous campaigns through their impact and success'. The date fixed for the conclusion of the campaign appears, in view of later events, remarkable: 30 June 1934. However, the campaign was not directed, or at least not in the first instance, against the SA, but above all against criticism from 'reactionary' and Church circles, in other words, opponents who were suspected of using the obvious tensions between the regime and the SA for their own purposes.[63]

However, the population was becoming tired of campaigns. They did not want to be mobilized yet again, and took the 'whinger campaign' for what in effect it was, namely a ban on all criticism. The response was indifference, apathy, and a further loss of trust.[64] At the same time the economic situation deteriorated still further. The foreign exchange crisis reached its climax in mid-June 1934 when Schacht announced the suspension of interest payments on all Reich bonds from 1 July,[65] and, a few days later, the Reichsbank abolished its monthly foreign exchange control system, in future allocating foreign exchange on an ad hoc basis. German foreign trade was in danger of collapsing; there was the threat of a trade war between Britain and the Reich.[66]

It was now obvious what was indeed about to happen. As a result of a shortage of raw materials there were interruptions in production, in fact even temporary shutdowns, and bottlenecks in deliveries.[67] The Reichswehr leadership responded to this situation by bitterly attacking the Reich Economics Minister, Kurt Schmitt.[68] The collapse of his health at the end of June after only a year in office proved quite convenient, paving the way for Hjalmar Schacht, who was to pursue a new course in order to protect the rearmament programme. However, before Schacht took up his appointment, on 30 June, Hitler was to solve the most serious crisis his regime had hitherto faced in his own very particular way.

The crisis comes to a head

On 13 July, Hitler told the Reichstag that, at the beginning of June, he had had a five-hour conversation with Röhm, during which he had reassured him that all rumours to the effect that he was planning to dissolve the SA were despicable lies. We do not know what was actually said during this conversation, but Hitler's comment suggests that it involved nothing less than the very existence of the SA. Moreover, Hitler added that he had complained to Röhm 'about the increasing number of cases of unacceptable behaviour', demanding that they should be 'stopped at once'.[69] After the meeting with Hitler, Röhm published a statement that he was 'going on leave for several weeks on the grounds of ill health', in order to take a cure, while during July the whole of the SA would go on leave. Röhm felt it necessary to add that after this break he 'would carry on his duties to the full' and that, 'after its well-earned holiday, the SA [would], unchanged and with renewed energy, continue to perform its great tasks in the service of the Führer and the movement'.[70]

In the meantime, however, Hitler's conservative coalition partners, who had been losing ground since spring 1933, saw in the conflict a chance to regain the initiative. The deteriorating economic situation, the general discontent, and the regime's insecurity, as demonstrated by the whingers campaign, encouraged this group to go on the offensive. Their hopes rested on the aged Hindenburg making a last stand. They assumed that if, with the aid of the President, they could get the Reichswehr to curb the SA, then this must have an effect on the balance of power within the government.[71] Moreover, the idea of possibly restoring the monarchy as a stabilizing factor was prevalent in these circles. In the middle of May, Papen informed Hitler that, at his suggestion, Hindenburg had prepared a will. Unaware of its contents, Hitler's entourage suspected that it might contain a recommendation to restore the monarchy. Hitler, therefore, prepared to prevent its publication after Hindenburg's death.[72] (It turned out that their fears were groundless, as Hindenburg had not followed Papen's advice.)[73] Meanwhile, during May, Goebbels had learnt from Blomberg that Papen was proposing to succeed Hindenburg himself.[74] However, the previous summer, Hitler had already decided that he would take over the Reich Presidency on Hindenburg's death.[75]

During the second half of July, the crisis intensified. On 17 June, Papen gave a speech at the University of Marburg, bluntly criticizing the Nazis' totalitarian ambitions and rule of terror.[76] Hitler (and not Goebbels, as Hitler told Papen) banned the press from publishing the Vice-Chancellor's speech.[77] Papen did not resign, pacified by Hitler's explanations of what had happened, and also because Hindenburg failed to support him, indeed disapproved of his action as a breach of cabinet discipline. When Hitler visited Hindenburg at Neudeck on 21 June, the Reich Chancellor and the Reich President were in full agreement.[78]

On 23 June, Hitler went down to the Obersalzberg and, during the following days, decided to combine the neutralization of Röhm, which he considered unavoidable, with a crackdown on 'reactionaries', who were becoming increasingly self-confident. In short, he determined to liquidate a number of second-rank people in the conservative camp in order to crush this emerging centre of opposition. This blow against the conservative opposition would take place in the shadow of the crushing of an alleged 'Röhm putsch'. By transforming his conflict with the SA leadership into an attempted putsch by the SA leader, he could justify his brutal settling of accounts with his opponents within the Nazi movement as 'an affair of state'. He claimed to be dealing with a 'national state of emergency', and he included the planned murder of members of the conservative camp under this heading. He could be certain that the majority of the population, and particularly the bourgeoisie, would welcome with relief the removal of the problems caused by the SA; indeed, that it would gain him respect. He reckoned that this support for the neutralization of the SA would lead the conservative elements in society to overlook the murder of a few of their number. He did not leave the sorting out of the SA to their major rivals, the Reichswehr, instead transferring it to the political police and the SS. In doing so, he was fulfilling the promise that he had made to the Reichswehr leadership at the start of his regime: in future, the Army would be kept out of domestic conflicts. At the same time, the neutralization of the SA would strengthen his alliance with the Reichswehr as the 'nation's sole bearer of arms' – the promise Hitler had made to it on 28 February 1933.

During the final days before the crackdown, there were plenty of warnings from the Party leadership. During the annual Gau Rally in Gera on 18 June, for example, Goebbels attacked 'saboteurs, grumblers, and malcontents' (while Hitler devoted his speech to foreign policy issues); and three days later, at Gau Berlin's solstice celebration, Goebbels announced that there would be a 'tough settling of accounts' with the 'posh gentlemen' and the 'whingeing pub strategists'.[79] On 25 June, Rudolf Hess warned the SA, in a speech broadcast via the Cologne radio station: 'Woe to him who breaks faith in the belief that he can serve the revolution by starting a revolt! Those people who believe that they have been chosen to help the Führer through revolutionary agitation from below are pathetic. . . . Nobody is more concerned about his [sic] revolution than the Führer.'[80] The following day, at a Party event in Hamburg, Göring railed against reactionary 'self-interested cliques' and 'barren critics', declaring that anyone who attempted to undermine people's trust in the regime, will have 'forfeited his head'.[81]

At this point, during the final phase of the crisis, the Reichswehr too got ready for action. From 28 June, the Army made preparations for an imminent violent struggle with the SA; on 29 June, Defence Minister Blomberg announced in the *Völkischer Beobachter*: 'the Wehrmacht and the state are of one mind'. In the same edition a speech of Göring's in Cologne was reported, in which he railed against 'people who are stuck in the past and who sow divisions', while in Kiel Goebbels attacked 'whingers and critics'.[82] Finally, on 30 June, Infantry Regiment 19 was prepared, if necessary, to restore law and order in the Tegernsee district; later on in the day, it was to take over securing the Brown House in Munich.[83]

A bloody showdown

On 28 June, Hitler attended the wedding of the Essen Gauleiter, Josef Terboven, and subsequently visited the Krupp steel plant. The previous day, he had told Rosenberg that he did not intend to move against so-called 'reactionaries' until after Hindenburg had died.[84] During his trip to Essen, however, he received news of some kind from Berlin that prompted him to consult with, among others, Göring and SA Obergruppenführer Viktor Lutze, who were accompanying him. Following these consultations, Göring flew back to Berlin, and Hitler ordered Röhm to convene a meeting of all the senior SA leaders in Bad Wiessee on the Tegernsee, where the latter was spending his holiday.[85] The following day, Hitler continued his tour of Westphalia and then travelled to Bad Godesberg, where he ordered Goebbels to fly in to see him from Berlin. During the previous days, Goebbels had been convinced that Hitler was preparing a blow against 'reactionaries', and so was very surprised to learn that he was planning to move against 'Röhm and his rebels' and was going to 'spill blood'. 'During the evening' according to Goebbels, they received more news from Berlin ('the rebels are arming'), prompting Hitler to fly to Munich that night.[86]

In his speech to the Reichstag on 13 July 1934, in which he gave a detailed account of the 'Röhm putsch', Hitler was to claim that he had originally intended to dismiss Röhm at the meeting in Bad Wiessee and to have the 'SA leaders who were most guilty arrested'. However, during 29 June, he had received 'such alarming news about final preparations for a coup' that he had decided to bring forward his flight to Munich, so that he could act 'swiftly', 'taking ruthless and bloody measures' to prevent the alleged coup. Göring had 'already received instructions from me that in the event of [sic!] the purge occurring, he should take equivalent measures in Berlin and Prussia'.[87] Hitler's comments, and the entry in Goebbels's diary concerning Hitler's surprising change of plan, suggest that Hitler did indeed decide to get rid of the SA leadership on 28 June, and, on 29 June, made the final decision on the extent, the precise targets, and the murderous nature of the 'purge'. The 'alarming news', of which Hitler spoke and which Goebbels summarized with the words the 'rebels are arming', presumably referred to the latest Gestapo information about the circle around Papen's colleague Edgar Julius Jung, who had been arrested on 25 June.[88] It suggested that this group was attempting to make a final approach to Hindenburg,[89] and Hitler was determined to preempt this at all costs through his double blow against the conservatives and the SA leadership. However, from 29 June onwards, he was no longer simply concerned with winning a domestic political power struggle; he was now determined to annihilate his opponents physically and create an atmosphere of terror and fear, which would in future prevent any opposition from forming at all.

However, to begin with Hitler carried out the Bad Godesberg programme that had been organized for him as planned.[90] Late in the evening of 29 June, he had two companies of SS sent to Upper Bavaria on the overnight train. During the night, he flew from Hangelar airport near Bonn to Munich, accompanied by his adjutants, Brückner, Schaub, and Schreck, his press chief, Otto Dietrich, and Goebbels. Once there, he learnt that, during the night, the members of an SA Standarte, around 3,000 men, had been put on the alert, some of whom had marched rowdily through Munich. It seemed there was a possibility that preparations for the planned measures had leaked out or had been intentionally leaked. Hitler, therefore, now decided to further accelerate the measures. He drove to the Interior Ministry, ordering SA leaders August Schneidhuber and Wilhelm Schmid to meet him there, and then personally tore off their insignia.[91]

Hitler's decision to liberate the regime from a serious crisis through a double blow against the SA leadership and the circle round Papen had been maturing over a period of weeks. However, events now culminated in a dramatic confrontation and the more the situation escalated the more furiously angry he became. However, his behaviour was not simply a clever tactic to provide himself with a justification for his actions. For, given his anger, a cool calculated decision to have a number of old comrades murdered could have appeared to be a crackdown arising out of the situation. It is also explicable in terms of particular personal characteristics that determined how he saw the situation. If this is the case, then the question as to whether Hitler really believed the SA intended to carry out a putsch is of secondary importance. He saw any putative attempt by the conservatives to approach Hindenburg as a threat to his power, which, together with the growing SA problem, could lead to a serious political crisis. This growing threat to his position and prestige – for him an intolerable thought – was already *itself* the feared 'putsch', the threatened coup d'état. His response to this threat, as he saw it, was to unleash a tidal wave of violence.

In this mood he did not wait for SS reinforcements to arrive in Munich from Berlin and Dachau. Instead, he drove to Bad Wiessee, accompanied by

Goebbels and a small group of SS and criminal police, where he found the SA leaders still in bed. Hitler insisted on carrying out the arrests himself.[92] Afterwards, he returned to Munich, on the way stopping cars bringing the remaining SA leaders to Wiessee and arresting some individuals.

On 8 July, Rudolf Hess provided an account of what happened in the Brown House during the next few hours in a speech at a Gau Party Rally in Königsberg that was broadcast on the radio. To begin with, Hitler spoke to the political leaders and SA leaders who were present, after which he withdrew to his study to pass 'the first sentences'.[93] He then dictated various instructions and statements concerning the 'change of leadership' at the top of the SA. These included the announcement of Röhm's dismissal and the appointment of Lutze as his successor, as well as a 'statement from the NSDAP's press office', which provided an initial summary of the events and an explanation of the measures that had been taken.

According to the statement, the SA had been increasingly developing into a centre of opposition, and Röhm had not only failed to prevent this, but had actually encouraged it, with his 'well-known unfortunate inclinations' playing an important part. Röhm had also, along with Schleicher, conspired with a 'foreign power' (France). This was another accusation for which no proof was produced.[94] Hitler had then made up his mind to 'go to Wiessee in person, together with a small escort', 'in order to nip in the bud any attempt at resistance'. There they had witnessed 'such morally regrettable scenes' that, following Hitler's orders, they had acted immediately, 'ruthlessly rooting out this plague sore'. Moreover, he had ordered Göring 'to carry out a similar action in Berlin and, in particular, to eliminate the reactionary allies of this political conspiracy'. Around midday, Hitler had addressed senior SA leaders, on the one hand emphasizing 'his unshakeable solidarity with the SA', but, at the same time, announcing his 'determination, from now onwards, pitilessly to exterminate and destroy disobedient types lacking discipline, as well as all anti-social and pathological elements'.[95]

The next press statement, which went out on 30 June, was a so-called eye-witness report, in which Hitler's personal intervention against the 'conspiracy' was praised as a truly heroic deed, while the 'disgusting scenes taking place when Heines and his comrades were arrested' were left to the readers' imagination. Edmund Heines, the SA leader in Silesia, was one of the SA leaders whose homosexuality was relatively well known.[96]

Also on 30 June Hitler issued an 'order of the day' to the new SA chief of staff, Lutze, containing a catalogue of twelve demands to the SA. Among other things, Hitler demanded 'blind obedience and absolute discipline', exemplary 'behaviour' and 'decorum'. SA leaders should in future set 'an example in their simplicity and not in their extravagance'; there should be no more 'banquets' and 'gourmandizing'; 'expensive limousines and cabriolets' should no longer be used as official cars. The SA must become a 'clean-living and upright institution' to which mothers can entrust their sons without any reservations'; the SA must in future deal ruthlessly with 'offences under §175'.* When it came to promotions the old SA members should be considered before the 'clever late-comers of 1933'. In addition, he demanded 'obedience', 'loyalty', and 'comradeship'.[97]

These statements referred to treason and mutiny, to a conspiracy by the SA leadership and 'reactionary forces'. Yet these initial announcements did not state that Germany had been facing the immediate threat of a putsch that had been in preparation for a long time, as Hitler was later to claim. Instead, the main justification for the crackdown was disgust at the alleged moral depravity of the SA leadership.

Around five o'clock in the afternoon, Hitler summoned Sepp Dietrich, the commander of his personal bodyguard, the SS Leibstandarte, ordering him to go to Stadelheim prison with his unit and shoot six SA leaders whose names were marked with a cross on a list. Dietrich carried out the order. The victims were Obergruppenführer August Schneidhuber (Munich) and Edmund Heines (Breslau), the Gruppenführer Wilhelm Schmid (Munich), Hans Hayn (Dresden) and Hans-Peter von Heydebreck (Stettin), and Röhm's adjutant, Standartenführer Count Hans Erwin Spreti. The shooting of these people was also announced by the NSDAP press office.[98]

Around eight o'clock in the evening, Hitler flew from Munich to Berlin. Göring was waiting for him at the airport and, according to Goebbels, who was still accompanying him, reported that everything in Berlin had 'gone according to plan'. Indeed, in the meantime, the Gestapo had carried out a series of murders involving a number of prominent individuals: General von Schleicher, who had been shot at home together with his wife (which Goebbels referred to as a 'mistake') and his closest colleague, Major-General Ferdinand von Bredow; in addition, Papen's colleague, Herbert von Bose, Erich Klausener, who had been dismissed as head of the police department in the Prussian Interior Ministry in February 1933, and was also the head of the Berlin diocesan section of the Catholic lay organization, Catholic

---

* Translators' note: This refers to the paragraph in the Penal Code dealing with homosexuality.

Action, and Edgar Jung, who was already under arrest. The following day, Göring reported to Hitler on how the executions were proceeding. Goebbels noted in his diary: 'Göring reports: executions almost completed. Some still necessary. That's difficult, but essential. Ernst, Strasser, Sander, Detten †.' Goebbels was referring to the Berlin SA Gruppenführer, Karl Ernst and his chief of staff, Wilhelm Sander, to Hitler's long-time colleague and Party opponent, Gregor Strasser, and to the head of the SA's political office, Georg von Detten, who lived in Berlin. Goebbels, who spent the whole afternoon with Hitler, noted: 'the death sentences are taken very seriously. All in all about 60.'[99] It is clear from Goebbels's diary that Hitler remained in close contact with Göring from the time of his arrival in Berlin on the evening of 30 June, and determined himself the later murders that took place, just as it was he who had personally ordered the execution of the six SA leaders in Munich.

After the initial executions in Stadelheim, the murders continued in Munich. They involved, in the first place, Röhm's entourage: the chief of his staff guard, two adjutants, two chauffeurs, the manager of his favourite pub, and his old friend, Martin Schätzel.[100] Secondly, Hitler focused on getting rid of a number of people who had crossed his path in earlier times and antagonized him. We can be certain that they were among the 'death sentences' Goebbels definitely attributed to Hitler. Among them were Otto Ballerstedt, the former chairman of the long-forgotten Peasant League. In September 1921 (!) Hitler had used violence to break up one of his meetings and been sent to prison for three months. He had had to spend four weeks inside, a humiliation which he hated mentioning. Hitler naturally blamed Ballerstedt for his punishment and from then onwards kept claiming that this marginal figure was a very dangerous opponent.[101] Gustav von Kahr was murdered. He was the man whom Hitler had wanted to force to join his putsch on 8 November 1923, but who after a few hours had managed to escape and then played a significant role in the collapse of the whole enterprise. For Hitler, Kahr, who had long since withdrawn from politics, was, more than ten years later, still the 'traitor' he blamed for his greatest humiliation.[102] Fritz Gerlich, a politically engaged Catholic, was also murdered. In his journal, *Der Gerade Weg*, he had mounted a campaign against Nazism, including bitter personal attacks on Hitler. In June 1932, for example, he had subjected Hitler to an 'examination' on the basis of the various racial criteria put forward by the Nazis, and reached the conclusion that, on the basis of his appearance and attitudes, Hitler should be classified as an 'inferior', 'eastern–Mongolian' type.

Gerlich had already been placed in 'protective custody' in March 1933.[103] Another case worth mentioning in this context is that of Bernhard Stempfle, a völkisch writer who, despite his ideological affinity to Nazism, during the 1920s developed a strong personal animosity towards Hitler. Shortly after its publication, he wrote a devastating review of *Mein Kampf* that appeared in the völkisch newspaper, the *Miesbacher Anzeiger*.[104]

The murders of Ballerstedt, Kahr, Gerlich, and Stempfle all followed the same pattern. To begin with, the victims were taken to Dachau concentration camp and then either killed there or nearby. The head of the Munich Student Welfare Service, Fritz Beck, was also murdered, possibly because he was assumed to have a close relationship with Röhm (in 1933 he had made the SA chief of staff honorary chairman of the organization).[105] The music critic, Wilhelm Schmid, was the victim of mistaken identity. In addition, there were at least five more victims: a communist, a Social Democrat, two Jews, and the private secretary and girlfriend of the former editor of the *Münchener Neueste Nachrichten*, who had had a row with the Party.[106] In Berlin the murder campaign involved not only those people already mentioned, but half a dozen colleagues of the local SA leader and Röhm's press chief, Veit-Ulrich von Beulwitz, as well as three other people who were eliminated for various reasons that did not necessarily have anything to do with the 'Röhm putsch'.[107]

Apart from Munich and Berlin, Silesia was a third centre where similar measures were taken on 30 June. A dozen SA leaders who were linked to the SA chief, Heines, were murdered on the orders of the responsible SS Oberabschnittsführer, Udo von Woyrsch. There were others who for some reason were targeted by the SS, including four Jewish citizens of Hirschberg.[108] A fourth focus for the murder campaign was Dresden, where three SA members were killed.[109]

Elsewhere, other people fell victim to the purge for various reasons. In some cases, it appears that 'old scores were being settled' by individuals acting on their own initiative. Among these were, for example, Freiherr Anton von Hohberg und Buchwald, who had been dismissed from the SS as a result of a row with the East Prussian SS leader, Erich von dem Bach-Zelewski, who had him murdered, and Hermann Mattheiss, who had been dismissed as head of the Württemberg political police in May 1934 because he refused to submit to the new head of the political police in Württemberg, Heinrich Himmler; instead, he wanted to continue to rely on SA support for the police. Mattheiss was shot in the SS barracks in Ellwangen.[110]

Adalbert Probst, Reich leader of the Deutsche Jugendkraft, the umbrella organization of the Catholic gymnastic and sports associations and one of the most prominent representatives of those Catholic associations that were in conflict with the state, was arrested in Braunlage in the Harz and murdered at an unknown location. Probst had made a name for himself as an advocate and organizer of paramilitary sport within the Catholic associations, and so was considered a representative of a truly 'militant' Catholicism. At the end of June, he had taken part in the Concordat negotiations in Berlin, which were dealing, among other things, with the future of the Catholic associations.[111] Kurt Mosert, the leader of SA Standarte Torgau, was taken to Lichtenberg concentration camp and murdered because of personal quarrels with SS guards in the camp,[112] as were three members of the SS who had been imprisoned for ill-treating prisoners.[113]

On 1 July, Hitler arranged for Röhm to be given a pistol in his cell in Munich-Stadelheim. When he failed to use it, Hitler sent the commander of Dachau concentration camp, Theodor Eicke, and the commander of the Dachau guards, Michael Lippert, to Stadelheim to shoot him in his cell.[114] The regime then put out a laconic press release: 'The former chief of staff of the SA, Röhm, was given the opportunity of facing up to his treason. He failed to do so and consequently has been shot.'[115]

On the evening of 1 July, Goebbels described the recent events in a broadcast, adopting the tone of moral indignation that had been prominent in the official statements of the previous day. He accused those who had been murdered and their associates of 'leading a dissolute life', of 'ostentation' and 'gourmandizing'; they had been liable to place the whole of the Nazi leadership under suspicion of being associated with 'disgraceful and disgusting sexual abnormality'. All their doings and actions had been dictated purely by 'personal lust for power'.[116]

On 2 July, Hindenburg sent telegrams to Hitler and Göring expressing his 'warm appreciation' that 'through your resolute intervention and courageous personal engagement you have managed to nip these treasonous machinations in the bud'. On the same day, Hitler issued a press statement announcing the conclusion of the 'purge'.[117]

When considering the events of 30 June, it is often overlooked that the murderous campaign was not only directed against the SA leadership and the conservatives (as well as a number of 'old' enemies), it was also intended as a warning to 'political Catholicism'. Moreover, this was at a time when a political compromise between the Nazi system and the Catholic Church was actually emerging. This aspect throws further important light on Hitler's decision to neutralize various opposition forces through a brutal and sweeping blow.

In October 1933, negotiations had already begun between the Reich and the Vatican concerning the implementation of various points in the Concordat of July 1933. They concerned, in particular, the future of those Catholic associations whose activities were not purely religious in nature; the issue was basically whether the Catholic youth organizations should retain a degree of autonomy, for example through being integrated into a state youth organization, or whether, as the Party wished, they should be absorbed into the Hitler Youth.

The final round of these negotiations was scheduled for the end of June in Berlin after the Vatican had instructed the German episcopacy to engage in direct talks with the regime.[118] On 27 June, Hitler, accompanied by Frick and Buttmann, received the delegation of the German bishops and he appears to have impressed his visitors with his sympathetic and responsible manner and his rejection of another 'cultural struggle'.[†] Indeed, he even stated that he was prepared to ban the advocacy of a 'Germanic religion' and 'neo-heathen propaganda'[119] (a promise, which, significantly, he immediately withdrew when he met Rosenberg, the main exponent of this doctrine).[120] Evidently, Hitler felt the general political situation obliged him to go to some lengths to conciliate the Catholic Church.

Two days later, they made an agreement, determining that the associations that served purely religious, cultural, or charitable purposes should be subordinated to the Catholic lay organization, Catholic Action, and so be integrated into the Catholic Church's hierarchy.[121] On 24 June, when the Berlin diocese celebrated Catholic Day, Erich Klausener, the head of Catholic Action in Berlin, urged his enthusiastic audience of 60,000 Catholics proudly to stand up for their Catholic faith in their daily lives. This rally must have been viewed by the regime as a demonstration of Catholic opposition; it looked as though, in addition to the SA and the conservative opposition, another domestic threat was now emerging on the horizon.[122] As a result of the impending implementation of the Concordat, Klausener's organization was now going to be strengthened and receive state recognition. Six days later, Klausener was murdered, as was the well-

---

† Translators' note: This refers to the 'Kulturkampf' waged by Bismarck, the Prussian government, and the Liberals against the Catholic Church during the 1870s.

known Catholic journalist, Fritz Gerlich, and the head of the Deutsche Jugendkraft, Adalbert Probst, like Klausener both representatives of a self-confident and militant Catholicism; Probst had also taken part in the Concordat negotiations at the end of June.

Seen in context, these three murders were a targeted blow against the emergence of a political opposition movement. There is a suspicion – it cannot be proved because of a lack of documentation – that these murders were intended at the last minute to block the compromise on the implementation of the Concordat worked out by the Interior Ministry because the Party disapproved of it. This was facilitated by the fall from power of Vice-Chancellor, Papen, the government minister who was most supportive of a modus vivendi between Catholicism and the regime. The compromise solution, which had appeared to the regime unavoidable on 29 June, could be revised on 30 June because of a completely changed political situation.

Bearing in mind how directly involved Hitler was in the issuing of the 'death sentences' on 30 June and 1 July, it appears improbable that the arrest and murder of these three prominent Catholics in different locations was the result of unauthorized actions by subordinate agencies. It is much more likely that they too were victims of Hitler's 'death sentences'.

The Catholic Church was horrified by the murder of the three Catholics, but it did not use the murders as an excuse for breaking off negotiations with the Reich government. This is probably one reason why the link between the Concordat negotiations and the murder of prominent Catholics has hitherto been neglected in historical accounts of the events of 30 June. In a letter to Cardinal Bertram, Eugenio Pacelli described the agreement reached on 29 June as unacceptable and referred, in an oblique way typical of representatives of the Vatican, to the events of 30 June. This 'writing on the wall' would hopefully 'convince the holders of ultimate power in Germany . . . that external force without the corrective and the blessing of a God-directed conscience will not prosper but bring disaster to the state and the people'.[123]

It was only several days after 30 June 1934, and then remarkably hesitantly, that Hitler's regime went beyond the confused statements that had been made in the immediate aftermath of the events and provided a properly thought-through justification for the murders.

To begin with, on 3 July, Hitler gave a detailed explanation of the action against Röhm at a cabinet meeting, taking 'full responsibility for the shooting of 43 traitors' (even if not every on-the-spot execution had been ordered by him personally').[124] The Reich cabinet then approved a Law concerning Emergency Measures, whose single clause read: 'The measures taken on 30 June and 1 July 1934 to suppress high treason and treasonable actions are, as emergency measures to defend the state, legal.'[125] According to Goebbels, Papen suddenly appeared at the meeting, looking 'quite broken'.[126] Although his colleagues, Edgar Julius Jung, who had written the Marburg speech, and Herbert von Bose had been among the victims, by appearing at the meeting Papen was indicating that he intended to continue with his official duties. The cabinet was particularly busy that day, issuing a total of thirty-two laws.[127]

On 3 July, Hitler visited Hindenburg at his Neudeck estate. On the following day, he returned to Berlin, but then did not appear in public for over a week.[128] He also did not take part in the meeting of Gauleiters on 4 and 5 July 1934 in Flensburg, where, according to the *Völkischer Beobachter*, Hess only briefly referred to recent events; apart from that, the Gauleiters discussed organizational and economic issues.[129] On 11 July, the Deutsches Nachrichtenbüro, the official German news agency, issued the text of an interview Hitler had given to Professor Pearson, a former US diplomat, which had appeared in the *New York Times*. Here, he had defended his measures on the grounds that he had acted to prevent a civil war.[130]

Hitler did not appear in public again until 13 July. In the meantime, he had decided to justify his actions on 30 June as emergency measures, required to counter an elaborate conspiracy, and now appeared before the Reichstag with this imaginatively concocted story. He began his speech by listing the opposition groups in the Reich: first, the communists; secondly, political leaders who could not come to terms with their defeat on 30 January 1933; thirdly, he dealt with those 'revolutionary types, whose earlier relationship to the state had become disrupted in 1918, who had become rootless and, as a result, had lost any connection with a regulated social order'; the fourth group he described as 'those people, who belong to a relatively small social group who, without anything else to do, while away their time in chatting about anything liable to bring variety into their otherwise completely trivial lives'.

Hitler then outlined a scenario in which a conspiracy was thwarted at the very last minute. He did this by ingeniously combining a number of issues that had been causing controversy during recent months and assigning key roles in them to particular individuals who had been murdered. The rumour of an impending dissolution of the SA had been used, he claimed, as an excuse for a 'second revolution', during which, among other things, Papen was to be killed; Röhm was planning to subordinate the Wehrmacht to the SA and to make Schleicher Vice-Chancellor; von Bredow had established contacts with foreign countries and Gregor Strasser had been 'brought into' the conspiracy. If anyone 'reproached him for not using the law courts to try' the conspirators, his answer was: 'In this hour I was responsible for the fate of the German nation and so I was the German people's supreme judge!' He gave the number of people who had been executed as seventy-seven.[131] The actual number of those murdered was higher. Up to the present, a total of ninety-one people have been proved to have died; it is possible that there were further victims.[132]

Hitler gave a very different justification for the measures taken on 30 June 1934, one much closer to the truth, in a secret speech to the Party's district leaders at the Ordensburg Vogelsang on 29 April 1937. He stated: '...to my great sadness I had to break that man and I destroyed him and his followers' and gave as his justification: 'the need to show the most brutal loyalty' to the army, whereas the SA's idea of a militia would have resulted in a 'militarily completely useless bunch of people'.[133]

On 20 July, Hitler ordered that, 'in view of its great services, particularly in connection with the events of 30 June 1934', the SS was to be promoted to be an 'autonomous organization within the NSDAP'. The leader of the SS, who previously had been subordinate to the chief of staff of the SA, would in future be directly subordinate to him in his capacity as 'Supreme SA leader'[134]. In this way Hitler prepared the path for SS chief, Heinrich Himmler, one of his most important allies during the 30 June action, to build up his 'Black Order' to become one of the main centres of power in the Third Reich.

The crisis of spring and early summer 1934 had resulted from a whole number of factors, as we have seen: against the background of the Reichswehr's rapid rearmament, the SA had been quickly forced out of its military role and was searching aggressively but unsuccessfully for new tasks. This was a process that was bound to lead to numerous conflicts and, above all, raised the question of the goals of the 'National Socialist revolution', one which could never be decisively answered. In addition, there were supply problems as well as a shortage of foreign exchange; the unresolved conflict within the Protestant Church and the equally unresolved issue of the Catholic associations; the discontent with the high-handed behaviour of the local Party bosses; and, finally, the growing self-confidence of the conservatives around Vice-Chancellor von Papen, who wanted to take advantage of the confused situation while Reich President von Hindenburg was still alive. Basically, a power struggle was developing between the regime, the Reichswehr, and the SS/political police on the one hand and the two very different centres of opposition around the SA and Papen's circle on the other.

Hitler's response to this complex pattern of conflicts was typical of him: radical, almost hysterical, driven by his wish to avoid the threat of a loss of face. The orgy of violence, including the settling of old personal scores, went beyond the need to deal with the actual political conflicts that existed. Hitler wanted to make it clear once and for all how he proposed to deal with opponents of any kind and to take revenge for past humiliations. Consequently, he subsequently took responsibility for the murders, under the cover of an incredible tissue of lies.

By removing his opponents in the SA leadership and the Papen circle, and simultaneously intimidating the Catholic Church, he had gained considerable room for manoeuvre; he had succeeded in shifting the political balance of forces in his favour. Yet most of the causes of the crisis remained and would, as a result, re-emerge in another temporal context and in a different constellation. This is confirmed by the official regime reports on the mood of the population and by the observations of the Social Democratic underground movement. Apart from the shock and horror the events had produced, the reports initially reflected the 'positive' interpretation put out by the regime's propaganda. For large sections of the population Hitler once more appeared as the decisive political leader, who in his 'resort to drastic measures' had the 'welfare of the state' at heart. However, 'relief' at being liberated from the irksome and loutish behaviour of the SA lasted only a short time; for it soon became clear that 30 June was not, as many hoped, the start of a general purge of the Party of all the 'bigwigs', the beginning of an energetic drive against the misuse of power and corruption. It was not long before there was a general revival of 'whingeing' and grumbling'.[135]

The Austrian putsch

A few weeks after his victory over his domestic political opponents, Hitler thought he could solve another major problem facing the young Third Reich: the so-called Austrian question. He was convinced that he had secured the most important precondition for the solution of this problem: Mussolini's agreement to an Anschluss.

On 14 June, Hitler had carried out his first state visit to Italy. He and his Foreign Minister Neurath had met the 'Duce' and the most important Italian politicians in Venice.[136] Austria had been at the top of the agenda during the two detailed discussions Hitler had with Mussolini in Venice. The 'Führer' had made it clear: 'the question of the Anschluss was not a matter of interest since it was not pressing and, as he well knew, could not be carried out in the present international situation'. However, he demanded an end to the Dollfuss regime: 'the Austrian government [must] be headed by a neutral personality, i.e one not bound by party ties', elections must be held, and then Nazis must be included in the government. All matters affecting Austria must be decided by the Italian and German governments. While the Italians agreed these points, Mussolini responded to Hitler's insistence that Italy should 'withdraw its protective hand from Austria' by merely 'taking note' of it. It is incomprehensible how Hitler could have gained the impression from these conversations that Mussolini would not respond to an attempted coup by the Austrian Nazis, authorized by Hitler a few weeks later. For Mussolini, under pressure from the Reich, had let it be known that he would at best tolerate the Austrian Nazis, forcing new elections to be held and a reconstruction of the government. However, he was by no means prepared to accept a bloody coup d'état; indeed, in view of Hitler's explicit renunciation of an Anschluss, he was bound to consider it a breach of faith. This fateful mistake, a complete misunderstanding of his 'friend', delayed for years both the alliance with Italy, to which he had aspired since the 1920s, and his Austrian plans. It can only be explained in the light of the euphoria and wishful thinking gripping Hitler during the domestic political crisis of early summer 1934. Thus, he believed that two basic aims of his foreign policy were about to be realized: the alliance with Italy and the 'coordination' of Austria, goals that he had had to play down the previous year. Yet neither Hitler's wishes nor his ideas reflected reality.

The meeting in Venice was the starting point for the Austrian Nazis' preparations for a putsch. They were organized by Theodor Habicht, the 'Landesinspekteur' for the Austrian NSDAP, appointed by Hitler, and by the leader of the Austrian SA, Hermann Reschny, who, after the ban on the Austrian NSDAP, had established an 'Austrian Legion' in the Munich area, composed of SA members who had fled Austria. The third figure in the conspiracy was the former SA chief, Pfeffer. He was now a member of the

NSDAP's liaison staff in Berlin and, apart from his role as Hitler's representative for Church questions, was now given the task of solving the Austrian question by force. In the historical literature there has been much speculation that the affair was basically triggered by competition between Habicht and Reschny.[137] According to these historians, cooperation between the SA and SS had been so damaged by the events of 30 June that Reschny, an SA leader, had not properly supported the actual putsch force, an SS unit. Hitler had remained largely passive and had simply 'let things drift', as Kurt Bauer put it a few years ago in a substantial work on the July putsch.[138] This perspective reflects the 'functionalist' interpretation of a dictator, who, as a result of his wait-and-see style of leadership, encouraged his subordinates, who were trying to 'work towards him' and at the same time competing with each other, to make great efforts to do what they perceived as his bidding. This, in turn, allegedly led to a radicalization of the decision-making process. In this model Hitler appears, above all, as one factor among many others within the system's own dynamic; it is the system that acts and not the dictator.

However, this version can be refuted with the aid of Goebbels's diary for the summer of 1934, which was published in 2006. For it is clear from Goebbels's diary that, on 22 July, accompanied by Goebbels, Hitler received in Bayreuth, first, Major-General Walter von Reichenau, Chief of the General Staff in the Defence Ministry, and then the three organizers of the putsch: Habicht, Rechny, and Pfeffer.[139] Concerning the content of these negotiations, Goebbels noted: 'Austrian question. Will it succeed? I'm very sceptical.'[140] Goebbels's scepticism was to prove justified. On 25 July, members of an Austrian SS Standarte carried out the putsch that Hitler had ordered. They occupied the Austrian broadcasting station and the Federal Chancellor's office, seriously injuring Chancellor Dollfuss and letting him bleed to death in his office. However, on the same day, the putsch was crushed in Vienna by troops loyal to the government,[141] and, during the following days, the uprising, which had spread quite widely, was completely suppressed.[142] The Goebbels diaries show in detail that, while in Bayreuth, Hitler was carefully and anxiously following developments in Austria.[143]

On 26 July, Habicht and Pfeffer appeared in Bayreuth to give their report. Habicht was forced to resign and, a few days later, the Austrian NSDAP headquarters was dissolved. Mussolini's immediate support for the Austrian government was decisive for the failure of the putsch.[144] Hitler was extremely disappointed; he could not bring himself to admit that he had completely misunderstood Mussolini in Venice.[145] On 26 July, in order to cover up the involvement of German agencies, Hitler issued a statement that 'no German agency had anything to do with these events'. The fact that the putsch had been supported by reports from the Munich radio station was a mistake for which Habicht was held responsible.[146] Hitler also decided to appoint Papen, who had lost his post as Vice-Chancellor, as the new ambassador in Vienna. His close connections with the Catholic Church were intended to help restore the damaged relationship with Austria.[147]

The death of Hindenburg

The signing of Papen's accreditation document as special ambassador on 31 July was the last official act Reich President von Hindenburg was capable of carrying out. For having withdrawn to his Neudeck estate at the beginning of June on grounds of ill health, at the end of July his condition worsened.[148] Hindenburg's imminent death gave Hitler the opportunity decisively to expand his power. As is clear from Goebbels's diary, he had already discussed the steps to be taken with senior cabinet members and the Reichswehr leadership. They involved the Reichswehr and the cabinet 'declaring Hitler to be Hindenburg's successor immediately after [Hindenburg's] demise. Then the Führer will appeal to the people'.[149] On 1 August, Hitler flew to East Prussia, where he saw Hindenburg, still alive but barely responsive.[150] Back in Berlin, on the evening of 1 August, Hitler told the cabinet that, within 24 hours, Hindenburg would be dead. At that point it was decided – not as originally envisaged immediately after the President's death – to issue a law stating that on Hindenburg's death his office would be combined with that of the Reich Chancellor, and so the presidential powers would transfer to the 'Führer and Reich Chancellor Adolf Hitler'. This totally contradicted the Enabling Law of 24 March 1933, which expressly stated that the rights of the Reich President remained unaffected.[151]

As a result of this legal change, Hitler also became head of the armed forces. At the cabinet meeting, Defence Minister von Blomberg announced, evidently on his own initiative, that, after Hindenburg's death, he wished the Reichswehr to swear allegiance to Hitler personally, although the constitution stipulated an oath of allegiance to the President. The following day, news of Hindenburg's death arrived,[152] and, only a few hours later, throughout the Reich soldiers swore 'absolute obedience to the Führer of the

German Reich and people, Adolf Hitler, Supreme Commander of the Wehrmacht'. The Reichswehr leadership hoped that, by getting soldiers to swear allegiance to Hitler *personally*, they would strengthen the special relationship between the dictator and the armed forces, thereby underlining the position of the army as the 'Führer's' most important instrument of power.[153] The new form of oath clearly revealed the dissolution of the constitutional bonds binding the Supreme Commander and the armed forces. The armed forces had sworn allegiance to a Supreme Commander who no longer exercised this function within the context of a constitutional office, but in his capacity as 'Führer of the German Reich and people', in which he was not bound by constitutional law. The cabinet met again that evening. They agreed that Hindenburg should have a magnificent state funeral and decided, at Hitler's request, to have the succession, which had already been legally confirmed, ratified by a plebiscite.[154] On the same day, Hitler issued an instruction to the Reich Interior Minister that in future he did not wish to bear the title of Reich President, but to be known as before as 'Führer and Reich Chancellor'.[155]

By combining the offices of head of the government and head of state, and taking over the supreme command of the armed forces, Hitler had successfully finished concentrating power in his own hands. And this was only a few weeks after, having raised himself to the status of 'Supreme Judge', he had settled accounts with the SA leadership and finally neutralized his conservative 'coalition partners'. Through the offices of Party chief, Chancellor, President, and Supreme Commander of the armed forces he exercised an enormous amount of real power. But, in addition, by combining these offices in his position as officially legitimized 'Führer', he had created an omnipotent position, which was not limited by any constitutional organ or body whose approval he was required to seek. He had succeeded in a little more than eighteen months in establishing a dictatorship of which he was solely in command. This decisive step has rightly been described as the 'usurpation of state sovereignty for his own person'.[156]

Hitler had good reason to celebrate Hindenburg's departure as the farewell to a bygone age. On 6 August, at a memorial ceremony in the Reichstag, he paid tribute to the merits of the deceased President,[157] and on the following day, he spoke again at Hindenburg's funeral. Despite Hindenburg's wish to be buried in Neudeck, the funeral took place at the memorial to the Battle of Tannenberg, in other words at the place in East Prussia, where, through his victory over a Russian army in 1914, he had established the basis

Figure 5. As this example from the Spreewald shows, not even the smallest village escaped the propaganda campaign in the plebiscite for Hitler as Reich President, although in some places, as here, the creation of posters was left to local Party officials.
Source: Scherl/Süddeutsche Zeitung Photo

for his aura as a national hero.[158] The interment in the castle-like grounds saw a display of the uniforms and flags of the old army; the funeral was a farewell in a very comprehensive sense: 'It's the last turn-out of old Germany', noted Goebbels.[159] In his funeral sermon the senior Protestant Wehrmacht chaplain, Franz Dohrmann, described Hindenburg in the way the latter had seen himself, as a nationalist conservative Protestant nationalist who had been marked by a simple faith in God, raising him above all animosity. In his address, Hitler, by contrast, concentrated on paying tribute to the 'military commander', and in his final sentence intentionally introduced a contrasting emphasis: 'Great commander, in death now enter Valhalla'.[160]

Despite careful preparation and assiduous manipulation of the electoral process, the result of the plebiscite that followed on 19 August was, as far as the Nazis were concerned, disappointing. Only 89.9 per cent of the valid votes were for 'yes'; if one includes those who did not vote and those whose votes were invalid, only 84.5 per cent of those entitled to vote were in favour, more than 5 per cent fewer than in autumn 1933,[161] and this in a process that was designed to secure unanimity. This clear reduction in voter support was discussed by Hitler and his immediate entourage as a matter of concern.[162] The regime's popularity was in decline as power became increasingly concentrated in Hitler's hands.

PART IV

Consolidation

17

Domestic Flashpoints

By the summer of 1934 Hitler had stripped the SA leadership of power, removed the conservative opposition, and taken over the office of Reich President, thereby achieving a significant increase in his own power. But the price was high. Within the SA, an organization that, in spite of many conflicts, had provided Hitler since 1921 with important, indeed vital back-up, 30 June had resulted in general frustration. The middle classes were happy about the removal of the SA and the disruption it caused, but this response was mixed with consternation at the bloody, disproportionate, and unlawful methods Hitler had employed and at the many victims in the conservative camp. From every point of view, the failed putsch in Austria had been a political catastrophe, and, however much Hitler tried to distance himself from events there, the standing of his regime had been damaged. In addition, he had persistent economic problems arising from rearmament, as well as the unresolved issue of the 'reform' of the Protestant Church. Over all, this was not what one would call success.

Responding to this, in many respects dispiriting, situation, Hitler adopted a strategy in the late summer and autumn of 1934 of 'business as usual'. He carried out once again the programme of engagements planned for the previous year. At the beginning of September he made a total of eight speeches at the Party Rally in Nuremberg, which had been expanded since the previous year by additional parades put on by the women's organization, war victims, the Labour Service, and the armed forces.[1] In his speech to 100,000 SA and SS men he attempted to remove the 'shadow' of 30 June from the SA as an organization. His relationship with his SA men was, he assured them, 'exactly the same as it had been for the past 14 years' and he continued to regard the SA and SS as 'guarantors of the National Socialist revolution'.[2] Hitler also seized the opportunity offered by the Party Rally to claim for himself the role of supreme authority in cultural policy, which was yet another battleground within the Party. Conflict had arisen between Goebbels and Alfred Rosenberg, whom Hitler had appointed in January 1934 to be 'responsible for supervising all matters relating to the intellectual and ideological training and education of the NSDAP'. Whereas Rosenberg insisted dogmatically on what was traditionally 'Teutonic' and wished to ban from the German cultural scene anything 'alien' and modern, Goebbels repeatedly advocated integrating specific modern elements. In his speech on culture for this year Hitler criticized both tendencies, the modern 'destroyers of art' as well as those who 'looked backwards' and their 'Germanic art'. This left open the question of what National Socialist culture actually was.[3]

The Party Rally was followed on 30 September by the second Harvest Thanksgiving on the Bückeberg near Hameln, then by the inauguration of Winter Aid on 9 October.[4] On 8 November, at the Munich commemorations of the November 1923 putsch, he once again made a memorial speech in the Bürgerbräukeller, using this opportunity to defend the mistake he had made eleven years previously.[5] This year there was no commemorative march through the city, for 30 June had left gaps that were all too visible.

During the summer and autumn of 1934 the German population was, however, preoccupied with other problems.

The economy in the shadow of rearmament

Although the incipient economic boom at the beginning of 1933 and the impact of work creation measures had at first led to some increase in employment levels, the German economy soon became dangerously unbalanced again. The culprit was the massive rise in expenditure on armaments; it is difficult, however, to provide more than an estimate of spending on armaments in the individual fiscal years because military allocations ceased to be included in the budget and there were numerous instances of concealed armaments spending, for example on infrastructure. Economic historians thus arrive at a variety of results. The British historian Adam Tooze nevertheless gives us a realistic idea of the scale of spending. According to his calculations, the proportion of national income spent on the military rose from less than 1 per cent in 1933 to almost 10 per cent in 1935. This unprecedented development, quite out of line with the norm for a capitalist market economy in peacetime, on the one hand produced a boom in the sectors of the economy directly or indirectly affected and on the other caused serious distortions that the regime had difficulty in controlling.[6]

During the summer and autumn of 1934 the wider population felt the impact of these in the form of price rises as well as through the restricted supply and declining quality of consumer goods. The pressure on foreign exchange caused restrictions on imports, which then led to shortages and disruptions to production in the consumer goods industry.[7] The situation became so critical that at the end of September Hitler was prompted to call on the Reich Minister for Food to produce a report on the development of fat and milk prices. A few months previously he had had a detailed briefing from Darré about the food situation.[8] In addition, since the spring of 1934 the unemployment figures had been reducing only slowly; from April 1934 to spring 1935 they dropped from 2.6 to 2.2 million.[9] This trend was already clearly visible in the summer of 1934, so that Göring, for example, wrote to Seldte, Minister of Labour, on 20 August concerned about the possibility of the unemployment figures rising.[10] Although this did not happen, in the winter of 1934/35 the labour market showed a sharper seasonal fall than in the previous year.

The key role in the steady process of gearing the entire economy to rearmament was played by the new Minister of Economics, Hjalmar Schacht. In his dual capacity as President of the Reichsbank and Reich Economics Minister Schacht's first task was to get a grip on the serious social and economic crisis affecting the country during 1933/34 following the drop in exports. He could then create the conditions for achieving his main aim, one that he shared with Hitler, namely ensuring that rearmament could proceed at the fastest pace possible. Schacht had a decisive hand in a series of measures that marked the start of the regime's new economic strategy. His 'New Plan', agreed with Hitler in August 1934[11] and announced shortly afterwards at the Leipzig Fair,[12] was based on limiting the import of manufactured and consumer goods in favour of essential foodstuffs and animal feeds, and also raw materials and goods needed for armaments.[13] The state moved to a system of rigorous import controls implemented through a closely coordinated network of 'supervisory offices' and at the same time gave subsidies to German exports, which led to businesses being obliged from July 1935 onwards to pay an export contribution.[14] Additionally, foreign trade was reoriented towards countries that were able to deliver raw materials and food, with the result that a system of offsetting could be developed that as far as possible avoided foreign exchange payments. Trade with the United States, Britain, and France was systematically wound down in favour of trading partners who were close geographically, in particular in south-east Europe, as a defence against any future blockade. The oil supplies essential to the Reich from Romania could, for example, be increased five-fold between 1933 and 1936. Thus between 1934 and 1936 Germany succeeded in marginally reducing imports over all, while reducing imports of manufactured goods by a considerable amount.

In the meantime significant progress was made under Schacht in gaining control of business organizations. This process had begun in the summer of 1933, when Schmitt was Minister for Economics, and was an essential precondition for Schacht's increasingly dirigiste approach.[15] He set about gradually imposing an 'organic' structure on the German economy (as it was called, to distinguish it from notions of a corporatist structure), in effect the imposition of membership of an organization embracing all businesses and companies. It encompassed the associations for specific industries, while what had hitherto been chambers of commerce at regional level were concentrated into district chambers of commerce. This created a relatively tightly structured instrument with which the state could control business and commerce.[16] What turned out to be crucial for the financing of the enormous costs of rearmament, however, was the system invented by Schacht of artificially expanding the money supply, the so-called Mefo bills.[17]

These measures went hand in hand with immense efforts to replace imports with home-produced goods. At the Reich Peasants' Rally in Goslar in November 1934 Darré, the Minister of Agriculture and peasants' leader, declared that an agricultural 'production battle' with regard to food production was commencing. In spite of great effort its success was modest, as increased spending power and a growth in population were leading to higher consumption of food. From the end of 1935 onwards foreign exchange had therefore to be diverted from imports of raw materials for industry to imports for the food sector.[18] As part of the desired move to 'autarky' in the German economy, in autumn 1934 Hitler gave his economic advisor Keppler a 'special responsibility for raw materials' and the task of implementing all 'economic measures necessary in the light of the foreign exchange situation to replace raw materials from abroad with those produced at home'.[19] Then in December 1934 Schacht received the legally binding order to conduct a 'thorough search of Reich territory for exploitable resources' and to secure the cooperation of owners of private property in this plan.[20]

Domestic oil extraction was almost doubled between 1933 and 1936.[21] In addition, through the 'petrol contract' of December 1933 and more especially through the establishment of Lignite-Petrol [Braunkohle-Benzin] as a public company by law the following year the Reich took a decisive step towards expanding its production of petrol from coal by means of the so-called hydrogenation process. Yet even so, by 1936 domestic extraction and synthetic fuel accounted for only a quarter of consumption (which was increasing year on year).[22] Considerable effort was also invested in creating 'German textiles' (artificial silk and spun rayon) and in the production of artificial rubber using the so-called Buna process. Between 1933 and 1936 German iron ore extraction increased by a factor of two and a half, but the economy's growing need for iron ore far exceeded what could be extracted. The same was true of most non-precious metals: the increased demand created by the armaments boom could be met only by increasing imports.[23]

The large-scale interventions by the state to boost the economy encouraged inflationary pressures. In order to keep prices under control (wages were already to all intents and purposes frozen) in November 1934 Hitler appointed a Reich commissioner to monitor them. Carl Friedrich Goerdeler, the Oberbürgermeister of Leipzig, was chosen for this role. A former member of the DNVP, he had already held the post, though with considerably fewer powers, under Brüning until the end of 1932. By now the population's dissatisfaction with rising prices when wages were stagnant had become a matter of personal prestige for Hitler. In cabinet on 5 November 1934, when the law to appoint the commissioner was under discussion, he declared he had 'given workers his word not to allow prices to rise'. If he were not to take steps to curb them, employees would 'accuse him of breaking his word'. The result would be 'revolution'.[24]

Failure to 'unite' German Protestantism

Shortages of goods and price increases were not, however, the only causes of dissatisfaction among the population. The regime's policies regarding the Churches were also giving rise to concern.

Although in his speech to the Reichstag of 30 January 1934 Hitler had made much of continuing the 'work of unifying' the Protestant Church, this initiative ultimately led to a dead end. Reich Bishop Müller continued to pursue his 'policy of integration' and, supported by August Jäger, appointed his legal administrator (who since 1933 had been the State Commissioner for the Protestant Churches in Prussia), he was in fact able to bring the majority of the state [Land] churches into line.[25] In the process, however, it became increasingly clear that Jäger (who secured the support of the German Christians) and Müller were not aiming to unite the fragmented Protestant Church but rather to create a supra-confessional German 'National Church', which in the final analysis would mean the replacement of both Christian confessions in Germany by some kind of völkisch 'Germanic Christianity'.[26]

Since the beginning of 1934, however, a broadly-based opposition to the German Christians and Müller's integration policy was forming within the Protestant Church.[27] On 13 March the bishops of the state churches in Württemberg (Theophil Wurm) and Bavaria (Hans Meiser), both members of this opposition movement within the Church, met Hitler,[28] and told him that cooperation with Müller was impossible because he did not abide by existing agreements. Thus they no longer regarded themselves as bound by their declaration of loyalty of 25 January. At a Protestant synod that met from 29 to 31 May 1934 in Wuppertal-Barmen a 'Theological Declaration on the present situation of the German Protestant Church' was issued rejecting the 'erroneous teachings' of the German Christians. After this synod a plethora of confessing congregations was formed, overseen by informal governing bodies called 'councils of brothers', which refused to be governed by the official Church leadership.

After 30 June 1934 Hitler considered that the time had come finally to push through the plan for a unified Protestant 'Reich Church' under Nazi control. On 18 July he received Jäger and Müller and in an official statement announced his support for the continuation of the 'task of unification'.[29]

In his speech opening the Reich Party Rally on 5 September Hitler again emphasized, this time with explicit reference to Martin Luther, that he was determined to put an end to the 'purely organizational fragmentation' of the German Protestant Churches by establishing 'one great Protestant Reich Church'.[30] In a show of support, Hitler made an appearance alongside Müller, whose Reich Church leadership had used a National Synod in August to empower itself to bring rebellious state Churches to heel.[31] In response to complaints from Bishops Wurm and Meiser about the policies of the Reich Church, Hitler had Otto Meissner, the state secretary in the President's office, inform them on 11 September that Müller's measures met with his approval.[32] After the Party Rally and before the end of September the Reich Church leadership appointed Reich commissars in the regional Churches of Württemberg and Bavaria, where German Christians continued to be in the minority. Bishop Meiser in Munich and Bishop Wurm in Stuttgart were both placed under house arrest by the police and it was announced they had been removed from office.[33] In both states, however, Protestant churchgoers, among them many members of the Nazi Party, strongly objected to these measures. There were demonstrations and letters of protest, delegations were sent to the state capitals, and there were threats of mass exits from the Church and the Party.[34] At the beginning of autumn 1934 these conflicts were reaching their climax.

In response to a speech made on 18 September in Hanover on a 'Rome-free German Church' in which Müller demanded a united German national Church bringing together Protestants and Catholics,[35] Foreign Minister Neurath decided to intervene. He summoned Müller and, in view of the consternation caused in Protestant Churches abroad, told him that 'no Church institution could be permitted to threaten the Reich's whole political strategy'. Hitler, continued Neurath, was letting Müller know that 'if he were to continue making speeches like the one in Hanover he would find he no longer had the support of the Reich Chancellor and would have no further access to him'.[36] Although Frick and Meissner were present as representatives of the state when, a few days later, Müller was formally installed as Reich Bishop, Hitler could not bring himself to send so much as a greeting.[37] In the light of the dramatic events in Württemberg and Bavaria the leaders of the Church opposition proclaimed an 'ecclesiastical emergency' at their second confessional synod on 19 and 20 October 1934 in Berlin-Dahlem, on the grounds that the Reich Church leadership had 'removed the Christian foundation of the German Protestant Church'. It was declared that the Reich Church had no authority and a Reich Brotherhood Council was established as the sole 'legitimate' source of leadership within the Church.[38]

Hitler, on the other hand, was still set on the idea of completing the 'work of unification' by means of a symbolic act of submission by the 'Reich Church' to him as the highest authority.[39] A bill was hurriedly prepared providing for an oath of loyalty to be taken by the new leader of the Protestant Church to the 'Führer of the German Reich and nation...as is fitting for one appointed to serve in the German Protestant Church'.[40] It was not until 19 October, the day the Dahlem synod began, that Hitler decided to give up the idea of swearing in the Reich Bishop and postpone the reception to 25 October.[41] He left unanswered the increasingly urgent requests of the Bavarian government to release Meiser from his house arrest.[42] During this period he was shown reports from the German ambassador in London stating that the Archbishop of Canterbury had clearly indicated that public protests from Protestant Churches outside Germany were on the cards, if the bishops were not immediately set at liberty.[43] Hitler discussed the matter at length three times with Goebbels but could still not make up his mind to abandon the Reich Bishop, as his Propaganda Minister urged.[44] Then on 24 October a submission by the Reich Justice Minister Gürtner tipped the scales; he had the task of telling Hitler that a Supreme Court trial, in which Pastor Martin Niemöller was challenging his dismissal from his post in Dahlem, would probably be decided in Niemöller's favour. The expectation was, according to Gürtner, that in the explanation for its judgment the Court would cast doubt in principle on the legal basis underlying the Reich Church leadership's 'work of unification'. This would represent a public rebuke to Hitler, since he had given such open support to Müller's and Jäger's strategy.[45]

On 25 October – the Reich Bishop was due to be received at 5 p.m. – Hitler decided literally at the last minute to cancel the appointment and remove the former SA leader Pfeffer, who since March had been Hitler's special appointee for Church matters. Müller had no choice but to announce at the last moment to the senior Church functionaries who had gathered for the ceremony that Hitler was suffering an attack of toothache and could regrettably not be present. Jäger's resignation was inevitable, whereas Müller, though clearly damaged, was able to continue in office.

On 25 October the house arrest imposed on Meiser and Wurm was lifted. Both Church dignitaries as well as August Marahrens, bishop of the Hanover state Church and similarly representing a Church not dominated by German Christians, were invited to a meeting in the Reich Chancellery. There Hitler told them that the measures taken against the state Churches had been in breach of the Church constitution and were null and void. Hitler then conceded that his plan to set up a 'Unified Reich Church' had failed. He would now withdraw from active Church politics and leave the Churches to go their own way, though they could no longer count on any financial support from the state.[46]

At a conference of Reich Governors on 1 November Hitler justified his retreat primarily as the result of his having gained the impression that the Church constitution had been contravened by the Reich Church. According to the minutes, he as 'Führer' and Reich Chancellor had 'intended to create a single, strong Protestant Church. Evidently, some of the clergy did not want that.'[47] In the months following he consistently refused to receive representatives of the Protestant Church and tended to treat Church issues in a dilatory manner.[48]

Yet it was in fact Hitler himself who had caused the 'unification' of the Protestant Church to escalate to the point where strong opposition forced him publicly to admit the failure of his policy, to abandon the Müller/Jäger partnership that he had supported, and in effect to apologize to the bishops opposing his policy. This was caused by his inadequate understanding of the actual power relationships in the Protestant Church, by his indecisive attitude towards Müller and Jäger, and finally by his indecision about whether he should create a strong Reich Church by intervening in Church policy or whether he should not rather be guided by his radical anti-Christian views and aim to weaken the Churches. That would have fitted in with the slogan he produced in August 1933: 'We shall become a Church.'

A crisis of confidence and a show of loyalty

The conflicts over the 'Reich Church' had damaged Hitler's reputation, showing him to be anything but an omnipotent 'Führer', including in circles that were not directly affected by the constitution of the Protestant Church. For these people had taken precise note of his ultimately fruitless dithering between his supposed neutrality in these matters and his radical impulses. Although the concerns discussed above about economic developments became less acute towards the end of the year (fears of what the winter might bring proved in the event illusory), they were replaced by other sources of discontent. Thus the 'purge' that had taken place on 30 June had not removed from public consciousness the problems caused by the arrogant bearing of Party functionaries and their over-zealous methods. On the contrary, criticism of individual functionaries as 'bigwigs' was now increasingly being applied to the whole 'movement'. Moreover, during the final months of 1934 tensions between the armed forces and the Party were growing. The establishment in the autumn of 1934 of an armed SS unit, which was Hitler's way of recognizing the key role played by the SS on 30 June 1934, was inevitably regarded by the military as a breach of Hitler's assurance that the army was 'the nation's sole bearer of arms'. In the end they had to put up with the SS's plans to set up an SS division equipped for military combat, but they attempted through tough negotiating to delay it. At the same time, criticism of the military was being voiced in Party circles, because it was unwilling to submit to the Party's claim to total power. From the standpoint of the Party machine, the regime's plan to introduce conscription was a reason to fear a further increase in the armed forces' influence, and since the autumn of 1934 this conflict of interests had led to frequent clashes between forces' personnel and members of Nazi organizations. Rumours circulated of plans for a military putsch or of a 'major move' by the SS and appeared in the foreign press.[49] Adding to the confusion was the fact that between the end of November and the middle of December Hitler reduced the frequency of his public appearances, causing speculation about an assassination attempt.[50] An official statement issued on 27 November, contradicting rumours spread by foreign newspapers about Blomberg, Commander-in-Chief Werner von Fritsch, and Walter von Reichenau (effectively the Chief of the General Staff), and also denying reports of tensions between Goebbels and the army, inevitably seemed to any newspaper reader who had learned to read between the lines to be a positive confirmation of those assertions.[51]

On 1 December in a speech in Rheinhausen Göring felt obliged to warn about 'traitors' who were trying 'to undermine the nation's confidence in the Führer'. The announcement two days later of the dismissal of the Gauleiter of Silesia, Helmuth Brückner, for 'behaviour damaging to the Party' and the following day of Gottfried Feder, state secretary in the Ministry of Economics (the 'economic theorist' of the Party since its earliest days was totally unacceptable to Schacht, the new Minister for Economics), did nothing to calm the situation, in particular because in both cases no details about the reasons for the dismissals were given.[52] Well-informed readers of the *Völkischer Beobachter* might well ask themselves why Defence Minister Blomberg thought it necessary to use an interview printed on 27 December in the main Party organ to declare once again his 'complete agreement' with Lutze, chief of staff of the SA, about the armed forces' role as 'the nation's bearer of arms'.[53]

It was evident that the regime was facing a situation in which it was losing control of public opinion. Local incidents, actual and manufactured conflicts, planned intrigues, general discontents, cryptic news reports about the dismissal of functionaries, fears and rumours, vague and yet significant denials, and defiant posturing all went into the pot to produce a negative mood. Added to the general nervousness was the widespread fear among the population that, as on 30 June 1934, the regime might be working up to a shock move that would solve the accumulated problems by violent means.

This situation of diverse and conflicting interests was precarious not least because at the end of 1934 a further major event, the consequences of which were impossible to discern, cast a long shadow. On 13 January 1935 in the Saar region a referendum was due to take place on whether in future the disputed territory, which under the Versailles treaty was subject to the League of Nations, should be part of Germany or France or should finally be given its independence. After the failure of the Austrian putsch, the Reich's international situation was in any case extremely tense. For many people the imminent referendum raised the spectre of an armed conflict with France and there were signs of a developing 'war psychosis'.[54] The regime intervened massively in the referendum campaign, and with Reich support the Nazi 'German Front' succeeded in taking almost complete control of the campaign in the region, with its population of 800,000, and in largely neutralizing the Unity Front (consisting for the most part of SPD, KPD, and parts of the Centre), which was advocating independence for the Saar region. At the same time mass demonstrations in support of the annexation of the Saar region took place in south-west Germany. The initial climax was a mass rally at Ehrenbreitstein in Koblenz; on 26 August 1934 Hitler spoke there to a crowd of 200,000, more than half of whom had been transported specially for the occasion from the Saar.[55]

The uncertain situation prompted the regime to hold a surprise 'rally of German leaders' at the Berlin State Opera House ten days before the vote.[56] Cabinet ministers, Gauleiters and Reichsleiters,* along with other top Party functionaries and military leaders took part. Speaking about the coming vote in his address, Hitler went 'into detail about the flood of lies' that had again been 'unleashed of late against the Reich' and appealed to the unity of the nation in its 'indissoluble solidarity in sharing one destiny'. Demonstrations of loyalty from Göring and Hess rounded off the noteworthy occasion.[57] All the same, Hitler was still worried, as he confided to Goebbels: 'After the Saar Paris will keep trying to blackmail us. 1935 will be a difficult year. We shall have to keep our nerve.'[58]

---

* Translators' note: The title 'Reichsleiter', lit. Reich Head was rather arbitrarily given to a number of top Party functionaries in charge of various departments.

By any sober assessment, two years after the 'seizure of power' the regime was at a low ebb. Hitler's plan to reset the domestic political agenda in line with his own thinking by means of the shock tactic of 30 June 1934 had failed. Foreign policy developments in the following months were, however, to push the deep-rooted domestic problems into the background.

18

Initial Foreign Policy Successes

On 13 January 1935 Hitler could chalk up one important success on the way to revising the post-war order, for on that day almost 91 per cent of those eligible to vote voted for the Saar territory to be annexed to the German Reich.[1] On the Tuesday after the referendum, when the results of the voting were known, Goebbels organized extravagant celebrations all over the Reich at which the population had to gather in 'large and spontaneous [sic!] demonstrations on the occasion of the Saar election victory'.[2] This victory was not, however, a sign of confidence in the regime, as the propaganda chief wished to persuade everyone, but rather reflected above all the population's own sense of which nation they belonged to and their desire to put the Treaty of Versailles behind them. For most natives of the Saar region it was unthinkable to be annexed to France, even for the Catholics and members of left-wing parties, and any future as an independent entity promised to be politically unstable and economically uncertain. Blatant National Socialist election propaganda during the campaign had played its part in convincing people in the end that reintegration with Germany was the only viable option. As he had already assured the French in talks in the run-up to the vote, Hitler also stated in a radio broadcast to the German people in the evening on 13 January that 'the German Reich will make no further territorial demands on France'. In the days following he was to repeat this declaration emphatically in press interviews with foreign journalists.[3]

Hitler attached great expectations to the victory in the Saar. On 20 January he discussed foreign policy with Goebbels, who noted: 'Far-reaching project regarding England. Protection of Empire, in return alliance for 30 years. Still developing. He's very taken up with it.... Poland is firmly on our side. France and England are getting ready to blackmail us. But we'll not give way.' As Goebbels noted the day after the previous lunchtime conversation,

'Foreign policy and armaments are still the main problems today. We must get more power. Everything else will fall into place.'[4]

Because of the Saar referendum the Geneva disarmament talks had been suspended in November 1934. Now France and Britain made new efforts to get negotiations moving again. On 3 February 1935 both governments put forward a proposal to replace the disarmament terms of the Treaty of Versailles with an international arms agreement and to initiate a defence pact to counter air attacks. The Reich government's response was broadly positive and it suggested talks with representatives of the British government.[5] The Foreign Secretary Sir John Simon and Lord Privy Seal Anthony Eden were invited to Berlin for 7 March. When, however, at the beginning of March the British government published a White Paper naming German rearmament as the reason for increasing British military expenditure, Hitler cancelled the talks at short notice, giving as an excuse that he was recovering from a throat infection.[6]

According to official reports, Hitler had caught a cold on 1 March at the extensive 'liberation celebrations' that had taken place to mark the official return of the Saar to the Reich by the League of Nations. On a day of persistent rain in Saarbrücken he had attended a march-past of Party formations, police units, and his personal bodyguard and made a speech in the town hall square in which he again called on the French to maintain peace.[7] Hitler then went to Berchtesgaden for a week to recover, after which he spent a few days taking a cure in Wiesbaden. Hitler's persistent cold was in fact more than just a diplomatically motivated indisposition. On 23 May he had to undergo an operation. The real cause of the hoarseness he had suffered from in recent months was a polyp, which was removed from his right vocal cord. The postponement of the British politicians' visit was, however, due above all to the fact that Hitler had been planning two 'surprises' ahead of it: the official announcement of the existence of a German air force and the introduction of conscription, both decisions that he wanted finally settled before beginning talks with the high-ranking British delegation.[8]

Since February there had been agreement between Hitler and the military leadership to stop concealing the expansion of the air force. They now judged that the new arm could be used to strengthen the Reich's hand in foreign policy. On 26 February the cabinet approved a secret Führer decree prepared by Göring about Reich aviation and justifying an air force as a third branch of the Wehrmacht;[9] on 10 March in an interview for the *Daily Mail* Göring officially announced the existence of a new German air force.[10]

Only a few days later, on 14 March, Hitler surprised his army adjutant Friedrich Hossbach by telling him he intended to introduce conscription very soon. The timing seemed right, he said, for the next day the French National Assembly would increase military service from one year to two and this would serve as the perfect pretext for German 'counter-measures'. When Hitler asked how large the leaders of the military were aiming to make the army, Hossbach gave the figure of thirty-six divisions, although in fact, according to their internal discussions, they were not aiming to achieve this for several years. Hitler, however, seized on Hossbach's figure without further consultation with military leaders and officially established thirty-six as the number of divisions the German army should be aiming to create.[11]

At first Blomberg, the Minister of Defence, and Werner von Fritsch, the head of the army high command, were doubtful about the wisdom of this rapid expansion, and Blomberg is reported to have made this clear on the evening of 15 March at a meeting chaired by Hitler of a number of cabinet colleagues. Yet the very next day both Blomberg and Fritsch withdrew their objections after personal interviews with Hitler,[12] for in the final analysis the introduction of conscription was a prerequisite for the generals' plans to enlarge the army.[13] The official decision was made at a cabinet meeting on 16 March, at which Blomberg got so carried away that he called for three 'Heil Hitlers'.[14] The next day at the ceremonies to mark 'Heroes' Memorial Day', as the National Day of Mourning had been officially renamed the previous year,[15] Blomberg took the opportunity of his speech in the Berlin State Opera House to assure his audience that Germany would now once more be able to 'take its rightful place among the nations'. Still prevented by hoarseness from speaking in public, Hitler observed proceedings from the royal box, after which he took the salute at a military parade in Unter den Linden.[16]

On 18 March, a Saturday afternoon, Hitler received the ambassadors of France, Britain, Italy, and Poland and told them of the Reich government's decision.[17] The British ambassador asked whether the Germans were still willing to attend the talks agreed in the communiqué of 3 February, and, when Neurath said they were, gave an assurance that the British ministers' visit would go ahead. This response gave a clear indication to the Germans that they need fear no political backlash from Britain. The same day Hitler announced his decision to the German nation in a lengthy declaration.[18] At the talks that Simon and Eden held as planned with Hitler on 25 and 26 March they realized that he could not be persuaded to commit to anything binding regarding Germany's possible participation in international agreements or arms limitations.[19] During the two days of negotiations Eden found Hitler's manner 'decidedly more authoritative' than at their first meeting more than a year previously; boosted by German rearmament he had constantly, and longwindedly, ratcheted up his conditions for a return to the League of Nations or binding armament restrictions, while offering nothing worthwhile in return.[20]

At a conference convened in Stresa in the middle of April, the heads of government of Italy, France, and Britain issued a joint declaration, stating that 'any unilateral termination of treaties' would be dealt with by 'all appropriate means'.[21] On 17 April the Council of the League of Nations confirmed this declaration with the statement that Germany had contravened the Treaty of Versailles and was endangering the security of Europe.[22] On 2 May 1935 France and the Soviet Union concluded a military pact. Yet none of these, on the whole moderate, responses to German remilitarization made Hitler change his rearmament policy in any fundamental way. On the contrary: as Goebbels, with whom Hitler discussed the foreign policy situation on various occasions following the British visit, records in his notes, the Chancellor was instead looking for opportunities to divide his opponents.

Hitler took Mussolini to be only bluffing when, according to Ulrich von Hassell, the German ambassador in Rome, the Italian leader claimed that war between the western powers and Hitler was inevitable. Even so, Hitler's response was, 'We're not ready. We need peace for a long time yet.'[23] He did not discount the possibility that Mussolini might 'suddenly do something stupid and set things off'. According to Goebbels's diary entries, Hitler was concerned that the French might intervene. They could be prompted to do so if Mussolini 'did something rash': 'So we must be careful and not allow ourselves to be provoked.'[24] Mussolini's own unmistakable preparations for war against the Ethiopian Empire were, however, also liable to create an international crisis from which the German Reich could profit, if it offered Mussolini support.[25] The Propaganda Ministry had been repeatedly warning the German press since February 1935 not to criticize Italy's policy towards Abyssinia.[26] On 15 May Goebbels recorded the following from a discussion with Hitler: 'Mussolini seems to have got himself entangled in Abyssinia.... He's seeking our friendship again.'[27]

The aim of removing Italy from the Stresa front was a vital motive for Hitler's speech, again styled a 'peace speech' by German propaganda, to the Reichstag on 21 May.[28] On this occasion Hitler made the declaration Italy had long been hoping for, that he respected Austria's borders. Mussolini responded immediately to this signal, referring in a meeting with the German ambassador to the possibility of German–Italian rapprochement.[29] On 25 May the German press received an instruction 'in future to avoid any friction with Italy on any subject'.[30] Hitler's speech on 21 May also contained an important concession to Britain; among other things he declared that Germany was prepared to limit its naval tonnage to 35 per cent of Britain's. On the other hand, he attacked France by asserting that Germany's western neighbour was threatening the Locarno Treaties by making a treaty with the Soviet Union (which Hitler called a 'military alliance'). In addition, he called into question the demilitarization of the Rhineland by referring to the continuing 'expansion of troop numbers' on the French side. He rejected the resolution of the League of Nations of 17 April on the reintroduction of conscription. He also expressed his support for détente in Europe in countless different formulations and produced a dazzling array of confidence-inspiring proposals: non-aggression pacts with other neighbours, an aviation treaty, agreements on arms limitation and a total ban on particular weapons systems, a limit on gun calibres and shipbuilding, an international non-intervention treaty, to name but a few. In reality, however, this speech, ostensibly about peace, was an attempt to divert the Stresa powers from Germany's policy of massive rearmament and to divide it as a 'front'.

This becomes especially clear given that on the afternoon immediately before the speech the cabinet had passed a defence law that, amongst other things, entitled Hitler to prescribe the duration of active military service in peacetime. The same day he used a Führer decree to introduce a period of service of one year.[31] At the same meeting the cabinet signed off specific laws (not meant for publication) that provided for far-reaching measures in the event of a war. They concerned the transfer of executive power to the Chancellor if war was imminent, the arrangements for mobilization, the appointment of a plenipotentiary for the war economy, also the creation of a Reich defence council in the event of war, the introduction of civilian conscription, as well as an obligation on the part of citizens to contribute materially and financially to the war effort.[32] The contrast with Hitler's assurances about peace could not have been more stark.

Nor did Hitler's offer to Britain to limit the size of the German navy to 35 per cent of that of the British navy indicate any actual self-restraint. As the background to this proposal makes clear, it was in fact only a staging post on the journey to planned naval expansion and in no way ruled out a later maritime arms race.

Towards the end of the Weimar Republic the German navy had already begun a programme of rearmament calculated to exceed the restrictions imposed by the Treaty of Versailles. The plan was to restore Germany as a future sea power, on exactly the same lines as the naval policies of the pre-war period.[33] After writing *Mein Kampf* Hitler had in fact opposed any large-scale expansion of the German navy and held to this view up to 1933.[34] After coming to power, however, he supported naval rearmament for he had been persuaded by the naval chiefs' argument that an effective navy was a precondition for Germany being able to prove to the British that it was 'fit to be an ally'.[35]

After the signing of the non-aggression treaty with Poland in January 1934, naval chiefs began to concentrate more on issues relating to war in the North Sea rather than in the Baltic. Early in 1934 the navy commissioned a series of warships that blatantly exceeded the tonnage stipulated in the Treaty of Versailles, and in March a schedule for construction was set up that raised the number of warships far above the limit the Treaty imposed and was heading for parity with the French fleet. The project was couched in terms of the future German navy being strengthened to the point of being a third the strength of the British navy, the most powerful naval fighting force in the world. The ratio of 3 to 1 (strictly speaking of 100 to 35) governing the strength of the British navy in relation to the French or Italian navy was the key agreement reached by the sea powers at the naval conference in Washington in 1922. The naval chiefs, and under their influence Hitler, had been aiming since the spring of 1934 to reach this magic 35 per cent too. The general expectation was that the next international naval conference, scheduled for 1935, would finally make the restrictions of the Treaty of Versailles obsolete.[36] At the same time, Hitler agreed in June 1934 with Neurath and the military chiefs that they should keep a low profile at this conference and establish the desired quota by means of a bilateral agreement with Britain, their strategy being that such an agreement on the part of the most important naval power in the world would in effect sanction this open flouting of a further set of provisions in the Treaty of Versailles.[37]

On 27 June, a short time after this meeting, Admiral Raeder persuaded Hitler that the tonnage of two cruisers under construction should be greatly increased and that they should be more heavily armed.[38] The outcome of this discussion makes it clear that at this point both men envisaged a fleet that within a few years would be more than one-third the size of the British fleet. Among naval chiefs there was already talk of a ratio of 1 to 2, parity with France once again being used as a justification. According to his own notes on the meeting, Raeder also expressed the view that at some future time the fleet would have to be deployed against Britain. Thus the notion of being 'fit to be an ally' could be understood in a variety of ways.

Officially, however, the 3 to 1 ratio was still being observed. Hitler's meeting on 27 November 1934 with Sir Eric Phipps, the British ambassador, marks the point at which talks began with Britain.[39] During the visit of Simon and Eden in late March 1935, the issue of a ratio of 100 to 35 was then discussed in detail,[40] and, after the British had taken cognizance of Hitler's proposal of 21 May, Ribbentrop, who had been appointed by Hitler to be a 'special representative and ambassador at large',[41] commenced negotiations in London on 4 June. They led relatively quickly, in fact by 18 June, to a naval treaty based on the ratio of 100 to 35.[42]

Whereas Hitler had assumed since the 1920s that he could achieve an alliance with Britain without a sizeable navy, from 1933 onwards, influenced by the naval chiefs, he gradually changed his view. Now a fleet, albeit still restricted, of large warships was to make the Reich 'fit to be an ally'. In the final analysis, however, the continued German naval rearmament was designed to challenge the dominance of the British fleet. Now the alliance Germany was aiming for was to be gained precisely through the pressure of naval strength. Thus Germany's naval policy culminated in open rivalry with the world's greatest sea power, bringing with it an increasing risk of a maritime war, although without anyone on the German side having a clear idea of how such a war might be waged.

For this arms race demonstrated that the thinking behind German policy, both with regard to material resources and to the opportunities of deploying the new weaponry in a war situation, was largely illusory. The gathering momentum of rearmament dragged German naval policy along with it. Hitler meanwhile did all he could to quicken the pace, on the one hand through his megalomaniacal plans, based on rapidly changing and hypothetical networks of alliances, to give Germany the status of a great power, and on the other hand by his absorption in the minutiae of naval technology and grandiose fantasies of warships.

As far as Britain was concerned, the naval agreement was not a first step, as Hitler had hoped, towards an alliance. The British government viewed it rather as the first step towards tying Germany for the long term into a collective European security system, for the sake of which it was prepared to give up the idea of an alliance to contain Germany. Although in breaking up the 'Stresa front' through the naval agreement, Hitler had achieved an important foreign policy success, what he was aiming for, namely to establish separate spheres of interest for Britain (its colonial empire) and Germany (hegemony in continental Europe) was precisely what Britain would not accept.

In addition to rapprochement with Britain and his hopes of friendly relations with Italy, Hitler focused his ambitions in 1935 on another country, the Polish Republic, with whose help he hoped finally to break out of Germany's international isolation.

After signing the German–Polish non-aggression pact in January 1934, the German leadership had taken the initial steps towards developing a far-reaching alliance with its new partner, based on their joint expansion at the expense of the Soviet Union. The policy being pursued can be found in a memorandum composed in May 1934 by Rosenberg and endorsed by Hitler. In the event of a clash between the Soviet Union and Japan, Rosenberg wrote, a genuine cooperation between Britain, Poland, and Germany might result and Poland could be guaranteed expansion towards the Black Sea. Rosenberg's intention was to offer Poland this option as part of a general overhaul of German–Polish relations. In other words his aim was to use Ukrainian territory as compensation for a revision of the German–Polish border.[43]

These ideas were by no means just castles in the air but practical political considerations. At the end of January 1935 Göring travelled to Poland in response to a hunting invitation, but in reality he was on a serious political mission. He had been instructed by Hitler to indicate to his Polish hosts that a shared policy of German–Polish expansion in eastern Europe was a possibility, with Poland standing to gain territory in the Ukraine and Lithuania and Germany expanding 'north-eastwards'. The extension of Polish territory was quite obviously intended as compensation for the return of former German territory in western Poland. Göring had in fact hinted the same to the Polish ambassador Lipski and the Polish leader, Pilsudski. The Poles had not responded, however.[44]

When Marshall Pilsudski died on 12 May 1935, the German leadership began to doubt whether Poland would continue to cooperate with Germany.[45]

Hitler hastened to send President Ignacy Moscicki a long telegram of condolence during the night of 12/13 May.[46] On 13 May Goebbels spoke to Hitler about the situation arising from Pilsudski's death and the following day they continued the discussion and were joined by Göring and Hitler's foreign policy adviser, Joachim von Ribbentrop. Goebbels's notes make clear how volatile Hitler and the most senior leaders considered the international situation to be. 'Poland crucial. 1936 and in particular 1937 dangerous. We're getting ready for anything. Even for the remotest possibility. Rearm. Rearm!'[47]

On 18 May Hitler and numerous other prominent Nazis paid their respects to the deceased, who was after all the head of the only state friendly to Germany, at a memorial service at St Hedwig's Cathedral in Berlin. Throughout the Reich flags were flown at half-mast. Hitler sent Göring to the funeral in Warsaw. He returned to Berlin with reassuring news: as Goebbels again noted, the Foreign Minister Jozef Beck had confirmed to Göring that Poland was 'sticking firmly to its treaty with us'.[48] Yet during his journey Göring had come to the conclusion that the Polish government was still seeking close relations with France and that further rapprochement between Germany and Poland and any adoption of a common policy such as he had outlined in January were possible only after a settlement to the dispute over Danzig [Gdansk]. This was the message he gave Hitler when he returned and in the months following he took on the role of coordinator of German policies regarding Poland and Danzig.[49]

On 22 May, after the memorial service, Hitler received Lipski, the Polish ambassador. In his 'peace speech' to the Reichstag the previous day he had commented positively and at some length on German–Polish relations. Now in his meeting with Lipski he again brought up the 'space question' as the crucial problem for the future. Germany, he said, was searching for territory for its growing population, space that Poland did not possess and was not in a position to offer. By comparison with these problems the issue of the Polish Corridor was of lesser importance. One day in the future, not today but perhaps in about fifteen years, they could consider a special railway line and a motorway link. This idea, which Hitler came out with fairly casually, soon afterwards became central to his thinking about German–Polish relations, not to mention the starting point for a policy of threats and blackmail that intensified as relations with Germany's eastern neighbour cooled during the following years.[50] When at the beginning of July 1935 Beck came on an official visit to Berlin he was at least in accord with Hitler in wanting to deepen relations on the basis of the agreement of January 1934.[51]

Since January 1935 Hitler's regime had achieved some important foreign policy successes. The Saar territory had been regained with the support of an overwhelming majority; conscription and an air force had been introduced without any significant negative consequences in foreign policy terms. Above all, it looked as though Germany's international isolation could be overcome. The Anglo–German naval agreement was one concrete result, while relations with Poland and now with Italy were shaping up well.

It would, however, be a mistake to assume that these foreign policy successes had any lasting positive impact on the domestic situation in Germany. Although for a few months they obscured the various problems (the Churches, criticism of the Party, economic difficulties, to name but a few) that had caused such trouble at the end of 1934, these and other unsolved problems were soon back on the political agenda.

19

The Road to the Nuremberg Laws

On 7 April elections were held in the Free City of Danzig, a Nazi stronghold. Although the NSDAP achieved 59.3 per cent of the vote, 9.2 per cent more than in 1933, the result still lagged far behind the extremely high level of approval that had become usual in the Reich and seriously disappointed the leadership.[1] Not only had the Danzig NSDAP received massive help from the Reich Party, the Nazi government of Danzig had given significant support to the NSDAP and tried to sabotage the electoral campaigns of the opposition parties. When the opposition contested the election result, the Danzig high court established that there had been considerable electoral interference, indeed nothing short of vote rigging. Although no rerun of the election was ordered,[2] the NSDAP's result was reduced by several percentage points. If this vote rigging is taken into account, approval ratings for the Party in 1935 were barely higher than in 1933, in fact they were probably lower. The Danzig result indicates that the Nazis had made little progress in taking support from their political opponents or in engaging the mass of the politically apathetic.

That may well have been true of the Reich itself, for euphoria there about the incorporation of the Saar, the establishment of an air force, and the reintroduction of conscription soon dispersed and international responses such as the Stresa front and the Franco–Soviet alliance aroused instead apprehension and the fear of war. Although gradual economic growth had been discernible since February and seemed to produce a general mood of spring optimism,[3] the imbalance between price rises and low wages coupled with very modest standards of living remained unchanged. Among many sections of the population the impression was taking hold that the regime was not prepared to pass on the benefits of the economic upturn to the mass of the people. The gulf between reality and the 'national community' that was invoked so frequently by the regime was only too evident. Although elections to the 'councils of trust',★ declared by the regime to be a demonstration of loyalty to the regime, secured a higher turnout than in the previous year, the official 80 per cent recorded as being positive most probably far exceeded the real result. The spirit of optimism that the regime produced in its initial phase through a constant round of propaganda campaigns, mass rallies, and ceremonial, had long since dissipated.[4]

Hostility to Jews, the Churches, 'reactionaries': unrest among Party members

The positive messages issued during the previous months had, however, succeeded in creating a triumphalist mood, particularly among the radical Party activists. It was therefore no accident that the first months of 1935 saw an increase in attacks on those groups that the rank and file of the Party already had in their sights from the previous year, namely Jews, the Churches, and 'reactionaries'.

Although the boycott of Jewish businesses in April 1933 had been limited officially to one day, Party activists had never ceased disrupting the work of Jewish business people to a greater or lesser extent. Away from the major cities it is fair to say that something like guerrilla warfare was being waged against Jewish businesses, resulting in frequent violent assaults on Jewish citizens.[5] During the Christmas period in 1934 these attacks had grown worse. After the Saar referendum and the reintroduction of conscription in March, they were deliberately provoked, with the Party press actively inciting people to violence. In the Party there were increasingly strident demands for Jews to be excluded completely from the economy, as well as for so-called 'racial disgrace', in other words sexual relations between Jews and non-Jews, to be stopped. In municipal swimming pools, parks, and on the entry to towns and villages all over the Reich signs with the words 'Jews not welcome' sprang up, a phenomenon Hitler expressly sanctioned when asked about it by his adjutant.[6] The campaign was matched by a series of

★ Translators' note: These were a regime substitute for the 'works' councils' dominated by the left-wing parties.

anti-Jewish measures introduced by the authorities from the beginning of 1935 onwards.[7]

The campaign against the Churches began in the middle of January, immediately after the Saar referendum, during which the Party had been glad of support from the Catholic Church in particular.[8] Yet when, two weeks after the Saar vote, the next round of negotiations over the Concordat began, the Papal Nuncio was forced to acknowledge that, as far as the future status of Catholic associations was concerned, Hitler was not remotely prepared to relinquish the position that had been reached in 1934. At that time the Vatican had deemed what had been negotiated to be unacceptable; Hitler now demanded further concessions from the Church: its, to him, objectionable associations were to disappear completely as independent entities. The activities they had been involved in hitherto, now restricted to narrowly defined religious and pastoral matters, could continue at best in individual parishes.[9] In addition, since the beginning of 1935 the regime had been trying to squeeze out Church-sponsored state primary schools, even though they were in fact protected by the Concordat, in favour of community schools,[10] and in March it began systematically to investigate Catholic priests on the grounds of alleged or actual infringements of currency regulations arising from international money transactions by Catholic religious orders. These investigations led to a series of trials.[11]

In February and March the German Faith Movement, composed of adherents of emphatically non-Christian groups espousing a völkisch religion, became active with the regime's approval. These believers in a völkisch religion took up an aggressively anti-Christian and anti-Church stance at numerous events.[12] When in March 1935 the Confessing Church wished to engage critically with this 'new paganism' the Interior Ministry forbade any reference to it in churches and had hundreds of clergy arrested.[13] In March the Protestant Churches in Prussia also had to accept the state intervening in their internal disputes by creating special finance departments that took over the distribution of money.[14]

The growing confidence of radical Party activists also emerged through further conflict with the 'forces of reaction'. The main objective was finally to neutralize the Stahlhelm.[15] From April onwards the organization had faced a ban on its activities in a number of regions and in May it was forbidden to parade anywhere in the Reich.[16]

Yet from April/May 1935 onwards the regime began to restrain anti-Semitic attacks[17] and shortly afterwards started being less aggressive towards the Churches. One reason for this change of direction was the fear that these campaigns would in time damage business. Schacht, the Economics Minister, warned Hitler emphatically at the beginning of May about threats to German exports, naming the conflict with the Churches, the 'Jewish question', and the activities of the Gestapo as the three most critical aspects of the problem.[18] The other more crucial reason had to do with foreign policy. The formation in April of the Stresa Front, coupled with the Franco–Soviet military pact in May, exacerbated Germany's political isolation internationally, and at the same time the regime did not want anything to upset the current naval negotiations with Britain. Clear signals were coming from Britain that German persecution of the Jews would prove an obstacle to Anglo–German relations.[19]

The measures being taken against Christians in Germany, as well as reports of the persecution of the Jews, led to growing concern in a number of Protestant Churches outside Germany, which had been alerted in particular by members of the Confessing Church. George Bell, the Bishop of Chichester and President of the Ecumenical Council for Practical Christianity, had long been the central figure in this movement of protest and solidarity.[20] In June 1935, while Germany's naval negotiations with Britain were in train, Bell wrote to Ribbentrop, Hitler's special envoy, warning him that outrage in the Anglican Church over the oppression of Christians in Germany might result in 'the opportunity for friendship between Britain and Germany being lost for a very long time'.[21] Bell expressed the same sentiment in a letter to *The Times* on 3 June.

These warnings had an impact. All the Protestant clergy who had been detained in concentration camps were released by the end of May,[22] after which Hitler also called a temporary halt to the foreign currency trials in June.[23] On 20 June Ribbentrop listened to Bell's complaints when they met and assured him that he was very anxious that public opinion in Britain should not turn against Germany.[24]

Meanwhile, the summer of 1935 showed clearly how precarious many Germans thought the economic situation to be.[25] In July Interior Minister, Frick, responding to reports from various parts of the Reich, informed Hans Heinrich Lammers, the head of the Reich Chancellery, that for three months there had been a surge in prices, 'which in view of wage stagnation has a very negative impact on the population's mood, particularly among the working classes.'[26] In August the Agriculture Minister also sent the Chancellery detailed and worrying reports about increases in the price of food.[27] In spite of this public mood, a month later the trustees of labour opposed any wage increases: 'Fighting unemployment and rearming the German nation must take priority...'[28]

At the end of September Hitler had in his hands a detailed analysis produced by the Reich Chancellery of the development of incomes, prices, and food supplies.[29] According to this, while wages had not risen, the cost of living on 21 August 1935 as compared with the summer of 1933 had increased by 5.4 per cent and the price of food by 8.1 per cent. Deciding how these price rises could be brought under control led to conflict within the regime. In view of the precarious situation Goerdeler, the Prices Commissioner, whose fixed term of office came to an end on 1 July 1935, asked Hitler to extend it and also to expand his powers. A number of ministers expressed their reservations. Hitler at first set aside any discussion of these disagreements and gave instructions at the beginning of August that Goerdeler's powers should for the time being be exercised by the relevant ministries.[30]

Against the background of this tense situation, in June Party activists had resumed the anti-Jewish campaign they had interrupted during the Anglo–German naval negotiations. Events in Berlin served as a catalyst. Goebbels, the Gauleiter of Berlin, had long been pondering the possibilities of taking more radical steps against the Jewish residents of the capital and had tried repeatedly to secure Hitler's approval. His impression was that he had been successful.[31] In June members of the Hitler Youth were repeatedly forming gangs outside Jewish shops in Berlin. On 30 June Goebbels raised the temperature at the Gau Party Rally by publicly denouncing the fact that 'at the moment Jews are trying to throw their weight around on every street'.[32] In the middle of July he saw his opportunity to create a blatant pogrom atmosphere in Berlin. The pretext for doing so was a Swedish anti-Semitic film that had allegedly been booed by Jewish members of the cinema audience. The Party press immediately seized on this incident and the Berlin NSDAP organized a 'counter-demonstration'. On the evening of 15 July 'outraged national comrades' attacked Jewish citizens, which led amongst other things to confrontations between Party members and the police, for the latter were unsure how to handle this 'outburst of spontaneous national indignation'. In the international press the assaults were reported as 'violent incidents in the Kurfürstendamm'. Goebbels managed to pin the blame on Magnus Levetzow, the Berlin police chief, whom he had long been trying to get rid of, and succeeded in having his friend Wolf-Heinrich von Helldorff appointed his successor. The 19 July edition of *Der Angriff* indicated the direction Goebbels intended to take: 'Berlin cleansed of communists, reactionaries, and Jews. Dr Goebbels makes a clean sweep in his Gau.'

The Berlin events prompted Party activists to mount similar attacks all over Germany, repeating the kinds of actions they had carried out in the winter and spring of 1934/35, while the Party press once more set the tone of anti-Jewish incitement.[33] The attacks, however, once again gave rise to serious concerns, voiced primarily by Schacht, the Economics Minister, about the negative effects they could have on what was already a precarious economic situation.[34] At the end of July/beginning of August leading members of the Party and government therefore began a campaign to calm things down and prevent 'individual initiatives'. On 9 August Hitler via Hess called for a complete stop to all violent incidents,[35] but further bans from Frick (taking his authority expressly from Hitler), Himmler, and other leading Nazis were needed before the attacks actually diminished in September.[36] At the same time, new plans for anti-Semitic legislation were made public.

As far as the Churches were concerned, Hitler assumed more of a mediating role in the summer of 1935. During May and June Interior Minister Frick, claiming authorization from Hitler, drafted a bill giving him the power 'to bring clarity to the legal position' within the Protestant Church.[37] However, Hitler soon after intervened with an alternative solution; his edict of 16 July assigned responsibility for Church matters to Reich Minister Hanns Kerrl.[38] After the Prussian Ministry of Justice was dissolved in June 1934, Kerrl had remained in the Reich cabinet as a minister without portfolio and during the earlier negotiations conducted by Frick had already been named as a potential Churches commissar by a Nazi ecclesiastical functionary. Frick had warmly welcomed this suggestion as Kerrl was 'a man the Führer trusted'.[39]

At a meeting at the beginning of August for state ministers responsible for Church matters and all the heads of the Prussian provinces (Oberpräsidenten), Kerrl sketched out the path he intended to take with regard in particular to the Protestant Church. It was, he said, to be brought to heel by the imposition of state supervision of its financial and property administration, as was already happening in Prussia. It had been a mistake in the past to back the German Christians one-sidedly, he continued, and the Church was instead to be open to clergy of all persuasions. This would prompt people to distance themselves of their own accord from 'quarrelsome priests'.[40] In mid-August Kerrl attended a meeting of leading Party comrades in Nuremberg, to get Hitler to confirm this policy.

Hitler's decision to introduce the Nuremberg Laws

The purpose of the meeting Hitler held on 17 August in Nuremberg was to establish the overall line to be taken at the Party Rally, which would in turn, via the regime's control of the public sphere, help to overcome the crisis in the national mood. To that end Hitler made a series of policy decisions, for which Goebbels's diaries provide our source.[41]

First of all, he announced that he wanted to 'make peace with the Churches', although with the important proviso that Goebbels records: 'At least for a while'. As Hitler explained to Goebbels two days later, Kerrl would 'let the warring clerics simmer'. Armed with these instructions, Kerrl had separate meetings a few days later with the Reich Bishop and the leaders of the German Christians as well as with representatives of the Confessing Church, telling them his aim was to bring 'order' to the Church but not to get involved in matters of faith. That was clearly his way of letting the warring parties 'simmer'.[42] In late September/early October the legal framework for this new Church regime was to be worked out. A Reich Church Committee was created replacing the Church governing body under Müller that had existed up to that point and had been controlled by the German Christians.[43] Keeping the peace on the Church front for the time being also determined Hitler's reaction to a memorandum sent to him by the Catholic Church on 20 August. It posed crucial questions concerning the regime's future Church policy, to which Hitler did not respond. He also ignored a pastoral message from the bishops to the 'hard-pressed' Catholic associations, 'faithful even through trials and tribulations'.[44]

Secondly, on 17 August Hitler announced the dissolution of the Stahlhelm. This step came as a surprise to nobody. Five days earlier, as the *Völkischer Beobachter* had reported, he had met the leader of the Stahlhelm, Seldte, to 'discuss the future' of the organization. In fact the only issue was *how* the expected dissolution should proceed.[45]

Hitler's third stipulation was that the overriding theme of the Party Rally should be 'Anti-Comintern': in other words it should paint as alarming a picture as possible of the 'Bolshevist threat'. The primary reason for this was not only to provide a distraction from domestic concerns but to emphasize the associated 'great foreign policy opportunities', as Hitler pointed out on 17 August to those who were going to speak at the Rally. The following day, during an excursion to Upper Bavaria, Hitler gave Goebbels more detail on these 'opportunities'. In essence, he meant forming a common policy in alliance with Britain and Italy against the Soviet Union.[46]

On 17 August Hitler spoke briefly about the negative mood in the country. However, he evidently made no mention of the problem that had caused so much concern in the previous months, namely the attacks on Jews prompted by the Party rank and file's expectation of radical measures to tackle the 'Jewish question'.[47] He evidently assumed that the instructions he had already issued to refrain from 'individual initiatives' were sufficient. It was Schacht, above all, who during this period was pressing for the attacks to be halted once and for all, not least because of their effect on the economy, and for a set of legal guidelines to tackle a problem that the regime had itself created. In a speech in Königsberg on 18 August, extracts from which were circulated in the press, he opposed further 'random initiatives by individuals'.[48]

On 20 August Schacht chaired a top-level meeting where there was substantial agreement that there must be an end to public disorder. Instead they intended to pass a series of anti-Jewish laws. Prominent in their deliberations were a ban on 'racial disgrace', a special form of citizenship for Jews, and certain economic measures. No concrete decisions were made, however.[49] Thus, in the run-up to the Party Rally there was movement towards the creation of an extensive legal framework for dealing with the 'Jewish question', though no details had been fixed, nor any timetable set. Hitler, who at this time was remarkably uninvolved with the 'Jewish question', appeared to be letting matters take their course.

As expected, Hitler's proclamation at the opening ceremony of the Party Rally placed the whole event under the banner of the fight against 'Jewish Marxism and the parliamentary democracy linked with it', against 'the politically and morally corrupting Centre Party', and against 'certain elements within an incorrigible and stupidly reactionary bourgeoisie'.[50] Hitler also referred to 'temporary shortages of certain kinds of food'. He had, he said, been forced to 'use every means of holding prices down' and to refuse any wage increases, as he wanted to avoid inflation at all costs; anyone who thought it necessary to respond to shortages of goods by raising prices would be targeted 'brutally and ruthlessly' and in certain circumstances sent to a concentration camp.[51] In fact Hitler already knew a few days before this proclamation that there was no prospect of preventing increases in food prices from the detailed report analysing the rises that had taken place over the previous two years. At the same time, he had been unable to decide whether to make Goerdeler Prices Commissioner with extraordinary powers, as the latter had suggested. Thus the threat of a concentration camp had to take the place of the absent state measures to control prices. Otherwise, on 11 September, Hitler delivered his usual speech on Art at the Party Rally, once again targeting modern art, and during the following days went on to address the various Party organizations at their rallies and conferences.[52]

Yet while he was carrying out this programme of events, which by now had almost become a ritual, Hitler decided to give prominence to a different topic from the one originally planned. On 8 September, shortly before the Rally began, he had decided to summon a special session of the Reichstag, in order to pass a 'Flag Law'. The swastika flag was now to be declared the only national flag. This new measure was prompted by an incident in New York, where demonstrators had taken down the swastika flag from a German ship as a protest against the regime's policies. The new law was designed both ostentatiously to raise the status of this Nazi symbol and also be a slap in the face to the forces of 'reaction', as it was no longer to be permitted to fly the black, white, and red flag of the old German empire, which had hitherto been used as the national flag in addition to the swastika.[53] Barely two months later Hitler was to announce almost casually the long expected dissolution of the Stahlhelm – a third-class burial for his partner in the government of 'national concentration' formed in 1933.[54]

The highly charged anti-Semitic atmosphere in the run-up to the Party Rally also influenced the drafting of the Reich Flag Law, which was to contain a provision forbidding Jews to display the swastika national flag. In addition, on 13 September 1935 Hitler also decided to have the Reichstag pass a set of anti-Jewish laws that had been planned for some time. He may possibly have been prompted to do this by a speech made the previous day by the Reich doctors' leader, Gerhard Wagner, who had announced that a law would 'soon' be passed 'to protect German blood', although he had no inkling that such a law could come into effect only two days later.

Following Hitler's instructions of 13 September the Interior Minister, Frick, with the help of a number of officials from his ministry who were present at Nuremberg, seems at first to have pursued the plan of drafting one single comprehensive bill. This project in its constantly changing versions was debated animatedly during 14 September by Hitler, Frick, Hess, Goebbels, and the doctors' leader Wagner, along with experts from the Interior Ministry, among them state secretaries Wilhelm Stuckart and Hans Pfundtner, and the 'desk officer for Jewish questions' Bernhard Lösener, who was flown in specially from Berlin. In the end the complex of issues was disentangled to form a series of individual laws. Thus a law against 'racial disgrace' (the so-called blood protection law) was drafted, also a citizenship law. The issue of the flag returned, as originally intended, to being a law on its own, while the introduction of a 'certificate of eligibility to marry' for non-Jewish Germans [involving a medical examination] was also discussed but withdrawn at Hitler's request. According to Lösener's account, Hitler chose the most lenient version of the four drafts of the blood protection law, although personally crossing out the introductory sentence, 'This law applies only to full Jews'. In doing so he himself was raising the problem of how to define and treat 'half Jews' and 'quarter Jews', an issue that would continue to exercise bureaucrats up until the end of the Third Reich.[55]

The drafting of these bills had been planned for some time. Now Hitler decided to have them produced quickly and to get them passed in demonstrative fashion by the Reichstag (which had been excluded from the legislative process since 1933). In so doing he was removing the drafting of anti-Jewish laws, already in train, from the ministerial bureaucracy, thereby preventing civil servants from delaying them, from adding complications, or from loading them down with rulings allowing for exceptions. This initiative sprang from domestic considerations. On the one hand, Hitler had considered any radical measures regarding Church politics to be inopportune in late summer 1935 and, as far as his battle with the forces of 'reaction' was concerned, he was doing no more than bringing about the overdue dissolution of the Stahlhelm and the downgrading of the black, white, and red flag; on the other hand, he had nothing substantial to announce on the problem that was troubling the population the most – rising prices and food shortages; so he turned the spotlight on to the 'Jewish question'. Thus he not only pacified the Party activists pressing for more radical measures against the Jews but also showed he was listening to ministerial bureaucrats and business circles, of which Schacht had made himself spokesperson. For the latter group was keen to settle the 'Jewish question' by legal means and thus avoid further disruption to the economy. As in June of the previous year, in September 1935 Hitler was again attempting to take control of a complex set of domestic problems through a spectacular and surprising decision and thus reset the political agenda. Although he could not solve existing problems, in particular those affecting the economy and Church policy, this tactic allowed him, for a time, to push these unwelcome subjects into the background.

Although the equal status of Jews as citizens had been seriously undermined since 1933, the Reich citizenship law passed on 15 September 1935 finally put an end to it by introducing a distinction between 'subjects of the state' and 'Reich citizens'. Being a 'Reich citizen', in other words possessing full citizenship rights, was open only to those 'of German or ethnically related blood' who proved 'by their behaviour and attitude that they were willing and suitable to serve the German nation and Reich loyally'. 'Reich citizenship' was to be conferred in the form of a 'Reich citizenship document', although this never happened. The 'Law to protect German blood and German honour' banned marriages and extra-marital sexual relations between 'Jews and citizens of German or ethnically related blood'. Jews were not allowed to employ Aryan women under 45 years of age as domestics and they were not permitted to hoist the Reich flag, a discriminatory provision that was designed once again to emphasize the Reich Flag Law that was being passed at the same time. The timing and method of announcing the anti-Jewish laws were surprising, but in content the so-called Nuremberg Laws were in line with what the rank and file of the Party had been demanding for months, as well as with the subsequent announcements that had come from the government. The exclusion of Jews from economic life, which the Party on the ground had also been demanding vigorously, was the only measure that as yet the government was not introducing.[56]

At the special session of the Reichstag in Nuremberg on 15 September Hitler made a short speech about the new laws, which were then passed.[57] In it he blamed 'Jewish elements' first and foremost for the 'international agitation and unrest' that Germany was being made to suffer. Incited by this international agitation, he said, the Jews in Germany had become involved in provocative acts, and he highlighted the incidents in Berlin after the screening of an anti-Semitic film. In order to prevent such occurrences turning into 'very determined and individually unpredictable acts of self-defence on the part of the enraged population', he had had no choice but to 'deal with the problem through legislation'. Hitler then interpreted the discriminatory laws as an attempt 'by means of one epoch-making solution perhaps to create the conditions that might enable the German nation to form a sustainable relationship with the Jewish people'. If the problem of German–Jewish coexistence could not be solved through legislation then the National Socialist Party would have to be 'given legal responsibility for finding a final solution'.[58]

The Party Rally then continued as planned. On 16 September Hitler made a speech to mark 'Army Day' and the following day closed proceedings with a long speech in which he rejected the frequent practice of critics of the regime of driving a wedge between the Party and the 'Führer'; 'The Führer is the Party and the Party is the Führer' was his pithy formulation.[59]

In the Hotel Deutscher Hof, at the end of the official programme, Hitler addressed Party leaders and once again expressly forbade any more 'individual initiatives' against Jews. Goebbels, significantly, doubted whether this instruction would be obeyed.[60] With the Olympic Games scheduled for 1936, Hitler did in fact wish to avoid anything that might further damage his regime's international reputation. For the same reason, after the Party Rally greater restraint was imposed on propaganda. For the time being the 'Jewish question' was not to be mentioned.[61]

The passing of the Nuremberg Laws did not resolve the problem of how the Jewish population could be precisely defined.[62] In particular there was disagreement between the Interior Ministry, which wanted 'half Jews' classified as Reich citizens, and the Office of the 'Führer's' Deputy, in this instance Reich doctors' leader Wagner, who wanted them generally to be classified as Jews. On 24 September, according to Goebbels's notes, Hitler spoke at a conference of NSDAP leaders in Munich against creating a 'hybrid race of non-Aryans', a phrase by which he sidestepped the basic question of whether citizens with two Jewish grandparents were 'Jews' or 'Aryans'.[63] A few days later Goebbels records Hitler as still being 'undecided' over the 'Jewish question'.[64] By getting rid of the provision that the law should be limited to 'full Jews', as originally intended, Hitler had created a problem that he now consistently refused to resolve. For him what had been important was the big splash the Nuremberg Laws would make and their impact at home. He had not thought through how it would be possible to define the 'Jewish race'. Given that propaganda made such an issue of 'racial mixing', this surprising fact once again demonstrates how nonsensical and misleading any attempt to differentiate the German population according to its 'racial' components was bound to be.

As Hitler continued to delay any decision,[65] the negotiating teams from Party and state eventually proposed a compromise, namely the definition of a Jew contained in the 'First Decree implementing the Reich Citizenship Law'.[66] A Jew was defined as someone who had 'at least three fully Jewish grandparents according to race' and was thus excluded from Reich citizenship. People were to 'count as Jews' (and thus be treated as Jews) if they were 'Mischlinge' [lit. 'mongrels'] with two Jewish grandparents, and if they were also adherents of the Jewish religion, were married to a Jew or were the product of an extramarital relationship with a Jew entered into after the Nuremberg Laws came into force. The remaining 'Jewish Mischlinge' (those with one or two Jewish grandparents) were to be given 'provisional Reich citizenship'. Thus the 'hybrid race' was created that Hitler had wanted to avoid. The classification and decision regarding the fate of 'Jewish Mischlinge' was from this point on to give the bureaucracy a huge amount of work. Although final regulations were discussed in 1936/37, they were never enacted.[67]

In addition to the anti-Jewish legislation, the Nazi regime's racism was expressed during the first years after 1933 primarily through the codification of 'racial hygiene'. Hitler was important in shaping this also. As early as July 1933 he had pushed the sterilization law through cabinet in spite of Papen's resistance. At the Party Rally in 1934 he authorized the Reich doctors' leader, Wagner, to have abortions carried out on 'eugenic' grounds even without a legal basis; he, Hitler, would guarantee Wagner would not be punished. Wagner then gave instructions to the relevant offices in the health service.[68] In July 1935 Hitler wanted an investigation to be carried out into whether sterilizations could be performed by radiation in order to reduce fatalities. After he had seen a report from an expert claiming that women could be sterilized through the use of x-rays, a change in the law in early 1936 made this possible.[69] At the end of 1935 he explicitly ruled out extending the sterilization law to include 'foreigners with inherited diseases' living in Germany, as there was no reason to improve other races by applying eugenic measures.[70] In the case of the compulsory sterilization in 1937 of the so-called Rhineland bastards, some 600 to 800 young people who were the product of liaisons between French colonial troops and German women, a 'special order' from Hitler provided for this measure to be carried out without a legal basis.[71] These examples show that Hitler pursued the demands he himself had voiced in *Mein Kampf* for 'racial hygiene' with a positively obsessive attention to detail.

20

A Foreign Policy Coup

At the beginning of October 1935, shortly after Hitler had made his annual Harvest Thanksgiving speech, Italy mounted its long anticipated invasion of Abyssinia [Ethiopia]. By imposing sanctions on Italy, the League of Nations then created the diplomatic situation for which Hitler had been hoping.[1] Learning in August of the Italians' imminent attack he had given Goebbels 'an outline of his foreign policy plans' that went far beyond a revision of the international order established by the Treaty of Versailles and the restoration of Germany's position of power in Central Europe: '...a permanent alliance with England. Good relations with Poland. A limited number of colonies. On the other hand, expansion eastwards. The Baltic States are ours. Control of the Baltic Sea. Conflicts between Italy and England over Abyssinia, then between Japan and Russia. That is, in a few years perhaps. Then our great historic moment will arrive.'[2]

Now, in October, Hitler instructed Goebbels to gear the press to be more strongly pro-Italian.[3] A few days later, after Hitler gave an address in the Reich Chancellery to a meeting of ministers and military leaders, Goebbels noted that Hitler had set out 'the full seriousness' of the situation: 'Mussolini's in a desperate situation. England will try to include us in a system of sanctions. Then the Führer will offer to mediate. Appeal to world opinion. All this is coming three years too soon for us. Führer sees things very clearly. Knows what he wants too. Apart from this, rearm and be prepared. Europe's on the move again. If we play our cards right, we'll come out on top.'[4]

The international sanctions against Italy, which came into force in the middle of November,[5] did not in fact have a serious impact on its ability to fight the war, and by May 1936 it had defeated Abyssinia. The war gave Hitler an opportunity, however, to exploit the quarrel between Italy and the western powers by continuing to rearm using the conflict as a cover.

Yet this rearmament, which was boosted in 1935 and was cranked up even further at the turn of 1936, deepened Germany's economic problems and could not be sustained at the desired pace, as became evident in the autumn of 1935 and during the following winter.[6]

At the end of October Hitler took note of a memorandum from Goerdeler, written at the instigation of the Reich Chancellery. Goerdeler exploited his resignation as Prices Commissioner to make fundamental criticisms of the way the government was forcing the pace of rearmament and of autarky. The notorious shortage of butter, he said, would oblige the government, if it did not provide foreign exchange to import fats, to introduce 'an orderly system of distribution from the producer to the consumer'. Goerdeler made no bones about his belief that such a step would be disastrous.[7]

Yet in spite of the difficult foreign exchange situation, at a meeting of army chiefs on 18 October 1935, the Defence Minister, Blomberg, had suspended the limit on armaments expenditure set by Schacht and in force hitherto. The Reich Bank considered this increased demand by the army for raw materials would inevitably put an intolerable strain on the foreign exchange situation. At a meeting with Hitler on 26 November Schacht provided an overview of the likely development of the foreign exchange situation over the coming six months, stating that the foreign exchange requirements of industry, the food industry, and commerce would produce a deficit of 376 million Reich Marks.[8] On 24 December 1935 Schacht wrote a letter to Blomberg setting out clearly that he was unable to satisfy the army's requirements for foreign exchange to buy lead and copper.[9]

These demands placed on Germany's foreign currency reserves had a particularly destabilizing effect on the food situation. The diminishing productivity of German agriculture (while the population was growing) could only be compensated for by increasing imports of food and animal feed. Yet Schacht, who had sharply reduced agricultural imports since 1933, refused to make the necessary foreign exchange available in order to safeguard the rearmament programme. Thus a direct conflict was arising between the production of 'guns or butter', which for the German people meant that they were forced to continue coping with food shortages.[10] Hitler, however, now intervened personally. Having already spoken at the Party Rally about problems surrounding the supply of food and rejected wage rises by arguing that they increased the risk of inflation, he now tackled critics of his food policies on 6 October at a mass rally of German farmers on the Bückeberg and then four days later, when opening the 'Winter Aid' programme, emphasizing the idea of 'national solidarity', which was bound to involve 'sacrifices' for the 'national community'.[11]

Following this lead, Goebbels mounted a vigorous campaign on this subject during the next few months. The Propaganda Minister told his audience in a speech at the beginning of October that the temporary shortage of butter had to be accepted so as to enable the import of raw materials as part of the battle for jobs and to prevent millions becoming unemployed.[12] Propaganda insisted that rearmament must continue at all costs; 'guns instead of butter' was the slogan.[13] The Winter Aid collections were boosted by propaganda throughout the cold season; from October 1935 to March 1936 the Party continuously organized meetings to 'enlighten' people about the food situation.[14] As a result of this campaign any sort of criticism of food shortages was branded as sabotaging the rearmament effort, with the result that such complaints were rarely expressed openly and, officially at least, did not particularly depress the public 'mood'.[15] An additional factor was that around the New Year in 1936 the food situation eased slightly. Hitler had brought in Göring as mediator in the ongoing conflict between Schacht and the Minister of Agriculture, Darré, over the provision of foreign exchange for the food industry. Göring saw to it that during December and January at least there was foreign exchange for the purchase of oil-seed.[16] This did not, however, lead to a perceptible lightening of the 'mood'. Among the working classes in particular low wages were continually being contrasted with the privileges of Party bigwigs and the rising incomes of more affluent classes and perceived as examples of a blatant lack of social justice. As a precaution Goebbels and Ley decided at the beginning of February 1936 during the campaign for the elections to the councils of trust not to ask Hitler to speak, as this would 'be too much of a commitment and so be too great a risk'.[17] In the end the elections were called off altogether.[18]

The Winter Olympics, which were held in February 1936 in Garmisch-Partenkirchen, offered the regime a welcome opportunity to divert attention from the precarious food situation and the unenthusiastic mood at home and present itself to the international media as open-minded and peace-loving. Yet this scenario was suddenly threatened when on 4 February, two days before the opening of the Games, a Jewish student named David Frankfurter assassinated Wilhelm Gustloff, the leader of the NSDAP in Switzerland.[19] No retaliatory action could be taken against German Jews at this moment. For weeks before the Olympic Games the German media had been primed to exercise restraint precisely with regard to the 'Jewish question'. Their response to the assassination was therefore relatively moderate.[20] Hitler opened the Games as planned. He waited until his address at Gustloff's funeral in Schwerin on 12 February to direct his rage at the 'hate-filled power of our Jewish enemy'.[21]

As far as foreign policy was concerned, the deep divisions between Italy and the western powers caused by the Abyssinian conflict were, from Hitler's perspective, producing their first positive results. On 6 January Ulrich von Hassell, the German ambassador in Rome, was able to report to Berlin that Mussolini had told him that it was possible 'to make fundamental improvements in German–Italian relations' and clear away the 'only cause of disagreement, namely the Austrian problem'. As Hassell reported, Mussolini was offering Germany a treaty of friendship that would enable it to draw Austria 'in Germany's wake' as far as foreign policy was concerned. If as a result Austria, although formally an independent state, became in effect a satellite of Germany, Mussolini would not object.[22]

Until that point, however, several more months were to pass. In the meantime Hitler saw an opportunity to exploit Mussolini's accommodating attitude in connection with a much more pressing problem. For at the start of 1936 the progress of German rearmament came up against a major obstacle that Hitler absolutely had to remove if he intended to realize his foreign policy goals, namely the demilitarization of the Rhineland as laid down in the Treaty of Versailles. This prevented Germany from protecting the heartland of German heavy industry, the Ruhr, against French intervention. However, by marching into the Rhineland Hitler would be violating not only the Treaty of Versailles but also the Locarno Pact and running the risk of reuniting its guarantors, Belgium, France, Britain, and Italy. Occupying the Rhineland was therefore not in the offing, as Hitler told Goebbels on 20 January 1936, so as to avoid 'giving the others the opportunity of turning their attention away from the conflict in Abyssinia'.[23] This was a clear indication of the significance of the conflict in Africa for Hitler's strategy. On 25 January, however, when Mussolini used an unattributed newspaper article to raise doubts about the continuation of the Locarno Pact because of talks between the British and French general staffs, Hitler began to revise his view of the Rhineland issue.[24]

In addition, by the middle of February Hitler had come to the conclusion that the imminent ratification of the Franco–Soviet mutual assistance pact agreed in May 1935 might provide a suitable pretext for the occupation. Using this argument, he attempted to persuade Mussolini to adopt a neutral stance regarding this violation of the Locarno Pact. The moment seemed right because in February the war in Abyssinia turned in favour of the Italians. This was bringing the international crisis to its climax, thus minimizing the likelihood of the Locarno powers acting in concert in the event of Germany occupying the Rhineland.[25]

Both Goebbels's diaries and the notes kept by the German ambassador in Rome, whom Hitler summoned unexpectedly to Munich on 14 February and equally unexpectedly to Berlin on 19 February, furnish some revealing insights into the process leading Hitler finally to decide at the beginning of March to occupy the Rhineland. In Munich Hitler revealed to Hassell that from a military perspective the occupation of the Rhineland was 'an absolute necessity'. Up to now, he said, he had planned it for the spring of 1937, as German rearmament would be more advanced by then. The right 'psychological moment' had arrived, however, because Britain and France were hardly in the mood to respond with military action. Hassell also gained the impression that domestic politics were an essential part of Hitler's motivation.[26] Neurath confirmed to Hassell that in view of the disaffected national mood Hitler was searching for 'a national cause that would fire up the masses again'.[27] The question of whether such domestic considerations were more important in determining Hitler's actions in February/March 1936 than strategic foreign policy ones is, however, of secondary importance. For Hitler's political style and strength lay precisely in his ability to combine such disparate motives and finally come up with a surprise move that took both domestic circumstances and the international situation into account. After a discussion between Hassell and Hitler over lunch on 19 February Goebbels noted: 'The Führer is again ready to pounce. He ponders and broods and then suddenly he acts.'[28]

Armed with instructions from Hitler, Hassell returned to Rome and a few days later he was able to relay Mussolini's answer to Berlin. Mussolini had assured him that, although he did not see the French–Soviet pact as a reason to leave the Locarno Pact, he would not join Britain and France in imposing sanctions if the Germans occupied the Rhineland.[29] In spite of this highly satisfactory response, it seems that at the end of February Hitler was not yet prepared to make a move. He discussed the matter once again with Goebbels and Göring and reached the conclusion that it was in fact 'somewhat too soon'.[30] The following day Goebbels recorded a further discussion in which Hitler was 'wrestling' with a decision, after the French parliament ratified the agreement with the Soviet Union.[31]

Out of the blue Hitler then asked Goebbels to go with him to Munich that same evening; he wanted Goebbels with him on account of his 'difficult decision concerning the Rhineland', as Goebbels, who was flattered, records.[32] During the train journey, on which they were joined by Magda, and the next day in Munich Hitler returned repeatedly to this topic, although without coming to a decision. Yet the following day, 1 March, on a visit to Goebbels in his Munich hotel Hitler declared he intended to act the next week and not wait for the impending final ratification of the 'Russian pact' by the French Senate on 12 March,[33] as Goebbels and also Neurath had advised him to do.[34]

Back in Berlin, on 2 March Hitler summoned Goebbels, Göring, Blomberg, Fritsch, Raeder, and Ribbentrop to the Reich Chancellery to tell them that on the following Saturday he would proclaim the remilitarization of the Rhineland in the Reichstag, combining this with a wide-ranging offer to the western powers of an understanding. He was convinced that neither France nor Britain was likely to put up serious resistance and he did not need to take account of Italy. In addition, Hitler announced that he intended to dissolve the Reichstag and hold fresh elections 'with foreign policy slogans'. To keep things secret, the deputies should be summoned to Berlin on the Friday evening on the pretext of a beer evening.[35] Hitler did not officially notify all the members of his cabinet until the morning of that same day, 6 March.[36]

On 7 March Hitler announced to the Reichstag that Germany was no longer bound by the Locarno Pact. The treaty, signed in 1926, was, he said, incompatible with the Franco–Soviet military pact. In the future France might come under communist rule and in the event of a crisis the centre of decision-making would therefore 'no longer be Paris but Moscow'. The climax of the speech came when a memorandum to the signatories to the Locarno Pact was read out: the German government declared that it had 'as from this day re-established full and unrestricted Reich sovereignty in the demilitarized zone of the Rhineland'. Simultaneously German troops, though a relatively small number, were marching into the territory on the left bank of the Rhine.[37] As in Hitler's 'peace speech' of 21 May 1935, there followed a comprehensive list of proposals to 'set up a system ensuring peace in Europe': demilitarized zones on both sides of the borders to France and Belgium; non-aggression pacts with neighbouring countries in the east and west; an aviation pact to prevent surprise air attacks. Finally, he declared his willingness to rejoin the League of Nations, although he linked this step to 'colonial equality', for in the preceding months he had begun to lay more emphasis on the restoration of German colonies than he had during his first three years in power, in order to boost further Germany's increased international importance.[38] At the end of the speech Hitler announced he had decided to dissolve the Reichstag and called on the German nation to support him during the coming elections 'in his struggle for genuine peace'.

The day after this military move the regime held its Heroes' Remembrance Day,[39] after which the propaganda for the 'election' got into full swing.[40] The mobilization of the masses was finally to put an end to discussions about food shortages and social injustices, to relieve the fear of war that the occupation of the Rhineland had reawakened, and to demonstrate the nation's solidarity, in order to stiffen the government's resolve to face the diplomatic battles ahead.[41] The regime could assume that the Rhineland remilitarization, which had passed off without incident, would in fact be welcomed by the majority of the population as an important step towards a complete dismantling of the restrictions arising from the Treaty of Versailles. During the 'campaign' Hitler made speeches between 12 and 28 March in a total of eleven towns and cities. He emphasized his claim to be working for peace, but his appeal to a reawakened national self-confidence set the tone for the campaign.[42]

The campaign reached its climax on the two days preceding the vote, when Hitler spoke at particularly large-scale events.[43] On the afternoon of 27 March he visited the Krupp works at Essen and made a speech that was broadcast on all German radio stations. Goebbels introduced the event, giving the order for the flags to be hoisted, whereupon, as the *Völkischer Beobachter* reported, 'the whole of Germany . . . was like a hurricane of swastika banners'. After Gauleiter Terboven welcomed Hitler, the traffic in Germany stopped for a minute and employees of firms stopped work so that they could listen to the speech.[44] In his Essen speech Hitler once again declared his determination to ensure peace, appealing to the nation's unity and finally calling on the people to judge 'whether you [using the singular familiar form 'du'] believe I have worked hard, that I have done my best for you during these years, and that I have made proper use of my time when serving this nation'. After this there were further events throughout Germany featuring prominent Party comrades.[45] The next day, which the regime had declared the 'German National Day for Honour, Freedom, and Peace',

Hitler made a speech in the major Rhineland city of Cologne that was once again broadcast by every radio station.

The *Völkischer Beobachter* gave a detailed schedule for the whole evening: 'On Saturday at 18.30 millions of people in the Reich capital will pour onto the streets and, like people all over Germany, will head for the assembly points, from which huge processions will set off. From 19.45 onwards the columns of people will stand silent, waiting solemnly for the signal to move off. At 19.50 the whole of Germany will be filled with the sonorous tones of the bells of Cologne Cathedral, and then Adolf Hitler will speak from the Cologne Fair exhibition halls.'

Ever since it was finally completed in the nineteenth century, Cologne Cathedral had been a popular national symbol of a strong Germany, united against France. Hitler used the ringing of the cathedral bells to present the election as the culmination of a project of national unity blessed by God. He appealed to the 'Almighty' to 'give us the strength to win the fight for freedom and our future and for the honour and peace of our nation, so help us God!'[46] After these closing words, his listeners and the millions who had gathered across Germany sang the old Dutch hymn 'We gather together' (the *Völkischer Beobachter* referred to a 'gigantic choir of 67 million Germans'), while the sound of the bells of Cologne Cathedral carried over the airwaves during the singing was, according to the newspaper, 'an exhortation to the German nation to give the Führer wholehearted thanks on Sunday'.[47]

Thus primed, the Germans went to vote that Sunday. The *Völkischer Beobachter* carried the banner headline 'German nation, now do your duty!'[48] The results of this election too were rigged as far as possible, for rather than reflecting the people's assent to the regime's policies they are evidence of how, in a 'public sphere' created artificially by the regime and carefully monitored by it, assent was manufactured and reproduced in stage-managed elections. 'Terror, electoral tampering, and electoral fraud' had on this occasion, 'grown to unprecedented proportions', as the Social Democrat underground reporter put it.[49] The official announcement was that 99 per cent of voters had supported the list. The number of 'No' votes was not, however, given as a separate figure but rather rolled up with the invalid ballot papers. Ballot papers handed in unmarked were counted as 'Yes' votes. In spite of strong pressure more than 400,000 people had refused to take part in the election.[50]

Nevertheless, the election result strengthened Hitler's position vis-à-vis the western powers, who in any case had been unable to muster the will to produce a serious response. Although on 19 March the council of the League of Nations had passed a resolution identifying the occupation of the Rhineland as a clear breach of the Treaty of Versailles and making specific demands of Germany, such as forbidding it to build fortifications in the occupied zone,[51] Germany rejected a proposal on these lines from the Locarno Pact members on 24 March.[52] The Italian government was a party to these resolutions, but as no sanctions resulted Mussolini was not reneging on the declaration of support he had made to Hassell in February.[53]

On 1 April, three days after the elections, Hitler went on the counter-attack. He had Ribbentrop, his special envoy, deliver a 'peace plan' in London. The plan contained a whole range of proposals designed to promote peace without devoting a single word to the demand that there should be no for-tifications in the Rhineland.[54] The British government responded to this peace plan with a set of detailed questions, the precise formulation of which indicated that it was more than a little sceptical about the Germans' fulsome protestations about wanting peace.[55] Hitler was extremely put out by the fact that the British government simultaneously passed on the set of ques-tions to the press; at a meeting with the British ambassador on 14 May he made it apparent that he was concerned about being thus paraded before an international public. He also stated categorically that Germany would cre-ate whatever fortifications it considered necessary in the reoccupied territory.[56]

Ultimately it had become clear that Hitler's coup had succeeded. The western powers imposed no sanctions and the threatened consultations by the Locarno Pact's military leaders in March led to no practical outcome.[57] The acceptance of the German occupation was tantamount to the collapse of the security system set up at Locarno. That summer Britain and France were to attempt once again to revive it, but Hitler responded with indifference.[58]

21

'Ready for War in Four Years' Time'

From Hitler's point of view, the surprise coup of the Rhineland occupation had been successful in every respect. The military position of the so-called Third Reich had been strengthened, the western powers had, as he had expected, proved incapable of acting, and the emerging German–Italian rapprochement had not suffered. Encouraged by this success, during the following months Hitler proceeded with a series of measures to lay the groundwork for his future policies on armaments, the economy, domestic affairs, and foreign relations. These did not all necessarily arise from a single, thought through, and comprehensive plan, and yet taken together they converged in one objective, namely to broaden decisively the basis for Germany's future policy of expansion.

At the beginning of 1936 Germany was once again going through an acute and serious foreign trade and foreign exchange crisis. The armaments industry required increasing quantities of raw materials at the same time as their price was rising on the world market. The demand for agricultural imports was also rising, as under the aegis of the Reich Food Estate agricultural production was declining, while both the population and consumer spending power were increasing. As Schacht, the Economics Minister and President of the Reichsbank, felt unable to make significant amounts of foreign exchange available to pay for agricultural imports, Hitler gave Göring the task of solving the problem. During the winter he had already committed foreign exchange to secure the supply of food,[1] and Hitler took the same line in the spring when, in the face of Schacht's objections, he allocated to Darré a further 60 million RM from foreign exchange reserves for the import of vegetable oils that were urgently needed to sustain the production of margarine.[2] This marked a notable change of direction, for since the autumn of 1935 Hitler and above all Goebbels had followed the slogan of 'Guns before butter' and presented criticism of the food situation as tantamount to sabotage of the rearmament effort. By the spring, however, Hitler had finally come to see the sense of giving some support to Göring's initiatives to make foreign exchange available *also* for urgently needed food imports. Hitler and the regime had therefore come to the conclusion that it was no longer butter that threatened to slow down rearmament but that dissatisfaction among the population was in danger of growing into a serious crisis of confidence.[3]

At the same time Hitler and his regime began to change their attitude to 'national morale' in a fundamental way. At the beginning of April 1936 Göring, as Prime Minister of Prussia, put a stop to the reports on the public mood produced by the Prussian administration and the Gestapo, alleging that these reports generalized too broadly on the basis of individual negative findings and contributed 'to a deterioration in morale' because they were distributed widely within the administration. Now that he was intervening more and more frequently in economic matters, Göring had no more use for these reports, which he had exploited previously to direct criticism at his fellow ministers. Hitler's attitude was the same; he told his adjutant Wiedemann, who dates the comment to 1936, that he attached no importance to any (negative) reports he received because he could form a better judgement himself of the national mood. To be quite sure that critical voices were completely banished from the Nazi-dominated 'public sphere', Hitler, when appointing Heinrich Himmler Chief of the German Police in June, also gave him the task of introducing stronger police measures against those who created or encouraged a 'negative mood'. Thus the regime implemented a dual strategy in response to the population's dissatisfaction about food shortages: it was removed from public debate, but at the same time substantial material concessions were made.

The pace of rearmament was to be maintained as a top priority. This was the view taken above all by Schacht. In a memorandum of February 1936 he had pointed out that the shortage of raw materials would most probably lead to significant halts in production in the course of the year, thus jeopardizing rapid rearmament.[4] In view of the particularly pressing problems surrounding the supply of petrol, Göring, whose air force was seriously affected, had put himself forward in March as Commissar for Fuel. Schacht, who regarded an alliance with Göring as a means of strengthening his position against opposition from the Party, supported him and the two men were able to gain

Hitler's assent to a more wide-ranging solution. On 4 April 1936 Hitler authorized Göring to use all means necessary to resolve the crisis surrounding raw materials and foreign exchange.[5] On 12 May, however, at a meeting of the so-called Ministerial Council, a cabinet committee chaired by Göring, it became apparent that Göring and Schacht had very different ideas. Schacht explained that Hitler had emphasized on numerous occasions that the rapid pace of rearmament had to be maintained up to the spring of 1936, whereupon Göring objected that he had 'heard nothing about this time limit'. In addition, at the meeting Göring advocated stepping up exports while at the same time increasing 'the exploitation of domestic sources of raw materials', which Schacht questioned on the grounds of cost.[6]

It was precisely this ruthlessness that from Hitler's point of view made Göring the perfect person to resolve the raw materials and foreign exchange crisis. Schacht, on the other hand, swiftly fell in Hitler's estimation during the following weeks, the latter refusing his demand for Göring to have this responsibility taken from him. Hitler stated privately at the end of May, 'in the long run' Schacht would 'have to go'.[7]

To support him in his new task Göring set up a team and from early July began to style himself 'Reich Commissioner' for raw materials and foreign exchange. He very quickly used the task Hitler had given him of mediating between the various consumers to claim 'general economic authority' and try to seize control of the entire armaments economy.[8] Thus in appointing Göring Hitler had started a chain reaction with far-reaching consequences for the armaments industry.

In addition to looking for ways to boost exports, the raw materials and foreign exchange team directed its main attention towards developing Germany's raw materials resources, in particular with regard to the extraction and production of petroleum.[9] In the short term these initiatives did not alleviate the crisis and in the summer of 1936 it intensified. The projected foreign exchange deficit for the second half-year was half a billion Reich Marks and the German munitions factories could work only to 70 per cent of their capacity because of uncertainties in the supply of raw materials. At the same time, the Ministries of Food and Defence were both demanding significant increases in imports.[10] Göring set about scraping together the last foreign exchange reserves.[11] In addition, in July he appointed the Chief of the Security Police, Heydrich, as head of a new 'Foreign Exchange Recovery Office', as a means of securing the finance administration's support in plundering Jewish assets.[12]

During this period Hitler made a decision of principle regarding the economy which, although it appeared to be aiming in a quite different direction, was in fact part of his efforts to prepare for war. In July 1936 he initiated the Volkswagen project. At the opening of the International Automobile Show in March 1934 he had already encouraged the industry to develop a cheap small car that would appeal to 'millions of new buyers'.[13] In response, in May 1934 the Reich Association of German Motor Manufacturers had established a working group to develop a 'people's car' and entrusted this task to the design engineer Ferdinand Porsche.[14] Even before this decision was made Hitler had been in favour of appointing Porsche and provided him with detailed ideas about the technical construction of the car.[15] In addition, when asked by the Association he had decided in favour of a four-wheel, full-size car and not the tiny three-wheeler favoured by the Ministry of Transport. In 1935 and 1936 Hitler continued to highlight the project at the International Automobile Show, assuring people that the new car would not create unwelcome competition in the industry but would give broad sections of the population their first opportunity to acquire a car of their own and thus produce mass motorization. The 'luxury for the very few' must become 'an everyday product for everyone'.[16]

On 11 July 1936 the Obersalzberg Porsche was finally in a position to present Hitler with two prototypes. On this occasion Hitler set the price for the car at 990 RM, although there was no actual calculation to underpin this, and he decreed that an independent company (and not, as originally envisaged, the automobile industry) would produce the cars at a dedicated factory. It was to have the first batch of 100,000 cars ready after only nine months, after which it must produce 300,000 cars per year. A possible location, Hitler said, was the area around the River Elbe in central Germany. Start-up finance would be needed from a wealthy partner. The car would then be on the market in time for the International Automobile Show in 1938.[17] A good two weeks later the leaders of the automobile industry had been made aware of these key dates,[18] although now the anticipated price had been raised to a maximum of 1200 RM. The, to put it mildly, less than enthusiastic response of the industry to the prospect of competition from a state-sponsored mass-produced car seems at first to have put a question mark over the venture. Hitler at any rate criticized the industry's resistance to it quite sharply in his speech at the 1937 Automobile Show.[19] By this time, however, he had found the partner he needed with the necessary finance for the project. The German Labour Front (DAF) would not only advance the money for the factory but also take on the marketing of the Volkswagen.[20] After personally deciding on the location,[21] on 26 May 1938 he finally laid the foundation stone at Fallersleben in Lower Saxony for the works where what was now called the 'Strength through Joy [KdF] car' would be built.[22] Insufficient progress was made before the outbreak of war, however, and instead during the war a light jeep was built as a military version, an option Hitler had kept open from the start.[23]

The fact that Hitler made crucial decisions concerning the mass production of the Volkswagen in the summer of 1936, at a stage when a serious crisis was looming in the supply of raw materials, in particular steel and petroleum, the fact too that in the years following he promoted the project and doggedly pushed ahead with it,[24] even though it was bound to divert resources from the armaments programmes, calls for an explanation. Hitler's main objective with the Volkswagen project, and with the motorway project[25] that ran parallel with it and consumed a great deal of money, was to gain credence through concrete measures for the vision he was repeatedly conjuring up of a nation that was motorized. The long-term perspective was crucial here. In the course of 1936 he gave unmistakable indications that he was expecting a major military conflict at the beginning of the 1940s.[26] The motorization of the masses, however, and the completion of the motorway network (for which there was no immediate military need) were goals for the period 'afterwards'. In the later 1930s the Germans could not fail to see the massive preparations for war and were therefore deeply worried. These projects were designed to give the population the idea of a future that would be characterized by prosperity, consumer power, and a significant degree of individuality. If resources had to be diverted from rearmament, that for Hitler was secondary. In addition, the numbers of vehicles envisaged for the future and conjured up by Hitler in his Automobile Show speeches (in 1936 it was three to four million, in 1938 six or seven) show clearly that he was not aiming for a general motorization but rather that he wanted above all to create a status symbol for the middle classes.

At the same time that rearmament was at its height, the regime was promoting other 'people's' products in addition to the Volkswagen, such as the 'people's fridge', as consumer goods for the more affluent middle classes. Only the 'people's radio' was fairly successful.[27] Even the subsidised mass tourism provided by Strength Through Joy principally benefited white-collar workers, civil servants, and small businessmen. With rearmament as the main focus of the economy it was impossible to move towards mass consumerism encompassing all sections of the population. The regime's strategy of boosting consumer goods was thus mainly aimed at the future.

On 17 June Hitler appointed the SS leader, Heinrich Himmler, 'Reich SS Leader and Head of the German Police in the Reich Ministry of the Interior'.[28] In taking this step shortly after delegating special authority to Göring in economic matters, he was conferring blanket powers on another, in his eyes particularly dependable, leading functionary and laying the foundation for a police force that had been removed from the regular state administration and had become closely linked to the SS. For, in spite of the choice of title, Himmler was in practice to ignore any connection with the Interior Ministry and receive his instructions from Hitler, to whom he was directly responsible as head of the SS. By dividing the police and placing the two sections under new 'head offices', the Security Police under Reinhard Heydrich and the Order Police under Karl Daluege, he created an organization that foreshadowed the desired conflation of SS and police.[29]

By 1936 the Gestapo, Himmler's main sphere of operations up to this point, had largely fulfilled its primary task of smashing the communist underground. On the alert for new responsibilities, Himmler now set about changing the Gestapo's focus to so-called preventative action against the opposition, a development with far-reaching consequences, for which he had already obtained Hitler's approval in principle in October 1935.[30] The aim, as Hitler and the new police chief agreed every time they met, was to track down 'intriguers', 'agitators', and 'subversive intellectuals'. They did not assume that such people were to be found only in left-wing circles but also among Freemasons, clergy with a 'political agenda', and above all among the Jewish population. The Gestapo now began to clamp down even on low-level opposition. From now onwards people who spread rumours or jokes, or who voiced criticisms or dissatisfaction in their daily lives were in the authorities' sights. Clearly this change in police work was directly linked to the Prussian administration's decision in April to cease its 'reports on the public mood'. Instead of discontents being noted so that they could influence political decision-making, the police were to attribute deteriorations in mood to particular groups or individuals and proceed against them. In a parallel initiative the new police chief, Himmler, refocused the activities of the criminal police from 1936 onwards on 'preventative crime-fighting', which to the Nazi mind meant the 'eradication' of marginalized social groups, who were regarded as carriers of allegedly inheritable 'asocial' characteristics and a tendency towards criminality. Thus a disparate collection of

Figure 6. Control and surveillance could not prevent all public protest. In Essen in 1937 this highly visible slogan, 'Down with the Labour Service and remilitarization', was difficult to remove and so the lettering was distorted to make it illegible.
Source: Anton Tripp/Fotoarchiv Ruhr Museum

'subhumans' found themselves in the firing line of the Gestapo, criminal police, and general police. All these developments amounted to one thing: arbitrary rule by the police.[31]

To this end Himmler set about the reform of the concentration camp system in the second half of 1936. Up until the summer of 1937 he had been gradually replacing small camps, with the exception of Dachau, with larger ones. In July 1936 work began on Sachsenhausen camp near Berlin and a year later the construction of Buchenwald was started and Dachau was extended.[32] This enlargement of the concentration camp network was clearly carried out with a view to a future armed conflict. At the beginning of 1937 Himmler announced that 'in the event of a war we must be clear that we shall be forced to put a significant number of unreliable types into them'.[33] Consequently the camp system was designed to take between 30,000 and

50,000 prisoners.[34] After the reform there was no change to the arbitrary practice of sentencing people to protective custody or to the use of terror inside the concentration camps. In November 1935, after Frick, the Interior Minister, made a complaint, Hitler stated unequivocally that he did not wish to see any change in the arrangements. Thus in Hitler's Germany it remained the case that anyone at all could be locked up, without legal proceedings or legal assistance and without any concrete evidence of a crime having been committed, and exposed to the most appalling torture even to the point of death.[35]

A new alliance

Hitler saw Mussolini's victory against Abyssinia in May 1936, his annexation of the country, and his proclamation of the King of Italy Emperor of Abyssinia as an opportunity to make a lasting change in power relations in Europe. On the one hand, he hoped to achieve a closer relationship with Italy's humbled opponent, Great Britain. Thus Goebbels records the 'Führer's' immediate reaction to the 'Duce's' triumph as being that Mussolini's 'drum-banging' was 'very useful for us', for 'it will lead to the alliance of the two Germanic nations'.[36] The ultimate outcome that might emerge from such an alliance, as Hitler told Goebbels at the end of May, was a 'United States of Europe under German leadership'.[37]

On the other hand, as a result of the Abyssinian conflict Mussolini appeared to be more or less isolated internationally and found himself obliged to develop ever closer ties with Germany, as his January message regarding Austria and his neutrality concerning the occupation of the Rhineland had already made clear. At the end of March 1936 a German–Italian police conference was held which concentrated on joint action against communism and Freemasonry, culminating in a treaty. In the spring of 1936 there were further visits in connection with other policy areas.[38] In June 1936 Mussolini replaced his Foreign Minister Suvich, who advocated a policy of cooperation with France and Britain, with his son-in-law Count Galeazzo Ciano.

In addition, during March and April Mussolini had withdrawn his support from the Austrian home defence forces, the Schuschnigg government's most important internal instrument of power. Pressured by Mussolini, Chancellor Kurt von Schuschnigg felt obliged to reassess his country's relations with the

German Reich. Although the published part of the so-called July Agreement between the two countries envisaged Germany recognizing Austria's sovereignty, at the same time the agreement committed the Austrian government to a political course determined by the principle that Austria was a 'German state'.[39] In an unpublished supplementary document it was agreed to lift restrictions on travel (that applied above all to the German imposition of the 1,000 RM visa on German visitors), to grant an amnesty to Austrian National Socialists in custody, and to include representatives of the 'nationalist opposition' in the Austrian government.[40] Schuschnigg complied with the last stipulation as early as 11 July by appointing the military author Edmund Glaise-Horstenau and the diplomat Guido Schmidt, both 'National Socialist agents' to his cabinet.[41] For Hitler, however, the agreement was no more than a starting point from which to undermine further the authority of the Austrian government and create the conditions for Anschluss. At the beginning of May he had told Goebbels: 'We've got to maintain the tension in Austria and Czechoslovakia. We can't let peace get established. We can only gain an advantage through turbulence. The wounds have to smart.'[42]

In the summer of 1936 there also seemed to be some prospect of closer co-operation with Japan against their common enemy, the Soviet Union. In the spring of 1935 Ribbentrop – going against the stance adopted by the Foreign Ministry of promoting German–Chinese relations – appears already to have put out feelers to the Japanese.[43] In October 1935 Oshima Hiroshi, the Japanese military attaché in Berlin, had produced proposals for an anti-Soviet neutrality agreement to which Hitler is believed to have agreed in principle at the end of November.[44] This project had been pushed into the background mainly by domestic developments in Japan, where in February 1936 there was a revolt by the military, but in the summer of 1936 Hitler turned his attention to it again. Hitler's fundamental rejection of the 'yellow race' did not affect his attitude to Japan. He admired the Japanese first and foremost as a fearless warrior nation that had special qualities because it had never been 'softened' by Christian influence and was the sole great power to have no Jewish minority.[45]

Hitler outlined the long-term prospects for potential cooperation with Japan on 8 June 1936 to Papen, Ribbentrop, and Goebbels. 'Führer sees conflict coming in the Far East,' Goebbels noted. 'And Japan will hammer Russia. And that colossus will start to wobble. And then our great moment will have arrived. Then we'll have to grab territory to keep us going for 100 years. I hope we'll be done then and the Führer will still be living. Let's get started.'[46] Hitler made these statements the evening before a meeting with the Japanese ambassador at which mutual assurances were again exchanged that Bolshevism represented a common threat. It was impossible, Hitler said, to 'reject communism as an ideology and at the same time maintain friendly relations with Soviet Russia'.[47]

On 8 July he received Herbert von Dirksen, the German ambassador in Tokyo, and asked about Japan's reliability as an ally. Dirksen replied positively.[48] On 22 July Hitler and Ribbentrop met Oshima in Bayreuth. Without going into detail Hitler indicated at this meeting that he would support a German–Japanese agreement[49] and a few weeks later Ribbentrop, who had been given responsibility for further negotiations, was able to report that agreement in principle had been reached with the Japanese.[50]

During his regular summer attendance at the Bayreuth Festival and only a few days after his meeting with Oshima, Hitler made a further momentous policy decision.[51] On 17 July 1936 officers in Spanish Morocco had rebelled against the left-wing popular front government in Madrid. Although the conspirators had little trouble gaining the support of Spanish forces in North Africa, they failed in their attempt to spread the rebellion quickly to the home country. The coup was in danger of collapse if aircraft could not be found immediately to transport the Spanish Africa troops to the European mainland.[52] The leader of the coup, General Francisco Franco y Bahamonde turned for help to the German government, many of whose members were in Bayreuth at this time, from where they were following events in Spain with great interest.[53] On 25 July Hitler granted an audience to two envoys from Franco, expatriate Germans and Franco sympathizers, and at the following night-time meeting he tasked Göring and Blomberg with supporting the coup, in particular by sending transport planes.[54]

This decision, taken, as in the case of the negotiations with Japan, without the involvement of the Foreign Ministry, was motivated by a number of considerations. Hitler regarded intervening in Spain first and foremost as an opportunity to inflict a defeat on World communism and to use support for Franco to develop a shared German–Italian policy and so strengthen the alliance with Rome. Göring was the man holding the various strings of Germany's intervention policy and his main concern was to test out the capability of his air force, while in his capacity as 'Commissar for Raw Materials' securing access to vital raw materials (particularly iron ore and iron disulphide) in return for Germany supplying weapons.[55]

Before the end of July Luftwaffe transport planes began to fly Spanish rebel units from North Africa back home, while German ships carried the first German troops to Spain. All of this was kept largely secret. At first the German units were forbidden to take an active part in the fighting, for incidents were to be avoided during the Olympic Games,[56] and only when the Games were over at the end of August did Hitler lift restrictions on the deployment of German troops. At the same time, he created elaborate smoke screens on the diplomatic front. In August Germany joined an arms embargo initiated by France and since September had been taking part in the conferences of an international non-intervention committee.[57] During the following months this new direction in foreign policy led to the subject of 'Anti-Bolshevism' being given even greater prominence in German propaganda.

These decisions – rapprochement with Italy, still largely isolated as a result of Abyssinia; the resulting increase in German influence in Austria; the co-operation with Japan against the Soviet Union; the intervention in the Spanish Civil War as a German contribution to the fight against international 'Bolshevism' – that Hitler initiated in the summer of 1936 and that determined the regime's direction make clear how far he had already broken free of the Foreign Ministry's traditional revisionist policies and begun to establish a new position for Germany among the major powers.

Summer Olympics

The summer Olympic Games, held between 1 and 16 August in Berlin, offered the regime a unique opportunity, in spite of the occupation of the Rhineland and intervention in the Spanish Civil War, to parade itself before the world's media as a peace-loving member of the family of nations and as a contented people, united behind their 'Führer'.[58] The 'Olympic Ideal' gave the Nazis plenty to work with. The Games were used in propaganda to support a massive campaign to improve and to glorify physical fitness. The still relatively strong military element in many sports such as riding, fencing, shooting, or the modern pentathlon suited the regime's purposes, as did the emphasis on the classical world through references to the Ancient Greek Olympic tradition. The famous torch relay, carried from Olympia to Berlin 3,000 kilometres away, was staged for the first time in 1936. Typically, the torch's arrival was celebrated by uniformed members of the Hitler Youth and SA in a ceremony of 'dedication' in the Lustgarten.

Berlin had been nominated to host the Games in 1931, but violations of human rights and racist measures in the Third Reich had quickly given rise to objections to their being held in Germany. Thus in the summer of 1933 the new government was forced to pledge to the International Olympic Committee (IOC) that it would uphold the rules enshrining the Olympic Ideal and not discriminate against any participants on the grounds of race or religion and respect the independence of the German organizing committee. The committee chair, Theodor Lewald, was not seen as close to the regime and, according to the Nuremberg Laws introduced later, he was also classed as a 'half Jew'.[59] In spite of these assurances, calls for a boycott of the Games persisted. In December 1935, advocates of a boycott only just lost a vote taken by the American Amateur Athletic Union.[60]

During that summer, anti-Semitism, normally ubiquitous in German public life, was banished. 'Jews not welcome' signs were temporarily removed and news reports about trials for 'racial disgrace' were suspended during the Games, although, significantly, they were resumed immediately after the close.[61] Shortly before the opening ceremony any Sinti and Roma living in Berlin were confined to a camp on the outskirts of the city so that there would be no chance of anyone even seeing upsetting signs of discrimination against another social group.[62]

One of the regime's diversionary tactics was to allow just a few normally 'unwelcome' people to be part of the German team as proof of the regime's 'tolerant attitude'. Helene Mayer, subsequently a silver medallist in fencing and according to racial laws a 'half Jew', was allowed into the German team, but this was the only concession made to the principle of equal treatment for all German sportspeople that the regime had officially accepted. The high jumper Gretel Bergmann, a Jew, was not chosen, in spite of having an excellent chance of a medal.[63] On the other hand, Werner Seelenbinder, several times German champion in wrestling and a former member of the KPD, was allowed to take part as a concession from a regime trying to cover its tracks.[64]

As mentioned above, from the outset Hitler had seen to it that the Games as a whole had a more prestigious character and were on a much larger scale than had been envisaged by the last Weimar governments. The forty-nine nations and almost 4,000 sportsmen and sportswomen who participated, coming to Berlin in spite of the demonstrations mounted by an international boycott movement, established a new record.

From the first moment onwards Hitler was the centre of attention for the public and the media. On the day of the opening ceremony he began by receiving the members of the IOC in the Reich Chancellery, where he made the grand gesture of announcing that German archaeological excavations at Olympia would be resumed. Then with his entourage and the members of the IOC he drove in a motorcade through the streets of the capital, lined with hundreds of thousands of people and decorated with Olympic and swastika flags, to the new Reich stadium in the west of the city, where, amidst great pomp, the opening ceremony took place. Richard Strauss conducted a 3,000-strong choir that sang the national anthem, the Horst Wessel Song, and an Olympic anthem composed by Strauss. The spectators cheered the teams as they marched in, particularly those, for example the French, who when passing the podium gave the 'Olympic salute', an outstretched right arm. The sporting participants accepted that it was similar to the Nazi 'German salute', while most of the spectators were unable to tell the difference. As head of state Hitler had the privilege of officially declaring the Games open. In the days following he attended a variety of events, among them the yacht races that took place in Kiel on 10 August. During this time Hitler presented himself as being fascinated by and enthusiastic about the Games, a generous host, and benevolent national figurehead, everywhere cheered by the masses.[65]

In addition, Hitler used the Games to hold numerous receptions and meetings in the Reich Chancellery. He met, among others, the Tsar of Bulgaria, Boris III; the Crown Prince of Italy; the Italian Propaganda minister Dino Alfieri; the Polish State Secretary Jan Count Szembek, and various Hungarian and Yugoslav ministers. Although Sir Robert Vansittart, the long-standing Permanent Under Secretary in the British Foreign Office, had come for an 'unofficial' visit, it was significant that none of the western countries was represented by a cabinet minister.[66] The Reich capital, where Nazi flags were flying for the duration of the Games, offered all kinds of fringe events such as theatre and music performances, exhibitions, additional sporting events, numerous conferences and congresses, as well as dazzling receptions and lavish parties, thus presenting itself to international visitors as the centre of a confident, peaceful, and sophisticated National Socialist state.[67]

As far as the sporting events themselves were concerned, things turned out well for Germany. With thirty-three golds it was top of the medals table. The most successful athlete of the Games with four gold medals was, however, Jesse Owens from the United States. The fact that Owens was black was naturally problematic from the point of view of Nazi racial policy. German spectators and German newspapers had some difficulty in accepting these achievements without betraying racist attitudes that would damage the impression the regime wanted to give of the Games being 'open to the world'.[68]

As far as their treatment by the media was concerned, the Berlin Summer Olympics represented a milestone in the development of the Olympic idea. In the run-up to the Games there had been an international campaign to raise public interest. In Berlin the reporters found excellent facilities and the most up-to-date technical equipment[69] and for the first time the events were broadcast live on the radio to the whole world.[70] Leni Riefenstahl's lavish film, which was promoted by Hitler personally and showcased by being premiered on his 49th birthday in 1938, set new aesthetic standards for a film about sport.[71] Another first was the showing of the Games on television, even if only on a small local network.

In spite of the huge efforts to use the 1936 Olympic Games for propaganda purposes, the response abroad was mixed, something the regime was forced to recognize through its monitoring of foreign media. The spacious buildings, the perfect organization, the lavish accompanying programme, the German sporting successes, and even the people's cheers for their 'Führer' were generously acknowledged and to some extent admired, but foreign media often suggested that everything had turned out to be too perfect and well-organized in a way that was oppressive. Foreign reporters became aware that the Berlin population's friendliness and hospitality towards international visitors was the result of being positively drilled by the regime. The 'Nazi Olympiad' looked to many journalists like a dictator's military parade, or a Potemkin village, serving as a façade behind which the regime continued its brutality and preparations for war. Special attention was paid to chauvinist tendencies on the part of the German crowds and the disdain for black sportspeople. Thus, in spite of the due respect paid to the Games, international criticism of the political system of the Third Reich was not softened but rather became more pronounced.[72] It is hardly surprising that many foreign visitors took home predominantly positive impressions of their stay in Germany but this was not primarily due to a successful propaganda campaign. As a rule, anyone who travelled to the 'Nazi Olympiad' felt some sympathy with the system there or was indifferent to the political situation in Germany.

The impression created at home by propaganda from the German media was that the Games had positively transformed international opinion. This extravagant exaggeration had a long-lasting effect; the myth of the 'Festival of Nations' lived on in Germany for decades.

Hitler's Four-Year Plan

As two weeks of 'the endless toing and froing of the Olympiad' had made Hitler 'somewhat stressed', as Goebbels noted,[73] he left immediately after the Games closed for rest and recuperation in Berchtesgaden. In July the extensive building alterations to his refuge there had been completed. Wachenfeld, a country villa, had been transformed into the Berghof, a grand house.[74] Hitler used his time there, which lasted until the start of the Party Congress on 8 September, to ponder on the directions he had set in the preceding months in foreign and rearmament policy, to assess their initial consequences, and to link together their various strands. His deliberations resulted in essence in the creation of the Four-Year Plan and the introduction of two years' conscription, which was directly connected with that Plan. Both were preconditions for further accelerating the pace of rearmament.

At the end of July Hitler had still been willing to allow Göring to announce what he was planning with regard to foreign currency and raw materials in a 'major speech' at the September Party Congress. With the slogan 'The Party's Great Production Battle' Göring wanted to set in motion a 'raw materials propaganda campaign'.[75] After the Olympic Games, however, Hitler changed his mind, composing a long memorandum, presumably at the end of August, in which he himself specified how the shortage of raw materials was to be dealt with. In it he emphasized and defined the tasks Göring had taken on in the spring, when he had become Commissioner for Raw Materials and Foreign Exchange. At the same time, the memorandum was designed to keep Schacht, the Economics Minister, in line. For on 20 August Schacht had once again spoken out frankly to the Reich governors about his fears concerning the economic situation, had demanded Goerdeler's reinstatement as Prices Commissar, and warned against any 'new decisions on dealing with the Jewish question'.[76] Hitler at any rate only informed Schacht at the end of August, that is, after the event, about the fundamental decisions on economic policy that he had taken.[77]

Hitler divided the memorandum into two parts. The first was a detailed exposition of familiar pet topics of his regarding 'world view' and world history. After a few introductory sentences, Hitler made his first core statement, naming the enemy against whom they all had to struggle: 'Since the outbreak of the French Revolution the world has been moving ever faster towards a new conflict, of which the most extreme resolution is Bolshevism, and the essence and goal of Bolshevism is the elimination of the hitherto dominant social strata of humanity by world-wide Jewry....Since Marxism, through its victory in Russia, has established one of the greatest empires in the world as a basis for its future operations this issue has become a menacing one.' In Europe, he wrote, Germany and Italy are 'at the moment the only two states that can be regarded as standing firm against Bolshevism'. All others are 'corrupted by their democratic ways, infected by Marxism...or ruled by authoritarian governments' and thus 'incapable of ever waging a successful war against Soviet Russia'. Outside Europe only Japan could be 'considered as a power standing firm in the face of this threat to the world'.

To judge by this, an alliance with Britain was not central to Hitler's considerations, even if he had by no means abandoned the idea. On 12 August, in other words during the Olympic Games, he had sent Ribbentrop as the new ambassador to London with the task of bringing about the desired alliance, and in the coming months he was to return repeatedly to the idea that *in the long term* it would come about.[78] The assumption in the memorandum, however, is that in the short term the anti-communist bloc Hitler was striving to create would have to do without British involvement. And the threat that he evoked so vividly was horrifying. If 'Bolshevism' were to triumph this would lead to the inevitable 'destruction, indeed annihilation of the German nation'. If 'in a very short time the German army...cannot be turned into the foremost army in the world, Germany will be doomed!'

Germany's economic situation, the second topic of the memorandum, was marked by over-population, too narrow a base in food production, and a shortage of raw materials. The 'ultimate solution' to all these problems lay in 'extending our nation's living space and its food and raw materials base'. While this problem remained unsolved and Germany continued to be dependent on imports (which could not be increased because of the limited export opportunities) the priorities that had to be set were clear. It was 'impossible to use foreign exchange earmarked for raw materials to buy food', if this were to be done 'at the expense of national rearmament'. In addition, he strongly objected to the notion of 'bringing about any "enrichment" of raw materials that might benefit Germany in the event of war' by putting restrictions on national rearmament, in other words on the production of arms and munitions. In the polemic that followed against this, to him misguided, idea – a polemic clearly directed against the Economics Minister,

Schacht – Hitler became somewhat bogged down in detail. Then, however, he advanced a concrete 'programme' for the next few years:

I Parallel with the military and political rearmament and mobilization of our nation must go its economic rearmament and mobilization and this must be effected in the same tempo, with the same determination, and if necessary with the same ruthlessness as well…

II To this end, foreign exchange must be saved in all those areas where German products can cover our needs, so that we can concentrate it on those requirements that can be met only by imports.

III In line with this, we must now push ahead with German fuel production as fast as possible and fully complete the task within eighteen months…

IV It is also clear that the mass production of synthetic rubber must be organized and achieved.

A series of individual instructions followed, peppered with polemical remarks aimed at the, in his view incompetent, bureaucrats dealing with economic matters. 'German iron production' had to be 'stepped up massively', the 'distillation of potatoes into alcohol' had to be 'banned forthwith', supplies of industrial fat had to be obtained from domestic coal, and the extraction of domestic non-ferrous ores had to be increased 'regardless of cost'.

Hitler summarized thus: 'In short I consider it necessary that with iron determination 100% self-sufficiency should be achieved in every sphere where it is feasible and that as a result not only should the nation become independent of foreign countries for its supplies of these most essential raw materials, but it should be able to conserve the foreign exchange that it needs in peace time to be able to import our foodstuffs.' In addition, he demanded that 'there be an immediate review of the outstanding debts in foreign exchange owed to German business abroad' for they concealed the 'malign purpose' of 'holding as a safeguard reserves of foreign exchange abroad that were being withheld from the grasp of the domestic economy'. This amounted to 'deliberate sabotage of the Reich's capacity to assert or defend itself'. For this reason laws were required: '1) a law providing for the death penalty for economic sabotage and 2) a law making the whole of Jewry liable for all damage inflicted by individual specimens of this criminal community on the German economy and thus upon the German people.' Thus the argument he had advanced at the beginning of the memorandum through his polemic against 'Jewish' Soviet Russia had come full circle. His measures, at home and abroad, to prepare for war were in the final analysis directed at the same enemy, namely the Jews. At the end of the memorandum he states succinctly that there are two tasks:

I The German army must be operational within four years.

II The German economy must be ready for war within four years.[79]

The most important message of the memorandum is certainly Hitler's absolute determination – a determination rooted in his political programme and ideologically charged to a high degree – to maintain the rapid pace of rearmament and thus to go to war. However, in addition to this he defined and emphasized the tasks linked to the 'general authority' in economic matters that Göring had obtained for himself in the spring and early summer. Thus Hitler intervened directly in the development of the policy to create economic 'autarky' in Germany and focused Göring's energies in particular directions. In the months to come these interventions by Hitler were to result in concrete measures. Thus the memorandum is not only important evidence of Hitler's programme and ideology but above all shows him as an active politician.[80]

Since the beginning of the summer, in other words even before Hitler's memorandum, rearmament had been stepped up. It was quite clear that the military had understood Hitler's giving responsibility to Göring in the spring of 1936 for alleviating the raw materials and foreign exchange crisis as an explicit sign that they should do all they could to force the pace of armaments production, and they were only too ready to respond to it. Thus as early as June 1936 state secretary Erhard Milch gave the order to arm the Luftwaffe to maximum capacity by the spring of 1937 rather than by 1938, as originally planned.[81] On instructions from the commander-in-chief of the army the General Army Office produced an armaments plan on 1 August 1936 that provided for a peacetime force totalling 43 divisions and a wartime force of 102 divisions to be in place by 1 October 1939.[82] In early December 1936 the commander-in-chief declared this plan would form the basis for all further armaments planning.[83] There is a clear connection between these projects and the demands of Hitler's four-year plan. The schedule for mobilization, during which the army was for the first time to reach its new size, began on 1 April 1940. In other words, the German army was to be ready for full deployment in four years,[84] and on 1 September 1939 103 divisions were in fact mobilized.[85] The introduction from 24 August 1936 of two years' conscription (Hitler issued the decree without at first giving it much media attention) was an integral part of these war preparations.[86]

The Party Rally, whose slogan was 'Rally of Honour' began on 8 September. It was opened by a proclamation, read out as usual by Gauleiter Wagner, announcing the 'Four-Year Programme'. 'In four years' time', Hitler told the Party, 'Germany must be completely self-sufficient in all the materials that we can supply in whatever way possible through our own skills, our chemical and machine industries, and our mining industry!' The foreign exchange saved in this way, as he particularly stressed in order to reassure his listeners, would be used to guarantee food supplies *and* to import raw materials that could not be produced in Germany.[87] In fact, the value of German agricultural imports rose in 1937 from 1.5 to 2 billion RM, which led to the food sector being markedly less strained.[88] In addition, there was an announcement about the extension of conscription from one to two years that Hitler had decreed at the end of August. As in the previous year, he also spoke out against wage increases.[89] In his closing speech on 14 September Hitler's main topic was 'Communism as a threat to the world'. He gave dramatic descriptions of alleged atrocities committed in Spain by the communists and predicted that if Bolshevism triumphed 'European culture' would be 'replaced by the most brutal barbarity ever known'.[90]

Thus during the spring and in the late summer of 1936 Hitler, influenced by political developments abroad, took a number of fundamental domestic decisions to boost preparations for war. Chief among these were the appointment of Himmler as Chief of the German Police, which was linked to a reorientation of police activity as a whole towards 'preventive' measures, and the two-stage establishment of a clear economic policy: in the spring through the appointment of Göring as Commissar for Raw Materials and Foreign Exchange, and in the summer through the implementation of the Four-Year Plan. By establishing this clear policy direction he succeeded in resolving the conflict between the rapid pace of rearmament and the need for food supplies, for which more foreign exchange was now available. At the core of this new economic strategy was the aim of 'autarky', in other words supplying the demand for goods as much as possible from domestic production and in particular from the production of substitute raw materials, regardless of cost. Preliminary decisions about how the plundering of Jewish property might be extended were directly linked to this. The fact that Hitler launched the Volkswagen project at the same time demonstrates that in view

of the strains being put on the economy he wished to provide a predominantly middle-class audience with a glimpse of the future prosperity of the
Nazi state.

Following on from 30 June 1934 and the Nuremberg laws of September
1935, Hitler's interventions in the spring and summer of 1936 represented
the third important change of direction in domestic politics. As he had done
before, although in both cases only after prolonged crises and equally long
periods of hesitation, Hitler established clear domestic priorities in order to
maintain the pace of rearmament. The foreign policy measures he took in
parallel with these indicate clearly that he was now convinced he had overcome the weakness of his position during his first years in office and could
now begin to engage much more confidently in power politics.

Plans for the anti-communist bloc

While Hitler had spent the late summer above all on pushing ahead with
rearmament, in the autumn foreign policy was top of the agenda. The steps
he now took were the result of a process of gradual reorientation that had
begun during the preceding months.

Whereas up to the spring of 1936 Hitler's ideas on foreign policy had
been determined by the view that as a result of Italy's conflict with Abyssinia
and the reactions provoked by it among the western powers the opportunities in the medium term for some kind of cooperation with Italy and in the
long term for an alliance with Britain had improved, in the summer he
believed he could see a pro-communist bloc forming and aimed to respond
by setting up a 'counter-bloc'. The formation in France in June 1936 of a
popular front government ruling with the support of the communists conjured up for him the threat of an alliance led by the 'Bolshevist' Soviet
Union. Spain might possibly join it and, for safety's sake, Czechoslovakia
should be regarded as part of it. The fact that the new French prime minister
Léon Blum was a Jew confirmed Hitler's deeply rooted prejudice. For him
Blum was a 'conscious agent of the Soviets, a Zionist, and a destroyer of the
world'.[91] As a counterweight to this he had visions of a pact, founded on a
German–Italian alliance, that would include Poland, parts of south-eastern
Europe, conceivably Spain, now that it had been 'rescued' from communism,
and in the longer term Britain. In addition, Japan would be a partner in East
Asia. On the other hand, he was dilatory in responding to a proposal made

in July 1936 by the three Locarno powers, Britain, France, and Belgium, that Germany and Italy should be part of a successor to the Locarno Pact. Such a 'Western Pact' was diametrically opposed to his thinking at that time.[92]

During the autumn of 1936 he spoke on numerous occasions to Goebbels of the 'fight against Bolshevism' as the regime's coming great challenge, reprising in other words the topic that he had emphasized so strongly at the Party Rally and which since then had been used heavily in propaganda.[93] Confrontation would, he said, be unavoidable at the latest if France became communist, which he considered likely. German rearmament would, however, only be completed in 1941,[94] and thus a danger period was opening up of several years. He put his main efforts, therefore, into rapidly consolidating relations with Italy and Japan. During the Peasants' Rally on the Bückeberg at the beginning of October Hitler had a private conversation with the Italian Propaganda Minister Alfieri. As Hitler told Goebbels regarding this discussion, he would be 'glad to see Italy out of Geneva. Then we would be free to act. He won't move against Italy. He wants ideological détente. He's invited Mussolini to Germany. They'll talk things through face to face.' Alfieri in turn let Hitler know that for their part the Italians had decided to send Giuseppe Renzetti, who from the 1920s to 1935 had acted as Mussolini's personal go-between with the Nazis in Berlin, back to the German capital. He had been withdrawn from California, where he had been Consul General, because of the cooling of relations with the United States.[95]

A short time later, still in October, the Italian Foreign Minister, Ciano, made an official visit to Germany. First of all he agreed a joint protocol with Neurath in which both states bound themselves in writing to cooperate on a series of issues: the League of Nations, their shared opposition to 'Bolshevism', and their policy towards Spain and Austria.[96] On 24 October Hitler received Ciano at the Berghof, where, if Ciano's record is to be believed, Hitler opened up to his guest much broader possibilities of German–Italian cooperation. Their future alliance was to be at the heart of a European front against Bolshevism. In addition, Hitler told Ciano, Germany would be ready for war in three to five years' time and he sketched out the two powers' spheres of interest: Germany was to expand into eastern Europe and Italy in the Mediterranean. The invitation to join forces in a large-scale war of aggression could hardly have been framed more clearly.[97] Mussolini took only a week to respond. In a speech made in Milan he spoke of a Berlin–Rome axis, around which 'all European states can move if they have a desire for cooperation and peace'.[98]

Parallel to his courting of Italy, Hitler was also trying to win Japan as a partner in his future strategy of conquest. On 25 November the so-called Anti-Comintern Pact with Japan, negotiated by Ribbentrop, was signed in Berlin. According to it the Communist International was to be opposed through the exchange of information. In a secret appendix both states gave mutual assurances that they would remain neutral in the event of an attack by the Soviet Union and in addition pledged not to conclude any treaties that ran counter to the 'spirit of the agreement'.[99] Since the summer of 1936, the German government had been trying to involve Poland in the emerging Anti-Comintern Pact but Poland had shown no interest. These efforts, which were ultimately fruitless, can be traced up to the autumn of 1937.[100] Hitler regarded Czechoslovakia, on the other hand, as first and foremost an ally of the Soviet Union, as a Soviet 'aircraft carrier', as it was referred to in propaganda.

It is striking that from the end of the summer Hitler (and Göring) had been dropping hints to Balkan politicians close to Germany that they should prepare for an imminent conflict between the 'authoritarian' states and the Soviet Union. These hints also pointed unmistakably to a coming conflict with Czechoslovakia. When the Hungarian head of state and Regent, Miklós Horthy, made a private visit to Germany in August 1936 Hitler spoke to him about the inevitable imminent conflict between the 'countries ruled by Bolshevism and those ruled by conservative authoritarian governments'.[101] Two months later, while in Budapest to attend the funeral of prime minister Gömbös, Göring declared quite openly to the Foreign Minister that Germany would annex Austria sooner or later and not stand by any longer while 'the Sudetenland, which is German to the core, is bleeding to death under Czech rule'.[102] In mid-December Hitler announced to the Hungarian Interior Minister, Miklós Kozma, that he was working to 'build a united front' against 'Bolshevism', to which Italy, Austria, Hungary, Romania, Poland, Yugoslavia, and the Baltic States should belong. In connection with this he also attempted to direct Hungary's revisionist policy and desire to regain lost territory towards Czechoslovakia, which was digging 'its own grave' by its pro-Soviet stance.[103] A month previously Hitler had expounded similar ideas to the Romanian politician Gheorghe Bratianu.[104]

In spite of such threats, in autumn 1936 Hitler appears to have sanctioned an initiative by Albrecht Haushofer, who at this time worked with Ribbentrop in the latter's Berlin 'office', to gauge the possibilities for fundamentally improving bilateral relations by means of informal talks with the Czech government.

Hitler's reaction to Haushofer's report of 25 November on his talks with President Eduard Beneš and Foreign Minister Kamil Krofta has been preserved. Haushofer had proposed a ten-year non-aggression treaty with Prague (Hitler had made a similar offer in his 7 March speech occasioned by the occupation of the Rhineland). Hitler now rejected this. He appeared completely uninterested in measures to improve the situation of the Sudeten Germans. Instead, the possibility of concluding a trade agreement was his main concern, as well as the issue of how Czech neutrality could be guaranteed in the event of a Soviet attack (a treaty of mutual support had existed since the previous year between Czechoslovakia and the Soviet Union) and the activities of German-speaking emigrés in Prague curtailed. Haushofer continued to put out feelers, but in January 1937 Hitler made it clear to him that he was not interested in pursuing the matter. At the beginning of 1937 he was utterly convinced that Czechoslovakia belonged in the enemy camp. He had evidently regarded Haushofer's efforts as a test that finally persuaded him that he was right to take an aggressive line with Czechoslovakia.[105] The episode demonstrates that Hitler was altogether prepared to allow some temporary ambivalence in German foreign policy, as long as he was still in control.

At the end of 1936 and beginning of 1937, as we can infer from a series of statements made by Hitler or by those around him, his perception of foreign policy suddenly became sharply focused.

In an address lasting three hours on 1 December, Hitler expounded to the cabinet his estimation of the situation. No other record of this appears to exist apart from the account contained in Goebbels's diary. According to Goebbels, Hitler claimed that Europe was already divided into two camps. Soon France and Spain would capitulate to the communist drive for expansion. If communist regimes were to be established there, a Europe-wide crisis would result. They (the Germans) could only hope that this crisis could be 'delayed until we are ready'. Therefore: 'Rearm. Money must be no object.' In the final analysis, however, the 'authoritarian states (Poland, Austria, Yugoslavia, Hungary)' could not be relied on. The only 'firmly anti-Bolshevist states' were 'Germany, Italy, Japan' and 'agreements' could be made with them. 'England will get involved if a crisis develops in France.' At least with his closest followers, therefore, Hitler maintained the impression that his increasingly aggressive foreign policy would in the end lead to the hoped for alliance with Great Britain.[106]

The measures approved by the cabinet on 1 December emphasized the seriousness of the situation and the need underlined by Hitler to ramp up even further the hectic pace of rearmament. One of the measures was a law against economic sabotage that provided for heavy penalties, even the death penalty, for those who moved wealth abroad.[107] The other provided for a legal change in how foreign exchange was handled; so-called security measures were introduced against persons suspected of transferring wealth abroad.[108] Both laws laid the foundation for the practice of confiscating Jewish property more or less arbitrarily and sentencing its owners to long prison terms as 'economic saboteurs'.[109] The anti-Semitic impulse behind these new laws reveals once again the ideological context uniting Hitler's domestic and foreign policy. German Jews were to be expressly targeted to finance rearmament for the fight against 'Jewish Bolshevism'. In addition, at the end of November 1936 the government issued a law imposing a general price freeze, following on from the appointment in October of Gauleiter Josef Wagner as the new Reich Prices Commissioner.[110]

On 17 December 1936, at a gathering of 'leading German businessmen' in Berlin, Hitler demanded an increase in production in every sector. His challenge ended in the slogan 'With this there's no such word as "impossible"'. Hitler commended Göring to his audience as a man of 'unbending will' to whom he had given the task of delivering the Four-Year Plan. For his part, Göring spurred the industrialists on to achieve the utmost to support rearmament. It was a matter of 'victory or destruction'; if Germany won through, 'business would be well recompensed'.[111]

The military prospects for any future war between Germany and its allies and the Soviet Union and its satellites now assumed increasing importance in Hitler's mind. A conversation that took place in January 1937 between Goebbels and Ribbentrop, two of his most loyal admirers among the leadership, repeated Hitler's line, including voicing the hope he still maintained that Britain would join them. Japan was 'a firm ally. . . . Everyone is hostile to Russia', as Goebbels noted. In the process 'Czechoslovakia will be caught in the crossfire . . . Everything in flux. England holds the key to a solution. In the end it must be on our side.'[112]

Goebbels's diary also tells us that at the end of January 1937 Hitler attended a presentation lasting several hours by Blomberg in the War Ministry about a study carried out by the army on the likely scenarios of a war between 'Germany and its fascist allies' and 'Russia, Czechoslovakia, and Lithuania'. At the lunch following the presentation Hitler defined these 'fascist allies' as being in future 'Romania, Yugoslavia, and, increasingly likely, Poland' in addition to Italy. This indicates some change in the negative views he had expressed in December about Yugoslavia and Poland as potential partners. It is striking that the Soviet Union's strongest potential ally, France, was missing from the theoretical war scenario (which, according to Goebbels, Hitler was hoping to delay 'for another six years'). In a conversation with Goebbels Hitler also said that he was not excluding the possibility of a 'reconciliation' with France, provided that 'we are strong enough'.[113] Hitler's reflections on alliances were therefore by no means over.

In the speech he made to the Reichstag on 30 January, the fourth anniversary of the seizure of power, Hitler strove above all to create the impression that the reintroduction of conscription, the creation of the Luftwaffe, and the occupation of the Rhineland had 'restored Germany to equal status' with other nations. His last unilateral step towards a final annulment of the Treaty of Versailles was to announce that he was 'solemnly' withdrawing the signature at the end of the treaty that, amongst other things, forced Germany to accept that it had been to blame for the war. This, however, signalled 'the end of these so-called surprises'. In eight points he again put forward his thoughts on a new 'peace programme' that covered a reform of the League of Nations, a general agreement on arms limitation, and security for national minorities. He took issue vigorously and at length with a speech made on 19 January to the House of Commons by the British Foreign Secretary, Eden. He opposed Eden's demand for a moderate arms limit on the part of the European powers with a longwinded exposition of the dangers of Bolshevism. Finally, he turned to the subject of the British note of 7 May 1936, which was to his mind an outrageous interrogation of his precise intentions and so he had thus far left it unanswered. His response to the question posed by the British government of whether Germany now considered itself capable of concluding 'real treaties' was that 'Germany will never again sign a treaty that is in any way in conflict with its honour, the nation's honour, and that of the government representing it, or that in other ways is incompatible with Germany's vital interests and therefore could not be upheld in the long run.'[114]

He also issued a detailed demand to Britain for the restitution of German colonies. This additional demand did not, however, signify that at this point Hitler had already abandoned his cherished ambition of forming an alliance with Britain. Although in *Mein Kampf* and his pre-1933 speeches he had indeed rejected any return to German colonial policies in order to encourage rapprochement with Britain, German colonies were for him reserved for the future when Germany would pursue 'world power policies' in different political circumstances. In the first years after 1933 he had therefore exercised restraint in this matter, particularly as his conservative coalition partners regarded the restoration of the colonies as being of indisputable national importance. Although he repeatedly emphasized that Germany would not settle for the loss of its colonies, he also made it clear that his government's foremost foreign policy concerns lay elsewhere.[115]

At the beginning of 1936, however, Hitler had begun to lay more emphasis on the restoration of the colonies.[116] At the same time, he had coordinated the various colonial organizations in Germany, which were predominantly conservative, integrating them in the Reich Colonial League, which was close to the NSDAP, for he wished to ensure that a single line was followed in the political handling of the demand for restitution.[117] In his speech of 30 January 1937 he focused again on this subject, although the tone of his demand was moderate and, as was usual in such instances, the press was instructed to show restraint in reporting it.[118] As far as the issue of colonies was concerned, however, Hitler had not changed his view and continued to regard it in the light of the desired alliance with Britain, in other words tactically. But now he was no longer prepared to hold back on his demands in order to bring about this partnership, but rather intended to achieve it from a position of strength and if necessary through pressure. Just like the expansion of the German fleet, this more confident stance with regard to colonies was from his perspective one component in the complex of issues he intended to employ to prepare the way for an alliance with his future British 'partners'. Surrendering claims to German colonies was no longer a small token but a major pledge that the British had to match.[119]

Hitler's 'courtship' of Britain was thus becoming increasingly confident and assertive, with threats of sanctions. Bearing in mind also that Hitler's calculations were based on a completely false notion of British policy, which was in no way aiming for an alliance with Germany but rather attempting to lock it into a system guaranteeing European security, the path to open rivalry was inevitable.

Domestic consequences of the preparations for war

This fixation on war had a direct impact on domestic politics, leading to more radical measures against the Jews, while at the same time Hitler tried under the banner of the fight against communism to find a modus vivendi with the Catholic Church.

Hitler's direct influence can be traced even in the details of these anti-Jewish measures. The ministerial bureaucracy resumed its efforts to remove Jews from economic life at a conference of senior civil servants on 29 September 1936. The Olympic Games had closed a few weeks before and so there was no more reason to hold back on the persecution of the Jews.[120] Now the regime's main concern was to exclude them from the economy but in such a way as not to slow down the dynamic of rearmament. As Hitler had demanded in the Four-Year Plan memorandum, the state began to appropriate Jewish property. The enormous efforts focused on rearmament made the economic situation precarious, however, and as a result the measures taken could not for the time being be too drastic. Although discrimination (for example exclusion from certain professions) was intensified, any further measures were delayed while the economy was at risk. Such measures included, for example, the proposed general ban on Party members having business dealings with Jews, a general ban on public bodies giving contracts to Jews, or the exclusion of Jews from land transactions and from economic involvement in the cultural sphere.

The demand Hitler had made in the Four-Year Plan memorandum for a 'special Jewish tax' was one of a bundle of anti-Semitic draft bills discussed by the ministerial bureaucracy at the turn of 1936/37.[121] Although at the end of 1936 he had ordered that this tax be enacted in law by the time sentence was pronounced in the trial in Switzerland of Wilhelm Gustloff's assassin, which was expected imminently, in December 1936 the plan was deferred, when the ministerial bureaucracy was unable to meet this deadline; Göring had vetoed the tax because of the continuing precarious economic and foreign exchange situation.[122] Then, in the spring of 1937, Hitler made a personal decision to delay the process of identifying Jewish businesses, which had been pursued by the relevant ministries up to that point. In the summer work on the details of the Reich Citizenship Law, which had been announced in 1935 as part of the Nuremberg Laws, was also delayed.[123] Instead Jewish businesses were to be identifiable indirectly through the adoption of a trade emblem for non-Jewish businesses. As these examples show, Hitler was more than ready to modify the methods used to persecute the Jews, and if necessary to adapt their pace, to suit other political objectives. Whereas an emblem for Jewish businesses and a special tax for Jews were in fact introduced in the autumn of 1938, a 'Reich citizenship document' as envisaged in the Reich Citizenship Law was, as stated above, never implemented.

Hitler also altered his policy with regard to the Catholic Church as a result of his drive to prepare for war. In contrast, however, to the radicalization seen in his persecution of the Jews, during the summer and autumn of 1936 he temporarily moderated his aggressive policy towards the Catholic Church and even appeared willing to compromise.

Less than three weeks after the elections of 29 March 1936 the regime had resumed its policy of hostility towards the Church. All private pre-schools were forbidden by law, which was a measure aimed principally at monastery schools.[124] The Ministry for Churches was still unwilling to engage in negotiations over the as yet unresolved issue of Catholic organizations, while the regime exploited the uncertain legal position in order to put more pressure on them.[125] The prosecutions of Catholic orders for foreign exchange offences were resumed in the spring.[126] The regime also initiated a campaign against Catholic priests and lay brothers for alleged cases of sexual abuse. In a magazine article in mid-April Heydrich wrote of 'over 100 monks' who would be brought to book for 'the vilest and most disgusting moral crimes'. The trials began at the end of May and were accompanied by a campaign against monasteries as 'hotbeds of vice'.[127]

This campaign was largely Hitler's doing. To Goebbels he expressed the view that homosexuality pervaded the whole Catholic Church: 'It must be eradicated.'[128] Even so, in mid-July Hitler told the Justice Minister to halt the trials until the Olympic Games were over.[129] After the Games, however, he was undecided about whether to proceed with them again[130] and in October decided to suspend them for the time being.[131] Important factors in this decision were the emerging alliance with Italy and also the consideration that during the Spanish Civil War there had been graphic descriptions of alleged atrocities perpetrated by communists on Catholic believers; these would cease to be credible if priests in Germany were being systematically persecuted.

The German Catholic Church for its part was altogether aware of and actively pursued the opportunity to use the struggle against 'Bolshevism' in Spain as a bridge to the regime and to expand its own scope once more. In their pastoral letter of 19 August, in other words at the precise point when the Olympic Games were over and the renewed prosecution of priests was looming, the German bishops made a clear overture to the government, for we read regarding Bolshevism: 'With God's help may our Führer succeed in dealing steadfastly with this immensely difficult problem through the loyal cooperation of all national comrades!'[132]

On 4 November 1936 the Munich Cardinal Michael von Faulhaber had a three-hour meeting with Hitler on the Obersalzberg, intended by both sides to gauge whether the 'fight against Bolshevism' constituted a sufficiently robust foundation for the future relationship between the regime and the Church. After Hitler and Faulhaber had agreed that 'Bolshevism' was their common 'mortal enemy' discussion moved to the regime's future Church policy. Hitler brushed aside Faulhaber's complaints about Nazism's hostility to the Church, namely, in addition to the prosecutions of priests, the secularization of schools, the activities of the German Christians, and the exclusion of Church associations. Faulhaber was surprised that Hitler distanced himself from Rosenberg's *Myth of the Twentieth Century* in extremely negative terms. Yet Hitler went on the offensive against Faulhaber when the topic of the 'Church's fight against racial laws' was raised (at which point the hitherto calm discussion threatened to become heated), justifying compulsory sterilization as being essential for the good of the nation as well as being 'God's will'. Apart from this particular bone of contention, Faulhaber was generally very impressed with Hitler: 'The Führer has a command of diplomatic and social formalities that is better than a born sovereign's', he noted. He did not let events take him by surprise, as governments in the Weimar Republic had done, but rather 'he moves deliberately towards them'. He expounded 'his ideas vigorously and confidently with self-control'. At various moments, however, he could become 'very solemn and almost emotional'. He had, for example, said: 'The individual does not count. The individual will die. Cardinal Faulhaber will die. Alfred Rosenberg will die. Adolf Hitler will die. That makes one reflect and be humble before God.' There was no doubt that Hitler had a 'faith in God' and recognized Christianity as the 'cornerstone of western culture'. 'Less clear', however, was his 'view of the Catholic Church as a divine institution with its divine mission independent of the state, with its immutable dogmas, and with its historical and cultural greatness'.[133]

Immediately after this meeting the regime had to accept a painful defeat in its conflict with the Catholic Church. In Oldenburg the state government had at the beginning of November ordered that crucifixes should be removed from schools, but massive protests from the Catholic population had forced it to reverse this decision.[134] In addition, on 1 December 1936 the law concerning membership of the Hitler Youth came into force – a direct attack on the Church's youth work. By means of this law, 'German youth within Germany' would be brought together 'in its entirety' and would be 'educated physically, intellectually, and morally in the spirit of National Socialism to be of service to the nation and the national community'. The law explicitly stated that parents and schools were also required to participate in the programme of education, thus making it indirectly clear that (even if membership of the HJ was not at this stage made compulsory) the state would not tolerate any other agencies providing education. It was evident that Church youth work was being ruled out.[135]

A few weeks after his discussion with Hitler, Faulhaber composed a pastoral letter from the German bishops in which, possibly encouraged by the opposition in Oldenburg, he summed up the essence of the meeting from his point of view: The Church's support for the regime's efforts to 'guard against Bolshevism' was dependent on the upholding of the Concordat.[136] Faulhaber sent Hitler the draft on 30 December 1936, referring to the contents as the product 'of our agreement' reached when they had met at the beginning of November.[137] He concluded the letter with the words, 'May Providence continue to preside over your doings!'

Hitler, however, took a rather different view from Faulhaber. As far as he was concerned, there was no 'agreement', but rather he intended to use his Church policy as a means of exerting pressure on the Catholic Church to continue supporting his 'fight against Bolshevism'. What he understood by support was, however, an unreserved commitment to his regime.[138] Faulhaber's pastoral letter, which set conditions for this support, inevitably aroused his displeasure. As he explained on 4 January to his lunch guests, the Catholic bishops had 'yet again fired off a pastoral letter opposing us'. Tirades against the Churches then followed, culminating in the statement that Christianity was 'doomed'. Its destruction might 'take a long time, but it will come'.[139] These words marked a new phase in Church policy, which was to lead in 1937 to the most serious conflict to date with the Churches.

22

Conflict with the Churches
and Cultural Policy

On 30 January 1937 the Reichstag met for a session intended by Hitler to demonstrate to the world that the regime had consolidated its position. At the ensuing meeting of ministers in the Reich Chancellery, however, there was a scandal. Hitler thanked the members of the cabinet formally for their work and announced that he intended personally to receive all ministers who were not yet Party members into the NSDAP and confer on them the 'Gold Medal'. Then, as Goebbels noted, the 'unimaginable' happened: Paul von Eltz-Rübenach, the Reich Minister for Transport and Post, flatly refused this offer, citing as his reason the regime's policy towards the Churches and demanding that Hitler explain himself, which the latter refused to do.[1]

Although Hitler claimed to be affronted by this disruption of the event, he was in fact aware that Eltz-Rübenach, a Catholic, was opposed to his Church policy. At the beginning of December he had voted for the Hitler Youth Law in cabinet only on condition that no 'religious values' would be destroyed; a few days earlier he had asked for the same assurance in a two-and-a-half-hour personal meeting with Hitler, which he then reported to Cardinal Faulhaber.[2] Hitler was extremely suspicious of his Transport Minister: 'When he sneezes, soot comes out, he's so black', he told Goebbels on 4 January.[3] Inevitably, Eltz-Rübenach was immediately required to resign from his posts. In the months following Hitler took the opportunity to use the cabinet circulation procedure to gain consent for a further law that had previously met with resistance from Eltz-Rübenach.[4] The planned Reich Schools Law, which aimed to impose the community schools favoured by the National Socialists, was intended to complete the process, already in train, of doing away with Church schools.

Eltz-Rübenach's public opposition to Hitler's Church policy was a clear signal that the regime was heading for a fundamental conflict with the Churches, and not only with the Catholic Church but with the Protestant Churches too. From the end of 1936 it was becoming increasingly clear that the efforts of Reich Churches Minister Kerrl to unite the fragmented Protestant Church would fail. Then, on 12 February 1937, the Reich Churches Committee, created by Kerrl in 1935, resigned. Kerrl announced that the Churches would be subordinated to state governance,[5] and Hitler, who at a lunch in January had left Kerrl in no doubt about his dissatisfaction with the latter's Church policy,[6] then summoned Kerrl, Frick, Hess, Himmler, and Goebbels, as well as the state secretaries Hermann Muhs (Churches) and Wilhelm Stuckart (Interior), at short notice to a meeting on 15 February on the Obersalzberg.

At the meeting Hitler severely criticized Kerrl; at this point, as Goebbels records, Hitler claimed he could 'do without a conflict with the Churches. He's expecting the great world struggle in a few years. Germany can lose only one more war, then that will be it.' For this reason the measures Kerrl was planning, which amounted to the creation of a *summus episcopus* (in the shape of the Minister for Churches), were out of the question for they could only be implemented 'with the use of force'. In the short term Hitler accepted a suggestion from Goebbels that the Party and the state should keep out of disputes within the Protestant Church and that a synod should be elected to create a constitution so that the quarrels could take place in that arena. Within a year, Goebbels claimed, 'they'll be begging the state for help against each other.'[7] Hitler therefore decreed that a general synod be elected so that the Protestant Church could create for itself 'a new constitution and with it a new organizational structure with complete freedom and according to the wishes of the Church members'.[8] The project was immediately given a propaganda spin as 'the Führer's conciliatory move to aid the Protestant Church'.[9]

After only a few days, however, Hitler changed course. Although at a meeting of high-ranking functionaries on 22 February about the 'Churches issue' he again justified his policy with reference to his wide-ranging foreign policy objectives, in contrast to the previous week he no longer wanted to keep the peace with the Churches in order to be able to survive the imminent 'great world struggle', but rather to neutralize them beforehand. 'Separation of Church and State, an end to the Concordat', was Goebbels's summary. 'Not the Party against Christianity. Instead we must declare ourselves to be the only true Christians. Then the full power of the Party will be turned on the saboteurs. Christianity is the watchword for priests to be destroyed, just as socialism was once the call to destroy the Marxist big wigs. For the time being, though, we'll wait and see what the other side does.'[10] Even so, it was five months, the end of July, before the preparations for the Church elections were finally discontinued. The idea was never taken up again.[11]

In the meantime relations with the Catholic Church had also, and dramatically, deteriorated. Annoyance at the Hitler Youth Law, the threat of the Reich School Law, the prosecutions for currency and sexual abuse offences, the seemingly endless negotiations about the conditions for implementing the Concordat, also the state's clear lack of interest in putting its policies towards the Church on a legal basis[12] finally prompted the Vatican to state its position clearly. On 21 March the Pope issued the encyclical 'Mit brennender Sorge' (With Deep Anxiety). It had been composed by Faulhaber in consultation with Pius XI and Cardinal Secretary of State Pacelli personally and was widely circulated among German Catholics. It marked the nadir of relations between the regime and Catholicism. The Pope spoke out against the harassment of the German Churches, the Nazi notion of 'belief in God', and racial ideology.[13] Hitler demanded that the document be 'completely ignored' and on 23 March the Ministry for Churches banned its dissemination.[14]

At the beginning of April Hitler geared himself up to retaliate. In a telephone call he told Goebbels he now intended to 'let rip against the Vatican'. In concrete terms this meant the resumption of the prosecutions of priests for sexual offences, which had been suspended in the summer of 1936. The judicial authorities were given their instructions.[15] They were to start with a group of prosecutions that were already with the public prosecutor in Koblenz. As the 'overture' Hitler was considering 'the gruesome sexually motivated murder of a young boy in a Belgian monastery'.[16] Naturally the propaganda media responded to this prompting and used the Belgian murder (which, it transpired, had occurred in quite different circumstances and had not even been committed in a monastery) as the start of an extensive campaign against the Catholic Church, which provided an effective backdrop to the series of trials in Koblenz that began at the end of April.[17] In total more than 200 members of religious orders and priests were found guilty in 1936/37 of sexual abuse. While the prosecutions (as with the case of currency offences) were instigated for political reasons, on the whole they were based on altogether credible accusations.[18]

A few days into the campaign Hitler professed himself to Goebbels to be satisfied with 'the radical turn in the prosecution of priests' and went on to make a number of fundamental statements concerning future policy towards the Churches. 'Does not want any religious dimension to the Party. Does not want to be made into a god himself either. Gives Himmler a good roasting over this. We must bring the Churches to heel and make them serve our ends.' Celibacy was to cease and the Church's wealth be surrendered. Men were not be allowed to study theology before the age of twenty-four and religious orders had to be dissolved: 'That's the only way we'll bring them into line within a few decades. Then they'll be eating out of our hands.'[19] Hitler also used his speech on 1 May for a broadside against the Churches: 'As long as they stick to their religious matters the state will not trouble them. If they try by whatever means such as letters, encyclicals, and so on to claim rights that are the business of the state alone, we will force them back into the spiritual and pastoral activities appropriate to them. Nor is it their business to criticise the state's morality when they have more than enough reasons to look to their own morals. . . . It's up to the leaders of the German state to look after the morals of the German state and German nation . . .'[20]

What was meant by this was stated more precisely by Goebbels in the Sportspalast on 28 May in a speech that is generally regarded as the high point of the campaigns against the Churches.[21] Hitler had in fact dictated the core statements to him. Even the Propaganda Minister was surprised at the sharp tone of the 'declaration of hostilities' that Hitler put in his mouth.[22] In this speech, which was given great prominence in the media, Hitler announced through Goebbels that 'perpetrators of sex offences and those behind them pulling the strings' would be brought to book. Goebbels had no scruples about adopting the pose of the disgusted father and detailing examples of 'hair-raising moral depravity': 'After confession under-age young people were forced into sexual acts in the sacristies; the victims of seduction were rewarded for their compliance with the immoral desires of these sex criminals with pictures of saints, and after being violated these young people were blessed and the sign of the cross was made over them.' 'This sex plague must and will be eradicated, root and branch', Goebbels announced, and if the Church showed itself too weak to tackle the matter, the state would see to it. His appearance culminated in the threat that it might be deemed necessary 'to force some very prominent members of the clergy to give an account of themselves under oath in court'.[23]

Only one day later Hitler had the German chargé d'affaires in the Vatican deliver a note in which he complained bitterly about the Chicago Cardinal George William Mundelein, who had voiced criticisms of conditions in Germany.[24] In Hitler's view his speech 'removed the basis for normal relations between the German government and the Curia', as the Vatican was allowing 'those sweeping public attacks on the head of the German state by one if its most eminent officials to go unchallenged' and was thereby supporting them.[25]

The Churches Ministry was prompted by this incident to suggest to Hitler that he terminate the Concordat.[26] After some hesitation, at a meeting with Kerrl he gave instructions that first a law concerning the relationship of Church and state should be drafted including provisions to abolish Church Tax and also state support for the Churches; then on Reformation Day he would make a keynote speech to the Reichstag, after which he would send a note terminating the Concordat.[27] Yet in the end he decided not to take such a radical step.

On 2 June Hitler gave a speech to the Gauleiters in the Air Ministry about Church policy, once again setting out some fundamental principles. He wanted 'no Church in the Party. He had no desire to be a Church reformer to regenerate the Churches.[28] Make them submit to the state's laws. No new religions to be founded.'[29] Accordingly, the propaganda campaign against the Catholic Church continued.[30]

Even though Hitler did not intend to found a new religion, during these months he was nevertheless more than usually preoccupied with religious matters and metaphysical problems. And in the process he appears to have concluded, independently of any religious affiliation or concrete notion of God, that he himself was the instrument of a superhuman providence. The idea that the course being followed by the NSDAP was in harmony with 'providence' occurs again and again in Hitler's speeches from 1933 onwards. In August and October 1935 and in his 'election appearances' after the occupation of the Rhineland he had on numerous occasions expressed in public the conviction that he was the instrument of providence.[31] The formulations he used on 27 June at the Gau Party Congress in Würzburg, however, are far more explicit than those in the speeches referred to above. However weak the individual may be, Hitler explained to the crowd gathered in front of the Residenz, 'he becomes immeasurably strong the moment he acts in accordance with this providence! Then the power that has marked out every great event in the world pours down upon him.' Hitler of course related this phenomenon to himself: 'And when I look back on the five years that lie behind us I may surely say: "That was not merely the work of men!" If providence had not shown us the way, I would often have failed to find these vertiginous paths. . . . For deep in our hearts we National Socialists are believers too! We cannot be otherwise; no-one can make national or world history if he does not have the blessing of this providence on his intentions and actions.'[32]

It is possible to speculate about whether by invoking providence Hitler wanted to fill the gap he may have felt in his own inner life as a result of his rejection (reiterated so vehemently during the conflict with the Churches) of any concrete notion of religious faith. What is certain, however, is that 'providence' was designed to help win the political and ideological struggle against the influence of the Churches. They were not to be allowed sovereignty in metaphysical matters; on the contrary, the regime was allied to omnipotent supernatural powers!

In July, however, while still at the Bayreuth Festival, Hitler issued an order to halt the prosecutions of priests. The situation with regard to the Protestant Church had escalated at the beginning of July, when Pastor Niemöller, the main representative of the Confessing Church, was arrested. However, in the meantime Hitler had once more moved away from his idea of neutralizing the Churches before the start of the 'great world struggle'. In fact it was his anticipation of those decisive foreign conflicts that persuaded him that it was more important to find a modus vivendi with the Churches in the interests of national unity.[33] Although in August Goebbels provided him with material for more 'priest trials', he decided for the time being not to act on it.[34] The same was true of the termination of the Concordat and the vexed question of the Schools Law.[35]

In August the Reich School Law was on Hitler's desk to be signed off; after Eltz-Rübenach's resignation every minister had signed the draft by the summer. By now, however, Hitler was dithering over whether to sign. Although by 1938 the regime had to a large extent succeeded in imposing community schools, it was crucial in the light of Hitler's conflict with the Churches that the initiative for them did not appear to come from the Reich government but rather from the states and local authorities.[36] When in November Goebbels suggested further measures against the Churches Hitler spoke in favour of 'reticence': 'Let's not disturb the Christmas season with such things.'[37] At the beginning of December at lunch Hitler expatiated 'once more on the problem of the Churches', defending his failure to act on tactical grounds: 'He's getting closer and closer to a separation of Church and state. But then Protestantism will be destroyed and we'll no longer have any counterweight to the Vatican.'[38] From Hitler's perspective, in view of the massive rearmament and preparations for war, there could be no question of upsetting the status quo regarding the Churches. As he explained to Goebbels later in December, he wanted 'peace for the moment... with regard to the Churches'.[39]

More than that, since the temporary truce in the conflict, Hitler had considered it expedient to declare himself, to some extent, 'positively disposed', in his personal attitude to religion and Christianity. Opening the Winter Aid programme on 5 October 1937, for example, he claimed to believe in a 'Christianity based on action' that had 'more right than other kinds to say "That is the kind of Christianity that comes from an open and honest profession of faith..."'[40] Talking confidentially to Party associates the tone was different. As one of those present recorded, he declared to Party propaganda chiefs at the end of October that after serious inner conflict and fully conscious that his life expectancy was limited he had liberated himself from all childish religious ideas he might still hold. 'I now feel as fresh as a foal in a meadow.'[41]

On 23 November he declared to the Party's district leaders and Gau functionaries that a state was being established that 'does not see its foundations as being in Christianity or in the idea of a state, but in a united national community'. This new state would be 'merciless in its treatment of all opponents and any religious or party-based fragmentation'. He promised the Churches 'absolute freedom in matters of doctrine or in their conception of God. For we are quite certain that we know nothing about that.' One thing, however, 'was firmly settled: the Churches might have some influence on individual Germans in the hereafter, but in the here and now these individuals were in the hands of the German nation via its leaders. In a time of rapid change only such a clear and clean separation can make life viable.' This did not mean, however, that he wished to deny the existence of a God. Rather, humanity was confronted 'with an immensely powerful, an omnipotent force, so strange and profound that we as human beings cannot grasp it. That's a good thing! For it can give people consolation in difficult times. It avoids that superficiality and arrogance that leads people to assume that, although they are no more than tiny microbes on this earth and in this universe, they can rule the world and determine the laws of nature, when they can at best study them. So we want our nation to remain humble and really believe there is a God.'[42]

Consolation and humility for the nation: this was religion conceived in purely instrumental terms. It was clearly irrelevant for a man called by a mysterious providence to lead the nation.

Cultural politics

It was no coincidence that during 1937, and in parallel with his bitter conflict with the Churches, Hitler endeavoured to determine the course of Nazi cultural politics. By presenting himself as a generous supporter, indeed as the creator, of a new National Socialist culture he was obviously aiming to counteract the negative responses his 'cultural campaign' against the Churches had provoked at home and abroad and in particular to limit the damage to his personal image. Above all, however, his efforts to inaugurate 'true' German art and to give a radical new face to German cities through massive building projects were linked to a desire to provide meaning. Nazi art and architecture were to herald the start of a cultural renaissance, symbolize the founding era of a great empire, and set the standard for millennia. It is hardly accidental that Hitler began his cultural offensive at the point when he was embarking on his policy of expansion. The conqueror also wanted to found a culture.

Hitler began 1937 with a significant cultural announcement: In the Reichstag session on 30 January he announced through Göring that he had created a lucrative 'German National Prize for Art and Learning' that henceforth would be conferred annually on 'three worthy Germans'. The prize was a response to the conferring of the Nobel Peace Prize in November 1936 on the pacifist Carl von Ossietzky, who was in a concentration camp. This gesture had prompted Hitler to issue a decree forbidding all Germans 'at any time in the future' to accept a Nobel Prize, the most important international recognition of achievements in scholarship, science, and the work for peace. The German National Prize was intended to be a fitting substitute.[43]

The first laureates were named by Hitler in September 1937 at the Party Congress.[44] In addition to the Party's ideology expert, Alfred Rosenberg, these were the conductor Wilhelm Furtwängler, the surgeons Ferdinand Sauerbruch and August Bier (who shared the prize), the Antarctic explorer Wilhelm Filchner, and (posthumously) the architect Paul Ludwig Troost. Hitler then presented the prizes as part of the ceremonies marking 30 January 1938.[45]

The opening in summer 1937 of the House of German Art with the 'First Great German Art Exhibition', a prestigious show of art works created under National Socialism, was designed to establish the future direction of art in the 'Third Reich'. Since 1933 Hitler had regularly used his annual speech on culture at the Reich Party Congress to pass judgement – sarcastically, dismissively, angrily, – on any kind of modern art. Yet apart from general evocations of the artistic achievements of past epochs, in particular of the classical world, which he especially admired, he had never made any serious attempt to develop what might be called a National Socialist aesthetic. This is what he wanted to do now by making the exhibition and its opening ceremony his personal concern.

On 5 June Hitler flew to Munich accompanied by Goebbels to inspect the Führer building, designed by Troost, on Königsplatz as well as the recently completed House of German Art. He was determined to take a personal look at the selection the jury, led by the chair of the Reich Chamber of Fine Arts, Adolf Ziegler, had arrived at for the exhibition. He was, however, far from pleased with the jury's work, as Goebbels records. The choice of paintings was in part 'catastrophic' and some of them 'were positively horrific'. He would rather postpone the exhibition by a year than 'exhibit such garbage'.[46] In the end Hitler decided to reduce the number of exhibits, leaving the choice to his personal photographer, Heinrich Hoffmann, whose taste in art he had long known and for the most part shared.[47]

The difficulty of securing works for display that provided evidence of the allegedly high level of artistic achievement under Nazism gave Hitler and Goebbels the idea of mounting a parallel exhibition of the kind of art that was *not* wanted in the Third Reich. At the end of June Hitler gave his approval to Goebbels's suggestion that the exhibition of 'the art of the era of decline' originally planned for Berlin be moved at short notice to Munich.[48] Management of the exhibition was to be taken on by Ziegler and by Hans Herbert Schweitzer, the former cartoonist from *Der Angriff*, although Hitler expressed some reservations about the latter's suitability.[49] On the basis of 'the Führer's express authority' Goebbels granted Ziegler special permission to 'secure' the relevant art works ('the art of German decline since 1910') from all the museums in public ownership in Germany.[50] The commission thereupon visited thirty-two collections and requisitioned 700 works of art.[51]

On 11 July Hitler once again visited the Führer building and the House of German Art. He was again accompanied by Goebbels, who had been made to interrupt a holiday on the Baltic coast with his family a few days before and resume it at Hitler's villa on the Obersalzberg.[52] Hitler's obvious purpose was to give Goebbels, who had the reputation of not being completely indifferent to modern artistic trends, a thorough lesson in the aesthetics of Nazi art. During this visit Hitler appeared much more satisfied with the works chosen for the Great German Art Exhibition.[53] The same was true of the exhibits for its negative counterpart, which he inspected on 16 July in the Hofgarten arcades, very close to the House of German Art, a few days before the official opening of the exhibition, which had been given the title 'Degenerate Art'. In the end, after Ziegler's rapid raids on German museums, there were 600 works, including those by Emil Nolde, Max Beckmann, Marc Chagall, Max Ernst, Otto Dix, Paul Klee, George Grosz, Wassily Kandinsky, Ernst Ludwig Kirchner, Lyonel Feininger, and Franz Marc. In order to reduce the impact of the pictures they were hung very close together and arbitrarily. The titles and comments were painted on the walls. By the end of November this exhibition had attracted over two million visitors, after which it went on tour to other cities.[54] The fact that many visitors did not come to the exhibition to get worked up about 'degenerate art' but rather to say farewell to these works that met with official disapproval does not appear to have disturbed Hitler, by contrast with Goebbels.[55] Hitler was pleased by the number of visitors and gave instructions for a catalogue to be issued.[56] Meanwhile, Ziegler still had the task of 'cleansing' the public museums and in 1938 this was put on a legal basis. The requisitioned works were sold on the international art market.[57]

On 18 July Hitler finally opened the Great German Art Exhibition and along with it the House of German Art. A total of 1,200 works were shown, a mixture of sculpture, painting, and graphic art, predominantly historical and genre paintings, landscapes, various 'Blood and Soil' themes, heroicizing depictions of the Nazi movement and its rise, portraits and busts of 'great Germans'. Hitler was the subject of no fewer than twelve.

In his speech opening the exhibition Hitler declared that National Socialism intended to provide 'German art' to contrast with the 'cultural decline' of the Weimar period. This art would be 'eternal'. But what did 'German' mean in this context? 'To be German is to be clear', he suggested. This principle, which he had in fact stressed in his culture speech at the 1934 Party Congress,[58] meant that 'to be German is thus to be logical and above all to be genuine'. National Socialism, he said, had created the material but more particularly the ideological preconditions for a recovery of this 'genuine

German art', for art itself had now been given 'new and great tasks'. The opening of the exhibition marked 'the start of putting an end to idiocy in German art and thus of the destruction of our nation's culture. From now on we shall wage a merciless war to purge every last element responsible for corrupting our culture.' In then expressing the wish that the new gallery might be granted the opportunity 'of again revealing many works by great artists to the German nation in the centuries to come', he was clearly indicating that he was deeply dissatisfied with the artistic products of the *present*.[59] The speech that followed by Goebbels was similar in tone.[60] The ceremonies in Munich were rounded off with a parade on the theme '2000 Years of German Culture'.

Now that he had the House of German Art at his disposal, Hitler repeatedly took the opportunity until the outbreak of war to make programmatic statements on matters of art and culture. In July 1938 and 1939 he again opened the Great German Art Exhibition in person, in September 1937 and 1938 he gave his 'culture speech' at the Party Congress, and on 22 January 1938 in the House of German Art he opened the first Architecture and Crafts Exhibition, which then went on to be held annually. As early as December 1938 he spoke in the run-up to the second exhibition.

Even though he repeatedly attacked modern art in these speeches, in 1938 he saw himself as particularly under pressure to justify in detail the campaign against 'Degenerate Art' begun the previous year. In view of the criticism levelled not only abroad but also in artistic circles in Germany at the ruthless 'purging' of German museums, he did not wish to appear a cultural barbarian.[61] Once again he used convoluted explanations to indicate that he was in no way satisfied with the level of what was on display. His aim was rather to maintain 'a nation's broad artistic heritage on a solid and respectable foundation' so that 'true geniuses can then emerge'.[62]

However, one year later, as is shown by his speech at the third Great German Art Exhibition in 1939, there had been no progress beyond a 'respectable general standard'. What was needed was 'the application of more stringent criteria from one exhibition to the next and the selection of the outstanding work from the generally competent products'.[63] In saying this Hitler was pinning his hopes on the idea that the new Nazi art would one day be capable of connecting aesthetically with the nineteenth century,[64] with the art he himself particularly admired and of which he claimed to be a good judge and a connoisseur.[65] If we look more closely at Hitler's preferences in this field the biographical links and the political and ideological premises of his understanding of art become clear. In addition to the Romantic artist Caspar David Friedrich, Hitler's favourites included the 'German-Romans' Arnold Böcklin and Anselm Feuerbach as well as a whole series of later Romantic and genre painters. He thus particularly admired Moritz von Schwind (whose work he most likely knew from his days in Linz and Vienna)[66] and he enjoyed Carl Spitzweg's small-town idylls, Eduard Grützner's carousing monks, and Franz Defregger's scenes of peasant life. He was also very taken with the Munich landscape painter Carl Rottmann and with Rudolf von Alt, whose views of the city of Vienna had at one time served as Hitler's models for his own watercolours.[67] He also admired the great Munich portrait painters Friedrich August von Kaulbach and Franz von Lenbach, Hans Makart, whose prestige paintings had contributed to Vienna's artistic life in the period when the Ringstrasse was built, and Adolph Menzel, above all for his historical depictions of Frederick the Great, whom Hitler revered.

It is not difficult to discern in this selection the influence of the taste predominant in Vienna and even more so in Munich at the turn of the century. In Munich, for example, the Schack Gallery, which Hitler knew well and which came to play an important role in his museum plans, housed works by Böcklin, Feuerbach, Lenbach, Rottmann, Schwind, and Spitzweg.[68] In addition to these Viennese and Munich influences the great 'Exhibition of the Century' of 1906 in the Berlin National Gallery, in which German painting from the first half of the nineteenth century was rediscovered and made available to a wide public as an important phase in the development of German art, had left a deep impression on him. At the time popular art journals of the kind Hitler read carried extensive articles on this exhibition.[69] From Hitler's point of view the artists he favoured distinguished themselves through the fact that they had worked before or outside Modernism in art and that they had not been produced by the academies of art that he so hated (although in a number of cases he was wrong about this). Instead he assumed that for the most part the artists he admired had either pursued their own path as unrecognized geniuses in the face of opposition or had only achieved the fame they deserved after their deaths. The points of contact with his own perception of himself as a man of genius who was prevented by adverse circumstances from pursuing an artistic career but who had brought his 'artistic' abilities – imagination and intuition – into politics, are only too obvious.

Hitler built up a collection of paintings of his own mirroring these preferences. The way these pictures were hung in his various official and private
residences betrays a strong awareness of display and effect. The pictures in
his Munich flat reflected completely his personal taste in art, while any
visitor was likely to imagine he was seeing the collection (which stopped
at the end of the nineteenth century) of a wealthy Munich citizen. The
Prinzregentenplatz was home to Böcklin's dramatic 'Battle of the Centaurs',
which depicts an elemental and barbaric struggle between two blond and
three dark centaurs, Lenbach's portrait of Bismarck in the uniform of a
cuirassier, a portrait of Richard Wagner, Feuerbach's 'Tristan and Isolde', also
a Brueghel, a country scene by Defregger, two Grützners, Böcklin's 'Spring
Dance', several Spitwegs, and a portrait of Geli by Ziegler.[70]

In the imposing Great Hall at the Berghof the positioning of the paintings was based on matching prominent nineteenth-century works with
their models, old Italian masters – a combination that was designed to demonstrate to visitors their host's expert knowledge of art history.[71] Feuerbach's
portrait of a woman, 'Nanna', was there (most likely chosen by Hitler at
least in part because of the obvious similarity to Geli), also Schwind's 'The
Arts in the Service of Religion', 'Venus' by Titian's pupil Paris Bordone,
Bordone's 'Lady with an Apple' (which replaced 'Nanna' in 1938), a number
of works by Giovanni Paolo Pannini, the most important Italian painter of
ruins in the eighteenth century, which pleased Hitler by showing how
buildings could have 'value as ruins', and a Madonna tondo from the sixteenth century. Two portraits of Hitler's parents by an amateur artist completed the display. In Hitler's office at the Berghof there was a portrait of
Field-Marshal von Moltke by Lenbach, while in the entrance halls there
were two Bismarck portraits by the same painter.

In the Führer building in Munich the paintings were mainly on loan
from the Schack Gallery and the Bavarian State Collection. Adolf Ziegler's
triptych 'The Four Elements', an attempt to find images for Nazi ideology,
was one of the few contemporary pictures from Hitler's own collection that
he had put up in a significant location in the Party headquarters. The pictures in Hitler's office offered a visual lesson in politics and history: once
again a portrait of Bismarck by Lenbach, a picture by Menzel of Frederick
the Great, and Defregger's 'From the Wars of Liberation 1809', a scene from
the Tyrol uprising, and also a Spitzweg.[72]

In the Reich Chancellery Hitler was keen to add dignity to his immediate working environment by adding portraits of historical figures. His office was graced by a full-length portrait from the state collection of Bismarck, an earlier incumbent; in the drawing room there was an oval, contemporary portrait of Frederick the Great in old age that Hitler had acquired and which he kept by him up to 1945, wherever he was living. In addition, in 1935 he acquired portraits by Lenbach of Kaiser Wilhelm I and Friedrich III for the office. In the function rooms in the Reich Chancellery there were three works whose somewhat obscure symbolism inevitably attracted the attention of visitors. The dining room was dominated by Friedrich August Kaulbach's 'Triumph of Music' from Hitler's private collection. For the large reception room created in 1935 Hitler chose Feuerbach's 'Plato's Feast', a painting three metres by six in size on loan from the Kunsthalle in Karlsruhe. In 1936 he acquired Böcklin's ominous painting 'Island of the Dead', which hung over the fireplace in the reception hall.[73]

In the new Reich Chancellery, inaugurated in Berlin in 1939, Speer put together a collection of paintings consisting mainly of loans from the Kunsthistorisches Museum in Vienna. The tapestries and paintings, ranging from the sixteenth to the eighteenth century and predominantly based on classical themes, were designed to underline the claim of the 'Greater German Empire' to historical greatness.[74]

When the Anschluss in February 1938 brought Austria into the German Reich, Hitler was in a position to consider realizing the plans we know he had pursued since the 1920s for an important gallery of nineteenth century German painting in Linz.[75] While on a journey to Italy in May 1938, he made extended visits to museums and these may well have given him the decisive impetus to turn these plans into reality. He regarded his own collection as the basis for the Linz project, which naturally called for a new building, and so he extended it significantly. He issued an instruction securing for himself first refusal on the confiscated Jewish art collections in Austria and made use of this prerogative via an expert on Hess's staff.[76]

As a result of his visit on 18 June 1938 to the Dresden State Art Gallery with its superb collection of Old Masters, Hitler enlarged considerably his plans for a museum in Linz. The very same day he issued a confidential instruction reserving for himself the decision on how works confiscated from their Jewish owners would be dealt with. He used this instrument primarily to secure Old Masters for the Linz museum. The first floor of this building was now to house a collection of European Masters up to the end of the eighteenth century, while the second floor would contain German art of the nineteenth century. He reinstated Hans Posse, the longstanding

director of the Dresden Gallery, who a short time before had been pen-
sioned off after disputes with the Nazis in Saxony, in his former post and
charged him with the task of setting up the 'Führer's Museum', as the project was called, in Linz.[77] Hitler did not envisage a large-scale, world-class
museum. Instead the Linz gallery was to be regarded as an important addition to the existing range of museums in what was now the Greater German
Reich and as the generous gift of a passionate and knowledgeable collector.
He was confident that posterity would turn a blind eye to the fact that his
passion as a collector rested on criminal impulses.

'The Third Reich's Master Builder'

Given the fact that even he was not truly convinced by the works of the
artists in his Reich, Hitler used his frequent speeches on culture (for example
his addresses to the Party Rally in 1935 and 1936) to highlight Nazi achievements in the field of architecture and to emphasize how excellent and unique
they were.[78] 'Never in German history were greater and nobler buildings
planned, begun, and completed than in our time', he declared at the 1937
Party Rally. They should not be 'thought of as designed to last to 1940, not
even to 2000, but rather they shall reach up like the cathedrals of our past
into future millennia.'[79]

   In fact, 1937 was the year in which he gave renewed and decisive impetus
to Nazism's great architectural projects, some of which had been initiated in
1933. In doing so, Hitler was not only emphasizing his role in cultural politics
but was aiming as 'Master Builder of the Third Reich'[80] to give expression
through imposing building projects to his ambitions for Germany as a great
power in this decisive phase of his plans for expansion. His aesthetic model
for realizing these plans was the classical world, for to his mind this era, by
contrast with the gloomy mysticism of Christianity, stood out by virtue of
its 'clarity, greatness, and monumentality'.[81] In his view, this approach
was called for if only because of his conviction that the Greeks, Romans,
and Teutons, the real 'founders of culture', all belonged to the same Aryan
'original race' and it alone was capable of 'immortal' achievements.[82] This
attitude was at the root of Hitler's preference for classicizing architecture. Yet
unlike Karl Friedrich Schinkel,[83] whom he considered exemplary, Hitler
pursued an idea of classicism determined solely by the desire to use architecture as an embodiment of power. The style he favoured as dictator and

prescribed to his architects, such as Troost and Speer, looked out of proportion, and oversized, in other words it conveyed the impression of an impoverished and gloomy classicism that almost seemed a caricature of its classical 'models'.

Hitler's main building project, the large-scale remodelling of Berlin, had not, however, proceeded in the previous years on the scale and at the pace he required. Because of persistent problems with the city administration and his difficult relationship with its head, Julius Lippert, Hitler came up with the idea in 1936 of creating a new body to be responsible for the development. He had probably given the first commission by March 1936 to Albert Speer.[84]

In his 1937 speech to the Reichstag marking 30 January, Hitler announced that Speer had been appointed General Buildings Inspector for the Reich capital; it was to be his responsibility 'to bring into the chaotic Berlin sprawl those magnificent clean lines that will do justice to the spirit of the National Socialist movement and the essence of the Reich capital'. Twenty years were envisaged for the execution of the plans. Speer, who was given extraordinary powers, was not subordinate to any ministry or regional authority but was answerable to Hitler alone.[85] Within one year these powers were increased by law and extended to other cities also, Hitler expressly reserving the right to determine which cities should be included during what period in Speer's redevelopment programme.[86]

At the end of April 1938 Hitler announced in the Munich press how he envisaged the redevelopment of the 'Capital of the Movement'. By constructing a new railway station three kilometres to the west of its previous location, space would be created where the platforms and tracks had been for a 'a street of truly monumental buildings', as the official press release put it. These prestigious new buildings would lead up to a 'monument to the Movement' at least 175 metres high. In addition there were plans for the Party offices to be extended in the Maxvorstadt district and for a complete overhaul of the traffic arrangements.[87] The memoirs of the architect Hermann Giesler reveal that since November 1938 Hitler had been discussing the plans for Munich in great detail.[88] At the end of December he officially included the city in the redevelopment programme and appointed Giesler as 'Director of Works' with overall responsibility.[89]

At an early stage Hitler already had plans to redevelop Hamburg, the second largest city in the Reich.[90] When visiting the city in June 1935, he appears to have ordered a viaduct to be built. In June 1936 he showed a preliminary sketch to Fritz Todt, who was responsible for planning, and in July 1939 the basic outline of the redevelopment plan had been established. Essentially it amounted to creating a north–south axis in Altona with prestigious buildings ending at the River Elbe in a tower 250 metres high that would be the Gau headquarters of the NSDAP.[91]

At the turn of 1938/39 Hitler charged the Munich professor Roderich Fick with taking forward the plans to redevelop Linz, thus realizing the architectural fantasies that the teenage Hitler had produced for his home town. From the autumn of 1940 onwards Fick was increasingly in competition with Giesler, whose planning for Munich had in the meantime won him Hitler's special trust. For that reason Hitler gave him more and more responsibility for the Linz project.[92]

Finally, in February 1939 Hitler included the Gau capitals Augsburg, Bayreuth, Breslau, Dresden, Graz, and Würzburg in the redevelopment plans.[93] At the beginning of 1941 Speer could already count twenty-seven towns and cities that Hitler had designated by decree as 'cities to be restructured'.[94] The redesigned provincial city centres adhered to a standard format; the Gau headquarters, a large hall for meetings, and a free-standing bell tower were to be grouped in the centre round a 'Gau forum', a parade ground. In Weimar this arrangement had been in existence since 1936 and it served as the model for planning (which usually got no further) in other cities. The new parade ground was located as a rule at the end of a broad approach road with additional monumental buildings. In this way a symbol of the new order would develop alongside the historic city centre.[95] In the later 1930s NSDAP local politicians and town planners were already also beginning to apply this model (parade ground, Party offices, axis road) to county towns and smaller communities.[96] Nazism's architecture of domination was to cover the Reich. Furthermore, Hitler made the remodelling of even provincial towns a personal concern of his, intervening in the planning and contributing sketches.[97]

In the spring of 1937 building work began in Berlin on the first large prestige project embarked on in anticipation of the extensive redevelopment plans, namely the New Reich Chancellery, Hitler's monumental official seat.[98] Since moving into Wilhelmstrasse Hitler had been extremely unhappy with his official residence, which fell far short of his expectations of grandeur. In an article he published in 1939 in the journal *Art in the Third Reich* concerning the building of the New Reich Chancellery, he complained that the historic Chancellery had been in a sorry state, while the modern extension created between 1928 and 1930 looked like 'a warehouse or a municipal fire station'.[99] As early as autumn 1933 Speer had begun extensive alterations, in part based on Troost's plans, to the various parts of the building used by Hitler for official business, for state occasions, and as his private apartments. After he also assumed the office of Reich President in 1934, an annexe was added for receptions and in 1935 a balcony on the street side, for which Hitler himself had supplied a sketch.

In July 1935 Hitler then proposed that the new building be constructed along Vossstrasse, in other words built onto the old Chancellery building on the west side.[100] A preliminary sketch from that year exists with essential features of the new building, although not yet on the scale it acquired later.[101] At the start of 1936 Speer, on instructions from Hitler, began to make concrete plans that in turn were approved stage by stage by Hitler personally.[102] Although originally the work was scheduled not to begin until 1939, in October 1936 Hitler decided to bring it forward. It was to be completed in phases over three or four years. Hitler's decision to provide himself with an impressive official residence was thus strikingly aligned with his decisions to implement the Four-Year Plan.[103]

The first phase began in the spring of 1937, Hitler giving instructions at the same time for work to be accelerated. It is significant, however, that the scale of the project as a whole was at first not made public.[104] It was only when the topping out was celebrated on 2 August that Hitler was prompted to make the project public. In a speech not published verbatim and made in the Deutschland Hall to the workers involved in the project, Hitler explained the extraordinary speed of construction by referring to his wish to hold a reception for diplomats there in the coming January and to show the world how his state tackled projects of whatever kind with 'German speed'.[105] In fact the building was completed on time on 7 January 1939 and five days later the annual reception for diplomats did take place there.[106] The monumental building in the Nazi classical style stretched for more than 400 metres along Vossstrasse. Official visitors were received in a grand courtyard and then had to walk more than 200 metres through a series of lavishly appointed rooms – foyer, mosaic room, circular room, marble gallery, reception room – before reaching the hub of the complex, Hitler's office, a space 27 metres long and 14.5 metres wide and almost ten metres high.[107]

In the meantime Speer's plans for the capital, begun in 1936, were far advanced. In November 1937 Hitler considered that the time had come to make an official announcement about the redevelopment of Berlin. At the ceremony on 27 November 1937 to lay the foundation stone for the new Defence Faculty at the Technical University, he made it known that it was his 'unalterable will and decision to equip Berlin with those streets, buildings, and public squares that will make it appear fitted and worthy for all time to be the capital of the German Reich. The size of these developments and projects is not to be judged according to the needs of 1937, 1938, 1939 or 1940, but shall be determined by the knowledge that our task is to build the nation a city to last a thousand years for the incalculable future ahead of it; that nation has existed for a thousand years and has a thousand years of history and culture behind it and must have a city of commensurate stature.' In the years following he often reiterated the claim to be building for millennia, in particular in his official speeches on art.[108] The new plans for Berlin were presented in their entirety to the public in January 1938.[109] In addition to the east–west axis, the expansion of which had already begun in 1937 and was inaugurated on Hitler's birthday on 20 April 1939, a north–south axis 120 metres wide was planned and lined with the most important monumental buildings. At the intersection of these axes a domed hall 320 metres high and able to hold more than 150,000 people would be built as the new landmark of the city. The 'Führer Palace', planned to stand close to the domed hall and opposite the old Reichstag building, would have been considerably bigger than the New Chancellery. The 'diplomats' walk' would have been more than 500 metres long, while there were plans for a dining room for 2,000 as well as its own theatre.[110]

In December 1938, in a speech at the opening of the second Architecture Exhibition in Munich, Hitler responded to criticism of his mania for building with reflections on power politics: 'Another objection is to ask, "Must we build so much just at this moment?" Yes! We must build now more than ever before because in times past nothing was built or things were built depressingly badly. And secondly:...People will associate it with the era in which the German nation had its greatest resurrection and founded a huge, great, strong empire!'[111] For, as he explained on 10 February 1939 to army officers he had invited to inspect the Reich Chancellery, it was not megalomania that prompted these building projects. Rather, he based his thinking 'dispassionately' on the assumption 'that it is only through such imposing projects that a nation can be given the self-confidence' to believe it is not 'of second-class status'. In Hamburg, for example, he was building the 'biggest bridge in the world' as well as 'skyscrapers...as mighty as American ones', to show that the Germans were not lagging behind the Americans. 'We can do just as well'.[112]

Politics but not a cult

Hitler's decision during the course of 1937 to place new emphasis on culture can, as already mentioned, be considered an attempt to impress on the Churches the cultural and ideological superiority of National Socialism precisely at the point when it was in conflict with them. In the process Hitler had for tactical reasons avoided making any public statement about his obviously anti-Christian attitude; instead, it seemed to him more opportune for the time being to present Nazis as the better Christians. At the same time, however, in the summer of 1937 he had appeared to be claiming the support of supernatural forces in the form of 'providence', and at internal Party events in the autumn he had clearly distanced himself from Christianity. By his own admission, his somewhat pessimistic estimate of his own life expectancy made him feel resentful at that time, reinforcing this anti-Christian attitude. Even so, the idea of developing Nazism into a sort of religion, a quasi-religious 'myth' or 'cult', something like a Germanic faith, did not appeal to him. He refused to be the founder of a religion, nor did he wish to be made into a god. His comments on the matter do, however, show that there were those around him who toyed with this idea.

Yet his standpoint on this subject during previous years had not been entirely consistent. From 1933 onwards, big Nazi rallies had increasingly employed quasi-religious rituals and Hitler had not only not rejected this trend but had actively promoted it. This was particularly true of the Nuremberg Party Rallies, one example being the ritual honouring of the dead, which always took place on a Sunday during the SA and SS roll call in the Luitpold Arena. Hitler, accompanied only by the SA chief of staff and by the Reichsführer SS, would cross the arena where the SA and SS formations were assembled and stand before an enormous wreath and, flanked by two lighted sacrificial bowls, pay silent homage to the dead at the city of Nuremberg's war memorial. The ritual of touching the new Party flags with the 'Blood Flag' from 1923, which Hitler initiated, was clearly influenced by liturgical practice.[113] Since 1935 a choric element had been integrated into the mustering of the Reich Labour Service (RAD), a so-called 'hour of consecration' or, as Hierl, the RAD leader called it in his speech in 1938, a 'service'. Hitler nevertheless avoided speaking about these ritual elements in his addresses to the RAD men. From 1934 onwards, when the evening March of the Political Leadership onto Zeppelin Field took place, they were framed by a 'cathedral of light' created by anti-aircraft searchlights.

Robert Ley, the head of the Party organization, had been emphasizing these rituals since 1936 and Hitler's speeches to the Party functionaries reflected this trend.[114] Thus in 1936, for example, he conjured up the mythical connection between himself and his audience, speaking to them as if they were a group of disciples whom he had brought into the light: 'In this moment, how can we not again feel conscious of the miracle that brought us together! You heard a man's voice back then and it touched your heart. It awakened you and you followed that voice. You carried on for years without even having seen the owner of that voice; you only listened to one voice and followed it. When we meet here we are filled with the wonder of this gathering. Not every one of you can see me and I cannot see every one of you. But I sense you and you sense me! We are now one.' In this night-time setting the mythic union of 'Führer' and retinue, evoked by Hitler to create a rhetorical climax, acquired positively erotic dimensions.[115]

In 1935 he resumed the solemn march in remembrance of 9 November 1923 and even extended the ceremony.[116] This had first taken place in 1933 and had then been shortened the following year because of its proximity to the events of 30 June. After his speech in the Bürgerbräukeller on the evening of 8 November he went first to the Feldherrnhalle, where the coffins of the sixteen 'Fallen' of 1923 had been set out and commemorated them in silence as part of a night-time act of mourning. He then made a further speech to members of the SS who had assembled in front of the hall to be sworn in.[117] The next day, as in 1933, the march of remembrance took place from the Bürgerbräukeller to the Feldherrnhalle, where the marchers were saluted with sixteen salvos fired by an army artillery detachment. Hitler then laid a wreath and the coffins were taken to Königsplatz on gun carriages and there placed in bronze sarcophagi in the two newly constructed 'temples of honour'. In 1936 a new element in the form of a kind of gesture of reconciliation was added: The Minister for War, Blomberg, and the general in command of the Munich district, Reichenau, joined the march of remembrance from the Feldherrnhalle to Königsplatz. From then on the format for this event did not change.

It is not difficult to discern in this ritual not only features reminiscent of military and civilian ceremonial, but also essential elements of Christian liturgies of sacrifice and resurrection. The annual speech Hitler made on the evening of 8 November to the 'old fighters' in the Bürgerbräukeller was reminiscent of the ritualized last supper of the faithful. This was followed the next day by the march of remembrance to the city centre, a solemn procession at which a symbol of salvation (the 'Blood Flag') was held aloft. The reading out of the names of all the victims of the 'time of struggle' over loudspeakers on pylons erected for this purpose along the route recalled the Stations of the Cross, and at the end Hitler, who marched at the head of the procession, conducted the act of commemoration on the 'altar' of the Feldherrnhalle. Then the procession took on the character of a triumphal march ending at Königsplatz at the temples honouring the victims. On arrival, Hitler entered the sunken interior of both temples in something like a descent to the shades. The construction of the two temples, which consisted of pillars and were open to the skies, can be interpreted as deriving from the religious notion of resurrection, though with very much an earthly meaning, as Hitler showed when they were inaugurated in 1935: '...as they marched then as defenceless civilians, may they now lie exposed to the elements – winds, storms, and rain, snow and ice, and also sunshine.... To us they are not dead and these temples are not crypts but rather two sentry posts, for here they stand guard over Germany and our nation.'[118] In the roll-call of the dead that followed a thousand voices called out 'Here' after each name. This was done by members of the Hitler Youth assembled on Königsplatz who had become members of the Party that day. The idea that the dead lived on in the public avowals of the young also underlay the idea of using the same day to swear in first the new army recruits and at midnight the new members of the SS in front of the Feldherrnhalle.

Yet from Hitler's point of view this well-rehearsed 'Cult of dead heroes' did not primarily serve to transfigure, as it were, the events of the past. The external form of this cult of death and resurrection was designed to emphasize a political message that was central to legitimizing his position as leader of the movement and to moulding the Nazi past as a success story. The failure of the putsch, as he repeated in endless variations like a mantra, already bore the seeds of future success. In 1923 he, Hitler, had not made a serious tactical error. He had not failed, but rather his courageous actions had prepared the ground for the later rise of National Socialism. The martyrdom of the sixteen victims had not been in vain! This message, which, reinforced by the bombastic commemoration, was raised to the status of a dogma, was in the final analysis the result of an avoidance strategy on Hitler's part. What was a debacle at the time was through exaggerated, quasi-religious veneration to be transformed in people's memories into a myth of sacrifice and heroism.

At the 1938 Party Rally, however, Hitler did set clear boundaries with regard to this trend towards introducing quasi-religious elements into Party ceremonies, even though he had tolerated it and even promoted it in previous years. In his address on culture he attacked 'any mysticism that goes beyond the purpose and goal of our doctrine'. National Socialism was 'certainly a popular movement but under no circumstances a religious movement' and represented a 'völkisch political doctrine derived exclusively from our understanding of race'. The NSDAP had 'no places of worship but only halls for the people', 'no places of worship, but rather places for people to assemble and parade grounds', 'no sacred groves but rather sports stadia and playing fields'. No 'cult activities' were put on but rather 'only people's rallies'. If therefore any 'mystically inclined devotees of the occult with their eyes on the afterlife' were to 'insinuate themselves' into the movement this could not be tolerated. For 'religious activities are not our responsibility, but that of the Churches!' It was quite a different matter, however, to preserve certain types of ceremony as belonging to Party 'tradition'.[119]

Thus, however much Hitler liked to make use of quasi-religious forms, his concern was not at all with metaphysics or with the founding of a new or substitute religion. Rather, his aim was to develop something like a Party tradition that could be passed on and create a clearly defined framework for public Party events. Speer, who created the Nuremberg that served as a backdrop, recalled while a prisoner in Spandau that in 1938 Hitler had explained to him how he intended to establish the Nuremberg ceremonial practices so firmly during his lifetime that they would become 'an unchanging ritual'. If a weaker man succeeded him he would then have at his disposal a framework that would 'support him and give him authority'.[120]

Ultimately, therefore, in Hitler's mind cultic or quasi-religious rituals were rooted in politics. Their purpose was purely functional as a means of securing and extending his own power.

23

Hitler's Regime

In assuming the office of Reich President in August 1934, Hitler, whose official title from now on was 'Führer and Reich Chancellor', had finally established himself as sole dictator. Moreover, the Nazis believed their regime had a clear constitutional basis. For in their view Hitler's position did not depend on his having been appointed by the President in 1933 and then becoming President himself after a plebiscite, but on the principle that, because of his historic mission, only he was capable of enacting the 'will of the nation' in a 'pure and unadulterated' manner. This was the view of Ernst Rudolf Huber, one of the leading constitutional lawyers in the Third Reich.[1] According to Huber, this regime was based not on popular sovereignty but on the sovereignty of the 'Führer': 'The Führer unites in himself all sovereign power in the Reich; all public power exercised within the state and in the movement is derived from the Führer's power.... For political power is not invested in the state as an impersonal entity, but rather it is invested in the Führer as the one who implements the common will of the Volk [ethnic nation]. The Führer's power is comprehensive and total; it unites in itself all the agencies that shape the political sphere; it extends to all areas of the ethnic nation's life; it encompasses all national comrades, who in turn have a duty of loyalty and obedience to the Führer.'[2] Thus the personal will of the 'Führer' had taken the place of the government. His word could have the force of law. As Huber put it, 'In truth there is only one lawgiver in the German Reich and that is the Führer himself...'[3]

Hitler had paved the way for this development from an early stage. Even in 1933 the government's importance had diminished relatively quickly. After the cabinet had ceased to be a coalition in mid-1933 the Chancellor called meetings less and less frequently. The last routine cabinet meeting was on 9 December 1937, although on 5 February 1938 ministers assembled once again to hear a statement from Hitler on the Blomberg–Fritsch crisis.[4]

After that Lammers, the head of Hitler's Reich Chancellery, made repeated attempts to set a date for a meeting, but Hitler always found new reasons to put it off.[5] In effect he simply let cabinet meetings peter out; no official decision to abandon them was ever announced.

Instead, Hitler increasingly used Lammers to clarify draft legislation directly with the ministries concerned. Formal approval was then given through the 'circulation procedure'*.[6] Thus the Reich government was soon no longer working as a single committee but fragmented into a 'polycratic' collection of specialist departments, all of which were individually subordinate to the head of government.[7] The marginalization of the cabinet as a collective body meant that the work of producing legislation increasingly lost its unity; government legislation was gradually replaced by decrees issued by individual ministries, and by Hitler himself, for he had 'Führer decrees' or 'Führer edicts' published in the *Reichsgesetzblatt* and these were regarded as having the force of law. As far as Lammers could manage it, they too had been agreed beforehand with the responsible departments, but if he had not managed it, repeated mistakes and awkward situations ensued.[8]

This increasing lack of clarity prompted the Interior Minister to try in 1937 to secure a ranking order among the ministries with regard to their responsibility for legislation. The project, tellingly, came to nothing because of opposition from Hitler, who decided instead to extend the Enabling Act [which was limited to four years] as a less complicated solution.[9] However, he appears to have recognized that this act was not a substitute for establishing his dictatorship permanently on a constitutional basis, for, on a number of occasions, he referred to plans to create a senate that would determine the succession and establish the outlines of a future constitution. As early as 1930 a 'senate chamber' had been set up in the Brown House, but in the end no such institution to lead the Party was created, any more than a senate was established to be the highest constitutional body in the Third Reich.[10] Hitler had in any case already settled his succession late in 1934, although this had not been made public. In December 1934 he had nominated deputies to stand in for him in the event of his being unable to carry out his responsibilities as Chancellor and President: Blomberg would be responsible for army and defence matters, Hess for Party matters, and Göring for 'all other government matters'. Also in December 1934 he had issued a decree naming

---

* Translators' note: Lammers circulated draft bills to the relevant departmental ministers for comment and approval in writing in lieu of a cabinet meeting.

Göring as his successor if he should die. Both sets of provisions were top
secret. In addition, to make the process even more secure, he subsequently
enacted a law that was never made public, giving him the power to determine his own successor.[11]

The 'Führer' between state and Party

As in the years before 1933, Hitler continued to lead the Party in a way that
allowed him to pursue his policy of avoiding as far as possible any rigid
structures that might limit his own position in it or restrict it through institutions. In particular, he prevented the formation of any collective leadership body or the creation of a central office with comprehensive powers to
direct the Party.

With the aid of a rapidly expanding bureaucracy (the staff of the 'Führer's'
Deputy led by the dynamic Martin Bormann) Rudolf Hess, Hitler's deputy
for Party matters, did in fact succeed in 1934/35 in assuming a central role
within the complex of offices within the NSDAP headquarters. Yet Hess
had no general authority to give instructions either to the Gauleiters or to
the Reichsleiters whom Hitler had appointed in June 1933.[12] Hess derived
his powers with regard to the Gauleiters and Reichsleiters only from the
'authority' assigned to him in 1933 as Hitler's deputy. As this authority was
not specified (and Hitler was careful not to be more precise) Hess and
Bormann worked on the basic assumption that their offices, in line with
Hitler's omnipotence, had 'unlimited' scope. On the other hand, Robert Ley,
the head of the Reich Party organization and Hess's most important adversary within the Party leadership, was constantly trying to define areas of
responsibility within the leadership and thus restrict Hess's freedom of
action. The Reichsleiters and also the numerous heads of the central main
offices of the NSDAP who did not hold the rank of Reichsleiter were in any
case dependent on Ley's agreement when making decisions on organizational, personnel, and financial matters, although in other respects they were
answerable only to Hitler.[13]

The position of the Party Treasurer, Franz Xaver Schwarz, who was head
of the biggest office within the Party headquarters, also remained out of
reach of the 'Führer's' Deputy. On 16 September 1931 Hitler had assigned
him sole authority to act for the Party in legal affairs involving property, and
this was expressly confirmed by Hess on 2 July 1933.[14]

Hess and Bormann managed, however, to take control of the personnel matters of those Party functionaries whose appointment or dismissal Hitler had reserved for himself. This involved all office holders from district leader upwards and also the political leaders in the Reich Party headquarters. As a result, they both acquired considerable influence over Hitler's personnel policy. In addition, by greatly increasing the number of regulations and reports, Hess's office attempted to make the Party apparatus the vehicle by which it carried out its own policies,[15] while also asserting its claim to be the sole representative of the Party in its relations with the state. In concrete terms this meant that during 1934/35 Hess successfully insisted on being involved in the legislative process and in the appointment of senior Reich and state [Land] civil servants. Whenever political issues of 'fundamental' importance arose with regard to the state, his office insisted on its right to intervene.[16]

As a result of the limit imposed in 1933, the number of NSDAP members was stable at around 2.5 million. (It was not until 1937 that this restriction was gradually lifted; by the outbreak of war the Party had a total of 5.3 million members and finally, by the beginning of 1945, eight to nine million.)[17] There was a remarkable concentration of functionaries in the Party. On 1 January 1935 there were more than 500,000 members of the political cadre (two-thirds of whom had only joined after the seizure of power) out of about 2.5 million members in all. In other words, one member in five held some kind of post in the Party.[18] This ratio remained for the most part constant. At the beginning of 1940 there were more than 1.2 million members of the political cadre in the NSDAP.[19] More than 90 per cent of Party functionaries held their office as unsalaried volunteers. On top of that the various sections and organizations linked to the Party, such as the NS Welfare Organization and the German Labour Front, made use of many additional helpers (so-called wardens), whose numbers had already grown to more than 1.3 million by the start of 1935 and went on rising.[20]

The greatest concentration of functionaries in the Party organization was at local level, where over 90 per cent of them were active.[21] In 1936 the organization of the Party's work at local level was revised. Unlike in the period before 1933, the 'period of struggle', the Party structure was no longer to be geared to the number of members, but rather it was to establish a network covering the whole of Germany that would be as dense and as evenly spread as possible, so that the whole population would be accounted for, supervised, and controlled.[22] 'Education' and 'surveillance' were the tasks Hitler had sent the political cadre home with from the Party Rally of 1935.[23]

To this end the following benchmarks informed the reform of the Party structure in 1936. The 'block', the smallest unit of the Party organization, was to be responsible for forty to sixty households. To maximize the level of surveillance, the block leader (often called the block warden) could be given additional helpers. 'Cells' consisted of between four and eight blocks and were overseen by local branches, which were not to cover more than 3,000 households. The leader of the local branch had a staff with a variety of responsibilities (secretary, treasurer, head of organizational matters, head of personnel, head of training, head of propaganda, press liaison officer). All these jobs were done on a voluntary basis.[24] As a visible sign of their power, the leaders of local branches were also allowed to carry a handgun.[25] In 1938 there was a further reform, the main purpose of which was to increase the number of local groups to make the network even more dense.[26]

For the population this meant that they were systematically 'processed' by countless Party workers. Thus the boundaries between education, supervision, surveillance, and intimidation were fluid. Local groups were instructed to concern themselves with people's everyday worries by giving individual counsel and so, for example, they helped people in dealing with various government agencies or with rental disputes. They also pressed those for whom they were responsible for donations, or urged them to put up flags, or pictures of Hitler in their homes, to use the officially recognized greetings, to attend meetings, or to cast their vote in elections. They also put pressure on them to be actively involved in National Socialism. A dissenting or even just a reserved attitude towards the Party's representatives or comments on political events and the like were not only carefully documented in the local branch's files, but awkward 'national comrades' or those who drew attention to themselves were kept under constant observation and could, for example, be summoned to an 'interview' with the local branch leader.[27]

The local branches drew on this fund of information when they had to provide details of people's political attitudes, such as in the case of promotions in the civil service, when people were claiming various kinds of state aid (such as loans for married couples or child support), or if they were applying to be admitted into state licensed professions. Enquiries might also come from private companies who wanted reassurance from the Party before appointing or promoting people.[28] Detailed information in the reports of local branches make clear to what extent the local branch leaders, helped by volunteer assistants and informers from the neighbourhood, were capable of keeping tabs on the everyday life of 'their' national comrades. It is therefore hardly surprising that local branches were urged to assist the Security Service (SD) as a matter of routine.[29] It has also been shown that when starting investigations the Gestapo relied on information held by local Party offices.[30] The Party organization, in other words, prepared the ground for a police state that ruled by terror.

The significance of this surveillance, carried out close to home by an army of several hundred thousand Party functionaries, cannot be overestimated when it comes to explaining the conformity and docility of the overwhelming majority of the population under the Nazi dictatorship and the way in which the Nazi vision of a 'national community' actually worked.

In addition to the political organization proper, the NSDAP had formations (which had no individual legal status and no funds of their own), associated organizations (which had both but were under the financial supervision of the Reich Party Treasurer), and other groups supervised by it but whose relationship to the Party was not clearly defined from a legal point of view.[31] Formations and associated organizations and other groups were as a rule structured in a similar hierarchical way to the Party and were thus represented by their own head offices within the Reich Party headquarters. Their 'offices' within the Gau and district headquarters and the organizations within the local Party branches were subordinate to this head office in matters relating to their specialist role. At the same time, these offices were subordinate in political matters to the various territorial Party leaders in charge at the different levels of the Party hierarchy [Gau, district, local branch]. This dual structure inevitably caused problems in practice but it also produced a finely graduated, stable, and at the same time flexible organizational machine.

Examples of such formations and associated organizations were the SA, which after 1934 became much less important, and the SS, which gained from the SA's loss of status and, after being combined with the police, formed the core of a self-contained, continuously expanding fiefdom. Particularly relevant here are the mass organizations that after 1933 had set about supervising individual sectors of German society and since then had greatly expanded. In a speech in December 1938 to NSDAP district leaders, Hitler described his view of how 'national comrades' were to be gathered into the fold. We shall 'train' the 'new German youth', he said, 'from an early age for this new state'. After four years in the Jungvolk and four in the Hitler Youth 'we shall admit them immediately to the Party, the Labour Front, the

Figure 7. A private celebration watched over by the 'Führer'. This wedding group from 1936 used a family photo to make a clear statement of loyalty.
Source: IMAGNO/Skrein Photo Collection

SA or the SS, or the NSKK, and so on. And when they have been in them for two years or a year and a half they will be put in the Labour Service and will have the edges knocked off them for another six or seven months. . . . And whatever they still have in the way of class consciousness or social superiority after six or seven months will be worked on for another two years by the army, and when they return after two, three, or four years we'll take them back immediately into the SA, SS etc., so that there's no chance of them backsliding, and then we'll have them for life.'[32] The individual organizations were to devote themselves zealously to this task.

The German Labour Front (DAF), which in October 1934 Hitler charged with 'forming a true German national and productive community',[33] succeeded gradually in encompassing the great majority of people in employment. Membership rose from seven to eight million in the middle of 1933 to around 14 million in March 1934, over 22 million in 1939, and finally 25 million in 1942.[34] It became impossible to imagine everyday working life without the DAF's practical involvement in it and it was very difficult to avoid becoming a member. It offered legal advice and special mentoring programmes for working women and young people. It was active in the provision of healthcare in the workplace and also in vocational training.[35]

Alongside those activities, the DAF built up a business empire that included, among other things, insurance companies, building societies, book clubs, and its own bank – all from the enterprises it had acquired through the incorporation of the trades unions.[36] The 'Strength through Joy' [KdF] organization, which was a subsidiary of the DAF, was concerned amongst other things with improving working conditions ('Beauty of Work') and it organized the 'German firms' productivity competition', promoted workplace sport and participation in sports, and organized holidays, even including cruises on its own KdF cruise ships.[37]

The National Socialist People's Welfare Organization (NSV) also continued expanding rapidly after 1933. In addition to its labour-intensive general welfare work it expanded the assistance it gave through institutions such as the Mother and Child organization, which ran aid and advice centres and also arranged stays in the countryside for city children to improve their health, the German People's Recuperation Support, which did the same for adults, or the NSV Youth Support. Alongside this, the NSV also created its own nursing service and took over a large number of German nursery schools.[38] By the end of 1939 more than 12.4 million members had joined the NSV. Only a small fraction of these were active, however, while the majority merely supported the organization by contributing money, attempting in this way to show they were doing their bit for the 'national community' in an area that, ostensibly at least, was relatively 'unpolitical'.[39]

The Hitler Youth under Baldur von Schirach, 'Youth Leader of the German Reich,' had since 1933 set about drawing the whole of German youth into its ambit.[40] In addition to the regular Hitler Youth commitments – 'home evenings' involving ideological instruction every Wednesday and sport on Sundays – the organization offered a broad range of activities. It ran music groups, marching bands, and special units of the Hitler Youth such as the aviation, mounted, naval, or motorized units (in particular to provide training in the immediate run-up to military service). It also gave members the opportunity to engage in sports that at the time were still exclusive such as tennis or fencing. At the same time the Hitler Youth was engaged in all kinds of 'services', such as taking part in collections or helping out at big rallies. The Hitler Youth's own patrol service was in effect a kind of youth police that disciplined the members when they were off duty and kept a watchful eye on the other youth organizations.[41]

Hitler himself gave the watchword for how the Hitler Youth was to be trained in his speech to the Reichstag in 1935: 'In our eyes the German youth of the future must be slim and supple, swift as a greyhound, tough as leather, and hard as Krupp steel. We must train up a new type of man so that our nation is not ruined by the degenerate features of our age.'[42] In line with these requirements, children and young people were taught to value loyalty, a sense of community, strength of will, and toughness and this was done by means of a 'community experience' totally geared to appeal to the mentality of the young. One of the principles was that 'youth leads youth' and thus the Hitler Youth was turned into a vast training ground where the NSDAP could shape the next generation. The Hitler Youth produced a total of 2 million male and female voluntary leaders for the Party.[43] At the beginning of 1935 3.5 million young people belonged to the organization and from 1936 onwards all ten-year-olds became members on 20 April of each year. By the end of 1936 the membership had risen to 5.4 million, and by 1939 to 8.7 million, by which time 98 per cent of young people were members.[44] In December 1936 a law was enacted making membership obligatory for all young people, male and female. The Youth Leader of the German Reich was elevated to the status of a Supreme Reich Authority and was answerable directly to Hitler.[45] It was not, however, until March 1939 that compulsory youth service was introduced.[46]

In 1933/34 the National Socialist Women's Organization [NS-Frauenschaft], which had existed since 1931, had difficulty in finding a distinctive role in the new state and there were numerous changes of leadership. Moreover, in the autumn of 1933 the German Women's Organization [Deutsches Frauenwerk] was founded as an umbrella organization for the middle-class women's associations that had been coordinated. It was not until early in 1934 that the regime's somewhat confused efforts to organize women were stabilized, when Gertrud Scholtz-Klink took over the leadership of both organizations.[47] Hitler's speech to the NS Women's Organization at the Party Rally in 1934 can be read as giving the new women's leader some essential pointers regarding her tasks. In it he attacked the 'term "the emancipation of women"' as 'a term invented by Jewish intellectuals' and went on to defend a conservative view of women's roles where men and women occupied distinct spheres. A woman's world, he said, is 'her husband, her family, her children and her household. . . . Providence has allotted to women the care of this, her very own, world, out of which men can then fashion and construct their world.' These two worlds should, however, remain strictly 'separate'.[48]

At the beginning of 1935 the NS Women's Organization and the German Women's Organization now linked to it had 1.4 million and 2.7 million members respectively.[49] Both organizations shared responsibility for the Reich Mothers' Service, which in particular organized motherhood courses in which by 1939 more than 1.7 million women had taken part.[50] The Reich Women's Leadership's department for economics/home economics provided consumer advice and courses in effective household management. In view in particular of the food shortages and the Four-Year Plan's policy of autarky, these played a significant part in the regime's food policy.[51]

The NS Motor Vehicle Corps [NS-Kraftfahrkorps], which in the wake of coordination combined all the existing automobile clubs in one association, also grew steadily from more than 70,000 members in May 1933 to more than 520,000 in 1941. The organization catered for technical buffs and promoted mass motorization in a variety of ways. It took over motor racing in its entirety, gave pre-military training in its motor racing schools to future army drivers, and was active in intensive road safety training with an ideological flavour. The 'traffic community' that had been trained to behave correctly in traffic situations was intended to represent a solid component of the national community.[52]

There were further formations and associated organizations that took responsibility for 'supervising' individual professions, such as doctors, lawyers, teachers, academics, and students.[53]

In the light of all this activity, it is easy to appreciate the extent to which everyday life for people in the Third Reich, in the sense of the dictum Hitler propounded in 1938, came within the purview of the Party and its satellite organizations. The NSDAP was capable of covering the entire country with numerous overlapping and, in the main, dense networks that monitored and educated the population in line with NS ideology, selecting those 'national comrades' worthy of advancement while systematically excluding 'community aliens' from support and disciplining them.[54] An important aspect of this wide-ranging 'supervision' consisted in the various charitable and social benefits provided, the numerous leisure, further education, and other opportunities offered to 'national comrades' by the various Nazi organizations, which were in part a replacement for the many clubs and associations the Nazis had either closed down or coordinated. Individuals had a wide range of motives for joining the organizations mentioned above, such as obedience to a regime whose aim was as far as possible to organize the whole population; determination to take advantage of the available opportunities;

the desire to play an active role in the creation of the new 'national community'; the attempt to gain recognition by taking on tasks in the neighbourhood, and, last but not least, to work one's way up the Party as a volunteer
and so put oneself in line for a salaried post.

The massive expansion of the Party organization meant that it increasingly assumed the duties of the state. Party functionaries took on posts in
the state, often carrying them out in conjunction with their Party functions
or propelling themselves into positions of control over the state administration. Examples of people who combined state and Party functions at Reich
level were Goebbels (Head of the Party's Reich Propaganda/Reich Minister
of Propaganda), Darré (Head of the Party's Agriculture Office/Reich Minister
of Agriculture), Himmler (Chief of the German Police/Reichsführer SS),
and Hess ('Führer's' Deputy/Party Minister).

Of the total of thirty Gauleiters in the Reich[55] the majority also held state
offices in their particular region. In 1933 ten Gauleiters had been given
supervisory powers over the states in their office as Reich governors, and two
were also state prime ministers. In 1935 six Gauleiters were Oberpräsidenten,
in other words simultaneously heads of the administration in Prussian provinces, while two were also heads of Bavarian government districts, and Josef
Bürckel, Gauleiter of the Palatinate, also held the post of Reich Commissar
in the Saarland.[56] When the German Local Government Law came into
force in January 1935 the NSDAP district leaders were appointed 'representatives' of the Party in local councils who 'took part in' the appointment of
mayors and local councillors.[57]

Historians have regarded these developments in the main as representing
the 'usurpation' of state functions by the Party. Viewed from this perspective,
the well-organized state apparatus, bound by laws and by the established
practices of administration and directed by staff with appropriate professional qualifications, was plundered by a clique of power-hungry, fanatical,
and often corrupt functionaries. The result was a 'progressive undermining
of hitherto binding legal norms', a 'dissolution of the fabric of the state'.[58]
These findings illuminate only one aspect of the relationship between Party
and state in the Third Reich, however. It is important to recognize that the
prevalent conflation of state and Party functions was the means by which to
ensure that the system as a whole had the necessary cohesion. This admittedly happened in a largely arbitrary manner, with the result that the relationship between the Party and state apparatus remained in a sort of limbo.[59]
Although it was quite normal for one person to hold Party and state offices

simultaneously, this state of affairs was never openly acknowledged as being a matter of policy and on occasions it was even expressly prohibited.

Hitler's attitude to the issue of a comprehensive reform of the administrative structure of the Reich and states and the associated problem of finally clarifying the relationship between Party and state provides a typical example of his tactical procrastination over matters to do with the formal organization of his regime. The administrative experts, most prominently Interior Minister, Frick, were agreed that a 'Reich reform' was urgently called for. Crucial issues were the extension of the powers of the Reich and the reorganization of its states into around fifteen to twenty administrative units of roughly the same size, which would have led to the dissolution of Prussia into its component provinces and the abolition of small states, and rested on the assumption that the boundaries of the state administration would be coterminous with the Party Gaus. This would have meant that all Gauleiters were integrated into a clear Reich structure. At first Hitler seemed open to such plans, but at the beginning of 1935 he put them on the back burner.[60] The lack of clarity in the existing structure of power – in which the old states (of extremely varying sizes) continued to exist, Reich governors were in place alongside state governments, and the Party was made up of Gaus and districts covering geographical areas that did not correspond to those of the state apparatus – was much more congenial to him. For the provisional nature of his regime helped to stoke rivalries and in the end offered him more opportunities to intervene than any 'reformed' Reich as recommended by the administrative experts.

Intervening and directing

Thus far, we can now draw a clear conclusion: Whereas under Hitler's regime the government dissolved as a collective body, with individual ministries gaining greater autonomy, at the same time Hitler as dictator dispensed with any coherent control over a Party apparatus that was proliferating more and more and trespassing on state territory. Even if this attitude can be attributed to the 'Führer', who was in any case removed from the everyday matters of government, being reluctant to involve himself in internal disputes, his unwillingness to make decisions inevitably led in the end to rivalries and open hostilities emerging about issues of responsibilities and powers. Hitler as the ultimate source of authority was increasingly faced with these situations.

To guarantee the effectiveness of his regime, Hitler resorted to a number of strategies through which to intervene in and direct events.

First of all, in critical areas Hitler repeatedly appointed special commissioners (also called general inspectors, commissars, plenipotentiaries), equipping them with extraordinary powers. Although the use of such appointees to solve specific problems that could be dealt with more expeditiously outside the routine business of the state bureaucracy was certainly part of the tradition of administration in Germany, it had up to that point happened mainly on a temporary basis and within the constraints of the constitution. Under the permanent state of emergency with regard to the constitution that prevailed in the Third Reich and in view of the decline of collective government, special commissioners acquired particular significance. This practice was above all in line with Hitler's anti-bureaucratic maxim of not tackling problems by bringing in the experts, but instead by investing powers to do so in men he trusted and who were personally responsible to him.

Special commissioners were, for example, given responsibility to direct large-scale projects that threatened to burst the confines of existing structures. The appointment of Fritz Todt as General Inspector of German Roads was a case in point, and the appointment of Speer early in 1937 as General Building Inspector for the Reich Capital was another. Hitler, however, invested special powers in people in particular to gain some measure of control over the economic and social crises arising from the rapid pace of rearmament. This was true of the appointment of Goerdeler as Reich Prices Commissioner in autumn 1934 and of the special powers given to Göring that culminated in summer 1936 in the Four-Year Plan. Schirach's appointment as Youth Leader of the German Reich was linked to a special commission from Hitler to ensure that the Hitler Youth would supervise youth organizations in their entirety.[61] Joachim von Ribbentrop was active in foreign affairs as a special commissioner; from 1934 onwards he was foreign policy adviser and the Reich government representative for disarmament matters as well as being the representative for foreign policy matters within the office of the 'Führer's' Deputy. As a result of this dual task, the foreign affairs office he set up to deal with these responsibilities (the Ribbentrop Bureau) was a curious hybrid creation existing between the state and the Party apparatus.[62] Josef Bürckel's task from 1935 as Reich Commissioner for the Reincorporation of the Saarland served as a pilot for later special powers granted in connection with annexations and the establishment of occupation regimes.

At least until the outbreak of war, however, the number of special commissioners directly responsible to Hitler remained limited; they were used deliberately to cope with particular urgent issues and it would be wrong to assume that in the 1930s his style of government was determined by an impenetrable tangle of special powers. It is telling that the ambitions of those who aspired to be 'empowered by the Führer' were not always realized. For example, Konstantin Hierl, the Commissioner for the Labour Service, who in 1933 was appointed director of the state Labour Service within the Reich Ministry of Labour, failed in his attempt to make this function into a Supreme Reich Authority as a result of opposition from the Reich Interior Ministry. In July 1934 Hierl became Reich Commissioner for the Labour Service but under the Reich Interior Minister.[63] Most commissioners were attached to a ministry or were appointed by Göring after 1936 to help him deliver the Four-Year Plan and therefore did not enjoy the privilege of being answerable 'directly to the Führer'.

Special commissioners allowed Hitler to focus on specific political issues quickly and with the minimum of red tape and to coordinate tasks that were spread over a number of different ministries. He could use this strategy to intervene in the existing administrative structure without making any fundamental changes to that structure. As the special commissioners directly answerable to Hitler were carrying out 'commissions from the Führer', their success was dependent on Hitler's support and this dependence enabled the dictator to give effective and clearly visible expression to his desire to shape political developments. This created the impression of a supreme leader who tackled problems vigorously and decisively.[64]

Secondly: Hitler's personalized leadership style, his tendency to allocate responsibilities not according to people's qualifications to do the job but according to whether he considered them loyal, led to a situation where individual senior functionaries were charged with a whole series of tasks. These could be state matters, Party matters, or other kinds of 'special tasks' assigned by Hitler and could well involve several political areas. Thus during the first years of the dictatorship two extensive and very heterogeneous empires arose under the aegis of Göring and Himmler. In addition to his powers as Prime Minister of Prussia, Prussian Minister of the Interior (up to 1934), Reich Minister of Aviation and Supreme Commander of the Luftwaffe, Göring had been given not only responsibility for the whole of forestry (including hunting), but in particular in 1936 the special task of implementing the Four-Year Plan. On top of all that he also had a special

role in Third Reich foreign policy.[65] Reichsführer SS Himmler had gradually
succeeded in placing the entire police apparatus under his command as
a centralized Reich police force and putting himself in charge of all the
concentration camps. He was working on uniting the SS and the police to
form a single 'state protection corps'. Since 1936/37 Himmler had also been
intervening decisively in the regime's policies towards ethnic Germans,
for in his view German ethnic minorities abroad represented important
outposts for a future 'Greater Germanic' policy.[66]

Other Nazi functionaries also combined several offices: Darré, the Reich
Agriculture Minister, was not only Reich head of the Party's Agriculture
Office but also head of the 'Reich Food Estate' (the 'corporate' organization
that regulated the production and marketing of agricultural products) and
head of the SS Race and Settlement Main Office. Goebbels was not only
Reich Minister of Propaganda and head of propaganda for the Party but also
President of the Chamber of Culture as well as Gauleiter of Berlin. Robert
Ley was not only head of the Party's Reich organization but also head of the
German Labour Front and, from 1940 onwards, Reich Commissar for Social
Housing Construction. As a result, power blocs arose that, as the individual
political spheres involved often had little in common or were at odds with
each other, were held together only by the men who headed them and
whose power resided chiefly in the personal regard Hitler bestowed on them.

Thirdly: In order to guarantee a minimum of coherence within his
regime, Hitler, as in the 'time of struggle', summoned the Party's Reichsleiters
and Gauleiters to meetings, sometimes separately and sometimes all together.
Between 1933 and the outbreak of war alone he did so twenty-seven times.
These meetings sometimes lasted several days and as a rule focused on specific subjects. There was an agenda for the day, with presentations and discussions. Up to the beginning of the war they were regularly chaired by
Hitler, who delivered lengthy addresses to 'give clear direction' to the Party
elite. The speeches and content of discussions were confidential. Their purpose was to give senior Party figures essential information about the policies
of the leadership and to bring them into line. In addition, these meetings
offered an important opportunity to pass on information, informally as well
as formally. As numerous Reichsleiters and Gauleiters were simultaneously
in state posts these meetings extended far beyond the confines of the Party.
Yet according to everything we know about these occasions there remained
one taboo, namely any open questioning of Hitler's policies or putting him
under pressure to justify them.[67] And the most crucial aspect: no decisions

were made here. Even within the sphere of the Party, Hitler was therefore careful not to make himself dependent on any supreme body.

In addition, Hitler met ten of the Gauleiters as part of their state functions at Reich governor (Reichstatthalter) conferences, which were held a number of times in the early years of the regime in order as far as possible to achieve consistency in the way policy was directed in the various states.[68] There were also regular conferences of functionaries, consultation exercises, and the like at all levels of the Party hierarchy, quite apart from informal exchanges of information, which frequently took place at social gatherings. The 'decline' and 'dissolution' of the Party and state apparatus therefore went hand in hand with redoubled efforts to create opportunities to exchange information and opinions.[69]

It was therefore characteristic of Hitler's regime that, on the one hand, the dictator allowed established organizational structures and hierarchies to wither away or where possible prevented them from developing, while, on the other, he created strategies to make it easier for him to intervene directly in individual parts of the power structure. He accepted the lack of clear direction, clarity, and consistency, also the conflicts over areas of responsibility and the rivalries. For the increasing lack of structure to his regime, the 'chaos of offices' frequently cited by historians, strengthened his personal position. In other words, Hitler had discovered the form of government that allowed him (by means of special commissions, the concentration of several roles in a few loyal followers, targeting information, or disinformation, at appropriate functionaries, as well as the dual system of Party and state) to enforce his political will directly as an autocratic dictator.

This form of government was also consonant with his own life-style and work-style, in which, by contrast with prevalent theories of rule, there was no clear separation between office and private sphere.

Although during his first months as Chancellor he had submitted to a disciplined work-style and a regular daily routine, read files, and arrived at cabinet meetings well prepared, he then discarded these habits the more he grew into his position as omnipotent dictator. As far as possible he avoided being incorporated into the working routine of the apparatus of power; instead he retreated from the requirements of discharging his responsibilities according to a regular timetable, and expected those in the political leadership to adapt to his largely unstructured rhythm. Hitler's day at the Reich Chancellery has frequently been described as positively indolent.[70] He would not arrive in his office suite until the late morning, would then often make his guests – a varying group of two or three dozen office holders, who would turn up each day – wait a long time for lunch, which in turn would be extended until late in the afternoon as a result of long, rambling conversations. This was often followed by confidential discussions with individuals. In the evening there was a meal, at which discussion of political matters was frowned upon, often followed by a film (mostly a piece of light entertainment) and ending as a rule with a smaller circle of people such as adjutants, colleagues, and guests, whom Hitler liked to treat to his monologues far into the night.

Another aspect of his life were his frequent absences from Berlin. He lived for several weeks a year on the Obersalzberg and was relatively often in Munich, which as the 'capital of the Movement' remained the seat of the huge and expanding Party headquarters and where he still kept his private apartment. In addition, there were the annual lengthy stays in Bayreuth at the Wagner Festival and in Nuremberg for the Party Rally. Hitler also liked to travel about the country, in part to enjoy seeing it as a tourist. Even for ministers and important functionaries, therefore, direct access to him was a distinct privilege that he handed out via an opaque camarilla of adjutants. Hitler preferred confidential meetings with individuals, which often arose spontaneously out of conversations at the lunch table, in the comparatively relaxed atmosphere on the Obersalzberg or somewhere on one of his journeys, to big work sessions or regular meetings of committees and boards. His life-style thus created an almost perfect environment for his personalized style of leadership.

Hitler's charisma

In Nazi eyes the Führer state was based on the mysterious identity of 'Führer' and nation, on the assumption, in other words, that 'the nation's will can be expressed in a pure and unadulterated manner only through the Führer'.[71] Although not every action by the 'Führer' was dependent on the consent of the nation – for that would have been democratic[72] – the regime was ultimately compelled to offer proof that in the medium and long term the policies pursued by the man at the top enjoyed the nation's support and were acknowledged as being successful.

Thus the legitimacy of Hitler's position derived essentially from his charisma; in Nazi terms he was the 'Führer' because the 'nation' ascribed to him extraordinary abilities and a historic mission, and because (in the eyes of his adherents) in the final analysis he was able to fulfil these expectations. This charismatic relationship, it should be noted, is a construction that served to *legitimize* the Führer state; it must not be confused with the *actual* basis of Hitler's power, nor does it tell us anything about his *actual* abilities and successes.

First and foremost, Hitler's regime was in fact a dictatorship. Basic rights had been abolished since February 1933; anyone was liable to be dragged off to a concentration camp for an unspecified length of time, without due process of law and without any verifiable reason, and was there at the mercy of the guards. Torture, torments of all kinds, and the murder of prisoners were part of this system and were not prosecuted. Although in the mid-1930s the number of concentration camp prisoners amounted to only a few thousand, the terror inspired by the camps left a deep impression on anyone who no more than toyed with the idea of resisting the dictatorship. The concentration camps were one part of a comprehensive system of repression that from 1936 onwards had been unified and centralized under Himmler's direction; other branches of it were the Gestapo, the criminal police, the uniformed order police, the SS with its own intelligence service (SD), as well as armed organizations. Special courts were standing by and could be relied on to find people guilty of political crimes as defined by the regime.

All potential sources of resistance that might have prevented the system from degenerating into a dictatorship had been eliminated. The separation of powers, the carefully calibrated balance of power between the individual constitutional institutions in the Reich as well as between the Reich and the states was suspended, as was the independence of local government. The independence of the judiciary was an illusion, for the judiciary had become a tool of the regime. There were no parties apart from the NSDAP, no social organizations that were not controlled by the National Socialist movement. The Churches as a source of moral authority had been compromised. There was no longer a free press.

Secondly, the regime enjoyed an organizational monopoly. We have seen that the entire country was covered by several overlapping networks of Party organizations that guaranteed effective, close-range supervision of people's everyday lives, without the need as a rule to deploy more muscular methods of repression.

Thirdly, the regime had taken control of the whole of the public sphere. This came about not only because it controlled the media and was continually waging propaganda campaigns, but also because Nazism (with its symbols, flags, uniforms, rituals, and involvement in very diverse activities, not least its architecture) put its stamp on public spaces and the public face of the so-called Third Reich and thus governed people's behaviour in those public spaces. In addition to their general propaganda, the Nazis educated the young and were also involved in the continuous 'instruction', in other words indoctrination, of large sections of the population. Conversely, opposition voices were to a great extent excluded or made to retreat into the private realm or semi-public contexts. The machinery of repression saw to this, as well as the surveillance of the population described above carried out by the Party and its satellite organizations.

Fourthly, if the Führer state rested in the final analysis on the identity of 'Führer' and 'nation'/'people' ('Volk'), the concept of the nation underpinning it must not be confused with the actual population and its attitudes. 'Volk' in Nazi ideology was a mythic category. Huber, the National Socialist constitutional historian, summed it up: 'The nation that shares a common ethnic descent is a supra-personal ethnic unit linking past, present, and future. It is a natural, elemental, organic, and at first unconscious entity. It is the nation as given by nature. The nation in this sense operates as the basic constituent in all political phenomena and all historical epochs, even if it has not come into people's consciousness as such. It has frequently been overlaid, obscured, degraded, but even in these distorted and obscured forms it remains the real and crucial core.'[73] In other words 'Volk' in Nazi thinking was always a closed unit. If the Nazis' key domestic aim was to create a 'national community', then the society of the Weimar Republic, which in their eyes had been divided and made degenerate by, among other things, liberalism, democracy, and Jewish influence, should be brought back to its authentic roots and the nation as an 'entity' should be restored.

What this 'national community' should look like in detail was never clearly defined, as is evident from the rather rare comments Hitler made on the subject.[74] Yet this lack of definition for one of Nazism's key terms was in fact its strength. On the one hand the vision of a 'national community' was certainly attractive to many people, for it held the promise of a nation as a united, homogeneous community with a shared ethnic background that, politically and ideologically at one with itself, was working to bring about national revival. In that process social tensions would be put aside, barriers of class and status torn down, and new chances of advancement opened up. The promise of the 'national community' was something people were supposed to be able to catch a glimpse of already, for example in the cheering masses at big National Socialist Rallies, through 'socialism in action', as the Winter Aid campaign was presented in propaganda, or in the experience of community in indoctrination and holiday camps, or during the Party Rallies.

For millions of people the extension of the Party's complex organizational machine and its satellite organizations, the creation of new administrations for specific projects, the assembling of large military forces, and the armaments boom meant concrete career opportunities and resulted over all in a rise in prosperity. The extensive political and racial purges in the realms of culture and higher education meant that intellectuals on the political right found they had new scope for working in many fields opening up under the headings of 'Race' and 'Nation'. For young people the regime seemed through the Hitler Youth to be offering a new form of autonomy. It is therefore not surprising that many younger Germans in particular gained the impression that this new regime would liberate German society from outmoded class differences and rigid and anachronistic structures and herald a more mobile type of 'national community' based on merit.[75]

On the other hand, the vagueness of the term enabled the regime to marginalize 'alien' minorities in this community and thus to encourage people to seek to belong to the majority community. While those Germans, such as the Jews, who were alleged to belong to an alien 'race' were the primary target of such exclusions, they could also be applied arbitrarily and in specific situations, such as when campaigns were mounted against 'whingers', intellectuals, or 'Jewish sympathizers'. Thus the 'national community' had two aspects: it was both a visionary promise of a marvellous future and an important tool in domestic policy, for by this method the basis of the Führer state's legitimacy could be redefined arbitrarily and in response to changing situations. No one who opposed the regime could belong to the 'national community' and such people were excluded from the mythical unity of 'Führer' and 'nation'.[76]

The machinery of repression, the close surveillance of national comrades, the control of the public sphere, as well as the central project of the 'national community' – these created the essential framework for the operation of Hitler's charisma within the Nazi regime. In fact, no 'pure' or actual relationship existed between the 'Führer' and the 'nation', but rather we are dealing with the strategy by which a dictatorship that had at its disposal an extensive array of instruments to create and underpin charisma, sought to legitimize itself. The fact that Hitler had a mass following and enjoyed a high degree of popularity for considerable stretches of his period in power does not alter this situation. The fact too that in reports on the national mood and in everyday comments by Germans Hitler was often not included in criticism of the regime (summed up in the set phrase, 'If only the Führer knew...') is not a confirmation of his charisma but instead must be regarded as an instinctive response to his sacrosanct position as projected by the regime's propaganda. Whatever criticism might be voiced about the inadequacies of the regime, belief in the 'Führer' had to be unsullied by doubts. That was, as it were, the operational basis on which Hitler's regime rested.[77] In reality, however, Hitler's dictatorship was not dependent on the consent of the majority of Germans.

The history of the period from 1933 to 1937 as presented in the preceding chapters of this book provides more than enough evidence that the identity of 'Führer' and 'nation' propagated by the National Socialists, the charismatic position occupied by Hitler as the agent of the true will of the nation, does not stand up to critical scrutiny. Even so, while the regime was not dependent on the consent of the majority, it could not simply ignore the mood of the country. Discontent was simmering beneath the surface and repeatedly flared up, to be countered by propaganda campaigns and repressive measures on the one hand, but also by material concessions and spectacular and astonishing interventions in domestic policy, although these did not divert Hitler from his fundamental political aims.

Since 1933 Hitler had been pursuing two central political objectives. In foreign policy he was out to establish a dominant position for Germany in Central Europe as the precondition for expansion and for acquiring 'living space' (although the timescale for this was still undecided). In domestic policy his aim was to produce the highest degree possible of unity and cohesiveness within the German nation, by whatever means possible. These two aims were inextricably linked. Internal unity at home was designed to demonstrate strength to the outside world and help to pave the way for expansion abroad, while foreign policy successes were designed to strengthen the regime domestically.

During the first months of his rule Hitler had already begun to push through his own ideas on foreign policy in opposition to the Foreign Ministry's traditional and cautious revisionist policy. In the first instance his aim was principally to create close alliances with Italy and Britain. In order to achieve his long-term expansionist goals, from the start Hitler's preference was to rearm at all costs and in so doing he rapidly exceeded the restrictions imposed by the established international system for arms control. His policy, however, not only put excessive strains on the economy and led to negative repercussions at home, but also quickly isolated Germany, an effect he could counteract only by means of the unexpected agreement with Poland. The alliance he sought with Italy was pushed into the distant future by his risky Austrian policy, while Britain's very receptive attitude to limited German rearmament turned out not to herald any kind of alliance but rather represented a British attempt to draw Germany back into the international security system by making concessions. To that extent his policy towards Britain was based on a fundamental miscalculation, in spite of the naval agreement concluded in 1935.

Hitler did, however, achieve early foreign policy successes with the reincorporation of the Saarland in 1935 and the occupation in 1936 of the demilitarized Rhineland, which did not provoke any serious sanctions. In addition, relations with Italy improved to the extent that he could now set about making Austria dependent on Germany. In the course of the summer of 1936 he expanded his view of international relations, viewing them increasingly in terms of the emergence of blocs. He perceived as a threat the possibility of an alliance led by the Soviets, of which France (which had been governed by a 'popular front' since June 1936), Czechoslovakia, and Spain would be members. His decision to intervene in the Spanish Civil War was also motivated by a wish to prevent Spain from becoming 'Bolshevist'. Instead he hoped to incorporate the country into a counter-alliance led by Germany, to which Italy, Poland, possibly Romania and Yugoslavia, and in the longer term Britain, and in East Asia Japan would also belong. The creation of such a bloc, which he pursued vigorously, was to his mind the decisive lever that would enable him to overcome purely revisionist policies, such as those supported by the conservative elites. Yet international recognition for his regime was still limited. The 1936 Olympic Games, with their projection of an image of Germany as a peace-loving country, did not alter this. In fact, the western powers responded to Hitler's political initiatives by rearming on a large scale.

Although Hitler's foreign policy successes had gained him some standing, his audacious foreign policy gave rise at the same time to considerable apprehension concerning Germany's continued isolation and to fears of war. Above all, the accelerated pace of rearmament, which was the basis for his foreign policy, placed considerable burdens on his regime domestically and was at odds with his second great political aim, namely to weld the Germans together into a unified 'national community'. This can be seen occurring in several phases between 1933 and 1937.

By July 1933 the so-called seizure of power had for the time being come to a close. From the late summer onwards the regime had saturated the population with an unremitting flood of mass rallies and propaganda campaigns and in October had used a referendum and fresh elections to confirm its decision to leave the League of Nations. Yet by the beginning of 1934 it was evident that propaganda was unable to disguise the reality of the problems any longer. Although in its first year in power the regime had succeeded in halving the number of statistically verifiable unemployed (a reduction that continued largely as a result of the armaments boom), the frequent assumption that the working classes, now able to support themselves, would feel grateful to the regime does not appear to have been borne out by reality. Instead people compared their circumstances with those before the crisis and came to the conclusion that they had been better off in 1928. The overheated boom created by rearmament had led, in conjunction with other factors, to distortions in the German economy, among them a fall in exports, a shortage of foreign exchange, problems with the supply of certain foodstuffs and everyday necessities, and rising prices at a time of wage stagnation. Large swathes of the population saw their standard of living fall and from 1934 onwards this situation was a constant source of complaints and dissatisfaction.

The economic situation of the masses was especially precarious during three phases: between spring and autumn 1934, in the summer of 1935, and at the beginning of 1936. In 1934 the fall in German exports led to a devastating lack of foreign exchange. For the average German this meant above all price rises coupled with shortages and a drop in quality in consumer goods. In addition to Schacht's total reorganization of foreign trade, in November the regime responded by appointing a Prices Commissioner. In July and August 1935 a wave of price rises, alongside wage stagnation, again provoked considerable discontent among the population. The regime's attempt in the autumn of 1935 to counter this mood with the slogan 'Guns before butter' soon petered out and had to be abandoned. When at the start of 1936 Germany once again found itself in an acute and serious export and foreign exchange crisis that threatened the pace of rearmament, the regime changed course: on the one hand it made more foreign exchange available to enable imports of food and on the other, led by the new Chief of Police,

Himmler, it took more vigorous steps to combat 'whingers'. In addition, the most important series of reports on the population's mood, namely the surveys conducted by the Prussian Gestapo and by the district presidents [Regierungspräsidenten], were halted on Göring's instructions. Thus critics of the deficiencies in food supplies, whose views were widely recorded in these reports, lost their most powerful organ inside the regime. The March 1936 elections to the councils of trust were called off as a precaution. Dissatisfaction with the regime was also spreading to broad sections of the small business population and to agriculture, in other words to population groups that before 1933 had voted in larger than average numbers for the NSDAP, for the regime was doing little to keep its promises to retailers and artisans. Agriculture was suffering as a result of pressure on costs, indebtedness, and a labour shortage.

In all sections of society there were complaints that Party functionaries were fat cats. Amongst practising Christians Hitler's policy towards the Churches also provoked negative responses. In spite of the explicit promise of protection contained in the Concordat, the Catholic Church found itself under considerable pressure to limit the activities of its associations or even to give them up. Since 1935 the regime had been taking action against state-maintained Church schools, while in 1935, 1936, and again in 1937 large numbers of priests were accused of currency violations (and then also of sexual offences). And Hitler's immense efforts to bring together the Protestant Churches of the individual states in one single Reich Church were unsuccessful in their 'unifying' aim, while managing to provoke bitter conflicts within the Church.

These facts point to one conclusion: the regime's repeated claim during the first years of Hitler's rule that the 'national community' was united was an illusion created by propaganda.

At the same time, however, Hitler developed an impressive ability to assert his leadership with confidence, in spite of the shaky ground on which he stood at home. This was an ability that had marked him out as Party leader since the earliest days of the NSDAP. From his position of extraordinary power he succeeded above all in finding spectacular solutions in tune with his own aims to profound political crises.

Between 1934 and 1936 such crises arose three times, when the precarious economic situation coincided with other factors putting a strain on domestic politics. In all three instances Hitler first bided his time and then intervened decisively to bring the complex situation under his control and reset the political agenda. In 1934 the conflict with the SA arose against the background of the foreign exchange crisis. It was also exploited by right-wing conservative circles around Papen to advance their own demands. Hitler ended the conflict with a double blow to the leadership of the SA and the conservatives and, during its aftermath, also saw off political Catholicism. In the summer of 1935, when the economic situation was once again precarious, the problems with the Churches reached crisis point, while at the same time the regime was facing its final confrontation with 'reaction' and the rank and file of the Party was using anti-Jewish street violence to press for the implementation of the NSDAP's anti-Semitic programme. Hitler dealt with the situation by initiating the Nuremberg Laws, which made the 'Jewish question' the focus of the domestic political agenda. In 1936 the lack of foreign exchange not only led to gaps in the supply of certain foods but was threatening to halt the rearmament programme. The result was serious disagreement within the regime about future economic policy. Hitler took two measures to solve the crisis: in April he appointed Göring as Commissar for Raw Materials and Foreign Exchange and in the summer initiated and 'promulgated' the Four-Year Plan.

The key to Hitler's effectiveness, as these developments demonstrate, did not lie in achieving overwhelming consensus by means of the power of his charisma, but rather in his ability to reshape extraordinarily complex situations through skilful, flexible, and (albeit after considerable hesitation) decisive political action. One should not forget, however, that he achieved this because as dictator he had at his disposal a range of instruments shaped by and geared to the implementation of *his* personal political vision.

PART V

Smokescreen

24

Resetting Foreign Policy

During 1937, Hitler finally gave up hope of an alliance with Britain, which he believed had declined as a world power; he now focused entirely on securing an alliance with Italy.[1] He still received prominent British guests and tried to convince them of his earnest and heartfelt desire for friendship, but he increasingly showed his disappointment and incomprehension that his advances met with no response.[2]

In Hitler's view, the new alliance was being forged above all by German and Italian cooperation in the Spanish Civil War. For this cooperation would inevitably provoke tensions (and, therefore, common diplomatic interests) in the relationship of both powers with Britain, which was continuing to try to reduce the conflict through a Non-Intervention Committee, in which Germany was also represented. From April 1937 onwards, German warships were taking part in international naval patrols in order to impose an embargo on the two civil war belligerents; but simultaneously, since summer 1936, Germany had been supplying Franco with weapons and actively supporting him with a unit of the Condor Legion composed of Wehrmacht soldiers and airmen.

On 29 May, the heavy cruiser 'Deutschland', docked in Ibiza harbour, was bombed by a Spanish Republican plane, a raid which caused thirty-one deaths and numerous casualties. Hitler used this as an excuse to launch a 'revenge attack' on 31 May, using several German warships to bombard Almería harbour. Germany also suspended its cooperation with the Non-Intervention Committee until 12 June.[3] On 23 June Germany withdrew its ships from the international naval patrols after the cruiser 'Leipzig' was torpedoed, presumably by a Republican submarine, and the committee failed to agree on a common response.[4] Hitler also postponed indefinitely a planned trip to London by Foreign Minister Neurath.[5]

Hitler believed that the now firm alliance with Italy would allow him to absorb Austria and Czechoslovakia into the Reich in the not too distant future; he would no longer need to take account of the views of Britain, his previous alliance candidate. In autumn 1936, he had already persuaded a number of Balkan politicians to agree to a German move against Czechoslovakia on the basis that a fundamental clash was developing between a communist-led bloc and an emerging bloc of 'authoritarian' states led by Germany. In March he had already told Goebbels bluntly that 'we must have [Austria and Czechoslovakia] to round off our territory'.[6] The Propaganda Minister had already altered German propaganda vis-à-vis Czechoslovakia a fortnight earlier. Now, the emphasis was no longer on its alleged bolshevization, but rather on the unfulfilled demands of the Sudeten Germans, which from now onwards were going to be used as a lever against the government in Prague.[7]

During 1937, Hitler also increased the pressure on Austria. In the course of his visit to Italy in January 1937, Göring had openly raised the issue of the Anschluss with Mussolini; however, the upshot of the exchange of views was unclear. The Italians relied on Göring's remark that Germany was not planning any 'surprises' in relation to the Austrian question; Göring relied on Mussolini's promise that he would not deploy any troops to the Brenner pass in the event of an Austrian crisis. In any event Göring was left with the impression that the 'Duce' had not been totally opposed.[8] Visits to Rome by Göring in April and Neurath in May convinced the Germans that a move on Austria would not provoke Italian intervention.[9] Over the next few months, the Austrian government was forced to make further concessions to the Austrian Nazis and the Reich Germans living in Austria.[10] During consultations in Vienna, which took place a year after the July 1936 agreement, the Germans managed to push through additions to the previous arrangement,[11] and, on 12 July, Hitler appointed his economic adviser, Keppler, who had taken part in the negotiations, to be his representative for Austrian affairs.[12]

The choral festival in Breslau, which Hitler opened at the end of July, saw a strong emphasis on 'Greater German' solidarity: 30,000 singers from abroad, mainly from Austria and Czechoslovakia, took part in the two-day event. In his address to the participants Hitler made a significant reference to the '95 million Germans' of whom only two-thirds lived within the borders of the Reich.[13] Back in Berlin and evidently still under the impression of the event in Breslau, Hitler told Goebbels in a private conversation that one day he would 'make tabula rasa [in Austria]. . . . This state isn't a state. Its people belong with us and will join us.' Goebbels commented: 'The Führer's entry into Vienna will one day be his greatest triumph.' But Hitler's ambitions were not limited to Austria: 'Czechoslovakia also isn't a state. It will be overrun one day.'[14] A few weeks later, just after the end of the Party Rally, Goebbels noted:[15] 'He says that Austria will one day be dealt with by force. That will be the final judgement of world history.'*

The Party Rally in Nuremberg, which began on 7 September, clearly demonstrated the regime's growth in self-confidence. Anti-Bolshevism and anti-Semitism were the main themes of the event, and Hitler linked them together in his concluding speech. He warned that the Bolshevik movement, which was directed from Moscow, had an 'international character'. In Russia, 'by taking over the leadership of the Russian proletariat, the Jewish minority' had succeeded in 'not only deposing the previous leadership of society and the state, but in exterminating it without further ado'. As a result, Russia was now nothing but the 'brutal dictatorship of an alien race'. By exploiting democracy and getting control of the communist movement, this 'racial germ' was now striving to dominate other nations. In describing this 'threat to the world' Hitler developed a positively apocalyptic vision: the Jews were taking 'the torch of Bolshevist revolution right into the heart of the bourgeois–democratic world. . . . Just as when, in the past, the masses, driven wild by incitement, and supported by asocial elements released from prisons and penitentiaries, exterminated the natural and racially pure educated classes of various nations, bleeding them to death on the scaffold, the Jew will remain as the sole bearer of an albeit pathetic store of intellectual knowledge.' Since the Jews were a 'totally uncreative race', 'if they want to establish permanent rule somewhere, they have to exterminate quickly the existing intellectual elites of the other nations'.[16] In his speech to the Party Rally Goebbels too claimed 'the Jews...[are] mainly responsible for the spread of the Bolshevik world revolution'. However, Hitler struck out the passage in the script of his speech where Goebbels had claimed that Germany was the leader in the 'world struggle against Bolshevism', telling Goebbels he had done so 'out of consideration for Mussolini, who is sensitive about this matter'.[17]

The visit of Benito Mussolini at the end of September represented the hitherto most important state visit in the history of the Third Reich, a high

---

* Translators' note: Adapted from a line in Schiller's poem 'Resignation'.

point in the regime's attempts to acquire international recognition. The 'Duce' arrived in Munich on 25 September, where he was ceremonially received by Hitler at the railway station. The programme for his visit included, among other things, a visit to Hitler's private apartment, a wreath-laying ceremony at the 'Temples of Honour' on Königsplatz, and a visit to the House of German Art. During this first meeting, Mussolini gained the impression that they were in such full agreement on the need for German–Italian cooperation that further political discussions between him and Hitler could be omitted from the programme.[18] Thus, the main emphasis of the visit was on the joint appearances of the two dictators. During the following days, Mussolini, accompanied by Hitler, visited Wehrmacht manoeuvres and the Krupp armaments works.[19]

At the end of his visit Mussolini went to Berlin, where the reception accorded the 'Duce' was intended to put everything that had gone before in the shade. 28 September was declared a national holiday. The centre of Berlin was elaborately decorated. Hitler's interpreter, Paul Schmidt, had the impression of being an 'extra in a gigantic opera production. Huge flags hung from attics down to the ground in rows along the fronts of houses. In the dusk big searchlights brought out the last bit of colour in the green-white-red Italian flags and the red of the Nazi swastikas.'[20] The whole population was urged by the press to participate in the spectacle and, thanks to the Party organization, the majority of Berliners did join in: a total of three million people were assembled on the Olympic grounds as well as on the approach route.[21] Hitler was the first to speak to what was officially termed this 'Demonstration of 115 Million People'. He emphasized that 'the current strength of these two nations represents the strongest guarantee of the survival of a Europe that still possesses a sense of its cultural mission and is not prepared to allow destructive elements to cause it to collapse!' Mussolini underlined 'German–Italian solidarity'; it was the 'expression and result of sharing natural bonds and common interests'. The visit ended the following day with a military parade.

On 20 October, four weeks after Mussolini's visit, the German ambassador in Rome, Ulrich von Hassell, approached the foreign minister Ciano with the suggestion that Italy should join the German–Japanese Anti-Comintern Pact as third partner. Ciano was surprised by this idea and asked urgently whether there were secret clauses, since the text of the agreement seemed to him suspiciously thin. Hassell mendaciously denied this was the case, but Ciano remained unconvinced.[22] Nevertheless, the Italian government accepted the idea and, on 6 November in Rome, Ribbentrop signed the document in which Italy declared its agreement to join the Anti-Comintern Pact.[23]

Meanwhile, on 5 November, Hitler signed a German–Polish Minorities Declaration, in which each state committed itself to protect the national group of the other, not to discriminate against their members in any way, and to respect their cultural autonomy. On the occasion of the signing of this agreement, Hitler received members of the Polish minority in Germany, declaring that it was the aim of his government to ensure that 'the Polish ethnic group can live harmoniously and peacefully together with German citizens', in order in this way to further strengthen friendly relations between the two countries. Moreover, Hitler met ambassador Lipski and a communiqué was issued stating 'that German–Polish relations should not be damaged by the Danzig question'.[24]

The idea of also including Poland in the Anti-Comintern Pact, which had been mooted since the previous year, was not raised during these conversations. But it had not been dropped; in January 1939, Ribbentrop was to return to this project once again with foreign minister Beck.[25]

Hitler's plans to acquire living space

It was not by chance that, at the beginning of November 1937, Hitler initiated a major change in his foreign policy. The mass demonstrations at the Breslau Choral Festival, the Party Rally with its strongly anti-communist theme, the consolidation of the friendship with Italy, and indeed the prospect of forging an alliance under Germany's leadership, all encouraged him in his decision now to embark on a policy of overt expansion. This policy was directed initially at Austria and Czechoslovakia.

In Hitler's view Czechoslovakia was an artificial construct created by the Allies after the end of the First World War and he quite simply refused to recognize as a legitimate nation state. The anti-Czech prejudices of his youth played a part in this as well as geopolitical considerations. A glance at a map showed that, after the planned Anschluss with Austria, Czechoslovakia would be like a stake penetrating deep into the future 'Greater Germany'. Protected by a strong ring of fortifications, it was a relatively well-armed state, which in May 1935 had made a defensive pact with the Soviet Union and was closely allied with France. As far as Hitler was concerned, it represented an important potential pillar of an anti-German bloc that was in the process of being constructed under communist leadership. Moreover, he was acting on the assumption that, by neutralizing this alleged threat, he would be expanding the 'living space' of his Reich by incorporating territories to which, from a traditional 'Greater German' perspective, there was already a historic claim.[26] During 1937, Hitler became increasingly convinced that the alliance he was seeking – with Italy at its core, but with Poland, Hungary, Romania, Yugoslavia, Spain, and possibly the Baltic states as potential candidates – would give him superiority over the 'Bolshevik' camp and so he could now go on the offensive. Franco's military advances in the Spanish Civil War and France's domestic political difficulties strengthened him in this view. The fact that the alliance with Britain had not come about seemed to have made many things easier.

The German minority in Czechoslovakia now provided Hitler with an important factor that could be utilized for undermining and violently breaking up Germany's unloved neighbour. Using the pretext of securing the legitimate minority rights of ethnic Germans, the Reich government now began to exploit the Sudenten German Party (SdP), the German minority's most important political organization, to implement its aggressive policy aimed at undermining Czechoslovakia.[27]

Germany's relations with Czechoslovakia, which since the spring had been a target of its press propaganda, rapidly deteriorated during autumn 1937. The Propaganda Ministry exploited an incident in Teplitz-Schönau, in which Karl Hermann Frank, the leader of the strong Nazi group within the SdP and a member of the Prague parliament, became involved in a violent confrontation with the Czech police, to launch a new press campaign against Czechoslovakia.[28] At the same time, Konrad Henlein, the chairman of the SdP, sent a protest to Prime Minister Beneš, in which he demanded autonomy for the ethnic Germans. The Czech government responded immediately to these developments, which had clearly been coordinated, by postponing the local government elections scheduled for 22 November and banning all political meetings. On 3 November, Goebbels stopped the campaign after Henlein had explained to him in a private conversation that he was afraid that events might get out of control, which the Reich government did not want to happen at that particular juncture.[29] A 'press truce' was eventually agreed through negotiations with the Czech government[30] lasting into the early months of 1938.[31] Meanwhile, Henlein, who had been forced into a serious confrontation with the Prague government by the Nazis in his party, had concluded that the only way out of this difficult situation was total subordination to Hitler.[32]

On the afternoon of 5 November, in other words immediately after the agreement with Poland and a day before Italy's signing of the Anti-Comintern Pact, Hitler invited War Minister Blomberg, Foreign Minister Neurath, and the commanders-in-chief of the army, navy, and air force to a meeting in the Reich Chancellery, at which he informed them in a lengthy address of his strategic plans. His Wehrmacht adjutant, Colonel Hossbach, took notes of the two-hour monologue for his own purposes.[33] Right from the start, Hitler tried to convince his audience of the exceptional importance of what he was going to say by stating that, 'in the event of his death, his words should be regarded as his last will and testament'. During this autumn, he was evidently seriously concerned that he might not have much time left to him. At the end of October, he had already told the Party's propaganda chiefs that, as far as could be judged, he did not have much longer to live. Based on this assumption, in his address he described the 'solution to the need for space' as the German nation's most important future problem with its 'over 85 million people'. He estimated that a solution could only be 'sought for a foreseeable period of about one to three generations'.

Before reaching the core of his reflections and sketching the war scenarios he was planning, Hitler spent a long time rejecting possible alternatives. 'Total autarky' could not be achieved even if domestic raw materials were fully exploited and substitutes were mass-produced, and it would in any case be impossible to provide sufficient foodstuffs. Increasing participation in the 'world market' would be equally incapable of providing real solutions to Germany's existential problems. This had been his standard argument since the 1920s.

Hitler was thereby conceding the fact that, a year after the launching of the Four-Year Plan, Germany's own sources of raw materials, essential to the expansion of the Wehrmacht, had not been significantly increased. On the contrary, the rearmament programme had stalled during 1937, forcing the three branches of the Wehrmacht, which had originally been gearing their rearmament planning to achieve full-scale mobilization by 1940, to extend the schedule. The main reason was the shortage of steel in Germany, which in February 1937 had, among other things, required the introduction of a quota system and prompted Göring to establish his own steel concern. The 'Hermann Göring Works' were designed to exploit the (comparatively low-grade) deposits of German iron ore. However, all these efforts had failed to solve the steel crisis. On 3 September, Blomberg had told Göring that 'there [is] no way that either the plan or the schedule for the Wehrmacht to be totally prepared for action, in accordance with the directives issued by the Führer and Reich Chancellor,...can be achieved'.[34]

Thus, in his address Hitler was obliged to deal with the political consequences stemming from the altered schedule for the rearmament programme. Basically, Hitler stated, German policy must reckon with two 'hate-inspired opponents', Britain and France, for whom 'a strong German colossus in the middle of Europe was a thorn in their side'. Neither country would accommodate the establishment of German bases overseas nor willingly give up former German colonies. After thereby conceding the failure of his previous British policy, he attempted to downplay the strengths of this new 'hate-inspired opponent' by asserting that Britain could not maintain power over the Empire in the long run 'on the strength of 45 million English'. France's position by comparison was relatively favourable, but it was faced with massive 'domestic problems'.

Finally, Hitler came to the main point of his address. The 'lack of space', of which he complained, 'could only be solved through the use of force', which, however, 'was never without attendant risk'. Taking this into account, the only remaining issues to be decided were 'when' and 'how'. The latest date for a German war of conquest was during the years 1943–45, in other words after the completion of rearmament; after that, time would be working against Germany. In addition to this first scenario, however, there were two other possible ones that would justify striking earlier: if the French armed forces were tied up by either a serious domestic crisis (scenario 2) or a war against Italy (scenario 3). In both cases 'the time for action against Czechoslovakia [would have] come'. If France was embroiled in a war then Austria should be simultaneously 'crushed'. However, it was quite possible that this eventuality might already occur during 1938. And that was the decisive message of this conference of 5 November: the extension of the rearmament period by no means implied that the move towards expansion was being postponed into the distant future.

Thus, the speech revealed Hitler's short-, medium-, and long-term foreign policy ideas. In the first place, Hitler told his military leaders that, in the short term and under certain favourable conditions, he had decided to move against Austria and Czechoslovakia through surprise military attacks. When Henlein decided to subordinate himself to Hitler and, on 19 November, wrote to him offering the assistance of his party in incorporating the 'whole of the Bohemian-Moravian-Silesian area' into the Reich, the dictator failed to respond. Evidently, at this stage, Hitler was still thinking of a purely military move against Czechoslovakia. He only accepted Henlein's offer the following spring. Secondly, Hitler made it clear in his address of 5 November that he was absolutely determined to deal with the 'space issue' by 1943–45, in other words during his lifetime, and to do so through the incorporation of Austria and Czechoslovakia. On this occasion, however, he did not refer to the realization of far-reaching plans for conquests in eastern Europe, such as he had developed in the 1920s, or to a great 'world conflict', which he had predicted for the period 1942–43 in a conversation with Goebbels in 1937.[35]

Hitler's limitation of his plans to Czechoslovakia and Austria resulted from the fact that he was engaged in a comprehensive analysis of the attitude of powers that might potentially intervene during the 1943–45 war scenario, referring specifically to the positions of Russia and Poland. In his view it was unlikely that they would intervene in a German war against Czechoslovakia and Austria. Thus, Hitler was concerned to develop a future scenario in which a war against Russia and Poland could be avoided rather than one involving the conquest of these states.[36]

Had he, therefore, postponed or given up his plans for acquiring living space in eastern Europe? He certainly gave his audience the impression that these plans would no longer be realized during his lifetime, but at best in the distant future after a period of between one and three generations. However, it would be a serious mistake to interpret Hitler's address of 5 November 1937 in the first instance against the background of his far-reaching plans for living space for that would be to confuse his utopia with his actions as a politician. For Hitler's aim in making this speech was not primarily to provide insights into his far-reaching plans for conquest. Rather, in view of the growing shortage of resources for rearmament, as a practising politician he was faced with the need to present his military leaders with more or less realistic short- and medium-term goals, and he did this by ordering them to prepare for aggressive action against Czechoslovakia and Austria, at the latest by 1943–45, and at the earliest during the following year. For the moment this task offered a political goal that would provide the context for further rearmament measures. As he evidently did not intend to stop full-scale rearmament after a war in the coming year, he was in fact keeping all his options open.

However, Hitler's address provoked misgivings and objections from his audience, not to the extent of fundamentally challenging his aim of going to war, but in questioning some of his premises. Blomberg and Fritsch argued 'that we should not let England and France become our opponents'; in the event of a war with Italy France would only have limited forces tied down on the Alpine frontier and would be able to direct its main forces against Germany. At the same time, the strength of Czech fortifications should not be underestimated. Neurath argued that a conflict between Italy and France and Britain was 'not yet so close…as the Führer seems to assume', to which Hitler responded that he was thinking of summer 1938 as 'the possible time'. He was 'convinced', and this was aimed at Blomberg and Fritsch, that 'England would not take part' and for that reason did not believe 'in military action by France against Germany'. Since he had not absolutely committed himself to a war during the following year, but had linked it to various conditions, he was able to calm the misgivings that had been expressed.[37]

The second part of the meeting was concerned with the armaments bottlenecks, which had been the real reason why it had been convened. The content was not recorded in as much detail as the first part. We know, however, that Blomberg gave a comprehensive account of the Wehrmacht's raw materials and armaments situation followed by attacks by Blomberg and Fritsch on Göring.[38] Thus it was Göring, as the main person responsible for the distribution of the limited amount of raw materials, who was in the firing line and not Hitler, who in his address had modified his aims to the extent that he had not been forced to admit failure as far as the armaments bottlenecks were concerned.

However, the generals soon overcame their misgivings. In the new version of the deployment order for 'Operation Green' of 21 December 1937 Blomberg took account of Hitler's statements of 5 November. The previous military plans for a two-front war against France and Czechoslovakia had been purely defensive and in his basic directive for the Wehrmacht's war preparations of June 1937 Hitler himself had still been operating on the assumption that Germany was not threatened and did not intend to launch a European war.[39] Now the new version stated that when Germany had achieved complete readiness for war in all spheres 'the military preconditions will have been created for an offensive war against Czechoslovakia, so that the solution of Germany's problem of space can be carried to a victorious conclusion even if one or other of the great powers intervenes against us'. The assumption was that the war against Czechoslovakia would occur 'simultaneously with the resolution of the Austrian question, in the sense of incorporating Austria into the German Reich'. However, the directive also envisaged a war against Czechoslovakia (and Anschluss with Austria) *before* Germany had achieved its full wartime strength, if intervention by the Western powers was not anticipated, either as a result of a lack of interest (Great Britain) or because of involvement in other conflicts (France).[40]

On 19 November, two weeks after the meeting with the military leadership, Hitler received an important member of the British cabinet in Berchtesgaden in the shape of the Lord President of the Council and future Foreign Secretary, Lord Halifax.[41] Halifax put forward the idea of closer cooperation between the four main European powers, France, Great Britain, Italy, and Germany, in order to lay the foundations for lasting peace in Europe. Hitler would have seen in this proposal the first step towards a revival of a system of collective security, which he had been strongly resisting since 1933. Thus, his response to Halifax was sceptical verging on aggressive. In particular, he pointed out to his British guest that, since 1919, Germany had not been treated as an equal by the Western powers, but rather had been humiliatingly discriminated against. The main point dealt with in the further discussions was the German demand for colonies. While Halifax cautiously indicated a willingness to discuss the issue, he referred in what was more of an aside to Germany's wish for a revision of the frontiers in Central Europe. He noted 'possible alterations in the European order, which might be destined to come about with the passage of time. Amongst these questions were Danzig, Austria, and Czechoslovakia'. His government was 'interested to see that any alterations should come through the course of peaceful evolution and that methods should be avoided which might cause far-reaching disturbances that neither the Chancellor nor other countries desired'. Hitler only responded briefly to these comments and declared that the agreement with Austria reached in July 1936 would lead to the 'removal of all difficulties', while it was up to the Czech government to deal with the existing problems by treating the German minority well. He did not refer to the question of Danzig.[42] However, the signal that Hitler had received from Halifax was clear: a revision of the German borders was possible provided it occurred through 'evolution', in other words not by Germany using force without the agreement of other powers.[43]

Two days later, at the fifteenth anniversary celebration of the founding of the Rosenheim Nazi Party local branch, Hitler significantly and after a long interval once again used a public speech to demand living space. 'Our people's living space is too small,' he insisted: 'One day the world will have to respect our demands. I have not the slightest doubt that, just as we were able to raise up our nation domestically, in foreign affairs we shall be able to gain the same rights to live as those possessed by other nations.' After that he once again dropped the subject for a long time.

It is clear from the Hossbach memorandum and his behaviour during his meeting with Halifax that, during the course of 1937, Hitler had finally given up the idea of an alliance with Britain. The reception of the Duke of Windsor at the Berghof in October, officially described as 'private', represented for Hitler an opportunity to reconcile himself to the idea that an alliance with Britain was impossible, as in the past he had vested great hopes in the British monarch, who had abdicated in December 1936.[44] The notion that he had still had at the beginning of 1937 of forcing Britain to make an alliance by threatening naval rearmament and demanding colonies had, in the meantime, been reduced to the aim of keeping Britain from intervening in a war in central Europe.

In his detailed 'Note for the Führer' of 2 January 1938 Ribbentrop, who had been sent as ambassador to Britain in the summer of 1936 in order to clinch the alliance with Britain,[45] reinforced Hitler's decision to move away from the idea of an alliance. Indeed, Ribbentrop went a step further. He proposed that, while 'outwardly our declared policy should be an understanding with England', in fact Germany should construct 'secretly, but with absolute determination''a network of alliances against England' by 'strengthening our friendship with Italy and Japan' and also by 'drawing in all states whose interests either directly or indirectly coincide with our own'.[46] In other words, the German alliance with Italy and Japan, which according to Hitler's original ideas was supposed to be open to future British membership, was to be built up into an anti-British alliance. Slightly more than a month later, Hitler appointed Ribbentrop as his Foreign Minister.[47]

After his meeting with Halifax had confirmed Hitler's view that Britain had no fundamental objections to a revision of the German–Czech border, in November 1937 he set about approaching a number of governments that were also interested in destroying Czechoslovakia, for that, rather than 'liberating the Sudeten Germans', was his real aim.

At a reception in the Reich Chancellery on 25 November he recommended to the Hungarian Prime Minister Kálmán Darányi and his Foreign Minister Kálmán Kánya that Hungary should not dissipate its policy but rather concentrate it on one target and this target was Czechoslovakia. Kánya agreed with this in principle, but emphasized that Hungary had a considerable interest in winning back Slovakia and also Carpatho-Ukraine, where there was a significant Hungarian minority that until 1918 had belonged to the Kingdom of Hungary.[48]

On 14 January 1938, Hitler received the Polish Foreign Minister, Beck, in Berlin. He expressed the fear that 'a Bolshevik infection would almost automatically spread from a Red Spain to France and then would grip Belgium and Holland, and so a new and powerful centre of Bolshevik activity' would be created. Germany, Hitler emphasized, did not want a change to the status quo in Danzig. He was anxious to develop further Germany's relationship with Austria in a peaceful fashion. The only case in which he would intervene immediately and without considering the attitude of France and Britain would be in the event of a 'Habsburg restoration'. As far as Czechoslovakia was concerned, the Germans were seeking 'initially only better treatment of the German minority'. Apart from that, 'the Czech state was, in terms of its whole construction, an aberration and, because of the mistaken policy of the Czechs in Central Europe, it too was in danger of becoming a source of Bolshevism'. Beck agreed 'wholeheartedly' with this view. Poland was above all interested in annexing the Olsa region with its Polish-speaking majority and was, therefore, pursuing the plan of removing Slovakia from the state of Czechoslovakia and placing it under a Polish protectorate. Hitler's soundings had begun to pay off.[49] Shortly afterwards, Göring left the impression in Warsaw that the Reich was willing to coordinate a move against Czechoslovakia with Poland and would respect its interests in the Olsa region.[50]

At the beginning of 1938, the Yugoslav Prime Minister, Milan Stojadinović was anxious to move his country closer to Italy and Germany, and paid a visit of several days to Germany. On 17 January, Hitler warned him of the danger of a 'slow Bolshevization of Europe'. Czechoslovakia was a 'source of trouble', but nevertheless he 'still had hopes that Prague would come to its senses'. As far as Austria was concerned, he would 'crush with lightning speed any attempt by the Habsburgs to return to Vienna'. Göring interjected: 'Yugoslavia could rely on the fact that if Austria one day joined Germany and so Germany became Yugoslavia's neighbour, it would never make any territorial claims on Yugoslavia'. Hitler expressly confirmed this remark.[51]

Thus, in terms of foreign policy, 1937 was entirely dominated by Hitler's move away from the idea of an alliance with Great Britain, while he increasingly turned towards Italy, thereby putting added pressure on Austria. It now seemed to him feasible to 'crush' Czechoslovakia the following year if France became paralysed domestically or as a result of conflict with Italy, thereby creating the opportunity for a surprise military intervention.

25

From the Blomberg–Fritsch
Crisis to the Anschluss

Hitler's intensive preparations for war during the last months of 1937 took place against a background of accelerating decline in morale in the Reich. The reports of the Social Democratic Party agents (Sopade reports) for 1937 show that the mood had significantly deteriorated during 1937. As far as the population was concerned, the old problems persisted: rising prices and low wages, shortages of raw materials, leading to repeated interruptions to production and to shortages and often to a decline in the quality of goods. Blatant corruption among Nazi Party functionaries continued, and the aggressive policy towards the Churches, in particular during the first half of the year, annoyed many.[1] Above all, however, the continuing unstable international situation, hectic rearmament, and sabre-rattling propaganda resulted in a growing fear of war among the majority of the population. On the other hand, the reports showed that hard-line supporters of the regime, particularly among young people, as well as diehard opponents welcomed the prospect of war.[2]

According to the Sopade reports for November, after almost five years of Nazi rule, it was 'impossible to establish an even vaguely uniform assessment of Hitler on the part of the population'. Support and rejection also 'do not correspond to the groups of supporters or opponents of the National Socialist regime. Indeed, it is precisely among the ranks of the "old fighters" that a significant number of opponents are to be found'. Many reports emphasized that the practice hitherto of expressly excluding Hitler from criticism ('if only the Führer knew . . .') was in decline; on the contrary, now Hitler too was 'included in criticisms of the regime'.[3]

At the beginning of 1938, Hitler's regime experienced its most serious test since 30 June 1934: the so-called Blomberg–Fritsch affair upset the relationship between the officer corps and Hitler and led to a serious leadership crisis. However, through a dramatic reshuffle, within a few days the dictator had succeeded in resolving the situation in his favour.

The pre-history of the extensive personnel changes carried out in February 1938 goes back to autumn 1937. Reich Economics Minister Schacht had been observing the critical foreign exchange situation produced by the rearmament drive with growing scepticism. As a result, during 1936 he was already being increasingly marginalized by Göring, who was emerging as a quasi-economic dictator, as well as provoking Hitler's disapproval. In the autumn of 1937, Hitler decided to dismiss Schacht.[4] His successor was to be Walter Funk, a state secretary in the Propaganda Ministry.[5] However, at the end of November, Hitler temporarily assigned the Economics Ministry to Göring for a few weeks so that Göring could coordinate it with his Four-Year Plan organization.[6] However, when Funk finally acquired his new office in February 1938, his appointment was part of a far more comprehensive reorganization of the Third Reich's leadership. The case of War Minister Blomberg was the trigger for the rush of events that followed.[7]

In January 1938 Blomberg had married a much younger woman who came from a humble background. Hitler and Göring had acted as witnesses, thereby giving their official approval to a marriage that was considered inappropriate according to the norms of the officer corps. This put them in an extremely embarrassing situation.[8] For, shortly afterwards, it emerged that Frau Blomberg had several previous convictions for 'leading an immoral life' and, albeit some years before her marriage, had been registered as a prostitute by the police.[9] Göring provided Hitler with the incriminating evidence not entirely disinterestedly, since he hoped to succeed Blomberg.[10] The affair led, on 27 January, to the latter's inevitable resignation. Moreover, at the end of January, Hitler recalled an old Gestapo file on the commander-in-chief of the army, Werner von Fritsch, which he had been shown some time before. The file contained material raising the suspicion that Fritsch was a practising homosexual, an accusation that at the time Hitler had not wished to pursue.[11]

Hitler decided to handle the matter personally, confronting Fritsch with his sole accuser in an extremely embarrassing scene in the Reich Chancellery. The young man, who had numerous previous convictions, identified Fritsch as the person he had blackmailed some years previously for having homosexual relations with an acquaintance. Fritsch vigorously denied these accusations.[12] However, as a result of this situation, the relationship of trust between Hitler and the commander-in-chief of the army had been destroyed.

Goebbels's diary entries for these days provide an insight into Hitler's state of mind. According to Goebbels, Hitler appeared 'very serious and almost sad', 'very pale, grey, and shocked'.[13] These observations, which were confirmed by other members of Hitler's entourage,[14] contradict the argument that he welcomed these affairs involving his two highest-ranking generals as enabling him to get rid of them as possible opponents of his next, highly risky, diplomatic moves. On the contrary, given the looming threat of a serious loss of prestige, Hitler's deep depression appears entirely plausible. Whether Hitler's depressed mood was assumed or authentic, however, he managed to use the crisis to his own advantage.

At the end of January, Hitler was considering possible successors to the two generals. In discussions with Goebbels and Hossbach the names of Ludwig Beck, Walther von Brauchitsch, Gerd von Rundstedt, and Count Friedrich von der Schulenburg were mentioned as successors to Fritsch, while Hitler began to contemplate taking over the Supreme Command of the Wehrmacht himself, with subordinate ministries for the individual branches. He rejected the idea of giving Göring the War Ministry because of the concentration of power that would result. Hitler told Goebbels that, in addition, there would have to be a whole series of appointments 'in order to obscure the whole affair with a smoke screen'.[15] However, to begin with nothing happened. The crisis grew from day to day, rumours began to spread through the Reich, and speculation was rife in the foreign press.[16] However, during the following days Hitler failed to act; indeed, he appeared paralysed in the face of the threat to his personal and political reputation.[17] This year, the celebrations for the anniversary of 30 January took place without the usual special session of the Reichstag.[18]

However, on 4 February, at the eleventh hour, Hitler finally made up his mind. He announced that Blomberg and Fritsch were now resigning for health reasons. Hitler himself took over command of the Wehrmacht; Wilhelm Keitel became head of a new Wehrmacht command centre [Oberkommando] with the rank of a Reich minister, directly subordinate to Hitler, thereby taking over the responsibilities of the former Reich War Minister. Göring received the title of Reich Marshal. More important, however, was the fact that in a secret Führer decree, Hitler ordered that, in the event of his being prevented from carrying out his official functions, Göring should deputize for him 'in all my offices'. This replaced the regulation issued at the end of 1934, which had divided authority between Göring (state), Hess (Party), and Blomberg (Wehrmacht).[19] Brauchitsch was appointed Fritsch's successor as commander-in-chief of the army.[20] Hitler's foreign policy advisor, Ribbentrop, became Neurath's successor as Foreign Minister; Neurath became president of a newly created 'Secret Cabinet Council', which was never to meet. In addition, there were substantial personnel changes in the officer corps, the Economics Ministry, and the Foreign Ministry, involving among others, the replacement of the ambassadors in Rome, London, and Vienna.[21]

Hitler had managed not only to solve the crisis, but to emerge significantly stronger from it. For now, all the key positions important for carrying out the policy of aggressive expansion on which he was bent were in the hands of obedient followers. As in June 1934, in the summer of 1935, and in the period between spring and autumn 1936, after a critical period of delay, Hitler had exploited a serious crisis in the regime by finally intervening on a massive scale to reorder the political agenda in his own interest, thereby overcoming the crisis. It is not surprising that, at the end of January, right in the middle of the crisis, he launched another project, assigning Speer the task of completing the extension to the Reich Chancellery within a year.[22]

On the evening of 5 February, Hitler gave an account of the whole affair to the cabinet; according to Goebbels, 'sometimes his voice trembled as if he was on the verge of tears'.[23] This theatrical performance was Hitler's last appearance in front of his ministers; after 5 February, he never again convened the cabinet. In future he was to be spared such embarrassing appearances before his ministers. Putting an end to cabinet meetings enabled Hitler to avoid soon having to confess to a further mistake, which in this case could not be rectified. When, in March, the trial of Fritsch took place in the Reich Military Court under Göring's chairmanship, the only prosecution witness had to confess that he had confused the general with someone else and the case was dismissed.[24] Fritsch's rehabilitation was kept very low key. After his innocence had been proved, there was simply a brief press release on 1 April stating that 'the Führer and Supreme Commander of the Wehrmacht... has sent Colonel-General von Fritsch a personal message with his best wishes for the recovery of his health'.[25] Later, in August, in a half-hearted gesture to restore Fritsch's reputation, Hitler gave him command of an artillery regiment.[26]

Austria

The annexation of Austria was one of Hitler's main foreign policy objectives. Since the failure of his attempted putsch in 1934, he had intended to bring the country under German control through a combination of internal and external pressure and then, with the crucial assistance of the Austrian Nazis, to coordinate it. The formal constitutional annexation would then be only a matter of time. In view of Italy's attitude to the Austrian question, Hitler had sometimes been inclined to adopt a cautious approach, but Nazi politicians such as Göring did not allow that to prevent them from repeatedly and demonstratively asserting Germany's claims to its neighbour.[27] It was not a question of rival foreign policy conceptions; rather such different approaches were part of Hitler's political system: strident statements by Nazis (such as Göring) were matched by more moderate voices, such as that of the German ambassador in Vienna, Papen, and it was Hitler's prerogative to choose between these 'options', depending on the situation.

During the summer of 1937, Germany had succeeded in improving the July 1936 agreement in a number of ways in its favour and, through a press agreement, in disseminating Nazi propaganda throughout the country.[28] During Mussolini's state visit to Germany in September 1937, Hitler left it to Goring to discuss the Austrian question with their guest. He gave the relevant instructions to Göring in Berlin in the presence of Neurath. He did not approve of the 'too tough line' Göring had adopted 'hitherto'; he, Hitler, was by no means intending that 'Germany should bring the Austrian question to a head in the foreseeable future, but rather that they should continue to pursue an evolutionary solution'.[29] While Hitler avoided the topic in discussions with his Italian guest, when Mussolini visited him in Carinhall on 28 September, Göring spoke to him, as he put it, 'in no uncertain terms about the merger issue' (but not about an Anschluss).[30] Mussolini responded by making it clear that he wanted to see Austria maintained as an independent state, but only in a 'formal sense', which was the equivalent of giving his approval to the coordination of Austria, roughly along the lines of Danzig, for example,[31] whereupon, Göring continued his campaign of threats against Austria.[32]

With Italy joining the Anti-Comintern pact at the beginning of November, the risk of a negative Italian response to a German intervention in Austria was further reduced.[33] On 5 November 1937, according to Hossbach's memorandum, Hitler had made clear to the heads of the armed forces his intentions vis-à-vis Austria. Austria was to be 'crushed' as part of an assault on Czechoslovakia. Thus, in addition to the idea of a 'coordination' or a 'merger', which had been pursued for some time by Nazis on both sides of the border, he had introduced a military option as a solution to the Austrian question.[34]

At the end of 1937, German propaganda began a campaign against the Austrian government, while the Austrian Nazis tried to destabilize the country through an increasing number of activities.[35] During a visit to Berlin in mid-December, Papen proposed to Hitler a plan for getting rid of Schuschnigg,[36] an objective which he had already suggested to him in September.[37] They were still thinking in terms of getting a new government in place that would be more sympathetic to the German regime. However, as Papen subsequently informed Ernst von Weizsäcker, the head of the political department in the Foreign Ministry, in a letter, they had agreed that a 'solution by force', by which was meant military intervention, should be avoided for the time being, but only 'so long as this is undesirable for European reasons'.[38] On 25 January, German policy objectives were exposed through a police search of the illegal Vienna Gau headquarters of the NSDAP: the extremely compromising material revealed that Austria was to be coordinated with the Reich through a combination of external and internal pressure.[39]

Since Germany's policy towards Austria had entered a decisive phase in November 1937, Göring had kept bluntly demanding a 'merger' of the two countries. The Third Reich's economic dictator was thinking of binding Austria into a customs and currency union with Germany, an idea he held on to until well into February 1938 and for which, in the meantime, he had gained Hitler's approval.[40] The fact that Austria was annexed three weeks later was a development that Göring had not foreseen, let alone had played a leading part in initiating. The final Anschluss was, rather, largely Hitler's initiative.

As part of the personnel changes in the wake of the Blomberg–Fritsch affair, at the beginning of February, Papen was recalled from Vienna. Nevertheless, before he left, Papen managed to agree a date for a long-planned invitation from Hitler to Schuschnigg.[41] Hitler was aware of Schuschnigg's willingness to make considerable concessions to Germany as the latter had previously discussed details of his negotiating position with Arthur Seyss-Inquart, one of his associates in Austria's German nationalist camp, who had then passed these details on to Berlin.[42] Hitler received the Austrian Chancellor on 12 February at the Berghof and put him under massive pressure. He threatened him with a German military invasion – the presence of a number of generals of a particularly martial appearance was intended to lend credence to this threat – thereby forcing him to sign an agreement in which, among other things, he agreed to allow the Austrian Nazis to act freely within the framework of the Schuschnigg regime's single party, the

'Fatherland Front', conceded an amnesty for convicted Nazis, and the appointment of Seyss-Inquart as Minister of the Interior.[43] Only a few days after his 'sorting out' of the Blomberg–Fritsch crisis, Hitler was now concerned to achieve success in what for years had been one of his main objectives. The 'coordination' of Austria, which he had now set in motion, was intended to prove the effectiveness of the recent changes in diplomatic and military personnel and consign the recent crisis to the past.

A few days after this meeting Hitler informed Goebbels of a number of details of his conversation with Schuschnigg: the latter 'now had the choice. He can resolve the issue. If he does the Führer will keep him, along with Miklas [the Austrian Federal President P.L.]'. Hitler wanted 'to deal [with Prague] in a similar way if a favourable opportunity arises'.[44] While Goebbels arranged for the German newspapers to focus on a 'press feud with Austria',[45] Hitler gave the Wehrmacht instructions to increase the pressure on Austria by carrying out manoeuvres for a few days in order to deceive the Austrians into thinking that Germany was preparing for military intervention.[46] On 16 February the Austrian cabinet reshuffle was announced: Seyss-Inquart became Federal Minister of the Interior and Security and Edmund Glaise-Horstenau, Schuschnigg's link man to the Nazis, Minister without Portfolio.[47] In addition, the Austrian government announced an amnesty for all political offences committed before 15 February 1938. On 17 February Seyss-Inquart arrived in Berlin to receive further instructions.[48]

Thus, the main demands of the 'agreement' of 12 February had been fulfilled. Nevertheless, during the following weeks Hitler increased the pressure in relation to the Austrian question, starting with his speech to the Reichstag on 20 February. It began with an endless list of statistics demonstrating the successful performance of the German economy. Hitler then dealt briefly with the Blomberg–Fritsch affair, emphasizing that the Wehrmacht and the Nazi movement were in full agreement. He then embarked on a lengthy disquisition on foreign policy full of polemics, pointing out that there were 'over 10 million Germans' living in 'two states that share our borders' and forming a historic community 'with the German nation as a whole'. The fact that they were living in separate states from the Reich could 'not be allowed to lead to a denial of their ethnic political rights'. Such a situation, he threatened, was 'intolerable for a self-confident world power'. However, Hitler also made a conciliatory gesture, expressing satisfaction with the agreement that he had forced on Schuschnigg, and his 'sincere thanks' to the Austrian Federal Chancellor.[49]

On 21 February, the day after his Reichstag speech, Hitler replaced the leader of the Austrian Nazi party, Josef Leopold, with Hubert Klausner. He combined this move with sharp criticism of the previous leadership of the Party in Austria, which had been too overtly conspiratorial, insisting that it 'must [move] from the illegal to the legal field of activity'. The Party should model itself on Bürckel's 'Deutsche Front', which in 1935 had organized the pro-German propaganda during the Saar plebiscite.[50] At the meeting Göring once again brought up his plan for a currency union without encountering any opposition.

On 24 February, Schuschnigg responded to Hitler's Reichstag speech in a statement to the Austrian Federal Assembly, in which he announced his commitment to Austrian sovereignty with the rallying cry 'Red–White–Red to the death'. He banned Nazi demonstrations and deployed the army to crush an attempted uprising in Graz.[51] However, despite this challenge, on 26 February, Hitler told leaders of the Austrian NSDAP that he 'wanted them to choose the evolutionary path, even if it was not yet possible to see whether or not it would work. The agreement signed by Schuschnigg was so far-reaching that if fully implemented the Austrian question would be automatically solved. At the moment, he did not want a solution through force if it could be somehow avoided…' While Goebbels continued to restrain the German press from criticizing Schuschnigg,[52] Hitler instructed Wilhelm Keppler, his agent for Austria, to visit Vienna regularly to ensure that the Berchtesgaden agreement was being fulfilled,[53] without, however, infringing Austria's formal sovereignty.[54] In the meantime, Hitler had moved away from Göring's plan for a currency union, now preferring a fixed rate of exchange between the Schilling and the Reich Mark.

A few days later, on 3 March, Hitler told the British ambassador that the Austrians must be asked their opinion about the political future of their country and the Sudeten Germans in Czechoslovakia must be given autonomy. If these demands were not met, then 'the moment would come when they would have to fight'. However, this threat of force was evidently not a matter of urgency as far as Hitler was concerned, for he responded to a query by the ambassador as to whether he wanted a plebiscite in Austria by saying that he wanted a process of peaceful 'evolution'. Apart from that, Hitler made it clear that he was not in the least bit interested in pressing Germany's demand for colonies, to deal with which Sir Nevile Henderson had brought a whole set of proposals.[55]

Hitler understood the 'peaceful evolution', to which he had referred in his meeting with Henderson, in terms of the process of coordination, which had now reached a decisive stage. On the same day, Keppler travelled to Vienna, in order to be on the spot to check 'the complete implementation' of the Berchtesgaden agreement and to coordinate the activities of the Austrian Nazis. He was to become the hub for further 'coordination from within'.[56] He now made more demands of Schuschnigg, such as the lifting of the ban on the *Völkischer Beobachter* and the legalization of the NSDAP, which, under the Berchtesgaden agreement, was permitted to operate only under the umbrella of the Fatherland Front.[57] In view of these unreasonable demands, Schuschnigg decided to take the bull by the horns. During the night of 8/9 March, he secured a cabinet decision to ask the Austrians in a referendum to come out 'in favour of a free and German, independent and social, Christian and united Austria'. The newly appointed Nazi Interior Minister, Seyss-Inquart, had not been present when this decision was made.[58] It was only now that, during the course of a few days, Hitler reached the decision to seek a rapid and radical solution to the Austrian question going beyond the coordination policy that he had pursued hitherto.

On the evening of 9 March, Goebbels and Göring were summoned to Hitler's presence. Goebbels noted: 'We consider either abstention or 1,000 planes dropping leaflets over Austria and then actively intervening.' Later that evening, – in the meantime Glaise-Horstenau, on a visit to south Germany, had been hurriedly summoned to Berlin,[59] and Bürckel, who, after the Saar plebiscite was considered an Anschluss expert, had also arrived – Goebbels noted the following remarks by Hitler: 'Italy and England won't do anything. France might, but probably won't. Risk isn't as great as during the Rhineland occupation'. The impending 'action' would, 'if it happened at all, be very brief and drastic'.[60]

On the following day, 10 March, Hitler had still not managed to come to a decision. Goebbels noted several options. They could either recommend the Nazi supporters to take part and vote 'yes', in order to devalue Schuschnigg's referendum. Or, they could demand an electoral law along the lines of the Saar plebiscite of 1935 (which could not be achieved quickly and would give the Austrian Nazis more time to prepare). If Schuschnigg refused to agree, the Nazi ministers, Glaise-Horstenau and Seyss-Inquart, could resign, and they could call for an uprising by dropping massive numbers of leaflets from German planes and then, in order to clarify the situation, march into the country.[61] Goebbels's report shows that Schuschnigg's surprise move had taken Hitler off-guard.[62] After overcoming the Blomberg–Fritsch crisis in February, he had been trying to make significant progress towards solving the Austrian question through 'coordination'. In November 1937, in his address to the heads of the Wehrmacht he had made any use of force against Germany's neighbours, Austria and Czechoslovakia dependent on France being neutralized, and, in March 1938, this was not the case, nor had Mussolini agreed to German military intervention in Austria. In view of the new situation, Hitler hesitated; he considered various options, wavering between them. His regime's failed interventions in Austria in 1933 and 1934 and the diplomatic risks were arguments against taking precipitate action. However, in the final analysis, his concern that Schuschnigg's surprise plebiscite could seriously damage his prestige proved decisive. It prompted him to adopt the most radical solution, finally solving the Austrian question through a triumphant victory over Schuschnigg and his supporters. It was only now that he abandoned his previous 'evolutionary' policy of a gradual coordination of Austria. He needed two full days before he reached his decision.

He informed his Propaganda Minister of it around midnight on 10 March; the invasion would take place on Saturday, 12 March.[63] That night two army corps stationed in Bavaria were hurriedly mobilized in order to be able to cross the border in the early morning of the 12th. The way in which the Anschluss, which had been proclaimed for so long by the Nazis, actually took place clearly demonstrated the extent to which the whole undertaking was improvised. Thus, the precipitate mobilization of Wehrmacht units resulted in numerous breakdowns and hold-ups during the occupation of Austria, making it clear to the military leadership that the Wehrmacht was not remotely ready for action and in no fit state to wage war in spring 1938.[64]

On 11 March, the day before the invasion, a number of leading Nazi politicians arrived in Vienna: Bürckel, Hitler's deputy Rudolf Hess, as well as Keppler, who was so active in this critical phase. They immediately began negotiations with senior Austrian politicians, increasing German pressure on the spot.[65] With Göring issuing massive threats and ultimatums to Vienna by telephone, on 11 March Schuschnigg decided to resign. Late that evening, the Austrian Federal President Wilhelm Miklas finally yielded to strong pressure from Berlin and the Austrian Nazis, appointing Seyss-Inquart as the new Austrian Chancellor.[66] Although it looked as if all German demands were going to be fulfilled, Hitler did not want to dispense with the military invasion. An Austrian 'appeal for assistance' was concocted, which Göring dictated over the telephone to Keppler for transmission to Seyss-Inquart, who then confirmed the content of the telegram by word of mouth.[67]

Hitler still had some concerns about the response of the Italian government. The SA leader and Oberpräsident [provincial governor] Prince Philipp of Hesse, a son-in-law of the Italian king, was dispatched as a special courier to Rome with a message for Mussolini. Mussolini should regard Hitler's intervention in Austria as 'an act of national emergency'. He assured Mussolini that his basic stance vis-à-vis Italy had not changed: 'The frontier is the Brenner'.[68] The prince was able to inform Hitler on the evening of 11 March by telephone of Mussolini's positive response. Hitler was hugely relieved and repeatedly asked Philipp to assure the Duce 'that he would never forget' his action; he would be prepared 'to go through thick and thin with him'.[69]

The following morning, German troops crossed the frontier as planned. German propaganda portrayed an overwhelming image of 'an invasion garlanded with flowers', an impression which still to this day dominates the public perception of the Austrians' contemporary response to the Anschluss. In fact, however, right to the last minute, the issue was so controversial in Austria that Hitler regarded Schuschnigg's plebiscite project as a serious threat to his own plans. He feared a considerable number of Austrians would support their country's independence. Thus, the pictures of the jubilant reception of the invasion are above all the result of the dominance of German propaganda, which was able to establish itself very rapidly with the aid of the Austrian Nazis; they are by no means a faithful reflection of reality.[70]

Around midday on 12 March, Goebbels read out a 'proclamation' from Hitler over the radio. In it Hitler announced that because of the unstable situation he had decided 'to provide help from the Reich for the 12 million Germans in Austria'. The Reich itself was ordered to 'hang out the flags for a period of three days'.[71] Before Hitler left Berlin on 12 March, he appointed Göring to be his deputy during his period of absence, in order to underline the fact that he was conducting the operation in Austria in person. Hitler then flew to Munich, from where he continued his journey in a procession of cars. In the afternoon they crossed the Austrian border with their first stop a visit to his birthplace, the town of Braunau, where he was greeted by a large crowd.[72] It was not surprising that there was also great enthusiasm among the supporters of Anschluss in Linz, where Hitler arrived in the evening. Here he gave a speech from the balcony of the town hall, declaring that 'providence' had 'long ago singled him out to come from this city to rule the Reich'.[73]

On the morning of the following day, while still in Linz, Hitler signed the Law for the Reunification of Austria with the German Reich, which he had unexpectedly given instructions to be drafted.[74] It made Austria 'a state [Land] within the German Reich' and decreed that a plebiscite on the Anschluss should be held on 10 April. In addition, Hitler appointed Bürckel 'acting head' of the Austrian NSDAP.[75]

Hitler's decision formally to annex Austria, rather than simply coordinating it by appointing a Nazi government or taking over the Austrian presidency in personal union with the Reich,[76] was evidently made spontaneously only a few hours before he signed the law.[77] His proclamation of 12 March mentioned only a plebiscite, in which the future of the country would be decided. Also, in his short address to the population of Linz on the evening of 12 March he had indicated that the timing of the Anschluss was still uncertain. Thus, not only did he make his decision to occupy the country to a large extent in response to the actual situation at the time, but the same was true of his decision on what constitutional form the Anschluss would take. It demonstrated how, after Schuschnigg's plebiscite initiative had set the ball rolling in the Austrian question, Hitler was then in a position to drive things forward, creating a dynamic, unstoppable train of events, while at the same time managing to keep it under his personal control. His actions were decisively influenced by the impetus given by the opportunity of solving a question that had preoccupied him since his earliest years in a positively triumphant way through a bold coup.

Since 1933, the Nazi government had worked towards the Anschluss with Austria, which was popular in both countries. It appeared essential for strategic, military, economic, and other reasons; the creation of a 'Greater Germany' was, after all, one of Nazism's main aims. However, the precipitate way in which Austria was annexed cannot be interpreted as simply the cumulative outcome of various attempts to achieve Anschluss; on the contrary, it shows how decisive were Hitler's motivation, initiative, and actions in the actual situation as it evolved.

During 13 March, Hitler remained in Linz; he interrupted his stay for a trip to Leonding, where he laid flowers on his parents' graves.[78] On 14 March, he travelled on to Vienna, once again greeted with jubilation. In the meantime, events there had been occurring thick and fast. On the previous day, the Seyss-Inquart government had ordained 'reunification' with the Reich through a federal constitutional law, prompting the resignation of President Miklas. The Austrian armed forces swore loyalty to Hitler.[79] At the same time, the regime's propaganda machine began to take over the Austrian capital; Goebbels established a Reich Propaganda Office and sent his state secretary, Otto Dietrich, to Vienna with instructions for the 'reform of the Austrian press'.[80]

The Anschluss was accompanied by mass arrests, directed in the first instance at members of the left-wing opposition, senior officials, functionaries of the Fatherland Front, and legitimists, who favoured a restoration of the monarchy. During March between 10,000 and 20,000 people were arrested.[81] Attacks on Jews represented a particularly striking development. In the wake of the jubilation at the Anschluss many were publicly humiliated; in particular, they were forced to wash off by hand the slogans on walls and streets painted by supporters of the plebiscite. Throughout the country Jewish homes and businesses were plundered, money was extorted from Jews, their cars were 'confiscated', they were forced to give up their homes, while Jewish firms were taken over by self-appointed 'commissars' from the ranks of the Austrian NSDAP. In Vienna alone several hundred of those affected committed suicide.[82]

On 15 March, a mass demonstration attended by several hundred thousand people was held in the Heldenplatz in front of the Hofburg. The Austrian Nazis had managed to bus in numerous supporters from all over the country in a very short time, while the declaration of a school holiday and an early end to the working day in Vienna increased the numbers who turned up.[83] In his address Hitler announced a new 'mission' for the 'Eastern Marches', which 'from now onwards [were] to be the German nation's, and so the German Reich's, youngest bulwark'. At the end of this speech he declared: 'As the Führer and Chancellor of the German nation and Reich I hereby announce before history the entry of my homeland into the German Reich.' During the afternoon there was a military parade of German and Austrian troops round the Ring lasting several hours.[84] Afterwards, Hitler received the Archbishop of Vienna, Cardinal Theodor Innitzer in his quarters in the Imperial Hotel; hitherto, Innitzer had been a supporter of Schuschnigg. He now told Hitler of his satisfaction with recent events and assured him of the loyalty of the Catholic population. Hitler was delighted with this response and began to wonder whether he could not harness the Catholic Church in Austria for his regime rather more easily than the one in the Reich.[85]

During the following days, Bürckel was able to persuade Innitzer and the Catholic bishops to issue a declaration in support of the new regime and to advocate a 'yes' vote in the coming plebiscite. This statement, together with Innitzer's use of the phrase 'Heil Hitler' in his official communication to Bürckel, then did indeed play an important role in the Nazi propaganda for the plebiscite to confirm the Anschluss. Although, during a visit to Rome in April, Innitzer was ordered by the Vatican to partially distance himself from the declaration, and to demand the upholding of the Concordat with Austria, at the same time he endeavoured to maintain contact with the Nazi leadership.[86]

Meanwhile, in Berlin Goebbels had been preparing a 'triumphal reception' for Hitler. As was usual for such major receptions for the 'Führer' in 'his' capital city, Goebbels used an announcement in the *Völkischer Beobachter* to instruct Berliners to close factories and businesses, to put up flags on their houses, and to arrive punctually at the meeting points, where they were to join the marching columns of the Party or the DAF. 'Everyone must be on the streets when the Führer's coming.'[87]

On the morning of 16 March, he switched on the 'people machine': according to official figures, he had mobilized a total of 2.5 million people, so that Hitler could make a 'triumphal entry' into the city, concluding with a brief speech to the crowds from the balcony of the Reich Chancellery. 'Germany', he declared, 'has become Greater Germany'.[88] The organized celebrations also reflected the relief felt by the German population that the military intervention had in the end not led to bloodshed or provoked a serious international crisis, as the Western powers had been unable to decide on any counter measures. The fear of war, which had been palpable in the border regions of the Reich during 10–11 March, now turned into a wave of euphoria; since 1918, after all, the demand for unification with Austria had been a matter of course for the majority of Germans. It is, therefore, quite conceivable that Ian Kershaw is right in his speculation that the successful 'solution' of this problem represented 'the absolute high point of Hitler's prestige and popularity'.[89]

As a result of the Anschluss, German territory increased by 84,000 square kilometers and the population by 6.7 million. The regime acquired large amounts of gold and foreign exchange from the Austrian National Bank and from private sources; it was able to incorporate 60,000 soldiers into the Wehrmacht, utilize 400,000 unemployed, and considerably improve its trading position in south-east Europe. Germany also took over a significant amount of raw material deposits, in the form of iron ore and oil, which were increasingly exploited during the following years. However, according to a report by the War Economy Office, in the short term 'the Greater German food and raw materials situation would deteriorate' because consumption in 'annexed' Austria exceeded the supplies that had been gained, and the construction of new production capacity would initially require additional rare raw materials.[90]

26

The Sudeten Crisis

After the incorporation of Austria, Hitler's next objective was the destruction of Czechoslovakia and the annexation of the Sudetenland. According to the Hossbach memorandum, in November 1937 he had only wanted to move against Czechoslovakia in the event that France was neutralized (through a civil war or a war with Italy). However, after the triumphant Anschluss, he was more and more determined to use force even without this precondition having been met.[1]

During these weeks, the way his mind was working gives an overwhelming impression of hubris. On 19 March, receiving Goebbels in his study, Hitler outlined his next foreign policy initiatives with the aid of a map: '...first on the list is Czechia. We shall divide it with Poland and Hungary. And we'll do it ruthlessly at the next opportunity.' While it is true that Hitler had already explained his intentions concerning Czechoslovakia to Goebbels in extremely aggressive terms on earlier occasions,[2] now, after the Anschluss, its incorporation had acquired a much greater urgency. Hitler also told Goebbels that, as regards Memel, which was being administered by Lithuania, 'we would want to grab it right away if Kovno got involved in a conflict with Warsaw', but the opportunity had not yet arrived. 'We are now a boa constrictor, which is digesting.' But Hitler's aims went even further: 'the Baltic, a slice of Alsace-Lorraine. France will have to sink deeper and deeper into its crisis. Above all, no misplaced [sic!] sentimentality.'[3]

Hitler's sudden interest in the Sudeten German minority was prompted by his determination to start a conflict intended to bring about the destruction of Czechoslovakia, using the pretext of the alleged threat to the existence of this ethnic group. He now recalled the offer, made in November 1937 by Henlein, leader of the Sudeten German Party [SdP], to subordinate himself to the German government. On 28 March he received Henlein, ordering him to put a series of maximum demands to the Czech government, which Prague would be unable to accept.[4] The SdP leader understood very well what was expected of him, summing it up as 'always demanding so much that we can never be satisfied'. Ribbentrop explained to him the following day that the aim of 'the negotiations to be pursued with the Czech government was basically to ensure that the scope of our demands, gradually spelt out in more and more detail, would prevent him from having to enter the government'.[5] On 24 April, speaking in the name of the SdP at a meeting in Carlsbad, Henlein declared his support for Nazism and announced an eight-point programme. It contained such far-reaching demands on behalf of the German minority that their fulfilment within the current constitutional structure of Czechoslovakia was inconceivable and they were duly rejected by the Prague government.[6]

On 21 April, Hitler revealed his plans to Keitel: a 'strategic attack out of the blue without any reason or possible justification' had to be ruled out. Instead, he was assuming that a war would be sparked either 'after a period of diplomatic conflict that gradually escalates' or 'through lightning action on the basis of some incident', for which he gave as a piquant example the 'murder of the German ambassador during an anti-German demonstration'.[7] The attack itself should be carried out through rapid advances into the heart of the country; the first four days of military action would be decisive. If they were not successful militarily, 'there would undoubtedly be a European crisis', and so they would have to create a 'fait accompli'.

At the beginning of May, Brauchitsch gave Hitler a memorandum by the Chief of the General Staff, Ludwig Beck, in which he expressed strong opposition to the 'Führer's' plans for war. Beck argued that, in the event of a move against Czechoslovakia, Germany risked intervention by the western powers and would be unable militarily to survive the lengthy war that would follow. Beck emphasized, in particular, the continuing strength of Britain as a 'world power' and its determination to resist a German policy of expansion in Central Europe. After consulting Keitel, Brauchitsch had ensured that Hitler received only the military conclusions, keeping back the foreign policy sections; however, it was clear that the memorandum was intended to provide a point-by-point rebuttal of Hitler's statement to the military leadership on 5 November 1937, namely that a move against Austria and Czechoslovakia during 1938 would be successful. Hitler was furious, making it clear that Beck no longer possessed his full confidence.[8]

On 18 March Hitler made another speech to the Reichstag in order to celebrate his triumph: 'Germany has once again become a world power.

However, what power in the world can in the long run tolerate millions of its own countrymen being seriously mistreated right in front of its own gates? There are moments when it becomes impossible for a self-confident nation to go on accepting it!' Apart from that, he was 'happy to have been the one who has fulfilled this supreme historical mission'; and he specifically thanked 'the leader of the great Fascist state, who is a personal friend of mine and whose understanding attitude [I] will never forget'. Finally, Hitler announced a plebiscite on the Anschluss with Austria and simultaneous elections to the Reichstag for 10 April.[9]

Between 25 March and 2 April Hitler made election speeches in Königsberg, Leipzig, in the Berlin Sportpalast, in Hamburg, Cologne, and Frankfurt, as well as in Stuttgart and Munich, then in Graz, Klagenfurt, Innsbruck, and, finally, on 9 April in Vienna. There he was initially received in the city hall, where, at 12 noon, Goebbels proclaimed from the balcony 'Greater German Reich Day'. At his command, broadcast over the radio at 12 noon exactly, throughout the Reich swastika flags were raised to the sound of factory sirens. A mass of 30,000 carrier pigeons were released from the city hall square to fly back to their lofts all over Germany; squadrons of aeroplanes flew over the city.[10]

Later, in their hotel, Hitler outlined to Goebbels the far-reaching aims he was pursuing in his meeting with Vienna's Cardinal Innitzer, arranged for the same day. 'We need a prince of the Church, if we want to get away from Rome. And we must do that. There must be no authority outside Germany that can issue orders to Germans.' After the meeting, Hitler reported to Goebbels that Innitzer had been 'very depressed', a state of mind that could be attributed to the fact that he had come into conflict with the Vatican over his publicly declared support for the Anschluss.[11] Innitzer had stated that he did not want to be dissuaded from his 'commitment to the German cause'. Hitler commented: 'this could be our chance to organize a dissenting movement and liquidate the Counter-Reformation.' Goebbels's diary shows that, even if only for a moment, Hitler was toying with the idea of a national Catholic Church free of papal influence under Innitzer's leadership, another bizarre example of his plans for ecclesiastical reorganization.[12] These ideas were then reflected in his next speech, which he gave from the hotel balcony. Hitler claimed to be God's instrument by stating 'that it was also the will of God to send a boy from here to the Reich, to allow him to become powerful, to raise him up to become leader of the nation, in order to enable him to bring his homeland into the Reich'.[13]

Arriving back in Berlin late in the evening of 10 April, Hitler was able to revel in the overwhelming election result: with an electoral participation rate of 99.6 per cent, no less than 99 per cent had voted 'yes'; in Austria it was the incredible figure of 99.75 per cent.[14] Nearly two weeks later, on 23 April, he appointed his Anschluss specialist, Josef Bürckel, to be 'Reich Commissar for the Reunification of Austria with the German Reich'.[15] At the same time, Hitler decided to abolish the 'state of Austria', which he had created in March – the aim was to minimize any remaining sense of Austrian identity as far as possible – and to divide the Austrian Party organization into Gaus. On 23 May, he appointed Gauleiters and made a few border corrections, which he later reversed.[16]

This reorganization of the Party in Austria provided the basis for the creation of so-called Reich Gaus. It had been initiated by Hess's office, effectively the Party headquarters and, after lengthy ministerial discussions, Hitler approved it in April 1939. The reorganization affected the intermediate-level state administration within the territory of the former state of Austria (and in the Sudetenland, which had been annexed in the meantime), with the borders of the provinces now made coterminous with those of the Party Gaus. Reich Gaus were also introduced into the annexed Polish territories after September 1939. Under the new system the Party Gauleiter simultan-eously ran the state administration at Gau level as Reich Governor (subordin-ate to the Reich Interior Ministry and the various departmental ministries), thereby allegedly ensuring the much vaunted 'unity of Party and state'.[17] The constitution of these new Reich Gaus then became the model for the Party's demand for a transfer of power from state officials to the Gauleiters in the 'old', that is, pre-1938, Reich as well. The whole process clearly shows how Hitler, in his role as the final authority, actively supported Hess's office in carrying out an 'administrative reform' in stages, by which the traditional state bureaucracy was gradually disempowered through the Party's claim to 'lead the administration'. In this sphere too the 'Führer' was by no means simply a puppet in the hands of Party functionaries operating in the back-ground, with him merely nodding through their proposals, but rather a decisive politician, who, during the development phase of his regime, sin-gle-mindedly and with lasting effect, changed the structures by which he ruled and turned them in a particular direction. However, when, during the war, powerful elements in the Party wanted to use the impending administrative rationalization for further structural reforms in its favour, Hitler proved less accommodating. He followed the pragmatic principle of avoiding unnecessary upheaval in the administrative apparatus during difficult times.

On 2 May, Hitler embarked on a state visit to Italy with a large entourage, including Goebbels, Hans Frank, Lammers, Keitel, and Himmler. During the following days, he had to get through a very full programme: receptions, the laying of wreaths, parades, and sightseeing. He visited Rome, Naples, where there was an impressive naval review, and then went back to Rome. On 8 May, he attended a display of the Italian air force near Civitavecchia and then travelled on his special train to Florence, in order to visit the Pitti Palace, the Uffizi, and also the Palazzo Vecchio.[18]

As far as the political aspects of the visit were concerned, the German delegation had failed in its aim of getting the German–Italian relationship confirmed in a written 'agreement'. The Italians were wary of entering such an agreement for fear of impairing their relations with Britain.[19] However, the Reich government assumed that the results of the visit were basically reflected in the two speeches that Hitler and Mussolini had made on 7 May in the Palazzo Venetia.[20] Apart from their joint reaffirmation of German–Italian friendship, the most important political statement was Hitler's announcement that it was his 'unshakeable determination and his testament to the German people that...they will always regard the Alpine border, which nature has established between us, as inviolate'.[21]

After the conclusion of the visit to Italy, Ribbentrop informed German embassies about its most important results. The 'Rome–Berlin axis' had proved to be a 'thoroughly reliable component of our future policy'. Austria had 'ceased to be a problem between Germany and Italy'. The essential precondition for this had been Hitler's renewed commitment to the 'inviolate status of our common border'.[22] State secretary von Weizsäcker noted 'for internal use' another essential point, though it too had only been communicated orally, namely that Mussolini and Ciano had unambiguously stated 'that, in the event of a conflict between Germany and Czechoslovakia, Italy would remain neutral'.[23]

'The week-end crisis'

After his Italian ally had made clear his intention to remain neutral, Hitler intensified his pressure on Czechoslovakia. As a result, only a few days after his return from Italy, a serious crisis developed, in which the propaganda machine, the Wehrmacht leadership, the Foreign Ministry, and Sudeten German activists all played the roles assigned to them. On 19 May, Goebbels launched a massive propaganda campaign against Czechoslovakia while at the same time the SdP provoked more incidents.[24] Meanwhile, on 20 May, Hitler received the draft plan for a military operation against Czechoslovakia that he had requested from Keitel on 21 April. Its first sentence confirmed what Hitler had told Keitel of his intentions at the time: 'It is not my intention to crush Czechoslovakia by military action in the immediate future without provocation unless an unavoidable development of the political situation within Czechoslovakia forces the issue, or political events in Europe create a particularly favourable opportunity, one that may never present itself again'.[25]

The 'provocation', without which Hitler did not wish to attack Prague, the 'unavoidable development' within Czechoslovakia, on which he was basing his future policy, then unexpectedly occurred. Alarmed by the German press campaign and made nervous by false reports of alleged German troop movements near the frontier, on the evening of 20 May the Czech government decided to order a partial mobilization of its armed forces for the following day, a Saturday. This resulted in a 'week-end crisis' that brought Europe to the brink of war. On 21 May, the British ambassador twice called on Ribbentrop, warning him unequivocally about military operations against Czechoslovakia. The French ambassador indicated that France would fulfil its alliance obligations.[26] While the Reich government refrained from taking military counter-measures, its propaganda fanned the flames. From 21 May onwards, it reported new incidents occurring in Prague, Brünn, and Eger. Hitler expressly ordered Goebbels to 'take a hard line'.[27] This was the start of a press campaign against Czechoslovakia lasting several months.[28]

The week-end crisis marks an important, indeed dramatic turning point in Hitler's policy. For he now began to reckon on war with the western powers. Colonel-General Alfred Jodl, chief of the Wehrmacht Leadership Office, and thus one of the most important generals in Hitler's entourage, noted in his diary that the crisis had led 'to a loss of prestige for the Führer as a result of Germany's failure to act' that he 'is not prepared to put up with a second time'.[29] Hitler had gained the impression that the Czech mobilization and the diplomatic intervention by the western powers had been deliberately designed to expose German policy towards Czechoslovakia as a series of empty threats. This intolerable loss of face for Hitler was the decisive

psychological moment, prompting him to press ahead with the rapid elimination of Czechoslovakia. Its destruction was intended, above all, to prevent
it from presenting a threat to Germany's rear in a future war against the
western powers. And that was the most important aspect of this new turn in
his aggressive foreign policy.

On 28 May, Hitler invited the military leadership, together with Neurath
and Ribbentrop, to a meeting in the Reich Chancellery.[30] Beck's are the
only notes of this meeting to have survived. According to him, Hitler began
by insisting on the need for 'increasing our space', a task, which 'our generation' must carry out. He named France ('it will always be our enemy'),
Britain, and 'Czechia' as Germany's opponents in this attempt at territorial
expansion. In November 1937, Hitler had still been telling the military and
political leadership that Austria and Czechoslovakia were the targets for territorial expansion that he had envisaged for his time in government. He had
assumed that, provided the Germans acted quickly and had effectively
secured their western borders, they would avoid intervention by the main
western powers. Now, however, he was envisaging a very different scenario,
namely an inevitable war with Czechoslovakia *and* France *and* Britain. For
Hitler 'Czechia' was no longer a primary target for his territorial spatial
policy, but the main threat in the event of a war with the western powers:
'It stands in the way of certain success in the West'. He now described the
strategic goal for the 'war in the West' against Britain and France as 'the
extension of our coast line (Belgium, Holland)'.

Thus, if Czechoslovakia had to be neutralized first, he said, there were
many reasons why 'quick action' was necessary. In two or three years the
Czechoslovak fortifications would be too strong; they had to exploit
Germany's lead over the western powers in armaments (British rearmament would not 'have an effect before 1941/42', and the French would also
'take many more years'); the present tensions between France and Britain,
on the one hand, and Italy, on the other, also had to be exploited. Finally, he
went into some detail about the need for extensive fortifications on the
western frontier, and then described the kind of sudden attack he envisaged
launching on Czechoslovakia. In his address Hitler was quite evidently talking about two wars: a Blitzkrieg against Czechoslovakia, with the western
powers prevented from intervening by large-scale fortifications in the
West; and then the 'war in the West', made possible by the neutralization
of Czechoslovakia. This war would have to be launched within the next
three years.

The notes show that, by comparison with the comments he had made to the leadership six months before as recorded in the Hossbach memorandum, Hitler's aggressive intentions towards the western powers – at that point still relatively 'moderate' – had in the meantime decisively hardened. The triumph of the Austrian Anschluss and the hubris that it encouraged undoubtedly played a very significant role in radicalizing Hitler's diplomatic and military aims. For him, however, the decisive psychological factor was the intolerable humiliation of the week-end crisis. It led to him ordering a number of specific armaments measures and naming a date for the occupation of Czechoslovakia. The growing readiness for war he had shown during the previous months had now become a programme.

During the following months, Hitler kept emphasizing the significance of the week-end crisis for his war policy. In a number of important speeches he repeatedly returned to the measures he had taken on 28 May. Thus, on 12 September, he declared that, in response to Czechoslovakia's 'dastardly attack' in May, he had 'hugely expanded' the army and Luftwaffe and had 'ordered the immediate strengthening of our fortifications in the West'.[31] On 10 November, in a secret speech to representatives of the press, he told them that 'after 21 May it had been quite clear that this problem had to be resolved'.[32] Similarly, in his speech on 30 January 1939, he stated that Beneš had intended 'first, to provoke the German Reich, and, secondly, to damage Germany's international reputation'. Despite his assurances to the Czech president that this was not the case, Beneš had 'maintained the fiction' and spread the message that it was 'only through his decisive measures [that Germany] had been put back in its proper place', which had undoubtedly led 'to a serious loss of prestige for the Reich'. As a result of this 'intolerable provocation', he had decided, on 28 May, to give the order 'to prepare for military action against this state on 2 October' and to order 'the vast and accelerated extension of our line of defence in the west'.[33] And, in his address to the Reichstag on 28 April 1939, he declared that 'giving in to this Czech mobilization' would have meant 'accepting a shameful defeat' and that had led him 'to resolve this question' and, at the latest, by 2 October 1938.[34]

Following the meeting on 28 May, Hitler did in fact take a number of far-reaching decisions on military and armaments matters. They resulted in another major expansion of rearmament, seriously distorting the whole economy, and requiring new state regulations, all of which represented, in effect, the start of a war economy.

Decisions on military policy

On 30 May, Hitler signed the 'Führer directive re: Case Green', to which he added the first sentence: 'It is my unalterable decision to crush Czechoslovakia by military action in the near future'.[35] This meant that the existing military preparations for 'Case Green', in other words the attack on Czechoslovakia, had effectively become a war plan ordered from the top.[36] In his directive Hitler further stated that it depended on the 'decisive utilization of a favourable moment', on 'acting with lightning speed in response to an incident'. In the event of such an opportunity arising then within the first three or four days a situation must already have been created such that 'the opposing states who are longing to intervene' realize the hopelessness of Czechoslovakia's military situation, while the countries with territorial claims on her, in other words Hungary and Poland, would have an incentive to intervene. It is clear from Keitel's accompanying statement that Hitler had ordered that the requisite planning for 'Green' be completed by 1 October at the latest.

On the day after Hitler's address of 28 May, Beck, Chief of the General Staff, composed a memorandum, in which he supported a war against Czechoslovakia in principle, but vigorously disputed Hitler's premise that Britain and France could be kept from intervening through strong fortifications in the West. Above all, according to Beck, a war against the western powers would rapidly develop into a European war, indeed into a world war. Although Germany would certainly win a campaign against Czechoslovakia, it would lose the war. In a further statement, dated 3 June, Beck described the plans for 'Green' as disastrous and declined to accept any responsibility on behalf of the General Staff.[37]

At a meeting of forty senior military commanders, which took place on 13 June in Barth near Stralsund, Brauchitsch outlined Hitler's view that the Czech question could be resolved only by force. Unlike Beck, he did not comment on it but also indicated that this was not his war. During the afternoon, Hitler appeared at the meeting and in an emotional speech informed the generals of his motives in the Fritsch case, stressing his satisfaction that, in the meantime, the commander-in-chief had been found innocent. However, unfortunately, the basis of trust between them had been so damaged that he could not reappoint him to his old post and so, as a kind of symbolic rehabilitation, intended to assign him command of an artillery regiment. Hitler concluded his speech by asking them to continue to put their trust in him.

The military commanders were content for the Fritsch case to be closed and to devote their energies to the tasks facing them as a result of the impending war that had just been announced by Brauchitsch.[38] During the middle of June, a war game carried out by the General Staff came to the conclusion that Czechoslovakia would be crushed so quickly that substantial military units could be transferred in time to defend the western front.[39]

Hitler appointed Fritz Todt to be in charge of the construction of extensive fortifications along Germany's western frontier, intended to prevent any French intervention or to delay it sufficiently to enable him to carry out a lightning attack on Czechoslovakia. Since 1933, Todt had proved himself in the 'Führer's' eyes as Inspector General of German Roads, in particular through his supervision of autobahn construction. The appointment of Todt, a non-military man and high-ranking Nazi, who was head of the Nazi Engineers Association, represented a complete change in the plans for fortifications on the western front, which had hitherto been in the hands of the army. Instead of the large bunkers envisaged by the army and already partially constructed, now a dense network of mainly small-scale standardized bunkers stretching across a distance of over 600 kilometres was to be built in the shortest possible time, with a deadline of 2 October. To achieve this, and using a special authorization from Hitler, Todt created a new organization, using private firms for which, on the basis of a decree of 22 June 1938, civilian workers could be conscripted. By September, nearly a quarter of a million workers were already engaged on this gigantic building project. Propaganda was constantly coming up with impressive figures and pictures conveying Germany's military strength, in order to portray the scheme as a practical example of Nazi drive and initiative. In fact, the impact of this propaganda at home and abroad was probably the most important result of this West Wall project. For the fortifications were not nearly ready on 1 October, nor even by the outbreak of war in 1939, and in 1944 they did not provide a significant obstacle to the advancing Allied forces.[40]

Hitler took a keen interest in the minutiae of the fortifications for the West Wall. During the night of 30 June/1 July he prepared a detailed memorandum on these questions for the Wehrmacht High Command (OKW) and the high commands of the three branches of the Wehrmacht. This was clearly intended to instruct the military, whom he considered simply incapable of implementing his ideas for the fortifications. The point of fortifications, Hitler pontificated, was 'not to ensure that the lives of a certain number of troops were preserved at all costs, but to maintain their combat strength'.

Firepower was more important than cover. The memorandum then communicated Hitler's detailed guidelines for the construction of the bunkers. In his view (and this may have reflected his own experience of the trench warfare of 1914–1918) decentralized small scale fortifications were to be preferred to large bunkers.[41] During the coming weeks and months, he was heavily involved with fortification issues, keeping himself regularly informed on the progress of the work on the West Wall.[42]

At the same time, after the week-end crisis, Hitler initiated a further increase in rearmament. For the armaments boom unleashed by the Four-Year Plan had largely collapsed by 1937 as a result of a shortage of raw materials; the three branches of the Wehrmacht were a long way from completing their armaments plans.[43] On 28 May, Hitler fixed even more far-reaching armaments goals. The precondition for these was the provision of larger amounts of steel for armaments. On 17 June, Hitler personally raised the monthly allocation of iron and steel for the Wehrmacht, which, as a result, increased its proportion of total German steel consumption from a sixth to a third. Also, during the same period, the Wehrmacht doubled its quota of non-ferrous metals.[44] On 30 May, Göring informed the generals that they need have no worries concerning the financing of rearmament: 'the completion of this project is the task of the political leadership'.[45] Two weeks later, Göring went even further in a speech to Wehrmacht officers: 'Finance does not play a decisive role in the present situation . . . the collapse of certain sectors of the economy will not make any difference'.[46]

This enormous redirection of resources enabled the three branches of the Wehrmacht considerably to extend and accelerate their armaments programmes. During the second half of 1938, army, navy, and air force engaged in massive armaments programmes that were directly focused on an imminent war. Already in late May Hitler was sending a clear message to the army by setting it targets for the production of particular weapons.[47] The army leadership obeyed this instruction and, at the end of May, set itself the goal of increasing armaments production for the land forces so that the wartime army of 102 divisions would be fully equipped by 1 April 1939, in other words a year earlier than envisaged in the 1936 plans. In fact, before May 1938, the army leadership had reckoned that, because of delivery bottlenecks, rearmament would not actually be completed until 1943. The construction of the Ju[nkers] 88 as the new standard bomber was at the heart of the Luftwaffe programme. It was intended to be built through division of labour, following the example of American mass production methods, which required a reorganization of the aircraft industry.[48] In fact, during 1938, aircraft production fell compared with the previous year as a result of shortages of raw materials and the difficulties involved in the reorganization of production to cope with the technically advanced Ju 88.[49] In this situation Göring made a direct appeal to the leading representatives of the aircraft industry, who had been unsettled by the Air Ministry's continually changing demands. On 8 July, he made a speech painting a gloomy picture of the international situation and, in view of the threat of a world war, demanding that the industry improve its performance, using among other things wild threats of expropriation.[50] The navy chiefs were prompted by Hitler's 28 May speech to focus on Britain as the main opponent and to press on with the programme of ship construction, which had stalled, a subject to which we shall return.[51]

Economic consequences and a crisis of morale

In the light of the hugely increased armaments production, during the summer of 1938 Göring was obliged fundamentally to reorganize the Four-Year Plan, which had now been operating for two years. During the first year of its existence alone, between autumn 1936 and autumn 1937, around 1.3 billion RM had been invested under the plan in the 'expansion of industry'. This applied above all to the production of petroleum in the hydrogenation plants, and the production of basic chemicals, as well as, amongst other things, synthetic rubber (Buna) and synthetic textiles. However, despite this massive investment, which continued during the following months, by 1938, given the increase in consumption, Germany's dependence on imports of raw materials from abroad had not been significantly reduced. The attempt to secure economic 'autarky' had proved an illusion.[52] Now it was above all a question of producing the goods the Wehrmacht needed immediately in order to wage war.[53]

The production goals were contained in the 'Defence Economy's New Production Plan' of July 1938. The plan, which was revised a number of times, concentrated on munitions and light metals, oil, and rubber, with a deadline of 1942/43. The implementation of the Four-Year Plan was to be guaranteed by the appointment of general plenipotentiaries and special commissioners with the authority to issue directives to Reich government agencies. This system already contained typical elements of a command economy.[54] State intervention was also occurring in other spheres to a massive extent. The state-controlled steel firm, Reichswerke Hermann Göring, which Göring had established in the summer 1937, was hugely expanded during 1938.[55] The Reichswerke incorporated numerous firms involved in heavy industry, particularly in Austria and the Sudetenland, moved into weapons and machine production, and took over large sections of the German inland shipping industry.[56]

The armaments boom led to full employment. A growing shortage of labour required decisive measures to control the allocation of labour – 'labour deployment' [Arbeitseinsatz] in Nazi terminology.[57] The administrative preconditions had already been created with the introduction in 1935 of the so-called 'work book', which ensured a thorough monitoring of individual employees. At the beginning of February 1937, the employment of metal workers was made dependent on the approval of the Labour Office.[58] During the early summer of 1938, the regime went a decisive step further. On 22 June 1938 Göring issued the 'Decree for Securing the Provision of Labour for Tasks of Special Political Importance', enabling the regime to conscript civilian workers for particular projects. This form of conscription was initially applied to the West Wall project; however, from September 1938 onwards it was increasingly extended to other areas (initially, above all, agriculture, the food industry, and shipping). By the outbreak of war, around 800,000 workers had been conscripted, around half of them for the West Wall.[59]

Despite conscription, the supply of labour, particularly in agriculture, remained precarious. In particular, the boom in the armaments industry and the continuing backwardness of living conditions in rural areas had caused around 400,000 agricultural workers to leave for the cities between 1933 and 1938.[60] Thus the people remaining on the land had to work harder, while the wages gap between industry and agriculture became ever wider. Together with other factors, the labour shortage led to a reduction in agricultural production and a decline in the profitability of farms. The attempts by the Reich Food Estate to cope with the crisis in agriculture by increasing regulation reduced the freedom of action of the peasantry and led to numerous disputes. Peasants, according to the SD's annual report for 1938, 'feel oppressed'; there was a 'mood partly of resignation, but partly of a real revolt against the agricultural authorities'.[61] The labour shortage in agriculture also resulted in a decline in the birth rate in peasant families, a development that was particularly disturbing from the point of view of Nazi ideology.[62]

The shortage of labour was also responsible for the 'Reich Workshy Action' of June 1938. The criminal police arrested over 100,000 'asocials', placing them in 'preventive custody' in concentration camps, a measure that was justified above all by the 'rigorous implementation of the Four-Year Plan'. At the same time, the SS began to establish production sites in the concentration camps such as brick factories and granite quarries. Although this form of 'labour deployment' was inefficient, the main aim was to make it clear to the population that nobody could escape the transformation of the labour market into a compulsory system directed by the state. The system's terror had reached the world of work.[63]

The decree for the control of wages, which was issued on 25 June, in other words three days after the introduction of labour conscription, gave the Trustees of Labour the possibility of setting binding upper wage limits in the individual sectors of the economy. Hitherto, the Trustees' role had been largely limited to maintaining wage tariffs at the existing level, while businesses were not prevented from paying more than was laid down in the tariff. However, businesses in the economic sectors that were particularly affected by the labour shortages managed partially to evade this new wage freeze through promotions, special payments, and other additional benefits.[64] The possibility of finding another job or threatening to resign provided workers with further opportunities for increasing their individual incomes. From their point of view this was highly desirable, for between 1933 and 1937, according to the Reich Bank's calculations, the cost of living had increased by around 20 per cent, whereas during the same period, the hourly wages of industrial workers had gone up by only 8 per cent. Workers had been able to keep up with the increase in prices only by extending their hours of work. Average net weekly wages had gone up 18 per cent in the same period, although there were big differences between the individual branches.[65] On the outbreak of war, purchasing power had at best reached the level of 1929.[66]

The strengthened position of workers as a result of the labour shortages and their attempts to evade the wage freeze by one means or another and to bargain with employers for extra benefits, when combined with the introduction of an increased work rate and tougher measures to discipline workers, produced an extremely tense atmosphere in many plants.[67] The widespread assumption that full employment automatically led to an improvement in workers' living standards and increased their loyalty to the regime completely ignores the social reality of the armaments boom economy of 1937–39.[68]

The armaments boom also had a negative impact to some extent on the urban middle class. Commerce suffered significantly from delivery problems, while in small artisan workshops raw materials shortages and the loss of workers to industry could quickly become existential issues.[69] The fact that the economy was being overstretched impacted in many different ways on people's lives. For example, the commitment of much of the construction industry to armaments production and the West Wall prompted Göring to decree, in 1938, that all public building projects that were not for the defence of the Reich or the 'redevelopment of the cities' required express approval; private house-building, apart from exceptional projects, was, in principle, to be halted.[70] As a result of the inadequate allocation of raw materials, the Reich railways were not in a position to maintain the track and rolling stock in a state to meet increased transport requirements. Freight transport was suffering from a shortage of goods wagons and the inadequate performance of the railways even manifested itself in the timetables, with increased journey times for passenger trains.[71]

The permanent overstraining of the economy through the rearmament drive also made itself felt in a decline in the health of the population. In July 1938, the Reich Bank's economic and statistical department produced a memorandum showing that cases of scarlet fever, diphtheria, polio, dysentery, puerperal fever, and infant mortality had risen continuously since 1933. Although no conclusions were drawn in this report, it is obvious that this deterioration in the health of the population was caused by poor nourishment and declining standards in the health system. Its authors pointed out that the number of doctors and midwives had declined slightly (in proportion to the size of the population) since the crisis year of 1931.[72]

According to the annual report of the Security Service, the general economic situation was marked 'by a growing tension between the German economy's potential and the demands being placed on it'. Any increase in those demands posed the 'danger of a reduction in performance'. The exorbitant public investment, namely through rearmament, together with the transfer of workers into heavy industry, had a negative impact on the production of consumer goods, leading to a 'reduction in living standards', in particular of the working class.[73] Complaints about food shortages were a constant refrain in the Sopade reports, particularly for the years 1937–39.[74]

The tense labour situation and the measures taken by the state to relieve it, outlined above, as well as the continuing inadequacies in the provisioning of the population, occurred at a time of growing concern about the international situation, with little enthusiasm for, indeed growing anxiety about war.[75] In its annual report for 1938, the SD, looking back, even referred to a 'war psychosis', which had lasted from May till the end of September, and in this context castigated 'defeatism', 'deep pessimism', as well as 'general depression'.[76]

This mood was not alleviated by a propaganda campaign that Hitler planned to launch in May, in order to prepare the population psychologically for the impending conflict with Czechoslovakia. Goebbels gave a speech along these lines in Dessau on 29 May (the text of which Hitler personally scrutinized)[77] and, with Hitler's agreement, intended to get the press once more 'agitating and putsching'.[78] However, during the following weeks it became clear that the campaign could by no means be continued with the same intensity.[79] When Goebbels learnt from Hitler in mid-June that the latter was 'determined . . . to get to grips with Czechoslovakia at the next good opportunity',[80] he immediately took it on board and, the following day, gave a speech in Königsberg attacking 'certain foreign circles' who were trying to 'spur Prague on, instead of calling it to order'.[81] Even so, during the following weeks the Sudeten crisis no longer played a dominant role in the German press.[82] On 31 July, Hitler dealt with the topic indirectly when he temporarily broke off his annual stay in Bayreuth for a day, in order to attend the 'Gymnasts' Festival' in Breslau. With 40,000 ethnic Germans taking part, including, at Hitler's express request, many from the Sudetenland, the event, like the Singers' festival the year before, was intended to be a 'great German popular festival', a demonstration of Greater German unity.[83] This time, however, Hitler did not make a speech.

This relative reserve about the Sudetenland was not simply the result of consideration for the SdP, which at the time was engaged in difficult negotiations with the Czech Interior Minister. In terms of domestic politics, it was not easy to maintain a mood of crisis over a lengthy period, without providing the population with the prospect of a solution to the problem.[84] This showed how far the preparations for war, particularly as regards the West Wall and rearmament, had made the population sensitive to and afraid of the risk of war. The Propaganda Minister believed that stoking this atmosphere of crisis in this situation would be counter-productive.

The campaign against the Berlin Jews

Hitler's move towards an aggressive foreign policy, which he had outlined to the military leadership in November 1937, for which he had created the essential preconditions through his personnel changes in March 1938, and which was now geared to the plan for an attack on Czechoslovakia in autumn 1938, was accompanied by a radicalization of Jewish persecution. This had already been foreshadowed in his anti-Semitic speech at the Party Rally.[85] At the end of November 1937, Hitler had told Goebbels: 'The Jews must get out of Germany, in fact, out of the whole of Europe. That will take some time, but it will and must happen.'[86] Since the start of 1938, the ministerial bureaucracy had once again begun to prepare more anti-Jewish regulations.[87] In spring 1938, in the wake of the Anschluss, the Austrian Nazis began to take a very tough line towards the 200,000 Jews living in the country,[88] and this immediately resulted in an increase in Jewish persecution in the Reich. The hard-line anti-Semites among the Party's rank and file invested great hopes in this wave of violence. In April 1938, encouraged by Hitler,[89] Goebbels started a major campaign against the Berlin Jews. His declared aim was to drive them out of the city through systematic chicanery. To achieve this, he had the police chief in Berlin, Wolff-Heinrich von Helldorf, prepare a comprehensive catalogue of anti-Semitic measures that aimed to exclude the Jews to a large extent from public life.[90] Hitler specifically approved this project, but wanted its start postponed until after his return from his trip to Italy. According to Goebbels's account of Hitler's further plans, he wanted 'all the Jews to be gradually deported'. They must negotiate with Poland and Romania. 'Madagascar would be the best place for them.'[91] In fact, as early as May, Party activists began to vandalize Jewish businesses and synagogues in Berlin. Goebbels now used these expressions of 'popular anger' in order to win Hitler's support for his 'Jewish programme for Berlin'.[92] On 31 May, the police arrested 300 people, mainly Jews, during a big raid on a café on the Kurfürstendamm and Goebbels urged the police to undertake further measures.[93]

Goebbels had Hitler's full support for his radical policy. The 'Führer' ordered that, as part of the Reich-wide campaign against 'asocials', beginning on 13 June, a large number of 'criminal' and 'asocial' Jews should be arrested.[94] In Berlin alone, which was the main focus of this special initiative, 1,000 people were involved, among them those who had previous convictions for only minor infringements. Hitler soon found himself obliged to change course, however. In view of the serious international tension caused by the Sudeten crisis, he could not afford to have more negative headlines in the international press, which was following the Berlin events closely. Thus, on 22 June he personally ordered a provisional halt to the police action against the Berlin Jews.[95] However, it is clear from Goebbels's diary that he was simultaneously encouraging Goebbels[96] to continue his anti-Semitic policy of using the Berlin authorities to cause administrative problems for the Jews.[97]

Hitler also did not prevent the anti-Semitic campaign from continuing outside Berlin. For in the wake of the Berlin excesses, similar attacks by Party activists took place in a number of other cities, while the Party press once again stepped up its anti-Semitic propaganda.[98] Moreover, at the beginning of June, the Bavarian Interior Ministry ordered the main Munich synagogue to be pulled down. It was not until September, when the Sudeten crisis came to a head, that further anti-Jewish measures were, for the time being, curtailed.[99]

Discontent among the military leadership

Hitler spent the summer as usual in a relaxed atmosphere. After attending German Art Day and Bayreuth, he went to the Obersalzberg.[100] In the meantime, however, it was becoming clear that his current political objective of crushing Czechoslovakia by military means and so risking a major war was faced with a military leadership that was hesitant, if not resistant; in particular, the Chief of the General Staff, Ludwig Beck, was actively opposing him. Beck, in turn, was in contact with the head of the Abwehr [Military Intelligence], Admiral Wilhelm Canaris, and the state secretary in the Foreign Ministry, Ernst von Weizsäcker, both of whom, like Beck, were not opposed to the dismantling of Czechoslovakia in principle, but nevertheless wished at all costs to avoid a war at this point.[101]

In the middle of June, Beck returned to his criticism of 'Case Green', producing a lengthy memorandum for the commander-in-chief of the army, Brauchitsch. In it he restated his view that a 'military move by Germany against Czechoslovakia [would] automatically lead to a European or a world war', which would 'end not only [in] a military but a general catastrophe for Germany'.[102] In a note for Brauchitsch Beck proposed that, in order to persuade Hitler to change his mind, 'the most senior Wehrmacht commanders' should threaten to resign en bloc. However, Beck then went a step further. In an addendum to his note – the meeting with Brauchitsch took place on 19 July – he stated that he also wanted to bring about 'a confrontation with the SS and the [Party] bigwig bureaucrats that was unavoidable if proper legal conditions were to be restored', at the same time explaining that 'this struggle will be fought for the Führer'. At the end of this document Beck wrote a number of pithy sentences that indicate he was anticipating a domestic political conflict in which they would have to appeal directly to the people with popular slogans.[103]

Ten days later, Beck had another meeting with Brauchitsch. On the previous day, he had learnt from Hitler's adjutant, Fritz Wiedemann, that Hitler was arguing that they 'would have to fight a war with Czechoslovakia, even if France and England intervene', although Hitler was not anticipating this. Beck also told Brauchitsch on 29 July that a major conflict with domestic political opponents was on the cards. The army must prepare for 'an internal conflict, which need only take place in Berlin'.[104] Thus, Beck appears to have envisaged a power struggle with certain radical elements in the regime, but probably not to the extent of carrying out a coup. In particular, Hitler's position was not to be affected.[105] Beck also presented Brauchitsch with a draft speech, persuading the generals to refuse absolutely to accept a war with Czechoslovakia.[106] However, when he met the top generals on 4 August, Brauchitsch was simply not prepared to follow this script, although he did permit Beck to read out his 16 July memorandum. While concern about an impending war with Czechoslovakia was expressed in the subsequent discussion, there was no mention of their agreeing to a joint intervention with Hitler.[107]

Hitler, who was making increasingly negative remarks about Beck,[108] learnt about the meeting and summoned Brauchitsch to the Obersalzberg, where he subjected him to a tongue-lashing.[109] On 10 August, he gave a speech to a number of general staff officers of the army and Luftwaffe, whom he had invited to the Berghof, in order to convince them that, contrary to Beck's view, the western powers would not intervene if Germany moved against Czechoslovakia. However, Beck had talked to the officers beforehand, convincing them that the views contained in his memorandum were correct, with the result that, on 10 August, Hitler was forced to listen to them expressing Beck's concerns. Hitler was furious and reprimanded them for contradicting him.[110] On 15 August, he gave another speech to generals in the mess at the Jüteborg military training area, reassuring them that an intervention by the western powers was not going to happen. It was very clear that he was implicitly criticizing the Chief of the General Staff, who was not present.[111] Beck responded by submitting his resignation, which Hitler accepted three days later, insisting that it should not be made public 'for foreign policy reasons'.[112]

Beck's successor as Chief of the General Staff, Franz Halder, shared the concerns of his predecessor about military action against Czechoslovakia, wishing at all costs to avoid the risk of a general war. Apart from his attempts to block Hitler's move towards war, carried out in cooperation with Weizsäcker, Canaris, Schacht, and other top functionaries, in other words through opposition and obstruction from within the regime's power structure, Halder was also involved in plans for a coup, although he and his fellow-conspirators regarded this as a last resort. These plans were being put forward, above all, by members of the Abwehr associated with Lieutenant-Colonel Hans Oster. They also involved a number of Wehrmacht commanders, the head of the Reich criminal police, Arthur Nebe, as well as the Berlin police chief, Helldorff, and his deputy, Fritz-Dietlof von der Schulenburg. These plans centred on removing Hitler, in order to prevent a war with the western powers, and beyond that, the elimination of Nazism. It is very difficult to assess how realistic they were, as our knowledge of them largely depends on the post-war statements of participants who survived. Reviewing the whole 'September conspiracy', one must conclude that, for a short time during summer 1938, various groups and individuals came together for whom the lowest common denominator was their hostility to the impending war, but who were divided about their intentions beyond that. It was typical of the heterogeneity and lack of commitment of these plotters that they failed to agree on whether they should arrest Hitler and put him on trial or simply kill him. When as a result of the Munich conference war was, for the time being, avoided, the network of conspirators rapidly disintegrated.[113]

The Sudeten Crisis intensifies

On 22 August, the Regent of Hungary, Admiral von Horthy, arrived in Germany for a five-day state visit. The ostensible occasion for his visit was the launching of a German cruiser in Kiel, which was to be given the name

'Prinz Eugen'. During the course of his career, Horthy, the last commander-in-chief of the Austro-Hungarian navy, had commanded a battleship with the same name. After a programme in north Germany with a strongly naval flavour, the state visit ended in Berlin. However, the real aim of the visit was to get the Hungarian delegation, which included prime minister Béla Imrédy and foreign minister Kánya to support a German intervention in Czechoslovakia. Göring, with his usual insouciance, had already sounded out the Hungarian ambassador during June and July.[114] Slovakia, which contained a large Hungarian minority, had been part of the Kingdom of Hungary until 1918 and was the target of Hungarian revisionism. During their visit the Hungarians appeared somewhat hesitant about supporting a German move against Czechoslovakia. However, in response to Hitler's clear comment that 'he was not expecting anything from Hungary in the affair... but those who want to sit at the table must also join in the cooking', Kánya finally stated that Hungary would be prepared to participate in such a move from 1 October onwards.[115]

During Horthy's visit the vicious propaganda attacks on Czechoslovakia temporarily ceased; afterwards, however, the German press campaign began again in earnest.[116] The negotiations being carried on by Lord Runciman were accompanied by sensationally blown-up reports of incidents allegedly provoked by the Czechs. He had been sent to Prague by the British government as a mediator to try to persuade the government to concede most of the SdP's demands.[117]

On 1 and 2 September, Hitler received Henlein on the Obersalzberg; he had already met him during the summer in Bayreuth and presumably also in Breslau.[118] Henlein now informed the 'Führer' about the state of the negotiations with the Prague government. Hitler favoured a continuation of the negotiations, but with the aim of demonstrating the Czech government's unwillingness to compromise and so providing a pretext for attacking.[119] Significantly, on 3 September, Hitler conferred with Brauchitsch and Keitel on the plans for the attack on Czechoslovakia.[120]

A few days earlier, on 26 August, Hitler had assigned Henlein's deputy, Karl Hermann Frank, the task of organizing 'incidents' in Czechoslovakia.[121] Some days later, when, on 7 September, the Prague government had largely conceded the SdP's demands with its so-called Fourth Plan, the Party provoked a large-scale confrontation with the police in Mährisch-Ostrau, as a pretext for breaking off negotiations. The incident came, as Goebbels noted, 'just at the right time'.[122] The German press were instructed by the Propaganda

Ministry to play down the Prague offer and concentrate on the events in Mährisch-Ostrau.[123]

The Reich Party Rally from 6 to 13 September, which this year was held under the slogan 'Greater Germany', provided Hitler with a suitable backdrop for making further threats concerning the Sudeten question. The Nuremberg Rally, with its numerous special trains for the participants, also served to conceal the military build-up,[124] which Hitler discussed intensively with his top generals during the rally, giving them precise directives for the attack.[125] To begin with, Hitler adopted a moderate tone in his usual speeches at the rally before declaring in his final speech that the Sudeten Germans were being 'intentionally ruined' by Czechoslovakia 'and thereby subjected to gradual extermination'; the Czechs wanted to 'destroy' them. 'Herr Beneš', Hitler declared, 'has no right to bestow presents on these Sudeten Germans; they have the right to live their own lives just like any other nation.' But if the democracies were convinced that they had 'to shield the suppression of the Germans, using every means at their disposal', then this would have 'serious consequences'. Hitler refrained from making concrete demands of the Prague government and intentionally left open what he might be planning to do next. Goebbels's comments reveal Hitler's thinking: 'Herr Beneš should ensure justice. How he does it is up to him. He won't be told what justice means. But if he doesn't deliver it, and we're the ones who'll decide on that, then we'll intervene.'[126]

Hitler's speech at the end of the Party Rally seems to have been intended as the signal to start, quite intentionally, ratcheting up the crisis into an open conflict. For immediately after his return from Nuremberg, Karl Hermann Frank presented the Prague government with an ultimatum. He demanded the suspension of martial law, which had been imposed on western Bohemia following the disruption caused by the Sudeten Germans.[127] This manoeuvre was obviously designed to create a pretext to justify intervention by the Reich to 'protect' the Sudeten Germans. The German press was instructed to attack Czechoslovakia, 'giving it a big spread and using the toughest language'.[128]

In the end, Hitler was not prepared to act on Frank's provocation. Without German support and because of the tough measures taken by the Czech authorities the unrest soon collapsed.[129] However, on the evening of 14 September, a sensational development occurred. The British prime minister, Neville Chamberlain, declared that he was ready to come to Germany the following day for discussions, whereupon Hitler invited him to the

Obersalzberg. This was rather a mean gesture, since it meant that Chamberlain, who had never flown before, was being forced to travel to meet Hitler in the furthest corner of the Reich. In the meantime, press and radio continued to heat up the threatening atmosphere, reporting on the mood of panic that had allegedly gripped Czechoslovakia and on Prague's military measures, to which Germany would respond.[130] This formed the intimidating background to the negotiations that followed.

The Munich Agreement

Chamberlain arrived in Berchtesgaden on the afternoon of 15 September. He was received in an atmosphere of strained friendliness underlaid with tension, as what was at stake was nothing less than war or peace.[131] During a conversation between the two statesmen – only the interpreter, Paul Schmidt, was present – Hitler began with a long monologue about all the humiliations that Germany had suffered since 1918 and about his foreign policy, calling into question the 1935 Naval Agreement. Given Hitler's determination to solve the Sudeten question 'one way or the other', Chamberlain asked why in that case he had let him come to see him. The 'Führer' then adopted a more constructive tone, demanding the cession of the Sudeten territory on the basis of the right of self-determination. Chamberlain replied that he would have to refer that back to London for clarification, but basically, he personally recognized the 'principle of the separation of the Sudeten territories', particularly since Hitler had told him during their conversation that this was the 'last major problem that remained to be solved'.[132]

After the meeting, Hitler told Weizsäcker that 'by brutally announcing his intention of solving the Czech question now, even at the risk of a general European war, and by stating that he would then be content with the situation in Europe', he had achieved his main goal, namely of getting Chamberlain to declare that he would support the cession of the Sudetenland to Germany. He 'had not been able to refuse' a plebiscite, a logical consequence of his own demand for 'self-determination'. If 'Czechia' rejected it then 'the way would be clear for the German invasion'; if it gave in, then 'it would be the next in line, but later, for example, next spring'. 'The settlement of the first stage in the Sudeten German question by peaceful means had its advantages too.' Weizsäcker noted that 'during this confidential conversation the Führer did not disguise the fact that he was calculating on a future war and had more far-reaching plans'.[133] Hitler could not have outlined more clearly his tactical calculations and the true motives concealed behind his policy purportedly designed to 'protect' the Sudeten Germans. He made very similar comments to Goebbels.[134] Hitler's instruction not to give the British a copy of the transcript of the meeting, prepared by the interpreter, Schmidt, was a breach of diplomatic protocol and a further example of his devious behaviour towards his British visitor. Chamberlain had correctly assessed the situation when he informed the Germans that he was 'upset' about this behaviour and, since he could not possibly remember all the details of this two-and-a-half-hour conversation, was left feeling 'like someone who had been cheated'. However, despite being duped, for the sake of maintaining peace, he did not let this prevent him from continuing the negotiations with Hitler.[135]

On 18 September, Hitler told Goebbels, who had been summoned to the Obersalzberg the previous day, that he believed that in the meantime 'public opinion in Paris and London had come to accept the idea of a plebiscite'. Would Prague give way to the pressure? 'The Führer thinks it won't; I think it will.'[136] On the following day, news arrived on the Obersalzberg that the British and French governments had agreed that the areas where Germans formed the majority should be ceded to the Reich without the need for a plebiscite. As compensation, they were going to guarantee the territorial integrity of the rest of Czechoslovakia. Moreover, Chamberlain now declared that he would be willing to come to Germany for a second meeting with Hitler.[137]

Hitler decided that at this meeting he would 'make quite categorical demands' and began to outline his territorial demands on a map.[138] The previous day he had begun to mobilize the other parties who had an interest in the destruction of Czechoslovakia, inviting the Hungarian prime minister, Imrédy, and his foreign minister, Kánya,[139] as well as the Polish ambassador, Lipski, to visit the Obersalzberg on 20 September, where he encouraged them to make their demands on Czechoslovakia.[140] The Hungarians wanted a role in determining the future status of the Hungarian minority in Czechoslovakia; the Poles claimed the whole of the Olsa region, which, in 1918, had been divided between Poland and Czechoslovakia. The Slovaks also began to stir and, on 20 September in Prague, demanded full autonomy within the state of Czechoslovakia, which they then managed to achieve at the beginning of October.[141] On 21 September, the Czech government gave way to French and British pressure, announcing that they accepted the proposals of the two governments 'with a sense of pain'.[142]

The German press was instructed to play down Prague's now evident willingness to compromise and instead to point out that the territorial demands on Czechoslovakia raised by Poland and Hungary in the meantime had created a new situation. The press was thereby already adopting the position that Hitler was going to take during his next meeting with Chamberlain.[143] Moreover, it continued to play up the bogus 'frontier incidents'.[144]

On 22 September, Hitler and Chamberlain continued their discussions, this time in Bad Godesberg. Hitler employed shock tactics at his first meeting with the British prime minister in the Hotel Dreesen. He confronted Chamberlain, who had come in order to sort out the modalities of the cession of the territories with mixed populations, with an ultimatum for the withdrawal of Czech troops from all the disputed territories and with the announcement that the Werhrmacht would invade if the matter had not been settled to Germany's satisfaction by 1 October. A plebiscite and appropriate frontier corrections could take place at a later date. Hitler adopted a threatening tone: 'At any moment, while we're having these discussions, an explosion may occur somewhere in the Sudeten territory, which would render all attempts at a peaceful resolution redundant'. Hitler then presented the map on which he had already marked in the territories that were to be ceded.[145] Chamberlain was extremely 'disappointed and puzzled', since, as he told Hitler, he had 'put his whole political career at risk' to achieve this solution.

Chamberlain did not appear at the meeting scheduled for the following morning, but instead sent a message initiating an exchange of correspondence between him and Hitler that lasted until the evening. In the late evening they met again in the Hotel Dreesen.[146] During these negotiations on 23 September, Hitler did not show the least willingness to compromise, but instead presented an ultimatum, according to which Czechoslovakia should withdraw from the disputed territories between 26 and 28 September; frontier corrections could follow later on the basis of a plebiscite. Chamberlain finally agreed to pass on this document to the Czech government; he succeeded only in getting Hitler to postpone the Czech withdrawal he was demanding to 1 October.[147]

On 25 September, once more in Berlin, Hitler discussed the crisis with Goebbels. He said he was convinced that Beneš would give way; Goebbels, however, was sceptical.[148] While on a walk together, Hitler told him of his immediate plans. The military build-up would be completed by 27–28

September. He would then have five days with room for manoeuvre in which finally to clarify the question of the Sudeten German territories. Then, he planned to order the full mobilization of the Wehrmacht during a period of eight to ten days in order to attack Czechoslovakia.

On the following day, 26 September, Hitler received the news from Sir Horace Wilson, Chamberlain's closest advisor, that the Prague government had rejected his ultimatum.[149] Hitler firmly dismissed Chamberlain's proposal, through Wilson, that he should continue negotiating with Prague;[150] indeed, according to the interpreter, Schmidt, 'it was the one and only time that Hitler lost his temper in my presence', furiously attacking Beneš and the Czechs.[151]

On the same day, Hitler gave an account of the crisis to an audience in the Berlin Sportpalast. His speech was expressly intended to provide a detailed justification for the coming war with Czechoslovakia and to give his position quasi-plebiscitary support from an enthusiastic public. Goebbels noted in his diary that he had prepared the meeting 'down to the last detail'. 'The audience is intended to represent the people.'[152] In his speech Hitler used the backdrop provided by Goebbels to project himself as the executor of the 'people's will': 'Now it is no longer the Führer who is speaking or an individual, now the German people is speaking!' He insisted on a solution of the Sudeten question in the interests of Germany, but also promised that, afterwards 'Germany will no longer have any territorial issues in Europe!' After the Sudeten issue had been resolved he would no longer have any interest in Czechoslovakia: 'We don't want any Czechs at all!' Beneš now had the choice between 'war and peace'.[153] The press were instructed viciously to attack the president of Czechoslovakia in order to drive a wedge between him and his population.[154]

Fired up by his speech, Hitler replied to Chamberlain in a letter he handed to Wilson on the morning of the 27 September.[155] In it he rejected the reasons the Czech government had given for its refusal to accept the German ultimatum as spurious. During the meeting at which the letter was handed over, Wilson produced another personal communication from Chamberlain stating that France would stand by its commitments to Czechoslovakia and Britain would support her. But Hitler was unimpressed and began making threats against Czechoslovakia, which, if its government rejected his demands, he would 'crush'.[156]

In the meantime, Göring and Ribbentrop were pressing the Hungarian government to take part in a joint military engagement. The Hungarians, however, remained hesitant, having become convinced that that they would be able to win back at least the Magyar-speaking southern areas of Slovakia and Ruthenia without the use of military force, which involved the risk of a confrontation with Romania and Yugoslavia. Göring, with whom Horthy was staying during this period in order to hunt, reported to Hitler on 26 September in the Reich Chancellery on a conversation he had had with the Hungarian regent: his behaviour had been 'totally feeble and cowardly'.[157]

On the afternoon of 27 September, on Hitler's orders, a motorized division paraded through the centre of Berlin.[158] Contrary to Hitler's expectations, however, the Berlin population did not respond to this display of military strength and readiness for war with the same enthusiasm as had 'the people' in the Sportpalast. The population ostentatiously ignored the troops; it was obvious that they were depressed about the prospect of an impending war.[159] Hitler's Luftwaffe adjutant, Nicolaus von Below, noted in his memoirs that Goebbels 'could have organized more cheering'.[160] The distinct lack of enthusiasm for war could indeed be explained by the fact that this time Goebbels did not turn on the 'people machine', as he was dubious about Hitler's war policy, and the parade was not going to prompt spontaneous jubilation from Berliners. To add to the pressure, the following day, at Hitler's regular lunch party in the Reich Chancellery, Goebbels declared that the population was not in favour of war.[161] This scene in Berlin mirrored the widespread rejection of war by the majority of the population throughout the Reich. This 'war psychosis', which was being openly referred to by the authorities, reached its high point in the second half of September.[162]

Hitler appears to have taken note of the lack of enthusiasm for war, particularly since this situation represented a significant decline in his prestige. He declared his willingness to participate in a last round of negotiations, proposed on 28 September by Mussolini, acting above all on behalf of Chamberlain. On the same day, the four governments of Britain, France, Italy, and Germany agreed on a conference to solve the problem, to be held in Munich.[163] The German leadership was divided: while Ribbentrop was strongly in favour of war, Goebbels and Göring were much less enthusiastic. 'The situation does not provide a springboard for war', Goebbels noted. One cannot fight a world war over 'modalities'.[164]

On the evening before the Munich conference, the regime organized a wave of demonstrations, involving several million people, throughout the Reich under the slogan 'Enough of Beneš'. Goebbels spoke at the main event in Berlin to a crowd of 500,000 people. He noted in his diary that he had been unable to say anything about the Munich conference, as 'there would undoubtedly have been demonstrations too obviously in favour of it'.[165] He did not want to give the Berlin population another opportunity publicly to demonstrate their opposition to war.[166] The great enthusiasm with which the Munich population greeted the participants the following day was also interpreted by numerous observers mainly as a clear expression of a desire for peace. The cheering was directed above all at Chamberlain, who was greeted much more warmly than Hitler.[167]

During the night of 29–30 September, Chamberlain, Daladier, Mussolini, and Hitler, meeting in the so-called Führer building in Munich, agreed the draft treaty proposed by Mussolini, according to which the Wehrmacht would enter the Sudeten German territories on 1 October and complete their occupation in stages by 10 October. An international committee composed of representatives of Germany, Britain, France, Italy, and Czechoslovakia was to define those territories where, as a result of an ethnically mixed population, a plebiscite appeared necessary. It was to supervise the plebiscites and, on the basis of the results, define the final borders. Every individual would have the right to decide whether he or she wished to stay in the disputed territories and the Czech government was to amnesty Sudeten German prisoners. Britain and France gave a guarantee for the remainder of Czechoslovakia and Germany and Italy agreed to join this guarantee as soon as the issue of the 'Polish and Hungarian minorities within Czechoslovakia had been sorted out'. No decision had been reached about the future of the non-German minorities after Hitler, in his opening speech, had declared that he could only speak for the interests of the Germans in Czechoslovakia.[168] The agreement covered an area of 29,000 square kilometres with a population of 3.6 million, of whom 3.1. million were German-speaking.[169] Following a Polish ultimatum of 1 October, Prague was also forced to cede the Olsa region to Poland.[170] By contrast, Hungary, for the time being, did not subject Czechoslovakia to any territorial claims.[171] However, under the so-called First Vienna Award of 2 November 1938, proclaimed by Ribbentrop and Ciano, Hungary received parts of Slovakia as well as a part of Carpatho-Ukraine.[172]

On the 30 September, the day after the long night of negotiations, Chamberlain visited Hitler around midday in his private apartment on Prinzregentenplatz. The interpreter, Schmidt, later recalled that, while listening to what Chamberlain had to say, Hitler looked pale, irritable, and distracted, and, unusually, did not respond with lengthy counter arguments.[173]

Chamberlain presented Hitler with the draft of a brief Anglo-German peace declaration that met the demands Hitler had made in his Sportpalast speech of 26 September and which he now felt obliged to sign. The declaration stated, in particular, that 'all other questions that affect our two countries, should be dealt with through the method of consultation'.[174] At the beginning of December, Ribbentrop agreed with his French counterpart, Georges Bonnet, a Franco-German consultation declaration, which also recognized the frontiers between the two countries as 'final'. Both declarations were without political consequences and served only – temporarily – to reassure the western powers.[175]

Although in the eyes of most of his contemporaries Hitler had achieved a remarkable success, he had not succeeded in annexing the whole of Czechoslovakia, for which the demand for a solution to the Sudeten German question had always only been a pretext. Indeed, he had to accept that, with his increasingly strident demands for the 'liberation' of the Sudeten Germans, he had manoeuvred himself into a cul-de-sac. For the western powers had taken him at his word and fulfilled all his demands based on ethnicity. They anticipated binding him into a four-power guarantee for the rest of Czechoslovakia, a development that he wished to avoid at all costs. For such a four-power guarantee threatened to lock him into a four-power bloc, thereby preventing him from continuing his expansionist policy. Moreover, on the domestic front he had been deeply disappointed to discover that not only were the German people not enthusiastic for war, but were actually afraid of it. The population had been so jubilant about the Munich Agreement not because they had seen it as a national success but rather because it averted war at the very last minute. Equally disappointing for Hitler was the lack of enthusiasm for his war policy among sections of the regime's leadership, in particular the military and the diplomats.

During the weeks following Munich, Hitler came to the conclusion that he must rectify the failure to crush Czechoslovakia at the earliest possible moment after the winter was over. The remaining months had to be used to prepare domestically for war.

27

After Munich

After Munich Hitler was determined to go ahead as soon as possible with the plan he had been nursing since May 1938 of destroying Czechoslovakia, a plan that, for the time being, had been thwarted by a combination of domestic and foreign opponents. To achieve this, from October onwards, he set about destabilizing Czechoslovakia through internal and external pressure, making the border established in Munich appear merely provisional. Above all, however, during the Munich conference he was already engaged in strengthening ties with Japan and Italy, in order to avoid the Reich being integrated into a European four-power bloc, into which he was being forced against his will, and to establish a rival bloc against the western powers. At the same time, he wanted to achieve a 'general settlement' with Poland in order to place the alliance with this important partner on a permanent basis. However, in order to achieve greater diplomatic freedom of action and to continue his power politics he had to accelerate rearmament, which he also set in motion during the Munich conference. Apart from that, he was determined to take radical steps to overcome the German population's evident lack of enthusiasm for war, as spectacularly demonstrated in September, and to underline the Party's leadership role through a reorientation of domestic politics.

At Munich the issue of the cession of Czechoslovak territories mainly populated by Poles and Hungarians to these two countries had been initially postponed for three months. Germany and Italy were going to guarantee the integrity of Czechoslovakia only after this matter had been settled; the two western powers had already done so. Hitler was determined at all costs to avoid Germany having to give such a guarantee, for his aim was instead to encourage the ongoing disintegration of Czechoslovakia. Thus, during the coming months, he pursued the policy of declaring that the question of the non-German minorities in Czechoslovakia had not yet been 'finally' settled, the internal situation in Czechoslovakia must return to normal and so on, and, therefore, that the guarantee could not yet be given.[1] He also soon found supporters of his destabilizing policy within Czechoslovakia itself.

Hitler gave up his previous plan of handing Slovakia over to Hungary after an autonomous Slovakian government was established on 6 October under Jozef Tiso, which succeeded in securing recognition from the central government in Prague. The opportunity of acquiring the Slovakian prime minister as a loyal ally, by supporting him against Prague and Budapest, and then using him to further German expansionist policy, was too tempting. Moreover, in view of Hungary's passive stance during the Munich crisis, Hitler saw no further need to support its territorial claims.[2]

Hitler acquired another totally dependent ally and a land bridge to Romania through the creation, a few days later, of an autonomous government in Carpatho-Ukraine, the easternmost part of Czechoslovakia. Here too he gave up, albeit only for a few months, his previous plan of giving this territory to Hungary in order to meet Poland's and Hungary's wish for a common frontier.[3] A further motive for this temporary change of policy was probably the thought that Carpatho-Ukraine could become the centre of a Ukrainian nationalist movement and therefore offer the possibility – albeit at this stage very vague – of influencing the Ukrainian minority in eastern Poland and in the Soviet Ukraine. At any rate, from 10 October onwards, German radio stations began broadcasting programmes in Ukrainian and supporting the cause of Ukrainian independence.[4]

Negotiations between Czechoslovakia and Hungary about a new definition of the border had just been broken off when, on 14 October, Hitler received the new Czechoslovak foreign minister, František Chvalkovský, and the former Hungarian prime minister, Kálmán Darányi, whom Budapest had sent as an emissary, for separate talks in Munich. During these talks, Hitler pressed both states to reach a rapid agreement about the future border based on ethnic criteria. He was determined to avoid at all costs this question being settled at an international conference, a second Munich, in other words once again having to submit to a process in which he would have to appear as an equal among equals.

Two weeks after Munich, Chvalkovský now hastened to inform Hitler of the 'complete change of attitude' and the '180% [sic!] alteration in Czechoslovak policy' in favour of Germany. Hitler told Chvalkovský that, at that moment, Czechoslovakia had two choices: a settlement with the Reich 'in a

friendly manner', or the adoption of a hostile attitude, which would inevitably lead to a 'catastrophe for the country'. He made it clear that he wished
to leave the settlement of the future border to further Czech–Hungarian
negotiations.[5] In his meeting with Darányi he expressed his dissatisfaction
with Hungary's passive attitude during the Sudeten crisis;[6] indeed, he and
Ribbentrop were to criticize Hungary frequently during the coming
months.[7] Apart from that, he told his Hungarian guest that he wanted to
keep out of the territorial disputes between the two countries. By contrast,
during his first meeting with the Slovak Prime Minister, Tiso, Ribbentrop
expressed strong German support for Slovak autonomy.[8]

After it proved impossible to settle the issue of the border between
Hungary and Czechoslovakia in bilateral negotiations, the governments of
the two countries decided to submit themselves to the arbitration of the
two Axis powers, Italy and Germany. Hitler was unenthusiastic, but suppressed his doubts probably because, at the time, he was trying to get Italy
to join a three-power pact. On 2 November, the so-called Vienna Accord
was announced, involving the cession of territory that hitherto had been
part of Slovakia and Carpatho-Ukraine to Hungary. Hitler left it to Ribbentrop
and Ciano to make peace between Slovakia and Hungary in Schloss Belvedere
in Vienna.[9] When, in the middle of November, Hungary attempted a military
occupation of the whole of Carpatho-Ukraine, Hitler forced the Hungarians
to call it off. The Hungarian occupation of Carpatho-Ukraine would
'humiliate the Axis powers . . . whose arbitration Hungary had accepted
without reservation three weeks ago'.[10]

It appeared at first as if Munich would bring Poland and Germany closer
together as beneficiaries of the defeat of Czechoslovakia. The cooperation
begun between the two countries in 1934 had borne fruit as far as the Nazi
regime was concerned and ought to be intensified. On 24 October, acting
on Hitler's instructions, Ribbentrop had received ambassador Lipski in
Berchtesgaden in the presence of Walter Hewel, his liaison with the Reich
Chancellery, in order to propose a 'general settlement' of German–Polish
relations.[11] He made the following proposals: Danzig should be returned to
the Reich, in compensation for which Poland would receive a series of concessions in the Danzig region; an extra-territorial railway line and autobahn
should be built through the Corridor; the two countries should guarantee
each other's borders; the German–Polish treaty of 1934 should be extended;
and Poland should join the Anti-Comintern pact. Initially, Lipski responded
only to the question of Danzig: an Anschluss with the Reich was ruled out

for domestic political reasons alone.[12] This was confirmed by the Polish government in their official response, which Lipski passed on to Ribbentrop on 9 November. Instead, the Warsaw government proposed that the League of Nations statute should be replaced by a Polish–German agreement, underpinning the status of Danzig as a free city.[13]

Poland's negative response convinced Hitler of the urgent need to secure a closer alliance with Italy and Japan. Responding to initial Japanese feelers put out in June, Ribbentrop had used the Munich conference to liaise with Ciano in pursuing a German–Italian–Japanese pact, behind the backs of Chamberlain and Daladier. This was intended to represent a firming up and expansion of the Anti-Comintern Pact, of which Italy had been a member since 1937.[14] During Ribbentrop's visit to Rome in October, Mussolini had given his approval in principle to this idea,[15] and, at the beginning of January, Ciano indicated that Mussolini was prepared to sign it. While in Rome, Ribbentrop had explained to Ciano that the alliance reflected Hitler's view that 'in four to five years' time armed conflict with the western democracies must be considered to be within the realms of possibility'.[16] Ciano concluded that Ribbentrop was heading for a war in three or four years' time under the cover of his proposed defensive alliance. Originally, the agreement was to be signed in January 1939, but this was prevented by the Japanese, who initially blamed communication problems,[17] and then sent a committee of experts to Europe to discuss further details.[18]

At the end of November, Hitler had issued detailed directives for 'Wehrmacht discussions with Italy'. The idea was to prepare the basis for a joint war against France and Britain 'with the aim of initially crushing France' – Hitler's first outline of the later 'western campaign'. However, when the discussions first got started some months later, Hitler issued new instructions, involving a much more general exchange of information rather than the working out of a common war plan. He wanted to conceal from the Italians that he had no intention of launching a war in three or four years' time, but rather aimed to do so at the next available opportunity, dragging Italy into this war through another surprise move.

A further increase in rearmament

Immediately after the Munich agreement, Hitler ordered a further exceptional increase in rearmament, a sign of his deep frustration that he had been

forced to accept 'the salvation of peace'. General Georg Thomas, chief of the
Wehrmacht rearmament programme, informed his armaments inspectors
some time later that, on the same day as Munich, he had received a directive
to concentrate all preparations on a war against Britain, 'Deadline 1942'.[19]

On 14 October, Göring announced to a meeting of the General Council
of the Four-Year Plan, which coordinated the work of the various ministries
involved, that Hitler had directed him 'to carry out a gigantic programme that
will dwarf what has been achieved so far'. He had been assigned 'by the
Führer the task of hugely increasing rearmament, with the main focus on
the Luftwaffe. The Luftwaffe had to be quintupled as fast as possible. The
navy too had to rearm faster, and the army had rapidly to acquire large
quantities of offensive weapons, in particular heavy artillery and heavy tanks'.
But priority should also be given to 'chemical rearmament', in particular
fuels, rubber, gunpowder, and explosives. In addition, there was the need for
'accelerated road construction, canal improvements and, in particular, railway
construction'. Moreover, the Four-Year Plan had to be revised in two ways:
'1. All building work to do with rearmament should be prioritized, and, 2.
Facilities had to be created that really saved foreign exchange'. Göring stated
that he was confronted with unexpected difficulties, but, 'in order to achieve
this goal, if necessary he would turn the economy round using the most
brutal methods.... He would make barbaric use of the general powers the
Führer had assigned him.'[20]

In the second part of his speech on 14 October, Göring talked about the
'Jewish problem'. He considered the expropriation of Jewish property as
undoubtedly one of the ways of resolving the economic difficulties: 'The
Jewish question had now to be tackled with every means available, for they
had to be excluded from the economy'. However, he totally rejected a 'free-
for-all commissar economy', as had occurred in Austria, where Party members had simply arrogated to themselves the right to take over Jewish
property. For 'Aryanization' was nothing to do with the Party, but 'solely a
matter for the state. However, he was not in a position to make foreign
exchange available for deporting Jews. If necessary, ghettos would have to be
established in the larger cities.'

Hitler's decision to increase rearmament, as reported by Göring, prompted
the propaganda ministry and OKW to launch a major campaign 'to make
the Wehrmacht popular'. Using a combination of media, 'the people's confidence in their own strength and in Germany's military power was to be
enhanced'.[21]

Hitler combined his directive for a further exceptional increase in rearmament with concrete political goals. During October, he made frequent brief visits to the recently occupied Sudeten territories, in order to receive applause, visit Wehrmacht units, and inspect the Czech fortifications.[22] On 21 October, he directed the Wehrmacht to set itself three tasks for the immediate future:

'1. To secure the borders of the German Reich and provide protection against surprise air attacks.

2. To liquidate the remainder of Czechoslovakia.

3. To take over Memel.'

As far as 'liquidating the remainder of Czechoslovakia' was concerned, preparations 'were to be made already in peacetime and geared to a surprise attack so that Czechia has no opportunity for a planned response'.[23]

Pogrom: 'The Night of Broken Glass'

Immediately after the signing of the Munich agreement, a strong anti-Semitic mood developed once more among Party activists. It followed on from the anti-Jewish excesses of summer 1938, for which Goebbels's Berlin campaign had been mainly responsible, but which had been suppressed by the regime during September for diplomatic reasons.

Now, in October 1938, Party activists evidently intended to find a scapegoat for the mood of depression that had spread throughout the Reich during September as a result of the threat of war. Once again, 'the Jews' would have to bear the brunt of the Party members' frustration. After the conclusion of the Munich agreement diplomatic concerns no longer applied, and so anti-Jewish excesses could begin again: Jewish shops and synagogues were daubed with graffiti and destroyed.[24] According to the SD, during October, a real pogrom atmosphere developed among Party activists.[25] However, this was by no means a spontaneous unleashing of emotion on the part of radical anti-Semites; it chimed in exactly with the policy the SD itself had been pursuing since the summer of 1938.

In response to the massive expulsion of Jews from Germany and, in particular from Austria after the Anschluss, in July 1938, an international refugee conference had been convened in Evian on the initiative of President Roosevelt. However, it had only revealed the unwillingness of participant countries to admit large contingents of Jewish refugees. The sole concrete result had been the creation of an Intergovernmental Committee on Political Refugees, which was supposed to work out future arrangements in consultation with Germany. This enabled Germany to turn the expulsion of Jews from the Reich into a 'problem' requiring an international solution.[26] Thus, there was an incentive to speed up expulsions in order to put pressure on the Committee to act.

In the meantime, Adolf Eichmann, the SD's desk officer for Jewish affairs appointed to deal with Jewish matters in Austria, had developed a scheme for accelerating Jewish expulsion. With the aid of Bürckel, in August he established a 'Central Agency for Jewish Emigration', through which the chaotic Jewish persecution in Austria was turned into an 'orderly' process for the comprehensive economic plundering and expulsion of the Jews.[27] For this procedure to be adopted throughout Germany, however, a new anti-Semitic 'wave' was required, a spectacular radicalization of Jewish persecution that would necessitate a Reich-wide reorganization of persecution and expulsion.

This was already happening at the end of October. On 26 October, Himmler ordered the expulsion of Polish Jews living in Germany. During the coming days, 18,000 people were arrested and driven over the Polish–German border, the first mass deportation of the Nazi era. On 7 November, 17-year-old Herschel Grynszpan shot the German diplomat, Ernst vom Rath, in Paris in revenge for the expulsion of his parents from Germany, thereby offering the regime a welcome pretext for unleashing a pogrom.[28]

On 7 November, the same day as the assassination attempt, the German propaganda media began a campaign, in which Grynszpan was declared to be the tool of an international Jewish conspiracy. The assassination of Gustloff by Frankfurter in 1936 was naturally portrayed as a prior example.[29] During the night of 7/8 November and on the following day, Party activists in the Kassel area (a traditional centre of German anti-Semitism) carried out large-scale attacks on Jewish businesses and synagogues. This campaign was probably launched by the Gau propaganda chief.[30] However, for these attacks to be turned into a Reich-wide pogrom against German Jews a central directive was required, and that, as was always the case when the regime's so-called Jewish policy was to be radicalized, could come only from Hitler.

Goebbels, one of the most important hard line anti-Semites, made a significant contribution towards preparing the way for this and he had personal reasons for doing so. A serious crisis in his marriage, caused by his affair with the actress Lída Baarová had damaged his relationship with Hitler,

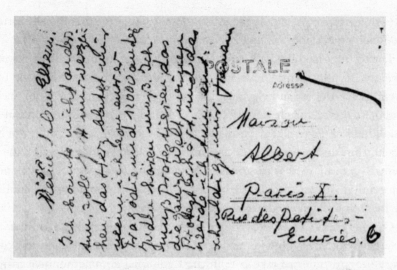

Figure 8. On 6 November Herschel Grynszpan wrote a final postcard to his
parents: 'Dear parents, I had to do it, may God forgive me. My heart bleeds when
I hear of the tragedy you and 12,000 other Jews have suffered. I simply have to
protest and make the whole world take notice of my protest, and that's what
I intend to do. Forgive me. Hermann'
Source: akg-images

and he also wanted the differences of opinion he had had with Hitler over
the Sudeten crisis to be forgotten. For Goebbels had not only been among
those who wanted to avoid a war at all costs, but had made no secret of his
unwillingness to use his propaganda machine to overcome the population's
lack of enthusiasm for war. Now, as Party activists in the provinces once
again began large-scale attacks on Jews, Goebbels saw the chance radically
to change the image of an all too 'peace-loving' German population through
a Reich-wide pogrom. And here Goebbels's desire to rehabilitate himself
coincided with the intentions of the Jewish persecutors in the SD and SS,
as well as with Hitler's own. During these weeks, the 'Führer' was trying to
find an issue that would enable him to bring about a fundamental change
in the Third Reich's public persona, a shift towards maximum solidarity,
ideological radicalism, and readiness for war. An open eruption of a hitherto
inconceivable degree of anti-Jewish violence would provide him with the
platform for this fundamental reorientation. He calculated that this would
cause a panic-stricken flight of Jews from Germany, with the international
community coming under pressure to take them in. Moreover, the most
radical expulsion possible of Jews from Germany would, as with Austria,

offer the prospect of rapidly acquiring Jewish property, thereby alleviating the Reich's precarious foreign exchange and financial position.

Thus, Hitler launched a pogrom against the Jews from a variety of very different motives and interests. His decision to step up the radicalization of Jewish persecution can be seen – following 30 June 1934, the Nuremberg laws of 1935, the switch to the Four-Year Plan in 1936, and the solution of the Blomberg–Fritsch crisis in 1938 – as one more stage in the history of his dictatorship, one of those situations in which he allowed a complex crisis to come to a head, so that he could then intervene in a spectacular way and apparently reorder it, focusing attention on an issue he could use to dominate the political agenda during the following weeks.

On the evening of 8 November, participants in the failed 1923 putsch, together with Party bigwigs, gathered in the Bürgerbräukeller, as they did every year, in order to take part in the traditional commemorative march the following day. Meanwhile, the anti-Jewish press campaign was continuing.[31] In addition, during the course of the day more reports were coming in of anti-Jewish riots in Kassel and Dessau.[32] In the late afternoon of the following day, while staying in his flat in Prinzregentenplatz, Hitler received the news that vom Rath had died of his injuries.[33] That evening, the usual celebrations took place in Munich's old town hall and, on the sidelines, Hitler conferred with Goebbels, who later noted the following in his diary: 'I explain the matter to the Führer, He decides: "Let the demonstrations continue. Withdraw the police. For once the Jews'll feel the people's anger." That's as it should be. I immediately give appropriate instructions to the police and the Party. Then I speak briefly along those lines to the Party leadership. Storms of applause. Everyone dashes straight off to telephone. Now the people will act.'[34]

Hitler had left the town hall before Goebbels's speech, but it is clear from Goebbels's note that it was Hitler who gave the go ahead for the pogrom. However, it was up to Goebbels to inform the Party leadership of the decision in his harangue and, during the next few hours, to take the lead as a hardliner, so that many people considered him responsible for the pogrom. This distribution of roles was fully intended by Hitler, who remained very much in the background during the events that followed.

During the night, high ranking Party functionaries, Gauleiters, SA Gruppenführer, and the like, urged on by Goebbels, unleashed the pogrom in hundreds of towns and cities. Party members and SA men in civilian clothes, who, throughout the Reich, had been meeting to commemorate

9 November, now went about destroying synagogues, setting them on fire, smashing the windows of Jewish businesses, and plundering shops; they gained forced entry to Jewish flats, destroying the furnishings, stealing items of value, mistreating and dragging off their inhabitants.[35] Shortly before midnight, the Gestapo received instructions to prepare for the arrest of 20,000 to 30,000 Jews, an order that came directly from Hitler.[36] These mass arrests of more than 30,000 people took place on 10 November; the vast majority of victims, over 25,000, were placed in concentration camps, where most of them remained incarcerated for weeks or months while being subjected to cruel mistreatment.[37] It is not known how many died from this violence; the official number of dead was given as 91.[38] However, there were a considerable number of suicides, as well as hundreds of Jews who, during the following weeks and months, were murdered in concentration camps or were to die from the effects of their imprisonment.[39]

While the pogrom was raging in Munich, as in many other cities, Hitler remained in his flat in the Prinzregentenplatz.[40] Around midnight, he joined Himmler in attending the annual swearing-in of recruits for the armed SS and the SS Death's Head units at the Feldherrnhalle, while the city's synagogues were burning. The fact that Hitler did not refer to these events in his address to the recruits is another example of his attempt to distance himself from the violence.[41] At midday on 10 November, Hitler met Goebbels in his favourite Munich restaurant, the Osteria Bavaria in Schellingstrasse. He approved a draft prepared by the propaganda minister for an official announcement that 'all further demonstrations and acts of retribution against the Jews' were to cease immediately.[42] Clearly, the whole campaign was threatening to get out of control. Hitler informed Goebbels about the next important anti-Semitic measures: 'They must put their businesses in order themselves. The insurance companies won't pay them anything. Then the Führer wants gradually to expropriate Jewish businesses and give their proprietors bits of paper that we can devalue at any time.'

Hitler then received 400 representatives of the press in the Führer building on Königsplatz, in order to provide them with a certain amount of essential background information about his policies and to initiate a decisive change in the focus of propaganda.[43] Hitler explained to the journalists that he had hitherto been forced 'for years almost solely to speak of peace'. This had been the only way he had been able to achieve his foreign policy successes. This 'peace propaganda that had been going on for decades' had, however, given the people the false impression that he wanted 'peace at all costs'. To remove this mistaken impression, months ago he had begun 'gradually to make clear [to the people] that there are things...which have to be achieved by force'. The propaganda media would have to do more to reflect this point of view.[44]

Thus, while in this speech Hitler was making clear his discontent with the German population's lack of readiness for war that had become apparent a few weeks earlier, he was using the unprecedented mobilization of force during the previous thirty-six hours as a platform for the transition to overt war propaganda. This change of course was not, however, intended to happen abruptly, but in stages. Hitler's next big speeches, beginning with his Reichstag speech of 30 January 1939, were to set the new tone. To start with, anti-Semitism was to be a main propaganda theme; the subsequent justification of the pogrom was intended to mark the shift in the process of getting the population ready for war, a war that was to be directed not merely at the western powers but also against a 'Jewish world conspiracy'. For, as with the hurried preparations for war at the end of September, in general the German population had not approved of the pogrom. In particular, the violence and destruction of 9 November had prompted widespread disgust and censure, although these sentiments were not as a rule openly expressed. Ultimately, the events had been accepted. However, it was precisely this passive attitude, often rooted in indifference, which was to be overcome by a more aggressive tone in propaganda, now concentrated on mobilization.[45]

During the following days, Hitler gave his express support to the Propaganda Ministry's anti-Semitic press campaign,[46] which focused above all on the middle class, whose response to the regime's violent Jewish policy had been distinctly unenthusiastic.[47] It continued into January 1939, although it began to face difficulties and lose momentum.[48] A campaign of Party meetings to 'enlighten the whole population about Jewry' was even intended to go on until March, an indication that the alleged 'popular anger' against the Jews needed considerable propaganda to stoke it.[49]

On 12 November, while the propaganda campaign to justify the pogrom was getting under way, over 100 representatives of the Party, the state, and economic organizations gathered in the Reich Air Ministry to consider, under Göring's chairmanship, how the further persecution of the Jews was to proceed. It was no accident that it was Göring who now took on the leading role in clearing up the mess left by the 'Night of Broken Glass' [Reichskristallnacht], and producing 'orderly policies'. Right from the start, the expropriation of Jewish property had been one of the basic objectives of the Four-Year Plan, for which, in 1936, Hitler had made Göring responsible. The meeting agreed on a legal 'solution', which was precisely in line with Hitler's requirements. As an 'atonement fine' for the death of vom Rath, Jews were to be forced to pay a billion RM (as Hitler had demanded in his Four-Year Plan memorandum of 1936). Also, as Hitler had told Goebbels in the Ostaria Bavaria on 10 November, they were to be excluded from German economic life, their insurance claims for the damage caused were to be confiscated by the state, and they were to be compelled to repair all damage immediately.[50] During the coming weeks, a large number of other anti-Semitic regulations were issued.[51] Moreover, Göring announced at the meeting that Hitler wanted 'finally to take a diplomatic initiative, first of all vis-à-vis the powers who were raising the Jewish question', in order then to move on towards a resolution of the 'Madagascar question'. He had explained all that to him on 9 November. Hitler wanted to tell the other states: 'Why are you always talking about the Jews? Take them!'[52]

Nearly, four weeks later, on 6 December, Göring had another substantial meeting with the Gauleiters, Reich Governors, and provincial presidents, in which he explained to them the most recent guidelines for Jewish policy, which the 'Führer' had given him a few days earlier, and whose implementation Hitler wished him to oversee, without his role becoming public. Göring's reputation should not be compromised too much at home and abroad. Hitler's concern about the former's prestige indicates why he himself did not want to be associated with the implementation of the anti-Jewish measures that were to follow. However, it was in fact Hitler who determined the future development of Jewish policy right down to the details. The main emphasis, as Göring explained once again on 6 December, was above all on 'vigorously pushing emigration'.[53]

As the regime had intended, the pogrom provoked a wave of Jewish emigration from Germany. Hitler was working on the assumption that this panic-stricken flight would put pressure on potential immigration countries that during the Evian conference were still refusing to admit more Jews. When, on 24 November, the South African defence and transport minister, Oswald Pirow, visited Hitler at the Berghof, in order, among other things, to offer his services as a mediator for an international solution to the German 'Jewish question', the 'Führer' told him that the 'Jewish problem' 'would soon be solved'; this was his 'unshakeable will'. It was not only a 'German', but also a 'European problem'. Hitler went so far as to issue an open threat: 'What do you think would happen in Germany, Herr Pirow, if I were to stop protecting the Jews? The world couldn't imagine it.'[54]

At the beginning of December, concrete steps were taken to turn the wave of Jewish emigration into a systematic policy of expulsion. These measures derived from Hitler's directives, as is clear from Göring's statements of 12 November and 6 December. At the start of December, building on an idea of the Austrian Economics Minister, Hans Fischböck, Schacht put forward a plan to finance Jewish emigration through an international loan, which would be guaranteed by the property left behind in Germany by Jewish emigrants and paid off by granting relief for German exports.[55] Hitler accepted this proposal,[56] and, in January, Schacht began negotiations with the chairman of the Intergovernmental Committee for German Refugees, George Rublee.[57] However, this truly fanciful plan was not put into effect, as negotiations were pursued only half-heartedly by all those involved.[58] During 1939, however, a number of countries, including Britain and the United States, indicated that they would be willing to take larger contingents of Jewish refugees.[59]

At the end of 1938/39, in order to increase the pressure to emigrate, the regime concentrated on trying to restrict Jewish life as far as possible. At the meeting on 6 December, Göring had, among other things, announced a number of concrete decisions by Hitler relating to Jewish policy. According to Göring, Hitler had set priorities for 'Aryanization': Jews were to be expropriated, in particular where they represented an obstacle to the 'country's defence'. Hitler also decided that Jews should not be visibly labelled, an issue that had been discussed in the meeting of 12 November, because he feared anti-Jewish excesses.[60] There should be no prohibitions on selling to Jews; however, Jews could be banned from entering certain localities. Göring then made clear his determination to continue to hold a certain percentage of Jews hostage: 'I shall not permit certain Jews, whom I could easily allow to emigrate, to do so, because I need them as a guarantee that the other riff raff* abroad will also pay for the Jews without means.'[61]

On 28 December, after a meeting with Hitler, Göring announced to senior Party and state officials another binding Führer decision concerning further anti-Jewish measures.[62] In accordance with this list, during the coming months a further wave of discriminatory provisions was issued. Thus, in response to Hitler's wishes, Jews were forbidden to use sleeping and dining

---

* Translators' note: Göring used the Yiddish term 'Muschpoke'.

cars,[63] rental protection for Jews was substantially suspended,[64] and Jews were largely prohibited from staying in seaside resorts and spas.[65] During the first months of 1939, there were a considerable number of additional measures.[66] The main focus was on the complete 'Aryanization' and expropriation of Jewish property. When it became clear that they could not all be rapidly expelled, there was a move towards the imposition of forced labour and restrictions on their freedom of movement and housing, with a clear trend towards ghettoization. All in all, German Jews were being subjected to a coercive regime, while in the event of war their incarceration in camps was being considered the appropriate 'intermediate solution' to the 'Jewish question'.[67]

Economic bottlenecks

In November 1938, Hitler and the regime's leadership began to deal with the impact of the 'Führer's' order, issued after the Munich conference, for an enormous expansion of the rearmament programme.[68]

At first, it appeared as if, for the first time, Hitler wanted to try to place his rearmament plans on a more realistic basis. On 11 November, at any rate, Keitel informed the Wehrmacht branches that, after hearing from their respective commanders-in-chief, Hitler intended 'to organize rearmament organically in accordance with uniform principles and priorities, using a timespan of several years, and to bring it into line with the available resources in men, raw materials, and finance'.[69] On 18 November, at the first meeting of the Reich Defence Council, created in September 1938 by statute, Göring as chairman gave a lengthy statement supposedly inaugurating this new course.[70] This was a committee intended to coordinate the war plans of the various ministries. Göring, working on the basis of a tripling of the rearmament programme, put forward a maximum programme for the civilian sector covering a range of areas.: expansion of the transport system; an increase in agricultural production; more exports to improve the foreign exchange situation; an increase in industrial production, above all through rationalization; an austerity programme to sort out the financial situation, which looked 'very critical'; cutbacks in the administration; a rigorous wage freeze; and the comprehensive control of all labour resources. This was designed to make such an enormous increase in armaments production feasible.

A few days and weeks after the meeting, the first measures were introduced:[71] a revision of price controls, aiming to reduce excessive profits from

armaments contracts;[72] the appointment of Colonel Adolf von Schell as
General Plenipotentiary for Motor Transport, whose task it was to introduce standardization throughout the motor industry;[73] and, finally, the
appointment of Fritz Todt as General Plenipotentiary for the whole of the
construction industry.[74]

In the meantime, however, the armaments' plans of the individual armed
forces had long since begun to go their own way. Since October, the
Luftwaffe had been planning a new construction programme that aimed to
build over 30,000 aircraft by spring 1942, in order to achieve a total of
21,750 combat-ready aircraft (excluding reserve, training, and test aircraft).[75]
The deadline was then slightly extended, but the plan was retained: around
30,000 aircraft were to be built by 1 April 1942, which, given the industrial
capacity and raw materials available, was completely unrealistic.[76]

The navy had similar gigantomaniacal plans. Responding to Hitler's
demand, already issued in May 1938, for increased armaments, a naval
planning committee convened in August produced a plan at the end of
October envisaging a fleet of 10 battleships, 15 pocket battleships, 5 heavy,
24 light and 35 small cruisers, 8 aircraft carriers, and 249 submarines. This
represented a considerable increase compared with the old construction
plan of December 1937, which, for example, had included only 6 battleships and 4 aircraft carriers.[77] Hitler approved the plan on 1 November,
but demanded that the construction of the battleships should be accelerated
to be ready by 1943. The navy chief, Admiral Raeder, produced a new schedule on this basis, the so-called Z programme, and put it to Hitler at the end
of January 1939. Hitler then ordered the construction of six battleships by
1944, giving the navy priority over the other armaments' programmes as
well as exports. Raeder, however, declared that he would not need this
fleet before 1946.[78] According to a calculation by the economics department of the Naval High Command (OKM), the fuel requirement for the
Z fleet when completed would be larger than the total German annual
consumption of oil products.[79] These plans greatly exceeded the limits
laid down in the Anglo-German Naval Agreement. Hitler's abrogation of
the agreement in April 1939, which we return to below, was in response
to advice from the naval High Command.[80] Raeder assumed that, with the
completion of this plan, from 1942 onwards the navy would be in a position
to fight a large-scale submarine war and, from the end of 1944, with its large
ships would 'even be a serious opponent for a major naval power such as
Great Britain'.[81]

The new armaments' programmes resulted in a massive expansion of the Wehrmacht's budget. In November, a memorandum by the OKW's liaison officer with the Economics Ministry and the Reich Bank estimated that, since 1934, 38.9 billion RM had been spent on rearmament, in other words already around 4 billion RM more than had been planned in 1934 for the next four years. The budget for 1939 had a deficit of over 8 billion RM.[82] There was such an urgent demand for exports in order to acquire foreign exchange that, on 9 November, the Wehrmacht economics staff were compelled to inform the Wehrmacht branches that industry had been instructed to give priority to export contracts, including those for machine tools and armaments, over all domestic orders. This also applied to the Wehrmacht itself.[83] During the final months of 1938, in view of a deficit amounting to billions, the Finance Minister found himself confronted with the alternative of either declaring bankruptcy or printing money.[84]

Thus, at the beginning of December, Hitler was obliged to inform the commanders-in-chief of the three Wehrmacht branches that 'the Reich's tense financial situation' made it necessary to reduce the Wehrmacht's expenditure until the end of the financial year (31 March 1939). All Wehrmacht branches should give priority to the acquisition of weapons systems over munitions.[85] In February, Brauchitsch was forced to inform Hitler in two 'reports' that, as a result of the cuts and the ban on issuing new contracts in the steel sector, he would be unable to meet the army's armaments' targets.[86] However, the naval Z Plan was to be exempted from these cuts in accordance with Hitler's January order.

In January 1939, after Schacht had given various warnings of the danger of inflation during autumn 1938,[87] the Reich Bank directorate sent a memorandum to Hitler. It stated that the 'foreign exchange and financial situation' had 'reached a danger point, requiring urgent measures to avert the threat of inflation'. 'The unlimited expansion of government expenditure is ruling out any attempt at achieving a balanced budget, and, despite a huge increase in taxes, is bringing the nation's finances to the brink of collapse, thereby undermining both the Reich Bank and the currency.' It was vital, in order to avert the threat of inflation, that new expenditure should be financed solely through taxes or loans (but then only if these did not disturb the long-term capital market). The whole of the financial sector must be put under the strict control of the Reich Finance Minister, the Reich Bank, and the Reich Prices Commissioner.[88] Two weeks later, Hitler dismissed Schacht.[89] With his departure all restrictions on the increase in the money supply disappeared.[90]

Visits from foreign statesmen

While the anti-Semitic propaganda campaign continued uninterrupted, in January Hitler received the foreign ministers of Poland, Hungary, and Czechoslovakia on the Obersalzberg, in order to prepare his further expansion plans. The uninhibited manner in which he discussed the 'Jewish question' during these meetings demonstrates the close connection that in Hitler's view existed between expansion and the further radicalization of Jewish persecution.[91] Before the meetings began, Hassell, the former German ambassador in Rome, had learnt from state secretary Weizsäcker during a visit to Berlin in the middle of December that German foreign policy was moving towards war; it was only a question of whether they should move straight away against Britain and secure Polish neutrality, or whether they should 'act first in the East to deal with the German–Polish and Ukrainian questions'. That was precisely the issue that Hitler wanted to clarify with the Poles in January.

During the meeting with the Polish foreign minister, Beck, on 5 January, the main focus was above all the future of Carpatho-Ukraine, where a government had established itself with German support and was pursuing a pronounced 'greater Ukrainian' policy, in other words the aim of creating the core of a future Ukrainian state to include the Ukrainians in the Soviet Union as well as those in Poland.[92] This alarming prospect was sufficient reason for Beck to advocate the territory being joined to Hungary.

In his reply Hitler began by emphasizing that 'nothing whatsoever had changed' in Germany's relations with Poland since the 1934 Non-Aggression Pact. As far as the Carpatho-Ukraine issue was concerned, he could assure him that, with reference to 'the intentions ascribed to Germany in the world press', Poland had nothing at all to fear. With his mention of 'ascribed intentions' Hitler was referring to speculations in the British and French press that Germany was planning to use Carpatho-Ukraine as a springboard for further conquests in the east.[93] In fact, Hitler stated, the Reich had 'no interests beyond the Carpathians'. He then raised the question of Danzig and the Corridor. He told his Polish guest that he was thinking in terms of a formula whereby 'Danzig would belong politically to the German community, but would remain economically with Poland'. Danzig was after all 'German, would always remain German, and would sooner or later join Germany'. If Poland agreed to Danzig returning to the Reich and if 'entirely new solutions' could be applied to settle the problem of the link with East Prussia – Hitler was referring to the project for extraterritorial transport links through the Corridor – then he was prepared to guarantee Poland's borders through a treaty. Beck took note of Hitler's wishes with regard to Danzig, but added that this question 'seemed to him extremely difficult'.

Hitler then raised another issue 'in which Poland and Germany had common interests', the 'Jewish problem'. According to the minutes, he said that he was 'determined to get the Jews out of Germany . . . if the western powers had shown more sympathy for Germany's colonial demands, he might have . . . provided a territory in Africa that could have been used for settling not only the German, but also the Polish Jews'.[94]

The following day Ribbentrop once again set out Germany's list of proposals: 'Return of Danzig to Germany', 'guaranteeing all Poland's economic interests in the Danzig region as well as an extraterritorial link through the Corridor; in return: recognition of the Corridor by Germany and permanent mutual recognition of their borders'. However, Ribbentrop mentioned another point on which he made himself much clearer than Hitler had done. He could imagine that, if these problems could be satisfactorily resolved, Germany would be willing 'to regard the Ukrainian question as a matter for Poland and to give it its full support in dealing with this question. However, this would involve Poland adopting a very clear anti-Russian position, since otherwise their interests would hardly coincide'. In this context Ribbentrop returned once more to the question of Poland's adherence to the Anti-Comintern Pact. Beck, however, had no intention of committing himself to a common policy towards the Soviet Union.[95]

Beck continued to stick to this position when Ribbentrop travelled to Warsaw at the end of January, in order to renew the German 'offer' of a settlement of the Danzig/Corridor issue together with a common approach to the Soviet Union and Poland's annexation of the Soviet Ukraine.[96] However, the Polish foreign minister was not prepared to make any concessions involving the subordination of his country to a risky alliance policy dictated by Germany.

Thus, the project for a joint war against the Soviet Union, which Germany had been proposing to Poland for years, had finally collapsed. Hitler, however, had already made clear to Beck that his regime did not need Poland's cooperation in order to use Carpatho-Ukraine to form the nucleus of a Ukrainian state. As we have seen, Germany had frequently revealed this ambition during the preceding weeks and months, and it had preoccupied not only the international press, but also neighbouring states. Both King Carol II of Romania and the Hungarian Regent, Horthy, had already spoken

to the German government about its plans for Ukraine.[97] At the end of
January 1939, Goebbels learnt from Hitler that he wanted to spend time on
the Obersalzberg 'reflecting on his next diplomatic moves. It might be
Czechia again, for this problem has only been half solved. But he's not quite
certain. It might also be the Ukraine.'[98]

If Hitler was still contemplating taking over the Ukraine in whatever
form, it indicates that at this juncture he was already considering the prerequisite for this step, namely the crushing of Poland. It is possible that he
thought that, by attacking Poland, he could prompt the Ukrainian minority
to start an uprising and, with solid German backing, extend it into the
Soviet Ukraine. In any case, at this point he certainly did not have a concrete plan. His comment to Goebbels, however, shows that, apart from
destroying Czechoslovakia, he was contemplating other options of how to
reorder the political landscape of eastern Europe, now in flux, and believed
that the issue of Carpatho-Ukraine could be exploited vis-à-vis Czechoslovakia, Poland, Hungary, and Romania, as well as the Soviet Union. This is
a good example of the extent to which Hitler's foreign policy, particularly
during this critical phase, was marked by multiple approaches and an unwillingness to commit himself, in short by an intentional unpredictability.

On 16 January, he rebuked the Hungarian foreign minister, Count István
Csáky, for his government's behaviour during the Sudeten crisis and for its
attempt in November, despite the Vienna Award, to take over Carpatho-
Ukraine. However, Hitler was magnanimously prepared to give Hungary a
second chance to prove itself a loyal ally by participating in the final destruction of Czechoslovakia, a move which would involve departing from 'ethnographic principles'. Now that the German, Hungarian, and Polish claims on
Czechoslovakia, based on bringing home the respective minorities, had
been met, another justification had to be found, a 'political-territorial one',
for forcibly occupying and directly subjecting it to his rule.[99] In the second
half of December, Hitler had rejected a treaty that had been prepared in the
Foreign Ministry following the Munich Conference with the aim of subordinating Czechoslovakia to the Reich.[100] He was not interested in a dependent
relationship based on a treaty.

On 21 January, Hitler once again received the Czechoslovak foreign minister, Chvalkovský, whom he also berated. The Czech state had not carried
out a thorough purge of Beneš supporters; it had not come to terms with
the fact that Czechoslovakia's fate was now indissolubly linked to Germany's.
He bluntly announced that 'if there was a change of course its first result

would be the destruction of Czechoslovakia'.[101] Two days later, Ribbentrop also gave Chvalkovský a long list of German complaints.[102] This was clearly intended as a 'last warning', which, when the time came, would have to serve as justification for a German attack on Czechoslovakia.

Hitler also referred to the 'Jewish question' in his discussions with Csáky and Chvalkovský, who did not remain silent. Csáky asked whether this question could not be 'solved internationally'; Romania had contacted him about reaching a common solution. Hitler responded by outlining Germany's plan 'to solve this problem through a financial scheme'. He was, however, clear about the fact that every last Jew had to disappear from Germany.[103] Chvalkovský was told: 'Our Jews will be annihilated. The Jews did not perpetrate 9 November 1918 for nothing; this day will be avenged.' Hitler's subsequent comment that 'the Jews were poisoning the people' in Czechoslovakia as well prompted his guest to launch into a lengthy anti-Semitic diatribe.[104]

The threat of 'annihilation' evidently did not mean the physical destruction of the Jews, but rather the end of their collective existence in Germany through expulsion. At the end of January, the responsible Reich authorities prepared for the planned negotiations between Schacht and Rublee concerning the organized emigration of the Jews soon to lead to concrete results. After a series of meetings of government representatives on 18 and 19 January,[105] Göring ordered the creation of a 'Reich Central Office for Jewish Emigration', (along the lines of Eichmann's emigration office in Vienna) under Heydrich, and simultaneously forced all Jewish organizations to be subsumed in a new compulsory single organization. This was the origin of the 'Reich Association of the Jews in Germany'.[106]

A day after the creation of the Reich Central Office, the Foreign Ministry, which had appointed a liaison officer to the new organization, informed all German missions and consular offices abroad: 'The final goal of German Jewish policy is the emigration of all Jews domiciled in Reich territory.'[107]

Hitler as 'Prophet': War against domestic and foreign enemies

In his speech to the Reichstag to mark the sixth anniversary of the seizure of power Hitler once again took a hard line on the 'Jewish question'. At the same time, he sketched out a war scenario similar to that in his secret speech of 10 November 1938, in which he had announced a change from talk of peace to the preparation of the population for war. The speech on 30 January 1939 marks the culmination of the anti-Semitic propaganda following the November pogrom and, at the same time, the point at which Hitler began to prepare the population for a war that might arise from the confrontation with 'Jewry' at an international level.

He began by dealing in detail with the negotiations concerning the organized expulsion of the Jews, joking about the 'democracies'' lack of enthusiasm in accepting Jews; Germany, at any rate, was absolutely determined 'to get rid of these people'. After heaping scorn on the Jews, he came to the core of what he had to say. The following statements were influenced to a considerable extent by feelings of inferiority rooted deep in the past and a resultant unsatisfied desire for revenge. He had, he said, in the course of his life, 'very often been a prophet and was generally laughed at for it', in particular by 'the Jewish people', who 'simply laughed at my prophecies that I would one day assume the leadership of the state and thereby of the entire people and then, among many other things, achieve a solution of the Jewish problem. Their laughter was uproarious, but I think that for some time now the Jews in Germany have been laughing on the other side of their faces. Today, I want to be a prophet once again: if international Jewish financiers inside and outside Europe should succeed once more in plunging the nations into a world war then the result will be not the Bolshevization of the world and therefore the victory of Jewry, but the annihilation of the Jewish race in Europe.'

Was Hitler announcing publicly and to the whole world his intention to murder the Jews in a coming war? At this juncture, the word 'annihilate' cannot be unequivocally interpreted in this sense. A few days earlier, Hitler had also spoken to the Czech foreign minister about 'annihilating' the Jews, but had meant their expulsion, quite apart from the fact that he had also warned Chvalkovský of the 'annihilation' of Czechoslovakia. When interpreting this passage, as with many other Hitler statements, one should be aware that Hitler was not simply announcing a decision taken in isolation, but rather that his 'prophecy' had several potential layers of meaning. Above all, in the first place, one must take into account the tactical motive of his speech, which should be seen in the context of the international negotiations concerning Jewish emigration.

His annihilation threat was intended, first of all, to increase the pressure on German Jews to emigrate and on foreign countries to receive them. Secondly, the announcement that the Jews in the German sphere of influence in Europe would be annihilated in the event of a world war was part of a long-term strategy for assigning blame for the outbreak of an impending war. When Hitler claimed that 'international Jewish financiers' within and outside Europe might attempt to bring about a world war (and not simply a war), the main target audience of his prophecy was the United States. He was contemplating a scenario in which the western powers, supported by the United States, could intervene in order to prevent him from continuing his expansionist policy in Europe, to which he was totally committed. In this case, blame for the war would rest unequivocally with the enemy, who had been incited by 'international Jewish financiers'. And, thirdly, if a war begun by Germany turned into a world war as a result of intervention by the western powers, Jews within Germany's sphere of influence would automatically become hostages over whom would hang the threat of annihilation. Thus, if his threats had no effect, if, in other words, emigration did not make much progress, and if, in the event of a war, the western powers were not deterred from intervening, then they would be responsible for the further intensification of Jewish persecution predicted in his 'prophecy'. Thus, Hitler was keeping all options open for further radicalizing his Jewish policy.

Hitler made clear his determination to continue his expansionist policy over the medium and longer term in another section of his speech. Having not referred to it for a long time, he once again emphasized, and in a very prominent place in the speech, 'how important the expansion of our people's living space' was in order permanently to secure their food supplies.[108] However, since 'for the time being [sic!]...on account of the continuing blindness of the former victor powers' this expansion 'is not yet [sic!] possible', they were compelled 'to export in order to buy food', and they had to export even more in order to acquire the raw materials for those exports. However, it was clear from these words that, as far as he was concerned, this could not provide a lasting solution. At some point, his argument suggests, German living space would 'expand', and indeed elements within the Party were already making no bones about demanding it.[109] This demand for living space, while simultaneously stressing Germany's commitment to peace, soon became part of the standard repertoire of German propaganda, although Hitler kept a 'statesmanlike' distance from it.[110]

Apart from that, his speech contained a number of other important statements. Thus, in the section of the speech concerned with the Sudeten crisis, he admitted quite frankly that he had already committed himself to military action against Czechoslovakia on 28 May 1938 with the deadline of 2 October 1938, more clear evidence of his determination to go to war. In referring to 'a serious blow to the prestige of the Reich' and an 'intolerable provocation', he clearly revealed that the motive for this decision was his fear of personal humiliation as a result of the May crisis. But above all, he wanted to point out that the incorporation of the Sudetenland came about not as a result of diplomatic efforts, but rather the great powers had come to an agreement only as a result of his 'determination to solve this problem one way or the other' (in other words to risk a war).

The speech also contained a lengthy passage, also intransigent in tone, on the relationship with the Churches. Hitler threatened a complete separation of Church and state, with the inevitable serious financial consequences for both confessions, and he made it clear that clergy who were critical of the regime or abused children would be brought to book like any other citizen.[111]

Two weeks later, Hitler dealt with the internal and external enemies of his regime in another major speech. On 14 February, he spoke at the launch of the new battleship, 'Bismarck' at the Blohm and Voss shipyard in Hamburg. The prospect that in the 'Bismarck' the German navy would have the most powerful battleship in the world gave additional weight to his words. Hitler used the opportunity for a comprehensive assessment of the 'Iron Chancellor', of whose 'little German' [i.e. without Austria] policy he was in fact basically critical. Now, however, he celebrated him as 'the pioneer of the new Reich'. He had created the preconditions for the creation of the present 'Greater Germany', as well as domestically laying the foundations 'for the unity of the National Socialist state'. Essentially, this assessment implied that the 'Iron Chancellor's' great historical achievement was to be the predecessor of Hitler, who was now completing his work. Bismarck had been the 'creator of a German Reich . . . whose resurrection from deep distress and whose miraculous enlargement have been a gift of providence'. Dealing with domestic policy, in particular, in his speech Hitler portrayed himself as an Über-chancellor. Bismarck had been largely unsuccessful in his struggle against the 'international powers', 'the politically engaged Centre Party priests' and 'Marxism'. By contrast, Nazism now possessed the 'intellectual, ideological, and organizational wherewithal . . . required to destroy the enemies of the Reich, both now and in the future'.[112]

The occupation of Prague

At the end of January, when discussing with Goebbels whether he should move against Czechoslovakia or focus on the Ukraine, Hitler had appeared undecided. However, shortly afterwards the next foreign policy move was decided; it involved solving the 'Slovakian question'. This was an issue that he himself did much to push forward at the beginning of 1939 and was to lead to the demise of Czechoslovakia.[113] Since the beginning of the year, there had been growing collaboration with the government in Pressburg [Bratislava][114] and, on 12 February, this culminated in a meeting between Hitler and Voytech Tuka, the influential leader of the fascist wing of the Slovakian People's Party, the most powerful political force in Slovakia, which had been autonomous since the previous autumn. Tuka was accompanied by the leader of the German ethnic group in Slovakia, Franz Karmasin. Hitler used the meeting to declare his sympathy for Slovakian demands for more independence and his mistrust of the Czechoslovak government, against which he would if necessary 'act swiftly and ruthlessly'.[115] On the following day, state secretary Weizsäcker, recorded that Hitler intended to deliver 'the deathblow to what remains of Czechoslovakia' in 'about four weeks'.[116]

Thus Hitler was taking active steps to implement the policy of incorporating Czechoslovakia, mooted in November 1937, and finally decided on in May 1938. The unwelcome Munich Agreement had merely postponed the project; but, with the aid of the Slovaks, he had succeeded in using the winter to further destabilize Czechoslovakia (particularly since in Hitler's view military operations in Central Europe during the winter were inadvisable). Encouraged by Hitler's support, the Slovak government now demanded an extension of their independence from the Prague central government, thereby provoking a political crisis. On 9 March, the Prague government dismissed the Tiso cabinet in Pressburg, in order to prevent Slovakia from finally leaving Czechoslovakia, a move that was being strongly supported by Germany. On 10 March Goebbels noted: 'Now we can completely resolve the issue that we only half resolved in October'.[117] Around midday, he, Ribbentrop and Keitel were summoned to the Reich Chancellery and it was decided to march into Prague on 15 March. The German press were now instructed openly to support Slovakia's claims to independence, and to launch a new campaign against the government in Prague. During the following days, the Propaganda Ministry exercised tight control over the reporting of the new crisis.[118]

In the late afternoon of 10 March, Hitler and Goebbels drafted an announcement to the effect that, before its dismissal, the Tiso government had appealed to the Reich for help. However, in the course of the night it became clear that Tiso was not yet willing to sign it.[119] During the night of 11/12 March, a German delegation of around twenty people, including the Anschluss specialists, Seyss-Inquart, Bürckel, and Keppler, arrived in Pressburg, and presented what was virtually an ultimatum to the Slovak ministers present, demanding that they declare Slovakian independence. They, however, rejected it, whereupon Tiso was summoned to Berlin.[120] Heroes' Memorial Day was being celebrated in the capital on 12 March and the atmosphere already hinted at Hitler's impending move against Czechoslovakia. During the official celebrations, Admiral Raeder declared, in Hitler's presence that Germany was the 'patron of all Germans both within and beyond our frontiers'.[121] On the same day, Hitler ordered the armed forces to prepare for the occupation of Czechoslovakia on 15 March.[122] Simultaneously, he decided to allow Hungary to occupy Carpatho-Ukraine, which he had refused them as recently as November.[123] The government of this hitherto autonomous region had declared its independence on 13 March, placing itself under the protection of the Reich.[124] However, from Hitler's point of view, during its short period of existence since October, it had already fulfilled its function of contributing to the disintegration of Czechoslovakia; now it was more important to have the gratitude of Germany's ally, Hungary, whose troops began occupying its tiny neighbour on 14 March. It was left to state secretary Weizsäcker to inform the government of Carpatho-Ukraine on 15 March that the Reich government 'was regrettably not in a position to establish a protectorate'.[125]

Tiso arrived in Berlin on 13 March, where Hitler offered him 'assistance' in establishing an independent state. Tiso had a matter of 'hours' to make up his mind; if he did not accept, Hitler indicated that he would no longer oppose Hungary's ambition to occupy Slovakia. However, Tiso refused to commit himself.[126] Ribbentrop then worked on Tiso during a session lasting nearly six hours, finally presenting him with an ultimatum to declare his country's independence the following day and, for his return journey to Pressburg, gave him the text of a telegram, appealing for help from the German government.[127] Impressed by Tiso's report on his Berlin meetings, on 14 March, the parliament in Pressburg declared the independence of Slovakia and elected Tiso prime minister; however, the telegram requesting help was only released on 15 March[128] under German pressure.[129] On 17 March, the new state formally recognized its dependence on the German Reich in a 'treaty of protection'.[130]

The Czech president, Emil Hácha, and his foreign minister, Chvalkovský, arrived in Berlin on the evening of 14 March. Hitler forced them to wait for hours and then, during the night, and in the presence of, among others, Keitel, Göring, and Ribbentrop, subjected them to massive pressure, finally compelling them to capitulate.[131] They had to sign a declaration, committing themselves to placing 'the fate of the Czech people and country trustingly in the hands of the Führer of the German people', who in turn promised 'that he would place the Czech people under the protection of the German Reich and guarantee the autonomous development of its ethnic life in accordance with its particular character'.[132] The German invasion of Czech territory began in the early morning. Hitler followed his troops, arriving that evening at Prague Castle in a convoy of vehicles.[133] The following day he signed a decree establishing a 'Protectorate of Bohemia and Moravia',[134] placing the territories occupied by his troops under the Reich's 'protection'. The 'autonomy' granted to the Protectorate was to be supervised by a 'Reich Protector' residing in Prague, who was also responsible for confirming the members of the Protectorate's government. Hitler appointed the former Foreign Minister, Neurath, as Reich Protector.

Hitler left Prague on the afternoon of 16 March, in order to return to Berlin via Brünn, Vienna, and Linz.[135] On 19 March, the Party organized 'spontaneous demonstrations', as they were described in the Berlin press conference, throughout the Reich.[136] In the capital Goebbels prepared another triumphal entry for Hitler. According to the *Völkischer Beobachter*, 'never in the history of the world was a head of state paid such homage'. The boulevard, Unter den Linden, was transformed into a 'canopy of light' by means of anti-aircraft searchlights, above which there was a firework display.[137]

In fact, the new coup does not appear to have produced overwhelming enthusiasm among the German population. While, on the one hand, there was certainly admiration for the renewed proof of Hitler's abilities as a statesman, there was, on the other, also surprise, criticism, and the fear of war.[138] Even Hitler's Luftwaffe adjutant, Below, wondered: 'Was it necessary?' In doing so, he hit the nail on the head,[139] for, unlike their 'Führer', the majority of Germans did not consider the occupation of Prague, Bohemia, and Moravia as the fulfilment of longstanding plans for the future of a Greater Germany.

Hitler's decision to tear up the Munich Agreement and occupy the 'remainder of Czechoslovakia' prompted the British and French governments to undertake a fundamental revision of their attitude to Hitler's dictatorship. For, with the incorporation of non-German territories, it had become apparent that Hitler's justification for his previous policies, namely that, acting on the principle of national self-determination, he was only bringing all Germans together in a single Reich, was simply a pretext for a brutal policy of expansion, while unscrupulously ignoring the rights of other nations. London and Paris now realized that the line followed hitherto of trying to appease Hitler by making more and more concessions had been a miscalculation. Dealing with Hitler clearly required another language.[140] He, however, did not take seriously the warning voices and the formal protests from Paris and London; both countries recalled their ambassadors for consultations.[141] Instead, he declared himself convinced that the British prime minister was simply pretending to 'take action'.[142]

The fact that Hitler only informed Mussolini subsequently about the occupation of Prague was also not conducive to strengthening the relationship of trust between the 'Axis power', Italy, and its ally north of the Alps, and very probably contributed to Mussolini's decision not to coordinate with Hitler the next steps in his policy of expansion.

The annexation of Memel

Completely unimpressed by these protests, after his return from Prague Hitler immediately embarked on his next diplomatic 'coup', the incorporation of Memel into the Reich.[143] This territory, whose approximately 140,000 inhabitants were largely of German extraction, had been separated from Germany by the Versailles Treaty and had initially been under French administration; in 1923 it was occupied by Lithuania and, from 1924 onwards, had been administered by Lithuania as an autonomous territory on the basis of an international convention. In his directive of 21 October 1938 Hitler had already demanded the 'capture of Memelland', when the 'political situation' allowed it.[144]

On 1 November, under German pressure, the Lithuanian government had lifted martial law, which had been operating since 1926. A Memel German electoral list, dominated by Nazis, was then drawn up and, in an election on 11 December, was able to establish itself as the dominant political force, effectively coordinating the country with Nazi Germany and demanding its return to the Reich.[145] In December, Hitler, accompanied by Ribbentrop, received Ernst Neumann, a leading representative of the Memel Germans and told him that Memel would be incorporated into Germany in March or April the following year; until then, he must maintain discipline among the Memel Germans.[146]

On 20 March 1939, Ribbentrop gave the Lithuanian foreign minister, Joseph Urbsys, who was visiting Berlin, an ultimatum to give up the territory. Under pressure, Urbsys secured the agreement of the Lithuanian cabinet in Kovno and, on 22 March, signed the transfer agreement in Berlin.[147] The following morning, German troops moved into the territory without meeting resistance. Hitler, who had boarded the cruiser 'Deutschland' in Swinemünde the previous evening, sailed up the Lithuanian coast with an impressive fleet. Around noon he then switched to a torpedo boat, landing in Memel harbour, which had previously been secured by a unit of marines. In Memel he greeted the Memel Germans with a brief speech as new members of the 'Greater German Reich' and then signed the transfer treaty aboard the 'Deutschland'.[148]

On the evening of 24 March, now back in Berlin, and during a joint visit to the Wintergarten variety show, Hitler gave Goebbels an insight into his thinking on foreign policy: 'The Führer is contemplating a solution to the Danzig question. He will try again with Poland, using a certain amount of pressure, and is hoping it will respond. But we shall have to bite the bullet and guarantee Poland's borders.'[149]

28

Into War

Following the occupation of Prague and Memel, Hitler now focused once more on Poland.[1] On 21 March, its ambassador, Lipski, told Foreign Minister Ribbentrop that the Polish government was disconcerted about the German 'treaty of protection' with Slovakia, and that 'the announcement that the relationship was based on protection was clearly directed against Poland'. Ribbentrop played this down, proposing Beck should make an early visit to Berlin, in order to discuss with him ideas for a common policy. However, for Germany the return of Danzig was non-negotiable. It would recognize the Corridor, provided Poland agreed to an extra-territorial transport link between the Reich and East Prussia.[2] Germany would also agree 'to concur entirely with the Polish view of the Ukrainian question'. Two days later, Ribbentrop returned to the issue, instructing his ambassador in Warsaw to inform Beck that Germany was prepared not only to recognize the Corridor, but to guarantee the whole of the western border for a period of twenty-five years. Within the context of a common 'eastern policy', it would be prepared 'to allow Poland to take the lead in dealing with the problem of the Ukraine as a whole'. Thus Ribbentrop was trying once more to play the 'Ukrainian card' with Poland, despite the fact that, during his visit to Warsaw in January, Beck had made it clear to him that Poland had no intention of engaging in common action against the Soviet Union. In view of Poland's irritation about Slovakia, this was hardly the appropriate moment to renew an offer that had already been rejected. Hitler, for whom Ribbentrop's offers had already gone too far, then intervened, and Ribbentrop, to his embarrassment, was forced to withdraw his instructions to Hans-Adolf von Moltke, the ambassador in Warsaw, who then had to cancel his appointment with Foreign Minister Beck.[3]

In fact, Beck did not come to Berlin, and the German proposals were unambiguously rejected by the Polish government; on 26 March, Lipski

informed Ribbentrop, and on 28 March Beck informed the German ambassador in Warsaw. Instead, the Polish government demonstratively moved troop
reinforcements to the Corridor. It then turned to Britain with a request for
support, to which Chamberlain responded positively in a declaration to the
House of Commons on 31 March. At the end of the month, the Polish
Foreign Minister told the German ambassador in unambiguous terms that
if Germany used force to resolve the Danzig question it would mean war. A
quickly arranged visit to London by Beck led to the announcement at the
beginning of April of a mutual assistance pact,[4] which France joined shortly
afterwards.[5]

Meanwhile, even before Poland's rejection of the German government's
proposals had become known in Berlin, Hitler had informed the commanders-in-chief that, while he did not intend to resolve the 'Polish question' for the time being, the military should 'work on it'. 'Dealing with it in
the near future would need particularly favourable political preconditions.
Poland would then have to be crushed so that, for the next few decades, it
no longer needs to be considered as a political factor.'[6] War against Poland
had now become a clearly defined political option for Hitler.

The document also noted that 'the Führer doesn't want to get involved'
in the Ukraine. They might at some point establish a Ukrainian state, but it
was still an open question. Thus, Hitler had still not completely abandoned
his speculative plans for the Ukraine; the Ukraine option was to reappear on
a number of occasions during the following months.

Hitler's decision to attack Poland

Hitler's next move was to use the opportunity offered by the launch of the
battleship, 'Tirpitz', the sister ship of the 'Bismarck', on 1 April in Wilhelmshaven,
to deliver a tirade in the Rathausplatz attacking above all British 'encirclement policy'. This attack was preceded and followed up by a vigorous anti-
British press campaign.[7] The slogan 'encirclement', which was increasingly
used by German propaganda, was an overt reference to the situation at the
beginning of the war in 1914, which, according to the dominant view in
Germany, had been caused by an anti-German coalition led by Britain.
In his speech Hitler referred to several alleged parallels with the situation
in the summer of 1914, culminating in the threat to abrogate the Anglo-
German Naval Agreement.

In his Wilhelmshaven speech Hitler justified his actions vis-à-vis Czechoslovakia with the argument 'that for a thousand years this territory has been part of the German people's living space'; he had merely 'united what, on the basis of history and geography and, in accordance with all rational principles, ought to be united'. This obviously meant that the annexation of a large number of other European states could be justified by similar 'historical' and 'spatial-political' arguments.[8] Hitler then spent a few days on board the 'Strength through Joy' ship, the 'Robert Ley', which was in the North Sea on its maiden cruise.[9] Prior to embarkation, however, he authorized Keitel to issue in his name the 'directive for the Wehrmacht to prepare for war', which Keitel duly did on 3 April.

This directive provides documentary evidence that, under the impression of the Polish government's rejection of Germany's proposals at the end of March, and, in view of growing British–Polish cooperation, Hitler had radicalized his attitude towards Poland. Within a few days, the *possibility* of armed conflict, which he had sketched out at the end of March, had become a *war plan*.

In the directive of 3 April Hitler ordered the Wehrmacht to prepare for three scenarios, namely 'to secure the borders of the German Reich and protection against surprise air attacks', 'Case White', in other words war against Poland, and the 'seizure of Danzig'. In relation to Poland, Hitler stated that basically Germany's attitude was determined by the desire 'to avoid upsets'. However, were Poland to adopt an 'aggressive attitude' then a 'final reckoning [could] become necessary'. According to Hitler, in the event of a war with their eastern neighbour, Germany's leaders saw it as their task to 'limit the war to Poland'. This eventuality might occur in the not too distant future as the result of a 'growing crisis in France' and, 'in consequence, a growing reserve on the part of Britain'. This statement clearly shows that Hitler was not making his decision on whether or not to go to war dependent on 'Poland's threatening attitude', but, first and foremost, on the next available opportunity that would allow him to crush Poland, while simultaneously avoiding having to fight a war in the West. Equally, he pointed out that Russian intervention would be of no use to Poland 'because it would involve its destruction by Bolshevism'. The directive had already been printed when he also instructed Keitel that preparations would have to be made for 'Case White' such that 'it would be possible to implement it at any time after 1 September 1939'.[10]

Thus, Hitler's decision to fight a war with Poland at the first favourable opportunity after 1 September was made after Poland's rejection of his 'generous' offer at the end of March and its move towards dependence on Britain, in other words between 26 March and 1 April, the day on which he embarked on his short pleasure trip on the North Sea. During this week, it became clear to him that the destruction of Czechoslovakia, in other words his breach of the Munich Agreement, had led the western powers to adopt a hostile attitude towards his policy of aggression. It had also caused the loss of, and change of sides by, his hitherto most important partner, Poland, which was not prepared to submit to his revisionist demands. Hitler's response to this setback is comparable to his reaction to the Weekend Crisis nearly a year earlier. He determined to destroy the Polish state just as, in May 1938, he had determined to crush Czechoslovakia. As far as he was concerned, by rejecting his revisionist demands both countries had caused him a serious loss of face, for which they would have to pay with their elimination.[11] As in the previous year, he believed he could ignore the risk of intervention by the western powers. If this proved unavoidable the Reich was far better prepared militarily than it had been a year earlier. His decision was irrevocable, which is clear, among other things, from the fact that diplomatic relations with Poland were now frozen. It was told that there was nothing more to negotiate; Ribbentrop's offer had been 'unique'.[12]

In contrast to the generals' attitude to a premature war the previous year, the Wehrmacht now rapidly got to grips with its new task without raising any objections. War with Poland was studied by the general staff for the first time during a war game at the beginning of May; the assumption was that it would lead to a confrontation with the Soviet armed forces, which once again raised the question of a conquest of the Ukraine. Moreover, numerous agents from military intelligence, the Gestapo, and the SD were involved in stirring up the German minority in Poland, to get them to provoke incidents, thereby causing the Polish authorities to intervene, along the lines of the Sudeten crisis.[13]

Sabre-rattling and fear of war

The elaborate festivities to mark Hitler's birthday on 20 April were designed to demonstrate his power and authority. However, it was striking that the only official representatives from foreign countries who came to Berlin to congratulate the 'Führer' were delegations from Italy, Japan, Spain, Scandinavia, and the Balkans. Since the ambassadors from Britain, France, and the United

States were also absent – they had been recalled after the invasion of Czecho-slovakia – it was only too clear that Hitler's birthday celebrations were taking place in the midst of a growing international crisis.[14]

The festivities began on the afternoon of 19 April with a series of receptions and tributes, after which Hitler inaugurated the East–West Axis in Berlin. Designed by Speer, it was the first prestige avenue in Hitler's scheme to redevelop Berlin. Two million people lined the brightly lit, seven kilometre road, choreographed according to a plan that had been carefully refined over several years,[15] and witnessed a Wehrmacht tattoo and a 'torchlight procession of the [Party's] old guard from all over the Reich'. Around midnight, Hitler's closest colleagues offered him their congratulations in the Reich Chancellery.

The following day, which, at short notice, had been declared a public holiday,[16] the main festivities began with a march past of the SS Leibstandarte in front of the Reich Chancellery, followed by more people offering their congratulations. At 11 a.m., a parade of the Wehrmacht, lasting almost five hours, began along the East–West Axis, the biggest demonstration of mili-tary power in the regime's history. It was aimed at the European powers, but was also a signal to the German people, who were showing a lack of enthu-siasm for war. After further congratulations, the festivities concluded with a ceremonial oath-taking by newly appointed political functionaries of the Party. The celebrations were given unprecedented media coverage.[17] Hitler was glorified as an almost superhuman figure. Göring wrote in the *Völkischer Beobachter* that he was the 'greatest German of all time' and Rosenberg celebrated him in the same newspaper as the 'founder of the greatest con-tinental European empire'.[18] The journalist Willy Beer wrote in the *Deutsche Allgemeine Zeitung* that 'a mysterious aura emanates from the Führer and stirs something akin to it in our innermost being'.[19]

During all these celebrations, Hitler himself remained remarkably silent. Presumably he avoided making any statement on his birthday because he would then have been forced to comment on the critical international situ-ation, and that would hardly have been compatible with the elevated atmos-phere of the occasion. There is no record of his own feelings on this day on which he entered his sixth decade; it was not in his character to comment on such personal matters. One can assume, however, that on this day he was particularly conscious of his none too optimistic assessment of how long he had to live. Time was threatening to run out and this fear may well have reinforced his decision to attack Poland by the end of the year and his will-ingness to fight the western powers, at the latest in a few years' time.

The celebration of Hitler's birthday on 20 April was in marked contrast to the depressed mood of the population in spring 1939. SD reports blamed a general 'overstraining of the available...supply of labour, means of production, and raw materials'. In particular, there were complaints from the artisanal sector about discrimination in the awarding of public contracts, a growing flight from the land, causing a further reduction in agricultural production, as well as in the profitability of farms; this was leading to 'a degree of indifference and sullenness' on the part of the rural population. Moreover, there was growing concern about new tax laws and about the difficult foreign exchange and foreign trade situation; there was discontent over rail transport problems and the serious housing shortage, which persisted, as popular criticism pointed out, while prestige Party and state buildings were constantly being constructed.[20]

The reports gathered by the SPD in exile fully confirmed this criticism. But they also made it clear that although this widespread discontent was caused above all by the accelerated rearmament programme, it was also accompanied by a real fear of war.[21] This was an aspect of 'popular opinion' that was avoided in the official reports, as the previous November Hitler had, after all, made it clear that he wanted a propaganda campaign to strengthen the nation's 'willingness to fight'. In January the Social Democrats noted that, after a year of unexpected foreign policy successes, the population's attitude to the dictatorship had become more critical...than the year before'. The decline in morale had also affected the middle classes, for whom the 'nationalist' successes had been overshadowed not only by dissatisfaction with their material situation, but also by their negative response to Jewish persecution.[22] These reports on Hitler's real personal popularity, compiled by the SPD in exile at the time of his birthday celebrations, present a mixed picture.[23] Above all, however, they noted: 'In spite of all the flags and festive noise, the fear of war weighed heavily' on the population.[24]

On 15 April, the American President, Roosevelt, sent a message to Hitler asking him for reassurances that, during the following ten or twenty-five years, he did not intend to infringe the territorial integrity of thirty named states. This was in a response to Hitler's Wilhelmshaven speech, in which he had justified the annexation of Bohemia and Moravia with arguments based on history and living space. In sending his list Roosevelt was pointing out that, by using such arguments, Hitler represented a threat to most European states. Hitler responded to this démarche in a speech to a special session of the Reichstag on 28 April.[25]

He used this speech, for which Goebbels prepared the way with vicious anti-British attacks in the *Völkischer Beobachter*,[26] for a general reckoning with his foreign opponents. He expressed his disappointment at his failure to achieve an alliance with Britain and abrogated the 1935 Anglo-German Naval Agreement, as British 'encirclement policy' had undermined its basis. Moreover, he tore up the non-aggression pact with Poland, spelling out in detail the offer he had made to Poland a few months before.[27] Finally, he went on to deal with the American President and his message, laboriously and sarcastically rejecting this 'peculiar document' point by point.[28]

At the beginning of May, following the abrogation of the non-aggression pact, anti-Polish rhetoric in the German media was intensified. Among other things, the press was instructed continually to report border incidents caused by Poland.[29] 'Warsaw', Hitler told Goebbels on 1 May, 'will end up in the same place where Prague ended up'.[30] However, journalists were informed that the 'big Poland campaign' had not yet started.[31]

At the same time, the rearmament propaganda within Germany was stepped up once again in order 'to strengthen the self-confidence of the German people' and confirm their 'trust in our military power'.[32] Against the background of a growing international crisis, this propaganda, which was more and more obviously geared to preparation for war, together with Hitler's threatening speeches and gestures, meant that, during the final months before the outbreak of the Second World War, fear of war was no longer openly expressed in a public sphere controlled by Nazism. While the rejection of war in 1938 had been in tune with Hitler's rhetoric of peace, now such anti-war statements were no longer tolerated. Although it proved impossible to generate enthusiasm for war, since spring 1939 the majority of the population appear to have accepted its coming as inevitable.

Between 14 and 19 May, Hitler undertook a tour of the West Wall, a clear demonstration against the western powers. The journey took him from Aachen through the Eifel to the Saar, and then into the Upper Rhine up to the Swiss border. In Saarbrücken he was joined by the Party's Gauleiters and Reichsleiters. He concluded the six-day tour of inspection with an 'Order of the Day' addressed to the 'soldiers and workers of the western front'.[33]

At the end of May, after the government had received indications that the British were going to stick by their commitments to Poland, the propaganda machine began to shift the main focus of attack from Poland to Britain.[34]

Alliances

Meanwhile, the international situation had become even more critical, as the western powers were not prepared to allow Germany and Italy to consolidate their position in the Balkans any further. On 23 March, an economic agreement was signed between Germany and Romania through which Germany secured control of Romanian oil supplies,[35] and, on 7 April, Italy attacked Albania. This came as a complete surprise to Hitler, but he too had not hitherto considered it necessary to coordinate his attacks on foreign countries with his ally.

In response to these developments, on 13 April Chamberlain unilaterally guaranteed Greek and Romanian independence, offering the same protection to a number of other countries, including Turkey. France followed suit on the same day.[36] A British–Turkish mutual assistance pact was signed on 12 May.[37]

The decision to attack Poland and Britain's and France's countermeasures prompted Hitler and Ribbentrop to secure Italy's support. To do this they had first to overcome the annoyance felt in Rome about Germany's attack on Prague. For the Munich Agreement, torn up by Hitler, had after all been largely Mussolini's initiative.[38] Thus, to conciliate Italy following the invasion of Prague, Hitler decided to make a gesture over South Tyrol. Since the beginning of the 1920s, he had opposed a revision of the Brenner frontier; however, now he went further, ordering SS chief Himmler and the governor of Tyrol, Franz Hofer, to prepare for the removal of 30,000 ethnic Germans from the South Tyrol. This represented the first step in a comprehensive solution to the South Tyrol problem, which was to be agreed with Italy in October 1939. The South Tyroleans would have to decide between Germany and Italy, in other words either to move to the Reich, or, if they wanted to remain in their homeland, to adopt the Italian language and culture without reservation.[39]

Hitler believed that this arrangement would contribute towards cementing the political alliance with Italy. However, in the spring of 1939, the project of a tripartite pact between Germany, Italy, and Japan, which had been pursued since the summer of 1938, was in crisis. In March, the Japanese were backpedalling, insisting that the alliance should be directed only against the Soviet Union.[40] In April, they modified this proviso by accepting that a pledge of general mutual assistance could be defined in the form of a treaty, but, at the same time, they wanted to inform the governments of France, Britain, and the United States that the alliance was not directed against the western democracies.[41]

The German government responded by starting to explore the alternative of a dual pact,[42] carefully concealing its war plans vis-à-vis Poland from the Italians. It hoped that an alliance with Italy would help to minimize the risk of a war with the western powers arising from the attack on Poland, as Britain and France would be compelled to divert forces in order to protect their positions in the Mediterranean. Right from the start, therefore, Hitler and Göring tried to reassure the Italians that there was no immediate threat of a war with the western powers.[43]

Meeting at the beginning of May in Milan, the two foreign ministers, Ciano and Ribbentrop, finally agreed an alliance between Germany and Italy. Ribbentrop had been forced to promise the Italians that there would be no war during the next three years.[44] Ciano signed the so-called Pact of Steel in Berlin on 22 May.[45] The pact involved the two parties promising to offer each other assistance in the event of their becoming involved in a war with another power. While the treaty offered the prospect of a future wartime coalition, it was initially intended by Germany as a clear warning to the western powers not to intervene in the event of a war with Poland. Ribbentrop reassured Ciano once more in Berlin that Germany wanted to have a period of at least three years of peace.[46] A few days after the treaty had been signed, Mussolini sent Hitler a detailed statement, in which he repeated that Italy would not be ready for war before 1942. Thus Hitler could not assume that he would receive the active support of his Italian ally in his planned war against Poland.[47]

The joint meetings of the two general staffs, planned at the end of 1938, took place between April and June 1939, coinciding with the final stage of the negotiations over the Pact of Steel. Hitler set out the ground rules: the talks were to be general in nature, focused on tactical and technical questions. Political issues and the strategic and operational questions involved in joint military operations, which the previous November he had envisaged including in the talks, were not to be discussed. Thus, during the first round in Innsbruck at the beginning of April, Keitel advocated in general terms a joint 'surprise assault', but 'following instructions' he did not name a date for this action, indicating rather that the critical moment would not arrive for some years.

Also, after a lengthy visit by Brauchitsch to Italy and North Africa between 29 April and 10 May, it was agreed: 'There will be no joint operations for the time being.' Less than four months before the start of the Second World War, keeping Germany's war plans a secret was more important to Hitler than close military coordination with his main ally. The way the two allies had treated each other during these past months had not exactly increased trust between them.[48]

Although Germany had done everything possible to keep its Italian ally in the dark about its plans to attack Poland in the autumn, it could not prevent the Italians from obtaining from various sources a fairly accurate picture of Germany's preparations for war. What was particularly alarming from the Italian point of view was the, as far as they were concerned, completely unrealistic assumption of their German ally that the war could be localized and would not lead to intervention by the western powers and, as a result, to a bigger European war. Mussolini and Ciano decided on a counter strategy and, at the end of June, suggested to their German ally that a meeting between Mussolini and Hitler should be held at the Brenner on 4 August, at which they should propose a European peace conference. Hitler and Ribbentrop naturally rejected this idea of a second Munich, however, and so the Brenner meeting did not take place.[49]

During the summer of 1939, in addition to the German–Italian pact, Hitler endeavoured to persuade a number of medium-sized and smaller states to adopt a position of benevolent neutrality towards Germany, or at least tried to prevent them from drifting into the camp of the western powers. In order to demonstrate his desire for peace, Hitler to begin with took a number of steps to confirm his commitment to the territorial integrity of various countries, presumably in response to Roosevelt's intervention of 15 April. After Germany had already confirmed Belgium's neutrality in October 1937,[50] at the end of May 1939 it made a non-aggression pact with Denmark,[51] and on 7 June identical treaties with Estonia and Latvia. Similar offers were made to Norway, Finland, and Sweden,[52] who, however, declared that they did not need a specific confirmation of their neutrality.[53]

In response to the British and French guarantees for Turkey, Greece, and Romania in April, Germany concentrated above all on trying to draw Yugoslavia and Hungary into its sphere. In summer 1939, it tried to persuade Yugoslavia to withdraw from the League of Nations and so draw it onto the side of the Axis. However, the new government under prime minister Dragiša Cvetković, who had replaced the pro-Axis Stojadinović in February, resisted these attempts and sympathized more with the western powers.[54]

At the end of June, Hungary made an official approach to the Axis powers, requesting trilateral talks concerning economic matters during wartime. Four weeks later, however, the Hungarian prime minister sent a letter to the Italian and German governments informing them that while, in the event of a general conflict, his country would align itself with the Axis powers, 'on moral grounds it was not prepared...to engage in a military action against Poland'. This Hungarian position was of a piece with its hesitant behaviour during the previous year, when Germany had tried in vain to get it to adopt an aggressive policy towards Czechoslovakia.[55] During a meeting in the Berghof at the beginning of August, Hitler bitterly reproached the Hungarian foreign minister, Csáki, for his letter, threatening: 'If Germany were defeated in a war that would be the end of Hungary's revisionist dreams', whereupon the Hungarian government withdrew the statement it had made at the end of July.[56]

Hitler's war scenarios

On 23 May, the day after the signing of the Pact of Steel, Hitler made a speech in the Reich Chancellery to his top military leaders, the content of which has been preserved because his Wehrmacht adjutant, Rudolf Schmundt, took notes.[57] Hitler stressed once again that the main goal of German policy was the urgent issue of acquiring appropriate 'living space'. 'In 15 or 20 years the solution will be forced on us. No German statesman can avoid the issue for longer.' The first six years of National Socialist rule had been 'put to good use'; the 'political unification of Germans in the nationalist cause' had been, with minor exceptions, secured. Now, however, further successes 'could not be achieved without spilling blood'. Compared with his key statements of November 1937, contained in the Hossbach memorandum, Hitler's view of Germany's future policy as a great power had undergone a remarkable change. Whereas eighteen months before, he had considered the final solution of Germany's problem of living space as a task for future generations, now this period had been reduced to fifteen to twenty years; however, it still lay beyond Hitler's expectation of how long he himself had to live or his period as an active dictator.

Later in his speech, Hitler turned to the question of Poland. The country was not 'an additional enemy', but would always 'be on the side of our opponents'. 'It's not Danzig that's at stake'; it was about 'expanding our living

space in the East and securing our food supplies as well as solving the problem of the Baltic states'. Colonies could not provide a solution to the problem of food supplies because they were always vulnerable to blockade by
sea. In the event of a war with the western powers, it would be 'a good thing
to have a largish area in the East'. Although the population of territories
annexed by Germany would not be available for military service, it would
provide 'labour'.

In the following passage Hitler developed the plan for a preventive war
against Poland, making it clear that his main enemy was in the West. The
problem of 'Poland' could not be separated from the conflict with the West.
In the event of a war with the western powers there was the danger that
Poland would stab Germany in the back. This meant that Poland could not
be spared and so he had taken 'the decision to attack Poland at the first available opportunity'. A two-front war must be prevented at all costs. Thus the
following 'principle' must be followed: 'A confrontation with Poland, beginning with an attack on Poland, can be successful only if the West stays out
of it'. He had already pointed that out in his directive of 3 April.[58] But now
he went further. For, if that was not possible then it would be better 'to
attack the West and finish off Poland at the same time'. Thus he had developed a strategy to cope with a two-front war, which he basically wanted to
avoid. He had increasingly come to see the war against Poland as essential,
irrespective of how the West responded to it. The similarities with his treatment of the case of Czechoslovakia the previous year are only too obvious.
Hitler now expanded the possible scenario of an impending war by bringing Japan into play: 'If Russia goes on scheming against us, we can move
closer to Japan. An alliance of France–England–Russia against Germany–
Italy–Japan would prompt me to deal England and France some crushing
blows.'

Hitler went on to sketch out some ideas for a successful war against Britain.
He justified this by basically doubting 'whether a peaceful settlement with
England is possible . . . England sees in our development the establishment of
a hegemony that would weaken England. Thus England is our enemy and
the showdown with England will be a matter of life and death.' As Britain
would not be able to defeat Germany quickly, it would, together with
France, support Belgian and Dutch neutrality, but in fact try to use these
countries as a base for an attack on the Ruhr. As far as Hitler was concerned,
this meant that 'if England decides to attack us during the Polish war, we
must quickly invade Holland'. In the final analysis, Britain could be defeated

only by cutting off its supply lines by sea, in other words by using the German navy, supported by Luftwaffe units operating from advance bases in western Europe.

In preparing for war the Wehrmacht leadership should, if possible, aim 'at inflicting a heavy blow or even a knock-out blow right at the start'. 'Rights, wrongs and treaties are unimportant'. However, to be on the safe side, they ought to prepare for 'a long war as well as a surprise attack, destroying England's prospect of allies on the continent'. Hitler's hopes rested on such a surprise attack: 'If we can occupy Holland and Belgium and defeat France we shall have created the basis for a successful war against England.' Finally, in response to a query from Göring, Hitler ordered that the Wehrmacht branches should each determine what armaments they wanted. But the naval shipbuilding programme should remain unaltered and 'the armaments programmes ... be geared to 1943 and 1944'.

In this speech Hitler was evidently talking about three different wars: first, a rapid preventive war against Poland at the next available opportunity, if possible without intervention by the western powers; secondly, a war against the western powers, ideally from around 1943/44 onwards, beginning with a preventive strike against the Netherlands (and Belgium). However, at the start of his speech, Hitler had talked about a period of fifteen or twenty years for finally solving the 'problem of living space'. When he later spoke of the 'eastern area' that was going to be conquered as being useful for a conflict with the western powers, he was evidently thinking of Polish territory, but probably also of the Baltic states. However, in talking about the conquest of further living space in fifteen to twenty years' time he was certainly not referring to these territories. One can only conclude that he wanted to gain this living space at the expense of the Soviet Union, using Japan as an ally. However, he made only vague comments on this future war.

Developments in the armaments sector were one of the vital factors influencing Hitler's war plans during these months. For during 1939 it became clear that the enormous increase in armaments production Hitler had ordered in October 1938 had once again exceeded the available raw materials and foreign exchange.[59]

Brauchitsch approached Hitler directly in February, in order 'dutifully' to report 'that, in view of these circumstances, I am not in a position to rearm the army to the extent and within the time span you require'.[60] Hitler replied on 3 March that 'rearming the army' was 'to be regarded as a political

priority'.[61] On 15 April, Brauchitsch concluded in a report that the shortage
of steel was preventing the army from equipping itself with modern offensive weapons. To underline the devastating consequences Brauchitsch compared the situation with that in 1914, when the imperial army had failed to
secure a rapid and decisive victory because parliament had not approved the
sums urgently needed for armaments.[62] A few weeks later, he added that
the rationing of non-ferrous metals amounted to 'the end of the army's
rearmament'.[63]

On 24 May, Georg Thomas, the head of the army's armaments office, gave
a lecture to Foreign Ministry officials in which he made an unvarnished
comparison between the armaments expenditure of the democratic countries Britain, France, and the United States on the one hand, and the Axis
powers, Germany and Italy, on the other. According to him, the western
powers were not only spending two billion RM more in the current economic year, but – and this was the most alarming point – 'were in a far
better position to increase their spending than Germany and Italy'. At the
moment Britain and France were spending 12 and 17 per cent of national
income respectively on armaments, Germany 23 per cent, the United States
only 2 per cent.[64]

Moreover, there was another warning note. At the end of May, Britain
introduced conscription;[65] within a few years it would be in a position to
build up a considerable military reserve, thereby massively strengthening its
land forces. In response to a request from Hitler for a survey of the projected
state of German rearmament on 1 April and 1 October 1940, the Army
Weapons Office reported, on the basis of detailed figures, that, because of
the shortage of raw materials, in a few months' time the munitions programme
would collapse. Nor was there any sign of improvement.[66]

Thus, Hitler knew that it would be impossible to fight a lengthy war in
1939/40, However, the Army was in a position to survive a short war, if necessary against the western powers, with some prospect of success. Contrary to
his observations in May 1939, when Hitler told his generals that the ideal
time for a war against the western powers would be 1943/44, he seems, during the summer, to have come to the conclusion that such a long wait would
not have any decisive advantages. He was increasingly coming to accept that
the western powers would intervene in the event of an attack on Poland;
indeed, he may have concluded that this would be better than postponing
for several more years a conflict that he in any case believed inevitable.[67]

Summer performances

During the three months before the outbreak of war, Hitler conspicuously avoided Berlin; instead, he spent most of his time on the Obersalzberg and in Munich; as usual, he attended the Bayreuth Festival, and went on a number of trips within 'Greater Germany'. His summer programme during 1939 was totally geared towards conveying the impression to the world and his people of a cultured and relaxed dictator, but also one who was self-confident. His public statements tended to be statesmanlike; he kept emphasizing, not only in words but also through demonstrative gestures, Germany's military strength and readiness to repel all attacks from abroad. He left anti-British propaganda, which from the end of May increasingly superseded anti-Polish rhetoric,[68] largely to his propaganda minister. Behind this facade Hitler was preparing for the war against Poland.

On 2 June Hitler arranged an impressive military parade in Berlin, lasting two hours, in honour of the state visit of the King of Yugoslavia and his wife.[69] Two days later, on 4 June, he visited the 'Greater German Reich Warriors' Day' in Kassel, to reassure 500,000 veterans of the First World War that 'even if British encirclement policy has remained the same as before that war, Germany's defence policy has fundamentally changed!' Hitler confirmed his policy of 'educating the population in soldierly values and making it adopt a soldierly attitude as a matter of principle'. The press was recommended to use the speech as a 'means of further strengthening the nation's military preparedness and military consciousness'.[70]

On 6 June, he took the parade in Berlin of the Condor Legion returning from Spain. In his address he openly stated that he had decided to commit troops to the Spanish Civil War in July 1936, thereby admitting that, three years earlier, he had misled the international community about his Spanish policy. If the 'international warmongers should ever achieve their aim of attacking the German Reich', he insisted, they would meet with 'resistance of a kind of which the propagandists of encirclement appear not to have the faintest notion'.[71]

His began his relaxed summer programme a few days later with a trip to Vienna. On 10 June, he attended a performance of the opera *Friedenstag* at the Vienna State Opera on the occasion of the 75th birthday of its composer, Richard Strauss, and the following day a performance at the Burgtheater. After these two performances he spent the remainder of the two evenings in the company of artists. On 12 June, he visited the grave of his niece, Geli, in the Vienna Central Cemetery, and then flew on to Linz, from where he made a detour to Hafeld, where the Hitler family had lived for some time in the 1890s; he also visited his former primary school in Fischlham before returning to the Obersalzberg.[72]

Hitler's summer programme also, however, included overt demonstrations of Germany's political and military strength. On 23 June, Britain sent the German government a memorandum, making it clear that Hitler's unilateral repudiation of the 1935 Naval Agreement at the end of April was contrary to the terms of the Agreement, which could only be changed or abrogated with the consent of both parties.[73] Hitler responded two days later in a speech at a reception for Italian veterans, which was also published in the press. He declared himself convinced 'that we shall defeat any attempt by the democracies and capitalist plutocrats to prepare the fate they may imagine they have in store for us through the common strength of our two nations and revolutions, through the strength of our common ideals, our courage, and our determination'.[74]

These tough words were accompanied by the continuing anti-British propaganda campaign that the regime had begun at the end of May and continued into July.[75] The 'high point' of this campaign was a series of leading articles that Goebbels published in the *Völkischer Beobachter*, as well as a number of his high-profile speeches, above all a speech in mid-June in Danzig.[76] Apart from that, topics addressed included Germany's 'lack of space', the alleged 'encirclement', as well as the 'blank cheque' that Britain had given to Poland, the arrogance of the old imperialist nations, possessing a surplus of land, compared with the young, rising, 'have not' powers, and in general, the moral responsibility for war that Britain and the western powers were acquiring as a result of their behaviour.[77]

Behind the scenes, Hitler urged Goebbels not to ease up on the anti-British campaign, trying to convince him of the effectiveness of his threats to foreign nations. At the beginning of July, he told him: 'Work up hatred against England. The German people must come to see it as the core of the opposition to us. Then we can more easily wear it down. The Führer is hoping to have ten more years. His aim is to wipe out the Peace of Westphalia.' And, a few days later, Hitler commented: 'We must put pressure on the Poles by making some more quiet preparations. They will lose their nerve at the decisive moment. England will be ground down by incessant propaganda.'[78] In response to pamphlets sent to various Germans by the British politician and journalist Stephen King Hall, Hitler got Goebbels to publish a reply in the *Völkischer Beobachter*, which he edited himself.[79]

Apart from that, Hitler devoted himself to his usual summer pleasures. On 16 July, as in the previous two years, he gave an address in Munich on the occasion of German Art Day, spending a few days in the city. Then, after inspecting the progress of building work on the Party's parade ground in Nuremberg, from 25 July onwards he attended the Bayreuth Festival, as he did every year.[80] There he spent time sorting out the Goebbelses' marriage. For, in the meantime, Magda had been having an affair with Goebbels's state secretary, Karl Hanke, a liaison which Goebbels was not prepared to tolerate. Magda put the case to Hitler, who decided, as he had in the Baarova case, that the couple had to stay together at all costs.[81] After the end of the Festival he returned to the Obersalzberg for the next three weeks.

Based in his summer residence, Hitler set about trying to secure a pretext for war with Poland by creating a crisis over the status of Danzig. He had told his generals in May that the conflict was not going to be about Danzig, but about living space. However, he believed that, in order to provoke a war, rather than threatening the integrity of Poland itself, it would be better to challenge the privileges given to Poles within the 'Free City' under the complicated arrangements made at the end of the First World War. The long-standing differences between the two countries over the authority exercised by Polish customs inspectors in the city were now to provide the pretext for provoking Poland. The Reich government was portrayed as the defender of the 'German city', Danzig, just as, in the previous year, it had used the alleged subjugation of the Sudeten Germans to further its anti-Czech policy. Underlying this was the assumption that the western powers would not want to get involved in a war with Germany arising from a dispute over obscure legal quibbles. Hitler was calculating that, once war had broken out and Poland had been defeated within a few weeks, the western powers would in the end accept a fait accompli.[82]

At the beginning of August, the Danzig authorities escalated the customs dispute, but then very quickly had to backtrack.[83] German propaganda now intensified its attacks on Poland having, during the previous months, tended to treat the conflict with Warsaw more as a byproduct of British 'encirclement policy'.[84] From 7 to 9 August, the Gauleiter of Danzig, Albert Forster, was staying at the Berghof, where Hitler gave him detailed instructions about what to do next. The result of this meeting was a note sent by the Foreign Ministry to the Polish government on 9 August, stating that the

most recent development in the customs dispute was seriously compromising German–Polish relations. This was an indication that the Reich government now intended to intervene massively in the relations between Poland
and the Free City.[85] On the evening of 9 August, Hitler travelled from the
Berghof to nearby Salzburg to attend a festival performance of *Don
Giovanni*.[86] Gauleiter Forster flew back to Danzig, where, on the following
day, he gave a tub-thumping speech in the Langer Markt demanding: 'We
want to return to the Reich'.[87]

On the same day, Hitler invited the League of Nations High Commissioner
for Danzig, Carl Burckhardt, to come to Berchtesgaden the following day,
in order to convey a message to the western powers about the crisis he had
just provoked. He received his visitor in the Eagle's Nest, his luxurious Tea
House, 1,800 metres up on the Kehlstein, near the Berghof. There, against
the imposing backdrop of the Berchtesgaden Alps, he endeavoured to impress
Burckhardt with a mixture of furious threats and apparent willingness to
negotiate in a rational manner.[88] Burckhardt noted down one of Hitler's key
remarks: 'Everything I am doing is directed against Russia; if the West is too
stupid and too blind to understand this, I shall be compelled to come to
terms with the Russians, to defeat the West, and then, after its defeat, to turn
against the Soviet Union with all my forces. I need the Ukraine, so that we
can't be starved out, as in the last war.'[89] Burckhardt passed on the essential
points of the meeting to the French and British foreign ministries, which
evidently did not feel the need to offer an immediate response.

On 12 August, Hitler received Ciano on the Obersalzberg.[90] He began
the meeting by talking at length about the Reich's military situation and
concluded by saying that 'at the present moment, the rapid liquidation' of
Poland could 'only be beneficial for the inevitable conflict with the western
democracies'. Ciano showed considerable surprise at his host's determination
to go to war. There had been no mention of imminent war either during
Ribbentrop's visit to Milan or during Ciano's stay in Berlin on the occasion
of the signing of the Pact of Steel (both meetings had been in May).
Accordingly, Mussolini had geared his plans for a war with the West, which
was naturally 'unavoidable', to occur in two or three years' time; this would
undoubtedly be a more favourable juncture from the Italian point of view.
Ciano spent the rest of the meeting explaining to Hitler in detail how inadequately Italy was prepared for war. Hitler, however, emphasized even more
how committed he was to war. In response to the 'next Polish provocation'
he would use the opportunity 'to attack Poland within 48 hours and in this

way solve the problem'. Ciano, however, concentrated on outlining a proposal of Mussolini's for international consultations in order to resolve the
European conflicts that were threatening peace. As regards the war Hitler
was planning to launch in less than three weeks, the two allies could not
have been further apart.

That also became apparent when the discussions were continued the following day. Hitler stuck to his aim of attacking Poland as soon as possible
(he now gave the end of August as the preferred date) and of following the
'old Germanic path to the East'. Ciano 'thanked the Führer for his exceptionally lucid statement of the situation', adding that Mussolini would 'presumably not have to make a decision, since the Führer had said that he was
convinced that the conflict with Poland could be localized'. This was a
diplomatic way of saying that Italy would not be joining Germany in the
event of war with Poland.[91]

Getting the generals on board for war

On 14 August, Hitler once again gave a speech fully geared to the coming war
to the commanders-in-chief on the Obersalzberg.[92] Referring to Stalin's
speech of 10 March 1939, Hitler told them that Russia was not prepared to 'pull
[the West's] chestnuts out of the fire' and would thus not intervene in a war.
Norway, Sweden, Denmark, Switzerland, the Netherlands, and Belgium would
remain neutral. Italy had 'no interest in a major conflict'; but wanted to revise
its borders. Victory for the democracies would mean the 'destruction' of Italy.[93]
Thus Britain and France would have to bear the whole burden of a war with
Germany. An attack on Germany's western frontier between Basle and
Saarbrücken would be useless. Hitler exuded confidence: 'The brains of
Munich [he meant Chamberlain and Daladier, P.L.] won't take the risk.' Had
England given it assurances, 'Poland would be being much bolder.' However,
Hitler was worried – he was naturally thinking of Munich – that the British
might complicate 'the final settlement by making offers at the last moment'. In
any event, the Germans had to show the world they were ready for war. They
would have 'sorted out Poland within 6–8 weeks', even if Britain intervened.
However, Hitler kept reassuring the generals that this would not happen.

That evening he continued with his summer cultural programme: he
appeared at Salzburg in order to attend the Festival production of Mozart's
Die Entführung aus dem Serail.[94]

Figure 9. In August 1939 propaganda photos such as these were used by the regime to make the German population ready to accept the imminent outbreak of war. Although this 'ethnic German' woman and her children have supposedly fought their way through barbed wire, they are shown looking remarkably neat and tidy and are given friendly assistance by the German border police.
Source: ullsteinbild / TopFoto

On 11 August, in other words the day after his meeting with Burckhardt, Hitler ordered the propaganda campaign against Poland to be at '80% volume', and four days later, to start the 'final sprint'.[95] Following these instructions, the German media launched strident attacks on Poland, while at the same time the German population was being persuaded that war was unavoidable.[96] On 19 August, Hitler gave instructions for propaganda to be cranked up to 'full volume' in two days' time.[97] Now the German media concentrated on blaming the impending outbreak of war on the attitude of Poland and the western powers.[98]

Meanwhile, following consultations with the Foreign Ministry, Gauleiter Forster had opened the negotiations between Danzig and Poland over the customs dispute with such provocative demands that the Poles broke them off, as he had intended.[99]

On 24 August, Forster had the Danzig Senate declare him 'Head of State', a unilateral promotion, intended to provoke the Poles and underline the fact that the Germans considered the position of the League of Nations High Commissioner of no importance.[100] On the same day, Forster got Hitler to approve further provocations. They were contemplating removing the Polish customs officials from the city and the customs border between Danzig and East Prussia. If this proved insufficient to provoke the Poles into taking counter measures, the next step would be to 'deal with the Westerplatte'.[101]

German–Soviet rapprochement

At the end of the summer, Hitler was about to embark on a complete reorientation of his foreign policy. The Berlin–Rome–Warsaw alliance he had envisaged up to spring 1939 had not come about because of Poland's refusal to submit to his demands. The Berlin–Rome–Tokyo alliance the Germans had sought in spring 1939 had proved abortive because of Japanese reluctance, and the alliance with Italy that finally emerged, the Pact of Steel, was extraordinarily unreliable on account of Italy's lack of commitment to war. In the light of the whole direction of Hitler's policy since the mid-1920s, what remained was a positively breathtaking option.

During the spring of 1939, the Foreign Ministry had already taken note of various signals from Moscow indicating an interest in normalizing relations with Germany. Stalin's speech to the XVIII Congress of the Communist Party of the Soviet Union on 10 March 1939, in which, referring to the West, he declared that he would not 'pull the chestnuts out of the fire' for warmongers, could be interpreted as such a signal,[102] and was followed by others.[103] The replacement of the foreign minister, Maxim Litvinov, by Vyacheslav Molotov also appeared to point in the same direction. The opening of talks about a trade agreement provided the opportunity for improved relations.

In response to the German occupation of Prague, in the middle of April the Soviet Union had offered Britain and France a tripartite pact to secure the status quo in eastern Europe, and negotiations had been continuing since May. The more the conflict between Nazi Germany and the western powers intensified, however, the more Russia was inclined to seek a separate arrangement with Germany, stay out of the impending war, and possibly use the conflict to regain former Russian territories it had lost in the First World War.[104]

The Germans' initial response to the first cautious Soviet feelers was mistrustful and reserved.[105] The uncertainty stemmed from the fact that the Soviet Union was already involved in negotiations with France and Britain, which suggested that it might be planning to start talks with Germany simply in order to strengthen its negotiating position with the western powers. There was also a need for caution given the fact that Japan could regard a German agreement with the Soviet Union as a breach of the Anti-Comintern Pact.

A change came about with Hitler's decision at the end of May to sound out the willingness of the Soviet Union to negotiate via a meeting between Weizsäcker and the Soviet Chargé d'Affaires in Berlin.[106] Although this test proved positive and further signals of the Soviet willingness to negotiate were received,[107] at the end of June, Hitler suddenly decided not to pursue the trade talks any further, as the Soviet conditions attached to them were unacceptable. However, a few days later, this position was reversed and the German embassy in Moscow received detailed instructions to begin trade negotiations and, on 22 July, the Foreign Ministry informed it that the 'pause' that had been inserted to allow for discussion of political questions was now over.[108]

Germany now became actively engaged. After the first approach by a member of the economics department of the Foreign Ministry to the Soviet Chargé d'Affaires in Berlin, Georgi Astachov, at the end of July,[109] Ribbentrop told Astachov in the course of a lengthy conversation that the Germans wanted a 'reshaping of German–Russian relations', and, according to his own account of the meeting, he gave a 'slight hint' that Germany wanted to 'reach an understanding with Russia about the fate of Poland'.[110]

After Molotov too had signalled his willingness to negotiate,[111] on 14 August, Ribbentrop instructed his ambassador, Count Friedrich Werner von der Schulenburg, to arrange a meeting with Molotov and inform him that the Reich government considered 'that there was no issue between the Baltic and the Black Sea that could not be arranged to the entire mutual satisfaction of both countries', including, in particular, 'the Baltic, the Baltic states, Poland, and south-eastern issues'. He, Ribbentrop, was willing to come to Moscow for a lengthy visit.[112] Ribbentrop felt under pressure, not least because, two days earlier, a Franco–British military delegation had begun further discussions in Moscow about the project for a trilateral pact with the Soviet Union, which was still a live issue.[113] On 16 August, Schulenburg reported to Berlin that Molotov had specifically asked about the possibility of a non-aggression pact.[114] Ribbentrop told Schulenburg that Germany was prepared to enter such a pact and to guarantee the Baltic states jointly with the Soviet Union. And Ribbentrop then passed on the message that was decisive for Molotov: 'The Führer believes that, in view of the present situation and the possibility of serious events occurring (please explain to Herr Molotov that Germany is not prepared to go on putting up with Polish provocations indefinitely), a fundamental and rapid clarification of German–Russian relations and of the attitude of both countries to current issues would be desirable.'[115]

Molotov replied that they welcomed Germany's 'reorientation' and, to begin with, wanted a trade and credit agreement that could smooth the way for a non-aggression pact.[116] Ribbentrop's reply of 18 August revealed Germany's impatience: 'German–Polish relations were deteriorating every day. We believed that incidents could happen at any time, leading inevitably to the outbreak of hostilities.' Thus, Hitler considered it necessary to clarify German–Soviet relations before the outbreak of a German–Polish war. Once again, Ribbentrop made clear his wish to visit Moscow, sketched out the non-aggression pact that was envisaged, and proposed a special 'protocol' in which, for example, 'the spheres of influence in the Baltic region, the question of the Baltic states etc.' could be clarified.[117] The following day, 19 August, a credit agreement was signed,[118] and Ribbentrop was invited to Moscow.[119] The Soviets also presented a draft agreement with an attached protocol ready for signature.[120]

The following day, Ribbentrop delivered a letter from Hitler addressed to 'Herr Stalin, Moscow'.[121] Hitler 'warmly' welcomed the signing of the trade agreement 'as the first step in the reshaping of German–Soviet relations'. A non-aggression pact would represent for him 'a long-term commitment of German policy. Germany was once again adopting a political approach, which in past centuries had been beneficial to both countries'. He accepted the Soviet draft and was convinced that the attached protocol could 'be substantially agreed in a very short time'. Hitler continued: the 'tension between Germany and Poland' had 'become intolerable'. Germany was determined, 'in view of this unreasonable behaviour, from now onwards to defend the Reich's interests with all means at its disposal'. Hitler now proposed that they should 'lose no more time' and that Ribbentrop should go to Moscow as soon as possible. His foreign minister would be bringing 'full and comprehensive powers to draw up and sign a non-aggression pact as well as the protocol'.

The following day, Stalin telegraphed his agreement and, late in the evening of 21 August, Germany was able to announce to the world – including its astonished allies, Italy and Japan[122] – the surprising news that it was about to sign a non-aggression pact.[123]

War aim: 'The destruction of Poland'

Assuming that there would shortly be an agreement with the Soviet Union that would seal Poland's fate, on 22 August Hitler once again spoke to around fifty high-ranking officers he had summoned specially to the Berghof. We do not have an actual copy of Hitler's speech, which was of vital importance for the outbreak of the Second World War,[124] but its contents can be reconstructed from the notes made by various members of his audience.[125]

Hitler explained to the generals that he had already taken the decision to attack Poland in the spring following the occupation of Memel. At first, he had thought that in few years' time he would first move against the West and only after that against the East. But then he had realized that, in the event of a conflict with the western powers, Poland would attack Germany. He had to preempt that.[126]

He justified his decision to go to war at this particular point in time by explaining that both Germany and Italy currently had exceptional leaders. His own supreme self-confidence is revealed in one of the transcripts of the speech: 'Essentially, everything depends on me, on my existence, because of my political talents. Also, the fact that probably no one will ever again have the confidence of the whole of the German people in the way that I have. In future, there will probably never again be a man who has more authority than I have. Thus, my existence is a factor of great value. But I can at any time be eliminated by a criminal or a lunatic.' After praising Mussolini and Franco in a similar fashion and declaring that Italy's loyalty as an ally and Spain's neutrality depended on these friendly leaders, he went on to mention another key point: 'as a result of the constraints on us, our economic situation is such that we can only hold out for a few more years . . . we have no other choice, we must act.'

The 'political situation' also made it advisable to act now. 'In the Mediterranean rivalries between Italy, France, and England, in East Asia tension between Japan and England, in the Middle East tension that is alarming the Moslem world.' Another factor was that the position of the [British] Empire and France had deteriorated since the end of the First World War. In addition, in the Balkans, 'since Albania . . . [there was] a balance of power'. Yugoslavia and Romania were in an extremely weak position, Turkey was ruled by 'weak and feeble men with small minds'. 'In two or three years' time' all these 'favourable circumstances [will] no longer' prevail. 'And no-one

knows how much longer I shall live. So, it's better to have a conflict now.'[127]
The founding of Greater Germany, Hitler continued, was 'politically a great
achievement, but militarily it was questionable, as it was achieved through
bluffing by the political leadership'. It was now necessary 'to test the military' by 'getting it to carry out individual tasks'.[128]

The relationship with Poland had become 'intolerable'. It was Britain's
fault for intervening and blocking his initiative in the Danzig and Corridor
question. It was time to act, he repeated, as 'it was still highly probable' that
the West would not intervene. In any event, they would be taking 'a great
risk' that would demand 'iron nerves' and an 'iron resolve'.

Britain and France, he continued, were not ready for war. Neither a blockade, nor an attack from the Maginot line would be successful and an attack
through neutral states was out of the question. If, contrary to expectation,
the western powers did intervene, they would defend the West until they
had conquered Poland.[129] Hitler went on to describe his rapprochement
with Russia, which excluded any risk from that quarter.[130] All in all, there
was only one final risk left, that some 'chap' ('Schweinehund' in another
version)[131] would screw it up with an offer to mediate.[132]

He told the generals he would 'provide a propaganda pretext for starting
the war, however implausible. The victor is never asked afterwards whether
or not he told the truth. When starting and waging a war it's not being in
the right that matters, but victory.' And he went on: 'Close your hearts to
pity. Act brutally. 80 million people must get what is their right. Their existence must be made secure. The stronger man is in the right. The greatest
harshness.' For the generals this meant: 'The military goal is the total destruction of Poland. Speed is of the essence. Pursuit to the point of complete
annihilation.' He announced that the war would 'probably' start on Saturday
26 August.[133] The process of military mobilization began accordingly.[134]

Hitler interrupted his speech briefly to say goodbye to Ribbentrop, who
was going off on his trip to Moscow.[135] His entourage consisted of some
thirty persons, including, apart from the diplomats, Hitler's personal photographer, Hoffmann.[136]

Arriving in Moscow on 23 August, Ribbentrop immediately began the
final stage of the negotiations with Stalin and Molotov.[137] They quickly
came to an agreement: the non-aggression and consultation pact was to last
ten years and stated that, in the event of military measures undertaken by a
third power against one of the two treaty partners – the word 'attack' was
carefully avoided – this third power would not be supported by the other

treaty partner. More important, however, was the additional secret protocol, envisaging the partition of Poland and the Baltic states into Soviet and German spheres of interest. Although he had been given plenary powers, Ribbentrop sought Hitler's approval for a concession in the division of spheres of influence: Stalin was demanding the Latvian ports Libau (Liepāja) and Windau (Ventspils). The 'Führer' agreed and the treaty was then signed.[138]

Hitler was now not only certain that, in the event of an attack on Poland, he had excluded the Soviet Union as a potential opponent, but he would also be able to let his new ally share in the spoils.[139]

War or peace?

The conclusion of the Nazi–Soviet pact was followed by a week of hectic diplomacy, involving Germany, Poland, Britain, France, and Italy: notes were exchanged, emissaries sent, and there were last-minute attempts at mediation. The decision over war and peace lay entirely in Hitler's hands. His attitude during this last phase before the outbreak of war was contradictory and wavering, which led to speculation among his contemporaries and later historians about his motives. Had Hitler become the victim of a miscalculation arising from his own disparate aims, so that he stumbled more or less blindly through the crisis, which then ended in a two-front war he had not intended? Or had he been aiming for a war with the western powers from the very beginning, believing that it would be better to face the inevitable confrontation in 1939 rather than a few years later?

When, immediately after the conclusion of the Hitler–Stalin pact, Chamberlain told Hitler in writing that Britain would go to war if Germany attacked Poland, Hitler responded in his written reply just as decisively: he would not withdraw his demands on Poland and if this meant war with Britain then Germany was 'ready and determined' to fight.[140]

While Weizsäcker believed that Hitler was reckoning on a 'localized war',[141] the latter left Goebbels the same day with a somewhat uncertain impression as to whether the western powers would intervene: 'At the moment one can't be sure.... It depends on the circumstances. London is more committed than in September 1938 . . . England probably doesn't want a war at the moment. But it has to save face.' At present Paris was holding back, but there too 'one can't be absolutely certain'. Italy was not enthusiastic, 'but it will probably have to join in; it has hardly any other choice.'

Hitler dismissed the fact that the new alliance with Stalin completely contradicted the regime's post-1933 anti-Bolshevik policy with a terse comment:
'The question of Bolshevism is at the moment of minor importance. Also,
the Führer believes he's in a tight spot...' 'It's an emergency and beggars
can't be choosers'. Finally, during the night, the long-awaited communiqué
arrived in the Berghof from Moscow, confirming the final version of the
alliance with Stalin.[142]

The following day, 24 August, Hitler flew from Berchtesgaden to Berlin,[143]
in order to begin the final preparations for the attack. That evening, accompanied by Göring and state secretary Weizsäcker, he met Ribbentrop, who
had just returned from Moscow.[144] The foreign minister declared that in
Moscow 'he had felt as if he was among old Party comrades', and Hoffmann
praised Stalin as intelligent, amiable, and cunning.[145]

Hitler only found the time to inform Mussolini, his most important ally,
about the conclusion of the non-aggression pact with Stalin and the background to it in an official letter sent on 25 August. As far as the impending
war was concerned, Hitler merely wanted to tell Mussolini that they had
been 'in a state of alert for weeks', that the German measures were naturally
'keeping pace with Polish mobilization' and 'that I will take immediate
measures if Polish actions become intolerable'.[146]

Later on that day, Hitler met the British and French ambassadors. He told
Henderson that he could put up with Britain declaring war on Germany,
if Germany attacked Poland.[147] However, Hitler was evidently impressed
by the firmness with which the British government, supported by its population, was sticking to its policy, and offered Britain comprehensive cooperation for the period after this 'problem had been solved'. He was determined,
he said, to play a decisive role in protecting the British Empire, was willing
to accept restrictions on armaments, and had no intention of altering the
borders in the West. However, not even Propaganda Minister Goebbels considered this offer convincing: 'England won't buy that any more.'[148] Nor did
Hitler's meeting with the French ambassador lead remotely to a de-escalation
of the situation. Robert Coulondre told Hitler 'on his word as an officer' that,
if Germany moved against Poland, France would fulfil its responsibilities.[149]

In the early afternoon, in other words immediately after his meeting with
Henderson, Hitler gave Keitel the final order to attack Poland the following
morning,[150] 26 August. This was the date for the attack that he had already
given to his generals on 22 August. Thus he did not even bother to wait for
the British government's response to his 'generous' offer of an alliance.

Evidently, it was merely designed to embarrass the British government the following day, a few hours after the start of the German attack.

At that point, however, a dramatic development completely upset Hitler's calculations. In the early evening, ambassador Bernardo Attolico shocked Hitler to the core with a message from Mussolini to the effect that, for the time being, Italy was not in a position to take part in the war. Mussolini reminded Hitler that 'during our meetings...the war was envisaged for after 1942' and, in accordance with this understanding, he would then naturally have been 'ready on land, at sea, and in the air'; but, at this point, Italy was not ready for war.[151] This message shook Hitler, who was visibly affected and downcast.[152] Moreover, during the afternoon, news arrived that the military pact between Britain and Poland, which had been agreed on 6 April 1939, had just been ratified in London.[153] This made it unlikely that, the day after Germany had started a war, Britain would seriously engage with Hitler's offer of an alliance. Thus, Hitler responded to this new situation by continuing the clandestine mobilization, but, in order to win time for final diplomatic negotiations and for troop reinforcements on the western and eastern frontiers,[154] the attack planned for the coming night was postponed for several days.[155] On 26 August, the Army was given 31 August as the new date for the start of the war.[156]

On 25 August, Hitler, who was not content with Mussolini's negative response, enquired of the 'Duce' what war *matériel* and raw materials he needed in order to be ready for war.[157] The following day Mussolini's reply arrived containing an enormous list of *matériel* and raw materials that Italy desperately needed in order to be ready for war. Mussolini could not have made his lack of enthusiasm for war any clearer.[158] Hitler responded immediately by giving his ally the chance to save face, while simultaneously diverting attention from his own miscalculation. In a lengthy reply he dealt in detail with the 'Duce's' wish list, but wrote that 'to my regret, your wishes...cannot be fulfilled for purely organizational and technical reasons'. He wrote that he understood Mussolini's situation and requested that he should 'as promised, tie down English and French forces through active propaganda and appropriate military demonstrations'.[159] Mussolini responded the same evening with a letter to Hitler in which he agreed to his request, but advocated a political solution to the conflict.[160]

In the meantime, Göring had asked an acquaintance, a Swedish businessman, Birger Dahlerus, to try to mediate in London. Dahlerus had already made an attempt to facilitate discussions between the British and German

governments.[161] He returned from London on 26 August with a letter from
Halifax to Göring, underlining Britain's willingness to negotiate. Göring
immediately passed the letter on to Hitler, and that night Dahlerus was
summoned to the Reich Chancellery, where Hitler initially regaled him with
a lengthy account of his efforts to reach an understanding with Britain.
Dahlerus's attempts to turn the monologue into a conversation were only
partially successful.[162]

According to Dahlerus, Hitler's eloquence 'was undeniable, his ability to
make his own opinions appear convincing impressive; however, he suffered
from the regrettable inability to acknowledge or respect his opponent's views'.
Hitler appeared to Dahlerus extremely tense and unstable; the scene late at
night, with the dictator pacing up and down in his study, in the end uttering
wild threats, in fact actually screaming them – all this made an alarming
impression on his Swedish visitor.

Finally, Hitler gave Dahlerus a concrete offer to take away with him:
Germany sought an alliance with Britain and was prepared to participate in
defending the Empire. It was exactly the same proposal that he had made to
Henderson. Hitler now increased his demands, however: for the first time
he now demanded, in addition to Danzig, most of the Corridor (apart from
a strip providing access to Gdingen, which would remain Polish), whereas
hitherto he had declared himself content with an extraterritorial transport
link through the corridor. Moreover, according to Hitler, Germany would
be prepared to guarantee Poland's borders. At the same time, it wanted
guarantees for the German minority in Poland and a settlement of the colonial question. By increasing his demands relating to the Corridor, making
it impossible for Poland to agree, while, at the same time, suggesting to
Britain his willingness to negotiate, he was trying to drive a wedge between
Poland and its guarantor, Britain. This tactic is revealed in a note by Halder,
who, in the late evening of 26 August, wrote: 'Faint hope that we can get
Britain to accept demands through negotiation that Poland is rejecting:
Danzig-Corridor.'[163]

This was therefore Hitler's last attempt before the attack on Poland to use
a diplomatic manoeuvre to prevent Britain from intervening, even though
she had repeatedly threatened to do so in the event of such an attack. Britain
was to be persuaded to accept the German demand for the Corridor, and
Germany's negotiations with Poland were then, using some pretext, to be
broken off. It was hoped that, in this event, the British government would
pull back from starting a European war and, without Britain, France would

not move. If this failed, then he would still be able to put the blame for the war on the other side, as he had, after all, shown himself willing to negotiate right up to the last minute.

On 26 August, a letter from Daladier to Hitler also arrived, in which he implored him to solve the problems in dispute through negotiation.[164] Goebbels noted Hitler's view that the letter was unimportant and evidently written only 'for the possible future issue of war guilt'.[165] Hitler replied the following day with a long letter indicating that he was determined to seek a solution to the Danzig and Corridor questions 'one way or the other'. He made it clear that he was no longer interested in the idea of an extra-territorial transport link, but rather in a much more extensive annexation: 'Danzig and the Corridor must return to Germany.' Although the Germans had promised the French confidentiality, they published the correspond-ence on 28 August.[166]

On the afternoon of the 27 August, Hitler received the Reichstag deputies, who had been summoned to Berlin, in the Reich Chancellery. Originally, he had envisaged using this day, which had been intended to be the second day of the war, for an address to the Reichstag justifying the opening of hostilities. As a kind of substitute he made a speech to the deputies in the Ambassadors' Hall and Halder took notes: 'Situation very serious. Determined. Eastern question to be solved one way or the other. Minimum demand: return of Danzig, solution to the Corridor question. Maximum demand: "depends on military situation." If minimum demand not fulfilled, then war: Brutal! He would be in the front line. The Duce will do his best for us. War very difficult, perhaps hopeless. "So long as I live there will be no talk of capitulation." Soviet pact perhaps misunderstood by Party. Pact with Satan, to drive out the devil. Economic situation.' According to Halder, 'the applause was as required but thin.' Halder's general impression of Hitler was not good. 'Bleary-eyed, haggard, his voice cracking, distracted'.[167] Goebbels, by contrast, had encoun tered his boss on the same day 'in the best of moods and very confident'.[168]

On the afternoon of 27 August, Hitler received a telegram from Mussolini, replying to his request to keep the Italian decision secret and to continue with military preparations for appearance's sake, in order to tie down the Allies.[169] Germany too declared Italy's refusal to act a state secret.[170] The 'Duce' accepted the German proposals, informing Hitler of what moral and military support Italy was prepared to give.

During the late evening of 27 August, Dahlerus returned from Britain, bringing with him the British government's reply to Hitler's proposals.[171]

Britain declared that, in principle, it was prepared to sign a treaty with Germany, but urged direct negotiations with Warsaw over the questions of Danzig, the Corridor, and the German minority in Poland. The Polish borders ought to be jointly guaranteed by Russia, Germany, Italy, France, and Britain. It rejected Germany's claim for the return of her colonies, but was prepared to discuss the matter after the crisis had come to an end and following Germany's demobilization. The German offer to take part in defending the Empire was 'incompatible with the dignity and interests of the British empire'.

The official response of the British government, brought by ambassador Henderson the following evening, explicitly referred to Britain's alliance commitments to Poland,[172] prompting Hitler to postpone the attack scheduled for 31 August by a further day.[173]

On 29 August, during a stormy meeting, Hitler gave Henderson his reply: there was little point in any further negotiations with Poland; he was, however, prepared to receive 'a Polish emissary with full powers' for talks in Berlin, but he must arrive by the following day, in other words on the 30th.[174] Goebbels was afraid that if the Polish foreign minister, Beck, actually came, people's sudden hopes of peace might lead to 'an unstoppable wave of optimism, which would ruin the government's whole position'.[175] This he summed up as 'possibly still managing to prise London away from Warsaw and finding a pretext to attack'.[176]

During 29 August Attolico, the Italian ambassador, brought a letter and an oral message from Mussolini, offering his services for mediation with Britain. According to the interpreter, Schmidt, Hitler's response was distinctly cool: he himself was already in direct contact with the British and had offered to receive a Polish negotiator.[177] He wanted to avoid another Munich at all costs.

Late in the evening of this same 29 August, Göring summoned Dahlerus, asking him once again to go to London to underline Germany's willingness to negotiate, and to announce that further German proposals would be made the following day.[178]

On the morning of 30 August, Hitler received the Danzig Gauleiter, Albert Forster, to give him final instructions for the intended take-over of Danzig. In addition, on 30 August he signed the 'Führer Decree for the Formation of a Ministerial Council for the Defence of the Reich', creating a committee composed of Göring, Hess, Frick, Funk, Lammers, and Keitel, which was entitled to issue decrees with the force of law.[179]

During the afternoon, Chamberlain sent a message that the British government was examining the German note in detail and would reply in the course of the day.[180] Meanwhile, Hitler was already working on a memorandum designed above all to demonstrate to world opinion that Germany had been willing to negotiate in good faith, even though, as intended, the negotiations had collapsed. The memorandum, comprising a total of sixteen points, demanded the annexation of Danzig, and a plebiscite in the Corridor, with the losing side being provided with extraterritorial links.

At midnight on 30 August, Ribbentrop received Henderson to tell him, in the course of a very heated conversation, that they had prepared proposals for settling the dispute with Poland. However, these were now redundant, as Germany's demand for a Polish emissary to arrive that day had not been met. Ribbentrop then quickly read out the 16-point memorandum without giving Henderson a copy.[181]

Hitler also summoned Goebbels at midnight in order to give him details of his 'proposals for negotiation' and to fill him in on the background: 'The Führer thinks it's going to be war.' Hitler told Goebbels that he wanted 'to release [the 16-point proposal] to the world at a suitable opportunity', demonstrating once again that his memorandum had been intended purely as propaganda. Neither Poland nor Britain was to be permitted to respond to the German proposals before the outbreak of war.

In the early morning of 31 August, Hitler confirmed the order to attack Poland the following day. At 12.40 he signed the 'Directive No. 1 for the Conduct of the War', in which he ordered the attack to begin at 4.45 a.m. In the West, German forces were to remain strictly on the defensive, so that 'England and France unequivocally bear the responsibility for beginning hostilities'. Around midday, Halder noted: 'Involvement of the West now said to be unavoidable, but Führer still decides to attack.' A few hours later, however, the fact that Hitler had initially countermanded the comprehensive evacuation of the frontier zone in the west that had been planned was leading Halder to conclude 'that he [Hitler] reckons that France and England won't be marching'.[182]

On the afternoon of 31 August, the Polish ambassador contacted state secretary von Weizsäcker with a request to be received by Hitler or Ribbentrop. Hitler did not wish to see him, however, and when that evening Lipski visited Ribbentrop to present his government's response to the British proposal for starting direct negotiations, the German foreign minister terminated the meeting on the pretext that they had waited in vain on the

30th for a Polish emissary with plenipotentiary powers. In fact, Lipski had to concede that even now he did not possess powers going beyond those he already had as ambassador. Shortly afterwards, the Foreign Ministry sent the 16-point programme to the British, French, Japanese, American, and Soviet ambassadors, declaring that Poland had not taken advantage of the opportunity for negotiations.[183] Shortly before, around 21.00, both this statement and the memorandum were broadcast on the German radio.[184] At this point, Hitler gave Goebbels the impression that he did not believe 'that England will intervene'. But, Goebbels continued, 'at the moment no one [can] say' whether or not this forecast would prove correct.[185]

Whereas in 1936 Hitler saw himself on the defensive against a looming communist alliance, in 1937 he began to act from a position of strength. Cooperation with Italy, which might turn into an alliance, subsequently extending to east and south-east European states, appeared to him to change the balance of power in Central Europe. At the end of 1937 he was already envisaging the possibility, in certain circumstances, of annexing Austria and Czechoslovakia, without having to fear intervention from France, Britain, or the Soviet Union, an assumption that was not, however, shared by the military. The fact that the alliance with Britain that he had originally sought had not come about appeared initially to increase his diplomatic room for manoeuvre.

The transition to an expansionist foreign policy during 1938 was not, however, part of a long-term plan, but in fact improvised. In February 1938, looking for a foreign policy success immediately after the Blomberg–Fritsch crisis, Hitler forced the Austrian Chancellor Schuschnigg to make substantial concessions that amounted to the 'coordination' of Austria. The further move towards the Anschluss of Austria by mid-March 1938 was not originally envisaged by Hitler as coming about in this way; it arose out of the unexpected countermoves by Schuschnigg and Hitler's determination to break this resistance through intervention. He only decided to annex Austria immediately when the invasion was already in progress.

This exceptional success encouraged Hitler to accelerate the break-up of Czechoslovakia. The so-called Weekend Crisis of May 1938, which he interpreted as a major loss of prestige resulting from the devious cooperation between Czechoslovakia and the western powers, dramatically radicalized his thinking and actions. For Hitler now became convinced that war with the western powers was unavoidable in the medium term. As far as he was concerned, the destruction of Czechoslovakia was now, unlike in 1937, no longer an option in the event that France was paralysed, but had become for him the precondition for a later war against the western powers, for which he wanted to protect his rear. Thus, at the end of May, he fixed the deadline for a move against Czechoslovakia as 2 October, at the same time initiating a massive increase in rearmament and the building of the West Wall to provide security against an attack by the western powers.

Hitler achieved a remarkable bloodless success when, after several months, the Sudeten crisis was settled by the Munich Agreement at the end of September 1938. However, he interpreted the Agreement as a defeat because he had not succeeded in destroying Czechoslovakia. The 'bringing home' of the Sudenten Germans had simply been the pretext for attacking Czechoslovakia. Moreover, the lack of enthusiasm for war, not only among the population, but also among his regime's political and military leadership, had become very evident. In response, he launched an exceptional rearmament programme and switched the focus of propaganda to preparing the population for war. Finally, in March 1939, as soon as possible, he destroyed the rest of Czechoslovakia, soon afterwards forcing Lithuania to return Memel to Germany.

After the destruction of Czechoslovakia, however, all Hitler's plans to compel Poland, his partner since 1934, to accept his terms for the settlement of the Danzig question and to join an anti-Soviet alliance failed. Instead, Poland preferred the safety of the Anglo-French guarantee. As in the previous year vis-à-vis Czechoslovakia, and strengthened by the Pact of Steel with Italy in May, Hitler fixed a specific date, 1 September 1939, for military action against Poland. This time he was certain that no new 'Munich' would get in the way of his military triumph. The coup of the Non-Aggression Pact with Moscow of August 1939 seemed to him, in all probability, to rule out a military intervention by the western powers.

Hitler's approach was, as so often when it came to important decisions in his career, ambivalent. On the one hand, he counted on being able to keep the western powers out of the war at the last minute through a combination of assertions of strength and generous offers. On the other hand, he was quite prepared to accept the possibility of a major war, in which case he assumed that, by ostentatiously showing his willingness to negotiate, he would be able to place the blame for the war on his opponents. During these decisive days, this dual-track approach enabled him to behave towards the western powers sometimes as if he were cynically determined to go to war and, at other times, as if he were hesitant and concerned to preserve peace, while allowing him also to take account of the different views among the military and political leadership. He led his regime by means of a dramatic decision-making process, at the end of which a result emerged that was irrevocable and was accepted by those who had been sceptical about going to war.

Within a period of one and a half years, his policy of conquest had brought him to the brink of a major European war. Reviewing the most important stages in this process, one is compelled to conclude that Hitler was the decisive, driving force in this process. He was not dragged into war by either the political or the military leadership, nor was he the victim of a rearmament dynamic that finally left him with no other option than war.[186]

Analysis of the SD and Sopade situation reports for the years 1938/39 shows that the Germans were far removed from forming a great, united Nazi national community. On the contrary, the sources at our disposal show a picture of a decidedly disunited society suffering under great burdens imposed by an accelerated rearmament programme. The various sections of society were particularly sensitive to perceived social injustices placing great emphasis on preserving their social status. Clashes between the interests of particular social groups were often publicly expressed, such as between employees and employers, producers and consumers, country and city. Above all, German society was far from becoming a united, national 'community of struggle', willing to make great sacrifices in order to restore Germany to great power status, if necessary through war. However, this had been the main aim of Hitler's domestic policy since 1933, and, in this respect at least, the majority of the population had failed to follow him.

The decisive point about the national enthusiasm generated by his foreign policy successes was that it was always overshadowed by the fear of war caused by his risky policies. Jubilation over the Anschluss with Austria broke out only when it was evident that there were not going to be any serious international repercussions. During the critical diplomatic situation between May and October 1938, it became clear that the regime was having difficulty in imposing great material burdens on the population, while simultaneously keeping it in a constant state of tension. When the crisis reached its climax at the end of September 1938, the population reacted with an obvious lack of enthusiasm for war, while applauding the preservation of peace following the Munich Agreement.

Slightly more than five weeks later, the Nazi activists unleashed their frustration at the German population's lack of enthusiasm for war, for which they blamed 'the Jews', in the November pogrom. Hitler, who played the key role in launching the pogrom, used the orgy of violence to initiate a general change of course in the field of propaganda. The population was to be gradually got ready for war. In his Reichstag speech on 30 January, Hitler put down an important marker for the new course by combining the themes of war and anti-Semitism in his threat that a world war would lead to the annihilation of the 'Jewish race' in Europe. His anti-British 'encirclement' speech of 1 April, referring to the outbreak of the First World War, as well as his Reichstag speech of 28 April, in which he abrogated the Anglo-German Naval Agreement and the Non-Aggression pact with Poland, determined the course of propaganda, which was now intended to prepare the population for a new war. During the months that followed, Hitler tended, however, to keep a low profile, and handed the role of chief agitator to his Propaganda Minister, Goebbels. Although it proved impossible to whip up enthusiasm for war during the August crisis, by this time the population had evidently come to accept what appeared likely to be a limited war.

PART VI

Triumph

29

The Outbreak of War

The attack on Poland began as planned at 4.45 a.m. on the morning of 1 September. The pretext was provided by Polish border provocations – in fact, incidents organized by the SS. The most notorious was the 'attack' on the Gleiwitz radio transmitter. At the same time, the German battle cruiser 'Schleswig-Holstein' opened fire on the Westerplatte, the fortified Polish arms depot at the entrance to Danzig harbour.[1] Hitler announced in a proclamation to the Wehrmacht read out over the radio at 5.40 a.m. that, because of the persecution of Germans in Poland with 'bloody terror' and, in view of the 'intolerable border violations', he had had 'no alternative other than, from now onwards, to meet force with force'.[2] He offered the same justification in a speech to the Reichstag on the morning of 1 September that culminated in the statement: 'Since 5.45 fire has been returned.'

He outlined his goals as follows: 'I am determined: to solve 1. the Danzig question, 2. the Corridor issue, and 3. to ensure that a change occurs in Germany's relationship with Poland, thereby securing peaceful cooperation.'[3] He reiterated that he had made no demands on France or Britain; the border with France was 'final'; he had repeatedly offered Britain 'friendship' and the 'closest cooperation'. However, he solemnly continued, 'love is not a one-sided affair; it must elicit a response from the other person'.[4] He then made public the directive he had already issued at the end of 1934, but had not published at the time: if anything were to happen to him, Göring would be his 'first successor'. And, in a vital addition to his directive, if Göring were no longer available, Hess should take over his offices. If anything should happen to Hess as well, the succession should be decided by a senate, which he now wished to establish by legislation, although in fact this never happened. He told the deputies that he had 'once again put on the uniform that has always been most sacred and dear to me'. In fact he had appeared for his speech not in his usual Party uniform, but, for the first time, in a grey military style uniform, and he used this occasion to make an emotional promise: 'I shall not take it off until after victory – or – I shall no longer live to see the end!'[5] The Reichstag then passed a law legalizing Gauleiter Forster's unilateral annexation of Danzig.[6]

Immediately after the Reichstag session, Hitler wrote to Mussolini once more, outlining the reasons for his actions – Poland's rigid attitude, the frontier violations and so forth – and trying to explain to him why he had not accepted the latter's offer to mediate.[7] Hitler now undertook a last attempt to try to prevent Britain from entering the war. He instructed Dahlerus to convey to Britain his willingness to negotiate; however, the response merely confirmed Britain's preconditions.[8] On the evening of 1 September, Ribbentrop then received Henderson, who handed over a British ultimatum: if Germany did not immediately halt its attacks on Poland, Britain would fulfil its treaty obligations towards Poland. On the following morning, the French ambassador gave Ribbentrop an identical message from his government.[9] On 2 September, Mussolini, in an effort to mediate, repeated his proposal of a four-power conference, which, however, the British government was only prepared to accept provided there was an immediate withdrawal of German troops. Hitler naturally refused.[10] The same was true of further mediation attempts by the Italians.

The upshot was inevitable. On 3 September, the British and French governments issued ultimatums to the effect that, unless they received assurances that Germany was prepared to withdraw from Poland by a certain time, a state of war would exist between their countries and Germany.[11] According to his interpreter, Schmidt, when Hitler received the news he was 'thunderstruck' and said to Ribbentrop: 'What now?', but he still remained composed. Around midday, Goebbels even thought Hitler appeared 'very confident'.[12] During the following days, Goebbels gained the impression that 'Hitler could do without a long war' and, after defeating Poland, was hoping for a quick peace with the West.[13]

War and terror in Poland

On the evening of 3 September, Hitler left Berlin in a special train that was to be his headquarters for the following weeks. Apart from two secretaries and his immediate personal staff, he was accompanied by various adjutants, an OKW military staff led by Keitel and Jodl, liaison officers with the three branches of the Wehrmacht and the SS, liaison staff from the Foreign Ministry, as well as Hess's deputy, Martin Bormann, who had become increasingly indispensable to him, and, finally, his personal photographer, Heinrich Hoffmann.[14] The train was, initially, parked at various places in Pomerania, later moving to Silesia. Hitler left his headquarters roughly every other day to visit military staffs or units by car or air; these visits were reported by the propaganda machine as 'trips to the front'.[15]

In terms of troops and equipment, the Wehrmacht possessed a clear superiority over the Polish forces. Poland was surrounded by Reich territory and by Slovakia, which also took part in the attack, in a pincer-like grip. On 3 September, troops from Pomerania had already established a land bridge with East Prussia through the Corridor. Strengthened by these troops, the 3rd Army, stationed in East Prussia, could reinforce its attack southwards, while simultaneously three armies advanced eastwards and north-eastwards from Silesia. On 8 September, German units reached the outskirts of Warsaw, which, by the 15th, was completely surrounded. During the following siege, the city was largely destroyed by artillery and bombing. On 17 September, under German pressure, the Soviet Union began occupying the territory in eastern Poland that it had been promised under the Nazi–Soviet Pact.[16] Poland's situation had now become completely hopeless.

Only two days later, Hitler moved his headquarters to the Casino Hotel in the Danzig seaside resort of Zoppot. The following day he made a speech in the Danzig Artushof, the first since his Reichstag speech of 1 September and broadcast by every radio station, in which he declared himself the victor.[17] Poland had been 'crushed in a matter of barely 18 days', thereby 'creating a situation that may perhaps make it possible to speak calmly and sensibly with representatives of this nation.... The final political arrangements in this large territory will, in the first instance, depend on the two countries that have engaged their most vital interests here.' However, he insisted he had no war aims as far as Britain and France were concerned. On 26 September, Hitler returned to Berlin.[18]

Right from the start, the Germans fought the war against Poland with extreme brutality; indeed, in embryo, this war already bore the hallmarks of a campaign of racial annihilation. It is important to recall in this context the directives given by Hitler to his generals on 22 August: 'destruction of Poland', 'elimination of the active forces', 'close your hearts to compassion', 'proceed brutally'. The most important instruments for the 'elimination of

the active forces' were the Einsatzgruppen [task forces] of the Security
Police created for this war. The five Einsatzgruppen (two more were established after the start of the war) were each assigned to one of the armies.[19]
These units, which comprised in total around 2,700 men, officially had the
task, agreed with the Army High Command (OKH) at the end of July, of
'combatting elements hostile to the Reich and to Germans in enemy territory operating behind the troops engaged in combat'.[20] In fact, the tasks of
the Einsatzgruppen were far wider in scope. It is clear from post-war inter-
rogations of Einsatzgruppen leaders that they were already being told by
Himmler and Heydrich at a briefing in August that it was up to them to
decide how the Polish intelligentsia should be neutralized.[21]

During the war, these directives from the SS leadership were duly implemented. On 3 September, Himmler told the Einsatzgruppen to shoot armed
Polish insurgents out of hand and, where such insurgents appeared, to take
the heads of the local Polish administration hostage.[22] On 7 September,
Reinhard Heydrich, the chief of the Security Police and SD, gave instructions to a meeting of heads of department that 'the leading circles in the
Polish population should be rendered harmless as far as possible',[23] and he
told the same audience at a meeting on 14 October that the 'liquidation of
the Polish elite' that was already under way should, if possible, be completed
by 1 November.[24] On 29 September, Halder noted à propos a conversation
between the Quartermaster General, Eduard Wagner, and Heydrich: 'A general clearing of the ground: Jewry, intelligentsia, clergy, nobility.'[25]

In a memo of July 1940 Heydrich reflected that, before the war, the
Einsatzgruppen had received instructions that were 'extraordinarily radical
(e.g. the order to liquidate numerous Polish ruling circles, which affected
thousands)'. He stated there had been problems cooperating with the army
because, at the time, they had not been able to reveal that the brutal actions
engaged in by the Einsatzgruppen were not arbitrary; on the contrary, as
Heydrich's comments make unmistakably clear, these exceptionally radical
orders came directly from Hitler himself.[26]

Right from the start of the war, they led to the mass shooting of members
of the intelligentsia, the clergy, the nobility, as well as Jews, the mentally ill,
and those suspected of being 'guerillas'.[27] The pretext for these murders was
the alleged Polish atrocities perpetrated on ethnic Germans, which, according to German propaganda, had cost the lives of more than 50,000 people.
In fact the number of ethnic German civilian victims who lost their lives
during the war, either in riots such as the 'Blomberg Bloody Sunday' or in

Figure 10. Decidedly unenthusiastic: Members of fighter squadron Hindenburg 1
listen to Hitler's declaration of war on Poland on 1 September 1939.
Source: bpk / Benno Wundshammer

the course of military operations, had been multiplied by a factor of ten.[28]
The Einsatzgruppen were supported by 'Ethnic German Self-Defence'
units, a force that had been rapidly created by the SS after the start of
the war from members of the German minority.[29] During the month of
September alone, the Einsatzgruppen and 'Self-Defence' units, but also the
uniformed police,[30] Waffen SS,[31] and, last but not least, Wehrmacht units[32]
had shot over 16,000 Polish civilians.[33] These murders were systematically
encouraged and backed by Hitler.

On 9 September, thanks to his knowledge of the attitude of the top leadership, General Halder had already concluded that it was Hitler's and
Göring's intention 'to annihilate and exterminate the Polish people'.[34] On
12 October, Hitler pressed the army commanders to issue a decree concerning the possession of weapons that would order all scattered soldiers who
were continuing the struggle against the Wehrmacht behind the front to
be treated as 'guerillas' and executed.[35] When, on 12 September, Admiral

Canaris, the head of military intelligence, asked the head of OKW, Keitel, about 'extensive shootings' in Poland, Keitel replied that 'this matter [had] already been decided by the Führer'. Hitler had made it clear that 'if the Wehrmacht did not want to have anything to do with this, it would have to put up with the SS and the Gestapo working alongside it'.[36] After a meeting with Hitler on 20 September, the commander-in-chief of the army, Brauchitsch, informed the commanders of the army groups and armies that, on Hitler's orders, the Einsatzgruppen would be 'carrying out certain tasks relating to ethnic politics in Poland' lying outside the Wehrmacht's area of responsibility.[37]

However, as various members of the SS had been court martialled for their actions, on 4 October Hitler issued a (secret) decree ordering that offences 'that were committed from bitterness at the atrocities carried out by the Poles' were not to be pursued by the courts and, if necessary, to be amnestied.[38] On 12 October, he went a step further and ordered the SS and police to be removed from civil and military jurisdiction. Crimes committed by members of the SS and police were in future to be tried within Himmler's sphere of jurisdiction, and would either be punished or not in accordance with the principles of the 'ethnic struggle' that prevailed there.[39]

Mobilization for war and ministerial decisions

In the meantime, Hitler's regime had begun to adjust the living conditions in Germany to wartime requirements. This manifested itself, on the one hand, in increased repression, on the other in a reduction in private consumption. At the same time, the SD had resumed keeping careful watch on the 'voice of the people' throughout the Reich, a practice which had been stopped in 1936. The regime's official situation reports, together with many individual reports from the first weeks of the war, were in agreement that, while the population showed no signs of enthusiasm about the war, it was none the less in a calm and confident mood. Naturally, the general fear of war, which had been so ubiquitous in recent years, had not disappeared overnight; however, in a public sphere that it dominated, the regime succeeded in keeping the expression of negative feelings under control and in interpreting the population's resignation, apathy, and paralysing fear as sober-mindedness and calm.[40] It was no accident that in his Reichstag speech of 1 September Hitler had told the Party functionaries: 'I don't want anybody telling me morale's bad in his Gau, or in his district, or in his local branch or cell. You're the ones responsible for morale!'[41] Goebbels frequently intervened in the reporting of the national mood when it seemed to him 'wrongheaded'.[42]

Apart from the local control of 'national comrades' exercised through the Party organization, which was constantly being expanded,[43] the threat of any public expression of discontent with the war was dealt with by an increase in repression. To facilitate this, shortly after the outbreak of war, the apparatus of police repression – criminal police, Gestapo, and the Party's intelligence service, the SD – was concentrated in a new organization, the Reich Security Head Office (RSHA) under Heydrich.[44] In addition, a decree of 4 September made listening to foreign broadcasts a criminal offence; passing on news received from this source in public could even lead to the imposition of the death penalty. While this did not prevent unwelcome information from being spread through foreign broadcasts, it did mean that anyone referring in public to a foreign broadcast as the source of their information was taking a serious risk.[45] The War Economy Decree of 4 September also provided for the punishment of 'behaviour damaging the war effort', such as hoarding food or slaughtering animals for the black market. Here too, in serious cases the death penalty could be imposed.[46] The National Vermin Decree of 5 September introduced lengthy sentences of penal servitude and the death penalty for crimes committed by taking advantage of wartime conditions (evacuation, the blackout, and so forth), or which in general posed a threat to the 'German people's military capabilities'.[47] Also, the Decree against Violent Criminals of 5 December introduced lengthier sentences.[48]

This was not all, however. After the outbreak of war, Hitler began personally to order the shooting of criminals if he concluded that the crime was particularly damaging to the home front. In some cases the victims had already been given prison sentences; other cases simply involved suspects. There was no legal authority for these arbitrary actions. News of these executions, which were usually carried out in concentration camps, was made public to act as a deterrent.[49] A few days after the outbreak of the war, Himmler asked Hitler what should be done with Polish prisoners of war who had 'friendly or even sexual relations' with German women. Hitler ordered that the prisoners should all be shot and the women be shamed by having their hair cut off in public and then be sent to a concentration camp.[50] The comprehensive War Economy Decree of 4 September, and the subsequent decrees implementing it, not only imposed drastic sanctions, but also placed substantial financial burdens on the population. Thus a 15 per cent surcharge was imposed on income tax; the consumption of beer, tobacco, and sparkling wines was subject to a special war tax, and the tax on brandy was increased. Also, overtime payments for night and Sunday work were cancelled, as well as all holiday entitlements. Thus, the various benefits introduced during the previous few years to get round the official wage freeze were being removed. At the beginning of September, food rationing was introduced; every citizen received a ration card.[51] .Clothing and articles of daily use were also rationed.[52]

During the autumn of 1939, however, the drastic measures introduced by the War Economy Decree were already proving counter-productive and unpopular; they affected, above all, workers in the armaments industry, who were already under pressure. Meanwhile, the closure of plants not vital to the war effort was causing a rise in unemployment because many of their workers could not quickly find employment in armaments plants at a time when war production was only gradually increasing. The population's discontent with the added burdens was soon reflected in the official situation reports. Questioning the war was still taboo, and so people found an outlet for their unhappiness in particular complaints.[53] Declining work discipline and an increase in ill health were clear symptoms of widespread dissatisfaction. The regime responded and various cuts were withdrawn; for example, the overtime payments for night and Sunday work and annual holidays were reinstated, planned structural changes to the wages system were dropped, and elaborate plans for tax increases postponed. This 'soft' policy of October and November 1939 occurred at a time when the regime had to accustom the population, which was not exactly enthusiastic about the war, to the idea of it going on for some time. That did not mean that it was in principle unwilling to impose burdens on the population during the war. Over the long term, private consumption was cut by shortages and rationing. Thus, consumer expenditure in 1943 was already 18 per cent below that in 1938. The shortage of goods meant that people's savings increased, with this money flowing 'noiselessly' into the government's coffers to finance the war.[54]

The Ministerial Council for the Defence of the Reich, which had been created by Hitler's edict of 30 August, was responsible for introducing (and partially revoking) all these radical measures. Under Lammers's chairmanship, this body consisted of Keitel, Hess, Frick, and Funk as permanent members; other ministers took part in particular sessions, the state secretaries [top civil servants] on a regular basis. The Ministerial Council was intended to provide uniform direction of the economy and the administration and had the authority to issue decrees with the force of law; as such, it had the role of replacing the defunct cabinet. Newly appointed 'Reich Defence Commissioners', who coordinated the civilian war effort in the military districts and were supposed to direct the various branches of the administration, were subordinated to the Ministerial Council. The fact that only Gauleiters were appointed to these posts was intended to indicate the increasing importance of the Party on the 'home front'. However, the Ministerial Council never became an effective organization for directing the economy, let alone a war cabinet, as Göring had no particular interest in the new body, which increasingly became a battleground for inter-ministerial conflicts. He allowed it to meet only a few times until November 1939, and dealt with the necessary legislative activity by circulating draft laws and decrees for the approval of the ministries involved.[55]

The establishment of the Ministerial Council was intended to emphasize to the public that Hitler was concentrating on the actual running of the war and to highlight Göring's status as second-in-command. In fact, however, Hitler kept control of the Ministerial Council, thereby securing his hold over the whole of domestic policy and legislation. He placed the business of the Ministerial Council in the hands of the Reich Chancellery (and not Göring's), maintained the right to dissolve it, claimed the right to legislate through the Reich government and the Reichstag (and made use of that right), had Ministerial Council decrees submitted to him on a regular basis, and intervened at will in the Ministerial Council's legislative practice.[56]

Thus the outbreak of war altered relatively little in the government's style of operating. Government bodies coexisted in an uncoordinated way, or to put it another way, there was endemic conflict between rival ministries, Party agencies, special delegates, as well as the Wehrmacht and its three individual branches, all engaged in battles over responsibilities. In particular, the division of the economy into a civilian branch, for which the Reich Economics Ministry was responsible, and an armaments sector under the jurisdiction of the Wehrmacht guaranteed friction. The fact that, on 7 December, Göring removed Economics Minister Funk from power as General Plenipotentiary for the Economy, declaring himself to be the person who wielded supreme authority over the war economy, made no real difference to this situation.[57] The opacity, the lack of clear structures for leadership and decision-making, as well as the conflicts between the individual authorities ensured Hitler's untrammelled power, providing him with numerous opportunities for intervening from issue to issue in a system whose functional flaws were the precondition for his own omnipotence.

Continuation of the war

Hitler initially behaved as if he was uncertain how to proceed with the further conduct of the war with the western powers. His entourage gained the impression that, at the end of September, he was still toying with the idea of a peace treaty. Thus, on 23 September, Goebbels learnt from the Reich press chief, Dietrich, who had just come from Hitler's headquarters, that, in view of the impending victory over Poland, he was not 'averse to making peace'; he wanted 'to separate France from Britain', in other words make contact with the French government. Dietrich immediately added, however, that Ribbentrop 'didn't really [have] any contacts' in Paris.[58] On 28 September, Hitler told Dahlerus, who had still not given up his attempts at Anglo-German mediation, that the precondition for peace was that he was allowed 'a completely free hand with Poland'.[59]

With such remarks Hitler was evidently trying gradually to convince those among the leadership who were unhappy with the idea of a major war of the inevitability of his course of action. For Hitler was already focusing on the possibility of a German offensive in the West. He appears to have already made a remark along these lines on 12 September, although without informing the army leadership of these plans.[60]

On 27 September, the day on which Warsaw surrendered, Hitler told a meeting of army commanders that, like it or not, they must get used to the fact that the war was going to continue. The other side would benefit most from the passage of time and so it was important not to 'wait until the enemy comes to us'; they had to go onto the attack themselves and 'the sooner the better'. The troops were quite capable of quickly having another go; the campaign in Poland had basically been an exercise, a manoeuvre. The war aim was to 'force England to its knees', and to crush France.[61] The war in the West must begin between 20 and 25 October and be fought initially in Belgium and Holland.[62] However, the military leadership was sceptical about, indeed opposed to, Hitler's plan to launch an attack in the West.[63]

Two days later, Hitler explained to Goebbels and Rosenberg, who was also present, how occupied Poland was to be dealt with in the future. Up until now, in view of the possibility of negotiations taking place with the western powers, he had left open the question of what they were going to do with a defeated Poland, not excluding the possibility of allowing a rump Polish state to continue to exist. This was, in fact, basically a phantom project, as is clear from the fact that that no serious attempts had been made to appoint a provisional Polish government.[64] Now, however, with victory in sight and peace with the western powers a long way away, his ideas acquired a clearer focus. Although the notion of some kind of a Polish rump state had not been abandoned, it was now going to be much smaller and, in addition, become part of a brutal plan for a reorganization of the region along racial lines. As Goebbels noted, according to this plan, Poland was going to be divided into '3 zones': 'the old German territory', which was to be 'totally Germanized' and, with the aid of 'military peasants', was to become 'core German territory' again; a strip of territory stretching eastwards up to the river Vistula, where 'the good Polish element' would live and enjoy a certain autonomy within a 'protectorate' (in his notes Rosenberg used the expression 'a Polish statehood'); and the new territory beyond the Vistula, which would contain the 'bad Polish elements and the Jews, including those from the Reich'.[65] He had already taken a fundamental decision to 'resettle' the Jews from the Reich a few days before.[66] Hitler reflected that they had gained 'a huge amount of territory', but at the same time had to accept that 'Moscow's influence in the Baltic states had been strengthened'. However, he was 'convinced of Russia's loyalty', particularly since Stalin was pocketing 'a big prize'.[67]

Hitler was referring to the Treaty of Borders and Friendship with the Soviet Union, signed by Ribbentrop in Moscow on 27 September, which had altered the spheres of influence agreed in August.[68] The Soviets wanted Lithuania, with Germany being compensated by receiving the central Polish territory between the rivers Bug, Vistula, and San.[69] This implied that the Soviet Union had no interest in the heart of Polish territory and was relaxed about the possibility that a rump state might be established there.[70] In a secret additional protocol it agreed to allow those Reich citizens and persons of German heritage living within its sphere of influence to go to Germany.[71]

Both nations stated in a joint declaration that they believed that peace between Germany and the western powers 'would be in the true interests of all nations'. Both governments declared that they would seek to bring an end to the war and, if their efforts proved unsuccessful, this 'would show that England and France are responsible for continuing the war', and both governments would 'consult together about the appropriate steps to take'.[72] Finally, in Directive 5 of 30 September, Hitler established a military administration in occupied Polish territory. He reserved the right to settle the 'political arrangements' in the part of Poland that had neither been annexed by Germany nor was occupied by the Soviet Union.[73]

At the beginning of October, fighting in Poland gradually came to an end. After the occupation of Warsaw, on 2 October, Hitler ordered the bells to be rung throughout the Reich for one hour for a whole week. Three days later, he visited the city in order to take a victory parade by the Wehrmacht. In Schloss Belvedere, the residence of Marshal Piłsudski until his death, he paid tribute to a statesman whom he had long revered. The gesture was intended to demonstrate that he considered the Polish leadership that had taken over following Piłsudski's death and abandoned the rapprochement with Germany to be responsible for the war.[74]

On 6 October, Hitler made a 'peace offer' to the western powers in a speech in the Reichstag. This move was motivated above all by domestic considerations, responding to the German population's pronounced yearning for peace, which continued even after victory over Poland. Hitler's image as a 'peace Chancellor', which had been carefully cultivated during the years before the war, was to remain during the early phase of the conflict and not be immediately replaced by his pose as a 'warlord'. The logic underlying Hitler's proposal was both simple and at the same time insolent. The western powers should stop the war, since the original reason for their intervention, the German attack on Poland, had been removed as a result of the collapse of the Polish state. A 'reordering of the ethnographic situation' in the whole of eastern and south-eastern Europe, that is to say a 'resettlement of nationalities', was necessary, so that 'there are better lines of separation than is the case today'. However, the 'final reorganization of this area' was a problem that only Germany and the Soviet Union could solve. Provided the western powers accepted this, then they could move on to deal with future problems together. Hitler sketched out a comprehensive European security system, and proposed limits on armaments and a convention to protect civilian populations. He stressed once again that his government had no interest in a further revision of the German borders, but simply demanded the return of Germany's colonies.[75]

With this 'offer' Hitler had quite cleverly made the restoration of peace appear to be up to the enemy. If, as was probable, the western powers did *not* accept his offer, he would have the basis for a propaganda campaign blaming Britain and France for continuing the war. In this way the German people could be gradually weaned off their widespread illusions about the possibility of peace and get used to the reality of a lengthy war. The assumption was that this would not damage the image of Hitler as the 'peace chancellor'. And, indeed, asserting that Germany was not guilty of a war started by the western powers became an established ritual leitmotif in numerous diplomatic and public statements by Hitler during the coming months and years.

On the morning of 10 October, it became clear just how strong the hopes for peace were. According to the SD reports 'almost overnight, a rumour that the English government had resigned and the English king had abdicated and that an armistice had been declared spread all over the Reich'. The rumour spread so quickly, among other things, because postal and railway officials had informed their colleagues throughout the Reich of the sensational news by telephone and telegraph. There were outbursts of spontaneous jubilation, in some plants the work breaks ran over time because the employees were busy discussing the new situation. According to the SD, the official denial of the rumour, broadcast on the radio, produced deep depression.[76]

The 'ethnic reorganization' of Poland

From 5 October onwards, Hitler took a number of more or less precipitate decisions, leading, before the month was over, to the replacement of the military occupation in Poland by a civilian administration. The waning prospects for peace with the western powers provided him with the opportunity of subjecting Poland to an 'ethnic reorganization'. This was to be undertaken by radical elements from the Party and SS rather than by the army, which began increasingly to protest against the SS terror in Poland. This had the effect of further damaging the relationship between Hitler and the generals, already under strain as a result of Hitler's plan to attack the West in the autumn.[77]

Around a half of the Polish territory occupied by Germany was directly 'incorporated' into the Reich by enlarging the Prussian provinces of Upper Silesia and East Prussia, as well as by creating two new 'Reich Gaus', West

Prussia and Posen, soon renamed Danzig–West Prussia and the Wartheland. The official line was that this was not in fact a restoration of the territorial situation existing prior to the First World War, an idea shared by the Foreign Ministry and the Interior Ministry.[78] Instead, in accordance with Hitler's instructions,[79] and following Göring's initiative, territory twice the size of the previous area was integrated into the Reich, territory that, with the exception of Danzig, was overwhelmingly inhabited by Poles. The Danzig Gauleiter, Albert Forster, and the president of the Danzig senate, Arthur Greiser, took over power in the two new Reich Gaus as Reich governors [Reichsstatthalter]. The Reich governors were entitled to control the whole of the Reich administration in the two Gaus and, through their position as Gauleiters, to secure the influence of the Party. Hitler specifically insisted on the Gauleiters being made as powerful as possible.[80] This provided the pre-conditions for a ruthless 'Germanization policy' in the two Reich Gaus.[81]

As far as the treatment of the remaining Polish territories was concerned, with his decision during this period to establish a 'General Government' [Generalgouvernement] Hitler set the course for a radical 'ethnic political' reorganization of central Poland. On 7 October, he signed an edict 'For the Consolidation of the Ethnic German Nation' with which he assigned the Reichsführer SS the task of organizing the resettlement of Reich and ethnic Germans living in the Polish and Baltic territories occupied by the Soviet Union, the 'elimination of the corrupting influence' of 'alien population elements' and the 'establishment of new areas for German settlement through a programme of resettlement'.[82]

On 17 October, Hitler explained to a small group in the Reich Chancellery the basic guidelines for the government and administration of the future General Government. Those present included Keitel, Himmler, Hess, Frick, Lammers, Stuckart, and Frank, in other words all those members of the leadership who were involved. Basically, according to Hitler, the General Government should not 'become part of the German Reich or an adminis-trative district of the Reich'. The German administration did not have the task of 'creating a model state exemplifying German order or to reform the country economically and financially'. At the same time, they must prevent 'a Polish intelligentsia from forming a leadership cadre'. The standard of liv-ing should be kept low so that labour could be recruited for the Reich. The new German administration should work with its own clear lines of respon-sibility and must not be dependent on the Berlin ministries. The type of rule exercised would be that appropriate to 'a tough ethnic struggle' and would not be limited by 'any legal restrictions'. 'The methods will be irreconcilable with our normal principles.' The territory is important above all militarily as an 'advance glacis' and, for this reason, the infrastructure must be maintained. Beyond that, however, 'a consolidation of the conditions in Poland' was not desirable. Those in charge of the territory must also enable 'the *Reich territory* to be cleansed of Jews and Polacks'.[83]

Hitler had thereby set out the decisive guidelines for German rule in the General Government. It was a colonial type administration free from legal norms and bureaucratic rules, which was to assert German interests brutally and arbitrarily against an indigenous population that was classed as 'racially inferior', and to do so simply by issuing orders. In speaking of this as 'devil's work' he made his intentions very clear. The constitutional status of the General Government remained intentionally vague. It was not subject to the Berlin government, but (via the Governor General) to Hitler directly; it was neither Reich nor foreign territory, but, according to a term increasingly used, an 'adjacent territory of the Reich'.

Hitler's decision to establish the General Government marked the conclusion of a decision-making process that had begun, less than two months before, with talk of maintaining an autonomous Polish rump state and moderate annexations. Now the country had been split up and handed over to rulers who were aiming to establish a racist regime. State authorities (Wehrmacht, the Foreign Ministry, Interior and Food Ministries) were excluded from the process of reorganization, which was mainly in the hands of Party functionaries and the SS. A completely new form of civilian occupation administration was constructed in the General Government that specifically overturned traditional administrative principles, while 'in the East' Himmler secured for himself a base where he wielded almost absolute power. And, with the new 'Reich Gaus', a new type of regional administration had been created (at the time the term 'middle level' was used) in which power lay in the hands of the Gauleiters as Reich governors.

Now, after the end of the war, Hitler began making contemptuous comments about Poles and Jews. His attempt to make Poland an accomplice in his plans for a war against the Soviet Union, brusquely rejected in spring 1939 by Beck, had proved to be a pipe dream. Given Hitler's racist world view, it did not take him long to categorize his recalcitrant neighbour as 'subhuman'. The Poles were 'more animals than human beings, totally dull and stupid',[84] 'frightful material'; Jews were 'the most ghastly people one can possibly imagine'.[85] These comments show that he now considered himself fully justified in the aim with which he had entered the war – to eliminate the 'active forces there' – and now wanted to implement it.

As a result, after the end of the war, the new rulers increased and systematized their employment of terror in Poland. From the end of October, Einsatzgruppen and 'Self-Defence' units, formed from members of the German minority, carried out the so-called 'Intelligentsia Action',[86] which was coordinated by the RHSA and involved mass arrests and executions, particularly of teachers, members of the professions, former officers, civil servants, clergy, landowners, leading members of Polish nationalist organizations, politicians, and, above all, Jews.[87]

During the autumn of 1939 and the following winter, SS units murdered at least 7,700 patients in mental hospitals in the newly annexed Polish territory, but also in the neighbouring Gau, Pomerania, in the 'old Reich'.[88] This action was independent of the 'Euthanasia' murder campaign, beginning at the same time in the Reich itself, to which we shall return. Most of the victims were shot. However, in Fort VI within the Posen fortifications the Gestapo built a gas chamber, in which Polish patients were murdered with carbon monoxide, the first use of gas by the Nazis. Himmler is known to have visited the site in December 1939 in order to inspect the murder procedure.[89] In total the 'Self-Defence' forces and the Einsatzgruppen murdered tens of thousands of people during the first months of the German occupation in Poland.[90]

The files from Heydrich's office show that, responding to proposals from Himmler, between 14 and 21 September Hitler made the basic decision to deport all the Jews in the annexed territories and from the whole of the Reich itself to a 'Jewish state under German administration' on the eastern border of German-occupied Polish territory. As their 'final destination' he contemplated moving these Jews to the eastern part of Poland occupied by the Soviet Union.[91]

After the spheres of influence of the Soviet Union and the Reich had been redefined on 28 September, the region between the Vistula and the Bug, the later district of Lublin in the General Government, came under German occupation, creating space for the future 'reservation'. However, according to the statements Hitler made on 29 September concerning the future division of Poland, this 'Reich ghetto', as Heydrich called it, was now to take in not only Jews, but also all 'elements which are in any way unreliable'.[92]

Hitler made no secret of the idea of a 'Jewish reservation'. On 26 September, he was already mentioning it to the Swedish industrialist, Dahlerus;[93] on 1 October he explained the idea of an 'ethnic cleansing' to the Italian foreign minister;[94] and, in his speech to the Reichstag on 6 October, he announced 'a resettlement of nationalities', linked to the 'attempt to sort out and regulate the Jewish problem'.[95] The German press was informed confidentially about the plans for a reservation and immediately speculation about a Jewish 'reservation' emerged in the foreign press.[96]

The so-called Nisko action was the first attempt to implement Hitler's order for substantial deportations to be carried out.[97] The plan, prepared by Eichmann on the authority of the Gestapo chief Heinrich Müller was to deport 70,000 to 80,000 Jews from the new Silesian district of Kattowitz (Katowice) and from Mährisch-Ostrau (in the Protectorate). Eichmann considered these deportations, which initially affected 4,700 people,[98] as only the first step in the expulsion of all Jews from Reich territory that was to be set in motion in a few weeks, following a further order from Hitler.[99] He was referring to an instruction from Hitler that had already been given 'to resettle 300,000 Jews from the old Reich and the Eastern Marches'. This was to be implemented following an initial field report, which was presumably going to be submitted to Hitler.[100] To achieve this, Eichmann ordered Berlin officials to prepare a list of all Jews who had been registered in Germany and which Jewish religious communities they belonged to.[101] However, the deportations had hardly begun, when they were halted again by the RSHA on 20 October.[102] The Berlin authorities feared that a continuation of the Nisko transports would get in the way of the major resettlement of ethnic Germans from the Soviet occupied territories recently launched by Himmler.[103] Moreover, in the meantime, Hitler had begun to have military concerns. On 17 October, he told Keitel that the future General Government 'has military significance for us and can be used for forward deployment'. This objective clearly could not be reconciled with creating a Jewish reservation. Nevertheless, Hitler insisted that in the long term 'control of this territory... must enable us to cleanse Reich territory of Jews and Polacks'.[104]

Although the Nisko project was quickly halted, it provides an insight into the SS's ideas at the time on how to implement Hitler's deportation order. The deportation trains ended up in Nisko on the river San, directly on the border with the district of Lublin, where the reservation was to be established. However, the majority of those involved were not put in the 'Transit

Camp', which, as a result of the precipitate way in which the project had been launched, was still being built, but forcibly driven away and left to fend for themselves. Had the deportations been continued and, after a few weeks, extended to all Jews throughout the Reich, the arrival of winter would have created catastrophic conditions, resulting in a high death rate and a mass flight over the line of demarcation into Russian-occupied territory.[105] The 'Jewish reservation' would have become a death zone.

'Euthanasia'

With the support above all of the SS and the Party, Hitler used the war against Poland to unleash a radicalization of racial policy, which, as we have seen, took shape above all in occupied Poland. This is reflected in the systematic mass murders, the imposition of a civilian administration with which to implement the most brutal 'Germanization plans', and the, albeit stalled, mass deportation of Jews into a death zone. On the outbreak of war, another murder project was begun: the systematic extermination of handicapped people carried out under the misleadingly named 'euthanasia' programme.

The euthanasia murders have a long pre-history. After the end of the First World War, there were growing demands for the 'humane' killing of people who were incurably sick and also 'useless' psychiatric patients. A number of factors were responsible for such ideas being seriously discussed during the post-war period, both among experts and among the general public. The millions of deaths during the First World War, but also the high rate of deaths in the 'lunatic asylums' because of war shortages resulted in utilitarian taking priority over humanitarian considerations. There was particular discussion as to whether the high costs of care for patients in asylums in the crisis-ridden post-war period were sustainable. Nevertheless, during the Weimar Republic the advocates of the killing of the mentally ill remained in the minority.[106]

From 1933 onwards, however, a more radical 'eugenic approach' became increasingly dominant within German psychiatry. After the mid-1930s, 'useless' patients incapable of work were increasingly systematically neglected, leading to a marked increase in the death rate in asylums.[107] At the same time, the demand for the 'elimination of lives unworthy of life' did not go unchallenged. From 1933 to 1937, in the debate among specialists conducted in public, the killing of the incurably sick or of 'inferiors' was a highly controversial issue.[108] This was also true within the judicial sphere. The Nazi Minister of Justice in Prussia and later Reich Minister for Churches, Hanns Kerrl, declared in a memorandum published in 1933 that the killing of incurable mental patients by organs of the state should not be regarded as an offence in itself.[109] However, the official commission on revising the penal code, meeting during 1934, declined to respond to the demand for the 'elimination of lives unworthy of life' to be free from prosecution, and it only surfaced again in August 1939 in the form of a draft law.[110]

If we look more closely at what was a decidedly nuanced debate, it becomes clear that 'euthanasia' was advocated above all in the event of a general emergency, in time of war, and in the case of malformed children; the granting of permission for abortions for eugenic reasons in 1934/35, expressly supported by Hitler, led the way in this matter.[111] However, the fact that the debate remained undecided until 1939 resulted above all from the lack of a clear statement by the 'Führer'.

Hitler had already dealt extensively with eugenic issues in *Mein Kampf* and, among other things, demanded sterilization and birth control.[112] In view of his comments about natural selective breeding, the right of the stronger, and the threat of degeneration through protection of the weak, a commitment to the 'elimination of lives unworthy of life' would not have been surprising, particularly as discussion about it had been relatively widespread after the publication of the book with that title by Karl Binding and Alfred Hoche in 1920.[113] Hitler avoided taking up that position, however. In his speeches during the years 1925–29, only once, at the Party Rally in 1929, did he go so far as to claim that 'if a million children were born annually in Germany and 700,000 to 800,000 of the weakest people were eliminated this might in the end increase our strength'.[114]

From 1933 onwards, as we have seen,[115] Hitler had actively supported a serious 'hereditary health policy', starting with the Sterilization Law of July 1933. He is alleged to have promised the Reich Doctors' Leader, Gerhard Wagner, at the 1935 Party Rally, to introduce 'euthanasia' in the event of war; but the only evidence for this is a post-war statement by Hitler's personal physician, Karl Brandt.[116] Whether or not this conversation took place, Wagner was in fact one of the leading advocates of the 'euthanasia' project in the Third Reich. On the other hand, in the large number of Hitler's statements surviving from the years 1933–38 there is not a single one suggesting that he was a supporter of the idea of 'euthanasia'.[117]

It was no accident that the mass murders of the sick began with a programme of children's 'euthanasia', in other words with the group of victims,
whose killing, since 1933, had been repeatedly described by its advocates as
a humanitarian move and as a 'release'. And, significantly, it began in August
1939 at a time of intensive preparation for war. The 'emergency' of a war
with an anticipated large loss of 'valuable' human life was considered, from
a 'demographic–biological' perspective, to provide the justification for the
radical 'culling' of 'inferior elements'. It appeared plausible that these murders could be carried out 'more smoothly and easily' (as the 1935 argument
attributed to Hitler put it) under the exceptional conditions of wartime.

According to the post-war statements of a number of those responsible
for the killings, the launch of the children's 'euthanasia' programme was
prompted by an individual case. In response to a petition from parents to the
Führer's Chancellery, which was responsible for dealing with such requests,
Hitler authorized his personal physician, Brandt, to have their seriously
malformed child killed.[118] At the same time as this individual assignment,
Hitler authorized Brandt, together with Philipp Bouhler, the head of the
Führer's Chancellery, to develop a procedure for dealing with similar cases.
The ambitious Bouhler, determined to extend his office's responsibilities to
a new sphere of activity, together with his deputy, Viktor Brack, then set up
a small group of experts. For the purposes of disguise, the murder programme was run by the 'Reich Committee for the Scientific Registration of
Serious Hereditary and Congenital Illnesses', which had originally been
established, to deal, among other things, with problematic sterilization cases.

On 18 August 1939, the Reich Interior Ministry issued a 'highly confidential' circular introducing 'a duty to report deformed etc. births'. Medical
personnel were obliged to report to the Public Health Offices 'serious congenital defects' in children up to the age of three. These reports were then
sent to the Reich Committee, which passed the forms on to three assessors,
who examined them in turn. If the decision was negative, after the parents
had given their consent to the children being hospitalized, they were sent to
one of thirty so-called child specialist clinics, where they were murdered. It
has been estimated that by 1945 there were around 5,000 victims of the
children's 'euthanasia' programme.[119]

As already mentioned, alongside the start of this children's murder programme during the autumn of 1939, the SS began another 'euthanasia'
programme involving asylums in Poland. The third murder programme
under the rubric of 'euthanasia', the killing of adult patients in the Reich,

was being prepared from the summer of 1939 onwards. After Hitler had given his approval in principle at a meeting in the summer of 1939, attended by Lammers, Bormann, and the state secretary in the Health Ministry, Dr Leonardo Conti, Bouhler and Brack managed to seize control of this project as well. In the summer of 1939, Bouhler held a meeting of around 15 to 20 physicians in which he announced the start of a general programme of 'euthanasia'. This move was justified in terms of the need to free up hospital space and nurses for the coming war. With the aid of the Reich Criminal Police Department's Technical Institute, which had already supplied the poison required for the children's 'euthanasia' programme, an appropriate method for killing was found in the form of carbon monoxide gas.[120]

An organization to carry out the project was established at a meeting in the Führer's Chancellery on 9 October. Party functionaries, civil servants, and doctors agreed that around one in five psychiatric in-patients should be killed, in other words between 65,000 and 70,000 people. It was probably also on 9 October that Hitler wrote a note on a piece of his personal writing paper giving Bouhler and Brandt 'the authority to extend the powers of specific doctors in such a way that, after the most careful assessment of their condition, those suffering from illnesses deemed to be incurable may be granted a mercy death'. Significantly, he backdated the note to 1 September 1939, in order to emphasize once again the link between the war and the 'destruction of worthless life'.[121] As Hitler had not given his assent to the procedure being legalized on the grounds of the need to keep it secret,[122] this note provided those responsible for the 'euthanasia' programme with the necessary legitimation.

From October 1939 onwards, mental hospitals in the Reich were instructed to report all patients who were suffering from specific mental defects and who 'cannot be employed in the asylum or only in purely mechanical tasks'. Furthermore, all patients, regardless of their diagnosis or employability, were to be reported if they had 'been in asylums continuously for at least five years, are confined as criminal lunatics, or do not possess German nationality or are not of German or related blood'; this provision was directed, in particular, at Jewish patients.

To carry out the 'euthanasia murders' the Führer's Chancellery constructed an elaborate cover organization with the title T4, after the Führer Chancellery's headquarters address in Berlin, Tiergartenstrasse 4. The victims were selected through an elaborate procedure. The forms provided by the mental hospitals were examined very superficially by three assessors, and a senior assessor then gave the final verdict, on the basis of which the head-quarters organized the 'transport to transfer' those affected. Initially, in order to cover their tracks, the patients were transferred to intermediate institutions, from where they were sent to one of six centres specially equipped to kill them. There they were murdered in gas chambers.

During the first half of 1940, the 'euthanasia' murders under the T4 programme were gradually extended to the various individual states and provinces within the Reich until eventually virtually the whole of the country had been included. The quota they were aiming for of 20 per cent of patients was in some places considerably exceeded and in others sometimes under-shot. In autumn 1940 this prompted the planners considerably to increase and then, in April 1941, to reduce the projected total of victims, until, having reached the planned figure of 70,000 murders, in August 1941 the T4 programme was halted.[123] We shall examine the reasons for this decision later.

With its mass shootings in Poland and the murder of mental patients, Hitler's regime had already embarked on a policy of systematic, racist-motivated extermination nearly two years before the start of the mass murder of the Jews. To implement the 'euthanasia' programme they had devised a complex, bureaucratic procedure involving a division of labour. The key elements were the 'selection' of the victims, their deportation to special murder sites, gas chambers, and mass executions (Poland). The victims were misled until the very last minute, and the perpetrators were enabled to evade the issue of personal responsibility, as they appeared to be performing only limited functions in a process that was taking place under scientific auspices and made necessary by force of circumstance. As with the murder of the Jews, the 'euthanasia' programme can be described as an 'open secret'. While the murder of mental patients was subject to stricter secrecy, the extent of the operation made it impossible to disguise.[124] Moreover, by making barely concealed references to the 'elimination' of 'inferiors', the regime showed it had few qualms about admitting it, thereby confirming the rumours that were in circulation.[125] The fact that, from the summer of 1940 onwards, all Jewish inmates of asylums, around 4,000–5,000 persons, were murdered irrespective of the state of their mental illness or their ability to work, illustrates the close connection between the 'euthanasia' programme and the Holocaust.[126]

Finally, there is a further parallel between the 'euthanasia' programme and the Holocaust: Hitler bore the main responsibility for both. Whereas in the case of the 'euthanasia' programme this is proved by the piece of personal writing paper with his signature, in that of the murder of the European Jews it can be reconstructed through a mass of detailed evidence. However, two years after the start of the 'euthanasia' programme and directly after it was stopped, Hitler came to prefer the 'unwritten order' to its written version.

30

Resistance

During the months following his rapid victory over Poland, Hitler gradually adjusted to what was a completely changed situation. He was now the ally of his arch-enemy, the Bolshevik Soviet Union, and found himself at war with Britain, which, since the 1920s, he had regarded as his ideal partner. Failure to bring the war to a rapid conclusion on the basis of the new status quo would mean a renewal of hostilities by the western powers, and yet he lacked the resources for a lengthy war. Thus, without waiting for the response of the British government to his 'peace offer' of 6 October, Hitler pressed forward energetically with his plan to attack in the West that autumn. A day after the speech, he told Halder that 'when the autumn mists arrive' Belgium would appeal to France for help and they must preempt that with a 'decisive operation'.[1]

On 9 October, he prepared a memorandum, setting out in detail his reasons for an attack in the West. The following day, he read out and commented on this document at a meeting with Brauchitsch and Halder. His basic ideas were then incorporated in his 'Directive No. 6 for the Conduct of the War'. He told the generals that, if the western powers did not soon indicate a willingness to make peace, he would attack France through the Netherlands and Belgium, if possible during the autumn, in order to smash the French armed forces and those of her allies. He would then establish a base within the conquered territory for a war on land and sea against Britain. Hitler claimed that, as far as could be seen, Russia would remain neutral; however, this could change in '8 months, in a year, let alone in a few years' time'.[2]

When Chamberlain rejected Hitler's proposals of 6 October in a speech on 12 October, the 'Führer' immediately responded with an exceptionally polemical government statement claiming that the Prime Minister had spurned 'the hand of peace'.[3] As a result, for the time being, all further attempts at mediation were pointless. While, at the end of September, he had appeared outwardly optimistic about Britain's willingness to negotiate, he now went to the other extreme. He even told Goebbels that he was now glad that 'we can go for England'.[4] His rapid change of stance indicates that the peace offer was made primarily for domestic political reasons, and Hitler now regarded its rejection as an opportunity to place the blame for the continuation of the war on Britain and France.

Hitler's determination to extend the war met with some reservations among members of the regime. Apart from Göring, the army leadership in particular was sceptical. The generals considered the prospects of success as minimal; in their view, the state of the armaments economy alone sufficed to rule out another major offensive. During October, for a short time, the opponents of the regime within the government machine were boosted by the continuing anti-war mood among the population. They once again established contact with one another and even contemplated a coup. At the centre of the conspiracy was a group of young officers within the army leadership, who looked to Franz Halder, the Chief of the General Staff, for support. He does appear to have considered a violent change of regime as a last resort if the war in the West could not be prevented.[5]

On 14 October, Halder discussed the situation with Brauchitsch, who suggested three options: 'Attack, wait and see, fundamental changes', although it was clear that none of these possibilities offered 'certain prospects of success'. 'Fundamental changes' evidently meant a coup d'état, an idea the two generals considered the least attractive of the three options, 'because basically it would have negative and damaging repercussions'.[6] On 16 October, Hitler told Brauchitsch that he had given up hope of an agreement with the West, and fixed the period from 15 to 20 November as the earliest possible date for an attack.[7]

Hitler's Directive No. 7 of 18 October permitted, for the time being, the 'crossing of the French frontier by reconnaissance units' and the over-flying of French territory by fighters.[8] The Directive Yellow, issued by the commander-in-chief of the army on 19 October, reflected Hitler's plans for the campaign. The aim was to defeat the Allied forces with an offensive through Belgium and the Netherlands and, 'at the same time, to capture as much Dutch, Belgian, and northern French territory as possible in order to provide a base for an effective sea and air campaign against England'.[9]

In view of the widespread scepticism (to put it mildly) within the military about his plans for an attack, Hitler tried to convince the civilian and military leadership through a series of speeches and interviews. On 21 October, he made a speech lasting several hours to the Party's Reichsleiters and Gauleiters. He told them he was determined to conduct the war, which he now considered 'almost unavoidable', 'ruthlessly and with all means until victory has been achieved'. According to another record of the meeting, Hitler had told them he would launch a major offensive in the West in about 14 days' time. Then, when he 'had forced England and France to their knees' he would 'once again turn to the East and sort things out there, for at the moment, as a result of the present difficulties, the situation had become disordered and confused. It had become clear that the Russian Army was not up to much, that its soldiers were badly trained and armed. Once he had achieved this goal, then he would create a Germany as of old, in other words, he would incorporate Belgium and Switzerland.'[10]

On 22 October, Halder, who was in a state of anxiety about the, in his view, insoluble task he had been set, learnt that Hitler wanted to attack on 12 November.[11] On 25 October, Hitler discussed his plans for the offensive with his military chiefs and found himself confronted with the concerns of the professionals.[12] He ordered that the commander-in-chief's Directive 'Yellow' of 19 October should once more be revised. The occupation of the Netherlands, originally in the plan, was dropped; the directive now envisaged 'destroying' (and no longer 'defeating') the Allied forces north of the Somme, and driving through to the Channel coast. In other words this meant no longer forcing the enemy out of Belgium, but surrounding them through an advance reaching deep into northern France.[13]

Hitler placed the military leadership under pressure not only as far as the launch of the attack was concerned. In contrast to his lack of interference in operational matters during the Polish war, he now began increasingly to intervene actively in the purely military planning of the attack. On 27 October, Brauchitsch once again tried to get Hitler to agree to change the date for the attack to the end of November; however, the 'Führer' insisted on sticking to 12 November.[14]

In the meantime, Halder tried to recruit opponents of the attack. At the end of October, he sent his deputy, Carl-Heinrich von Stülpnagel, to the commanders of the three army groups in the West, to secure their backing in the event of an open conflict with Hitler. Only General Wihelm von Leep, the commander of Army Group C, responded positively. However, the generals all shared Brauchitsch's and Halder's critical assessment of an attack in the West. After a trip to Army Groups A and B, undertaken with

Brauchitsch at the beginning of November, Halder concluded from his meetings: 'We cannot anticipate a decisive success in a land war.'[15]

On 5 November, a serious confrontation occurred between Hitler and Brauchitsch. Hitler was furious when, in order to justify his doubts about a western offensive, Brauchitsch referred, among other things, to certain weaknesses shown by the infantry in Poland. Hitler demanded proof of this assertion, declaring that he would fly to the front himself in order to assess the troops' morale. After this confrontation Brauchitsch left, totally demoralized.[16]

The combination of Brauchitsch's evident weakness, Hitler's threat that he would soon deal with the 'spirit of Zossen' (the headquarters of OKH), and his order now definitely fixing the date of the attack as the 12 November, sufficed to persuade Halder, who feared the exposure of his soundings about a coup, to cease his opposition. From now onwards he concentrated solely on his military duties. The real regime opponents, basically the group of youngish officers in the OKH, who were much more committed to acting, then abandoned their plans. The result of this confrontation had shown that Hitler had no challenger among the military leadership who could mount a serious opposition to his war plans, and was prepared to act to prevent him from implementing what was regarded as a catastrophic policy. Thus, autumn 1939 can be considered only with reservations as the second phase of the conspiracy against Hitler.

On 8 November, Hitler appeared at the celebrations in the Bürgerbräukeller, which had been significantly curtailed as a result of the war, in order to give his usual speech.[17] This time the speech was dominated, above all, by an attack on Britain and designed to spread confidence in victory. However, it was much shorter than expected because Hitler had been forced at short notice to alter his plans for the return to Berlin, and had to catch the regular night train, to which his special train was attached. During the stop in Nuremberg a message was passed to the train, which to begin with Hitler simply could not believe. Shortly after he had left the Bürgerbräukeller, there had been a big explosion resulting in eight deaths and sixty injured.[18]

Hitler immediately agreed with Goebbels, who was accompanying him, that had he not left early he would certainly have been assassinated.[19] German propaganda began immediately to blame the British Secret Service for the attack.[20] For days, Hitler and his entourage speculated about who could have done it, without having any definite information.[21] When, after a few days, the culprit was revealed to be a carpenter, Georg Elser, Hitler and Goebbels were convinced that he was merely the 'creature' of the Nazi Party renegade, Otto Strasser, who was living in Switzerland, and who, in turn, had been acting at the behest of the British Secret Service.[22] Hitler then took a few days before deciding to issue a communiqué about Elser's arrest. German propaganda now attempted to establish a connection between Elser, Strasser, and the Secret Service by including 'revelations' about two British agents, Richard Stevens and Sigismund Payne Best, who had been abducted from Venlo in Holland on 9 November.[23] Naturally, the fact that a single individual had almost succeeded in assassinating Hitler and important members of the Nazi leadership could not be revealed in the media, nor be allowed to become public through a court case. The same was true of Elser's motives. For this loner was not acting on behalf of any political organization and was simply aiming to get rid of Hitler as the main cause of the war. Elser was by no means alone in his conviction that, if this war were not quickly brought to an end, it would be fatal for Germany.

The spectacular abductions at Venlo and the regime's decision to accuse the Secret Service of carrying out the assassination attempt produced such strong responses from the western powers and the neutral states that the success of the surprise attack was put in further doubt. It had already been postponed from 12 to 15 November at the earliest, and now had to be postponed again, not for the last time that year.

Preparations for the attack in the West

On 23 November, Hitler gave a speech to the military leadership in which he made clear his determination to expand the war at all costs, even against the advice of his hesitant generals, and took the opportunity to humiliate the commander-in-chief of the army in front of the top brass.

In his speech he projected the image of a ruthless conqueror. After Munich, he said, it was clear to him 'from the very first moment that I could not be satisfied with the Sudeten German territory. That was only a partial solution. The decision to march into Bohemia was made. There followed the establishment of the Protectorate and with that the basis for the action against Poland was laid, but I was not quite clear at the time whether I should start first against the East and then in the West or vice versa.' Then Hitler moved on to his favourite topic: 'the adjustment of living space to the size of population'. A solution to this problem was possible only 'with the sword'. At this time, they were engaged in a 'racial struggle'. Basically, he had 'not built up the Wehrmacht in order not to fight. I always wanted to fight. I wanted to solve the problem sooner or later.' In view of the overall situation, he had decided to attack first in the East. After the defeat of Poland, they were now in the fortunate position of not having to fight a two-front war. For the moment Russia was not dangerous; it was weakened 'by numerous internal issues'; its army was 'of little account'. This situation would last for one or two years. The fact that he had survived the assassination attempt had convinced him that Providence had chosen him to lead the German people to victory in this war. As a result, his willingness to take a risk had considerably increased.

'As the final factor I must in all modesty name my own person. I am irreplaceable . . . I am convinced of the power of my intellect and my determination.' This was particularly important, for 'wars are always ended only by the destruction of the opponent. Anyone who believes otherwise is irresponsible. Time is on the side of our adversaries. . . . The enemy will not make peace if the balance of forces is not in our favour. No compromise. We have to be tough with ourselves. I shall strike and not capitulate.' The 'fate of the Reich' depends 'on me alone', and he would act accordingly. Their forces were still more numerous and stronger than those of their opponents in the West. They had to preempt a possible attack on the Ruhr through Belgium and the Netherlands, particularly since the occupation of both countries by German troops was an essential prerequisite for the further air and sea war against Britain. 'My decision is unalterable. I shall attack France and England at the most favourable opportunity. Breaching the neutrality of Belgium and Holland is irrelevant. No one will question that when we've won'.[24]

Then he moved on to deal with Brauchitsch. The latter's questioning the effectiveness of the troops, which is how Hitler interpreted the recent confrontation with his army commander-in-chief, had 'hurt him deeply'. As far as Fedor von Bock, the commander-in-chief of Army Group B, was concerned, the whole speech was marked by 'a certain degree of discontent with the army leadership'. According to Bock, Hitler knew 'that, at this point, the majority of the generals did not believe the attack could achieve a decisive success.'[25] Following the speech, Hitler reproached Brauchitsch and Halder for the generals' negative attitude; however, when Brauchitsch offered his resignation, Hitler refused to accept it, and so the army commander-in-chief remained in office under a cloud.[26]

The 'pause' that occurred after the defeat of Poland did, however, give Hitler's regime the opportunity of reorganizing the armaments sector during the winter of 1939/40. The outbreak of war had produced significant shortages of raw materials. However, during the following months, despite the Allied blockade, they could be partially compensated for with the help of neutral states and, not least, through the trade agreement with the Soviet Union.[27]

In the economic sphere, experts did not consider that the camouflaged mobilization, carried out at the end of August and beginning of September, had been a success. This was because many planned economic measures had not been implemented at the start of the war, and even during the following weeks the rapid victory over Poland made such changes appear unnecessary. The economics staff of the OKW, the Economics Ministry, and the Reich Food Estate were banking on it being a long war. The economy had to be adapted to wartime conditions: investment in infrastructure was needed to survive the blockade; exports had to be increased to enable the import of vital goods; the basis of the food supply had to be further expanded. All this meant that it was necessary to refrain from undertaking major military operations and remain on the defensive.[28]

Hitler, however, who was banking on a rapid and decisive military success against the West, had other priorities. On 21 August 1939, he had already signed a Führer order, prepared by Göring, putting the Ju-88 programme, which had stalled during 1939, once again into high gear; up to 300 of this type of aircraft were to be built every month. However, Hitler cannot, at this point, have foreseen the results of his order. He had signed a general order, enabling the Luftwaffe to secure a substantial quota of raw materials (for example around half the consumption of aluminium) and a large part of Germany's industrial capacity.[29] The navy's Z-Plan, which since 1939 had dominated German armaments production and was only going to be completed by the mid-1940s, was now replaced by a relatively modest programme of U-boat construction.[30]

Above all, however, during the autumn of 1939, Hitler launched a massive munitions programme. In November he demanded a tripling of the munitions production planned by the Army Weapons Office. This was a fundamental change of course compared with his previous interventions, which had focused, above all, on increasing the supply of weapons for the Wehrmacht. He also issued various specific orders concerning the production of artillery and munitions.[31] By the end of the month, he had made his intentions more precise through a 'Führer demand', the final version of which he signed on 12 December. It contained planned monthly production quotas for artillery of particular calibres, and revealed that Hitler's ideas concerning the campaign in the West were strongly influenced by his own experiences in the First World War: artillery barrages would achieve the breakthrough.[32] The munitions and Ju-88 programmes were set to absorb two-thirds of armaments capacity during the first ten months of the war.[33]

In 1940 Hitler's decisions began to have an impact. The redirection of raw materials and the new armaments priorities led to a sharp increase in German armaments production and an 11 per cent per capita reduction in private consumption. This reduction was to continue increasing until the end of the war. Thus, the claim that the regime was attempting to avoid imposing too much of a burden on the population for political reasons is unsustainable. Hitler wanted a quick and decisive end to the war in 1940 not because he did not believe the German people were up to fighting a long war, but simply because Germany's economic basis, even if exploited to the limit, was incapable of sustaining a long war.[34]

By July 1940, the output of armaments had doubled compared with that in January. However, the information given to Hitler in February 1940 did not yet show this increase, but instead conveyed the impression that armaments production had stagnated since the outbreak of war. Hitler, therefore, decided on a reorganization. On 17 March, he appointed Fritz Todt, the General Plenipotentiary for Construction, successful builder of the autobahns and the West Wall, and head of the Wehrmacht's construction organization named after him, as the newly created Reich Minister of Munitions.[35] Thus, the reputation Todt acquired in the following months as a successful armaments manager derived less from the rapid organizational changes in the munitions sector that he introduced immediately after his appointment, and more from the new priorities in the distribution of raw materials, which had been set before his appointment.[36]

The year 1940 began with an event that forced Germany to revise completely its plans for the western offensive, resulting in the plan of operations that in May 1940 led to a rapid and surprising victory in the West. On 10 January a Luftwaffe courier plane, which was off course, made an emergency landing in Belgium. Documents being carried by a paratrooper officer on board fell into the hands of the Belgian military authorities, revealing details of the German plans for the attack in the West, including a paratroop assault on Belgium.[37] The affair prompted Hitler to issue a 'basic order', which had to be posted up in every office in the Wehrmacht. It stated that 'No one. No office, no officer must have knowledge of any secret matter, unless for official reasons it is essential'; no one was to be allowed to know *more* than was absolutely necessary for carrying out their task, and no one was to be put in possession of this information earlier than necessary.[38] The aim of Hitler's clamp-down was drastically to reduce the number of people who had access to his strategic-operational decisions and to channel the flow of information. In Halder's view, expressed after the war, Hitler's objective was to prevent the military leadership from forming an independent assessment of the situation based on a comprehensive picture of it.[39]

That incident in Mechelen in Belgium also prompted Hitler to review his most recent decision to attack in the West. It dated from 10 January, and envisaged 17 January as the date of attack.[40] A few days later, he cancelled the attack, telling Jodl he wanted to place the whole plan of the operation on 'an entirely new basis, in particular in relation to secrecy and the element of surprise'. On 20 January, Hitler told the army and Luftwaffe chiefs that, in view of the fact that the enemy had acquired concrete ideas about German intentions, and these had been confirmed by the 'airman affair', the war could now be won only if they ensured with a 'fanatical determination' that 'operational ideas [remained] secret'. The period between the giving of the order and the attack must be radically shortened in order to maintain the element of surprise.[41] The following day he demanded from Brauchitsch and Halder 'permanent readiness for action, in order to make use of possible favourable weather conditions in February'.[42] The army leadership ensured the implementation of his directive: from 1 February 1940 onwards, the army in the West was on standby to launch an offensive within twenty-four hours.[43]

The renewed postponement of the campaign provided the German leadership with the opportunity fundamentally to alter the plan of attack. The original plan of the OKH envisaged the main attack as focused on two armies advancing north and south of the Belgian fortress complex of Liège. From now onwards, however, Hitler began increasingly to intervene in the operational planning.

In November 1939, Hitler had responded to the Luftwaffe's arguments that, in the event of war, they would have to reckon on the transfer of enemy air force units to the Netherlands, by insisting that the army should partially occupy the country, although without 'Fortress Holland' in the centre and with only limited forces. At the same time, in November, Hitler had demanded that the army shift the main focus of attack to the southern flank of the front.[44] The Chief of Staff of Army Group A, Erich von Manstein, was thinking along the same lines, also wanting the main focus of the attack to be in southern Belgium. The enemy would not anticipate a tank offensive through the Ardennes, which, despite the obstacle presented by the wooded hills, would be entirely feasible. German forces should advance towards the Somme, and then along it towards the Channel, thereby cutting off and destroying the enemy forces in Belgium and northern France.[45] On 17 February, Hitler's Wehrmacht adjutant, Schmundt, arranged a meeting between Hitler and Manstein, whereupon the 'Führer' adopted Manstein's ideas, ensuring that the operational plans were revised accordingly. On 24 February, the OKH issued a new directive, moving the main focus of attack to the southern flank, and also ordering the rapid occupation of the Netherlands with much larger forces.[46]

Mussolini, a reluctant ally

In January, Goebbels noted down comments Hitler made at a small soirée about his future plans: he was 'determined to fight a major war against England'; it must be 'swept out of Europe and France must be deposed as a great power'. Then Germany would have 'hegemony and Europe would have peace'. After that he wanted 'to spend a few more years in office, carry out social reforms and his building plans, and then withdraw'. He would then 'simply hover over politics as a benign spirit' and write down all the things that still preoccupied him, 'the gospel of National Socialism, so to speak'.[47] A few days later, Goebbels noted Hitler's remarks about the 'the old Holy Roman Empire', whose imperial tradition he wished to continue and with a clear goal: 'on the basis of our organization and our elite we must automatically one day come to rule the world'.[48]

However, there was still a long way to go. In terms of foreign policy, at the beginning of 1940 the main objective was to repair the damaged relationship with Hitler's main ally, Mussolini. For the 'Duce' was clearly still very uncertain about whether or not to enter the war on Hitler's side. At the beginning of January, Hitler received a long letter from Mussolini in which he subjected the policies of his German ally to very frank criticism on a number of points. The Poles, the 'Duce' told him, deserved to be 'treated in a way that did not provide subject matter for enemy speculation'. He should

create 'a Polish state under German supervision', in order to remove the
western powers' main argument for continuing the war. This state could get
rid of all the Jews; he thoroughly approved of Hitler's plan to deport them
all to a large ghetto near Lublin. Hitler must, Mussolini continued, 'on no
account seize the initiative on the western front'; victory in the West was
more than doubtful, for 'the United States would not permit the complete
destruction of the democracies'.

As far as the alliance with the Soviet Union was concerned, Mussolini
warned Hitler not 'to keep sacrificing the principles of your revolution to
the political requirements of a particular political situation'; he must not
'abandon the anti-Semitic and anti-Bolshevik banner... that you have held
high for 20 years'. This was followed by a clear warning: 'Any further move
towards Moscow would have catastrophic repercussions in Italy'. 'The solution to your problem of living space lies in Russia and nowhere else.... Four
months ago Russia was still world enemy No.1; it can't have become world
friend No. 1 and it isn't.' Italy, wrote Mussolini in a more conciliatory tone,
wanted to be Germany's 'reserve', 'from a political and diplomatic point of
view', 'from an economic point of view', as well as from a 'military point of
view'.[49]

Hitler, who, in his discussions with his entourage, made no bones about
his dissatisfaction with his Italian ally,[50] waited two months before replying.
His response was twice as long as Mussolini's lengthy epistle.[51] Above all, he
tried to persuade Italy to enter the war, saying that if Italy did not fight now,
it would, in a few years' time, be compelled to fight against the same opponents. By referring in the same paragraph to the problem of delivering
German coal to Italy as a result of the British blockade, and promising an
alternative solution, he was underlining the dependence of his ally on
Germany for supplies of an essential raw material. He defended his alliance
with Russia as a 'clear division of spheres of influence' with Stalin's
empire. It was possible to establish a 'tolerable situation' between the two
countries because the Soviet system was in the process of getting rid of its
'Jewish-internationalist leadership' and developing 'a Russian nationalist
state ideology and economic theory'. This statement shows that Hitler was
resorting to the (optimistic) idea of a 'nationalist Russia' that he had believed
in at the beginning of the 1920s on the basis of developments in the early
days of the Soviet Union. During these months, Hitler frequently discussed
the unnatural alliance with Moscow with Goebbels, often referring to the
allegedly inferior racial composition of the Soviet leadership. At the end of

December, he expressed the view that Stalin was 'a typical Asiatic Russian. Bolshevism had removed the West European leadership in Russia'.[52] Two weeks later, he claimed that for Germany that had been a 'very good thing. Better a weak partner as neighbour than an alliance treaty, however good'.[53] In March, he asked himself: 'Will Stalin gradually liquidate the Jews? Perhaps he only calls them Trotskyists to fool the world.'[54]

In his letter Hitler rejected Mussolini's request that he should establish a Polish state; he claimed that if Poland had been left to itself after the victory there would have been a 'ghastly chaos', which he clearly enjoyed sketching out in detail. He attempted to persuade Mussolini to ignore the mission to Europe that the deputy American Secretary of State, Benjamin Sumner Welles, had embarked on at the end of February. This concern was presumably the reason why Hitler answered Mussolini's letter at all and dealt with his criticisms in a relatively conciliatory tone. He did not, he wrote, rule out the possibility that the point of the mission was mainly to enable the Allies to gain time. Welles had been sent by the President to find out from the British, French, German, and Italian governments the prospects for peace. After an initial meeting with Mussolini and Ciano in Rome, Welles went on to Berlin in April, and then returned to Rome.

Hitler had issued his own guidelines for the meetings Welles had with Göring, Ribbentrop, and Hess. He ordered that they should be 'reserved' and, 'if possible, avoid' answering specific questions, such as whether there was going to be a Polish state in the future. Apart from that, they should say that the war had been forced on Germany and that they were determined to 'break the destructive will of the western powers'. The American diplomat should not be left under any illusion that Germany was interested in discussing the possibility of peace. As a result, according to Welles, the meetings with German officials led nowhere.[55] On 2 March, Hitler himself received Welles and, as was his wont, delivered a lengthy monologue, convincing the latter that the Germans had decided to continue the war.[56]

On 10 March Ribbentrop handed over Hitler's 8 March letter to Mussolini during a visit to Rome; he had been assigned the task of at last getting Italy to enter the war.[57] Ribbentrop told Mussolini that Germany was aiming to attack France and Britain during the course of the next few months. Its rear would be protected because Stalin had given up the idea of world revolution and, after the departure of Litvinov, all Jews had been removed from key positions. During another meeting the following day, Mussolini gave his agreement in principle to enter the war, although only after prompting by Ribbentrop.[58] Hitler expressed himself 'very satisfied' with the success achieved by Ribbentrop in Rome,[59] and met Mussolini at the Brenner Pass on 18 March. The 'Duce' used the few minutes left to him after Hitler's usual lengthy monologue to reaffirm his decision to enter the war, but without naming a specific date. However, he emphasized that the Italian forces needed at least three or four months to be ready for war.[60]

'Weserübung' [Weser Exercise]

At the end of 1939/beginning of 1940, Hitler began increasingly to consider the idea of expanding the war to Scandinavia. The 'Weserübung' [Weser Exercise], the occupation of Denmark and Norway, which Hitler decided on in March, had a long pre-history.[61] On 10 October 1939, the commander-in-chief of the navy, Raeder, alerted Hitler to the possibility of using U-boat bases in Norway, which he hoped to secure with the aid of pressure from the Soviet Union; Hitler agreed to consider the idea.[62]

On 30 November 1939, the Soviet Union attacked Finland, after it had refused to agree to Soviet demands to concede certain bits of territory.[63] The tough Finnish resistance against the numerically far superior Soviet forces met with sympathy from the western powers, and an expeditionary force was prepared to support Finland, which was also intended to enter Swedish territory, cutting off German imports of iron ore.[64] In this conflict Hitler was definitely on the side of his Soviet ally, acknowledging the fact that in the German–Soviet treaties of 23 August and 28 September Finland had been declared to be part of the Soviet sphere of influence. The prospect that British and French troops could be shortly landing in Scandinavia meant that he was hoping for a rapid Soviet victory, particularly as he resented the fact that, in spring 1939, the Finnish government had rejected his offer of a German–Finnish non-aggression pact. A leading article in the *Völkischer Beobachter*, presumably written by Hitler, attributed this decision to the influence of the 'the English warmongers'.[65]

The Soviet attack on Finland ensured that Norway now increasingly entered the calculations of the belligerent powers. Apart from the fear that the British might establish themselves in Norway and so close off the North Sea, the fact that Germany received two-thirds of its iron ore from Sweden via the ice-free port of Narvik was of decisive importance. In mid-December, Admiral Raeder arranged a meeting between Hitler and Vidkun Quisling, the leader of the Norwegian National Socialist splinter party, Nasjonal

Samling, and succeeded in getting Hitler to order the OKW to discuss with Quisling plans for the occupation of Norway, either peacefully (following a Norwegian request for assistance) or by force.[66]

In January, a special staff N was established in the OKW and, on 27 January, Keitel told the chiefs of the three Wehrmacht branches that Hitler wanted the 'N Study' to be produced under his personal and direct influence, and to be coordinated as far as possible with the overall conduct of the war'. Thus the order was clearly intended, on the principle of *divide et impera*, to exclude the top military leadership as far as possible from the planning process involved in extending the war to the north.[67] The 'Altmark' incident of 16 February, in which a British commando operation in Norwegian waters captured a German naval supply ship, freeing three hundred imprisoned British sailors on board, once again made it clear how important control of the Norwegian coast was for Germany's conduct of the war.[68]

On 21 February, Hitler appointed General Nikolaus von Falkenhayn to command 'Weserübung'; the army general and his staff were directly subordinated to the OKW (rather than the OKH), probably primarily in order to exclude the army leadership from the operation and to secure Hitler's 'personal and direct influence' on it.[69] On 1 March, he signed the directive for 'Operation Weserübung'[70] and, on 5 March, conferred with the commanders-in-chief of the Wehrmacht branches about it at a meeting in the Reich Chancellery. According to Jodl, Göring 'was furious', as he had not been 'previously consulted', and pushed through some changes in the plan of attack.[71]

In the middle of March, the Finnish–Russian war surprisingly came to an end, removing the motive for Allied intervention.[72] However, Hitler was now determined to create a situation in Scandinavia favourable to Germany. Apart from wanting to secure Germany's supplies of iron ore and extend the basis for the war against Britain, he appears to have had far-reaching plans for the region. The involvement of Quisling and the Norwegian National Socialists offered the prospect of politically coordinating Norway and incorporating it into a future 'Greater Germanic Reich'.[73] On 26 March, Hitler fixed 9 April as the date for the invasion of Denmark and Norway. He did not inform Goebbels about the impending operation until 8 April, giving him little time to prepare German propaganda for the new situation.[74]

The Wehrmacht began the invasion early on the morning of 9 April. A coordinated, large-scale operation involving army, navy, and Luftwaffe was a new experience for the German armed forces and carried considerable risk. Whereas the German troops took control of Denmark on the same day, events in Norway did not develop as expected. The plan for a

surprise takeover of Oslo failed, giving the Norwegian government sufficient time to organize military resistance and escape capture. The landings
in the other Norwegian ports largely succeeded, but with the navy suffering heavy losses.

The Goebbels diaries show that Hitler allowed himself to be dazzled by
the Wehrmacht's initial military successes. On 9 April, he was positively
euphoric. At midday on the first day of the invasion, he considered the
whole operation a success; it would go down 'as the most daring piece of
impudence in history'.[75] On the following day, he told Goebbels he was
thinking of a north German 'confederation . . . not a protectorate, more an
alliance. A unified foreign, economic, and customs policy. We shall acquire
the most important military bases, take on the military defence, and the two
states will give up having any kind of military capability.'[76] He informed
Mussolini about the invasions only on 10 April.[77]

However, during the next few days it became clear that Hitler had been
too optimistic in his assessment of developments. On 13 April, a Royal Navy
task force succeeded in sinking ten German destroyers in the Narvik fjord,
or forcing them to scupper.[78] Germany had been clearly put on the defensive. Hitler had already decided to evacuate German troops from Narvik;
Jodl was talking about 'chaotic leadership'.[79] At a small gathering in the
Reich Chancellery to celebrate Hitler's 51st birthday, the 'Führer' studiously
avoided this issue, preferring to discuss the coming war with the West. On
24 April, Hitler appointed the Gauleiter of Essen, Josef Terboven, as Reich
Commissar in Norway. It was only at the end of the month that the military
situation gradually improved for Germany. German troops were able to
advance from the Oslo region towards Trondheim, where a German invasion force had meanwhile been trapped by an Anglo-French pincer movement; these Allied forces were now compelled to withdraw and re-embark.
However, there was still concern about the situation in Narvik in the north,
where, at the end of April, Anglo–French forces had landed and were soon
reinforced.[80]

Viewed in the round, the surprise attack on Norway had failed. The
expedition force had become involved in battles that continued until June
and could be successfully concluded only because of military victories in
western Europe. The navy suffered relatively high losses and the large
Norwegian merchant fleet joined the Allies. Despite gaining bases on the
Norwegian coast, Weserübung had, therefore, not secured any significant
strategic advantages for the conduct of the war against Britain.

31

War in the West

The war in the West had been repeatedly postponed. In February, the preparations for the war in Scandinavia had influenced the plans for western Europe. Then, at the beginning of March, Hitler, who had hitherto been inclined not to start Weserübung until there had been some initial successes in the war in the West, decided to reverse the order, by first launching the campaign in Scandinavia before attacking in the West a few days later.[1] The difficulties encountered in Norway, however, made it seem advisable once again to postpone the campaign in the West.[2] Then, the weather intervened until, finally, on 9 May, the irrevocable decision was taken to attack the following day.[3]

The Wehrmacht began the war on 10 May. On the same morning, memoranda were sent to the governments in Brussels, The Hague, and Luxemburg, justifying the attacks on the grounds of alleged violations of their neutral status by Belgium and the Netherlands.[4] The first 'special operations' against airfields and bridges in the Netherlands and the Belgian fortress of Eben-Emael were largely successful. However, the attempt to take over the Dutch seat of government in The Hague from the air failed.[5] The 18th Army, which invaded the north of the Netherlands, secured the capitulation of the Dutch armed forces on 15 May. The 6th Army, which together with the 18th formed Army Group B, tied down large Allied forces in northern Belgium. Meanwhile Army Group A, which with three of its armies managed to achieve a surprising breakthrough in the Ardennes, succeeded as early as 13 May in breaching the French defensive lines on the Meuse near Sedan and advancing westwards in a sickle-shaped manœuvre.

Hitler had already moved to his headquarters, the Felsennest (Rock Eyrie) near Münstereifel, on 10 May.[6] He had made it clear in Directive No. 11 that, by contrast with the war against Poland, he intended this time to take over direction of the operations in the West himself.[7] During the following days, when the campaign reached decisive stages, the first major clash occurred between Hitler and the army leadership over the right way forward. It became apparent that Hitler judged the risks of too rapid and extensive an operation to be much greater than did the commander-in-chief of the army, Brauchitsch, or the chief of the general staff, Halder.

Twice, on 17 and 24 May, Hitler intervened massively in the operations of Army Group A, both times halting its advance. The army leadership had wanted to press on with rapid thrusts, in order to decide the outcome of the war there and then.[8] Hitler's first order to halt, made when visiting Army Group A headquarters at Bastogne, was prompted by his desire to protect the Army Group's southern flank against possible French counterattacks. Halder noted that Hitler had 'an incomprehensible anxiety about the southern flank. He shouts and screams that we are about to ruin the whole operation and are risking defeat.'[9] The second order to halt of 24 May resulted in the British and French being able to consolidate their bridgehead at Dunkirk.[10] There has been speculation that, by intervening in this way, Hitler wanted to preserve the British expeditionary corps, the core of their professional army, from destruction, in order to keep alive the prospects for peace through this generous gesture. However, if his decision of 24 May is viewed against the background of the clash between the army leadership and Hitler that had been going on since 17 May, a completely different picture emerges.

Hitler and the army leadership were still disagreeing about the question of whether the German panzer units should advance southwards to the east of Paris (Hitler) or in a big sweep to the west of Paris (army leadership),[11] when Hitler, visiting Army Group A on 24 May, learnt of an order issued by Brauchitsch a few hours earlier. According to this, the 4th Army, in which all the panzer units of Army Group A were concentrated, was to be subordinated to Army Group B, in order to surround and destroy the enemy forces in the Dunkirk–Ostend region.[12] Hitler summoned Brauchitsch and countermanded the order.[13] Moreover, he backed the decision of the commander of Army Group A, Gerd von Rundstedt, who was in command of all the panzer forces on the western front, to conserve the panzers and not to deploy them for the destruction of the Allied bridgehead at Dunkirk–Ostend. However, Hitler left the decision to Rundstedt, who did indeed hold back the panzers from engaging on terrain that did not appear suitable for tank operations. This order to halt backed by Hitler's authority was in force for two days.

Hitler's decision was designed above all to demonstrate his power. He was making it clear that he was in a position to give direct orders to lower ranking commanders, in this case the commander of Army Group A, bypassing Brauchitsch and Halder. His message was that, in the event of a dispute, as supreme commander he had the authority to take control of the panzer forces, the army's spearhead, and would make use of it, if the army leadership failed to do what he wanted.

On 26 May, Hitler gave the go-ahead for the panzers' advance towards Dunkirk to continue,[14] Belgium capitulated on 28 May, and Dunkirk fell at the beginning of June, albeit only after the enemy had succeeded in evacuating more than 300,000 British and French soldiers across the Channel.[15] On 30 May, the Italian ambassador Alfieri conveyed a note from Mussolini to the effect that Italy was now ready to enter the war on 5 June, or later if Hitler wanted it.[16] The 'Führer' then told the 'Duce' that he preferred a somewhat later entry, since they were preparing a major operation against French air force bases,[17] whereupon Mussolini postponed Italy's entry until 11 June.[18]

In the second phase of the campaign, on 4 June Army Group B first advanced towards Rouen and the lower Seine, and, five days later, Army Group A moved in the direction of the Marne. Finally, on 14 June, Army Group C crossed the frontier near Saarbrücken, breaching the Maginot line. Once again there was disagreement between Hitler and the army leadership. While Halder and Brauchitsch proposed a second expansive sickle movement in central France, Hitler feared the risks and was initially content with occupying the Lorraine iron ore region, but then, a few days later, came round to the army's plan.[19] On 5 June, he summoned Goebbels to his headquarters to explain his further plans. He wanted 'if possible to spare Britain' and a 'generous peace would be best'. Belgium 'should disappear as a state, not Holland, otherwise we would lose its colonies'. The aim should be to have 'a kind of protective relationship'. He hoped to have dealt with France within four to six weeks and its future looked 'very gloomy'; it would be 'severely cut back'. 'As far as the Jews are concerned,' he explained, 'we'll soon sort them out after the war', and 'then it will be made immediately and brutally clear to the Churches that there is only one authority in the state, the source of all authority, and that is the state itself'.[20]

Paris fell on 14 June,[21] and Hitler ordered 'flags to be flown and bells to be rung for three days'.[22] On 12 June, Marshall Pétain took over the French government and requested an armistice. Hitler was now concerned above all to portray the end of the war as his personal triumph and to place his ally, Mussolini, one step below him on the victors' podium. Thus, on 18 June, during an encounter in Munich, at which Mussolini made only too clear his wish to partake in the booty of victory, he informed the 'Duce' only in very general terms about the armistice, and opposed Ciano's suggestion that they should hold parallel armistice negotiations. He would, however, only sign the German–French armistice agreement after the conclusion of the Franco–Italian negotiations.[23]

Hitler gave orders that the armistice negotiations should take place in Compiègne in northern France,[24] where, on 11 November 1918, the armistice ending the First World War had been signed in Marshall Foch's railway carriage. The negotiations began on 21 June in the same famous forest clearing. To begin with, Hitler himself was present in the historic railway carriage, which had been specially retrieved from the museum that had been built in the 1920s and brought to the historic November 1918 location. Hitler, who was accompanied by Göring, Raeder, Brauchitsch, Ribbentrop, and Hess, left the announcement of the armistice conditions to Keitel.[25] There was a preamble to the document composed by Hitler himself,[26] making it clear what he intended to achieve. He wanted 'an act of restorative justice', in order 'once and for all to erase a memory that was not exactly the most glorious episode in France's history, and was felt by Germans to be the deepest disgrace of all time'. After Keitel had read out the preamble, Hitler departed with his entourage, leaving it to Keitel to inform the French delegation, led by Colonel Hunzinger, of the conditions of the armistice. The same day, he ordered the carriage, the memorial stone displayed in Compiègne, and the 'monument to Gallic triumph' to be brought to Berlin and the rest of the site to be destroyed. The monument to Marshall Foch, however, was left untouched.[27]

The negotiations continued until the evening of the following day, until Keitel ended them by issuing an ultimatum. The agreement that was finally signed imposed on France – in contrast to the humiliating circumstances of the signing in Compiègne – what were, from the German point of view, relatively moderate conditions, raising French hopes for a later peace treaty. It was envisaged that the south of France would be excluded from the occupation and that a French government should be allowed to continue to exist. The French armed forces were to be largely demobilized and dissolved; the French navy, by contrast, was to remain partly intact and the compulsorily decommissioned units left in French hands. This was intended to prevent French ships from joining the enemy.[28] The Germans refrained from making colonial demands, fully aware that the overseas territories could easily transfer their support to the enemy.

Under Hitler's leadership, the Wehrmacht had succeeded in only six weeks in winning decisive victories over the western powers in the European theatre of war. Given the more or less identical strengths of the two sides, this was unexpected. However, Germany's rapid military success is entirely explicable. It was due above all to the effectiveness of German military leadership, which applied the operational theories developed by the Prussian general staff to the modern war of movement, aiming to bring about a decisive battle where the enemy least expected it. The main elements of this type of warfare involved a willingness to take significant risks, the element of surprise, the speed of operations, the courage to concentrate one's forces at particular points, the aim of achieving a breakthrough with massed forces, subsequent deep thrusts at the risk of exposing flanks, and rapid enveloping movements. All of this was feasible only because officers were given great freedom of action through 'mission-type tactics' [Auftragstaktik] and were used to leading from the front. Moreover, they had learnt to apply traditional principles of leadership to modern panzer tactics, where panzers with accompanying armoured, or at least motorized, forces cooperated in wide-ranging operations with the concentrated tactical support of the Luftwaffe.[29]

After the victory in the West, Hitler found himself in a political and strategic situation that provided him with completely new options for continuing the war. With France's Channel and Atlantic coast he had conquered a platform for the war against Britain; with the take-over of France he had changed the balance of power in the Mediterranean; he could now make use of the economic resources of a highly developed western Europe, and so survive a lengthy war. His authority over the military, which had been so sceptical about his preparations for a war in the West, was now unchallengeable.

From 'Sea Lion' to 'Barbarossa'

On 23 June, two days before the armistice came into effect, Hitler fulfilled a long-held dream: he visited Paris, not as a conqueror but instead secretly, in the pose of a cultured tourist. He was accompanied by his architects, Giesler and Speer, his favourite sculptor, Arno Breker, General Karl-Heinrich

Bodenschatz, his doctor, Karl Brandt, Bormann, and his adjutants, Engel, Brückner, and Schaub.[30] This bizarre sightseeing tour in a city that, in the aftermath of the war, was dead, took place in the early morning and covered the major sights at speed so that, in the case of most buildings, Hitler had to content himself with a view of the exterior. The only interiors he was able to look at were of the Opera and Les Invalides, where he spent a short time in front of Napoleon's tomb. At the Trocadero, the group left their vehicles and Hitler viewed the site of the 1936 World Fair and, in the distance, the Eiffel Tower. Newspapers and the newsreels only reported the visit some time later.[31]

This flying visit by the 'supreme commander' at the height of his triumph, which was intended to remind people of his true 'artistic' nature, had a lasting effect on the 'Führer'. During his later table talk, he kept referring to the impression Paris had made on him. He compared the French capital (unfavourably) with Vienna and Rome, commenting that one day Berlin must surpass Paris.[32] Immediately after his return from Paris, he ordered work on the rebuilding of Berlin – the 'most important current building project in the Reich' – to begin again, and gave instructions that the building work in Munich, Linz, Hamburg, and on the site of the Party Rallies in Nuremberg should continue.[33]

In contrast to his low-key Paris visit, a big show was put on for Hitler's entry into Berlin. Indeed, the reception of the 'victorious Führer' in the Reich capital on 6 July was one of the most striking mass demonstrations in the history of the Third Reich. The Propaganda Minister surpassed himself and the event was minutely planned. Factories and shops shut at midday and the employees were directed along carefully planned routes to their assigned places in the heart of the city; 8,000 people had been involved in decorating the streets and houses, and boys from the Hitler Youth and girls from the BDM turned Hitler's route into a sea of flowers.[34] On 7 July, Hitler explained the point of the spectacle to his Italian guest, Ciano: he had 'come to the Reich capital' in order, with his entry, 'to demonstrate to the rest of the world what the German people think of me.' Contrary to reports on British radio, they were not 'crushed and demoralized', but 'fighting fit'.[35]

The fact that the campaign in the West had not resulted in another lengthy war with enormous casualties, which many people had feared, but had ended within a few weeks in a triumphant victory, undoubtedly produced an enormous sense of relief, consolidating Hitler's reputation as a decisive statesman and a 'Führer' with exceptional abilities. It appears doubtful, however, whether the fear of war that marked the pre-war years had suddenly been transformed into enthusiasm for war. The very reserved response of the German people to the attack on the Soviet Union the following year suggests that the much-described euphoric mood of the summer of 1940 derived instead from the expectation of a quick end to the war. It is, at any rate, going much too far to interpret the jubilation of the Berlin crowds as an unambiguous expression of enthusiasm for Hitler and the war.[36]

On 8 July, still in the euphoric state induced by his success, Hitler outlined his future occupation policies to Goebbels. In Norway he wanted to found 'a great German city, probably named "Nordstern" [Northern Star]', and to link it to Klagenfurt with an autobahn traversing the whole of the Reich. France, on the other hand, must 'never again become a military power' and must 'be reduced to a subordinate position'. As far as Britain was concerned, he was 'not yet ready to deliver the final blow'. At the beginning of July, he had decided to give a speech to the Reichstag, which would 'offer London a last chance'; if Britain rejected it, 'then, immediately afterwards, it will be dealt a devastating blow'. He had made a number of similar statements to Goebbels from 24 June onwards.[37] A 'boundless Germanic empire' would be created under his leadership; the tasks for the future, Goebbels noted, would be 'of grandiose dimensions'.[38]

On 9 July, Hitler withdrew to the Obersalzberg, to work on his Reichstag speech. Having originally planned to give it on 8 July, he postponed it several times, in order to await developments in Anglo–French relations. These had been severely damaged when, on 3 July, the Royal Navy sank part of the French fleet in its Algerian base of Mers-el-Kébir, in order to prevent it from falling into German hands.[39] In addition, he wanted to push on with preparations for the war against Britain. On 2 July, even before his ceremonial entry into Berlin, he had given the military a directive to prepare an invasion of Britain under the code name 'Seelöwe' [Sea Lion].[40]

During his stay at the Berghof, Hitler was very preoccupied with this topic as, so to speak, an alternative to his plan for a 'peace offer'. On 11 July, he conferred with Keitel and Raeder about the possibility of an invasion. Hitler and Raeder, who had already discussed this in May and June,[41] were in agreement that it could be considered only as 'a last resort', in order to force Britain 'to make peace'. On this occasion, Hitler agreed in principle to Raeder's proposal to revive the large naval construction programme (on the basis of the Z plan), which had not been further pursued since the start of the war.[42] On 13 July, Hitler instructed Halder to begin the actual planning for Sea Lion and made certain practical suggestions. However, one gets the sense from Halder's notes that Hitler was primarily concerned with the question of 'why England is not prepared to make peace'. 'He sees the answer', Halder noted, 'as we do, in the fact that England still has hopes of Russia. Thus, he reckons that he will have to compel England to make peace by force. But he does not like the idea. Reason: "If we smash England's military power, the British Empire will collapse. That is of no use to Germany. German blood would be shed to achieve something of which America and others would be the beneficiaries."'[43] Nevertheless, on 16 July, Hitler issued Directive No. 16 'to prepare and, if necessary, carry out a landing operation against England'. He had previously politely turned down Italy's offer to participate.[44]

Hitler was also preoccupied with the future relationship with the Soviet Union, for Stalin had used the period when German troops were engaged in western Europe to secure for Russia the territorial gains that had been agreed in the Nazi–Soviet pact. In June 1940, the Soviet Union occupied the Baltic States, which were part of its 'sphere of influence', and prepared to annex them. Then, at the end of the month, it moved against Romania, occupying both the former Russian territory of Bessarabia, in which, in the secret protocol attached to the Hitler–Stalin pact, Ribbentrop had declared Germany's 'complete lack of political interest', and northern Bukovina.[45] This move did not come as a surprise to the German government,[46] particularly since it had been warned about it beforehand by Molotov.[47] Thus Hitler responded coolly to King Carol, advising him to accept the Soviet territorial demands and reminding him of 'the anti-German attitude' that Romania had maintained 'for decades'.[48] In order to prevent an outbreak of hostilities, Hitler also persuaded Romania to make territorial concessions to Hungary and Bulgaria, which occurred in August and September.[49]

Not least as a result of the impression made by the Soviet moves against the Baltic States and Romania, Germany began a fundamental reappraisal of its policy towards the Soviet Union. The idea of attacking and crushing the Soviet Union, the only remaining major power on the continent that did not belong to the Axis, loomed ever larger. Soviet actions during recent weeks had made it abundantly clear that Russia was still a power to be reckoned with. This reappraisal will have occurred to a large extent during Hitler's stay in the Berghof during July. The question of whether the initiative came from him – the view of traditional 'intentionalist' scholarship – or from the military, as recent German military scholars maintain, appears to be of secondary importance, bearing in mind Hitler's normal way of dealing with his subordinates. It is conceivable that Hitler sent out certain signals, to which the military then responded with proposals and memoranda or which, in the spirit of 'working towards the Führer', they even anticipated. The lack of relevant sources prevents us from reaching a definitive conclusion. The war against the Soviet Union being contemplated in July 1940 was, in any event, not the war of racial extermination of 1941; it was envisaged as a short campaign, leading to the annexation of a considerable amount of territory in the west of the Soviet Union, and to a significant limitation of the power of what was left of Russia.[50]

This reappraisal of German policy can be reconstructed from a number of references, indicating that a decision-making process of far-reaching significance was taking place. At the end of June, following a meeting with state secretary Weizsäcker, Halder had noted: 'Eyes focused on the East', also commenting that Britain needed another 'demonstration of our military power... before it will give way, thereby protecting our rear for a move East'. It is not clear from the minutes whether these remarks were Weizsäcker's own views, or whether he was informing Halder about Hitler's thinking.[51] In any case, at the beginning of July, Halder noted in a conversation with the head of his operations department that the 'central question with regard to the East' was, 'How can a military campaign against Russia be mounted in order to force it to recognize Germany's dominant role in Europe?'[52]. During July, operational plans for a war against Russia were also being prepared in the OKH and the OKW, which we shall look at in more detail.

On 19 July, Hitler returned to Berlin. He told Goebbels, who found him to be in an 'excellent mood and health', that he would make a 'brief, terse offer to England, without a precise proposal', although 'with a clear message that this was his last word'.[53] He then made his speech to the Reichstag the same day in the pose of the triumphant military victor. He began by announcing a series of promotions: Göring became 'Reich Marshal of the Greater German Reich', a newly created military rank; he also promoted twelve generals to the rank of field-marshal and promoted a number of other generals. Only then did he move on to the political core of his speech. He stated that the German–Russian relationship was 'permanently fixed'; it was determined by a 'cool balancing of mutual interests'. If Britain was hoping for a deterioration in the German–Russian relationship, then this was a 'mistake'. At the end, he made a brief and imprecise appeal to 'reason in England', pointing out that he was 'after all not appealing to them as the defeated one, but as the victor, who was only speaking in the name of reason'.[54] This 'appeal to reason' was intended to be understood as Britain agreeing, as the precondition for peace, to recognize the situation on the continent created by his military success; as a quid pro quo, he was offering to respect the integrity of the British Empire. Like Hitler's 'appeal for peace' in October 1939, this 'offer' was motivated primarily by domestic political considerations. Since his speech on the occasion of the Heroes' Memorial Day in March he had not spoken to the German people, and now had to address the still open question of how he was planning to carry on the war. If it failed to see 'reason', the enemy was now to be blamed for the continuation of the war and the German population was finally going to have to get used to the inevitability of a lengthy war.

Three days later, Hitler had to face the fact that Britain had officially rejected his 'peace offer', as Lord Halifax made clear in a radio address.[55] Even before this definitive rejection, Hitler had already indicated that he rated the chances of his approach as being very slim. At any rate, on 21 July, during a meeting with Brauchitsch (Halder produced detailed minutes), he said that Britain would continue the war, as it was pinning its hopes on the one hand on the United States, and, on the other, on the Soviet Union. He considered an invasion to be a 'major risk'; it would be an option only if all other possibilities 'of coming to terms with England' were ruled out. If Britain decided to fight on, then they would have to try to confront her with a solid political front: Spain, Italy, Russia. 'If we decide to attack, Britain must be finished off by mid-September.' Stalin was 'flirting' with England, in order to exploit Germany's being tied down by her military engagement in western Europe, and 'to take what he wants, and what he won't be able to take when peace comes'. However, Hitler continued, at the moment there was 'no sign of Russian activity directed against us'. And so they must 'get to grips with the Russian problem'. It is clear from Halder's minutes that in the preparations for an attack on the Soviet Union referred to in this conversation Hitler could rely on preliminary work already being carried out by the OKH.[56] This had reached the following conclusions: the deployment would last four to six weeks; the military goal would be to defeat the enemy or at least to 'capture sufficient Russian territory' to prevent air attacks on Berlin and the Silesian industrial region. The political aim was: 'a Ukrainian empire, a Baltic confederation. White Russia – Finland. Baltic states – a thorn in the flesh.' They reckoned on needing 80–100 divisions for the attack, against which Russia would have only 50–75 'good' divisions.[57]

Thus, Hitler's attitude to the Soviet Union at this stage was decidedly ambivalent. On the one hand, in order to counter Stalin's territorial ambitions, he had let the military prepare war plans; on the other hand, he toyed with the idea of utilizing his ally for the continuing war with Britain. During the next ten days, however, after further discussions with his generals, Hitler made a fundamental decision with far-reaching consequences. On 25 July – in the meantime, he had made a trip to the Bayreuth festival[58] – he once again discussed the possibility of an invasion of Britain with Keitel, Jodl, Raeder, and Todt. When, at the end of July, Hitler asked Jodl whether it would be possible to mount a successful attack on the Soviet Union during the current year, Jodl dismissed the idea. Jodl's staff had, however, already prepared a preliminary plan for such an attack,[59] and planning for a war in the East continued in the OKH as well. There was now a consensus that the operation should be postponed to the following spring.[60] At the end of the month, both Brauchitsch and Halder agreed that neither the invasion of Britain nor an attack on the Soviet Union should receive priority. At a meeting on 30 July, both the commander-in-chief of the army and the chief of the general staff came to the conclusion that an invasion of Britain in the autumn was unlikely to succeed, whereas, were it postponed to the following spring, the enemy would be stronger. A solution to this dilemma would be to shift the focus of the war to the Mediterranean, in order to attack Britain in Gibraltar or Egypt; or another option: 'Russia could be prodded towards the Persian Gulf'. Both generals were basically sceptical about the idea that if Britain could not be beaten, the Soviet Union, as its potential ally, should be attacked first. In their view a two-front war should be avoided and it would be better to 'remain friends with Russia'.[61]

On 31 July, Hitler discussed the options for continuing the war against Britain with his senior generals. Among the topics covered were: the prospects for an invasion of Britain, involving Spain in the war, reinforcing the Italians in North Africa with German panzer divisions, and the continuation of the sea war.[62] Finally, Hitler made the order for an invasion of Britain dependent on the progress of the air war. However, the army should definitely prepare for an invasion on 15 September. Then, as is clear from Halder's brief notes, Hitler got to the main point of his deliberations: 'England's hopes are pinned on Russia and America. If they can no longer hope for help from Russia, then America too will fall by the wayside because, with Russia gone, Japan would be hugely strengthened in the Far East. Russia is England's and America's Far Eastern sword pointed at Japan. Here an ill wind is blowing for England. Like Russia, Japan has her own agenda, which she wants to carry out before the end of the war.... With Russia smashed, England's last hope would be crushed. Germany will then be the master of Europe and the Balkans.' His 'decision' was fixed. 'Russia's destruction must therefore be made a part of this struggle. Spring '41. The sooner Russia is crushed the better.' The aim of the operation was the 'destruction of Russia's vital strength' through an offensive in two main directions. On the one hand, towards Kiev, on the other through the 'border states' in the direction of Moscow. Hitler named the political goals as: 'Ukraine, White Russia, Baltic States to us. Finland extended up to the White Sea.'[63] While the army leadership thought they would need 80–100 divisions, Hitler reckoned on 120 divisions for the offensive, in other words two-thirds of the number of major units that would be available in the coming spring.

The meetings with his generals during July reveal that, having taken on board that, for the moment, the war against Britain could not be concluded, Hitler was responding with a megalomaniacal strategy of expansion. He was now developing a global scenario for continuing the war.

Madagascar

In the summer of 1940, after the victory over France and anticipating a peace agreement with Britain, Hitler considered the situation ripe for pursuing another territorial solution of the 'Jewish problem'. Instead of Poland he now considered the French colony of Madagascar as a suitable target area.[64] This was by no means an original idea. The notion that large numbers of European Jews could be resettled in tropical Madagascar had been very popular in anti-Semitic circles since the end of the nineteenth century.[65]

During the war against France, this idea received important encouragement from Himmler, who had submitted a memorandum on the 'Treatment of Ethnic Aliens in the East' to Hitler on 25 May 1940. In it he had announced his intention[66] of 'seeing the "Jew" as a concept completely extinguished... through the possibility of a substantial emigration of all Jews to Africa or to some other colony'. Hitler agreed with the memorandum in principle, suggesting that Himmler should show it to Governor General Frank 'in order to tell him that the Führer considers it the right thing to do'.[67] During the summer, he often spoke of the Madagascar project with approval, for example (via Ribbentrop) to Ciano on 18 June, on 20 June to Raeder, the commander-in-chief of the navy, at the beginning of August to Otto Abetz, the German ambassador in Paris, and, in the middle of the month, to Goebbels.[68]

Backed by such unequivocal statements from the 'Führer', during the summer of 1940, various bodies began to work out the details of the project. On 3 July 1940, Franz Rademacher, the new head of the desk for 'Jewish affairs' in the Foreign Ministry, proposed in a memorandum that France must place Madagascar at Germany's disposal as a mandate 'for the solution of the Jewish question'. 'The part of the island that has no military importance will be placed under the administration of a German police governor, who will be subordinate to the Reichsführer SS. The Jews will be able to run their own administration within this territory.' The aim was for 'the Jews to become bargaining counters to guarantee the future good behaviour of their racial comrades in America'. The Madagascar project was thus intended to act as a form of 'hostage taking', as had also been the case with the 'Polish reservation'.[69] Another document of Rademacher's, dated 2 July, contains further information about his intentions: from the German point of view Madagascar represented 'the creation of a huge ghetto'. Only the Security Police was capable of coping with such a project; it had 'experience in carrying out such appropriate punishment measures as may become necessary in the event of hostile actions against Germany by Jews in the USA'.[70]

During the following weeks, Göring had the 'possibilities for settlement' on the island confirmed by a report from the Reich Office for Area Planning.[71] At the same time, the Reich Security Head Office, which was involved in the planning process,[72] put together its own version of the Madagascar Plan, which was ready by the middle of August. It proposed the establishment of a 'police state' in Madagascar for the four million Jews currently living under German rule. The RSHA estimated a period of four years as necessary for transporting the Jews by ship to the east coast of Africa.[73]

On the question of transport, Viktor Brack, the organizer of the 'euthanasia' programme in the Führer's Chancellery, made a proposal, noted by Rademacher,[74] that 'the transport organization he had established to carry out the Führer's special mission during the war should later be used for transporting the Jews to Madagascar'. The fact that a further key figure in the 'euthanasia' programme, the head of the Führer's Chancellery, Philipp Bouhler, was to become governor of the future German colony in East Africa[75] makes it clear that the experience that had been gained in the mass murder of the mentally ill was now going to be used for the next stage of the solution to the 'Jewish question'. For years, millions of European Jews would have been deported to Madagascar, where a large number would have fallen victim to Rademacher's proposed security police 'punishment measures', as well as to the hostile living conditions. In reality it was a project for the physical extermination of the Jews living under German rule. How far it was implemented would in part be dependent on the United States' 'good behaviour', which was to be exacted by means of a genocidal threat. The fact that in his memorandum Rademacher referred to a figure of 6.5 million Jews to be settled suggests that the Jews of south-eastern Europe as well as those in the northern French colonies were now also being included in the plan.

Despite appearing to be pure fantasy and irrespective of whether it had a chance of being implemented, the Madagascar project meant that the RSHA was able to continue with its plans for a 'Jewish reservation'; even though such a reservation could no longer be created in the General Government, planning under the rubric 'Madagascar' could go on until another 'solution' to the 'Jewish question' emerged. After Hitler's agreement in principle to Himmler's memorandum, the Madagascar project had emerged independently in the plans of the Foreign Ministry and those of the RSHA, but Hitler remained in control of what was actually going to happen. Thus, under the influence of the Madagascar plans, from July 1940 onwards, Goebbels was preparing for the deportation of all Berlin Jews; but for this to occur he would need Hitler's express approval.[76]

The Madagascar plan was also probably responsible for the fact that, immediately after the armistice, the German occupation forces began expelling Jews and other 'undesirable' French citizens from Alsace and Lorraine; by September 23,000 people had been deported from these provinces to southern France. This measure, together with Hitler's appointment, on 2 August, of the Gauleiters Josef Bürckel (Palatinate) and Robert Wagner (Baden) to head the administrations of Lorraine and Alsace, was clearly intended to prepare for the annexation of these two territories.[77] On 28 September, Hitler specifically told the Gauleiters that in ten years' time they were to report that the French territories of which they were in charge were 'German, and that means completely German', and he would not enquire about 'what methods they had used'.[78] The two Gauleiters extended their 'purges' to their own Gaus; at the beginning of October, the Jews still living in Baden and the Saar-Palatinate, a total of around 6,500 people, were also deported to southern

France, a measure that was expressly approved by Hitler and can be seen as a late consequence of the Madagascar Plan.[79]

The prospect of deporting the European Jews to Madagascar had a direct impact on Jewish policy in Poland, and once again Hitler was involved. On 8 July 1940, as Hans Frank informed his colleagues a few days later, Hitler had assured him that, in the light of the Madagascar project, there would be no further deportations to the General Government.[80] The following day, Himmler issued an internal directive halting further deportations into Frank's territory.[81] This put an end to the idea of creating a 'Jewish reservation' in the General Government. However, within only a few months, the Madagascar plan had become a fantasy project, a 'somewhere, anywhere' to provide a 'solution' to the 'Jewish problem', for which there was in fact no clear scheme. It continued to be used by Hitler in this sense, as a purely imaginary place, as late as spring 1942, although it was officially abandoned in February 1942 and, in the meantime, the murder of the Jews in death camps had already begun.

The Blitz

On 24 July, after Britain's rejection of his 'peace offer', and following his usual visit to the Bayreuth festival, Hitler indicated that he was going to prepare an air offensive to force her to make peace.[82] On 1 August, when final 'feelers' put out via non-belligerent states had met with no response,[83] he issued Directive No. 17 for the conduct of naval and air warfare against Great Britain. According to the directive, starting on 5 August, the Royal Air Force was to be 'defeated' and the air war was then to be directed mainly at ports (with the exception of those on the south coast, which would be needed for the invasion) and against facilities used for storing foodstuffs. 'I am reserving the decision as to whether to carry out terror raids in retaliation.'[84] Also, a massive propaganda campaign was to be launched to create a fear of invasion in Britain, 'in order to confuse the enemy'. Hitler made it clear to his Propaganda Minister, however, that an 'invasion was not planned'.[85] During the following weeks in various meetings with his military chiefs,[86] Hitler told them that Operation Sea Lion was a threat that might, in certain circumstances, be the last resort to force Britain to make peace.

In fact, the massive air raids were delayed. Bad weather meant[87] that – after the first large-scale air battles over the Channel[88] – the long-awaited major raid with almost 1,500 aircraft could not take place until 13 August. On the following days too there were a considerable number of raids,[89] but once again bad weather set in and large-scale raids could not be mounted until the end of the month.[90]

The German raids elicited a response. Two days after the Luftwaffe had bombed residential districts in the East End of London on 24 August, British aircraft were flying over Berlin,[91] and, on 28 August, the RAF mounted its first raid on the city, causing ten deaths.[92] Following further British raids (the bombing of an hydrogenation plant near Stettin resulted in seven deaths), in his speech in the Berlin Sportpalast opening the Winter Aid programme on 4 September, Hitler promised 'retaliation': 'And if they [the British, P.L.] drop two, or three, or four thousand kilogram bombs, then in a single night we shall drop 150,000, 180,000, 230,000, 400,000, a million kilograms. If they announce they will mount large-scale raids on our cities, we shall obliterate their cities!'[93] The following day, he gave the go-ahead for raids on London and other British cities, which meant that he had begun intervening in the air war at the tactical level.[94] The German press, which printed pictures of the damage to German cities, also began to demand 'retaliation'.[95]

On 14 September, at a meeting with the commanders-in-chief of the three branches of the Wehrmacht, Hitler insisted that there was a 'chance of totally crushing the English'; only four or five more days of good weather were required in order to force a military decision.[96] During the following night, London was once again attacked by 200 bombers. However, despite continuing raids in the second half of September, the hoped-for result was not achieved; Britain could not be forced by the air terror to surrender. In the meantime, on 19 September Hitler had ordered the disbanding of the ships assembled in the 'invasion harbours', although the ships had to be available again within a few days, so that the option of an invasion of Britain was, in theory, retained.[97]

At the beginning of October, after a meeting with General Otto von Waldau, the Chief of the Luftwaffe Leadership Staff, Halder noted that they had 'underestimated the British fighters by about 100 per cent'. They would be considerably reducing the air raids during the winter; in the spring they would be no stronger than they were at the start of the air war against Britain; but, in order to 'smash the English' they would need four times the strength.[98] The German 'blitz' had failed. 'A two-front war impossible' was thus Halder's conclusion.

32

Diplomatic Soundings

Germany's victories in the West had implications for the balance of power that went far beyond Europe. Having had to backtrack on his aim of forcing Britain to make peace, Hitler's main challenge over the next few months was to recognize this fact, respond to it, and exploit it.

After Germany's victory in western Europe, Japan was hoping to inherit the Dutch and French colonies in south-east Asia. But Britain's colonies were also now vulnerable, as it was engaged in a life-and-death struggle with Germany and could not defend them as vigorously as before. With its eyes on these colonies, the Japanese government decided that it would be advisable to seek a rapprochement with the Soviet Union.[1] Japan also concluded that it would make sense to improve relations with Germany, as these relations had been negatively affected by the Nazi–Soviet pact, in order to ensure that Germany did not attempt to take over the colonies of the defeated powers. A clear demarcation of their respective spheres of influence was required. Hitler was initially opposed to a formal alliance with Japan.[2] However, he changed his mind in the light of Britain's rejection of his peace offer and the threat of the United States entering the war, and in August came out in favour of such an alliance.[3] The aim was to force the United States to focus on the Pacific region, putting Britain under greater pressure to accede to Germany's 'desire for peace'.[4]

The emerging cooperation between Italy, Japan, and Germany prompted the German government to begin developing more far-reaching plans. Ribbentrop, in particular, put forward the idea of an anti-British continental bloc from Spain to Japan.[5] Romania, Hungary, Bulgaria, Slovakia, and Yugoslavia would all be incorporated into the triple alliance of Japan–Italy–Germany, and also Spain, enabling Gibraltar to be conquered and the Mediterranean to be thereby blocked off from the West. In addition, France was earmarked to play an active part in the war against Britain, and, finally, the Soviet Union was to be incorporated into the alliance; this would require the expansionist ambitions attributed to Stalin to be directed away from Europe and towards Iran and India.

Ribbentrop's initiative was similar to ideas being discussed by the Naval High Command. In two situation conferences with Hitler in September, Raeder proposed eliminating the British military presence in the Mediterranean and the Near East. Germany should seize Gibraltar and the Suez Canal and advance through Palestine and Syria towards the Turkish border. Then Turkey would be 'in our power' and the 'Russian problem' would 'look very different'. It would then be questionable whether 'moving against R from the north would still be necessary'. If they established a link to Italian East Africa, Britain's position in the Indian Ocean would be weakened. In addition, the establishment of naval bases in Dakar, Casablanca, and in the Canary Islands would improve Germany's position in the Atlantic. This in turn would benefit her situation vis-à-vis the United States, in the event of its entering the war, which the Naval High Command considered likely. Hitler, who on 11 July had already approved the navy's request for a large naval construction programme along the lines of the Z plan, responded positively to Raeder's proposal at the situation conference on 26 September, which took place tête-à-tête; he would consider, he said, whether to implement the plan with Spain or with France, more likely France.[6]

Between September and December, Hitler and Ribbentrop were actively engaged in diplomacy to realize the continental bloc idea. The problem was trying to reconcile the different interests of the various parties.

This required, in the first place, sorting out the sensitive relationships in the Balkans.[7] During the middle of August, after massive intervention by Hitler and his foreign minister, Romania had begun negotiations with Bulgaria and Hungary about their territorial demands.[8] However, after a few days the meetings between Romania and Hungary were broken off, and Hungary began to threaten to use force to resolve the conflict.[9] Germany and Italy were determined to secure a quick resolution, in order to integrate both adversaries into the Axis; this was agreed at a meeting at the Berghof between Hitler and Ciano on 28 August.[10] After a hurriedly convened conference in Vienna on 29 and 30 August 1940 in Schloss Belvedere, attended by the foreign ministers of Italy, Hungary, Romania, and Germany, Ribbentrop and Ciano imposed the so-called Second Vienna Award.[11] Romania had to give up a large part of Transylvania to Hungary, whose territory now stretched deep into Romania. In recompense, Germany and Italy guaranteed the integrity of Romania's remaining territory.[12] This produced a wave of anger in Romania, leading to the abdication of King Carol II in favour of his son, Michael. General Ion Antonescu became prime minister with German backing, had himself nominated 'head of state',[13] and was forced by Hitler to give up further territory; on 7 September, South Ossuja was awarded to Bulgaria. In return, Hitler agreed to Antonescu's request[14] for a German military mission to be sent to Romania. To outward appearances this was to assist Romania in establishing and training its armed forces. However, its 'real task' was to protect the oil fields from 'being seized by a third power', and to enable the Romanian armed forces 'to carry out...certain tasks', as well as to prepare 'for the deployment from Romania of German and Romanian forces in the event of war being forced on us by the Soviet Union'.[15] To start with, the German military mission was kept secret by both countries; Hitler also saw no need to inform his main ally, Mussolini.

In the late summer of 1940, alongside this incorporation of Romania into his preparations for war against the Soviet Union, Hitler reappraised his policy towards Finland. Aiming to secure an important ally on the northern flank of his planned invasion, and to integrate the country into his preparations for war as a base for operations and supplies, he abandoned the distant approach adopted towards Finland during the Russo–Finnish war and the succeeding months.[16] He ordered a substantial concentration of German forces in northern Norway,[17] and, at the beginning of August 1940, approved the revival of arms exports to Finland.[18] In return, on 12 September, a German–Finnish transit agreement was signed, permitting German troops and supplies to be transported from Finnish ports to northern Norway and the permanent stationing of German troops along the transit route.[19]

From July onwards, Hitler had been toying with the idea of mounting a surprise attack on Gibraltar, an operation that was inconceivable without Spain's support.[20] Spain was also expected to allow Germany to establish bases on the Canary Islands. In the subsequent negotiations, Hitler followed the maxim: 'Promise the Spaniards everything they want, even if not all their wishes can be fulfilled'.[21] During the second half of September, Hitler and Ribbentrop promised to deliver large quantities of food and raw materials, and agreed to the Spanish request to hand over the French colony of Morocco.[22] However, Franco stalled when, during the following weeks, Hitler refused to commit himself on Morocco. At a meeting with Mussolini on 4 October, Hitler said that 'there was an issue as to whether it might not be possible to get France and Spain to come to terms and, thereby, secure a continental coalition against England'. For that it would be essential to come to an agreement with France. But this was not going to happen. During an internal discussion before the meeting with Mussolini, Hitler put his finger on the core of the problem: reconciling the conflict of interests between France, Italy, and Spain in Africa would only be 'possible through grandiose deceit'.[23]

This was Hitler's aim when he set off at the end of October on a trip to Montoire (north of Tours) and to Hendaye on the Franco–Spanish border. He told Prime Minister Pierre Laval that a refusal by France to support Germany in the war against Britain would lead to a reduction in France's colonial possessions. According to his interpreter, Schmidt, Hitler did not even bother to respond to a proposal by the French president, Marshal Philippe Pétain, for a Franco–German peace treaty. As far as the French were concerned, this meant there was no point in discussing Franco–German cooperation further; the possibility of France's inclusion in an anti-British bloc was not even touched on.[24]

In Hendaye Hitler had to inform Franco that, because France might enter the war, the prospect of his receiving the French colony of Morocco was now uncertain.[25] Hitler told the Spanish dictator that if they failed to come to an arrangement with France, there was a danger of the French north African colonies breaking away, which would mean they would be lost to the Axis. Subsequently, Ribbentrop and the Spanish foreign minister, Serrano Súñer, discussed a secret German–Spanish protocol, which was finally signed by Ribbentrop, Súñer, and Ciano in November 1940. It confirmed Spain's willingness to join the Tripartite Pact and the Pact of Steel. After the victory over Britain, apart from Gibraltar, Spain was to receive French colonial possessions in Africa, and France would gain British colonies.[26] However, after his return, Hitler told Goebbels that he did 'not have a good opinion of Franco. A lot of bravado, but no commitment'.[27] Hitler's adjutant, Engel, told Halder that Hitler had called Franco a 'Jesuit swine'.[28]

During the same period, Ribbentrop involved himself in another project. Between 19 and 22 September, during a visit to Rome, he tried to persuade Mussolini and Ciano of the advantages of a pact between Italy, Germany, and Japan.[29] While the existing alliance between the three powers, the Anti-Comintern Pact of 1936/37, had a clear anti-Soviet slant, Ribbentrop suggested to his interlocutors a very different perspective. They should start by waiting for the Soviet Union's response to the new pact and then, 'at an appropriate moment, [offer] Russia a free hand to achieve its aims in the south in the direction of the Persian Gulf or India'.[30] At this point, the negotiations with Japan had already been substantially completed.[31]

On 27 September, the ceremonial signing of the Tripartite Pact took place in Berlin.[32] In the agreement, which was valid for ten years, Japan recognized 'Germany's and Italy's leading role in the creation of a new order in Europe', while the two European powers recognized Japan's similar role in the 'greater Asian area'. The three powers promised each other mutual support in the event that one of them was 'attacked by a power that is not at present involved in the European war or in the Sino–Japanese war'. Article 5, in which the three powers declared that the agreement did not affect their current respective positions vis-à-vis the Soviet Union, clearly shows that the promise of mutual support was aimed primarily at the United States.

Hitler tried to reassure Mussolini about the threat from the United States at the Brenner meeting referred to above.[33] To begin with, he outlined in detail to the 'Duce' his plans for defeating Britain: 'Only five days of decent weather were needed to achieve air superiority. Then, 8 to 10 days of calm weather for crossing the sea...'. But so far they had been waiting in vain for four weeks for this period of good weather. Britain's hopes of an intervention by the United States or the Soviet Union were, according to Hitler, unfounded. The United States would merely provide armaments – and even that to only a limited extent – and he reckoned a military intervention by the Soviet Union was 'out of the question'. In any case, they were fully prepared for a Soviet intervention. The Russians, according to Hitler, represented 'no problem for Germany even under the worst-case scenario'.

At this meeting Hitler still did not consider it necessary to inform Mussolini that a German military mission had been sent to Romania. It was only eight days later, on 12 October, that Germany's engagement in Romania was made public in an official announcement. According to an entry in Ciano's diary, Mussolini was so furious about this fait accompli that he decided to give Hitler a similar surprise by attacking Greece, thereby restoring the balance between the two allies.[34] Thus Hitler learnt that the Italians had decided to attack Greece against his wishes only on his return from his visit to France at the end of October.[35] On hearing the news. he had his special train redirected to Florence, where he met Mussolini on 28 October, only hours after Italy had launched the attack from Albania.[36] In fact, the advance soon stalled and the Italians had to withdraw to Albanian territory. The German leadership realized that, if they were to prevent Britain from sending troops and establishing a foothold in the Balkans, they would have to intervene militarily themselves.[37] Preparations were under way in November.[38]

Molotov: A tough opponent

The visit of Molotov, the Soviet Foreign Minister, to Berlin in the middle of November represented the climax of the diplomatic soundings and negotiations that Hitler initiated during the autumn of 1940. The Soviet visitor was given a cool reception in Berlin. Goebbels had ensured that the visit took place with little involvement on the part of the Berlin population.[39] The interpreter Schmidt noted that no 'cheering crowds' had been organized to welcome him.[40]

A few days before the visit, at a meeting with Keitel, Jodl, and Halder, Hitler told them that Russia 'was the main problem for Europe. Everything must be done to prepare for the great showdown.'[41] Immediately before the visit, Hitler issued Directive No. 18 of 12 November 'for the conduct of war in the near future', in which he definitively stated that, regardless of the results of the discussions with Molotov, 'all preparations for the East that have already been orally ordered, [are] to be continued'. France 'for the time being [will] have the role of a non-belligerent power'. The primary task of the French was 'the defensive and offensive protection of their African possessions... against England and the de Gaulle movement'. From this task 'the participation of France in the war against England [may] develop to a full extent'. Spain would shortly be joining in the war; the Italian offensive against Egypt would, if sufficient success was achieved, be supported by the Wehrmacht, in particular in order to mine the Suez Canal from the air. In addition, preparations were to be made for a German advance from Bulgaria into northern Greece, so that Luftwaffe units could be deployed in the eastern Mediterranean. An invasion of Britain in the course of the spring was conceivable.[42]

Thus, directly before the start of the negotiations with Molotov, Hitler was making it clear that he was committed, in the first instance, to an anti-British alliance without the Soviet Union, and that, irrespective of the consultations with Molotov, he was sticking to his plans for an attack on Moscow. From his point of view, therefore, the discussions had, above all, the function of keeping channels to the Soviet Union open, in order to prevent a possible Anglo-Soviet rapprochement. In view of his attitude in the conversations that followed, it must be doubted whether he was seriously contemplating an even temporary incorporation of the Soviet Union into an anti-British alliance. After a preliminary meeting between Ribbentrop and his Soviet counterpart,[43] Hitler opened the discussions with Molotov on 12 November with a general, wide-ranging survey of the international situation.[44] Molotov, however, was little interested in such a tour d'horizon; instead, he preferred to confront Hitler with a series of specific questions about the aims of German foreign policy. In fact, he largely succeeded in putting the 'Führer' on the spot, making him take refuge in vague statements and evasions. According to the interpreter, Schmidt: 'No foreign visitor had ever spoken to him in such a way in my presence.'[45]

Molotov's forceful approach during the negotiations is explained by the fact that Stalin had given him a detailed set of instructions and questions to work through and clarify before the Russian dictator was prepared to sign up to a 'four-power pact' – an agreement he certainly did not dismiss out of hand.[46] Molotov now asked Hitler what significance the Tripartite Pact actually had, and in what way the Soviet Union was going to be integrated into the new order in Europe and Asia. In addition, there were issues relating to Russian interests in the Balkans and the Black Sea concerning Bulgaria, Romania, and Turkey that needed clarification.

Hitler replied that the Tripartite Pact was 'intended to regulate relationships in Europe as regards the natural interests of the European countries' and that, consequently, Germany was now approaching the Soviet Union in order that she might express her views concerning the areas of interest to her. On no account would a settlement be made without Soviet Russian cooperation. The Tripartite Pact 'represented the first concrete step, so to speak, towards comprehensive collaboration, with due consideration for the problems of Western Europe that were to be settled between Germany, Italy, and France, as well as for the issues of the East, which were essentially the concern of Russia and Japan, but in which Germany offered its good offices as mediator.'

Molotov indicated that he was quite open to the idea of the Soviet Union participating in the Tripartite Pact, but wanted Russia to be treated not as an 'object' but as a 'partner'. Hitler then broke off the meeting by mentioning the threat of an air raid; it was continued the following day. In the evening – the raid did not occur – Ribbentrop gave a reception in honour of Molotov in the Hotel Kaiserhof, which Hitler did not attend; nor did he appear at the reception Molotov gave the following day in the Soviet embassy.[47]

The following day, Molotov continued to put his probing questions to Hitler. He complained that Germany's activities in Finland contravened their previous year's treaty, in which it had been agreed that Finland would be in the Soviet sphere of influence; in particular, Molotov objected to the stationing of German troops in the country. Hitler replied that these were simply troops being transported to Norway on a temporary basis. The discussion then reached a decisive point. While Molotov claimed for the Soviet Union the right to occupy Finland, which belonged to its sphere of influence,[48] Hitler emphasized that he was not prepared under any circumstances to put up with a Finnish–Soviet war in the Baltic region: 'A new war in the Baltic would put a serious strain on German–Russian relations and on future collaboration.' Hitler stated that he was afraid that, in the event of such a war, Britain might try to intervene in Finland; in fact, of course, he was primarily interested in using Finland as a base for his planned war on the Soviet Union.

Molotov, however, stuck to his guns by making it clear that, by rejecting the use of force by the Soviet Union in Finland, Hitler was calling into question the demarcation of spheres of influence that had been agreed in 1939. The 'Führer' now tried to divert attention from this contentious issue by opening up a new perspective for Soviet expansion. Once the British Empire had been defeated, 'a gigantic, bankrupt, world-wide estate of 40 million square kilometres would be up for grabs. This bankrupt estate would provide Russia with access to the ice-free and really open ocean.' Molotov, however, was not prepared to engage with this point, as his instructions stated that the four powers – Germany, the Soviet Union, Japan, Italy – should issue a declaration guaranteeing the existence of the British Empire (with the exception of Gibraltar and Egypt). Thus the Soviet Union was solely interested in eliminating Britain's dominant position in the Mediterranean, and otherwise wanted to retain it as a major player in the international balance of power.[49] Molotov kept returning to particular critical issues in German–Soviet relations, demanding definite commitments from Hitler. Among other things, he complained – 'if I may be permitted to express myself so bluntly' – that the German–Italian guarantee of Romania was directed against the Soviet Union, and asked 'how Germany would respond if Russia gave Bulgaria, the country nearest to the Straits, a guarantee with the same conditions'.

Hitler once again tried to evade the issue: it would have to be raised with the Bulgarians as well as with Germany's Italian allies. When Molotov persisted, he refused to see what Molotov was getting at. Once again, Hitler ended the meeting by mentioning the possibility of a British air raid.[50] Later on that evening Ribbentrop continued the discussion with Molotov in the air-raid shelter. He gave his Soviet colleague the draft of a Four-Power Pact, de facto an extension of the Tripartite Pact to include the Soviet Union. However, Molotov now had the bit between his teeth, bombarding Ribbentrop with a list of questions the Soviet Union definitely needed clarifying in order to determine its policy towards Germany. Apart from their relationship with Turkey, Romania, and Bulgaria, there was the issue of the two powers' policy in relation to Poland, Yugoslavia, Greece, Sweden, and the question of access to the Baltic, all of which had to be sorted out. Ribbentrop finally gave up, admitting to his Soviet guest that he was 'at a loss'.[51]

On 26 November, after Molotov's return to Moscow, the Soviet government submitted its conditions for participating in the Four-Power Pact sketched out by Ribbentrop on the 13 November: the withdrawal of German troops from Finland; the conclusion of a Soviet–Bulgarian mutual assistance pact; Turkey's agreement to the construction of Soviet bases on the Bosphorus and the Dardanelles; the recognition of the area south of Batum and Baku 'in the general direction of the Persian Gulf' as 'the main focus for the further southwards expansion of the Soviet Union', and Japan's renunciation of coal and oil concessions in North Sakhalin.[52]

The Soviet proposals did not receive a response. Hitler and his foreign minister were forced to conclude that their bid to tempt the Soviet Union into an anti-British coalition, even if only temporarily, with the vague prospect of participating in the break-up of the British Empire had failed as a result of the concrete conditions set by the Soviets for such an alliance. For these could not be fulfilled, as the Germans did not want to risk weakening their position prior to an attack on the Soviet Union. Also, given the highly specific conditions set by the Soviets, there was no point in continuing the negotiations, for they would almost certainly soon have to be broken off, leading to a fundamental diplomatic reorientation of the Soviet Union vis-à-vis Germany. The Germans wanted to avoid this at all costs and so the matter was left in abeyance.

After Molotov's departure, Hitler continued to try to expand the Tripartite Pact – without the Soviet Union. On 18 November, he received various candidates for the alliance one after the other at the Berghof. The first was King Boris of Bulgaria, who was on a private visit to Germany. According to Jodl's notes, they discussed the impending attack on Greece (which was going to cross Bulgarian territory).[53] However, Hitler does not appear to have succeeded in binding Bulgaria any further to the Axis, as is clear from a letter he wrote to Mussolini two days later.[54]

Only a few hours after Boris had been received by Hitler, Molotov offered the Bulgarian government a wide-ranging pact,[55] which, however, was rejected.[56] But, at the same time, Bulgaria was not prepared to damage its relations with the Soviet Union any further.[57] At the beginning of December, Hitler tried in vain to convince the Bulgarian ambassador that if Bulgaria joined the Tripartite Pact, 'Russia [would] automatically keep its hands off Bulgaria'.[58] On 18 November, the Spanish foreign minister, Súñer, also came to the Berghof, where Hitler urged Spain to enter the war soon.[59] However, Súñer avoided making a clear commitment, raising a whole series of difficulties. As ever, it was a question of deliveries of foodstuffs, which Spain was hoping to receive from both belligerents as a result of its temporizing tactics, and also the territorial concessions in Africa, which Germany was expected to make to Spain at the expense of France. Hitler responded that it would be 'unwise to make demands, which, if they became known, would inevitably mean Morocco going over to de Gaulle'. Súñer repeatedly urged Hitler to be more precise about what territorial concessions in Africa Germany was prepared to make to Spain. Hitler, however, declined to do so.

Although he had not received a clear commitment from Spain, after Súñer's visit Hitler issued orders to prepare for the implementation of Directive No. 19 (Operation 'Felix'). This involved not only the conquest of Gibraltar, but also holding three divisions ready to neutralize a possible British counter-attack through Portugal. Preparatory studies had shown that, because of the poor road conditions and difficulty of maintaining supplies, the German attack on Gibraltar, which was intended to involve a reinforced division and over 200 artillery pieces, could only take place twenty-five days after the frontier had been crossed, and so there was no chance of carrying out a sur-prise attack.[60] Although Franco gave his approval for the operation at the end of November,[61] the German ambassador learnt from Súñer that he had attached various conditions to it, indicating his scepticism.[62]

Hitler received Ciano on the same day, spelling out to him the negative impact of Italy's unsuccessful attempt to go it alone in Greece, which he then explained to Mussolini in detail two days later in a letter. He pointed out the 'negative psychological consequences' of Italy's action: the unwill-ingness of Bulgaria to enter the Tripartite Pact, the increased Soviet interest in the Balkans, and other problems. The construction of British air bases in

Greece, from which they could reach the Romanian oil fields, had a nega-tive military effect.[63] In view of this situation, a whole series of measures had become necessary. Spain had to enter the war, which 'it can be assumed will happen in six weeks or so'; this would enable the Mediterranean to be cut off from the West. They must try to 'lure Russia away from the Balkans and direct it towards the East'; they had to persuade Turkey to reduce its pressure on Bulgaria. Yugoslavia must be persuaded to accept the Axis line on the Greek issue. Hungary had to accept the transporting of large German forces to Romania across its territory and, finally, Romania must accept an increase in the number of German forces stationed there. If British forces moved into Greece he, Hitler, was willing to counter them, but not before next March. The Italians ought to advance towards Egypt and establish an air base in the Mersa Matruh region, from which aircraft could reach the Suez Canal. Mussolini should also remove his aircraft based on the French Channel coast and deploy them against British targets in the Mediterranean.

If the two air forces fought a coordinated campaign, Hitler continued, 'within three or four months the Mediterranean would be the graveyard of the British fleet', and that was 'the decisive precondition for the military operations, which, as far as Greece itself is concerned, in my opinion cannot start before the beginning of March'.[64] In his reply of 22 November Mussolini endeavoured to justify the weak performance of his armed forces against Greece. As far as Hitler's proposals for coordinated action in the Mediterranean were concerned, he wrote that he was quite prepared to cede Saloniki to Yugoslavia.[65]

The position of the Axis appeared to have been strengthened when, on 20, 23, and 24 November respectively, Hungary, Romania, and Slovakia joined the Tripartite Pact.[66] On 23 November, Hitler received Antonescu in Berlin. The Romanian leader was supremely self-confident, launching into a lengthy monologue to equal any of Hitler's usual tirades, glorifying the heroic history of the Romanians and complaining about the decisions of the Second Vienna Award. This was despite the fact that, prior to the interview, Ribbentrop had upbraided him for his critical comments.[67] Hitler seems to have been impressed by the 'Conducator', indicating that, despite the Vienna Award, the issue of the Hungarian–Romanian border was still unfinished business.[68]

Although the Tripartite Pact had been successfully strengthened, in December it became clear that the attempt to form an anti-British continental bloc, even in the reduced version left by the failure to achieve an alliance with the Soviet Union, had proved abortive. Plans for a comprehensive anti-British Mediterranean strategy, outlined in Hitler's letter to Mussolini of 20 November, soon became obsolete. For on 7 December Franco vetoed the Gibraltar operation proposed by Hitler for 10 January. He explained his reasons for this to the Abwehr chief, Canaris, in Madrid, adding that Spain was prepared to enter the war at a later date; but it was clear that he had little enthusiasm for doing so.[69] The Spanish position was elucidated by the German ambassador in Madrid. Franco was concerned about a threat to his regime if he failed to respond to the concerns of his military chiefs about entering the war; the catastrophic food situation added to the problem.[70] Hitler's attempt to persuade Spain to enter the war by promising them colonies *after* Britain had been defeated had failed. He, therefore, cancelled Operation 'Felix'.[71]

On 8 December, Hitler met Alfieri, who explained to him at length the precarious situation of the Italian army, which, in the meantime, had gone on to the defensive in Albania. Hitler advised Alfieri 'immediately to create order at the front by using barbaric methods such as shooting generals and colonels...and decimating the troops'. In addition, he promised to provide German transport aircraft, but regretted being unable to intervene with troops until March.[72]

On 10 December, in his Directive No. 19, Hitler acted on his failure to persuade France to join the anti-British bloc. He ordered the 'rapid occupation' of the hitherto unoccupied part of France in the event of the French colonies beginning to 'defect'.[73] He interpreted the dismissal of the French Prime Minister, Laval, on 13 December, as a clear rejection by France of a policy of cooperation with Germany. On receiving Laval's successor, Admiral Darlan, in his special train during a brief visit to German occupation troops on 24 December, the 'Führer' bluntly rejected Darlan's request for a continuation of the policy of cooperation with France.[74]

On 13 December, Hitler signed Directive No. 20 concerning Operation 'Marita', involving the occupation of Greece during the coming spring, which he had promised Mussolini;[75] but the grandiose Mediterranean strategy, of which the operation had originally been a part, the plan to exclude Britain from the Mediterranean all the way from Gibraltar to Suez, had failed.

How serious then was Hitler about the idea of a continental bloc? Was he at any point really prepared to abandon the attack on the Soviet Union that he had conceived in the summer of 1940, a war that had been in his mind since the mid-1920s as a solution to Germany's 'problem of a lack of space'?

It appears that the outlines of a plan for a continental bloc had simply represented one option for Hitler, which he tried out temporarily, possibly as an 'intermediate solution in world politics'.[76] He thought it necessary just in case the Soviet Union, seeing the alliance between Germany, Italy, and Japan, should seek an accommodation with Britain. In fact, as it became clear that the continental bloc had no future, Hitler was confirmed in his goal of engaging in a final confrontation with the Soviet Union. For Halder, Hitler's comment on 13 December that 'the question of future hegemony in Europe will be decided in the war with Russia' contained the quintessence of his views.[77] This war was no longer planned, in the first instance, to force Britain to make peace and to boost Japan in the Far East against the United States; now, this war had become in Hitler's mind a war of annihilation and a war to achieve living space.

On 16 December, he signed his Directive No. 21 to defeat the Soviet Union. The preparations for 'Case Barbarossa' were to be completed by 15 May 1941.

33

The Expansion of the War

On 8 and 9 January Hitler held lengthy discussions at the Berghof with Jodl, Keitel, Brauchitsch, and other army, navy, and Luftwaffe chiefs.[1] He stated that 'it's not yet clear how Russia will respond to Germany's planned action in Bulgaria. Russia needs Bulgaria for any move towards the Bosphorus. Britain is being kept going by its hope that the United States and Russia will intervene.' Britain was trying 'to get Russia to move against us.' Stalin should be 'seen as an ice-cold extortionist', but also as a 'smart guy; he won't openly go against Germany, but we must assume that in tricky situations he will increasingly make difficulties for us'. Entry into the war by the United States and the Soviet Union would represent 'a very serious challenge to our conduct of the war'; this danger had to be eliminated from the start. 'Once the threat from Russia has been removed we can continue the war with England under quite manageable conditions; the collapse of Russia will be a great relief to Japan and an increased threat to the United States.' Up until now, Hitler continued, he had always acted on the principle of destroying the most important enemy positions in order to be able to move on. 'So we must now crush Russia.'[2]

During a two-day meeting with Mussolini in Salzburg and at the Berghof, which began on 19 January, Hitler tried to coordinate the military efforts of the two allies more closely or, to put it more precisely, to integrate Italy's hitherto 'parallel war' into an overall war strategy determined by Germany.[3] At the first meeting, Hitler held the floor as usual. To begin with, he dealt mainly with France and the position of the Axis powers in the Mediterranean. On the second day, he gave a comprehensive address to a larger group – apart from Mussolini, Ciano, and Ribbentrop, there were numerous German and Italian generals present – in which he went into military details. He described Russia as a serious threat to his future policies, as it pinned down substantial German military resources. 'So long as Stalin is alive, there is probably no danger; he is clever and cautious. But when he is no longer there, the Jews, of whom there are a number in the second and third echelons of the regime, can once again rise to the top.' As far as the situation in the West was concerned, Hitler stated that he would launch an attack on Britain only when 'success was completely assured', as, given the huge military resources involved, if such an operation failed, it could not be repeated.[4] Mussolini left the meeting with the impression that Hitler had given up the idea of an invasion.[5] The Italians learnt nothing about the preparations for the attack on the Soviet Union.

In January, Hitler also decided to have another go at persuading Franco to enter the war.[6] Ribbentrop took on the task and the German ambassador in Madrid had repeated audiences with Franco, giving him a virtual ultimatum to do what had so long been expected of him. In a letter to the 'dear Caudillo' Hitler had bluntly threatened that Spain would 'never be able to gain such good friends as it now has in Germany and Italy'.[7] Franco evaded these peremptory demands, however, though without definitively refusing to enter the war.[8]

In the meantime, the army leadership remained distinctly sceptical about the prospect of war with the Soviet Union. In a note about a meeting with the commander-in-chief of the army on 28 January 1941 Halder recorded his own opinion of 'Barbarossa': 'The purpose isn't clear. We won't strike at the English that way. It won't significantly improve our economic potential. Risk in the West shouldn't be underestimated.' The collapse of Italy following the loss of its African colonies could not be ruled out, so that a new southern front might emerge.[9] When meeting them at a lunch, Brauchitsch too expressed doubts about the overall political and military situation to Halder and the Army Group commanders, Leeb, Bock, Witzleben, and Rundstedt.

On 1 February, at a meeting with Hitler, Bock told him that, while they could no doubt defeat the Russians, it was questionable whether they would be able to force them to make peace. Hitler responded by saying 'that if the occupation of the Ukraine and the fall of Moscow and Leningrad did not bring about peace', then they would simply have to go on to Ekaterinburg (the Soviet city in the Urals).[10] However, on 3 February, Halder gave a detailed outline of the military plans for Barbarossa and Marita (the operation against Yugoslavia and Greece) to Hitler, Brauchitsch, and other military chiefs at the Berghof without expressing any basic concerns. Hitler then approved Halder's plans, emphasizing once more the significance of the thrusts towards the Baltic states and the Ukraine. This was where the war would be decided, he said, and not on the central front. The attack was still planned for the middle of May.[11]

At this meeting Hitler also decided to give the Italians in Libya more support than hitherto. He was influenced by the conquest of the port of Tobruk by British forces on 22 January. Since September, the British had taken 130,000 Italian prisoners, and there was a danger of Italy suffering a total defeat in North Africa.[12] All German and Italian forces in North Africa – after initial hesitation, Hitler had sent a panzer unit of 8,000 men in January[13] – were to be subordinated to a general command under German leadership. Hitler appointed General Erich Rommel, who had distinguished himself as an unconventional commander of a panzer division in the campaign in Western Europe, to head up this command.[14]

Hitler's 'warning' and the radicalization of anti-Jewish policy

Hitler's speech in the Sportpalast on 30 January 1941 to mark the anniversary of the 'seizure of power' revealed his far-reaching goals for the war against the Soviet Union. On the one hand, there was the 'settling of accounts' with Britain, whose political and economic elites he made the object of his mockery and scorn.[15] On the other, the 'Führer' made it clear that the, in his view, close association between the conduct of the war and anti-Jewish policy was acquiring entirely new dimensions with the preparations for Barbarossa. Hitler referred to the 'warning' he had given exactly two years before 'that, if the rest of the world were to be plunged into a general war, the whole of Jewry will have played out its role in Europe!' Now he added, 'they may now be laughing about it, just as they used to laugh at my prophecies. The coming months and years will show that here too I've been right'. 'Nation after nation' was becoming convinced by the 'racial expertise' of the Nazis, and he was convinced that this would help establish 'the front against the international Jewish exploitation and corruption of nations'. However, Hitler erroneously gave the date of his previous 'prophecy' as 1 September 1939, in other words claiming it was issued during the Reichstag speech marking the outbreak of the Second World War. With this 'error', which was possibly deliberate, he was in effect underlining his association of the war with the violent persecution of the Jews.

In fact, Hitler's anti-Semitic tirade of 30 January 1941 represented, above all, a reference to the deportation of the Jews, which he had recently ordered and was now under way. At the beginning of November 1940, he had instructed that over 150,000 Poles and Jews were to be deported from the annexed eastern territories into the General Government.[16] In view of the strong objections of Governor General Frank to further 'resettlement',[17] Hitler had announced that 'later on we'll get rid of the Jews from this territory as well'.[18] To start with, however, Frank had to accept more Jews. At the beginning of December, Hitler had given the Gauleiter, Schirach, the permission he had been requesting since autumn 1940 to begin deporting the Viennese Jews.[19] During February and March 1941, 5,000 Jews were to be deported from Vienna to the General Government as the first stage in the planned removal of 60,000 Jews.[20]

However, in the meantime, the RSHA had begun to prepare a much more comprehensive project, which was intended to provide Frank with the 'relief' promised by Hitler in his November announcement. During the final weeks of 1940, Hitler had assigned Heydrich the task of working out an overall plan for the deportation of all Jews from the area controlled by Germany at the end of the war. Heydrich submitted this plan, which has not survived, to Hitler at the beginning of January 1941. It involved deporting to the conquered parts of the Soviet Union all the Jews living in the areas that would be dominated by Germany after the successful conclusion of Barbarossa.[21] There are various indications that suggest the regime continued to pursue these ideas until the late summer of 1941.[22] Given the various announcements by Hitler about 'annihilating' the Jews and the regime's increasingly brutal Jewish policy, it is clear that, after the conclusion of the deportation programme, there was no plan to settle these people in the Soviet Union in adequate living conditions. Everything points to the fact that, at the beginning of 1941, the regime was preparing in the long term to annihilate the European Jews through forced deportation to the east. Hitler had no more of a clue about how this was to happen than did his 'Jewish experts'.

Final preparations for the war in the Balkans

Yugoslavia and Bulgaria had to be won for the Axis before the attack on Greece could take place. From December onwards, the Wehrmacht began

to establish its own bases in Bulgaria,[23] and the Bulgarian government gradually came round to dropping its objections to joining the Tripartite Pact.[24]
As a reward, Germany offered to secure Bulgaria access to the Aegean at the
expense of Greece.[25] On 13 February, Hitler issued orders for the Wehrmacht
to march through the country, combined with instructions for the German
troops to mount an 'offensive in the direction of Istanbul' in the event of the
Turks beginning hostilities against Bulgaria in response to Germany's intervention.[26] However, this threat was minimized as a result of the Bulgarian–
Turkish Non-Aggression Declaration of 17 November, signed under strong
German pressure.[27]

After Bulgaria's ceremonial accession to the Tripartite Pact on 1 March,
Hitler took immediate action. The very next day, German troops marched
into Bulgaria 'to deal with measures taken by Britain in south-east Europe,
of which we have become aware' as the official German announcement put
it.[28] In the course of the accession celebrations on 1 March, Ribbentrop had
given the Bulgarian Prime Minister a note confirming that 'as part of the
rearrangement of the borders in the Balkans, the Axis powers are prepared
[to give] Bulgaria access to the Aegean'.[29] That afternoon, during a meeting
with Ciano and Ribbentrop concerning an official reception for the Bulgarian
Prime Minister, Bogdan Filoff, Hitler had confirmed that 'all the continental states would gradually be brought together to form an anti-English
bloc'.[30] The next goal was to bring Yugoslavia into the pact,[31] and Germany
was already working on it. On 14 November, at the Berghof, Hitler had
informed the Yugoslav Prime Minister, Dragiša Cvetković and the Foreign
Minister, Aleksandar Cincar-Marković, that the Soviet Union had promised
Bulgaria 'a generous grant of territory in Macedonia' at the expense of
Yugoslavia, 'in order to provide it with access to the Aegean'. Yugoslavia must
'in its own interest...take part in the new order envisaged by Germany and
Italy by immediately joining the Tripartite Pact'.[32] Hitler made the same
demand of the Yugoslav Prince Regent, Paul, whom he received at the
Berghof on 4 and 5 March. As a reward, Hitler promised Paul access to the
Aegean at the expense of Greece, in fact the annexation of Saloniki, which
Mussolini had agreed, on 22 November 1940, to give up. If Yugoslavia did
not seize the chance, 'then it would risk, in the end, finding a third power
blocking its path to the Aegean'. He had, after all, already promised Bulgaria
access to the Aegean.[33]

After a certain amount of hesitation, Yugoslavia finally agreed to join the
Tripartite Pact on 25 March. Before the ceremony took place, Germany

made a number of demands. Among other things, Ribbentrop made it clear to the pro-British prince regent that he might 'not be there in six months' time if he didn't follow our advice'.[34] Despite these attempts at intimidation, on the Prince Regent's return to Belgrade, the Yugoslav government insisted on a number of guarantees: of the country's territorial integrity; of the agreement not to call on Yugoslavia for military support; and of the promise to provide access to the Aegean through the granting of Saloniki, to all of which both Hitler and Mussolini agreed.[35]

Joining the Tripartite Pact was a highly contentious issue in Yugoslavia. Two days after the signing, the Cvetković government was overthrown by a military coup organized by pro-British officers. King Peter II, who was a minor, ascended the throne in place of the Prince Regent, Paul.[36] At midday on 27 March, at a hurriedly convened meeting of the military leadership in the Reich Chancellery, which Ribbentrop also joined later, Hitler announced that he was determined 'to crush Yugoslavia militarily and as a state with merciless severity' in a 'lightning operation'.[37] Yugoslavia was an 'uncertain factor' for the attacks on Greece and the Soviet Union. In addition, however, to Hitler's disappointment and anger at this sudden development, which he considered a blow to his prestige, and which posed a threat to his further military plans,[38] he had an old and deep-seated hostility to Serbia and Slovenia. They had never been 'pro-German'. As a result of the nationalities problem and the existence of 'a camarilla of officers who were prone to carry out coups, their governments had never been secure'. However, in view of this new operation, the attack on the Soviet Union would have to be postponed by up to four weeks. Hitler gave his approval in principle to a plan for a Balkan campaign that Halder had hurriedly sketched, and Brauchitsch was able to reassure the 'Führer' that the attack on Greece could still go ahead on 1 April as intended.[39]

As far as Greece was concerned, during the course of the month, Hitler had given way to the demands of the Luftwaffe and the navy and decided to occupy the mainland down to the Peloponnese (and possibly also the peninsula itself). As this would require stronger forces, he had intervened in the planning for Barbarossa, removing the whole of the 12th Army from the southern sector of the invasion, and deploying it to the Balkans, where it was to remain. As a result, the southern flank of the German invasion of the Soviet Union was significantly weakened.[40]

On 27 March, in his Directive No. 25, Hitler announced his intention 'to destroy the Yugoslav forces and to detach the southernmost part of Yugoslavia from the rest of the country, in order to use it as a base for the continuation of the German–Italian offensive against Greece'.[41] On the same day, he summoned the ambassadors of Hungary and Romania to the Reich Chancellery to demand that their governments take part in the war against Yugoslavia.[42] He offered both envoys the prospect of territorial gains.[43] The following day ambassador Döme Sztójay returned, bringing with him Horthy's agreement.[44] During the next few days, the issue of military intervention provoked a government crisis in Budapest, culminating in the suicide of the Prime Minister, Pál Teleki. Under Teleki's successor, Lászl Bárdossy, Hungary continued to support Germany, although with the stipulation that it could intervene only when the dissolution of Yugoslavia offered a pretext for doing so.[45] Bulgaria decided not to join in the war.[46]

Meanwhile, Hitler wrote a letter to the Italian dictator informing him of the impending war with Yugoslavia.[47] He also requested the 'Duce' to halt his offensive in Albania, which he agreed to do.[48] Mussolini also acknowledged that Hitler would assume supreme command of the coming operations himself. The 'Führer' managed this by communicating his 'proposals and wishes' in personal letters to Mussolini and Horthy, thereby 'taking account of the Allies' sensitivities'.[49] Ciano and Ribbentrop decided to ignore the Yugoslav foreign minister's statement that Belgrade continued to recognize the international treaties it had signed, including the Tripartite Pact.[50]

The Balkan War

Hitler set the date for the attack on Yugoslavia as 6 April 1941. On 5 April, the day before the attack, the Soviet Union concluded a friendship and non-aggression pact with the new Simović government in Yugoslavia.[51] Late in the evening, Hitler summoned Goebbels, who noted: 'He estimates the whole operation will take about 2 months. I think it'll be shorter.' Goebbels went on: 'The war against the Serbian arsonists will be fought without mercy. The Führer is expecting a sniper war with a lot of casualties.'[52]

On the first day of the war the Luftwaffe bombed Belgrade, causing heavy losses among the civilian population, despite the fact that the Yugoslav government had declared the capital to be an 'open city', in other words that it would not be defended. Hitler's decision to bomb the city nonetheless reflected his desire for retribution for Yugoslavia's 'betrayal'. It was no accident that the code word for the bombing of Belgrade was 'Tribunal'.

However, he did ban air raids on Athens. Indeed, Hitler became quite sentimental about the Greeks. Goebbels noted that the 'Führer' admired the courage of the Greeks and regretted having to fight them: 'Perhaps there's still something of the ancient Hellenes in them.'[53] For Hitler the Balkan war was, above all, an anti-Serbian war of revenge, with old Austrian resentments playing a not unimportant part. The following day he told Goebbels the Serbs 'had always been troublemakers. Now we must go in for the kill'. In contrast to the failed diplomatic methods of the Habsburg Monarchy they had to 'sort things out in a big way'.[54]

The campaign made rapid progress. From 6 April onwards, the 12th Army advanced through Bulgaria towards northern Greece; the 2nd Army, along with a separate panzer unit, attacked Yugoslavia from Carinthia, Styria, Hungary, Romania, and Bulgaria. As planned, the Wehrmacht was supported by Italian and Hungarian forces. By 10 April Zagreb had already been captured.[55] Hitler left Berlin and established his headquarters in a special train south of Vienna Neustadt, near a tunnel that could offer protection in the event of air raids.[56] On 12 April, he was already issuing 'Provisional Directives for the Partitioning of Yugoslavia'. The parts of Slovenia that had originally belonged to Austria were assigned to Carinthia and Styria.[57] Croatia became an 'independent state' with a puppet regime. On 14 April, Anton Pavelić, the leader of the secret nationalist organization, Ustacha, who had hitherto been living in exile in Italy, took over the government as 'head of state' (Poglavnik).[58] A military administration was established in Serbia, while the other Yugoslav territories were divided up between Italy, Hungary, and Bulgaria.[59]

However, the war was not yet over. In response to the Yugoslav request for an armistice, the German leadership demanded unconditional surrender. On 13 April, the day German troops entered Belgrade, Hitler issued Directive No. 27, ordering the 'annihilation' of the Yugoslav armed forces, which had already been largely defeated.[60] After almost all Yugoslav requests for concessions had been rejected, the surrender was completed on 17 April.[61]

The war in Greece went on for a few more days. The Greeks concentrated on holding their positions against the Italians in Albania, and were prepared to surrender only when the German troops were in their rear. On 21 April, evidently in response to a request from the Greeks, Hitler ordered the armistice to be conducted by the 12th Army without the participation of their Italian allies. However, as Mussolini protested, a second armistice was arranged on 23 April and this time the Italians took part.[62] On 25 April,

Hitler signed his directive for Operation Mercury, the conquest of the Greek island of Crete, where British troops had established bases.[63] The attack eventually began on 20 May, carried out by paratroopers and glider forces. The military engagements, which involved heavy losses, continued until 2 June, leading to the evacuation of the British forces and the complete occupation of the island by German troops.[64]

In the meantime, German forces were making significant progress in North Africa. Following Hitler's decision to bolster the almost hopeless Italian positions in North Africa, in February German troops under General Rommel arrived in Libya. Rommel moved against the British forces in Cyrenaica, pushing them back eastwards and conquering Benghazi, and, by the middle of April, he was outside Tobruk.[65] This advance was made possible not least because of the transfer of British forces to Greece.

On 28 April, Hitler made a triumphal entry into Berlin. On the same day, he met the German ambassador, Friedrich Werner von der Schulenburg, who had just arrived from Moscow, in the Reich Chancellery. Schulenburg attempted in vain to allay Hitler's deep-seated mistrust of Soviet policy. He assured him that the Soviet agreement with Yugoslavia was not directed against Germany. Moreover, there was no indication that the Soviet Union had been behind the putsch in Belgrade, or that the Soviets were seeking a rapprochement with Britain. Hitler evidently resented being contradicted, for he abruptly ended the meeting.[66] Two days later, on 30 April, Halder briefed Hitler about the state of the preparations for Barbarossa. It was on this occasion that the date of the attack was fixed for 22 June.[67] On 4 May, Hitler gave a report to the Reichstag on the Balkan campaign. 'The German Wehrmacht', he told them, 'will always intervene, whenever and wherever required'.[68]

Failure to secure a strategic agreement with Japan

In the middle of the preparations for the war in the Balkans, Hitler had tried to secure Germany's position in the impending war with the Soviet Union by reaching a strategic agreement with his ally, Japan. A unique opportunity was provided by the visit of the Japanese Foreign Minister, Matsuoka Yosuke, who arrived in Berlin at the end of March, having already held talks in Moscow.[69] As he had already made clear in his Directive No. 24 of 5 March, Hitler wanted to 'get [Japan] to take action in the Far East as soon as possible', in order to pin down British forces and to get the United States to focus on the Pacific. He was, however, determined to keep the Barbarossa operation secret from the Japanese, thereby considerably limiting his room for negotiation.[70]

During his first meeting with Matsuoka on 1 April, referring to Germany's relationship with the Soviet Union, Hitler stated that, although, 'as was well-known [the Reich] had made a treaty', 'more important than this was the fact that, if necessary, it had 160–180 divisions ready to defend itself against Russia', although he did not believe it would come to a war. Matsuoka was surprised by this statement, since the Japanese leadership assumed that Germany was still working to construct a 'continental bloc' including the Soviet Union. However, for Japan the stabilization of its relationship with the Soviet Union was the decisive prerequisite for its plans to expand in South-East Asia.

Hitler pressed his guest, arguing that there would probably never be a more favourable opportunity for the Tripartite powers to act together: Britain was pinned down by the war in Europe; America was only just beginning to rearm; and the Soviet Union could not take the initiative because of the German forces on its western frontier; Japan was the strongest power in East Asia, and there were no conflicts of interest between Germany and Japan. However, Matsuoka remained reserved. They would attack Singapore sooner or later, but at the moment he could not 'make any commitment on behalf of Japan'.

Ribbentrop, who met Matsuoka on a number of occasions during these days, was much more direct, trying to convince his Japanese colleague that Japan's next step ought to be 'a quick attack on Singapore'. Ribbentrop even went so far as to make the highly disingenuous claim that the conquest of Singapore would 'perhaps be the best way of keeping America out of the war because the United States would hardly dare risk sending its fleet into Japanese waters'. The argument was only too transparent. For German policy in Europe was banking precisely on America becoming entangled in a conflict in East Asia.[71] And the Japanese guest was by no means prepared to accept the argument that the impending confrontation between Germany and the Soviet Union would leave Japan with a free hand in East Asia. Matsuoka even asked Ribbentrop 'whether the Führer had ever contemplated a Russian–Japanese–German alliance'. Ribbentrop denied this and 'described a closer cooperation with Russia as an absolute impossibility, as the cultures of the armies and of the two populations were completely contrary to one another'.[72]

As Matsuoka was intending to continue his talks in Moscow on his way back to Tokyo, Ribbentrop advised him 'not to get in too deep with the Russians'. Indeed, he went considerably further: 'If Russia were ever to attack Japan, Germany would immediately fight'. Hitler had already given the same 'guarantee' a few days earlier when talking to Oshima Hiroshi, the Japanese ambassador in Berlin.[73] Thus Japan could 'move southwards towards Singapore without any fear of possible complications with Russia'. Ribbentrop believed, however, that 'Russia would not get involved in any military entanglements'. He went to the absolute limit of what Hitler had permitted to be mentioned about Barbarossa when adding that 'in any event, he wanted to point out to Matsuoka that a conflict with Russia was at least within the bounds of possibility'.[74] Interpreter Schmidt noted that in the course of the talks the German negotiators 'referred increasingly openly to the impend-ing conflict with the Soviet Union, without, however, ever actually spelling it out in so many words'.[75]

On 4 April, Hitler had another conversation with Matsuoka, who in the meantime had been in Rome. He emphasized 'that if Japan got into a con-flict with the United States, Germany would immediately take appropriate action'.[76] Germany's declaration that, if Japan became involved in a war with the United States or the Soviet Union it would immediately intervene, naturally implied that, in the event of a Soviet–German war, Japan would be expected to open a front against the Soviet Union. Matsuoka quickly made clear what he thought of this assumption. On his way back to Japan, he successfully pressed Moscow to agree a Japanese–Russian pact of neutrality, which was signed on 13 April, and was to remain in force throughout the whole of the war between Germany and the Soviet Union. Germany's attempt to incorporate the attack on the Soviet Union into a global war was thus doomed from the start.

The Hess affair

A few weeks later, on 10 May, the 'Führer's' deputy, Rudolf Hess, climbed into a fighter plane, which he had had placed at his disposal for test flights. Taking off from the airfield at the Messerschmidt works in Augsburg, he flew along a carefully prepared route over the North Sea, landing late in the evening by parachute on the estate of the Duke of Hamilton in Scotland. The two men had been acquaintances since the 1936 Olympic Games.

According to his own account, Hess was pursuing a peace mission and aiming to advance it by establishing direct contact with Britain's aristocracy. In this, however, he failed, as he was immediately arrested.

The German leadership, which was initially unaware of Hess's arrest, was in total shock. On 12 May, Hitler announced on the radio that Hess, 'whom he had banned from flying on account of a progressive illness he had been suffering from for years', had nevertheless undertaken a flight. 'A confused letter he left behind showed signs of mental derangement, which has given rise to fears that Party comrade Hess had been suffering from delusions.' It was to be feared that Hess 'had crashed, or had met with an accident'.[77] 'The Führer', noted Goebbels, 'is totally shattered'. 'What a spectacle for the world; the second man in line after the Führer mentally deranged. Appalling and inconceivable.'[78] The press was instructed 'not to give [the matter] undue prominence beyond the need to inform people of the basic facts'.[79]

Hitler had everybody arrested or interrogated who was in any way connected with the flight: adjutants, secretaries, engineers, and Professor Karl Haushofer, who was a friend of Hess, and Haushofer's son, Albrecht. In addition, Bormann, Hess's chief of staff, and Goebbels began a large-scale campaign against astrologers, fortune-tellers, faith healers, occultists, and other alternative 'teachings', as it was assumed that Hess, who was very interested in such abstruse ideas, had been encouraged to act by people who belonged to these circles. Bormann could refer to Hitler, who had long been trying to reason Hess out of his 'superstition'.[80] On 12 May, Hitler abolished the position of Deputy Führer, renaming Hess's previous office the Party Chancellery, appointing Bormann to head it, and, at the end of the month, making him a Reich Minister.[81] Unlike Hess, however, he was not named as Hitler's second successor after Göring. Instead, Göring was named as his sole deputy, responsible for carrying out Hitler's functions in the event that he was prevented from doing so.[82]

On 13 March, however, when the BBC announced that Hess was in British hands, Hitler had to issue another statement. Hess, he said, seemed 'to have been deluded in thinking that, by approaching English acquaintances, he could somehow still manage to bring about an understanding between Germany and England'. Moreover, Hess, who had been suffering for some years from health problems, had recently 'increasingly sought help from various mesmerists, astrologers etc.', and might have been negatively influenced by such people. It was also conceivable that 'Hess was lured into a trap by the British'. It was possible that the 'idealist' Hess had come to imagine that, by making a personal sacrifice, he would be able to prevent the British Empire's downfall.[83] A few days later, Goebbels ordered German propaganda to cease referring to the affair.[84]

The motives that prompted Hess to fly to England are still unclear. A peace mission undertaken on Hitler's behalf can most probably be ruled out. He was unable to provide the British authorities with any kind of authority to negotiate, nor did he have any proposals for an Anglo–German peace that went beyond Hitler's vague 'appeal to reason' of 19 July 1940. Moreover, Hitler's statements of 12 and 13 May declaring that Hess was mad put paid to his role as a potential negotiator. Hess does seem, however, to have regarded himself as a peace emissary, acting on Hitler's behalf, even if without his specific authorization. He was motivated by the idea that, by making contact with members of the aristocracy, he could bring about a change in Britain's attitude before Germany became involved in a two-front war by attacking the Soviet Union. It appears that the Deputy Führer's flight to Britain was a solo effort, which can only be understood against the background of his growing isolation within the Reich leadership.[85]

Towards the war of racial extermination

Hitler's decision to launch a war against the Soviet Union had originally been taken in the summer of 1940. The attack was intended to resolve the dilemma into which Hitler, notwithstanding his brilliant victory in the West, had manoeuvered himself. In spite of all his attempts, Britain had neither been defeated nor compelled to agree a peace in accordance with his wishes. It possessed its own overseas resources with which to fight the war as well as those of the United States. Germany had to assume that the United States would enter the war and would do so just when German pressure on Britain was increasing. Hitler's Soviet ally was waiting in the rear of the Reich, and Germany had to maintain a substantial military force to compensate for Russia's growing military power. In short, time was working against Hitler's Reich.

Thus Hitler had come to believe that a war against Russia would cut the Gordian knot. After victory over the Soviet Union, he would be in a position to concentrate all his forces on Britain, while Japan would be free from a threat to its rear and enabled to pin down American forces in East Asia. After toying during the final months of 1940 with alternatives to a war against the

Soviet Union in the shape of an 'anti-British continental bloc', by the end of 1940 his decision to fight a war in the East was irrevocable.

As the practical preparations for the attack began, in addition to military and strategic considerations, he became increasingly concerned with ideological goals. Since the beginning of the 1920s, he had been preoccupied with gaining 'living space' in the East, and we have seen that during the 1930s he had toyed with a project for the Ukraine. The space to be conquered had to be settled, economically exploited, and controlled. In accordance with his ideological premises, this had to occur on the basis of a racially determined hierarchy. The precondition for this was the destruction of the Soviet system and the violent elimination of the alleged Jewish leadership cadre in the Soviet Union. This would result in the destruction of the core of international 'Jewish Bolshevism', Hitler's main bogeyman since the end of the First World War.

From March 1941 onwards, Hitler made a series of decisions that were largely responsible for ensuring that the war against the Soviet Union acquired the character of a war of racial conquest and extermination. His role is documented in numerous statements, hints, and orders, which generally did not meet with reservations or opposition from the military, but rather, during the coming weeks and months, were faithfully turned into orders. To begin with, on 3 March, Hitler ordered Jodl, the chief of the Wehrmacht leadership staff, to revise the OKW draft directives for the occupation administration in the territories that were to be conquered. Hitler's new directive stated: 'The forthcoming campaign is more than just an armed conflict; it will lead to a confrontation between two ideologies. Given the extent of the area involved, bringing this war to an end will require more than defeating the enemy's armed forces.... The Jewish–Bolshevik intelligentsia, as the people's "oppressor" up to now, must be eliminated.'[86] A week before, the head of the OKW armaments office, General Thomas, had already heard of a comment made by Hitler and relayed by Göring that 'first of all, the Bolshevik leaders' had to be 'finished off quickly'.[87]

In accordance with Hitler's directives of 3 March, on the 13 March Jodl issued the 'Guidelines for the Special Areas relating to Barbarossa', in which he stated: 'The Führer has given the Reichsführer SS special tasks within the zone of army operations to prepare for its political administration, tasks deriving from the necessity of finally resolving the conflict between two opposing political systems. In carrying out these tasks the Reichsführer SS will be acting independently and on his own responsibility'.[88] What was envisaged by these 'special tasks' is clear from Jodl's instructions for finalizing the guidelines of 3 March. Referring to the directives given him by Hitler, they emphasized the need 'immediately to neutralize all Bolshevik chiefs and commissars'.[89]

On 17 March, Hitler made himself equally clear in a meeting with Halder and the Quartermaster General, Wagner: 'The intelligentsia installed by Stalin will have to be liquidated. The Russian Empire's leadership apparatus must be destroyed. We shall have to use force of the most brutal kind in Greater Russia.'[90] On 30 March Halder noted very similar key points made by Hitler at a meeting with generals: 'Clash of two ideologies. Devastating assessment of Bolshevism, equivalent of social delinquency. Communism is a huge threat for the future. We must get away from the idea of comradeship among soldiers. The communist is from first to last no comrade. This is a war of annihilation. If we don't see it in these terms, we may beat the enemy, but in 30 years' time we shall again be facing the communist enemy. We're not waging war to preserve the enemy. . . . Battle against Russia: annihilation of Bolshevist commissars and of the communist intelligentsia. . . . The struggle must be fought against the poison of disintegration. This isn't a matter for military courts. . . . Commissars and GPU people are criminals and must be dealt with as such. . . . This struggle will be very different from the fight in the West. In the East being harsh today means being mild in the future.' At the same time, Hitler indicated, at least in outline, how he envisaged reorganizing the area he was planning to conquer: 'Northern Russia will go to Finland. Protectorates for the Baltic states, Ukraine, White Russia. . . . The new states must be socialist states, but without their own intelligentsias.'[91]

Hitler's statement that military justice would not apply in Russia was quickly put into writing. The 'Edict on the Application of the Law and on Special Measures carried out by the Army' was initially drafted by the OKH, tightened by the OKW, and finally signed off by Hitler on 13 May. It ordered that criminal offences perpetrated by members of the Wehrmacht against civilians would no longer be automatically subject to disciplinary measures, but only in exceptional cases. In the case of offences committed by enemy civilians, the Wehrmacht's judicial system should not become involved at all; instead, punishment should be carried out by the troops on the spot. Localities where the Wehrmacht had been attacked 'in an insidious and underhand manner' should be subject to 'collective measures' if 'circumstances [prevent] the rapid identification of the individual perpetrators'.[92]

In tandem with the edict on military justice and in accordance with Hitler's requirement of 30 March ('annihilation of Bolshevist commissars and the communist intelligentsia'), by the beginning of May the OKH had prepared guidelines for the systematic murder of political functionaries of the Communist Party. When Rosenberg opposed the murder of all the functionaries on the grounds that it would complicate the administration of the occupied territories, the OKH sought a Führer decision. The result was contained in the 'Guidelines for the Treatment of Soviet Commissars' signed by the chief of the OKW, Keitel, on 6 June, which took account of Rosenberg's concerns. Commissars in the Red Army were 'to be finished off' by the troops; civilian commissars who opposed the troops were to be 'dealt with' in accordance with the Edict on Military Justice; the fate of those who were not guilty of any hostile act would be decided after the establishment of the occupation regime. On the question of 'guilty or not guilty' 'the impression a person makes . . . must be considered more important than the facts, which may prove impossible to verify'.[93] The 'Guidelines for the Conduct of the Troops in Russia' of 19 May, demanding 'ruthless and energetic measures against Bolshevist agitators, irregulars, saboteurs, Jews', and the 'total elimination of all forms of resistance', clearly indicate Hitler's radical views on the way to conduct the war in the East. The guidelines were distributed in sealed envelopes down to battalion level and were to be given to the troops 'on the arrival of the order to attack'.[94]

A week before the start of the invasion, Hitler reiterated his general views on the war in the East at a meeting of the commanders of the army groups and armies. In his statement to the Nuremberg Tribunal Keitel mentioned the key points, which are familiar from Hitler's previous remarks: it was a struggle between two conflicting ideologies, so that the traditional form of warfare governed by military justice had to be abandoned and all types of resistance be dealt with ruthlessly.[95] In addition, during the months preceding Barbarossa, a 'division of labour' was established between the army and the SS. This was in response to the guidelines of 13 March, which had been substantially altered at Hitler's request. The execution of civilians not involved in combat operations was, to a large extent, to be left to the SS murder squads. For this purpose the Army High Command and the Reichsführer SS came to an agreement, contained in the OKH order of 18 April 1941, to deploy 'special commandos of the Security Police and SD within the area of operations', which were to perform 'their tasks under their own responsibility'.[96] They were entitled, 'within the remit of their assignment, to carry out executive measures involving the civilian population'. This formula ensured that, unlike during the war with Poland, the SS special commandos were no longer subordinate to the OKW, and, although supported by the military, could operate independently of it.

On 21 May, Himmler announced that 'to implement the special orders that I have received from the Führer' (he was using the formula from the edict of 13 March) I intend to appoint Higher SS and Police Leaders in the territories that are to be conquered', to whom Einsatzgruppen [task forces], order police battalions, and units of the Waffen SS would be subordinated. 'They will carry out tasks specifically assigned to me.'[97] During the following months, these units received unequivocal orders, involving the murder of a vaguely defined Jewish leadership cadre in the Soviet Union, as well as communist functionaries and all those who appeared in the least suspect.[98]

Victory and beyond: Hitler's plans for world power

As we have seen, by the end of 1940, Hitler's plan to establish a base in North-West Africa and to cut off the Mediterranean from the west by occupying Gibraltar had failed, after he had been unable to achieve the necessary agreement of Spain or Vichy France. However, in 1941, alongside the preparations for Barbarossa, the German government began to consider how they could exploit the expected rapid military success in the East in order to weaken Britain's position in the Mediterranean (though not only there). For they now understood that an invasion of Britain during this year was as unrealistic as it had been in the previous one, and a naval blockade would not prove decisive.[99]

At the end of February, Hitler once again gave orders for the conquest of Gibraltar; the final plan was ready on 10 March. The attack was to be carried out in October (in other words after Barbarossa) with troops brought over from the East.[100] At the beginning of May, he also ordered 'Operation Isabella', a German counter measure against a possible British invasion of Spain and Portugal, which was to be undertaken by the German occupation forces in France.[101] However, Hitler had even more far-reaching ideas: in February, he ordered the OKW 'to prepare a study covering an advance from Afghanistan into India' after Barbarossa.[102] In response to these initiatives, at the beginning of April, Halder produced a plan, according to which, after Barbarossa, the army would be reduced to 136 divisions, of which only thirty-six would remain in the East as an army of occupation, a further eight in Scandinavia, thirty in the West, and six in the Balkans. In addition, seven would be assigned for an operational group in Spanish Morocco, eight for the advance in North Africa–Egypt, seventeen for the Afghanistan operation, and, assuming Turkey entered the war, fourteen for Anatolia, in order to intervene in the Near East from here as well.[103] The remaining ten, of which no details were given, were evidently intended as a reserve. They believed they had already secured a partner for their Afghanistan project in the Afghan economics minister, Abdul Majid Khan, who was sympathetic to the Nazi regime and was staying in Germany during the spring and early summer, allegedly for medical treatment. In May he declared that he was willing to collaborate with the Axis by supporting a partisan war across the Indian frontier. But, under the impression of the debacle suffered by the Axis in Iraq, to which we shall soon return, he quickly distanced himself from the plan.[104]

Hitler, however, had by no means given up the idea of deploying German forces to Afghanistan. After defeating the Soviet Union, he reckoned there would be plenty of willing partners in this region.[105] His aim was not, of course, the 'liberation' of India, but rather to threaten the British position in India, forcing Britain to make peace on his terms. The Indian nationalist leader, Subhas Chandra Bose, who had fled to Berlin, requested Hitler to issue a proclamation in favour of a 'Free India'. Although the 'Führer' had approved it in the spring, he was not in the end prepared to issue it.[106]

Rommel's successful offensive and the German campaign in south-east Europe also had an impact on the Arab world. In April, King Farouk of Egypt approached Hitler directly with a message that he was 'at one with his people in looking forward to seeing the German troops victorious in Egypt as soon as possible and as liberators from the intolerably brutal English yoke'. Hitler's reply was non-committal: Germany wanted the 'independence of Egypt and of the whole of the Arab world'.[107] In Iraq, from which Britain had transferred troops to Libya and Crete, there was a change in the balance of power in favour of the Axis. The former prime minister of Iraq, Raschid Ali al-Gailani, who had been overthrown at the end of January 1941, managed to regain power through a coup at the beginning of April. Hitler now got state secretary von Weizsäcker to reply to a letter which had been sent to him in January by the Grand Mufti of Jerusalem, Amin al-Husseini. The Grand Mufti was one of the central figures in anti-British resistance in the Arab world and was now living in Baghdad. Hitler promised in general terms to provide the assistance requested by Husseini for their common struggle with the 'English and the Jews', assuring him that he recognized the Arab states' struggle for independence.[108] Much encouraged by Hitler's support, in April Gailani resisted British pressure to allow the permanent stationing of substantial British forces in Iraq. This prompted a military confrontation at the beginning of May, as Britain was determined to eliminate this nascent Axis outpost. The German attempts to support the Iraqis by sending a few aircraft and weapons, in particular from Syria, which was under a French mandate, could not prevent Britain from bringing the whole country under its control by the end of the month.[109] Hitler had made it clear in his directive that the Iraq operation could have, at best, symbolic significance: 'whether and how' the British position in the Near East could be eliminated would only become apparent after Barbarossa.[110]

The weapons deliveries from Syria, which was under the control of Vichy France, had been made possible only after lengthy negotiations with Admiral Darlan, who had been Deputy Prime Minister since February. Darlan hoped that this concession (together with the sale of a large number of lorries to the German forces in North Africa) would re-establish direct contact with the German leadership, thereby improving Franco–German relations, which had been frozen since the end of 1940.[111] In fact, his concession did indeed secure him an invitation to Berchtesgaden. On 11 May, at the Berghof, Hitler agreed limited military cooperation with Darlan.[112] In the subsequent negotiations between the two countries' military authorities, French support for Iraq from Syria was confirmed and the prospect was raised of granting the use of the port of Bizerta in Tunisia for supplying the German forces in North Africa and the use of Dakar in Senegal for German naval operations in the Atlantic.[113] However, the agreement did not come into force because Germany was unwilling to respond to the French request for a peace agreement. Here too Hitler was working on the assumption that, after the impending victory over the Soviet Union, his position vis-à-vis France would have radically changed to his advantage. The support given to Iraq by the French mandate administration in Syria prompted Britain to attack Syria with the help of Free French troops and, despite resistance from Vichy forces, they managed to occupy it by the middle of July.[114] This demonstrated to Vichy France only too clearly that cooperating with the Axis carried a high risk.

The post-Barbarossa planning and, in particular, the idea of continuing to 'besiege' Britain by cutting off its access to the Mediterranean once again increased the importance of the navy in Germany's overall conduct of the war. In his address to the generals on 30 March Hitler had announced that, after Barbarossa, the programme of constructing capital ships would be renewed. The naval leadership did its best to emphasize the value of a high seas fleet. Since the autumn of 1940, the navy had begun using not only U-boats to attack merchant shipping, but also capital ships. The first were the cruisers 'Hipper' and 'Scheer'; they were followed in February by the battleships 'Scharnhorst' and 'Gneisenau'; and then, in May, the largest German battleship, the 'Bismarck', arrived in the North Atlantic.[115] Its sister ship, the 'Tirpitz', which had come into service a few months before, was intended to perform the same role.[116] Raeder told Hitler on 22 May that the naval high command considered that the use of Dakar would significantly enhance the conduct of naval warfare in the Atlantic. Hitler also approved Raeder's proposal to support the Spanish navy in building up their defences on the Canary Islands, so that they could be held 'at all times against the English and Americans'. When Hitler raised the possibility of occupying the Azores, Raeder told him that, even if they deployed the whole of the navy, they would still be unable to hold them. Nevertheless, Hitler stuck to the idea of using the islands, from autumn 1941 onwards, as a base 'for attacking the United States with long-range bombers'.[117]

It was, in fact, becoming increasingly clear that Germany would soon be confronted by an Anglo-American alliance and a strategic partnership between the two countries. The Lend-Lease law of 11 March gave the American President the power to supply Britain with considerably increased amounts of armaments. In response, Hitler extended the area of operations round the British Isles as far as Iceland.[118] The United States responded by sequestering all German ships in American ports and declaring the Atlantic west of 30 degrees longitude to be a security zone, subject to regular American patrols. On 20 April, Hitler ordered the navy to abide by this American move affecting the North Atlantic.[119] During these critical months before Barbarossa, he wanted at all costs to avoid an American entry into the war as a result of incidents on the high seas, an attitude he stuck to during the first months of the war in the East.[120] In any case, the sinking of the 'Bismarck' by the Royal Navy on 27 May and the destruction of the floating German supply bases in the Atlantic by the British produced a change in Germany's conduct of naval warfare. The naval high command had to abandon its idea of fighting a war in the Atlantic with capital ships.[121]

In his Directive No. 32 of 11 June Hitler once again clearly set out his goals for the period after the eastern campaign.[122] He was working on the

assumption that, after the Soviet Union had been destroyed, Germany and
Italy would no longer face a significant threat from hostile land forces on
the continent of Europe. Thus, the army could be significantly reduced to
the benefit of the navy and Luftwaffe. The increase in 'Franco–German
cooperation' would enable the Atlantic coast of North and West Africa to be
protected against 'Anglo-Saxon attacks'; in other words, the possible threat
from the United States was already being taken account of. Thus, in the first
place, the British positions in the Mediterranean and in the Near East could
already be eliminated in the autumn of 1941 or during the following winter
by a 'concentric attack' from three directions: first, through a continuation
of the German–Italian attack from Libya towards Egypt, through a second
offensive via Bulgaria and Turkey towards Suez, as well as 'in certain circumstances a further offensive through Transcaucasia and Iran towards Iraq'.
Secondly, after victory in the East, it would be easy to overcome Spanish resistance to a military operation in Gibraltar. Afterwards, German forces would
have to go over to Spanish Morocco, whereas they would leave the defence of
the Atlantic coast of North-West Africa and the elimination of the British and
Free French bases in West Africa to the French. The German navy and Luftwaffe
would then use the French bases on the West African coast and contemplate
occupying the islands in the Atlantic. Thirdly, the 'siege of England' would continue. An invasion of the island should be prepared in order to 'provoke and
complete . . . England's collapse, which is already under way'.[123]

The directive makes it clear that the conquest of an empire providing
living space in the East, regarded by most scholars as the 'core' of Hitler's
policy, did not represent his final goal. From his point of view, it was only
the prerequisite for a continuation of the war against Britain and its possessions on three continents. By occupying the western and eastern entries to
the Mediterranean, by establishing bases in North-West Africa and on the
Arabian peninsula, as well as by having the option of attacking India, the
Axis powers would have been in a position militarily to seal off continental
Europe, initially from Britain (although it was hoped that Britain would
soon be forced to make peace), and then from the United States. Protected
from the possibility of intervention by outside powers, the Axis powers
could then reorder the whole of the continent, including British possessions
in North Africa and the Near East, and possibly Central Asia as well. That
was the vision that Hitler was pursuing in 1941.

Had Hitler actually defeated the Soviet Union in 1941, these goals might
well have been feasible. What was megalomaniacal was not so much the idea

of establishing Wehrmacht bases as far away as Senegal, the Azores, Iraq, or Afghanistan, but rather the notion that the Soviet Union could be defeated in a matter of a few months.

During the final weeks before Barbarossa, Hitler evidently sought to secure the loyalty of his allies, although he was very reticent about informing them of his plans for the war. On 2 June, he once again met Mussolini at the Brenner. To Mussolini's annoyance,[124] the meeting, which was also attended by Ribbentrop, was arranged by Hitler at extremely short notice. The 'Führer' expatiated on every conceivable military and political aspect of the war, but, on the subject of his intentions vis-à-vis the Soviet Union, according to the interpreter, Schmidt, he did not 'utter a single syllable'; on the contrary, the aim of the meeting was, not least, to divert attention from his war plans.[125] He also appears to have left the Croatian head of state, Pavelić, whom he met at the Berghof on 6 June, in the dark about the impending war.[126] At this point Croatia's entry into the Tripartite Pact had already been agreed and was completed in Venice on 15 June.[127]

On 7 June, Hitler received King Boris of Bulgaria at the Berghof in the presence of Ribbentrop,[128] and, on 12 June at the Führer building in Munich he met the Romanian head of state, General Antonescu, whom he informed of his plan to attack the Soviet Union, although without revealing the details.[129] He justified it on the grounds that, by maintaining large troop concentrations on their common border, Stalin was pinning down large Wehrmacht units, preventing them from being used to win the war. While he considered a direct attack by the Soviet Union on Germany unlikely, he would be obliged to intervene in the much more probable event of a Soviet attack on Finland or Romania. The treaty the Soviet Union had made with Yugoslavia in April underlined the Soviet leadership's anti-German attitude. He could no longer tolerate the risk of an attack, and so had determined to engage in military action. Tempted by Hitler's offer of the prospect of territorial 'compensation', Antonescu declared that, in the event of a military conflict, Romania would be willing to fight alongside Germany from the very first day. A few days later, on 18 June, Hitler informed Antonescu that the behaviour of the Soviet Union, 'above all its preparations to attack, which are being stepped up daily, will compel me shortly to commit the German Wehrmacht in order to remove this threat to Europe once and for all'.[130]

On 14 June, eight days before the planned attack, he held a final military briefing.[131] On the following day, he summoned his Propaganda Minister to the Reich Chancellery in order to spell out to him in detail his reasons for the war with the Soviet Union, which he reckoned would last for four months. According to Hitler, Moscow wanted 'to keep out of the war until Europe was exhausted and had bled to death. Then Stalin would act, bolshevize Europe, and come into his own.' But, looked at from a global perspective, it was also necessary to expand the war: 'Tokyo would never get involved in a war with the United States so long as Russia is still a presence in its rear. So this is another reason why Russia must be eliminated.' Russia 'would attack us if we became weak, and then we would be faced with a two-front war, which we shall avoid with this preventive action. It's only then that our rear will be secure.'

Thus, Hitler described the attack on the Soviet Union as a 'preventive action', not because he felt threatened by an immediate attack from this quarter, but because he was afraid that, at a later date, Stalin could exploit Germany's potential weakness after a lengthy war in the West. This threat had to be prevented. Finally, the Soviet Union had to be attacked, in order, as Hitler put it, 'to free up people'. So long as the Soviet Union existed, Germany would be compelled to maintain 150 divisions, whose personnel 'are urgently needed for our war economy', in order to carry out the 'armaments, U-boat, and aircraft programmes, so that the United States can no longer threaten us'. Hitler was reiterating that in his view the successful continuation of the war against Britain and its empire depended on the defeat of the Soviet Union, as, with the European continent dominated by Germany and sealed off from intervention by the United States, Britain would be deprived of any hope of successfully defending itself. 'If Russia were defeated, then we could demobilize whole cohorts and build, rearm, and prepare. Only then can we begin a major Luftwaffe offensive against England. An invasion is, in any case, barely feasible. And that means we need to find other means of achieving victory.' Finally, Hitler reached the core of his argument: it did not matter 'whether we are in the right or in the wrong, we have to win.... We've in any case got so much to answer for, that we really must win, otherwise our whole nation, and we at the head of it, would be wiped out, with all that we hold dear.'[132]

34

Operation Barbarossa

Late in the evening of 21 June, Hitler summoned Goebbels, who had spent the day looking after a completely unsuspecting delegation led by his Italian colleague, Pavolini. Goebbels left his guests to their own devices and hurried to the Reich Chancellery. Here, he and Hitler walked up and down for three hours in the drawing room while the 'Führer' informed him about the latest arrangements for the attack on the Soviet Union, which had been planned for months. The time of attack was fixed for 3.00 a.m. They both agreed that, for propaganda purposes, they should claim 'that Russia's ambiguous attitude has hitherto prevented us from defeating England'. At 2.30 a.m., Hitler dismissed Goebbels, who now informed his colleagues, whom he had summoned to the Propaganda Ministry, about the forthcoming attack. In the early morning, Goebbels read out a proclamation, drafted by Hitler, over the radio. It was introduced by an excerpt from 'Les Préludes' by Franz Liszt, which he had just agreed with Hitler should be the music played before special announcements from this new theatre of war.[1]

In this proclamation Hitler gave a lengthy review of German–Soviet relations, providing an elaborate justification for his decision to make an alliance with Stalin in August 1939. He claimed that there had been increasing signs that the Soviet Union wanted to use the agreement to strengthen its position at the expense of Germany. He cited the Soviet claim to Lithuania in September 1939, the attack on Finland, as well as the occupation of the Baltic States in June 1940. He, of course, kept quiet about the fact that all these 'violations' corresponded to the 'demarcation of spheres of influence' agreed with Stalin in 1939. He knew that the Soviet Union had no interest in revealing the secret agreement that had been reached at the time, in which the two dictators had cold-bloodedly overridden the sovereignty of a total of six states.[2] Above all, according to Hitler, it had become increasingly clear that the Soviet Union was secretly cooperating with Britain.

Thus, by mobilizing large numbers of troops in 1940, it had tied up large German forces in the East, with the result that Germany had been unable to achieve a final military victory over Britain. Continuing his catalogue of the Soviet Union's sins, he claimed that, with some difficulty, he had managed to prevent the Soviet Union from absorbing Romania by agreeing to the latter's cession of Bessarabia; in reality, he had already ordered Ribbentrop to agree to this annexation in 1939.

At the Berlin meeting with Molotov in December 1940, Hitler continued, the former had clearly revealed Soviet ambitions in Romania, Finland, Bulgaria, and the Bosphorus. He wisely concealed the fact that, during these meetings, he himself had offered the Soviet Union the opportunity of helping itself to parts of the 'bankrupt' British Empire, if it cooperated with Germany. Both the Romanian coup of January 1941 and the Yugoslav putsch in March had, according to Hitler, been engineered by Moscow with far-reaching intentions. For it was only the victory of the Axis powers in the Balkans that had prevented Germany from becoming bogged down in months-long campaigns in the Balkans during the summer. This would have allowed the Soviets to complete the mobilization of their armies, increasing their readiness for war. Then, together with Britain, and supported by supplies from the United States, they would have been able to throttle and crush the German Reich and Italy. This was not a description of the imminent Soviet attack that he later repeatedly alleged as his justification for war, but rather of a Soviet strategy of attrition, forcing Germany to maintain increasingly large forces in eastern and south-eastern Europe. The massive Soviet mobilization and the allegedly repeated frontier violations had now made it necessary 'to confront this plot by the Jewish-Anglo-Saxon warmongers and the equally Jewish rulers in the Bolshevik headquarters in Moscow'.[3]

Ribbentrop summoned the Soviet ambassador to the Foreign Ministry for 4.00 a.m., in order to inform him officially of the start of hostilities, shortly before the official proclamation, but an hour after the war had actually begun.[4] Half an hour later, Schulenburg, the German ambassador in Moscow, met Molotov to hand over the official German note.[5] His previous visit to the Soviet Foreign Minister had been only a few hours earlier. On the evening of 21 June, Molotov had invited him in order to find out the reasons for Germany's possible 'dissatisfaction' with Soviet policy; there were, he said, even rumours of war flying about. Schulenburg, who only found out about the attack on the morning of 22 June, replied that he was unable to answer the question.[6] Hitler informed his main ally about the 'toughest decision of my life' in a letter that a German diplomat delivered to Ciano at 3.00 a.m.[7] Despite his annoyance, Mussolini, who was informed of the contents of the letter by Ciano in a telephone call to his holiday resort, Riccione, decided to declare war on the Soviet Union as well. In the meantime, he had become so dependent on his German ally that he had little choice other than to take this risky step.[8]

At a conference within the ministry on 23 June, Goebbels told his most important colleagues the essential reasons for the expansion of the war that were to be emphasized in propaganda. In the first place, as Hitler had pointed out in his proclamation, the military potential of the Soviet Union in Germany's rear prevented Germany from 'mounting a major offensive against England'. Secondly, the attack provided the opportunity of acquiring a huge 'increase in supplies of petrol, petroleum, and grain'. This was, however, such a blatant admission of plunder as a motive, that even Goebbels thought it was 'more suitable for word-of-mouth propaganda than for the media'. Thirdly, the fundamental 'conflict with Russia' could not be avoided, as 'in a Europe that had been pacified for decades, Bolshevism [could] not exist side by side with National Socialism'. Given this premise, it was better to have 'the confrontation now' rather than wait until the Soviet Union had completely rearmed.[9] These comments reflected the statements Hitler had made to Goebbels on 15 June, although with the important difference that he made no reference to continuing the war against the United States.

It was not until July that Goebbels changed the propaganda line in accordance with new instructions from Hitler. The attack, according to Hitler's new justification for it,[10] had occurred in order to preempt an imminent Soviet invasion. The Wehrmacht's initial major military successes suggested something quite different, however, namely that, in summer 1941, the Red Army was in no fit state for a war.[11]

Initial military operations and conflicts

From 23 June 1941 onwards, Hitler stayed in his East Prussian headquarters, the Wolf's Lair. This was a series of secluded bunkers and barracks in a remote and thickly wooded area near the small town of Rastenburg. From here he directed the war in the East.[12] The Wehrmacht entered the 'Eastern Campaign' with over three million soldiers, 600,000 motor vehicles, 3,350 tanks, over 7,000 guns, and 3,900 aircraft. In addition, the Romanian, Finnish, and Hungarian allies had, between them, some 500,000 men, although with a relatively limited amount of heavy weaponry. This force was confronted on the Soviet Union's western border by around three million members of the Red Army, which was far superior to the aggressors in tanks, artillery, and aircraft, but was not combat ready.[13]

The German offensive was carried out by three Army Groups with, initially, seven armies and four panzer groups. Two of the panzer groups, in which the army's panzer divisions and motorized units were concentrated, in other words the spearheads of the German offensive, were assigned to Army Group Centre, while one each was attached to the Army Groups North and South. This arrangement corresponded to Hitler's Barbarossa directive of December 1940, according to which the main thrust was initially to be in the centre, in order to destroy the enemy forces in White Russia; after that, the panzer units were intended to move north and, together with Army Group North, defeat the enemy in the Baltic region. Although the army had implemented this directive in its deployment arrangements in January 1941,[14] since the summer of 1940, Halder, the Chief of the General Staff, had been working on another plan. He wanted to win the war through a thrust by Army Group Centre towards Moscow and, having failed to get his way, hoped that, after the major successes that were anticipated in the initial phase of the campaign, he would still be able to win Hitler over to his point of view.[15] This basic conflict between Hitler and Halder was to determine the first stage of the war in the East. It now became clear that, whereas during the war in the West, Hitler had intervened only sporadically in military operations, he was now insisting on running them on a daily basis.

By the end of June, with two pincer movements, first near Bialystock and then near Minsk, Army Group Centre had succeeded in surrounding and then destroying or taking prisoner substantial Soviet forces. In the meantime, Army Group North had advanced rapidly through Lithuania and Latvia: Dünaburg (Daugavpils) and Riga were captured by the end of June. Army Group South, which had been weakened by the withdrawal of the 12th Army to Greece, at first only attacked on its northern flank, making slow progress because of relatively strong resistance from the Red Army.[16] While Halder was pressing for Army Group Centre to continue the rapid advance towards Smolensk and thus in the direction of Moscow, Hitler hesitated, wanting to clear the pocket between Bialystock and Minsk completely and protect the flanks of the panzer units. This resulted in differences over the planning of operations, leading to quite absurd situations. Thus, in accordance with Hitler's wishes, the commander-in-chief of the army ordered Army Group Centre merely to secure the strategically important city of Brobujsk, whereas Halder was hoping that Guderian's panzer group, deployed there, would take the initiative to capture the city, and then advance to the river Dnieper, which was only about 50 kilometres away. 'We must hope', Halder noted on 29 June, 'that the mid-level commanders will do the right thing on their own initiative without having received specific orders, which we are unable to give them because of the Führer's instruction to the C-in-C Army.'[17]

Thus Halder was aiming to bypass the Supreme Commander's directives by issuing broadly framed orders and hinting at what he wanted. He relied on the commanders at the front intuitively acting in tune with the basic intentions of the general staff. When, a few days later, Hitler wanted to intervene once again in the conduct of operations, Halder noted critically that resolving matters of detail should be left to army and corps commanders. However, 'people at the top don't understand the need to place their trust in the people on the ground, though that is one of the most valuable features of our style of leadership. This is because they're unaware of the value of the education and training that our leadership corps has gone through together.'[18]

In the end, during July, this conflict came out into the open, as both continued to pursue their different approaches. Halder remained committed to capturing Moscow, whereas Hitler considered Leningrad and Kiev to be the more important goals. Hitler was concerned, on the one hand, to destroy the Soviet Union's main military forces,[19] and, on the other with economic issues affecting the war. Leningrad had to be captured in order to prevent the Soviet fleet from blocking Germany's access to iron ore through the Baltic, while in the Ukraine he wanted to seize the Donets basin, a centre of Soviet heavy industry, and cut off oil supplies from the Caucasus. On 30 June, he told Halder that, to begin with, he wanted 'to make a clean sweep' in the north with panzer units and that he reckoned that 'Moscow could wait until August and then be taken with infantry units'.[20] Halder responded on the same day by getting Brauchitsch to sign off a memorandum setting out the opposite point of view, namely that a rapid thrust towards Moscow would prove decisive in ending the war.[21] Essentially, this dispute during the summer of 1941 involved the deployment of the panzer groups 2 and 3, which Halder wanted to continue to use in Army Group Centre's advance

on Moscow, whereas Hitler intended to deploy them to support the operations of Army Groups North and South. In any case, in early July, both
Hitler and Halder believed that the war in the East had already been won.[22]

On 4 July, Hitler was still preoccupied with the question of the future
deployment of the panzer units, without being able to reach a decision: 'It
will be the most difficult decision of this campaign'.[23] After a presentation
by Halder and Brauchitsch, on 8 July he decided that Army Group Centre
should carry out another pincer movement in order to clear the way for the
advance on Moscow. However, the two panzer units should then remain
behind so that they could take on tasks in the north and south. Leningrad
and Moscow should be 'razed to the ground, to prevent people from continuing to live there whom we would then have to feed during the winter'.
That would be the task of the Luftwaffe.[24]

The further the German forces advanced, the more urgent became the
question of the future deployment of the panzer units. This inevitably sharp-
ened the disagreement between Hitler and the army leadership over the
main focus of the operations.[25] Halder's diary entries for 14 July show that,
at this point, the growing discontent with Hitler's interventions in matters
of detail in the military operations was reaching a critical stage: 'Hitler's
endless interventions in matters he does not properly understand are turning into a real menace, which is becoming intolerable.'[26]

In his Directive No. 33 of 19 July Hitler left no doubt about his
determination to get his way on the conduct of the war. It emphasized the
need to 'continue to prevent substantial enemy forces from escaping into
the depths of Russia and to destroy them'.[27] His message was that in cases of
doubt he was not interested in engaging in operations deep into enemy territory, but rather in eliminating Soviet units that were contained in small
pockets in front of the German lines. After Brauchitsch had spoken to Hitler
on 22 July, he supplemented Directive No. 33. After the situation in the
south had been sorted out, Army Group Centre was now ordered to 'capture Moscow' and no longer simply to continue its march on Moscow, as
had been stated in Directive No. 19 of 19 July. However, this was merely an
apparent concession to the army leadership, as at the same time he removed
the panzer units from Army Group Centre for this operation.[28]

After a further vain approach to Hitler, undertaken together with
Brauchitsch,[29] Halder now tried to get the general staffs of the army groups
to modify Hitler's directive so that its application was more in tune with his
own approach.[30] When, on 26 July, Hitler had the idea of deploying the

tanks of Army Group Centre against an enemy concentration near Gomel, Halder rejected it on the grounds that it represented a 'move from strategic to tactical operations'. If they were going systematically to eliminate all the pockets lying between the various thrusts, this would restrict movement and they would end up engaging in static warfare.[31] However, Hitler insisted on the destruction of this enemy group, telling Halder during a meeting on 26 July that 'Russians couldn't be defeated by operational successes, because they simply didn't recognize them. So they had to be smashed piecemeal in what might be considered small tactical envelopments.' Halder was prepared to admit that this point had 'some merit', but with this kind of thinking they were 'leaving the initiative to the enemy'; 'what had hitherto been a dynamic operation would start becoming bogged down'.[32] Although Brauchitsch succeeded in mobilizing Bock and Jodl in his support,[33] on 28 July, Hitler once again insisted 'that the industrial area round Kharkov is more important to him than Moscow'. Expansive operations had to be subordinated to 'the elimination of enemy forces ahead of the front line'.[34] Thus, in his Directive No. 34 of 30 July he ordered that Army Group Centre should temporarily go on the defensive, thereby postponing for the time being the decision on the main focus of future German operations.[35] In short, the German armies had within a few weeks penetrated deep into Soviet territory without the political–military leadership being able to agree on what their further military goals should be.

At the beginning of August, Halder's method of working on the generals in the field behind Hitler's back and getting them to follow his line began to pay off. Hitler was increasingly confronted with requests from his generals to begin an offensive on Moscow, in some cases cleverly using his own arguments to persuade him to adopt the army leadership's approach.[36] On 12 August, Hitler finally issued his supplement to Directive No. 34: Army Group Centre's 'aim must be to deprive the enemy of the whole of the political, armaments, and transport hub around Moscow before the onset of winter'. However, he made this objective dependent on a set of preconditions that could hardly be met. In the first place, Army Group Centre had to remove the threat that Hitler believed existed on its two flanks, and re-equip its panzer units. In addition, he insisted that, before the offensive against Moscow could begin, 'the operations against Leningrad must be concluded'.[37] On 14 August, he appeared to be 'seriously disturbed' about an enemy breakthrough near Staraja Russa in the area of Army Group North, demanding that Halder deploy a panzer corps made up of elements from Army Group Centre. This prompted the latter to note that 'responding in this way to pinpricks undermines any attempt at producing an operational plan and focusing on strategic targets'.[38]

The conflict was now coming to a head, although, during this period, Hitler was partly out of action as a result of contracting dysentery.[39] After a presentation by Brauchitsch, on 15 August he ordered that Army Group Centre should, for the time being, cease any further offensives in the direction of Moscow. First of all, the offensive by Army Group North had to be brought to a rapid and successful conclusion and, for this purpose, powerful elements of Panzer Group 3 were to be transferred to it. The advance on Moscow could be continued only after the successful conclusion of the northern operations.[40] Halder responded by preparing a proposal for the advance by Army Group Centre to continue alongside those of Army Groups North and South,[41] which Brauchitsch adopted, and which was further supported by an assessment from the OKW.[42] According to Halder, Army Group Centre had to secure the 'destruction of the strong enemy forces in front of it' and 'capture the industrial area round Moscow'. This would 'prevent the enemy from re-equipping its armed forces and from building up military units capable of mounting serious offensives against us'. Hitler, now recovered, responded on 21 August with a new Führer Directive in which he definitively stated that the 'Army leadership's proposal is not in accord with my views'. The most important goal to be achieved before the onset of winter was 'not the capture of Moscow', but the conquest of the Crimea and the Donets basin, the cutting off of the Soviet oil supplies from the Caucasus, as well as the isolation of Leningrad. The next task for Army Group Centre was, together with Army Group South, to surround and destroy the 5th Soviet Army.[43] Hitler justified his rejection of Halder's proposal in more detail the following day by arguing that more important than the conquest of industrial sites was the 'destruction or rather removal of essential sources of raw materials' and 'to deal the enemy a knock-out blow'. He made a detailed critique of the army leadership's conduct of operations hitherto, telling them in no uncertain terms that the motorized units could 'under no circumstances be considered integral parts of a particular army group or army'; they were at the exclusive disposal of the Supreme Command.[44]

Halder considered the situation resulting from Hitler's intervention as 'intolerable' and his treatment of Brauchitsch as 'unheard of'. He suggested to the commander-in-chief that they should both resign, which Brauchitsch, however, declined to do.[45] At the end of the month, a conversation took place between Hitler and Brauchitsch, in which the 'Führer' told his army commander-in-chief that 'he hadn't meant it like that', thereby apparently putting an end to the dispute for the time being.[46] During a visit to Fedor von Bock, the commander of Army Group Centre, on 23 August, he and Halder agreed that the offensive should be continued towards the east, in the direction of Moscow, and not to the south. Heinz Guderian, the commander of Panzer Group 2, who was brought into the discussion, stated that his troops were simply not in a position to carry out the offensive ordered by Hitler.[47] On the same day, at Halder's and Bock's suggestion, Guderian went to see Hitler in order to press the arguments for an advance on Moscow. However, Hitler was not prepared to change his priorities and, in the end, Guderian suppressed his concerns and acquiesced – much to Halder's and Bock's disappointment.[48]

In the end, however hard the army leadership had tried to bypass Hitler's directives by issuing flexible orders or by dressing up their aims as, in reality, identical to his own goals, by continually intervening, the 'Führer' had managed to get his way in this major dispute over strategic objectives. It was inevitable that these disagreements had damaged the basis of trust between the political and military leadership. The army believed that Hitler's constant interventions were hampering a bold military operation, while from Hitler's perspective the army was showing no awareness of the requirements of the war economy. What lay behind this dispute was the basic problem posed by Germany's 'Eastern Campaign', for, despite its remarkable success, during the first weeks it was already becoming apparent that Germany had underestimated both the quality and quantity of the Soviet armed forces. In the middle of August, Hitler told Goebbels that he had 'estimated the number of Soviet tanks as 5,000, whereas in reality they had around 20,000. We thought they had about 10,000 aircraft, in fact they had over 20,000...'[49] In the meantime, his opponent, Halder, had reached the same conclusion: they had 'underestimated...the Russian colossus. At the start of the war we reckoned with about 200 enemy divisions. Up to now we have already counted 360.'[50] Despite its heavy losses in the pockets produced by encirclements, the Red Army had nonetheless succeeded in withdrawing a large part of its forces, and in managing to mobilize and re-equip new units. Behind the dispute about strategic objectives lay the unspoken realization that the Soviet Union could not be defeated before the onset of winter. Neither offensives by the flanks towards Leningrad and Kiev, nor an advance on Moscow in the centre could achieve this goal.[51]

Hitler's further war plans

During the first phase of this war, Hitler was already energetically pursuing his goals, as summed up on 11 June, for the period after Barbarossa.[52] To facilitate further conquests he was even prepared to withdraw troops, which in reality were urgently needed in the eastern theatre. On 8 July, he ordered brand new tanks to be kept in reserve in Germany, in order to have new units ready for action outside Russia.[53] Six days later, he issued guidelines in the form of a Führer Directive for a reduction in the size of the army. It began with the statement: 'After the defeat of Russia our military control of the European area will shortly enable us significantly to reduce the size of the army.' The panzer arm was, however, to be expanded (among other things by '4 more tropical panzer divisions'), while the main focus of rearmament was to be shifted from the army to the Luftwaffe. Naval rearmament was to be limited to those measures that 'directly apply to the war against England and the United States, assuming it enters the war'.[54] With this restriction of naval rearmament largely to U-boat construction – in June he had been treating the navy on a par with the Luftwaffe – he was taking account of the setbacks that the German navy had been increasingly suffering in the Atlantic since the sinking of the 'Bismarck' in May.[55] Big capital ships were no longer an option for 'besieging' Great Britain. On 4 August, during a visit to Army Group Centre, Hitler announced that, in order to deal with a possible British invasion of the Iberian peninsula, or landing in West Africa, but also to meet 'other eventualities', a 'mobile reserve' must be created in the Reich. This required retaining two panzer divisions and the creation of new panzer units in Germany.[56]

At the end of August, Hitler approved the OKW memorandum 'Concerning the Strategic Situation in the Late Summer of 1941 as the Basis for Further Political and Military Goals' and had it sent to the chiefs of the Wehrmacht branches and the Foreign Minister. This was an indirect admission that his original plan of bringing the whole of the Mediterranean under his control and establishing bases on the Atlantic coast, following a rapid victory over the Soviet Union, was no longer feasible, at least during 1941. For in the memorandum, albeit discreetly expressed, the OKW was no longer assuming that the war in the East could be won during that year.[57] The detailed memorandum made it clear that, without this victory, almost all further German war plans, such as had been developed during the first half of 1941 – the cutting off of the Mediterranean with Spanish and French assistance, the 'besieging' of Britain through an intensification of the 'Battle of the Atlantic', the offensive through Turkey, and the advance through North Africa towards the Suez Canal – could not be carried out. These options were still kept in view, but they could not now be realized before spring 1942 at the earliest. The only way of threatening Britain's position in the Near East *before* complete victory over the Soviet Union would be to mount a successful offensive via the Caucasus.[58] The earliest this could start would be May 1942, as a continuation of a successful offensive in the south of the eastern front. An invasion of Britain would not be possible before autumn 1942, as a final option in case the 'siege' of the island did not prove decisive.

Thus, by the end of August, Hitler was having to face the fact that not only his idea of a 'lightning war' against the Soviet Union, but also the rapid realization of his other war plans – to undermine Britain's position in the Mediterranean during 1941, to bring Britain to its knees through an increase in naval warfare, and to establish a position from North Africa through the Near East to the Urals, from which he could calmly face the prospect of a war with the United States – were all doomed to failure. Now that he had been unable to consolidate his future empire he had to fear that the United States, whose entry into the war appeared from month to month more likely, would be able to build a base in the Mediterranean, from which, together with Britain, it could mount an attack on the weak southern flank of the Axis. During the first months of the war in the East, as relations with the United States rapidly deteriorated, Hitler had placed great emphasis on trying to delay its entry into the war for at least some months. When, on 9 July, during one of his presentations, Raeder had asked him whether the recent occupation of Iceland by the United States meant its 'entry into the war', Hitler replied that 'he was extremely anxious to postpone the entry of the United States for one or two more months'. For one thing, he needed the whole of the Luftwaffe for the war in the East, while 'the success of the eastern campaign would have an enormous effect on the whole situation, including on the attitude of the United States'.[59]

Whereas during the visit of the Japanese foreign minister to Berlin at the end of March/beginning of April 1941, Hitler and Ribbentrop had been

putting huge pressure on Japan to attack Singapore,[60] now their concern
was to prevent the Japanese from precipitately going to war with the United
States. In the medium term, after the victory over the Soviet Union, such a
war would of course be very welcome. Thus Berlin was wary of a potential
American–Japanese rapprochement.[61] This set of aims formed the background to Hitler's meeting with Oshima on 15 July. 'We shall not', he told
Oshima, 'be able to avoid a conflict with America'. And then he came to the
point: 'The only way of keeping the United States out of the war would be
by defeating Russia, and only then if Japan and Germany act with clear and
ice-cold determination.'[62] He added: 'And if there was going to be war with
the United States then he would be leading it'. By this he did not mean the
global war deploying the 'Z fleet' and long-range bombers, which he considered the task of his successors.[63] Instead, he was thinking of a European
continent under German rule being able successfully to defend itself against
an American invasion. However, this must not occur during the next few
months; first of all, the Soviet Union had to be defeated. The United States
was not ready for war, Hitler opined in August.[64] In the middle of September,
he instructed Raeder that, 'incidents must not be allowed to occur in the
trade war' before the middle of October, since, at the end of September, 'the
Russian campaign would reach a major turning point'.[65] At that stage he
was already aware that his post-Barbarossa plans could no longer be realized
before the middle of 1942. He nevertheless gave the appearance of being
confident of victory and, on several occasions when speaking to Goebbels,
played down the threat of the United States entering the war.[66] He must,
however, have been fully aware that he was running out of time.

While the entry of Japan into a war with the United States was now to
be postponed in order to prevent the latter from becoming engaged in
Europe, Hitler became all the more desperate for a Japanese attack on the
Soviet Union. This would have immediately eased the situation on the eastern front, opened a realistic prospect of victory over the Soviet Union and,
in the process, increased the likelihood of preventing American intervention.
Immediately after the start of the war with the Soviet Union, Ribbentrop
had put the Japanese under huge pressure to take this step.[67] But month
after month went by and the Japanese government failed to act; on the contrary, it had decided in August to stay out of the war with the Soviet Union.[68]
At this time, Hitler still behaved as though he was convinced that Japan
would enter the war with the Soviet Union.[69] In contrast to the Foreign
Ministry, he did not want to put any pressure on Japan because that could

appear a sign of weakness.[70] By September, he was only hoping for such an intervention; in November he believed it might come about 'in certain circumstances'.[71]

Occupation fantasies

In a series of endless monologues while at his headquarters in East Prussia during the summer and autumn of 1941, Hitler developed his vision of a German-dominated 'eastern area'. His audiences were members of his intimate entourage or visitors who were present at lunch or dinner; often these monologues lasted late into the evening. He invariably began by emphasizing the 'racial inferiority' of the indigenous population. He was convinced that 'the Russian does not naturally seek to create a higher form of society'. Russia only managed to establish a 'state form' by using compulsion. It was only possible to get Russians, who were by nature work-shy, to work 'by creating a really tough organization'. The Russian was 'incapable of organizing himself; he can only be organized'.[72] The Ukrainians were 'just as lazy, disorganized and, nihilistic–anarchistic'.[73] In short, 'the Slavs are a mass of born slaves crying out for a master'.[74] The fact that Stalin had managed 'to forge a state out of this Slav rabble' [lit. 'rabbit family'], albeit 'only by using the toughest form of compulsion and with the aid of the Jews', made him in Hitler's eyes 'one of the greatest men alive'.[75]

Given these opinions, Hitler's views on how to rule this newly conquered territory were appropriately barbaric. No military power, no 'Bolshevist form of state must be allowed to exist on this side of the Urals, not even an urban power centre'.[76] He kept describing in detail how the great Soviet cities were to be destroyed. In August, he announced that he did not even intend 'to take Petersburg and Kiev by force of arms, but to starve them out'. He wanted to surround St Petersburg, in those days Leningrad, and then 'smash' it with the Luftwaffe and artillery.[77] In fact, the total destruction of Leningrad became one of Hitler's favourite topics.[78] It was necessary, he told Goebbels, for this city 'totally to disappear'.[79] They could not feed the 'mass of 5 million people squashed together there. Thus, it's very much in our interest if Leningrad resists for a time. We can then destroy this city of millions street by street, quarter by quarter, and then, when we occupy it, the ruins that remain can be blown up until it has been razed to the ground. The most gruesome urban drama that history has ever known is developing here. Bolshevism, which began with hunger, blood, and tears will perish in hunger, blood, and tears. Though it is a cruel nemesis, historically it is a just one.' The significance of the destruction of the city for the future should not be underestimated. 'The plough must once again pass over this city. It was conceived by Asiatic Slavs as a gate of entry to Europe. This gate of entry must be closed.'[80] In November, he committed himself to the destruction of the city in a speech broadcast by the media.[81] He ignored the navy's interest in using its docks and armaments facilities.[82]

Hitler's comments clearly show that his determination to conquer the city had less to do with the economic motives with which he was always trying to justify it, such as protecting iron ore supplies from the Gulf of Finland from the Red Army, and more to do with his desire to destroy the city that bore the name of the founder of the Soviet Union. Prestige and visceral hatred determined his attitude. The same was true of Moscow, which also 'had to disappear from the face of the earth'.[83] In principle, he told his audience, there should be no fixed boundary to Germany's living space in the east; even the Urals were not the final frontier with Asia, but rather 'the place where settlements of Germanic-type people will cease and pure Slavdom begins. It is our task to push this frontier as far as possible to the east and, if necessary, beyond the Urals.'[84] West of the Urals 'no organized Russian state can be allowed to exist!'[85] He was even prepared to make a peace treaty with the remnant of the Soviet Union that would be left in Asia, but only after the Red Army had been completely crushed.[86]

This ruthless colonial policy was justified by 'nature's eternal law of the stronger, which gives Germany the right before history to subjugate these racially inferior peoples, to rule them, and to force them to undertake productive labour. Although this is a long way from Christian ethics, the very fact that it corresponds to the older and more tried and tested laws of nature ensures its permanence.'[87] 'After all, the great migrations... came from the East and, with us begins the ebb tide flooding from the West back to the East....The laws of nature require uninterrupted killing in order for the superior to survive.'[88] Seen in a longer-term historical perspective, his aims were not 'exorbitant', for they only involved 'territories where Germanic peoples had been settled in the past'.[89]

He developed practical ideas for settling the conquered territories,[90] which he delighted in elaborating on to his audience. Priority was to be given to the construction of great transport networks: big canal projects,[91] autobahns, as well as a broad-gauge railway of three metres, which he was particularly interested in.[92] As centres of settlement, 'German cities' would be linked together along these arterial roads 'as in a pearl necklace'. The 'German agencies and authorities will be housed in splendid buildings, the governors in palaces.... Around the cities to a depth of thirty to forty kilometres we shall have a belt of attractive villages, linked together by high quality roads.'[93] The 'monotonous appearance of the Russian Steppe' would be gradually transformed into a cultural landscape on the Central European model. In ten years' time, four, in twenty years, at least ten, perhaps even twenty, million 'Germans' would settle there,[94] not only from the Reich, but also from America, Scandinavia, the Netherlands, and Flanders. The Swiss, however, could only be used as hotel managers.[95]

The main focus of the German settlement programme was to be the southern Ukraine; he wanted to turn the Crimea, whose attractive landscape he praised,[96] into an Eastern Goths' Gau, with the best 'human material' from all the 'Nordic-type' nations.[97] In his fantasies he had pictured life in the new eastern territories down to the last detail. Thus he kept talking about installing retired NCOs, discharged after twelve years' service, as peasant settlers. They would be given fully-equipped farms, but would have to commit to marrying 'country girls not town girls'.[98]

The model for all these visions of the future, which he kept coming back to, was British rule in India, as he understood it. He remarked in admiration that 250,000 Englishmen ruled 400 million Indians without having to exercise a tight control over the lives of the inhabitants.[99] He considered this way of ruling the 'colonial territory' in the East, in which there was no intention of introducing civilized Central European standards, absolutely ideal.[100] The main aim, after all, was to keep the indigenous population in a primitive state. The 'natives' would be 'screened'. 'We shall get rid of all the dangerous Jews.' He did not want to be bothered with the Russian cities; they 'must all die out'. There was no need to have 'pangs of conscience' about it; they had 'absolutely no responsibility for the people involved'. It was enough for them 'to recognise the traffic signs, so that they don't get in the way of our vehicles!' The main task was 'Germanization, by bringing in Germans and treating the natives like Red Indians'.[101]

Given the extensive ground their colonial rule would cover, their methods were bound to be draconian. 'Of course the police there will have to be trigger-happy. Party officials will know what to do.' 'A new type of man will emerge, ruler-types, though we shan't of course be able to use them in the West: Viceroys.'[102] If the natives started a revolution 'then we only need to drop a few bombs on their cities and that will be that. Once a year we shall take a group of Kyrgizes through the capital in order to impress them with the grandeur of its monuments.'[103]

He was approaching this matter with an 'ice-cold attitude. I feel I am merely the executor of the will of history. I don't care in the least what people think of me at the moment. Law is an invention of human beings. Nature can't be contained by human planning or statutes. The heavens only acknowledge strength. The idea that everybody should love one another is a theory that has actually been most effectively refuted by those who believe it.' 'The German people [have] now secured... what they need to be of world importance'. He was very pleased 'that, as a result of this development, we have been drawn away from the Mediterranean' and in future would be living in a 'Northland'. The Ukraine and then the Volga basin would one day be the 'granaries of Europe'.[104] The Crimea had citrus fruits and they would plant rubber plants and cotton on a large scale. They would get reeds from the Pripet marshes. 'We'll supply the Ukrainians with scarves, glass beads, and whatever else colonial peoples like.' The Germans living in the east would have to 'form a closed society, like a fortress; the least of our stable lads must be superior to any native'.[105] On the railways Germans would have to travel in 'the first or second class' to distinguish themselves from the 'natives'.[106]

Possession of the vast eastern space would enable Europe under German leadership to practise autarky, making it independent of world trade and secure against blockade. 'When we're the masters of Europe we shall dominate the world.'[107] In future, in addition to the '130 million' in the Reich there would be ninety million in the Ukraine, as well as the other states of the 'new Europe', altogether 400 million people. With their characteristic mixture of megalomaniacal building projects, romantic ideas about colonial settlement, and brutal methods of rule, Hitler's extravagant fantasies about future life in 'Germany's eastern area' were not merely pipe dreams. Within a short time, he was taking steps to turn them into reality.

Occupation policy

On 16 July, three and a half weeks after the start of the war, at a meeting in his headquarters, Hitler took the vital decisions affecting the direction and structure of future occupation policy in the east; Göring, Keitel, Rosenberg,

and Bormann were present. To begin with, Hitler explained that the occupation phase would enable them to carry out certain measures – he referred
to 'shootings, resettlement etc.' – designed to prepare for the final domination
of the territory, without revealing Germany's long-term aims. It was, however, already clear that they would never give up the conquered territories.
'Basically', Hitler continued, 'we now have the task of cutting up the giant
cake according to our needs, in order to be able, first, to dominate it, second,
to administer it, and, third, to exploit it.' According to Hitler, Stalin's call for
partisan warfare had an advantage: 'It enables us to exterminate everyone
who opposes us'. He also declared: this 'huge area' could best be 'pacified' if
'we shoot everybody who even looks askance'. 'It must never again be possible to construct a military power west of the Urals, even if we have to
wage war for a hundred years.' They must never permit anybody but
Germans to carry arms, as otherwise Germany would inevitably one day
become the target.

The 'newly-won eastern region [Ostraum]' had to become a 'Garden of
Eden'. A considerable portion of the occupied territories would have to be
incorporated into the Reich. This included the whole of the Baltic states, as
well as the Crimea (which had to be completely cleared of its indigenous
population), together with a substantial hinterland in the north of the peninsula, as well as the Volga colony, in other words the autonomous 'Soviet
Republic of the Volga Germans' on Russian territory bordering Kazakhstan.
The area round Baku was also to become Reich territory, as was the Kola
Peninsula with its extensive reserves of nickel. Galicia would be subordinated
to Governor General Frank. According to Rosenberg, Hitler even took the
trouble to sketch in the new frontiers on a map.[108]

These plans for annexations were very different from the announcements
Hitler had made to his generals on 30 March. At that time, he had still been
talking about a protectorate over the 'Baltic countries' as well as the acquisition of the Ukraine and White Russia. Indeed, Hitler's statement of 16 July
even exceeded the settlement plans that Himmler as Reich Settlement
Commissar had worked out in response to Germany's rapid advances.
Hitler's new statement had made these plans obsolete and, during the following months, they had to be completely revised.[109] These 'spontaneous'
commitments by Hitler followed a familiar pattern. As with his earlier conquests (Austria, Poland, France, and the Balkans), the 'Führer' had decided
on his plans for the new order only in the course of, or after, the occupation.
Now, once again, in summer 1941, he allowed himself to be carried away by

his euphoria at an (apparent) victory and to commit himself to much more 'elaborate' plans than he had originally envisaged.

In the middle of June, Hitler was determined to carry out his settlement plans in the 'eastern region' by embarking on huge mass expulsions while eliminating potential resistance in the most brutal way. As we have seen, he also wanted to destroy completely the main urban centres of the Soviet Union, to depopulate them, and then do nothing to feed their former populations. This resulted in a policy geared to the systematic starvation of the population of the Soviet cities. A meeting of state secretaries at the beginning of May 1941 had already agreed that the Soviet Union must feed the whole of the Wehrmacht, which would undoubtedly 'result in the starvation of tens of millions of people'.[110] In accordance with his pre-war instructions, the Jewish–Bolshevik leadership, as he envisaged it, was to be liquidated. In addition, at the end of the war he intended to deport Europe's Jews to the 'eastern territories'; he had repeatedly 'prophesied' their 'annihilation'. By brutally purging this territory he would create an empty space that could be colonized with Germans and exploited economically. These principles established by Hitler for future occupation policy in the East help explain how those who were to carry out this policy during the coming months set about 'ruling' the 'eastern region'.

On 17 July, the day after the notorious meeting with Göring, Bormann, Keitel, and Rosenberg, Hitler signed the Führer edict concerning the administration of the occupied territories, which contained further conclusions of the previous day's conference. After the end of military operations, a civil administration was to be established, for which Rosenberg would be responsible as Reich Minister for the Occupied Eastern Territories. The occupied territories were to be divided into Reich commissariats subordinate to Rosenberg.[111] A few days later, as had been decided at the meeting of 16 July, Gauleiters Hinrich Lohse (Schleswig-Holstein) and Erich Koch (East Prussia) were appointed Reich Commissars in the Ostland (Baltic states and White Russia) and the Ukraine respectively. By appointing the 'masterful' Koch, despite Rosenberg's objections,[112] Hitler ensured that Rosenberg's idea of limited cooperation with local populations would not apply in the Ukraine.[113] The edict also obliged Rosenberg to acknowledge that Göring and Himmler had been assigned special responsibilities for the Four-Year Plan and 'police security operations' respectively. The names Göring and Himmler stood for ruthless exploitation and brutal repression.

On the same day, Hitler issued a further edict defining Himmler's powers.[114] For the purpose of carrying out 'police security operations' in the Reich commissariats he was authorized to issue instructions to the Reich commissars, to each of whom he was also to assign a Higher SS and Police Leader. With the term 'police security operations' Hitler had defined Himmler's assignment in the occupied East more narrowly than the latter had anticipated. A few weeks earlier, the Reichsführer SS had proposed to Lammers that he should take over 'police *and political* security operations' in the occupied territories, in order, in his role as Reich Settlement Commissar 'to be able to ensure the pacification and consolidation of the political situation'.[115]

Himmler was evidently not prepared to put up with this setback. He responded by expanding his 'police responsibilities', combining them with those that he claimed in the East in his role as Settlement Commissar. For the assignment he had been given in October 1939 included not only the 'establishment of new areas for German settlement through a resettlement programme', but also the 'elimination of the damaging influence of...alien populations'. Himmler now interpreted this assignment, and the edict of 17 July concerning 'police security operations',[116] as making him responsible for 'solving the Jewish question' in the occupied eastern territories and thereby providing him with an important opportunity to extend his power.

During the first days of the 'Eastern Campaign', the Einsatzgruppen, operating directly behind the advancing troops, had already started shooting large numbers of Jewish civilians in the conquered territories. This was in response to clear instructions, issued by Hitler and Himmler, before the start of the campaign.[117] On the one hand, they initiated pogroms with the aid of members of the local populations, in particular in Lithuania, Latvia, and western Ukraine; on the other, they carried out mass executions themselves. To begin with, the main victims were men belonging to an only vaguely defined Jewish upper class, in some places all men of military age. The justification put forward for the mass murder was the need forcibly to remove the most important support within the population for the Bolshevik system. During 1939/40, tens of thousands of members of the Polish elites had already been shot by special units.

Now, in July 1941, Himmler seized the initiative to expand this terrorist mass murder, accounted for by the need to get rid of the Soviet system and on the grounds of 'security', into genocide. At the end of July/beginning of August 1941, the Einsatzgruppen, police battalions, and two SS brigades (which were subordinated to a special Reichsführer SS command staff) extended the shooting of Jewish civilians to include women and children; within a short time they started making villages, towns, and whole regions 'free of Jews', as they put it, in other words murdering the vast majority of the Jewish civilian population. Only a minority was left alive to be confined in specially established ghettos in order to undertake forced labour. By the end of the year, the murder units had already killed well over 500,000 people.[118]

These murders were undertaken less from 'police motives' and more from the belief in a racial hierarchy. The murder of the Jews during the war was intended to be the first step in a gigantic reordering of the new living space on a 'racial' basis, as Hitler had outlined in his instructions of 16 July; it was a topic he was to return to on several occasions during the first months of the 'Eastern Campaign'.[119] Himmler recommended himself to Hitler as the man, who, with his SS, possessed the requisite brutality to tackle this task; he clearly carried it out with Hitler's approval and backing. A radio telegram from Heinrich Müller, the Gestapo chief, dated 1 August 1941, according to which 'particularly interesting illustrative material' was to be sent to Berlin, demonstrates the fact that Hitler was being kept continually informed: 'The Führer is going to receive regular reports from here on the work of the Einsatzgruppen.'[120]

The propaganda war

Apart from conducting military operations in the East and establishing the guidelines for Germany's future occupation policy, during the summer of 1941 Hitler was preoccupied to a considerable extent with the repercussions of the extension of the war for the 'home front'. From the very beginning, he kept a careful eye on the development of the 'mood' in Germany and maintained personal control over the main themes of propaganda. He was able to do both through more or less continuous contact with Goebbels, his Propaganda Minister. At the start of the campaign, the propaganda machine was in a precarious state. The German population was not in the least prepared for the 'Eastern Campaign'; to begin with, the unexpected extension of the war provoked anxiety and concern.[121] Moreover, for reasons of secrecy, during the first days after the launch of the invasion, the OKW report contained no concrete details about military developments.[122] This propaganda blackout soon produced exaggerated rumours about the Wehrmacht's success.[123] After urgent representations from Goebbels, Hitler gave instructions[124] that, on Sunday 29 June, a week after the start of the campaign, a series of special announcements should be made about German military successes.[125] They did not, however, match up to expectations; many people had assumed that the Wehrmacht's spearheads had penetrated even further into the Soviet Union.[126]

On 4 July, Hitler instructed Goebbels 'to begin the great anti-Bolshevist campaign'.[127] The media were told 'to launch a big attack', with the 'conspiracy between Bolshevism and the Jews' as its main theme.[128] This was prompted by the discovery of a massacre of political prisoners and Ukrainian insurgents that the Soviets had carried out in the local prison on their withdrawal from Lemberg [Lvov].[129] On 8 July, Hitler received Goebbels in the Führer headquarters for the first time since the start of the campaign against the Soviet Union. The 'Führer' told him he was convinced that 'two thirds of the Bolshevik armed forces had already been destroyed or severely damaged'. He used this opportunity to order his propaganda minister to focus even more on anti-Semitism in his propaganda, 'to reveal the cooperation between Bolshevism and plutocracy, and also to emphasize more and more the Jewish character of this alliance'.[130] On the following day, therefore, Goebbels instructed the press to make 'the Jews are to blame' 'the main theme of the German press'.[131] The press, but also the other media, now began a hitherto unexampled chorus of anti-Jewish hatred. As ordered by Hitler, the aim was to include the war against 'Bolshevik' Russia and against 'plutocratic' Great Britain in a single propaganda slogan, and to portray it as the decisive struggle against the 'Jewish world conspiracy'.[132]

The United States was also increasingly described in German propaganda as the puppet of Jewish world domination and prophylactically included among the Reich's enemies. In this way the leadership thought they had invented a convincing slogan to prepare the German people for the entry of the United States into the war. 'Churchill – Stalin – Roosevelt : The Pan-Jewish Triple Star'* was, for example, the *Völkischer Beobachter*'s headline on 13 July. The Atlantic Charter of 14 August, in which Roosevelt and Churchill had established common principles for the peaceful coexistence of nations, following 'the final destruction of National Socialist tyranny', provided a

---

* Translators' note: The term 'triple star' (Dreigestirn) derived from the 'rulers' of the annual Cologne Carnival festivities: a prince, a peasant, and a maiden.

further target for propaganda attacks. Although Hitler mocked it as a cheap propaganda trick by the western powers,[133] this overt gesture of solidarity by the United States towards Britain was interpreted by German propaganda as confirming its claim of a Jewish world conspiracy. In the summer of 1941, Hitler's regime was already engaged in a global propaganda 'war against the Jews'.

In the meantime, as a result of the military successes against the Soviet Union, the German population was coming to expect victory within a matter of weeks, and thus a relatively calm atmosphere prevailed during July. Significantly, during the course of the month the situation on the eastern front took up less and less space in the SD reports on the public mood.[134] Instead, complaints about the everyday difficulties of life in wartime took centre-stage. People were worried about problems in the supply of food and about the British air raids on the cities in western Germany,[135] while 'vacation evacuees' (better-off people escaping the cities and seeking refuge in holiday resorts) damaged the image of a national community totally committed to the war.[136] In addition, there was the fear that the war could go on indefinitely.[137]

Towards the end of the month, when, despite all the military successes, victory was still not yet in sight, the mood deteriorated sharply.[138] Goebbels felt obliged to take a 'tougher' line in his propaganda.[139] Apart from the negative influences on the public mood already referred to,[140] the growing concern, in particular among churchgoers, about the arbitrary expropriation of Church property was having a negative impact on morale. In July, therefore, Hitler decided officially to halt the expropriation,[141] although in practice this was widely ignored.[142] In addition, information and rumours were being spread about the so-called euthanasia programme.[143]

The situation changed in August when radio broadcast a series of special announcements about important successes on the eastern front, producing a generally very positive picture and resulting in the 'reports on morale' once more becoming optimistic in tone. This high point in morale was not, however, destined to last long.[144]

35

The Radicalization of
Jewish Policy

Meanwhile, it had become clear that the mood of the German population was subject to major fluctuations depending on the course of the war in the East and that people were acutely sensitive to domestic political issues; trust in the regime's conduct of the war was distinctly lacking. The German people had gone to war without enthusiasm and, after the successes of the first twenty months, had hoped it would end rather than be extended. Lack of reports of successes from the front line was sufficient to produce a mood of pessimism, concern, and anxiety. In addition, Hitler, who was running the war from the isolation of his East Prussian headquarters, had not appeared in public for months, with the result that the propaganda machine could not deploy the usual ritual of mass support for the 'Führer's' policies.

In this difficult situation, during the course of two weeks in the second half of August, Hitler took two decisions with significant domestic political repercussions: the introduction of a Jewish badge and a halt to the 'euthanasia' programme. Both decisions affected the core of his ideological concerns and could not have been more different in their implications. Jewish persecution was to be further radicalized, while the 'elimination' of so-called 'life unworthy of life' was – officially at least – to be stopped. As the regime had entirely geared its propaganda to the campaign against a Jewish world conspiracy that was allegedly uniting Germany's enemies, it made sense to extend this campaign to the Jews still living in Germany, dubbing them the enemy within. This would underline the radical 'ideological' character of the war. The message that Germany was engaged in an existential struggle against the Jewish 'world enemy' was to dominate a 'public opinion' that was controlled by the regime, thereby pushing into the background the day-to-day worries and burdens of the war. Shortages, air raids, and fears about the military situation had to be borne stoically in the face of this life-and-death struggle.

The marking of German Jews with a yellow star represented the start of this campaign. The initiative came from Goebbels, who revived suggestions that had come from the security police and the Party leadership after 'Kristallnacht' and again during 1940.[1] In Poland the marking of Jews had already been compulsory since November 1939. On 15 August, Goebbels held an inter-ministerial conference in the Propaganda Ministry at which, among other things, the marking of the Jews was discussed.[2] When Goebbels, while visiting Hitler at his headquarters on 18 August, suggested marking the Jews so that they could no longer avoid detection as 'grumblers and fault-finders', the dictator immediately agreed both to that and to a reduction in their food rations. Moreover, he now reassured Goebbels 'that the Berlin Jews [are to be] deported from Berlin to the East as quickly as possible as soon as transport becomes available. They will be worked over in the harsher climate there'.[3] However, Hitler insisted that this should not happen until the campaign in the East had come to an end.[4]

In the course of the discussion Hitler also told Goebbels that his prophecy of 30 January 1939 that a new world war would end in the 'annihilation' of the European Jews was now becoming true during these weeks and months with a certainty that was almost uncanny. For 'the Jews in the East must pay the bill; in Germany they have already paid part of it and in the future they will have to pay more.' This statement makes it clear that, under the impression of the mass murder in the occupied eastern territories, Hitler was now prepared to take a tougher line with the Jews in Germany itself. His 'global war against the Jews' was not simply a propaganda fantasy; it was increasingly becoming reality.

At the same time as dealing with the 'Jewish question' Goebbels focused on another issue that threatened to affect the public 'mood': the conflict with the Churches. The Catholic population was not only concerned about the continuing confiscation of Church property by the state,[5] there was also growing opposition to the 'euthanasia' programme, which, despite attempts to keep it secret, was becoming known to broad sections of the population.

At the beginning of July a pastoral letter objecting to the killing of innocent people was read out in Catholic churches.[6] On 3 August 1941, the Bishop of Münster, Clemens August von Galen, who had already criticized the policy of confiscating Church property, preached a sermon opposing the systematic murder of patients in mental hospitals. News of this protest quickly spread throughout the Reich during the following days.[7] The fact that Münster, like other predominantly Catholic cities in north-west Germany, was a prime target for British air raids during the summer of 1941 increased the regime's concern about the potential emergence of a particular threat to the home front, a concern heightened by the fact that Galen cleverly hinted at the raids being divine punishment.[8] On 11 August, the chairman of the German Catholic Bishops' Conference, the Breslau cardinal Adolf Bertram, wrote to the Minister for Churches, Hanns Kerrl, requesting his comments on the issue of 'euthanasia'. Kerrl did not reply.[9] Goebbels was clearly concerned about the situation.[10] During his visit to the Führer headquarters on 18 August he agreed with Bormann that in future they should exercise restraint on religious issues. After he had obtained Hitler's approval for this position, on 24 August he issued a circular to the Gauleiters and Reichsleiters to that effect.[11]

On the same day, Hitler finally ordered a stop to the 'euthanasia' murders being carried out through the T4 programme because he clearly wished to avoid further discontent among the church-going population.[12] In fact, at this point the T4 programme had already achieved its original goal of killing 70,000 asylum patients,[13] and the murder of patients did not then cease, but rather, from 1942 onwards, continued throughout the war in a decentralized form. In fact, during this second phase of 'euthanasia' more people were murdered than under the T4 programme.[14] Moreover, as a direct consequence of the halt to 'euthanasia', Hitler decided to establish a large number of emergency hospitals near to certain areas threatened by air raids (he was naturally thinking in the first place of north-west Germany, which had been badly hit). The existing mental hospitals could be used for this purpose and their patients moved elsewhere. He put his personal physician, Karl Brandt, who had been responsible for the first case of child euthanasia, in charge of the project. The transfer of the patients was to be carried out by the Community Patients Transport Ltd, which had hitherto been involved in transferring the victims of 'euthanasia'. The overall coordination of the transfer of patients was in the hands of a civil servant, Herbert Linde, who had been responsible for the Interior Ministry's role in the T4 programme. As concern grew among the population that the plan for the transfers simply represented a continuation of the 'euthanasia' programme, they were to be reassured by, for example, the introduction of measures such as visits to the patients. Thus Hitler skilfully responded to the population's concern, aiming to neutralize the protests against the murder of patients through targeted assistance to the cities affected by air raids, even doing so using personnel from the old T4 organization.[15]

In this critical phase the regime did everything possible to avoid a confrontation with the Catholic Church. During the summer, protests and even demonstrations occurred in Bavaria against the order, issued by the Bavarian Interior and Culture Minister and Gauleiter Adolf Wagner, to remove all crucifixes from schools. Wagner was forced to withdraw the edict on 28 August.[16] During the following months as well, Hitler reiterated his position that there should be no conflicts with the Churches during the war. After the victorious conclusion of the war he would then set about achieving a fundamental solution to the Church problem.[17]

In September the war in the Soviet Union was dominated by the events in the southern sector of the front. As ordered by Hitler, elements of Army Group Centre, including Guderian's panzer group, turned southwards and, operating together with sections of Army Group South, surrounded substantial Soviet forces east of Kiev. The city itself was conquered on 19 September. The battle in the greater Kiev area was concluded around 25 September with more than 600,000 Red Army soldiers taken prisoner. In contrast to the clashes of opinion during August, there was widespread agreement between Hitler and the army leadership concerning these operations. After their conclusion Army Group South pressed forward towards the Crimea and the Caucasus.[18] These military successes were exploited by propaganda with the result that morale, which had deteriorated, not least as a result of the lack of reports from the front,[19] improved once again during the second half of September.[20] At the end of the month the official announcements recorded an almost euphoric mood, as reports of victories gave many people hope that the war in the East would be over before the start of the winter.[21]

When Hitler once more received Goebbels in his headquarters on 23 September, he assured him that, while up until around 15 October they would 'still have serious battles to fight, from then onwards he believed he would have the Bolshevists on the run'. All necessary arrangements had been made for the troops to survive the winter; he was even contemplating disbanding a number of divisions. If Stalin were to offer him a separate peace at this stage he would of course accept such an offer. 'For if the military power of Bolshevism is broken it will no longer pose a threat; it will then be driven back into Asia.'

After the conclusion of operations in the Kiev area the focus of events moved to the central part of the front. Strong Soviet forces had established themselves between Army Group Centre and Moscow.[22] The Wehrmacht's autumn offensive began on 2 October in full strength. With the conquest of Moscow the aim was to achieve a decisive success in the war against the Soviet Union before the end of the year so that during the coming year the main focus could once again be the war with Britain and, as was becoming increasingly probable, the United States.[23] On the day after the start of the offensive Hitler appeared in Berlin to make a speech in the Sportpalast to open the Winter Aid campaign, his first public appearance since 4 May 1941. He used it for a series of detailed justifications of his policies. He declared theatrically that his alliance with Stalin in 1939 could only be described as the 'biggest humiliation...that I have ever had to put up with'. But the decision to attack the Soviet Union had been 'the most difficult decision of my whole life'. 'Every such step opens a door behind which secrets are hidden and only posterity can know how it came to pass and exactly what happened'. With this he was preparing for the main point of his speech – the announcement that the military operations in the East were about to reach a decisive stage: 'I am talking about it today because I can say today that this enemy is broken and will not rise again'.[24] With this statement he was disguising the fact that that, even after the impending decisive blow against the Soviet Union, the war in the East would be continued.

According to Rosenberg's liaison officer, on his return from Berlin on 4 October Hitler was still 'in a remarkably good mood'.[25] At dinner on 8 October he referred to the 'tremendous and decisive change in the military situation during the last three days' and Jodl added that, in view of the great progress made by their operations 'one could say without exaggeration that Germany had won this war'.[26] Hitler ordered a special announcement to be made that in the Viasma area 'several Soviet armies had been surrounded and faced inevitable destruction'.[27] And, on 9 October, under the impression of the euphoria in the Führer headquarters, Reich Press Chief Dietrich even went so far as to call a press conference in Berlin at which he declared that the war in the East had been decided. According to both Hitler's and Dietrich's own statements, the 'Führer' had authorized him to make this announcement.[28]

By 12 October, in two large encirclements near Briansk and Viasma, the Wehrmacht had in fact succeeded in surrounding a significant number of Soviet divisions and taking over 600,000 prisoners. As a result, Army Group Centre calculated that there were no longer any significant concentrations of enemy forces in front of Moscow.[29] On 12 October, Hitler gave instructions that any offer to surrender the city of Moscow should be rejected. German soldiers were not to set foot in either Leningrad or Moscow.[30]

The 'war against the Jews'

Between the middle of September and the middle of October Hitler succeeded in encouraging his immediate entourage to believe that Germany was about to achieve a great military success, and this sense of euphoria was transferred to the media and the 'popular mood' as reflected in the official reports, even though Goebbels tried to counteract it with a more realistic approach.[31] On 15 September, in the midst of this victorious mood, the wearing of a yellow star, ordered by Hitler a month before, became compulsory for Jews. This move was prepared by a new anti-Semitic propaganda campaign. The yellow star badge was portrayed as necessary in order to mark out the Jews as participants in an international Jewish conspiracy. It was designed to ensure that the German population kept its distance from Jews still living in the country and, thereby, publicly demonstrated its support for the radical war against the Jews.[32]

A central role in this campaign was played by a booklet published in the United States by a certain Theodore N. Kaufman, in which among other things he had demanded that the German people should be sterilized.[33] With Hitler's express approval,[34] the booklet was extensively quoted and commented upon in a pamphlet that was widely distributed.[35] In it Kaufman, who was in fact a private individual with no connections to the American government, was described as an advisor to President Roosevelt. His booklet, which had been published at the beginning of January 1941, was claimed to be one of the 'intellectual inspirations' for the Atlantic Charter. In addition, propaganda tried to explain the need for the Jewish star in the light of the struggle against 'international Jewry', the war in the East, and the alleged Jewish atrocities committed there in Lemberg and other places.[36] Similar arguments were made in particular by the Party press.[37] Finally, to justify the star the Propaganda Ministry produced a leaflet ('Recognize the

Figure 11. The 'Jewish star' openly stigmatized German Jews. Contrary to the regime's intention, the non-Jewish population did not altogether welcome this move. More people than expected made small gestures of sympathy to those forced to wear them. 'German philistines are shits', thundered Goebbels.
Source: Scherl/Süddeutsche Zeitung Photo

real enemy!')[38] that was distributed to every household along with their food ration coupons. However, the response of the German population to the compulsory Jewish star left much to be desired. While the official announcements of victories were undoubtedly a welcome confirmation of many people's hopes, it is clear that the propaganda accompanying the introduction of the Jewish star met with little enthusiasm.[39] It was probably for this reason that a planned 'campaign of enlightenment against the Jews' did not take place.[40]

However, it was precisely during these days immediately before and after the introduction of the yellow star that Hitler took the decision to deport the German Jews. He had been preoccupied ever since the beginning of September with the idea of starting the deportations before the end of the war. After a meeting with the 'Führer', Himmler had discussed the matter on 2 September with Friedrich-Wilhelm Krüger, the Higher SS and Police Leader in the General Government, and, following his negative response, on 4 September with the Higher SS and Police Leader in the Warthegau, Wilhelm Koppe. On 10 September Koppe wrote to him referring to the deportation of 60,000 Jews to Łódź.[41] During the coming days, the idea for a project involving the mass deportation of Jews was put to Hitler on several occasions. Himmler's soundings were evidently having an impact.

In addition, however, there was a new development. Probably on 8 September, the German leadership learnt of the Soviet government's decision of 28 August to deport the Volga Germans to Siberia. From the point of view of the Nazi leadership this clearly represented an example of 'ethnic cleansing' that demanded 'counter measures'.[42] On 11 September, Rosenberg proposed to Hitler that he 'inform Russia, England, and the USA through a radio broadcast that if this mass murder [sic!] were carried out Germany would make the Jews of Central Europe suffer for it'.[43] Probably on 16 September, at a meeting with Himmler, the German ambassador in Paris, Otto Abetz, proposed deporting the Jews living in France and in the rest of occupied Europe to the occupied eastern territories, an idea to which Himmler, who at this point was heavily preoccupied with dealing with the 'Jewish question' and 'eastern settlement', responded positively.[44] The same day, Abetz spoke with Hitler, who used the opportunity for a lengthy discourse on his future eastern empire. On 17 September, Hitler met Ribbentrop, with whom he discussed the deportations, and afterwards Ribbentrop met Himmler.[45]

The decision was taken the following day. Himmler informed the Gauleiter in the Warthegau, Artur Greiser, that Hitler wanted 'the Old Reich and the Protectorate to be cleared and liberated of Jews from west to east as soon as possible. As a first stage I am, therefore, anxious to transport the Jews of the Old Reich and the Protectorate, if possible this year, to the eastern territories that came into the Reich two years ago, before deporting them further eastwards next spring. For the coming winter I intend to put around 60,000 Jews from the Old Reich and the Protectorate into the Litzmannstadt [Łódź] ghetto, which, as I have heard, has sufficient capacity.'[46] Only a few days later Hitler informed Goebbels that Berlin, Vienna, and Prague would be the first places to be made 'free of Jews' and the Propaganda Minister prepared to transport 'a significant number of Berlin Jews to the East before the onset of winter'.[47]

There is only an indirect record of Hitler's decision to start the deportations after all, before achieving victory in the East, namely through Himmler's letter to Greiser. The reasons prompting him to make this decision must be deduced from the regime's assessment of the overall situation in which it found itself at this stage. The fact that within the occupied eastern territories, the 'final destination' for the deportations, SS, civil administration, and Wehrmacht had in the meantime expanded the mass murder of Jewish civilians into a comprehensive genocide was a fundamental precondition for Hitler's decision to begin deporting the Jews from Germany and the rest of Europe. The racial war of extermination being pursued in the East – in the regime's view, a fight for Germany's very existence – inevitably resulted in a radicalization of the whole conduct of the war. After Himmler, on Hitler's initiative, had started at the beginning of September to sound out the feasibility of deportations, the Soviet decision to deport the Volga Germans provided the opportunity to justify them as retaliation, to accelerate the whole process, and to exploit them for foreign policy purposes.

For Hitler clearly saw the chance of using the deportations as a means of threatening the United States and as a clear warning – only comprehensible in terms of his radical anti-Semitic tunnel vision – that the threatened entry of the United States into the war would have consequences for the European Jews. Since 1939 he had after all been announcing repeatedly 'the annihilation' of the Jews in Europe in the event of a 'world war'. On 21 September, he threatened 'in the event of America's entry into the war' to impose further 'repressive measures on the German Jews because of the treatment of the Volga Germans'.[48] The Nazi leadership had been using 'repressive measures' against the German and European Jews as a means of putting pressure on the United States ever since the 1933 'Jewish boycott'. The November 1938 pogrom had been designed to increase the willingness of the United States and other nations to accept Jewish emigrants, and the Madagascar project was very likely aimed at blackmailing the United States with mass deportations.

The deportations were intended mostly to take place in daylight and in the public eye,[49] to become known through the neutral and American media, and so to provide a 'warning' to the United States.[50] Goebbels himself was responsible for ensuring that foreign correspondents were given access to information.[51] Domestic propaganda, on the other hand, was not to deal *directly* with the deportations of Jews, taking place in broad daylight, from the biggest cities in the Reich,[52] but rather emphasize the 'guilt of the Jews for the war' in general. It was, however, inevitable that the deportations, officially 'non-events', would provoke discussion.[53]

This leads us on to the domestic motives that lay behind Hitler's decision to deport the Jews. In general, as already outlined, the intention was to gear the German population to their involvement in an 'ideologically' based struggle for existence. In addition, however, the propaganda machine subtly used the growing intensity of the British air raids since autumn 1941 to portray Jews as the alleged string pullers behind the bombing war and the deportations as retaliation. The air war also helped the regime to justify the speeding up of the eviction of Jews from their homes, which had already begun in a number of cities during the summer of 1941.[54] This local policy of displacement, the repeated appeals from Goebbels and various Gauleiters to Hitler finally to make their areas 'free of Jews', will certainly also have influenced Hitler's decision to begin the deportations.[55] At the same time, tens of thousands of inhabitants of the big cities were moving into the 'Jewish homes' that had been vacated and securing household goods at favourable prices, and so had become beneficiaries of the deportations and complicit in the injustice inflicted on the Jews.

With his decision to begin the deportation of Jews from the Reich, Hitler had prompted preparations for the deportation of Jews from the occupied territories. This was motivated by the increasing tension in the occupied territories during autumn 1941. Following the attack on the Soviet Union, resistance movements began to form throughout Europe, often led by communists. The German occupation authorities generally responded by shooting hostages, in July in Serbia, in September in France, Belgium, and Norway, and, from the end of September, in the Protectorate. Here, Reinhard Heydrich, who had been recently appointed as Deputy Reich Protector, immediately declared martial law and, during the following two months had over 400 men and women shot for alleged resistance activities on the basis of sentences pronounced by summary court martials.[56]

This policy of massive repression had Hitler's full backing. In September he not only advocated 'draconian punishments, but in more serious cases...shootings' and, at the beginning of October, contemplated replacing the military commander in Belgium, Alexander von Falkenhausen, whom he considered too soft, with someone who would act more ruthlessly.[57] He also intervened personally, for example giving instructions to extend the shootings in France.[58] At this point the military had already developed a systematic basis for the radicalization of hostage-taking in Europe. The OKW Order of 16 September 'Concerning the Communist Resistance Movement in the Occupied Territories' decreed that, as atonement for the killing of one German soldier, the execution of 50–100 communist hostages should be considered 'appropriate'.[59]

As far as the Nazi leadership was concerned, communists and Jews were more or less identical. In the increasingly brutal war against 'Jewish Bolshevism' it was thus only logical to act ever more ruthlessly against Jewish minorities. And so the phantom of a Europe-wide Jewish–communist resistance movement soon had repercussions: in October 1941 the Wehrmacht in Serbia began systematically shooting all male Jews as 'retaliation' for attacks.[60] As far as the various occupation authorities were concerned, the complete removal of the Jews came to be regarded as an essential prerequisite for the restoration of internal 'security' in their area. Hitler himself had confirmed this policy, when, at the beginning of October, he explained to his dinner guests how he envisaged 'sorting out the Czechs', namely by shooting hostages among the rebellious work forces, while at the same time allocating food to peaceful work forces – above all, however, by the deportation of all Jews from the Protectorate to the occupied eastern territories. For in the final analysis the Jews were 'everywhere the link through which all enemy news reports spread like wildfire into every corner of the nation'.[61] On 20 October Himmler offered the Slovakian government the opportunity of deporting the Slovakian Jews to a specially allocated part of the General Government.[62] In France at the end of the year the military authorities stopped shooting Jewish and communist hostages and began plans to deport them 'to the East'.[63]

The various motives that lay behind the decision no longer to postpone the deportations until the end of the war had one thing in common: in the autumn of 1941 Hitler and the Nazi leadership began to conduct the war on all levels as a war 'against the Jews'. The deportation of the German Jews – a project that had been pursued since the autumn of 1939 – was intended to emphasize this commitment and to underline to the German people, to the populations in the occupied territories, and to international public opinion the seriousness with which the Germans regarded their racial war aims. The concept of a war of racial extermination, introduced in the Russian campaign, was now being transferred to the conduct of the whole war and focused particularly on the Jews. The decision in September to begin the deportations should not, therefore, be attributed primarily to the 'euphoria of victory' as in Christopher Browning's influential interpretation, but rather to the fact, that under the impression of the events of summer 1941, Hitler and the Nazi leadership had revised their whole concept of the war.[64] 'That race of criminals', Hitler told his guests, Himmler and Heydrich, at a meal on 25 October, 'has the two million dead of the First World War on its conscience, and now already hundreds of thousands more. Let nobody tell me: We can't send them into the swamps [of Russia]! Who's worrying about our own people. It's a good thing if the fear that we're exterminating the Jews goes before us.'[65]

At this time the first deportation trains were already on their way. At the beginning of October, following objections from the regional authorities to the originally planned transfer of 60,000 Jews to the Łódź ghetto,[66] the RSHA had modified the plans: now 20,000 Jews and 3,000 Gypsies were to be deported to Łódź and 25,000 each to the ghettos in Riga and Minsk.[67]

In fact, the first wave of deportations began on 15 October. By 9 November, around 20,000 Jews from Reich territory and 5,000 Gypsies (Sinti and Roma) from the Burgenland had been deported to Łódź,[68] between 8 November 1941 and 6 February 1942 a total of almost 25,000 people to Riga[69] and Kovno (as a substitute for Riga)[70], and by December almost 8,000 people to Minsk (where winter weather caused a halt to the deportations).[71] Already in November 1941 the RSHA was acting on the assumption that the deportations would continue in the spring in a third wave. In fact, those trains were to go to the Lublin area, in other words to the district in the General Government where already in 1939 there had been a plan to establish a Jewish reservation [the Nisko project]. The deportations were then intended to occur 'city by city', a procedure to which Hitler had given express approval.[72] Following his fundamental decision of mid-September 1941 to begin the deportations, the 'Führer' continued to concern himself with the concrete details of the 'evacuations'.

This decision also involved the idea of deporting those who had already been 'evacuated' that autumn 'further east' in the coming spring. Thus, with the aid of the local civilian authorities, the SS immediately began preparations for the reception of the deportees at their intended destinations. The intention now was to begin by murdering the indigenous Jews in those localities. Himmler had given a clear signal for this at an early stage. The relevant documents suggest that Reich Governor Greiser's 'agreement' to receive 25,000 deportees in the Łódź ghetto had been secured in exchange for Himmler's permitting him to murder 100,000 local Jews.[73] This programme of mass murder was to be carried out by gas, which had been used in the T4 'euthanasia' programme, halted in August 1941. Hence there was considerable experience of this method. The gas wagons of the 'Special Commando Lange', which had murdered Polish mental patients in the Warthegau during

1940, were now deployed in the Łódź district to murder the existing ghetto inhabitants.[74]

Considering the various developments as a whole, it is clear that, after Hitler's September decision to deport the German Jews, the SS worked out a comprehensive deportation and murder plan. The mass murder of Jews, already under way in the Soviet Union, was now to be extended to particular key districts in Poland. As in the case of the murders in the Soviet Union, Himmler was the decisive figure, issuing the necessary orders in the areas involved and pulling everything together.[75] In the middle of October he assigned the SS and Police Leader in the Lublin district, Odilo Globocnik, the task of building an extermination camp (Bełżec).[76] In December he met Viktor Brack, one of the key figures in the 'euthanasia' programme, who shortly afterwards dispatched his murder experts to Globocnik.[77] In October preparations began for the construction of extermination camps in Riga,[78] and apparently also in the Minsk district (Mogilev).[79] In other words, preparations were being made for the murder by means of gas of the local Jews at all four of the planned destinations for the deportees from Germany: in Łódź, Riga, Minsk, as well as the district of Lublin (Bełżec).

In addition, at the beginning of October, the security police in the district of Galicia began to shoot large numbers of Jewish men, women, and children. This new district had been created on 1 August from Soviet-occupied Polish territory and was attached to the General Government. The security police engaged here in the same murderous activity as in the other German-occupied Soviet territories.[80]

The parallel with Serbia, where also in October the Wehrmacht was extending its repressive measures into a comprehensive campaign of extermination aimed at the Jewish population, is evident. And it was doubtless no coincidence that, shortly afterwards, the German military administration in France began directing its reprisals for resistance activities against Jews (in addition to communists), with the aim of deporting them as hostages to the East.

There is no written record of the 'decision' to embark on this programme of deportations and murder; it is an assumption based on a reconstruction of a series of events. The programme was developed by Himmler directly after Hitler's order for the deportation of the German Jews, issued in the middle of September, and then subsequently carried out. Hitler provided the impulse and initiative and the backing and confirmation for it, as is clear from his recorded table talk of 25 October. To what extent he became involved in issuing detailed orders for it, and how far he arranged for Himmler, who was a regular visitor to his headquarters, to report to him on its progress is unclear. However, this circumstance is of no significance in evaluating the assertion that has sometimes been made that Hitler's henchmen carried out the murder of the Jews without his knowledge, or even against his will. For if one considers Hitler's treatment of the 'Jewish question' over a lengthy period, it is clear that it was always he who set the agenda for the various stages of radicalization and controlled developments. With his unchallengeable authority he ensured that the SS could rely on the cooperation of the various administrative agencies (civilian occupation authorities, local government in the deportation cities, the Reich railways, the finance administration, and numerous other agencies), which were involved in this comprehensive deportation and murder programme. Himmler, Heydrich, and the SS leadership focused on its actual implementation, but the final responsibility lay with the 'Führer'.

36

The Winter Crisis of 1941/42

In the middle of October 1941, Army Group Centre's offensive towards Moscow appeared to be on the brink of success. In a state of euphoria Hitler and his generals were not only assuming that they would soon have Moscow surrounded, but would be able to continue the offensive beyond the Russian capital before winter arrived. Thus the OKH envisaged withdrawing significant forces from the projected siege of Moscow and deploying them in wide-ranging movements to the north and south of the capital.[1] Confident of victory, Hitler strongly supported removing powerful panzer forces from the advance on Moscow in support of these operations.[2]

In the middle of October, on the assumption that the Russian operations would soon be successfully concluded, the OKH ordered the transfer of five divisions from the central sector of the front to the West.[3] At the end of the month, Hitler informed Mussolini in a letter that the campaign in the East had not only been 'won, but...had basically been finally decided'. A few days before, Ciano had made the generous offer for Italian troops to take part in future campaigns in India.[4]

During the second week in October, however, the usual autumn weather set in in the occupied eastern territories: heavy rain ensured that the mostly unpaved roads soon became quagmires, thereby seriously hindering all army operations as well as the supply of the troops.[5] Quartermaster General Wagner, who bore the main responsibility for army supplies, wrote to his wife on 20 October: 'We can no longer ignore the fact that at the moment we are literally stuck in the mud.'[6] Under the impact of the poor weather conditions the advance on Moscow slowed and, by the end of the month, had effectively come to a halt.[7] This meant that the German 'Blitzkrieg' in Russia had ultimately failed. The Wehrmacht had to gear itself to a winter war in Russia and the German population be prepared for the fact that the victory that had been declared in October had been postponed.

As a result of the altered war situation, the whole propaganda approach had to be revised. Hitherto the popular 'mood' had been buoyed up by the overwhelming impression of great military victories. Their failure to materialize inevitably made it sink, as reflected in the official reports.[8] In order to prevent the emergence of a general sense of depression, Goebbels now set about trying to alter the public's expectations. Over-optimistic reports, above all those that suggested that the war in the East would soon be over, were banned; instead, a moderately positive attitude was adopted. Above all, the population was geared to expect greater hardships and burdens in the future.[9] At the same time, over-pessimistic and negative statements were to be completely excised from the official reports on the population's mood, so that internal sources for rumours, pessimism, and nervousness could be blocked.[10] At the beginning of January, Hitler intervened personally to ban reports on the mood on the eastern front.[11]

From November onwards, Goebbels supervised this reorientation of propaganda in close consultation with Hitler. The new line was inaugurated in the speech Hitler gave on 8 November in Munich commemorating the 1923 putsch.[12] To begin with, Hitler spoke about 'international Jewry', the 'inspirer of the world coalition against the German people and against the German Reich'. This fitted in with the propaganda line that was dominating these weeks. Then he once again offered a detailed justification for his decision to attack the Soviet Union, describing the progress that had been hitherto achieved in this 'struggle for existence'. Finally, however, he made it clear that the war in the East could not be concluded before the end of the year: 'If our opponents say: well then, the fight will go on until 1942 – it can go on as long as it likes – the last battalion in the field will be a German one!'[13]

The following day an article written by Goebbels,[14] which had been discussed with Hitler and approved by him,[15] appeared in the weekly, *Das Reich*, and took a similar line. A special edition was distributed in millions of copies to the soldiers at the front.[16] As far as the matter of the end of the war was concerned, it stated, the important thing was not *when* the war would come to an end, but *how*. If it were lost then 'our national life would be completely and entirely' lost. All further discussion of how long the war would last was pointless and damaging; every effort must be concentrated on achieving victory.[17] That represented a clear ban on any further discussion of the length of the war. A few days later, Hitler once again expressly approved as a propaganda theme the need for 'toughness' in the conduct of the war as emphasized in the article.[18]

On the day the article appeared Hitler gave a confidential speech to the Reichsleiters and Gauleiters in Munich.[19] He used it to demand from the Party elite an 'uncompromisingly tough attitude'. Should a real crisis engulf the Fatherland 'they would find him with the last division'. At this point it was not a matter of 'when the war was going to end', but 'how it would end'. He was hoping within four weeks 'to have achieved the goals that could still be achieved before the onset of winter, and then the troops would take up their winter quarters'. He thought that, under favourable weather conditions, within a matter of ten days or a fortnight, they would be able to seal off the Caucasus, encircle Moscow, and reach the Volga in several places'. They would take up the offensive again in the spring. 'One couldn't say how long the war against the Soviet Union would last. Whether a peace treaty would ever be signed was entirely unclear.' In certain circumstances they could still be fighting in the East for years without that affecting living conditions in the rest of Europe. 'On the contrary, it would be really good for our youth to be continually trained and toughened up in the process'.

A week later, on 16 November, another important article appeared in *Das Reich* with the title 'The Jews are to Blame!'[20] It was an official reply to the negative responses of the population to the deportations from Germany that were taking place in full public view. In the light of the deteriorating military situation this potential source of discontent and criticism had to be stifled. In this article Goebbels referred back to Hitler's prophecy of 30 January 1939: 'At present we are experiencing the realization of this prophecy and so the Jews are meeting with a fate that may be harsh but is also more than deserved. In this case pity or regret is completely inappropriate.' 'World Jewry', Goebbels continued, is now 'suffering a gradual process of annihilation'. Referring specifically to Hitler's approval, this provided a sufficiently clear answer to the question of what was happening to the Jews who were being deported from Germany.

The article, which received a wide circulation,[21] contained a list of detailed regulations governing people's behaviour towards those Jews still living in Germany. Among other things, it stated: 'If someone is wearing a Jewish star he is marked out as an enemy of the people. Anyone who has private contact with him, belongs with him and must immediately be regarded and treated as a Jew'.[22] This made it clear that Hitler's regime was determined to proceed against all 'friends of Jews' and critics of its anti-Semitic policy.

In the meantime, Hitler's army adjutant was noting that the top commanders were increasingly uncertain and unable to make decisions about how to continue operations in the East.[23] In fact, the situation of the German armies in Russia was far from satisfactory. On 19 November, General Halder gave Hitler a summary of the overall situation. According to his account, it was proving impossible to maintain an unbroken line on the eastern front, but only a series of advance posts in fortified positions, which were having to attempt somehow to control the territory between them. Instead of 73 trains per day bringing supplies, in the past two weeks on average only 50 trains were arriving at the stations where the supplies were unloaded. Of the 50,000 motor vehicles in the eastern armies 30 per cent were beyond repair and 40 per cent in need of maintenance.[24] The OKH estimated that, at the beginning of November, of the 3,580 assault guns and panzers in the eastern armies 2,009 had been lost and only 601 had been replaced.[25] By 6 November, over 20 per cent of the troops in the eastern armies (686,000 men) were either dead, injured, or missing.[26] The combat strength of the infantry divisions had been reduced by an average of one third, that of the panzer divisions by two thirds.[27]

In the middle of November, Army Group Centre resumed its offensive towards Moscow. Hitler and the military leadership were under the false impression, almost amounting to self-deception, that the Red Army had more or less been defeated and that a decisive blow would prevent it from reviving during the winter. The depressing impression created by Hitler's admission during his speech of 8 November that the war could not be won that year was to be compensated for by the triumphal announcement of the capture of Moscow. At the start of the campaign Hitler had assigned priority to the conquest of Leningrad and of the sources of raw materials in the south of the Soviet Union over the capture of Moscow; now, having failed to achieve those goals, he clung to the hope of achieving a prestige success by capturing the enemy's capital.[28]

However, not only that: both Hitler and the military leadership continued to believe in their October plan whereby, in addition to capturing Moscow, two spearheads of Army Group Centre, advancing north and south of the capital, would be able to link up with the offensives of the other army groups. Before the winter had set in with full force, they could capture

Stalingrad and, in the north, cut the railway line between Moscow and Leningrad, thereby blocking the supplies of Allied war matériel.[29]

To begin with, the offensive towards Moscow did in fact make some progress. However, as a result of the onset of frightful winter conditions in the middle of November, the exhaustion of their own troops, and the tough resistance of their opponents, the advance came to a halt at the beginning of December.[30] The same thing happened with the other army groups. Since the middle of October, in the Leningrad area Army Group North had been trying to link up with the Finns east of Lake Ladoga through an offensive by the 16th Army. Tichwin was captured on 8 November but it was impossible to advance further.[31] In the south of the front the 1st Panzer Army captured Rostov on the Don on 20 November.[32] In the middle of November, the 11th Army succeeded in conquering most of the Crimea, including Kerch. Only the fortress of Sebastapol remained in Soviet hands.[33]

The attempt by the German forces to achieve further territorial gains, despite the onset of winter, resulted in the troops having no time to prepare fortified winter quarters. When they were forced to retreat a few weeks later, they found no line of defence in their rear, prepared for winter conditions, to which they could retire. The autumn offensive, with its requirement for more supplies, had also resulted in the winter equipment not arriving in time at the front, despite assurances given by the Quartermaster General to Hitler.[34] Displays of winter equipment in five major German cities, with which the population was to be mentally prepared for the winter war, were initially postponed and then cancelled.[35]

As victory had proved impossible before the onset of winter, Hitler concentrated on preparing plans for continuing the war during the following spring. On 19 November, he told Halder of his intention to launch an offensive towards the Caucasus and Russia's southern border between March and April the following year. The Soviet Union's combat strength had been seriously depleted, he claimed. All in all, his surprising conclusion was that 'the recognition that the two combatants were unable to destroy each other [would] lead to a negotiated peace'. It appears that, following a renewed southern offensive, he was contemplating recognizing the existence of a rump Soviet state. In any event, there was no more talk of totally destroying Bolshevism and driving it east of the Urals.[36] While Goebbels was still preoccupied with gearing up the population for another winter of war, at the end of November Hitler gently prepared his Propaganda Minister for the fact that the war was certainly not going to be concluded during the coming year; 1942, Hitler told him, would be 'difficult', while 'during 1943 a much better situation would emerge'. After all, in the European part of the Soviet Union there were 'huge amounts of foodstuffs' as well as 'sufficient quantities of almost all raw materials' so that 'our victory can no longer be endangered'.[37] His remarks clearly demonstrate Hitler's extraordinary ability to put a positive gloss on bad news.

In the middle of November the Red Army launched a counteroffensive in the northern and southern sectors of the front.[38] In the south it initially succeeded in recapturing Rostov on the Don.[39] When, at the end of November, the 1st Panzer Army began to withdraw from Rostov westwards, Hitler intervened, demanding that the panzer army hold a line lying further eastwards than the army commander and Army Group South had envisaged. In the course of the dispute Hitler relieved the commander of Army Group South, Gerd von Rundstedt, of his command, replacing him with Walter von Reichenau, and subjected Brauchitsch to bitter accusations.[40] However, Reichenau too was neither willing, nor indeed able, to hold the line Hitler was insisting on, which, in the end, the 'Führer' had to accept. At the beginning of December, he flew to the headquarters of the 1st Panzer Army, subsequently visiting Army Group South, in order to form a picture of the situation for himself on the spot, a clear demonstration of his lack of trust in the army's commander-in-chief.[41]

Back in his headquarters, on 6 December Hitler gave Halder his views of the situation. He did not regard the figure for the effective (i.e. not replaced) loss of 500,000 personnel from the eastern armies as dramatic, as he reckoned the Soviet losses were eight to ten million. He considered the fact that some of their divisions were forced to hold thirty kilometre-long sectors of the front as 'proof of the enemy's weakness. Thus numbers prove nothing.' In the north of the front they must keep trying to link up with the Finns; in the south it was a matter of capturing the oil fields of Maykop. Only in the centre was he prepared to accept a shortening of the front line. Germany had no lack of soldiers but only of workers, and so Russian POWs must be increasingly employed. He did not want any reduction of the forces in the West. If the situation altered in North Africa then enough divisions must be made available for the occupation of southern France. In Norway even two or three extra panzer divisions were required, in case the British should attempt to land. They were also unable to withdraw troops from the Balkans.[42]

However, Hitler had fundamentally underestimated the Red Army's offensive capabilities. On 9 December, it managed to recapture Tichwin on the Leningrad front and, by the end of December, had driven the German troops back to the point from which they had started their offensive in October.[43] On 7 December, the Red Army in the central sector launched a major offensive with over 100 divisions, forcing the German aggressors, whose forward units had come within 30 kilometres of Moscow, to retreat on a broad front.[44]

Responding to the first alarming reports from the north and the centre, Halder concluded that the local commanders should be given the freedom to make their own decisions as to what territory should be given up. According to Halder, Hitler treated Brauchitsch like a 'postman'. 'The most awful thing, however, is that the top leadership doesn't understand the condition our troops are in and prefers to try and simply patch things up, when major decisions are required.'[45]

On 8 December Hitler issued Directive No. 39, a rather bizarre attempt to avoid having to admit the failure of the 'Blitzkrieg' against the Soviet Union. On the contrary, according to the directive, following the creation of an orderly defensive position, forces were to be assembled in order to return to the offensive as soon as possible.[46] In the first sentence of the directive Hitler blamed the crisis on the 'surprisingly early onset of winter in the east', which required 'the immediate halting of all major offensive operations and a move onto the defensive'. It is clear from further statements in Hitler's directive that it was based on the assumption that the eastern army could withdraw to prepared defensive positions, where it would be protected from the winter and able to minimize losses. Moreover, above all, it would be in a position to withdraw the panzer and motorized divisions and 'refurbish' them in the rear areas in preparation for the planned offensive in the coming spring. However, as part of the 'defensive warfare' during the winter the following 'special tasks' had to be fulfilled: in the southern sector of the front Sebastapol, which was under siege, had to be taken. But, above all, the Army Group must do everything possible, during the winter, to capture the lower Don–Donetz line, thereby creating the preconditions for the 'spring offensive towards the Caucasus'. Army Group North should link up with the Finns, thereby at long last securing the encirclement of Leningrad.

The directive was based on a totally false perception of the situation on the eastern front. The German army in the East had used up its last reserves of energy in offensive operations and was now in retreat, in some cases abandoning its heavy weapons. During the final weeks, it had lacked the capacity to construct fortifications and so there were none to fall back on. Thus, the troops were forced to defend themselves under the most difficult winter conditions in the open or in ad hoc strongpoints that no longer formed a coherent front line. In these circumstances the idea of preparing resources during the winter for a spring offensive, let alone of mounting an offensive was completely absurd.

War with the United States

On 7 December the crisis on the eastern front was temporarily overshadowed by a new development. News of the Japanese attack on the American fleet in Pearl Harbour reached Führer headquarters.[47] It was not unexpected. Since the beginning of November 1941, Japan and the United States had been negotiating about the lifting of the oil embargo that the United States had imposed on Japan in July 1941. In this way the United States had been trying to force the Japanese to abandon their aggressive policy in Indochina. The negotiations could be seen as having failed when, at the end of November, the US Secretary of State, Cordell Hull, demanded that, in return for the lifting of the embargo, Japan withdraw all its troops from China and Indochina. The Japanese government was not prepared under any circumstances to agree to this demand, which would have meant conceding the failure of its policy of expansion. It now prepared to conquer the oil-rich British and Dutch colonies in South-East Asia, which entailed the threat of a war with the United States. Thus, in order to preempt a possible American intervention, the Japanese government decided to attack the main base of the American Pacific fleet in Hawaii.

On 17 November, Ribbentrop had already been informed by the German embassy in Tokyo that an imminent Japanese attack was very probable and the German Foreign Minister then indicated to the Japanese the possibility of a German declaration of war on the United States.[48] When ambassador Oshima prepared Ribbentrop for the failure of the negotiations with the United States, the German Foreign Minister urged the ambassador to declare war on the United States, as 'the situation can hardly ever be more favourable for Japan than it is now'.[49] According to his telegram, intercepted by the American secret service, Oshima reported to Tokyo that Ribbentrop had added the reassurance that, in the event of Japan becoming involved in a military conflict with the United States, Germany would immediately join in the war. A separate peace with the United States would, he said, be inconceivable for Hitler.[50] Presumably, Ribbentrop had secured this assurance from the 'Führer' during a meeting immediately preceding Ribbentrop's interview with Oshima, as Hitler was in Berlin to attend the celebrations to mark the expansion of the Anti-Comintern Pact.[51]

During the first days of December, the Japanese government informed its allies in Rome and Berlin about the impending war with America, requesting them to respond with rapid declarations of war and to make a tripartite agreement committing themselves not to agree a separate peace with the United States.[52] Having received Hitler's approval, Ribbentrop responded on 5 December with a draft tripartite agreement.[53] As far as the 'Führer' was concerned, the fact that this agreement bound the Japanese not to quit a war with the United States, thereby pinning America down in East Asia for a lengthy period, was sufficiently valuable to make it worth his while to declare war on the United States.[54]

Thus, behind the decision to declare war on the United States lay a calculation that formed part of Hitler's war strategy. His claims, following 7 December, to have been completely surprised by the Japanese attack could only have referred to its timing and location. Since the end of November, he must have been anticipating such a move during the next few days or, at the most, weeks.[55] However, Hitler not only expressed his surprise, but attempted to portray the developments in the Pacific as a liberation. For he and his entourage assumed that the war in the Pacific would prompt the United States to reduce its arms deliveries to Britain and its increasingly massive presence in the North Atlantic in recent months. Thus, the Japanese attack would provide Germany with sufficient time to bring the continent completely under its control before any American intervention in Europe was possible.

On 11 December, Hitler announced the declaration of war on the United States in a major speech to the Reichstag.[56] At its core was a lengthy personal attack on President Roosevelt. Since his Chicago speech of October 1937 (in which he had demanded that those powers that interfered violently in the internal affairs of others should be placed under 'quarantine') Roosevelt had openly opposed the German Reich and increasingly interfered in 'European matters'. Hitler went on to list the various stages of President Roosevelt's 'increasingly hate-inspired and inflammatory policies', accusing him of having, since the outbreak of war, systematically led the United States into the camp of Germany's enemies. Moreover, he declared that he was 'mentally disturbed' – just as Woodrow Wilson had been. There could only be one explanation for the fact that this man had been able to maintain himself in power: behind Roosevelt was the 'eternal Jew', who, like Roosevelt, was aiming 'simply to destroy one state after another'. As the climax of the speech, Hitler announced the declaration of war on the United States, while at the same time, reading out the terms of the Japanese–German–Italian agreement, which had been signed that same day. It contained the commitment of all three powers to pursue the war with the United States and Great Britain to its victorious conclusion and not to seek a unilateral armistice or a separate peace.[57]

On the afternoon of the following day, Hitler then spoke to the Reichleiters and Gauleiters assembled in the Reich Chancellery. According to Goebbels's detailed account, Hitler began by describing the situation created by the war against the United States, which for the Reich had fallen 'like a gift into its lap'. For 'the German people would have been very disturbed by a declaration of war by us on the Americans, without it being counterbalanced by the East Asian conflict. Now everybody regards this development as almost inevitable'. He tried to downplay the difficulties on the eastern front by announcing that the Wehrmacht was in the process of 'adjusting the front line' and he was determined 'next year to finish off Soviet Russia at least [sic!] as far as the Urals.'

Following on from that, Hitler referred once again to his 'prophecy' that he would 'annihilate' the Jews in the event of a world war, an issue that, as he emphasized, 'should be treated without any sentimentality'. At first sight, his statement appears to contain nothing really new. For months Hitler had considered himself engaged in a 'war against the Jews' and, during the past months, had announced their impending annihilation on several occasions, and both Goebbels and Rosenberg had said the same thing.[58] However, now that, with the declaration of war against the United States, the war had expanded into a real 'world war' Hitler's 'prophecy' inevitably came closer to its realization. With his increasingly anti-Semitic rhetoric, which he also maintained during the coming days and weeks in conversations with Rosenberg,[59] Himmler,[60] and Goebbels,[61] Hitler was indicating to his entourage in December 1941 that he was determined that the mass murder of the Jews, which had already begun in the Soviet Union, Poland, and in Serbia, should be further intensified and extended.[62]

At the end of his speech Hitler stated 'that we must achieve victory, because otherwise as individuals and as a nation we shall be liquidated'. 'Such an enormous loss of life as is currently occurring can only be historically and ethnically [völkisch] justified through the conquest of land and soil on which future generations of peasants can serve our national life'.[63]

Conflict with the generals

Back in his headquarters, Hitler was forced to respond to the alarming progress being made by the Soviet offensive against Army Group Centre. On 13 December, he had told Oshima he wanted to withdraw his best divisions from the front and re-equip them in the West.[64] Now this was out of the question.

On 15 December, he warned his Army group commanders that withdrawals during the winter had the 'most serious consequences' and ordered the immediate transfer of divisions that were being created from the reserve army or were in the West to the eastern front. 'Exceptional efforts had to be made' to improve the 'transport situation in the east'.[65] Any units capable of combat that could be put together had to be sent to the front by air.[66] A day later, Hitler issued a general order banning any retreat. Officers were ordered 'to do their personal utmost to compel the troops to engage in fanatical resistance in their positions, irrespective of whether the enemy had broken through on their flanks or in the rear'.[67] Thus, on this day, 16 December, Hitler was effectively taking over the functions of commander-in-chief of the army.[68]

On the same day, the commander of Army Group Centre, Fedor von Bock, informed Hitler that if he withdrew there was the danger of his having to leave behind his heavy weapons. At the same time, given the order to hold their ground, 'I am concerned that in some places the troops may withdraw without having received the order to do so'. Bock was not the only commander, who, now that the enemy had taken the military initiative, was at a loss and unable to cope.[69] Late in the evening of 16 December Hitler telephoned Bock, explaining that withdrawing into a rear position without artillery and matériel was pointless. 'The only decision that could be taken was not to withdraw an inch and to fill the gaps and hold the line'. When Bock replied that there was a danger that the Army Group's front might be penetrated, Hitler replied that that was a risk they had to take.[70]

During a meeting in the middle of the night of 16/17 December, Hitler told Halder and Brauchitsch, who was anxious to resign, that there 'can be no question of a withdrawal'. There was only one problem at the front: 'The enemy has more troops. He doesn't have more artillery. He is worse off than we are.'[71] The following day Hitler agreed to Bock's request for leave on health grounds. He had made the request earlier, but Bock was surprised at the speed with which Hitler had now granted it. He was replaced as commander of Army Group Centre by Field-Marshal Günther von Kluge, the commander of the 4th Army.[72] Brauchitsch, who for some time had not felt up to the job, also tendered his resignation as commander-in-chief, which Hitler accepted on 19 December, officially on the grounds of Brauchitsch's 'heart problems'.[73]

Hitler had been critical of Brauchitsch for some time, but had told Goebbels in September that he could not 'sack the army's commander-in-chief in the middle of a campaign'.[74] However, the situation on the eastern front had now become so critical that Hitler not only got rid of Brauchitsch, but, after Bock and Rundstedt, was also determined to dismiss the third army group commander on the eastern front, the commander of Army Group North, Field-Marshall Wilhelm von Leeb. In the middle of January, Leeb was replaced by Colonel-General Georg von Küchler. A few days earlier, because of Reichenau's sudden death from a heart attack, Hitler had had to reappoint Bock to the post of commander of Army Group South.[75] In the middle of December he also decided to get rid of Colonel-General Falkenhorst, who was in charge of operations in northern Finland, and had dismissed him by the end of the year.[76]

Hitler decided not to name a successor to Brauchitsch, but instead to take over command of the army himself. While during the past weeks he had been repeatedly intervening in the operations of the armies and army groups over the head of Brauchitsch, now he could claim the right to do so in accordance with the military hierarchy.[77] On 20 December, he instructed Halder to 'hold position and fight to the last man'. There must be no withdrawal. If enemy troops broke through their lines, they must be 'finished off in the rear'. 'Dynamic officers' should be assigned to the critical points to speed up the delivery of supplies and to organize those soldiers who had become separated from their units and deploy them in combat. The battle had to be fought with the most brutal means: 'Prisoners and local inhabitants should be ruthlessly stripped of their winter clothing...all abandoned farmsteads are to be burnt down.'[78]

On the same day, Hitler received panzer general Guderian at the latter's request for an audience that lasted five hours. Hitler banned Guderian from withdrawing his troops to a position in which they had the prospect of surviving the winter, a step the general had been advocating and in fact had begun to carry out. Instead, Hitler insisted his troops 'dig in and [defend] every square metre'. When Guderian dared to object that digging in was impossible because the ground was frozen hard, Hitler countered that they could use artillery to blast craters, as had been done in Flanders during the First World War. However, Guderian pointed out that the winter conditions in the two countries were completely different. Being forced to remain in his current position would mean a switch to positional warfare and, during the coming winter, the 'cream of our officer and NCO corps would be sacrificed'. Hitler responded that no doubt Frederick the Great's grenadiers had not wanted to die, but the king had been justified in demanding that they sacrifice their lives, and he was now claiming the same right. Guderian argued that the sacrifices were not comparable; most of his troops were dying from the intense cold. Hitler responded by accusing him of lacking perspective and having too much compassion for his soldiers.

Guderian's attempts to give Hitler a realistic description of conditions at the front proved unsuccessful because the 'Führer' considered his reports exaggerated. The general's suggestion, made later on in the meeting, that Hitler replace his senior staff officers with men with front-line experience was brusquely rejected. Six days later, Guderian was dismissed at the instigation of his new superior, Kluge, and placed in the OKH reserve.[79]

During the winter crisis, Hitler dismissed a number of other generals, in some cases in dramatic circumstances. When, at the end of December, the Red Army succeeded in landing troops on the Kerch peninsula and at Feodossiya on the south coast of Crimea and forcing the Germans to withdraw from Kerch,[80] Hitler dismissed the commanders of the two corps involved, Helmuth Förster and Count von Sponeck.[81] Sponeck was sentenced to death by a court martial; Hitler changed the sentence to life imprisonment, however.[82] On 17 January, he dismissed the commander of the 8th Army, Col-General Adolf Strauss.[83] The commander of 28th Corps, Freiherr von Gablenz, was also relieved of his command.[84] On 8 January 1942 he discharged Colonel-General Erich Hoepner from the Wehrmacht with loss of pension rights without a court martial or any other legal basis because, on his own responsibility, Hoepner had withdrawn a corps that had almost been cut off.[85] On 20 January, he relieved the commander of the 4th Army, Georg von Küchler, of his command; the general had confessed in a private conversation that he no longer felt up to the job.[86]

The decisive result of this crisis was that Hitler had consolidated his authority over his generals. He believed that his interventions in the winter crisis, his strict order banning any retreat, and his ruthless decisions on personnel had prevented the German army in the East from suffering a total catastrophe in the winter of 1941/42. However, by banning any withdrawal he had prevented the military from developing and deploying other options such as the use of delaying tactics, evasion of contact with the enemy, or a major withdrawal. The conflict with his generals resulted in the military leadership suffering a permanent loss of operational freedom of manoeuvre; from now onwards, they had to put up with constant interventions by Hitler even in matters of tactics.[87]

Feeling confirmed in his role as a military commander, on 19 January, Hitler told Goebbels that in his relations with the generals he had 'often felt like someone whose main function was to pump up rubber men from whom the air had all escaped'. He had needed 'to exert all his energy' 'to resist this general collapse in morale'.[88] He was, however, overlooking the fact that (continuing the simile of the generals as 'rubber men') he was the one who had let the air out in the first place.

By the end of 1941, the Red Army offensive in the area of Army Group Centre[89] had driven the Wehrmacht some 100–150 kilometres back to the west and a coherent front line no longer existed. After lengthy hesitation,[90] on 15 January Hitler finally felt compelled to issue a Führer order withdrawing the whole Army Group Centre on a broad front. He emphasized that, even with this 'move backwards', 'the troops' sense of superiority over their opponents and the fanatical will to inflict the greatest possible damage' must be sustained.[91]

In January, in the area of Army Group North,[92] the Red Army succeeded in advancing over the river Volchov, which links Lake Ilmen with Lake Ladoga, although the 18th Army managed to contain the breakthrough. As a result of the German tactic of holding ground at any price, Soviet offensives south of Lake Ladoga in January succeeded in surrounding a German combat group in the district of Cholm. By the end of February, six German divisions had been surrounded in the district of Demyansk, which Hitler was desperate to hold onto as the base for a later offensive. The pockets were supplied by air and could only be reopened in spring 1942. In the southern sector of the front,[93] a major Soviet offensive, launched towards the Dnieper on 20 January, was blocked, and, at the beginning of March, a further Soviet attack on Kharkov came to a halt in the spring thaw. The Soviet counter-offensive had stalled. The winter crisis had considerable repercussions for the domestic situation in Germany. As a result of the lack of concrete news from the eastern front since December[94] and Hitler's surprise take-over of command of the Army, there were growing concerns about the military situation in the East. There were worrying rumours about the eastern front, encouraged by letters from the front and stories told by soldiers on leave. Moreover, after Germany's declaration of war on the United States, there were concerns about the expansion and extension of the war. Official propaganda was faced with a profound crisis of credibility.[95]

Hitler, however, was not prepared to comment publicly on the evident difficulties and reverses by providing 'a word of reassurance'. He evidently wished to avoid associating himself personally with the crisis. By remaining silent in the greatest crisis of his regime, he was taking the risk that his 'charisma', the exceptional leadership qualities attributed to him, would suffer yet more damage. In order to get on top of the growing mood of crisis, the regime adopted a strategy of diverting attention and providing people with something to do.

On 17 December, Hitler assigned Goebbels the task of organizing a 'collection of woollen articles for the troops on the eastern front', which the Propaganda Minister had in fact already discussed with the OKH a few days earlier.[96] On 20 December, Goebbels announced the collection in a radio broadcast. After his speech,[97] he read an appeal from Hitler: 'If the German people want to give their soldiers a Christmas present then they should give up all the warm clothing they can do without during the war and which can in any case be replaced during peacetime'.[98]

To emphasize the seriousness of the scheme Hitler also issued a Führer decree imposing the death penalty on anyone who dared to steal any of the 'winter items' that had been collected.[99] On Hitler's suggestion,[100] at the beginning of January Goebbels extended the collection period once again by another week, so that they would have a 'positive' propaganda topic until the middle of what was the most critical winter month. According to the result, announced with a fanfare of propaganda, in a Reich-wide 'major action' lasting a little over three weeks, the Party had managed to collect scarves, socks, pullovers, and ear muffs, in all a total of 67 million 'winter items and woollens'.[101]

The fact that, as a result of the lack of winter clothing for the troops, Hitler and Goebbels were forced to embark on an improvised campaign appealing to their own population represented, in reality, an incredible declaration of bankruptcy by the regime, which was used to making proud claims for its efficiency. According to the SD reports, the population was indeed initially shocked by the announcement.[102] The campaign was extremely dubious from a practical point of view as well, and in fact prompted speculation among the population about its effectiveness. For there was already adequate winter clothing for the troops. The main problem was the difficulty of transporting it to them, and that applied equally to the items that had been collected. After the conclusion of the collection Hitler judged that it had been a purely 'political measure'. They had been clear all along that 'nothing from the collection of woollens would get to the front' and that 'the things would have to be mothballed'.[103]

However, from the point of view of the regime it was not the practical aspects but rather propaganda considerations that were decisive. The aim was to emphasize the strong link between front and homeland during the emotionally critical Christmas period by mobilizing the population through a 'major action' organized by the Party and thereby taking their minds off their worries. Goebbels wrote that, with the collection of winter clothing, 'the people are at least engaged in a positive task and the Party also has something to do and won't have to spend its time indulging in speculation about the situation'.[104] Thus, it was not surprising that, despite the initial shock, during these weeks the SD reports focused on the overwhelming impact of the winter clothing campaign rather than on the population's concerns.[105]

The collection of woollens became the pilot project for a fundamental adjustment of propaganda to take account of the seriousness of the war situation. The period of Blitzkrieg victories was finally over; now they were engaged in a world war whose length could not be foreseen and which would demand exceptional efforts from both the front and the homeland. During the course of autumn 1941 and the following winter, the national mood had changed from a semi-intoxicated triumphalism to a gloomy pessimism. Propaganda now focused on getting the population used to the altered war situation, to the 'toughness of the war', to a struggle for existence that in the final analysis was about the very survival of the German people.[106]

During January, German propaganda had remarkably little to say about the situation on the eastern front.[107] Instead, it was dominated by the Axis successes in East Asia. After Hong Kong had fallen on 25 September, on 2 January the Japanese succeeded in conquering Manila and, by the end of January, they had completely occupied British Malaya.[108] However, for the German population whose husbands, fathers, and sons were fighting on the eastern front, Luxor and Kuala Lumpur were far away. And on this subject the Wehrmacht reports had little to say. Only occasionally were battles mentioned that could be located through place names.[109]

From the end of January, the situation in North Africa once again moved in favour of the Axis and this gave some comfort. On 30 January the Wehrmacht report was able to announce the taking of Benghazi.[110] Propaganda now set about turning Rommel into a war hero in order to divert attention from the situation on the eastern front.[111]

Thus there were signs that the crisis was being overcome when, on the afternoon of 30 January, Hitler gave a speech in the Sportpalast to mark the ninth anniversary of the take-over of power. It is clear from the SD reports, however, that the population was only partly reassured by his appearance following the uncertainty caused by his silence over the past weeks.[112] Hitler attacked Winston Churchill, his main opponent in the West, subjecting him to crude insults. He described him as a 'windbag and drunkard', 'this mendacious creature', this 'sluggard of the first order', one of the 'most miserable Herostratic characters in world history', 'incapable of doing or achieving anything positive, capable only of destruction'. 'I don't even want to mention his philistine comrade in the White House, for he is simply a pathetic imbecile'. He never subjected Stalin, whom he respected as a brutally efficient dictator, to similar abuse.

Hitler's speech highlighted the toughness of the winter war, while at the same time emphasizing that the crisis had almost been overcome. 'These fronts are firmly held and wherever, at certain points, the Russians have broken through, and wherever they thought they had succeeded in capturing places, they were in fact no longer places, but simply piles of rubble.... God give us the strength with which to retain our people's, our children's and grandchildren's freedom, and not only that of our German people but also that of the other peoples of Europe.' For they were engaged in a 'fight for the whole of Europe and, thereby, for the whole of civilized humanity'. At the same time, in his speech he had declared the war to be a decisive battle between 'Jews' and 'Aryans', referring once again to his 'prophecy' of 30 January 1939: 'We are clear that the war can only end either with the extermination of the Aryan peoples or with the disappearance of the Jews from Europe.' 'The hour will come, when the *most evil enemy of the world of all time* will have played his *last part in Europe for at least a thousand years*.'[113] This passage was given due emphasis by the press and, according to the SD reports, was understood by the public to mean that 'the Führer's fight against the Jews is being fought mercilessly to the end, and that soon the last Jews will have been driven from European soil'.[114] Hitler had once again made clear that, in his view, the further course of the war was inextricably bound up with the fate of the Jews under his regime.

On 20 January 1942, a few days before Hitler's speech, Heydrich had invited state secretaries, senior officials, and SS functionaries to an SS villa on the Wannsee lake in Berlin to discuss in detail the current state and further development of Jewish persecution. It is clear from the minutes of the so-called Wannsee Conference that two versions of the 'Final Solution' were discussed. On the one hand, there was Heydrich's old plan, which had emerged during 1941 and had been approved by Hitler, of deporting the European Jews to the German-occupied Soviet Union and murdering them there. On the other hand, representatives of the occupation authorities in the General Government and the occupied eastern territories at the conference put forward an alternative plan of killing the largest Jewish population in German-occupied Europe, namely that in the General Government, on the spot. This 'new plan' was based on the preliminary work done by the SS and Police Leader, Globocnik, in his district of Lublin. Here, in autumn 1941, construction of the first death camp had started, although initially it was only intended to kill the local Jews. However, a final decision to replace the 'old' plan with the 'new' one was not taken either at the Wannsee conference or during the following weeks. The reason for this was that Hitler had approved the old plan and Heydrich had referred to this authorization during his address at the conference. The new plan, on the other hand, had not yet been approved.[115]

During the following weeks, however, Hitler made it clear in a number of statements that he was not prepared to allow the prolongation of the war to result in the postponement of the 'Final Solution' to the distant future. On 14 February, he told Goebbels that 'Jewry will undoubtedly suffer its great catastrophe along with Bolshevism'. He was 'determined...to deal ruthlessly with the Jews in Europe'.[116] Also, at the celebration of the founding of the Party on 24 February, which for the first time he did not attend himself, he had Gauleiter Wagner read out a statement announcing that 'my prophecy will be fulfilled, namely that through this war it will not be Aryan humanity but rather Jewry that will be exterminated'.[117] The 'Führer' was evidently interested in a 'solution' that was as radical and rapid as possible.

37

The Pinnacle of Power

In the middle of February, Hitler was already reassuring Goebbels that the crisis of winter 1941/42 had in essence been overcome. On the eastern front 'the worst aspects of the winter had been dealt with'. Given the continuing bitter cold in the east, this was a distinctly optimistic assessment; his propaganda minister, was, however, happy to hear it. The situation in North Africa was also under control, Hitler said, and he considered that the Japanese military successes in East Asia were a harbinger of a serious crisis for the British empire.[1] During the night of 11/12 February, the battleships 'Scharnhorst' and 'Gneisenau' and the heavy cruiser, 'Prinz Eugen', managed to sail from Brest through the English Channel to the North Sea without the Royal Navy and the RAF being able to prevent them. The aim was to strengthen the German naval forces in Norway against the threat of an invasion. Hitler, who was receiving a visit from the recently appointed Norwegian Prime Minister, Quisling, at the time, considered it 'a tremendous boost to Germany's prestige and a corresponding blow to Britain's reputation'.[2] Hitler felt all the more triumphant because he had insisted on the risky operation against the advice of the navy.[3]

In fact, from the middle of February onwards, the situation on the eastern front began to improve.[4] On 18 February, Hitler discussed the 'overall situation' with Halder and with the commanders of the Army Groups North and Centre. He issued the watchword 'not a yard back'; the most important goal was to maintain the siege of Leningrad. He confidently told his generals that the threat of a panic, similar to that during Napoleon's retreat of 1812, had now been averted.[5] After the German press had remained silent for weeks about the situation on the eastern front, on 22 February it was told to focus once more on the performance of the German Army on the eastern front.[6] These reports and the news about Japanese advances in East Asia ensured that the regime's assessments of the national mood during February and March provided a somewhat more positive picture.[7] This situation continued during April, despite difficulties in the supply of food and consumer goods[8] and an increase in the number of British air raids.[9] In his speech on 15 March, on the occasion of Heroes' Memorial Day, Hitler not only emphasized that the winter crisis was now over, but solemnly announced that 'this summer we shall annihilate the Bolshevik hordes'.[10]

However, the crisis had in fact left its mark on Hitler. Thus, on a visit to Führer headquarters on 19 March Goebbels found him showing clear signs of strain. The 'Führer' commented that 'recently he had been feeling rather ill' and, from time to time, had had to cope 'with serious attacks of dizziness'. According to Goebbels, the long winter 'had had such an effect on his spirits, that it had left its mark on him. . . . I notice that he has become very grey and simply talking about the concerns he'd had during the winter made him look much older.' Had he 'given way to a moment of weakness', Hitler told Goebbels, 'the front would have begun to collapse, causing such a catastrophe as would have put that of Napoleon in the shade'. Goebbels, at any rate, was convinced 'that during this winter it was the Führer who alone saved the eastern front'.

However, it was above all Hitler himself who believed in the myth that he spread to the effect that he alone was responsible for preventing the collapse of the front through his iron determination to hold the army's positions, despite opposition from his incompetent generals. Indeed, he was to keep returning to this key point.[11] This perspective was to have far-reaching consequences for his influence on the operational conduct of the war. For if, in his view, it had only been possible to hold the front line because he himself had taken over the day-to-day leadership of the army in the East, then it stood to reason that he would have to control the tactics and not just the strategy of the future offensive.

Hitler told Goebbels that his further objectives for 'the coming spring and summer' were 'the Caucasus, Leningrad, and Moscow. If we can achieve these goals, by the beginning of next October he definitely wants to call it a day and go into winter quarters. He may possibly construct a massive defensive line and call a halt to the eastern campaign.' In any event, there was not going to be another winter crisis. It might come 'to a hundred years' war' in the East: 'We shall then be in the same position vis-à-vis Russia as England is in relation to India. . . . It will then be our task to keep preventing the creation of any new state beyond our defensive line.' In effect, Hitler was admitting that he no longer considered it feasible to complete the 'annihilation of the Bolshevik arch enemy', which he had announced in his Heroes' Memorial Day speech. Some kind of rump state would remain, and he tried to project a positive future in terms of the need to be continually fighting this 'remnant of Russia', in order to prevent the emergence of a new power. In the course of the conversation Hitler admitted having 'a certain respect' for the Soviet enemy and described Stalin as a model: 'Stalin's brutal measures saved the Russian front. We must use similar methods in our conduct of the war...'[12]

Hitler, however, had not changed his view that the planned major offensive in the east would be decisive for the future of the war. For the construction of a defensive position far in the East against a greatly weakened Soviet Union would enable him to divert considerable resources to the war against the Western Allies. He appears to have become convinced that a successful offensive in the East would, after all, allow him to realize the strategic concept with which he had entered the war with the Soviet Union in June 1941. This was to establish a position in the East, enabling him to continue the war against the British Empire and the United States for years ahead. Following a major military success in the East, he would not only have the option, which he had been pursuing since 1940, of driving Britain out of the Mediterranean, but the entry of Japan into the war even opened up further perspectives: a weakening of the American position in the Atlantic on the assumption of Japanese naval superiority in the Pacific, and combined operations with Japan against British positions in the Near and Middle East. In spring 1942, Hitler envisaged the construction of an empire dominating the continent not as the final result of the war but rather as the decisive precondition for its continuation. The end of this global conflict would see a new partitioning of the world. However, all these far-reaching plans had one precondition: a decisive victory on the eastern front by autumn 1942.

These premises determined a series of important decisions Hitler took during the next few months. His military plans required, on the one hand, a rapid reorganization of the armaments sector, which was by no means fully efficient. This, in turn, involved finding a solution to the labour shortage through the forced recruitment of millions of workers from the occupied territories. Secondly, he wanted to increase his power at home by reducing the influence of the state bureaucracy, which he loathed, even further. By removing the remaining independence of the judiciary, he aimed to turn it into an arbitrary tool of his racial policies and an agent in realizing

the core of his project: the creation of an empire spanning the whole of
Europe and organized along racial lines. Only on this basis would the new
colossus be capable of successfully conducting global warfare. This would
inevitably have fateful consequences for the regime's Jewish policy, which
had already become a campaign of mass murder.

The development of rearmament

Hitler's efforts in July 1941 to switch the main focus of armaments production to support the Luftwaffe and tank production, on the assumption that
Barbarossa would soon be successfully concluded, rapidly turned out to be
unrealistic. During the summer and autumn of 1941, it proved impossible to
increase aircraft production. From November onwards, it even proved
impossible to replace the planes that were being lost in the East. During
autumn 1941, industry had also been unable to meet the army's armaments'
priorities. The main reason for this was a shortage of raw materials. The
regime was unable to realize its plans to exploit the resources of the Soviet
Union on a large scale while the war was continuing. Here too Hitler's
assumptions were proving false.[13] In view of this situation, in his edict of
3 December concerning 'the rationalization and improvement of the
performance of our armaments production' Hitler had demanded that 'mass
production should be introduced and manufacturing processes be organized accordingly'.[14] However, in view of the winter crisis, even Hitler soon
realized that such rationalization measures were insufficient to deal with the
problem.

Hitler's plan for dealing with the second major obstacle for increasing
armaments production, the shortage of workers, by employing millions of
Soviet prisoners also proved unsuccessful. On 15 October, he had decided
to use Soviet prisoners for road works and other forms of heavy labour and,
on 31 October, he agreed to their 'extensive deployment' in the war industries.[15] Millions of 'racially inferior' slave workers were to be brought into
the Reich to make up for the war-induced shortage of males. Given Hitler's
racial views, this was a remarkable decision. However, the scheme came to
naught, for systematic undernourishment and appalling treatment resulted
in the death of large numbers of prisoners of war. The survivors had to be
gradually 'given a boost' in order to restore their strength. In March 1942, of
the 3.3 million prisoners only 5 per cent were in work.[16]

Already, at the beginning of the year, Hitler had issued a Führer command demanding an increase in armaments production and giving priority
to the army. Fritz Todt, the Minister for Armaments and Munitions,[17] had
been introducing measures to increase armaments production and make it
more efficient when, on 8 February, following a visit to Führer headquarters, he was killed in a plane crash. The following day, Hitler surprisingly
transferred Todt's offices to his personal architect, the 36-year-old General
Building Inspector for the Reich Capital, Albert Speer. Thus, Speer became
Reich Minister for Armaments and Munitions, General Inspector for the
German Road Network, General Inspector for Water and Energy, General
Plenipotentiary for the Regulation of the Construction Industry within the
Four-Year Plan, and head of the Todt Organization, the official construction
organization created by his predecessor.[18]

By making this appointment Hitler was, not least, hoping for psychological
impact. Speer was regarded as dynamic, a good organizer, and had considerable experience with large-scale building projects, particularly in the armaments sector.[19] He radiated youthful energy and optimism, and the fact that
he clearly had the Fuhrer's confidence indicated right from the start that he
would have considerable clout within the regime. Speer's appointment was
designed to create a mood of optimism both within the confused and disorganized armaments sector, but also among the general public. From the
very beginning, Speer's activities were hyped in an extraordinary propaganda campaign, with which Hitler was personally involved, and which
systematically constructed the legend of the 'armaments miracle' under
Speer, the brilliant organizer.[20] Reinforced by Speer's own personal propaganda after the war and often uncritically accepted, the legend has had a
lasting effect right up until the present day.[21]

With Speer's appointment, Hitler was following his principle of solving
problems by appointing particular individuals who possessed his confidence,
and who were directly responsible to him. A few weeks later, on 21 March,
he applied this principle again by creating a new office with plenary powers
in the shape of the General Plenipotentiary for Labour Mobilization, to
which he appointed Fritz Sauckel, the Gauleiter of Thuringia. Sauckel was
assigned the task of 'organizing the deployment of all available supplies of
labour, including foreigners and POWs, in accordance with the requirements of the war economy, as well as mobilizing all labour that is still not
being utilized in the Greater German Reich, including the Protectorate, as
well as in the General Government and in the occupied territories'.[22]

Dr Robert Ley, the head of the German Labour Front, had tried to acquire this appointment, but both Bormann and Speer had objected to such an excessive concentration of power in Ley's hands. Sauckel, Hitler's eventual choice, was neither professionally qualified nor temperamentally suited to the post. However, by appointing an average Gauleiter, Hitler (no doubt under the influence of Bormann) intended to continue shifting the balance of power away from the state bureaucracy towards the Party apparatus. For in order to provide Sauckel with the necessary administrative machine, with his edict of 21 March Hitler removed two departments from the Reich Labour Ministry, subordinating them to Sauckel, who then went on to appoint the Gauleiters to be his 'authorized representatives for labour deployment' in their areas.

The General Plenipotentiary for Labour Mobilization was subordinated to the Four-Year Plan (above all, in order not to damage Göring's prestige), and not, as Speer had wished, to the Armaments Ministry. Moreover, as a Gauleiter, Sauckel was directly responsible to Hitler. Thus, Hitler's two important personnel appointments of February and March 1942 had created a new relationship calculated to produce conflict.

In his reorganization of the armaments sector Speer applied his own ideas, which, in close collaboration with Hitler and backed by his authority, he implemented during the following weeks. Like his predecessor, Todt, the new minister aimed to work in close cooperation with industry. Apart from ammunition, for which he was responsible for the whole of the Wehrmacht, to begin with his authority was limited to the equipment needs of the army. His main aims were: to secure a degree of clarity in the whole production process; to extend his authority to the whole of the Wehrmacht's armaments production; to expand the armaments sector at the expense of the production of civilian goods and to make it more effective; and, above all, rapidly to increase armaments production, in order to achieve a decisive victory in the East, if possible before the end of the year, in other words before American resources could be mobilized.

A few days after his appointment, at an armaments conference in the Air Ministry, Speer was already making blatantly clear his claim to the central role in the whole of the armaments sector. Hitler, with whom he had discussed the path he intended to follow the previous day, strengthened Speer's position by inviting the participants to a meeting in the Reich Chancellery, where he spoke for an hour about Speer's appointment. Five days later, on 18 February, at a further armaments meeting, Speer got those present to provide written confirmation of their acceptance of the leadership role he was seeking. Having had the results of this meeting approved by Hitler in the course of a lengthy discussion, on 24 February he spoke to a meeting of Gauleiters in Munich, seeking their support.[23]

Speer took over from Todt the system of 'Committees', in which the firms responsible for the final stage of the production of particular armaments were brought together, and extended this system with Hitler's express approval.[24] Around these committees the 'Rings' were then reconstructed, bringing together the firms that provided the relevant parts for those particular armaments. In this way, under the slogan of the 'self-responsibility' of industry, the representatives of the various firms worked together in a complex, but unbureaucratic system made up of Main Committees, Special Committees, Main Rings, and Special Rings. These bodies were responsible, in the first instance, for the allocation of orders to the individual firms, giving preference to the most efficient ones, encouraging the exchange of best practice among the firms involved, and in general ensuring the continual optimization of production.[25]

Speer also created a tough disciplinary instrument through Hitler's Decree for the Protection of the Armaments Economy of 21 February, for which he had presented Hitler with a draft on the 19 February. Under it he could order the punishment of those who intentionally gave false statements about their labour or raw materials requirements, or about the size of their labour force or stocks of raw materials and the like.[26] In May Speer secured the bureaucratic apparatus he needed by using a Führer edict to remove the Armaments Office from the OKW's Military Economic and Armaments Office and transfer it to his Ministry. This gave him control over the Armaments Inspectorates in the Reich and the occupied territories.[27]

By April 1942, backed by Hitler's authority, Speer secured Göring's agreement to the creation of a 'Central Planning' committee [Zentrale Planung]. This new committee, of which Speer, Göring's state secretaries, Erhard Milch (Luftwaffe)and Paul Körner (Four-Year Plan) were the permanent members, became the central coordinating body for the allocation of raw materials. To avoid damaging Göring's prestige, Speer, as a formality, had subordinated himself to him as 'General Plenipotentiary for Armaments Production within the Four-Year Plan'. In effect, however, this meant that Speer was responsible for all armaments projects within the Four-Year Plan.[28]

In September 1942, Speer created a new intermediate authority by establishing regional armaments commissions, in which all the various agencies involved in armaments production in the various regions were represented. These regions followed the borders of the Gaus, not those of the military districts, that is, of the armaments inspectorates, and assigned a decisive role to the Gauleiters as chairmen of the commissions. This new arrangement prepared the way for a reorganization of the system of Reich Defence Commissioners. While hitherto only fifteen Gauleiters had held this office, which corresponded to the military districts, on 16 November 1942 Hitler appointed all Gauleiters Reich Defence Commissioners. From now onwards, these power-hungry regional Party bosses had the task of coordinating and promoting the war effort within their Gaus.[29]

Speer now visited Hitler every two weeks, during the first months even more often, in order to discuss the armaments situation with him in detail, sometimes over a period of several days. These so-called 'armaments meetings', which began on 19 February 1942, contained on average several dozen agenda items. From Speer's point of view, they served above all to secure Hitler's agreement to his proposals and in most cases they succeeded in doing so. In June 1942, Hitler assured Speer 'that everything that came from me would always be signed off'.[30] However, the minutes show that, in a considerable number of cases, Hitler opposed Speer's proposals or wanted changes, above all in technical matters, which in some cases even involved going into detail. Thus, the idea that, during these armaments meetings, Hitler adopted a passive stance, merely nodding his agreement with Speer's detailed expositions, is mistaken. On the contrary, the minutes reveal a dictator who was keen to make it clear that he knew what he was talking about in armaments matters, capable of making suggestions for improvement, and was reserving for himself the role of 'effective head of armaments production'.[31]

It is important to note, however, that the continuing discussions between Hitler and Speer concerning armaments involved decisions on particular issues; they did not pursue a general programme based on an overall view of the various armaments and of the most important factors involved in production – industrial capacity, labour supplies, raw materials, transport availability and so on. Significantly, during these meetings, Speer did not provide a series of statistical pictures of the armaments sector as a whole, but used individual figures, whose reliability was difficult to verify but which evidently often impressed Hitler, who was a numbers enthusiast.[32]

Speer's method of always giving Hitler the opportunity of commenting on particular armaments issues and making decisions on the production of particular armaments without any reference to the overall situation corresponded exactly to the 'Führer's' arbitrary armaments policy. This involved permanently overstraining the whole armaments sector with over-ambitious projects and abrupt changes of priorities, as well as putting pressure on those responsible by then referring to the resultant shortages and inadequacies. Had Hitler established a rationally functioning armaments operation, which matched his requests with the available resources, this would in time have created a control mechanism that might have acted as a veto over his overambitious military and strategic plans. However, Hitler had no interest in doing that, and Speer was aware of the limits of his power within Hitler's system.

The reorganization of armaments production was already having an effect during 1942. Apart from expanding the motorized units of the army, Hitler's basic directive of 10 January 1942 had, above all, envisaged boosting the supplies of army munitions by six times compared with the figure consumed in August 1941. This was the main challenge facing the new Reich Minister for Armaments and Munitions.[33] At the end of June, Hitler also told Speer what the monthly production figures for the most important types of munitions must be. As usual, his demands exceeded many times over the available productive capacity.[34] To achieve this goal, the allocation of steel to the munitions industry had to be rapidly and considerably increased. However, this was impossible within the existing allocation system, which had become completely distorted because of the excessive demands being made on it. Thus, in order to reorganize the whole steel sector, on 1 June Speer created the Reich Iron Association, and Hitler 'recommended' as chairman Hermann Röchling, a leading figure in heavy industry whom he admired.[35] To begin with, Röchling managed to sort out steel allocation on a clearer basis; but increasing steel production was much more problematic, in particular because of the need for a significant increase in coal supplies. On 11 August 1942, Hitler told a high-level meeting[36] that 'if, as a result of a shortage of coking coal, the production of steel cannot be increased as envisaged, the war will be lost'.[37] In this way he forced Paul von Pleiger, the chairman of the Reich Coal Association, to pledge to deliver the required amount of coal. Sauckel agreed to provide the necessary number of workers. However, in the autumn these promises were revealed to be worthless. The impending crisis – a collapse in steel production – with catastrophic results for armaments production across the board – was in the end avoided through a 10 per cent cut in private coal consumption. Speer commented laconically that it was better 'for people to feel a bit chillier at home than that armaments production should collapse'. As a result, and through an improvement in the allocation system, it even proved possible to increase steel production during winter 1941/42, which meant that Speer's key goal, the increase in munitions production, could still be achieved.[38]

As far as the armaments actually produced during 1942 were concerned, the balance shifted as follows: the most important products were aircraft, which made up 46.1 per cent of total production at the beginning of 1942, although only 36.3 per cent by the end. While warships increased their percentage from 9.3 per cent to 10.9 per cent, the production of tanks, motor vehicles, and weapons, during what was after all the year of the decisive eastern offensive, only increased from 18.3 per cent to 19.5 per cent of the total. The highest percentage increase was achieved by munitions, namely from 26.3 per cent to 33.3 per cent.[39]

Meanwhile, Sauckel had been engaged in ruthlessly implementing the 'Reich mobilization' of foreign labour in the occupied territories. This occurred through a combination of more or less voluntary recruitment, conscription by the local administrations, and compulsory recruitment by the occupation authorities, in some cases by simply deporting people who were pressganged off the streets.[40] At the end of 1942, the total of all foreign workers in the Reich had already reached over 5.6 million, among whom there were over a million Poles, over 900,000 French POWs, as well as almost 50,000 Soviet POWs, and over 1.2 million Soviet civilians.[41]

Conditions in the Soviet POW camps were still horrendous, so that the death rate was extremely high.[42] Civilian workers from the Soviet Union, who had been promised more or less equal treatment with that of German workers, ended up in camps surrounded by barbed wire, poorly fed, badly paid, and subject to disease. Clearly marked out by the 'eastern worker' badge they were forced to wear, they were in general treated as 'sub-humans' by the German guards and foremen. The edicts issued by the RSHA, which imposed on the eastern workers a strict and repressive regime, declared them to be 'enemies of National Socialist Germany'.[43]

In March, Hitler told Speer that he 'did not approve of the poor nourishment of the Russians' and was surprised that the civilian workers were treated the same as the POWs. Speer had to explain that this was the result of his own instructions, but the 'Führer' claimed not to be aware of it.[44] However, even when Hitler realized that the miserable situation of the eastern workers impaired their productivity for the war economy, as with the

Soviet POWs, he did not make any serious attempts to change the situation fundamentally. The categorization of the eastern workers and the members of the Red Army as second-class humans was a direct result of the aggressive racism that was fundamental to the regime's policies. Treating the Soviet workers in the Reich humanely would have threatened the foundations of his war policy. Thus he was obliged to accept that the 'deployment of Russians' would not achieve the desired results.

The radicalization of the murder campaign

It is striking that the gradual overcoming of the winter crisis and the move to a military offensive in the spring and summer of 1942 is chronologically linked to the further radicalization of Jewish persecution. The mass murders that began in the summer of 1941 and, during the autumn, were extended to Poland and also Yugoslavia, were now expanded by the Nazi state into a comprehensive plan, set in motion between May and July 1942, to murder all European Jews. Thus the military plans for the eastern offensive and the preparations for the 'Final Solution' occurred during the same period. Moreover, the planned schedule for the 'Final Solution' shifted: It was now no longer to be concluded *after*, but rather *during*, the war. The questions of 'where' and 'how' were also changed at the same time as the issue of 'when': no longer in the Soviet territories, but instead in Poland; no longer through a combination of deportation, debilitating forced labour, executions, and gas vans, but rather through stationary gas chambers in special death camps.

The concrete decision-making process and Hitler's role within this process can only be partially reconstructed from documents. He had, however, played a central role in all the previous phases of Jewish policy. Moreover, as dictator, he alone possessed the requisite authority: (a) to coordinate the various radical plans for a 'Final Solution' that had been worked out during 1941/42 within the SS-police apparatus, the Party organization, the Foreign Ministry, and the other offices and administrative agencies of the Third Reich; (b) to combine them in a murder programme covering the whole of Europe; and (c) to set this in motion, ordering the participating organizations to carry out their various tasks within the extermination project.

To understand the fateful move towards the 'Final Solution' one should bear in mind the 'Führer's' central role in determining the regime's policies, his war aims, his out-and-out racist ideology, and his imperialist views.

Governed by these various ideological perspectives, during spring and summer 1942, he developed and implemented his radical ideas for 'solving the Jewish question'. For Hitler's Europe, which now appeared to be taking shape, was to be reorganized along racist lines, that is to say to be dominated and exploited in order to fight a global war. He was determined that there should be no more Jews living in this empire. By breaching all the norms of civilization through its programme of murder, carried out by hundreds of thousands of perpetrators not only in Germany but within the occupied and allied states as well, this regime had burnt all its bridges.

The historical causes of the Holocaust are varied and cannot be reduced to the figure of Hitler. Anti-Semitism and racism were widespread in Germany and Europe; they had been firmly institutionalized within the administrative apparatus of the Nazi regime. Interest in a radical 'solution to the Jewish question' existed within the regime in different forms and with a variety of motivations – ideological, political, economic; and, for a number of reasons, the war encouraged the radicalization of Jewish persecution. However, the Holocaust cannot be explained solely by the coming together of these various factors, by structures and functions, however important these may be.

For a systematic anti-Semitic policy to emerge out of the widespread hostility to the Jews and for this policy to be geared to the most radical possible solution required the engagement, the coordination, the driving force of the authoritative man at the top of the regime, and *in a particular historical situation, as he perceived it.*

During the middle of March, Globocnik began supervising deportations of the Jews in the districts of Lublin and Galicia to the Belzec death camp, which had been under construction since autumn 1941 and was now ready. By the middle of April, around 60,000 people had been murdered there, the majority of whom had been designated as 'incapable of work'.[45] Thousands of people had also been killed during the course of the bloody clearance of the ghettos. The mass murder in these two districts represented the first step in the 'Final Solution' in the General Government, as envisaged in the Wannsee Conference.

The deportation of the Jews from Reich territory, which had been interrupted during the winter, was also resumed in March. By mid-June, around 55,000 people had been deported to the General Government in a 'third deportation wave'. In general, the trains from the Reich were halted in Lublin, where men who were considered 'capable of work' were sorted out and assigned to the camp at Majdanek.[46] The other deportees were placed in Polish ghettos (above all, Izbica, Piaski, Zamość),[47] whose inhabitants had been murdered shortly beforehand in Belzec.[48] The majority of the Jews deported from the Reich succumbed to the miserable conditions in the ghettos during the following months; most of the survivors were deported to death camps. This pattern of systematic murder was a repetition of what had already happened in Łódź , Riga, and Minsk: the indigenous Jews were murdered and the Jews from the Reich then provisionally accommodated in the 'freed–up' ghettos.

By now, deportations were occurring in other countries. On the basis of an agreement that Himmler had made with Slovakia in autumn 1941,[49] between March and June 1942 Slovakian Jews were deported for forced labour in the district of Lublin and in Auschwitz in Upper Silesia.[50] At the end of March, following a decision by the military administration already made in December 1941, an initial train with a thousand Jewish men from France also went to Auschwitz. This was termed a 'hostage transport' and regarded as a reprisal for the actions of the French resistance. However, in March, the RSHA envisaged deporting a further 5,000 Jews from France to Auschwitz.[51] And, at the beginning of April, preparations were made for the deportation of a further half a million Jews from the Reich, Slovakia, the Protectorate, the Netherlands, Belgium, and France.[52]

Hitler's comments on the 'Jewish question', which Goebbels noted in March and April, can be read as a kind of commentary on these events: 'The Jews must be got out of Europe, if necessary by using the most brutal means.'[53] When, at the end of March, Goebbels learnt of the existence of the Belzec death camp, he had no doubt that Hitler was responsible for the murders being carried out there, since the 'Führer is the protagonist and advocate of a radical solution, which, in view of the situation, is necessary and therefore appears unavoidable'.[54] And in April, after a further meeting with Hitler, he noted: 'He wants to drive the Jews out of Europe completely. That is absolutely right. The Jews have caused so much misery in our part of the world that the toughest punishment that one can possibly inflict on them is still too mild.'[55]

However, the people whom the RSHA were deporting from central Europe to Poland were not yet being killed in the death camps that already existed. At this point, it was Polish Jews, designated as 'incapable of work', who were being murdered in the gas chambers of Belzec and the gas vans of Chelmno. In Auschwitz, where the first gassings took place in Crematorium

I from September 1941 onwards, the main victims were sick prisoners, Soviet POWs, as well as sick and exhausted Jewish prisoners from forced labour camps in annexed Upper Silesia.[56]

Evidently, the RSHA was still sticking to the plan, outlined by Heydrich at the Wannsee Conference, of deporting the majority of Jews from western and central Europe to the occupied Soviet territories after the final military victory in the East. However, during the following months, on the basis of their initial experience with the gassings in Poland, this old plan was finally abandoned.

Crisis in the judiciary

It was not pure chance that, between spring and late summer 1942, Hitler engaged in a power struggle with the hated state bureaucracy over domestic affairs. For this was precisely the phase when, on the basis of renewed victories, he became increasingly convinced that he was about to achieve his dream of an empire providing Germany with living space. Hitler had not held any cabinet meetings since 1937, with the result that the government no longer existed as a collective body; the individual ministries went their own way. Hitler ruled with the aid of his chancelleries, above all with the support of the indispensable Martin Bormann, head of the Party Chancellery, who communicated Hitler's wishes not only to the Party agencies but also to the ministries and to the special commissioners appointed by Hitler.

In spring 1942, Hitler decided to deal a further blow to the state administration, which was already in the process of disintegration. In a system governed by the absolute authority of the Führer's will it was burdensome to continue to operate within legal rules and bureaucratic procedures. Instead, the principle of the arbitrary, politically-determined 'measure' was finally to triumph over the 'state governed by norms'. Hitler chose the judiciary as the target for the further emasculation of the state bureaucracy. He now homed in on it, to begin with in comments to his entourage.[57]

Hitler's attacks began in February and March 1942. On 8 February 1942, for example, he declared: 'Our judiciary is still too inflexible!'. The judiciary failed to understand that, during wartime, crimes that were committed in the blackout represented a particular threat to public security and, therefore, should be given exemplary punishment. It was also completely pointless sentencing soldiers to years of imprisonment if this meant that they avoided service at the front. 'In any case, after ten years of penal servitude a person is of no further use to the national community. Who's going to give him work? Someone like that should either be given a life sentence in a concentration camp or be killed.' The judiciary, on the other hand, spent its time poking around 'in their law books to come up with a sentence that fits in with their way of doing things in peacetime. It's vital that such sentences are suspended!'[58]

On 19 March, Hitler told Goebbels that he was determined to 'get the Reichstag once again to provide him with special powers for a thorough overhaul of the conduct of political and military affairs'. It is clear from Goebbels's report that Hitler did not simply want to attack the alleged abuses, thereby undermining the existing judicial system, but aimed to use his 'criticism of the judicial system' as a platform for securing a symbolic enhancement of his position as Führer vis-à-vis the state bureaucracy as a whole. These 'special powers' were specifically intended to give him the authority to intervene arbitrarily throughout the military and civilian sectors, and to make an example of officers or civil servants irrespective of their legal rights, dismissing or punishing them. Hitler referred in this context to the 'Hoepner case', that of the general he had dismissed from the Wehrmacht in January without regard to Hoepner's legal rights as an officer, making it clear which way the wind was blowing. Two days after this conversation, Hitler signed an edict concerning the simplification of the administration of justice, intended to speed up the processing of cases as much as possible.[59]

All that was now required was a pretext to launch the attack on the judiciary and the civil service. An article in the *Berliner Illustrierte Nachtausgabe* of 21 March alerted Hitler to the Schlitt case. A week earlier, the 29-year-old Ewald Schlitt had been sentenced by the district court in Oldenburg to five years' penal servitude after his wife had died in an asylum. Schlitt had been abusing his wife for a long time, and, three months before, had subjected her to a brutal attack. The court considered this incident responsible for the woman's physical decline and eventual death, sentencing Schlitt to five years' penal servitude for manslaughter.[60] However, in Hitler's view the only appropriate punishment was the death penalty. Up until now, Hitler had not in fact had a legal basis for peremptorily dismissing judges with whose sentencing policy he disagreed.[61] Now, that night, he telephoned state secretary Franz Schlegelberger, since Gürtner's death in January 1941 the acting Minister of Justice, demanding that the sentence be revised.

Moreover, he threatened to take the 'toughest measures' if the judiciary did not mend its ways.[62] The head of the Justice Ministry responded to Hitler's criticism by referring the Schlitt case to the Reich Supreme Court in Leipzig.[63] On 31 March, Schlegelberger was able to inform Hitler that Schlitt had been condemned to death, and the sentence was carried out on 2 April.[64]

On 29 March, during dinner, Hitler sketched out his ideas as follows: 'The whole of current jurisprudence [is] nothing but a systematic abdication of responsibility'. Thus, he would do everything he could to make 'the study of the law, that is the study of that kind of legal thinking, appear as contemptible as possible'. Moreover, 'apart from a select group of up to 10 per cent of judges, he would replace the whole of the judiciary'. The 'totally bogus system of using lay judges', which simply enabled judges to evade their responsibility, would be abolished.[65] Four days later, Hitler issued an edict toughening the Wehrmacht's sentencing policy: 'Dubious elements must be prevented from using the opportunity of avoiding front line service by sitting out their sentence in prison.' Instead, military units for prisoners had to be immediately created and 'must where possible be deployed with the fighting troops to undertake the toughest duties under dangerous conditions'.[66]

Around a month later, on 26 April, Hitler outlined his criticisms of the judicial system in a speech to the Reichstag. He began by explaining how the winter crisis had been overcome, once again blaming the deterioration of the military situation on the 'international world parasite'. He effectively confirmed the widespread rumours about the fate of the Jews by declaring that, during 'recent years, one state after another' in Europe had been compelled by 'its instinct for self-preservation to introduce measures that were designed to provide permanent protection against this international poison'.[67]

As the climax of his speech, Hitler requested the Reichstag expressly to confirm that he possessed 'the legal powers to oblige everybody to do their duty' and 'to subject to military degradation or dismiss from their office and position' anyone who failed to perform their duty, irrespective of his 'acquired rights'. As he had discussed with Goebbels at the end of March, Hitler assumed the right to dismiss officials regardless of their rights and privileges as civil servants, including their right to a pension.[68] Hitler concluded his speech with sharp criticism of the judicial system and, without naming names, quoted in detail the sentence in the Schlitt case, which he 'found incomprehensible'.

Hitler's request was immediately accepted by the Reichstag. Its resolution, which repeated the main passage in Hitler's speech, was given official status by being published in the official legal journal, the *Reichsgesetzblatt*.[69] It stated that Hitler, without being bound by existing legal provisions, was 'entitled at any time ... if necessary, to dismiss from his office, his rank or his position any German, whether a simple soldier or an officer, a low- or a high-ranking official or judge, a senior or a junior Party functionary, a blue- or a white-collar worker, without the need to follow prescribed procedures'. Hitler possessed this right 'as Führer of the nation, as the supreme commander of the Wehrmacht, as head of government and possessor of supreme executive authority, as the supreme judge, and as leader of the Party'. The listing of all his official functions was designed to underline the fact that this empowerment of Hitler reflected his sovereign and autocratic position. The resolution was a demonstration of power targeted at the civil service, and designed to put it under psychological pressure and publicly humiliate it. However, it represented above all a symbolic degradation. For, in practice, Hitler's special powers did not acquire any legal significance.[70]

Although the Security Service was expected to report positively on the reception of Führer propaganda, it could not disguise the confusion in the population's response to Hitler's speech of 26 April. After all, his assurance that they were well equipped for war during the coming winter implied that it was unlikely that the war would be over by the autumn. Moreover, many asked themselves why on earth a further extension of his powers was necessary when, in effect, he already possessed absolute authority. Thus his action was interpreted as a sign of weakness.[71]

This confusion was increased by the rarity of Hitler's public appearances. The reason for this was not only his intensive preoccupation with military affairs, which absorbed most of his energy, but presumably also his awareness that he would damage his prestige as a charismatic leader and warlord if he kept banging on in public about the tough demands made by the war and the need to stand firm. Moreover, the winter of 1941/42 had taken its toll on his energies and resilience. He failed to attend the celebrations of his 53rd birthday on the evening before 20 April. Goebbels tried to gloss over the fact by drawing attention to the parallels between King Frederick the Great of Prussia and Hitler, which were stressed in the film *Der grosse König* [The Great King], premiered in March 1942. In his speech, which he had got Hitler to approve,[72] Goebbels praised the king as someone who, 'despite crushing blows that sometimes brought him to the brink of collapse, kept finding the strength to triumph over testing times and defeats, and to act as a shining example of steadfastness in adversity, to his people, to his soldiers, to sceptical generals, wavering ministers, conspiring relatives, and recalcitrant officials'. Like Frederick the Great, Hitler was engaged in a 'titanic struggle' for 'the life of our people'.[73] The film showed Frederick as prematurely aged by grief and the burdens of responsibility, a clear indication that Führer propaganda was undergoing a profound transformation.

The conduct of war in spring 1942

In his Directive No. 41 of 4 April 1942 Hitler had assigned the forces in the East the primary task in the southern sector of 'securing a breakthrough into the Caucasus region'. In the course of this offensive the enemy was 'to be destroyed in front of the Don', and Hitler gave detailed instructions as to how the pincer movements were to be carried out, referring to Stalingrad as a goal of the operations. Afterwards, they were to conquer the oil region further east, considered by Hitler essential for the continuation of the war, and the Caucasus. However, the Kerch peninsula and Sebastopol were the initial targets and the Izyum region, where the Red Army had established a salient, also had to be cleared. Following the conclusion of operations in the south, his second major operation for the coming year was to be the capture of Leningrad.[74]

Thus, in effect the directive represented an admission that, following Germany's failure to defeat the Red Army during the previous year, and its great difficulty in overcoming the winter crisis, the armies in the East were now only capable of mounting a limited offensive. Only one of the three army groups was going to carry out a wide-ranging offensive. Moreover, even if all its goals were achieved, while the Soviet Union would have been considerably weakened by the cutting off of its important sources of raw materials, it would still not have been completely defeated. In other words, the war in the East would have to be continued during 1943, although Hitler hoped that he would be able to free up a considerable number of troops in order to provide a counterweight to America's growing military potential. The military leadership supported the basic premise of the offensive, but was fully aware that, fundamentally, the resources were inadequate even for this advance in the south, on which every effort was now to be concentrated. In fact, the initial successes of the summer offensive were due primarily to the fact that the Soviet leadership had anticipated a resumption of the attack on Moscow, concentrating large forces in the central sector of the front. In short, the summer offensive was a final effort on the part of the already seriously weakened eastern armies, which were no longer capable of mounting another major campaign.[75]

Halder was obliged to report to Hitler that, as a result of the winter battles, there had been a 'wastage' of 900,000 men, of which it had been possible to replace only half. Of the total of 2,340 tanks lost during the winter only 80 per cent could be replaced.[76] The army's general staff estimated that only 5 per cent of divisions were capable of carrying out all tasks, 8 out of 162; in June 1941 it had been almost two thirds: 134 out of 209. The transport situation in the East was precarious; the shortage of fuel was undermining the army's mobility.[77]

These weaknesses could only be partially compensated for by further enlisting the services of allies. During the previous months the German leadership, and Hitler in particular, had made strenuous efforts to get Italy and Hungary to promise to increase their respective contingents to the size of an entire army, while the Romanians had promised two armies. All these contingents arrived on the southern sector of the eastern front during the summer.[78]

A development that occurred during the planning phase of the summer offensive illustrates the extent to which Hitler overestimated Germany's military potential. In February, the commander-in-chief of the navy suggested an alternative strategy to Hitler. The main focus of the war during 1942 should not be on the Soviet Union. Instead, through a dual offensive in North Africa and the Caucasus, and with a simultaneous campaign by the Japanese via the Indian Ocean, the attempt should be made to destroy the British position in the Near East.[79] Hitler had basically approved these ideas in March, but, significantly, for *after the conclusion* of the summer offensive (and not as an alternative).[80] Thus, he was returning to his far-reaching plans for the post-Barbarossa phase, although with the decisive difference that he now wanted to advance in the Near East without having first defeated the Soviet Union.

On 8 May, the Wehrmacht began a series of attacks on the eastern front, intended to prepare the ground for the real summer offensive.[81] Within a few days the Kerch peninsula in eastern Crimea was conquered. However, the fortress of Sebastopol, which was strongly defended, managed to hold out until the beginning of July.[82] By the end of May, the Wehrmacht was able to cut off a Soviet advance from the Izyum salient towards Kharkov, which began on 12 May, with a counter offensive, which captured 240,000 Red Army troops. However, a further German offensive to sort out the whole situation round Izyum lasted until the end of June and, as well as the tough Soviet resistance in Sebastopol, resulted in the great summer offensive, originally planned to begin on 15 June, being delayed for two weeks.[83]

The news from the eastern front aroused great expectations among the German population for the success of a major summer offensive, but also fears that, despite all their military efforts, it would not succeed in finally defeating the Soviet colossus. Concerns about the uncertain length of the war, the continuing enemy air raids, and, last but not least, the precarious food situation, were in fact creating a rather tense atmosphere.[84]

While in the East the initial signs were promising, Hitler's attention was focused on the start of the major offensive in the southern sector of the front, which he believed would prove decisive for the war. An opportunity for him to report to the Party leadership on the great events that were impending was provided on 22 May 1942, when the Gauleiters and Reichsleiters attended a memorial ceremony for the Gauleiter of Weser-Ems, Carl Röver, who had died suddenly.[85]

After the ceremony Hitler gave a speech lasting two hours. Goebbels's notes give the impression of a very serious and crisis-laden atmosphere, in which Hitler endeavoured to provide new hope in the light of the coming offensive. He remarked that the members of the leadership corps were now all between 45 and 60 years of age and 'it may well be unfortunate for the National Socialist movement that we are all of the same age and so, when death comes to our ranks, it could have a devastating effect....He himself hoped that he would outlive the war, as he was convinced that nobody else would be in a position to deal with the problems created by it.' Hitler then talked about the 'world situation', in particular the dramatic crisis of the past winter. In a long-winded discourse he blamed it on the Wehrmacht leadership, the leadership of the Reich railways, the judiciary and the civil service. 'He is also of course aware that the Jews are determined under all circumstances to win this war, since they know that defeat would also mean personal liquidation for them.' It was a case of 'triumph or downfall'. In addition, according to Goebbels, Hitler said that he was 'determined to give the Soviets the coup de grace this summer'. Victory in the East was the basis for the 'creation of a new Eastern Marches', for which Hitler sketched out grandiose future prospects: 'There we shall hugely extend our land. There

Figure 12. By the middle of 1942 queues such as this at fruit and vegetable stalls were an everyday sight. Food shortages, which had occurred repeatedly from the beginning of the so-called Third Reich and grew more acute during the war, depressed the public 'mood'. The regime's assurances of a glorious future could not alleviate the gloom.
Source: Scherl/Süddeutsche Zeitung Photo

we shall acquire coal, grain, oil and above all national security.... A shrewd population policy, above all using the resettlement of ethnic Germans, could within sixty, seventy years easily increase the German population to 250 million.' However, according to Hitler, they should 'not believe that with this war all war would be abolished. In future too, war would still be the father of all things.'[86]

The concentration of military forces in the East during the spring also meant that the Luftwaffe in the West was not in a position to provide an effective defence against the RAF or to mount a substantial counterattack on Great Britain. Hitler was increasingly compelled to get to grips with this problem. After the destruction of the densely populated historic centres of Lübeck and Rostock at the end of March and beginning of April,[87] he ordered attacks on cities in Britain that were primarily of cultural rather than military significance, as the Luftwaffe was too weak for major raids on Britain's industrial centres. He hoped that these so-called 'Baedeker raids', as British propaganda dubbed the attacks on cities like Exeter, Bath, Norwich, or York,[88] would at least have a psychological effect.[89] The RAF had, however, only just begun its major offensive against German cities. During the night of 30/31 May, it launched the first 1,000-bomber raid in military history on Cologne, which, contrary to expectations, did not wipe out the city, but destroyed 13,000 dwellings and killed almost 500 people, more than any previous air raid. Two nights after the bombing of Cologne, the RAF launched a big raid on Essen, carried out by almost 800 bombers and, during the remaining seven months of the year, the RAF took part in over fifty more raids on German cities, with several hundred bombers involved each time.[90] Moreover, in July, the Luftwaffe largely had to abandon its 'retaliation' attacks on Britain because of heavy losses.[91] As the Luftwaffe was unable to defend Germany effectively against British raids, in Hitler's view 'retaliation' was the only feasible way of stopping the British air offensive. Thus, he increasingly placed his hopes in new rocket systems on which Luftwaffe and army engineers were working flat out. He was hoping they would bring about a change in the air war during 1943.[92]

Heydrich's death and its aftermath

During May and June, alongside the preparations for the summer offensive, the regime initiated a concrete programme for the murder of the European Jews. How this decision was reached is unclear;[93] the result, however, was unambiguous. The distinction made hitherto between East European Jews, who were shot or gassed, and the West and Central European Jews, who were deported to the East and deployed in forced labour, vegetating in ghettos under miserable conditions, was no longer applied. Now the trains from the Reich, from Slovakia, and, from July onwards, also from other European countries went directly to Auschwitz and to the other death camps that had been constructed in the meantime.[94] In May, Himmler, to whom Governor General Frank had already transferred significant responsibilities in March, secured the appointment of the Higher SS and Police Leader in the General Government, Friedrich-Wilhelm Krüger, as state secretary for security issues in Frank's regime. This appointment specifically covered all 'matters involving Jews'.[95] Himmler now set about gradually extending the murder programme to every district in the General Government and to occupied Upper Silesia.[96] At the same time, a second wave of murders was unleashed in the occupied parts of the Soviet Union.[97] This meant that the original plan, which had still been referred to in Heydrich's statement at the Wannsee Conference, namely to deport the Jews to the Soviet territories that had not yet been occupied, had finally been abandoned.

However, during May and June, certain events occurred which are likely to have accelerated the shift to a Europe-wide deportation programme. On 18 May 1942, a left-wing Berlin resistance group, the majority of whose members were of Jewish origin, carried out an arson attack on a propaganda exhibition, 'The Soviet Paradise', which the Propaganda Ministry was putting on in Berlin's Lustgarten. Those involved were soon arrested. As a reprisal, on 27 May, the Gestapo arrested a large number of Berlin Jews. A total of 154 were transferred to Sachsenhausen concentration camp and shot, together with another 96 Jewish inmates. In addition, a further 250 Jews were also transferred to Sachsenhausen and held there as hostages. The Jewish community in Berlin was informed that, in the event of another 'act of sabotage', these people would also be shot.[98]

On the same day, 27 May, Heydrich, both head of the RSHA and, as deputy Reich Protector, Hitler's strong man in Prague, was seriously injured in an attack by Czech resistance fighters, trained by British Intelligence and dropped by parachute. To begin with, it looked as if Heydrich's condition was stabilizing, but after a few days it deteriorated.[99] On the same day as the assassination attempt, Hitler ordered that everybody who had helped those involved should be 'shot together with his whole family'. In addition, 10,000 suspect or politically compromised Czechs, not already incarcerated, were to be arrested and all of them shot 'in concentration camps'. In fact, however, the following day Karl Hermann Frank, Heydrich's state secretary, was able to persuade Hitler to drop this part of his order.[100]

The next day, 29 May, Hitler told Goebbels that they must take 'vigorous and ruthless action against those [in the Protectorate], who are supporting assassination attempts'. [101] When Goebbels then responded by mentioning his aim of 'deporting all the Jews from Berlin', since 'there were now 40,000 Jews hanging around in the capital of the Reich who have nothing more to lose' (he was referring to the attack on the Soviet Paradise exhibition), Hitler immediately agreed. He ordered Speer to replace Jewish workers with foreign workers and in September raised this issue again.[102]

To a wider audience during the lunch that followed, Hitler insisted that they must 'liquidate the Jewish threat, whatever the cost'. He did not want 'the Jews to be evacuated to Siberia', thereby distancing himself from Heydrich's old plan. The best thing would be to 'resettle [them] to Central

Africa', where there was a climate that 'certainly would not make them strong and hardy'. However, in view of the military situation, this goal was completely unrealistic – at the beginning of May the British had landed in Madagascar, the deportation destination for Jews favoured by Germany's 'Jewish experts' in 1940. Hitler was evidently trying to gloss over the real situation. In any case, he continued by saying that it was his aim 'to make western Europe completely free of Jews'.[103] These comments show that it is possible that at this stage no final plan for murdering the *western* European Jews had been decided. In fact, large-scale deportations from France to Auschwitz began only in July, whereas deportations from Central Europe to a death camp (Maly Trostinets near Minsk) had already started in May.[104]

On 4 June, Heydrich died of septicemia, and, a few days later, an elaborate state memorial ceremony was held in Berlin for him.[105] In his commemorative address Himmler committed himself to 'atone for his death, take over his task and now more than ever destroy the enemies of our people without mercy or weakness'.[106] Finally, Hitler paid tribute to Heydrich in a short address. He had been 'one of the best National Socialists, one of the strongest defenders of the idea of the German Reich, one of the greatest opponents of all the enemies of this Reich'.[107]

Following the ceremony, in the presence of Lammers, Bormann, Karl Hermann Frank, and other top functionaries, Hitler received the Czech Protectorate government, led by President Hacha, who tried to distance themselves from the assassination. Hitler made a speech in which he threatened his guests that he would 'deport a few million people from Bohemia and Moravia...if necessary during the war'.[108] Immediately after this meeting Frank ordered the commander of the security police in Prague – referring specifically to a 'meeting with the Führer' – to carry out retaliatory action against the Czech village of Lidice near Kladno, despite there being no proof of any support for the assassins coming from this village. In pursuit of this order, on 10 June, the security police murdered all 199 men, deporting the women to Ravensbrück concentration camp, and the children to the Chelmno death camp after the 'racially valuable ones' had been sorted out.[109] A few weeks later, during his table talk, Hitler referred to this brutal action with approval.[110]

However, the retaliation for the death of Heydrich, the organizer of the Einsatzgruppen murders and the deportation programme, above all affected the Jews, in other words those against whom, in the first instance, the regime was fighting the war. On 10 June 1942, a thousand Jews from Prague were deported to Majdanek and to camps in the surrounding area, where they were incarcerated.[111] Much more serious, however, was the fact that, following Heydrich's assassination, the Nazi leadership was evidently determined to intensify and accelerate the expansion of the mass murder of Jews throughout Europe that was already under way.

During these critical days, Hitler was having unusually frequent meetings with Himmler. Between 27 May, the day of the assassination attempt, and the memorial ceremony on 9 June they met a total of eight times. Once again we do not know the content of their conversations, but we can presume that they were closely connected with Himmler's actions to speed up the 'Final Solution' that immediately followed.

Himmler's efforts were not hindered by a transport ban in the General Government between 19 June and 7 July as a result of the coming summer offensive; on the contrary, it simply prompted the reorganization of the deportation and murder programme. While the transports from the Reich to Maly Trostnets near Minsk had to be interrupted, in June they were already being replaced by an increase in transports to the 'old people's ghetto' in Theresienstadt.[112] The transports from Slovakia that were originally intended to go to the Lublin district were now rerouted to Auschwitz where, on 4 July, for the first time, a selection of Jews 'incapable of work' took place, who were then murdered immediately after their arrival.[113] In addition, the deportations from western Europe to Auschwitz were now significantly expanded. On 11 June, deportation quotas were fixed for a total of 135,000 people from France, Belgium, and the Netherlands and, before the end of the month, Himmler established the target of achieving 'sooner rather than later the total liberation of France from Jews'.[114]

After the lifting of the transport ban on 7 July the deportations from the Reich to Maly Trostnets, and thus the murder of German Jews, were resumed.[115] In July the security police also began the deportation of Croatian Jews, of whom 5,000 were murdered in Auschwitz during August.[116] Also in June, the SS arranged with the Antonescu regime for the deportation of the Romanian Jews[117] (which the Romanians then, however, prevented), and Himmler tried to persuade the Finnish prime minister, Johan Rangell, to deport the Finnish Jews, albeit in vain.[118] Above all, the deportations within the General Government to the three death camps that were now available – Belzec, Sobibor, and Treblinka – were being carried out on a large scale.[119] After lengthy meetings with Hitler on 11, 12, and 14 July, Himmler used his liaison officer in the Führer headquarters, Karl Wolff, to press for an even larger transport capacity for deportations to the death camps. Then, having visited Auschwitz and Lublin's Higher SS and Police Leader, Globocnik, on 19 July he ordered that the 'resettlement [i.e. murder] of the whole of the Jewish population of the General Government be carried out and completed by 31 December 1942'.[120]

While we can only presume that, in the middle of July, Hitler discussed the murder of the Jews in the General Government with Himmler, we have clear written proof for the so-called second wave of murders in the Soviet Union, which had already begun in May and to which around half a million people fell victim. On 28 July, Himmler wrote to Gottlob Berger, the head of the SS Head Office: 'The occupied eastern territories [i.e. the Soviet territories] are being made free of Jews. The Führer has placed the implementation of this very difficult order on my shoulders.' The document clearly demonstrates that Himmler was not acting on the basis of a general authorization, a single Führer order, but evidently received an explicit order from Hitler for each of the occupied territories.[121]

In July 1942, when the SS began to involve the whole of Europe in the programme for murdering the Jews, Hitler also decided to give Himmler the responsibility for combatting Soviet partisans. Behind this decision lay the idea of also murdering the surviving Jews in the East, in other words to follow the method he had already proposed to Himmler in December 1941: 'to exterminate Jews – as partisans'.[122]

On 18 August, Hitler signed Directive No. 46, 'Guidelines for the Enhanced Combatting of Partisan Activities in the East'. In it he set Himmler the task of making sure that 'by the start of the winter...these bands [must have been] basically exterminated'.[123] Himmler reported to Hitler regularly on the 'successes' of the 'fight against the bandits'. At the end of 1942, he passed on to Hitler a report from Hans-Adolf Prützmann, the Higher SS and Police Leader in southern Russia, in which Prützmann stated that in the course of 'combatting bandits' in his area of responsibility, which included the Ukraine and Bialystock, during the period from 1 September to 1 December 1942, he had 'executed' a total of 363,211 Jews. A note in the margin indicates that Hitler had read this document.[124]

The summer offensive

Meanwhile, since January Rommel had been gradually moving onto the offensive in North Africa and, by the beginning of February, had conquered

Cyrenaica. At the end of May, he launched an attack on the British position in Gazala and, using an enveloping movement, forced the British to retreat. In June, he advanced on the port of Tobruk, capturing it on 21 June[125] and, in view of these successes, Hitler promoted him to field-marshal.[126] By the end of June, he had reached a point around a hundred kilometres from Alexandria;[127] during the so-called first battle of El Alamein, which lasted the whole of July, he was, however, unable to break through the British lines.[128] In fact, his resources had already become overstretched.

In the meantime, by the end of June, considerable progress was being made on the eastern front. On 28 June, Army Group South launched the real summer offensive. By the beginning of July, it had reached the River Don and, at the end of the month, had established a broad front along the river. However, although the first goal of the operations had been reached, the underlying intention of destroying the enemy forces west of the Don had not been achieved. The Red Army had managed to avoid being surrounded by retreating to the south-east.[129]

At the beginning of July, Hitler divided Army Group South into two independent Army Groups, A and B, and then, on the 13th, dismissed Field-Marshal von Bock, whom he blamed for what he considered the unnecessary delay in the advance of Army Group B. The dismissal of the independent-minded and self-confident Bock was a foretaste of the major confrontations between Hitler and his generals that were to occur during the course of the campaign.[130]

Based on the reports of success from the front, on 16 July, Hitler moved his headquarters to a new location around 10 kilometres north of Vinnitza in the Ukraine. The relatively extensive complex, with the codename Werwolf, was in a dark forest and basically consisted of simple wooden houses and a few bunkers. It was from here, in the middle of conquered enemy territory, that, during the coming weeks, Hitler intended to inflict a decisive defeat on the Soviet Union. This would then open the way for the creation of his racial empire and enable him to fight a global war against the western powers. The base was more than 1,500 kilometers from Berlin; its residents were out of touch with the realities of wartime life in the Reich, suffering from the summer heat, and subjected to a plague of flies and mosquitos and the monotony of daily routine. Its remoteness and seclusion created a surreal atmosphere and, during the coming weeks, encouraged Hitler's growing illusions about the prospects for victory. As his military advisors did not share this optimism, there was growing tension, and, because there were no distractions or ways of avoiding each other, this increasingly led to aggressive confrontations. Hitler remained in Vinnitza until 31 October 1942, a stay broken only by a visit to Berlin for several days between the end of September and the beginning of October.[131]

Initial success in the advance toward the Caucasus had convinced Hitler that the Soviet Union would soon be cut off from its sources of oil, and from supplies from the west via Iran, and he now set about trying to block its northern supply route. His Directive No. 44 of 21 July ordered preparations to be made for an attack on the Murman railway in the far north of Russia, in order to cut off transports from the port of Murmansk. He was working on the assumption that a renewed assault on Leningrad would lead to its capture at the latest by September. To achieve this he transferred the 11th Army under Erwin von Manstein, which had played a major part in the conquest of Sebastapol, to the Leningrad front. He had not changed his mind about the city's future. He told the commander of Army Group North at the end of August that, right from the start, the attack must focus on its 'destruction'. However, Soviet counterattacks in the Leningrad sector frustrated Hitler's wide-ranging plans in the north.[132]

The division of Army Group South into two Army Groups (A under Field-Marshal Wilhelm von List and B under Bock) at the beginning of July was the product of an increasing diversification of the operational goals of the summer offensive. In the middle of July, Hitler forced the army leadership to agree to Army Group A sending strong panzer forces south in order to envelop a large concentration of enemy forces round Rostov. Rostov was indeed taken on 23 July, but the majority of enemy units once again evaded capture. While Halder believed that the enemy was withdrawing intentionally in order to avoid a decisive battle, Hitler assumed the enemy forces were at the end of their tether and urged that they should be rapidly pursued.[133]

Hitler's over-optimism was reflected in his Directive No. 45 of 23 July, in which he divided further operations between the two groups.[134] Army Group A, which now became the main focus of the offensive, was ordered to envelop and destroy the enemy forces withdrawing over the Don in the Rostov area, and then, in a wide-ranging operation to the south, capture the east coast of the Black Sea, thereby securing the sea route for further operations. Finally, a group of light infantry and mountain infantry divisions were to advance through the Caucasus to Baku on the Caspian Sea. Meanwhile, Army Group B was to take Stalingrad and then advance along the Volga towards Astrakhan.

Halder, on the other hand, wanted to concentrate the offensive initially on Stalingrad, as Hitler had originally intended, and to postpone the advance on the Caucasus. However, Hitler, who, in the light of the overall war situation, was seeking a rapid victory in the East, thought he could achieve both war aims – Stalingrad and the Caucasus – *simultaneously*.[135]

On 23 July, after Hitler had 'ranted and raved, heaping serious reproaches on the military leadership', Halder noted bitterly: 'This chronic tendency to underestimate the enemy's capabilities is gradually assuming grotesque proportions and becoming dangerous. The situation is increasingly intolerable. Serious work is no longer taking place. This so-called "leadership" is marked by pathological responses to impressions of the moment and a complete lack of judgement when it comes to the military command and its potential.'[136]

The reorganization of the judicial system

In August 1942, at the climax of the summer offensive, Hitler brought to an end the crisis in the judicial system he had initiated in the spring. On 20 August, he appointed the President of the People's Court, Otto Georg Thierack, Reich Minister of Justice and state secretary Schlegelberger, who had been acting Justice Minister, was retired. Hitler had already contemplated replacing him with a hard-line Nazi the previous February.[137] At the same time, the previous President of the Hanseatic High Court in Hamburg, Curt Rothenberger, became a state secretary in the Justice Ministry,[138] while the previous incumbent, Roland Freisler, was appointed President of the People's Court.

Hitler also appointed Thierack to succeed Hans Frank as President of the Academy for German Law and leader of the Nazi Lawyers' Association. Frank also resigned as head of the Nazi Party's Reich Legal Office, which was dissolved. According to the official explanation of these changes, Frank had requested to be relieved of these offices so that he could devote himself 'entirely to his duties as Governor General'. Frank's removal as head of the Nazi Lawyers' Association was in fact the result not only of his involvement in a corruption affair, but also because, in a number of speeches, he had spoken out in favour of the independence of the judiciary and the 'upholding of the law'. In the light of Hitler's Reichstag speech, this represented a direct provocation of the 'Führer'.[139] At the same time, Hitler authorized the new Justice Minister, Thierack, 'to develop a new National Socialist legal system and to take all necessary measures to secure it'. It was expressly stated that, in doing so, he was permitted 'to depart from established law'.[140]

On the day of Thierack's appointment Hitler received him, Rothenberger, and Schlegelberger in his headquarters in order to spell out once again his views on the tasks of the judicial system.[141] He displayed a purely utilitarian understanding of the law. According to him, the judge was in the first instance 'an agent for ethnic self-preservation'. The war was inevitably leading to a process of 'negative selection' since the bravest were the ones killed at the front, while the law-breakers were conserved because of the relatively light prison sentences they received. If one did not 'ruthlessly exterminate the scum then one day there will be a crisis. I'm definitely not a brutal person but on this matter I'm a rational one.'

In future judges must represent a 'select cadre of the nation', who will receive from the 'highest authority' 'an insight into the aims and intentions of legislation and into the whole policy background that must inform their sentencing'. They must 'get rid of the idea that the judge is there to deliver justice, whatever the cost'. Rather 'the primary task...is to preserve the social order'. For this purpose the current detailed penal code should instead be replaced by framework legislation, within which judges, having been politically instructed, could make uniform judgments.[142]

Thierack got the Reich Chancellery to send him the minutes of this table talk and used Hitler's statements, in some cases word for word, in his address to the presidents of the regional high courts on 29 September 1942.[143] Less than a month after his appointment, Thierack was already applying Hitler's idea of a negative selection occurring during the war in the most brutal fashion. On 18 September, Thierack and Rothenberger agreed with Himmler that, in future, all 'inadequate sentences' should be 'corrected' by 'police special treatment'. All 'asocial elements serving prison sentences', in particular, all prisoners in preventive detention, all Jews, Gypsies, Russian, Ukrainians, Poles sentenced to more than three years, Czechs, and Germans sentenced to more than eight years who were still in prison should be transferred to concentration camps to be 'liquidated through labour'. Moreover, it was agreed that, in future, Jews, Poles, Gypsies, Russians, and Ukrainians should no longer be tried in the normal courts; rather they should be 'dispatched by the Reichsführer SS'.[144]

Thus, in summer 1942, Hitler pushed through a 'reform' of the penal system, according to which 'racial inferiors' were now no longer to be taken to court, and those already sentenced were no longer to be kept in prison, while the remaining criminal justice system was to be subordinated to political priorities. Together with his 'authorization' of April 1942, enabling him in future to call anybody to account for failure to fulfil their wartime duties, irrespective of legal provisions, these actions inflicted significant damage on those elements of the rule of law that were still operating in the 'Third Reich'. They also represented a clear signal that, in future, his rule would be based even more on the Party, the SS, and special commissioners and was in the process of finally abandoning traditional forms of state authority.

As we have seen, it was not by chance that these changes occurred during a period in which Hitler was seeking to achieve a decision in the East that would enable him to free up substantial military forces in order to prevent a British–American invasion in the West and to wage a global war alongside his successful Japanese partner. He now aimed to order his nascent empire in such a way that it could provide the basis for a successful continuation of the war. The decision forcibly to recruit millions of slave workers from abroad belongs in this context, as does the extension of the systematic murder of Jews throughout his whole territory. Hitler was making it clear that his war was a racial war, that he was waging it systematically, and from it there was no way back either for him or for all those who were supporting him. A few days after the fateful agreement between Thierack and Himmler, during the armaments meeting of 20–22 September, Hitler ordered Speer to complete 'the removal of Jews from the armaments plants in the Reich' in order substantially to conclude the deportation of German Jews to the death camps. In doing so, he was once again clearly reinforcing this approach.[145]

38

Hitler's Empire

In June 1942, in other words at the moment when Hitler was launching the great eastern offensive intended to decide the outcome of the war, Himmler gave his settlement planners the task of producing an 'overall settlement plan' for continental Europe. He outlined the basic principles underlying it to SS functionaries in two important speeches given in his headquarters during August and September 1942. German settlement policy was to embrace not only occupied Poland, but also parts of the Ukraine, Byelorussia, Estonia and Latvia, the Crimea, the 'Ingermanland' (in other words the region round Leningrad), but also Alsace and Lorraine, Upper Carniola and South Styria, and the Protectorate of Bohemia and Moravia. In his August speech, in relation to the occupied eastern territories, he referred specifically to a Führer command. However, we can naturally assume that the other settlement programmes had also been discussed with the 'Führer'.[1]

These plans represented the core of the future 'Greater Germanic Reich'. As far as the further 'reorganization of Europe' was concerned, Hitler himself only made extremely vague comments about the future arrangement of this extended empire, concerned not to tie himself to any commitments about the post-war order that might result in future claims or prove contradictory. However, two models can be reconstructed from his comments and from the preliminary plans of his entourage. On the one hand, there was the idea of uniting under German leadership all 'Germanic' European nations in a 'Greater Germanic Reich', which would have included Norway, Denmark, Sweden, the Netherlands, and Flanders, perhaps also Switzerland, in addition to the territories involved in Himmler's settlement policy. Hitler did not commit himself as to what form the integration of these states into the Greater Germanic Reich would have taken, whether they would have been allowed to keep some form of sovereignty or would simply have become

'Reich Gaus' as in the case of the Austrian, Czech, and Polish territories. The two leaders of the fascist movements in Norway and the Netherlands, Quisling and Mussert, did not get very far in their attempts to gain some kind of commitment for the post-war order. Quisling was bluntly informed that Hitler was unable to discuss his proposed peace treaty while the war was still going on,[2] and Mussert's proposal of a 'Germanic confederation' was given equally short shrift.[3] Hitler also did not wish to make any firm decision about the future of Belgium. The question of whether Flanders was to become a 'Reich Gau' and the future status of Wallonia, in which Nazi racial 'experts' increasingly claimed to be discovering 'Germanic elements', remained equally unclear.[4]

On the other hand, the regime began using the slogan, the 'New Europe', in order to suggest to its allies the vague prospect of some participation in the post-war order. Thus, in November 1941, Hitler had ceremoniously admitted several countries to the 1936 Anti-Comintern Pact, which he extended by five years, even though they had been unwilling to join the Tripartite Pact or enter a military pact with Germany. Apart from Germany, Italy, Japan, Hungary, Manchukuo, and Spain, now Bulgaria, Denmark, Finland, Croatia, Slovakia, and the Japanese puppet government in Nanking all signed the agreement 'against the Communist International'.[5] However, the agreement did not contain any concrete arrangements for the post-war order.[6] However much German propaganda bandied about the slogan 'New Europe', Hitler continued to insist that there should be no public discussion of the details of this European concept. In November 1942, he banned all European 'demonstrations', such as 'congresses' or inter-state associations.[7] At the end of 1942, Ribbentrop presented him with a plan for a European peace settlement prepared by his ministry, according to which, among other things, Czechs and Poles would regain their independence; but Hitler rejected such efforts as superfluous.[8] While Hitler gave Goebbels permission in January 1943 to prepare a 'Programme for Europe', he later cut a passage from a Goebbels speech dealing with the subject,[9] and was equally unwilling to pursue an idea put forward by Ribbentrop in March 1943 for a 'European confederation'.[10]

The relationship between the two concepts, the 'Greater Germanic Reich' and the 'New Europe', also remained completely obscure, as did that between the 'non-Germanic' nations and 'Greater Germania'. Thus, for example, Hitler intentionally left the role that France would play in a future Europe unresolved; it was made clear to the French that this would depend on their behaviour towards the German occupation. Although Hitler was aware that substantial support by the Vichy regime for the Reich, ideally participation in the war against the western powers, would require reciprocation, in particular a peace treaty, he was not prepared to make any such commitment.[11] At the same time, it was made clear in no uncertain terms to Germany's 'allies' in south-east Europe that, when it came to the crunch, 'Greater Germanic' policy had priority over recognition of their sovereignty. Thus, from 1941/42 onwards, Himmler compulsorily recruited tens of thousands of so-called ethnic Germans in Croatia, Slovakia, Hungary, and Romania for the Waffen SS, despite the fact that these men were citizens of the countries concerned; their governments simply had to put up with it.[12]

Despite Hitler's failure to create uniformity in his empire – significantly, there was no central authority for the occupied territories, for final decisions rested with him – certain basic distinctions can be discerned. Territories that were considered to be part of the future 'Greater Germanic Reich' were subjected to civilian administration, that is to say the Party and SS wielded considerable influence and they were directly subordinate to Hitler via a Reich Commissioner. In the west this applied to the Reich Commissariats in the Netherlands and Norway, where an attempt was already being made during the war to begin the process of 'Germanization' with the aid of allied fascist movements. In the case of Denmark, which the Nazis considered 'Germanic', a special arrangement was made. To maintain the fiction of a 'peaceful' occupation of the country and to protect its resources, the German ambassador was appointed 'Reich Plenipotentiary', who, aided by a small staff, then informed the Danish government of his 'wishes'. The General Government and the occupied former Soviet territories were also subjected to civilian administrations. However, here there was no interest in involving indigenous elements except at local level. These administrations acted as exploitative and repressive colonial-type regimes. Here, during the war, extensive 'resettlement' programmes were initiated in order to prepare for the post-war order. The territories outside the sphere of the future Greater Germanic Reich remained under military administration. Hitler's idea of treating the various occupied territories on the basis of racial criteria was thus clearly reflected in the types of their occupation administrations. He was primarily concerned to prevent the emergence of established supranational structures, which, in the form of an occupation or alliance 'system', would bind him to promises, commitments, and obligations. Instead, he wanted to keep things fluid, responding to problems in the occupied territories on a case-by-case basis.

He judged the effectiveness of his occupation policy not least in terms of the considerable economic contribution that the countries he controlled made to his conduct of the war. Between 1941 and 1943, more than half the German supplies of iron ore came from annexed and occupied territories (above all from Lorraine, Luxemburg, and Norway). Through the annexations that had occurred by summer 1940, German steel producers increased their capacity from 23 million to 39 million tons per annum, in fact an amount too big to be utilized. From summer 1941 onwards, the largest manganese deposits in Europe in Nikopol in the Ukraine were able largely to supply the requirements of German industry for this rare non-ferrous metal. From 1941 onwards, chromium was provided by mines in Yugoslavia and Greece,[13] while supplies of bauxite and copper came largely from France.[14] The occupied territories in the Soviet Union, Poland, France, and Denmark played the most important role in supplying Germany with food during the war. During 1942/43, they provided more than 30 per cent of the grain and around a third of Germany's meat consumption.[15] By the end of 1943, the number of foreign civilian workers had reached over 5.4 million; a third were Soviet 'eastern workers', and more than a million came from the General Government.[16] Moreover, by the end of 1943, there were more than 1.8 million POWs involved in the 'labour mobilization' programme, including over 564,000 from the Soviet Union and more than 664,000 from France.[17] Germany also demanded heavy occupation payments from the occupied territories, which greatly outweighed the costs of their occupation forces. In fact, these payments, along with the German clearing debts that had not been paid, covered a substantial part of Germany's war costs.[18]

Thus the Nazi regime's wartime economic policy in Europe was basically a gigantic programme of plunder and exploitation. The massive intervention in the economies of the occupied countries, which were also cut off from foreign trade relations with states outside the German 'bloc', resulted in inflation and reduced production. Significantly, Germany only partially succeeded in utilizing the industrial capacity of the occupied countries through the distribution of orders to produce armaments for the Wehrmacht.[19] In addition, the removal of food stocks worsened the supply situation, even causing famines, particularly as agricultural production in almost all the occupied countries declined during the war.[20]

Meanwhile, resistance was growing, particularly after the attack on the Soviet Union, and was dealt with by the German occupation authorities and police agencies with extreme brutality. In combatting partisan movements, underground organizations, strikes, or cases of civil disobedience, German forces had no compunction about involving wide sections of the population. The ruthless combatting of 'bands' and their alleged supporters, the so-called 'reprisals', in other words the shooting of hostages and the destruction of villages and urban districts, was characteristic of this approach. It also involved the large-scale deportation of local people to concentration camps, draconian sentences imposed by special courts, and, in the second half of the war, 'counter-terror', in other words the assassination of well-known personalities considered hostile to the German occupation.[21] At the same time, local collaborators with the German occupation and its allied regimes in south-east Europe became complicit through their involvement in the criminal policies of the regime, namely the persecution and deportation of Jews. As a result, they felt compelled to remain completely and utterly loyal to Germany.

German occupation policy and its treatment of its allies, which clearly bore Hitler's signature, had one overriding aim: to secure the Nazi regime's total control over the whole of Europe and the racial 'reordering' of the continent. It was not interested in mobilizing the resources of the occupied and allied countries through incentives, rewards or binding pledges. Instead, it ruthlessly took what was required for the war: raw materials, food supplies, people. Hitler's rule over the continent was based on military superiority vis-à-vis its foreign opponents and unlimited force against its internal ones.

The regime at home

The heterogeneity of the German occupation administrations and the lack of clarity about the organization and constitution of the future empire were basically a reflection of the internal workings of Hitler's regime during the war.

After 1937 Hitler had effectively abolished the government as a collective body, and his attempt, on the outbreak of war, to create a kind of war cabinet in the shape of the Ministerial Council for the Defence of the Reich had also come to nothing.[22] In January 1942 Lammers failed to persuade Hitler to issue a Führer edict instituting regular ministerial meetings under the former's chairmanship; the 'Führer' considered that such an arrangement was 'unnecessary'.[23] Thus, the individual ministries continued to have to legislate through the 'circulation procedure', leading to long-winded written consultations. As a result, legislation inevitably continued to lack coherence. In any case, Hitler took the view that legislation should primarily take the form of framework laws, with the detail being filled in through decrees dealing with particular issues,[24] and, in June 1940, he banned all new laws not considered important for the war effort.[25] In consequence, the main emphasis shifted from governmental legislation towards a proliferation of decrees issued by the individual ministries.[26]

Under this system, Hitler possessed unlimited authority to create law by issuing a Führer edict. However, there were problems. This was particularly the case when edicts were not submitted to the Reich Chancellery for comments by the government departments affected prior to their being signed off by Hitler, but instead were secured through personal audiences with the 'Führer' arranged by powerful individuals in what Lammers termed an 'ambush procedure' [as distinct from the regular 'circulation procedure']. Hitler banned this practice, insisting that he did not wish to be approached about an edict or a decision without the Reich Chancellery and the departments affected having been asked to comment on the matter. However, as he had to repeat the injunction it was clear that the practice was continuing.[27] Also, the fact that Führer edicts were not published could give rise to considerable difficulties.[28]

Thus Hitler's regime increasingly departed from the forms of traditional state practice, in other words from a governmental process marked by the distribution of functions to officially responsible departments, by adherence to the law and to bureaucratic rules, and by a fixed civil service hierarchy based on qualifications and performance criteria. Instead, his regime was increasingly becoming a Führer autocracy, in which he assigned particular tasks to individuals whom he could trust, at his discretion. The result of this personal rule, which was progressively undermining the existing governmental apparatus through ad hoc assignments, was opaque lines of responsibility leading to bitter and lengthy conflicts within the power structure. The fact that Hitler often declined to get involved in such conflicts, instead leaving their resolution to the relative assertiveness of the individual disputants, further encouraged the regime's fragmentation.

As far as this development during the war was concerned, the following factors stand out:

First: Hitler's continuing practice of appointing 'special representatives', often with the title 'Reich Commissioner/Commissar' or 'General Plenipotentiary', to deal with particular political issues in a rapid and unbureaucratic fashion. The 'Führer' gave these special assignments to a small and easily manageable group and this small coterie of top functionaries, most of whom performed both state and Party functions, created complex power structures, whose 'bosses' owed their position entirely to their personal relationship to Hitler.

Göring's power base essentially derived from his responsibilities as Prussian Prime Minister (now a largely prestige position), commander-in-chief of the Luftwaffe, head of the Four-Year Plan, and, from 1939 plenipotentiary for the war economy. He extended the responsibilities of the last-named position to include the occupied territories. During the winter of 1941/42, however, it became clear that his policy of ruthlessly plundering raw materials and agrarian products, particularly from eastern Europe, could not cope with the requirements of a lengthy war, and, with the rise of Speer from 1942 onwards, Göring lost his preeminent position within the economy. In addition, Hitler largely excluded him from decision-making on foreign policy issues, and the failure of the 'Blitz' on Britain and, above all, the increasing British air raids during 1941/42, damaged his prestige as commander-in-chief of the Luftwaffe. Despite his loss of power and influence, he remained Hitler's designated successor, although from 1942 onwards he appears to have given up, increasingly withdrawing from politics to pursue his various other interests.[29]

During the war, the Reichsführer SS and Chief of the German Police, Heinrich Himmler, created an apparatus of repression encompassing the whole of Europe. He built up his own military force in the Waffen SS, as Reich Settlement Commissar pursued an elaborate settlement policy based on racial criteria, and used his various responsibilities to subject the conquered territories to a gigantic programme of deportation, resettlement, and extermination resulting in millions of victims. In the process Himmler and the SS became the decisive driving force in creating the 'New Order'. In addition, in 1943 he took over the Interior Ministry and, in 1944, was appointed commander of the Reserve Army.[30]

Apart from his positions as head of the Party's propaganda department, Propaganda Minister, President of the Reich Chamber of Culture, and Gauleiter of Berlin, during the war Goebbels acquired additional functions in the civilian sector, particularly involving critical issues on the home front. To begin with, in 1942, Hitler assigned him the task of coordinating aid for bombed cities, an activity that in 1943 was extended to organizing preventive measures. Finally, in July 1944, he was appointed Plenipotentiary for Total War with the authority to 'overhaul' the civilian sector.[31]

As successor to Todt, Speer took over the latter's various functions (Minister of Munitions, General Inspector of the German Road Network, General Inspector of Water and Energy, General Plenipotentiary for the Regulation of the Construction Industry) and, in possession of Hitler's full confidence, quickly brought the whole of the armaments sector under his control. In addition to these tasks, in autumn 1944, as General Inspector of Construction, Speer extended his responsibilities to include the rebuilding of war-damaged cities.[32]

Although other leading Nazi figures also accumulated responsibilities during these years, they were less successful in their attempts to build up independent power bases. In November 1940, Dr Robert Ley, the head of the Party's national organization and of the German Labour Front, was appointed Reich Commissar for Social Housing and, in October 1942, given additional responsibilities, as 'Reich Housing Commissar'. In February 1940, he had also secured a Führer edict authorizing him to prepare an 'Old Age Welfare Plan', which he aimed to turn into a comprehensive programme of social reform. However, Hitler ordered a halt to Ley's project during wartime; his major house-building plan could not be implemented during the war; the Labour Front was declining in importance; and the office of head of the Party's national organization lost out in its internal struggle with Bormann's Party Chancellery. As a result, Ley proved unable to integrate his various responsibilities to form a coherent empire.[33] The Party's chief ideologist, Alfred Rosenberg, apart from being Minister for the Eastern Territories, continued to head the Party's Foreign Policy Office and maintained the Bureau Rosenberg to support his work as the 'Führer's' 'Representative for the Supervision of the Intellectual and Ideological Indoctrination and Education of the NSDAP'. In summer 1940, Hitler also assigned him the task of confiscating libraries, art collections, and other cultural artefacts in the occupied territories. The Rosenberg Taskforce was established to carry out this comprehensive campaign of plunder. However, as Minister of the East, Rosenberg was unable to get his way in the face of the Reich Commissars and the various Reich agencies operating in the occupied eastern territories, and he was unsuccessful in coordinating his other activities. In addition, in March 1942 Sauckel was appointed General Plenipotentiary for Labour Mobilization; in July 1942, Karl Brandt became Plenipotentiary (from 1943 Commissar General) for Health Services; and, in May 1942, the Hamburg Gauleiter, Karl Kaufmann, was appointed Reich Commissar for Shipping. All these appointments were special representatives 'directly responsible to the Führer'.[34]

Secondly: those who were merely Reich ministers, and whose position was not underpinned by a power base in the Party or by other special assignments from Hitler, generally declined in importance. Foreign Minister Joachim von Ribbentrop managed to achieve a privileged position within the leadership clique vis-à-vis Hitler on account of the regime's foreign policy 'successes' during the years 1938–41, because of his total subservience to the 'Führer', and the fact that, by 1938, he had succeeded in excluding the usual 'special emissaries' from foreign policy making. However, he was unable to intervene actively in occupation policy, and, with the almost complete absence of foreign policy after 1942, his influence waned.[35] Interior Minister, Wilhelm Frick, the 'lawyer of the lawless state', lost all influence in the course of the war because of his attempt to maintain legal procedures within the administration and support for a reform of the Reich's federal structure. Hitler considered him tired and worn out, finally replacing him with Himmler in August 1943, and appointing him to the largely figurehead post of Reich Protector of Bohemia and Moravia.[36]

In 1942, Hitler made significant changes at the top of three ministries without appointing new ministers. In May 1942 he transferred effective power in the Reich Agriculture Ministry from the minister, Walther Darré, to Darré's state secretary, Herbert Backe. Backe was a confidant of Himmler's and, like Darré, an agricultural ideologist, but, unlike him, also a pragmatic technocrat. He played a key role in imposing Nazi racial ideology in the agricultural sphere and, in particular, was responsible for the systematic starvation policy pursued in the occupied eastern territories.[37] In May 1942, the portfolio of the long-serving transport minister, Julius Dorpmüller, was effectively taken over by Albert Ganzenmüller, a tough railway expert, who had been a keen Nazi in his youth, and now, at Speer's instigation, was appointed state secretary.[38] Backe and Ganzenmüller, experts in the critical areas of food supplies and transport, both enjoyed Hitler's particular favour. The Ministers Walther Funk (Economics), Franz Seldte (Labour), Bernhard Rust (Education), and Lutz Schwerin von Krosigk (Finance) remained in office with much reduced authority. Hitler replaced state secretary Schlegelberger (justice) by the biddable Thierack as part of his attempt to reform the judicial system, with the aim of removing the last vestiges of an independent judiciary.[39]

Thirdly: Hess's chief of staff, Martin Bormann, who after Hess's flight to Britain in May 1941 took over the Staff of the 'Führer's' Deputy under the new title of Party Chancellery, rapidly established himself as the leading figure within the Party. He proved more effective at exercising the Party's control functions vis-à-vis the state bureaucracy, in particular when it came to participating in legislation, the appointment of officials, but also in relation to all 'fundamental political issues'.[40] Above all, however, his permanent proximity to Hitler, who continued to entrust him with his personal affairs, gave him a key position. Through his responsibility for Hitler's schedule, Bormann was able, to a considerable extent, to control access to the 'Führer', as the latter preferred interviews to studying documents. Thus, he was able to direct the flow of information reaching Hitler, particularly in the sphere of domestic policy. He also relayed Führer assignments and Hitler's opinions on other matters, all given orally, to leading members of the regime. Moreover, Bormann's intermediary role was by no means limited to Party matters, which meant that the Reich Chancellery under Lammers, hitherto the main link between Hitler and the state bureaucracy, acquired a serious competitor. Bormann's power was by no means unlimited, however. Military matters were outside his sphere of competence, and he was not permitted to intervene in matters for which those top politicians who had immediate access to Hitler, namely Göring, Goebbels, Himmler, Speer, and Ribbentrop, were responsible. He was able to take the initiative in the sense of emphasizing particular opinions of Hitler only in issues involving the NSDAP and its place within the power structure, the radicalization of racial policy, and the attempt to exclude the Churches from almost all areas of life.[41]

During the war, the Gauleiters further increased their importance. In the two new 'Reich Gaus', which had been established in the annexed Polish territories on the model of the 'Sudeten Gau', Gauleiter Albert Forster (Danzig-West Prussia) and Gauleiter Artur Greiser (Warthegau), as Reich Governors, possessed the right to issue directives to various branches of the state administration. They took full advantage of this, establishing a virtual dictatorship in their Gaus, and invoking Hitler's assignment to justify carrying out a ruthless 'Germanization' of their districts.[42]

Hitler regarded the extended responsibilities of the Gauleiters/Reich Governors in the annexed territories as the model for a future reform of the 'old Reich'. He justified this by noting that, during the 'time of struggle', he had given the 'Gau kings' the greatest possible freedom of action and in future wanted them to have the same freedom as far as their state functions were concerned. He envisaged a network of regional power holders, who combined Party and state responsibilities and were directly responsible to him.[43] In 1939, he applied this idea by appointing fifteen of the thirty-nine Gauleiters to be Reich Defence Commissioners, giving each of them responsibility for civil defence issues in their particular military district. They were organs of the new Ministerial Committee for the Defence of the Reich established on the outbreak of war, were officially supervised by the Reich Interior Ministry, and were responsible for overseeing the work of the various branches of the administration in their military district in accordance with the directives of the ministries concerned.[44] This measure contained a clear political message: 'authority on the home front' was to be transferred to the Party.[45] Since the borders of the military districts did not coincide either with those of the Gaus or with those of the federal states and the Prussian provinces, the Reich Defence Commissioners/Gauleiters and the Reich Governors/Gauleiters of the annexed Polish territories were in effect privileged vis-à-vis the other Gauleiters, a situation which led to friction. In November 1942, all forty-two Gauleiters were appointed Reich Defence Commissioners and the borders of their jurisdictions were adjusted to correspond to those of the Gaus rather than the military districts. However, since the borders of the federal states and the Prussian provinces did not correspond to those of the Party Gaus, that is, the jurisdictions of the Reich Defence Commissioners/ Gauleiters, friction between the various political and administrative bodies with their overlapping boundaries inevitably continued.

As the war went on, there was an increasing tendency for the Gauleiters to regard more and more administrative spheres as matters relating to 'Reich defence' and to intervene in matters hitherto controlled by the regional state authorities. They claimed that the Gauleiters should be responsible for coordinating the various branches of the cumbersome state administration, providing it with flexible leadership and, whenever necessary, using the Party apparatus to carry out certain functions. Their direct subordination to Hitler would avoid the need to go through laborious official channels.[46] This shift in the balance of power towards the Gauleiters clearly showed what the political structure of the so-called 'Third Reich' would have looked like, had Germany won the war. Hitler intended that the Gauleiters, who had risen within the Party hierarchy and were directly subordinate to him, would provide a counterweight to the concentration of power in the hands of the few individuals whom he trusted at Reich level. They already represented an important personnel reserve for special assignments. Apart from Goebbels and Sauckel, who have already been mentioned, Josef Terboven (Essen), Hinrich Lohse (Schleswig-Holstein), Erich Koch (East Prussia), and Josef Grohé (Cologne-Aachen) all received new tasks as Reich commissars in the occupied territories. Alfred Meyer (Westphalia: North) became state secretary in the Ministry for the Eastern Territories, and a number of Gauleiters were appointed as 'heads of the civilian administration' in territories occupied by the Wehrmacht, in order to prepare for their annexation.[47] The regular Gauleiter and Reichsleiter meetings continued during the war. They were designed not for making decisions but for the informal exchange of information and Hitler often used them for lengthy 'tours d'horizon'.

At local level, in particular, the Party increased its supervision and monitoring of the 'national comrades' with the aim of nipping in the bud any form of unrest in a population that was unenthusiastic about the war and subjected to increasing burdens.[48] To this end, the Party mobilized its members, whose number increased from 5.3 million at the start of the war to well over 8 million by the end, to undertake a wide range of tasks.[49] It became involved in the distribution of foodstuffs and important supplies; it organized the accommodation of the homeless and evacuees from the air war; it took on responsibilities for air raid protection (such as control of the blackout), for providing immediate aid after air raids, for the provision of accommodation for, and the supervision of, foreign forced workers, who were to be separated as far as possible from the German population, and for looking after Wehrmacht soldiers and their families, including the arrangement of funeral ceremonies for those who had been killed. Thus the Party was heavily involved in all matters affecting the population's 'mood', and could immediately intervene to sort things out when tricky situations arose at local level and even in people's domestic sphere.

Thus, during the early years of the war, the system of Führer autocracy had been perfected. Hitler ruled through direct personal contact with his entourage as well as through directives issued via the increasingly competing chancelleries or liaison officials based in the Führer headquarters. He was careful to avoid the creation of new, or the revival of old, collective decision-making bodies. Direct contact with the 'Führer', which was so vital for securing decisions, was restricted to a few top functionaries – Bormann, Göring, Goebbels, Ribbentrop, Himmler, Ley, and Speer, although the Reich Youth Leader, Baldur von Schirach, Sauckel, and Brandt, and, to a limited extent, the Gauleiters also enjoyed this privilege.[50] The Party's influence was increasing at all levels, above all with the aim of strengthening its control over the state bureaucracy, improving the latter's performance and commitment, and concentrating Menschenführung* [lit. 'the leadership of people'] in its own hands.

* Translators' note: Menschenführung denoted political control in every sphere of life. Together with Betreuung ['supervision'], Menschenführung was the term used to define the Party's role in relation to the German people.

Figure 13. Full mobilization: Ten sons belonging to the Schmidt family from Köpprich in Lower Silesia gather in uniform for a group photograph on 8 April 1941. The two boys are in the Hitler Youth. The son on the front right is in the Fire Police and all seven sons in the back row are in the Wehrmacht.
Source: bpk / Joe Heydecker

Within this Führer autocracy that he had created, Hitler not only kept tight personal control of the key areas of policy, but made decisions on matters of detail, sometimes on a day-to-day basis. This applied first of all to the actual conduct of the war, which, as supreme commander of the Wehrmacht and commander-in-chief of the army, he controlled through daily situation conferences often lasting for hours. With the help of his Reich press chief, Otto Dietrich, and in close consultation with Goebbels, he also set the guidelines for propaganda, had the whole of foreign policy under his aegis (mainly through the liaison officer with the Foreign Ministry, Walter Hewel), monitored armaments production, trying to control it through detailed directives, and kept an eye on the civilian side of the war (air raid precautions, labour conscription, transport, and so on). Any alteration in the allocation of food rations required his approval. He took personal charge of all measures affecting the constitution and administrative structure not only of the Reich itself but also of the occupied territories, repeatedly intervened in the details of occupation policy, and directed the radicalization of Jewish policy at every stage to the point of mass murder, as well as reserving for himself all important decisions relating to 'racial policy'.

However significant the damage resulting from this style of government may have been as a consequence of the friction and inefficiencies caused by the opaque lines of responsibility, the closing off of channels of information, and the internal power struggles, the fact remains that Hitler had at his disposal the kind of regime he needed in order to achieve his main goal: the establishment of a European empire on a racial basis under his virtually total control.

Hitler's charisma in the Second World War

It has already been argued at length[51] elsewhere that the basis of, and legitimation for, the 'Führer state' was Hitler's 'charisma', in other words the allegedly total consensus between 'people' and 'leadership', finding expression through the actions of the regime. Great efforts were required in order for this to be sustained. It was only through the apparatus of repression, local monitoring of the 'national comrades', and control of the public sphere by the propaganda machine that Germany's many-voiced and multifaceted society could be subsumed into a 'national community' and people's behaviour be adjusted to the norms set by the regime. This was the context within which the 'Führer' was continually renewing his putatively charismatic position. On the one hand, he gave expression to the alleged expectations, longings, and hopes of the German people in major speeches and with grand gestures. On the other hand, he reacted to negative shifts in the 'national mood' by responding to certain concerns and promising remedial action, while declaring others to be unacceptable, publicly banning critical voices from the national community and thereby silencing them. Sometimes he would then reset the domestic agenda by making a sudden dramatic move.

With his shift towards expansion and war during 1938/39, Hitler continued this constant interaction with the 'people', an indispensable element of 'Führer' charisma. He regained the initiative with his comprehensive reshuffle in February 1938. The unparalleled violence of the November pogrom, through which the regime mobilized the 'people's anger', then introduced a complete reorientation of propaganda in order to prepare the German population, which was hardly ready for war, for tougher times to come. After 1 September 1939, voices opposed to, or sceptical about, the war were banned from the public sphere through increased controls and repression, while Hitler himself initially sustained people's hopes of a short war. Even if there were no signs of enthusiasm for the war, propaganda took the line that the population was contentedly and confidently going along with the leadership's war policies. In November 1941, the parameters for Hitler's charisma were readjusted. In view of the difficulties on the eastern front, discussions about how long the war was going to last were banned and even presented as sabotaging the war effort. The almost simultaneous public declaration that Hitler's 1939 'prophecy' about the annihilation of the Jews was now in the process of being realized underlined the message: all bridges had been burnt and the 'people' had no alternative but to entrust themselves to Hitler's purportedly superhuman leadership qualities and support his conduct of the war until victory had been achieved.

At the same time, there were now an increasing number of lengthy breaks in the interaction between 'Führer' and 'people'. Hitler's charisma was, to a certain extent and for a certain time, suspended. This occurred for the first time between 10 March and 19 July 1940, in other words between Heroes' Memorial Day and Hitler's peace offer to Britain. This was the period during which he was preparing and carrying on the wars in northern and western Europe. His absence may have caused concern; but, by the summer of 1940, his victories and apparent willingness to make peace, which was a response to the population's desire for an end to the war, revived his charismatic leadership role. More serious was the fact that between May 1941 and 3 October 1941, in other words the period when he was preparing for war against the Soviet Union and engaged in the major eastern offensive, he had effectively disappeared from public view. This immediately resulted in ups and downs in the public 'mood', for the authoritative voice capable of allaying the widespread concerns about the course of the war was absent. At the beginning of October 1941, Hitler tried to remove this uncertainty with his public promise of imminent victory. During the following weeks, this did not occur and, instead, the advance of the armies in the East stalled. The 'Führer' responded by announcing on 11 December that, as the war had become a world war, an entirely new situation had arisen, in the light of which the temporary hold-up in the East was insignificant. Afterwards Hitler decided to remain silent until the end of January 1942, although the most serious crisis of the war hitherto had suggested that his whole strategic concept for the war was in serious jeopardy. Instead of making a blood, sweat, and tears speech, he left it to his Propaganda Minister to get over the critical period by organizing a collection of socks and warm underwear for the soldiers at the front. However, by patently failing to perform his leadership role at the height of the crisis, he had in fact seriously damaged the 'charismatic' basis of his regime.

With the gradual improvement in the military situation, Hitler spoke twice in public in March and April 1942, before becoming preoccupied with the preparations for and conduct of the summer offensive and disappearing once more from view until the end of September. In this difficult and, in the view of many, decisive phase of the war, his charisma could only have been salvaged if he had been able to return to the public stage to announce a decisive victory. It was such a victory that Hitler was pinning all his hopes during 1942 and this fixation was ultimately to shatter his charisma.

PART VII

Downfall

39

The Turning Point of the War and Radicalization

On 23 July 1942, Hitler divided the offensive in the southern sector of the eastern front into two spearheads. On the northern flank, Army Group B began advancing towards the Volga, reaching the river north of Stalingrad on 23 August.[1] At the military briefing on 1 September, Hitler ordered that, on 'entering the city the whole male population is to be got rid of because Stalingrad, with its million-strong and totally communist population, is particularly dangerous'.[2]

Meanwhile, by mid-August, the second spearhead, Army Group A, had advanced around 500 kilometres southwards; however, this offensive into the northern Caucasus now began to stall.[3] It managed to capture Maikop, the first of the Caucasus oil fields, but the Soviets had comprehensively destroyed its installations, and it would take at least six months to restart oil production in significant quantities.[4] Moreover, at the end of June, a Soviet offensive had begun in Army Group Centre's sector of the front, compelling the German forces to yield a significant amount of territory. The situation around Rzev proved particularly critical. Hitler aggravated the crisis by refusing a request from Kluge, the army group's commander, for reinforcements, preferring to deploy troops for a counter-offensive in the southern sector of Army Group Centre. Hitler considered the fact that the front near Rzev was then held as confirming his view that such crises could be overcome by strong nerves and by sticking to his guns, specifically in defiance of his generals.[5]

When Goebbels visited Hitler in Vinniza on 19 August, the 'Führer' appeared extremely optimistic as far as the progress of the summer offensive was concerned, but, at the same time, seemed worn out, which Goebbels attributed to an attack of dysentery from which he had only just recovered.

Hitler told him that 'recently he had been on his own a great deal' and had 'almost completely given up socializing in his headquarters', in order to devote himself entirely to his duties.[6] The extreme nervous tension after more than seven weeks of the offensive, the continual disputes with his generals, and his self-imposed isolation in his headquarters were taking their toll. However, Hitler had by no means given up hope of being about to achieve a success that would decide the war. He told Goebbels that in two or three days' time he would begin the major attack on Stalingrad, and in the autumn conquer Leningrad, in order 'to raze this city to the ground'. At the same time, he was planning to reach Krasny and Baku in the south. But that was not all, for his aim was 'to break through to the Near East, conquer Asia Minor, and overwhelm Iraq, Iran, and Palestine, thereby cutting England off from its last oil supplies, it having already lost its East Asian ones'. In Africa Rommel would 'sooner or later break through the El Alamein line and reach Cairo'.[7]

These were not simply fantasies intended to impress his propaganda minister. For on 9 September, during a military briefing, he ordered the commander-in-chief in the West to prepare eight divisions for use in the tropics, 'to form the attack group in the Caucasus for deployment in the Near East'.[8]

On 24 August, the tensions in Führer headquarters exploded in a furious row between Halder and Hitler, who accused his chief of the general staff of always approaching him with the same request – to withdraw. During the subsequent exchanges, Halder complained about the massive and senseless loss of life at the front, whereupon Hitler brought up his personal experience as a front-line soldier in the First World War, pointing out that Halder had spent the whole of that war and the present one as a staff officer![9]

In the meantime, at the end of August, a Soviet counter-offensive in the northern sector of the front, south of Lake Ladoga, undermined the prospects of capturing Leningrad before the onset of winter.[10] At the military briefing on 30 August, Hitler stated he was 'very dissatisfied with the performance of Army Group A', summoning its commander, List, to Führer headquarters for the following day.[11] List was severely reprimanded and ordered to advance in three places towards the Black Sea coast. However, on his return to his headquarters List had doubts about the third of these spearheads; he was afraid his troops could be wiped out.[12] Hitler refused to alter the directive,[13] but List succeeded in winning over Jodl. When, however, the latter approached the 'Führer' about the issue on 7 September, Hitler, according to Keitel, responded with 'an indescribable fit of rage'.[14] On the following day, he dismissed List, taking over command of the army group himself.[15] It was this confrontation that led to the final and irreparable breach between Hitler and his generals.[16]

Hitler's army adjutant, Gerhard Engel, sensed Hitler's 'suppressed rage', but also 'his uncertainty: What now?' The 'Führer' indulged in furious tirades against the officer corps, which he accused of 'failures of judgment, lack of a sense of responsibility, of civil courage', and also 'of ideological conviction'. He said he was contemplating adopting the Soviet system of political commissars, in order 'to ideologically pep up' the military commanders.[17] Keitel had the impression that he had 'lost all credit with Hitler'.[18] In fact, at this point, Hitler had almost certainly realized that he would be unable to achieve his eastern goals during 1942. This was serious; it amounted to accepting the failure of his whole strategic concept. For according to his original plans decisive success in the East would have enabled him to concentrate his forces against the western powers before the United States had had time to mobilize all its resources. But his policy of going for broke had failed. At this point, Hitler may have become aware for the first time that his war was now unwinnable.

From now onwards, he restricted his daily contacts with the military to what was necessary. He justified this almost total self-isolation on the grounds of his anger with the generals, who had allegedly let him down; but this was almost certainly a façade to shield him from the intolerable realization that his military entourage had lost all respect for him. This produced a ludicrous situation. He refused to shake hands with his generals and no longer appeared at lunch or dinner. Instead, he barely left his windowless barracks. The military briefings took place in an 'icy atmosphere' and, as Halder later recalled, Hitler was often in a state of white hot fury.[19]

Hitler now ordered a group of shorthand typists from the Reichstag to his headquarters with the job of noting down every word that was spoken.[20] In the middle of September, he was for a time determined not only to dismiss Halder, but Jodl and Keitel as well.[21] However, his pent-up rage finally exploded at Halder, whom he dismissed on 24 September under 'humiliating circumstances', as Engel put it.[22] Hitler justified it to Halder on the grounds that the latter's nerves were shot. There was also the 'need to inculcate in the general staff a fanatical belief in our ideology'. He, Hitler, was determined 'to impose his will even on the army'.[23] Halder was replaced by Major-General Kurt Zeitzler, hitherto the chief of staff of the commander-in-chief of the forces in the West, eleven years younger than Halder, and known to be absolutely loyal to Hitler.[24]

Shortly afterwards, Hitler left the oppressive atmosphere of his headquarters for a few days and travelled to Berlin. On 28 September, he once again gave a speech to army officer recruits in the Sportpalast, and two days later spoke at a 'people's demonstration' there to mark the start of the Winter Aid programme, his first public engagement since the end of April.[25] In this speech he described in detail the successes of the summer offensive and announced the impending capture of Stalingrad; he had already permitted an announcement to be made at the official Berlin press conference on 15 September that the city was about to fall.[26] Hitler told the Sportpalast audience that, for the time being, he did not wish to comment further on his military objectives. Instead, he spoke at length on his plans for the 'organization of this gigantic space',[27] and about the need to get transport, agriculture, and industrial production going again. There was no more talk of defeating the Soviet Union before the end of the year.

On 25 October, however, in addition to the critical situation on the eastern front, where the 6th Army was still fighting its way into the centre of Stalingrad, Hitler had once more actively to engage with developments in the North African theatre. For, on that day, British forces began their counter-attack on Rommel,[28] whom, shortly before, during a meeting in the Reich Chancellery, Hitler had honoured with a field-marshal's baton.[29] On 2 November, the British managed to achieve a breakthrough at El Alamein; some of Rommel's forces were surrounded and destroyed, the majority having to retreat westwards along the Mediterranean coast.[30]

On 8 November, Hitler was preparing as usual to commemorate the failed Munich putsch when news arrived of the large-scale landing of Allied forces on the coasts of Algeria and Morocco.[31] During his speech that evening to the 'old fighters' in the Munich Löwenbräukeller, Hitler did not, however, refer to these reports from Africa.[32] Instead, he once again announced the capture of Stalingrad, saying that as far as he was concerned the actual timing of it was 'irrelevant'. He was relaxed about possible Soviet counter-offensives. And he did not forget to remind his audience about his 'prophecy' of 30 January 1939, although he no longer spoke of the 'annihilation' but rather of the 'extermination of European Jewry'. 'Of those who laughed then countless numbers are no longer laughing now, and before long those who are still laughing may no longer be doing so.'[33]

As in autumn 1940, Hitler was now trying to persuade the Vichy government to join in the war on the side of Germany.[34] He had Prime Minister Laval flown in during the night of 9/10 November. It was already becoming clear, however, that the military resistance to the Allies being put up by the French in their North African colonies was going to be merely symbolic.[35] In response, on 11 November, Hitler ordered the occupation of the south of France, which was completed in a few days.[36] Although the Wehrmacht managed to build a bridgehead[37] on the new western front of the African theatre, Rommel was at the same time forced to continue his retreat towards the Tunisian border, and Tobruk surrendered on 13 November.[38]

Stalingrad

In the meantime, the 6th Army's offensive had clearly begun to slacken, as it fought its way through the rubble wasteland of Stalingrad towards the Volga. The troops were exhausted. For Hitler, however, the conquest of the city that bore the name of his Kremlin opponent, had become a matter of prestige.[39] Thus, on 17 November, he issued an order to the commanders of the forces engaged in Stalingrad to put all their energy into securing some at least of their goals within the city; it sounded like an admission of the collapse of his ambitious plans for more conquests.[40]

On 19 November, the Red Army opened its massive winter offensive against the southern sector of the German front. Within a few days, using a pincer movement, it had managed to encircle the 6th Army, based in the Stalingrad area, and large parts of the adjacent 4th Panzer Army.[41] Even before the encirclement of the 6th Army was complete, Hitler had ordered it to stand its ground, come what may.[42] When the 6th Army's commander, Friedrich Paulus, kept requesting permission to abandon the existing front line and break through towards the south, the 'Führer', who, responding to the news from the eastern front, had returned to his headquarters in East Prussia from the Obersalzberg on 23 November, kept rejecting these requests. Instead, he was determined to supply the troops in the Stalingrad pocket from the air, despite the fact that the Luftwaffe's experts were highly dubious about Göring's assurances on the feasibility of that plan.[43] On 20 November, Hitler had already assigned Field-Marshal von Manstein the task of taking over a newly created Army Group Don, made up of the troops that were already surrounded, the parts of the 4th Panzer Army outside the pocket, and two Romanian armies. Manstein rapidly concluded that, during any relief operation, the 6th Army must have the option if necessary of abandoning its positions in Stalingrad and making an orderly move back towards its own front line. Hitler approved this plan at the beginning of December.[44] However, he continued to believe that the abandonment of Stalingrad could be avoided, for otherwise this would mean 'giving up the most significant success of this year's offensive'.[45]

Thus Hitler continued to stick rigidly to the original goal of the summer offensive: to cut off the Soviet Union from its sources of raw materials in the Caucasus, for which the blocking of the most important transport link, the Volga, was a decisive prerequisite. For him these fundamental considerations outweighed the concerns of his generals, who, for operational reasons, advocated abandoning Stalingrad.

During December and January, Hitler's Luftwaffe adjutant, Nicolaus von Below, showed Hitler private letters from the chief of staff of the 6th Army, Arthur Schmidt, in which he provided sober descriptions of the plight of the besieged soldiers, who were not only suffering heavy losses, but whose powers of resistance were being reduced by hunger and the bitter cold. According to Below, Hitler took note of the contents, but did not comment on them. He only once referred darkly to the 'obligation' that the fate of the 6th Army represented 'in the struggle for the freedom of our people'. Below had the impression that Hitler was now aware that they could no longer cope with a war on two fronts.[46]

In the middle of December, an attempt by the 4th Panzer Army to relieve the besieged troops failed. Hitler rejected Manstein's request, supported by Zeitzler, for permission for the 6th Army to break out and try to join up with the 4th Army's Panzer spearheads. Even Manstein's objection that this was the last chance to save at least the mass of the troops and the army's mobile weapons failed to sway Hitler.[47] This meant that the fate of the 6th Army was finally sealed. A few days later, in this desperate situation, Zeitzler at least managed to overcome Hitler's continuing resistance to the withdrawal of Army Group A from the Caucasus. The threat of a still more extensive envelopment of the German forces, which were in an exposed position far to the east, was simply too great.[48] Thus, on 28 December, the 'Führer' ordered a gradual withdrawal of Army Group A, which had advanced far into the south-east. However, Army Group Don, which lay west of the besieged 6th Army, was only to withdraw further 'if it is absolutely necessary'. The Army Groups Don and A were now reunited under Manstein's command to form Army Group South.

On 18 December, Hitler received the Italian foreign minister, Ciano, in his Wolf's Lair headquarters, 'in the gloom of that damp forest' as Ciano put it in his diary, where the necessity of living together in those barracks produced a seriously depressed mood.[49] Hitler told Ciano that they were engaged in a 'life-and-death struggle'. He did not refer directly to the fact that, immediately prior to their meeting, the Italian army had collapsed in the central sector of the eastern front, but an unspoken reproach for Italy's military failure hung over the whole meeting. Acting on Mussolini's instructions, Ciano broached the question of peace with the Soviet Union and, in this connection, referred to Brest–Litovsk, the peace settlement through which, in 1918, Imperial Germany had forced the Soviet Union to accept a substantial loss of territory. However, Hitler explained in great detail why such an arrangement would be pointless. He was not prepared to make do with the Baltic States and Poland, but determined to claim a line further to the east, enabling him to exploit the raw materials there. But the Soviet leadership would not agree to that. Moreover, a peace treaty would not allow him to withdraw significant numbers of troops from the eastern front, as he would have to insure himself against the enemy restarting the conflict.

'Bearing'

Meanwhile, Goebbels set about preparing the German population for another winter of war. In a lead article in the weekly, *Das Reich*, he emphasized that, in view of the burdens of war, it was not the 'mood' of the population that was important, but its 'bearing'. 'Mood is mostly temporary; bearing, however, is sustained'.[50] It is clear from this statement that, in future, the population's support for the regime's policies was to be judged on the basis of a different set of criteria. The short-term manifestations of the 'mood barometer', as recorded in the official reports, were no longer going to be decisive, but rather the population's fundamental 'bearing', expressed above all in the fact that it doggedly continued to carry out its daily tasks and duties. This required a change in the wartime role of the Party machine. Unlike during the first phase of the war, it was no longer to be preoccupied with demonstrating the population's enthusiastic support for the regime through endless displays of excessive adulation, mass demonstrations, or the collective show of flags; instead, it was to focus entirely on keeping the nation steady through tight control and supervision. This also required an increase in civilian involvement in the war effort.

At the end of 1942, Hitler finally decided to put in place the measures that had long been mooted for implementing total war. On 25 December, he discussed with Bormann in the Führer headquarters the preparations for the celebration of the tenth anniversary of the seizure of power, and mentioned the distinctly bleak prospects for the coming year. According to a note by Bormann, it was a question of 'to be or not to be', and so they must set about ensuring the 'total involvement of the German people in this our most decisive struggle for existence'.[51] Afterwards, Bormann, who now took on an important role in implementing this demand, travelled to Berlin, at Hitler's request, for discussions with Lammers and Goebbels on how to boost the war effort.[52] Goebbels had for a long time been making suggestions to Hitler, such as labour conscription for women or shutting down industries not important for the war effort. Now, he ordered his ministry to prepare concrete proposals for 'making the war total'.[53]

On 1 January 1943, the Party Chancellery received a draft decree from Sauckel, the General Plenipotentiary for Labour Mobilization, which envisaged conscripting all men and women not yet engaged in the war effort.[54] On 8 January, Goebbels, the head of the Reich Chancellery, Lammers, the head of the Party Chancellery, Bormann, the head of OKW, Keitel, Economics Minister Funk, and Sauckel all agreed on the draft of a Führer edict that went far beyond Sauckel's proposals.[55] The 'Führer's' edict 'concerning the comprehensive mobilization of men and women for tasks involving the defence of the Reich', which Hitler signed on 13 January, was designed to redeploy all those engaged in work not essential to the war effort to either the armaments industry or the Wehrmacht. All those who had exemptions from the Wehrmacht were to have their status re-examined; all those who had not yet been 'mobilized for work' were obliged to register; and plants not essential to the war effort as well as superfluous administrative agencies were to be shut down.[56] On being presented the draft by Lammers and Bormann, Hitler raised the minimum age for registration for women from 16 to 17.[57] A few days later, he ordered that the maximum age for the registration of women be reduced from 50 to 45.[58] These interventions indicated that Hitler did not wish to push the people's 'total involvement in the war' too far for fear of provoking popular discontent at the burdens being imposed on them.[59] According to the edict, a so-called 'committee of three' would oversee the implementation of these comprehensive measures. Its members would include Keitel, Lammers, and Bormann, in other words the heads of Hitler's three key chancelleries, but not Goebbels, who, according to the edict, would maintain 'close contact' with the committee.[60] Bringing the three chancelleries together established a new body that created the opportunity to overcome at least the most egregious consequences of the existing 'polycracy of government departments', and to form the core of a more coordinated and effective government.

To strengthen his influence, Goebbels began a propaganda campaign for total war through which he aimed to bring the more hesitant members of the Nazi leadership around to his point of view. It was also intended to provide a propaganda response to deteriorating morale resulting from the uncertain situation on the eastern front.[61]

The destruction of the 6th Army

In the meantime, the Stalingrad pocket was being progressively squeezed by the overwhelmingly superior Soviet forces. The relief flights were not remotely capable of covering the needs of the troops, and the wounded were remaining untreated. As a result, the physically exhausted soldiers were becoming increasingly demoralized.[62]

It was not until 16 January that the OKW report admitted (albeit only indirectly) that the 6th Army had been encircled, despite this having actually occurred nearly two months before.[63] However, an observant reader and radio listener could have spotted that, from then on, there had been hardly any reports on the fate of the besieged soldiers and, instead, propaganda had begun to portray the army as engaged in an heroic and epic struggle, a line that was evidently intended to prepare the population for its defeat.[64] On 15 January, Hitler had ordered the Luftwaffe's state secretary, Erhard Milch, to fly 300 tons of supplies daily into the pocket. However, on 23 January, the last airfield was lost,[65] so that, from then onwards, it was only possible to drop supply canisters. Moreover, on 23 January, a Soviet thrust split the pocket in two.[66] Once again, officially, this was only indirectly admitted; the Wehrmacht report of 31 January now referred to two combat groups in the north and south of the city. On 22 January, Hitler had flatly rejected proposals from both Paulus and Manstein to negotiate a surrender with the Red Army.[67]

There were only modest celebrations of the 'seizure of power' on 30 January and Hitler did not participate. Goebbels had the task of reading a proclamation from the 'Führer' to mark its tenth anniversary, in which, significantly, he no longer referred to 'destiny' but instead to the 'Almighty'. 'It is our task, however, to do our duty in such a way that we are able to stand before Him as the creator of the universe, in fulfilment of his law of the struggle for existence, and such that we will never give up, show no mercy, and shirk no toil in order to preserve the future life of our nation.'[68]

In the meantime, the situation in Stalingrad was becoming catastrophic. The southern section of the pocket, which contained Paulus's headquarters, surrendered on 31 January, followed two days later by the northern one.[69] On 30 January, Hitler had appointed Paulus field-marshal, in order to confer on the defender of Stalingrad a final honour before he was expected to die a hero's death by committing suicide. Hitler considered the fact that he had then allowed himself to be taken prisoner by the Red Army a serious blow to the prestige of the Wehrmacht leadership. Thus, at a military briefing on 1 February, he commented: 'Shooting oneself' in such a situation was 'a matter of course'. What sort of a motivation would ordinary soldiers have to go on fighting in the next pocket with Paulus's example in front of them?[70] Over 200,000 soldiers of the 6th Army became POWs.[71]

On 3 February, the radio finally announced the loss of the city. According to the SD reports, the news produced 'deep shock'; people were saying openly that this represented a turning point in the war.[72]

Immediately after the fall of Stalingrad, on 5 and 6 February, a meeting of Gauleiters and Reichsleiters took place in Posen, focusing mainly on the topic of 'total war mobilization'.[73] The following day, Hitler summoned the Party elite to Führer headquarters where, in a two-hour speech, he tried to convince them of his confidence in victory, thereby simultaneously implying that victory was now by no means inevitable. He blamed the situation on the eastern front on the 'total failure' of the allies, 'first the Romanians, then the Italians, and then the Hungarians'. At the same time, after a long-winded statement, he reached the surprising conclusion 'that basically the crisis could be regarded as having been overcome'. Goebbels summed up Hitler's comments in his diary: the enemy had 'an advantage in that they were held together by international Jewry. The Jews operated as a driving force in all the enemy states, and we have nothing comparable to set against it. This means that we must eliminate the Jews not only from Germany but from the whole of Europe.' The speech implied a final confrontation. According to Hitler's statement to the Gauleiters, in the event of the Reich collapsing, this would 'also mean the ending of his life'. And, 'If the German people proved to be so weak, they would deserve nothing more than to be wiped out by a stronger people. Then one could have no sympathy for them'. He added, however, that he considered 'such a development as completely out of the question'.[74]

Goebbels's total war

Hitler's renewed public silence during this, the most serious, crisis of his regime – his last broadcast on the radio had been on 8 November – had serious repercussions. The whole system of the Führer state, which was geared to continuing demonstrations of public support for the 'Führer's' policies, risked losing its charismatic focus and running out of steam. There was a dearth of occasions on which to organize the usual official demonstrations of mass support for Hitler's policies, and this gap was inevitably registered by the official reports on the national mood as a leadership crisis. Thus, during the second half of the war, maintaining the façade of the Führer state without the 'Führer' became a key problem for the regime. One way of alleviating this situation was to move other leading politicians, namely the propaganda chief, Goebbels, further into the limelight, and thus somehow preserve the charisma through his performing a kind of deputy's role in the name of the 'Führer'. The masses were no longer to applaud Hitler's 'successes', but instead, through their positive 'bearing', express their unbroken trust in his leadership *potential*, which his closest confidants publicly confirmed. Moreover, the critical situation provided the opportunity to declare the war a life-and-death struggle, and demand the continued loyalty of the masses with the slogan 'victory or death'. In addition, repression and the Party's tight control over everyday life ensured that the regime and the military machine continued to function even without a 'Führer' in the public eye. The regime had in any case never been dependent on the support of the majority of the population.

Goebbels took advantage of his opportunity to continue urging support for total war.[75] He had already used the celebration of 30 January to advocate his own programme, telling his audience in the Sportpalast that 'from the length and breadth of our nation we're hearing a call for the most total commitment and effort, in the broadest sense of the words, in this war'.[76] He interpreted the huge applause, usual on these big occasions, as an endorsement of further efforts to secure radical war policies in the domestic sphere.[77]

His aim was to overcome the widespread depression among the population through increased 'mobilization' for the war, to transform the public image of the Third Reich so that it reflected a tough, realistic attitude to the war, and, at the same time, to strengthen, or rather restore, the regime's authority. This scenario of total commitment to the war could allow no scope for 'fluctuations in mood'.

However, strong opposition to the total mobilization of the home front emerged within the leadership, in particular in connection with the planned shutting down of businesses and plants, and with the systematic implementation of female labour conscription.[78] Moreover, the opponents of tough measures on the home front, among them Göring, Lammers, and Sauckel, could even appeal to Hitler, who was only halfheartedly backing the campaign for total war. Thus, for example, Hitler took the view that they should proceed cautiously with the policy of closing down businesses not essential to the war effort in order to avoid causing unnecessary unemployment.[79] At the beginning of February, he also objected to the drafting into the Wehrmacht of a group of 3,500 men from the cultural sphere, hitherto exempted, for fear of its negative impact on film, music, and the theatre. Just at this very moment, Hitler told his propaganda minister, 'when we are calling on our people to make increased efforts and big sacrifices' we must have 'at least something left more or less intact...to prevent the nation from succumbing to a grey hopelessness'. Theatre, concerts, and film were to remain completely out of bounds.[80]

However, Goebbels was determined, 'through using a certain degree of intimidation' by the Party, to get to grips with those who 'have kept trying in various way to avoid taking part in the war'.[81] On 14 February, in the weekly *Das Reich*, he insisted: 'The people know the hard truth and are now demanding that we draw the hard conclusions....In other words, total war in every sphere is the order of the day.'[82]

Finally, on 18 February, after extensive preparations by the propaganda ministry, Goebbels gave his notorious speech on total war in the Sportpalast before an audience carefully selected by the Party.[83] At this point, the regime had conceded the 'planned withdrawal' from Rostov and Voroshilovgrad, and the Red Army had advanced into the Donbas area, capturing Kharkov. Goebbels used the slogan, which he had introduced to the public a few days before, declaring total war to be 'the order of the day' and that 'in this fateful struggle' it was time to put aside 'bourgeois scruples'. Goebbels spoke to his audience as the representatives of the German people. He portrayed the carefully organized and staged public applause as plebiscitary approval for his policies: 'I can, therefore, assure you that the leadership's measures are in full agreement with the wishes of the German people at home and at the front.... It's time to get the slackers moving.'

The event culminated in ten rhetorical questions, to which the audience responded with a collective shout of 'yes'. The message was that the nation not only agreed with total war, but was actually demanding it: 'Do you want total war? If necessary do you want a war more total, more radical than anything we can begin to imagine today...? Do you approve, if necessary, the most radical measures against a small group of shirkers and black-marketeers? Do you agree that those who harm the war effort should lose their heads?'[84]

Goebbels was pleased to note that, at a party he had given on the same evening for leading Nazis, those present had 'expressed the view that this rally had represented a kind of peaceful coup d'état'. Total war was 'now being supported by the people'.[85] However, when it became apparent, during the next few days, that neither the SD reports nor the reports of his own propaganda machine were recording the impression of a nation committed to total war, he refused to accept this evidence.[86]

Hitler deliberately declined to comment. On 24 February, he ordered Gauleiter Adolf Wagner to issue a proclamation on the occasion of a celebration of the anniversary of the Party's foundation in Munich, appealing in the first instance to the 'fanaticism' of the old Party comrades. Apart from once again referring to his being chosen by 'destiny', and repeating his announcement of the 'extermination of the European Jews', he simply made a vague statement that the German people would now be making a huge and exceptional effort. He put more emphasis on the announcement that the occupied territories would be 'forced to become more involved in this fateful struggle', that 'foreign lives would not be spared', and that, together with their allies, they would 'carry out an unparalleled mobilization of European spiritual and material values'. That effectively summed up Hitler's alternative programme to total war on the home front. During the coming months, it was to become clear that he was not in the least prepared to make any political compromises in this attempt to mobilize resources from outside Germany.[87]

Hitler's total war

At the end of February 1943, a thaw began, and the Soviet winter offensive came to a standstill. On 10 March, Hitler flew to Manstein's headquarters in

Saporoshe.[88] In this southern sector of the front the situation had significantly improved during recent weeks. Manstein's 4th Panzer Army was closing in on Kharkov.[89] During his visit, Hitler emphasized how important the possession of the Donbas was. If this region were lost for good 'then we would be unable to sustain our own war production'. Because of its manganese reserves the loss of Nikopol would even mean the end of the war.[90]

On 10 March, Hitler returned to his headquarters in Vinnitsa and received Rommel, who had just flown in from Tunis.[91] With defeat looming, Hitler relieved him of his command in North Africa and, against his wishes, sent him to take a lengthy cure. Hitler wanted above all to avoid damaging Rommel's image as the most successful field-marshal in the Wehrmacht by involving him in a defeat. Rommel had to remain untarnished to be able to command future operations.

On 13 March, Hitler flew to Rastenburg. He stopped off in Smolensk on the way in order to visit the headquarters of Army Group Centre, where he met Field-Marshal von Kluge. He was not aware that a group of officers led by the chief of staff of the army group, Colonel Henning von Tresckow, had determined to get rid of him; we shall return to this conspiracy in detail.[92] In any event, Tresckow succeeded in placing a bomb on Hitler's aeroplane; however, the detonator failed and the plane landed without incident in Rastenburg.

The following day, Kharkov was recaptured by Manstein's forces and, from around the middle of March onwards, the situation on the eastern front appeared more or less stable from the German point of view.[93] This development gradually had a positive effect on the reports on the popular 'mood'. During March, it appeared to have become increasingly 'firm' and, during April, improved still further.[94] However, these reports were reflecting not so much the population's improved morale, but, above all, the fact that Goebbels was continuing to alter the criteria for the reports by emphasizing that it was not a matter of temporary fluctuations in mood but about people's 'bearing'.[95] Above all, the propaganda minister ensured that the 'Reports from the Reich' prepared by the SD, which for a long time he had considered too critical, were stopped. In June 1943, these SD reports were replaced by 'Reports on Domestic Matters', which went to a smaller group of recipients.[96]

On 21 March, Hitler gave a ten-minute speech, the first for over four months, in the Berlin Zeughaus to mark Heroes' Memorial Day, and, to everyone's relief, the feared British air raid did not happen.[97] In his speech, which contained violent anti-Semitic abuse, Hitler emphasized the difficulties of the recent campaign, but appeared confident of victory. He gave the total number of German war dead as 542,000, a number that, although it was probably fairly accurate,[98] according to Goebbels, was 'generally regarded by the German people as too low'.[99] There could hardly have been a clearer sign of the decline in respect for the 'Führer'.[100]

Hitler then went on to visit a special exhibition in the Zeughaus of weapons that had been captured on the eastern front. He was accompanied by a Colonel Freiherr von Gersdorff, who was working with the conspirators round Tresckow. They had decided to make another attempt to kill Hitler with a bomb, and Gersdorff activated the detonator, which had a ten-minute timer. However, the 'Führer' went through the exhibition at the double as if he sensed the danger, and Gersdorff only just managed to deactivate the detonator in time.[101]

Since the situation on the eastern front had stabilized, Hitler was increasingly unwilling to support radical plans for the implementation of total war. While not changing course in principle, he ensured that many of the measures that had been taken came to nothing. This was true of a considerable number of plans to amalgamate or close down government departments, which he suspected were intended to preempt decisions about a future reorganization of the administration.[102] For Hitler believed that to a certain extent the opacity characteristic of the administrative structure of the Third Reich was something worth maintaining. Indeed, the idea of one day being confronted with an administrative machine rationally organized at every level, with simple and transparent decision-making procedures, contradicted his policy of *divide et impera*. Moreover, with a distinctly populist instinct, he objected to interference in people's everyday lives aimed at restricting the elevated life-style of the so-called 'better off' or at removing the small pleasures enjoyed by the mass of the population. Thus, through an intervention with Hitler, Lammers succeeded in getting women with children exempted from labour conscription, even in cases where they had child care.[103] That affected, above all, families who could afford nursemaids. Hitler was also unwilling to adopt Goebbels's proposal to close down all horse racing – in Goebbels's eyes a manifestation of an elite life-style that was no longer appropriate in wartime.

Hitler told Goebbels in March that they should 'not be small-minded in the matter of total war measures and above all make sure not to put women's backs up'. They should be allowed to go on having beauty treatments, for example. For, after all, 'it wasn't a bad thing for women to make themselves look nice for men, and the National Socialist programme does not ban either make-up or dying one's hair'.[104] He was also not prepared to reprimand members of the political leadership who broke the rationing regulations. At the beginning of 1943, the Berlin police discovered extensive profiteering by the owner of a delicatessen, who illegally provided prominent figures such as the Reich Interior Minister, Frick, the Foreign Minister, Ribbentrop, the Education Minister, Rust, and the Agriculture Minister, Darré, with expensive and strictly rationed foodstuffs.[105] Hitler, however, did not wish to make it a 'matter of state'.[106] Instead, he ensured that the case was dealt with without any damage to the prominent individuals involved. During the course of the spring and summer, Goebbels and the other advocates of a tougher domestic policy finally gave up their efforts.[107] This was prompted, on the one hand, by Hitler's lack of enthusiasm for pushing total war too far while the military situation had stabilized, and, on the other by the failure of Goebbels's attempt, during March and April 1943, in cooperation with Göring and Speer, to revive the Ministerial Council for the Defence of the Reich and thereby emasculate the Committee of Three.[108]

Hitler's was a different kind of total war. 'Most of our contemporaries', Goebbels reported Hitler as saying in March 1943, 'don't understand that the wars of the twentieth century are racial wars, and that, in the case of racial wars, it's always a matter of survival or destruction; in other words we must be clear about the fact that this war will also end like that'.[109] Hitler's decision of September 1942 to remove all the Jews from armaments production was followed, on 27 February 1943, by mass arrests throughout the Reich. In Berlin alone, in the course of this so-called Factory Action, the SS Leibstandarte arrested around 7,000 people at their workplaces or in their homes. During March, over 13,000 people, some of them highly qualified workers, were deported from the Reich to Auschwitz.[110] At this point, there were only 31,897 Jews officially still living in the Reich, of whom more than 18,515 were in Berlin.[111] From now onwards, there were only a few more deportations.[112]

Goebbels's diary entries record how Hitler responded to the change in the war situation by pursuing the surviving minority with vicious hatred. On 8 and 14 March, he reaffirmed to Goebbels that they 'must get the Jews out of Berlin as quickly as possible'.[113] On 20 March, he remarked how 'happy' he was that 'most of the Jews have been evacuated from Berlin', noting with satisfaction 'that the war has enabled us to find a solution to a whole number of problems that under normal circumstances we would never have been able to solve'. A few days later, Hitler was 'extremely put out' to discover that there were still 17,000 Jews in so-called mixed marriages living in Berlin, and, as Goebbels had learnt, had 'instructed Frick to facilitate the divorce of such marriages, and to authorize a divorce even if just one party expresses the wish for it'.

In Hitler's view the increase in the war effort demanded by the regime's functionaries should not take the form of petty restrictions on people's everyday lives, and pledges to occupied or allied European neighbours were also inopportune. Thus, as has already been mentioned,[114] at the beginning of 1943, he ignored proposals by Ribbentrop and Goebbels for a 'European' initiative in the sense of general pledges for the post-war period, as well as the 'Proclamation to the East', which Goebbels had proposed in February 1943. The idea of promising the inhabitants of the occupied eastern territories religious freedom and a certain level of participation in the 'New Europe' would only be seen as signs of German softness and weakness.[115] Hitler was much more concerned to portray the war as a life-and-death struggle against the Jewish 'enemy of the world'. Thus, during the spring, he directed the energies unleashed by the shock of Stalingrad away from the reform of the home front towards the 'racial war'. And it was not only German Jews who were affected. In February, the mass graves of Polish officers who had been shot in 1940 by Soviet 'agencies' were discovered in Katyn near Minsk,[116] and Hitler gave Goebbels permission to exploit the topic in his propaganda. For him the most important point was 'that in the process the Jewish question will once more become a big issue'.[117] During the following days, Hitler, who had been informed about the state of the European 'Final Solution' in a report by the SS statistician, Richard Korherr,[118] paid great attention to the propaganda treatment of the Katyn incident and kept demanding an intensification of anti-Semitic propaganda.[119]

What followed was the most vicious anti-Semitic campaign since the start of the regime. On 14 April, the whole of the press reported the opening of the mass graves with banner headlines, and the massacre was described as the work of Jewish NKVD commissars. After a few days, propaganda had adopted the slogan of 'Jewish mass murder' (as in *Der Angriff* on 16 April) and continued to pursue this topic relentlessly.[120] The regime considered the breach between the Polish exile government in London and the Soviet Union as a result of the Katyn murders as the first concrete success of this campaign.[121] The Warsaw ghetto uprising, which began on 19 April, also fitted into the picture of a Jewish threat, which was blown up massively by propaganda. The Katyn propaganda campaign was expanded further and its statements became more extreme. According to Goebbels in a leading article in *Das Reich* on 9 May, the Jews were 'the glue that is holding the enemy coalition together'.[122] Their war aim was to destroy the German people and so the Jews had to be destroyed before they could achieve their goal.

The start of the Katyn campaign occurred in the middle of a series of meetings, taking place at the Berghof or at Schloss Klessheim near Salzburg, which Hitler used to try to put some backbone into his remaining vassals, or to exert pressure on them. He considered that Jewish policy was an excellent way of achieving this, particularly in the case of his south-east European retinue.[123]

The first visitor was King Boris of Bulgaria, who was told by Ribbentrop – the minutes of Hitler's meeting with Boris have not survived – that, in Germany's opinion, 'in dealing with the Jewish question the most radical solution is the only right one'.[124] Up until then, the Bulgarian government had not been prepared to adopt it. Shortly beforehand, it had agreed to the deportation of the Jews from its occupied territories in Greece and Yugoslavia, but had firmly resisted handing over its own Jews to Germany. And, despite increased German pressure, it was to stick to this position.[125] However, after the meeting with Hitler the Sofia Jews were compulsorily resettled in the countryside.[126]

After King Boris, Benito Mussolini arrived. He was severely depressed and, once again, suggested that Hitler should seek a compromise peace with the Soviet Union.[127] This would put him in a better position to fight the western powers, given that defeat in North Africa was on the horizon. The 'Duce' was then forced to listen to a lengthy monologue that stretched over several days, and, on leaving Salzburg, appeared to have overcome his doubts. However, in a few months' time, Hitler's refusal to end the war in the East or to support his Italian ally against the threat of an impending Allied invasion of southern Europe was to have far-reaching consequences for Italian politics.[128] While in Salzburg, the Italian delegation also brought up the question of a 'European declaration', but the Germans did not want to make any commitments about their planned 'New Order'. Also, possibly while under German pressure in Salzburg, Mussolini conceded the prospect of interning the Jews in his country, a request that he had hitherto always resisted.[129]

Romania's dictator, Antonescu, who appeared at Hitler's court on 12 and 13 April, was subjected to severe reproaches on account of alleged peace feelers put out by Romanian diplomats to the western powers and lectured on the link between a radical Jewish policy and commitment to the war effort. 'Having solved the Jewish question, we in Germany have at our disposal a united people with no opposition.'[130] That was a clear reference to the fact that the Romanian government had reneged on its promise of July 1942 to deport the Romanian Jews to German concentration camps.[131]

On 16 April – meanwhile, the Katyn campaign was in full swing – Hungary's Reich governor, Admiral Horthy, was next in line. Hitler tried to get him to deport the Hungarian Jews to German death camps, but Horthy refused. Hitler told him that 'he simply couldn't understand Hungary's pro-Jewish attitude'. Once again it was left up to Ribbentrop to spell out the link between Hungary's doubtful loyalty as an ally and the lack of activity on the 'Jewish question': 'Every Hungarian Jew should be regarded as a British agent', the German foreign minister remarked.[132] The Jews, continued Hitler the following day, were 'pure parasites'. But 'in Poland they had dealt thoroughly with this situation. If the Jews there wouldn't work, they were shot. If they couldn't work, they starved. They had to be treated like tuberculosis bacilli that could infect a healthy body.... Nations that don't protect themselves from Jews become degenerate.'[133] Horthy was also reproached for the fact that Hungarian individuals abroad had put out peace feelers.

There is no information on Quisling's visit on 19 April, but one can assume that the Norwegian prime minister was acutely disappointed at the inadequate response to his wish for Norway to be treated as a junior partner in a future Greater Germanic Reich.

On 22 April, Hitler received the Slovakian president, Josef Tiso, and began by outlining 'how little action the Hungarians had taken against the Jews'. He then described to Tiso in detail the 'solution' to the 'Jewish question' in Germany and concluded that 'every country that did not defend itself against the Jews would be ruined by them'. Tiso was expected to apply these comments to his own country, since his government had provisionally halted the Jewish deportations in October 1942.[134]

On 27 April, the Croatian head of state, Pavelić, was the next in the queue, Hitler subjecting him to a lengthy anti-Semitic tirade while at table. The audience that followed was relatively unimportant politically, as Pavelić was a submissive ally, who had put himself completely at Hitler's mercy by agreeing to the deportation of Croatia's Jews in the summer of 1942.[135]

Two days later, Hitler also received the French prime minister, Pierre Laval. A few weeks before, the latter had requested Hitler to make 'a magnanimous statement about France'. What he meant was a guarantee of France's future place in Hitler's Europe, for Laval a precondition for a closer association between France and Germany. However, Hitler rejected this request, for, in his view, such a declaration would only strengthen the resistance of the anti-German elements in France. In the end, they agreed on a formula in the communiqué to the effect that an assessment would be made of the 'contribution that would be expected of France to the effort and sacrifice the Axis Powers had committed themselves to in order to construct the new Europe' and 'what advantages France would receive from this participation'. This was hardly a 'magnanimous' statement. To make clear his contempt for the French, on the day before Laval's departure, Hitler informed President Pétain, via the French embassy, that he was strongly opposed to a reconstruction of the French government and the possible dismissal of Laval. This was clearly a warning not to exploit Laval's absence for a palace revolution.[136]

Reviewing Hitler's attitude to his allies in the light of these meetings, on the one hand, it is clear that he rejected any attempt, whether in the shape of Mussolini's peace proposals or of the wishes of the Italians, the French, or the Norwegians in regard to the planning of the post-war order, to impose restrictions on his future political freedom of action; on the other hand, he put massive pressure on his south-east European vassals (and possibly on Mussolini) in relation to the 'Jewish question', in order to bind these countries closer to him. He had already turned Laval and Quisling into accomplices in the murder of the Jews; for the deportations from Vichy France and from Norway (from where in October 1942 over 700 Jews had been deported) committed the two leaders irrevocably to remaining 'loyal allies'.

It was clear from these meetings that, for Hitler, anti-Semitism was much more important than merely propaganda. He regarded his radical Jewish policy as the basis of his political hold over Europe. For by creating an alliance system that was founded on complicity in a crime against humanity, he had burnt all his bridges. He was no longer prepared to consider alternative ways of motivating his allies to give more support to the war effort; peace feelers, pledges about a post-war order (such as requested by France), and an easing of the occupation regimes were all rejected.

Immediately after he had made this clear to his 'allies', he made the same point to the leaders of the Nazi Party. This occurred when the Reichsleiters

and Gauleiters met on 7 May to attend the memorial ceremony held in
Berlin for the SA leader, Viktor Lutze, who had been killed in a car crash.
After the ceremony Hitler gave a speech to the Party leaders in which he
stated that he had a growing respect for, and felt a degree of envy of, Stalin
and his ruthless methods. As far as the 'intellectual basis of the fight against
the Soviet Union' was concerned, 'anti-Semitism, as the Party used to practise and propagate it in the time of struggle, [must] once again be at the
heart of our intellectual confrontation with our enemies.' Citing the
example of Horthy, who had in fact used 'perfectly humane counterarguments', Hitler made it clear that, as far as he was concerned, refusal
to compromise on the 'Jewish question' was in future to be an essential
criterion for judging the reliability of his allies. Horthy's soft attitude had
confirmed him in his view 'that the mass of petty states that still exists in
Europe must be got rid of as quickly as possible'. This was a remarkable
statement, once again underlining the hollowness of his 'European' policy.
Hitler used this opportunity to make clear to the Party leadership the centrality of his 'Jewish policy': 'The fact that eastern Bolshevism is now largely
led by Jews and that Jews also have a significant presence in western plutoc-
racies must form the core of our anti-Semitic propaganda. The Jews must
get out of Europe.'[137]

When, on 12 May, Goebbels referred to the Protocols of the Elders of
Zion, doubting the authenticity of this propaganda piece, Hitler contradicted him. On the contrary, they could 'claim absolute authenticity . . . nobody
could describe the Jewish drive for world power so brilliantly as the Jews
themselves'. He continued with a long disquisition on the 'Jewish race' and
its 'world conspiracy'. Hitler only allowed for one solution: 'Modern nations
have no other alternative than to exterminate the Jews. They will do all they
can to oppose this gradual process of annihilation. One of these methods is
war. Thus, we must be clear that, in this confrontation between Aryan
humanity and the Jewish race, we shall face very difficult struggles because
Jewry has managed, whether consciously or unconsciously, to recruit major
Aryan nations into its service.'[138] It is important to note that behind this
paranoid tour de force and apocalyptic vision lay a clear political calculation.
Hitler was convinced that, if rigorous anti-Jewish policies were extended to
the whole of Europe, this would inevitably have the effect of binding
Germany's empire together. As he had already explained to Antonescu, there
was 'no way back from the path once it has been embarked upon'.[139] In the
process, Nazism and its leader had acquired political resources that had not

hitherto been tapped: 'Those nations that were the first to recognize the Jews for what they are and have been the first to combat them will replace them as rulers of the world.'[140]

Meanwhile, in accordance with Hitler's specific instructions, the anti-Semitic campaign was continuing with full force in all the media.[141] The Katyn issue was played down in the second half of May,[142] but was replaced by other anti-Semitic attacks, for example the assertion that the Allied air raids were, above all, the work of Jews,[143] or that the Allied plans for the post-war period had been designed by Jews to ruin Germany.[144] Thus, in the light of these threats, the annihilation of the Jews was an act of self-defence.[145]

However, this propaganda, implying that, in the event of defeat, the German people would be faced with 'Jewish retaliation', failed to achieve its object of mobilizing the last reserves. On the contrary, the fact that so much was being made of enemy 'atrocities' – Katyn and the bombing of German cities – produced, if anything, incomprehension among the population, which was more or less well informed about the crimes of its own regime. In addition, there were worries about the POWs in the Soviet Union, as well as horror and despair at the idea that they themselves were going to be slaughtered in the event of defeat.[146] The negative response was so great that not only was the campaign phased out at the end of May 1943, but Goebbels felt obliged to defend his propaganda against criticism from the Party in a circular[147] to the Gauleiters.[148]

Hitler's attempt in his speech of 7 May once again to convince the Party elite of the importance of his Jewish policy as a political instrument within the context of alliance and occupation policy, the remarks to his foreign guests, as well as the anti-Semitic spin he gave to the Katyn campaign, all inevitably led to a radicalization of anti-Jewish policy.

After the Allied landings in North Africa in November 1942, the Germans had already responded by stepping up Jewish persecution in the territories they controlled in the south of Europe. From the beginning of 1943, there is evidence of preparations that led shortly afterwards to a new wave of deportations to the death camps. From February 1943 onwards, Jews from the recently occupied south of France were affected (but also from other parts of the country),[149] and, from March, the Jews in Saloniki[150] as well as from the areas of Greece and Yugoslavia occupied by Bulgaria.[151]

Only a short time later, in April 1943, Hitler used Katyn and the Warsaw ghetto uprising to reemphasize the 'Jewish threat', with the result that, during the following weeks, he unleashed a further Europe-wide radicalization of Jewish persecution. This had an impact during the spring and early summer above all in Poland, where ghettos and labour camps were increasingly 'cleared', but there was also an increase in persecution in western and south-east Europe. In the Netherlands the deportations were expanded and now included, among others, a thousand children. The Reich Security Head Office also demanded that they should now start deporting Jews with Belgian citizenship, and implemented Himmler's order of 8 June to deport Jews who had lost their French citizenship by 15 July. In May 1943, the Germans pressed for the Croatian deportations to be concluded, and in Slovakia they began a new initiative during spring 1943 to get the government to restart deportations.[152]

Further setbacks

On 13 May, the German and Italian forces surrounded in Tunis surrendered, a total of 250,000 men.[153] Thus, only a little more than three months after Stalingrad, the regime had suffered another catastrophic defeat. A communiqué that was approved by Hitler, but which, on his orders, was not broadcast over the radio,[154] stated that the 'heroic struggle' had reached an 'honourable conclusion'. Despite the defeat, it was suggested that the engagement of the Axis troops had not been in vain because they had pinned down the Allied forces for months, and so had enabled the alliance to gain valuable time.[155] Hitler did not comment publicly on the defeat. As already mentioned, in order not to damage Rommel's prestige as a victorious field-marshal, Hitler had recalled him from North Africa two months earlier, but without informing the German public. The press now published a two-month old photograph of Rommel being received at Führer headquarters with the explanation that the field-marshal had been recalled from Africa in March for health reasons and decorated by the 'Führer' with the Knight's Cross with oak leaves, swords, and diamonds. Now he was fit again and ready to be given new tasks.[156] As a popular figure, Rommel had hitherto raised people's spirits,[157] and it was hoped the same thing would occur now. But the opposite happened. This all too blatant propaganda trick simply worsened an already depressed atmosphere.

After the defeat in Africa, Hitler was convinced that the Allies would soon attempt a landing on the European continent. He thought that Sardinia, but also Sicily and the Peloponnese were possible targets. He was convinced that, in any case, he would have to defend the southern borders of his empire and thus must not, under any circumstances, withdraw from Italy. He had very little faith in Italy's loyalty as an ally, however. He was afraid that the Royalist elements would succeed in getting their way against the Fascists and that, if the Allies attacked, Italy would not mount an effective defence. As a result, he accepted that, in the event of an Allied attack, he would if necessary have to defend Italy or the Balkans without Italian assistance. Thus he appointed an army staff under Rommel to prepare for a German invasion of Italy.[158]

Hitler arrived in Berlin from Rastenburg on 20 March and spent the next two months either there or at Berchtesgaden. On 22 May, he suddenly changed his mind and, instead of returning to East Prussia, retired to Berchtesgaden until the end of June, allegedly for health reasons.[159] Among the depressing truths that he was forced to confront there was the realization that, in the meantime, the campaign in the North Atlantic had also been lost. Radar, air support, improvements to the convoy system, the ability to read German naval code messages, and other factors that worked in favour of the Allies forced the German Naval High Command, in view of increasing losses, to halt the deployment of U-boats in the North Atlantic and order them to move to more peaceful waters. On 31 May, Admiral Dönitz, who had taken over from Raeder as naval commander-in-chief, was obliged to inform Hitler about the new situation. They were agreed that the U-boat war should be continued, even if temporarily scaled down. Hitler remarked that the Atlantic 'is my western glacis and so, even if I'm on the defensive there, it's better than having to defend the European coastline itself'. They hoped to solve the problem in the medium term through an increase in U-boat production and technical improvements that would compensate for the Allied advantage in defence against U-boat attacks.[160]

All these setbacks had a devastating effect on morale in the Reich. And there was more bad news. In May 1943 the regime was forced to announce to the population a massive reduction in the meat ration,[161] which as late as March Hitler had been hoping to postpone beyond 1 June.[162] Now the meat ration for ordinary consumers amounted to only around half of what they had been eating during the first year of the war. Even if Germans did not starve, with the increasing loss of occupied territory the food situation was to continue to deteriorate until the end of the war.[163] Moreover, the 'air battle over the Ruhr', which the RAF had launched with a big raid on

Essen, had now reached its climax. Almost all the major cities of the Rhine–
Ruhr area had been badly hit and the attack on the Möhne and Eder dams,
during the night of 16/17 May, had caused serious flooding. The RAF continued this series of raids until the end of July.[164] Hitler, however, never carried out the visit to the affected areas that he had promised to Goebbels and
Speer.[165] He thought that visiting a city that had been turned into rubble
and then possibly being photographed or appearing on film would damage
his prestige as 'Führer'.

According to the SD's 'Reports from the Reich' for the end of May, the
population, already burdened by day-to-day worries, was becoming increasingly preoccupied with the question of how the war was going to end.[166] It
now became clear to what extent the slogan 'victory or downfall', which
had been part of the Katyn propaganda campaign, had encouraged a climate
of fatalism and apathy.[167]

Another demonstration in the Sportpalast on 5 June 1943, at which Speer
and Goebbels were the main speakers in place of Göring, and the subsequent propaganda campaign were intended to reconcile the population to
the regime's policies. Whereas Speer, who a few weeks earlier had impressed
Hitler with a comprehensive 'report' on armaments production, now boasted
about Germany's armaments output,[168] Goebbels, on the other hand, focused
on their success in overcoming the winter crisis and on the situation in the
areas affected by air raids.[169] Hitler vetted both speeches and cut Goebbels's
in particular.[170]

However, the confidential reports on the impact of the event, which had
been widely covered in the media, while referring to the alleged increase in
people's confidence in victory, also contained a marked degree of scepticism. Some of Speer's figures were not believed, and his announcement that
production would have increased still further by the spring prompted discussion about how long the war would last. Goebbels's grandiose statements
about Germany's chances of victory appeared to a section of the public as
seriously exaggerated.[171] The further reports on morale show that the demonstration in the Sportpalast had not done anything to increase the plausibility of official announcements; on the contrary, more and more people
were now trying to evade the flood of propaganda.[172]

In view of the heavy blows the Western Allies were inflicting on him in
the Mediterranean, in the Atlantic, and in the air war, Hitler was hoping that
on the eastern front, at least, he would be able to regain the initiative with
a new offensive in one sector of the front and prevent the Red Army from

finally acquiring a dominant position. However, he knew that the Wehrmacht was no longer in a position to mount a major offensive like those of 1941 and 1942.[173] The core of this new plan, 'Operation Citadel', a major attack in the Kursk region, was originally supposed to begin in the middle of May.[174] Hitler had then postponed it, however, in order to retain the option of transferring forces from the eastern front to the Mediterranean.[175] For the same reason, in the middle of June, the OKW advised aborting it altogether, which Hitler declined to do. After the numerous defeats and increasing loss of public trust, he urgently needed a clear victory. The start of the offensive was fixed for 3 July and then postponed by two days.[176]

On 5 July, 1.3 million men with over 3,000 tanks attacked the Soviet salient from the north and the south. However, the Red Army had been informed about the German plans and inflicted severe losses through a multiple layered defence.[177]

On 1 July, Hitler had told his generals that their flank in southern Europe was adequately secured.[178] But, then, on 10 July, at the climax of the battle for Kursk, the Western Allies carried out Operation Husky, landing in Sicily and rapidly driving out the Italian and German forces.[179] When the Red Army began an offensive north of Kursk on 12 July,[180] Hitler was forced to call off the battle for Kursk, in order to free up troops for the southern theatre, and, a few days later, withdrew the 2nd SS Panzer Corps from the front for this purpose.[181] The German army in the East was now forced to go onto the defensive, with the situation becoming critical when, on 3 August, a further Soviet offensive began, attacking the German forces south of Kursk.[182] Thus, Hitler's attempt, in summer 1943, to regain the initiative by securing a military success in the East had proved a complete failure.

The dismissal of Mussolini

On 19 July, Hitler met Mussolini near the town of Feltre in the Veneto. As usual when the two statesmen met, Hitler subjected the exhausted 'Duce' to an endless monologue, during which news came in that Rome had been bombed for the first time. Mussolini was so upset that he could barely follow what Hitler was saying.[183] The Germans were already aware that dramatic changes in the Italian political leadership were about to take place in Rome. Goebbels, for example, had been informed in November 1942 that there were those within the Italian leadership who were seeking to make contact with the enemy.[184] Immediately after the Feltre meeting, Himmler informed Bormann and Ribbentrop that Mussolini was about to be overthrown, and, after a conversation with Roberto Farinelli, a confidant of Mussolini, the German ambassador, Hans von Mackensen, reported to Berlin that the old Fascists were planning to persuade Mussolini to get rid of a number of ministers.[185]

In fact, the historic session of the Fascist Grand Council took place on the evening of 24 July. After a long debate, it ended with a resolution in which King Victor Emanuel III was requested to take over command of the armed forces from Mussolini. With this move the king and the military leadership intended to put an end to the Fascist regime. The following day the king received Mussolini, who was still in the dark about the extent of the coup, and dismissed him as head of the government, replacing him with Marshal Pietro Badoglio. Mussolini was arrested and moved to a secret and heavily guarded location.[186]

Hitler immediately recognized the significance of these political developments in Italy and, on 25 July, based in his headquarters, began to prepare the first measures to counter this 'treachery'. He was determined to launch a coup against Rome. Since September 1942, he had ordered his military briefings to be minuted, and so his comments have been recorded in all their vulgarity. A German division was to move into the city; the 'whole government, the king, the whole bunch of them [must] be immediately put under arrest; above all the crown prince must be arrested at once, together with that rabble of his; Badoglio and his gang [must] be put under lock and key. Then you'll see, they'll just bottle it, and in two or three days there'll be another coup.'[187] A few hours later, he decided to use the opportunity to occupy the Vatican: 'We'll grab it. What's more, they've got all the diplomatic corps there. I don't give a damn. They're scum. We'll get the whole lot of swine out...'.[188] Based on military plans drawn up in May, Hitler also began preparing comprehensive measures to deal with the possibility of Italy breaking with the Axis. Rommel was now officially given command of a new Army Group B, which was to be responsible for the whole of the Italian theatre, and various divisions were sent to Italy from Germany and France. Meanwhile, in the Balkans and the south of France preparations were made to take over those areas occupied by Italian troops.[189]

On the morning of 26 July, Goebbels, Göring, Ribbentrop, Rommel, Dönitz, Speer, Keitel, and Bormann arrived at Führer headquarters to discuss the new situation. Hitler assumed that Badolgio had already been negotiating with the Allies before the coup. Above all, he advocated rapid action before the new government had become firmly installed.[190] After conferring with Göring and the military leadership, Hitler decided to send a paratroop division to the Rome area, in order to cut off the city on all sides ready for the planned coup against the Italian government.[191] Ribbentrop and Goebbels had great difficulty in persuading him not to use this opportunity to take over the Vatican as well.[192] The next day, paratroopers did indeed land near the Italian capital; however, during the following days, the Italians deployed six divisions round Rome, thereby thwarting Hitler's plan.

The German leadership adjusted to the new situation, making extensive plans in the event of Italy leaving the Axis. During August, German–Italian relations were in a state of uncertainty. Formally, the alliance between the two states remained intact, and Italian and German forces continued to fight together against the Allies. At a meeting in Tarvisio on 5 August, Ribbentrop and the new Italian foreign minister, Raffaele Guariglia, emphasized their desire to continue cooperating.[193] However, shortly afterwards, during an evening conversation with Ribbentrop, Goebbels, and Dönitz, Hitler more or less pronounced Italian Fascism dead. 'Basically, [it had] not been a proper state; it hadn't developed an effective method of selecting leaders and, in the end, came to grief as a result. Mussolini took over power too quickly and, as a result, was unable to select from the broad mass of the people a minority who were prepared to stand by him when it came to the crunch. He also got to grips with the Jewish question too late, which inevitably seriously corrupted Fascism.' Mussolini was 'naturally a huge personality', but, 'in the end, he hadn't been able to prevail against the Italian aristocracy'. The person mainly responsible was Ciano; 'the catastrophe had begun with his marriage to Mussolini's daughter.' On another occasion, Hitler commented that Mussolini's dismissal by the Fascist Grand Council had shown that his decision many years before not to create a 'senate' composed of public figures had been the right one.[194]

On 17 August, the Allies completed the occupation of Sicily; the majority of the German troops stationed there had been evacuated over the Straits of Messina a few days before.[195] An Allied landing on the Italian mainland was now only a matter of time. As Hitler had suspected,[196] the Italians had been engaged in serious negotiations with the Allies since 12 August about ending the war, while the Wehrmacht was gradually increasing the number of its troops in Italy.

On 28 August, King Boris of Bulgaria, who two weeks earlier had been in Rastenburg, died suddenly. There is no record of what he had been discussing with Hitler. It is possible that the 'Führer' had asked his ally to take part in military action, something he had avoided doing hitherto. Since Boris was married to a daughter of the Italian king, Hitler may have feared that the events in Italy might have repercussions for Bulgarian politics. This situation led to speculation that Hitler had had Boris poisoned. Hitler, on the other hand, suspected that Princess Mafalda, the wife of Prince Philipp of Hesse, who had been staying in Sofia at the time, had poisoned her brother-in-law on behalf of the Italian royal family. Such speculations cannot be proved, particularly as the removal of the king did not create a new situation beneficial to German interests.[197] The king was succeeded by his six-year-old son, Simeon II; a regency was established composed of Prince Kyrill, prime minister Bogdan Filoff, and the minister of war, Nicolai Michoff, and Bulgaria remained a military ally of Germany without being actively involved in the war.

The intensification of the air war and 'retaliation'

After the 'Battle of the Ruhr', the series of major air raids by the RAF between March and July 1943, Bomber Command and the USAF mounted a number of large-scale attacks on Hamburg, Germany's second largest city, from 24 July to 3 August. The aim of 'Operation Gomorrah' was to destroy this port city on the River Elbe. The British used a new technique to neutralize the German air defences: by dropping reflecting metal strips, they prevented German radar from picking up the bombers. As a result, 'Operation Gomorrah' became the most devastating attack on any German city throughout the Second World War. It caused fires over a wide area, producing actual firestorms, with many people dying in air raid shelters. There were over 40,000 deaths, far more than in previous city air raids. After the raids the majority of the inhabitants of Hamburg were homeless, and public life in the severely damaged city broke down.[198]

The substantial destruction of Hamburg prompted hectic preparations for air defence in the capital, which was expecting the worst. And, indeed, from late summer onwards, the RAF concentrated on Berlin. Bomber Command began its air raid campaign on Berlin with three major raids between 23 August and 4 September, continuing it with full force from

November 1943 onwards.[199] The German air defences had great difficulty in countering these attacks by the RAF and, increasingly, the USAF.

Among his entourage Hitler tried to play down the damage caused by these air raids on German cities, which during 1943 had acquired completely new dimensions; indeed, he even tried to portray it as an opportunity for a large-scale rebuilding project. At the end of June, he told Goebbels à propos the raids on the Ruhr that 'the loss of people', however regrettable, unfortunately had to be accepted in the greater interest of fighting the war'. The loss of works of art was 'terrible, but even that is not of decisive importance compared with the possibility that, by being weak, we would lose the war'. The fact that 'churches are being destroyed in the process is not even such a bad thing. In so far as they have cultural value they can be rebuilt, and, if not, then we shall have to do without them.' 'Looked at from a broader perspective', the fact that the industrial cities of the Ruhr had been so badly hit 'was not such a bad thing'. Most of the industrial cities had been 'badly planned, boringly and poorly built'; the British air raids would 'create space' for a generous rebuilding programme and transport projects.[200]

Above all, however, Hitler was relying on 'retaliation attacks' stopping the Allied bombing war. In addition to the (illusory) notion of still being able to construct an offensive air force, during 1943 his hopes became more and more focused on new kinds of offensive weapons, some of which had been a long time in development. Since 1936, the army had been working on constructing a large rocket for military purposes, the so-called Aggregat 4. A large-scale base for its development had been established in Peenemünde, on the northern point of the Baltic island of Usedom. Hitler had been initially sceptical about the project.[201] After a lecture by Walter Dornberger, the head of the project, on 20 August 1941, Hitler had declared the rocket was of 'revolutionary importance for the conduct of war throughout the world',[202] but he had not abandoned his doubts about the project.[203] It was only the Luftwaffe's inadequate performance in the air war against Britain that prompted him, at the end of 1942, to order the serial production of the A4, which at this point was still in the testing phase and showing mixed results.[204] Meanwhile, the Luftwaffe had begun to develop its own 'long-range weapon',[205] the unmanned jet-propelled flying bomb, Fi 103. At the end of May 1943, there was a 'comparison launch' in the presence of Speer, Milch, Keitel, and senior military figures at Peenemünde, with the result that both projects were given the go-ahead.[206]

Faced with the heavy air raids on the Ruhr, at the beginning of July, Hitler set a completely unrealistic production target of 2,000 A4 rockets per month. On 25 July, he signed a Führer edict concerning the 'largest possible output' of rockets, giving Speer a special mandate to achieve it.[207] At the same time, and equally precipitately, the mass production of the Fi 103 was started, although it was not yet ready for service.[208]

The British air raid on the top-secret facility in Peenemünde, on the night of 17/18 August, aborted the plan to construct a factory to produce the A4 rockets next to the development base. Exploiting the assumption that there must have been a treasonous leak of information, Himmler became involved in the project, persuading Hitler to move production to protected sites under the aegis of the SS and to use concentration camp labour. This order led to the construction of the 'Mittelwerk Dora' near Nordhausen in Thuringia, in which both A4 and Fi 103 rockets were assembled by tens of thousands of concentration camp prisoners under appalling living and working conditions.[209] However, although Hitler invariably appeared optimistic about soon being able to inflict terrible blows on London with rockets and flying bombs, the deployment of the new weapons had to be repeatedly postponed.[210]

In the meantime, Hitler focused increasingly on another long-range weapon project, with which he hoped to terrorize the population of London: the so-called High Pressure Pump, also called the Millipede, a gun with a range of 160 kilometres that had been in development since 1942. Because of the exceptional length of the barrel, of up to 140 metres, the immobile gun installation had to be set up on a slope.[211] At an armaments meeting in the middle of August 1943, Hitler ordered the production of the gun, although the results of the test firing had not yet come through.[212] When these finally indicated that the project was unviable, he nevertheless let it continue in a pared down form.[213] However, during the summer of 1944, the site in Calais intended for the supergun was overrun, with London now out of its range.[214]

On 6 July 1943, Goebbels, who was aware of the risk that the repeated postponement of 'retaliation', let alone its possible cancellation, could lead to a propaganda disaster, issued a directive to the press instructing it no longer to refer to retaliation.[215] However, the fact that there were numerous rumours about 'retaliation' in circulation throughout the Reich indicates that the regime had been conducting word of mouth propaganda, in order to maintain at least a faint belief that a counter-blow could bring about a turning point in the war.[216]

Hitler did not, however, adhere to the directive issued by his propaganda minister; instead, during a radio broadcast on 10 September, he responded to the widespread expectations about 'retaliation' by hinting at counter-measures against the air raids.[217] This announcement by the 'Führer' revived the rumours about retaliation. The SD observed that retaliation 'was for many people the crucial point underpinning their hopes for victory'. However, it was fully aware of the risks this propaganda posed: 'If retaliation doesn't happen, or doesn't happen in the way I think it will', as the report summed up people's feelings, 'then I don't see any way of winning the war'.[218]

Italy capitulates

On 3 September, British troops landed on the Italian mainland in Calabria.[219] Hitler assumed at first that the landing was a diversionary tactic, and that the main invasion was about to happen in western Europe.[220] On 8 September, he then received the news of Italy's unconditional surrender, which had already happened on 3 September and had initially been kept secret.[221]

The 'Führer' now launched the measures to occupy Italy that had been prepared weeks beforehand. On 9 September, he told a small group including Goebbels, Göring, Ribbentrop, Himmler, Lammers, Bormann, and Eduard Dietl that at the moment they could not 'afford' to install the kind of regime they would really like to have; at the present time, they did not want to 'antagonize' 'the Italian people and, above all, the Fascists'. Hitler was indicating that, now that Italy had forfeited its role as Germany's main ally, he was determined to abandon a cornerstone of his previous Italian policy, the 'renunciation' of South Tyrol.[222]

On 10 September, after a long period of hesitation,[223] Hitler commented in a radio broadcast on the situation in Italy. The collapse of his most important ally had long been foreseen. He emphasized the 'pain I personally felt in view of the historically unique injustice' that Mussolini had suffered. Apart from that, he said that he was convinced that the 'military effect of the loss of Italy would be minimal', as for months Germany had been bearing the brunt of the fight for this country.[224] Within a few days German troops had occupied the majority of the Italian mainland, and the Italian forces were disarmed.[225] German troops also moved into the Italian occupation zones in the south of France and the Balkans and interned the Italian soldiers. On 20 September, Hitler ordered that, if they were not prepared to continue fighting as allies, they were to be treated as 'military internees'.[226] Thus this group of around 600,000 men were denied the status of prisoners of war. They were interned in camps in the Reich and eastern Europe and subjected to forced labour, most often under deplorable conditions.[227]

On 9 September, British and American troops landed at Salerno. After bitter fighting the German troops were finally compelled to withdraw. The Wehrmacht now began a war of attrition during which it slowly withdrew northwards from one line of defence to the next.[228]

In the meantime, on 12 September, a German special commando unit had liberated Mussolini from the mountain hotel on the Gran Sasso, where he was being held captive.[229] Two days later, Hitler was able to greet him at the Rastenburg air field. During the following days, in the course of lengthy sessions, he tried to boost the 'Duce's' morale.[230] Finally, on 15 September, Mussolini announced the re-founding of the Fascist Party and militia.[231] Shortly afterwards, in a radio broadcast from his provisional residence in Munich, he proclaimed the creation of a Republican–Fascist government under his leadership and the continuation of the war alongside Germany.[232] On 28 September, a new 'Fascist–Republican' government was established at Salo on Lake Garda.[233] However, Hitler had little faith in this revival of Fascism. In confidence he told Goebbels that they were now 'gradually going to have to write off the Duce politically'.[234]

During the Italian crisis, the situation on the eastern front had become increasingly critical. On 16 August, the Red Army had begun its operation to retake the Donbas in the far south of the front and, a few days later, had captured Kharkov. At the end of August 1943, it had begun another major offensive further north, parallel to Kursk, as well as attacks throughout eastern Ukraine, forcing Army Group South to retreat over the Dnieper. However, the Red Army in pursuit managed to establish several bridgeheads on the west bank[235] and, in the middle of September, began another offensive against Army Group Centre, which in the end led to the capture of Smolensk.[236]

With His Back to the Wall

Following Italy's exit from the Axis, the Wehrmacht had occupied a large part of Italian territory, as well as the Italian occupation zones in France and south-east Europe. Hitler had thus succeeded, at least for the time being, in securing the southern flank of 'Fortress Europe'. After Italy's defection, as a precaution, he had military plans prepared for the occupation of Hungary and Romania under the code names 'Margarethe I' and 'Margarethe II'.[1]

This increase in the territory directly controlled by Germany in late summer 1943 led to an increase in repression throughout its sphere of influence. Not only in Italy, but a few months later in France, and, during spring 1944, finally in Hungary as well, radical indigenous forces came to the fore under German protection and became willing assistants in implementing German policies, employing terror above all in the process. Hitler's regime thus acquired accomplices whose fates were tied irrevocably to that of their German masters. In the course of this radicalization of their occupation policy and their relationship with their allies, the Germans managed, once again, to extend their systematic murder of the Jews to several new areas. From Hitler's point of view, a further increase in mass murder and terror appeared to be the most effective means of preventing the German 'bloc' from disintegrating. By implicating indigenous forces in this terror regime he could compel the absolute 'loyalty' of his remaining allies. His personal interventions in the further development of Jewish policy were motivated not only by his vitriolic anti-Semitism and destructive impulses, they were also intended to secure the survival of his regime. In other words, he was less concerned about dragging his arch-enemies down with him to what was now almost inevitable destruction, than that their violent deaths should serve to extend the period of his rule. Thus, by continuing to murder the Jews in the last phase of the war, Hitler was not least pursuing *political* goals. It was precisely those four states that successfully resisted the most extreme form of German Jewish policy (Badoglio's Italy, Romania, Finland, and Bulgaria)[2] that managed, between September 1943 and 1944, to escape from their alliance with Germany by securing separate armistices. This inevitably confirmed the German government in its determination not to make any compromises in their Jewish policy.

On Hitler's orders, the 'Social Republic of Italy', proclaimed by Mussolini on 15 September, whose government was based at Salo on Lake Garda, was to be supervised by a Plenipotentiary of the Greater German Reich, the envoy Rudolf Rahn.[3] In addition, a German military government, branches of various economic agencies, and an SS and police apparatus were established. Thus, the Social Republic was firmly under Germany's thumb. The Italian troops remained interned, Italian civilians were deported to Germany as forced labour, and a strike movement, which had spread through northern Italy from August onwards, was suppressed with the aid of Fascist forces. Hitler intervened personally and, in March 1944, ordered that 20 per cent of the striking workers be immediately deported to Germany and placed at the disposal of the SS as forced labour.[4] However, the order was then withdrawn and, instead, 1,200 alleged ring leaders were deported to concentration camps in Germany.[5] In addition, the occupiers used terror to combat the partisan movement that was now springing up everywhere in opposition to the new Fascist republic.[6]

Above all, however, the Reich Security Head Office was now determined ruthlessly to deport the over 33,000 Jews living in this part of the country.[7] The first stage was the deportation of the Jews in Rome. In October 1943, Ribbentrop told the Foreign Ministry that 'in accordance with a Führer directive, the 8,000 Jews living in Rome are to be moved to Mauthausen (upper Danube) as hostages'.[8] This Führer directive eventually led on 16 October to a round-up in the Italian capital that the majority of Rome's Jews managed to evade; even so, more than 1,000 of them were deported to Auschwitz. Up to the end of 1944 a total of 6,000 Jews from Italy arrived there. They were initially deported by Germans, but by the beginning of the following year the Italian authorities were also assisting. Thus, the Fascist state was drawn into complicity in murder with the Third Reich. After the Wehrmacht moved into the Italian-occupied zones in Greece, Croatia, Albania, Montenegro, and the Dodecanese (a group of islands in the eastern Aegean in Italy's possession since 1912), around 10,000 Jews were deported during 1944 from these territories to Auschwitz and murdered there.[9]

When German troops moved into the Italian-occupied zone in the south of France, on 8 September, following the Italian–Allied armistice, German special units immediately began to pursue the Jews who had hitherto been living there in safety.[10] They concentrated above all on Nice, where between 20,000 and 25,000 Jews, mostly refugees, were living. However, without the support of the French authorities, in three months the special units managed to catch only a small proportion of them, deporting 800 to the camp in Drancy.[11]

However, the removal of the Italian occupation regime in the south of France, which had been established in 1940, provided the security police with the opportunity of radicalizing Jewish persecution throughout the whole of France. Since August 1943, the Gestapo had been increasingly getting the French police to arrest Jews throughout the country for alleged breaches of France's anti-Semitic laws, and then deporting them.[12] However, the French authorities were not prepared to take part in systematic and comprehensive persecution of French Jews. The political preconditions had to be created for this stance to change.

At the end of 1943, Hitler once again made a massive personal intervention in the French situation. Marshall Pétain, the French President, was planning a constitutional reform, according to which the French National Assembly, which had not met since 1940, would appoint his successor. Via Ribbentrop, Hitler informed Pétain that this was ruled out. Moreover, the French government would have to be reshuffled in accordance with Germany's views, the Vichy civil service had to be purged, and future French legislation would be subject to a German veto.[13] In fact, at the beginning of 1944, the Laval government was substantially reshuffled under considerable German pressure, and degraded into becoming merely an executive arm of the occupying power.[14] This had a direct impact on the persecution of the Jews. From now onwards, under instructions from the security police, the French police increasingly took part in arresting French Jews in the provinces.[15] On 14 April 1944, the commander of the security police in France, Helmut Knochen, ordered the arrest of all Jews irrespective of their citizenship, with the exception of those living in 'mixed marriages'. During the four months before the deportations stopped in August 1944, more than 6,000 people were deported.[16]

The fact that the Nazi empire had begun to crumble on its southern flank, while the eastern front was in retreat and a landing was expected in western Europe, encouraged resistance in the north.[17] Thus, during the summer of 1943, acts of sabotage, strikes, and disturbances began to proliferate in Denmark. In August Hitler decided to declare martial law there.[18]

In view of this, the Reich Plenipotentiary, Werner Best, a former Reich Security Head Office official, decided that the best solution would be to allow the situation to deteriorate in a controlled fashion, in order to justify abandoning the previous cooperation with the Danish government. Then, in line with the general tightening of German occupation policy in Europe, the occupation administration should be transformed into a police regime under his leadership.[19] He thus proposed to his superiors in the Foreign Ministry that the Danish Jews be deported,[20] in order to demonstrate the general change in German policy towards Denmark.

Best's proposal coincided with the announcement of the Italian armistice, and Hitler's consent to the transformation of the Danish occupation into a police regime coincided with the period when the 'Führer' was implementing measures to occupy Italy and its occupation zones. These measures, in turn, were motivated by his desire to eliminate once and for all the pernicious 'Jewish influence' prevalent there. However, it soon became clear that the preparations for the deportation of the Danish Jews could not be kept secret, and that Best did not have the numbers of police troops required to carry out the arrests 'at a stroke'. Meanwhile, he had become convinced that he did not need a dramatic event such as an anti-Jewish 'action' in order to be able to transform the occupation regime.[21] After he had failed to convince the German leadership of his misgivings,[22] and with the planned arrests threatening to turn into a fiasco, Best decided to leak the timing.[23] The flight of the great majority of Jews living in Denmark to Sweden, made possible through a remarkable rescue operation mounted by the Danish population, seemed to him the preferable option.[24] Thus he claimed to the Foreign Ministry that the flight of the Jews had been a success, as, one way or the other, Denmark had been 'dejewified'.[25]

Hitler (also Ribbentrop and Himmler) did not regard Best as having sabotaged their Jewish policy, but, in the end, accepted it. Although it contradicted Hitler's radical ideas about the 'annihilation' of the European Jews, during this phase of the war Jewish persecution had become for him, above all, a function of occupation and alliance policy. The collaboration of indigenous forces in the countries under German control in this matter was intended to increase the resilience of his 'Fortress Europe'. If an occupation regime in a small country like Denmark could, as an exception, be stabilized by allowing the flight of a few thousand Jews then this was evidently acceptable.

Power struggles

In the meantime, Hitler made a number of changes in the regime's power structure. On 20 August 1943, he appointed Himmler as the new Interior Minister; his predecessor, Wilhelm Frick, whom Hitler had long regarded as burnt out, was given the insignificant, and purely ceremonial, post of Reich Protector of Bohemia and Moravia.[26] Appointing Himmler a minister was intended further to strengthen his authority as the central figure in the apparatus of repression; at the same time, it was a sign that the internal administration of the state was now finally under the control of the Party.

In terms of domestic politics, Himmler's appointment marked the end of the influence of the 'Committee of Three', the alliance of the powerful heads of Hitler's most important chancelleries, Lammers, Keitel, and Bormann. Bormann was the only one who managed to retain his position of power under the new circumstances, and indeed, if anything, to extend it. The particular position of trust that he enjoyed with Hitler is reflected in his appointment as 'Secretary to the Führer' in April 1943. The new title makes it clear that Bormann, even apart from his position as head of the Party Chancellery, had the right to pass on 'Führer directives and opinions to leading and senior figures of the state, as well as to state agencies, on behalf of the Führer'.[27] As a result, Lammers, the head of the Reich Chancellery, lost influence, as from now on he rarely met Hitler and, on occasions, had to wait weeks for an interview.[28] In his new post of Interior Minister Himmler refrained from carrying out a comprehensive reform of the administrative structure, which many, particularly in the Party, were hoping for and had anticipated. Speculation that Himmler might use his new position to subordinate the Gauleiters in their role as Reich Defence Commissioners (who were already subject to 'official supervision' by the Reich Interior Minister) unequivocally to the authority of the Reich [i.e the state] also proved incorrect.[29] Himmler was acting cautiously and no doubt realized that Hitler was not prepared to support far-reaching administrative reorganization during the war. As a result, right up until the end of the regime, the Party's 'territorial princes' remained in an intermediate position politically between Party and state and this, in many respects, unclear status, requiring frequent decisions by the 'Führer', had the effect of strengthening Bormann's position.

Apart from Himmler's appointment, the second major change in the regime with which Hitler responded to the crisis in the summer of 1943 was the increase in Speer's authority in the armaments sector. From June 1943 onwards, Speer had been trying to take over the Reich Economics Ministry's responsibility for the production of consumer goods, which made up over 50 per cent of Germany's total production. To achieve this he had secured the cooperation of Hans Kehrl, the official in the Economics Ministry responsible for industry.[30]

At the beginning of September, Hitler signed a Führer edict 'concerning the concentration of the war economy',[31] and, by the end of October, the responsibilities of Speer's ministry had been reorganized and its title changed from 'Ministry for Weapons and Munitions' to 'Ministry for Armaments and War Production'. A new planning office, 'Central Planning', was established under Kehrl with extensive powers,[32] and the responsibility for industries producing consumer goods, hitherto exercised by the Reich Economics Ministry, was transferred to Speer's system of rings and committees.[33]

While Goebbels considered that his own plans for 'making the war total' were being realized through these measures, and he backed the 'organizational genius' Speer,[34] the Armaments Minister made an alliance with the other beneficiary of the summer 1943 crisis, Heinrich Himmler.[35] This became clear at the Reichsleiters' and Gauleiters' conference in Posen on 6 October, where Speer gave a tough warning to the Gauleiters not to continue obstructing his total war measures, in particular the extensive closing down of factories geared to civilian production. He referred specifically to the arrangement he had made the previous day for the SD to provide him with the requisite information about the production of goods that were not essential to the war effort. He announced that, if necessary and with Himmler's support, he would intervene ruthlessly in their Gaus.[36] The meeting was marked by Himmler using the opportunity, as the new Interior Minister, to talk 'quite openly' about the murder of the Jews. He also specifically justified the systematic murder of Jewish children, since he did not want them to grow up as 'avengers'.

In a comment, meant ironically, Himmler drew a parallel between the forced closing down of production in the Warsaw ghetto after the crushing of the April uprising and the closure programme Speer had been referring to. This powerful demonstration of the collaboration between Speer and Himmler made it clear that Speer's warning to the Gauleiters was not simply an empty threat.[37] The Gauleiters were furious about Speer's statements and the added weight given to them by Himmler's comments, and complained to Hitler via Bormann. They claimed Speer had threatened them with police intervention and concentration camp.[38]

Speer responded by turning Hitler's attention to the area that formed the real basis of their personal relationship – architecture and town planning. Five days after the Posen speech, Speer persuaded Hitler to issue an edict, entitling him, even during the war, to start planning for the rebuilding of bombed cities 'by preparing plans for urban reconstruction'.[39] Speer was given extensive special powers, imposing significant restrictions on the ambitions of the Gauleiters in this sphere, a deliberate demonstration of his power and one that anticipated the position he was hoping to acquire after the war. A circular of November 1943, containing his Posen speech to the Gauleiters, and once again emphasizing their responsibility for implementing the measures to ensure increased armaments production, reinforced the message. It underlined once more his claim to leadership on the home front.[40]

Hitler also set boundaries to Speer's ambitions, however. For example, at a meeting about the labour shortage in the German war economy on 4 January 1944,[41] Hitler opposed his armaments minister, who wanted to solve the problem by reallocating orders to France. Speer had already held talks with the French in September 1943, which he had got Hitler to approve.[42] However, Hitler now decided to support Sauckel's solution to the labour problem through forced recruitment, and, during the coming months, the latter did what he could to try to get hold of workers from the French firms that Speer had wanted reserved for German contracts.

At the end of 1943, Himmler too was on a collision course with Speer. He ensured that in the course of the reorganization of the Reich Economics Ministry, from which Speer removed certain important responsibilities, two of his closest colleagues were given key positions. Otto Ohlendorf, the head of the SD's Home Department, took over the important Main Department II of the Economics Ministry, and Franz Hayler, head of the Reich Group Commerce, became the new state secretary. This intervention was designed to ensure that, in preparing for the post-war economy, the Economics Ministry would be in a position to impose limits on the kind of economic planning Speer was introducing.[43]

It now became clear that Speer had overplayed his hand. He had alienated the Gauleiters, Sauckel, and Bormann; the alliance with Himmler had failed, indeed the latter had built up a counterweight to him within the Economics Ministry; and Goebbels too began to distance himself.[44] Moreover, Hitler was bound to regard the fact that Speer was on his way to becoming the second most powerful man in the regime as a challenge to start thinking again about his successor. Although Hitler had declared Göring to be his deputy in 1939, and had confirmed this decision in 1941,[45] the latter's grow-ing weakness and declining prestige meant this settlement of the succession now appeared highly problematic. Any further strengthening of Speer's pos-ition might compel Hitler to appoint a new deputy. This would involve disavowing Göring as well as having to make clear to other candidates, such as Himmler or Goebbels, why they were not qualified to become 'Führer'. There was thus something to be said for leaving open the question of suc-cession, and for putting Speer, who was making such efforts to become the second man in the regime, in his place.

The opportunity arrived very soon. On 18 January, Speer had to undergo a knee operation. However, during his stay in the Hohenlychen clinic, which was run by Professor Gebhardt, an intimate of Himmler's, his health rapidly deteriorated. While Speer believed that he was the victim of delib-erately poor treatment by Gebhardt, and thought that Himmler had been trying to have him killed, it is more plausible that it was in fact years of stress and overwork that had led to his physical and psychological collapse.[46]

During his absence from the ministry, Speer's opponents, both within and outside his ministry, set about trying to destroy the crown prince's position, and Hitler did not back him. Already during the autumn, and increasingly after Speer became ill, Bormann passed on to Hitler complaints about the closing down of particular businesses and about other measures taken by the Armaments Ministry, with the aim of damaging Speer's reputation. Ley and Göring intrigued against him, and, within his ministry, a growing number of colleagues wanted to settle scores with their often arrogant boss.[47] A few days after his operation, Speer sent several memoranda to Hitler, in which, above all, he asked for more responsibilities in the armaments sphere at the expense of the Gauleiters and the Plenipotentiary for Labour Mobilization. He was no doubt intending to demonstrate his undiminished commitment and to counteract what he feared was Hitler's loss of trust in him. Significantly, however, Hitler did not respond to these initiatives.[48] When, after more than three months, Speer returned to the political stage, regaining his previous position of power was to cost him considerable effort.

How to proceed?

During the autumn of 1943 Hitler had succeeded in consolidating his regime once more, both internally and externally, after the loss of his main ally, and indeed had even significantly extended the territory under his direct rule. It was nevertheless obvious that, if a war on two fronts continued or a third front opened up in western Europe, military defeat was inevitable.

During September and October 1943 Goebbels spoke to Hitler on several occasions about the possibility of making separate peace deals. Although Hitler clearly agreed, he nevertheless dismissed any concrete steps at the present time. On 9 September he came out with the conjecture that it would be 'easier to do something with the British than with the Soviets'. He also said he was sure that the British would be unwilling to surrender their conquests in the Mediterranean − Sicily, Calabria (Corsica and Sardinia would no doubt be added) − and on the basis of these territorial gains 'might be more open to an arrangement'. The tensions between the Soviet Union and the Anglo–Americans were, however, not yet developed enough to be successfully exploited, he said, and so they had to go on waiting, although a crucial factor would be 'to restore order to our fronts'. When Goebbels once again brought up the subject of separate peace deals on 27 October − in the meantime Badoglio's Italy had declared war on Germany − Hitler explained to him that he was now tending 'more to the Soviet side'. Allegedly, both sides, the Soviets and the Western Allies, had made 'secret overtures', he said, but Hitler had not responded to them because, as he confided to Goebbels, 'we must not negotiate when things are going so badly for us'.[49] This change of attitude on Hitler's part in favour of possible talks with the Soviet Union was in fact based on real events: In September there had been tentative contacts (but not talks or official meetings) in Stockholm involving German and Soviet go-betweens.[50]

But if regaining the military initiative was the precondition for peace talks, how might that be achieved? In the winter of 1943/44 Hitler set his mind to it, focusing above all on the Allies' landing in western Europe, which was feared to be imminent. He was convinced that this constituted the greatest threat, but that it also offered opportunities to bring about a decisive turn in the entire war situation.[51] For militarily the failure of a large-scale landing in western Europe would set the Allies back years. It was possible, as he had explained to Goebbels in September, that Britain would settle for its strengthened position in the Mediterranean and be prepared to make a separate peace.

That prospect made him willing to accept setbacks on the eastern front, which was still more than 500 kilometres from the old Reich border, although these setbacks could not be allowed to jeopardize his strategic position in eastern and southern Europe. Since the winter of 1942/43 there could be no more talk of 'annihilating' the Soviet Union or of forcing it back behind a secure frontier established far to the east, and, by discontinuing the Battle of Kursk offensive in the summer of 1943, the Wehrmacht had surrendered its last chance of regaining the initiative on at least part of the front. What remained was a defensive battle that had to be continued until the hoped for decisive turn in the West. Only then, on Hitler's reckoning, could he send reinforcements to the East and in this way possibly force a draw with Stalin. This was the background to the comment he made to Goebbels in October about possible approaches to the Soviet Union.

For the time being, however, he had to accept the Soviet advance. By late September/early October Army Groups Centre and South had withdrawn to the so-called Panther line, which meant among other things the loss of Smolensk and the Donbas. Only Army Group North remained in its old position outside Leningrad, thus forming a curved front that protruded dangerously far eastwards.[52]

In October the Red Army began its attack on Army Group South, positioned on the far side of the Dnieper; on 6 November it took Kiev. To the south of the Dnieper the Red Army attacked Army Group A reaching the Black Sea by 5 November and cutting off the Crimea from the north. Army Group South was holding the Dnieper line in only two areas between these successful Soviet thrusts, the wedge stretching far to the east on the lower Dnieper being particularly precarious.[53]

When Field-Marshal von Manstein, the commander-in-chief of the army group, met with Hitler on 7 November, he told him plainly that the Kiev situation was already irretrievable. Instead it was crucial that they secured the 'victory that could be won on the lower Dnieper'. What in the eyes of the military was a salient that could no longer be defended, in Hitler's deluded mind had to be held, whatever the cost. His explanation was that it was absolutely necessary to safeguard access to the sources of manganese ore in Nikopol and from there to re-conquer the gateway to the Crimea. The enemy must on no account take possession of the peninsula, which might then be used as the base for air attacks on the Romanian oilfields.[54]

Hitler was not prepared to follow the military logic of army professionals; instead, his view of how to conduct the war as a totality was to gear it to political and strategic objectives, to give it an ideological foundation, and, not least, to include economic factors. The day after his meeting with Manstein, Hitler underlined this position in his customary speech to mark

8 November. This time he was less concerned to project confidence in victory, concentrating instead on the allegedly small band of 'criminals' who
did not have faith in Germany's victory and threatening to 'do away with
them': 'What happened in 1918 will not happen a second time in Germany.'
Hitler was making it clear that any 'stab in the back' delivered to the army
at the front, such as had caused Germany's defeat in the First World War (and
he was not alone in holding this view), would be prevented in this war because
of his decisive, politically and ideologically solid leadership. The speech was
recorded on magnetic tape and broadcast that evening, after Goebbels, with
Hitler's consent, had had 'a very few slightly awkward formulations' cut.[55]
Goebbels was relieved that after months Hitler was once again being heard
in public.

On 24 December the Red Army in the Kiev area again launched a large-
scale offensive on the northern flank of Army Group South.[56] Manstein
once more felt he must press Hitler to surrender not only the Dnieper salient, which stretched far to the east, but also the Crimea, in order to free up
troops for a counterattack in the north of his army group. When on 4 January
he presented this view to Hitler at the latter's headquarters, Hitler flatly
refused.[57]

During this visit Manstein tried one more time to introduce his proposal
for a change to the military leadership structure, in other words to find one
in which Hitler was to a greater extent 'relieved of the burden' of operational
leadership of the army in the east. Manstein recalled after the war that he
had hardly mentioned the subject before Hitler began to fix him with his
stare:

> He stared at me with a look that gave me the feeling that he intended to crush
> my will to say anything further to him. I cannot remember ever having seen
> a look on someone's face that so strongly expressed the power of his will. . . .
> Suddenly the notion of an Indian snake charmer flashed across my mind. It
> was a sort of wordless battle that took place between us within the space of
> a few seconds. I realised that he must have used that look in his eyes to intimi-
> date a good many people, or to use a vulgar but in this case fitting expression,
> to 'break them'.

When Manstein, according to his account, stood his ground, Hitler declared
that he alone had the authority to decide what troops should be made available for individual theatres of war.

Colonel General Guderian, who had been dismissed by Hitler in the
winter crisis of 1941/42 but had been brought back in the spring of 1943 as

General Inspector of panzer divisions, also attempted in January to raise with Hitler the appointment of a Wehrmacht Chief of the General Staff (he had already put the same proposal to Jodl in November 1943), but Hitler stonewalled.[58]

The controversies involving Manstein and Guderian showed that during this winter of crises the tensions between Hitler and his top military men increased still further. However, whereas in the previous two winter crises military and strategic issues relating to the conduct of the war in the East had been dominant, this time Hitler was determined to subordinate the military to the primacy of his political leadership and to the ideological premises underpinning it. For him this was the crucial precondition for surviving this critical juncture, until they could regain the initiative in the war.

This improvement in troop morale was to be achieved by propagating a 'fighting will' unequivocally inspired by Nazism at all levels of the military hierarchy.[59] To this end Hitler, responding to proposals from Bormann, had decided to give the officers hitherto responsible for 'leadership in military values' at divisional level and with the higher-ranking staff officers the new title of 'National Socialist Leadership Officers',[60] as he rejected the old term as a relic of a pre-Nazi army that was still dependent on bourgeois values.[61]

In a Führer decree of 22 December Hitler ordered the creation of a National Socialist Leadership Staff within the OKW that, 'taking instructions directly from me' (in other words, over Keitel's head) and working in concert with the Party Chancellery, was to guarantee 'that the troops received the necessary political training and motivation'.[62] Further National Socialist Leadership Staffs were created in the three Wehrmacht branches, and in addition to the already existing full-time National Socialist Leadership Officers they covered the whole of the military hierarchy down to battalion level with a network of part-time National Socialist Leadership Officers. As the involvement of the Party Chancellery suggests, the aim was less to increase the Party's influence on the Wehrmacht but rather a new structure was supposed to ensure that the commanding officers showed no uncertainty or laxity as far as ideology was concerned.[63]

As Hitler explained at a briefing in January, the whole business was worthwhile only if it was clear 'that all complaints about and criticisms of directives involving ideology will be punished in exactly the same way as criticisms of tactical or other military matters and that it will cost the officer in question his rank and his neck.... He must not criticize any order he receives, particularly not in the presence of subordinates.'[64] In this briefing

Hitler made detailed use of his experiences as an 'education officer' in 1919, for as far as he was concerned 'the gradual saturation of the whole army with National Socialist ideas' was 'the most important thing of all'. Accordingly, he considered the propaganda activities of the League of German Officers, which had been formed in September 1943 under General Walther von Seydlitz from officers who were prisoners of war in the Soviet Union, to be the 'most dangerous thing occurring at the front at the moment'.[65]

On 27 January Hitler received his field-marshals and senior commanders at his Wolf's Lair headquarters.[66] His address to them there was the first in a series in which he aimed to demonstrate 'National Socialist leadership' of the army by instructing his commanders on ideological matters.[67] He was convinced that only if the military leaders focused on the primacy of political leadership would it be possible to conduct the war in such a way as to enable them to regain the initiative in the medium term. In addition, they were, he said, engaged in a 'struggle' that would 'end in the annihilation of the German nation if we do not prevail'. He also expressed the expectation that if his regime should find itself in a serious crisis the entire officer corps would stand before him to protect him, 'with their swords drawn'.[68]

Manstein took Hitler's call to mean he doubted the loyalty of his officer corps and was provoked by this 'deliberate affront' to interject, 'And that is what we will do, my Führer!' Hitler seemed to be slightly rattled by this, he recalled, and replied with an icy stare, 'Thank you, Field-Marshal von Manstein!' After the meeting he told him he would not tolerate such interruptions. Manstein, who had clearly intended to convey his annoyance at Hitler's long-winded 'ideological' lecture, was thus marked down by Hitler to lose his command.[69]

In the meantime the military situation around Army Group South was becoming more critical. After Hitler's refusal to withdraw forces from the Dnieper bend, in January 1944 Manstein had at first succeeded in blocking the Soviet assault on Uman,[70] but an extremely dangerous situation then developed in the Cerkassy area, where Army Group South held a stretch of terrain about forty kilometres long along the Dnieper, whereas it had been pushed back a long way from the river on other sectors of the front. Thus a 'balcony' extending for a hundred kilometres had formed, which, the military agreed, practically invited the Red Army to encircle the German forces positioned there. Yet Hitler was not prepared to abandon this salient, the sad remnant of the 'Dnieper Line', for he clung to the idea of launching an offensive from here in the coming spring aimed at Kiev.[71] At the end of

January the Red Army did in fact employ a pincer movement to encircle the German troops, consisting of two German corps, in the front of the salient. Yet even in this new situation Hitler refused to surrender this territory, in his eyes a 'fortress on the Dnieper', and forbade the troops to break out of the encirclement. Eventually, however, Manstein succeeded in getting his way: in the end the encircled German troops were able to break out of the pocket, supported by a relief operation from outside, and a second Stalingrad was prevented.[72]

In the meantime it had been impossible to halt the Soviet advance on the northern flank of Army Group South at the interface with Army Group Centre.[73] In January the Red Army reached the former Polish–Soviet border. A situation began to emerge there that had the potential to determine the fate of the whole of Army Group South, the northern flank of which was now positioned more than 500 kilometres further west than the units on the most southerly sector of the front.[74] A further Red Army offensive in February forced Army Group A to abandon the second position on the Dnieper still held by the Wehrmacht, the Nikopol bridgehead in the south of the front. Thus any hope of restoring a connection with the German troops cut off in the Crimea had become illusory.[75]

As a result of their offensive against Nevel and Gorodok between October and December 1943 the Red Army had, in addition, succeeded in driving a wedge in the front line between Army Groups Centre and North. In January it moved its main attack further to the north and compelled Army Group North to pull back its front from Leningrad and Novgorod to the Baltic. For Hitler this was reason enough to dismiss the commander-in-chief of Army Group North, Field-Marshal von Küchler, and appoint Colonel General Walter Model as his successor.[76]

The new year also brought further setbacks on the southern front in Italy. In mid-January the Battle of Monte Cassino began; the Allied attack was boosted by a landing behind the German front line in the Anzio area and the Allies were now only forty kilometres from Rome.[77] Speaking to Goebbels, Hitler blamed the military leaders for not managing to destroy the bridgehead at Anzio, in his view a clear sign 'that he . . . has to do everything himself'. Yet the German forces lacked the strength to attempt what he wanted, namely to mount a large-scale attack on the bridgehead.[78]

Meanwhile, the Allied landing in the West that Hitler was expecting from February onwards began to dominate his thoughts. In his view it would be decisive for the outcome of the war.[79] Yet in discussions with his military staff Hitler seemed very uncertain about where the 'invasion' would take place.[80] On the more than 5,000 kilometres of coastline between Norway and the Bay of Biscay, on the French Mediterranean coast, or, as a 'dummy invasion', in Spain or Portugal? On 4 March he announced to his generals that he considered Normandy and Brittany to be the most threatened areas.[81] He held to this view in the following months.[82] In spite of this, the bulk of the German defences were concentrated on the Pas de Calais.[83]

A sizeable fighting force had been assembled to fend off an Allied landing in western Europe. By 6 June 1944 it had grown to around sixty divisions, even though many of them had already fought in the East and so were battle-weary.[84] Hitler's hopes were focused on deploying the bulk of these troops, up to forty divisions, in an offensive in the East, once the Allied landing had been repelled. Uncertainty about where the landing would take place and the Western Allies' air superiority made it impossible, however, to concentrate these forces in the right place at the right time in order to push the Allied troops quickly back into the sea and shift the main war effort back to the threatened East. Even the ideological 'orientation' of the officer corps and Hitler's insistence on the primacy of his political leadership in the war could do nothing to change that.

The invisible 'Führer': Repercussions for the regime

While Hitler concentrated his efforts on regaining the initiative in the war by preventing an Allied landing in the West, and was working to bolster his primacy via-á-vis the Wehrmacht and strengthen it ideologically, his 'charisma', already seriously damaged in 1942, was rapidly losing its power. A crucial factor was that during the winter of 1943/44 the Reich was facing an ever-increasing threat from the air. The air raids, against which there was no defence and which were not being halted by 'retaliation', however much it was invoked, became the most significant burden affecting the 'home front'. Between November 1943 and March 1944 the RAF mounted its long-expected bomber offensive against Berlin. The first four raids in November alone killed 4,000 people and destroyed 9,000 buildings.[85] Hitler consoled Goebbels, the Gauleiter of Berlin, with the words: 'Berlin would never be able to claim for itself the moral right to lead the Reich in the future, if other cities in the

Reich had suffered much more than the capital itself.'[86] This message gave little comfort, however, to those who had been bombed out.

Shortly after this Hitler appointed Goebbels to head the 'Reich Inspection of Civilian Air War Measures' with the role of scrutinizing 'all local measures taken to prepare for, prevent, and alleviate air war damage' and of mobilizing suitable local personnel.[87] Goebbels's task was to maintain morale in cities affected by bombing by getting the Party involved and employing a mixture of supervision and propaganda.[88] In allocating him this task, Hitler had transferred to Goebbels yet one more part of his, now almost invisible, domestic leadership role. For his own part, he preferred to maintain silence on the consequences of the bombing war and to avoid the affected areas as far as possible.

In the second half of the war a wide range of developments led to a dissolution of the inner cohesiveness of German society: the bombing with its catastrophic effects; the evacuation of millions of actual or potential bombing victims to 'bomb-safe' areas; the years-long separation of many families as a result of the 'deployment' of millions of Germans to work far from their homes and of men being called up for military service; the growing problems caused by food shortages and the black market that sprang up as a result; the well-known privileges and corruption of the Party big wigs; the rigorous measures taken to suppress everyday contact with the millions of people deported to Germany as forced labour; the regime's battle with the emergence of unconventional opposition among young people. The concrete conditions of life in wartime produced in the majority of the population something like a caricature of the Nazi 'national community' that was far from developing into a united fighting community battling for its survival. The regime's attempt to mobilize people's last reserves of resistance, persuading them to adopt the slogan 'Victory or Downfall' by reminding them that Germany's crimes were widely known had already proved unconvincing in 1943. Although the apparatus of repression and the local Party's continuing close control of everyday life ensured that wartime society still functioned and the mass of the population obediently fulfilled their obligations, the idea that this was one 'nation' united behind the 'Führer' could no longer be maintained, not even as a façade.[89] The Führer propaganda of 1942 had frequently used Hitler's actual successes to boost the impression of his leadership qualities; however, these images had been exhausted by 1944 at the latest. As the war situation grew ever more critical, Hitler's absence from the public sphere posed a serious and growing problem of domestic political leadership. During 1944 he was rarely seen or heard in public.

Figure 14. The regime tried to preserve some experience of normality amid the destruction, and the public responded. If, as here in the winter of 1943/44, queues formed outside places of entertainment such as the Tauentzienpalast in Berlin the regime was able to use them in propaganda as evidence of 'the will to endure'.
Source: bpk / Hanns Hubmann

Goebbels concluded from reports he received from the Reich Propaganda Offices that Hitler's speech on 30 January 1944, which had been broadcast on the radio, had 'not quite had the desired impact'.[90] A speech he made on 24 February to 'old fighters' to mark the founding of the Party was judged by Goebbels to be unsuitable for a wider audience 'because of a series of psychological slips';[91] on 8 November the previous year he had just about managed to salvage the recording of a Hitler speech for a radio broadcast by making a few cuts, but this time he gave up.

In April Hitler admitted to Goebbels that he felt his 'health was not good enough' to permit him to 'speak with total assurance at a public rally'.[92] He had in fact fallen ill a number of times in the previous weeks and was now becoming positively frail. He had impaired vision in his right eye, the result of bleeding in the vitreous body, and was diagnosed with high blood pressure and progressive arteriosclerosis of the coronary blood vessels. For some time his movements had looked significantly restricted. He dragged his left leg, his left arm had a serious tremor, and his posture was becoming increasingly stooped.[93] These are clear symptoms of advanced Parkinson's disease, although it had not been recognized as such. The cocktail of medicines, tonics, and stimulants that his personal physician, Theodor Morell, provided him with every day assumed bizarre proportions.[94] In spite of the tense military situation, his worsening condition made Hitler withdraw to the Obersalzberg between mid-March and mid-July 1944 to recover. His already rare public appearances reduced still further. He would make only one more speech during 1944 that was broadcast on the radio, and that was immediately after the assassination attempt of 20 July. He now never appeared at major events.[95] The very fact that he was no longer a presence as 'Führer' in the public sphere was bound to have a seriously negative effect on his political effectiveness, quite apart from the issue of how far his physical frailty had a direct influence on his behaviour or his objectives. What is altogether evident, however, is that his physical decline went hand in hand with the growing rigidity with which he responded to the collapse of his authority. This rigidity was evident in his unbending insistence on 'holding on, whatever the cost' (which included his deliberate tactic of prolonging his regime by extending the mass murder of the Jews).[96]

From the second half of 1943 onwards an alliance was emerging between four top functionaries who were prepared by means of a network of agreements to compensate at least partially for Hitler's personal decline and that of his regime and thus finally to put an end to Göring's role as Hitler's deputy. During the winter crisis of 1942/43 the Committee of Three, composed of the 'Chancellery bosses', Lammers, Keitel, and Bormann, had attempted to take over this function, while Goebbels, with the partial support of Speer, had opposed their dominance. During the summer of 1943, however, this Committee of Three had ceased to exist. Once Himmler had taken over as Interior Minister (in addition to his many other offices), Speer had further consolidated his position in armaments, Goebbels, in the virtual absence of Hitler, was appearing ever more frequently as the most important public face of the regime, and Bormann had managed to supplant Lammers as the real coordinator and manager in Hitler's immediate entourage, a loose alliance of these four men, all with multiple responsibilities, began to form. The aim of this 'Gang of Four' was to gain control of all the functions within the Reich that were important for the continuation of the war and thus take over the leadership of the 'home front', given that Hitler was no longer capable of doing so effectively. The emergence of this alliance was, however, repeatedly overshadowed by rivalries, suspicion, and animosities.

Whereas Speer's relationship with Bormann and Himmler (with whom he had joined forces in the autumn of 1943 to oppose the Gauleiters) was always strained and he was forced in the early months of 1944 to put up with significant, if only temporary, damage to his position, his relationship with Goebbels worked relatively well, as was shown the previous year when the efforts to bring about 'total war' were stepped up.[97] For his part, Goebbels stated that he had an 'excellent personal and comradely relationship' with Himmler.[98] He had, as he put it, 'developed a good personal and working relationship' with Bormann; he valued him, he said, because he had been 'very useful' to him 'by speaking to the Führer directly about a huge number of issues'.[99] Bormann had complained to him many times that Himmler 'took charge of too many things',[100] a clear reference to the rivalry that existed between these two prominent figures. Goebbels was forced, however, to admit that Bormann was right in his opinion. It would not be until the summer of 1944, after further massive military setbacks, that the 'Gang of Four' was capable of taking coordinated action.

Crumbling alliances

While Hitler was awaiting the Allied landing in the West in the spring of 1944 and hoping that a defensive victory would bring him a decisive turn in the war situation, he was forced to focus on further military setbacks on the eastern front. His ally Hungary, which was in serious danger from the Red Army's advance, was threatening to break away. On 12 February Horthy requested that Hitler allow him to pull back his divisions positioned on the eastern front to the Carpathian border.[101]

Hitler told Goebbels on 3 March that he would now set about 'resolving the Hungarian question'. The Hungarians engaged in 'treachery the whole time'. He was therefore determined to depose the government in Budapest, take Horthy, whom he had long mistrusted,[102] into custody, and try to instal a regime using the former Prime Minister Imrédy. If the Hungarian army were disarmed, it would be possible 'to tackle the issue of the Hungarian aristocracy and above all the Jews of Budapest', for while 'the Jews are still in Budapest it is impossible to do anything with this city and with the country and in particular with public opinion'. Another factor was the prospect of significant amounts of plunder: the Hungarian army's equipment, the country's oil reserves, 'not to mention their food stocks'.

In addition, Hitler was convinced that the 'removal of the threat from Hungary' would have a positive effect on the Bulgarians, who would then 'buck up their ideas'. The occupation of Hungary would also give the Romanians hope that closer relations with Germany would sooner or later help them to secure their territorial demands vis-à-vis Hungary. When Hitler raised the matter of Hungary's unreliability with Antonescu at a meeting at the end of February, Antonescu strongly advocated intervening against his neighbour, agreeing to supply a much greater number of troops for their joint war against the Soviet Union once the 'Hungarian threat' was dealt with.[103]

By mid-March the issue of his ally Hungary became acute. On 14 March Hitler informed Goebbels that he had brought forward the move against Hungary 'because the Hungarians had smelt a rat'.[104] On 18 March Hitler met Horthy and high-ranking representatives of his regime at Schloss Klessheim and heaped reproaches on them, such as that the Hungarian government was involved in negotiations with the Western Allies and the Soviets and intended to get out of the war. Almost a million Jews could move about freely there, he said, which the Germans inevitably regarded as a threat to the eastern and Balkan fronts. There was a risk of another Badoglio emerging. The occupation of the country would therefore begin that very night. When Horthy refused to give his written consent, Hitler announced he would go ahead regardless. Horthy then threatened to resign, to which Hitler responded that in that case he could not guarantee the safety of Horthy's family. Horthy made to abandon the meeting and could be prevented only by false air raid warnings being put out. In the end Horthy gave in to the occupation and promised not to resist.[105]

On 19 March, very early in the morning, German troops crossed the border.[106] Contrary to Hitler's expectation, Imrédy was not prepared to form a new government and so the Hungarian ambassador in Berlin, Sztójay, was made the new Prime Minister. Edmund Veesenmayer was installed as the new German governor and given the title of Ambassador and Plenipotentiary of the Greater German Reich in Hungary.[107]

Stand firm, whatever the cost

At the beginning of March the Soviet offensive had begun both on the northern flank and on the completely overstretched southern flank of Army Group South.[108] To stop it Hitler pinned his hopes on holding out at all costs. By doing so he hoped to bridge the relatively short interval that, according to his plan, the army in the East would still have to hold out until the landings in the West were decisively pushed back. To this end he had issued Führer Order 11, which laid down that 'strongholds' were in future to form the backbone of the German defence. A 'specially selected, tough soldier', if possible a general, was to take over command in each instance and be responsible 'on his honour as a soldier for the fulfilment of his mission to the end'; if overwhelmed by an enemy attack he was to allow himself to be encircled, pinning down as much of the enemy's forces as possible and thereby creating the conditions for 'successful counter-operations'. 'Strongholds' were to be surrendered only with Hitler's express permission.[109]

In the area of the 4th Panzer Army the city of Tarnopol, which was being directly attacked by Soviet troops, had been declared a stronghold on 9 March, a decision Hitler would not budge from, in spite of protests from Army Group South that the city was too difficult to defend. On 23 March it was surrounded. The 4,600 men defending it held out for four weeks but by then they were completely worn down. In the end only fifty-five men escaped from the pocket.[110] A little further south the Red Army succeeded in encircling the entire 1st Panzer Army by the end of March. Clearly seeing that the army was in danger of being cut off, at a conference on the Obersalzberg on 19 March, Manstein, along with Kleist, commander-in-chief of Army Group A, demanded that the army group be pulled back to the Dniestr, so as to free up troops for Army Group South. Hitler, however, refused.

Manstein's stay at the Berghof took place in the context of a curious event. On 19 March Hitler received the field-marshals and senior commanders; the military elite presented him with a declaration distancing themselves from the propaganda activities against his regime carried on by General von Seydlitz and his League of German Officers based in Moscow, while at the same time pledging unconditional loyalty to their supreme commander. As has already been mentioned, Hitler and the army leadership saw the Seydlitz propaganda as extremely dangerous; in particular, a series of personal letters from Seydlitz to high-ranking commanding officers in the East had alarmed Hitler, prompting him to raise doubts about the loyalty of the officer corps.[111] The declaration, which was written by Schmundt in consultation with Goebbels,[112] was designed to rectify this situation. In fact, it was something of an impertinence towards the most senior officers to hold them collectively responsible for Seydlitz's actions, even though they had taken an oath of 'unconditional obedience' to Hitler. The ceremony was a visible expression of the subordination Hitler required of his commanding officers to his ideologically based absolute claim to leadership. A situation such as the one that had occurred when Hitler had last made a speech to his generals and Manstein had interjected a comment was never to happen again.[113]

It was very evident that Hitler was extremely pleased with this demonstration; as far as he was concerned there was complete harmony that day between him and his generals.[114] Schmundt for his part quickly set about making the entire officer corps aware of the declaration through a special decree.[115]

Only a few days later this harmony was again disturbed. The situation of the now almost completely encircled 1st Panzer Army became even more critical in the days that followed. Manstein gave notice that he would ignore Hitler's order to hold the position and would command the 1st Panzer Army to break out of the pocket that was forming around it on his own authority.[116] On 25 March Manstein was summoned once again to headquarters, where he had a heated argument with Hitler. Manstein stuck to his guns, however. Hitler terminated the discussion, whereupon Manstein told Hitler's chief adjutant that he would resign. By the evening, however, Hitler surprised him by changing his mind and being prepared to listen to Manstein's proposals. This startling willingness to give way prompted Manstein to put forward his ideas about how the eastern front might be stabilized and to recommend a German chief of the general staff for Antonescu. For 'political reasons', however, Hitler was unwilling to agree to that. On 28 March the 1st Panzer Army did finally begin to break out of the Soviet encirclement and after a few days this operation, supported by a relief attack mounted by an assault force hurriedly brought from France, was successful.[117]

On 27 March Hitler received Field-Marshal Ewald von Kleist at the Berghof, who asked Hitler to consent to his withdrawing with his Army Group A, which was operating to the south of Army Group South, from the River Bug to the lower Dniestr. He was astonished when Hitler agreed to this, although the latter demanded at the same time that, whatever happened, the Crimea should be held.

On two occasions within a short time Hitler had been reluctantly forced to give way to pressure from two of his most senior generals, which for him was an almost unbearable loss of face.[118] He therefore decided to dismiss Manstein and Kleist, instructing them to come to the Berghof on 30 March, where he received them individually, telling them they were to be dismissed at the same time as conferring on them the Knight's Cross with Oak Leaves and Swords.[119] In the East, Hitler explained to Manstein, 'the time for expansive operations' had come to an end; now what they needed to do was 'simply to hang on stubbornly' and for this 'new type of leadership' he needed 'a new name and a new watchword'. Walter Model, now promoted to the rank of field-marshal, was made Manstein's successor, while Kleist made way for Ferdinand Schörer, who was promoted to the rank of Colonel General; he was considered to be a particularly sound National Socialist.[120]

As Hitler had explained to Manstein, his removal did indeed signify clearly that mobile warfare had been abandoned. This modern concept of war, in which the holding of territory was subordinated to evasive manoeuvres and the rapid formation of foci of attack, had always seemed a little suspect to Hitler. He had always rather mistrusted the brilliant strategies of the officers of the General Staff with their, as he saw it, arrogant bearing and sophisticated jargon. Hitler was more inclined to trust his personal experience of four years of trench warfare.

His idea of doggedly holding on whatever the cost was not, however, primarily motivated by military and operational considerations but rather by political and strategic ones. As he had done the previous winter, he emphasized that he had to hold certain positions in order to be able to use them as bases for future offensives. The change in name of Army Groups South and A to 'North Ukraine' and 'South Ukraine' was meant to point to the possibility of the Germans going on the offensive in the near future, precisely because the German army was still in control of only the extreme western edge of the Ukraine. Yet even if he had succeeded in repelling a landing by the Western Allies and as a result had prevented them from launching an offensive for years, the German army would have been a long way from having the necessary strength to mount offensives in the East of the kind it had launched in 1941 and 1942.

In Hitler's view, however, the idea of going on the offensive again against the Red Army after repelling an invasion in the West, and of holding on to as much territory as possible in the East until that point, offered the only chance of escaping imminent defeat. As he had already been expecting an Allied landing in the spring of 1944, the need to hold on doggedly would, he thought, last for only a few months or even weeks. It must surely be possible simply to hang on for that length of time. On the other hand, he feared losing the operational base for the decisive offensive in the East if he were to give in to the ideas of his generals and respond flexibly to the Red Army attacks by shortening the front, surrendering territory, and adopting over all a more mobile approach. His generals were prepared to give up territory they had conquered in order to gain time. Hitler, by contrast, wished to make use of this time by bending every sinew to hold on to territory.

Hitler's order to stand firm was an expression of the paralysis that had been increasingly affecting the regime since the autumn of the previous

year. The rapid and large-scale operation to take control of much of Italy
and its zones of occupation had been the last show of strength of which it
was capable. Since then the focus externally had been on establishing the
defence of 'Fortress Europe', and internally on gearing everything to economic exploitation, total repression, and merciless implementation of the
programme to murder the Jews. The hope was that by conjuring up a ter-
rifying apocalyptic vision of the total destruction that would come about if
Germany were defeated, the regime would be able to mobilize people's
final reserves of stamina. No further allies had in fact jumped ship, enemy
forces were still far from Germany's borders, the air war had not been able
to paralyse armaments production, and although resistance and partisan
movements had grown to a significant size, they were not capable of posing
a threat to Hitler's empire. Hitler was aware, however, that this defensive
position would collapse in the medium term under Allied pressure. Hitler's
watchword 'Hold out, whatever the cost', which from a purely military point
of view was amateurish, in fact positively absurd, derived from a political
and strategic plan to go on the offensive that did indeed have an inner logic
and in theory offered a way out of the impasse of the war situation. In the
light of the relative strengths of the opposing sides, however, it was unrealistic, and in fact delusional.

On 8 April the Red Army began its offensive to reconquer the Crimea
and forced the German 17th Army defending the peninsula to retreat to the
fortress of Sebastopol. In spite of the hopeless situation, in mid-April Hitler
refused to allow the army to evacuate across the Black Sea, justifying this on
the grounds that such a move might drive neutral Turkey into the enemy
camp. At the end of April he removed the army's commander, Erwin Jaenecke,
from his command for his negative assessment of the situation. When, in
view of the by now catastrophic situation in the Sebastopol area, Hitler
finally gave his consent for the evacuation on 9 May, only 30,000 men out
of around 60,000 who had made up the force in this final phase could be
rescued. On 14 May the Army High Command was obliged to announce
the end of the fighting.[121]

Hungary: The last chapter in Hitler's Jewish policy

'Exterminate, so that you yourself are not exterminated.' This was the maxim
Hitler had impressed on the Reichsleiters and Gauleiters on 17 April after

the funeral of Gauleiter Adolf Wagner. The Hungarians were finally to be forced to adopt this ruthless precept. In April the German authorities in occupied Hungary pushed through a set of anti-Jewish laws along German lines. They laid the foundation for large-scale deportations that were organized from Budapest by a special RHSA task force led by Eichmann. As early as mid-April the Hungarian police were gathering the country's Jews together in ghettos and camps. At the end of April the first deportations to Auschwitz began, and from mid-May these became extensive and systematic. As a rule, four trains set off for Auschwitz daily with 3,000 people in each.[122] Up to the point when deportations were halted at the beginning of July 437,000 Jews had been deported in this manner to the extermination camp at Auschwitz, where the overwhelming majority were murdered immediately on arrival.

Hitler considered that the new Hungarian government was already so compromised by its involvement in Germany's policies towards the Jews that it could no longer leave the alliance. 'At any rate the Hungarians will no longer be able to escape the logic of the Jewish question', as Goebbels put it in his record of Hitler's comments on the subject at the end of April. 'If you say A, you must say B, and now that the Hungarians have got started with anti-Jewish policies they cannot apply the brakes any more. After a certain point these policies acquire their own momentum.'[123] This provides another example of the central role played by anti-Jewish policies in Hitler's efforts to bind his 'allies' to him.

Hitler continued to follow events in Hungary with great attention and intervened during the summer to prevent the deportations from stalling. At the beginning of July, in response to world-wide protests, Horthy decreed that the deportations should be halted, immediately before the Jews living in Budapest were also caught up in them. When Prime Minister Sztójay then asked Veesenmayer if they could take up the offers made by several states to permit Jews to immigrate or to transit, Hitler, when consulted, decided that this could be allowed if 'the deportation of Jews to the Reich, temporarily halted by the Reich Administrator', were 'completed immediately with all possible speed'.[124] Powerful German pressure made the Hungarian government finally agree at the beginning of August to a resumption of the deportations, but the rapidly approaching military defeat of the Axis powers (on 23 August Romania declared it had left the alliance and joined the anti-Hitler coalition) meant that this never happened.

In line with Hitler's maxim of using anti-Jewish policies as an indicator of the loyalty of those allies he still had, the Nazi regime attempted in the course of 1944 to draw other vassal states into its radical measures following the example of Hungary. Now it was Slovakia, which had halted deportations in October 1942, that was put under pressure: just like the previous year, on 12 May 1944 at Schloss Klessheim the Slovakian delegation under Tiso was browbeaten about 'the Hungarians' treachery' and the 'Jewification' of Hungary as a clear warning to the regime in Bratislava.[125]

As far as the regime was concerned, the mass murder of the Hungarian Jews essentially marked the end of the 'Final Solution' (even though Jews were hunted down literally right up to the end of the war and hundreds of thousands of Jewish concentration camp inmates were to die by the time it was over). Shortly before the start of the Hungarian deportations Hitler therefore decided to change the focus of propaganda, which up to then had concentrated on creating images of the Jews as the enemy. Since the summer of 1941 the Third Reich had been pursuing the war primarily as a 'war against the Jews', in other words conjuring up an enemy that would explain the existence of this unnatural alliance of 'plutocrats' and 'Bolsheviks'. But now that the Third Reich was finally on the defensive, Hitler no longer thought it opportune to go on with propaganda that focused on the distorted image of the Jews as the universal enemy. And given that the last Jewish communities in German-occupied Europe would soon be annihilated, the propaganda cliché of the Jew as the enemy within, who had to be defeated by Germany and her allies so that the foundations for a 'New Europe' could be laid, had necessarily reached the end of its useful life.

On 26 April 1944 Hitler told his Propaganda Minister 'that international Jewry is certainly not as sympathetic to Stalin as people generally suppose. In a number of respects he treats the Jews rather harshly.' In the same conversation Hitler expressed the view that the emergence of strikes in Britain was probably 'Trotskyite' and a sign of 'opposition to the war and to Stalin'. 'Jewish influence' was of course behind it, he said, and this could be 'very useful for our purposes at the moment'.[126]

These comments suggest that Hitler no longer held to the ideologically motivated dogma that had preoccupied him for twenty-five years, namely that Jewishness and Bolshevism were identical. This astonishing departure from a core element in his world view was the result of the political situation. Now that the Soviet Union was so unmistakably on the offensive, it was no longer important to present it as part of a 'world-wide Jewish conspiracy', thereby emphasizing how it could form an alliance with the west. On the contrary, now that Germany was on the defensive, it was vital to emphasize the differences in the enemy camp and bank on such a heterogeneous coalition breaking up. Thus, from then on anti-communist and anti-Semitic propaganda were kept separate. Anti-Semitic propaganda was geared towards American Jews, who were styled as the driving force behind the Western Allies' war; at the same time the 'Bolshevik' peril was evoked with all its terrors.[127]

On 26 May Hitler gave a speech in the Platterhof, the guesthouse on the Obersalzberg, to generals and senior officers who had just completed an indoctrination course in Nazi ideology at a Party college. This speech can be regarded as the culmination of Hitler's efforts to imbue the army with Nazi doctrine (a process he had begun by introducing National Socialist Leadership Officers). He first went back to 1918, but after the usual Party narrative he became more philosophical. Via discussion of the Ptolemaic and the Copernican systems he found a way into his Social Darwinist philosophy, according to which life was 'an endless struggle'. After discussing the alleged racial superiority of the Germans, he came to the key point of his speech: his policies towards the Jews, a chapter that, significantly, he treated as if already closed.

'By removing the Jews I have dealt with any possibility in Germany of some kind of revolutionary cell or nucleus forming. People may of course say to me: "Could you not have solved the problem more simply – or not more simply, because any other way would have been more complicated – but more humanely?" Gentlemen, we are engaged in a life and death struggle. If our enemies were to gain victory in this struggle the German nation would be exterminated. Bolshevism would slaughter countless millions of our intellectuals. Anyone who wasn't shot in the back of the neck would be carted off. The children from more elevated social groups would be separated out and disposed of.... Precisely in this situation, as in every other, humane policies would amount to the greatest cruelty to one's own nation. If I am making the Jews hate me I would at least be loath to miss out on the advantages of their hatred.' These advantages, Hitler continued, consisted in Germany having 'a cleanly organized national body, which cannot be influenced by alien forces.' Hitler had a negative example immediately to hand: Hungary. 'The whole country disintegrating and corroded, Jews everywhere, nothing but Jews up to the highest positions, and the whole state covered by, it has to be said, a dense network of spies and agents.... I have intervened here too and now this problem also will be solved.'[128]

41

Defeat Looms

In the summer of 1944 Hitler's regime faced what was up to that point its most serious crisis. The long-expected Allied landing had been successful, the Soviet offensive that began shortly afterwards led to the destruction of an entire German army group, air raids were bringing about the almost total collapse of German production of aviation fuel, and on 20 July 1944 Hitler only narrowly escaped an assassination attempt, planned as the first step in a comprehensive coup d'état. Hitler's response to this crisis was once again to carry out a restructuring of his regime and to equip the advocates of a radical course for the war – Speer, Himmler, Bormann, and Goebbels – with further powers. The influence of this 'Gang of Four' was already growing considerably during the spring as a result of the continuing deterioration in conditions within the Third Reich. A significant factor in this process was that the Armaments Minister, Speer, whose ambition had led him to overplay his hand at the end of 1943, was able from May 1944 onwards to strengthen his position once more. Speer's sudden loss of power and then meteoric recovery were the result of Hitler's personalized leadership style.

At the end of April 1944 Speer gradually resumed his official responsibilities after a break caused by illness in the first months of the year. The Armaments Minister, who in the past had been treated as Hitler's successor, was, however, forced to admit that he had much ground to make up.

Since the end of 1943 intensive air raids on the German aviation industry had led to a steep decline in aircraft production. Speer, prompted by Milch, had proposed the formation of a 'Fighter Staff' to Hitler in February. It was to be made up of representatives of state bodies and industry who, equipped with special powers, would re-energize the production of fighter aircraft. Whereas Speer, however, wished to entrust this task to his friend Karl Hanke, the Gauleiter of Silesia, Hitler appointed Karl Saur, Speer's rival, as head of the 'Fighter Staff'; in view of his illness, Speer's being assigned overall

control was at first purely a formality.[1] By employing ruthless methods
the Fighter Staff did, however, manage to increase fighter production from
its nadir of 1,323 planes in February 1944 to 3,558 in September.[2] Speer,
who since his return to work had been taking an active role in the Fighter
Staff, now claimed special credit for this success achieved by the ministry
he headed.[3]

Since 1943 there had been a plan to ensure that essential armaments production was safe from bombing; the work of the Fighter Staff gave new
impetus to this initiative. At the beginning of April Speer reported to Hitler
that by the end of the year he would be able 'to provide reliable protection
against bombing raids' to the 'most vulnerable factories' by 'making them
totally safe underground'.[4] Yet in April Hitler, on Göring's suggestion, gave
Franz Xaver Dorsch, Speer's deputy as head of the Todt Organization and,
as Hitler knew, one of Speer's main rivals,[5] responsibility for constructing six
extensive bunkers for fighter production.[6] By giving these special assignments to Saur and Dorsch, Hitler was giving a clear sign that he had no
scruples about dismantling Speer's power base.

Speer put up serious objections to Dorsch being given this task and
threatened to resign.[7] After an interview on 25 April at the Berghof, Hitler
pandered to Speer's considerable vanity and a solution began to emerge. At
the end of April Speer, with Hitler's approval, appointed Dorsch as head of
construction in the ministry and made him his deputy as plenipotentiary for
the building sector. This solution saved Speer's face.[8] Sauckel too was one of
the rivals trying to undermine Speer's position in the early months of the
year. At the end of April 1944 he succeeded in persuading Hitler to water
down the guarantees the latter had given Speer only in January to make
available the labour he required for his 'protected industries' in occupied
France and instead to support Sauckel's recruitment policies.[9]

Speer's rapid loss of influence was to a great extent the result of Hitler's
leadership maxim of not taking notice of people's established spheres of
responsibility but rather of making individual top functionaries personally
responsible for the whole of an assignment and then adjusting and realign-
ing areas of responsibility as he saw fit. Speer for his part was someone who
understood how to exploit this system. The key, which also secured his
spectacular recovery, was the 'Führer's' trust.

When Speer fully returned to work in his ministry on 8 May he was determined not only to restore his authority within his fiefdom but to extend it.
This was to occur at Göring's expense in particular, for Göring had been

the most active in undermining his power.[10] Speer could exploit the fact that Göring's prestige at this point was suffering huge damage from the sustained Allied bombing raids and the weakness of the fighter command's defence. In Hitler's regime, which was based totally on individuals, Göring's weakness provided the opportunity for Speer to start expanding his power.

In addition to their bombing of towns and cities,[11] on 12 May the Americans (and later the British) began an air offensive to target German hydrogenation plants, thus striking at one of the most vulnerable points in the German war machine. At a crisis meeting on 22 and 23 May, Hitler demanded more anti-aircraft guns and screening smoke to protect the plants being targeted; apart from this there were few ideas on how to put up a more effective defence.[12]

The next series of raids came on 28 and 29 May, reducing the daily production of aircraft fuel by more than half. Speer persuaded Hitler to sign a decree appointing a 'General Commissar' to restore fuel production. Equipped with extraordinary powers and supported by a staff drawn from industry and state agencies, Edmund Geilenberg, up to then the head of the main committee for munitions, attempted to deal with the Allied bombing campaign, though this seemed an almost hopeless task. In June the average production of aircraft fuel had fallen to 30 per cent of the March average.[13] Only the fact that from June 1944 onwards the Allied air forces were mainly concentrated on preparing for the forthcoming landings in France saved the German war machine in the summer of 1944 from grinding to a halt.[14]

Göring suffered a further serious loss of prestige when at a meeting with Luftwaffe chiefs on 23 May Hitler discovered that, although on numerous occasions he had ordered that the jet fighter Me 262 be developed into a 'lightning bomber',[15] this command had not been carried out.[16] He had ordered it against the advice of experts, his intention being to use the bomber to resist invasion and deliver 'retaliatory strikes' against Britain. When at the beginning of June Speer informed Hitler that he and Milch had both come to the conclusion that Luftwaffe armaments production should be incorporated into Speer's ministry, Hitler immediately agreed.[17]

During the same armaments briefing, Speer managed to convince Hitler that the various independent armaments initiatives of the SS ought to 'be subject to the same control' as 'the rest of armaments and war production'. It was unacceptable, he claimed, that every year Himmler imprisoned about 500,000 'runaway' foreign workers and prisoners of war in concentration camps after the police recaptured them, thus making them unavailable for much more important armaments projects. He spoke to Hitler about the clash with Sauckel, which was still unresolved: in doing so, his aim was, he said, to ensure that 'the main responsibility for everything connected with munitions and war production (and that includes labour) rests with me'.[18] Over the next few weeks control over armaments was indeed adjusted in Speer's favour. In the meantime, however, Hitler was forced to suffer yet more painful reverses.

In mid-May the British and Americans in Italy had broken through the German 'Gustav Line'. On 3 June the German defences in the Alban Hills south of Rome collapsed and the following day the Italian capital surrendered.[19] When Goebbels paid Hitler a visit on the Obersalzberg on 5 June, Hitler informed him cheerfully that the news about Rome's surrender had 'not dismayed him at all' for 'the decisive action will doubtless be in the West'. He 'awaited the invasion with complete confidence', he explained to Goebbels; the new flying bomb (by which he meant the Fi 103, later the so-called V1) would be ready for use against London in a few days, even if the A 4 [V2] would take some time longer.[20]

For months Hitler had been preparing intensively for the Allied landing in western Europe and had informed his entourage that Germany would still manage to bring about a turn in the war by achieving a great defensive success in the West. He had total confidence that, as so often in his career, the crisis would in the end turn into a triumphant victory. Had he not after all been proved right in being confident in 1923/25, 1932/33, 1934, or 1939/40?[21]

During the night of the 5/6 June the Allied landings began on the coast of Normandy. Once more Hitler, who was informed about the 'invasion' in the course of the morning at the Berghof, acted as though he was extraordinarily optimistic. The landings had, he claimed, taken place exactly where he had expected them and the enemy troops would be pushed back into the sea. During the previous months Hitler had in fact referred to Normandy as a possible landing zone, but his pronouncements about the coming 'invasion' had indicated great uncertainty about the question 'Where?'; the army had certainly not been concentrating its defences in Normandy. Thus his almost euphoric reaction to the landings was primarily designed to give confidence to those around him.

Although the landing forces managed to secure their five beachheads relatively quickly, link up with each other, and bring in continuous reinforcements, it still took until the end of July before they were able to break through the hastily formed German defensive line and advance deep into France. During those weeks Hitler went on propounding his old illusion that by beating back the landing he could initiate the desired turn in the war. Thus on 17 July at a meeting in Margival, north of Soissons, he explained to Rundstedt and Rommel, his commanding officers responsible for the invasion front, that the invasion army would soon find itself the target of huge numbers of jet fighter-bombers, while the use of the new 'catapult bomb' against London would have such devastating effects as to make Britain give up the war.[22] Attacks by the new flying bomb on London had actually begun during the night of 15/16 June, as Hitler had stipulated in mid-May.[23]

In spite of Goebbels's warning to hold back, hints about imminent 'retaliation' had found their way into German propaganda in the early months of 1944 and thus had awakened high expectations among the German population of some kind of counterattack.[24] On Hitler's instructions the Reich press chief Dietrich issued a press notice suggesting that the deployment of this new weapon meant that 'retaliation' had already begun. During the following days Goebbels, who was worried that such an over-optimistic presentation of the situation might arouse expectations that for the time being could not be met,[25] succeeded in softening this line and ensuring that there was scope for propaganda to provide more positive reports in the future.[26] Hitler's decision to name the weapon the V1 and thus to mark it out as the first of a series of 'weapons of retaliation' [Vergeltungswaffen] was also part of this propaganda tactic.[27]

Yet this new, purportedly decisive, weapon was not to have the anticipated impact. In fact, only a little more than 20 per cent of the bombs landed in the Greater London area. Because they were far apart both spatially and temporally and had a load of under one ton each, their impact was far less than that of the major Allied air raids, with their relatively high degree of accuracy and their combined load each raid of several thousand tons.[28] As a result, the population's disappointed expectations produced the depressed mood that Goebbels had feared.[29]

On 21 June, on a visit to the Berghof, Goebbels made another attempt to persuade Hitler finally to implement measures for 'total war', although Hitler objected that it was 'not yet the right time'. The same was true, he said, of moves to end the war by political means. As on the eve of the invasion,[30] he still did not believe it was possible 'to come to an arrangement with England'. Whether it might at some point come about with the Soviet Union was something he wished 'to leave an open question'; the present

state of the war would make it doubtful, though.[31] Instead, Hitler was relying completely on the V 2, as rocket A 4 was now being called. He assured
Goebbels it would be deployed at the beginning of August and though it
would not 'be immediately decisive for the war, it would probably bring a
decisive outcome closer'.[32] Until then propaganda would be forced to compensate for the bad news from all fronts with the prospect of imminent
'retaliation'.[33]

The very next day, on the third anniversary of the German invasion, the
great Soviet summer offensive against the front salient of Army Group
Centre began. Thus the strategy on which Hitler had based his entire conduct of the war since the end of 1943 had failed. He had assumed that a
successful defensive operation against the invasion in the West would free up
a large number of troops for an offensive in the East and might force a
'decisive end to the war'. Now, however, it became clear how much a war
on two fronts favoured his opponents. It was obvious that the Red Army
would quickly exploit the fact that German forces were tied down in the
West after the Allied invasion in order to mount its own large-scale offensive. The fact that Hitler had expected the Soviet attack to begin on 22 June,[34]
without being capable of any effective countermeasures, makes clear how
flawed his own strategy was.

By the beginning of July the Red Army had succeeded in almost completely destroying three German armies with twenty-eight divisions. On
3 July it recaptured Minsk, on 14 July Vilnius in Lithuania.[35] Hitler could do
nothing but watch these events helplessly. In view of the overall situation, a
fire-fighting operation by German units from other fronts was impossible.
He therefore fired his generals.

When on 29 July at the Berghof Rundstedt and Rommel attempted to
make clear to him the hopelessness of the situation in the West, Hitler at first
responded with a speech about the miracle weapons. The new weapons
would be the 'miracle that turned the war', just as the death of the Russian
Empress in the Seven Years' War had been for Frederick the Great.[36] Only
four days later, on 3 July, he had Rundstedt replaced and transferred the
supreme command in the West to Field-Marshal von Kluge.[37] This was followed by the dismissals of the commander of Panzer Group West, Leo Geyr
von Schweppenburg, and in August of the Luftwaffe Field-Marshall Hugo
Sperrles, responsible for air defence in the West.[38] The Chief of the General
Staff, Zeitzler, who in the previous months had increasingly suffered Hitler's
disapproval, was replaced at the end of July by Guderian,[39] while the

supreme commander of the defeated Army Group Centre, Field-Marshal von Busch, had already been forced to go in June. He was replaced by Field-Marshal Model.[40]

On 15 July Rommel took action. He explained in a letter to Hitler that 'the situation in Normandy' was becoming 'more difficult day by day' and was close to developing into a 'serious crisis'. After a bleak description of the extremely precarious position of his own troops, who could not hold out much longer, Rommel came to an unequivocal conclusion: 'I must ask you to recognise the position we are in and act without delay.'[41] The tone of the letter guaranteed that Rommel would face repercussions, were Hitler to react negatively to it. It did not come to that, however, because on 17 July Rommel was seriously injured during a low-flying air attack.

In mid-July Hitler had already taken measures in case of further advances by the Western Allies. On 13 July he replaced the existing military adminis-tration in Belgium and Northern France with a civilian administration and appointed Grohé, the Gauleiter of Cologne–Aachen, as Reich Commissar for this area.[42] In addition, on that same day he signed two decrees dealing with the authority of military agencies in relation to civil administrative bodies and Party offices in the event of the enemy's penetration of Reich territory.[43] Hitler was in other words already preparing to defend the Reich.

After four months there he finally left the Berghof on 16 July and returned to his Wolf's Lair headquarters. He was never to return to the Obersalzberg. The evening before he left he looked one more time at his paintings hang-ing in the great hall and then said goodbye to his guests in a manner that gave his Luftwaffe adjutant the impression that he was consciously taking 'leave for ever'.[44]

In June and July, during the dramatic military events following the Allied landings, fundamental changes were taking place in the armaments sector; in the wake of the 20 July plot, these changes would result in the shift in the balance of power that had been on the horizon for some time in favour of a group of four men, namely Speer, Goebbels, Bormann, and Himmler.

After his crucial decision at the beginning of June to hand Luftwaffe armaments to Speer, on 20 June Hitler ordered Göring himself to take charge of this transfer to Speer's ministry. Göring demonstrated his annoy-ance at this loss of power by dismissing his state secretary, Milch, from all his posts. Speer, however, immediately appointed Milch as his deputy.[45] In addition, on 19 July Hitler signed the decree drafted by Speer's ministry concerning the concentration of munitions and war production that transferred to

Speer all powers relating to the technical construction and rationalization of weapons and war matériel. Speer now held the key to controlling the whole production process.[46] Following Hitler's decree Speer streamlined the armaments ministry's regional organization, thereby strengthening his position vis-à-vis the Gauleiters.[47]

At the armaments conferences in Essen and Linz in June Speer demonstrated his key position to the industrialists and attempted to boost their damaged morale. This was also the purpose of a speech that Hitler made after the Linz conference on 26 June on the Obersalzberg to about 150 leading figures in the armaments industry. Its main point was to counteract dissatisfaction within the industry about Nazi tendencies to favour state control of the economy. Hitler assured them: 'If this war ends in victory for us then private initiative will be triumphant in the German economy!' While looking decidedly forlorn and battered,[48] Hitler tried to appear confident of victory, but his rambling references to his own charisma no longer convinced anyone present: 'The gods love someone who demands the impossible of them.... And if we achieve the impossible, providence will reward us.'[49]

During June and July Speer also succeeded in achieving total dominance over his rival Sauckel with regard to 'labour deployment', having already obtained Hitler's backing at the beginning of June.[50] First of all he made sure that inside the Reich itself the responsibilities of the heads of the regional armaments agencies, who were answerable to him, were substantially expanded in relation to the Gau employment offices, which were part of Sauckel's empire.[51] Shortly afterwards he made his second move by putting a stop to Sauckel's practice of compulsory recruitment. On 2 July 1944, almost four weeks after the Allied landings in Normandy, Sauckel was forced to report to Hitler that during the previous few weeks the recruitment of labour from Italy and western Europe had practically come to a standstill.[52] At the meeting of top officials then called by Hitler for 11 July 1944 it became evident that Sauckel would have to drop his existing policy of recruiting forced labour.[53] Thus Speer had managed to bring the whole of armaments production under his authority, at the same time resuming his role as crown prince. Yet it would soon be clear that this apparent resurgence was little more than a 'false dawn before the final downfall'.[54]

At this point Speer and Goebbels began a joint initiative, although one in which they had different roles, to step up the war effort. At the beginning of July in a leading article Goebbels had again taken up the slogan of 'Total War';[55] he had claimed in a speech in Breslau on 7 July that the nation faced its 'To be or not to be'.[56] After Hitler had rejected his June proposals to ramp up the war effort as premature, Goebbels attempted, as he had done the previous year, to get his way once again by making use of 'public opinion', which he could shape. At the same time, Speer drew Hitler's attention at an armaments briefing to the fact that, as far as the mobilization of labour was concerned, 'there were still possibilities to exploit on the home front and in the army'; doing so required a significantly 'more stringent . . . idea of what was meant by the country's total commitment'.[57] He therefore suggested that Hitler might speak to a small circle (Speer had Himmler, Lammers, Keitel, Sauckel, Goebbels, and himself in mind) about the 'requirements for this increased commitment'. Hitler agreed and the meeting was fixed for 22 July.

Speer and Goebbels then arranged to send Hitler memoranda they had previously worked out together.[58] Whereas Speer in his memoranda of 12 and 20 July put forward a detached, rational case on the basis of statistics,[59] Goebbels in his memorandum of 18 July adopted the tone of an old comrade and pointed out the psychological repercussions that might arise among the masses from too great an inequality in the distribution of the burdens of the war.[60]

In essence Speer and Goebbels were in agreement about the necessary measures: firms and businesses had to be shut down, women had to be mobilized, staff in desk jobs had to be reduced, the army's administration at home had to be sifted for extra manpower, and public life in general had to be purged of activities more appropriate to peacetime. These tasks should be carried out by somebody who enjoyed Hitler's implicit trust and who should be equipped with extraordinary powers. No name was mentioned, but it was understood that Goebbels should be chosen, for the previous year he had spoken so strongly in favour of 'total war'.

42

20 July 1944

The successful Allied landing in the West, the rapid advance of the Red Army in the East, and the devastating enemy bombing raids combined to make the Third Reich's military situation ultimately hopeless. The fact that Hitler's regime nevertheless managed to keep going and continue the war, despite great loss of life and the extensive destruction of German towns and cities, for almost another full year, to the point of total defeat, poses the key problem in the historiography of the final phase of the Third Reich. For it confronts us with the historical reality of a dictatorship that has overtaxed its strength in a war of conquest and is heading towards destruction finally summoning resources from the ranks of its own leadership and from the elites to fend off its downfall, even as that downfall becomes increasingly inevitable.

Yet these resources are not evident among the actual leaders of the regime, the top functionaries working directly under Hitler. There is, admittedly, plentiful evidence to show that many of these men were clear-sighted enough to recognize that total defeat was approaching, and, in confidence, they discussed this prospect and also the possibilities of ending the war by political means. Goebbels and Speer are examples of individuals who tried to extract more detailed information from Hitler about his intentions for the future conduct of the war. Yet at no point did the leadership – ministers, Reichsleiters, Gauleiters, or powerful special commissioners – even consider confronting Hitler as a united group to demand a binding statement concerning his plans to continue the war and if necessary to compel him to confront the implications of the defeat that was looming. To remove or topple the dictator was beyond their mental horizons.

One reason for the passivity shown by the leaders of the regime as they approached inevitable defeat without developing any kind of counter-initiative may be found in the leadership structure of the Nazi dictatorship.

The apparatus of power was fragmented, and below the 'Führer', who was responsible for all policy matters in the regime but was screened off behind a system of 'chancelleries', collective decision-making had ceased. It was also an apparatus of power in which the position of individual top functionaries depended on the degree of trust Hitler placed in them, a rare commodity for which they competed fiercely. These were just about the worst conditions for a conspiracy.

Another factor was that the political caste that made up the elite in the National Socialist state lacked any collective vision of a future after Hitler. They saw clearly that any political end to the war, even if they managed to avoid the unconditional surrender demanded by the Allies, could be achieved only at the price of dismantling the Nazi system. This would bring with it the predictable consequences of loss of power and punishment of the crimes against humanity for which they shared responsibility. This prospect made the top functionaries incapable as a collective of initiating any process of self-liquidation or transformation of the system. Their best chance of survival was as individuals.

Yet the regime's inability to avert its own downfall cannot be explained primarily by structures or the mentality of its leaders. Hitler himself was a crucial factor. For the structure of the regime, in which all power was concentrated in the dictator himself, was above all the result of the deliberate policy of the man who created it with the express purpose of achieving his own aims. Hitler was not the tool of structures and circumstances that inexorably led to self-destruction and total defeat; rather, the fact that people endured and fought on to the point of destruction was fundamentally the product of his political will.[1]

There was, however, resistance to Hitler's regime throughout the Nazi dictatorship in every political camp and right across German society. The motivation behind it varied and it manifested itself in very different ways. It included critical comments about the regime and non-conformist behaviour, the creation of underground organizations and the illegal dissemination of information, protest and non-compliance, sabotage and espionage, not to mention the many attempts that were made on Hitler's life. They could not, however, halt his progress.

During the final phase of the war, however, a serious threat was posed to his regime by resistance occurring below the highest level of leadership and organized by precisely those pillars of the regime who up to that point had served Hitler faithfully and shared responsibility with him, and who as partners in his power had access to resources and connections to match. Here was a series of figures who were not inclined to await their own downfall passively but who instead attempted to avert it by means of a palace revolution, a coup d'état. This resistance was rooted above all in the conservative elites, and I examine it here as part of Hitler's biography in order to show how his life was seriously threatened numerous times and how significant efforts were made to bring to an end the regime he had instigated.

During the years 1938 to 1940 plans had already been laid for a coup but Hitler's political and military successes had made the men in question abandon their resistance as hopeless for the time being. When the turn in the war came in the winter of 1942/43 they joined forces again to oppose the dangerous course Hitler was pursuing. The conservative politicians and high-ranking, in some cases retired, military men who had emerged as the principal resisters between 1938 and 1940 were now joined by a group of younger officers, who for the most part had seen active service at the front and who had frequently excelled there. These men now deliberately took a leading role in organizing a coup, after a whole series of generals had shown themselves too hesitant for this task. They had links, in particular via the Kreisau Circle (of which more later), with further civilian opposition groups, particularly within the two Churches, and even with individual Social Democrats and trade unionists who could still act, even though their organizations had been smashed. In addition, there were Nazis such as Count Wolf-Heinrich von Helldorff, the Berlin police chief, and Arthur Nebe, chief of the criminal police, who were developing an increasingly critical attitude to the regime's policies.

These disparate groups were united by the idea that the virtually inevitable military defeat must be prevented by a change of regime. The replacement of Hitler (however that might occur), the removal of the Nazi leadership, and the dissolution of the Party became indispensable preconditions for a political end to the war. This would salvage the essential structures of the German state and, significantly, preserve as far as possible the position of the traditional elites. The only organization capable of creating these preconditions was the German army. From the perspective of members of the traditional elites in the officer corps and in the civil service (and these included many members of the aristocracy), getting rid of Hitler and his regime became increasingly a matter of the survival of their class. Having forged a close alliance with the Nazis in 1933, they were now forced to make a radical break to avoid going down collectively and finally along with the regime.

Any discussion of resistance to Hitler and his motives therefore also means exploring the collective self-interest of the old ruling elites, which now consisted in distancing themselves clearly from Nazism and defeating it, in order to have some chance of taking on a distinct and independent role in the post-war order. This collective interest should be borne in mind when the individual motives of men and women in the German resistance are examined.

The most important information we have about the backgrounds of the members of the 1943/44 conspiracy against Hitler comes primarily from the post-war recollections of surviving conspirators and from those close to them. In the immediate post-war years the survivors and their families were forced to defend themselves against the charge of 'treason', until the history of the conspiracy against Hitler came more and more to be reinterpreted as the moral prehistory of the Federal Republic and 'resistance' was positively elevated to the status of a myth. It was unavoidable that in the course of this decades-long process the resistance fighters and their motives underwent a moral transfiguration and these men and women were made into heroes. This transfiguration, however, in no way rules out our seeing the history of the resistance as a response to concern among a section of the conservative elites to set a marker before the war ended and to distance themselves clearly from Hitler and his regime. Without 20 July the moral corruption of the traditional ruling elites, the aristocracy in particular, at the end of the Third Reich would have been total.

As we have seen, the plan to remove Hitler went back as far as the Sudeten crisis, when a conspiracy arose to prevent war against the western powers. This group of conspirators broke up after Hitler's foreign policy success in Munich. Some life was breathed into the conspiracy again in the summer of 1939, but in the wake of the intensive preparations for war against Poland it was effectively over. The crimes of the SS in Poland in 1939/40 provoked vehement protests among the generals of which criticism of the regime was a distinct element, but the success of the war in the West meant that for the time being the idea of getting rid of Hitler had disappeared.[2]

It was the course of the war against the Soviet Union, in particular after the rapid German advance had been halted in 1941, that gave new impetus to resistance among the military. Colonel Henning von Tresckow, the 1st general staff officer of Army Group Centre, who even in the pre-war years had become an implacable opponent of Hitler's policies, took on a key role. Since the start of 1941, when preparations for the war against the Soviet

Union had become apparent, he had been searching out like-minded men among his staff so that he could create a hub for preparations for a coup.[3] A second cell of military resistance was forming in the Abwehr, the military intelligence service, around its chief of staff Hans Oster and his colleague Hans von Dohnanyi.[4] Around the New Year of 1941/42 there was intensive contact between Oster and Friedrich Olbricht, the head of the General Army Office in the Army High Command, an opponent of National Socialism, who was to become the main organizer of the coup.[5]

Since the end of 1941 and beginning of 1942 these groups and individuals had been increasing contacts with each other and also with the leading members of the conservative resistance. Ludwig Beck, the former chief of the general staff, who resigned in 1938 in protest over Hitler's policies, belonged to this group; other members included the former Mayor of Leipzig, Carl Goerdeler, who had also resigned, the former German ambassador in Rome, Ulrich von Hassell, who lost his job in the course of the personnel reshuffle early in 1938, the Prussian finance minister Johannes Popitz, and the Berlin Professor of Politics and Economics Jens Jessen. In addition, these groups had many links to the 'Kreisau Circle', a fluid grouping around Counts Helmuth James von Moltke and Peter Yorck von Wartenburg that had been meeting since 1940 on Moltke's estate in Silesia. Influenced by shared experiences in the youth movement and motivated by ideals such as humanitarianism, social justice, and international reconciliation, Christians of both confessions, Christian socialists, Social Democrats, and others came together to share ideas on how to develop a programme of renewal for Germany after the fall of the dictatorship. Precisely because of its heterogeneous composition the circle had multiple and close links with other opposition and resistance groups.[6]

At the end of March 1942 Beck, Hassell, Oster, Olbricht, Goerdeler, and Jessen had a meeting at which they decided that Beck should coordinate planning for the coup. Since July Beck and Goerdeler had been in constant contact with the group of conspirators in Army Group Centre via Tresckow's ADC, First Lieutenant Fabian von Schlabrendorff. Schlabrendorff also maintained contact with the group around Oster and with other resistance cells. At a meeting in Berlin around the New Year of 1943, Olbricht made a commitment to Tresckow and Goerdeler to lay the groundwork for a coup in Berlin, Vienna, Cologne, and Munich with support from the Reserve Army.[7] Olbricht therefore worked out detailed plans to topple the regime, which were ready by the end of March. They were primarily based on the official

'Valkyrie' plans, which, in the case of a domestic uprising, provided for the Reserve Army to take over all the key nerve centres in the country and in doing so to override the Party and the SS if necessary.[8]

The coup was to be set in motion by the assassination of Hitler. In 1943 several promising attempts were made:

- In February Hubert Lanz, general of the mountain troops and commander of the army battalion named after him, developed a plan, along with his chief of staff Major General Hans Speidel and the commander of a tank regiment, Colonel Count von Strachwitz, to arrest Hitler when he visited the headquarters of Army Group Centre in Poltawa and, if his entourage should prevent this, to shoot him. Hitler's visit to Army Group B was, however, cancelled at short notice.[9]
- During a visit by Admiral Canaris, head of the Abwehr, to the headquarters of Army Group Centre in Smolensk Hans von Dohnanyi, an Abwehr officer who was accompanying him, discussed details of a possible attempt with Tresckow. On 13 March Hitler visited the headquarters of the army group, but the original plan to shoot him there was dropped, possibly out of consideration for Kluge, the commander of the army group, who was sympathetic to the conspirators and whose life they did not wish to endanger.[10]
- Instead, Tresckow, as described earlier, attempted to bring down the 'Führer's' plane on its flight home by smuggling a bomb on board. This was, however, unsuccessful.
- A good week later, as also mentioned above, during an inspection of captured weaponry in the Zeughaus in Berlin and following the ceremonies marking Heroes' Memorial Day, Colonel Gersdorff attempted to blow himself and Hitler up. This attempt was also unsuccessful.

As the year went on, the conspiracy suffered some damaging setbacks. The Gestapo began to investigate members of the conspiracy and those who knew about it, a group that was becoming ever more numerous and widespread. The Reich Security Head Office (RSHA) uncovered foreign exchange transactions by means of which the Abwehr had enabled a group of Jews to flee to Switzerland and had given them economic support. It now took wide-ranging measures against the Abwehr, finally managing to incorporate it in February 1944 and thereby smashing this group of conspirators. In the autumn of 1943 Tresckow was transferred out of his key position in Army Group Centre. Attempts to persuade front-line generals to support the plan were fruitless. The commander-in-chief of Army Group South, Manstein, although worked on persistently by various members of the resistance, refused to take part in a coup, while Kluge, the commander-in-chief of Army Group Centre, knew Tresckow's views, but although supportive in principle was not able to make up his mind to act.[11]

Some prospect of change began to emerge with the arrival on 1 October 1943 of Colonel Count Claus Schenk von Stauffenberg as chief of staff in the General Army Office under Olbricht. Stauffenberg, who had lost his left eye, right hand, and two fingers on his left hand in the Africa campaign, had developed into an implacable opponent of Hitler and was dynamic enough to become the force that drove the conspiracy forwards. He had a great many contacts among the civilian members of the resistance, including in particular former trade union leaders and Social Democrats, and kept in close touch with von Moltke and the Kreisau Circle.[12] He succeeded in building a network of close associates in the various military areas, whose task it would be to make sure that the Valkyrie instructions issued by operational headquarters were actually followed. There were also operational centres for conspirators in Vienna and Paris, and, in addition to these military liaison individuals, there was a network of designated political agents in the military areas.[13]

Stauffenberg then set about finding a potential assassin among those with access to Hitler. He identified a series of suitable candidates, but although preparations, often concrete preparations, were made to kill Hitler, for a variety of reasons they all came to nothing. The conspirators inevitably began to feel that Hitler had a sixth sense for when he was personally in danger and intuitively avoided critical situations.[14] Opportunities to carry out the assassination suddenly increased, however, when Stauffenberg was appointed chief of staff to the commander of the Reserve Army, which gave him access himself to military briefings with Hitler.

On 6 July Stauffenberg was at the Berghof, attending two briefings with Hitler on forming army units. Stauffenberg had a parcel bomb with him but for unexplained reasons he did not detonate it.[15] On 11 July he again flew to Berchtesgaden and took part in the morning briefing. Again, he had the explosives with him but again did not detonate the bomb, possibly because Himmler was not present.[16] On 15 July he again flew to the morning briefing, this time at headquarters, which had in the meantime been moved back to East Prussia. Once again Stauffenberg was carrying explosives, yet evidently found no opportunity to set the detonator in time. Around midday he telephoned Berlin, presumably to clarify whether he should go ahead with the assassination attempt, even though Himmler was not present. After some deliberation he was advised not to; even if Stauffenberg had still been determined to act, so much time had been lost that the opportunity had passed. That morning in Berlin a number of Valkyrie units had already been alerted; when the attempted assassination was called off they were told this had been an 'exercise'.[17]

Stauffenberg was once again summoned to a briefing on 20 July in the Führer headquarters, where he arrived during the morning.[18] As a visit from Mussolini was planned for the afternoon, the briefing was brought forward and the entire schedule thereafter became rushed. As a result, Stauffenberg and his adjutant Haeften managed to set the detonator for only one of the two bombs they had brought with them and to place it in Stauffenberg's briefcase. It remains a mystery why Stauffenberg did not put the second bomb in his briefcase, even without setting the detonator, for by failing to do so he limited the impact of the explosion.

The briefing in the so-called situation hut had already begun when at about 12.35 Stauffenberg arrived and was announced to Hitler by Keitel. Stauffenberg placed the briefcase under the heavy oak table and after a few minutes made an excuse to leave the hut. At about 12.40 the bomb exploded, throwing the table and Hitler, who at that moment was leaning over it, into the air. He suffered bruising to his right arm and back, grazes to his left hand, and his eardrums were damaged. Of the total of twenty-four people present at the briefing four were so badly injured that they subsequently died, while all the rest were injured to varying degrees.

Stauffenberg had observed the explosion from a safe distance and had come to the conclusion that it must have achieved its aim. He immediately set off with Haeften by car for the airport. En route Haeften threw away the second parcel of explosives, though the driver of the car noticed this. Stauffenberg's hurried departure quickly aroused suspicion; then the discarded parcel of explosives was found. Early in the afternoon steps were taken to have him arrested. At 18.30, after Hitler had received Mussolini at the Wolf's Lair, an official announcement was broadcast on the radio that an attempt had been made on Hitler's life but that, apart from minor cuts and bruises, he had 'suffered no injuries'. He had returned to work 'without delay'.[19]

Given that Hitler had survived, the attempted coup had failed before it got started. The entire plan was built on the assumption that the dictator's death would prompt many officers who were sceptical about the regime but who nevertheless felt bound by their oath to support regime change. In addition, the conspirators in Berlin had no reliable information about the situation and so delayed setting Valkyrie in motion. As a result, Führer headquarters had several hours in which to initiate effective counter-measures.

It was not until Stauffenberg and Haeften were back in Berlin that afternoon and confidently announced that the attempted assassination had succeeded that the Valkyrie order was issued – on the authority of the chief of staff of the Army Office, Mertz von Quirnheim, in the face of resistance from the head of the Reserve Army, General Friedrich Fromm, who was detained by the conspirators as a result.[20] Although the Valkyrie measures were in fact set in motion in Berlin, in several military areas (in particular Kassel, Prague, and Vienna), and in Paris and led to units being alerted and in some cases mobilized, and although a number of radio stations and public buildings were occupied and in Vienna and in Paris some SS members were arrested, Führer headquarters quickly gained the upper hand in the decisive power struggle that now ensued.[21]

In Berlin the tipping point in the attempted putsch came around 19.00, when the Propaganda Minister, Goebbels, organized a telephone call from Hitler to the commander of the guard regiment, Major Remer, which made it clear that Remer's orders (namely that, because Hitler was dead, the army must implement security measures to prevent internal riots) were based on a deception. The guard regiment was now deployed to quash the uprising, a task that it completed by late evening.[22] Now released from his captivity, General Fromm allowed Beck to shoot himself (when Beck only seriously injured himself, Fromm ordered that he be given the coup de grâce). He then had the leaders, Mertz, Olbricht, Stauffenberg, and Haeften, executed in the courtyard of the Bendler block, the headquarters of the conspiracy. Fromm was deeply implicated in the conspirators' preparations and aimed by this means to get rid of those who knew it.[23]

That evening Hitler himself gave an address that went out over all German radio stations. 'A tiny clique of ambitious, ruthless, and at the same time criminal and stupid officers plotted to get rid of me and at the same time to destroy practically the whole leadership of the German army.' Apart from minor injuries, he said, he was 'completely unharmed'. He took the fact that he had survived the assassination attempt 'as confirmation of the task providence has given me to continue pursuing my life's aim, as I have done up to now'.[24] Hitler announced the appointment of Guderian as the new chief of the general staff and during the night of 20/21 July issued a special order to the army containing a sort of declaration of confidence in the troops.[25]

Hitler's injuries subsequently turned out to be much less minor than they had at first appeared. At the beginning of August Goebbels noted he was 'still somewhat unwell and out of sorts', which he put down to the 'serious physical and emotional trauma inflicted by the assassination attempt'. More than a month after the attack his ear was still bleeding and in retrospect Goebbels referred to the 'serious physical shock' Hitler had suffered on 20 July.[26]

43

Total War

The attempted coup played into the hands of those who were advocating a more radical course. On 20 July Hitler had appointed Himmler as commander of the Reserve Army 'in order finally to create order', for this was where the conspirators' hub had been. The same day Bormann was given the task of making 'the necessary arrangements' within the Party 'to bring about commitment to total war'.[1] Thus the path was cleared for the measures so forcefully demanded by Speer and Goebbels to step up the war effort in the state sector.

At a meeting of department heads on 22 July attended by Lammers, Keitel, Bormann, Goebbels, Speer, Funk, and Sauckel, among others, a package of measures to achieve this was put together. Lammers made the now unsurprising suggestion of equipping Goebbels with special powers in the civilian sector and Himmler in the military.[2] As Goebbels recorded in his diary, these decrees, which the group intended to present to Hitler the next day, created something 'tantamount to a home front dictatorship'. At the crucial meeting in the Führer headquarters on 23 July Hitler declared himself basically in agreement. Göring, who as commander of the air force saw the proposals affecting his area of responsibility as evidence of his being ignored, sought a compromise with Hitler by suggesting that the decree Lammers had drawn up should for the time being apply only to the army. After a statistical report from Speer, Hitler spoke on the subject of total war, and, as Goebbels noted smugly, in doing so adopted to a large extent the ideas contained in his memorandum of 18 July 1944. Hitler left the meeting early, while the final version of the 'Führer's decree concerning total war' was being prepared. To maintain Göring's prestige it was stated that the Reich Marshal was to assume the task of 'gearing public life completely to the requirements of total war'. To this end he was to propose to Hitler the appointment of a 'Reich Plenipotentiary for Total War' who would be responsible for 'delivering the maximum resources for the armed forces and armaments production'.[3] That meant Goebbels, although Lammers succeeded in incorporating into the final version a number of exceptions and safeguards that placed significant restrictions on the 'Reich Plenipotentiary's' powers.[4]

A few days later the reorganization of the armaments ministry, which had begun in June, was completed. On 1 August Speer concentrated all the urgent armaments tasks in his ministry in a new armaments staff along the lines of the Fighter Staff, taking charge of it personally with the assistance of Saur.[5]

Meanwhile, the military situation was changing dramatically. At the close of their offensive against Army Group Centre, the Red Army had advanced at the end of July almost to Warsaw. On 1 August it established a bridgehead to the south of the city on the west bank of the Vistula, while further to the north it had already reached the East Prussian border.[6] In the Lemberg [Lviv] area, which had been taken by the Red Army on 22 July, the front of Army Group North Ukraine became destabilized and was able to restore the situation only with great difficulty.[7] On 26 July on the western front the Americans finally launched their offensive and by the beginning of August achieved a crucial breakthrough at Avranches. The German army in Normandy was in danger of being encircled.[8]

At a conference for Reichsleiters and Gauleiters that Bormann had arranged in Posen for 3 and 4 August Speer, Himmler, and Goebbels outlined their plans for using their extended powers to achieve total war.[9] After the conference the Party functionaries went to the Wolf's Lair, where Hitler addressed them. He used the speech to present the failed 20 July plot as the result of years of betrayal and perfidy. These were now over; 'these traitors', this 'powerful clique' had, he said, 'been continuously sabotaging the efforts and struggles of the nation, not just since 1941 but since the National Socialist seizure of power'. Hitler interpreted the events of 20 July as a 'stroke of fate and a personal liberation', for at last it had been possible 'to expose this elusive internal resistance and remove the criminal clique'. 'In the end' it would be 'clear that what at the moment seems a very painful event was perhaps the greatest blessing for the entire future of Germany'. It was, he continued, the precondition for the single-minded 'mobilization of all the resources of our nation'. 'Precisely as a result of 20 July' he had 'acquired a confidence I have never experienced before. We shall therefore ultimately be victorious in this war.'[10]

On 22 July Hitler gave Goebbels the task of 'launching a great wave of rallies throughout Germany'[11] which, according to the guidelines issued, 'should be a spontaneous expression of the nation's determination'[12] that the conspirators be dealt with mercilessly. It is hardly surprising that official reports during the days following emphasized the population's general disapproval of the attempted coup.[13] In addition, Hitler told Goebbels of his determination 'to exterminate root and branch the entire generals' clique opposing us and so demolish the dividing wall that it has artificially erected between the army on the one hand and the Party and nation on the other'.[14]

Hitler had made up his mind to have all those involved in the conspiracy condemned in show trials.[15] In order to remove them from the jurisdiction of the military courts, where they actually belonged, and place them under the People's Court, Hitler summoned a special army court of which General Keitel, General von Runstedt, Colonel General Guderian, and four other generals were members.[16] The court met four times in August and September and proposed to Hitler that a total of fifty-five officers, including those who had been shot or had killed themselves on 20 July, should be expelled from the army and a further twenty-nine be dismissed. Hitler made an exception only in the case of Rommel. After extensive investigations Hitler issued an order for him to commit suicide. In order to avoid connecting the popular field-marshal publicly with the conspiracy he was given a state funeral with full honours.[17]

Leaving nothing to chance, Hitler and Goebbels spelled out in detail in advance what was to happen at the first trial, conducted on 7 and 8 August before the People's Court, involving eight key members of the conspiracy. Hitler insisted that the accused were to have no opportunity to explain their motives; it was to be clearly demonstrated that the conspirators were members of a 'small clique' and 'under no circumstances' should there be a witch-hunt against the officer class itself, against the generals, against the army, or against the nobility', although Hitler would, as he said, 'deal later' with the aristocracy, this 'cancerous growth on the German nation'.[18]

As presided over by the arrogant and enraged Freisler, the first trial turned into a travesty of justice and ended as expected with eight death sentences.[19] The execution was filmed and very probably shown to Hitler.[20] His need for personal revenge is at any rate attested in the case of Helldorff, the former chief of the Berlin police, who was condemned to death in a further trial in mid-August; Hitler ordered that before his execution Helldorff be obliged to witness the hanging of three fellow prisoners.[21] Trials of further members of the conspiracy, in total more than 150 people, were still being heard by the People's Court in April 1945; over a hundred death sentences

Figure 15. In the wake of 20 July 1944 the regime took people into custody across Germany. The French-language translator Irmgard Reinemann and Anita Weber were held from 4 to 18 November in the cellar of the notorious EL-DE House, the headquarters of the Cologne Gestapo. 'Chin up, even if it's hard', noted Weber. In January 1945 Reinemann was sentenced to five years' imprisonment for listening to foreign radio broadcasts, spreading 'enemy propaganda,' and for failing to report a planned act of high treason.
Source: © Rheinisches Bildarchiv Köln

were pronounced and carried out.[22] In addition, after the assassination attempt thousands of actual or presumed opponents of the regime were taken into custody as part of 'Operation Thunderstorm', many of whom remained in custody until the end of the war. A good few of them were murdered without trial.

On 15 August American and French troops landed on the south coast of France.[23] The same day Hitler replaced Field-Marshal von Kluge as commander-in-chief of Army Group West with Field-Marshal Model. Hitler suspected that Kluge, who in any case was under suspicion of having cooperated with the conspirators, was conducting negotiations for surrender with the Allies on his own initiative. Kluge wrote a letter to Hitler justifying in detail his military decisions of the previous weeks and drawing the conclusion that the position of the army in the West and the military situation in the Reich as a whole was hopeless. Adopting a distinctly respectful tone and acknowledging Hitler's 'genius' Kluge asked him now to show his greatness by 'putting an end, should it be necessary, to the hopeless struggle'. The next day Kluge committed suicide.[24]

The new commander-in-chief, Model, was similarly powerless to stop the Allies from encircling much of the German 7th Army at Falaise in Normandy on 21 August and then destroying it.[25] On 25 August Paris was liberated; the city's commandant, General von Choltitz, did not heed Hitler's order to defend it like a fortress and not to let it fall into the enemy's hands until it 'lay in ruins'.[26]

The German army now withdrew rapidly from France, Belgium, and Luxembourg and by mid-September was holding a line that in the north ran along the Meuse and in the south included Alsace and other French territories; in Belgium and Luxembourg the Allies were already at the German border.[27] In late August and early September Hitler was compelled to issue directives for defensive positions on the western border of Germany to be extended, which included the order to prepare the West Wall, built in 1938/39, for defensive action. Field fortifications were to be constructed on the German border by mobilizing a 'national task force' led by the Gauleiters.[28] On 7 September he appointed von Rundstedt to be the new commander-in-chief in the West and gave him command over the 'German western fortifications'.[29]

At the same time, the German position in south-east Europe began to collapse like a house of cards. Early warning of this development was given by the Turkish National Assembly's decision on 2 August to break off diplomatic relations with Germany.[30] The successful Soviet offensive in eastern Romania beginning on 20 August led to rapid political change in the country. On 23 August King Michael of Romania removed Antonescu from power and announced he intended to conclude a cease-fire with the Allies.[31] In view of the immediate threat posed to Romania by the Red Army, on 5 August Antonescu, while at the Wolf's Lair, had asked for more help from Germany. Regretfully, Hitler had been obliged to decline.[32] Now that a German combat group was attempting to occupy Bucharest and the German air force was bombing the city, on 25 August Romania declared war on Germany.[33] On 5 September the Soviet Union declared war on Germany's ally, Bulgaria, which had never actually played an active role in the war. Bulgaria put up no resistance to the invading Soviet troops and declared war on Germany with effect from 8 September.[34] Romania's and Bulgaria's termination of their alliance with Germany and the ensuing collapse of the German front in the Balkans also required German troops (about 300,000 men in all) to beat a swift retreat from Greece. The German troops began to withdraw in September, pursued in October by British forces, who began to occupy the country.[35]

In September Hitler also lost his ally Finland. After initial Finnish–Soviet talks between February and April 1944 on ending the war, which the Germans were aware of but which came to nothing, the Finnish government decided at the beginning of September to accept the Soviet precondition for a cease-fire and call on its former ally, Germany, to withdraw its troops from the country. In the months following, 200,000 German troops retreated to Lapland.[36]

As General Plenipotentiary for Total War, Goebbels had set a target of transferring 1.2 million men from the civilian sector to the front. He intended to fill the resulting gaps in the armaments industry and in vital services with people who had hitherto not been employed at all or were being used in occupations not important to the war effort. The whole of civilian life was to be fundamentally overhauled through widespread shut downs, restrictions, and rationalization to facilitate this transfer of labour. The net result of these efforts, insofar as they can be reconstructed, clearly lagged far behind the targets set, even though Goebbels was constantly announcing successes to Hitler in a positive avalanche of Führer bulletins. In fact, however, the labour that was made available in this way could not simply be put to use immediately in armaments production, while the removal of skilled and experienced armaments workers for military service left gaps in production that were hard to fill. This situation gave rise to conflict between Goebbels and Speer, with Hitler being called on several times to arbitrate, even though he could not resolve the fundamental contradiction between 'more soldiers' and 'more arms'.[37] In addition, it became clear that the Wehrmacht was completely incapable of absorbing and training larger numbers of recruits within a short time.[38]

Even though these restructuring measures were only partially successful, there was another intention underlying the concept of total war. The aim was to gear the entire public sphere to the war in an immense collective effort; people should simply be deprived of any chance to reflect in case they doubted the need to continue the war.

Even in 1944, however, Hitler was still reluctant to approve the most radical measures as a consequence of total war; his view was that pettifogging and unpopular interventions in everyday life and the complete suspension of cultural activities should be avoided so as not to place further burdens on the 'home front'. Thus he objected to music halls and theatres being closed down,[39] to art journals no longer being published,[40] to a ban on the sending of private parcels and telegrams,[41] and to the suggestion that the production of beer and confectionary should be suspended: soldiers on the march were 'dependent on drops' and any ban on beer-brewing would surely result in 'very negative psychological consequences in Bavaria', he suggested.[42]

As in the previous year, Hitler opposed above all attempts to use the situation of 'total war' to introduce aspects of the 'great reform of the Reich' planned for after the war;[43] the complex interlacing and opacity of his power structure were the product of his style of leadership and deliberately created to be an important source of that power. Although Goebbels did finally succeed in dissolving the Prussian Finance Ministry, Hitler, having at first agreed[44] to Goebbels's proposal to get rid of the office of prime minister of Prussia, then opposed it with counterarguments supplied by Lammers and Bormann.[45] He similarly resisted the dissolution of the Reich Economics Ministry and other Reich-level government departments.[46] More extensive changes, such as those put forward by Stuckart, the state secretary in the Interior Ministry, to consolidate the fifty or so ministries and Reich government agencies into about ten ministries and to cut down radically the many 'special commissions' dispensed by Hitler were not taken further.[47]

Whereas the Western Allies had focused their bombing raids since June primarily on the invasion area and the rest of France, in September the intensive bombing of Germany began again. On the one hand, the raids on German hydrogenation plants were continued and, on the other, not only Berlin[48] but towns and cities in the west of Germany came increasingly under air attack. The effects were devastating: On 11 September more than 8,000 people were killed in Darmstadt, on 14/15 October more than 2,000 in Duisburg, between 23 and 25 October over 1,600 in Essen, in the night of 4/5 November more than 2,000 in both Bochum and Solingen, another 2,000 in Freiburg on the night of 27/28 November, and on 4/5 December more than 5,000 in Heilbronn.[49]

On 17 September American and British forces launched Operation 'Market Garden'. The plan was to use combined paratroop and tank attacks across the southern Netherlands to cross the Rhine and directly threaten the Ruhr area. Although the Germans' relatively strong resistance held back this first direct attack on German soil, in the meantime American troops had advanced into the Aachen area and the city had to be partially evacuated.[50]

In the last ten days of September rumours about the possibility of making a separate peace with the Soviet Union, for which Japan offered to act as mediator, prompted Goebbels to send Hitler a memorandum suggesting he should take advantage of the Japanese offer. Goebbels received no response from Hitler; he simply heard from the latter's adjutant, Schaub, that he had read it carefully, though without commenting on its contents.[51] From Hitler's perspective – and he had told his Propaganda Minister this often enough – the preconditions for a peace initiative did not exist because of the military situation. It is, however, altogether possible that he himself was the source of rumours about Japanese attempts at mediation, his aim being to create a political context for his attempt to mount a final big military offensive in the West leading to the break-up of the enemy coalition.[52]

In contrast to Hitler, Horthy, Hungary's regent, was doing his best to arrive at a peace agreement with the Soviet Union. After Romania had changed sides, Soviet and Romanian forces had begun their offensive against Hungary, the Romanians motivated by the prospect of regaining the territories they had lost in 1940. Horthy instigated negotiations in Moscow and in the end gave way to the Soviet Union's insistence on Hungary's declaring war on Germany as a precondition. The Germans were fully aware of these developments and immediately ensured that power in Hungary was transferred to the fascist Arrow Cross party.

First of all, on Hitler's orders Otto Skorzeny, who had freed Mussolini, abducted Horthy's son Nikolaus on 15 October and brought him to Germany in order to prevent Horthy from issuing the declaration of war on Germany. When Horthy reacted by deciding to ask the Soviet Union for a cease-fire, on 16 October Skorzeny's unit occupied the castle at Budapest, Horthy's seat of office, and compelled him to abdicate in favour of Szálasi, leader of the Arrow Cross. Horthy was then also taken to Germany and held captive until the end of the war. The Hungarian army was now fighting on its own soil on the German side under the unpopular Szálasi regime and against the advancing Soviet army. In addition, the Germans were trying to involve the Arrow Cross in their Jewish policy, in order to bind it more closely to them. After Horthy had put a stop to deportations in July there were still 200,000 Jews in Budapest. The Szálasi government agreed to surrender a first contingent of 50,000 Jews, who were marched in brutal fashion in the direction of the Austrian border. In October, however, Germany not only lost Hungary as an ally, but on 10 October Army Group North was definitively cut off in Courland in Latvia, defending its position there until the end of the war.[53] The Allies were now approaching German soil on the eastern as well as the western front.

In the middle of October the Red Army crossed the East Prussian border for the first time, thus posing a direct threat to Hitler's headquarters. Hitler reduced its personnel but banned any references to giving up or evacuating the headquarters.[54] By the beginning of November the Soviet advance had been beaten back.[55]

On 21 October the city of Aachen surrendered after heavy fighting. Although American troops on this section of the front did not at first manage to make significant progress towards penetrating further into Germany, on the southern section of the front they, together with French units, were able to advance to the Upper Rhine at the end of November. In the Saar they had already taken a strip of German territory.[56]

On 8 November, amid celebrations to mark the anniversary of the 1923 putsch, the Wehrmacht reported that V2 rockets were being deployed and had been, according to the communiqué, for several weeks. The bombing of targets in Britain, France, and Belgium had in fact started in September and since the middle of October been concentrated on London and Antwerp. However, the very fact that these new rockets had been in use for some time clearly indicated that they lacked the devastating power to change the course of the war, in spite of all the hopes invested in continuing and escalating 'retaliation'. Although the rockets landed without warning and there was no defence against the V2, the scattered impacts, as in the case of the V1, did not have sufficient force to be truly devastating.[57] Thus the last hope of a miracle weapon of retaliation had been destroyed.

On this occasion Hitler's physical frailty made him decide not to make a speech to mark 9 November.[58] Instead, he had Himmler read out a long-winded proclamation in Munich the following Sunday. Much was said about the 'treason' of former allies, the '20 July criminals' were castigated, and Hitler also stated clearly that he was determined to fight up to the very last: 'as long as I live, Germany will not suffer the same fate as those European states engulfed by Bolshevism'.[59]

Although in the middle of November Hitler was telling those around him that he would not leave East Prussia as the war was in any case lost,[60] he nevertheless left the Wolf's Lair on 20 November in order to undergo a further operation on his vocal chords in Berlin.[61] In the previous few

months he had suffered from 'chronic hoarseness' as the result of a polyp.
But it was not only this handicap that had prevented him from appearing in
public[62] for he was making only a slow recovery from an attack of jaundice
that had developed at the end of September or beginning of October and
greatly weakened him physically.[63] Meanwhile, his absence had given rise to
rumours that he was seriously ill or even already dead.[64]

After a short final private visit to the Goebbelses in Lanke on 3 December,[65]
Hitler moved to his headquarters at Ziegenburg near Bad Nauheim. From
there he intended to lead the military operation that had been intensively
planned during the previous few weeks and which he hoped would bring
about a turn in the war. The Ardennes offensive was designed to inflict a
painful defeat on the Americans, which Hitler hoped would bring about a
rupture in the enemy coalition. On 11 and 12 December he gathered twenty
or thirty generals in order to explain to them in detail the goals of the operation. Hitler's speech of 12 December, which has been largely preserved,[66]
indicates that he was not using this occasion to batter the generals with slogans about endurance; instead, the address was measured in tone, with Hitler
setting the highly risky offensive in the overall context of his war policy, for
which he gave detailed historical justification.

In his lengthy historical introduction, Hitler described his war as the continuation of the Wars of Unification from 1864 to 1871, the aim of which,
now as then, was to bring all Germans together into a unitary state. He then
defended his rearmament and foreign policy since 1933 once again in detail.
The introduction of conscription, the huge rearmament programme, the
remilitarization of the Rhineland, the 'incorporation' of Austria, and the 'sorting out' of Czechoslovakia and Poland had been designed to put 'German
Reich territory into a state in which it could be defended': 'These were the
preconditions for a peace that could be maintained for the future', the process of 'territorial arming' in the light of Germany's 'tiny living space'. He
had of course been aware that these policies were liable to lead to conflict
and war: 'If they led to war then that war had to be put up with. For it was
better to accept it immediately at a moment when we were equipped for it
as never before.' Interestingly, however, he concluded his review of his war
policy at this point and did not repeat yet again the arguments, all too familiar to his audience, that had been crucial to his decision to invade the Soviet
Union and extend the war by declaring war on the USA.

Finally, he explained his decision to go on the offensive again, in spite of
the generally precarious situation. Even if they were on the defensive over

all, they had to try 'from time to time to bring home to the enemy by means of ruthless attacks that they had not gained anything but rather that the war would be continued regardless'. Similarly, the enemy must be made to understand that they 'can never, ever count on capitulation' and will 'never under any circumstances' bring things 'to a successful outcome'. Then, according to Hitler, 'at the end of the day their resolve will finally collapse'. This was particularly true of the enemy coalition, as it was made up of 'such heterogeneous elements with such completely irreconcilable objectives'.

On the morning of 16 December the last great German offensive of the Second World War was launched. Three German armies advanced through the snow-covered Ardennes and attacked the sparsely defended American lines. Poor weather conditions at first prevented the deployment of Allied aircraft and allowed the German spearheads to penetrate up to a hundred kilometres into Belgian territory. They did not, however, achieve their objective of pushing through to Antwerp, the Allies' vital supply port. By the end of December the Americans had already regained the initiative in the Ardennes. Hitler tried to intercept the American counter-offensive by launching a second offensive in northern Alsace (Operation Northwind), but it was quickly evident that this effort was in vain: In January the Americans gradually forced the German troops back to where they had started from.[67]

Thus Hitler's last attempt to regain the military initiative had failed. It was now clear that he would have no further opportunity to regain by military success the scope for action he had always said was a precondition for any initiative to end the war by political means. His adjutant Below reports that in the days following the failure of the Ardennes offensive Hitler for the first time made a completely despairing impression.[68] He had spoken of the war being lost, of being the victim of betrayal, and said it would be best if he killed himself. Yet this report, which cannot be corroborated by other evidence, appears untypical of Hitler during the last months of his life. In fact, up to his last days he communicated to those around him an imperturbable confidence, for he appealed to his (totally unfounded) hope that at the last moment there would be discord in the enemy camp, while at the same time preparing to turn the end of his regime, if its end should really be unavoidable, into a 'heroic' downfall.

44

The End

On 12 January the Red Army, with its huge numerical superiority, launched its winter offensive from its positions on the Vistula; during the previous days Colonel General Guderian, chief of the general staff, had asked in vain for troops to be transferred from the western front. Within three weeks the Soviet forces had succeeded not only in taking most of East Prussia and cutting it off, but in advancing to the River Oder on a broader front. By the beginning of February Soviet troops had captured the eastern part of Silesia with its valuable industry. Further north they had formed a bridgehead near Küstrin [Kostrzyn nad Odra] and were now only about sixty kilometres from the capital.[1]

In view of these developments Hitler had decided to move his head-quarters on 15/16 January from Ziegenberg in Hesse to Berlin. Once there, he ordered the 6th Panzer Army, stationed in the West, to the East, although not to the highly vulnerable front between the Baltic and the Carpathian Mountains, but rather to Hungary, in order to secure the Hungarian oil wells, which in his opinion were now vitally important for the war economy following the destruction of most of the hydrogenation works.[2]

The Red Army's rapid advance towards Berlin made it necessary to set up a new army group as quickly as possible to hold the Oder line in the Berlin area and also defend Pomerania and West Prussia. Hitler appointed Himmler, Reichsführer-SS and Head of the Reserve Army, as its commander-in-chief, with the intention of giving him the opportunity to prove his competence to be commander-in-chief of the army.[3]

Army Group North (renamed Army Group Courland in January) had since October 1944 been cut off in Courland and on Hitler's express orders had to remain in Latvia, forbidden to evacuate by sea or to break out towards East Prussia. Although massively reduced in numbers by continuous Soviet attacks, the army group was not defeated and did not capitulate until May 1945.[4]

Similarly, more than half a million Wehrmacht soldiers were still in 'Fortress Norway', which Hitler, even after the Allied landing in France, meant to defend against any further invasion attempts. Even in March 1945 Hitler was still unwilling to evacuate northern Norway because by doing so he thought the German U-boat positions in the south of the country would come under threat.[5]

From the point of view of the military leadership it was absurd to retain large intact formations on the periphery while there was no operational reserve force left to defend the Reich. Thus, at the beginning of February 1945, Guderian sought an interview with Hitler and as a precondition for launching a counter-offensive in the East he asked for the evacuation of troops from the Balkans, Italy, Norway, and in particular, and not for the first time, from Courland to be accelerated. Hitler's response was a fit of rage, which he repeated when Dönitz supported Guderian's request.[6]

The military could explain Hitler's attitude only on the grounds that he was blind to reality, a dilettante in military matters who could not give up his illusions of victory and who insisted rigidly and fanatically on holding the line, whatever the cost. This assessment has often been repeated in post-war historiography and in analyses of Hitler.[7] In reality, however, his insistence on holding on to distant and exposed territorial bargaining chips and his unwillingness to surrender opportunities to launch offensives, even if they appeared completely unrealistic at that particular point, was an essential part of his political and strategic thinking, although in conflict with the methods of the military leadership. The military leaders were pursuing a defensive strategy based on professional military principles, which amounted to pulling back the fronts gradually to the German border, in the process preventing as far as possible any sizeable formations from being cut off and destroyed. This strategy relied on attrition and delaying tactics, but it could only postpone eventual defeat; defensive action could not be sustained indefinitely, and, at the latest at the stage when enemy troops were at Germany's borders, the next move would have to be a political decision to end the war, as had happened at the end of the First World War. Their training and mentality made the generals regard themselves as military managers of a war whose conditions had been set by the political leadership: politicians determined the objectives as well as the point at which the war would begin and end and they carried the responsibility for it.

For Hitler, however, capitulation was unthinkable. Not for nothing had he been stressing for decades that the German defeat in 1918 had been the result of weakness, treachery, and lack of political leadership and that the war should have continued at all costs, even if the prospects of success were slim, for the sake of the nation's honour and dignity. Thus in 'his' war he put his trust in a strategy of 'all or nothing'. Well-timed counter-offensives would regain the initiative and would bring about a rupture of the 'unnatural' enemy coalition; this would open up the prospect of concluding a separate peace with one or other of the parties, and the war could then continue or be brought to an end (for the time being) under tolerable conditions. For this reason distant territories had to be held and troops kept in reserve in case an offensive war were resumed. The fact that they were not available to defend Germany was for Hitler a matter of secondary importance, as the defensive strategy in any case amounted only to a capitulation in stages. If the opportunity to go on the offensive did not arise or the offensive failed and the enemy coalition did not break up, then the war must not end in capitulation but rather (and this theme acquired increasing prominence) be fought to the point of total destruction.

If defeat was indeed inevitable, then it must not simply be accepted and suffered passively. If it could not be prevented, it must be consciously confronted in a 'heroic' struggle to the last bullet and the last man. A beacon had to be lit, an example that would inspire future generations; in this way total defeat contained within it the potential for a glorious resurgence.

The theme of heroic downfall planting the seed of a later 'glorious rebirth' (as he put it in his testament of 29 April 1945) was one that Hitler returned to throughout his political career. He was eager to adopt a tradition that had begun in Germany in the late eighteenth century with the Romantic rediscovery of the heroic Germanic sagas (which were among Hitler's favourite reading when he was young). At the time of the Wars of Liberation against Napoleon, it can be found in the emotionally charged work of poets who embraced death; it was enacted on stage in Wagner's operas; it was evoked in the enthusiasm for war shown in 1914 and in the Langemarck myth; it was reflected in the determination of many of the military in 1918 to continue the war regardless of losses; it was there in the debate during the Weimar Republic about a future 'total war'. Hitler tapped into this theme in his grim evocation of the 'fallen heroes', the cult of the dead he had deliberately staged for members of the 'movement' who had lost their lives. Hitler had already written in *Mein Kampf* that nations were not necessarily destroyed by losing wars, but rather only if 'military defeat is the fitting outcome of their inner corruption, cowardice, lack of resolve, in short of their unworthiness'.[8]

At the latest since the defeat at Stalingrad Hitler had been pursuing the notion of heroic downfall as a serious political option in the face of the superior power of his enemies. It would ensure Nazism's enduring glory beyond the end of the war and guarantee him a preeminent historic role after his death. By staging his own downfall in this way he could thus give expression to the idea he had entertained throughout his life of being in essence both a hero and an artist of genius whose importance would become fully apparent to posterity only after his death. To the last, however, his increasing tendency to flee from the reality of war and to raise himself and his imminent death to heroic heights did not rule out efforts to avoid defeat by taking robust advantage of any chance, however slim. As so often in his career, his behaviour was ambivalent: on the one hand, he hung on to political and strategic options to continue the war successfully (although even in his own estimation their feasibility was reducing from one day to the next); at the same time, he was working on an exit strategy that would be a kind of heroic *Götterdämmerung* designed to transfigure him. There is an unmistakable dual strategy in the way Hitler responded to the weighty challenges facing him, the result of the calculations and considerations of Adolf Hitler, the *politician*, who never ceased to search for options and alternatives.

At the same time, we clearly see his inability to accept reverses and his tendency to transform the threat of humiliation into megalomaniacal fantasies presaging his own triumph. 'The best person to have at the controls is someone who has not only burnt his bridges in fact but has come to terms with this personally', he announced to Goebbels at the beginning of February. 'Someone who has settled his scores with life tends to win the day.'[9] This idea that he was not engaged in a defensive strategy where the enemy determined his ever-diminishing room for manoeuvre was an expression of Hitler's fundamental need for the greatest possible freedom of action.

After Hitler's living quarters in the Reich Chancellery had been destroyed by an air raid on 3 February he moved into the large air-raid bunker situated under the Chancellery garden, where he had been spending the nights since his arrival in Berlin. At first he could still use his offices in the Chancellery and it was there that the daily military briefings took place.[10]

We know from Goebbels's diaries that since the end of January Hitler had been determined to remain in Berlin and take charge of the city's defence himself, citing as his example Stalin's role in the defence of Moscow in the winter of 1941/42. Eva Braun, his partner, who since November had been living with him in the Reich Chancellery, was also unwilling to leave Berlin, as Hitler told Goebbels, describing her attitude as worthy of 'the greatest respect and admiration'.[11] At the end of January Goebbels had already declared to Hitler that Magda was determined to see things out with him in Berlin and to keep her children with her. Although Hitler could not consider this view 'correct', he regarded it as 'admirable'.[12]

From the beginning of February to the beginning of April, while Hitler's main focus was the military situation in the West,[13] the Red Army was extending the positions it had established in the January offensive. Of the great German counter-offensive that Hitler had announced to Goebbels at the beginning of February nothing remained beyond a limited operation mounted by the Army Group Vistula, whose task in mid-February was to push back from the north the Red Army's wedge towards Berlin. This attack was preceded on 13 February by a noisy altercation during the military briefing, in the course of which Guderian managed to insist, in the face of opposition from an enraged Hitler, that the novice army group commander, Himmler, should be joined by Walther Wenck, an experienced general. This defeat in the presence of the assembled military leadership was for Hitler an unbearable breach of loyalty; Guderian was suspended.[14] As it turned out, even Wenck could do nothing to alter the fact that the army group's attack had to be abandoned after only a few days because of overwhelming Soviet superiority. From 24 February onwards the Red Army launched an offensive across Pomerania towards the Baltic, which it reached on 1 March near Köslin, thereby cutting off the German divisions still positioned in West Prussia and Gdansk. During February the Red Army also conquered Lower Silesia and by the end of the month had reached the River Neisse.[15]

In the meantime things were moving again on the western front. On 9 February the German army surrendered its bridgehead on the left bank at Colmar on the Upper Rhine; the Americans and French were now positioned on the Rhine from the Swiss border northwards to Strasbourg.[16] On 8 February British, Canadian, and American forces began their offensive in the northern part of the western front; by 10 March they had managed to push the German army back across the Rhine between the Dutch border and Koblenz and on 7 March the US First Army captured an intact bridge over the Rhine at Remagen and established a bridgehead on the eastern side of the river.[17] Hitler's response to this sudden advance was to fly into a violent rage and immediately set up a 'flying drumhead court martial', which two days later sentenced five officers alleged to be responsible to death, four of whom were immediately executed. Field-Marshal Albert Kesselring, who on 9 March had been appointed by Hitler to succeed von Rundstedt as commander-in-chief in the West, had the verdict announced to the lower ranks to serve as a warning.[18] By 25 March the German army was forced to pull back to the east bank all its divisions that were still west of the Rhine and yet it was still not able to hold a defensive line. On 22 March the Americans had already crossed the river at Oppenheim and the British followed by crossing at Wesel on 24 March.[19]

At the beginning of March the offensive in Hungary led by SS General Sepp Dietrich began. Hitler's aim was to recapture the Hungarian oilfields, but by the middle of the month progress had been halted.[20] On 16 March the Soviet counter-offensive began in west Hungary, pushing rapidly towards Bratislava and Vienna.[21] Hitler used this deterioration in the German situation as an excuse to dismiss his self-assured chief of the general staff, Guderian, at the end of March.[22]

As Hitler's attempts to put out feelers to the West had been fruitless, he was now concerned to create the impression among those around him that he intended to seek a political solution in the East. Thus at the beginning of March he told Goebbels that he saw negotiations with Stalin as likely to yield greater opportunities to 'continue the struggle with Britain with maximum ferocity'.[23]

Himmler had fallen from favour with Hitler after the defeat of his Army Group Vistula in Pomerania[24] and had retreated to the SS sanatorium in Hohenlychen, claiming to be ill. He was unaware of this change of direction on Hitler's part and, as Goebbels learned when visiting him, was still supporting the view that it would be in the West rather than in the East that 'sooner or later a political opportunity will develop to turn [the war] in our favour'.[25] Goebbels did not inform Himmler that this was no longer Hitler's view; rather, he calmly contemplated the collapse in the standing of the man who, only a few months before, had been the second most powerful in the Reich.

On 11 March Hitler explained his point of view to Goebbels: a separate peace with the Soviet Union would 'not of course fulfil our aims of 1941', but he nevertheless hoped to be in a position to share Poland with Stalin, to bring Hungary and Croatia under German sovereignty, and to gain 'operational freedom in the west'. Even Goebbels, however, was convinced after this conversation that these ideas were completely unrealistic.[26]

On 21 March Hitler, according to Goebbels 'somewhat in despair' about military developments, declared to him that the enemy coalition would 'inevitably break up'; it was simply a case of whether this happened 'before we're finished or only after we're finished'. According to Hitler, the end of the enemy coalition would come 'from Stalin rather than from Churchill or Roosevelt'. Yet the following day, when Goebbels suggested establishing contact with the Soviet Union via Sweden, Hitler's response was negative. Later, in early April, Goebbels discovered the Foreign Ministry had been involved in initiatives in Switzerland, Sweden, and Spain to find out how far the two enemy camps were willing to negotiate, although these moves had not yielded any concrete results.[27]

Although Goebbels's diaries make it clear that he spoke to Göring, Speer, and Himmler (but not to Bormann) about the imminent defeat and the possibilities of averting it by political means, all four were waiting for a decisive signal from Hitler; the option of seeing him as a group, and pressing for an end to the war (in the same way that they had decided in summer 1944 to act in concert to advocate total war) was something that they evidently did not consider. Crucial reasons for not doing so were not only the complete collapse of the system of government into a polycracy, for this made it more difficult for leading representatives of the regime to act together, but also Hitler's unequivocal and openly declared view that he reserved for himself any issue of bringing the war to an end by negotiation and would regard independent initiatives as treason. It is typical of Goebbels's modus operandi that he did not seek solidarity with the other leading players, but instead aimed in these final months of the war to use his personal influence to undermine the positions of Göring, Speer, Himmler, and Bormann with Hitler.[28]

Hitler had little interest in these power struggles. He was moving increasingly towards the option of going out with an almighty bang. On 18 March Speer handed Hitler a memorandum stating that the war was lost. It was 'certain' that in four to eight weeks the German economy would finally collapse. When the enemy advanced into the Reich steps must be taken to prevent the destruction of industry and essential services, and of so many bridges that the transport network would collapse.[29]

Hitler, however, was heading in a completely different direction. On 19 March he issued the so-called Nero Order, which provided for the destruction of all 'military, transport, communications, industrial, and supply installations, as well as any material assets on Reich soil' that might be valuable to the enemy. As far as the civilian sector was concerned, he placed this orgy of destruction in the hands of the Gauleiters as Reich Defence Commissioners – a clear repudiation of the armaments minister.[30] In a personal conversation

Hitler is supposed to have expounded to Speer why it was unnecessary to consider how the German nation would survive in the future: it had shown itself inferior to the 'stronger nation in the east' and the war had left behind only 'those of inferior quality'. We admittedly have only Speer's own notes as evidence for these statements.[31]

In two highly charged discussions at the end of March Speer did, however, succeed in persuading Hitler to issue a further order that mitigated the Nero Order in some vital respects. The focus was no longer on destruction but on a temporary 'paralysing' of infrastructure and industry (which should keep going until the last possible moment). This new order also made Speer responsible for the implementation of all these measures.[32] In the plan for implementation, which he did not show to Hitler, Speer reinstated the instructions he had issued before the Nero Order to preserve industries and vital services.[33] The conflict resulted in an irreparable rupture in the personal relationship between Hitler and his armaments minister.

In proceeding as he did, Speer could be confident that a 'scorched earth' policy inside Reich territory was generally rejected by industry, workers, regional administrations, and also by local Party branches, as it would have jeopardized the very existence of the German nation. Even without Speer's intervention, therefore, it would have been virtually impossible for Hitler to implement a policy of total destruction. The Nero Order makes it clear, however, that contrary to his public and internal declarations, Hitler had to a great extent given up hope of a final turn in the war.

In March he made his last public appearances. Not least because he wished to avoid taking part in that year's 'Heroes' Memorial Day', he set out on 11 March for the River Oder on a 'journey to the front'; the newsreels and press gave extensive reports of his visit to the officers of an army corps and also to various military establishments, while Göring laid the customary wreath at the memorial in Unter den Linden in Berlin.[34] On 20 March, in the garden of the Reich Chancellery, Hitler along with Reich Youth Leader Axmann, received twenty members of the Hitler Youth who had been decorated with the Iron Cross for their service at the front. The surviving newsreels show him moving along the line of boys, his collar turned up, shaking hands and patting heads nervously. These are the last recordings of Hitler on film.

At the end of March Goebbels attempted to persuade him to make another speech; although he reluctantly agreed, it was never made.[35] 'The Führer seems to have a fear of the microphone that I can't understand at all', Goebbels's noted.[36]

On 1 April the Western Allied forces had succeeded in surrounding the Ruhr region along with the remainder of Army Group B. Meanwhile, Montgomery's forces (21st Army Group) drove on towards north Germany, the American 12th Army Group marched westwards towards Leipzig and Dresden, and the 6th Army Group, composed of American and French troops, turned southwards to occupy southern Germany. Prominent German cities – Frankfurt, Aschaffenburg, Kassel, Würzburg – were capitulating almost daily.[37] Even on 7 April Hitler was trying to respond to the situation in the West by a comprehensive 'adjustment of the structure of command in the western theatre of war'.[38]

On 12 April President Roosevelt died. The news seems to have given Hitler hope for a brief moment that the miracle for which he had waited for so long had now come; the President's death would rescue him from a crushing defeat, just as Frederick the Great had been saved from a crushing defeat in 1762 by the demise of Czarina Elisabeth. The news created a mood of euphoria in those around him, and yet after only a short time it became clear that Roosevelt's death would not result in any fundamental change in American policy.[39]

On 15 April Hitler issued instructions in the event of the army's area of operations being split in two as a result of the juncture of the forces of the Western Allies and the Red Army.[40] These instructions reveal that he was still keeping his options open as to whether he would base himself in the south or in the north (in other words in Berchtesgaden or Berlin). If he remained in Berlin, supreme command in the south was to be transferred to Kesselring, and if he moved to Berchtesgaden Dönitz was to take charge of the north.

At the same time as dealing with the army command in the north and south, Hitler issued a proclamation that was to be passed on to the troops on the eastern front at the start of the major Russian assault on Berlin. It appeared in the newspapers on 17 April. Threats combined with calls to hold fast were once again issued to motivate the soldiers to risk their lives. Hitler painted a drastic picture of the consequences of allowing the Russians to advance further: 'Old men and children will be murdered and women and girls will be turned into soldiers' whores. Everyone else will be marched off to Siberia.' On the other hand: 'The Bolsheviks will suffer the fate of the Asians of old, that is they must and will bleed to death at the gates of the capital of the German Reich.' Troops should deal summarily with defeatist superiors: 'Anyone who orders you to retreat, unless you know him well, must be arrested at once and if necessary killed on the spot, whatever his rank may be.'[41]

Meanwhile, the Red Army had been using the time since February to consolidate its position on the River Oder and at the bridgeheads on the western bank of the river, and to prepare for the decisive battle for Berlin.[42] The Soviet major offensive finally began on 16 April.[43] The 1st White Russian front did not, however, manage to destroy the German 9th Army units east of Berlin and quickly occupy the city, as originally planned; instead, after extraordinarily fierce fighting around the Seelow Heights, the German troops were pushed back towards the capital, where they joined with units of the Volkssturm to defend it block by block.

Meanwhile, on 18 April the encircled Army Group B in the Ruhr surrendered with more than 300,000 men to the Americans. Their commanding officer Field-Marshal Model committed suicide. At the same time, British troops were pushing deeper into the northwest German plain, on 15 April liberating the Bergen-Belsen concentration camp, and on 19 April reaching the River Elbe at Lauenburg. American troops swept through central and southern Germany, taking Magdeburg on 18 April, Leipzig on 19 April, and, after several days of fighting, Nuremberg on 20 April.[44]

From his headquarters in Berlin, Hitler followed the varying degrees of commitment with which the Gauleiters approached the final battle for their region. On 12 April he sent a telegram to Gauleiter Hanke, who was holding on in an encircled Breslau, to tell him he had been awarded the highest order of merit; he clearly intended to put Hanke under moral pressure to continue the hopeless defence of the city.[45] On 16 April he sent an encouraging telegram to Gauleiter Karl Holz in Nuremberg, who since the fall of Streicher had been in charge of the Franconian Gau and was now determined to defend the city to the last: 'That fanatical struggle that reminds us of our own struggle for power is now beginning.' Hitler conferred on Holz the Golden Cross of the German Order; four days later Holz died in the rubble of his Gau capital, presumably by suicide.[46]

20 April was Hitler's 56th birthday. This year there were no festivities. At midnight his closest colleagues gathered in the anteroom to his office, where he received their congratulations apathetically. He then withdrew again to his private quarters, leaving them in the afternoon for a short sortie into the garden of the Reich Chancellery, where further well-wishers, among them representatives of the Hitler Youth, the army, and the SS, had assembled. In the late afternoon those leaders of the regime who were still in Berlin also

gathered in the bunker to congratulate Hitler ahead of the military briefing. Among them were Goebbels, Bormann, Göring, Dönitz, Keitel, Jodl, Krebs, Ley, Ribbentrop, and Himmler. After the briefing people were generally keen to get away. Göring, Ley, Rosenberg, Himmler, and the other ministers quickly left Berlin.[47] Hitler charged Dönitz with taking over command of the 'Northern area'.[48] On the evening of 20 April he gave instructions for some of his personal staff to be flown out to Munich/Berchtesgaden and this was done during the next few days.[49]

On 21 April the first Red Army shells landed in the centre of Berlin. Hitler was incredulous to hear that the shelling came not from long-range railway guns but Soviet field artillery, which had already reached the suburb of Marzahn.[50] Without any more precise intelligence about the situation, he now gave orders for the city to be relieved by Army Group Steiner from the north and the 9th and 12th Armies from the south. Yet the idea that these decimated and war-weary remnants of armies, propped up by makeshift improvised units, could hold up the vastly superior Soviet troops quickly proved to be an illusion. When Hitler realized this at the military briefing on 22 April he became immensely agitated, heaped reproaches on his generals, and announced he would remain in Berlin and lead the defence of the city himself. Those around him had the impression that he was having a breakdown and now regarded the situation as hopeless.[51] This impression was reinforced by the fact that Hitler now had his adjutant Schaub destroy those personal papers of his that were in the bunker and the Reich Chancellery and then sent him to Berchtesgaden to do the same.[52]

On this same 22 April Goebbels and his wife and their six children moved into Hitler's bunker, occupying five rooms.[53] Goebbels had announced publicly on several occasions that in the event of defeat he planned to kill himself and his entire family.[54] When at the beginning of March he told Hitler of Magda's intention to remain in Berlin with the children, even if the city should be encircled, it was evident what the consequences of this decision would be. As Goebbels noted in his diary, Hitler had approved it 'after some hesitation'.[55] As in the case of every important decision in the life of the Goebbels family, Hitler's consent had to be sought for this final one. The dictator's substitute family was to go down with him.

On 23 April Goebbels announced that Hitler was in the capital and had assumed command of 'all the forces assembled to defend the city' in order to 'crush the deadly enemy, Bolshevism, wherever it appears'.[56] Hitler was recovering from his depression of the previous day and took part in briefings in the usual manner. In these he seemed not at all ready to give up, once again placing his hopes in the 9th and 12th Armies positioned to the south of the city. He regarded the fact that the enemy had almost encircled Berlin and was already in the outer suburbs as 'the best opportunity for us... to lure him into a trap.... In four days the matter must be decided.'[57]

The same day Speer arrived by plane in Berlin in order to take leave of Hitler. As he described the meeting in his memoirs, he had the sense of talking to 'someone whose life was over'. According to Speer's account, Hitler had been determined to remain in Berlin (which Speer supported) and to end his life there. In this confidential tête-à-tête there was no mention of any final chance of averting defeat.[58]

While Speer was in the bunker (he left the city the same evening) a radio telegram arrived in the afternoon from Göring, who had now reached Berchtesgaden. Göring asked if Hitler agreed that he, Göring, as Hitler's deputy should take over the overall leadership of the Reich 'with complete freedom of action internally and externally'. Göring added that if he should receive no answer by 22.00 he would assume that Hitler had 'lost his freedom of action' and that he, Göring, could therefore act independently as his deputy. In addition, it became known in the bunker that Göring had sent a telegram to Ribbentrop, summoning the foreign minister on the assumption that the plan for Göring to deputize for Hitler would go ahead. Bormann presented this matter to Hitler as Göring being highhanded and delivering an ultimatum, to which Hitler responded by flying into an uncontrollable rage: In his cabled reply he declared his decree of 29 June 1941 concerning his successor to be null and void, dismissed Göring as commander-in-chief of the Luftwaffe, accused him of treason, and ordered his arrest in Berchtesgaden.[59]

During the following days, Hitler attempted from his bunker to gain a clear picture of the progress of the operations of the two armies he had earmarked for the relief of Berlin. He was equally persistent in demanding that in the north of the city General Rudolf Holste and not General Steiner, whom he had in the meantime written off, should lead a corps to break through the Soviet encirclement. His bizarre orders had no effect, however; the troops were in no position to make any impact on the Red Army; instead, the commanders of the 9th and 12th Armies had been trying since 25 April to break out towards the west across the Elbe, so that they could become prisoners of war of the Americans.[60]

On the evening of 26 April Colonel General Ritter von Greim, up until then commander-in-chief of Air Fleet 6, arrived in the Chancellery bunker after an eventful flight along with his pilot Hannah Reitsch and was appointed Göring's successor. Reitsch and Greim only just managed to get their plane out of the embattled city again. Nevertheless, Hitler succeeded during those few short hours in conjuring up an optimistic image of the situation, such that after the meeting the new Luftwaffe commander-in-chief declared to his chief of staff that he felt he had been 'rejuvenated'. This is another episode that indicates that Hitler was capable, at least for limited periods, of overcoming his lethargic and depressed mental state.[61]

In his last recorded briefings Hitler again tried to create the illusion that he could defy the Red Army amid the ruins of Berlin. The hopeful message he was putting out was that a military success would create the opportunity to break up the enemy coalition. 'If I can strike a successful blow here and hold the capital, perhaps the British and Americans may begin to hope that there might still be a chance to stand up to this whole threat alongside Nazi Germany. And I am the only man for this task.'[62] If this could not be done – and this alternative was looming ever larger in his mind – he would, he said, at least have achieved an important victory for his own prestige, avoided 'disgrace and dishonour',[63] and set a marker for the future. This was the idea he now clung to.

On 28 April 1945 even Hitler could not pretend to himself that he would get out of the bunker alive. On this day Soviet forces penetrated the innermost defensive ring surrounding the government district, in places coming within almost 2,000 metres of the bunker, while the inner city was under heavy artillery fire. It was particularly depressing for Hitler to hear via international radio stations that the head of the SS, Himmler, up to that point his most loyal colleague, had set out the terms for a possible capitulation to the Western Allies. Hitler was furious and determined to eject Himmler from all his posts in the Party and the state. It was evidently during this fit of rage that he had Hermann Fegelein, the chief Waffen SS liaison officer in the Führer headquarters and Eva Braun's brother-in-law, shot for defeatism after he quitted the headquarters without leave.[64]

In view of his hopeless situation Hitler's behaviour in the forty-eight hours remaining to him was relatively circumspect and remarkably unheroic. First, he married his partner of many years, Eva Braun, during the night of 28/29 April.[65] He then dictated his political testament, openly acknowledging his responsibility for the murder of the Jews, urging the nation 'to adhere strictly to the laws of race', and dividing his succession between Admiral Dönitz (Reich President) and Goebbels (Reich Chancellor). He settled his personal property in a private testament. He then poisoned his Alsatian, for whom there could be no life in a world without him, spoke by radio during the night of 29/30 April with the remaining members of the OKW to convince himself one last time that his situation was completely hopeless, took comprehensive leave of his colleagues and staff, and finally gave instructions that his body should be burned. On the afternoon of 30 April 1945, while Eva Hitler died next to him of poisoning, he shot himself on the sofa in his office.

Conclusion

The so-called Third Reich capitulated on 8 and 9 May 1945, only a few days after Hitler's suicide. The final outcome of his years in power could hardly have been more devastating: war and genocide had claimed the lives of more than 50 million people, vast swathes of Europe lay in ruins, and the German population's support for this criminal regime now made them appear morally corrupt in the eyes of the world.

It is beyond question that no single individual was responsible for this catastrophic outcome of twelve years of dictatorship. Millions of committed Nazis had worked tirelessly for this regime; a huge army of willing helpers and opportunistic fellow travellers had given it unquestioning support; the elites had been only too glad to put their specialist knowledge and expertise at its disposal; officers and soldiers had carried out their military tasks obediently and with great commitment; the great majority of the German population had followed their 'Führer' devotedly and without protest. And yet these facts on their own are not adequate to explain what happened. There had to be a political figure who knew how to exploit these preconditions and forces, how to integrate them and channel them effectively into a political process designed to realize his own aims and ambitions. At the heart of the Third Reich there was a determined dictator who shaped this process at every level, focused all these energies on himself as an individual, and managed to acquire such extensive powers that he enjoyed unprecedented freedom of action.

The first decades of Hitler's life gave no hint of what was to follow. This book presents him as someone who up to the end of the First World War was simply insignificant, a nobody. Although this part of his life was later presented, first of all by himself, as the period when his 'genius' matured (Nazi propaganda seized on this glorification of Hitler's past and saturated the country with it in numerous forms), nothing in his first thirty years pointed to the formation of a character destined to pursue an exceptional political career. These first three decades are nevertheless revealing within any historical analysis, though for another reason. For in Hitler's early history we can discern (and to some extent explain) a series of personality traits that would be significant in the light of his later actions: his retarded emotional development and inability to form close ties with others; his lack of empathy and of a private self, which he compensated for by constructing a 'public image' fed by grandiose plans and complex fantasies; his intense anxiety about losing control, which expressed itself among other things in his refusal to be tied into structures of any kind; his exaggerated fear of humiliation, which made defeat intolerable and was the reason why he responded to real or supposed threats with excessive aggression to the point of annihilation.

Any sober appraisal of Hitler at the end of the First World War reveals someone who had failed repeatedly and would certainly not have assumed a public role, had it not been for the specific circumstances prevailing in Bavaria in the immediate post-war period. The start of his political career in Munich in 1919 was not therefore marked by his 'resolve' to save the fatherland, a claim he repeated like a mantra. His entry into politics was rather organized by external forces with a particular agenda. Hitler was trained by the army [Reichswehr] unit based in Munich as a propagandist and assigned as such to the German Workers' Party [DAP]. Behind this lay concrete political motives. For far from being no more than the insignificant debating society to which Hitler and Nazi propaganda reduced it in retrospect, in the autumn of 1919 the DAP occupied a key position within a network of army officers, völkisch journalists and newspapers, and extreme right-wing organizations, who were all united in the aim of building up a platform for anti-socialist agitation, above all within the working class, in post-revolutionary Munich. These activities were sponsored and encouraged by conservative forces in the state, in particular after Gustav von Kahr, the new Prime Minister, proclaimed in March 1920 that Bavaria was a 'cell of order'. During the following months, as plentiful evidence shows, influential figures on the extreme Right promoted and directed Hitler, who quickly rose to be the leading propagandist, principal speaker, and policy maker for the party. Even the conservative establishment lent him and the DAP their support.

What is remarkable is that Hitler was not content with the role he had been given. Instead, in the summer of 1921 he took over the leadership of the party with dictatorial powers, used exceptional skill to secure for himself further resources, both material and non-material, from the conservative establishment, and through cooperation with the Reichswehr in particular gained access to the latter's weapons arsenals. At the same time, throughout the various phases of Bavarian post-war politics he constantly alternated between conditional cooperation with those close to the government and radical opposition, always keeping 'his' party's independence in view and exploiting the extremely tense relations between Bavaria and the national [Reich] government. In this way, within a few years he established the NSDAP in Munich and Bavaria as a serious political force. What is more, from the end of 1922 he was growing increasingly in the eyes of his follow-ers as well as in his own into the role of leader ['Führer'] of the whole of the political extreme Right, in particular because the army, the state apparatus, political organizations, the right-wing press, and, increasingly, sections of the affluent commercial middle class gave him continued support. In the autumn of 1923, however, as the entire political Right in Bavaria mobilized for a coup, he was in danger of being instrumentalized by the government and the forces around it. This situation was incompatible with his self-perception as 'Führer'. Hitler feared that his adherents would consider him a failure if he did not follow up his voluble predictions of a coup d'état with real actions, and this was in essence the reason why in November 1923 he staged his own putsch. Viewed as Hitler's attempt to free himself through violent action from his dependence on conservative forces and to assume political leadership himself, the putsch was, however, doomed to fail in the context of the power relations in post-war Bavaria. The forces that had set Hitler up now turned against him when he exceeded his role as an agitator or 'drummer'.

However unequivocal his defeat, Hitler was not prepared to accept it as such. Rather, he recast his woeful failure of November 1923 as a grandiose failure and invented for himself the role of political martyr who had fallen victim to the intrigues of the conservative establishment. For him this was the only way possible to come to terms with his spectacular miscalculation of the actual political situation. And his followers were only too ready to accept this interpretation. For its part, the Bavarian judicial system (in order to avoid revealing the extent of the Bavarian state's collusion with right-wing extremists in the autumn of 1923) benevolently saw to it that, during the trial and the 'honourable' detention that followed it, he could present himself in a heroic light. From his prison cell Hitler complacently observed during this period of political abstinence how the völkisch-national socialist movement fell apart in his absence. He was aware that without a central political figure as leader it was structurally unable to act, and after his 'heroic stand' in the November putsch he was irreplaceable in that role. This failure nevertheless remained a festering wound in Hitler's self-perception. It was the reason why, once in power, he repeatedly tried to shore up his reinterpretation of the events of 8–9 November 1923 by means of bombastic rituals of commemoration.

Even when the Weimar Republic was stabilizing, the expectation of a 'Fuhrer' was built into the structure of the extreme right-wing movement and after his release Hitler was to succeed in fulfilling that expectation. He marginalized competing elements in the Party or brought them under his control, and, within a few years, built up the NSDAP into the most power-ful force in the extreme right-wing camp, even though it had little electoral success. It was not until the Weimar Republic was in political and economic crisis from 1929 onwards that this splinter party turned into a mass move-ment. The fact that the NSDAP under Hitler's leadership had become not only a national and tightly organized party but a 'movement,' in which para-military formations (SA and SS) were combined with special organizations for young people, women, and individual professions and occupations, now paid real dividends. Thus the Party could offer something to a wide range of groups among the discontented masses of the electorate. The wave of support for the NSDAP was prompted not only by the fact that the crisis had led to the impoverishment of large sections of society. Rather, the decline (or the increasing political impotence) of the liberal and conserva-tive milieus – a process that had begun in the mid-1920s – brought the Party large numbers of politically 'homeless' voters who were sceptical about Weimar democracy and therefore willingly accepted the authoritarian ideas of order propounded by the NSDAP, as well as its nationalism, militarism, and anti-Semitism. The various Presidential governments between 1930 and 1933 were an additional factor. On the one hand, they were unable to develop an effective strategy to tackle the crisis and thus gave broad swathes of the population the impression of being left in the lurch. On the other hand, they adopted an attitude to the NSDAP that was by turns distanced and supportive, because they were toying with the idea of using the Party to attract a mass base to support their policies.

Yet all of these factors are insufficient to explain why Hitler succeeded in his second attempt to gain power. He was neither swept into the office of Chancellor by the masses, nor was he simply adopted by President Hindenburg and those around him; 30 January 1933 was possible only because Hitler was very skilful in pursuing a number of strategies to gain power (at times in parallel with each other) and was finally able to combine them: the alliance with the right-wing conservatives (the so-called Harzburg Front); agreements with the Catholic Centre Party; the attempt to use the pressure of the streets to make a solo bid for power; finally, the demand (as leader of the strongest party) to become Chancellor of a government backed by the President. Admittedly, he was successful only because he had contacts in the conservative establishment. In the final years of the Republic they repeatedly made significant concessions to him and in the end, when all viable alternatives seemed to have been exhausted, they agreed on 30 January to a compromise that gave Hitler the scope he needed to 'seize power'. At the same time, he had pulled off the feat of holding together the rapidly expanding and very diverse National Socialist 'movement', within which there was a growing threat of internal conflict. In this he was aided by the 'Führer myth' that had been created around him and acted as an integrating factor. The 'visionary' Führer was relieved of the tiresome need to provide concrete detail about unclear points of the Party programme or to make frequent statements about the political issues of the day. Hitler prevented the creation of a leadership apparatus with clearly defined roles (which would have imposed obligations upon him) and instead preferred a leadership style that focused on individuals. Thus surrounded by an aura of unapproachability and unpredictability, he hovered as the ultimate arbiter above the, at times, warring Party factions and ensured that their disparate aims were, as far as possible, not openly fought over. For Party members, the Führer figure embodied the hope of imminent victory and this expectation could be kept alive over a considerable period of time, even if at the end of 1932 his supporters were showing clear signs of weariness.

By contrast, the 'Führer myth' seems to have played only a limited role in the NSDAP's election victories. Although a relatively coherent National Socialist milieu, in which 'belief in the Führer' was an essential element, did form around the Party, the majority of NSDAP voters probably did not vote for the Party because they saw Hitler as a saviour, the personification of their 'last hope,' but first and foremost because they wanted a way of registering a protest against the Weimar 'system' and hoped the Party, by now the strongest political force in Germany, would bring concrete improvements in the economic and social situation. Accordingly, in the final years of the

Weimar Republic NSDAP election propaganda focused primarily on 'issues', although they were given highly charged demagogic treatment. Hitler as 'Führer' was central to propaganda only in the Presidential elections of 1932 and the November elections of the same year, and both times he was unsuccessful: in the Presidential elections Hitler was the clear loser to Hindenburg and in November 1932 the Party lost 4 per cent of its vote.

Once he had become Chancellor (on the back, significantly, of conservative support), Hitler, unlike in 1923, was able to break out relatively quickly from the 'frame' designed to contain him. He had at his disposal millions of active supporters ready to bring the 'National Socialist revolution' to every part of society. But the fact that by the summer of 1933 the Nazis had neutralized all political opposition and by the summer of 1934 had set up a dictatorship is due in large measure to Hitler's extremely skilful direction of events. For, as circumstances demanded, he mobilized his diverse supporters or pulled them back, and, when necessary, eliminated less biddable sections of his support with brutal force. Once in possession of total power Hitler established a leadership style suited to his political requirements and his personality. Consistently evading any collective and formalized decision-making, he aimed to personalize the political process to an extreme degree, intending to shape it as an active dictator whose power could no longer be legitimately curtailed from any quarter. As 'Führer' who felt responsible for just about everything, he now had the mechanism with which to implement his wide-ranging ideas systematically with the support of his loyal followers.

While in the process of seizing power, Hitler had already intervened in foreign policy and brought foreign affairs relatively quickly under his control. At first his ideas on this subject seemed to conform fully to the policy, which enjoyed popular support, of revising the Versailles Treaty. Between 1933 and 1936 he swept aside the military restrictions imposed by Versailles and through the reincorporation of the Saarland managed to achieve the first of the revisionist territorial demands. Yet as early as 1933 and 1934 his 'revolutionary' attempt to 'coordinate' Germany's neighbour Austria from within showed that he intended to leave behind traditional revisionist policies. In order definitively to move beyond them, he worked from 1936 onwards to create an anti-communist bloc that would include Poland, Italy, several south-eastern European states, Japan, and even Great Britain. Keeping the creation of this bloc in view, during the course of 1937 Hitler increasingly developed a politics of acting from strength.

He accepted the reverses that followed from this, in particular the ultimate failure of his plan for an alliance with Britain, since, as a result, he no longer had to take account of Britain as a potential partner in his foreign policy. At the end of 1937, at any rate, he saw a favourable opportunity to annex Austria and Czechoslovakia the following year, without having to reckon with interventions from France, Britain, or the Soviet Union. After embarking on this course, he set in motion an accelerated process of forcible territorial expansion that culminated, via the annexation of Austria (the Anschluss), the weekend crisis of May 1938, the Munich Agreement, the defeat of Czechoslovakia, and the occupation of Memel, in a war against the western powers. In doing so, Hitler was in no way being swept along by events, but rather he dictated the objectives, the means to be employed, and the pace of events, in the face of serious misgivings among the leadership and the generals. What was crucial was his determination to achieve his foreign policy goals regardless of any conflict with the western powers. Indeed, he was resolved to embark on this, to his mind unavoidable, confrontation sooner rather than later, even though the set of alliances he had aimed to create did not materialize and the foreign agreements and alliances he did achieve turned out to be largely ineffective.

To guarantee support domestically for his decision to go to war he similarly made early and persistent interventions in the most important areas of policy. His overriding aim was to achieve, at any price and against all opposition, an extraordinary level of rearmament, the basis for his high-risk foreign policy, and at the same time to weld the German nation into a 'national community' prepared for war, united, racially homogeneous, and ready to serve. Every important stage in the rearmament process can be traced back in detail to Hitler's decisions. His generally exaggerated and, in view of the strained economic base, seemingly delusional demands sprang from his strategy of constantly demanding too much so that he would extract the maximum effort from the government rearmament team. At the same time, he kept a close eye on the economic distortions and social tensions that inevitably resulted, intervened, and repeatedly took counter-measures in order to ensure that rearmament remained the top priority and that the direction of his policy would meet with acquiescence. This is also the context in which we must view his personal backing for prestige projects such as the motorways and the Volkswagen, which were designed to give a population tired of austerity the prospect of prosperity in the affluent National Socialist society of the future. Convinced since the start of his career of its absolute effectiveness, Hitler reserved for himself the leading role in propaganda both at home and abroad and used it to determine even press headlines and topics for the cinema newsreels. He paid great attention to all fundamental issues concerning the structure of the administration and of public law and the 'constitution' of the Third Reich and was watchful that they were settled in line with his ideas, while in Party matters, although he left routine business to the Reichsleiters, he nevertheless took care to prevent either a powerful deputy or a governing body from emerging. He retained the authority to make final decisions about the structure, the allocation of spheres of responsibility, and appointments to senior positions within the NSDAP; at internal meetings he pledged the Gauleiters and Reichsleiters to his policies, and demonstrated his absolute claim to be 'Führer' at regular mass events (such as the Party Rallies in Nuremberg and the November commemorations in Munich) in a positively ritualized form. As supreme 'master builder' of the Third Reich, he attempted to assert his regime's claim to power through monumental building projects. Styling himself a serious artist and connoisseur of art, he intervened actively in Nazi cultural policy, for example in his 'cultural addresses,' which were heralded as being ground-breaking, and also in his role as a patron.

He also put serious effort into the regime's policy towards the Churches. As far as the Catholic Church was concerned, his aim was to eliminate 'political Catholicism', and although he gave an assurance in 1933 that German Catholicism would be preserved, he did in fact try to back-pedal in the years that followed. As early as 1934 he failed in his project of neutralizing German Protestantism by turning it into a Reich Church with the aid of the German Christians. From then on he wavered between two policies. On the one hand, he instigated campaigns against the Churches on several occasions (1935, 1936, and 1937) with the aim of bringing about a consistent separation of Church and state and marginalizing the Churches, but on the other hand he took a number of initiatives, in the interests of internal unity and rearmament, to establish a modus vivendi with them. When he ceased his attacks on the Churches in the summer of 1937 the second course of action in the end prevailed. Among his entourage, however, he made his fundamentally anti-Christian attitude only too evident, continually emphasizing that the ultimate 'day of reckoning' for the Churches was yet to come. By contrast, his policies with regard to all those – Jews, the 'racially inferior', 'asocials' – who could not belong to the homogeneous 'national community' he was aiming to create were significantly more consistent, although still influenced by tactical considerations. From the beginning Hitler, who since the start of his political career had accorded huge significance to these issues, controlled all fundamental decisions concerning the regime's anti-Semitic policies, gave decisive impetus to 'policy on hereditary illness', which included compulsory sterilization and abortion on 'eugenic' grounds, and in the final months before the outbreak of war personally initiated the so-called 'euthanasia' programme.

His virtually limitless power, the elimination of formal procedures for reaching decisions, and the extreme curtailment of decision-making pro-cesses, also his powerful presence both in foreign policy and in various core areas of domestic politics allowed Hitler – and this is crucial to the way he exercised power – to respond in critical situations to complex issues in an ad hoc and effective manner and one that had far-reaching consequences. In the process he combined technical and political issues in an extremely idiosyn-cratic way, wrong-footed everyone by shifting the emphasis onto new topics, and thus reshaped the political agenda to suit his purposes. Although he had his ideological *idées fixes*, he could nonetheless demonstrate an extraordinary degree of flexibility, which confounded both opponents and colleagues and made him unpredictable even to those who knew him best. His ability to combine domestic and foreign policy effectively became apparent as early as the autumn of 1933: in the midst of the series of large-scale events and propa-ganda campaigns that publicly marked the uniting of the German nation under his leadership he made the surprise decision to leave the League of Nations in spectacular fashion and immediately had this move confirmed by a plebiscite and fresh elections. The overwhelming support was hailed by the regime as the culmination of the process of national unification.

The reality was, of course, different. In the spring of 1934 the economic problems were coming to a head. There was widespread discontent and bitter conflicts broke out over the role of the SA, while a conservative opposition formed around the Vice Chancellor, Franz von Papen. Taken together, all these developments threatened to produce a serious crisis for the regime, one that Hitler 'resolved' by claiming that the real cause of these problems was a broadly based conspiracy, the alleged instigators of which he neutral-ized by a double blow struck at the SA leadership and various figures in the conservative opposition. In addition, he exploited this opportunity to cut the Catholic opposition, apparently regrouping, ruthlessly down to size. The following year he 'sorted out' internal political disputes that were emerging from the, once again, precarious economic situation and also from the continued attacks mounted by the Party mob on Jews, the Churches, and the forces of 'reaction'. He made the surprise move of having the Reichstag pass the Nuremberg Laws during the Party Rally in 1935, thereby using the 'resolution of the Jewish question' as the Nazis' political cure-all to which all other problems were subordinated.

When in 1936 the rapid pace of rearmament was threatened by the acute crisis surrounding the supply of raw materials and foreign exchange, Hitler again intervened decisively by cutting across the boundaries of individual areas of policy. In April he conferred special economic powers on Göring and charged him in the late summer with the implementation of the Four-Year Plan. In doing so Hitler made it clear that the additional finance required was to be raised from the Jewish minority. German intervention in the Spanish Civil War, entrusted to Göring in July of the same year, was not only a strategic decision but was also designed to secure Germany raw materials as a quid pro quo. The appointment of Himmler as Chief of Police in June and the agreement made with him for the police to move to a 'general prevention' strategy, resulting in more punitive measures being taken against 'troublemakers', was designed to further underpin the unpopular rearmament policy. His personal initiative in launching the Volkswagen project shortly after aimed to offer the promise of a prosperous future to offset the anxieties of the present.

Hitler exploited the embarrassing affair involving War Minister Blomberg and army chief Fritsch in February 1938 to carry out a purge of top diplomatic and military personnel securing him much greater power to intervene in foreign policy and the Wehrmacht. And he lost no time in testing out the effectiveness of these powers, not least to transform his loss of prestige following the crisis into a triumphant success. For only a week after the end of the Blomberg–Fritsch crisis he began to put massive pressure on the Austrian government as a prelude to the 'coordination' of Germany's neighbour. When he met with unexpected resistance, within a month he had orchestrated the occupation and the Anschluss, the annexation of Austria. Having thus used a domestic political crisis to initiate the policy of expansion by force that he had announced in November 1937, after only a little more than two months he took advantage of rapidly developing foreign policy tensions to intervene drastically in domestic affairs: He reacted to the week-end crisis of May 1938, which once again he perceived as a serious blow to his prestige, not only by deciding to crush Czechoslovakia in the near future but also by ordering the acceleration of rearmament. The implementation of this decision led very quickly to an unprecedented mobilization of the German economy and society for war. This involved a far-reaching refocusing of the Four-Year Plan on the production of the immediate requirements for war, the conscription of civilian workers, large-scale arrests of the 'work-shy', and the diversion of the resources of the German construction industry to work on the western defensive wall ['West Wall'].

At the height of the Sudeten crisis he was confronted with clear evidence of the limits to his expansionist policies; the anticipated crushing of Czechoslovakia had been frustrated after he was compelled to accept the Munich Agreement. The reluctance of the population to go to war had also become evident. Again he responded by striking a double blow. At the beginning of October 1938 he ordered yet another exorbitant increase in rearmament and only a few weeks later, on 9 November, he instigated the November pogrom. This allegedly spontaneous wave of anti-Semitic violence issuing 'from the people' was to change radically the all too peaceful veneer of the Third Reich. The very next day Hitler announced to the press that there was to be a general shift in propaganda from an emphasis on peace to preparation for war. In addition, he pushed ahead with the plan he had indicated back in 1936 of expropriating Jewish property by legal means as a way of financing arms production.

This series of far-reaching interventions demonstrates the extent to which, by the outbreak of the Second World War, Hitler had succeeded in freeing himself from the original constraints of his Chancellorship and taking control into his own hands – and the supreme confidence with which he had done so. He had established a regime in which he enjoyed virtually unrestricted freedom of action. The many deliberate and often brutal interventions also indicate, however, that Hitler's position of power was not primarily rooted in consent based on charisma. Admittedly, his 'successes' in the years after 1933 were in time acknowledged beyond his core support by the majority of the population: among these were the elimination of the political Left, the replacement of a weak democratic system with a dictatorship, the regaining of 'military sovereignty' and the gradual revision of the Treaty of Versailles, national unity as paraded by the regime under the banner of the 'national community' or the bombastic displays of renewed national confidence. It is also evident that, once in power, Hitler's regime had considerable success in galvanizing the population. Thus new energy and dynamism were released, not only by the development of the Party and state apparatus, the reestablishment of the army, and the armaments boom, but the Hitler Youth also offered the young new scope for activity; the key concepts of 'race' and 'nation' seemed to open up breathtaking new perspectives for young intellectuals in the cultural and academic spheres; committed careerists sniffed the chance to make their way regardless of traditional class barriers and social prejudice.

All these factors played their part in strengthening the dictatorship and Hitler's standing. But it would be wrong to assume that his position rested on the identity of 'Führer' and nation. For it must be remembered that Hitler failed to achieve his key domestic policy goal, namely to weld the Germans together into a united 'national community' conscious of its 'racial identity', one that would willingly make any sacrifice in order to form a united 'defence community' to take up the fight for 'living space' that, as the regime propounded, would ensure the future security of the nation. The immense pressures put on German society by the rapid pace of rearmament showed it even then to be distinctly disunited and disinclined to bear stoically the material deprivations expected of it. People's sense of belonging to particular social classes, groups, and milieus endured. Among large swathes of the population a well-developed awareness of their social status, as well as of conflicting social and economic interests, was undiminished, even if under the conditions of a dictatorship people in the main limited themselves to expressions of general dissatisfaction and annoyance. Confessional loyalties proved similarly stable and as a result Hitler did not succeed in his efforts to marginalize the Churches completely. Although the exclusion and persecution of the Jews, the central pillar of his 'racial policy', gave rise to mixed responses, it would be incorrect to claim that these were enthusiastically supported by the majority of the population. National enthusiasm for Hitler's foreign policy successes was in the end always overshadowed by the fear of war that his high-risk policies provoked. When in September 1938 he took Germany to the brink of armed conflict the population demonstrated a pronounced unwillingness to go to war.

In practice, therefore, Hitler's position was based not on charisma, whatever the regime liked to claim, but on the powers available within a dictatorship: control of the public sphere, which prevented the formation of any views outside the limits prescribed by the regime; a well-organized system of repression that spread an atmosphere of terror, combined with surveillance conducted locally by 'national comrades' through the omnipresent apparatus of the NSDAP and its affiliated organizations. By consistent use of these instruments Hitler as dictator secured himself maximum freedom of action. The conditions of war only intensified this state of affairs.

The Second World War was Hitler's war: he not only determined the individual moves extending the war, but he conducted it as a racially motivated war of extermination with the aim of establishing an empire built on the criteria of 'race' and 'space'. These key ideas determined his actions from the outset. Immediately after the outbreak of war he initiated a radical racial policy: he made the key decisions to subject Poland to a brutal policy of Germanization; it was his initiative to make a first attempt to deport the Jews from the 'Greater Germanic Reich' to a death zone in Poland; on Reich soil he instigated the systematic murder of patients in mental institutions, which by the summer of 1941 would claim 70,000 lives.

Hitler's determination to take the war to the western powers dictated his next moves to extend it: the invasion of Scandinavia, the war in western Europe, the unsuccessful attempt to construct an anti-British continental bloc and thus to neutralize the British Empire's power in the Mediterranean (Britain being unwilling to accept his conquests). They also included the war against Yugoslavia and Greece, which, in the wake of the failed campaign against Greece mounted by Germany's ally Italy, was designed to frustrate British attempts to establish a foothold in the Balkans.

From the summer of 1940 onwards he had also been pursuing a plan to attack the Soviet Union, motivated initially by the thought of depriving Britain of her last potential ally on the continent. During the preparations for Operation Barbarossa, however, he broadened his perspective and ensured that this war was conducted as a campaign of racial extermination to conquer 'living space'. He was now determined to turn the ideological goals he had been pursuing since the 1920s into reality. In the absence of institutions at the top of the regime to provide safeguards and counterbalancing powers, his far-reaching war plans inevitably led to hubris, not least because of his notorious overestimation of his own abilities. Thus as early as the spring of 1941 Hitler was making large-scale plans for the time after the anticipated rapid victory over the Soviet Union: he aimed to expand the Mediterranean strategy that had failed during the previous year and swiftly establish an unassailable position stretching from strategic bases on the west coast of Africa and the Atlantic islands via the south coast of the Mediterranean as far as Egypt and the Arabian Peninsula as well as to Transcaucasia and Afghanistan. He thus developed a vision of a blockade-proof empire that would extend over three continents and would be capable of defying not only Britain but any conceivable intervention by the United States.

Yet he was unable to achieve the crucial precondition for all this, namely rapid victory over the Soviet Union, while the United States' growing support for Britain indicated it would soon enter the war. Hitler responded in the summer and autumn of 1941 to the prospect of a war on two fronts by further radicalizing and intensifying the ideological element in his conduct of the war, which he now geared up to be a comprehensive 'war against the Jews'. This imaginary opponent, who was presumed to be behind the emerging enemy coalition, was to be utterly annihilated. Not only did he support Himmler's actions in extending the mass shootings of Jewish civilians in the Soviet Union to an out-and-out genocide, but he gave orders that the Jews in Germany and other European countries under German control should be deported to the East – a move that in his distorted, anti-Semitic vision of the world was 'retribution' for the threatened entry of the United States (which he claimed was controlled by 'the Jews') into the war. At the same time, in December 1941 he considered himself secure enough to declare war on the United States in the wake of the Japanese attack on Pearl Harbour, even though the German advance was grinding to a halt before Moscow in the winter of 1941. Hitler's calculation was that America would be diverted from Europe by an extended war in Asia, in particular because his declaration of war on the United States was linked to his agreement with Japan that they would wage war together to the end. Thus his plans to create an empire on three continents did still appear realizable, provided that the Wehrmacht succeeded in 1942 in delivering a crippling blow to the Soviet Union through its summer offensive on the southern sector of the front. In the spring and summer of 1942 his hubris appeared to be turning into reality.

By his own decree Hitler's empire was to be based on the ruthless plundering and exploitation of the human and economic resources of the occupied territories and on the brutal suppression of their populations. Jews had already been excluded. He himself established the different kinds of treatment meted out to the occupied territories in accordance with the racial 'value' of their inhabitants, by determining the structure, personnel, and political guidelines for the individual occupation regimes and repeatedly intervening in and adjusting the occupation policies for particular countries. It was Hitler who made the basic decisions regarding the colonization of conquered territory by German and 'Germanic' settlers and the expulsion of the native inhabitants, and it was he too who, in the spring and early summer of 1942, made the decisions intended to bring about the murder of all European Jews while the war was still in progress. On top of this, Hitler wanted to retain absolute freedom of action and thus flatly refused to give any assurances to the occupied and allied countries about their future position within the vague concept of a 'New Europe'. Even at this point his guiding principle remained to prevent the emergence of any structures he had not created himself or had total control over.

In the spring of 1942, when he thought he was on the point of realizing his dreams of an empire, he immediately set about eliminating the final remnants of the rule of law in Germany by abolishing the independence of the judiciary and securing a Reichstag resolution empowering him to suspend the laws governing the civil service in individual cases – measures intended to give symbolic expression to the 'Führer's' autocracy. And since the outbreak of war he had in fact managed to extend his powers even further: Carefully avoiding, even under the conditions of war, any form of collective decision-making, he ruled primarily by means of Führer decrees, aided by the various chancelleries, all vying with each other, as well as by direct instructions issued to a limited circle of intimates, who held the most important offices within the power structure. By means of these instruments Hitler monitored and directed not only the military conduct of the war, foreign and occupation policy, and the Europe-wide mass murder of the Jews, but also important areas of the war effort as it affected civilians, for example the provision of food; he continued to give the instructions for armaments production, reserved for himself the right to make any significant change to administrative structures in Germany, and set the parameters for the regime's propaganda.

In the course of the war, the population of his own country had also to be subjected to stricter discipline and the 'mood' more tightly controlled; sceptical voices were for the most part reduced to silence. At first Hitler carried on interacting with 'the people' in the way he had developed before the war, by repeatedly using his appearances at high-profile occasions to address topics of widespread interest and concern. Thus he knew how to combine his triumphs over Poland and France with the impression that in each case he was now looking for a way to bring armed hostilities to a rapid close. As early as October 1941 he made fulsome declarations that the war against the Soviet Union, which had created great anxiety in its first months, was won. When the promised victory refused to materialize, in the autumn of 1941 he banned the question of how long the war would last from public discussion and gave unmistakable signals that the war must not be lost, if only because the 'extermination' of the Jews, announced so many times, was now really happening and that as a result the regime and the nation had burnt their bridges. But from the winter of 1941/42 onwards, with the first telling reverses and defeats, he withdrew increasingly from the public eye and thereby gradually surrendered the charismatic façade to his power. Facing up to failures and defeats and taking responsibility for them fundamentally conflicted with his self-perception as a triumphal leader; his personality made it impossible. In the event, the regime, albeit with some difficulty, was able to create an appearance of the population's permanent 'consent' to its policies, even without the actual presence of the 'Führer'.

By the end of 1942, with the catastrophic defeat at Stalingrad and the Western Allies' successful offensive in North Africa, Hitler's plan to create an empire had finally failed. But contrary to what leading members of his regime were asking of him, Hitler responded to the turn in the war neither by demanding an unconditional 'totalizing' of the German war effort nor by making concessions to the occupied countries or political promises to his allies. Instead he advocated increasing repression and exploitation in the lands he controlled. His form of 'total war' focused on stepping up the persecution of the Jews more intensively and making it even more widespread and blatant; the extermination of this 'world enemy', a product of his own imagination, acquired top priority for both ideological as well as tactical reasons. Knowing about the persecution and being complicit in it were designed to sustain the German population's commitment to the war and also guarantee the loyalty of Germany's allies. He now put Hungary, Italy, Romania, and Bulgaria in particular under pressure to deliver up their Jews, with varying degrees of success.

At the same time, he placed his faith, above all, in Germany's ability on the eastern front to hold securely any positions they had captured. His motive was not simply to delay a defeat that, given the relative strengths of both sides, was now inevitable. He was rather pursuing the idea with which he was now obsessed, namely that he could regain the military initiative, if the moment was right, by defending particular areas. Thus he again responded to the loss of his main ally, Italy, with an offensive, occupying northern and central Italy and also the Italian zones of occupation in France and in the Balkans, in order to bring further territory under his control. When he suspected disloyalty among the Hungarian leadership, the country was immediately occupied. Faced with the threat of an Allied landing in western Europe, since the winter of 1943/44 Hitler had clung obsessively to the idea that, if he could successfully repel an 'invasion', a second landing by the Allies would be ruled out for a lengthy period. He would then be able to move a large number of troops from the West to the East. Thus he was still hoping to win a military victory in the East or at least to achieve a draw with Stalin. In response to the increasingly catastrophic effects of escalating air raids on Germany, he fostered the illusion that he could use new kinds of weapon systems to inflict such massive 'retaliation' that the enemy would be compelled to abandon its air offensive. To the last he went on believing that, by keeping opportunities for offensives open, he could drive a wedge between the enemy Allies and thus still manage to end the war by political means under tolerable conditions. He held on to this illusion up to his last days in the Berlin bunker.

By then Hitler's regime had long since been in ruins. Incapable of admitting his monumental failure, Hitler tried to cling to the notion of a heroic downfall, evidently linking it with the hope of salvaging the core elements of the National Socialist 'project' for the future. Meanwhile, the German Reich had already largely been captured by the Allies and Soviet troops had almost reached the Reich Chancellery. The 'Third Reich' could not actually collapse, however, until the dictator who had held it together finally took his own life.

Figure 16. After the defeat: The Allies conduct Germans round Wöbbelin camp, a subcamp of Neuengamme concentration camp.
Source: © CORBIS/Corbis via Getty Images

Notes

INTRODUCTION

1. Martin Broszat and Klaus Schwabe (eds), *Die deutschen Eliten und der Weg in den Zweiten Weltkrieg* (Munich, 1989), 25–71 (66).
2. On this line of argument see, among others, Eberhard Jäckel, *Hitlers Weltanschauung. Entwurf einer Herrschaft* (Stuttgart, 1991); Andreas Hillgruber, *Hitlers Strategie. Politik und Kriegführung 1940/1941* (Frankfurt a. M., 1965); Jäckel, 'Die "Endlösung" und das deutsche Ostimperium als Kernstück des rassenideologischen Programms des Nationalsozialismus', in Wolfgang Wippermann (ed.), *Kontroversen um Hitler* (Frankfurt a. M., 1986), 219–47.
3. Alan Bullock, *Hitler. A Study in Tyranny* (Harmondsworth, 1962).
4. Ian Kershaw, *Hitler,* 2 vols (Stuttgart, 1998/2000).
5. Hans Mommsen, 'Nationalsozialismus' in *Sowjetsystem und demokratische Gesellschaft. Eine vergleichende Enzyklopädie* vol. 4 (Freiburg, 1971), 702.
6. Joachim Fest's biography, *Hitler* (London, 1974), which was praised above all for its brilliant style and its author's intellectual range, now appears outdated in the questions it poses, its emphases, and its sources.
7. The focus on Hitler's 'private side' is one of the main concerns of Volker Ullrich's biography *Hitler,* the first volume of which, *Die Jahre des Aufstiegs. Biographie* (Frankfurt a. M.) appeared in 2013.

PROLOGUE: A NOBODY

1. There are two extensive collections of documents on Hitler's childhood and youth: BAB (Bundesarchiv Berlin), NS 26/65, collected by the Hauptarchiv der NSDAP, and LHA (Landeshauptarchiv) Linz, NL Jetzinger. The Social Democrat Jetzinger wrote the first important book about this period in Hitler's life. As a member of the Upper Austrian provincial government, he acquired Hitler's army file, which he managed to conceal until the end of the Second World War. See Brigitte Hamann, *Hitlers Wien. Lehrjahre eines Diktators* (Munich, 1996), 81ff. See also Wolfgang Zdral, *Die Hitlers. Die unbekannte Familie des Führers* (Bergisch Gladbach, 2008); Hamann, *Wien*; Kershaw, *Hitler* 1, 29ff.; Sidney J. Jones, *Hitlers Weg begann in Wien, 1907–1913* (Munich, 1999); Dirk Bavendamm, *Der junge Hitler. Korrekturen einer Biographie 1899–1914* (Graz, 2009), although the 'corrections' are

largely speculative; Bradley F. Smith, *Adolf Hitler. His Family, Childhood, and Youth* (Stanford, 1967).

2. Margot Schindler, *Wegmüssen. Die Entsiedlung des Raumes Döllersheim (Niederösterreich) 1938–1942. Volkskundliche Aspekte*, (Vienna, 1988) esp. 253ff. It concerns the military training area Döllersheim, today Allentsteig.

3. Franz Jetzinger, *Hitlers Jugend, Phantasie, Lügen – und die Wahrheit* (Vienna, 1956), 21ff.

4. See in detail: Hamann, *Wien*, 69ff.

5. On the suspicion about his Jewish descent see Jetzinger, *Jugend*, 28ff. The assertion is based on the memoirs of Hans Frank written while in prison in Poland after 1945. See Hans Frank, *Im Angesicht des Galgens, Deutung Hitlers und seiner Zeit auf Grund eigener Erlebnisse und Erkenntnisse. Geschrieben im Nürnberger Justizgefängnis* (Munich-Gräfelfing, 1953), 330f., but there is no evidence for it. See Hamann, *Wien*, pp. 73ff.; Kershaw, *Hitler* 1, 35f. See Jean Paul Mulders, *Auf der Suche nach Hitlers Sohn. Eine Beweisaufnahme* (Munich, 2009), on a DNA analysis carried out a few years ago confirming Hitler's descent from the Hiedler family.

6. On his career see Jetzinger, *Jugend*, 45ff.

7. Ibid., 48.

8. Ibid., 58ff.

9. Ibid., 69.

10. On Alois Hitler Jr see Zdral, *Hitlers*, 129ff.

11. Jetzinger, *Jugend*, 57.

12. *Linzer Tagespost (LT)*, 8 January 1903.

13. BAB, NS 26/17a, report by a member of the NSDAP-Hauptarchiv's staff of 21 June 1940 concerning an interview with senior Customs Inspector Hebenstreit in Braunau, and a report by the Hauptarchiv about an interview with Frau Rosalia Hörl, born 9 June 1862, in Braunau. On 18 September 1933, the *Wiener Sonn- und Montagszeitung* published the results of research carried out by a British journalist in Leonding, according to which a former classmate of Hitler's, Max Sixtl, reported that Alois had been very strict towards Adolf and his son had been afraid of him. According to Jetzinger, reporting after 1953, Hitler's guardian, Mayrhofer, had told him that, although Alois had not beaten Adolf, he had scolded and reprimanded him. Alois had had no use for religion, he said. See Jetzinger, *Jugend*, 69f.

14. The 'Freie Schule' (Free School) association was established in Vienna in 1905 and was largely supported by Liberals. The reference to the Freie Schule in the *Linzer Tagespost* can be regarded as evidence for these efforts, which were already under way. See Helmut Engelbrecht, *Geschichte des österreichischen Bildungswesens. Erziehung und Unterricht auf dem Boden Österreichs*, vol. 4, (Vienna, 1986), 128.

15. *LT*, 8 January 1903.

16. *Wiener Sonn- und Montagszeitung*, 18 September 1933; see Hamann, *Wien*, 22.

17. Because of the limited information about Hitler's childhood, psychoanalytical literature on this topic is highly speculative and reaches very different conclusions. Here are just some examples: Edleff H. Schwaab, *Hitler's Mind. A Plunge*

into Madness (New York and Westport, CT, 1992) claims that Hitler suffered from paranoia as a result of a traumatic childhood; Helmut Stierlin, *Adolf Hitler. Familienperspektiven* (Frankfurt. a. M., 1975), argues his mother subjected him to excessive and unrealizable expectations; Alice Miller, *Am Anfang war Erziehung* (Frankfurt a. M., 1980) blames the development in Hitler of a destructive personality on the extremely brutal educational methods of his father. Other authors do not see the reasons for Hitler's abnormal development as lying in his childhood. Thus, for example, Gerhard Vinnai, *Hitler – Scheitern und Vernichtungswut. Zur Genese des faschistischen Täters* (Giessen, 2004) blames a serious trauma caused by war service, while others focus, highly speculatively, on Hitler's alleged psychiatric treatment in the Pasewalk hospital (see footnote 213). We shall not explore any further the serious pathological disorders attributed to Hitler in the literature. However, Paul Matussek, Peter Matussek, and Jan Marbach, *Hitler – Karriere eines Wahns* (Munich, 2000), put forward a thesis that is not only plausible in the light of Hitler's family background, but also conforms with Hitler's behaviour in various periods of his life. It claims that Hitler's personality was characterized by a narcissistic fixation on his public self, combined with a repression of his private feelings, which resulted in his finding any public shame or exposure intolerable.

18. On his time in primary school see Jetzinger, *Jugend*, 88ff.
19. Adolf Hitler, *Mein Kampf* (286–290 edn) (Munich, 1938) (*MK*), 5ff.
20. LHA Linz, NL Jetzinger, No. 44, letter from Huemer, 12 December 1923, referred to as a statement in Hitler's defence in Jetzinger, *Jugend*, 100ff., quote 105. On his time in the Realschule see also pp. 96ff.
21. Elke Fröhlich and others (eds), *Die Tagebücher von Joseph Goebbels*, 2 parts, 9 and 15 vols (Munich, 1993–2006) (*Goebbels TB*), 3 June 1938; Werner Jochmann (ed.), *Adolf Hitler, Monologe, im Führerhauptquartier 1941–1944. Die Aufzeichnungen Heinrich Heims* (Hamburg, 1980) (8/9 January 1942).
22. Jetzinger, *Jugend*, 103.
23. On the illness see Hamann, *Hitlers Edeljude. Das Leben des Armenarztes Eduard Bloch* (Munich, 2008), 33. See also *MK*, 16; Jetzinger, *Jugend*, 148ff.; Hamann, *Wien*, 33; August Kubizek, *Adolf Hitler. Mein Jugendfreund* (Graz, 1995), 62.
24. *Österreichisches statistisches Handbuch*, 1900, 9: 58 778 (1900 Census) and 1910, 6: 67 859 (1910 Census).
25. Kurt Tweraser, 'Das politische Parteiensystem im Linzer Gemeinderat', in Fritz Mayhofer and Walter Schuster (eds), *Linz im 20. Jahrhundert*, vol. 1 (Linz, 2010), esp. 94–133; Kurt Tweraser, 'Dr. Carl Beuerle – Schönerers Apostel in Linz' in *Historisches Jahrbuch der Stadt Linz* (1989), 67–84; Evan Burr Bukey, *'Patenstadt des Führers'. Eine Politik- und Sozialgeschichte von Linz 1908–1945* (Frankfurt a. M./New York, 1993); Harry Slapnicka, *Oberösterreich unter Kaiser Franz Joseph (1861 bis 1918)* (Linz, 1982).
26. *Wiener Sonn- und Montagszeitung*, 18 September 1933; see Hamann, *Wien*, 22ff.
27. On the relatively complicated history of the various German nationalist organizations in the Habsburg Monarchy see in particular Lothar Höbelt, *Kornblume*

und Kaiseradler Die deutschfreiheitlichen Parteien Altösterreichs 1882–1918 (Vienna and Munich, 1993).

28. *Goebbels TB*, 27 April 1944. Although Hitler does not give the title, the evidence is clear. Hitler was complaining about the closure of the paper, which did in fact occur in January 1944. On the other hand, assertions that Hitler read extreme right-wing papers during this period are based on speculation. André Banuls, 'Das völkische Blatt "Der Scherer". Ein Beitrag zu Hitlers Schulzeit' in *Vierteljahrshefte für Zeitgeschichte* (*VfZ*) 18 (1970), 196–203, refers to an anti-Semitic satirical paper that appeared in Linz without, however, providing any evidence that Hitler actually read it. Hamann, *Wien*, 37, refers to the *Linzer fliegenden Blätter*, a strongly anti-Semitic 'Little Völkisch Satirical Magazine', as its subtitle put it. But the editor only made the claim that Hitler had read it in 1938 (BAB, NS 26/17a, Notizen für die Kartei, 8 December 1938).

29. Helga Embacher, 'Von Liberal zu National: Das Linzer Vereinswesen 1848–1918', in *Historisches Jahrbuch der Stadt Linz* (1991), esp. 79ff.

30. According to a spokesman for the Turnverein Linz. See *LT*, 16 March 1904.

31. See the *LT*, e.g. 26 June 1903, on the summer solstice of the Deutsche Bund für Oberösterreich, which was praised by the keynote speaker as a truly Germanic festival; 26 June 1904, on the summer solstices of various associations according to old German custom; the issue of 20 June 1905 refers to the vigorous awakening of the German national idea and German national consciousness in our German people of the Eastern Marches during recent years.

32. *LT*, 19 December 1905.

33. In 1900 the Verein Südmark held its general meeting in Linz. See Embacher, *Vereinswesen*, 98; in July 1902 the Austrian gymnasts held the VIIIth German-Austrian Gymnasts' Festival in Linz. See *LT*, 18–23 July 1902. In 1905 the Deutsche Schulverein held its 25th anniversary in the national colours of black, red, and gold in Linz; ibid., 9 June 1905. On the festival committee's announcement see numerous other articles during May and June. In May 1905 the centenary of Friedrich Schiller's death was commemorated in the Oberrealschule, which Hitler had left the previous year. His former history teacher, Poetsch, gave the ceremonial address on the topic 'Schiller – Role Model for and Educator of his Nation', in ibid., 6 April 1905, 9–11 May 1905; on the speech see the report of 10 May. In October a monument to Turnvater Jahn was erected in the same spirit. See ibid., 3 October 1905.

34. Slapnicka, *Oberösterreich*, 41; Hamann, *Wien*, 29ff.

35. *Österreichisches Statistisches Handbuch*, 1903, 14: 3535, and 1911, 13: 1953. They contain the census results for 1900 and 1910. See also Slapnicka, *Oberösterreich*, 42.

36. Slapnicka, 'Linz, Oberösterreich und die "Tschechische Frage"', in *Historisches Jahrbuch der Stadt Linz* (1977), 226.

37. *LT*, 10 December 1905, 'Tschechische Anmassungen in Linz' about a quarrel in an inn. See ibid., 23 December 1905, 'Unglaubliche Frechheit' about letters sent by the Bohemian Industrial Bank in Brünn to German businessmen 'addressed entirely in Czech'.

38. Described in detail in Slapnicka, *Oberösterreich*, 41ff.

39. *LT*, 17 and 18 March 1904.

40. Andrew G. Whiteside, *Socialism of Fools. Georg Ritter von Schönerer and Austrian Pan-Germanism* (Berkeley, Calif. and Los Angeles, 1975).

41. Embacher, *Vereinswesen*, 77ff.

42. Tweraser, *Beuerle*, 79.

43. *MK*, 54f.

44. Eleonore Kandl, Hitlers Österreichbild (Ms. Vienna, 1963), Appendix, has collected various statements from interviews with former classmates of Hitler. Three of the eight interviewed could remember an informal 'Jewish boycott' in the senior classes, which also had an impact lower down the school (Dietscher, XI, Stockhammer, XLII, Müller, XX), while one of the interviewees maintained that Jewish pupils had not been treated differently (Estermann, XXXI). However, overall it is clear that the pupils were much more hostile to the clergy and to Slavs (Keplinger, XXIV, Estermann, XXX). By contrast, Kubizek, *Hitler*, 94, gives more weight to anti-Semitism in the Realschule. Brian McGuiness, *Wittgensteins frühe Jahre* (Frankfurt a. M., 1988), 97, cites a note by Wittgenstein, which he made on joining the school in 1903: 'Realschule class. First impression: "Rubbish". Attitude to Jews'. There is no evidence for any contact between Hitler and Wittgenstein, who was in a more senior class.

45. RSA 3/2, Doc. 35. In Hitler, *Monologe*, 21 September 1941, he mentions similar quarrels with Czech fellow pupils in the Realschule in Steyr.

46. Kandl, *Österreichbild*, 25ff (on Poetsch) and 39ff. (on Huemer).

47. *MK*, 12f.; RSA 3/2, Doc. 46.

48. See Jetzinger, *Jugend*, 108; Kandl, *Österreichbild*, 38.

49. Jetzinger, *Jugend*, 106f.

50. *MK*, 13.

51. Ibid. 10; in his Table Talk Hitler described how he used to annoy his religion teacher by using black, red, and gold pencils (*Monologe*, 8/9 January 1942).

52. On the conditions at Hitler's school see Kandl, *Österreichbild*, 11ff.; Hamann, *Wien*, 23ff.

53. Jetzinger, *Jugend*, 131.

54. *MK*, 20.

55. BAB, NS 26/65, piano teacher Joseph Wend's (Prewratsky) memories of Hitler, whom he taught for four months.

56. LHA Linz, NL Jetzinger.

57. On criticism of Kubizek see Jetzinger, *Jugend*, 139ff. After 1945 Jetzinger worked with Kubizek but then fell out with him. Among other things, he accused Kubizek of using Jetzinger's material without permission in the book he published in 1953. For criticism of Jetzinger and Kubizek as sources see Hamann, *Wien*, 77ff. Hamann notes that Jetzinger is too critical of Kubizek and that his account of Hitler's youth contains a number of significant mistakes, for example, in particular, his assertion that Hitler was not present at the death of his mother in Linz. Also, his estimate of Hitler's income during his period in Vienna is too high.

58. Kubizek, *Hitler*, 28ff.

59. Ibid., 23f.

60. Because of a number of inconsistencies Jetzinger, *Jugend*, 142f., considers this account completely implausible and an invention of Kubizek's. However, forty years later Kubizek himself traced this lady and discovered that she had received an anonymous letter, the content of which suggests that it was from Hitler.

61. Kubizek, *Hitler*, 86.

62. Ibid., 71ff.

63. Ibid., 75ff.

64. In noting that Schwab was retelling the sagas of early German history Kubizek overlooked the fact that the popular edition of Schwab's work actually contains the sagas of classical antiquity. However, this confusion of classical antiquity and German myth is typical of Hitler's mental universe.

65. Kubizek, *Hitler*, 84.

66. Ibid. 97ff., quote on pp. 98 and 91ff. on his early interest in political topics.

67. Ibid., 44.

68. Ibid., 107ff., quote 108.

69. Ibid., 121ff. Hitler sent Kubizek four postcards from Vienna, which, although they cannot be clearly dated, are the most important source for this trip. See Jetzinger, *Jugend*, 151ff.; Hamann, *Wien*, 42ff.

70. Kubizek, *Hitler*, 124ff.

71. Hamann, *Wien*, 82.

72. *MK*, 18f.; on the circumstances of the examination see Hamann, *Wien*, 48ff. The rejection announcements from the Academy of Art (from the years 1907 and 1908) are quoted in Konrad Heiden, *Adolf Hitler. Eine Biographie*, vol. I (Zurich, 1936), 20. See also Jetzinger, *Jugend*, 174.

73. *MK*, 19; he also recalls the conversation with the Rector in Hitler, *Monologe*, 29 October 1941.

74. See below, p. 25.

75. Kubizek, *Hitler*, 135ff.; Hamann, *Wien*, 53ff. Jetzinger is definitely wrong in his statement in *Jugend*, 175ff., that Hitler appeared in Linz only after the death of his mother.

76. Hamann, *Hitlers Edeljude. Das Leben des Armenarztes Eduard Bloch* (Munich, 2008). Bloch's article appeared on 15 and 22 March 1941 in *Collier's Magazine*. Its content is identical to the memoirs he had already written on 7 November 1938 and made available to the NSDAP Hauptarchiv (BAB, NS 26/65). The fact that he submitted this text for publication in 1941, when he no longer had to be concerned about the Nazi authorities, suggests that his memoirs are authentic.

77. Hamann, *Wien*, pp. 57ff. corrects the account in Jetzinger, *Jugend*, 180ff. in particular in relation to the amount of the sums involved.

78. Correspondence in Institut for Zeitgeschichte (IfZ), F 19/19. See also Hitler, *Monologe*, 15/16 January 1942; Hamann, *Wien*, 59ff. and 87.

79. Kubizek, *Hitler*, 146ff.

80. Ibid., 156.

81. Ibid, 156ff.

82. Hamann, *Wien*, 98ff.

83. Kubizek, *Hitler*, 200ff.

84. Ibid., 163ff., quotes 165, and 173ff.

85. Ibid., 167.

86. Hamann, *Wien*, 59.

87. Kubizek, *Hitler*, 195ff., Quotes 195; Hamann, *Wien*, 89ff.

88. Kubizek, *Hitler*, 240ff., recalls a joint visit to parliament and Hitler's subsequent tirades about the nationalities question (240ff.), Hitler's complaint about the swamping of the city by non-Germans (248f.), a workers' demonstration in front of the parliament, whose violent dispersal they both observed (246f), and Hitler's attitude to Schönerer and Lueger (248).

89. Ibid., 250ff.

90. Ibid, 238 and 228ff.

91. Ibid., 234ff.

92. Ibid., 253ff.

93. Heiden, *Hitler*, 30; Hamann, *Wien*, 196. The author claims the Rector's alleged advice to study architecture came after the second rejection. However, according to *MK*, 19, Hitler received it before his mother's death.

94. Kubizek, *Hitler*, 19, 21, 69, 77 and 109.

95. Ibid., 125.

96. Ibid., 21 and 36f.

97. Birgit Schwarz, *Geniewahn. Hitler und die Kunst* (Vienna, 2009), 51ff., points out that around the turn of the century a cult, indeed a mania, for genius existed, whose representatives took their cue in particular from Schopenhauer, Hitler's favourite philosopher. There was a particular tendency to portray the unrecognized genius as a heroic man of will. Hitler took as his models for this role among others Anselm von Feuerbach, one of his favourite painters (whose alleged lack of recognition was in fact based on Hitler's misunderstanding of his biography) and Richard Wagner. In Wagner's case Hitler was influenced above all by Friedrich Pecht's biography and Houston Chamberlain's interpretation. Wagner also provided the basis for his anti-Semitic interpretation of his lack of recognition and Wagner's operas provided numerous examples of outsiders who asserted their will. See above all Fest, *Hitler*, 73ff; Wolfgang Weimer, 'Der Philosoph und der Diktator. Arthur Schopenhauer und Adolf Hitler' in *Schopenhauer Jahrbuch* 84 (2003), 137–67; Schmidt, *Geschichte des Genie-Gedankens*, vol. 2 (Darmstadt, 1985). Hitler's life as an artist and the influence of his self-image as an artistic genius on his role as a military commander are the main focus of the exceptionally fruitful book by Wolfram Pyta, *Hitler. Der Künstler als Politiker und Feldherr. Eine Herrschaftsanalyse* (Munich, 2015).

98. *MK*, 19f.; on the second rejection see Hamann, *Wien*, 196.

99. Jetzinger, *Jugend*, 218; Anton Joachimsthaler, *Hitlers Weg begann in München 1913–1923* with a Foreword by Ian Kershaw (Munich, 2000), 39f.

100. Entry in the accounts book, which at this time was being kept by Johanna Pölzl, Klara Hitler's sister: 'Lent Adolf Hitler 924 Kronen Johanna Pölzl' and 'Adolf 924 Kronen', quoted in Gerhard Marckhgott, '"…Von der Hohlheit des gemächlichen Lebens". Neues Material über die Familie Hitler in Linz' in *Jahrbuch des Oberösterreichischen Muselvereins* 138/1 (Linz 1993), 267–77; Hamann, *Wien*, 195f.

101. Hamann, *Wien*, 206; Joachimsthaler, *Weg*, 51.

102. *MK*, 20ff.

103. Ibid., 24f. and 40ff.; Eberhard Jäckel (ed.), Hitler. *Sämtliche Aufzeichnungen 1905–1924* (Stuttgart, 1980) (*JK*), No. 325; on the legend of Hitler as a building worker see Hamann, *Wien*, 206ff.

104. *New Republic*, 5, 1, and 19 April 1939; BAB, NS 26/64, My encounter with Hitler; ibid., Letters to Franz Feiler (Innsbruck), including a letter of May 1933. On Hanisch's report see Hamann, *Wien*, 222ff. and 265ff.

105. Ibid., 229ff.

106. Ibid., 239ff.; Joachimsthaler, *Weg*, 67ff.; Pyta, Hitler, 105ff.

107. Hamann, *Wien*, 245; Joachimsthaler, *Weg*, 69.

108. Hamann, *Wien*, 246ff.; Joachimsthaler, *Weg*, 69ff.; BAB, NS 26/64, Hanisch letters.

109. Hamann, *Wien*, 249f.

110. Ibid., 271ff. There is supposedly a report for the period February–April 1912, which appeared in Czech in the Brünn journal *Moraský Ilustrovany Zpravoda*. According to Hamann, the author is authentic, but the report does not contain anything significantly new. The book by Josef Grein, which appeared in 1947 is, however, pure fantasy, despite the fact that Heim was definitely living in the hostel in the Meldemannstrasse in 1910. See Hamann, *Wien*, 275ff.

111. Ibid., 250; Jetzinger, *Jugend*, 226ff.

112. BAB, NS 26/17a, Karl Honisch: Wie ich im Jahre 1913 Hitler kennenlernte, 31 May 1939. Printed in Joachimsthaler, *Weg*, 52–9; see also Hamann, *Wien*, 272f.

113. *MK*, 106ff.

114. Ibid., 134ff. and 74f.

115. Ibid., 13 and 118.

116. Ibid., 119.

117. Ibid., 82.

118. Ibid.

119. Ibid., 80ff.

120. Ibid., 1.

121. Henry Picker, *Hitlers Tischgespräche im Führerhauptquartier. Entstehung, Struktur und Folgen des Nationalsozialismus* (Berlin, 1997), 5 April 1942, evening.

122. *MK*, 93f.

123. Ibid., 135.

124. Whiteside, *Socialism*, 236ff.

125. *MK*, 110ff., quote 110.

126. Ibid, 106ff.

127. Ibid., 59, 107 and 109, on Lueger also 58f., 74 and 132f.

128. John W. Boyer, *Karl Lueger (1844–1910). Christlichsoziale Politik als Beruf* (Weimar, 2010).

129. *MK*, 59ff.

130. Ibid., 130ff.

131. Ibid., 61.

132. Ibid., 69f.

133. In his later speeches and writings there are passages that are similar to the ideas of the Viennese Germanic mystic, Guido von List, who tried to assert the racial superiority of an 'Aryan' master race from the far north. See Hamann, *Wien*, 301f. List's most important disciple, Lanz von Liebenfels, who demanded in numerous works that this heroic, noble race must be protected from the inferior race of half apes through planned racial breeding, was the main person claiming that he had influenced Hitler. See ibid., pp. 316ff. It is entirely plausible, but not provable and not claimed by Hitler, that, during his Vienna period, he became familiar with the anti-Semitism of Houston Chamberlain, whose main work, *Die Grundlagen des 19. Jahrhunderts*, was published in Vienna in 1899. It is certainly true that Pan-German literature quoted Chamberlain extensively. See ibid., 288. However, he could only have come across Chamberlain's work as such for the first time in Munich, possibly through Dietrich Eckart. A programmatic speech by Hitler in 1920 has many similarities with Chamberlain's ideas. See *JK*, No. 136. However, according to Hamann, the attempt to achieve a precise reconstruction of Hitler's debt to individual authors is a hopeless task. See Hamann, *Wien*, 333,

134. Joachimsthaler, *Weg*, 77ff. There is a lengthy description of his first stay in Munich by his first landlady, Anna Popp, which was published in 1934 in a very pro-Nazi English publication. See Heinz A. Heinz, *Germany's Hitler* (London, 1934). The whole book is based to a considerable extent on such personal memories and was intended to familiarize the reader with Hitler as a person. The very fact that, in accordance with the version in *Mein Kampf*, the landlady shifts the date of Hitler's stay in Munich from 1913 to 1912 shows that the whole Heinz project was part of the official construction of the Hitler legend.

135. Joachimsthaler, *Weg*, 83ff.

136. *MK*, 138ff., in the chapter about his pre-war stay in Munich (quote 170); *JK*, No. 325.

137. Joachimsthaler, *Weg*, 77ff.

138. *MK*, 138f. His decision to move to Munich may also have been influenced by the idea that Munich was a haven for artists who had failed in Vienna. See Schwarz, *Geniewahn*, 68ff.

139. *Hitler, Monologe*, 20 October 1941. Schwarz, *Geniewahn*, 82ff., points out that Hitler's idea of becoming an architect followed models like Rubens, Markert, Semper, Klenze, and above all Schinkel, who combined architecture, the decorative arts, and painting.

140. Army file in Jetzinger, *Jugend*, 253ff.; for a summing up see Joachimsthaler, *Weg*, 27f. See also *JK* No. 20.

141. The reporting during the first days of August by both the Social Democratic *Münchener Post* and the middle-class *Münchener Zeitung* convey this ambivalent impression and emphasize above all the concern felt by broad sections of the public.

142. Thomas Weber, *Hitlers erster Krieg. Der Gefreite Hitler im Weltkrieg – Mythos und Wahrheit* (Berlin, 2011), 30f.; Joachimsthaler, *Weg*, 98ff.

143. *MK*, 177.

144. Joachimsthaler, *Weg*, 100ff. It is possible that he had applied to another regiment beforehand and been rejected. His claim that, as an Austrian citizen, he had successfully appealed directly to King Ludwig III for admission to the Bavarian army seems implausible. See *MK*, 179. The report of the Bavarian military archive of 13 October 1924 about Hitler's admission to the Bavarian army is printed in Joachimsthaler, *Weg*, 103ff., Staatsarchiv München (SAM), StAnw. München, 13099, and in facsimile on p. 109 of Hitler's military personal file: Kriegsarchiv München (KAM), No. 4470/7111.

145. Hitler, *Monologe*, 13 October 1941, Midday.

146. Weber, *Krieg*, 31f.

147. Ibid., 35f.

148. For the quote see *JK*, No. 24: KAM, RIR 16, Bund 12, KTB 1. Btl., 8–10 October 1914; Franz Rubenbauer, 'Der Sturm auf Ypern. Freiwillige vor!' in Fridolin Solleder (ed.), *Vier Jahre Westfront. Die Geschichte des Regiments List. Reserve-Infanterie-Regiment 16* (Munich, 1932), 8ff. For the history of the regiment see also Walther Beckmann, *Bayerisches Reserve-Infanterie-Regiment Nr. 16 'Regiment List'* (Berlin, 1939); 'Erinnerungen'; List-Regiment. On the excessive demands placed on the troops see also KAM, RIR 16, Bund 3, Appendices to the KTB, 1 October–30 November 1914, Excerpt from KTB of the 10th Company (Graf Bassenheim), 3–17 October and 20 October, where the author complained that 'discipline had become very poor because of the marches and excessive demands'. Weber, *Krieg*, 41f. Joachimsthaler, *Weg*, 114f.

149. *JK*, No. 26. On transport see: KAM, RIR 16, Bund 12, KTB 1. Btl., 21 October 1914. See Joachimsthaler, *Weg*, 115. On the cheering crowds see also Weber, *Krieg*, 44f.

150. KAM, RIR 16, Bund 12, KTB 1. Btl., 23/24 October 1914.

151. Joachimsthaler, *Weg*, 118; Weber, *Krieg*, 62ff.

152. KAM, RIR 16, Bund 3, Appendices to the KTB, 1 October–30 November 1914, Excerpt from KTB 10th Company (Graf Bassenheim), 29 October 1914; IfZ, MA 732, NSDAP-Hauptarchiv, No. 47, Report of Raab, a member of the regiment Raab to the NS-Hauptarchiv (Uetrecht), 5 August 1939. See also Weber, *Krieg*, 68.

153. On the acquaintanceship see Joachimsthaler, *Weg*, 88f.

154. *JK*, No. 30, Orthography, punctuation, and grammar as in the copy. He had described the same battle to Joseph Popp in letters of 3 December 1914 and 26 January 1915 (Nos 26 and 29).

155. *MK*, 180f.

156. The legend is based on a section of the German Army report of 11 November 1918: Karl Unruh, *Langemarck. Legende und Wirklichkeit* (Koblenz, 1986). See also Joachimsthaler, *Weg*, 122; Weber, *Krieg*, 65.

157. Rubenbauer, 'Tage der Ruhe in Werwick-Comines', in Solleder, *Vier Jahre*, 62; Weber, *Krieg*, 71f. Thus, Hitler's assertion in his letter to Joseph Popp of 3 December 1914 (*JK*, No. 26), according to which there were only 611 men left out of originally 3,600, can be regarded as plausible.

158. Weber, *Krieg*, 69ff.; Joachimsthaler, *Weg*, 122f.; Rubenbauer, 'Sturm'.

159. Rubenbauer, 'Im Schützengraben vor Messines', in Solleder, *Vier Jahre*; Joachimsthaler, *Weg*, 124.

160. Rubenbauer, 'Oostaverne-Wytschaete', in Solleder, *Vier Jahre*; Joachimsthaler, *Weg*, 128.

161. Ibid., 129; Weber, *Krieg*, 72ff.

162. Hitler, *Monologe*, 1 August 1942: 'and then everything was washed out'. Weber, *Krieg*, 77.

163. *JK*, No. 29, Orthography, punctuation, and grammar as in the copy.

164. Wiedemann, 'Der zweite Kriegswinter bei Fromelles', in Solleder, *Die Jahre.*, esp. p. 99. See also the files of the regimental doctor (KAM, RD 6, Bund 147, Akt 6 und 11); Weber, *Krieg*, 78ff. and 97f.

165. KAM, No. 4470/7111, Hitler's personal file; Joachimsthaler, *Weg*, 123f.; Weber, *Krieg*, 75.

166. Ibid., 129ff.; Balthasar Brandmayer, *Zwei Meldegänger* (Überlingen am Bodensee, 1932) 54f., 70f., 77f., and 92f. Hitler's wartime comrade Lippert also reported to the NS Party archive on 28 March 1940 that Hitler had taken many messages to the commander of Bat. I/16, Major Leb, at his command post immediately behind the front line (BAB, NS 26/47).

167. For details see Weber, *Krieg*, 296ff.

168. Fritz Wiedemann, *Der Mann, der Feldherr werden wollte. Erlebnisse und Erfahrungen des Vorgesetzten Hitlers im 1. Weltkrieg und seines späteren Persönlichen Adjutanten* (Velbert/Kettwig, 1964), 23ff. On Hitler' experience as a runner see Weber, *Krieg*, 187ff.; BAB, NS 26/47, descriptions by his regimental comrades, Heinrich Lugauer, Hans Bauer, and Karl Lippert provided to the NS Hauptarchiv and dated 26 February, 15 May 1940, and 28 March respectively. On Lippert see Joachimsthaler, *Weg*, 340. KAM, RIB 12, Bund 25, 1, contains a list of the NCOs and men in lodgings in Fournes (i.e. in private accommodation), in which Hitler is mentioned by name. On this and on Hitler's wartime painting see Joachimsthaler, *Weg*, 133ff.

169. Wiedemann, *Mann*, 24; SAM, SprkAkte Amann K 20, Interrogation, 5 November 1947. On the possible reasons for his failure to be promoted see Weber, *Krieg*, 191ff.

170. Georg Eichelsdörfer, 'Sturm auf das beilförmige Waldstück', in Solleder, *Vier Jahre*, 75. Weber, *Krieg*, 76, refers to a report by W., 'Osttaverne-Wytschaete', 36, which was written earlier.

171. KAM, No. 4470/7111, Hitler's personal file, and RIR 16, KTB of 12 December 1914; List Regiment, 3, Joachimsthaler, *Weg*, 129; Weber, *Krieg*, 77.

172. *JK*, No. 26.

173. KAM, KTB 1. Btl., 12 March 1915, and KTB RIR 16, Bund 12, 12 March 1915. Georg Eichelsdörfer, 'Die Schlacht bei Neuve Chapelle', in Solleder, *Vier Jahre*; Brandmayer, *Meldegänger*, 19ff.; Weber, *Krieg*, 105ff.

174. Solleder, 'Zwischen'; KAM, RIR 16, KTB 1. Btl., and KTB RIR 16, 20 March 1915; Joachimsthaler, *Weg*, 133ff.; Weber, *Krieg*, 129ff.

175. Wiedemann, 'Der zweite Kriegswinter bei Fromelles', in Solleder, *Vier Jahre*; on the period in Fromelles see in detail Weber, *Krieg*, 111ff.

176. KAM, KTB 1. Btl., 9 and 10 May 1915; Georg Eichelsdörfer, 'Das Gefecht bei Fromelles, 9. und 10. Mai 1915', in Solleder, *Vier Jahre*; Weber, *Krieg*, 118ff.

177. KAM, RIR 17, KTB, 1. Btl., 19 and 20 July 1915; Fritz Wiedemann, 'Das Gefecht bei Fromelles am 19. und 20. Juli 1916', in Solleder, *Vier Jahre*; Weber, *Krieg*, 196ff.; Joachimsthaler, *Weg*, 162.

178. In *MK*, 209, Hitler conveys the impression that he had been wounded at the front and dates the event as 7 October. On the dating of 5 October see Joachimsthaler, *Weg*, 163 with the evidence from the military documents; Weber, *Krieg*, 208f.; Wiedemann, *Mann*, 29; Brandmayer, *Meldegänger*, 85 (he was not, however, present at the wounding). See also Wiedemann, 'Die Sommeschlacht', in Solleder, *Vier Jahre*.; KAM, KTB, 1. Bl., 5 October 1916 and for the following days of the attack.

179. On the whole journey see *MK*, 211.

180. Kershaw, *Hitler* 1, pp. 134f., considers such early anti-Semitic outbursts by Hitler plausible. Weber, *Krieg*, p. 239, however, points out that there is no solid documentary evidence that Hitler was a committed anti-Semite at the beginning of 1917.

181. *JK*, No. 47; Wiedemann, *Mann*, 30; Joachimsthaler, *Weg*, 167; Weber, *Krieg*, 246.

182. Ibid., 247f.

183. Freiherr von Tubeuf, 'Das Regiment hört auf den Namen Tubeuf', in Solleder, *Vier Jahre*, 275ff. KAM, RIR 16, Bund 9, Doc: Einsatz des Regt. in der Fünftagesschlacht bei Arras vom 11. bis 17. Mai 1917 (Appendices) and doc.: Ablösung des 16. Inf. Regiments am 11. Mai 1917 (Regimentsbefehl zur Ablösung des 20. Durch das 16. Rgt.); Weber, *Krieg*, 247ff.

184. Ibid., 252ff.

185. Ibid., 253 and 260ff.; KAM, RIB 12, KTB, Bund 1, June and July 1917; RIR 16, Bund 9, Doc.: battle reports 31 July/1 August 1917 and doc.: Reports 31 July–1 August 1917; Tubeuf, Regiment., 281ff.

186. Weber, *Krieg*, 264 and 269; KAM, No. 4470/7111, Hitler's personal file.

187. He sent various postcards from there: *JK*, No. 50–53. Joachimsthaler, *Weg*, S. 169; Weber, *Krieg*, 269ff.

188. Ibid., 274ff.; Tubeuf, 'Regiment', esp. pp. 296ff., 298. On the losses see Egid Gehring, 'Am Schicksalsstrom Deutschlands. Stimmungsbilder aus der zweiten Marneschlacht im Juli 1918', in Solleder, *Vier Jahre*, 316–24.

189. IfZ, ED 100/86, Letter from the deputy commander of the regiment von Godin of 31 July 1918, to the 12. Reserve Infantry Brigade, published in Joachimsthaler, *Weg*, 173f.

190. Weber, *Krieg*, 285ff.; Hitler, *Monologe*, 10/11 November 1941.

191. Weber, *Krieg*, 126ff., brings together various statements about Hitler's courage. See, in particular the collection in the Party archive (IfZ, MA 732); Ignaz Westenkirchen in the English language propaganda publication Heinz, *Hitler*, 64ff.; Hans Mend, *Adolf Hitler im Felde* (Diessen vor München, 1931); Brandmayer, *Meldegänger*. In 1922 Hitler himself collected positive references from former superiors BAB, NS 26/17a, Battalion commander Lieutenant-Colonel Freiherr von Lüneschloss, 20 February 1922 (who, however, only knew of Hitler's achievements from hearsay). BAB, NS 26/1223, Regimental commander Friedrich Petz, February 1922 (copy), published in Joachimsthaler, *Weg*, p. 159; BAB NS 26/17a, Oberst von Spatny, 10 March 1922, and the statement by Lieutenant-Colonel Freiherr von Tubeuf, 20 March 1922. On these officers see Joachimsthaler, *Weg*, pp. 159, 167f., and 347. Hitler's former regimental commander Baligand testified in Hitler's favour in the 1924 trial (published in ibid., p. 154) and for Christmas 1931 sent him a copy of the regimental history with a personal dedication. See Timothy Ryback, *Hitlers Bücher. Seine Bibliothek – sein Denken* (Cologne, 2010), 39. Michael Schlehuber, as a Social Democrat, i.e. a political opponent, also pointed out in 1932 that Hitler had been a good soldier. See Weber, *Krieg*, p. 135, with a quote from *Volksgemeinschaft*, 7 March 1932. On Schlehuber see Joachimsthaler, *Weg*, 339. However, during the early 1930s, a number of former comrades complained that Hitler had occupied a relatively privileged position. See note 208. The story that was often put about in the Third Reich that Hitler had captured a number of prisoners in summer 1918 is untrue. The origin of this legend is clear from Baligand's report in the official regimental history: in summer 1918 a six-man patrol from the regiment captured 18 prisoners. See Maximilian von Baligand, 'Ende wie Anfang', in Solleder, *Vier Jahre*, p. 336. This disproves Weber's speculation in *Krieg*, 289f. that Lieutenant Gutman was the leader of this daring coup.

192. *MK*, 181.

193. *JK*, No. 27 and No. 30, orthography as in the copy.

194. Hitler, *Monologe*, 25/26 September 1941.

195. Weber, *Krieg*, 165ff.; Brandmayer, *Meldegänger*, 103; BAB, NS 26/47, Einsendung Lippert, 28 March 1940.

196. The story of Hitler having allegedly had a son during the war, which was put about by Werner Maser in the 1970s, is unsupported by evidence. See Weber, *Krieg*, p. 167; Joachimsthaler, *Weg*, pp. 159f. Jean Paul Mulders in his book, *Auf der Suche nach Hitlers Sohn. Eine Beweisaufnahme* (Munich, 2009) refers to a DNA analysis he had carried out, which disproves the claim of a relationship between Hitler and the person concerned. Machtan's claim in Lothar Machtan, *Hitlers Geheimnis. Das Doppelleben eines Diktators* (Berlin, 2001), that Hitler was

homosexual lacks proof and will not be considered further here. The key document, the report of the alleged witness, Hans Mend, is highly unreliable. See note 203.

197. Brandmayer, *Meldegänger*, 102f.

198. SAM, SprkAkte Amann K 20, also Wiedemann, *Mann*, 27; there are numerous similar comments in the memoirs of his regimental comrades, Lugauer, Lippert, and Bauer. See note 168; Weber, *Krieg*, pp. 187ff.

199. A collection of the relevant material is in Joachimsthaler, *Weg*, 143ff.

200. Hitler, *Monologe*, 22/23 January 1942.

201. Weber, *Krieg*, 193ff.

202. Brandmayer, *Meldegänger*, 90f.

203. Ibid., 41. The later assertions by Hitler's army comrades, Hans Mend and Ignaz Westenkirchner, that Hitler had already expressed anti-Semitic sentiments during the war must be considered unreliable. Mend's book, published in 1931 (*Hitler*, 17 and 60f) was a glorification of Hitler. There is also a very negative assessment of Hitler by Mend, a fraudster convicted of falsifying documents. See Weber, *Krieg*, 185f.; Machtan, *Geheimnis*, 81ff. Westenkircher's statements are only recorded in Heinz's propaganda piece (Heinz, *Hitler*, 74) See Weber, *Krieg*, 239. Pyta, *Hitler*, 125ff., has discovered that Hitler maintained comradely contacts with German Jewish members of his regiment.

204. *MK*, 182.

205. *JK*, No. 30, orthography as in the copy.

206. See Weber, *Krieg*, 144f.

207. *MK*, 182.

208. Weber, *Krieg*, 136ff., with detailed contemporary quotes. On an anonymous correspondent, whom Weder identifies as Korbinian Rutz see also Joachimsthaler, *Weg*, 150ff.; US National Archives and Records Administration Washington (NARA) T 581-1, Ferdinand Widmann's, letter to Hitler, 9 March 1932.

209. Joachimsthaler, *Weg*, 174 (KAM, No. 4470/7111, Hitler's personal file); Weber, *Krieg*, 291.

210. Joachimsthaler, *Weg*, 174; Weber, *Krieg*, 293; *MK*, 219.

211. Ibid., 220.

212. Baligand, 'Ende', 336 describes the gas attack on the regimental staff. See also *MK*, 220f. On his gas injury see Joachimsthaler, *Weg*, 174f.; Weber, *Krieg*, 293f.

213. *MK*, 223ff. The claim often repeated in the literature (most recently in Weber, *Krieg*, 294f.) that his temporary blindness was a psychological response, a kind of war hysteria, cannot be proved any more than can the assertion that he was hypnotized during his treatment, which might explain the change in his personality. These speculations are all based on his medical notes, which have not survived but have supposedly been indirectly recorded:

1. in the novel, *Der Augenzeuge* (The Witness) by the émigré author, Ernst Weiss, who allegedly based his narrative on the report of the psychiatrist, Edmund Forster, who is supposed to have treated Hitler in Pasewalk;

2. through the statements of the émigré doctor, Karl Kroner, who gave a description of Hitler's treatment by Forster to the American secret service;

3. through the report of the neurologist, Otfried Förster, who is supposed to have told two American colleagues that he had seen the medical notes in 1932. See, in particular, Gerhard Köpf, 'Hitlers psychogene Erblindung. Geschichte einer Krankenakte' in *Nervenheilkunde* 24 (2005), 783–90; Bernhard Horstmann, *Hitler in Pasewalk. Die Hypnose und ihre Folgen* (Düsseldorf, 2004); Rudolph Binion, *'...dass ihr mich gefunden habt'. Hitler und die Deutschen*, 19ff. However, these theories have been convincingly refuted by Jan Armbruster, 'Die Behandlung Adolf Hitlers im Lazarett Pasewalk 1918. Historische Mythenbildung durch einseitige bzw. spekulative Pathographie', in *Journal für Neurologie, Neurochirurgie und Psychiatrie* 10/4 (2009), 18–23.

BACK IN MUNICH: POLITICIZATION

1. Kriegsarchiv München (KAM), No. 4470/7111, Hitler's personal file; Weber, *Krieg*, 305ff.; Joachimsthaler, *Weg*, 184ff.; Othmar Plöckinger, *Unter Soldaten und Agitatoren. Hitlers prägende Jahre im deutschen Militär 1918–1920* (Paderborn, 1920), 29.

2. Karl Bosl (ed.), *Bayern im Umbruch. Die Revolution von 1918, ihre Voraussetzungen, ihr Verlauf, und ihre Folgen* (Munich and Vienna, 1969); Allan Mitchell, *Revolution in Bayern 1918/1919. Die Eisner-Regierung und die Räterepublik* (Munich, 1967); Bernhard Grau, *Karl Eisner 1867–1919. Eine Biographie* (Munich, 2001).

3. KAM, 2. Inf.Rgt., Bund 19, Doc. 2, Order, 13 December 1918, on the election of barracks councillors on 17 December 1918, who relieved the provisional councillors of the immediate revolutionary period, see Plöckinger, *Soldaten*, 30ff.

4. KAM, 2. Inf.Rgt., Ersatzbataillon, Bund 7, battalion Order, 4 December 1918, Punkt 23; 2nd Inf.Rgt./I. u. II. First Btl., Bund 19, Orders, 3 and 4 December 1918, on Hitler's being ordered to Traunstein; on the recollections of Ernst Schmidt, who was at Traunstein with Hitler see Heinz A. Heinz, *Germany's Hitler* (London, 1934), 97ff. See also Franz Haselbeck, 'Das Gefangenenlager Traunstein-Au' in *Jahrbuch des Historischen Vereins für den Chiemgau zu Traunstein* 7 (1995), 241–90; Plöckinger, *Soldaten*, 34ff., 286–90. In Hitler, *MK*, 226, Hitler creates the impression that he had escaped to Traunstein to avoid the revolution, which he loathed.

5. Plöckinger, *Soldaten*, 35f.

6. See KAM, 2nd Inf.Rgt., Bund 19, Doc 7, battalion orders, February and March 1919, for the battalion's service rota, for example for guard duty at the main train station. See Joachimsthaler, *Weg*, 195ff.; Plöckinger, *Soldaten*, 37.

7. KAM, Nr. 4470/7111, Hitler's military personal file: Transfer to the demobilization company on 12 February 1919; 2nd Inf.Rgt., Bund 19, Doc. 3, Regimental order of 14 February 1919 to establish a demobilization battalion on 18 February 1919. Doc. 7 reveals the new title from 20 February. The 2nd Demobilization Company, which Hitler joined, was subordinated to the battalion on 4 March 191 (ibid.). See also Joachimsthaler, *Weg*, 186ff.

8. KAM, 2. Inf.Rgt., Bund 19, Doc 7: In the orders of the Demobilization Battalion to the 2nd demobilization company for a meeting on 4 April attended by Hitler in his function as a representative of his company he was referred to as Hüttler. The representatives were nominated on 1 April. Hitler was evidently nominated subsequently as a reserve. Joachimsthaler's supposition in *Weg*, 198f. that Hitler had already been elected around 15 February cannot be confirmed from the documents and contradicts the more recent detailed research by Plöckinger, *Soldaten*.

9. Ibid., 44.

10. KAM, 2nd Inf.Rgt., Bund 19, Doc 7: In a rider by the propaganda department to the regimental order of 7 February 1919, referring to the meeting of representatives in the city commandant's office on 21 February for a talk and discussion on the subject of 'Parliament or Councils?' In the battalion order of 4 April 1919 the representatives were ordered to participate in briefings on the three Socialist parties and to attend a memorial ceremony for Kurt Eisner. See Joachimsthaler, *Weg*, 202.

11. KAM, 2nd Inf.Rgt./I. u. II. Ers. Btl., Bund 7, order 15 February 1919. It is quite possible that Hitler took part in this demonstration.

12. On the further course of the revolution see Bosl (ed.), *Bayern*; Grau, *Eisner*; Georg Köglmeier, *Die zentralen Rätegremien in Bayern 1918/19. Legitimation – Organization – Funktion* (Munich, 2001); Johannes Merz, 'Auf dem Weg zur Räterepublik. Staatskrise und Regierungsbildung in Bayern nach dem Tode Eisners (Februar–März 1919)' in *Zeitschrift für Bayerische Landesgeshichte* 66 (2003), 541–84; Mitchell, *Revolution*; Michael Seligmann, *Aufstand der Räte. Die erste bayerische Räterepublik vom 7. April 1919* (Grafenau-Döffingen, 1989).

13. KAM, 2nd Inf.Rgt., Bund 19, Doc. 3, Rgt. Orders, order 25 February 1919. Weber, *Krieg*, p. 332, follows here the interpretation of the ZDF documentary 'Hitler' (Knopp/Remy) of 1995. The photo taken by Hoffmann is, for example, published in Ralf Reuth, *Hitlers Judenhass. Klischee und Wirklichkeit* (Munich and Zurich, 2009), 88.

14. Mitchell, *Revolution*, 290ff.; Köglmeier, *Rätegremien*, 288ff.; Seligmann, *Aufstand*, 105ff.

15. Joachimsthaler, *Weg*, 206f.

16. On the first Räterepublik: see Mitchell, *Revolution*, 305ff.; Seligmann, *Aufstand*, 207ff.; Köglmeier, *Rätegremien*, 316ff.

17. On the communist Räterepublik see ibid., 344ff.; Mitchell, *Revolution*, 318ff.

18. KAM, 2nd Inf.Rgt., Bund 19, Doc. 7, battalion order, 16 April 1919, with the election results of the 2nd Company for the battalion's council: Blüml 30, Hittler 19 votes. The file contains successive demobilization lists for the months of February to April, showing that Hitler's remaining in the battalion would have been seriously jeopardized had he not been elected. On the election and the varied political views of the soldier representatives see Plöckinger, *Soldaten*, 48ff. For the other references to Hitler's activities see Joachimsthaler, *Weg*, 199ff.

19. *MK*, 226; Plöckinger, *Soldaten*, 64.

20. *JK*, No. 269. In fact, not only Esser but a considerable number of later Nazis were Social Democrats or even further to the left during the Revolution. See Joachimsthaler, *Weg*, 187f.

21. Hitler, *Monologe*, 21 September 1941 and 1 February 1942.

22. See, for example, Heinrich Hillmayr, *Roter und Weißer Terror in Bayern nach 1918. Ursachen, Erscheinungsformen und Folgen der Gewalttätigkeiten im Verlauf der revolutionären Ereignisse nach dem Ende des Ersten Weltkrieges* (Munich, 1974), 78ff.

23. KAM, 2nd Inf.Rgt., Bund 19, Doc. 6a, order from the Munich city commandant's office 7 May 1919.

24. KAM, Nr. 4470/7111, Hitler's personal file; Joachimsthaler, *Weg*, 221. KAM, 2nd Inf.Rgt., Bund 19, Doc. 6a, order from the city commandant's office, 7 May 1919, according to which the soldiers to be demobilized were to be examined for possible involvement in Spartakist, Bolshevik, or communist activities, and order from the city commandant's of 9 May 1919 concerning the immediate convening of the commissions of investigation. Ibid., Doc. 3, regimental order of 9 May 1919: 'The investigation and demobilization commission is to be composed of Lieutenant Merklin, Sergeant-Major Kleber, Corporal Hitler'. On the work of the commission see Plöckinger, *Soldaten*, 86ff.

25. SAM, SprkAkte Amann K 20, Interrogation of Amann, 6 December 1946.

26. Plöckinger, *Soldaten*, 92f.

27. SAM, Staatsanwaltschaften Nr. 1979, Criminal proceedings against Georg Dufter, Protocol of the proceedings on 17 June 1919. Hitler is referred to here as Hiedler; see also Plöckinger, *Soldaten*, p 97.

28. On the reconstruction of political life under the military regime see Bruno Thoss, *Der Ludendorff-Kreis 1919–1923. München als Zentrum der mitteleuropäischen Gegenrevolution zwischen Revolution und Hitler-Putsch* (Munich, 1978), 86ff.; Horst G.W. Nusser, *Konservative Wehrverbände in Bayern, Preußen und Österreich, 1918–1933* (Munich, 1973), 75ff.; Hans Fenske, *Konservatismus und Rechtsradikalismus in Bayern nach 1918* (Bad Homburg v.d.H., 1969), 62ff.; Hillmayr, *Terror*, 158ff.; Plöckinger, *Soldaten*, 66.

29. On the political atmosphere in Munich after the crushing of the *Räterepublik* see Fenske, *Konservatismus*, 62ff.

30. On this see the information in the annotated list in Rudolf von Sebottendorf, *Bevor Hitler kam. Urkundliches aus der Frühzeit der nationalsozialistischen Bewegung* (Munich, 1933).

31. Uwe Lohalm, *Völkischer Radikalismus. Die Geschichte des Deutschvölkischen Schutz- und Trutz-Bundes* (Hamburg, 1970), 15ff. To begin with the organization was called the Deutscher Schutz- und Trutz-Bund.

32. Ibid., 122ff.

33. Ibid, 290ff.

34. *Münchener Beobachter* (MB,) 17 May 1919, published the appeal by the Deutsche Bürgervereinigung, signed by Eckart, on the front page. For details on this organization see Max Engelman, 'Dietrich Eckart and the Genesis of Nazism', PhD Washington University, St. Louis, MO, 1971, 142ff.

35. On his speaking activities see Lohalm, *Radikalismus*, 127. On Feder's ideas see Gottfried Feder, *Das Manifest zur Brechung der Zinsknechtschaft des Geldes* [1919] (Munich, 1932); Feder, 'Das Radikalmittel' in *Süddeutsche Monatshefte* 16 (1919), 307–20.

36. On Lehmann see Rainer Hering, *Konstruierte Nation. Der Alldeutsche Verband 1890 bis 1939* (Hamburg, 2003), 480; Bundesarchiv Berlin (BAB), NS 26/865a, Hering Diary, according to which Lehmann reported to the Thule Society on 19 October 1919 on an encounter with Ludendorff in Berlin.

37. Elina Kiiskinen, *Die Deutschnationale Volkspartei in Bayern (Bayerische Mittelpartei) in der Regierungspolitik des Freistaats während der Weimarer Zeit. Von nationaler Erneuerung zu nationalem Untergang* (Munich, 2005), 45ff., quote 48.

38. Dirk Walter, *Antisemitische Kriminalität und Gewalt. Judenfeindschaft in der Weimarer Republik* (Bonn, 1999), 23ff.

39. Stefan Meining, 'Ein erster Ansturm der Antisemiten: 1919–1923', in Douglas Bokovoy (ed.), *Versagte Heimat. Jüdisches Leben in Münchens Isarvorstadt 1914–1945* (Munich 1994), 59ff. Four hundred Jews were to be expelled, but, because of the temporizing policy of the Interior Ministry, in the end only eight of them were.

40. Material on anti-Semitism in the second half of 1919 can be found in particular in KAM, Gruppenkdo. 4, No. 204, Jewbaiting; SAM, PolDir. 6697, Reports on the public mood. See also Reuth, *Judenhass*, 135ff.; Walter, *Kriminalität*, 24f. and 52ff.; Plöckinger, *Soldaten*, 185ff.

41. In the older literature it was assumed that Hitler took part in the first course. Othmar Plöckinger interpreted a diary entry of Gottfried Feder's to mean that Hitler participated in the second course. See Othmar Plöckinger, 'Adolf Hitler als Hörer an der Universität München im Jahre 1919. Zum Verhältnis zwischen Reichswehr und Universität', in Elisabeth Kraus (ed.), *Die Universität München im Dritten Reich. Aufsätze*. Part 2 (Munich, 2008), 13–47 (34); *MK*, 227ff. For the order to attend the third course see KAM Auflösungsstab 102, Bund 2, Doc. 3, 2nd Inf.Rgt., 2 July 1919 (now Auflösungsstäbe 25), Reports of the commander of the demobilization office of the 2nd Inf.Rgt., List of participants, 7 July 1919. See Plöckinger, *Soldaten*, 107f. This correction also fits in with Müller's recollections. He claims to have encountered Hitler in the lecture theatre on the Promenadenplatz, where Course III in fact took place. See Karl Alexander von Müller, *Mars und Venus. Erinnerungen 1914–1919* (Munich, 1954), 338.

42. Plöckinger, *Soldaten*, 100.

43. *MB*, 24 May 1919, 'Thule-Gesellschaft'. The article states that, during the final phase of the Councils' regime, Captain Karl Mayer had taken over the military organization in Munich in collaboration with the Thule.

44. Joachimsthaler, *Weg*, 221ff.; on Mayr see ibid., p. 225 and p. 360; on the information department and its activities see Fenske, *Konservatismus*, 85ff. The alleged memoirs of Mayr, 'Boss', are not a reliable source. According to Plöckinger, *Soldaten*, 331, in September 1919 Mayr also passed on the so-called Gemlich letter to Eckart. According to Georg Franz-Willing, *Ursprung der HitlerBewegung*.

1919–1922 (Preußisch Oldendorf, 1974), 54, Mayr corresponded with Eckart in September concerning a list of subscribers to *Auf gut deutsch*.

45. Plöckinger, *Soldaten*, 240f. The Heimatdienst Bayern had been established separately from the Reichszentrale für Heimatdienst and was not its Bavarian offshoot, as was previously thought. See Klaus W. Wippermann, *Politische Propaganda und staatsbürgerliche Bildung. Die Reichszentrale für Heimatdienst in der Weimarer Republik* (Bonn, 1976). The leading figure was the publicist, Fritz Gerlich, a later opponent of Hitler, who was murdered on 30 June 1934.

46. *Auf gut deutsch* appeared from December 1918 onwards, at first weekly, later irregularly. From the fifth issue Bothmer provided regular, often anti-Semitic, contributions. To begin with Eckart had written all the articles himself. On the link between Bothmer und Eckart see Engelman, 'Eckart', 94ff.

47. Course III was – exceptionally – divided into officers (IIIa) and other ranks (IIIb). On the programmes see KAM, Gruppenkdo. 4, Nr. 312; Plöckinger, *Soldaten*, 108.

48. IfZ, ED 874, Feder-Tagebuch, 12 and 14 July (officers' course) and 15 July 1919 (other ranks' course).

49. On the programmes of Courses I and II see Deuerlein, 'Hitlers Eintritt. in die Politik und die Reichswehr', in *Vierteljahrshefte für Zeitgeschichte* (VfZ) 7 (1959), Doc. 2. On the activities of the Information Department see Joachimsthaler, *Weg*, 223ff. and 227ff. On the courses see KAM, Gruppenkdo. 4, Nr. 307, Command, 28 May 1919, Directives of 13 June 1919, letter from Bothmer re: Fees for Course I and report of 2 July 1919 (published in Joachimsthaler, *Weg*, 237ff.).

50. For details see Plöckinger, *Soldaten*, 210ff.

51. The historian, Karl Alexander von Müller, who was evidently recruited as a lecturer on the course for a short time reported in his memoirs that, after his talk, he had spotted Hitler surrounded by a small group. See Müller, *Mars*, 338.

52. Hitler's name can be found in various Information Commando lists. See KAM, Gruppenkdo. 4, No. 309, list of participants at Lechfeld with 26 names and a list of 22 July 1919 with 23 names; No. 315, Lechfeld list with 27 names, of which one was crossed out. Undated list of propaganda people with 70 names and Bestell-Liste II. For details see Plöckinger, *Soldaten*, 121.

53. KAM, Gruppenkdo. 4, No. 309, Report by Captain Lauterbach, 19 July 1919. List with 23 names (among them Hitler's) and list of 'Kdo Beyschlag' with a total of 26 names. On the training course see Joachimsthaler, *Weg*, 24ff. For more detail see Plöckinger, *Soldaten*, 113ff.

54. Ibid., 122.

55. KAM, Gruppenkdo. 4, No. 309, Reports of the commander of the Guard Commando Lieutenant Bendt, 21 and 25 August 1919, and excerpts from the reports of the course participants published in Deuerlein, 'Eintritt', Docs. 7–9. It is clear from Bendt's report of 25 August that the indoctrination was restricted to the permanent staff of the camp. See also ibid., provisional report on the course of 19–20 August, infantry soldier Beyschlag, 22 August 1919.

56. Plöckinger, *Soldaten*, 130ff. and 138.

57. KAM, Gruppenkdo. 4, No. 314, Gemlich letter and Mayr's accompanying letter.

58. For details see Plöckinger, *Soldaten*, 331ff. Plöckinger points out that in the literature distributed by the Reichswehr at that time anti-Semitism and anti-Bolshevism were not necessarily linked (248 and 341f.), which could explain why, while he was a soldier, Hitler was relatively cautious in his public statements on this matter.

59. Walter, *Kriminalität*, 34ff.

60. Heinrich Pudor, 'Kultur-Antisemitismus oder Pogrom-Antisemitismus?' in *Deutscher Volksrat*, 8 August 1919.

61. Plöckinger, *Soldaten*, 100ff. and 154f. Hitler can be shown to have been in the demobilization centre of the 2nd Inf.Rgt. since June (KAM, Nr. 4470/7111, Hitler's personal file).

62. On the 'stab in the back' legend see Boris Barth, *Dolchstoßlegenden und politische Desintegration. Das Trauma der deutschen Niederlage im Ersten Weltkrieg 1914–1933* (Düsseldorf, 2003); Rainer Sammet, *'Dolchstoß'. Deutschland und die Auseinandersetzung mit der Niederlage im Ersten Weltkrieg (1918–1933)* (Berlin, 2003).

63. On Hitler's anti-Semitism at this time see Kershaw *Hitler* 1, 168ff. and 197ff. Kershaw claims that Hitler only combined the topics of anti-Semitism and anti-Bolshevism in the summer of 1920. However, in fact he had already described the Jews as being the instigators of the revolution in his letter to Gemlich. Reuth's claim in *Judenhass* that Kershaw largely ignored the post-war phenomenon of anti-Semitic anti-Bolshevism in order to sustain his thesis of substantial continuity in German political culture from the Second Empire to the Weimar Republic does not do justice to Kershaw's nuanced argument (in particular 109ff.).

JOINING THE PARTY

1. Plöckinger, *Soldaten*, 140ff.

2. Ibid.,133ff. Plöckinger partly corrects the picture in Joachimsthaler, *Weg* 248ff.

3. Plöckinger, *Soldaten*, 151f. Baumann's presence is questionable. His name was mentioned not by Hitler but by Drexler and Lotter; the latter's statement cannot be verified by the surviving list of those present dated 12 September 1919, BAB, NS 26/80. Drexler's statement of 1936 that Hitler's first visit to the DAP and the dispute with Baumann might have taken place already in August 1919 also does not accord with it; ibid., NS 26/82, Memo. 23 January 1936.

4. BAB, NS 26/80, Attendance list; Plöckinger, *Soldaten*, 150. Bayerische Hauptstaatsarchiv (BHStA) V, Slg. P 3071, Drexler, Curriculum Vitae, 12 March 1935 and letter to Hitler, January 1940, published in Geschichtswerkstatt Neuhausen e.V. (ed.), *Neuhausen*, 231ff. and 235ff.; BAB, NS 26/78, Lotter, 1935 lecture, published in Joachimsthaler, *Weg*, 249 and 252f., and NS 26/78/3,

Drexler, letter to the NS-Hauptarchiv, 23 January 1936, published in part in ibid., 252ff. For Hitler's own account see *MK* (Munich, 1936), 237f. See also BAB, NS 26/76, minutes of the first DAP meetings. On this issue see Albrecht Tyrell, *Vom Trommler zum Führer. Der Wandel von Hitlers Selbstverständnis zwischen 1919 und 1924 und die Entwicklung der NSDAP* (Munich, 1975) 27f.

5. For example in Franz-Willing, *Ursprung*, 97ff.; Hagen Schulze, *Weimar. Deutschland 1917–1933* (Berlin, 1982), 331; Werner Maser, *Der Sturm auf die Republik. Frühgeschichte der NSDAP* (Frankfurt a. M, 1981), 157ff., to name only a few well-known works.

6. Hitler's membership card had the number 555 (only numbers from 500 onwards had been issued in order to give the impression of a larger number of members). However, the first membership numbers did not correspond to the order in which people joined the Party, but instead were given out altogether at a particular point in time, namely at the turn of the year 1919/1920, to existing members in alphabetical order. From membership number 714 onwards the membership numbers were given out in chronological order (BAB, NS 26/230, Membership list). Hitler's own claim to have been the seventh member to join the Party presumably refers to his role as a committee member. In this function he saw himself as the seventh member of the Party's hitherto six-member executive committee, of which, however, he was not formally a member. See Joachimsthaler, *Weg*, 254ff., see also 257, facsimile of a letter from Lotter to the Hauptarchiv, 17 October 1941 [BAB, NS 26/78/3].

7. Drexler had previously tried to win support for the extreme Right among the working class without much success. In March 1918 he had sought to spread propaganda for a victorious peace by setting up a Free Workers' Committee for a Good Peace. On Drexler see Tyrell, *Trommler*, 17ff.; Franz-Willing, *Ursprung*, 90ff. See also Drexler's piece 'Erwachen' (Awakening) with detailed statements about his political activities and his 1935 curriculum vitae (BHStA V, Slg. P 3071).

8. On Harrer see Tyrell, *Trommler*, 188; Reginald H. Phelps, '"Before Hitler Came". Thule Society and the Germanen Orden', in *Journal of Modern History* 35 (1963), 245–61.

9. Rudolf Sebottendorf, *Bevor Hitler kam. Urkundliches aus der Frühzeit der national-sozialistischen Bewegung* (Munich 1934, new edn. 1934), 81; the book appeared in 1934 in a slightly altered edition. BAB, NS 26/2234, Decision of the Bavarian Political Police on 1 March 1934 to confiscate the book on the grounds that it exaggerated the role of the Thule Society in the national renewal. In his 1935 cv (BHStAV, Slg. P 3071) Drexler gives 5 January 1919 as the date for the foundation of the National Socialist German Workers' Association e.V. It was established officially on 30 September 1920 (BAB, NS 26/76). This may have happened despite an earlier incorporation of the DAP as an association. On the founding process see Franz-Willing, *Ursprung*, 95.

10. BHStA V, Slg. P 3071, Drexler, Curriculum Vitae of 1935; Anton Drexler, 'Geburt und Werden der N.S.D.A.P', in *Völkischer Beobachter* (*VB*), 25 February 1934.

11. BAB, NS 26/76, minutes.

12. A. Drexler, 'Wie ein Arbeiter über die Schuldfrage denkt', in *Münchener Beobachter* (MB), 22 February 1919, and *Auf gut deutsch*, 29 August 1919.

13. Drexler, 'Erwachen', 37.

14. Joachimsthaler, *Weg*, 254; Kershaw, *Hitler* 1, 171. In *MK*, 238ff., Hitler portrays his joining the Party, presumably for dramatic effect ('it was the most important decision of my life'), as the result of a period of reflection lasting several days (244).

15. Plöckinger, *Soldaten*, 160ff.; KAM, SchützRgt. 41, Bund 5, Gebinde 229 (now Reichswehr SchützenRgt. 41, No. 5), Order of the Day, 12 November 1919, in which Hitler is mentioned. On the reconstruction of the propaganda material available to Gruppenkommando 4 see Plöckinger, *Soldaten*, 218ff.

16. KAM, Nr. 4470/7111, Hitler's personal file; *JK* Nos 75–78, No. 81f. and No. 84f.

17. Among these there was, in particular, a leaflet comparing the treaties of Brest-Litovsk and Versailles. See Plöckinger, *Soldaten*, 166; Text: *JK*, No. 72; *MK*, 525. Also: KAM, Gruppenkdo. 4, Nr. 314, Hitler file with references to Mayr's assignments to Hitler.

18. BAB, NS 26/230, No. 543.

19. Tyrell, *Trommler*, 195, fn. 77. According to Plöckinger, *Soldaten*, 149, the ex-prop-agandists were Ewald Bolle, Alois Knodn, Karl Schauböck, Johann Stricker, Heinrich Brauen, and Karl Eicher. BAB, NS 26/80, Attendance list; KAM, Gruppenkdo. 4, No. 309, re: Indoctrination commando, 22 July; No. 315, undated ms. Liste 'Lechfeld' and report on the indoctrination course in Lechfeld camp published in Deuerlein, 'Eintritt', 195 and 200.

20. Plöckinger, *Soldaten*, 145; BAB, NS 26/80, Attendance list.

21. Ibid.

22. SAM, SprkAkte K 379; BAB, NS 26/230, Membership list, No. 881, date of entry 8 March 1920.

23. Ernst Röhm, *Die Geschichte eines Hochverräters* (Munich, 1934), 113f.

24. BAB, NS 26/230, Membership list, No. 623; Röhm, *Geschichte*, 100f.; RSA 4/1, Doc. 67. On Röhm see Tyrell, *Trommler*, 197; Joachimsthaler, *Weg*, 256f.

25. KAM, Officer's personal file 61512: From this it is clear that Hierl was city com-mandant on 1 December 1919 and took up another post on 1 October 1920. Hitler's letter to Hierl of 3 July 1920 was sent to a private address and not to the commandant's office.

26. BAB, NS 26/230, Membership list, No. 524; Max Domarus (ed.), *Hitler. Reden und Proklamationen 1932–1945*, vol. 2 (Neustadt a.d. Aisch, 1963), 2111ff.; Winfried Heinemann, *Des Führers General. Eduard Dietl* (Paderborn, 2004).

27. BAB, NS 26/230, Membership list, No. 641; BAB, NS 26/80, Attendance list of 16 October 1919; SAM, SprkAkte, L 1711 (Schüssler), Judgment, 4 October 1948, and minutes of the session on the same day *MK*, 883; Tyrell, *Trommler*, 198; Joachimsthaler, *Weg*, 259.

28. BAB, NS 26/230, Membership list, No. 648.

29. BAB, NS 26/80, Attendance list, and NS 26/230, Membership list, No. 609.

30. Margarete Plewnia, *Auf dem Weg zu Hitler. Der völkische Publizist Dietrich Eckart* (Bremen, 1970), 28f. On Eckart see also Engelman, 'Dietrich Eckart and the Genesis of Nazism', PhD Washington University, St Louis, MO, 1971.

31. Eckart adopted Feder's demand for the breaking of interest slavery in a pamphlet, which he signed ('An alle werktätigen Deutschen'), BAB, NS 26/1318; it is published in Plewnia, *Weg*, 50.

32. Plewnia, *Weg*, 66; BAB, NS 26/76, Drexler to the Berlin banker, von Heimburg, 14 August 1919. Eckart gave another speech to a DAP meeting on 5 February 1920 on the topic of 'German Communism'. Deuerlein, 'Eintritt', Doc. 18.

33. Plewnia, *Weg*, 68ff.

34. BAB, R 8048/208, Gansser to Class, 21 July 1921: Eckart gave most of his fees from the staging rights to 'Peer Gynt' to the Party; as the play was staged in Berne in September 1921 this would have provided foreign exchange.

35. Rudolf von Sebottendorf, *Bevor*. Index.

36. Alfred Rosenberg, *Letzte Aufzeichnungen. Ideale und Idole der nationalsozialistischen Revolution*, 72ff., 83, and 91f.

37. NS 26/230, Membership list, No. 878, 11 March 1920. On Lehmann see Sigrid Stöckel (ed.), *Die 'rechte Nation' und ihr Verleger. Politik und Popularisierung im J.F. Lehmanns Verlag 1890–1979* (Berlin, 2002); on the Pan-German League see Hering, *Nation*, 482f.

38. BAB, NS 26/230, Membership list, No. 515.

39. BAB, NS 26/80, Attendance List; Tyrell, *Trommler*, 197.

40. *JK*, Nos 63 and 67.

41. Ibid., No. 93.

42. BAB, R 8048/258, Letter of thanks from Mayr to Class, 9 August 1920, and Class to Mayr, 18 August 1920; BAB, R 8048/392, Hopfen to Class, 1 August 1920, and Class to Hopfen, 18 August 1920 (published in Joachim Petzold, 'Class und Hitler. Über die Förderung der frühen Nazi-Bewegung durch den Alldeutschen Verband und dessen Einfluss auf die nazistische Ideologie', in *Jahrbuch für Geschichte* 21 (1980), Doc. 1).

43. For example, the League put an announcement in the *MB* for the DAP meeting on 16 October 1919 at which Hitler made his first big appearance. *MB*, 16 October 1919; Plöckinger, *Soldaten*, 158f.

44. BAB, NS 26/230, Membership list No. 670. Tafel wrote among others the pamphlets 'Das neue Deutschland', 'Parlamentarismus', and 'Volksvertretung' as well as 'Die Teuerung'.

45. BAB, NS 26/230, Membership list, No. 660, CV in Joachimsthaler, *Weg*, 367.

46. BAB, NS 26/230, Membership list, No. 531.

47. IfZ, ED 874/2, Feder Diary for 1920: 27 May and 2 June, 28 August, 16 September. The *MB* of 18 July reported on a further demonstration of the Kampfbund on 14 July in Munich.

48. *JK*, Nos 67 and 73; *MB*, 21 January 1920, Report on Feder's speech to the DAP on 18 January. There is evidence for more Feder speeches at NSDAP meetings on 18 May, 21 June, and 27 August 1920. See Deuerlein, 'Eintritt', 288f.

49. *MB*, 6 December 1919 on a meeting on 1 December in the concert hall of the Wagner Hotel.

50. BAB, NS 26/230, Membership list, No. 626.

51. Uwe Lohalm, *Radikalismus*, 295; SAM, SprkAkte K 1522.

52. Hermann Gilbhard, *Die Thule-Gesellschaft. Vom okkulten Mummenschanz zum Hakenkreuz* (Munich, 1994), 155.

53. *JK*, No. 63, No. 71 (appears here as 'Hesselmann, editor of the *Beobachter*') and No. 83.

54. Tyrell, *Trommler*, 72ff.

55. Sebottendorf, *Hitler*, 171ff.; Gilbhard, *Thule-Gesellschaft*, 154ff.

56. Manfred Weissbecker, 'Die Deutschsozialistische Partei 1919–1922', in Dieter Fricke (ed.), *Lexikon zur Parteigeschichte*, vol. 2 (Leipzig, 1984), 547–9.

57. *MB*, 25 October 1919.

58. BAB, NS 26/80, Attendance list; *JK*, No. 63; See Tyrell, *Trommler*, 197.

59. *JK*, Nos 66f. and 73; for the co-speakers see the footnotes to the individual documents.

60. Ibid., Nos 69 and 74.

61. Ibid., No. 262; BHStA V, Slg. P 3071, Drexler to Hitler, January 1940.

62. BAB, R 8005/26, Lindeiner report. His trip is mentioned in Elina Kiiskinen, *Deutschnationale Volkspartei*, 42; she does not, however, refer to Harrer's contacts.

63. *MK*, 390f. and 401.

64. BAB, NS 26/76, Rules of procedure, and NS 26/77, Organization of the committee of the Munich local branch. Tyrell, *Trommler*, 30f.; Joachimsthaler, *Weg*, 265f., with a facsimile of Hitler's signature; BHStA V, Slg. P 3071, Drexler to Hitler, January 1940.

65. Joachimsthaler, *Weg*, 265.

66. See *MK*, 390f. and 401; RSA 3/2, Doc. 62; RSA 4/1, Doc. 61.

67. Lohalm, *Radikalismus*, 293f.

68. *JK*, No. 83; complete reproduction of the police report in Phelps, 'Hitler', Doc. 2; *MK*, 400ff.; Joachimsthaler, *Weg*, S. 268; Kershaw, *Hitler* I, 186ff.

69. Agricola, 'Geldwahn'. Dingfelder published as Germanus Agricola with the Hoheneichen-Verlag as well as regularly in the *MB*. On his giving up the pseudonym see Fenske, *Konservatismus*, 325.

70. Drexler claimed retrospectively both to have been responsible for the mass meeting and also for co-authorship of the programme (BHStA V, P 3071, Drexler to Hitler, January 1940); see also Joachimsthaler, *Weg*, 267ff.

71. It corresponds fairly closely with the DSP's programme, which the *MB* had published on 31 May 1919 under the heading 'Our Political Programme!'

72. Ernst Deuerlein, *Der Aufstieg der NSDAP in Augenzeugenberichten* (Munich, 1974), 108ff.

73. Tyrell, *Trommler*, 191; *JK*, No. 168.

74. Johannes Erger, *Der Kapp–Lüttwitz-Putsch. Ein Beitrag zur deutschen Innenpolitik 1919/1920* (Düsseldorf, 1967).

75. Michael Kellogg, *The Russian Roots of Nazism. White Emigrés and the Making of National Socialism, 1917–1945* (Cambridge, 2005), 88. According to the report of the Augsburg industrialist and Nazi sympathizer Gottfried Grandel of 22 October 1941, Eckart was the central figure in the organization of the Kapp putsch in Bavaria (see BAB, NS 26/514).

76. Mayr to Kapp, 24 September 1920, published in Kurt Gossweiler, *Kapital, Reichswehr und NSDAP. Zur Frühgeschichte des deutschen Faschismus 1919–1924* (Cologne, 1982), 554ff.; on the indications that this link had already existed since the beginning of 1920 see Plöckinger, *Soldaten*, 174.

77. Mayr mentions the flight in his letter to Kapp, 24 September 1920, published in Gossweiler, *Kapital*, 554ff.; BAB, NS 26/514, Gottfried Grandel (Freiburg), Report, 22 October 1941.

78. Fenske, *Konservatismus*, 89ff.; Horst G. W. Nusser, *Konservative Wehrverbände in Bayern, Preußen und Österreich 1918–1933* (Munich, 1973), 196ff.

79. Bruno Thoss, *Der Ludendorff-Kreis 1919–1923. München als Zentrum, der mitteleuropäischen Gegenrevolution zwischen Revolution und Hitler-Putsch* (Munich, 1978), esp. 351ff.

80. On the cell of order see Karl-Ludwig Ay, 'Von der Räterepublik zur Ordnungszelle Bayern. Die politischen Rahmenbedingungen für den Aufstieg Hitlers in München', in Björn Mensing and Friedrich Prinz (eds), *Irrlicht im leuchtenden München? Der Nationalsozialismus in der 'Hauptstadt der Bewegung'* (Regensburg, 1991); Martin H. Geyer, *Verkehrte Welt. Revolution, Inflation, und Moderne. München, 1914–1924* (Göttingen, 1998), 112–17; Herbert Speckner, 'Die Ordnungszelle Bayern. Studien zur Politik des Bayerischen Bürgertums, insbesondere der Bayerischen Volkspartei, von der Revolution bis zum Ende des Kabinetts Dr. von Kahr', Dissertation. Erlangen, 1955.

81. Fenske, *Konservatismus*, 166.

82. Pamphlet, 29 February 1920, quoted in Fenske, *Konservatismus*, 166.

83. *JK*, Nos 242 and 259.

84. Speeches until the end of 1920 in ibid., Nos 87f., 90–115, 117–21, 123–31, 134, 136–41, 143–8, 150f., 153–5, 157–61, 164–73, and 177.

85. Ibid., No. 100 (Hofbräuhaus, 11 May 1920: 2,000), No. 118 (Bürgerbräukeller, 6 July 1920: 2,400) and No. 148 (Münchner-Kindl-Keller, 24 September 1920: 3,000–4,000).

86. Thus the main line taken in ibid., Nos 93, 100, and 108b.

87. Ibid., Nos 83 and 108b.

88. Ibid., Nos 91 and 103.

89. Ibid., Nos 69 and 146. On Hitler's foreign policy ideas during the early phase of his career see Axel Kuhn, *Hitlers außenpolitisches Programm. Entstehung und Entwicklung 1919–1939* ((Stuttgart, 1970), 32ff.

90. *JK*, No. 69.

91. Ibid., No. 109.

92. Ibid., No. 121; see also Nos 124 and 124b.

93. Ibid., Nos 272 and 380.

94. So long as he was a soldier (till the end of March 1920) he avoided using the, at the time, quite usual propaganda slogan of Jewish Bolshevism in public and, compared with his later tirades, was restrained in his anti-Semitic statements. See Plöckinger, *Soldaten*, esp. 342f., points out that his caution was a response to the official position of the Reichswehr.

95. *JK*, Nos 96, 103, 105, 121, and 124.

96. Ibid., Nos 103, 108b, 112, and 121.

97. Ibid., No. 139.

98. Plewnia, *Weg*, 94ff.

99. *JK*, No. 136. On this speech see also Kershaw, *Hitler* 1, 197.

100. *JK*, Nos 91 and 96.

101. Ibid., No. 91.

102. Ibid., No. 136; see also Nos 91, 112, and 159.

103. Ibid., No. 173.

104. Ibid., No. 129.

105. Ibid., No. 140.

106. Müller, *Wandel*, 144f.

107. Carl Zuckmayer, *Als wär's ein Stück von mir. Horen der Freundschaft* (Frankfurt a. M., 1971), 435f.

108. SAM, SprkAkte Amann K 20, Interrogation, 5 November 1947. On Hitler's exaggerated rhetorical style see also the notes of the opera singer, Paul Stieber-Walter, stage name Paul Devrient, who gave Hitler speech training in 1932. See Werner Maser (ed.), *Paul Devrient: Mein Schüler Adolf Hitler. Das Tagebuch seines Lehrers* (Munich, 2003).

109. *JK*, Nos 195 and 238.

110. Alfred Stein, 'Adolf Hitler und Gustav le Bon. Der Meister der Massenbewegung und sein Lehrer', in *Geschichte in Wissenschaft und Unterricht* 6 (1955), 362–8.

111. Tyrell, *Trommler*, 42ff., on the sources of Hitler's propaganda see also 53ff.; *VB*, 29 September 1919, 'Die Massenseele'.

112. *MK*, 107ff., 193 and 376.

113. Ibid., 194. He devotes a whole chapter to the war propaganda.

114. Ibid., 197.

115. Ibid., 198.

116. Ibid., 201.

117. Ibid., 649.

118. *JK*, No. 178.

119. *MK*, 649.

120. Ibid., 653.

121. Tyrell, *Trommler*, 37f.; on this, retrospectively: SAM, PolDir. 6778, Committee to Hitler 15 July 1921.

122. Tyrell, *Trommler*, 42ff. in detail on his political conception, also 65ff. on the impetus and reasons prompting Hitler to take over the Party chairmanship. On the leadership crisis in the summer of 1921 see Wolfgang Horn, *Der Marsch zur Machtergreifung. Die NSDAP bis 1933* (Düsseldorf, 1980), 53ff.; Kershaw, *Hitler* 1, 208ff.

123. On his unstable mental state and unpredictability see Tyrell, *Trommler*, 107ff.

124. Excerpt published in Petzold, 'Class', Doc. 10.

125. *JK*, Nos 96 and 95.

126. Ibid., No. 101.

127. Ibid., No. 185.

128. Ibid., No. 203.

HITLER BECOMES PARTY LEADER

1. Paul J. Madden, 'The Social Composition of the Nazi Party 1919–1930', Dissertation, University of Oklahoma 1976, 77.

2. *JK*, No. 97.

3. Donald M. Douglas, 'The Early Ortsgruppen. The Development of National Socialist Local Groups', Dissertation, Lawrence/Kansas, 1968, 55ff. and 93.

4. Lohalm, *Radikalismus*. 298 and 306ff.

5. *JK*, No. 116.

6. See Georg Franz-Willing, *Ursprung*, 286, Lehmann to Mayr, 24 June 1920 (according to Franz-Willing in 'private hands').

7. Plöckinger, *Soldaten*, 74.

8. Mayr to Kapp, 24 September 1920, published in Gossweiler, *Kapital*, 554ff., quote 556f.

9. KAM, Gruppenkdo. 4, No. 253.

10. BAB, NS 26/229, Entries 22 July, 24 October, 18 November, and 7 December 1920; see Tyrell, 175ff.

11. BHStA V, Slg. P 3071, Drexler to Hitler, January 1940. *JK* No. 175; BAB, NS 26/514, Grandel report, 22 October 1941. On the take-over of the paper see Tyrell, *Trommler*, 175ff.; Franz-Willing, *Ursprung*, 271ff.

12. BAB, R 8048/258, published in Joachim Petzold, 'Class', Doc. 2. The letter was intended for Class and for Paul Bang, another influential figure in the Pan-German League. From the letter it is clear that Hitler had got to know Class following a stay by the latter in Munich, which is confirmed by Class's unpublished memoirs. See Johannes Leicht, *Heinrich Class 1898–1953. Die politische Biographie eines Alldeutschen* (Paderborn, 2012), 287; also, Hitler had already visited Class in Berlin during 1920 perhaps in connection with his March trip to the capital. See ibid.

13. Petzold, 'Class', Docs. 3–5; the originals are all in the file BAB, R 8048/258. On this issue see also Leicht, *Class*, 287ff.

14. BAB, R 8048/258, Class to Tafel, 8 June 1921, Petzold, 'Class', Doc. 6.

15. Lothar Gruchmann and Reinhard Weber (eds), *Der Hitler-Prozess 1924. Wortlaut der Hauptverhandlung vor dem Volksgericht München I* (Munich, 1997), 447.

16. Adolf Hitler *MK*, 403.

17. Ibid., 558ff.; *JK*, No. 193.

18. Ibid., No 194. Eckart claimed in an article in *Auf gut deutsch* (Heft 5/6, 15 February 21, 65–71), that Hitler's appearance had been intentionally drowned out by music.

19. *JK*, No. 205 and No. 210.

20. Assessment by *JK*.

21. Ibid., No. 116, see also No. 66; Petzold, 'Class', No. 6; Ludolf Herbst, *Hitlers Charisma. Die Erfindung eines deutschen Messias* (Frankfurt a. M., 2010), 115; Karl Alexander von Müller, Wandel, vol. 3, 144: The audience at a Hitler speech in the Löwenbräukeller consisted 'largely of the downwardly mobile middle class in all its variations' (refers to 1923).

22. Police report of the meeting, 5 September 1920, published in Reginald H. Phelps, 'Hitler als Parteiredner im Jahre 1920', in *Vierteljahrshefte für Zeitgeschichte* (IfZ) 1 (1963), Doc. 13; Peter Longerich, *Geschichte der SA* (Munich, 2003), 23.

23. Graf claims that the 'Security Service' was established when the Party's evening meetings were moved from the Sterneckerbräu to the Högerbräu, which in fact happened in the summer/autumn of 1921 (*JK*, Nos 265 and 301). His aim was to bridge the period during which the Sturmabteilung (SA) (Storm Department), officially established in August 1921, was created from the 'Sportabteilung' ('Sports Department') (IfZ F 14, Wie ich den Führer kennenlernte, 19 August 1934). On his background and career see Joachimsthaler, *Weg*, 277; Albrecht Tyrell (ed.), *Führer befiehl . . . Selbstzeugnisse aus der 'Kampfzeit' der NSDAP, Dokumentation und Analyse* (Düsseldorf, 1969), 23.

24. SAM, PolDir. 10172 (Weber file), contains details of numerous investigations concerning his NSDAP activities. See, in particular, the interrogation of 18 May 1923. See also SAM, SprkAkte K 1910, Verdict of 20 February 1948; *VB* (Bayern), 25 August 1933, 'Pg. Christian Weber, der unerschrockene Kämpfer'; Thomas von Berg, *Korruption und Bereicherung. Politische Biographie des Münchner NSDAP-Fraktionsvorsitzenden Christian Weber (1883–1945)* (Munich, 2003); Markus Schiefer, 'Vom "Blauen Bock" in die Residenz', in Marita Krauss (ed.), *Rechte Karrieren in München. Von der Weimarer Zeit bis in die Nachkriegsjahre* (Munich, 2010).

25. SAM, SprkAkte K 1131, Protocol of the session on 13 May 1948.

26. Rudolf Hess, *Briefe 1908–1933* (Munich, 1987), Nos 280, 265; Erich Ludendorff, *Vom Feldherrn zum Weltrevolutionär und Wegbereiter deutscher Volksschöpfung*, vol. 1 (Munich, 1934), 161; Thoss, *Ludendorff-Kreis*, 257; Hans-Adolf Jacobsen (ed.), *Karl Haushofer. Leben und Werk*, vol. 1 (Boppard am Rhein, 1979), 225ff.

27. Heinz Kurz, former leader of the Kampfbund Thule, recalled in 1975, that Hess checked the applicants to the Kampfbund and later those to the Free Corps Oberland (interview in Gilbhard, *Thule-Gesellschaft*, Appendix. In a letter to his parents of 18 May 1919 Hess described his participation in the uprising against the councils' regime on 1 May (Hess, *Briefe*). Wulf Schwarzwäller, *Rudolf Hess. Der Stellvertreter* (Munich, 1987), 64ff., contains a number of details on Hess's conspiratorial activity for the Thule, but without evidence. On the audience with Kahr see Speckner, Ordnungszelle, 205; on the Hess letter to Kahr see Deuerlein, *Aufstieg*), 132ff.

28. Stephen G. North, *Rudolf Hess. A Political Biography* (Saarbrücken, 2010), 62ff.; Kurt Pätzold and Manfred Weissbecker, *Rudolf Hess. Der Mann an Hitlers Seite* (Leipzig, 1999), 34ff.

29. On the circle around Scheubner-Richter see Michael Kellogg, *The Russian Roots of Nazism. White Emigrés and the Making of National Socialism, 1917–1945* (Cambridge, 2005), esp. 41f., 79ff., 111f., and 122ff.; on the Russian emigrés in Munich see Johannes Baur, *Die russische Kolonie in München 1900–1945: Deutsch-russische Beziehungen im 20. Jahrhundert* (Wiesbaden, 1998) (on Scheubner-Richter esp. 253ff.); Ernst Piper, *Alfred Rosenberg. Hitlers Chefideologe* (Munich, 2005), 55ff.; Karsten Brüggemann, 'Max Erwin von Scheubner-Richter (1884–1923) – der Führer des "Führers"?'in Michael Gerleff (ed.), *Deutschbalten, Weimarer Republik und Drittes Reich*, vol. 1 (Cologne, 2001).The personal histories of Kursell, Rosenberg, Scheubner-Richter, and Schickedanz are brought together in *Album Rubonorum 1875–1972* (Neustadt a. d. Aisch, 1972). See also Otto von Kursell, *Erinnerungen an Dr. Max von Scheubner-Richter* (Munich, 1969).

30. Tyrell, *Trommler*, 96f.; *JK*, No. 129ff.

31. Letter to Riehl, 19 January 1921, in Alexander Schilling, *Dr. Walter Riehl und die Geschichte des Nationalsozialismus* (Leipzig, 1933), 266.

32. Tyrell, *Trommler*, 103ff.; *JK*, No. 262, refers to this event.

33. Joachimsthaler, *Weg*, 285.

34. Tyrell, *Trommler*, 110ff.

35. Ibid., 122f.The resignation statement is in *JK*, No. 262, with a detailed justification of his decision.

36. For details see ibid.

37. According to the persuasive analysis in Tyrell (*Trommler*, esp. 122f.), who rejects contrary interpretations in the older literature. See also Kershaw, *Hitler*, 1, 211.

38. *MK*, 658f.

39. *JK*, No. 262.

40. SAM, PolDir. 6778, Written statement by the committee, 5 July 1921.

41. Tyrell, *Trommler*, S. 129; Pamphlet: Deuerlein, *Aufstieg*, 138ff., quote, 138.

42. SAM, PolDir. 6778, Note about the two visitors of 15 July 1921.

43. *JK*, No. 267.

44. Tyrell, *Trommler*, 129ff.; *JK*, No. 270.

45. For the statutes see Tyrell (ed.), *Führer*, No. 9; for their interpretation see Tyrell, *Trommler*, 132ff.

46. On Weber see Berg, *Korruption*, 19f.; SAM, PolDir. 10172. On Amann: SAM, PolDir.6784, Amann statement, 27 December 1928, to the magistrates' court in Munich, according to which he joined the Party in August 1921.

47. RSA 4/1, Doc. 61. The rental agreement, dated 22 December 1919, for the 'Reichsrätezimmer' in the Sterneckerbräu; one of the signatures is Hitler's (BAB, NS 26/80).

48. *VB*, 4 August 1921.

49. Ibid., 11 August 1921.

50. Leicht, *Class*, 290.

51. Fenske, *Konservatismus*, 143ff.; Horst Nusser, *Konservative Wehrverbände in Bayern, Preußen, und Österreich 1918–1933* (Munich, 1973), 215ff.

52. SAM, PolDir. 6804, Membership list.

53. For the early history of the SA and the agreement between Hitler and Ehrhardt see Longerich, *Geschichte*, 22ff.; Andreas Werner, 'SA und NSDAP: "Wehrverband", "Parteitruppe", oder "Revolutionsarmee"? Studien zur Geschichte der SA und der NSDAP 1920–1933', Dissertation Erlangen-Nürnberg, 1965, 38ff.

54. Fenske, *Konservatismus*, 169f.; Ernst Rudolf Huber, *Deutsche Verfassungsgeschichte seit 1789* vol. 7 (Stuttgart, 1984), 206ff.; Gerhard Schulz, *Die Periode der Konsolidierung und Revision des Bismarckschen Reichsaufbaus 1919–1930*, 2nd edn (Berlin/New York, 1987), 364ff.

55. Martin H. Geyer, *Verkehrte Welt. Revolution, Inflation und Moderne. München 1914–1924* (Göttingen, 1998), 175f.

56. *JK*, Nos 274 and 280.

57. Fenske, *Konservatismus*, 170.

58. Kershaw, *Hitler*, 1, 225f. See, for example, *JK*, Nos 361f. and 376.

59. Deuerlein, *Aufstieg*, 145f.

60. *VB*, 1 October 1921.

61. Deuerlein, *Aufstieg*, 146f.

62. *JK*, No. 308.

63. Ibid., No. 313f. *MK*, 563ff., with a detailed account of the pub brawl.

64. Deuerlein, *Aufstieg*, 147ff.

65. Hitler, *Monologe*, 30 January 1942.

66. *VB*, 15 March 1922 asserts that, in response to a question from the Independent Socialist, Ernst Niekisch, Schweyer had announced that the Bavarian government was considering Hitler's deportation. On his sentence see Deuerlein, *Aufstieg*, 150f.; Kershaw, *Hitler*, 1, 224f.

67. *JK*, No. 352.

68. Ibid., Nos 350f. and 352 (for the quote). See also No. 347.

69. Douglas, Ortsgruppen, 123, 166ff. and 202f.

70. Madden, Composition, 77 and 86.

71. *JK*, No. 347.

72. Ibid., No. 353.

73. Julius K. Engelbrechten and Hans Volz, *Wir wandern durch das nationalsozialistische Berlin* (Munich, 1937), 52, a revised version of a report by Fritz Geisler; for the more detailed original see BAB, R 43 II/883a, 9 October 1936. See also *JK*, No. 330.

74. BAB, R 8048/208, Class to Hitler, 11 Mai 1922, published in Petzold, 'Class', Doc. 6.

75. BAB, NS 26/1223, Invitation, 26 May 1922, published in Joachimsthaler, *Weg*, 278. On Emil Gansser see ibid., 369f.; Henry Ashby Turner, *Die Großunternehmer und der Aufstieg Hitlers* (Berlin, 1985), 68f.

76. The report of this speech comes from an account based on recollections by Fritz Geisler (a shortened version [BAB, R 43 II/883a], published in *JK*, No. 387; for a longer version see Engelbrechten and Volz, *Wir wandern*, 53 (quote)).

77. For the content of the second speech see ibid., 54; on Burhenne see BAB, NS 26/1223, Letters to Burhenne 8 March, 2 August and 1 December 1922, published in Gossweiler, *Kapital*, 558ff.

78. Turner, *Großunternehmer*, 70f.

79. BAB, R 8048/No. 208, also published in Petzold, 'Class', Doc. 9, with the note '150.000'.

80. BHStA, MA 10374, Committee of Investigation, 87f. (Statement by Hermann Aust, 15 January 1924); SAM, PolDir. 6784, Copy of a statement by Aust, 16 February 1929, to the Munich magistrates' court. See also Turner, *Großunternehmer*, 69.

81. Engelbrechten and Volz, *Wir wandern*, 54.

82. Tyrell, ed., *Führer*, No. 14.

83. SAM, PolDir. 6697, Statement by Weber, 10 January 1924, in which, as former head of the NSDAP's transport department, he comments on the Party's use of motor vehicles. PolDir.6804 contains further material on the transport department. On the use of motor vehicles by the early NSDAP see Joachimsthaler, *Weg*, 301f.

84. Adolf Hitler, *Reden, Schriften, Anordnungen: Februar 1925 bis Januar 1933,* 17 vols (Munich, 1992–2003) (RSA) 4/1, Doc. 61.

85. Ernst Hanfstaengl, *Zwischen Weissem und Braunem Haus. Memoiren eines politischen Aussenseiters* (Munich, 1970), 52ff.

86. *JK*, No. 269.

87. In the anonymous pamphlet 'Adolf Hitler – Verräter?', published in Deuerlein, *Aufstieg*, 238f.

88. *JK*, Nos 329 and 269. See Tyrell, *Trommler*, 209; Kershaw, *Hitler*, 1, 20 (quote).

THE MARCH TO THE HITLER PUTSCH

1. Hans Fenske, *Konservatismus*, 179ff.; Gerhard Schulz, *Periode*, 374ff.; Ernst Rudolf Huber, *Verfassungsgeschichte*, 249ff.

2. *JK*, No. 399; *Münchener Neueste Nachrichten (MNN)* 17 August 1922: 'Bayern und das Reich'. At an internal Party meeting following the demonstration Hitler expressed his 'satisfaction at the successful demonstration'. See *JK*, No. 400. See also Kershaw, *Hitler*, 1, 226.

3. Fenske, *Konservatismus*, 179ff.; Ernst Deuerlein (ed.), *Der Hitler-Putsch. Bayerische Dokumente zum 8/9 November 1923* (Stuttgart, 1962) 40ff. The *MNN*, 25–27 August 1922, reported on the 'evening demonstration' but nothing about the plans for a putsch.

4. Kershaw, *Hitler*, 1, 226f.; *JK*, No. 403. On 27 February 1925, Hitler declared in the Pittinger slander trial at the magistrates' court in Munich: 'I'm prepared to prove that Herr Pittinger tried to do the same thing in 1922 that we failed to bring off in 1923.' See RSA 2, Doc. 3.

5. Published in Franz Menges, *Hans Schmelzle, Bayerischer Staatsrat im Ministerium des Äußeren und Finanzminister. Eine politische Biographie mit Quellenanhang* (Munich, 1972) 221ff.; see also Geyer, *Verkehrte Welt*, 319ff.

6. Kershaw, *Hitler*, 1, 227f.; Andreas Werner, SA, 57ff.; Longerich, *Geschichte*, 29; *JK*, No. 410; *MK*, 614ff.

7. Rainer Hambrecht, *Der Aufstieg der NSDAP in Mittel- und Oberfranken 1925–1933* (Nuremberg, 1976), 34f.

8. J. Paul Madden, 'Composition', 93, has 7,768 members for September 1922 and estimates the number at the beginning of 1923 as 8,100.

9. Douglas, Ortsgruppen, Lists, 229f. and 262f.

10. Fenske, *Konservatismus*, 165ff.

11. *JK*, No. 418; Kurt G. W. Lüdecke, *I Knew Hitler. The Story of a Nazi Who Escaped the Blood Purge* (London, 1938), 110.

12. Werner, SA, 61f.

13. *JK*, Nos 439–448.

14. Ibid, No. 449; Longerich, *Geschichte*, 30.

15. Kurt Sontheimer, *Antidemokratisches Denken in der Weimarer Republik. Die politischen Ideen des deutschen Nationalismus zwischen 1918 und 1933* (Munich, 1968), 214ff.; Klaus Schreiner, '"Wann kommt der Retter Deutschlands?" Formen und Funktionen von politischem Messianismus in der Weimarer Republik', in *Saeculum* 49 (1998), 107–60.

16. *Aufbau*, No. 21, 11 September 1919.

17. *Auf gut deutsch* 40/41, 5 December 1919, 613f.

18. *VB*, 8 November 1923.

19. Refers to the meeting of 30 November.

20. Kurt Pätzold and Manfred Weissbecker, *Rudolf Hess. Der Mann an Hitlers Seite* (Leipzig, 1999), Doc. 3.

21. *Auf gut deutsch* 44/45, 30 December 1919.

22. Henry A. Turner, *Großunternehmer*, 74ff.; Georg Franz-Willing, *Ursprung*, 266ff.

23. This is clear from a remark by Ernst Hanfstaengl in Hanfstaengl, *Haus*, 65.

24. Hitler, *Monologe*, 16/17 January 1942; Turner, *Großunternehmer*, 68.

25. Text of the agreement ('in private hands'), published in Franz-Willing, *Ursprung*, 289f. with the wrong spelling of the name as 'Frank'. Bayerisches Hauptstaatsarchiv (BHStA), MA 10374, Committee of Inquiry, 89 (Bechstein statement). Bechstein in the Hitler trial: *Hitler und Kahr* 2, 102; Hanfstaengl, *Haus*, 76; Anton Joachimsthaler, *Hitlers Liste. Ein Dokument persönlicher Beziehungen* (Munich, 2003), 63f.

26. BHStA, MA 10374, Committee of Inquiry, 77ff.

27. SAM, PolDir. 6784, copy of the statement by Gertrud von Seidlitz, 2 February 1929 to the Munich magistrates' court. BHStA, MA 10374, Committee of Inquiry, 89f.; Joachimsthaler, *Liste*, 136ff.

28. Turner, *Großunternehmer*, 443; BHStA, MA 10374, Committee of Inquiry, 90.

29. Lüdecke, *Hitler*, 71ff.

30. Ibid., 137ff.

31. On the suspicion of spying see RSA 3/3, Doc. 13; Deuerlein (ed.), *Hitler-Putsch*, 546ff.

32. Arthur L. Smith, 'Kurt Lüdecke. "The Man who Knew Hitler"', in *German Studies Review* 26/3 (2003), 597–606. On the relationship between Hitler and Lüdecke see also the (admittedly very speculative) account in Lothar Machtan, *Hitlers Geheimnis. Das Doppelleben eines Diktators* (Berlin, 2001), 305ff.

33. Hanfstaengl, *Haus*, 43ff.

34. Ibid., 59f. and 187f. The agreement was presented to the Bavarian Landtag's committee of enquiry (BHStA, MA 10374, S. 113f.).

35. Joachimsthaler, *Liste*, 301ff.

36. Friedrich Percyval Reck-Malleczewen, *Tagebuch eines Verzweifelten*, new edn (Stuttgart, 1966), 226ff.

37. Müller, *Wandel*, 129.

38. Hanfstaengl, *Haus*, e.g., 44f., 48f., and 70ff.

39. Rudolf Herz, *Hoffmann & Hitler. Fotografie als Medium des Führer-Mythos* (Munich, 1994), esp. 26ff. and 92ff. See also *Das Hitler-Bild. Die Erinnerungen des Fotografen Heinrich Hoffmann* (St Polten, 2008), which the journalist Joe Heydecker wrote after conversations with Hoffmann and was first published in 1954 in the *Münchener Illustrierte*. What purported to be memoirs of Hoffmann, who had died in 1957, appeared in 1974 under the title 'Hitler, wie ich ihn sah'.

40. Herz, *Hoffmann*, 92ff.

41. Hitler, *Monologe*, 20 August 1942; Anton Joachimsthaler (ed.), *Christa Schroeder, Er war mein Chef. Aus dem Nachlass der Sekretärin von Adolf Hitler* (Munich, 1983), 55; Hanfstaengl, *Haus*, 174.

42. *Hitler-Bild*, 157.

43. Hanfstaengl, *Haus*, 49ff.

44. Engelman, Eckart.; Plewnia, *Weg*, 88ff.

45. Schroeder, *Chef*, 6ff.; Hitler, *Monologe*, contains numerous recollections of Eckart, e.g. 16/17 January 1942.

46. Fenske, *Konservatismus*, 185.

47. *JK*, No. 464.

48. Ibid., No. 466, also No. 465. In No. 484 Hitler describes the negotiations from his point of view.

49. Ernst Röhm, *Die Geschichte eines Hochverräters* (Munich, 1934), 164f.

50. Reports on the twelve appearances in *JK*, Nos 467–478.

51. Ibid., Nos 463 and 479.

52. Ibid., Nos 480–483. On the Party Rally see Kershaw, *Hitler*, 1, 244f.; Werner, SA, 69ff.; *VB*, 31 January 1923: 'Deutschland erwache!'.

53. Röhm, *Geschichte*, 167.

54. On the military training by the Reichswehr see also Hitler's 1924 statement in Lothar Gruchmann and Reinhard Weber (eds), *Der Hitler-Prozess 1924. Wortlaut der Hauptverhandlung vor dem Volksgericht München*, vol. 1 (Munich, 1997), 188. Fenske, *Konservatismus*, 185ff.

55. Hitler recalled details during the war. See *Monologe*, 16/17 January 1942.

56. Alfred Kube, *Pour le mérite und Hakenkreuz. Hermann Göring im Dritten Reich* (Munich, 1986), 8f.; Hanfstaengl, *Haus*, 88ff.

57. Fanny Gräfin von Wilamowitz-Moellendorff, *Carin Göring* (Berlin, 1934), 58f. Apart from Hitler, the author cites as guests Dietrich Eckart, Hermann Esser, and Ernst Hanfstaengl.

58. Werner, SA, 72ff.; Longerich, *Geschichte*, 34.

59. Bruno Thoss, *Der Ludendorff-Kreis 1919–1923. München als Zentrum der mitteleuropäischen Gegenrevolution zwischen Revolution und Hitler-Putsch* (Munich, 1978), 281f.; Röhm, *Geschichte*, 180f.; *Hitler-Prozeß*, 188 (Hitler statement). Hitler can, however, be shown to have been in Munich on this day (*JK*, No. 493).

60. *Hitler-Prozeß*, 681 (Hitler statement).

61. Werner, SA, 103ff.; Longerich, *Geschichte*, 35f.

62. *JK*, No. 524.

63. Lothar Gruchmann, 'Hitlers Denkschrift an die bayerische Justiz zum 16. Mai 1923. Ein verloren geglaubtes Dokument', in *VjZ* 39 (1991), 305–38.

64. Geyer, *Welt*, 321ff.

65. On the 1923 crisis see among others Schulz, *Periode*, 404ff.; Fenske, *Konservatismus*, 207ff.; Heinrich August Winkler, *Von der Revolution zur Stabilisierung. Arbeiter und Arbeiterbewegung in der Weimarer Republik 1918 bis 1924* (Berlin, 1984), 505ff.

66. Thoss, *Ludendorff-Kreis*, 316ff.; Werner, SA, 123ff.

67. Ibid., 134ff.

68. On the pre-history of the putsch see Harold J. Gordon, *Hitlerputsch 1923. Machtkampf in Bayern 1923–1924* (Munich, 1978), 193ff.

69. Deuerlein (ed.), *Hitler-Putsch*, Doc. 16; Geyer, *Welt*, 338.

70. Ibid., 340f.

71. Ibid., 342ff.

72. *JK*, No. 572.

73. Gordon, *Hitlerputsch*, 206ff.; Fenske, *Konservatismus*, 207ff.

74. Gordon, *Hitlerputsch*, 224ff.

75. Ibid., 210ff.; Deuerlein (ed.), *Hitler-Putsch*, Doc. 42. On Ehrhardt's role and on the border defence operation see Wilhelm Hoegner, *Hitler und Kahr. Die bayerischen Napoleonsgrössen von 1923. Ein im Untersuchungsausschuss des bayerischen Landtages aufgedeckter Justizskandal* (Munich, 1928), 20ff.

76. Deuerlein (ed.), *Hitler-Putsch*, Doc. 61.

77. Kriebel, however, was present, representing the Kampfbund as a whole.

78. Deuerlein (ed.), *Hitler-Putsch*, Doc. 68; *Hitler-Prozess*, 161 (Hitler statement). On the military training of Nazis by the Reichswehr see in detail Hoegner, *Hitler und Kahr*, 105ff.

79. Gordon, *Hitlerputsch*, 229.

80. Ibid., 230; *Hitler-Prozeß*, 859f. (Seisser statement).

81. Ibid., 736ff. (Lossow statement).

82. Gordon, *Hitlerputsch*, 230.

83. *Hitler-Prozeß*, 737.

84. Madden, 'Composition', 34 and 93 (the author estimates the number of members at the beginning of 1923 at 8,100).

85. Michael Kater, 'Zur Soziographie der frühen NSDAP', in *VjZ* 19 (1971), 124–59.

86. From 13 April onwards, the announcement 'our Führer Adolf Hitler will speak' appeared regularly in the *Völkischer Beobachter*.

87. See Kershaw, *Hitler*, 1, 234ff.; *JK*, Nos 493, 521, 533.

88. Ibid., No. 525.

89. Ibid., No. 544.

CUNARD

Daily Crossword Puzzle

I	T	C	H		P	U	N	C	T	U	A	L
N		L		I		R		O		T		U
S	W	O	L	L	E	N		U	N	T	I	L
E		W		L				N		E		L
C		N		E		V		T		R		
U				G		A		R		L		B
R	O	T		I	N	L	A	Y		Y	O	U
E		E		T		U		W				S
	P	R	A	I	S	E	W	O	R	T	H	Y
S		R		M			M		E			B
K	O	A	L	A		S	H	A	M	P	O	O
I		C		T		E		N		I		D
D	E	E	P	E	N	E	D		E	D	D	Y

Across

1. Skin imitation (4)
3. Prompt (8)
9. Enlarged; puffy (7)
10. Up to the time when (5)
11. Room attached to a house (12)
14. Decay (3)
16. Embed; type of filling (5)
17. Not me (3)
18. Laudatory (12)
21. Australian arboreal marsupial (5)
22. Hair-cleansing product (7)
23. Intensified (8)
24. Circular movement of water (4)

Down

1. Lacking confidence (8)
2. Children's entertainer (5)
4. Ancient pot (3)
5. Female fellow national (12)
6. Totally (7)
7. Quieten down (4)
8. Unlawful (12)
12. Regard highly (5)
13. Meddlesome person (8)
15. Patio area (7)
19. Lukewarm (5)
20. Slide; Ioe grip (4)
22. Notice (3)

Crossword 1931

Sudoku

367	2	1367	4	5689	8			
4567	47	9	57	1	3	6	257	24578
4567	13467	8	567	5689	2			
	5			3	7			9
1				2	4			6
3			9	56	1		4	
		8	8	9	3			
6789	36789	5	2	4	5	1	679	7
299	149	124	3	7	6	2459	8	295

Crossword Answers

90. Ibid., No. 561.

91. Ibid., No. 580.

92. Ibid., No. 583a.

93. *VB*, 1 November 1922: 'Männer und Waschweiber'.

94. In Saxony the intervention occurred on 23 October, the 'Reich execution', in other words the appointment of a Reich commissioner, on 29 October; in Thuringia the troops marched in on 6 November, whereupon the communist ministers withdrew from the government. For details see Heinrich August Winkler, *Revolution*, 655ff.

95. Gordon, *Hitlerputsch*, 231; *Hitler-Prozess*, 78 (Weber statement) and 859 (Seisser statement).

96. Gordon, *Hitlerputsch*, 224f.; Seysser notes, 3 November 1923, in Deuerlein (ed.), *Hitler-Putsch*, Doc. 79.

97. Gordon, *Hitlerputsch*, 231ff.

98. Report of the 2nd Prosecutor Dr Ehard, 14 December 1923, about Hitler's interrogation the previous day (BHStA, Ehard Papers 94), in *Hitler-Prozess*, 299–307, quote 304.

99. *Hitler-Prozeß*, Doc. 6 (in the appendix to Part 1). On Hitler's statement see ibid., 47ff. Hitler claimed the two men were dead. See also Gordon, *Hitlerputsch*, 235.

100. For the events in the Bürgerbräukeller see Gordon, *Hitlerputsch*, 253ff.; for a reconstruction of the events see in particular *Hitler-Prozeß*, 309ff. (Indictment) and 49ff. (Hitler's statement).

101. Ibid., 310f. (Indictment); *JK*, Nos 594 and 595 (quote).

102. Gordon, *Hitlerputsch*, 262ff.

103. Ibid., 61ff.

104. Ibid., 261.

105. Walter, *Kriminalität*, 120ff.

106. Gordon, *Hitlerputsch*, 299f.; Walter, *Kriminalität*, 135f.

107. Gordon, *Hitlerputsch*, 298.

108. Ibid., 281ff.

109. Ibid., 313ff. Two other putschists were killed during an exchange of fire at the military district headquarters.

110. The policeman who arrested him found him wearing white pyjamas and completely abstracted. See Otto Gritschneder, *Bewährungsfrist für den Terroristen Adolf H. Der Hitler-Putsch und die bayerische Justiz* (Munich, 1990), 33. During his interrogation by the prosecutor, Hitler himself said that he had been initially prostrated by physical and mental anguish. See *Hitler-Prozess*, 59. On the arrest see Hanfstaengl, *Haus*, 5f. and 148ff.

THE TRIAL AND THE PERIOD OF THE BAN

1. Published in *Hitler-Prozeß*, 299ff.; see Kershaw, *Hitler*, 1, 269ff.

2. The memorandum, which has not survived, was available during the trial. See *Hitler-Prozeß*, 63f.; Othmar Plöckinger, *Geschichte eines Buches. Adolf Hitlers 'Mein Kampf', 1922–1945* (Munich, 2006), 21.

3. Ibid., 30f.; BAB, NS 26/1212.

4. During the trial Hitler created the impression that he had come to Munich 'in order to train as an architect'. He had given up this idea under the impression of his Pasewalk experience. See *Hitler-Prozeß*, 19 (quote) and 21.

5. See his hints at the start of the proceedings in ibid., 14.

6. *Bayerische Kurier (BK)*, 27 February 1924.

7. *Hitler-Prozeß*, 20ff., Quote 20.

8. Ibid., 41f.

9. Ibid., 1014, 1017, and 1024.

10. Ibid., 805ff.

11. Ibid., 915.

12. Ibid., 1034. At least Hitler was reprimanded by the chairman of the judges for this remark.

13. Ibid., 1017.

14. Gritschneder, *Bewährungsfrist*, 47.

15. *Hitler-Prozeß*, 45 and 63.

16. Ibid., 1023; on Neithardt see Bernhard Huber, 'Georg Neithardt – nur ein unpolitischer Richter?', in Marita Krauss (ed.), *Rechte Karrieren in München. Von der Weimarer Zeit bis in die Nachkriegsjahre* (Munich, 2010), 95–113.

17. *BK*, 1 March 1923, 'Angeklagte und Ankläger'.

18. *Hitler-Prozeß*, 1197f.

19. Ibid., 1585. For Hitler's self-perception as 'Führer' at the time see also Kershaw, *Hitler*, I, 275.

20. *Hitler-Prozeß*, 1573ff.

21. Ibid., 1581.

22. Ibid., 1591.

23. Ibid., Doc. 10 (in the appendix to Part 1). For criticisms of the judicial failures see, in particular, Gritschneder, *Bewährungsfrist*, 48ff.

24. *BK*, 2 April 1924; *Kölnische Volkszeitung*, 5 April 1924; *Berliner Tageblatt (BT)*, April 1924; *Münchener Post*, 4 April 1924.

25. Ernst Hanfstaengel in *Haus*, 157, writing about the food that was sent to the prisoners, refers to the prison as a delicatessen. See also Fobke's report about their daily routine in Werner Jochmann, *Nationalsozialismus und Revolution. Ursprung und Geschichte der NSDAP in Hamburg 1922–1933. Dokumente* (Frankfurt a. M., 1963), Doc. 26 and Hans Kallenbach, *Mit Adolf Hitler auf Festung Landsberg. Nach Aufzeichnungen des mitgefangenen Oberleutnant a. D. Hans Kallenbach*, ed. Ulf Uweson (Munich, 1933).

26. On the list of visitors see SAM, StAnw. 14344, Report on the prison.

27. Tyrell (ed.), *Führer*, No. 26.

28. Hitler, *Monologe*, 3/4 February 1942.

29. See *MK*, 226ff., quote 231f. The fact that Hitler was referring to himself in this passage is clear from the interpretation in Tyrell, *Trommler*, 167ff.

30. *Völkischer Kurier (VK)*, 25 April 1924, 'Eine glänzende Hitlergeburtstagsfeier'.

31. Georg Schott, *Das Volksbuch von Hitler* (Munich, 1924).

32. Heinrich Hoffmann (ed.), *Deutschlands Erwachen in Bild und Wort. Photographische Zeitdokumente.* Text by Marc Sesselmann (Munich, 1924), 16.

33. Plöckinger, *Geschichte*, 32.

34. Gordon, *Hitlerputsch*, 446.

35. David Jablonsky, *The Nazi Party in Dissolution. Hitler and the Verbotszeit 1923–1924* (London and Totowa, NJ, 1989), 54f.

36. Kershaw, *Hitler*, I, 283; Georg Franz-Willing, *Putsch und Verbotszeit der Hitlerbewegung November 1923–Februar 1925* (Preussisch Oldendorf, 1997), 214ff.

37. Jablonsky, *Nazi Party*, 55; Deuerlein (ed.), *Hitler-Putsch*, No. 229; Franz-Willing, *Putsch*, 229f.

38. Ibid., 228.

39. Donald R. Tracey, 'Der Aufstieg der NSDAP bis 1930', in Detlev Heiden and Günther Mai (eds), *Thüringen auf dem Weg ins 'Dritte Reich'* (Erfurt, 1996), 65–93 (69f.); Jablonsky, *Nazi Party*, 57.

40. Ibid., 10 and 22.

41. Kershaw, *Hitler* I, 283f.

42. Jablonsky, *Nazi Party*, 60 and Appendix B of the agreement in English translation.

43. Ibid., 60 and 63.

44. Ibid., 64f.

45. Mathias Rösch, *Die Münchner NSDAP 1925–1933. Eine Untersuchung zur inneren Struktur der NSDAP in der Weimarer Republik* (Munich, 2002), 548 (the percentages used by Rösch refer to those entitled to vote and were converted by the author).

46. Rudolf Buttmann, *Bayerische Politik 1924–1928* (Munich, 1928), 10ff.

47. *BK*, 7 April 1924.

48. Rösch, *NSDAP*, 548.

49. Jablonsky, *Nazi Party*, 86ff.

50. Ibid., 89; Jochmann, *Nationalsozialismus*, Doc. 16f.

51. Jablonsky, *Nazi Party*, 89.

52. Ibid., 93; Jochmann, *Nationalsozialismus*, Doc. 17 and Doc. 19.

53. Deuerlein, *Aufstieg*, 235f. He was compelled to repeat this request at the end of the month.

54. Jablonsky, *Nazi Party*, 96.

55. BAB, NS 26/857, Streicher/Esser circular, 29 July 1924, published in Tyrell (ed.), *Führer*, No. 31; Jablonsky, *Nazi Party*, 98ff.; Kershaw, *Hitler*, I, 289.

56. Rosenberg objected to this in particular in his Weimar speech in August. See Jochmann, *Nationalsozialismus*, Doc. 30.

57. Tyrell (ed.), *Führer*, No. 29a, uses the statement in the *Mecklenburger Warte*, 9 July 1924.

58. Jochmann, *Nationalsozialismus*, Doc. 28.

59. Ibid., Doc. 29.

60. Jablonsky, *Nazi Party*, 80; Werner, SA, 199ff.; Röhm, *Geschichte*, 321.

61. Jablonsky, *Nazi Party*, 90; Werner, SA, 206ff.; Longerich, *Geschichte*, 46; Röhm, *Geschichte*, 324.

62. Ibid., 325, Jablonsky, *Nazi Party*, 99ff.

63. Röhm, *Geschichte*, 325ff.; Gritschneder, *Bewährungsfrist*, 110ff. On the Frontbann see Jablonsky, *Nazi Party*, 116f., 126f. and 131ff.; Werner, SA, 245ff.

64. Jochmann, *Nationalsozialismus*, Docs. 29–32; Jablonsky, *Nazi Party*, 103ff.

65. Werner Jochmann, *Nationalsozialismus*, Doc. 33. Fobke himself criticized Hitler's 'obsession with neutrality'. Hitler was convinced he would be released on 1 October. See Jablonsky, *Nazi Party*, 111.

66. Jochmann, *Nationalsozialismus*, Doc. 34; Jablonsky, *Nazi Party*, 111.

67. *VK*, 8 August 1924; Jablonsky, *Nazi Party*, 112.

68. Huber, *Verfassungsgeschichte*, 502f.

69. *Frankfurter Zeitung* (*FZ*) (A), 19 August 1924, Leading article; *VK*, 17/18 August 1924. On the meeting see also *Goebbels TB*, 19 and 20 August 1924; Jablonsky, *Nazi Party*, 118ff.

70. Jochmann, *Nationalsozialismus*, Docs 36–38; Jablonsky, *Nazi Party*, 124f.

71. Jochmann, *Nationalsozialismus*, Doc. 43; Jablonsky, *Nazi Party*, 129ff.

72. Jochmann, *Nationalsozialismus*, Doc. 46; Jablonsky, *Nazi Party*, 136f.

73. Jochmann, *Nationalsozialismus*, Doc. 51f.

74. Jablonsky, *Nazi Party*, 146; Jochmann, *Nationalsozialismus*, Doc. 56.

75. Jablonsky, *Nazi Party*, 135 and 139ff.; Tyrell (ed.), *Führer*, No. 34; Franz-Willing, *Putsch*, 273.

76. *BK*, 1/2 November 1924, 'Der Streit im "völkischen Lager"'. See Jablonsky, *Nazi Party*, 141f.

77. Hanfstaengel, *Haus*, 163.

78. For the interpretation of the book see, above all, Eberhard Jäckel, *Hitlers Weltanschauung. Entwurf einer Herrschaft* (Stuttgart, 1991); Axel Kuhn, *Hitlers außenpolitisches Programm. Entstehung und Entwicklung 1919–1939* (Stuttgart, 1970); Klaus Hildebrand, *Deutsche Außenpolitik. Kalkül oder Dogma?* (Stuttgart, Berlin, and Cologne, 1990); Andreas Hillgruber, *Hitlers Strategie. Politik und Kriegführung 1940/1941* (Frankfurt a. M., 1965). The programmatic character of the book was disputed above all by the so-called structuralist school in the 1970s and 1980s. This view is represented predominantly by Kershaw, *Hitler*, I, 298ff. While the main focus of Plöckinger's study, *Geschichte*, is the book's reception, it also contains significant information on *MK*'s origins as well as its publication.

79. *MK*, 321.

80. For the characterization of the ideal 'Führer' see, in particular, *MK*, 650ff. A party organized on the basis of the Führer principle would succeed 'with mathematical certainty', 662. See also Schwarz, *Geniewahn*, 89ff.; on the fusion of the concept of the genius with the Führer principle after the First World War see Jochen Schmidt, *Geschichte des Genie-Gedankens*, 2 (Darmstadt, 1985), 194ff.

81. BAB, NS 26/2247, Advertising brochure of the Eher-Verlag with an overview of the impending book. Plöckinger, *Geschichte*, 42, assumes it appeared in June 1924.

82. In spring 1924 the Austrian and Bavarian authorities were still agreed on Hitler's deportation, but later the Austrian federal chancellor, Seipel, went back

on this agreement on the grounds that Hitler had lost his Austrian citizenship by serving in the Bavarian army. See Donald Cameron Watt, 'Die bayer- ischen Bemühungen um Ausweisung Hitlers 1924', in *VjZ* 6 (1958), 270–80; Österreichisches Staatsarchiv, Archiv der Republik, BKA/AA, GZI. 130.622/1932– 52 Varia-15VR, Upper Austrian provincial government to the Munich police headquarters, 20 April 1924; BKA/AA, Personalia Adolf Hitler, Minute 27 October 1924, re: Remarks about Hitler.

83. During the period of his imprisonment at least, Hitler wrote the manuscript in his own hand, which is clear from numerous references Plöckinger has put together in *Geschichte*. There is no evidence for contributions to the content from Hess, Maurice, or anybody else in Hitler's entourage. The idea that he dictated the book to Hess or Maurice is incorrect; the rhetorical style of the book is intentional. Hess and the editor of the *Völkischer Beobachter*, Stolzing-Cerny, only helped with publishing aspects. See Plöckinger *Geschichte*, 71f. and 121ff.

84. Various general statements by Hitler, when looked at more closely, can be seen as comments on internal Party discussions going on at the time about such matters as the reform of the Party programme, the issue of Nazi trade unions, and the relationship between the Party and the SA (Ibid., 105ff.).

85. *MK*, 772ff., quote 780.

86. Plöckinger, *Geschichte*, 90ff.

87. Ibid., 52, makes the point that Hitler introduced the term 'Lebensraum' into the manuscript shortly after Hess had asked Karl Haushofer for a definition of the concept following discussions among the prisoners about it. See Wolf Rüdiger Hess (ed.), *Rudolf Hess, Briefe 1908–1933* (Munich, 1987), No. 348, to Ilse Pröhl, 10 July 1924.

88. *MK*, 372.

89. Ibid., 772.

90. *JK*, No. 305.

91. Ibid., No. 167.

92. Ibid., No. 422.

93. Ibid., No. 452.

94. On the reassessment of Anglo–German relations from the end of 1922 onwards see ibid., No. 422. Hitler argued that the Anschluss with Austria was possible only with the support of Italy and Britain, although he left the future relation- ship with Britain open. See ibid., No. 452. In his conversation with Scharrer, Hitler stated that they must exploit Anglo–French rivalry. Britain would not allow Germany to 'regain its former high status', but would allow it 'some elbow room'. See also ibid., No. 512; *Hitler-Prozeß*, 188f.

95. *JK*, No. 626; see Kershaw, *Hitler*, 1 324f.

96. *MK*, 138ff., quote 154.

97. Ibid., 687ff.

98. Ibid., 707ff.

99. Ibid., 720ff., quote 724.

100. Ibid., 742 and 757.

101. Ibid., 751 and 743.

102. F. Lenz, 'Die Stellung des Nationalsozialismus zur Rassenhygiene', in *Archiv für Rassen- und Gesellschafts-Biologie einschliesslich Rassen- und Gesellschafts-Hygiene* 25 (1931), 302: 'I have heard that, of the serious books on racial hygiene, Hitler has read the second edition of Baur-Fischer-Lenz during his confinement in Landsberg'. Hitler's remarks reflect some passages in the book. Lenz was basing his assertion on Hitler's statements on the matter in *Mein Kampf*, 441ff.

103. Ibid., 279.

104. Ibid., 448.

A FRESH START

1. Wolfgang Horn, *Der Marsch zur Machtergreifung. Die NSDAP bis 1933* (Königstein i.Ts and Düsseldorf, 1980), 211.

2. There are various sources for these two meetings: Theodor Doerfler maintained in an action for slander, which he, together with Drexler, brought against Hitler in 1926 that Hitler had tried to curry favour with Held. See *RSA* 2 Doc. 9. Hitler strongly disputed this, but not the dates for the meetings referred to by Doerfler – 21 and 22 December (the second date was revealed by the press reports of the trial). The content of the meetings is also clear from comments made by Hitler on the night of 3/4 February 1942 in Hitler, *Monologe*, from a circular by Hermann Fobke of 10 February 1925 in Jochmann, *Nationalsozialismus*, Doc. 61, and from Held's statement to the Bavarian parliament on 15 December 1925, of which excerpts are contained in Tyrell (ed.), *Führer*, No. 36. The date of 4 January frequently referred to in the literature is almost certainly wrong.

3. Wolfgang Martynkewicz, *Salon Deutschland. Geist und Macht* (Berlin, 2009), 407ff.; Norbert Borrmann, *Paul Schultze-Naumburg 1869–1949. Maler, Publizist, Architekt. Vom Kulturreformer der Jahrhundertwende zum Kulturpolitiker im Dritten Reich. Ein Lebens- und Zeitdokument* (Essen, 1989), 198. See also Müller, *Wandel* 3, 301ff.

4. *Münchener Post*, 4 February 1925, published in Deuerlein, *Aufstieg*, 242f.; Tyrell (ed.), *Führer*, No. 37. See also the unsigned polemical article by Reventlow in the *Reichswart*, 7 February 1925, 'Hitlers Frieden mit Rom'; see also Jablonsky, *Nazi Party*, 156; Horn, *Marsch*, 212ff.

5. *VK*, 17 February 1924, 'Eine Kundgebung der deutsch-völkischen Freiheitsbewegung'; see also Graefe's statement of 18 February in the *VK*, in which he accused Hitler of going his own way with the refounding of his workers' party. See Jablonsky, *Nazi Party*, 156.

6. Jochmann, *Nationalsozialismus*, Doc. 61.

7. *VK*, 13 February 1925, 'Rücktritt der Reichsführerschaft der Nationalsozialistischen Freiheitsbewegung'; Horn, *Marsch*, 213; Jablonsky, *Nazi Party*, 158.

8. The bans were automatically lifted with the suspension of the state of emergency by the Bavarian government's decree of 14 February. See *VK*, 15 February 1925.

9. Ibid., 17 February 1925.

10. Tyrell (ed.), *Führer*, No. 39; see also Jochmann, *Nationalsozialismus*, Doc. 65. On the re-founding see Ian Kershaw, *Hitler*, 1 (Stuttgart, 1998), 341ff.

11. *RSA* 1, Doc. 1.

12. Ibid., Doc. 2.

13. Hitler had already made the same point to Hess during his imprisonment. See Hess, *Briefe* No. 359, to Ilse Pröhl, 11 December 1924.

14. Kershaw, *Hitler*, 1, 345f.; Noel D. Cary, 'The Making of the Reich President, 1925. German Conservatism and the Nomination of Paul von Hindenburg', in *Central European History* 23 (1990), 179–204; Hans-Jochen Hauss, *Die erste Volkswahl des deutschen Reichspräsidenten. Eine Untersuchung ihrer verfassungspolitischen Grundlagen, ihrer Vorgeschichte und ihres Verlaufs unter besonderer Berücksichtigung des Anteils Bayerns und der Bayerischen Volkspartei* (Lassleben and Kallmünz, 1965).

15. *RSA* 1, Doc. 14 and Doc. 13. On Hitler's tactics see Lüdecke, *Hitler*, 250ff.; Hanfstaengl, *Haus*, 179f.; Horn, *Marsch*, 218.

16. *RSA* 1, Doc. 41.

17. Longerich, *Geschichte*, 48.

18. Ibid., 51; Jablonsky, *Nazi Party*, 155 and 170f.; Lüdecke, *Hitler*, 259; Werner, SA, 305ff.; Röhm, *Geschichte,* 337ff.

19. Rosenberg, *Letzte Aufzeichnungen. Ideale und Idole der nationalsozialistischen Revolution* (Göttingen, 1955), 114; see also his comment to Lüdecke in Rosenberg, *Hitler*, 257f. For the speech see *RSA* 1, Doc. 6. See also Jablonsky, *Nazi Party*, 168; Horn, *Marsch*, 220.

20. Ibid., 216f.

21. Ibid., 218. *VK*, 8 March 1925, 'Auflösung der Ortsgruppe München der Nationalsozialistischen Freiheitsbewegung', and 10 March 1925, 'Auflösung des Völkischen Blocks'.

22. *RSA* 1, Docs 7 and 9.

23. Ibid., Doc. 11; *MNN*, 9 March 1925, 'Versammlungs-Verbot'. See also *VB*, 14 March 1925, 'Unsere Beschwerde gegen das Versammlungsverbot'.

24. According to Tyrell (ed.), *Führer*, 107f., based on reports in the *VB*, Hitler was banned from speaking in Bavaria from 9 March 1925 to 5 March 1927; in Baden from April 1925 to 22 April 1927; in Prussia from 25 September 1925 to 23 September 1928; in Hamburg from 8 October 1925 to 23 March 1927; in Anhalt from 30 October 1925 to November 1928; in Saxony from February 1926 to January 1927; in Oldenburg from February 1926 to 22 May 1926; in Lippe from March 1926, and in Lübeck from March 1926 to 19 May 1927. See also Horn, *Marsch*, 222.

25. On this see *RSA* 2, Doc. 9, references in the notes; Horn, *Marsch*, 219; *VK*, 1 May 1925, 'Gründung des National-sozialen Volksbundes'.

26. *Goebbels TB*, 23 February 1925; Gerhard Schildt, 'Die Arbeitsgemeinschaft Nordwest. Untersuchungen zur Geschichte der NSDAP 1925/26', Dissertation. Freiburg, 1964, 32ff. on Hamm and Harburg; Markus März, *Nationale Sozialisten in der NSDAP. Strukturen, Ideologie, Publizistik und Biographien des national-sozialistischen*

Straßer-Kreises von der AG Nordwest bis zum Kampf-Verlag 1925–1930 (Graz, 2010), 83ff.

27. Udo Kissenkoetter, *Gregor Straßer und die NSDAP* (Stuttgart, 1978), 20f.; Peter Hüttenberger, *Die Gauleiter. Studie zum Wandel des Machtgefüges in der NSDAP* (Stuttgart, 1969), 15ff.; Schildt, Arbeitsgemeinschaft, 36ff.

28. Ibid.; Hüttenberger, *Gauleiter*, 13ff.

29. Horn, *Marsch*, 225.

30. Hüttenberger, *Gauleiter*, 21.

31. Schildt, Arbeitsgemeinschaft, 40 and 45. *Goebbels TB*, 3 August and 28 September 1925.

32. Partly reproduced in Schildt, Arbeitsgemeinschaft, 38.

33. *RSA* 1, Doc. 52. See Philipp Bouhler, *Kampf um Deutschland. Ein Lesebuch für die deutsche Jugend* (Munich, 1938), 79f.; *RSA* 4/1, Doc. 61.

34. *RSA* 1, Doc. 52. See Ulrich Wörtz, 'Programmatik und Führerprinzip. Das Problem des Straßer-Kreises in der NSDAP. Eine historisch-politische Studie zum Verhältnis von sachlichem Programm und persönlicher Führung in einer totalitären Bewegung', Dissertation, Erlangen, 1966, 75; Schildt, Arbeitsgemeinschaft, 47. The statutes of 21 August 1925 laid down in §3: 'Membership of the association shall be acquired through the completion of the National Socialist German Workers' Party membership form and the payment of a membership fee ...' (*RSA* 1, Doc. 64).

35. Ibid., Docs 48–51 and Docs 54–61; *Goebbels TB*, 14 July 1925, on Hitler's appearance on 12 July 1925 in Weimar.

36. *RSA* 1, Doc. 51.

37. Ibid., Docs 51 and 54f.

38. Ibid., Doc. 63f.

39. *Goebbels TB*, 23 February 1925.

40. Ibid., 21 August 1925; BAB, NS 1/340, Strasser to Goebbels, 29 August 1925, and reply, 31 August 1925.

41. On the Working Group see Jochmann, *Nationalsozialismus*, Doc. 66; Schildt, Arbeitsgemeinschaft; Horn, *Marsch*, 232ff.; Wörtz, *Programmatik*, 78ff.; März, *Sozialisten*, 93ff.

42. BAB, NS 1/340, Goebbels, Report for Strasser 11 September 1925, reproduced in Schildt, Arbeitsgemeinschaft, VIIIff.

43. BAB, NS 1/340, Strasser to Goebbels (on the preparations for the meeting) and NS 26/899, Fobke circular, 11 September 1925; *Goebbels TB*, 11 September 1925. For the meeting on 10 September see Schildt, Arbeitsgemeinschaft, 105ff.; Wörtz, *Programmatik*, 80f.

44. *Goebbels TB*, 30 September and 2 October 1925.

45. Jochmann, *Nationalsozialismus*, Doc. 67. The statutes were agreed by the working group (AG) on 22 November in Hannover. See Schildt, Arbeitsgemeinschaft, 112f.

46. *Goebbels TB* 26 October 1925; Schildt, Arbeitsgemeinschaft, 108.

47. On Strasser's draft programme see ibid., 127ff.; BAB, NS 26/896, published in Reinhard Kühnl, 'Zur Programmatik der nationalsozialistischen Linken: Das

Straßer-Programm von 1925/1926', in *VjZ* 14 (1966), 317–33; on the meeting in Hannover see März, *Sozialisten*, 102ff. and 164ff.

48. Ibid., 110.
49. Jochmann, *Nationalsozialismus*, Doc. 71.
50. Schildt, Arbeitsgemeinschaft, 140ff.; März, *Sozialisten*, 114ff.
51. *Goebbels TB*, 25 January 1926.
52. Otto Strasser had strongly opposed compensation for the German princes in the *Nationalsozialistischen Briefe* of 15 December 1925, writing under the pseudonym Ulrich von Hutten. On the issue of compensation for the princes see Otmar Jung, *Direkte Demokratie in der Weimarer Republik. Die Fälle 'Aufwertung', 'Fürstenenteignung', 'Panzerkreuzerverbot' und 'Youngplan'* (Frankfurt a. M., 1989), 49ff.; Ulrich Schüren, *Der Volksentscheid zur Fürstenenteignung 1926. Die Vermögensauseinandersetzung mit den depossedierten Landesherren als Problem der deutschen Innenpolitik unter besonderer Berücksichtigung der Verhältnisse in Preussen* (Düsseldorf, 1978). For the decisions see Jochmann, *Nationalsozialismus*, Doc. 72.
53. Albrecht Tyrell, 'Gottfried Feder and the NSDAP', in Peter D. Stachura (ed.), *The Shaping of the Nazi State* (London, 1978), 69f.
54. Peter Longerich, *Joseph Goebbels. Biographie* (Munich, 2010), 76ff.
55. *RSA* 1, Doc. 101. According to Goebbels's diary (*TB*, 15 February), on this occasion Hitler was also advocating an alliance with Britain, but the manuscript version of the speech makes no mention of it.
56. *RSA* 1, Doc. 101; *Goebbels TB*, 15 February 1926. See also Horn, *Marsch*, 240ff.; Schildt, Arbeitsgemeinschaft, 155; Kershaw, *Hitler*, 1, 353; März, *Sozialisten*, 126ff.; Wörtz, *Programmatik*, 97ff.
57. See Kershaw, *Hitler*, 1, 357.
58. Jochmann, *Nationalsozialismus*, Doc. 74.
59. Schildt, Arbeitsgemeinschaft, 169ff.
60. *Goebbels TB*, 13 April 1926.
61. *VB*, 10 April 1926.
62. See BAB, BDC, Oberstes Parteigericht, Karl Kaufmann file, Kaufmann to Heinemann; an excerpt is published in Tyrell (ed.), *Führer*, No. 53.
63. *Goebbels TB*, 19 April 1926.
64. Peter D. Stachura, 'Der Fall Strasser' in Stachura, *The Shaping of the Nazi State*, 50; Kissenkoetter, *Strasser*, 30f.
65. Longerich, *Goeb/bels*, 81.
66. *RSA* 1, Doc. 143f.
67. Ibid., Doc. 145. The speech was published as a special edition of the *VB*. On the membership meeting see Kershaw, *Hitler* 1, 358f.
68. This is referred to in various entries in Goebbels's diary between 3 May and 14 June 1926; see Longerich, *Goebbels*, 83.
69. *Goebbels TB*, 16–21 June 1926. On Hitler's appearances during these days see *RSA* 1. For the membership meeting see Docs. 152–155 and 157f.

70. *Goebbels TB*, 10 and 12 June and 6 July 1926. See also Longerich, *Goebbels*, 84f.;
    Albrecht Tyrell, 'Führergedanke und Gauleiterwechsel. Die Teilung des Gaues
    Rheinland der NSDAP 1931', in *VjZ* 23 (1975), 352.

71. *RSA* 2, Doc. 3.

72. Ibid., Doc. 1.

73. Ibid., Doc. 3. This is similar to the statement in the 'Basic Guidelines' (Doc. 4).

74. Tyrell (ed.), *Führer*, No. 57a; *RSA* 2, Docs. 6 and 4. For an account of the Party
    Rally see *VB*, 6 July 1926, 'Weimar im Zeichen der kommenden Reichsflagge';
    Kershaw, *Hitler* 1, 359.

75. The motion put forward by the Pomeranian Nazi, Walther von Corswant, that
    the Party should no longer take part in elections was thus not considered by the
    special meeting on election issues. See *RSA* 2, Doc. 5. The Party leadership gave
    Hermann Fobke the opportunity to make a statement opposing participation
    in elections, to which the meeting responded, as Hitler wished, by passing a
    motion opposing the further discussion of this issue. Buttmann then issued a
    statement to the effect that, while the Party remained opposed in principle to
    parliamentary politics, in the current situation participation in elections could
    be useful. See *VB*, 6 July 1926; Horn, *Marsch*, 272.

76. *RSA* 2, Doc. 6. Although he was known to be prone to exaggerating, according
    to Goebbels there were as many as 15,000 there. See *Goebbels TB*, 7 July 1926.

77. *RSA* 2, Doc. 6.

78. Ibid., Doc. 7; *Goebbels TB*, 6 July 1926.

79. *Frankfurter Zeitung* (*FZ*) (M), 15 July 1926, 'Hakenkreuzler-Terror in Weimar'.

80. *Goebbels TB*, 24 July to 1 August 1926.

81. *Nationalsozialistische Briefe*, 15 September 1926, 'Die Revolution als Ding an
    sich'.

82. *RSA* 2, Doc. 29.

83. Horn, *Marsch*, 243; *Nationalsozialistische Briefe*, 1 October 1926.

84. *RSA* 2, Doc. 40.

85. Ibid., Doc. 44.

86. Ibid., Doc. 31.

87. Ibid., Doc. 28, also Doc. 53. See also the distancing from the paramilitary leagues
    in *MK*, 603ff.; on this issue see Longerich, *Geschichte*, 65ff.

88. Hitler had already established the incompatibility of membership of the Party
    and membership of the paramilitary leagues in his speech of 11 September 1926
    and a specific ban in writing followed on 5 February 1927. See *RSA* 2, Doc. 75.

89. On the use of this ambiguous tactic towards the paramilitary leagues in
    Thuringia see Tracey, 'Aufstieg', 81ff.; also Werner, SA, 433ff. On the paramili-
    tary leagues see, in particular, James M. Diehl, *Paramilitary Politics in Weimar
    Germany* (Bloomington and London, 1977), 233ff.

90. For the following characterization see, in particular, Kershaw, *Hitler*, 1, 358ff.

91. *Goebbels TB*, 21 August, 30 September and 2 and 19 October 1925.

92. Tyrell (ed.), *Führer*, No. 74 (Hitler was surrounded by a 'Chinese wall') and No.
    82 on Hitler's 'contempt for humanity'; see also Lüdecke, *Hitler*, 250ff.

93. On the rejection of open discussion within the Party see Albert Krebs, *Tendenzen und Gestalten der NSDAP. Erinnerungen an die Frühzeit der Partei* (Stuttgart, 1959), 131f.

94. Hanfstaengl, *Haus*, 177.

95. Ibid., 184f., refers in this context to Hitler's dislike of being seen when not fully clothed (for example when bathing). He rejected ballroom dancing lessons since dancing was 'an undignified activity…for a statesman' (174).

96. Rudolf Herz, *Hoffmann und Hitler. Fotografie als Medium des Führer-Mythos* (Munich, 1994), 94ff.

97. Krebs, *Tendenzen*, 135.

98. Kershaw, *Hitler*, 1, 364; see also Hitler, *Monologe*, 16/17 January 1942.

99. *RSA* 6, Doc. 16.

100. Oron James Hale, 'Adolf Hitler: Taxpayer', in *American Historical Review* 60 (1955), 837.

101. Ibid., 836; *RSA* 6, Doc. 5 (re: tax declaration 1925).

102. There is a considerable amount of evidence for this statement in a variety of formulations. See Joachimsthaler, *Liste*, 23ff.

103. Ibid., 213ff.; on the innocence of the relationship see Hanfstaengl, *Haus*, 64f.

104. Joachimsthaler, *Liste*, 356. This chapter is based on the statements made by Frau Schultze, née Klein, to Joachimsthaler or rather to Christa Schroeder (from whom Joachimsthaler heard them).

105. Ibid., 177ff.; Hitler, *Monologe*, 16/17 January 1942.

106. Joachimsthaler, *Liste*, 341 (however, only with limited information); *Goebbels TB*, 24 August, also 8 and 10 September 1927. The vague remark by Wagener in Otto Wagener, *Hitler aus nächster Nähe. Aufzeichnungen eines Vertrauten 1929–1932* (Frankfurt/M, 1978), 98, that Hitler felt 'something more…than affection' is an example of the rumours circulating in the NSDAP at the time.

107. Joachimsthaler, *Liste*, 203ff. In Goebbels's diary there are various references to her presence in Hitler's entourage, for example, on 19 December 1932.

108. Joachimsthaler, *Liste, passim*.

109. Ibid., 362f.; *Akten Partei-Kanzlei*, Regest 11158, Letter from Hertha Oldenbourg (Starnberg) to Hitler's adjutant Wiedemann, 18 November 1935, with a reference to a postcard sent jointly with the 'little princess' to Hitler.

110. Joachimsthaler, *Liste*, 309ff.; Anna Maria Sigmund, *Des Führers bester Freund. Adolf Hitler, seine Nichte Geli Raubal und der 'Ehrenarier; Emil Maurice – Eine Dreiecksbeziehung* (Munich, 2003).

111. Joachimsthaler, *Liste*, 322.

112. *Goebbels TB*, 31 January 1930 (Munich); Hanfstaengl, *Haus*, 237.

113. *Goebbels TB*, 15 January and 6 March 1931.

114. Ibid., 22 November 1929.

115. Ibid., 2 August 1929.

116. Ibid., 8 and 10 September 1927, 30 March, 15, 17, and 19 November 1928, also 3 May 1930.

117. Ibid., 20 July 1930.

118. Ibid., 19 October 1928.

HITLER AS A PUBLIC SPEAKER

1. *VB*, 29 July 1925, Hess directive concerning the recording of speeches in shorthand.
2. Horn, *Marsch*, 221f.
3. Kershaw, *Hitler*, 1, 369f.
4. *RSA* 1 Doc. 72; *RSA* 2, Doc. 67.
5. On 'Jewish Marxism' see *RSA* 1, Doc. 76; *RSA* 2, Docs 80 and 140.
6. *RSA* 1, Doc. 72.
7. *RSA* 2, Doc. 159.
8. Ibid., Doc. 59 (quote) and Doc. 60.
9. Ibid., Docs 53, 67–69, and 84.
10. *RSA* 1, Doc. 72.
11. Ibid., Doc. 94.
12. See, for example, *RSA* 2, Docs 67 and 197, also Docs 96, 243, and 248.
13. *RSA* 1, Doc. 103; see Kershaw, *Hitler*, 1, 367.
14. *RSA* 1, Doc. 157.
15. *RSA* 2, Doc. 55.
16. Ibid., Doc. 56.
17. Ibid., Doc. 112.
18. Ibid., Doc. 201.
19. Tyrell (ed.), *Führer*, No. 41.
20. *RSA* 2, Doc. 83; Deuerlein, *Aufstieg*, 268.
21. *RSA* 2, Doc. 84. The *VB* referred to an audience of 7,000, but the police reporter noted only 4,500.
22. Kershaw, *Hitler*, 1, 375. According to Rösch, *Münchener NSDAP*, 209, 60 per cent of the NSDAP mass meetings in 1927 were poorly, 20 per cent moderately, and only 15 per cent well attended.
23. See below p. 173.
24. *RSA* 2, Doc. 222.
25. *MK*, 757.
26. *RSA* 2, Docs 160 and 221.
27. Ibid., Docs 94, 119, and 187.
28. According to Otto Wagener, *Hitler*, 17, Hitler could not be understood at the 1929 Reich Party Rally because of the lack of loudspeakers. The British correspondent, Sefton Delmer, was present at one of Hitler's Berlin speeches (he gives the date as February 1929): 'It was by no means easy to gather what the man with the red face and agitated features, speaking with a hoarse voice in an Austrian accent, was so passionately trying to get across. Either the microphones were badly placed or he hadn't yet mastered the art of public speaking.' See Delmer, *Die Deutschen und ich* (Hamburg, 1962) 102f. See also: Cornelia Epping-Jäger, 'Lautsprecher Hitler. Über eine Form der Massenkommunikation im Nationalsozialismus', in Gerhard Paul and Ralf Schock (eds), *Sound des Jahrhunderts. Geräusche, Töne, Stimmen 1889 bis Heute* (Bonn, 2013); Hitler, *Monologe*, 4 January 1942, midday.

29. BAB, NS 18/5502, Himmler circular, 31 March 1928.

30. Rösch, *NSDAP*, 119. See Kershaw, *Hitler*, 1, 383, although he uses the figures in Tyrell (ed.), *Führer*, 225, and not those that have been established in the meantime and are contained in the *RSA* edition.

31. Müller, *Krieg*, 171.

32. BAB, NS 18/5502, questionnaires, directives, and extensive correspondence with the individual local branches. Directives published in Müller, *Krieg*, 173ff.

33. Beate Behrens, *Mit Hitler zur Macht. Aufstieg des Nationalsozialismus in Mecklenburg und Lübeck 1922–1933* (Rostock, 1998), 77f.; see also material in BAB, NS 18/5007.

34. See Müller, *Krieg*, 178ff.

35. Krebs, *Tendenzen*, 126f.

36. Deuerlein, *Aufstieg*, 269ff.

37. Krebs, *Tendenzen*, 126; Delmer (*Die Deutschen*, 103) noted that Hitler perspired during a speech so much that his cheap blue suit dyed his shirt collar.

38. On his exhaustion and retreat to his hotel see Krebs, *Tendenzen*, 127.

39. In the state elections in Saxony on 31 October 1926 the Party achieved 1.6 per cent, in the state elections in Thuringia on 30 January 1927 3.5 per cent, and in the state elections in Mecklenburg-Schwerin on 22 May 1927 only 1.8 per cent. In Mecklenburg-Strelitz the DVFP secured 5 per cent (the NSDAP did not put up candidates); however, in the election of 29 January 1928 this had fallen to 3.8 per cent. The NSDAP secured 1.5 per cent on 9 October 1927 in Hamburg, 3.7 per cent in the state of Brunswick on 27 November 1927. See Jürgen Falter, Thomas Lindenberger, and Siegfried Schumann, *Wahlen und Abstimmungen in der Weimarer Republik. Materialien zum Wahlverhalten 1919–1933* (Munich, 1986).

A NEW DIRECTION

1. *RSA* 2, Docs 161–63. See also Siegfried Zelnhefer, *Die Reichsparteitage der NSDAP. Geschichte, Struktur und Bedeutung der großen Propagandafeste im national-sozialistischen Feierjahr* (Nuremberg, 1991), 23ff.; Report of the Reich Commissar for the Supervision of Public Order published in Deuerlein, *Aufstieg* 279ff.

2. *RSA* 2, Doc. 168, Notes; Zelnhefer, *Reichsparteitage*, 29ff.; the *VB* of 23 August 1927, in referring to 100,000 participants, absurdly exaggerated the number.

3. On the Left after 1926 see März, *Nationale Sozialisten*, 219ff.; Reinhard Kühnl, *Die nationalsozialistische Linke 1925–1930* (Meisenheim a. Glan, 1966).

4. This is clear from an examination of the relevant statements in the collection in *RSA* 2.

5. Horn, *Marsch*, 248ff.

6. *VB*, 2 February 1927, Alfred Rosenberg, 'Nationaler Sozialismus', in *Nationalsozialistische Briefe*, 15 February 1927, Gregor Strasser, 'Nationaler Sozialismus' in ibid.

7. *RSA* 2, Doc. 83 (quote), also Docs 89 and 112.

8. Rösch, *NSDAP*, 157ff.; Longerich, *Geschichte*, 64. On Hitler's attempts to mollify them see *RSA* 2, Docs 125, 130, and 218.

9. *RSA* 2, Doc. 165. See Rösch, *NSDAP*, 167.

10. Longerich, *Himmler*, 97ff. Kershaw's claim in *Hitler*, 1, 384 that Hitler announced a 'change of course' towards trying to win over the middle class at a meeting of Gauleiters on 27 November 1927 is not confirmed by the summary of the speech he made there, which has survived. See RSA 2, Doc. 198; the comment by a functionary, Karl Dincklage, which is used by Kershaw as evidence for this (see Tyrell (ed.), *Führer befiehl*, 188), does not permit such a far-reaching conclusion to be drawn. Stachura's claim that the decision to change course was substantially taken at the leadership meeting in September 1928 is also not tenable. See Peter D. Stachura 'Der kritische Wendepunkt? Die NSDAP und die Reichstagswahlen vom 28. Mai 1928', in *VjZ* 26 (1978), esp. 95f. On the meeting of leaders see below p. 184f. See also Rösch, *NSDAP*, 165ff.

11. Gerhard Stoltenberg, *Politische Strömungen im schleswig-holsteinischen Landvolk 1918–1933. Ein Beitrag zur politischen Meinungsbildung in der Weimarer Republik* (Düsseldorf, 1962), esp. 107ff.

12. *RSA* 2, Doc. 203.

13. Ibid., Doc. 254; see Kershaw, *Hitler*, 1, 385.

14. Heinrich August Winkler, *Mittelstand, Demokratie und Nationalsozialismus. Die politische Entwicklung von Handwerk und Kleinhandel in der Weimarer Republik* (Cologne, 1972), 167ff.

15. On the early history of the NSDStB see Anselm Faust, *Der nationalsozialistische Deutsche Studentenbund. Studenten und Nationalsozialismus in der Weimarer Republik*, vol. 1 (Düsseldorf, 1973), 36ff.

16. *RSA* 2, Doc. 73.

17. Ibid., Doc. 195.

18. A pamphlet that was distributed among members of the leagues in 1927 referred to the 'general recognition of Hitler as being at present...the simplest and best solution to the whole leadership issue'. See Ernst Ritter (ed.), *Reichskommissar für Überwachung der öffentlichen Ordnung und Nachrichtensammelstelle im Reichsministerium des Innern. Lageberichte (1920–1929) und Meldungen (1929–1933)* (Microfiche, 1979), No. 123.

19. BAB, NS 23/374, Bouhler circular, 7 May 1928.

20. See, for example, *RSA* 2, Doc. 280; *RSA* 3/1, Docs 13 and 70.

21. See, for example, *RSA* 3/2, Docs 2, 6, 17, and 23.

22. *RSA* 2, Doc. 235.

23. Lewis Hertzman, *DNVP: Right-Wing Opposition in the Weimar Republic 1918–1924* (Lincoln Nebr., 1963); BAB, R 72/273, Circular from the headquarters of the Stahlhelm, dated 18 September 1928, referring to the decision of the executive committee of 9 March 1924.

24. On anti-Semitism in the Weimar Republic see Dirk Walter, *Antisemitische Kriminalität und Gewalt. Judenfeindschaft in der Weimarer Republik* (Bonn, 1999); Michael Wildt, *Volksgemeinschaft als Selbstermächtigung. Gewalt gegen Juden in der deutschen Provinz 1919 bis 1939* (Hamburg, 2007), 69ff.

25. He first used the term on 29 January 1928. See *RSA* 2, Doc. 225; see also ibid., Docs 230 and 244.

26. Ibid., Doc. 258.

27. Ibid., Doc. 268.

28. For the text of the poster see ibid., Doc. 278, note 9.

29. Ibid., Doc. 278.

30. Falter, Lindenberger, and Schumann, *Wahlen*, 89ff.

31. *RSA* 2, Doc. 279.

32. Kershaw, *Hitler*, 1, 393f.; Stoltenberg, *Strömungen*, 147ff.; Police report of 13 March 1929 about the burial of a victim published in Deuerlein, *Aufstieg*, 299ff. See also two articles in *VB*, 16 and 17 March 1929, which were signed by Hitler, but which, in view of the language, had at the least been heavily edited (*RSA* 3/2, Doc. 9f.).

33. Stephanie Merkenich, *Grüne Front gegen Weimar. Reichs-Landbund und agrarischer Lobbyismus 1918–1933* (Düsseldorf, 1998), esp. 255f.; Stoltenberg, *Strömungen*, 128ff.

34. *RSA* 2, Doc. 280.

35. New edition by Gerhard L. Weinberg in the form of vol. 2 A of the *RSA*.

36. Ibid., 123.

37. Ibid., 181.

38. Ibid., 182ff.

39. See the commentary by the editor, Weinberg (ibid. XXIf.), who also refers to other possible reasons.

40. On the USA see ibid., 84ff. (quote 92); on Germany's leadership role 181.

41. *RSA* 3/1, Doc. 2.

42. Ibid., Doc. 87.

43. Ibid., Doc. 91; *RSA* 3/2, Doc. 38.

44. Ibid., Docs 30, 32, and 37.

45. *RSA* 3/1, Doc. 91.

46. Gustav Stresemann, 'Die Entwicklung des Berliner Flaschenbiergeschäfts. Eine wirtschaftliche Studie', Dissertation, Leipzig, 1900.

47. *RSA* 3/1, Doc. 89.

48. *RSA* 3/2, Doc. 4.

49. *RSA* 3/1, Doc. 84.

50. *RSA* 3/2, Doc. 83.

51. Hitler to the cleric Magnus Gött, 2 March 1927, published in Paul Hoser, 'Hitler und die katholische Kirche. Zwei Briefe aus dem Jahre 1927', in *VjZ* 42 (1994), 487ff. Gött was a supporter of the NSDAP, but was concerned about atheistic tendencies in the Party. Hitler told him that he considered it in general unfortunate if religion in whatever form became mixed up in politics.

52. *RSA* 2, Doc. 183.

53. *RSA* 3/2, Doc. 4. The letter from the Investigation and Conciliation Committee, included here as an appendix, referred to a review by Dinter of Count Reventlow's book 'Die Gottfrage der Deutschen'; see also note 6.

54. *RSA* 3/1, Doc. 13.

55. Dinter's reply to Hitler, 19 August 1928, published in *Geisteschristentum* 1, Appendix, 369f. On the treatment of the motion at the leadership meeting see Kissenkoetter, *Strasser*, 38f.

56. Hitler to Dinter, 27 August 1928, published in *Geisteschristentum*, 1, 370.

57. Reply from Dinter's private secretary to Hess 30 August 1928, published in ibid., 371f.

58. Hess to Dinter, telegram of 31 August 1928, published in ibid., 372.

59. Ibid., 373ff.

60. Telegram from Hitler to Dinter, 8 October 1928, published in ibid., 375; also in *RSA* 3/1, Doc. 33.

61. *Geisteschristentum* 1, 379f.; also RSA 3/1, Doc. 35.

62. *VB*, Directive, 26 July 1928 and 27 July 1928, 'Kein Reichsparteitag 1928'.

63. *RSA* 3/1, Doc. 12 (quote) and Doc. 14f. on two further addresses on 2 September 1928; see also *Goebbels TB*, 1 September 1928.

64. *RSA* 3/1, Docs. 16–22 with the individual regulations and Doc. 25. See also Kissenkoetter, *Straßer*, 38f.

65. The thesis put forward by Stachura in 'Wendepunkt', that the switch from an urban to a rural strategy was agreed at the leadership meeting, is no longer tenable in view of the documents now available (*RSA* und Goebbels TB). In his diary entries of 1 and 4 September Goebbels emphasizes the banality of most of the contributions. Also, 'A lot of strife in the Party.'

66. *RSA* 3/1, Doc. 23.

67. Kurt Pätzold and Manfred Weissbecker, *Geschichte der NSDAP 1920–1945* (Cologne, 2009), 108f.

68. See Tyrell (ed.), *Führer*, 352.

69. *RSA* 3/1, Doc. 93.

70. Joachim Albrecht, *Die Avantgarde des 'Dritten Reichs'. Die Coburger NSDAP während der Weimarer Republik 1922–1933* (Frankfurt a. M., 2005), 116ff.

71. *RSA* 3/2, Doc. 49.

72. März, *Sozialisten*, 278ff. In 1926/27 Mücke had been a deputy in the Saxon parliament. See Andreas Hofer, *Kapitänleutnant Hellmuth von Mücke. Marineoffizier – Politiker – Widerstandskämpfer. Ein Leben zwischen den Fronten* (Marburg, 2003); Horn, *Marsch*, 255; Kühnl, *Linke*, 221ff.

73. Volker Berghahn, *Der Stahlhelm. Bund der Frontsoldaten 1918–1935* (Düsseldorf, 1966), 118ff.; Jung, *Demokratie*, 109ff.

74. Longerich, *Goebbels*, 130ff.; *Goebbels TB*, 24 and 28 March, as well as 5, 6, 16, and 30 April 1929.

75. *Der Angriff*, 13 May 1929, 'Gegen die Reaktion', and 27 May 1929, 'Einheitsfront'.

76. *RSA* 3/2, Doc. 29.

77. Ibid., Doc. 50f.; see also Jung, *Demokratie*, 110.

78. *RSA* 3/2, Doc. 55.

79. März, *Sozialisten*, 269ff.

80. RSA 3/2, Doc. 56.

81. Ibid., Doc. 60. Hitler repeated here word for word the directive for the specialist committees issued in 1926. In the announcement for the 1929 Party Rally

dated 1 March 1929 he had already issued a reminder that Party Rallies were not 'occasions for fruitless discussions, as was the case with other parties, but demonstrations comprehensible to everybody of the determination and the strength of this ideology and its organization'. See ibid., Doc. 1.

82. Goebbels referred here to discussions about 'the Mücke case'. See *Goebbels TB*, 2 August 1929.

83. Tyrell (ed.), *Führer*, No. 131. Rehm Motion in IfZ, MA 1550 (NSDAP-Hauptarchiv, No. 391).

84. *RSA* 3/2, Doc. 61 (quote) and Doc. 64f.

85. Ibid., Doc. 45 and Doc. 62. See also Zelnhefer, *Reichsparteitage*, 34ff. and 39ff., and the personal impressions of Otto Wagener, who was a guest. See Wagener, *Hitler*, 7ff.

86. *RSA* 3/2, Doc. 63.

87. Zelnhelfer, *Reichsparteitage*, 44ff.

CONQUERING THE MASSES

1. *Goebbels TB*, 19 and 22 September 1929; on the negotiations see Jung, *Demokratie*, 111ff.

2. Ibid., 116f.

3. *RSA* 3/2, Doc. 88.

4. Ibid., Doc. 89 and (on the accusation), Doc. 91.

5. Ibid., Doc. 99.

6. *Goebbels TB*, 20, 21, 23, and 28 October 1929.

7. Longerich, *Goebbels*, 127ff.

8. On the position of the Party's left wing see März, *Nationale Sozialisten*, 249ff.

9. Jung, *Demokratie*, 128ff.; Turner, *Grossunternehmer*, 141.

10. Jung, *Demokratie*, 122ff.

11. *RSA* 3/3, Docs 19 and 6.

12. Brandenburg: 5.6 per cent, Hanover: 6.8 per cent, Wiesbaden: 8.2 per cent, Saxony 5.8 per cent, Schleswig-Holstein 10.3 per cent; see Falter, Lindenberger, and Schumann, *Wahlen*, 102ff.

13. On the fruitful concept of milieu and the decline of milieus in the Weimar period see Cornelie Rauh-Kühne, *Katholisches Milieu und Kleinstadtgesellschaft. Ettlingen 1918–1939* (Sigmaringen, 1991); Wolfram Pyta, *Dorfgemeinschaft und Parteipolitik 1918–1933. Die Verschränkung von Milieu und Parteien in den protestantischen Landgebieten Deutschlands in der Weimarer Republik* (Düsseldorf, 1996); Helge Matthiesen, *Bürgertum und Nationalsozialismus in Thüringen. Das bürgerliche Gotha von 1918 bis 1930* (Jena, 1994); Matthiesen, *Greifswald in Vorpommern. Konservatives Milieu im Kaiserreich, in Demokratie und Diktatur 1900–1990* (Düsseldorf, 2000); Siegfried Weichlein, *Sozialmilieus und politische Kultur in der Weimarer Republik. Lebenswelt, Vereinskultur, Politik in Hessen* (Göttingen, 1996); Oded Heilbronner, *Die Achillesferse des deutschen Katholizismus* (Gerlingen, 1998); Joachim Kuropka (ed.), *Grenzen des katholischen Milieus. Stabilität und Gefährdung katholischer Milieus in der Endphase der Weimarer Republik und in der NS-Zeit* (Münster, 2013). In *Das*

konservative Milieu, Vereinskultur und lokale Sammlungspolitik in ost- und westdeutschen Regionen (1900–1960) (Göttingen, 2002) Frank Bösch provides an explanation, according to which the crisis did not lead to a collapse of the conservative milieu but rather to its mobilization, which was then exploited politically by the NSDAP.

14. Udo Kissenkoetter, *Straßer*, 48ff.; *VB*, 12 September 1929 on the creation of the Organization Department II; Tyrell (ed.), *Führer befiehl*, No. 132 and Nos 150a and 150b.

15. On the world economic crisis see Theo Balderston, *The Origins and Course of the German Economic Crisis, November 1923 to May 1932* (Berlin, 1993); Harold James, *Deutschland in der Weltwirtschaftskrise 1924–1936* (Stuttgart, 1988); Charles P. Kindleberger, *Die Weltwirtschaftskrise 1929–1939* (Munich, 1973); Rainer Meister, *Die große Depression. Zwangslagen und Handlungsspielräume der Wirtschafts- und Finanzpolitik in Deutschland 1929–1932* (Regensburg, 1991); Albert Ritschl, *Deutschlands Krise und Konjunktur 1924–1934. Binnenkonjunktur, Auslandsverschuldung und Reparationsproblem zwischen Dawes Plan und Transfersperre* (Berlin, 2002).

16. März, *Sozialisten*, 285f.

17. *RSA* 3/3, Doc. 11.

18. Günter Neliba, 'Wilhelm Frick und Thüringen als Experimentierfeld für die nationalsozialistische Machtergreifung', in Detlev Heiden and Günther Mai (eds), *Thüringen auf dem Weg ins 'Dritte Reich'* (Erfurt, 1996), 96ff.

19. *RSA* 3/3, Doc. 10.

20. Ibid., Doc. 11.

21. Neliba, 'Frick', 99ff.

22. Frick's decree for the purging of cultural life of 5 April 1930 was entitled 'Against Negro Culture. For German Ethnicity'.

23. Neliba, 'Frick', 110; Hildegard Brenner, *Die Kunstpolitik des Nationalsozialismus* (Reinbek b. Hamburg, 1963), 28ff.

24. Neliba, 'Frick', 114ff.

25. 1929: 39 speeches, 1930: 72 (according to the *RSA*).

26. *RSA* 3/3, Doc. 57. His refusal to comment on current political issues is also evident in *RSA* 3/2, Doc. 106; *RSA* 3/3, Doc. 63.

27. *RSA* 3/2, Doc. 61.

28. *RSA* 3/2, Doc. 106 (quote); *RSA* 3/3, Docs 44, 61, and 69; *RSA* 4/1, Doc. 5.

29. *RSA* 3/2, Doc. 106.

30. *RSA* 3/3, Doc. 57.

31. Ibid., Doc. 61.

32. Ibid., Docs 59 and 69.

33. Ibid., Doc. 18.

34. *RSA* 3/2, Doc. 103.

35. Numbers of unemployed in Balderston, *Origins*, 2.

36. Heinrich August Winkler, *Weimar 1918–1933. Die Geschichte der ersten deutschen Demokratie* (Munich, 1993), 359ff.

37. *Goebbels TB*, 1 and 2 April 1930.

38. On the DNVP see Gerhard Schulz, *Von Brüning zu Hitler. Der Wandel des politischen Systems in Deutschland 1930–1933* (Berlin/New York, 1992), 41ff.

39. *RSA* 3/3, Doc. 31.

40. *Goebbels TB*, 4 and 5 April 1930. On the exit from the Reich Committee see Horn, *Marsch*, 259.

41. *Goebbels TB*, 10 and 12 April 1930; Winkler, *Weimar*, 378.

42. *Goebbels TB*, 13 April 1930; for a similar statement after the failed vote of no confidence see ibid., 4 April 1930.

43. On this conflict see März, *Sozialisten*, 145ff.; Longerich, *Goebbels*, 99f. and 112f.

44. For example in the article 'Hinein in den Staat', which he gave Hitler to read in December 1929, but only published after the break with the NSDAP in July 1930. See Patrick Moreau, *Nationalsozialismus von links. Die 'Kampfgemeinschaft Revolutionärer Nationalsozialisten' und die 'Schwarze Front' Otto Straßers 1930–1935* (Stuttgart, 1985), 29f.

45. For details see Longerich, *Goebbels*, 135ff. See also the numerous entries in the Goebbels diaries between January and April 1930, which show, in particular, Goebbels's disappointment at Hitler's lack of support. He in turn commented on the Kampf-Verlag in the *VB* on 5 and 16 February 1930.

46. Moreau, *Nationalsozialismus*, 30.

47. For Goebbels's criticism see *Goebbels TB*, 28 April 1930. For Hitler's speech see *RSA* 3/3, Doc. 38.

48. *Goebbels TB*, 2 and 3 May 1930.

49. See ibid., 3 and 4 May 1930. On the Strasser crisis see also Kershaw, *Hitler*, 1, 412ff.

50. *Goebbels TB*, 20, 22, and 24 May 1930. 'He appears completely rootless and unorganic, an intellectual white Jew, a completely incompetent organizer, an archetypal Marxist' (22 May 1930).

51. Otto Strasser, *Ministersessel oder Revolution? Eine wahrheitsgemäße Darstellung meiner Trennung von der NSDAP* (Berlin, 1933); Tyrell (ed.), *Führer*, 314; Moreau, *Nationalsozialismus*, 30ff.

52. Ibid., 35f.; *Goebbels TB*, 12, 14, and 23 June 1930.

53. Andreas Wagner, *'Machtergreifung' in Sachsen. NSDAP und Staatliche Verwaltung 1930–1935* (Cologne, 2004), 106f.

54. *Goebbels TB*, 26 June to 1 July 1930.

55. *Der Angriff*, 3 July 1930, published a letter from Hitler dated 30 June 1930, in which the Party leader authorized him to carry out a 'ruthless purge' of the Berlin Party organization.

56. See his declaration in the *VB*, 3 July 1930; *Goebbels TB*, 1 July 1930; Kissenkoetter, *Strasser*, 44f.; Moreau, *Nationalsozialismus*, 36ff.

57. *Goebbels TB*, 3 July 1930.

58. *RSA* 3/3, Doc. 70.

59. Wagner, 'Machtergreifung', 108f.

60. On the dissolution of the Reichstag and the background to it see Winkler, *Weimar*, 378ff.; Schulz, *Brüning*, 103ff.

61. *Goebbels TB*, 20 July 1930.

62. Ibid.

63. *RSA* 4/1, Doc. 61.

64. *RSA* 3/3, Doc. 79 (quote). See also Goebbels's report in *Der Angriff*, 2 August 1930, 'Es kann losgehen'.

65. BAB, NS 18/5010, Goebbels's survey in the Gaus, May 1930; see also Daniel Mühlenfeld, 'Zur Bedeutung der NS-Propaganda für die Eroberung staatlicher Macht und die Sicherung politischer Loyalität', in Christian A. Braun, Michael Mayer, and Sebastian Weitkamp (eds), *Deformation der Gesellschaft? Neue Forschungen zum Nationalsozialismus* (Berlin, 2008), 98.

66. On the election campaign see Dirk Lau, 'Wahlkämpfe der Weimarer Republik: Propaganda und Programme der politischen Parteien bei den Wahlen zum Deutschen Reichstag von 1924 bis 1930', unpublished dissertation, Mainz, 1995, 420ff.; David Andrew Hacket, 'The Nazi Party in the Reichstag election of 1930', Dissertation, University of Wisconsin, 1971; Gerhard Paul, *Aufstand der Bilder. Die NS-Propaganda vor 1933* (Bonn, 1990), 90f.; BHStA, Varia, 1425, Circular, 15 August 1930.

67. Paul, *Aufstand*, 92.

68. For the audience numbers see *RSA* 3/3, Doc. 90: between 10,000 and 20,000 in Cologne (12 August); Doc. 96: between 13,000 and 15,000 in Ludwigshafen (26 August); Doc. 112: between 20,000 and 25,000 in Breslau (12 September).

69. Ibid., Doc. 87, similarly: Doc. 90.

70. Ibid., Doc. 90; similarly: Doc. 86.

71. Ibid., Doc. 90.

72. Ibid., Doc. 112.

73. Ibid., Docs 86, 90, and 92.

74. Turner, *Großunternehmer*, 144ff.

75. Ibid., 136ff.; for the Reichsverband der Deutschen Industrie distancing itself from the NSDAP during the 1930 election see Reinhard Neebe, *Großindustrie, Staat und NSDAP 1930–1933. Paul Silverberg und der Reichsverband der deutschen Industrie in der Krise der Weimarer Republik* (Göttingen, 1981), 73ff.

76. Georg Schröder, 'Das nationalsozialistische Wirtschaftsprogramm', in *Der Arbeitgeber*, 15 July 1930: 'Industrie'.

77. *Goebbels TB*, 8 August 1930.

78. Ibid., 30 August 1930; see also Longerich, *Goebbels*, 171ff.

79. *Goebbels TB*, 30 August 1930; *Der Angriff*, 31 August 1930: headline: 'Der Sieg wird unser sein!'

80. *Goebbels TB*, 1 September 1930.

81. *RSA* 3/3, Docs 99 and 101f.

82. Ibid., Doc. 100.

83. Jürgen Falter, *Hitlers Wähler* (Munich, 1991), 110ff.

84. Ibid., 139ff. and 169ff.

85. On non-churchgoing Catholics see, for example Heilbronner, *Achillesferse*.

86. Falter, *Wähler*, 194ff.

87. *RSA* 3/3, Doc. 123.

88. *Goebbels TB*, 23 September 1930.

89. Gerhard Granier, *Magnus von Levetzow: Seeoffizier, Monarchist und Wegbereiter Hitlers. Lebensweg und ausgewählte Dokumente* (Boppard am Rhein, 1982), No. 30 (quotes); Schulz, *Brüning*, 178f.; Turner, *Grossunternehmer*, 159f.

90. *Goebbels TB*, 30 September 1930 (about the 29th).

91. Schulz, *Brüning*, 179ff.; Heinrich Brüning, *Memoiren 1918–1934* (Stuttgart, 1970), 191ff., wrongly gives the date of the meeting as 6 October. On this see also Gottfried Treviranus, *Das Ende von Weimar. Heinrich Brüning und seine Zeit* (Düsseldorf and Vienna, 1968), 161.

92. *Goebbels TB*, 6 October 1930.

93. Ibid., 12 October 1930.

94. Winkler, *Weimar*, 392ff.

95. Ibid., 399ff.

96. Ibid., 398.

97. On the financing of the NSDAP see Turner, *Großunternehmer*; Turner, and Horst Matzerath, 'Die Selbstfinanzierung der NSDAP', in *Geschichte und Gesellschaft* 1 (1977), 59–92.

98. Turner, *Großunternehmer*, 157.

99. Ibid., 157f.

100. *RSA* 4/1, Doc. 17.

101. Turner, *Großunternehmer*, 164,

102. *RSA* 4/1, Doc. 36.

103. Turner, *Großunternehmer*, 162.

104. Ibid., 177ff.

105. Wagener, *Hitler*, 45ff.

106. *Der Angriff*, 28 September 1930, 'Weiter arbeiten', and 12 October 1930, 'Wirtschaftsprogramm'.

107. At the end of 1929 Hitler had already established a commission that was supposed to produce a 'Guide to National Socialist Economic Theory' (*RSA* 3/2, Doc. 117). Wagener, at the time still SA chief of staff, recalls a meeting with Hitler, Strasser, and Gauleiter Adolf Wagner in the 'early summer' of 1930 to discuss economic matters. See Wagener, *Hitler*, 105ff. On 2 and 3 August 1930 Organization Department II under Hierl had a meeting to discuss basic economic issues. See Joachim Petzold, 'Wirtschaftsbesprechungen der NSDAP in den Jahren 1930 und 1931', in *Jahrbuch für Wirtschaftsgeschichte* (1982), 200ff.

108. On its establishment see Avraham Barkai, *Das Wirtschaftssystem des Nationalsozialismus. Der historische und ideologische Hintergrund 1933–1936* (Cologne, 1977), 31ff.

109. Ralf Banken, '"An der Spitze aller Künste steht die Staatskunst". Das Protokoll der NSDAP-Wirtschaftsbesprechungen Februar/März 1931', in Johannes Bähr and Ralf Banken (eds), *Wirtschaftssteuerung durch Recht im Nationalsozialismus. Studien zur Entwicklung des Wirtschaftsrechts im Interventionsstaat des' Dritten Reichs'* (Frankfurt a. M., 2006), 545ff.

110. Ibid., 548ff.

111. Economic meetings of the Party leadership in February and March 1931, BAB, NS 51/10, edited by Banken, in 'Spitze'. The document of 16/17 February had already been edited with other documents from the same file. See Petzold, 'Wirtschaftsbesprechungen'. For further meetings see BAB, NS 22/1, 18 May 1931, on the topic, according to the invitation, of 'Revising social legislation, in particular social security'; ibid., 10 June 1931, according to the invitation, on the topic of 'Trade Policy'; ibid., 'The result of the meetings of 26 November and 1 December 1931 re: Economic issues: profit sharing, policy towards profit, social security, settlement policy, corporatism, trades union questions, regulation of wage, salary, and labour issues, technical training (through the corporate bodies), social security, and welfare. Participation in legal decisions affecting economic issues.'

112. *Goebbels TB*, 13 and 16 March 1931 (quote); Longerich, *Goebbels*, 154f.; Wagener's paper is published in Avraham Barkai, 'Wirtschaftliche Grundanschauungen und Ziele der NSDAP. Ein unveröffentliches Dokument aus dem Jahre 1931', in *Jahrbuch des Instituts für Deutsche Geschichte* 7 (1978), 373ff.

113. Turner, *Großunternehmer*, 170ff.

114. Hans Reupke, *Der Nationalsozialismus und die Wirtschaft* (Berlin, 1931).

115. *Goebbels TB*, 17 March 1931; Reupke, *Nationalsozialismus*; also, opposed to Reupke see *Goebbels TB*, 23 and 28 March 1931.

116. *VB* (B), 15/16 March 1931, 'Jüdisches Allerlei'.

117. *Goebbels TB*, 25 March 1931.

118. *RSA* 4/2, Doc. 60.

119. BAB, NS 22/1, Report on the meeting of the Reich Economic Council on 27 April 1932 and circulars from Wagener to the members of the Economic Council 4 May 1932; Wagener, *Hitler*, 178ff.

120. On the appointment see Longerich, *Geschichte*, 107f.

121. *RSA* 4/1, Doc. 54.

122. Ibid., Doc. 59 (quote), similarly Doc. 62.

123. Ibid., Doc. 67.

124. *Goebbels TB*, 30 and 31 March 1931.

125. *RSA* 4/1, Doc. 73.

126. *Der Angriff*, 1 April 1931, 'Hauptmann Stennes nicht abgesetzt!' (headline); *Vossische Zeitrung* (*VZ*), 2 April 1931, 'Führerkrise im Hitler-Lager' (headline). On the Stennes revolt see Longerich, *Geschichte*, 111; *Goebbels TB*, 2 April 1931.

127. Ibid., 2 and 4 April 1931.

128. *RSA* 4/1, Doc. 79.

129. Ibid., Doc. 80.

130. Ibid., Doc. 81.

131. Ibid., Doc. 87.

132. Ibid., Docs 89 and 91.

133. Ibid., Doc. 102.

134. *Goebbels TB*, 28 April 1931. According to Goebbels's entries of 22 and 25 April he had already toyed with the idea of resigning as Gauleiter.

135. Ibid., 10 and 20 May 1931.

136. Ibid., 9 May 1931.

137. Joseph Goebbels, *'Der Nazi-Sozi'. Fragen und Antworten für den Nationalsozialisten* (Munich, 1930), 18f.

138. RSA 4/1, Doc. 115. See also the detailed report in the *VZ*, 9 May 1931: "'Adolf Legalité". Hitlers Bekenntnis'. On the confrontation in the court room see Knut Bergbauer, Sabine Fröhlich, and Stefanie Schüler-Springorum, *Denkmalsfigur. Biographische Annäherung an Hans Litten (1903–1938)* (Göttingen, 2008), 146ff.

139. *Goebbels TB*, 9 May 1931. Goebbels, *'Nazi-Sozi'* (1931).

140. Brigitte Hamann, *Winifred Wagner oder Hitlers Bayreuth* (Munich and Zurich, 2006).

141. Hale, 'Hitler', 837.

142. *Goebbels TB*, 24 August 1931; for further details on the relationship see Longerich, *Goebbels*, in particular pp. 167ff.

143. *Goebbels TB*, 26 and 27 August 1931.

144. Ibid., 4 September 1931.

145. Ibid., 14 September 1931. During these days Goebbels had cut several pages referring to Magda out of his diary.

146. Ibid., 16 September 1931.

147. Ibid., 31 October 1931.

148. Wagener, *Hitler*, 392ff.

149. Joachimsthaler, *Liste*, 328.

150. *Goebbels TB*, 20 September 1931.

151. Österreichisches Staatsarchiv, Archiv der Republik, 04, 122291-14/1924, Bundespolizeidirektion Wien, 26 September 1931.

152. *Goebbels TB*, 5 February 1932.

STRATEGIES

1. Figures on unemployment in Balderston, *Origins*, 2; on unemployment and its consequences see, in particular, Richard J. Evans and Dick Geary (eds), *The German Unemployed. Experiences and Consequences of Mass Unemployment from the Weimar Republic to the Third Reich* (London, 1987); Peter D. Stachura (ed.), *Unemployment and the Great Depression in Weimar Germany* (New York, 1986); Heinrich August Winkler, *Der Weg in die Katastrophe. Arbeiter und Arbeiterbewegung in der Weimarer Republik 1930 bis 1933* (Berlin and Bonn, 1987), 19ff.

2. *RSA*, 4/1, Doc. 88.

3. Volker Berghahn, *Der Stahlhelm. Bund der Frontsoldaten 1918–1935* (Düsseldorf, 1966), 169 and 172f.; Gerhard Schulz, *Brüning*, 433ff.

4. *Goebbels TB*, 24 August 1931.

5. Gerhard Granier, *Levetzow*, No. 35.

6. Schulz, *Brüning*, 494.

7. See the notes of the DNVP politician, Otto Schmidt-Hannover, who was present at the subsequent meetings in Otto Schmidt-Hannover, *Umdenken oder Anarchie. Männer – Schicksale – Lehren* (Göttingen, 1959), 274f.

8. *RSA* 4/2, Doc. 27.

9. Maximilian Terhalle, *Deutschnational in Weimar. Die politische Biographie des Reichstagsabgeordneten Otto Schmidt(-Hannover) 1888–1971* (Cologne, 2009), 276f.

10. *Goebbels TB*, 5 October 1931.

11. Winkler, *Weimar*, 430.

12. Heinrich Brüning, *Memoiren 1918–1934* (Stuttgart, 1970), 391.

13. Granier, *Levetzow*, No. 36.

14. Brüning, *Memoiren*, 430.

15. Granier, *Levetzow*, No. 36; *Goebbels TB*, 12 October 1931; Brüning, *Memoiren*, 391; Wolfram Pyta, *Hindenburg. Herrschaft zwischen Hohenzollern und Hitler* (Munich, 2007), 636f.

16. *Frankfurter Zeitung (FZ)*, 10 October (announcement of Hitler's visit to Hindenburg) and 11 October 1931, 'Hitlers Besuch beim Reichspräsidenten'.

17. Pyta, *Hindenburg*, 631; Brüning, *Memoiren*, 391f. See also *Goebbels TB*, 12 October 1931.

18. Larry Eugene Jones, 'Nationalists, Nazis and the Assault against Weimar. Revisiting the Harzburg Rally of October 1931', in *German Studies Review* 29 (2006), 483–494; Schulz, *Brüning*, 554ff. See also Granier, *Levetzow*, No. 3.

19. *UF* 8, Nos. 1784a and c; Ilse Maurer and Udo Wengst (eds), *Politik und Wirtschaft in der Krise, 1930–1932. Quellen zur Ära Brüning* (Düsseldorf, 1980), No. 341.

20. Christoph Kopper, *Hjalmar Schacht. Aufstieg und Fall von Hitlers mächtigsten Bankier* (Munich, 2006), 191ff. Schacht's speech is documented in *UF* 8, No. 1784d.

21. *VB*, 13 October 1931, 'An der Spitze des Kampfes zur Überwindung des herrschenden Systems marschiert die N.S.D.A.P.!' (headline), and 14 October 1931, 'Die Kampfansage von Harzburg'.

22. Terhalle, *Schmidt*, 288.

23. *RSA* 4/2, Doc. 46.

24. Schulz, *Brüning*, 560ff.; Martin Schumacher, *Mittelstandsfront und Republik. Die Wirtschaftspartei – Reichspartei des deutschen Mittelstandes, 1919–1933* (Düsseldorf, 1972), 148.

25. A further meeting with Schleicher on 22 October 1931 did not result in progress. Speculations in the liberal press prompted Hitler to issue a denial and the Army Ministry a statement in which the contacts between Hitler and Schleicher were downplayed. See *RSA* 4/2, Doc. 65; *FZ*, 30 October 1931, 'Adolf Hitler bei General Schleicher'.

26. *RSA* 4/2, Doc. 48 (quote) and Doc. 49.

27. Granier, *Levetzow*, No. 37.

28. Winkler, *Weimar*, 434; Schulz, *Brüning*, 604ff.

29. *RSA* 4/2, Doc. 76, note 5.

30. Ibid., Doc. 78.

31. Ibid., Doc. 82.

32. Ibid., Docs 83, 87, 89, and 97–99.

33. *RSA* 4/3, Doc. 15. See also Turner, *Großunternehmer*, 261ff.; Schulz, *Brüning*, 733f.

34. Turner, *Großunternehmer*, 269f.

35. Ibid., 290ff.; see also the documentation compiled by Kurt Koszyk, 'Paul Reusch und die "Münchner Neuesten Nachrichten". Zum Problem von Industrie und Presse in der Endphase der Weimarer Republik', in *VfZ* 20 (1972), 75–103.

36. On Schacht's office see Neebe, *Großindustrie*, 122ff.

37. Turner, *Großunternehmer*, 293ff.; on the creation of the working group see also Emil Helfferich, *1932–1946. Tatsachen. Ein Beitrag zur Wahrheitsfindung* (Jever, 1969).

38. Turner, *Großunternehmer*, 244ff.; Hartmut Berghoff and Cornelia Rauh-Kühne, *Fritz K. Ein deutsches Leben im zwanzigsten Jahrhundert* (Stuttgart, 2000).

39. See Goebbels's shocked response in 'Uniform- und Abzeichenverbot. Facta in Deutschland. Der Anfang von Ende' (*Goebbels TB*, 9 December 1931).

40. Tilman Koops (ed.), *Die Kabinette Brüning I und II. Akten der Reichskanzlei* (Boppard am Rhein, 1982–1990), No. 599; Pyta, *Hindenburg*, 649. Brüning claimed in his memoirs that, surprised by this meeting, he had threatened to resign on account of 'these unconstitutional negotiations'. See *Memoiren*, 467.

41. *Kabinette Brüning I und II*, No. 617. On the attempts to achieve an extension of his term of office see Schulz, *Brüning*, 704ff.

42. *Kabinette Brüning I und II*, No. 626. See also Pyta, *Hindenburg*, 653f.

43. Brüning, *Memoiren*, 501.

44. *Goebbels TB*, 10 und 11 January 1932; Brüning, *Memoiren*, 504f.

45. For the relevant correspondence see *Kabinette Brüning I und II*, Nos 623 and 642; *RSA* 4/3, Docs 6, 8, and 12. On the background see *Goebbels TB*, 12 January 1932.

46. Ibid., 13 January 1932. See also the note by the German Nationalist politician Reinhold Quaatz of 14 January, for whom Hitler's behaviour was a debacle. See Hermann Weiss and Paul Hoser (eds), *Reinhold G. Quaatz. Die Deutschnationalen und die Zerstörung der Weimarer Republik. Aus dem Tagebuch von Reinhold Quaatz* (Munich, 1989), 168ff.

47. For this assessment see in particular Schulz, *Brüning*, 710f.

48. *RSA* 4/2, Doc. 84.

49. Longerich, *Goebbels*, 178f.

50. *Goebbels TB*, 20 and 28 January and 3 and 10 February 1932.

51. *RSA* 4/3, Doc. 23.

52. *Goebbels TB*, 23 February 1932; *Der Angriff*, 23 February 1932, 'Schluss jetzt! Deutschland wählt Hitler!' (headline); *VZ*, 23 February 1932 (M), 'Hitler und Duesterberg proklamiert'.

53. *RSA* 4/3, Doc. 28.

54. *Goebbels TB*, 1 March 1932.

55. BAB, NS 26/287, Memo by the Party's Reich propaganda HQ, 13 March 1932; Paul, *Aufstand*, 95ff. and 248ff.

56. *RSA* 4/3, Docs. 29, 32–41, 43, and 45.

57. Ibid., Doc. 41.

58. Ibid., Doc. 34.

59. Ibid., Doc. 32f. and Doc. 43.

60. Ibid., Doc. 45, see Doc. 38.

61. *Goebbels TB*, 14 March 1932.

62. *RSA* 4/3, Doc. 47f.

63. *Goebbels TB*, 16 March 1932.

64. Ibid., 20 March 1932.

65. *RSA* 4/3, Doc. 55 (quote), Doc. 56.

66. See the reporting in *Der Angriff*, which headlined this topic between 2 and 7 April 1932.

67. Hans Baur, *Ich flog Mächtige der Erde* (Kempten, 1956), 81ff.

68. Schulz, *Brüning*, 758.

69. Julius K. Engelbrechten, *Eine braune Armee ensteht. Die Geschichte der Berlin-Brandenburger SA* (Munich, 1937), 212.

70. *RSA* 4/3, Doc. 52 (quote) and Doc. 53f.

71. Excerpts appeared in the SPD supporting the *Münchener Post* of 9 March 1932.

72. *Goebbels TB*, 7 March 1932.

73. *RSA* 5/1, Doc. 15.

74. Ibid., Docs 30f. and 32 (for the word 'victory').

75. In the book version of his diaries, published in 1934 under the title *Kaiserhof*, Goebbels altered those passages that did not fit in with the image of a confident and decisive 'Führer' and included passages in which he praised Hitler's gifts of leadership. See in detail Longerich, *Goebbels*, 741f.

76. *RSA* 5/1, Doc. 1.

77. See the report of the British military attaché, Colonel Thorne, in *UF* 8, No. 1821b.

78. *Goebbels TB*, 15 April 1932. There are already references to the impending ban in the entries for 12 and 13 April 1932.

79. *RSA* 5/1, Doc. 36.

80. Ibid., Doc. 57.

81. Ibid., Doc. 51 (quote), Doc. 38 (16 April) to Doc. 63 (23 April); see also the reporting in the *VB* from 17 to 24 April 1932.

82. *Goebbels TB*, 25 April 1932.

83. Ibid., 29 April 1932.

84. Pyta, *Hindenburg*, 690f.

85. Ibid., 685.

86. Hagen Schulze, *Otto Braun oder Preussens demokratische Sendung. Eine Biographie* (Berlin, 1977), 732.

87. Pyta, *Hindenburg*, 691; Brüning, *Memoiren*, 575ff.

88. *Goebbels TB*, 5 and 7 May 1932.

89. Ibid., 9 May 1932.

90. Ibid.

91. *Politik und Wirtschaft*, No. 498; Brüning, *Memoiren*, 586.

92. *Goebbels TB*, 13 May 1932. Goebbels claimed that the resignation was Schleicher's first success and that the crisis was 'deepening according to plan'. See ibid., 14

May 1932. On Groener's resignation see Schulz, *Brüning*, 820f.; Johannes Hürter, *Wilhelm Groener. Reichswehrminister am Ende der Weimarer Republik (1928–1932)* (Munich, 1993), 348ff.; Pyta, *Hindenburg*, 687ff.

93. *RSA* 5/1, Doc. 68.

94. *Goebbels TB*, 19 and 25 May 1932.

95. Ibid., 25 May 1932.

96. Ibid.

97. Hermann Pünder, *Politik in der Reichskanzlei. Aufzeichnungen aus den Jahren 1929–1932* (Stuttgart, 1961), 126; Brüning, *Memoiren*, 593ff.; Otto Meissner, *Staatssekretär unter Ebert, Hindenburg, Hitler. Der Schicksalsweg des deutschen Volkes von 1918 bis 1945, wie ich ihn erlebte* (Hamburg, 1950), 224ff.; see also Schulz, *Brüning*, 853f.

98. Herbert Hömig, *Das preußische Zentrum in der Weimarer Republik* (Mainz, 1979), 258f.

99. Hans-Peter Ehni, *Bollwerk Preußen? Preußen-Regierung, Reich–Länder-Problem und Sozialdemokratie 1918–1932* (Bonn-Bad Godesberg, 1975), 247f.

100. *RSA* 5/1, Docs 69–75.

101. *Goebbels TB*, 28 May 1932.

102. On the background see Friedrich Martin Fiederlein, *Der deutsche Osten und die Regierungen Brüning, Papen, Schleicher* (Würzburg, 1967); Schulz, *Brüning*, 800ff.

103. *Kabinette Brüning I und II*, No. 773; Brüning, *Memoiren*, 597ff.; Pünder, *Politik*, 128f.; Schulz, *Brüning*, 843ff.

104. With 48.4 per cent of the votes. See Falter, Lindenberger, and Schumann, *Wahlen*, 100.

105. Walther Hubatsch, *Hindenburg und der Staat. Aus den Papieren des Generalfeldmarschalls und Reichspräsidenten von 1878 bis 1934* (Göttingen, 1966), No. 84; Meissner, *Staatssekretär*, 232f. However, Meissner's promise to provide the NSDAP with access to radio is referred to only in his memoirs, not in the note in his file. Following the meeting, Hitler also informed Goebbels. See *Goebbels TB*, 31 May 1932.

106. Ibid., 1 June 1932.

ON THE THRESHOLD OF POWER

1. Interior Minister Gayl and Agriculture Minister Braun; see Gerhard Feldbauer and Joachim Petzold, 'Deutscher Herrenklub', in Dieter Fricke, *Lexikon zur Parteiengeschichte. Die bürgerlichen und kleinbürgerlichen Parteien und Verbände in Deutschland (1789–1945)*, 2 (Leipzig, 1984), 107–15.

2. According to Papen in Franz von Papen, *Der Wahrheit eine Gasse* (Innsbruck, 1952), 187.

3. On the Papen government see Ulrike Hörster-Philipps, *Konservative Politik in der Endphase der Weimarer Republik. Die Regierung Franz von Papen* (Cologne, 1982); Joachim Petzold, *Franz von Papen. Ein deutsches Verhängnis* (Munich and Berlin, 1995).

4. *RSA* 5/1, Doc. 81; for his other appearances in Mecklenburg see ibid., Docs 76, 78f., and 82.

5. Hitler's remark to Goebbels. See *Goebbels TB*, 5 June 1932.

6. Schulz, *Brüning*, 879f.

7. *Goebbels TB*, 7 June 1932. On the negotiations see *Germania*, 18 July 1932; on a conversation between the Centre party and Papen on 8 June see Ilse Maurer and Udo Wengst (eds), *Politik und Wirtschaft in der Krise 1930–1932. Quellen zur Ära Brüning* (Düsseldorf, 1980), No. 530b.

8. *Goebbels TB*, 5 June 1932.

9. *RSA* 5/1, Doc. 85.

10. Ibid., Doc. 87.

11. Ibid., Doc. 86.

12. Ibid., Doc. 171.

13. *Goebbels TB*, 28 June 1932.

14. The speech was published as a pamphlet: Gregor Strasser: *Arbeit und Brot! Reichstagsrede am 10. Mai 1932* (Munich, 1932).

15. Kissenkoetter, 137ff.

16. Wagener, *Hitler*, 478ff.; Turner, *Großunternehmer*, 298f.; see also the report by Emil Helfferich, one of those attending the meeting, in Helfferich, *1932–1946. Tatsachen. Ein Beitrag zur Wahrheitsfindung* (Jever, 1969), 1932–1946, 13ff.

17. BAB, NS 22, Goebbels/Dietrich letter to all Party agencies, 4 June 1932, BAB, NS 22, to all Gauleiters and Gau propaganda chiefs, 27 June 1932, as well as individual directives, 5 July 1932; BAB, NS 26/289, undated memorandum concerning the Reichstag election and various signed circulars from the Reich propaganda headquarters; see also Paul, *Aufstand*, 100ff.

18. BAB, NS 26/89, Memorandum of the Reich propaganda headquarters concerning the Reichstag election of 1932.

19. Ibid., Circular from the Reich propaganda headquarters to all Gau, propaganda, and press departments, 19 July 1932.

20. *VB* (Bayern), 13 July 1932, 'Des Führers Freiheitsflug über Deutschland beginnt' (headline), and reports between 17 and 31 July 1932.

21. *RSA* 5/1, Docs 112–162.

22. Ibid., Doc. 158.

23. Individual examples in ibid., Doc. 121, note. 6; see also Winkler, *Weg*, 643f.

24. *RSA* 5/1, Doc. 122.

25. Ibid., Doc. 148.

26. *Goebbels TB*, 9 July 1932.

27. Winkler, *Weimar*, 486.

28. Léon Schirmann, *Altonaer Blutsonntag, 17. Juli 1932. Dichtungen und Wahrheit* (Hamburg, 1994).

29. Winkler, *Weimar*, 489f.

30. Decree of the Reich President concerning the Restoration of Public Safety and Order within the Territory of the State of Prussia 20 July 1932 in *Reichsgesetzblatt* (RGBl.) 1932 I, 377; Karl Heinz Minuth (ed.), *Das Kabinett von Papen (1932). Akten der Reichskanzlei* (Munich, 1989), Nos 57 and 59.

31. Schulz, *Brüning*, 920ff.

32. *Goebbels TB*, 21 to 23 July 1932.

33. Falter, *Wähler*, 110ff.

34. Ibid., 136ff.

35. *Goebbels TB*, 3 August 1932.

36. Papen declared on 1 August in an interview with Associated Press: 'The time has now come for the national socialist movement to cooperate in rebuilding the fatherland', an initial attempt to get the NSDAP to tolerate or join his government. See *Schulthess' Europäischer Geschichtskalendar* 1932, 136.

37. On the contacts between the Nazis and Schleicher see also IfZ, ED 93, Schäffer, Confidential report 5 August 1932.

38. *Goebbels TB*, 7 August 1932. The conversation took place on 6 August.

39. Hubatsch, *Hindenburg*, No. 87; *Kabinett von Papen*, No. 99; see also IfZ, ED 93, vol. 22a, Schäffer Diary, 10 August 1932.

40. *Goebbels TB*, 12 August 1932. The negative attitude is clear from Meissner's notes about the previous meetings concerning the question of forming the government. See Hubatsch, *Hindenburg*, No. 87.

41. On the wave of violence see Longerich, *Geschichte*, 156f.; for details see the daily reports in the *Vossiche Zeitung* (*VZ*) after 2 August 1932.

42. Decree of the Reich President against Political Terror, Decree of the Reich Government concerning the Creation of Special Courts, and the Decree of the Reich President concerning the Securing of Internal Peace, all dated 9 August 1932 (*RGBl.* 1932 I, 403ff.). For details on the process see *Kabinett von Papen*, No. 98.

43. Paul Kluke, 'Der Fall Potempa', in *VjZ* 5 (1957), 279–97; Richard Bessel, 'The Potempa Murder', in *Central European History* 10 (1977), 241–54.

44. *Goebbels TB*, 11 August 1932.

45. Ibid., 14 August 1932; Pyta, *Hindenburg*, 718f.; Pünder, 141.

46. *Goebbels TB*, 14 August 1932; *Kabinett von Papen*, No. 101; see also Schulz, *Brüning*, 963.

47. For details see *Kabinett von Papen*, No. 101, notes 5 and 102.

48. *Goebbels TB*, 14 and 15 August 1932.

49. *VB* (R), 17 August 1932. On the NSDAP crisis at the end of 1932 see Dietrich Orlow, *The History of the Nazi Party*, 1 (Newton Abbot, 1971), 286ff.; Horn, *Marsch*, 363ff.

50. On the coalition negotiations see Schulz, *Brüning*, 945 and 958; Rudolf Morsey (ed.), *Die Protokolle der Reichstagsfraktion und des Fraktionsvorstands der deutschen Zentrumspartei 1926–1933* (Mainz, 1969), 315ff.; on the willingness of the leadership of the Centre to negotiate see ibid. No. 8; IfZ, ED 93, Schäffer-TB, 11 August, concerning a meeting with Brüning. On the motives of the Nazi leadership see *Goebbels TB*, 14 August 1932.

51. *RSA* 5/1, Docs 174 and 175 (quote).

52. *Goebbels TB*, 26 August 1932. At a meeting with Schleicher Goebbels came to the conclusion that the former was continuing to pursue the idea of a presidential cabinet to include the Nazis only in order to lure the Party into a trap and

to be able to dissolve the Reichstag. The only thing left was the 'bitter idea of a coalition with the Centre in order to put Hindenburg and Schleicher under pressure'. Goebbels reported to Hitler along these lines. See ibid., 27 and 28 August 1932.

53. Ibid., 26 August 1932. On the meeting between Brüning and Strasser see Brüning, *Memoiren*, 623; Rudolf Morsey, *Der Untergang des politischen Katholizismus. Die Zentrumspartei zwischen christlichem Selbstverständnis und 'nationaler Erhebung' 1932/33* (Stuttgart/Zurich, 1977), 61.

54. Joint declaration by the Centre and the NSDAP of 1 September 1932, published in *Schulthess' 1932*, 151. There are various indications of the start of negotiations. See IfZ, ED 93, Confidential message to Schäffer, 21 October 1932; ibid., vol. 22, Schäffer-TB, 1 September 1932, on the meeting with Brüning see Morsey (ed.), *Protokolle*, No. 707. On the negotiations see Morsey, 'Die Deutsche Zentrumspartei', in Erich Matthias and Morsey (eds), *Das Ende der Parteien 1933* (Düsseldorf, 1960), 320f.; Morsey, *Untergang*, 60ff.; Schulz, *Brüning*, 967ff.

55. *Goebbels TB*, 30 August 1932. Brüning confirmed in his memoirs that at this meeting he had offered to mediate between the NSDAP and the central committee of the Centre Party (623f.). See also Schulz, *Brüning*, 968; Morsey, *Untergang*, 61, dates the start of the negotiations between the Centre and the Nazis to 28 August.

56. *Kabinett von Papen*, No. 120; Winkler, *Weimar*, 518f.

57. *Goebbels TB*, 1–9 September 1932.

58. Ibid., 9 and 11 September 1932. Morsey, *Untergang*, 61ff. on the negotiations and 65ff. on the subsequent attempt by the Centre to 'hide their tracks'. On the plan to bring down Hindenburg see also Pyta, *Hindenburg*, 736.

59. Brüning, *Memoiren*, 625f.

60. On the negotiations see Morsey (ed.), *Protokolle*, No. 709.

61. Pyta, *Hindenburg*, 737. The law, which was planned as a law to implement Article 51 finally, in December 1932 under altered circumstances, took the form of a law altering the constitution. See *RGBl.* 1932 I, 547.

62. *Goebbels TB*, 13 August 1932; *Die Verhandlungen des Reichstags*, 6. Wahlperiode, 13ff. The Centre Party parliamentary group believed that, in view of the majority held by the NSDAP and KPD, there was no point in opposing the dissolution. See Morsey (ed.), *Protokolle*, No. 711.

63. Schulz, *Brüning*, 973 and 993f.

64. *Goebbels TB*, 14 September 1932.

65. Paul, *Aufstand*, 104ff.; BAB, NS 26/263, Strictly confidential information from the Reich propaganda headquarters of 20, 25, and 27 October 1932.

66. Turner, *Großunternehmer*, 335.

67. Ibid., 344f.

68. Paul, *Aufstand*, 249f.

69. *RSA* 5/2, Doc. 5.

70. Hitler's election speeches in *RSA* 5/1, Doc. 187, and *RSA* 5/2, Docs 6–11, 13f, 16–22, 24f., 27–40, and Docs 42–60.

71. Ibid., Doc. 15.

72. Winkler, *Weg*, 765ff.; Klaus Rainer Röhl, *Nähe zum Gegner. Kommunisten und Nationalsozialisten im Berliner BVG-Streik von 1932* (Frankfurt a. M. and New York, 1994).

73. *RSA* 5/2, Doc. 58.

74. Ibid., Doc. 61.

75. *Kabinett von Papen*, No. 214. On the other meetings see ibid., Nos 211–13; Schulz, *Brüning*, 1013f.

76. *Kabinett von Papen*, No. 215; Schulz, *Brüning*, 1014f.

77. On the preparations for the meeting see *Goebbels TB*, 19 November 1932.

78. *Kabinett von Papen*, No. 222. On this meeting and what followed see Pyta, *Hindenburg*, 753ff.; Meissner, *Staatssekretär*, 247ff.

79. *RSA* 5/2, Doc. 67.

80. *Goebbels TB*, 22 November 1932; Pyta, *Hindenburg* 756f.; *Kabinett von Papen*, No. 224.

81. *RSA* 5/2, Docs 67 and 69.

82. Ibid., Docs 68–70; Hubatsch, *Hindenburg*, Nos 97 and 99.

83. RSA 5/2, Doc. 69.

84. *Goebbels TB*, 21 and 22 November 1932; in its *Partei-Correspondenz* the BVP had been very critical but not totally opposed to a Hitler chancellorship. See the *Bayerische Kurier* (*BK*), 22 November 1932, 'Eine neue Lage.', which Hitler immediately interpreted as a rejection.

85. *RSA* 5/2, Doc. 69.

86. *Kabinett von Papen*, No. 228.

87. Hubatsch, *Hindenburg*, No. 99.

88. *Kabinett von Papen*, No. 232. See also *Goebbels TB*, 24 November 1932.

89. Ibid., 29 November 1932.

90. Ibid., 1 December 1932.

91. *RSA* 5/2, Doc. 74.

92. *Goebbels TB*, 1 December 1932. Ott is wrongly referred to in this entry as Otte.

93. Ibid., 2 December 1932. In the later version published by him he added to the word 'toleration' the half sentence 'but that was out of the question'. In fact, at the beginning of December 1932, the Nazi leadership regarded this solution as a feasible option.

94. Hubatsch, *Hindenburg*, No. 103.

95. *Kabinett von Papen*, No. 239 b; for the war game see IfZ, ZS 279, Ott note, 1946. On Schleicher's soundings see Karl Dietrich Bracher, *Die Auflösung der Weimarer Republik. Eine Studie zum Problem des Machtverfalls in der Demokratie* (Königstein i. Ts., 1978), 667ff.; Thilo Vogelsang, *Reichswehr, Staat und NSDAP. Beiträge zur deutschen Geschichte 1930–1932* (Stuttgart, 1962), 318ff.; Kissenkoetter, *Straßer*, 162ff.; Friedrich Karl von Plehwe, *Reichskanzler Kurt von Schleicher. Weimars letzte Chance gegen Hitler* (Frankfurt a. M. and Berlin, 1990), 234ff.; Irene Strenge, *Kurt von Schleicher. Politik im Reichswehrministerium am Ende der Weimarer Republik* (Berlin, 2006), 182ff.

96. *Goebbels TB*, 6 December 1932.

97. See, for example the report of the *Tägliche Rundschau* of 8 December 1932. Local government election results are poorly documented.

98. *Goebbels TB*, 6 December 1932.

99. For details see Longerich, *Goebbels*, 200ff.

100. Moreover, motions for the introduction of winter aid for the unemployed and for the suspension of the whole emergency decree of 4 September 1932 were sent back to the committees. See Winkler, *Weimar*, 560.

101. On 3 December the Schleicher cabinet had already discussed the question of whether, as the chancellor put it, 'one couldn't relax the domestic emergency decree a bit'. See Anton Golecki (ed.), *Das Kabinett von Schleicher 1932/3. Akten der Reichskanzlei* (Munich, 1986), No. 1. These efforts led to the Reich President's Emergency Decree for the Maintenance of Domestic Peace of 19 December 1932, through which, among other things, the emergency decrees of 14 and 28 June, of 9 August, and of 2 November 1932 were suspended. See *RGBl.* 1932 I, 548, and the Reich government's decree of the same day suspending the special courts (ibid., 550).

102. *Kabinett von Schleicher*, No. 5.

103. He visited Goebbels on 4, 5, and 6 December. On 7 December he appeared at a soirée at Leni Riefenstahl's. See *Goebbels TB*, 5–8 December 1932.

104. On the letter see Peter D. Stachura, '"Der Fall Straßer". Gregor Straßer, Hitler and National Socialism, 1930–1933', in Stachura, *The Shaping of the Nazi State* (London, 1978), 113ff. On this event see also *Vossische Zeitung* (*VZ*), 9 December 1932, 'Konflikt Hitler–Straßer' (headline); *VZ*, 10 December 1932, Konrad Heiden: 'Schach oder matt? Gregor Straßers Rebellion' (Leading article).

105. *RSA* 5/2, No. 87. See also *Goebbels TB*, 9 December 1932, from which it is clear that this speech of Hitler's should not be confused with that of the following day, as is also clear from Kershaw's account in *Hitler*, 1, 496ff.

106. *Goebbels TB*, 9 December 1932.

107. *RSA* 5/2, Doc. 86.

108. Tyrell (ed.), *Führer*, 369f.; *RSA* 5/2, Doc. 93f. and Docs 96–98.

109. Ibid., Doc. 99, second part: Doc. 106 (quote). See also Hitler's directive of 14 December 1932 (Doc. 93), according to which the memo should go only to top Party functionaries.

110. *Goebbels TB*, 10 December 1932. The text of Hitler's speeches has not survived.

111. *RSA* 5/2, Doc. 100.

112. Jutta Ciolek-Kümper, *Wahlkampf in Lippe. Die Wahlkampfpropaganda der NSDAP zur Landtagswahl am 15. Januar 1933* (Munich, 1976); *Goebbels TB*, 5–15 January 1933.

113. See Otto Dietrich, *Mit Hitler in die Macht. Persönliche Erlebnisse mit meinem Führer* (Munich, 1934), 173ff.

114. Heinrich Muth, 'Das "Kölner Gespräch" am 4. Januar 1933', in *Geschichte in Wissenschaft und Unterricht* 37 (1986), 463–80.

115. *Goebbels TB*, 10 January 1933.

116. Henry Ashby Turner, *Hitlers Weg zur Macht. Der Januar 1933* (Munich, 1997), 70ff. (on the basis of a reconstruction from three reports: (a) and (b) from the journalists Dertinger and Reiner, (c) from an unknown hand published in ibid., 247ff.).

117. *Kabinett von Schleicher*, No. 56.

118. Pyta, *Hindenburg*, 780; Meissner, *Staatssekretär*, 261f.

119. *Kabinett von Schleicher*, Nos 50 and 51 (the resolution is recorded in note 16).

120. Meissner, *Staatssekretär*, 251f. on Strasser's reception by Hindenburg at the beginning of January. On the project of a Strasser vice-chancellorship see Schulz, *Brüning*, 1041f.; Turner, *Weg*, 116f.

121. *Kabinett von Schleicher*, No. 54.

122. Ciolek-Kümper, *Wahlkampf*.

123. *Goebbels TB*, 17 January 1933; Rudolf Jordan, *Erlebt und Erlitten. Weg eines Gauleiters von München bis Moskau* (Leoni am Starnberger See, 1971), 90.

124. Turner, *Weg*, 153ff.; Pyta, *Hindenburg*, 785ff. Joachim von Ribbentrop, *Zwischen London und Moskau. Erinnerungen und Letzte Aufzeichnungen* (Leoni am Starnberger See, 1953), 39, mentions Hitler, Frick, Göring, Körner, Meissner, Hindenburg, and Papen as his guests. According to this account Papen agreed to push through Hitler's chancellorship. On the meeting see Meissner, *Staatssekretär*, 263f. He does not, however, mention his own presence.

125. *Goebbels TB*, 25 January 1933.

126. Turner, *Weg*, 157f.

127. Ibid., 164f.; Pyta, *Hindenburg*, 772ff.

128. Turner, *Weg*, 180; Ribbentrop, *London*, 39; *Goebbels TB*, 26 January 1933.

129. Turner, *Weg*, 182; Ribbentrop, *London*, 40; Schmidt-Hannover, *Umdenken*, 332. According to *Goebbels TB*, 28 January 1933, Hugenberg wanted Schmidt as Hitler's state secretary and the DNVP press spokesman, Hans Brosius, as the new government's press spokesman. Also the Berlin police should be subordinated to the Reichswehr.

130. Ribbentrop, *London*, 40f.

131. *Kabinett von Schleicher*, No. 71f.

132. Turner, *Weg*, 184f., according to Ribbentrop, *London*, 41; see also Papen, *Wahrheit*, 267ff.

133. Turner, *Weg*, 185.

134. Ibid., 186f.

135. Ibid., 190f.

136. Papen, *Wahrheit*, 271; Kirstin A. Schäfer, *Werner von Blomberg. Hitlers erster Feldmarschall. Eine Biographie* (Paderborn, 2006, 97f.).

137. Turner, *Weg*, 192f.; Ribbentrop, *London*, 42.

138. Turner, *Weg*, 193ff.

139. Schmidt-Hannover, *Umdenken*, 334f.; Turner, *Weg*, 195f.; Theodor Duesterberg, *Der Stahlhelm, und Hitler* (Hamelin, 1950), 40f. Schmidt-Hannover, *Umdenken*, 334, makes it clear that the meeting took place on the 29th and not, as

Duesterberg has it, on the 26th. See also Ewald von Kleist-Schmenzin, 'Die letzte Möglichkeit', in *Politische Studien* 10 (1959) (the piece was written in 1934).

140. Turner, *Weg*, 202ff.; *Goebbels TB*, 30 January 1933.

141. To Blomberg's chief of staff, Walter von Reichenau, who had asked Hitler about his ideas on foreign policy and defence, to which Hitler had replied in December ('Hitler's letter') – and to the chaplain of the military district, Ludwig Müller.

142. Pyta, *Hindenburg*, 784.

143. On the appointment of commissars see Friedrich Hartmannsgruber (ed.), *Regierung Hitler 1933–1945*, 7 vols (Berlin and Munich, 1983–2015), 1, No. 14.

144. His proposal at the cabinet meeting of 3 February 1933 in ibid., No. 11.

145. Turner, *Weg*, 198ff.

146. Ibid., 204ff.; Duesterberg, *Stahlhelm*, 42.

147. Turner, *Weg*, 206ff.; Duesterberg, *Stahlhelm*, 43; Papen, *Wahrheit*, 275f. (with the false assertion that this was the first time that Hitler had demanded new elections); Meissner, *Staatssekretär*, 269f.

THE SEIZURE OF POWER

1. Kershaw, *Hitler*, 1, 547ff.; Hans Ulrich Thamer, *Verführung und Gewalt. Deutschland 1933–1945* (Berlin, 1986), 232.

2. Karl Dietrich Bracher, *Stufen der Machtergreifung* (Frankfurt a. M., 1983). From the extensive relevant literature see also Thamer, *Verführung*, 232ff.; Kershaw, *Hitler* 1, 547ff.; Irene Strenge, *Machtübernahme; 1933 – alles auf legalem Weg?* (Berlin, 2002); Michael Kissener (ed.), *Der Weg in den Nationalsozialismus 1933/34* (Darmstadt, 2009); Andreas Wirsching (ed.), *Das Jahr 1933. Die nationalsozialistische Machteroberung und die deutsche Gesellschaft* (Göttingen, 2009).

3. *Regierung Hitler* 1; Kershaw, *Hitler*, 1, 555.

4. *Goebbels TB*, 31 January 1933; Papen, 297.

5. On the negotiations see Rudolf Morsey, 'Hitlers Verhandlungen mit der Zentrumsführung am 31. Januar', in *VfZ* 9 (1961), Doc. 1f.; Morsey (ed.), *Die Protokolle der Reichstagsfraktion und des Fraktionsvorstands der deutschen Zentrumspartei 1926–1933* (Mainz, 1969), 613; Max Domarus, *Adolf Hitler, Reden und Dokumentationen 1932–1945. Kommentiert von einem deutschen Zeitgenossen*, 2 vols (Neustadt a. d. Aisch, 1963), 1, 190f.; Walther Hofer, *Der Nationalsozialismus – Dokumente 1933–1945* (Frankfurt a. M., 1957), 50f. See also Brüning, *Memoiren*, 648; Bracher, *Stufen*, 82ff.; Detlef Junker, *Die deutsche Zentrumspartei und Hitler 1932–1933. Ein Beitrag zur Problematik des politischen Katholizismus in Deutschland* (Stuttgart, 1969), 156ff.

6. *Regierung Hitler* 1, No. 2.

7. Ibid. (quote). On Gürtner see Lothar Gruchmann, *Justiz im Dritten Reich 1933–1940. Anpassung und Unterwerfung in der Ära Gürtner* (Munich, 1988), 9ff.; his appointment (basically a confirmation of his existing position) followed on 1 February. See *Regierung Hitler* 1, No. 1, Note 2.

8. Meissner, *Staatssekretär*, 279; Decrees on the dissolution of the Reichstag and on new elections in *Reichsgesetzblatt* (*RGBl.* 1933 I, 45).

9. *Regierung Hitler* 1, No. 5; Domarus 1, 191ff.; on the proclamation see also Kershaw, *Hitler*, 1, 558f.

10. Schulz, *Brüning*, 1000ff.

11. Domarus 1, 195f.; on Brecht's speech see *Frankfurter Zeitung* (*FZ*), 3 February 1933 (2nd morning edn).

12. The decree is dated 6 February 1933 in *RGBl.* 1933 I, 43.

13. *Regierung Hitler* 1, Nos 2, 9, 11, and 13. See also Schulze, *Braun*, 780ff.; Bracher, *Stufen*, 94ff.

14. Apart from the parliament, the 'three-man committee', composed of the prime minister and the presidents of the parliament and the state council, could also order the dissolution. In his position as Braun's replacement as prime minister, together with the Nazi president of the parliament, Papen now had a majority in this body.

15. *RGBl.* 1933 I, 35ff.; *Regierung Hitler* 1, Nos 11 and 9. This provision was a so-called 'decree in a drawer' (ibid., No. 3), which the Papen cabinet had already drawn up during the BVG strike in November 1932. See Bracher, *Stufen*, 91ff.; Winkler, *Weg*, 867ff.

16. In the manuscript replaced by 'to be exterminated'.

17. The speech exists in several versions. The most recently discovered one, quoted here, derives from the KPD's intelligence operation and had already reached Moscow by 14 February. See Andreas Wirsching, '"Man kann nur Boden germani-sieren". Eine neue Quelle zu Hitlers Rede vor den Spitzen der Reichswehr am 3. Februar 1933', in *VfZ* 49 (2001), 517–51. This version essentially confirms the well-known version in note form produced by Lieutenant-General Kurt Liebmann. See Thilo Vogelsang, 'Neue Dokumente zur Geschichte der Reichswehr 1930–1933', in *VfZ* 2 (1954), 397–436. See also Klaus-Jürgen Müller, *Das Heer und Hitler. Armee und nationalsozialistische Regime 1932–1940* (Stuttgart, 1969), 11ff.

18. The second Reichswehr armaments programme envisaged enabling the Reichswehr to fight a limited defensive war by 1938. See Michael Geyer, 'Das zweite Rüstungsprogramm (1930 bis 1934)', in *Militärgeschichtliche Mitteilungen* (*MGM*) 17 (1975), 121–86.

19. Hitler had emphasized that if possible the Reichswehr should not be deployed to crush a general strike, to which Blomberg responded positively in a brief note. See *Regierung Hitler* 1, No. 1.

20. Ibid., No. 17. In the cabinet meeting the discussion was about the construction of a reservoir in Upper Silesia.

21. Ibid. On Hitler's cautious approach to economic matters see Adam J. Tooze, *Ökonomie der Zerstörung. Die Geschichte der Wirtschaft im Nationalsozialismus* (Munich, 2007), 61.

22. Geyer, 'Rüstungsprogramm'.

23. *Regierung Hitler* 1, No. 19. In addition to the 140 million there was 360 million for the federal states and local authorities. In March 1933 this emergency

programme was increased by 100 million Reich marks, which were to be used for the rearmament programme. See ibid., No. 67. On the final allocation of the money see Jürgen Stelzner, *Arbeitsbeschaffung und Wiederaufrüstung 1933–1936. Nationalsozialistische Beschäftigungspolitik und Aufbau der Wehr- und Rüstungswirtschaft* (Bamberg, 1976), 67. The 50 million offered to the Reichswehr on 9 February had not hitherto figured in the plans, but was allocated for the so-called reorganization of the peacetime army.

24. Hans-Jürgen Rautenberg, *Deutsche Rüstungspolitik vom Beginn der Genfer Abrüstungskonferenz bis zur Wiedereinführung der Allgemeinen Wehrpflicht 1932–1935* (Bonn, 1973), 212ff.

25. Paul, *Aufstand*, 111ff. On the election campaign see also Bracher, *Stufen*, 108ff.

26. *Regierung Hitler* 1, No. 17.

27. Domarus 1, 202f.

28. Ibid., 203ff. (quote); on the speech see Kershaw, *Hitler*, 1, 573ff.

29. Ansgar Diller, *Rundfunkpolitik im Dritten Reich* (Munich, 1980), 65ff.; *Regierung Hitler* 1, No. 17; Eugen Hadamovsky, 'Großkampftage der Rundfunkpropaganda. Vom 30. Januar bis zum "Tage der erwachenden Nation"', in Hadamovsky, *Dein Rundfunk. Das Rundfunkbuch für alle Volksgenossen* (Munich, 1934), 82–90; Longerich, *Goebbels*, 213.

30. Erich Matthias, 'Die Sozialdemokratische Partei Deutschlands' in Matthias and Rudolf Morsey (eds), *Das Ende der Parteien 1933* (Düsseldorf, 1960), 153; Siegfried Bahne, 'Die Kommunistische Partei Deutschlands', in Matthias and Morsey (eds), *Ende*, 699ff.; Winkler, *Weg*, 876ff.; Johann Wachtler, *Zwischen Revolutionserwartung und Untergang. Die Vorbereitung der KPD auf die Illegalität in den Jahren 1929–1933* (Frankfurt a. M., Berne, and New York, 1983), 190ff. Allan Merson, *Kommunistischer Widerstand in Nazideutschland* (Bonn, 1999) 44ff. (for February); Kurt Koszyk, *Zwischen Kaiserreich und Diktatur. Die sozialdemokratische Presse von 1914 bis 1933* (Heidelberg, 1958), 49f. (for the Social Democratic Press). The KPD's main newspaper, *Die Rote Fahne*, was banned from 5–7 February, then again from 11–25 February 1933 and after the Reichstag fire. See Jürgen Stroech, 'Zur Herstellung und Verbreitung der illegalen *Rote Fahne* 1933–1938', in *Beiträge zur Geschichte der Arbeiterbewegung* 19 (1977), 81f.

31. *Regierung Hitler* 1, No. 22 (outside the formal agenda); Domarus 1, 210ff.

32. Morsey, 'Deutsche Zentrumspartei', 348ff.

33. *Germania,* 22 and 23 February 1933.

34. Domarus 1, 223.

35. Gerhard Schulz, *Die Anfänge des totalitären Maßnahmestaates* (Frankfurt a. M., 1974), 91ff. and 154f. According to Hans Buchheim, 'Die organisatorische Entwicklung der politischen Polizei in Deutschland in den Jahren 1933 und 1934', in *Gutachten des Instituts für Zeitgeschichte* vol. 1 (Munich, 1958), 307f., in February thirteen, in March twelve police presidents were dismissed.

36. *UF* 9, No. 1980b.

37. Ibid., No. 1980c; Bracher, *Stufen*, 116.

38. *Regierung* Hitler 1, No. 30; *RGBl.* 1933 I, 85ff.

39. On 17 February he spoke in the Dortmund Westfalenhalle, on the 19th, after a brief trip to Munich for meetings, in the Cologne exhibition hall, on the 24th at the celebration of the Party's foundation in the Hofbräuhaus in Munich and then in the exhibition halls. On the following day he appeared in Nuremberg. See Domarus 1, 212 and 214f.

40. Turner, *Großunternehmer*, 393ff.; Hitler's speech in *International Military Tribunal: Der Prozess gegen die Hauptkriegsverbrecher vor dem Internationalen Militärgerichtshof 14. Oktober 1945 bis 1. Oktober 1946 (IMT)*, 42 vols (Nuremberg, 1947–1949) 35, 203-D, 42ff., and 204-D, 48; *Goebbels TB*, 21 February 1933.

41. At the trial at the Leipzig Supreme Court, which lasted from September to December 1933, van der Lubbe was the only one convicted and he was sentenced to death. On the trial see Dieter Deiseroth (ed.), *Der Reichstagsbrand und der Prozess vor dem Reichsgericht* (Berlin, 2006).

42. On the controversy see Fritz Tobias, *Der Reichstagsbrand – Legende und Wirklichkeit* (Rastatt, 1962); Uwe Backes et al., *Reichstagsbrand – Aufklärung einer historischen Legende* (Munich and Zurich, 1986); Ulrich von Hehl, 'Die Kontroverse um den Reichstagsbrand', in *VfZ* 36 (1988), 259–80; Walther Hofer et al., *Der Reichstagsbrand – Eine wissenschaftliche Dokumentation* (Freiburg i. Br., 1992); Hans Schneider, *Neues vom Reichstagsbrand? Eine Dokumentation. Ein Versäumnis der deutschen Geschichtsschreibung* (Berlin, 2004); Deiseroth (ed.), *Reichstagsbrand*; Sven Felix Kellerhoff, *Der Reichstagsbrand. Die Karriere eines Kriminalfalls* (Berlin, 2008).

43. *Goebbels TB*, 28 February 1933. The telephone call is confirmed by Hanfstaengl, *Haus.*, 294f.

44. See the issue of 1 March (N), 'Jetzt wird rücksichtslos durchgegriffen'.

45. *Regierung Hitler* 1, No. 32.

46. Ibid., No. 34; *RGBl.* 1933 I, 83. Even if, as Otto Diels recalls, Hitler had an almost hysterical fit of rage on the evening of the fire, his decisions that followed were by no means impulsive or uncontrolled. See Rudolf Diels, *Lucifer ante portas. Zwischen Severing und Heydrich* (Stuttgart, 1950), 194; Kershaw, *Hitler*, 1, 581f.

47. These provisions were repeated in a further decree of 28 February against treason against the German people and high treasonable activities. See *RGBl.* 1933 I, 85.

48. Wachtler, *Revolutionserwartung*, 204ff. In the literature the figure of 10,000 people arrested in Prussia is often given, including 1,500 in Berlin alone, which has not been entirely confirmed. See, for example, Otto Winzer, *Zwölf Jahre Kampf gegen Faschismus und Krieg. Ein Beitrag zur Geschichte der Kommunistischen Partei Deutschlands 1933 bis 1945* (Berlin, 1955), 30. Horst Duhnke, *Die KPD von 1933 bis 1945* (Cologne, 1972), 104, gives a total of 4,000–10,000 arrests during the period from the end of February/March 1933. On the crushing of the KPD see also Winkler, *Weg*, 880f.

49. Koszyk, *Kaiserreich*, 50.

50. Winkler, *Weg*, 891.

51. Knut Bergbauer, Sabine Fröhlich, and Stefanie Schüler-Springorum, *Denkmalsfigur. Biographische Annäherung an Hans Litten (1903–1938)* (Göttingen, 2008), 229ff.; Bruno Frei, *Carl von Ossietzky: eine politische Biographie* (Berlin, 1978), 208ff.; Kai-Britt Albrecht, 'Renn, Ludwig', in *Neue Deutsche Biographie*, 21 (2003), 426f.; Chris Hirte, *Erich Mühsam. Eine Biographie* (Freiburg i. Br., 2009), 303. Kisch, a Czech citizen, was the only one set free after a few days. See Klaus Haupt, *Egon Erwin Kisch (1885–1948). Der Rasende Reporter aus dem Prager 'Haus zu den zwei goldenen Bären'* (Teetz/Berlin, 2008), 38f.

52. Domarus 1, 216f.

53. On the speech see *VB* (M), 8 March 1933, 'Die Glocken von Königsberg'.

54. See the reports on the meeting in *Der Angriff* on 4 and 6 March 1933, and the *VB* (B), 5/6 March 1933, 'Der Freiheitstag der erwachten Nation'.

55. *FZ* (M), 6 March 1933, 'Der Verlauf des Sonntags in Berlin'. The same picture is conveyed by the election leader of the *Vossische Zeitung* (*VZ*) of 4 March 1933 (A) and the local reports of the *Berliner Tageblatt* (*BT*) of 6 March 1933 (A).

56. *Regierung Hitler* 1, No. 44.

57. Thamer, *Verführung*, 260ff.; Bracher, *Stufen*, 190ff.

58. *Goebbels TB*, 9 March 1933.

59. Henning Timpke (ed.), *Dokumente zur Gleichschaltung des Landes Hamburg 1933* (Frankfurt a. M., 1964), 15ff.; Ursula Büttner and Werner Jochmann, *Hamburg auf dem Weg ins Dritte Reich. Entwicklungsjahre 1931 bis 1933* (Hamburg, 1983), 33ff.

60. Timpke (ed.), *Dokumente*, 31.

61. *Goebbels TB*, 9 March 1933; see also 8 March 1933 on the start of the coordination process in Baden.

62. The meeting between Schäffer and Hindenburg is recorded in a note of Meissner's dated 21 February. See *Regierung Hitler* 1, No. 23. On the conversation between Held and Hitler see Falk Wiesemann, *Die Vorgeschichte der nationalsozialistischen Machtübernahme in Bayern 1932–1933* (Berlin, 1975), Doc. 2.

63. Verbatim in ibid., 280f.

64. Meissner, *Staatssekretär*, 316.

65. On the take-over of power in Bavaria see Wiesemann, *Vorgeschichte*, 177ff.; Ortwin Domröse, *Der NS-Staat in Bayern von der Machtergreifung bis zum Röhm-Putsch* (Munich, 1974), 42ff. Held wrote an account immediately after these events, which was first published in 1948 and edited in Winfried Becker, 'Die nationalsozialistische Machtergreifung in Bayern. Ein Dokumentarbericht Heinrich Helds aus dem Jahre 1933', in *Historisches Jahrbuch* 112 (1992), 412–35.

66. Horst Matzerath, *Nationalsozialismus und kommunale Selbstverwaltung* (Stuttgart, 1970), 66ff.

67. Uwe Dietrich Adam, *Judenpolitik im Dritten Reich* (Düsseldorf, 1972), 46ff.; Avraham Barkai, *Vom Boykott zur 'Entjudung'. Der wirtschaftliche Existenzkampf der Juden im Dritten Reich* (Frankfurt a. M., 1988), 23ff.; Helmut Genschel, *Die Verdrängung der Juden aus der Wirtschaft im Dritten Reich* (Göttingen, 1966), 43ff.; Peter Longerich, *Politik der Vernichtung. Die Verfolgung und Ermordung der europäischen Juden 1933–1945* (Munich and Zurich, 1998), 26ff.

68. *VB* (N), 10 March 1933, 'Rücktritt des jüdischen Börsenvorstands gefordert'.

69. *VZ*, 11 March 1933.

70. Domarus 1, 219ff. See also the Reich Interior Minister's edict of 13 March 1933, which forbade the 'closing of and threats to individual retailers' (BAB, 1501, 13859) and published in *VZ*, 13 March 1933, and *VB*, 14 March 1933. In a letter to Papen, who had complained about disruptive behaviour by members of the SA, Hitler defended his SA and SS against 'the constant grumbling'. See *Regierung Hitler* 1, No. 5.

71. See Gruchmann, *Justiz*, 124ff.; Horst Göppinger, *Die Verfolgung der Juristen jüdischer Abstammung durch den Nationalsozialismus* (Villingen (Schwarzwald), 1963), 21f.; Tillmann Krach, *Jüdische Rechtsanwälte in Preußen. Über die Bedeutung der freien Advokatur und ihre Zerstörung durch den Nationalsozialismus* (Munich, 1991), 172ff.

72. Domarus 1, 220.

73. *Regierung Hitler* 1, No. 56.

74. Reich President's edict concerning the provisional regulation of the raising of flags, 12 March 1933, in *RGBl.* 1933 I, 103; radio address in Domarus 1, 221f.

75. Ibid., 222.

76. *Regierung Hitler* 1, No. 56; *RGBl.* 1933 I, 104. On the background to the appointment and Goebbels's expectations see Longerich, *Goebbels*, 211ff.; *Goebbels TB*, 14–16 March 1933.

77. Edict 13 March 1933 in *RGBl.* 1933 I, 104.

78. Ansgar Diller, *Rundfunkpolitik*, 76ff.

79. Henning Rischbieter, 'NS-Theaterpolitik' in Thomas Eicher, Barbara Panse, and Rischbieter, *Theater im 'Dritten Reich'. Theaterpolitik, Spielplanstruktur, NS-Dramatik* (Seelze-Veelbert, 2000).

80. Decree concerning the Tasks of the Reich Ministry for Propaganda and Popular Enlightenment of 30 June 1933 in *RGBl.* 1933 I, 446. On Hitler's support see *Regierung Hitler* 1, No. 196. On the organization of the propaganda ministry see Longerich, *Goebbels*, 230f.; see the continuing entries in Goebbels's diary.

81. BAB, R 55/414, Joint minutes of the propaganda ministry and the foreign ministry concerning the departmental meeting of 12 May 1933; *Regierung Hitler* 1, No. 138; *Goebbels TB*, 29 April, 5, 10, 11, 14, and 25 May, and 8 June 1933.

82. *Regierung Hitler* 1, No. 65. Schacht was elected by the General Council of the Reichsbank on 16 March. See ibid., 231. On Luther's resignation see Henry Picker, *Hitlers Tischgespräche im Führerhauptquartier, Entstehung, Struktur, und Folgen des Nationalsozialismus* (Berlin, 1997), 83ff., according to which Hitler dismissed Luther because the latter was unwilling adequately to finance his rearmaments plans. Luther disputed this account in his memoirs. See Luther, *Vor dem Abgrund 1930–1933. Reichsbankpräsident in Krisenzeiten* (Berlin, 1964), 304f. On the appointment of Reinhardt see *Regierung Hitler* 1, No. 80.

83. Martin Sabrow, 'Der "Tag von Potsdam". Zur doppelten Karriere eines politischen Mythos', in Christoph Kopke (ed.), *Der Tag von Potsdam. Der 21. März 1933 und die Errichtung der nationalsozialistischen Diktatur* (Berlin, 2013); Pyta, *Hindenburg*, 821ff.

84. Originally it had been envisaged as taking place at the Potsdam City Palace. See *Regierung Hitler* I, No. 32. On the preparation of the ceremonies see ibid., Nos 41 and 43; BAB, R 43II/291, Provisional Programme.

85. This is the argument of Sabrow in 'Tag von Potsdam'.

86. *Regierung Hitler* I, 158.

87. *Der Angriff,* 21 and 22 March 1933; *VB* (B), 22 March 1933. On Hitler's statement and the reply of the Church authorities see Domarus I, 225.

88. On the proceedings and the speech see ibid., 232 (quote).

89. *Regierung Hitler* I, No. 70 (on the preliminary meeting on 20 March see *Goebbels TB*, 21 March 1933); Reich President's Decree for the Prevention of Malicious Attacks on the Government of the National Uprising, 21 March 1933. See *RGBl.* 1933 I, 135 and the Decree of the Reich Government for the Creation of Special Courts 21 March 1933. See ibid., 136ff.

90. *Regierung Hitler* I, Nos 44, 60, and 68.

91. *RGBl.* 1933 I, 141.

92. See Frick's explanations to the cabinet on 15 March 1933 in *Regierung Hitler* I, Nos 60 and 68, note 6.

93. Bracher, *Stufen*, 213ff.; Thamer, *Verführung*, 272ff.; Winkler, *Weg*, 901ff. On the constitutional repercussions see Jörg Biesemann, *Das Ermächtigungsgesetz als Grundlage der Gesetzgebung im nationalsozialistischen Staat. Ein Beitrag zur Stellung des Gesetzes in der Verfassungsgeschichte 1919–1945* (Münster, 1985). On Kaas's informing the parliamentary group see Morsey (ed.), *Protokolle*, Nos 741–744 and 746.

94. For the speech see Domarus I, 229ff. (quote).

95. Both speeches quoted from ibid. 239ff. See also Winkler, *Weg*, 905; according to Friedrich Stampfer in *Erfahrungen und Erkenntnisse. Aufzeichnungen aus meinem Leben* (Cologne, 1957), 268, the manuscript of Wels's speech had been given to the press beforehand.

96. Klaus Drobisch and Günther Wieland, *System der Konzentrationslager 1933–1939* (Berlin, 1993), 39ff.

97. On the protective custody regulations issued in 1933/34 see ibid., 25ff.; on the concept of protective custody see Martin Broszat, 'Nationalsozialistische Konzentrationslager 1933–1945', in Hans Buchheim et al., *Anatomie des SS-Staates*, 2 (Olten and Freiburg, 1965), 13ff.

98. Estimate based on the assessments in Drobisch and Wieland, *System*, 38.

99. Ibid., 43ff.

100. *Regierung Hitler* I, No. 82; for similar complaints from the Reich Bank on previous days see BAB, R 43 II/397. On assaults by the SA on members of chambers of commerce see *Regierung Hitler* I, No. 88. BAB, R 43 II/1195 Frick circular, 13 March 1933, to the interior ministers of the states and to Reich commissars re the closure of and threats to retail businesses; Complaint from the Association of German Department Stores, 16 March 1933, re assault on the Wohl-Wert Verkaufsgesellschaft on 5 March 1933 in Dessau; Schacht to Lammers, 7 April 1933 concerning continuing interference in banks by Nazi

organizations; Reich Bank directorate to the Justice Minister, 20 April 1933, re claims by 'commissars' for the property of firms; 26 April 1933, ditto. This indicates that the difficulties were continuing.

101. The file BAB, R 43 II/1195, contains numerous complaints about such assaults on British, French, Greek, Italian, Yugoslav, Dutch, Polish, Soviet, Czech, and American citizens and diplomatic institutions.

102. Hannah Ahlheim, *Deutsche, kauft nicht bei Juden! Antisemitismus und politischer Boykott in Deutschland 1924 bis 1935* (Göttingen, 2011).

103. *Goebbels TB*, 27–29 March 1933.

104. On the preparations for the boycott see Barkai, *Boykott*, 26ff.

105. *Regierung Hitler* 1, 272.

106. *VB*, 29 March 1933.

107. *FZ*, 1 April 1933.

108. *VZ* and *FZ*, 1 and 2 April 1933. On the course of the boycott and the response of the population see Kurt Pätzold, *Faschismus, Rassenwahn, Judenverfolgung. Eine Studie zur politischen Strategie und Taktik des faschistischen deutschen Imperialismus (1933–1945)* (Berlin, 1975), 74ff.; Ian Kershaw, *Popular Opinion and Political Dissent in the Third Reich: Bavaria 1933–1945* (Oxford, 2002), 231f.; David Bankier, *Die öffentliche Meinung im Hitler-Staat. Die 'Endlösung' und die Deutschen. Eine Berichtigung* (Berlin, 1995), 85ff.; Longerich, *Politik*, 34ff.; Saul Friedländer, *Das Dritte Reich und die Juden*, 1 (Munich, 2000), 31ff.

109. *VB*, 4 April 1933.

110. Gruchmann, *Justiz*, 126ff.; Krach, *Rechtsanwälte*, 188ff.

111. *RGBl.* 1933 I, 175ff.

112. Barkai, *Boykott*, 36.

113. *RGBl.* 1933 I, 188. See Krach, *Rechtsanwälte*, 202ff.

114. Law against the Overcrowding of German Schools and Universities and the first implementation decree of 25 April 1933. See *RGBl.* 1933 I, 225f.

115. Adam, *Judenpolitik*, 72f.; Diemut Majer, *'Fremdvölkische' im Dritten Reich. Ein Beitrag zur nationalsozialistischen Rechtssetzung und Rechtspraxis in Verwaltung und Justiz unter besonderer Berücksichtigung der eingegliederten Ostgebiete und des Generalgouvernements* (Boppard am Rhein, 1993), 238f.; Michael Köhn, *Zahnärzte 1933–1945. Berufsverbot, Emigration, Verfolgung* (Berlin, 1994), 42.

116. *Regierung Hitler* 1, No. 93.

117. Sigrun Mühl-Benninghaus, *Das Beamtentum in der NS-Diktatur bis zum Ausbruch des Zweiten Weltkrieges. Zu Enstehen, Inhalt und Durchführung der einschlägigen Beamtengesetze* (Düsseldorf, 1996), 83, estimates a total of 30,000 cases brought under the law.

118. Provisional Law for Coordinating the States with the Reich. See *RGBl.* 1933 I, 153ff.

119. Ibid., 173.

120. On the removal of the sovereignty of the states see Bracher, *Stufen*, 237ff.; Martin Broszat, *Der Staat Hitlers. Grundlegung und Entwicklung seiner inneren Verfassung* (Munich, 1969), 144f.

121. Kube, *Pour le mérite*, 32f.; Sabine Höner, *Der nationalsozialistische Zugriff auf Preußen. Preußischer Staat und nationalsozialistische Machteroberungsstrategie 1928– 1934* (Bochum, 1984), 443f. Kerrl was appointed acting Justice Minister on 23 March. The first indication of Göring's plans to become Prussian Prime Minister can be found in Goebbels's diary. See *Goebbels TB*, 21 March 1933.

122. Avraham Barkai, *Das Wirtschaftssystem des Nationalsozialismus. Der historische und ideologische Hintergrund 1933–1936* (Cologne, 1977), 110ff.; Arthur Schweitzer, *Die Nazifizierung des Mittelstandes* (Stuttgart, 1970), 47ff.

123. Ibid., 49f.

124. *FZ*, 5 May 1933 (1 M and 2 M).

125. The property tax decree of 31 March 1933 permitted the states to impose a tax on chain stores and an increase in the tax on department stores. See *RGBl.* 1933 I, 157ff. This was updated by the law of 15 July 1933, ibid., 492. This regulation expired at the end of 1933. The finance minister's attempt to impose a permanent higher value-added tax on large-scale retail stores failed in May 1933. See *Regierung Hitler* 1, No. 127. The Law to Protect Retail Business of 12 May 1933 banned the establishment of 'sales outlets' and craft businesses in department stores. See *RGBl.* 1933 I, 267ff.; Decree of 11 July 1933, in ibid., 468f. The supplementary law of 15 July provided the opportunity to close catering outlets in department stores. See ibid., 493. See also Heinrich Uhlig, *Die Warenhäuser im Dritten Reich* (Cologne, 1956), 91ff.

126. BAB, R 43 II/362, Letter from the Reich Association to Hitler, 24 March 1933; Neebe, *Großindustrie,* 177.

127. As a member of the Liaison Staff, Wagener can be shown to have been his economic advisor since the end of April 1933. See *Akten der Partei-Kanzlei der NSDAP*, Teil I, Regesten 10035 and 10062 (from BAB, R 43 II/1352 and 1195). On this role see also Erich Czech-Jochberg, *Adolf Hitler und sein Stab* (Oldenburg i. O., 1933), 109.

128. BAB, R 43 II/362, Hugenberg directive, 24 April 1933. See also *FZ* 4 May 1933 (2 M), 'Die Umgestaltung des Reichsverbandes der Industrie'; Neebe, *Großindustrie*, 181ff.; Turner, *Großunternehmer*, 397ff.; Udo Wengst, 'Der Reichsverband der Deutschen Industrie in den ersten Monaten des Dritten Reiches', in *VfZ* 28 (1980), 94–110.

129. *Regierung Hitler* 1, No. 21; Decree of the Reich President concerning the Halt to Agricultural Foreclosure, 14 February 1933. See *RGBl.* 1933 I, 63; Reich presidential decrees for the support of agriculture and support for domestic cheeses dated 23 February 1933 (in ibid., 80ff.). The policy of debt relief took the form of a law to regulate agricultural debt of 1 June 1933 (in ibid., 331ff.), also in the Law for the Protection of Tenants of 22 April 1933 (in ibid., 221f.). On 16 February the Cabinet agreed to the Agriculture minister's proposals for 'new support measures for grain' (see *Regierung Hitler* 1, No. 23) and for an increase in import duties with the decrees for changes to customs duties of 18 February 1933 (in *RGBl.* 1933 I, 72) and 4 March 1933 (in ibid., 101). One of the main points of the Hugenberg programme was the 'Fats Plan', i.e. an

extension of the already existing compulsory measures of support for butter and for the reduction in margarine production. See the Decree for the Use of Domestic Oil Seeds of 24 February 1933 in ibid., 93; the Decree concerning the Commercial Production of the Products of Margarine Factories and Oil Mills of 23 March 1933, the Second Decree for the Support of the Use of Domestic Animal Fats and Domestic Feedstuffs of 23 March 1933 in ibid., 143 and 145f. On Hugenberg's agricultural policy see Gustavo Corni, *Hitler and the Peasants. Agrarian Policy of the Third Reich, and 1930–1939'* (New York, Oxford, and Munich, 1990), 41ff.

130. See Hitler's statements at the Cabinet meeting of 11 March 1933, in which he opposed the envisaged compulsory measures for switching from butter to margarine consumption because this would put too much of a burden on consumers. See also the cabinet meeting of 31 May 1933, in which Hitler objected, without success, to the high interest rate for mortgages in the debt relief law. See *Regierung Hitler* 1, Nos 57 and 150.

131. *FZ*, 5 April 1933 (1 M), concerning the 63rd plenary meeting of the German Agriculture Council.

132. On 4 April he became chairman of the newly formed Reich Leadership of German Peasantry (an amalgamation of the Reichslandbund, Christian Peasant Associations, and the agrarian department of the NSDAP). See *FZ*, 5 April 1933 [2 M], 'Zusammenschluß landwirtschaftlicher Organisationen unter nationalsozialistischer Führung'. On 19 April he became President of the agricultural cooperatives; on 12 May he took over as head of the German Agricultural Council and on 20 May as head of the German Association for Commerce in Land. See Claudia Frank, *Der 'Reichsnährstand' und seine Ursprünge, Struktur, Funktion und ideologische Konzeption* (Hamburg, 1988), 112; Horst R. Gies, *Walther Darré und die nationalsozialistische Bauernpolitik in den Jahren 1930 bis 1933* (Frankfurt a. M., 1966), 134ff.

133. Prussian Hereditary Farm Law of 15 May 1933 in *Preußische Gesetzsammlung* 1933, No. 34, 165.

134. Corni, *Hitler*, 48, points out that Darré had been carrying on a press campaign against Hugenberg since the spring. See BAB, NL 1231/36, Hugenberg note of his oral complaint to Hindenburg on 17 May 1933 that Darré was preventing him from fulfilling his duties as agriculture minister.

135. Hubert Gelhaus, *1933. 365 ganz normale Tage. Beobachtungen zum nationalsozialistischen Alltag in Cloppenburg und Umgebung (Südoldenburg)* (Oldenburg, 1988), describes this process in exemplary fashion for the state of Oldenburg. The same thing happened during these weeks throughout Germany. See, for example, Michael Schepua, '"Machtergreifung" und Etablierung des NS-Systems in einem Industriezentrum: Ludwigshafen und Oppau 1933–1938', in Hans-Georg Meyer and Hans Berkessel (eds), *Die Zeit des Nationalsozialismus in Rheinland-Pfalz* (Mainz, 2000).

136. On the coordination of German sport see Hajo Bernett, *Sportpolitik im Dritten Reich. Aus den Akten der Reichskanzlei* (Stuttgart, 1971); Bernett, 'Der deutsche

Sport im Jahre 1933', in *Stadion. Internationale Zeitschrift für Geschichte des Sports und der Körperkultur* VII/2 (1981), 225–283; Bernett, *Der Weg des Sports in die nationalsozialistische Diktatur. Die Entstehung des Deutschen (nationalsozialistischen) Reichsbundes für Leibesübungen* (Schorndorf, 1983); Lorenz Pfeiffer, '"…Unser Verein ist judenfrei" – Die Rolle der deutschen Turn- und Sportbewegung in dem politischen und gesellschaftlichen Wandlungsprozess nach dem 30. Januar 1933', in *Historical Social Research* 32 (2007), 92–109.

137. Arno Klönne, *Jugend im Dritten Reich. Die Hitler-Jugend und ihre Gegner* (Cologne, 2003), 20.

138. How this was supposed to happen in detail is described in E. Paquin, *Der Vereinsführer im neuen Reich. Praktischer Wegweiser für Führer von Vereinen, Verbänden, Innungen, Genossenschaften und sonstigen Organisationen* (Hösel, 1934).

139. A perfect example of the atomization of the whole community as a result of the coordination of the local associations is provided by William Sheridan Allen, '*Das haben wir nicht gewollt!*'. *Die nationalsozialistische Machtergreifung in einer Kleinstadt 1930–1935* (Gütersloh, 1966), 222ff. See also Herbert Freudenthal, *Vereine in Hamburg. Ein Beitrag zur Geschichte und Volkskunde der Geselligkeit* (Hamburg, 1968). Recent studies present a more nuanced picture in which conformity but also persistence play a greater role. For gun clubs see Henning Borggräfe, *Schützenvereine im Nationalsozialismus. Pflege der 'Volksgemeinschaft' und Vorbereitung auf den Krieg (1933–1945)* (Münster, 2010); Frank Bösch, *Das konservative Milieu. Vereinskultur und lokale Sammlungspolitik in ost- und west-deutschen Regionen (1900–1960)* (Göttingen, 2002), 134ff.; Reinhard Mann, *Protest und Kontrolle im Dritten Reich. Nationalsozialistische Herrschaft im Alltag einer rhei-nischen Großstadt* (Frankfurt a. M. and New York, 1987), 120ff. on coordination in Düsseldorf; Cornelia Rauh-Kühne, *Katholisches Milieu und Kleinstadtgesellschaft. Ettlingen 1918–1939* (Sigmaringen, 1991), 343ff.; Zdenek Zofka, *Die Ausbreitung des Nationalsozialismus auf dem Lande. Eine regionale Fallstudie zur politischen Einstellung der Landbevölkerung in der Zeit des Aufstiegs und der Machtergreifung der NSDAP 1928–1936* (Munich, 1979), 238ff.

140. *Regierung Hitler* I, Einleitung, XVIIf.

141. Ibid., No. 88. At the cabinet meeting Hugenberg complained about SA assaults against members of chambers of commerce who were members of the DNVP. See BAB, R 43 II/1295 for further complaints by Hugenberg on 12 April about attacks on DNVP members and a substantial collection of material on the issue. On 8 May 1933 Hugenberg approached Hitler again about discrimination against members of the German Nationalist Front in appoint-ments to economic bodies and in their role as civil servants. See Bundesarchiv Koblenz (BAK), NL 1231/36. On 17 May he complained to the Reich President that there were powerful forces in the NSDAP who were trying to undermine the 30 January 1933 pact between the NSDAP and the DNVP. See ibid., vol. 38. Files 85 and 89 of the Hugenberg papers contain further material on Nazi attacks on DNVP and Combat Front Black-White-Red members and their organizations between February and May.

142. On the attacks on Hugenberg see Walter Borchmeyer, *Hugenbergs Ringen in deutschen Schicksalsstunden. Tatsachen und Entscheidungen in den Verfahren zu Detmold und Düsseldorf 1949/50* (Detmold, 1951), 78ff.; *FZ*, 6 May 1933 (2 M), 'Probleme um Hugenberg' (headline). On Hugenberg's article in *Der nationale Wille* see Friedrich Frhr. Hiller von Gaertringen, 'Die Deutschnationale Volkspartei', in Erich Matthias and Rudolf Morsey (eds), *Ende*, 600 and Doc. 18. BAB, R 43II/1195, Complaint by Schacht, Hitler's response, and Wagener's announcement (Liaison Staff), 27 April 1933.

143. As the collection of material in note 141 demonstrates.

144. Berghahn, *Stahlhelm*, 263.

145. Hans Buchheim, 'Die Eingliederung des "Stahlhelm" in die SA', in *Gutachten des Instituts für Zeitgeschichte* (Munich, 1958), 1, 294–307. It is clear from Goebbels's *TB*, 7 April 1933, that at this time Seldte was already planning to subordinate the SA to Hitler and to get rid of Duesterberg.

146. *VB* (N), 20 and 21 April 1933; see also the reports of the *FZ*, 21 April 1933 (1 M); Fuhrer, 'Führergeburtstag'.

147. See, for example, *MNN* and the *Leipziger Neueste Nachrichten*, 21 April 1933.

148. Examples in Rolf Steinberg (ed.), *Nazi Kitsch. Mit einem dokumentarischen Anhang über den Kleinkitsch von 1933* (Darmstadt, 1975); Kershaw, *Hitler*, 1, 611f.

149. Domarus 1, 256; *Goebbels TB*, 17–21 April 1933. Magda contacted him on 19 April from Düren, to which she had travelled in the meantime.

150. Koszyk, *Presse*, 355ff.

151. Hildegard Brenner, *Die Kunstpolitik des Nationalsozialismus* (Reinbek bei Hamburg, 1963), 39f.; Julius H. Schoeps and Werner Tress (eds), *Orte der Bücherverbrennungen in Deutschland 1933* (Hildesheim, Zurich, and New York, 2008), 56ff.; Fred K. Prieberg, *Musik im NS-Staat* (Frankfurt a. M., 1982), 41ff.; Florian Odenwald, *Der nazistische Kampf gegen das 'Undeutsche' in Theater und Film 1920–1945* (Munich, 2006), 172ff.

152. Domarus 1, 211 and 232.

153. Publication of the correspondence, for example, in the *VZ*, 11 April 1933, reprinted in Joseph Wulf, *Musik im Dritten Reich. Eine Dokumentation* (Gütersloh, 1963), 86ff.; Fred K. Prieberg, *Kraftprobe. Wilhelm Furtwängler im Dritten Reich* (Wiesbaden, 1986), 78ff. See also *Goebbels TB*, 2, 10, and 11 April 1933.

154. Prieberg, *Musik*, 44ff.; Rischbieter, '*NS-Theaterpolitik*', 17.

155. Odenwald, *Kampf*, 179ff.

156. Eicher, '*Spielplanstrukturen*'.

157. Brenner, *Ende einer bürgerlichen Kunstinstitution. Die politischen Formierung der Preußischen Akademie der Künste 1933* (Stuttgart, 1972).

158. Ibid., Doc. 64.

159. Jan-Pieter Barbian, *Literaturpolitik im 'Dritten Reich'. Institutionen, Kompetenzen, Betätigungsfelder* (Frankfurt a. M., 1993), 80ff.

160. Brenner, *Kunstpolitik*, 49ff.

161. Christoph Zuschlag, '*Entartete Kunst'. Ausstellungsstrategien im Nazi-Deutschland* (Worms, 1995), 58ff. on the exhibitions and 45ff. on the Expressionism debate.

162. Law on the Establishment of Student Associations (*Studentenschaften*) at Institutions of Higher Education in *RGBl.* 1933 I, 215. In 1927 the Prussian Culture Minister had dissolved the German Student Association (Deutsche Studentenschaft) because many of its branches had been unwilling to represent Germans from abroad who were Jews. This law now resolved this long-standing dispute in favour of the German Student Association.

163. Helmut Heiber (ed.), *Goebbels-Reden 1932–1945* (Bindlach, 1991), No. 14 (quote); *Goebbels TB*, 11 May 1933.

164. The book burnings have been thoroughly and systematically researched. See Julius H. Schoeps and Werner Tress (eds), *Verfemt und Verboten. Vorgeschichte und Folgen der Bücherverbrennungen 1933* (Hildesheim, 2010); Schoeps and Tress (eds), *Orte*. This volume contains an informative introduction by Tress; see Werner Tress, 'Phasen und Akteure der Bücherverbrennungen in Deutschland 1933', in ibid., 9–28.

165. Wolfgang Jäger, *Es began am 30. Januar* (Munich, 1958), 47f. (based on the contemporary radio broadcasts).

166. Michael Grüttner, *Studenten im Dritten Reich* (Paderborn and Munich, 1995), 67ff., gives the universities of Kiel, Hamburg, and Heidelberg as examples, also Göttingen, Breslau, Frankfurt, Münster, and the Technical University of Darmstadt. On Berlin see Christian Jahr, 'Die nationalsozialistische Machtübernahme und ihre Folgen', in Michael Grüttner (ed.), *Geschichte der Universität unter den Linden. Biographie einer Institution*, 2 (Berlin, 2012), 301. On Halle see Henrik Eberle, *Die Martin-Luther-Universität in der Zeit des Nationalsozialismus 1933–1945* (Halle, 2002), 39f.

167. Birgit Vezina, *Die 'Gleichschaltung' der Universität Heidelberg im Zuge der nationalsozialistischen Machtergreifung* (Heidelberg, 1982), 58ff. (on Baden); Jahr, 'Machtübernahme', 320, quotes a Prussian edict of 21 April 1933 concerning the re-election of all rectors already in office prior to 1933.

168. Martin Heidegger, *Die Selbstbehauptung der deutschen Universität. Rede, gehalten bei der feierlichen Übernahme des Rektorats der Universität Freiburg i. Br. am 27. Mai 1933* (Breslau, 1933).

169. Vezina, 'Gleichschaltung', 71ff. (on Baden); Wolfgang Kahl, 'Die Geschichte der bayerischen Hochschulen', in Max-Emanuel Geis (ed.), *Hochschulrecht im Freistaat Bayern. Handbuch für Wissenschaft und Praxis* (Heidelberg, 2009), 1–26 (on Bavaria); Gerhard Kasper et al. (eds), *Die deutsche Hochschulverwaltung. Sammlung der das Hochschulwesen betreffenden Gesetze, Verordnungen und Erlasse*, 1 (Berlin, 1942/43), 33f. (on Prussia). See also Jahr, 'Machtübernahme', 321. After the establishment of the Reich Education Ministry in May 1934 this new arrangement was introduced uniformly throughout the Reich with an edict of 3 April 1935. See Kasper et al. (eds), *Hochschulverwaltung* 1, 34f. On the whole process see Hellmut Seier, 'Der Rektor als Führer. Zur Hochschulpolitik des Reichserziehungsministeriums 1934–1935', in *VfZ* 12 (1964), 105–46.

170. Michael Grüttner and Sven Kinas, 'Die Vertreibung von Wissenschaftlern aus den deutschen Universitäten 1933–1945', in *VfZ* 55 (2007), 123–86.

171. Claus Dieter Krohn et al. (eds), *Handbuch der deutschsprachigen Emigration 1933– 1945* (Darmstadt, 1998), including among others Wolfgang Benz, 'Die jüdische Emigration', sections 5–16; Alexander Stephan, 'Die intellektuelle, literarische und künstlerische Emigration', sections 30–46.

172. *Regierung Hitler* 1, No. 81; Law concerning Works Councils and Economic Associations, 4 April 1933 in *RGBl.* 1933 I, 161f.; Wolfgang Zollitsch, *Arbeiter zwischen Weltwirtschaftskrise und Nationalsozialismus. Ein Beitrag zur Sozialgeschichte der Jahre 1928 bis 1936* (Göttingen, 1990), 210ff.

173. *Regierung Hitler* 1, No. 93; Law concerning the Introduction of a Day of Celebration for National Labour, 10 April 1933 in *RGBl.* 1933 I, 191.

174. On the preparations see *Goebbels TB*, 18 April–1 May 1933.

175. Domarus 1, 258.

176. Ibid., 259ff.

177. Winkler, *Weg*, 921f.

178. *Goebbels TB*, 18 April 1933.

179. Winkler, *Weg*, 928f.; Dietrich Scheibe and Margit Wiegold-Bovermann, '*Morgen werden wir die Gewerkschaftshäuser besetzen*'. *Die Zerschlagung der Gewerkschaften in Rheinland-Westfalen-Lippe am 2. Mai 1933* (Essen, 2003).

180. *FZ*, 7 May 1933 (1 M), 'Dr. Ley mit der Bildung der Arbeiterfront beauftragt'; *VB*, 12 May 1933, 'Der erste Kongreß des deutschen Arbeitertums' and a report on Hitler's 'commitment'.

181. *Regierung Hitler* 1, No. 134; *RGBl.* 1933 I, 285.

182. Günter Morsch, *Arbeit und Brot. Studien zu Lage, Stimmung, Einstellung und Verhalten der deutschen Arbeiterschaft 1933–1936/37* (Frankfurt a. M., 1993), 70.

183. Law concerning the Transfer of the Tasks and Authority of the Reich Commissioner for Price Supervision of 15 July 1933 in *RGBl.* 1933 I, 490; *Regierung Hitler* 1, 667.

184. Dan P. Silverman, *Hitler's Economy. Nazi Work Creation Programs 1933–1936* (Cambridge, MA and London, 1998), 251.

185. Domarus 1, 208f.

186. *Regierung Hitler* 1, No. 94; Law concerning the Alteration of the Motor Vehicle Tax, 10 April 1933 in *RGBl.* 1933 I, 192f.; Heidrun Edelmann, *Vom Luxusgut zum Gebrauchsgegenstand. Die Geschichte der Verbreitung von Personenkraftwagen in Deutschland* (Frankfurt a. M., 1989), 160ff.

187. Buchheim, 'NS-Regime', esp. 384.

188. Edelmann, *Luxusgut*, 157ff.; Hansjoachim Henning, 'Kraftfahrzeugindustrie und Autobahnbau in der Wirtschaftspolitik des Nationalsozialismus 1933– 1936', in *Vierteljahrschrift für Sozial- und Wirtschaftsgeschichte* 65 (1978), 222ff.

189. Martin Kornrumpf, *Hafraba e.V. Deutsche Autobahn-Planung 1926–1934* (Bonn, 1990).

190. Estimate based on the figures given for 1 July 1932 in the *Statistisches Jahrbuch* for 1933, 157, and for 1 July 1933 in *Statistisches Jahrbuch* for 1934, 169 (cars, lorries, and buses).

191. *Regierung Hitler* 1, Nos 91, 92 (quote), 95 and 133 (quotes).

192. Ibid., Nos 158 and 166; Law concerning the Establishment of a Reich Autobahn Concern in *RGBl.* 1933 II, 509f. On Todt's appointment see *Regierung Hitler* I, 585. On the whole project and Todt's role see Karl-Heinz Ludwig, *Technik und Ingenieure im Dritten Reich* (Düsseldorf, 1974), 303ff.; Franz W. Seidler, *Fritz Todt. Baumeister des Dritten Reiches* (Frankfurt a. M. and Berlin, 1988), 97ff.; Hans-Erich Volkmann, 'Die NS-Wirtschaft in Vorbereitung des Krieges', in Wilhelm Deist et al., *Ursachen und Voraussetzungen des Zweiten Weltkrieges* (Frankfurt a. M., 1991), 282ff.

193. *Regierung Hitler* I, No. 211; on the actual development see Morsch, *Arbeit*, 131ff.

194. Jürgen Stelzner, *Arbeitsbeschaffung und Wiederaufrüstung 1933–1936. Nationalsozialistische Beschäftigungspolitik und Aufbau der Wehr- und Rüstungswirtschaft* (Bamberg, 1976), 63ff.; BAB, R 18/660, Reich Economics Minister to Schwerin-Krosigk, 4 April 1933.

195. *Regierung Hitler* I, No. 114.

196. In the decisive *Chefbesprechung* (top-level meeting) of 31 May Hugenberg was still objecting to all plans involving artificial work creation measures. See ibid., No. 149.

197. Stelzner, *Arbeitsbeschaffung*, 56.

198. *Regierung Hitler* I, No. 147; Stelzner, *Arbeitsbeschaffung*, 72ff.

199. *Regierung Hitler* I, No. 149.

200. Law for the Reduction of Unemployment of 1 June 1933 (*RGBl.* 1933 I, 323ff.); Law concerning Tax Reliefs, 15 July 1933 in ibid., 491f.; Detlev Humann, '*Arbeitsschlacht*'. *Arbeitsbeschaffung und Propaganda in der NS-Zeit 1933–1939* (Göttingen, 2011), 74ff. The contributions were effectively used for equipping the SA on a large scale. See Stelzner, *Arbeitsbeschaffung*, 83.

201. *RGBl.* 1933 I, 651ff.; *Regierung Hitler* I, No. 212. On the Reinhardt programme see Stelzner, *Arbeitsbeschaffung*, 76ff.; Volkmann, 'Aspekte der nationalsozialistischen Wehrwirtschaft 1933–1936', in *Francia* 5 (1977), 281f.; Humann, *Arbeitsschlacht*, 82ff.

202. Buchheim, 'Das NS-Regime und die Überwindung der Weltwirtschaftskrise in Deutschland', *VfZ* 56 (2008), 391; *Regierung Hitler* I, Nos 262 and 298; Humann, *Arbeitsschlacht*, 706.

203. *Regierung Hitler* I, No. 873; Michael Geyer, 'Das zweite Rüstungsprogramm (1930 bis 1934)', in *MGM* 17 (1975), 125–72. Also Michael Geyer, *Aufrüstung oder Sicherheit. Die Reichswehr in der Krise der Machtpolitik 1924–1936* (Wiesbaden, 1980), 347f.; *Regierung Hitler* I, Nos 90 and 97, Note 8.

204. Ibid., No. 93.

205. Ibid., No. 156; Law concerning the Outstanding Debts to Foreign Countries, 9 June 1933 in *RGBl.* 1933 I, 349.

206. Geyer, 'Rüstungsprogramm', 134. Tooze, Ökonomie, 76ff., takes 8 June 1933 as his date.

207. Geyer, *Aufrüstung*, 348f.

208. On the last point see, for example, the comments by Martin Broszat in 'Der zweite Weltkrieg: Ein Krieg der "alten" Eliten, der Nationalsozialisten oder

der Krieg Hitlers?', in Broszat and Klaus Schwabe (eds), *Die deutschen Eliten und der Weg in den Zweiten Weltkrieg* (Munich, 1989), esp. 32ff.

209. ̃On the speech see Domarus 1, 270ff.

210. Brüning, *Memoiren*, 669.

211. Winkler, *Weg*, 933f.

212. Brünung, *Memoiren*, 669.

213. Winkler, *Weg*, 907ff.; Matthias, 'Sozialdemokratische Partei Deutschlands', 168ff.

214. Winkler, *Weg*, S. 930f.

215. Ibid., 939.

216. Ibid., 946ff.

217. *Schulthess' Geschichtskalender 1933*, 194. The list was published in the *Deutscher Reichsanzeiger* and the *Preußischer Staatsanzeiger* No. 198 of 25 August 1933. A second list with thirty-seven names was published on 27 March 1934. A total of 360 lists of those deprived of their citizenship had been published by 1945. See Michael Hepp (ed.), *Die Ausbürgerung deutscher Staatsangehöriger 1933–1945 nach den im Reichsanzeiger veröffentlichen Listen*, 3 vols (Munich, 1985).

218. Anton Ritthaler, 'Eine Etappe auf Hitlers Weg zur ungeteilten Macht. Hugenbergs Rücktritt als Reichsminister', in *VfZ* 8 (1960), 193–219.

219. Gaertringen, 'Deutschnationale Volkspartei', esp. 599ff.

220. Domarus 1, 280.

221. Gaertringen, 'Deutschnationale Volkspartei', 610f.

222. *Akten der Deutschen auswärtigen Politik 1918–1945* (ADAP). Aus dem Archiv des Auswärtigen Amtes Serie C 1933–1937 (Göttingen, 1950), I, No. 312.

223. See Ritthaler, 'Etappe'. Doc. 2.

224. *Regierung Hitler* 1, No. 166.

225. He did not secure access to the president either through the deputy, Hergt, or through Oskar von Hindenburg. See Ritthaler, 'Etappe', 199f.

226. BAK, NL 1231, No. 711, published in Ritthaler, 'Etappe', Doc. 1.

227. Ibid., 201.

228. Ibid., 202f.

229. According to his own account in BAK, NL 1231, Nr. 711, Hugenberg note, published in Ritthaler, 'Etappe', Doc. 2.

230. Ibid., Doc. 4.

231. Ibid., 203f.

232. BAK, NL 1231, No. 711, published in Ritthaler, 'Etappe', Doc. 3. On the appointment of the state commissioner see below p. 323f.

233. See below p. 336f.

234. For Hitler's announcement of 26 June 1933 see Domarus 1, 281ff.

235. Buchheim, 'Eingliederung', 372f.

236. Domarus 1, 229ff., quote, 233.

237. Bernhard Stasieweski and Ludwig Volk (eds), *Akten deutscher Bischöfe über die Lage der Kirche 1933–1945* (Mainz, 1968), vol. 1, No. 14a (Berlin, 1977).

238. Ibid., No. 32/I; Klaus Scholder, *Die Kirchen und das Dritte Reich* (Berlin, 1977), vol. 1, 438ff.

239. On 22 April the Mecklenburg state government had pressed for the appoint-
     ment of a state commissioner for its Protestant Church, a step that Hitler
     regretted and had reversed. See ibid., 426ff.; Kurt Meier, *Der evangelische
     Kirchenkampf*, 1, (Göttingen, 1976), 91; Gertraud Grünzinger and Carsten
     Nicolaisen (eds), *Dokumente zur Kirchenpolitik des Dritten Reiches* (Gütersloh
     and Munich, 1971), 1, No. 17/33. At a meeting to clarify matters with the presi-
     dent of the Protestant Church Committee, Hermann Kapler, held on 25 April,
     Hitler tried to persuade him to support the project for a Reich Church and
     met with a positive response. See Scholder, *Kirchen* 1, 433ff., based on the mem-
     oirs of the chairman of the Hesse state Church Council, Johannes Kübel. See
     Johannes Kübel, *Erinnerungen. Mensch und Christ, Theologe, Pfarrer und Kirchenmann
     zum 100. Geburtstag*, ed. Martha Frommer (Villingen-Schwenningen, 1972),
     pp. 89f. and another written statement.
240. Scholder, *Kirchen* 1, 401ff. Müller's appointment was announced on 25 April;
     this was preceded by a lengthy meeting with Hitler on 17 April. See *Dokumente
     Kirchenpolitik*, 1, No. 19/33. For earlier contacts between Müller and Hitler see
     Goebbels TB, 8 October and 2 December 1932.
241. Scholder, *Kirchen* 1, 470ff.
242. Ibid., 506ff.
243. Ibid., 517ff.
244. Ibid., 522ff. According to the Gestapo's information, at the beginning of July
     Pastor Scharf read out his account of the meeting from the pulpit. For the
     meeting see *Dokumente Kirchenpolitik*, 1, No. 18/33.
245. Ibid., No. 27/33 XIII; Oskar Söhngen, 'Hindenburgs Eingreifen in den
     Kirchenkampf 1933. Heinrich Bornkamm zum 60. Geburtstag', in Heinrich
     Brunotte and Ernst Wolf (eds), *Zur Geschichte des Kirchenkampfs. Gesammelte
     Aufsätze* (Göttingen, 1965),
246. According to information from Walter Conrad, *Der Kampf um die Kanzeln.
     Erinnerungen und Dokumente aus der Hitlerzeit* (Berlin, 1957), 17, Conrad was a
     desk officer for Church issues in the Interior Ministry.
247. Scholder, *Kirchen* 1, 533ff.; Conrad, *Kampf*, 22.
248. Domarus 1, 291.
249. Scholder, *Kirchen* 1, 626ff.
250. The quote, which was orally recorded and exists in a number of variations, was
     subsequently confirmed and explained by Niemöller. See Hannes Karnick
     and Wolfgang Richter, *Niemöller. Was würde Jesus dazu sagen? Eine Reise durch ein
     protestantisches Leben* (Frankfurt a. M., 1986), 69ff.
251. See by contrast Kershaw, *Hitler* 1, 554, who in my view considerably
     underestimates Hitler's activity. 'Remarkable in the seismic upheavals of 1933–4
     was not how much, but how little the new Chancellor needed to do to bring
     about the extension and consolidation of his power. Hitler's dictatorship was
     made as much by others as by himself.' See also ibid., 611.
252. Domarus 1, 286f. (based on the *VB*, 8 July 1933); see also the text version in
     Regierung Hitler 1, No. 180, with similar formulations.

253. Domarus 1, 289f.

254. Barkai, *Wirtschaftssystem*, 121f.; Volkmann, 'NS-Wirtschaft', 261f.

255. Schweitzer, *Nazifizierung*, 36.

256. For the composition of the General Council see *VB*, 17 July 1933.

257. On Wagener's dismissal and Keppler's role see Barkai, *Wirtschaftssystem*, 104ff.; IfZ, 472-NI, Wollfs Telegraphisches Buereau, 13 July 1933.

258. Schweitzer, *Nazifizierung*, 36ff.

259. Barkai, *Wirtschaftssystem*, 121.

260. For the legal measures see note 125.

261. In March Hitler had already, despite considerable doubts, felt obliged to agree to advance a special credit to the Karstadt concern to avoid it going bankrupt. See *Regierung Hitler* 1, No. 80; in July he reluctantly agreed to the rescue of the Tietz concern through the granting of a credit note from the Akzept- and Garantiebank. See Uhlig, *Warenhäuser*, 115f.

262. On the exception, agriculture, see Barkai, *Wirtschaftssystem*, 131ff.; Volkmann, 'NS-Wirtschaft', 254ff.

263. Gustavo Corni and Horst Gies, *Brot, Butter und Kanonen. Die Ernährungswirtschaft in Deutschland unter der Diktatur Hitlers* (Berlin, 1997), 79ff.; Frank, Der 'Reichsnährstand', 115ff. Law concerning the Responsibility of the Reich for the Corporate Organization of Agriculture 15 June 1933 in *RGBl.* 1933 I, 495; Law concerning the Provisional Organization of the Reich Food Estate 13 September 1933 in ibid., 626f.

264. Frank, 'Reichsnährstand', 150ff.

265. *RGBl.* 1933 I, 479; on the cabinet meeting see *Regierung Hitler* 1, No. 193.

266. *RGBl.* 1933 I, 479; Otmar Jung, *Plebiszit und Diktatur. Die Volksabstimmungen der Nationalsozialisten: die Fälle 'Austritt aus dem Volkerbund' (1933), 'Staatsoberhaupt' (1934) und 'Anschluss Österreichs' (1938)* (Tübingen, 1995), 20ff.

267. *RGBl.* 1933 I, 480 and 538f.

268. Ibid., 517f.

269. Ibid, 529; Hans-Walter Schmuhl, *Rassenhygiene, Nationalsozialismus, Euthanasie. Von der Verhütung zur Vernichtung 'lebensunwerten Lebens 1890–1945, 2nd edn'* (Göttingen, 1992), 154ff.; Gisela Bock, *Zwangssterilisation im Nationalsozialismus. Studien zur Rassenpolitik und Frauenpolitik* (Opladen, 1986), 80ff.

270. *Regierung Hitler* 1, No. 193.

271. The figures are based on the documents in the files in *Regierung Hitler*. In contemporary usage a distinction was made between cabinet meetings, in other words meetings of ministers and state secretaries [the most senior civil servants trsl.] and ministerial meetings attended only by ministers, whereas here the two terms are used synonymously. When ministerial meetings and cabinet meetings overlapped they were counted here as one meeting.

272. *Goebbels TB*, 21 July 1933.

273. Domarus 1, 293.

274. Scholder, *Kirchen* 1, 638f. The section of Hitler's speech concerned with Church politics was confirmed by Hess in the form of a directive to all Reich Party

leaders and Gauleiters dated 12 January 1934 and not intended for publication. See *Dokumente Kirchenpolitik* 2, 5/34. See also Meier, *Kirchenkampf* 1, 127ff.

275. *Goebbels TB*, 7 August 1933.

276. Remarkably, Rosenberg, one of the strongest opponents of the Churches within the NSDAP, emphasized this distancing of the Party from all internal Church matters in a leading article in the *VB* of 16 August 1933, 'Politik und Kirche'; Hess announced this as the official Party line in a directive of 31 October. See *Dokumente Kirchenpolitik* 1, No. 47/33 III; see also Scholder, *Kirchen* 1, 646ff.

277. Domarus 1, 293, mentions among others Schmitt, Schacht, Lammers, Göring. See *Goebbels TB*, 25 August to 2 September 1933.

278. He had already made similar statements: 'The states must disappear' and 'in three years there won't be anything left of them' in ibid., 28 July 1933.

279. Ibid., 27 March 1933.

280. Ibid., 25 August 1933. Goebbels had already discussed this solution with Lammers in July. See ibid., 19 July 1933.

FIRST STEPS IN FOREIGN POLICY

1. Wolfram Pyta, *Hindenburg*, 783 and 798f. For Hitler's early foreign policy see Kershaw, *Hitler*, 1, 621ff.; Gerhard L. Weinberg, *Hitler's Foreign Policy 1933–1939. The Road to World War II* (New York, 2010), 23ff.; Thamer, *Verführung*, 310ff.

2. *Regierung Hitler* 1, No. 93. Neurath's statement was based on a memorandum by the state secretary. See Günter Wollstein, 'Eine Denkschrift des Staatssekretärs Bernhard von Bülow vom März 1933. Wilhelminische Konzeption der Außenpolitik zu Beginn der nationalsozialistischen Herrschaft', in *MGM* 13 (1973), 77–94.

3. See the views of Andreas Hillgruber in Hillgruber, *Kontinuität und Diskontinuität in der deutschen Außenpolitik von Bismarck bis Hitler* (Düsseldorf, 1969), which are still of fundamental importance. See also Reinhard Frommelt, *Paneuropa oder Mitteleuropa. Einigungsbestrebungen im Kalkül deutscher Wirtschaft und Politik 1918–1933* (Stuttgart, 1977).

4. On the course of the Concordat negotiations see Ludwig Volk, *Das Reichskonkordat vom 20. Juli 1933. Von den Ansätzen in der Weimarer Republik bis zur Ratifizierung am 10. September 1933* (Mainz, 1972), 90ff. The important role played by Kaas in the negotiations and the fact that the signing of the Concordat and the dissolution of the Centre Party occurred at the same time suggests – although this is controversial – that the Catholic Church was prepared right from the start to sacrifice the Centre Party in return for a guarantee of its own position. Indeed, this motive could even explain the Centre's willingness to support the Enabling Law. This view was put forward by Klaus Scholder in *Kirchen*, but strongly rejected, above all by Konrad Repgen in Repgen, 'Über die Entstehung des Reichskonkordats-Offerte im Frühjahr 1933 und die Bedeutung des Reichskonkordats. Kritische Bemerkungen zu einem neuen Buch', in *VfZ* 26 (1978), 499–534. This controversy was dealt

with most recently in Thomas Brechenmacher (ed.), *Das Reichskonkordat 1933. Forschungsstand, Kontroversen, Dokumente* (Paderborn, 2007).

5. On 26 April, before 16 June, and on 22 June. See Alfons Kupper (ed.), *Staatliche Akten über die Reichskonkordatsverhandlungen* (Mainz, 1969) Nos 14, 45, and 54; see also No. 47. Hitler was prepared in compensation to make a concession to the Church concerning religious instruction in state schools.

6. Ibid., No. 68, here article 32. Moreover, Hitler's concerns about the guarantee of social and professional associations contained in the draft were dealt with by a statement according to which a list of such associations would be agreed between the German government and the German episcopacy. See ibid., Nos 61 and 64. See also Volk, *Reichskonkordat*, 155ff.

7. *Staatliche Akten*, No. 75.

8. Volk, 'Episkopat und Kirchenkampf im Zweiten Weltkrieg', in Dieter Albrecht (ed.), *Katholische Kirche und Nationalsozialismus. Ausgewählte Aufsätze von Ludwig Volk* (Mainz, 1987), 92ff.

9. Volk, *Reichskonkordat*, 138f.

10. Rudolf Morsey, 'Zentrumspartei', 396f.; *Goebbels TB*, 29 June 1933.

11. *Dokumente Kirchenpolitik*, Docs 30/33; Volk, *Reichskonkordat*, 136f.

12. *Staatliche Akten*, No. 62.

13. On the dissolution of the Centre Party see Rudolf Morsey, *Der Untergang des politischen Katholizismus. Die Zentrumspartei zwischen christlichem Selbstverständnis und 'nationaler Erhebung' 1932/33* (Stuttgart and Zurich, 1977), 163ff.; on the demise of the BVP see Karl Schwend, 'Die Bayerische Volkspartei' in Matthias and Morsey (eds), *Das Ende*, 452–519.

14. *Staatliche Akten*, Nos 77a and 78; Volk, *Reichskonkordat*, 148.

15. *Regierung Hitler* 1, No. 193, Statement, 683.

16. Günter Wollstein, *Vom Weimarer Revisionismus zu Hitler. Das Deutsche Reich und die Großmächte in der Anfangsphase der nationalsozialistischen Herrschaft in Deutschland* (Bonn, 1973), 42ff; *ADAP* C 1, Nos 18, 20, and 26; Neurath's article in the *Leipziger Illustrierte Zeitung*, 11 May 1933 is published in Karl Schwendemann, *Abrüstung und Sicherheit. Handbuch der Sicherheitsfrage und der Abrüstungskonferenz. Mit einer Sammlung der wichtigsten Dokumente*, 2, (Leipzig, 1932/33), Appendix 12; *ADAP* C 1, No. 238; *Volk und Reich*, 3 March 1933, Konstantin von Neurath, 'Deutschlands bedrohte Sicherheit'; Weinberg, *Foreign Policy*, 34ff.

17. See the convincing analysis by Michael Geyer, *Aufrüstung oder Sicherheit. Die Reichswehr in der Krise der Machtpolitik 1934–1936* (Wiesbaden, 1980), 322. Hitler clearly revealed his fear of a preventive war in a speech to industrialists on 29 May 1933, see below p. 516.

18. Wollstein, *Revisionismus*, 59; *ADAP* C 1, Nos 46, 49 (with note 7), and No. 56.

19. Wollstein, *Revisionismus*, 93f.

20. Karl Schwendemann, *Abrüstung* 2, 127.

21. *Regierung Hitler* 1, No. 126.

22. Domarus, 1, 270ff.; see also Wollstein, *Revisionismus*, 97f. On the speech see Kershaw, *Hitler*, 1, 622f.

23. *ADAP* C 1, No. 251.

24. Wollstein, *Revisionismus*, 148.

25. *ADAP* C 1, No. 9; Wollstein, *Revisionismus*, 39.

26. *ADAP* C 1, No. 163; Wollstein, *Revisionismus*, 78f.

27. *ADAP* C 1, No. 19.

28. Domarus, 1, 296: 'Keiner will fremdes Volk uns einverleiben'.

29. *ADAP* C 1, No. 430; Wollstein, *Revisionismus*, 177f.; Robert W. Mühle, *Frankreich und Hitler. Die französische Deutschland- und Außenpolitik 1933–1935* (Paderborn, 1995), 119f.

30. Ibid., 99ff.; *ADAP* C 1, No. 92.

31. Mühle, *Frankreich*, 110ff.

32. Ibid., 120ff.

33. *Schulthess'* 1933, 179.

34. *ADAP* C 1, No. 258.

35. Ibid., No. 84, Nos 260 and 290. Text of the agreement in *Schulthess'* 1933, 490f. See also Wollstein, *Revisionismus*, 64ff., 88ff., and 154ff.; Jens Petersen, *Hitler – Mussolini. Die Enstehung der Achse Berlin-Rom 1933–1936* (Tübingen, 1973), 137ff.; Mühle, *Frankreich*, 82ff.; Sören Dengg, *Deutschlands Austritt aus dem Völkerbund und Schachts 'Neuer Plan'. Zum Verhältnis von Außenpolitik und Außenwirtschaftspolitik in der Übergangsphase von der Weimarer Republik zum Dritten Reich (1929–1934)* (Frankfurt a. M., 1986).

36. Norbert Schausberger, *Der Griff nach Österreich. Der Anschluss* (Vienna and Munich, 1978), 234ff.

37. Ibid., 248f. On the propaganda see *Beiträge zur Vorgeschichte und Geschichte der Julirevolte* (Vienna, 1934), 25ff.

38. *ADAP* C 1, No. 187.

39. *Regierung Hitler* 1, No. 142; Law concerning Restrictions on Travel to Austria, 29 May 1933 in *RGBl.* 1933 1, 311.

40. *ADAP* C 1, No. 390; Schausberger, *Griff*, 251.

41. Domarus, 1, 229ff., quote 236.

42. *ADAP* C 1, Nos 212 and 194, Note 1.

43. Ibid., No. 194.

44. Wollstein, *Revisionismus*, 106ff.

45. *ADAP* C 1, No. 428, Note 3.

46. Wollstein, *Revisionismus*, 209ff.; *ADAP* C 1, No. 409.

47. Ibid., No. 457. Bülow records Hitler's remarks in a more radical version than that in the official minutes; see ibid., No. 456.

'FÜHRER' AND 'PEOPLE'

1. Domarus, 1, 300. On the event see *Der Angriff*, 13 September 1933, 'Sozialismus der Tat' (headline).

2. On the Winter Aid programme see Herwart Vorländer, *Die NSV. Darstellung und Dokumentation einer nationalsozialistischen Organisation* (Boppard am Rh., 1988), esp. 44ff.

3. Ibid., 4ff.; on Hitler's directive see ibid., Doc. 12.

4. Ibid., 319.

5. Christoph Sachsse and Florian Tennstedt, *Der Wohlfahrtsstaat im Nationalsozialismus* (Stuttgart, 1992), 110ff.

6. On the coordination of welfare see Vorländer, *NSV*, 20ff. The Socialist Workers' Welfare organization was dissolved and its property transferred to the NSV; the Jewish welfare organization lost state support; most of the non-confessional welfare organizations were coordinated by the NSV. The self-help organizations of the handicapped also joined it. See Sachsse and Tennstedt, *Wohlfahrtsstaat*, 134.

7. *VB* (M), 25 September 1933, 'Adolf Hitler: Deutsche Arbeiter ans Werk!'.

8. Erhard Schütz and Eckhard Gruber, *Mythos Reichsautobahn. Bau und Inszenierung der 'Straßen des Führers' 1933–1941* (Berlin, 1996); Benjamin Steininger, *Raum-Maschine Reichsautobahn. Zur Dynamik eines bekannt/unbekannten Bauwerks* (Berlin, 2005).

9. Bernhard Gelderblom, 'Die Reichserntedankfeste auf dem Bückeberg 1933–1937. Ein Volk dankt seinem Verführer', in Gerd Biegel and Wulf Otte (eds), *Ein Volk dankt seinem (Ver)führer: Die Reichserntedankfeste auf dem Bückeberg 1933–1937. Vorträge zur Ausstellung* (Brunswick, 2002), 19–62. See also *Goebbels TB*, 1 and 2 October 1933.

10. Domarus, 1, 305.

11. *Der Angriff*, 28 November 1933, 'Das große Feierabend-Werk gegründet'.

12. Wolfhard Buchholz, 'Die nationalsozialistische Gemeinschaft "Kraft durch Freude": Freizeitgestaltung und Arbeiterschaft im Dritten Reich', Dissertation, Munich 1976, 7ff.; Shelley Baranowski, *Strength through Joy: Consumerism and Mass Tourism in the Third Reich* (Cambridge, 2004).

13. For details see Sachsse and Tennstedt, *Wohlfahrtsstaat*, 57ff.

14. Björn Weigel, '"Märzgefallene" und Aufnahmestopp im Frühjahr 1933. Eine Studie über den Opportunismus', in Wolfgang Benz (ed.), *Wie wurde man Parteigenosse? Die NSDAP und ihre Mitglieder* (Frankfurt a. M., 2009); Jürgen Falter, 'Die "Märzgefallenen" von 1933. Neue Forschungsergebnisse zum sozialen Wandel innerhalb der NSDAP-Mitgliedschaft während der Machtergreifungsphase', in *Geschichte und Gesellschaft* (1998), 595–616.

15. For details see Karl-Dietrich Abel, *Presselenkung im NS-Staat. Eine Studie zur Geschichte der Publizistik in der nationalsozialistischen Zeit* (Berlin, 1968).

16. In mid-July 1933 the cabinet passed the Law for the Creation of a Provisional Reich Chamber of Culture; see *RGBl.* 1933 I, 483 and Gerd Albrecht, *Nationalsozialistische Filmpolitik. Eine soziologische Untersuchung über die Spielfilme des Dritten Reiches* (Stuttgart, 1969), 19ff. At the same time Hitler accepted Goebbels's request for a chamber of culture. See *Regierung Hitler* 1, No. 196. On 24 August 1933 he approved Goebbels's drafts for a newspaper editors' law and a chamber of culture law. See *Goebbels TB*, 25 August 1933.

17. BAB, R 2/4870, Submission of the draft of a chamber of culture law and its explanation to the Reich Chancellery 18 August 1933, and the minute of 2 September about the joint ministerial meeting in the propaganda ministry. BAB, R 43 II/1241, renewed submission of the draft 15 September 1933; *Regierung Hitler* 1, No. 215. See also *Goebbels TB*, 14 and 25 August, and 20 and 23 September 1933.

18. Chamber of Culture Law, 21 September 1933 (*RGBl.* 1933 I, 661f.). The relevant legal regulations are published in Karl Dietrich Schrieber et al. (eds), *Das Recht der Reichskulturkammer. Sammlung der für den Kulturstand geltenden Gesetze und Verordnungen, der amtlichen Anordnungen und Bekanntmachungen der Reichskulturkammer und ihre Einzelkammern*, 2 vols (Berlin, 1943). On the establishment of the Chamber of Culture see Uwe Julius Faustmann, *Die Reichskulturkammer. Aufbau, Funktion und Grundlagen einer Körperschaft des öffentlichen Rechts im nationalsozialistischen Regime* (Aachen, 1995), 34ff.; Volker Dahm, 'Anfänge und Ideologie der Reichskulturkammer. Die "Berufsgemeinschaft" als Instrument kulturpolitischer Steuerung und sozialer Reglementierung', in *VfZ* 34 (1986), 53–84.

19. Complete text in *Die Reden Adolf Hitlers am Reichsparteitag 1933* (Munich, 1934), 22–31, quotes pp. 25 and 28f.

20. Timo Nüsslein, *Paul Ludwig Troost (1878–1934)* (Vienna, Cologne, and Weimar, 2012).

21. Domarus, 1, 315ff.

22. For further references to Hitler's architectural drawings prior to 1933 see Hanfstaengl, *Haus*, 80; *Goebbels TB*, 25 July 1926 and 3 February 1932; Otto Strasser, *Mein Kampf. (Eine politische Autobiographie)* (Frankfurt a. M., 1969), 72.

23. *MK*, 291.

24. Lars Olof Larsson, *Die Neugestaltung der Reichshauptstadt. Albert Speers Generalbebauungsplan für Berlin* (Stuttgart, 1978), 22; BAB, R 43 II/1181, Report on the conference on 19 September, 25 September 1933, in facsimile in Jost Dülffer, Jochen Thies, and Josef Henke, *Hitlers Städte. Baupolitik im Dritten Reich. Eine Dokumentation* (Cologne and Vienna, 1978), 90ff. On the 'Germania plans' see Alexander Kropp, *Die politische Bedeutung der NS-Repräsentationsarchitektur. Die Neugestaltungspläne Albert Speers für den Umbau Berlins zur 'Welthauptstadt Germania' 1936–1942/43* (Neuried, 2005), 80ff.

25. Letter from the Bürgermeister to Lammers, 5 December 1933, published in Dülffer, Thies, and Henke, *Städte,* 94ff.

26. BAB, R 43 II/1181, Minutes of the meeting in the Reich Chancellery 29 March 1934, in facsimile in Dülffer, Thies, and Henke, *Städte*, 97ff.

27. BAB, R 43 II/1181, Minutes of the meeting in the Reich Chancellery on 5 July 1934 in facsimile in Dülffer, Thies, and Henke, *Städte*, 101ff.

28. Wolfgang Schäche, *Architektur und Städtebau in Berlin zwischen 1933 und 1945. Planen und Bauen unter der Ägide der Stadtverwaltung* (Berlin, 1991), 111ff. and 160.

29. Dülffer, Thies, and Henke, *Städte*, 214f.; Siegfried Zelnhefer, *Die Reichsparteitage der NSDAP. Geschichte, Struktur und Bedeutung der größten Propagandafeste im nationalsozialistischen Feierjahr* (Nuremberg, 1991), 62 and 77ff.

30. See ibid., 78; Minutes of the meeting of 25 April 1934 and concerning the submission of a draft by Ruff to Hitler 1 June 1934 in Dülffer, Thies, and Henke, *Städte*, 219ff.

31. Albert Speer, *Erinnerungen* (Berlin, 1969), 97.

32. Heike B. Görtemaker, *Eva Braun. Leben mit Hitler* (Munich, 2010); Erin E. Gun, *Eva Braun-Hitler. Leben und Schicksal* (Kiel, 1994).

33. *Goebbels TB*, 16 April 1934.

34. Longerich, *Goebbels*, esp. 255ff. and 289ff.

35. On the relationship between Hitler and Speer see Speer, *Erinnerungen*; Speer, *Spandauer Tagebücher* (Berlin, 1975); Joachim Fest, *Speer. Eine Biographie* (Berlin, 1999); Fest, *Die unbeantwortbaren Fragen. Notizen über Gespräche mit Albert Speer zwischen Ende 1966 und 1981* (Reinbek b. Hamburg, 2005); Gitta Sereny, *Das Ringen mit der Wahrheit. Albert Speer und das deutsche Trauma* (Frankfurt a. M., 1996). On the 'Berghof society' in general see Görtemaker, *Braun*; Volker Ullrich, *Adolf Hitler. Die Jahre des Aufstiegs. Biographie* (Frankfurt a. M., 2013), 673ff.

36. Adolf Hitler, 'Die Reichskanzlei', in *Die Kunst im Dritten Reich* 3 (1939), 279.

37. Joachimsthaler, *Chef*, 132.

38. Speer, *Erinnerungen*, 114.

39. Ibid., 45; Speer, *Tagebücher*, 219.

40. Görtemaker, *Braun*, 132ff.; Ulf Schmidt, *Hitlers Arzt Karl Brandt. Medizin und Macht im Dritten Reich* (Berlin, 2009), 88ff.; Schroeder, *Chef*, 173ff. See below p. 669f.

41. On the relationship between Hitler and Hoffmann see *Das Hitler-Bild. Die Erinnerungen des Fotografen Heinrich Hoffmann* recorded by and published from the private papers of Joe J. Heydecker (St. Polten, 2008). Rudolf Herz, *Hoffmann & Hitler. Fotografie als Medium des Führer-Mythos* (Munich, 1994).

42. Joachimsthaler, *Liste*, 517ff.

BREAKING OUT OF THE INTERNATIONAL SYSTEM

1. *Regierung Hitler* 1, No. 208.

2. Longerich, *Goebbels*, 248f.

3. *ADAP* Series C, 1, No. 447.

4. Ibid., No. 475.

5. Dengg, *Austritt*, 291f.; Wollstein, *Revisionismus*, 190ff.; *ADAP* C, 1, No. 479. According to a marginal note, Neurath was informed three days later about this.

6. See *Goebbels Tbi*, 14 October 1933 on the cabinet meeting (possibly an informal ministerial meeting) on 12 October. The meeting is not recorded in the *Regierung Hitler* edition.

7. *Goebbels TB*, 16 October 1933; *Regierung Hitler* 1, No. 230.

8. *Goebbels TB*, 28 July 1933.

9. *Schulthess' 1933*, 473.

10. Domarus, 1, 307f.

11. Ibid., 308ff.

12. *Regierung Hitler* 1, No. 231.

13. Domarus, 1, 323ff.

14. Ibid., 327.

15. *Goebbels TB*, 11 November 1933, see also 1 and 8 November 1933.

16. Domarus, 1, 330.

17. Bracher, *Stufen*, 481ff.; see also the examples in Gerhard Hetzer, 'Die Industriestadt Augsburg. Eine Sozialgeschichte der Arbeiteropposition', in Martin Broszat (ed.), *Bayern in der NS-Zeit*, 3, part B (Munich, 1981), 137ff.; also the report on the complaints about the election prepared in the Reich Interior Ministry in Bundesarchiv (BAB, R 1501/5350).

18. Jung, *Plebiszit*, 35ff. and 50ff. on the result (according to the official Reich statistics).

19. Hans-Jürgen Rautenberg, *Deutsche Rüstungspolitik vom Beginn der Genfer Abrüstungskonferenz bis zur Wiedereinführung der allgemeinen Wehrpflicht 1932–1935* (Bonn, 1973), 305f. The author shows that in November Blomberg was still preoccupied with measures that reflected the 1932 plans.

20. Ibid., 212ff.; Michael Geyer, 'Das zweite Rüstungsprogramm (1930 bis 1934)', in *MGM* 17 (1975), 125–72.

21. *IMT* 29, 1850-PS, 5f.

22. Rautenberg, *Rüstungspolitik*, 220ff.

23. *IMT* 29, 1850-PS, 2ff.; this training was carried out by the Wehrmacht. See Wilhelm Deist, 'Die Aufrüstung der Wehrmacht', in Deist et al. (eds), *Ursachen und Voraussetzungen*, 484; Hans Meier-Welcker, 'Aus dem Briefwechsel zweier junger Offiziere des Reichsheeres 1930–1938', in *MGM* 14 (1973), esp. 88ff.; Müller, *Heer*, 92; Rautenberg, *Rüstungspolitik*, 339ff.

24. Hans-Jürgen Rautenberg, 'Drei Dokumente zur Planung eines 300,000 Mann Friedensheeres aus dem Dezember 1933', in *MGM* 22 (1977), 103–139, No. 3. See also Rautenberg, *Rüstungspolitik*, 306ff.; Geyer, *Aufrüstung*, 329ff. and 351ff. Rautenberg provides evidence for the plans through two other key documents.

25. *ADAP* C 2, No. 23; *Documents on British Foreign Policy (DBFP)* series 2: 1929–938, vol. 6, No. 485; Wollstein, *Revisionismus*, 239; Geyer, *Aufrüstung*, 329.

26. Covered in Domarus, 1, 333f.; see also Mühle, *Frankreich*, 161ff. It is also clear from a meeting between Hitler and the French ambassador on 24 November 1933 that a fundamental improvement in Franco–German relations was not in sight. See *ADAP* C 2, No. 86.

27. As late as November Nadolny had received an instruction, approved by Hitler, to seek improved relations. See Günter Wollstein (ed.), *Rudolf Nadolny, Mein Beitrag. Erinnerungen eines Botschafters des Deutschen Reiches* (Cologne, 1985), 143ff.; see also Wollstein, *Revisionismus*, 258ff. He prepared a proposal along these lines (*ADAP* C 2, No. 171), which was corrected by Neurath (ibid., No. 190); Nadolny, *Beitrag*, 167ff.; Wollstein, *Revisionismus*, 265ff.

28. German–Polish relations had initially been extremely frosty. In an interview with Hitler published in the *Daily Mail* on 6 February 1933 Hitler was quoted

as demanding the return of the Corridor, which was denied in a milder version of the interview published in the *VB* of 14 February 1933. See Domarus, I, 201f. Ambassador Wysocki had then told Ministerialdirektor Meer that Germany and Poland were on the brink of war. See *ADAP* C 1, No. 22. On 2 May 1933, however, Hitler, reassured the ambassador of his desire for peace (ibid., No. 201), and was equally friendly at the latter's leave-taking. See *Official Documents Concerning Polish–German–Soviet Relations 1933–1939* (New York, n.d.) Doc. 4.

29. *ADAP* C 2, No. 69f., the text of the communiqué approved by Hitler is quoted in Note 2 of No. 69. See also Józef Lipski, *Diplomat in Berlin, 1933–1939. Papers and Memoirs of Józef Lipski, Ambassador of Poland* (New York and London, 1968), Doc. 30; Marian Wojciechowski, *Die polnisch–deutschen Beziehungen 1933–1938* (Leiden, 1971), 70ff. Originally a ministerial meeting on 16 November 1933 had decided to make the agreement a treaty. See *ADAP* C 2, No. 70, note 5.

30. Ibid., No. 77f.

31. Ibid., No. 81, with the minute on Hitler's approval. On the rest of the negotiations see ibid., Nos 87f., 90, 168, and 203.

32. Lipski, *Diplomat*, Doc. 25; Report in the VB, 26 January 1934.

33. *ADAP* C 2, No. 219; *VB* (M), 27 January 1934, 'Verständigung mit Polen'.

34. Wojciechowski, *Beziehungen*, 102ff.

35. Hitler ignored Göring's doubts about the deportation. See *Regierung Hitler* 1, No. 310. Speaking to the Reichstag on 30 January 1934 Hitler had advocated a continuation of friendly relations with Russia. See Domarus, I, 357.

36. *ADAP* C 2, No. 390.

37. Nadolny, *Beitrag*, gives the date as the 'Sunday after Whitsun', i.e. it must have been 27 May.

38. Schwendemann, *Abrüstung* 2, Appendix No. 30; on the Franco–German exchange of notes of December 1933/January 1934 see Mühle, *Frankreich*, 164ff., Wollstein, *Revisionismus*, 238ff.; Rautenberg, *Rüstungspolitik*, 264ff.

39. Mühle, *Frankreich*, 196ff.; *ADAP* C 2, Nr. 314; Joachim von Ribbentrop, *Zwischen London und Moskau. Erinnerungen und letzte Aufzeichnungen*, ed. Annelies von Ribbentrop (Leoni am Starnberger See, 1953), 56f.

40. *ADAP* C 2, No. 392.

41. Schwendemann, *Abrüstung* 2.

42. Mühle, *Frankreich,* 208ff.

43. Petersen, *Hitler*, 262ff.; Schausberger, *Griff*, 263.

44. *ADAP* C 2, No. 126; see Petersen, *Hitler*, 286ff., on the visit see Schausberger, *Griff*, 263ff.

45. Ibid., 265ff.; Petersen, *Hitler*, 292ff.

46. Schausberger, *Griff*, 275; Dieter Ross, *Hitler and Dollfuss. Die deutsche Österreich-Politik 1933–1934* (Hamburg, 1966), 192; *ADAP* C 2, No. 329.

47. Petersen, *Hitler*, 319ff.; Schausberger, *Griff*, 275f. On the reaction of the Berlin government see Ross, *Hitler*, 195ff.

48. After the German-Hungarian trade treaty of June 1933 (see *Schulthess' 1933*, 152) there were further agreements in 1934. See *RGBl.* 1934 II, 111 and 727. In

May there was also a treaty with Yugoslavia (see ibid., 301). The existing agreement with Romania was renewed in December (see ibid., 1405).

BECOMING SOLE DICTATOR

1. Longerich, *Geschichte*, 183ff.
2. Friedrich Wilhelm, *Die Polizei im NS-Staat. Die Geschichte ihrer Organisation im Überblick* (Paderborn, 1997), 48.
3. Gerhard Schulz, *Die Anfänge des totalitären Massnahmestaates* (Frankfurt a. M., 1974), 138f.; Ortwin Domröse, *Der NS-Staat in Bayern von der Machtergreifung bis zum Röhm-Putsch* (Munich, 1974), 18ff. After summer 1934 the guards in the Prussian concentration camps provided by the SA were replaced by SS or police. See Johannes Tuchel, *Konzentrationslager. Organisation geschichte und Funktion der 'Inspektion der Konzentrationslager' 1934–1938* (Boppard am Rhein, 1991), 73ff.
4. Hitler even went a step further and on 17 October told the SA leaders that he was dubious about the Reichswehr training members of the SA because under the Versailles Treaty this could be compromised by espionage. Röhm then requested the Reichswehr to take responsibility for this. See *IMT* 29, 1850–PS, 10ff.
5. *VB*, 28 April 1933.
6. Peter Longerich, *Hitlers Stellvertreter. Führung der Partei und Kontrolle des Staatsapparates durch den Stab Hess und die Partei-Kanzlei Bormann* (Munich, 1992), 8.
7. *RGBl.* 1933 I, 1016; Martin Broszat, *Der Staat Hitlers. Grundlegung und Entwicklung seiner inneren Verfassung* (Munich, 1969), 263f.
8. Alfred Rosenberg made himself the spokesman for this view in an article in the *VB* on 9 January 1934 ('Totaler Staat?'). According to this, the new state was the 'tool' of the NS movement.
9. *Goebbels TB*, 1 and 2 December 1933.
10. *VB* (N), 3 December 1933, 'Stabschef Röhm über seine Aufgaben als Reichsminister'.
11. On his contacts among Berlin diplomats and the foreign press see Eleanor Hancock, *Ernst Röhm. Hitler's Chief of Staff* (New York, 2008), 142ff. and 148. On Röhm's largely abortive attempts to establish contact with François-Poncet see *ADAP* Series C, No. 129.
12. Wolfgang Sauer, *Die Mobilmachung der Gewalt* (Frankfurt a. M., Berlin, and Vienna, 1974), 318ff.
13. Longerich, *Geschichte*, 201f. For example, in October 1933 the Reich Interior Minister wrote to the Reich governors and state governments that there were 'repeated reports of assaults by low-ranking leaders and members of the SA. These assaults must now finally cease'. See BAB R 43 II/1202).
14. See Röhm's article 'Die S.A. im neuen Staat', in *Der SA-Mann*, 16 December 1933; see also the publication of a keynote speech by Röhm in ibid., 20 January 1934.
15. Texts in *VB* (N), 1/2 and 3 January 1934.

16. Ibid., 24 January 1934: 'Adolf Hitler bei seinen S.A. Führern'; *Schulthess'*, 1934, 21/22 January 1934.

17. Rudolf Hess, 'Partei und Staat', in *Nationalsozialistische Monatshefte*, January 1934, Reprinted in *VB* (N), 23 January 1934.

18. On the appointment see Piper, *Rosenberg*, 323ff. In making this appointment Hitler had specifically not responded to Rosenberg's demand to make the state a 'tool' of the NSDAP (*VB*, 9 January 1934, 'Totaler Staat'), as he limited Rosenberg's authority to the 'movement'.

19. Church law regarding the legal position of the clergy and Church officials, 6 September 1933, published as an extract in Joachim Beckmann (ed.), *Kirchliches Jahrbuch für die Evangelische Kirche in Deutschland 1933–1938* (Gütersloh, 1948), 24f. See also Scholder, *Kirchen*, 667ff.; Kurt Meier, *Der evangelische Kirchenkampf*, 1 (Göttingen, 1976), 116ff.

20. Klaus Scholder, *Die Kirchen und das Dritte Reich*, 2 (Berlin, 1985), 37.

21. Meier, *Kirchenkampf*, 1, 116ff.; Scholder, *Kirchen*, 1, 644ff. and 681ff.

22. *VB* (N), 15 November 1933, Resolution of the 'German Christians'.

23. Scholder, *Kirchen*, 1, 783f.; Meier, *Kirchenkampf*, 1, 122ff.; *Goebbels TB*, 29 November 1933.

24. Scholder, *Kirchen*, 1, 792ff.; Meier, *Kirchenkampf*, 1, 136f.

25. *VB* (N), 2 December 1934, 'Kein staatliches Eingreifen in den Meinungskampf in der Evangelischen Kirche'.

26. *Goebbels TB*, 8 December 1933.

27. On the meeting of 25 January 1934 see Meier, *Kirchenkampf*, 1, 146ff.; Scholder, *Kirchen*, 1, 814ff.; Scholder, *Kirchen*, 2, 59ff. More than eight years later Hitler referred to the bugged telephone call recalling that the Protestant dignatories had 'collapsed with shock'. See Picker, *Tischgespräche*, 7 April 1942.

28. Scholder, *Kirchen*, 2, 51.

29. *VB* (M), 29 January 1934, 'Die Kirchenführer hinter dem Reichsbischof' (statement of 27 January 1934); Scholder, *Kirchen*, 2, 57ff.; Meier, *Kirchenkampf*, 1, 161ff.; Jørgen Glenthøj, 'Hindenburg, Göring und die evangelischen Kirchenführer. Ein Beitrag zur Beleuchtung des staatspolitischen Hintergrundes der Kanzleraudienz am 25. Januar 1934', in Heinz Brunotte and Ernst Wolff (eds), *Zur Geschichte des Kirchenkampfs. Gesammelte Aufsätze*, 1 (Göttingen, 1965), 45–91. See also Hitler's account to Goebbels in *TB*, 28 January 1934.

30. On the speech see Domarus, 1, 352ff.

31. *VB* (N), 3 February 1934.

32. Krohn et al., *Handbuch*, including among others: Wolfgang Benz: 'Die jüdische Emigration', sections 5–16; Werner Röder, 'Die politische Emigration', sections 16–30; Hartmut Mehringer, 'Sozialdemokraten', sections 475–93; Klaus-Michael Mallmann, 'Kommunisten', sections 493–506; Jan Foitzik, 'Linke Kleingruppen', sections 506–18; Michael Schneider, 'Gewerkschaftler', sections 543–51.

33. Domarus, 1, 349ff.

34. *RGBl.* 1934 I, 75.

35. Broszat, *Staat*, 263ff.

36. *VB* (N), 25/26 February 1934 on the oath taking by Hess and 27 February 1934 on Hitler's Hofbräuhaus speech.

37. Ibid., 24 March 1934, 'Konferenz der Reichsstatthalter beim Führer'.

38. BAB, R 43 II/495, Frick to Lammers, 4 June 1934, and reply from Lammers, 27 June 1934; Broszat, *Staat*, 151ff.

39. The only Prussian ministry left was the Finance Ministry. On the details see Alfred Kube, *Pour le mérite*, 65ff.

40. IfZ, ED 1, Liebmann Notes, note about meetings on 2 and 3 February 1934; see Müller, *Heer*, 95f. Hitler had already put forward the idea of a 300,000–man army to the British ambassador on 24 October. See *ADAP* C 2, No. 23.

41. Müller, *Heer*, 94; see also IfZ, ED 1, Liebmann Notes, notes about a meeting of commanders on 15 and 18 January 1934, at which a number of such cases were discussed. These tensions were also noticed outside the SA and the Reichswehr. See *Deutschland-Berichte der Sozialdemokratischen Partei Deutschlands. Sopade 1934–1940* (reprinted Salzhausen et al., 1980) (*Sopade*) 1934, 14ff.

42. *UF* 10, No. 2366.

43. Müller, *Heer*, Appendix, Doc. 7; on the 28th February see ibid., 98ff. IfZ, ED 1, Liebmann Notes: Meeting of the Army commander-in-chief (Fritsch) and Hitler speech of 27 February 1934. It is unclear whether Liebmann gave the wrong date for the meeting or whether it refers to a preliminary meeting. Further statements by the witness, Stölzle, in the investigations into the case against Dietrich/Lippert (IfZ, Gm 07.06, vol. 4, 24 Jun 1949) concerning a subsequent 'fraternization breakfast' involving SA leaders and Reichswehr officers in the staff mess. After the officers' departure Röhm demanded absolute obedience of the order by the SA.

44. Ernst Röhm, *Die nationalsozialistische Revolution und die SA. Rede vor dem Diplomatischen Korps und der Auslandspresse in Berlin am 18. April 1934* (Berlin, 1934). See also a similar speech to Bavarian SA formations, which he had published in the *SA-Mann* of 19 May 1934.

45. Hancock, *Röhm*, 148f.; see also Engelbrechten, *Armee*, 288ff., about the 'Spring Inspections', for which the Berlin-Brandenburg SA paraded on 15 Sundays.

46. *IMT* 36, 951-D, S. 72f.

47. *VB*, 21 April 1934.

48. Photo report on this trip in *Reichsmarine* 6/1934, 57–9.

49. Peter Longerich, *Heinrich Himmler. Biographie* (Munich, 2008), 177.

50. Sauer, *Mobilmachung*, 343ff.; Heinz Höhne, *Mordsache Röhm. Hitlers Durchbruch zur Alleinherrschaft 1933–1934* (Reinbek b. Hamburg, 1984), 226ff.; Göring statement in *IMT* 9, 302: He collected information and passed it on to Hitler; IfZ, Gm 07.06, Dietrich/Lippert Trial, vol. 6, Witness interrogation Rudolf Diels, 22 October 1953; IfZ, ED 1, Liebmann Notes: Meeting of the Army commander-in-chief (Fritsch) with commanders on 7 May 1934 in Nauheim.

51. Tooze, *Ökonomie*, 93ff.

52. Silverman, *Economy*, 253. In March 1934 the 'quasi-unemployed' – emergency relief workers, public relief workers, school leavers who were initially employed

in agricultural work, and those in the volunteer labour service programme – amounted to a total of 1,075,000 workers, which was the maximum reached. In the period summer 1933 to summer 1934 the number of those employed through these state support measures represented between 20 and 40 per cent of those entering the work force. On these groups of employed see also Claudia Brunner, *Arbeitslosigkeit im NS-Staat. Das Beispiel München* (Pfaffenweiler, 1997).

53. Those removed from the unemployment insurance programme included, for example, housemaids and those employed in agriculture, forestry, and the coastal fishing industry. See Volker Herrmann, *Vom Arbeitsmarkt zum Arbeitseinsatz. Zur Geschichte der Reichsanstalt für Arbeitsvermittlung und Arbeitslosenversicherung 1929–1939* (Frankfurt a. M., 1993), 59. The statistics show clearly that during summer 1933 hundreds of thousands were coming onto the labour market who were not from the reserve army of the unemployed. When the numbers of employed once again declined by almost 800,000 at the end of the year, only around 300,000 of those affected were registered in the unemployed statistics. See Silverman, *Economy*, 251. Also, only a minority of those workers newly recruited from spring 1934 onwards had been formerly unemployed.

54. *VB* (N), 22 March 1934, 'Deutsche Arbeiter fanget an.' On the return to the 'battle of labour' motif in propaganda see also the various headlines in the *VB*: 23 March 1934, 'Der Bau von 1500 Kilometern Reichsautobahn freigegeben'; 5 April 1934, 'Die Leistungen der Gemeinden in der zweiten Arbeitsschlacht'; 6 April 1934, 'Über 250 000 Bauarbeiter neu eingestellt'; 10 April 1934, 'In einem Monat 570 000 Arbeitslose weniger'; 11 April 1934, 'Einzigartiger Aufmarsch am Tag der Nationalen Arbeit'; 22/23 April 1934, 'Musterschau deutschen Schaffens eröffnet'.

55. Morsch, *Arbeit*, 131.

56. Tooze, *Ökonomie*, 98ff.

57. Michael Ebi, *Export um jeden Preis. Die deutsche Exportförderung von 1932–1938* (Stuttgart, 2004), 97ff.; Tooze, *Ökonomie*, 103.

58. *Schulthess'* 1934, 108; Decree Against Price Increases of 16 May 1934 (*RGBl.* 1934 I, 389f.); see also Tooze, *Ökonomie*, 125.

59. Morsch, *Arbeit*, 146f.

60. For examples see Kershaw, *Opinion*, 120ff.

61. Tooze, *Ökonomie*, 125; Morsch, *Arbeit*, 214f.

62. Ibid., 178; *Sopade* 1934, 9, 13, 74f., and 99; on the deterioration in the mood in the first half of 1934 see Ian Kershaw, *Der Hitler-Mythos. Führerkultur und Volksmeinung* (Stuttgart, 1999), 86ff.; Kershaw, *Opinion*, 75ff. On the Councils of Trust see *Sopade* 1934, 36ff. and 136ff.

63. Domarus, 1, 382.

64. Morsch, *Arbeit*, 178; *Sopade* 1934, 105ff. and 187.

65. After a ministerial meeting concerning transfer issues on 7 June 1934, at which Hitler approved Schacht's approach. See *Regierung Hitler* 1, No. 359.

66. Tooze, *Ökonomie*, 96f.

67. Hans-Erich Volkmann, 'NS-Wirtschaft', 298f.

68. Rolf Barthel, 'Rüstungswirtschaftliche Forderungen der Reichswehrführung in Juni 1934', in *Zeitschrift für Militärgeschichte* 9 (1970), published a memorandum of the Army Weapons Office, dated 20 June 1934, demanding 'economic leadership by the Reich Chancellor', which meant de facto the appointment by Hitler of a strong economic representative.

69. Domarus, I, 418f.

70. Dated 7 June 1934 (ibid., 385); see also the similarly very self-confident order by Röhm of 8 June to the SA (ibid.).

71. Höhne, *Mordsache Röhm*, 231ff.; Karl Martin Grass, 'Edgar Jung. Papenkreis und Röhmkrise 1933/34', Dissertation, Heidelberg, 1966.

72. *Goebbels TB*, 15 May 1934.

73. Pyta, *Hindenburg*, 859ff. Papen, *Wahrheit*, 369ff., maintains that, after having gained Hitler's agreement, he prepared on Hindenburg's behalf the draft for such a testament, but Hindenburg decided not to include the recommendation in the testament but instead simply in a letter to Hitler.

74. *Goebbels TB*, 21 May 1934.

75. Ibid., 25 August 1933.

76. Text in *UF* 10, No. 2375.

77. Hitler's directive is revealed in *Goebbels TB*, 18 June 1934; PA 1934, 243.

78. Pyta, *Hindenburg*, 844f.; Joachim Petzold, *Franz von Papen. Ein deutsches Verhängnis* (Munich and Berlin, 1995), 209ff.; Papen, *Wahrheit*, 345f.

79. On Hitler's appearance in Gera see *VB* (N), 19 June 1934, 'Die Welt muss wissen: Die Zeit der Diktate ist vorbei', and 'Dr. Goebbels gegen die Nörgler'; *VB*, 23 June 1934, Report on the summer solstice celebration.

80. *UF* 10, No. 2376.

81. *VB* (N), 27 June 1934, 'Nirgend kann die Glaubenskraft des Menschen besser verwurzelt sein als im Nationalsozialismus'.

82. Ibid., 29 June 1934, 'Die Wehrmacht im Dritten Reich', 'Deutschland lebt, wenn Adolf Hitler es führt!' (Göring) and 'Goebbels in Kiel'.

83. Klaus-Jürgen Müller, 'Reichswehr und "Röhm-Affäre". Aus den Akten des Wehrkreiskommandos (Bayer.) VII. Dokumentation', in *MGM* 1 (1968), 107–44.

84. Rosenberg, *Tagebuch*, 43.

85. Domarus, I, 394; Aufzeichnungen ('Tagebuch') Viktor Lutze, published in part in *Frankfurter Rundschau*, 14 May 1957; IfZ, Gm 07.06, vol. 10, Dietrich/Lippert Indictment, 4 July 1956, 56, concerning the telephone call to Wiessee, and vol. 1, 98ff., letter from Robert Bergmann, Röhm's former chief adjutant, 14 May 1949.

86. *Goebbels TB*, 1 July 1934.

87. Domarus, I, 420f.

88. Grass, *Jung*, 242.

89. Fritz Günther von Tschirschky reports in his memoirs (*Erinnerungen eines Hochverräters* (Stuttgart, 1972), 176ff.) that, together with Bose and Jung, he had

NOTES 1065

developed the following plan: By referring to the Nazis' misuse of power Papen would persuade Hindenburg to declare a state of emergency, take over power, and establish a directory in which Hitler would be dominated by conservatives. It was thus a revival of the 'taming concept'. Papen had put this proposal to Hindenburg's son at the end of June during the latter's visit to the Vice-Chancellery. However, he had passed it on to Blomberg, thereby neutralizing the plot. There is no other evidence for the plan. Bose and Jung were murdered and Papen does not mention it in his memoirs.

90. Domarus, 1, 395; *Goebbels TB*, 1 July 1934.

91. Domarus, 1, 395; IfZ, Gm 07.06, vol. 10, Dietrich/Lippert Indictment.

92. Domarus, 1, 396; IfZ, Gm 07.06, Bd. 10, Dietrich/Lippert Indictment.

93. Domarus, 1, 397; *VB* (N), 10 July 1934, 'Die große Friedensrede des Stellvertreters des Führers'.

94. The available evidence for alleged meetings is based purely on second-hand reports and cannot be verified. See Sauer, *Mobilmachung*, 308f.

95. Domarus, 1, 398f.; Hitler's authorship is clear from the Hess speech of 8 July.

96. Ibid., 399f.

97. Ibid., 401f.

98. Ibid., 402f.; IfZ, Gm 07.06, vol. 10, Dietrich/Lippert Indictment, 64ff. The Berlin Gruppenführer, Karl Ernst, was reported as having been shot, although at this point he was on his way to Berlin. See also *Goebbels TB*, 4 July 1934, on the situation on 30 June.

99. Ibid.

100. Wolfram Selig, 'Die Opfer des Röhm-Putsches in München', in Winfried Becker and Werner Chrobak (eds), *Staat, Kultur, Politik. Beiträge zur Geschichte Bayerns und des Katholizismus. Festschrift zum 65. Geburtstag von Dieter Albrecht* (Lassleben, 1992), 351–6.

101. Hitler, *Monologe*, 30 January 1942. On Ballerstedt see above p. 91f.

102. Günther Kimmel, 'Das Konzentrationslager Dachau. Eine Studie zu den nationalsozialistischen Gewaltverbrechen', in Martin Broszat and Elke Fröhlich (eds), *Bayern in der NS-Zeit*, 2, Part A (Munich, 1979), 365.

103. *Der Gerade Weg*, 17 June 1932 (up to January 1932 the paper was called *Illustrierter Sonntag*). See Rudolf Morsey (ed.), *Fritz Gerlich – ein Publizist gegen Hitler. Briefe und Akten 1930–1934* (Paderborn, 2010); Hans-Günter Richardi and Klaus Schumann, *Geheimakte Gerlich/Bell. Röhms Pläne für ein Reich ohne Hitler* (Munich, 1993).

104. That alone was enough reason why he ceased to be the editor of *Mein Kampf*, as Othmar Plöckinger has convincingly shown in his *Geschichte*, 133ff. His personal relationship with Hitler was by no means sufficiently close for the reason for his murder to have been his knowledge of intimate details of Hitler's life.

105. Veronika Diem, 'Friedrich Beck (1889–1934) und die Gründungsgeschichte des Münchner Studentenwerks', in Elisabeth Kraus (ed.), *Die Universität München im Dritten Reich. Aufsätze*, Part 1 (Munich, 2006), 43–71.

106. Selig, 'Opfer', 349ff. They were Walter Häbich, Adam Hereth, Erich Gans, Julius Adler, and Ernestine Zoref.

107. They were Eugen von Kessel, who was believed to have carried out intelligence work for the former Gestapo chief, Rudolf Diels, Othmar Toifl, who had acted as an informant and in other ways for the SS and the Gestapo, and the SA doctor, Erwin Villain, who had been condemned for a violent attack on state secretary Leonardo Conti of the Interior Ministry, despite the opposition of the Berlin SA. See Frank Flechtmann, 'Casanova, Vidoq, Toifl, Mauss. Ein Beitrag zur Kulturgeschichte des Spitzels', in *Geschichte, Politik, und ihre Didaktik* 26 (1998), 281–6; Judith Hahn, 'Erwin Villain und Leonardo Conti: Scharmützel unter NS-Kameraden', in *Deutsches Ärzteblatt* 104/42 (2007) A 2862–A 2864.

108. Höhne, *Mordsache Röhm*, 285. Among the victims was the police president of Gleiwitz. See Daniel Schmidt, 'Der SA Führer Hans Ramshorn. Ein Leben zwischen Gewalt und Gemeinschaft (1892–1934)', in *VfZ* 60 (2012), 201–35. Apart from the SA leaders, the following were murdered: Kuno Kamphausen, head of the council building works department of Waldenburg (evidently because of a quarrel with an SS leader over a building matter), Emil Sembach, dismissed from the SS in spring 1934 because of alleged embezzlement, and Erich Lindemann, physician and one of the leaders of the Jewish Veterans Association in Silesia. On Lindemann's murder see IfZ, Gm 08.06, vol. 9, Osnabrück court indictment, 21 April 1956.

109. Ernst Ewald Martin, former head of Gauleiter Mutschmann's intelligence service, Lamberdus Ostendorp, member of the SA's internal police, and the leader of the Dresden SA Brigade, Joachim Schroedter. A further name on the list of deaths, Otto Pietrzok, is evidently an error. See Rainer Orth, *Der SD-Mann Johannes Schmidt. Der Mörder des Reichskanzlers Kurt von Schleicher?* (Marburg, 2012), 193ff.

110. Jürgen Schuhladen-Krämer, 'Die Exekutoren des Terrors: Hermann Mattheiss, Walter Stahlecker, Friedrich Mussgay, Leiter der Geheimen Staatspolizeileitstelle Stuttgart', in Michael Kissener and Joachim Scholtyseck (eds), *Die Führer der Provinz. NS-Biographien aus Baden und Württemberg* (Constance, 1999), 407ff.

111. Barbara Schellenberger, 'Adalbert Probst (1900–1934), Katholischer Jugendführer – Opfer des Nationalsozialismus', in *Düsseldorfer Jahrbuch. Beiträge zur Geschichte des Niederrheins* 69, 279–86; on Probst see also Dietmar Schulze, 'Der "Röhm-Putsch" in der Provinz Sachsen', in *Hallische Beiträge zur Zeitgeschichte* 15 (2005), 26f.

112. Ibid.

113. Tuchel, *Konzentrationslager*, 177.

114. IfZ, Gm 07.06, vol. 10, Dietrich/Lippert indictment, 77ff., and vol. 12/13, Minutes of the main trial. Statements by Walter Kopp and Johann Mühlbauer, both platoon leaders of the state police.

115. Domarus, 1, 404.

116. *Der Angriff*, 2 July 1934, 'Die Niederschlagung der Hochverräter'.

117. Domarus, 1, 405f.

118. Scholder, *Kirchen*, 1, 156f.

119. *Akten Bischöfe*, No. 160; Deuerlein, *Reichskonkordat*, 160f., provides Buttmann's relevant notes; another account is contained in a letter from Buttmann. See *Dokumente*. 2, No. 44/34. On this meeting see Klaus Scholder, *Kirchen*, 2, 246; on the whole issue involved in the negotiations see *Dokumente Kirchenpolitik* 2, No. 43/34.

120. Rosenberg, *Tagebücher*, 28 June 1934.

121. Scholder, *Kirchen*, 2, 247f.; *Akten Bischöfe* 1, No. 160.

122. Heinz Boberach (ed.), *Berichte des SD und der Gestapo über Kirchen und Kirchenvolk in Deutschland 1934–1944* (Mainz, 1971), No. 1, 13ff. On Klausener's position see Scholder, *Kirchen*, 2, 242f.

123. *Akten Bischöfe*, 1, Doc. 167a.

124. *Regierung Hitler* 1, No. 375.

125. *RGBl*. 1934 I, 529.

126. *Goebbels TB*, 4 July 1934.

127. It is clear from a letter from Papen to Hitler dated 4 July that Papen had explained to Hitler in a private meeting the day before that he could only rejoin the cabinet when 'my honour and that of my officials [has been] restored'. See *IMT* 35, 714-D, 392f. *Regierung Hitler* 1, No. 375: His name is contained in the list of those present dated 3 July, but was subsequently crossed out.

128. Domarus, 1, 406.

129. *VB* (N), 7 July 1934, 'Rudolf Hess auf der Reichs- und Gauleitertagung'. See also 8/9 July 1934, 'Rudolf Hess über die Aufgaben der S.A.' (interview), refers to the article 'SA und Partei' of 23 January 1934, which was intended as a warning shot to Röhm.

130. *Regierung Hitler* 1, No. 375.

131. For the speech see Domarus, 1, 407ff.

132. Höhne, *Mordsache Röhm*, 319ff., provides 85 names in his list of those killed (although some are not certain). See Orth, *SD-Mann*, 191f. This list can be added to (see ibid., 102ff.).

133. Hildegard von Kotze (ed.), *'Es spricht der Führer'. 7 exemplarische Hitler-Reden* (Gütersloh, 1966), 123–77, quotes 170f.

134. Domarus, 1, 426.

135. Morsch, *Arbeit*, 182f.; Kershaw, *Hitler-Mythos*, 109ff.; *Sopade* 1934, 197ff.

136. Petersen, *Hitler*, 344ff.; *ADAP* C 3, Nos 5 and 7.

137. Gerhard Jagschitz, *Der Putsch. Die Nationalsozialisten 1934 in Österreich* (Graz, 1976), 82ff., emphasizes this rivalry, as does Schausberger, 289, who claims that Hitler was inactive; also Hans Schafranek, *Sommerfest und Preisschießen. Die unbekannte Geschichte des NS-Putsches im Jahre 1934* (Vienna, 2006), 214, claims that Hitler did not 'raise any significant objections' to the putsch plans insofar as he was aware of them. Gerhard L. Weinberg, 'Die deutsche Außenpolitik und Österreich 1937/38', in Gerald Stourzh and Brigitte Zaar (eds), *Österreich und die Mächte. Internationale und österreichische Aspekte des 'Anschlusses' vom März*

1938 (Vienna, 1990), and Gottfried-Karl Kindermann, *Hitlers Niederlage, in Österreich. Bewaffneter NS-Putsch, Kanzler-Mord und Österreichs Abwehrsieg 1934* (Hamburg, 1984), 151f., by contrast argue that it is improbable that the putsch occurred without Hitler's knowledge. This view was confirmed by among others the memoirs of the Vienna Gauleiter, Alfred Frauenfeld. See Alfred Frauenfeld, *Und trage keine Reu'. Vom Wiener Gauleiter zum Generalkommissar der Krim. Erinnerungen und Aufzeichnungen* (Leoni am Starnberger See, 1978), 113.

138. Kurt Bauer, *Elementar-Ereignis. Die österreichischen Nationalsozialisten und der Juliputsch 1934* (Vienna, 2003), 120.

139. Longerich, *Himmler*, 187.

140. *Goebbels TB*, 23 July 1934. Prior to the publication of the Goebbels diaries the only thing known about the role of the Reichswehr in the preparations for the operation was the fact that on the morning of 25 July the commander of Military District VII was informed by Hitler of an impending putsch by the Austrian army. See Anton Hoch and Hermann Weiss, 'Die Erinnerungen des Generalobersten Wilhelm Adam', in Wolfgang Benz (ed.), *Miscelleanea. Festschrift für Helmut Krausnick zum 75. Geburtstag.* (Stuttgart, 1980), 32–62. At the beginning of June Reichenau had already taken part in a meeting in Hitler's private flat at which Rechny was also present. See Schausberger, *Griff*, 287f.

141. Jagschitz, *Putsch*, 99ff.; Bauer, *Elementar-Ereignis*.

142. Ibid.

143. *Goebbels TB*, 26 July 1934.

144. Bauer, *Elementar-Ereignis*, 120.

145. *Goebbels TB*, 30 and 31 July 1934.

146. Domarus, 1, 427.

147. Jagschitz, *Putsch*, 182.

148. On Hindenburg's death see Pyta, *Hindenburg*, 855.

149. *Goebbels TB*, 31 July 1934.

150. Ibid., 2 August 1934.

151. *Regierung Hitler* 1, No. 382; Law concerning the Head of State of the German Reich, *RGBl.* 1934 I, 747; *Goebbels TB*, 2 August 1934.

152. Ibid.

153. See the reflections in Müller, *Heer*, 134ff.

154. *Regierung Hitler* 1, No. 383.

155. Domarus, 1, 431.

156. Hans Buchheim, 'Die staatsrechtliche Bedeutung des Eides auf Hitler als Führer der nationalsozialistischen Bewegung', in *Gutachten des Instituts für Zeitgeschichte* (Munich, 1958), 328ff.

157. Domarus, 1, 434ff.

158. *VB* (B), 8 August 1934.

159. *Goebbels TB*, 8 August 1934.

160. Domarus, 1, 437f. Dohrmann's sermon was published. See Franz Dohrmann, *Predigt zum Feldgottesdienst am 2. Oktober 1935 bei der Weihe der Hindenburggruft im Reichsehrenmal Tannenberg* (Wuppertal-Barmen, 1935).

161. See Jung, *Plebiszit*, 61ff. on the plebiscite.
162. *Goebbels TB*, 20 and 22 August 1934.

DOMESTIC FLASHPOINTS

1. Domarus, 1, 447ff.
2. Ibid., 452ff.
3. The appointment occurred on 24 January 1934 (ibid., 348). For details of the dispute see Longerich, *Goebbels*, 282ff.; Piper, *Rosenberg*, 323ff.
4. Domarus, 1, 455.
5. Ibid., 457f.
6. Tooze, *Ökonomie*, 91. According to ibid., 89ff. in 1932 the Reich spent 0.3 billion RM on the armed forces, in 1933 around 0.5 billion, in 1934 about 2.9 and in 1935 around 5.5 billion RM. This compared with civilian expenditure of 1.3 (1932), 2.1 (1933), 2.8 (1934), and 2 billion (1935) RM. Volkmann, 'NS-Wirtschaft', 293f., provides the figures given by various historians; see also Willi A. Boelcke, *Die Kosten von Hitlers Krieg. Kriegsfinanzierung und finanzielles Kriegserbe in Deutschland 1933–1948* (Paderborn, 1985), 28.
7. Tooze, *Ökonomie*, 125ff. See also *Sopade* 1934, 398ff. on price increases; 408ff. on shortages of consumer goods and raw material problems; 631ff. on price increases; 633ff. on shortages of consumer goods; 634ff. on hoarding. According to Morsch (*Arbeit*, 184ff.), who relies mainly on Gestapo reports, during the summer concerns emerged about price increases and an economic setback from which by November there developed 'the most serious crisis in morale hitherto, particularly among the working class'. See ibid., 188. An important element in this was criticism of the NS movement in general and no longer merely of individual functionaries. See ibid., 191.
8. BAB, R 43 II/193, Lammers to Darré, 30 September 1935, Statement by Darré, 9 October 1935, and reports by Darré about grain and fat supplies, livestock and meat prices, and food supplies in general. (7, 8, and 9 May 1935).
9. Morsch, *Arbeit*, 129ff.
10. BAB, R 43 II/537.
11. Dengg, *Austritt*, 400f.
12. *Schulthess'* 1934, 221ff.
13. On the 'New Plan' see Volkmann, 'NS-Wirtschaft', 302ff.; Tooze, *Ökonomie*, 113ff.; Ebi, *Export*, 117ff.; Boelcke, *Kosten*, 100ff.
14. Ebi, *Export*, 159ff.
15. The Law for the Preparation of the Organic Construction of the Economy of 27 February 1934 had already transferred control over the economic associations to the Economics Minister. See *RGBl.* 1934 I, 185.
16. Barkai, *Wirtschaftssystem*, 123ff.
17. These complex financial manipulations are discussed in detail in Volkmann, 'NS-Wirtschaft', 294f.
18. Ibid., 314ff.

19. *Regierung Hitler* 2, 194, Note. 1.

20. Law concerning the Search of Reich Territory for Exploitable Sources of Raw Materials, 4 December 1933. See *RGBl.* 1934 I, 1223; on the extraction and production of domestic raw materials see Volkmann, 'NS-Wirtschaft', 319ff.

21. Ibid., 320f.

22. Wolfgang Birkenfeld, *Der synthetische Treibstoff 1933–1945. Ein Beitrag zur nationalsozialistischen Wirtschafts- und Rüstungspolitik* (Göttingen, Berlin, and Frankfurt a. M., 1964), 26ff.; Gottfried Plumpe, *Die I.G. Farbenindustrie AG. Wirtschaft, Technik und Politik 1904–1945* (Berlin, 1990), 275ff.

23. Bundesarchiv Freiburg (BAF), RM 19/82, Report on the economic situation, 1 October 1935. See Volkmann, 'NS-Wirtschaft', 327, 322ff.; Tooze, *Ökonomie*, 146ff.

24. *Regierung Hitler* 2, No. 37; Law concerning the Appointment of a Reich Commissioner for the Control of Prices. See *RGBl.* 1934 I, 1085f.; on the appointment and his role see Ines Reich, *Carl Friedrich Goerdeler. Ein Oberbürgermeister gegen den NS-Staat* (Cologne, Weimar, and Vienna, 1997), 221ff.

25. Kurt Meier, *Der evangelische Kirchenkampf*, 1 (Göttingen, 1976), 204ff.; Scholder, *Kirchen*, 2, 59ff.

26. Scholder, *Kirchen*, 2, 309f. During an appearance in Stuttgart on 8 September 1934, for example, Jäger publicly advocated a 'national Church' that would overcome the religious divisions within the German nation. At any rate, the Reich Council of Brothers quoted him to that effect in a demonstration on 18 September 1934. See Joachim Beckmann (ed.), *Kirchliches Jahrbuch für die evangelische Kirche in Deutschland 1933–1934* (Gütersloh, 1948), 72. On this project Jäger worked closely with the former SA chief, Franz von Pfeffer, appointed Hitler's representative for Church questions in March 1934. See Scholder, *Kirchen*, 2, 160.

27. Meier, Kirchenkampf, 1, 165ff.; Scholder, *Kirchen*, 2, 171ff.

28. Jørgen Glenthøj, 'Hindenburg, Göring und die evangelischen Kirchenführer. Ein Beitrag zur Beleuchtung des staatspolitischen Hintergrundes der Kanzleraudienz am 25. Januar 1934', in Heinz Brunotte and Ernst Wolff (eds), *Zur Geschichte des Kirchenkampfes. Gesammelte Aufsätze*, 1 (Göttingen, 1965), 88ff.

29. Meier, *Kirchenkampf*, 1, 502; Scholder, *Kirchen*, 2, 278; *VB*, 14 July 1934 (on the announcement of the reception).

30. *Dokumente Kirchenpolitik*, 2, No. 56/34.

31. Scholder, *Kirchen*, 2, 285ff. and 307.

32. Ibid., 312f.; Gerhard Schäfer, *Der Einbruch des Reichsbischofs in die württembergische Landeskirche 1934* (Stuttgart, 1974), 533 and 500ff on the letters of complaint from the bishops of 14 August 1934.

33. On the events in Württemberg see Scholder, *Kirchen*, 2, 311ff.; Meier, *Kirchenkampf*, 1, 445ff. On Bavaria see Scholder, *Kirchen*, 2, 315ff.; Meier, *Kirchenkampf*, 1, 462ff.

34. On the protests see Scholder, *Kirchen*, 2, 313ff. (Württemberg) and 330ff. (Bavaria); Meier, *Kirchenkampf*, 1, 453ff. (Württemberg) and 465ff. (Bavaria).

35. Scholder, *Kirchen*, 2, 320; Joseph Gauger (ed.), *Chronik der Kirchenwirren*, Part 2 (Wuppertal-Elberfeld, 1935), 310.
36. *Dokumente Kirchenpolitik*, 2, No. 60/34.
37. Scholder, *Kirchen*, 2, 323f.
38. Ibid., 335ff.; Meier, *Kirchenkampf*, 1, 221ff.
39. Scholder, *Kirchen* 2, 334.
40. BAB, R 43 II/163, Reich Interior minister to the Reich Chancellery, 18 October 1934.
41. Scholder, *Kirchen*, 2, 348.
42. The details are documented in *Dokumente Kirchenpolitik*, 2, No. 65/34.
43. *Regierung Hitler* 2, 1030 and 1036. On the presentation of the report to Hitler see BAB, R 43II/163, Lammers minutes, 16 and 24 October 1934.
44. *Goebbels TB*, 25 and 27 October 1934, on the meetings of 23, 24, and 25 October 1934.
45. See Scholder, *Kirchen*, 2, 351.
46. *Dokumente Kirchenpolitik*, 2, 65/34 IX, also 67/34 I and II. See also Scholder, *Kirchen*, 2, 196f. and 351f.
47. *Dokumente Kirchenpolitik* 2, No. 68/34.
48. Gerhard Besier, *Die Kirchen und das Dritte Reich*, 3 (Berlin, 2001), 24ff. and 61.
49. Krausnick, 'Vorgeschichte und Beginn des militärischen Widerstandes gegen Hitler', in Krausnick, *Vollmacht des Gewissens* (Frankfurt a. M., 1960), 248ff.; Müller, *Heer*, 147ff.; Bernd Wegner, *Hitlers politische Soldaten. Die Waffen-SS 1933–1945. Leitbild, Struktur und Funktion einer nationalsozialistischen Elite* (Paderborn, 1999), 84ff. The War Ministry's edict of 24 September published in Paul Hausser, *Soldaten wie andere auch. Der Weg der Waffen-SS* (Osnabrück, 1966), Doc. 1 was of fundamental importance for its establishment.
50. Domarus, 1, 461.
51. *VB* (M), 28 November 1934, 'Gegen ausländische Lügenmeldungen über das Reichsheer'.
52. Domarus, 1, 462. *VB* (N), 4 December 1934, 'Ministerpräsident Göring im Industriegebiet'; 5 December 1934, 'Der Gauleiter von Schlesien, Brückner, aus der Partei ausgeschlossen'; 7 December 1934, 'Gottfried Feder in den einstweiligen Ruhestand versetzt'.
53. *VB* (N), 27 December 1934, 'Eine Unterredung mit Reichswehrminister Blomberg'. It involved the publication of an interview by the US correspondent Louis Lochner.
54. Morsch, *Arbeit*, 188ff. The Sopade reports had been referring to a 'war psychosis' in Germany since October/November 1934 (682ff. and 723ff.) and noted that Hitler was no longer excluded from criticism (730ff.).
55. Gerhard Paul, *'Deutsche Mutter – heim zu Dir!'. Warum es mißlang, Hitler an der Saar zu schlagen. Der Saarkampf 1933–1935* (Cologne, 1984), 62ff. on the activities of the German Front and 114ff. on the mass meetings in the Reich; see also Patrick von zur Mühlen, *'Schlagt Hitler an der Saar'. Abstimmungskampf, Emigration und Widerstand im Saargebiet 1933–1935* (Bonn, 1979).

56. *Goebbels TB*, 4 January 1935.

57. Domarus, 1, 469ff.; *VB* (N), 5 January 1935, 'Adolf Hitlers Rede vor der deutschen Führerschaft'.

58. *Goebbels TB*, 6 January 1935.

INITIAL FOREIGN POLICY SUCCESSES

1. On the Saar plebiscite see Kershaw, *Hitler*, 1, 686ff.; Paul, *'Mutter'*; Mühlen, *'Schlagt'*.

2. *VB*, 15 January 1935, 'Der Dank des Führers an die Saar' (headline); on the mass demonstration in Berlin see ibid., 16 January 1935, 'Aufmarsch der 500,000'.

3. Domarus, 1, 472ff.

4. *Goebbels TB*, 22 January 1935.

5. Norbert Theodor Wiggershaus, *Der deutsch–englische Flottenvertrag vom 18. Juni 1935. England und die geheime deutsche Aufrüstung 1933–1935* (Bonn, 1972), 261ff.; Schwendemann, *Abrüstung*, 787ff. and 791ff.

6. British White Paper on Defence of 4 March 1935.

7. Domarus, 1, 484ff.; *VB* (N), 2 March 1935, 'Die Heimkehr der Saar ins Reich'.

8. Domarus, 1, 489f. and 497; *Goebbels TB*, 6, 8, 10, 16 (on conscription), 20, 22, and 24 March 1935. *VB*, 6 March 1935. Kershaw, *Hitler*, 1, 690, refers to Rosenberg's diary where he writes that he found Hitler in the best of spirits on the day when he became hoarse. See *Tagebuch* 74f. According to Hitler they had to pull in their horns for 14 days and rely on the time factor.

9. *Regierung Hitler* 2, No. 105. The cabinet accepted a secret Führer decree concerning Reich aviation prepared by Göring naming the Luftwaffe as the third branch of the Wehrmacht. See *ADAP* C 1933–1937 3, No. 507 (Appendix).

10. *VB* (B), 12 March 1935, 'General Göring über die deutsche Luftverteidigung' (Report on the Daily Mail interview). On the revelation of the existence of the German Luftwaffe see Karl Heinz Völker, *Die deutsche Luftwaffe 1933–1939. Aufbau, Führung und Rüstung der Luftwaffe sowie die Entwicklung der deutschen Luftkriegstheorie* (Stuttgart, 1967).

11. Friedrich Hossbach, *Zwischen Wehrmacht und Hitler 1934–1938* (Göttingen, 1965), 81f.; Kershaw, *Hitler*, 1, 691f.

12. Hossbach, *Wehrmacht*, 82f.; Müller, *Heer*, 208f.; Deist, 'Aufrüstung', 494ff. Hitler still remembered Fritsch's objections in 1942. See *Hitler, Monologe*, 16 August 1942 (in the evening).

13. IfZ, ED 1, Liebmann Notes, Comments by Fritsch at the commanders-in-chief meeting on 24 April 1935 that the introduction of conscription was essential for the expansion of the army.

14. *RGBl.* 1935 I, 369ff., Proclamation of the Reintroduction of Conscription and on p. 375 The Law for the Build-Up of the Army, 16 March 1935. On the Cabinet meeting see *Goebbels TB* 18 March 1935.

15. The Law on Public Holidays of 27 February 1934 (*RGBl.* 1934 I, 129) declared Heroes' Memorial Day, 1 May, and Harvest Thanksgiving to be public holidays, both of which would take place on a Sunday.

16. Domarus, 1, 495.

17. *ADAP* C 3, No. 538.

18. Domarus, 1, 491ff.; *VB*, 16 March 1935, Special edition.

19. *ADAP* C 3, No. 555; Wiggershaus, *Flottenvertrag*, 292ff.

20. Anthony Eden, *Angesichts der Diktatoren. Memoiren 1923–1938* (Cologne and Berlin, 1964), 167ff. On the atmosphere at the meetings see also Paul Schmidt, *Statist auf diplomatischer Bühne 1923–1945. Erlebnisse des Chefdolmetchers im Auswärtigen Amt mit den Staatsmännern Europas* (Bonn, 1949), 298ff.

21. Petersen, *Hitler*, 399ff. On the Stresa communiqué see British and Foreign State Papers 139 (1935). Microfiche Washington, 756ff., 14 April 1935.

22. *Schulthess'* 1934, 489ff.

23. *Goebbels TB*, 1 April 1935.

24. Ibid., 5 April 1935, see also 7 April 1935.

25. Aram Mattioli, *Experimentierfeld der Gewalt. Der Abessinienkrieg und seine internationale Bedeutung 1935–1941* (Zurich, 2005), esp. 55ff.; Petersen, *Hitler*, 385.

26. *NS-Presseanweisungen der Vorkriegszeit* (PA) 1935, 74, 94, 113, 245, and 320. See also Petersen, *Hitler*, 391.

27. *Goebbels TB*, 15 May 1935, see also 5 May 1935.

28. Petersen, *Hitler*, 112; Kershaw, *Hitler*, 1, 698f.; Domarus, 1, 505ff.

29. *ADAP* C 4, No. 109, also No. 120f.

30. *PA* 1935, 320.

31. *RGBl.* 1935 I, 609ff. and 615ff., Führer edict concerning the length of conscription in the Wehrmacht. See *Regierung Hitler*, 2, No. 159.

32. Ibid.: War Powers Law (No. 160); Law concerning the Security Situation regarding the Protection of People and Reich (No. 161); Reich Defence Law (No. 162); National Service Law (No. 164), further the decision to appoint a Reich Defence Council (No. 163).

33. Jost Dülffer, *Weimar, Hitler und die Marine. Reichspolitik und Flottenbau 1920–1939* 1939 (Düsseldorf, 1973), 229ff.

34. See ibid., 204ff.; *VB*, 21 October 1932: Hitler opposed the construction of warships unless preceded by discussions with Britain.

35. The naval chief, Raeder, had probably made Hitler aware of this aspect at the beginning of April 1933. See Michael Salewski, 'Marineleitung und politische Führung 1931–1935', in *MGM* 1971/2, 123ff. and 152ff. (facsimile of Raeder's notes for his presentations), Dülffer, *Weimar,* 244ff. On early naval rearmament see also the concise overview in Deist, 'Aufrüstung', 537ff. At a meeting with the British naval attaché on 29 November Raeder hinted at the possibility of an alliance referring to ideas held by the political leadership. See Salewski, 'Marineleitung', 131. On 5 December Hitler told the British ambassador that initially he simply wanted to limit the building programme to the size prescribed by the Versailles Treaty and await the impending naval conference. See *ADAP* C 2, No. 99.

36. Deist, 'Aufrüstung', 540ff.; Dülffer, *Weimar,* 250ff.; Salewski, 'Marineleitung', 132ff. The idea of parity based on one-third first appears in the naval files immediately after extensive discussions between Hitler and the military leadership

during a joint trip on the battleship 'Deutschland'. See Dülffer, *Weimar*, 279. Michael Salewski, *Die deutsche Seekriegsleitung 1935–1945*, 1 (Frankfurt a. M. and Munich, 1970), 13, quotes the directive of 4 June 1935, according to which the future fleet was to be based on the proportion of 1:3 in comparison with British tonnage. On the naval building plan see Dülffer, *Weimar*, 566.

37. Deist, 'Aufrüstung', 543f: Dülffer, *Weimar*, 286ff.; Salewski, 'Marineleitung', 139f.; *ADAP* C 3, No. 32. From the note quoted by Salewski from the files of the naval high command it is clear that, as a result of not being invited to the main conference, they felt free from all commitments. See 'Marineleitung', 139.

38. Ibid., 140ff. and docs 5 and 6 (the latter was composed retrospectively). See also Dülffer, *Weimar*, 289ff.

39. *ADAP* D 3, No. 358.

40. At the time the British considered 35 per cent an inappropriately high figure. See ibid., No. 555.

41. Domarus, 1, 515.

42. On the Anglo–German Naval Treaty see Klaus Hildebrand, *Das vergangene Reich. Deutsche Außenpolitik von Bismarck bis Hitler* (Berlin, 1999), 600ff.; Wiggershaus, *Flottenvertrag*, esp. 313ff. See also Ribbentrop, *London*, 61ff.

43. This is suggested by the half sentence: 'quite apart from whatever else Germany and Poland had to sort out between themselves'. See the memorandum of 12 May 1934, published in Rosenberg, *Tagebuch*, 163ff., quote on p. 166. From the entry dated 14 May in this diary it is clear that Hitler immediately read the memo and approved of its contents.

44. Wojciechowski, *Beziehungen*, 245ff.; see also Kube, *Pour le mérite*, 105ff.

45. *Goebbels TB*, 13 May 1935.

46. Domarus, 1, 504.

47. *Goebbels TB*, 15 (quote) and 13 May 1935.

48. Ibid., 21 May 1935.

49. On the trip see *ADAP* C 4, No. 97f.; Wojciechowski, *Beziehungen*, 198f.; significant new information in Kube, *Pour le mérite*, 111ff.

50. Lipski, *Diplomat*, Doc. 44. The document is available only in English.

51. Wojciechowski, *Beziehungen*, 203ff.

THE ROAD TO THE NUREMBERG LAWS

1. *Goebbels TB*, 8 April 1935.

2. The reductions amounted to 3 per cent in the urban and 10 per cent in the rural communities. For details see Ernst Sodeikat, 'Der Nationalsozialismus und die Danziger Opposition', in *VfZ* 14 (1966), 139–74. See also Friedrich Fuchs, *Die Beziehungen zwischen der Freien Stadt Danzig und dem Deutschen Reich in der Zeit von 1920 bis 1939. Unter besonderer Berücksichtigung der Judenfrage in beiden Staaten* (Freiburg i. Breisgau, 1999), 44ff.

3. Morsch, *Arbeit*, 198ff.; *Sopade*, 1935, 151ff.

4. Longerich, *Politik*, 70ff.; Morsch, *Arbeit*, 321ff.; Kershaw, *Hitler-Mythos*, 96ff.

5. Longerich, *Politik*, 53ff.; Michael Wildt, *Volksgemeinschaft als Selbstermächtigung. Gewalt gegen Juden in der deutschen Provinz 1919 bis 1939* (Hamburg, 2007).

6. Helmut Heiber (ed.), *Akten der Partei-Kanzlei der NSDAP*, 1 (Munich, 1983), MF 124 05038, Wiedemann to Bormann, 30 April 1935.

7. Longerich, *Politik*, 81.

8. Besier, *Kirchen*, 3 142f.

9. Ibid, 144; *ADAP* C 33, No. 470; BAB R 43 II/176a, Lammers's minutes of 9 and 15 February 1935, concerning the presentation of the draft, initialled in 1934, of an agreement with the Vatican. See *Regierung Hitler* 2, 1069.

10. Besier, *Kirchen* 3, 144ff.

11. Ibid., 159ff.; Petra Madeleine Rapp, 'Die Devisenprozesse gegen katholische Ordensangehörige und Geistliche im Dritten Reich. Eine Untersuchung zum Konflikt deutscher Orden und Klöster in wirtschaftlicher Notlage, totalitärer Machtausübung des nationalsozialistischen Regimes und im Kirchenkampf 1935/36', Dissertation, Bonn, 1981, 42ff., and 69ff.

12. Meier, *Kirchenkampf*, 2, 21ff.

13. Besier, *Kirchen*, 3, 61f.

14. Ibid., 67ff.; Meier, *Kirchenkampf*, 2, 21f.

15. Longerich, *Politik*, 77. Goebbels returned in the middle of April from a meeting of Reich party leaders convinced that the Stahlhelm had to be dissolved. See *Goebbels TB*, 13 April 1935. This was a step that Himmler had already announced on 11 February 1935. See Berghahn, *Stahlhelm*, 271.

16. Longerich, *Politik*, 612.

17. For details see ibid., 81ff.

18. Albert Fischer, *Hjalmar Schacht und Deutschlands 'Judenfrage'. Der 'Wirtschaftsdiktator' und die Vertreibung der Juden aus der deutschen Wirtschaft* (Cologne, Weimar, and Vienna, 1995), 152ff. Schacht had presented a memorandum, partly published in Hjalmar Schacht, *76 Jahre meines Lebens* (Bad Wörishofen, 1953), 436ff., in which he proposed a legal solution of the Jewish question instead of the so-called individual actions. The Jews should become 'inhabitants with reduced rights'. At the opening of the Leipzig Spring Fair he warned that 'Jews should not all be destroyed indiscriminately', which, despite the brutal language used, represented a criticism of the uncoordinated actions of the Party activists.

19. For details see Longerich, *Politik*, 83f.

20. On Bell's activities in Autumn 1934 see Besier, *Kirchen*, 3, 26ff.

21. Ibid., 86ff., quote 86.

22. Meier, *Kirchenkampf*, 2, 50.

23. Rapp, Devisenprozesse, 72. At the end of July the trials were restarted. See ibid., 79.

24. Besier, *Kirchen*, 3, 92f.

25. Morsch, *Arbeit*, 324ff.; *Sopade* 1935, 651f., 757ff., 895ff. (according to which the 'discontent with the regime' had reached 'an extent that one would never have imagined possible'), and 1011ff.

26. BAB, R 43 II/318, Frick to Lammers, 24 July 1935, with excerpts from situation reports and the passing on of further reports by Grauert on 2 August 1935.

27. Ibid., Minister of Food and Agriculture to the Reich Chancellery, 31 August 1935.

28. Ibid., Minutes of the trustees' meeting on 27 August 1935.

29. Ibid., note about the prices, incomes, and supply situation in Germany, 4 September 1935, minuted as 'submitted to the Führer'. See Kershaw, *Hitler*, 1, S. 727.

30. Jens Reich, *Carl Friedrich Goerdeler. Ein Oberbürgermeister gegen den NS-Staat* (Cologne, Weimar, and Vienna, 1997), 225ff. See also the correspondence concerning the relevant draft law in BAB, R 43 II/315a; Sabine Gillmann and Hans Mommsen (eds), *Politische Schriften und Briefe Carl Friedrich Goerdelers*, 1 (Munich, 2003), 236ff.

31. *Goebbels TB*, 29 April and 9 May 1933 (about meetings with Hitler) also 19 May and 5 June 1935.

32. Longerich, *Politik*, 85ff.

33. Ibid., 88ff.; Longerich, '*Davon haben wir nichts gewusst!' Die Deutschen und die Judenverfolgung 1933–1945* (Munich, 2006), 80ff., and the numerous reports in Otto Dov Kulka and Eberhard Jäckel (eds), *Die Juden in den geheimen NS-Stimmungsberichten 1933–1945* (Düsseldorf, 2004), for the months July to September 1935.

34. Fischer, *Schacht*, 158ff. Schacht's resistance reached its high point in July when he closed the Reichsbank branch in Arnswalde because its head had been publicly pilloried for shopping in Jewish shops.

35. For details see Longerich, *Politik*, 94. Hitler's order was distributed in the 'Führer's' deputy's circular in R 164/35.

36. Ibid., 100f.

37. Besier, *Kirchen*, 3, 76ff.; *Dokumente Kirchenpolitik*, 2 No. 21/35 and No. 30/35.

38. Edict concerning the Combining of the Responsibilities of the Reich and Prussia in Church Matters 16 July 1935 (*RGBl.* 1935 I, 1029).

39. *Dokumente Kirchenpolitik*, 2, No. 21/35, quote 305. The church functionary referred to was Erwin Noack, the president of the Saxon provincial synod. See ibid., 302.

40. Besier, *Kirchen* 3. 310; *Dokumente Kirchenpolitik* 3, No. 15.

41. *Goebbels TB*, 19 August 1935.

42. Besier, *Kirchen* 3, 311ff.

43. Law to Secure the German Protestant Church, 24 September 1935. See *RGBl.* 1935 I, 1178, and for the first decree to implement it dated 3 October 1935 (see ibid., 1225).

44. *Akten* 2 Nos 231/I and 229/IId.

45. Meissner's note on the meeting held on the Obersalzburg is published in Volker Berghahn, 'Das Ende des Stahlhelm', in *VjZ* 15 (1965), 446–51. What this future looked like was made clear to readers of the *VB* report by a further report placed right beneath it, according to which the Gronau branch of the Stahlhelm

had been dissolved as a result of 'activities hostile to the state'. See *VB* (M), 13 August 1935. See also Berghahn, *Stahlhelm*, 272f.

46. *Goebbels TB*, 19 August 1935.

47. Ibid.

48. IfZ, 4067-NG. Excerpts of the speech were published in the daily press and distributed by the Reichsbank as a special edition. The draft of the speech in the Reichsbank files dealt much more directly with the 'individual actions'. See BAB, 2501/6992; see also Fischer, *Schacht*, 161ff.; Kurt Pätzold, *Faschismus, Rassenwahn, Judenverfolgung. Eine Studie zur politischen Strategie und Taktik des faschistischen deutschen Imperialismus (1933–1935)* (Berlin, 1975), 234ff.

49. There are three versions of the minutes of the meeting, one by the Reich Interior Ministry (see BAB, R 18/5513, 27 August 1935; see also the handwritten notes by Lösener: IfZ, Fb 71/2), one by the Foreign Ministry (see *ADAP* C 4, No. 268), and one by the Gestapo (see OA Moskau, 500-1-379, 20 August 1935).

50. Domarus, I, 525ff., quotes 525.

51. Ibid., 527.

52. Ibid., 527ff.

53. Longerich, *Politik*, 102; *Goebbels TB*, 9 September 1935.

54. On the occasion of the swearing-in of the first annual cohort of those conscripted into the Wehrmacht under the newly-created Reich War Flag on 7 November 1935 *Hitler* sent the head of the Stahlhelm, Seldte, a letter. In a few laconic words he let him know that, in view of the Wehrmacht having returned to its role as the 'bearer of German arms and…protector of its tradition', he considered that the conditions for the continuation of the 'Stahlhelm' no longer existed. See Domarus, I, 549f.

55. In 1950 Lösener wrote a report that clearly described the improvised nature of the Nuremberg laws, while downplaying his own role and ignoring the fact that at this point a considerable amount of preparation for these anti-Jewish laws had already been carried out by the ministerial bureaucracy. See Lösener, 'Als Rassefererent im Reichsministerium des Innern', in *VjZ*, 9 (1961), 262–313.

56. On the Nuremberg laws see Cornelia Essner, *Die 'Nürnberger Gesetze' oder die Verwaltung des Rassenwahns 1933–1945* (Paderborn, 2002). On the immediate period of drafting, 113ff.; Saul Friedländer, *Das Dritte Reich und die Juden*, I (Munich, 2000), 158ff.; Helmut Genschel, *Die Verdrängung der Juden aus der Wirtschaft im Dritten Reich* (Göttingen, 1966), 114ff.; Longerich, *Politik*, 102ff.; Pätzold, *Faschismus*, 259ff.; Hans Christian Jasch, *Staatssekretär Wilhelm Stuckart und die Judenpolitik. Der Mythos von der sauberen Verwaltung* (Munich, 2012), 197ff.

57. *Parteitag der Freiheit von 10.–16. September 1935, Offizieller Bericht über den Verlauf des Reichsparteitages mit sämtlichen Kongressreden* (Munich, 1935), 254ff.

58. Domarus, I, 535ff., quotes 536f.

59. *VB* (M), 18 September 1935.

60. Domarus, 1, 538f.; *Goebbels TB*, 19 September 1935.

61. PA 1935, 675f., 713f., and 762.

62. BAB, R 18/5513; see Fischer, *Schacht*, 184f.

63. *Goebbels TB*, 25 September 1935. The *VB* (M) of 25 September commented in a brief note that Hitler had spoken about the directives to implement the Reich Citizenship Law. According to Lösener ('Rassereferent', 281), who was present at Hitler's address, the latter avoided making a decision.

64. *Goebbels TB*, 1 October 1935.

65. Hitler cancelled a meeting of departmental heads scheduled to discuss this matter at the beginning of November. See Adam, *Judenpolitik*, 132ff.; *Regierung Hitler*, 2, 918, note 1. See also *Goebbels TB*, 7 November 1935.

66. *RGBl.* 1935 I, 1333. On the background see Adam, *Judenpolitik*, 134ff.; Lösener, 'Rassereferent', 280ff.

67. See below p. 473.

68. Hans-Walter Schmuhl, *Rassenhygiene, Nationalsozialismus, Euthanasie. Von der Verhütung zur Vernichtung 'lebensunwerten Lebens' 1890–1945* (Göttingen, 1992), 163; Gisela Bock, *Zwangssterilisation im Nationalsozialismus. Studien zur Rassenpolitik und Frauenpolitik* (Opladen, 1986), 97ff.; BAB, R 43 II/720, Confidential circular by Wagner, 13 September 1935, and Lammers's minute of 16 October 1934: Hitler had approved the contents of the letter. This issue was finally settled in June 1935 in a law amending the Sterilization Law. See *RGBl.* 1935 I, 773.

69. BAB, R 43 II/720, Lammers's minute, 16 July 1935, and the Interior Ministry's provision of the relevant memorandum on 16 October 1935. Second Law amending the Law for the Prevention of Hereditarily Diseased Offspring. See *RGBl.* 1936 I, 773; Schmuhl, *Rassenhygiene*, 164.

70. BAB, R 43 II/720, Lammers to Reich Interior Minister, 6 December 1935 and 23 January 1936; Bock, *Zwangssterilisation*, 352f.

71. BAB, R 2/12042, Reich Interior Ministry minute, 26 April 1937; Bock, *Zwangssterilisation*, 354.

A FOREIGN POLICY COUP

1. See the diary entry for 5 October 1935 in *Goebbels TB* for Goebbels's enthusiastic response to the news of the attack. See also Aram Mattioli, *Experimentierfeld der Gewalt. Der Abessinienkrieg und seine internationale Bedeutung 1935–1941* (Zurich, 2005), 125ff.

2. *Goebbels TB*, 19 August 1935.

3. Ibid., 13 October 1935, see also 9, 11, and 17 October 1935. This change of course is, however, only marginally reflected in the press directives. See *PA* 1935, 665f. and 671f.

4. *Goebbels TB*, 19 October 1935, about 17 October. Hitler had issued invitations to this meeting on the evening before a cabinet meeting. See *Regierung* Hitler, 2, No. 246.

5. Mattioli, *Experimentierfeld*, 125ff.

6. The figures on this vary: according to Tooze, *Ökonomie*, 248, expenditure on armaments in 1934 amounted to 4.2 billion RM, in 1935 to 5–6 billion. See also the comparison of the various calculations in Volkmann, 'NS-Wirtschaft', 293, according to which armaments expenditure in 1936 exceeded 10 billion RM.

7. Goerdeler, *Schriften*, 387ff. In the memorandum Goerdeler demanded a reorientation of the economy towards a liberal economic system and Germany's return to the world market. The trust necessary to achieve this could be secured only by abandoning the repressive policies towards the Jews.

8. *IMT* 36, 293-EC, 291ff.

9. Ibid.

10. Dietmar Petzina, *Autarkiepolitik im Dritten Reich. Der nationalsozialistische Vierjahresplan* (Stuttgart, 1968), 30ff.

11. *VB* (N), 7 October 1935, 'Wir wollen das Rechte tun und niemanden scheuen'; 11 October 1935, 'Der Ruf des Führers an das deutsche Volk'.

12. Speech on 3 October 1935 in Halle. See *FZ*, 5 October 1935; see also the speech at the Wehrmacht Day in Karlshorst, 29 September 1935 in ibid., 30 September 1935.

13. Morsch, *Arbeit*, 306ff.; Helmut Heiber (ed.), *Goebbels Reden 1932–1945*, 1 (Bindlach, 1991), No. 29; Johannes Hohlfeld (ed.), *Dokumente der deutschen Politik und Geschichte von 1848 bis zur Gegenwart. Ein Quellenwerk für die politische Bildung und staatsbürgerliche Erziehung*, 9 vols (Berlin, 1951–56), 4, No. 1. See also Goebbels's 1935 New Year's Eve address in *Der Angriff*, 1 January 1936.

14. *Unser Wille und Weg*: November 1935, Gerhard Donner, 'Der Reichsnährstand sichert Deutschlands Ernährung', 372–5; February 1936, Hans Riess, 'Der erste Abschnitt des Winterfeldzuges 1935/36 – ein voller Erfolg', 47–51; June 1936, Walter Tiessler (Head of the Reich Ring for NS-Propaganda), 'Winterfeldzug 1935/36. Wirtschaftspolitische Aufgaben der Propaganda', 203f.

15. On the relaxation of the food supply situation see *Sopade* 1936, 320ff.

16. Petzina, *Autarkiepolitik*, 33.

17. *Goebbels TB*, 2 February 1936.

18. Morsch, *Arbeit*, 339ff.

19. *Goebbels TB*, 6 February 1936.

20. *PA* 1936, 12; Longerich, 'Davon', 101.

21. Domarus, 1, 573ff.

22. Esmonde M. Robertson, 'Zur Wiederbesetzung des Rheinlands 1936', in *VfZ* 10 (1962), 178–205; see Petersen, *Hitler*, 466ff.

23. *Goebbels TB*, 21 January 1936.

24. On Hitler's domestic and foreign policy motives see in detail James Thomas Emmerson, *The Rhineland Crisis, 7 March 1936: A Study in Multilateral Diplomacy* (London, 1977), 72ff.; on the decision-making see ibid., 82ff.; on the whole situation see Weinberg, *Foreign Policy*, 187ff. The assertion that the military had been informed of the impending step weeks beforehand is an oversimplification of the decision-making process based on hindsight. See Max Braubach, *Der Einmarsch deutscher Truppen in die entmilitarisierte Zone am Rhein im März*

1936. Ein Beitrag zur Vorgeschichte des Zweiten Weltkrieges (Cologne, 1956), 12ff., who refers in particular to Friedrich Hossbach, *Zwischen Wehrmacht und Hitler 1934–1938* (Göttingen, 1965), 83f. According to him Hitler returned to Berlin on 12 February 1936 determined to occupy the Rhineland. However, according to Hassell, a definitive decision had not been taken by mid-February. See Ulrich von Hassell, *Die Hassell-Tagebücher 1938–1944. Aufzeichnungen vom Andern Deutschland* (Berlin, 1994). According to Hitler's own account given to a secret meeting of district Party leaders in 1937, he had begun to contemplate the occupation at the end of February 1936. See Hildegard von Kotze and Helmut Krausnick (eds), *Es spricht*, 123–77, 133.

25. See Manfred Funke, '7. März 1936. Fallstudie zum außenpolitischen Führungsstil Hitlers', in Wolfgang Michalka (ed.), *Nationalsozialistische Außenpolitik* (Darmstadt, 1978), esp. 301ff.

26. Robertson, 'Wiederbesetzung', Docs. 3f. and 8.

27. Ibid., Doc. 8.

28. *Goebbels TB*, 21 February 1936.

29. Robertson, 'Wiederbesetzung', Doc. 5. On this development see Petersen, *Hitler*, 471ff.

30. *Goebbels TB*, 29 February, about 27 February 1936.

31. The parliament in Paris had already approved the treaty on 27 February. See *Goebbels TB*, 29 February 1936.

32. Ibid., 29 February 1936.

33. Robertson, 'Wiederbesetzung', Doc. 4.

34. *Goebbels TB*, 29 February and 2 March 1936.

35. Ibid., 4 March 1936.

36. *Regierung Hitler*, 3, No. 39.

37. Domarus, 1, 583ff., quote p. 593; Helmut-Dieter Giro, *Frankreich und die Remilitarisierung des Rheinlandes. Hitlers Weg in den Krieg?* (Essen, 2006), 69ff.

38. See below p. 472.

39. Domarus, 1, 597.

40. On election propaganda see *Goebbels TB*, 10–31 March 1936; *PA* 1936, 253f.

41. *Sopade* 1936, 300, according to which, far from producing great enthusiasm, the entry of the troops provoked 'above all fear of war and concern about counter-measures by the western powers'. See also ibid., 314ff. and 460ff., for comments that Hitler's successes had caused 'serious depression among the opposition'. It is inexplicable how Kershaw (*Hitler-Mythos*, 101) can conclude that the election result represented 'overwhelming support for Hitler and his foreign policy'. See also Kershaw, *Hitler* 1, 742.

42. Domarus, 1, 603ff.

43. *PA* 1936, 331ff., documents the careful preparation of this high point in the election campaign.

44. *VB* (B), 28 March 1936, 'Kommando an die Nation: Hißt Flagge!' (headline). See also 27 March 1936, 'Der Führer spricht zu den Arbeitern und Soldaten des neuen Reiches' (headline).

45. Ibid., 28 March 1935, 'Das ganze deutsche Volk hörte seinen Führer!', as well as further reports of various events.

46. Domarus, 1, 616.

47. *VB* (B), 28 March 1936: 'Letzter Appell des Führers am freien Rhein' (headline); see also ibid., 27 March 1936.

48. Ibid., 29 March 1936.

49. *Sopade* 1936, 407ff., quote p. 407.

50. Ibid., 407; *VB* (B), 31 March 1936, with the provisional election results. See *Goebbels TB*, 31 March 1936.

51. Friedrich Berber (ed.), *Locarno. Eine Dokumentensammlung* (Berlin, 1936), No. 62; Giro, *Frankreich*, 248ff.

52. Berber ed., *Locarno*, Nos 63, 68, and 74.

53. *ADAP* C 5, No. 174; Petersen, *Hitler*, 477f.

54. *ADAP* C 5, No. 242.

55. Ibid., No. 313.

56. Ibid., No. 326; see also Josef Henke, *England in Hitlers politischem Kalkül 1935–1939* (Boppard am Rhein, 1973), 52f., on Hitler's response.

57. Weinberg, *Foreign Policy*, 202ff.; Giro, *Frankreich*, 249ff.

58. See below p. 467.

'READY FOR WAR IN FOUR YEARS' TIME'

1. See above p. 439.

2. Dietmar Petzina, *Autarkiepolitik*, 34.

3. *Sopade* 1936, 671 (summing up), 689ff. (problems with the food supply), 1055ff. (continuing supply problems from autumn 1935), 1111f. and 1405ff. (food shortages).

4. BAF, RW 19/862, Re: Foreign exchange requirements 3 February 1936; on the raw material bottlenecks; see, in particular, Tooze, *Ökonomie* 250f.

5. Petzina, *Autarkiepolitik*, 39; Kube, *Pour le mérite*, 140ff.; Tooze, *Ökonomie*, 251; *Regierung Hitler*, 3, No. 64.

6. *IMT* 27, 1301-PS, 135ff. Schacht also opposed the exploitation of domestic raw materials no matter what the cost at the meeting of the ministerial council on 27 May 1936. See ibid., 144ff. Göring had announced the creation of the ministerial council at the top level meeting in the Prussian State Ministry on 4 May 1936 through a decree for implementing the Four-Year Plan, but only formally implemented it on 23 October. See *Regierung* Hitler, 3, No. 83. See ibid., note 1 to Doc. 89. These were not, therefore, as is sometimes stated in the literature, sessions of the Prussian government. For the minutes of the Ministerial Council of 12, 15, and 27 May 1936 see also *Regierung Hitler*, 3, Nos 89f. and 93.

7. *Goebbels TB*, 31 May 1936; see also 3 May 1936. On Schacht's move see also Carl Vincent Krogmann, *Es ging um Deutschlands Zukunft 1932–1939. Erlebtes diktiert von dem früheren Regierenden Bürgermeister von Hamburg* (Leoni am Starnberger See, 1976), 272.

8. Kube, *Pour le mérite*, 147f.
9. Petzina, *Autarkiepolitik*, 44f., emphasizes the concentration on the exploitation of resources, whereas Kube in *Pour le mérite*, 151 and 161f. stresses that the securing of domestic raw materials and the encouragement of exports should be seen as an overall strategy.
10. Petzina, *Autarkiepolitik*, 45ff.
11. For details see *IMT* 36,493–EC and 497–EC, 557f.; see also Petzina, *Autarkiepolitik*, 46f.; Tooze, *Ökonomie*, 255f.; Banken, 'Devisenrecht', 279ff.
12. By a decree of 16 July 1936. See Bundesarchiv Berlin (BAB), R 58/23a; Longerich, *Politik*, 124; on this activity in detail see Banken, 'Devisenrecht', 188ff.
13. Domarus, I, 369ff., quote 370.
14. Hans Mommsen and Manfred Grieger, *Das Volkswagenwerk und seine Arbeiter im Dritten Reich* (Düsseldorf, 1996), 60ff. Porsche had already produced a memorandum on 17 January 1934 taking a similar line and sent it to Hitler. See Herbert A. Quint, *Porsche. Der Weg eines Zeitalters* (Stuttgart, 1951), 183ff.
15. On the meetings with Porsche in 1933/34 see Mommsen and Grieger, *Volkswagenwerk*, 78f.
16. Domarus, I, 481 and 576ff., quote 577.
17. Mommsen and Grieger, *Volkswagenwerk*, 104ff.; Heidrun Edelmann, *Vom Luxusgut zum Gebrauchsgegenstand. Die Geschichte der Verbreitung von Personenkraftwagen in Deutschland* (Frankfurt a. M., 1989), 205.
18. Mommsen and Grieger, *Volkswagenwerk*, 107ff.
19. *VB* (M), 22 February 1937, 'Vierjahrsplan sichert Motorisierung' on the 20 February speech. During a train journey on 15 January Hitler had promised Porsche that he would pursue the project 'unwaveringly'. See Mommsen and Grieger, *Volkswagenwerk*, 117.
20. Ibid., 117ff., dates Ley's official appointment to the 1937 International Automobile Exhibition, in other words the end of February/beginning of March, whereas the Goebbels diary entry of 15 January already contains a reference to Ley's participation in the project.
21. At the latest in September 1937. See Mommsen and Grieger, *Volkswagenwerk*, 156.
22. Mommsen and Grieger, *Volkswagenwerk*, 182ff.; Domarus, I, 867f.
23. Mommsen and Grieger, *Volkswagenwerk*, 79 and, on the start of production, 383ff.
24. In particular in his speeches opening the International Automobile Exhibitions on 20 February 1937 and 18 February 1938. See Domarus, I, 680f. and 791f.
25. Erhard Schütz and Eckhard Gruber, *Mythos Reichsautobahn. Bau und Inszenierung der 'Straßen des Führers' 1933–1941* (Berlin, 1996), 12.
26. See below, pp. 467ff.
27. Wolfgang König, *Volkswagen, Volksempfänger, Volksgemeinschaft. 'Volksprodukte' im Dritten Reich. Vom Scheitern einer nationalsozialistischen Konsumgesellschaft* (Paderborn, 2004). Between 1933 and 1941 ownership of a people's radio increased from

25.4 to 65.1 per 100 households, although a considerable number were owned by official bodies and businesses and the coverage of rural areas was significantly worse. See ibid., 204; Florian Cebulla, *Rundfunk und ländliche Gesellschaft 1924–1941* (Göttingen, 2004).

28. Edict concerning the Appointment of a Chief of the German Police in the Reich Ministry of the Interior. See *RGBl.* 1936 I, 487f.

29. BAB, R 43 II/391, Himmler directive, 26 June 1936.

30. Longerich, *Himmler*, 207ff. The delay in the appointment was the result of lengthy negotiations with Interior Minister, Frick.

31. Ibid., 211ff.; Patrick Wagner, *Volksgemeinschaft ohne Verbrecher. Konzeptionen und Praxis der Kriminalpolizei in der Zeit der Weimarer Republik und des Nationalsozialismus* (Hamburg, 1996), 191ff.; Ulrich Herbert, *Werner Best. Biographische Studien über Radikalismus, Weltanschauung und Vernunft 1903–1989* (Bonn, 1996), 163ff.

32. Karin Orth, *Das System der nationalsozialistischen Konzentrationslager. Eine politische Organisationsgeschichte* (Hamburg, 1999), 35ff.; Johannes Tuchel, *Konzentrationslager*, 326ff.

33. *IMT* 29, 1992 (A)-PS, 206ff., quote 222.

34. Orth, *System,* 38.

35. BAB, NS 19/1269, two letters from Himmler to the Justice Minister, 6 November 1935; see also Longerich, *Himmler*, 209.

36. *Goebbels TB*, 11 May. Similarly, on 15 May 1936.

37. Ibid., 29 May 1936.

38. Petersen, *Hitler*, 481f.

39. *ADAP* C 5, 706f., Note. On the background to the agreement see Gabriele Volsansky, *Pakt auf Zeit. Das Deutsch–Österreichische Juli-Abkommen 1936* (Vienna, Cologne, and Weimar, 2001). Bruce F. Pauley, *Der Weg in den Nationalsozialismus. Ursprünge und Entwicklung in Österreich* (Vienna, 1988), 161ff.; Schausberger, *Griff*, 349ff.; Petersen, *Hitler*, 483.

40. *ADAP* C 5, 703ff., note; Petersen, *Hitler*, 483.

41. Schausberger, *Griff*, 358f.

42. *Goebbels TB*, 7 May 1936.

43. *ADAP* C 4, 929f., Editor's comment. No further details are known.

44. Bernd Martin, 'Die deutsch–japanischen Beziehungen während des Dritten Reiches', in Manfred Funke (ed.), *Hitler und die Mächte. Materialien zur Außenpolitik des Dritten Reiches* (Düsseldorf, 1976), 460ff., who bases himself on the papers of the German armaments dealer, Friedrich Wilhelm Hack. For a time, at the suggestion of the Chinese prime minister, the inclusion of China in the planned agreement was contemplated and supported in principle by Hitler. See *ADAP* C 4, No. 416.

45. Wolfram Pyta, 'Weltanschauliche und strategische Schicksalsgemeinschaft. Die Bedeutung Japans für das weltpolitische Kalkül Hitlers', in Martin Cüppers, Jürgen Mathäus, and Andrei Angrick (eds), *Naziverbrechen. Täter, Taten, Bewältigungsversuche* (Darmstadt, 2013), esp. 24f.

46. *Goebbels TB*, 9 June 1936.

47. *ADAP* C 5, No. 362. For the negotiations see Theo Sommer, *Deutschland und Japan zwischen den Mächten 1935–1940. Vom Antikominternpakt zum Dreimächtepakt. Eine Studie zur diplomatischen Vorgeschichte des Zweiten Weltkrieges* (Tübingen, 1962), 23ff.

48. Herbert von Dirksen, *Moskau, Tokio, London. Erinnerungen und Betrachtungen zu 20 Jahren deutscher Außenpolitik 1919–1939* (Stuttgart, 1949), 186.

49. Sommer, *Deutschland*, 34f., based on a manuscript by Hermann von Raumer, Ribbentrop's deputy in his foreign policy bureau.

50. *ADAP* D 5, No. 509.

51. On the stay in Bayreuth see *Goebbels TB*, 20–28 July 1936.

52. On Germany's intervention in Spain see Hans-Henning Abendroth, *Hitler in der spanischen Arena. Die deutsch–spanischen Beziehungen im Spannungsfeld der europäischen Interessenpolitik vom Ausbruch des Bürgerkrieges bis zum Ausbruch des Weltkrieges 1919–1939* (Paderborn, 1973); Manfred Merkes, *Die deutsche Politik im spanischen Bürgerkrieg 1936–1939* (Bonn, 1969); Christian Leitz, *Economic Relations between Nazi Germany and Franco's Spain, 1936–1945* (Oxford, 1996), esp. 8ff.; Wolfgang Schieder, 'Spanischer Bürgerkrieg und Vierjahresplan. Zur Struktur nationalsozialistischer Außenpolitik', in Wolfgang Michalka (ed.), *Nationalsozialistische Außenpolitik* (Darmstadt, 1978).

53. *Goebbels TB*, 20–26 July 1936.

54. Abendroth, *Hitler*, 29ff.

55. Hans-Erich Volkmann, 'NS-Wirtschaft', 375ff.

56. This caution is documented in *Goebbels TB*, 12 August 1936.

57. Abendroth, *Hitler*, 40ff. and 95ff.

58. On the Olympic Games see Arnd Krüger, *Die Olympischen Spiele 1936 und die Weltmeinung. Ihre außenpolitische Bedeutung unter besonderer Berücksichtigung der USA* (Berlin and Munich, 1972); David Clay Large, *Nazi Games. The Olympics of 1936* (London and New York, 2007); Richard Mandell, *Hitlers Olympiade. Berlin 1936* (Munich, 1980); Reinhard Rürup (ed.), *1936. Die Olympischen Spiele und der Nationalsozialismus. Eine Dokumentation* (Berlin, 1996); Karin Stöckel, *Berlin im olympischen Rausch. Die Organisation der Olympischen Spiele 1936* (Hamburg, 2009); Christopher Hilton, *Hitler's Olympics. The 1936 Berlin Olympic Games* (Stroud, 2006); Arnd Krüger (ed.), *The Nazi Olympics: Sport, Politics, and Appeasement in the 1930s* (Urbana, IL and Chicago, IL, 2003); Armin Fuhrer, *Hitlers Spiele. Olympia 1936 in Berlin* (Berlin, 2011).

59. Arnd Krüger, *Theodor Lewald. Sportführer ins Dritte Reich* (Berlin, Munich, and Frankfurt a. M., 1975).

60. Mandell, *Olympiade*, 72ff.; Krüger, *Spiele*, 109ff. (USA) and 151ff. (the other foreign countries); Large, *Games*, 69f.

61. *PA* 1936, 777 and 927. On the temporary restrictions on Jewish persecution see Longerich, 'Davon', 101.

62. Ute Brucker-Boroujerdi and Wolfgang Wippermann, 'Das "Zigeunerlager" Marzahn', in Wolfgang Ribbe (ed.), *Berlin Forschungen II* (Berlin, 1987).

63. Volker Boch, *Die Olympischen Spiele unter Berücksichtigung des jüdischen Sports* (Konstanz, 2002), 72ff.

64. Walter Radetz, *Der Stärkere. Ein Buch über Werner Seelenbinder* (Berlin, 1982).

65. *VB* (N), 2 August 1936, 'Adolf Hitler eröffnet die Spiele von Berlin'. On the opening ceremony see Mandell, *Olympiade*, 139ff.; Krüger, *Spiele*, 195f.; Large, *Games*, 191ff.

66. *Goebbels TB*, 1–17 August 1936; Domarus, 1, 632ff., with evidence of Hitler's public appearances during the Games; *VB* (N), 3–16 August on Hitler's appearances at the various sports venues and on his receptions.

67. On the various events surrounding the Games see Rürup (ed.), *1936*, 120ff.; Stöckel, *Berlin*, 180ff. See also *Der Angriff*, 17 August 1936, 'Märchen auf der Pfaueninsel'; *VB* (N), 15 August 1936, 'Gartenfest bei Generaloberst Göring'.

68. The press was repeatedly admonished to play down the 'racial aspect' when reporting the sporting successes and to restrain its enthusiasm about German victories. See *PA* 1936, 831f., 841, 881f., and 895.

69. Franz Becker, 'Schneller, lauter, schöner? Die Olympischen Spiele von 1936 in Berlin als Medienspektakel', in Friedrich Lenger and Ansgar Nünning (eds), *Medienereignisse der Moderne* (Darmstadt, 2008).

70. Stöckel, *Berlin*, 164f.

71. On the Olympia film and Hitler's support for Riefenstahl see Lutz Kinkel, *Die Scheinwerferin* (Hamburg, 2002), 107ff.; Jürgen Trimborn, *Riefenstahl. Eine deutsche Karriere. Biographie* (Berlin, 2002), 238ff.; Rainer Rother, *Leni Riefenstahl. Die Verführung des Talents* (Berlin, 2000), 87ff.; Steven Bach, *Leni. The Life and Work of Leni Riefenstahl* (New York, 2007), 141ff.; Cooper C. Graham, *Leni. Riefenstahl and Olympia* (Metuchen, NJ, 1986); Hilmar Hoffmann, *Mythos Olympia – Autonomie und Unterwerfung von Sport und Kultur. Hitlers Olympiade, olympische Kultur und Riefenstahls Olympia-Film* (Berlin, 1993).

72. On the international press response see Krüger, *Spiele*, 206ff.; for a comprehensive and relatively sober assessment of the foreign press see a report by the Foreign Ministry published and commented on in Jürgen Bellers (ed.), *Die Olympiade Berlin 1936 im Spiegel der ausländischen Presse* (Münster, 1986), and the postscript on the systematic drilling of the Berlin population. See Ralf Beduhn, 'Berlin 1936: Olympia im Potemkinschen Dorf', in Bellers (ed.), *Olympiade*, 198. Ewald Grothe, 'Die Olympischen Spiele von 1936. Höhepunkt der NS-Propaganda?', in *Geschichte in Wissenschaft und Unterricht* 59 (2008), 291–307, sums up the impact of the Games abroad as ambivalent. These conclusions contradict the picture sketched in Ian Kershaw, *Hitler*, 2 (Stuttgart, 2000), 39, of an impressive propaganda success abroad.

73. *Goebbels TB*, 16 August 1936.

74. Ulrich Chaussy, *Nachbar Hitler. Führerkult und Heimatzerstörung am Obersalzberg* (Berlin, 1995).

75. Institut für Zeitgeschichte (IfZ), 3890-PS, Minute of a meeting with Göring on 30 July 1936; see also Kube, *Pour le mérite*, 152.

76. BAF, RW 19/991, Result of the meeting between Schacht and the Reich governors, 20 August 1936.

77. *Goebbels TB*, 1 September 1936.

78. Hitler had already decided to appoint Ribbentrop on 21 July in Bayreuth. See *Goebbels TB*, 22 July 1936. For his mission see the unpublished manuscript by Hermann von Raumer, quoted in Wolfgang Michalka, *Ribbentrop und die deutsche Weltpolitik 1933–1940. Außenpolitische Konzeptionen und Entscheidungsprozesse im Dritten Reich* (Munich, 1980), 155. On 2 January 1938 Ribbentrop himself commented in retrospect that he had been sceptical about the enterprise at the time. See *ADAP* D 1, No. 93. On the appointment on 26 July 1941 see Hans-Adolf Jacobsen, *Nationalsozialistische Außenpolitik, 1933–1938* (Frankfurt a. M. and Berlin, 1968), 302f.

79. Quoted from Wilhelm Treue, 'Hitlers Denkschrift zum Vierjahresplan', in *VfZ* 3 (1955), 184–210. See also Kube, *Pour le mérite*, 153ff.; Petzina, *Autarkiepolitik*, 48ff.; Kershaw, *Hitler*, 1, 53ff.; Tooze, *Ökonomie*, 261ff.

80. Law concerning the Exploitation of Mineral Resources of 1 December 1936 in *RGBl*. 1936 I, 999f., authorizing mining authorities to compel those with mining rights to exploit them. Decree concerning the Use of Rye and Wheat for the Production of Brandy of 27 November 1936 in ibid., 954f.

81. Tooze, *Ökonomie*, 252.

82. Deist, 'Aufrüstung', 517ff.; Müller, *Heer*, No. 140.

83. Deist, 'Aufrüstung', 523.

84. Ibid., 525.

85. Ibid., 527.

86. Führer Edict concerning the Length of Conscription in the Wehrmacht in *RGBl*. 1936 I, 706; see also Deist, 'Aufrüstung', 525f.

87. *Reden des Führers auf dem Parteitag der Ehre 1936* (Munich, 1936), 11ff. and 19ff.

88. *Statistisches Jahrbuch* 1938, 255. The increase in imports of wheat and maize was excessive. Hitler asserted that he had just issued the instructions for the implementation of this gigantic German economic plan (*Reden Parteitag 1936*, 22), which was not actually the case. He only signed the Decree for the Implementation of the Four-Year Plan and formally assigned Göring the task on 18 October 1936. See *RGBl*. 1936 I, 887.

89. *Reden Parteitag 1936*, 25.

90. Domarus, 1, 645f., and 639ff. on the usual speeches on the various topics.

91. This is how he described him to the cabinet on 1 December 1936. See *Goebbels TB*, 2 December 1936.

92. *ADAP* C 5, 761f., note. Germany accepted the invitation a week later. See ibid., 489. On Germany's further delaying tactics see ibid., Doc. 596. Also *ADAP* C 6, Docs. 1, 107, and 258. See Weinberg, *Foreign Policy*, 204.

93. *PA* 1936, 1102, 1125f., 1182, and 1289ff.

94. *Goebbels TB*, 21 October and 15 November 1936.

95. Ibid, 5 October 1936; Schieder, 'Faschismus'.

96. *ADAP* C 5, Nr. 618, Nos 620–22 and No. 624.

97. *Documenti, Diplomatici Italiani* Series 8, 1935–1939, 5 (Rome, 1994), No. 277.

98. *Goebbels TB*, 3 November 1936; *Schulthess'* 1936, 402ff.

99. Agreement against the Communist International. See *RGBl*. 1936 II, 28ff.; Secret additional agreement *ADAP* D, 1 No. 463, note 1; see also Gerhard

Krebs, 'Von Hitlers Machtübernahme zum Pazifischen Krieg (1933–1941)', in Krebs and Bernd Martin (eds), *Formierung und Fall der Achse Berlin–Tokyo* (Munich, 1994). On further secret agreements in which Japan and Germany agreed reservations about their respective official agreements with the Soviet Union see Weinberg, 'Abkommen'.

100. Wojciechowski, *Beziehungen*, 326ff. Göring reassured the general inspector of the political armed forces, Marshal Rydz-Smigly, that Germany had no territorial claims and emphasized their common anti-Soviet attitude, see *ADAP* C 6, No. 22. In summer 1937 the question of Poland joining the Anti-Comintern pact was discussed further at a German–Japanese conference; in November it was revived in the context of Italy joining the pact.

101. *ADAP* C 5, No. 516.

102. Lajos Kerekes (ed.), *Allianz Hitler–Horthy–Mussolini. Dokumente zur ungarischen Außenpolitik* (Budapest, 1966), No. 14.

103. *ADAP* C 6, No. 98.

104. Ibid., No. 38.

105. Essential is Weinberg, 'Secret Hitler–Benes Negotiations in 1936–37', in *Central European Affairs* 19 (1959/60), 366–74; discussed among other things in Ronald Smelser, *Das Sudetenproblem und das Dritte Reich 1933–1938. Von der Volkstumspolitik zur nationalsozialistischen Außenpolitik* (Munich, 1980), 136ff.

106. *Goebbels TB*, 2 December 1936; see also 7 December 1936 about comments made by Hitler at midday on the previous day. On the diary entry of 2 December see Kershaw, *Hitler*, 2, 51, although he leaves out the passage about Britain. This explains his conclusion that by 'the end of the year Hitler had become indifferent to an alliance with Britain' (59).

107. *RGBl.* 1936 I, 999.

108. Law to alter the Law concerning Foreign Exchange Controls in ibid., 1000f.

109. Ibid., 1000f.

110. Law to Implement the Four-Year Plan – Appointment of a Reich Prices Commissioner 29 October 1936 in ibid., 927f.; Decree concerning the Ban on Price Increases 26 November 1936, and the first implementation decree in ibid., 955f.; *Regierung Hitler*, 3, No. 190. Volkmann, 'NS-Wirtschaft', 347ff.

111. Domarus, 1, 658; Göring: *Trials of War Criminals before the Military Tribunal (TWC)* 12, 051-NI, 460ff.

112. *Goebbels TB*, 23 January 1937.

113. Ibid., 28 January 1937. Kershaw, *Hitler*, 2, 82f., erroneously gives the date as 1938.

114. Domarus, 1, 664ff., quotes 667f. and 676.

115. Hildebrand, *Reich*, 252ff.

116. For example to the former British air minister, Lord Londonderry, in February 1936, in an interview with Ward Price in March, in his speech to the Reichstag on 7 March 1936 (on the occasion of the reoccupation of the Rhineland), in the German 'peace plan' of April 1936, and at the Reich Party Rally in September 1936. On Londonderry see Kershaw, *Hitlers Freunde in England*.

Lord Londonderry und der Weg in den Krieg (Munich, 2005), 169ff.; on Ward Price see Domarus, 1, 598ff. On the Reichstag speech of March 1936 and on the 'peace plan' see above pp. 443f and pp. 445f.

117. Hildebrand, *Reich*, 357ff.

118. *PA* 1936, 1076: The colonial issue was not acute, even though Hitler had referred to it at the Party Rally. See ibid., 1106 and 1126f.; *PA* 1937, No. 377.

119. Hildebrand, *Reich*, refers to a threat of 'colonial sanctions'.

120. BAB, R 18/5514, 29 September 1936; Barkai, *Boykott*, 127; Adam, *Judenpolitik*, 159ff. (also on the passage of further legislation).

121. IfZ, 3939-NG, Reich Interior Minister to state secretary Fritz Reinhardt (Finance Ministry), 18 December 1936; Adam refers to this in *Judenpolitik*, 161.

122. Barkai, *Boykott*, 127, on the basis of the file BAB, R 2/31.097.

123. Adam, *Judenpolitik*, 163ff.

124. Besier, *Kirchen*, 3, 706f.; Law to alter the law on Grundschulen and the Abolition of Pre-schools, 18 April 1936 in *RGBl.* 1936 I, 372; *Regierung Hitler*, 3, 189, note 1: The minister of education proposed that the law should only be published after the Reichstag election.

125. Besier, *Kirchen*, 3, 710ff. In May 1936 the DAF issued a ban on simultaneous membership of the DAF and the Catholic Kolping Association. The Catholic youth associations in particular were subject to pressure during the sex abuse trials.

126. Rapp, *Devisenprozesse*, 81. The currency trials were, however, soon halted, probably in view of the much more promising prospects offered by the sex abuse trials.

127. See Frick's polemic in the *VB* of 29 June 1936; it represented the provisional high point of a press campaign, which, however, was not pursued with full force. See *PA* 1936, 533f., 546, 626, 657, and 670. See also Hockerts, *Sittlichkeitsprozesse*, 64f. and 82f.; Reinhard Heydrich, 'Die Bekämpfung der Staatsfeinde', in *Deutsches Recht*, 15 April 1936, 121–3.

128. *Goebbels TB*, 29 May and 4 July 1936. Otherwise, during this period, the campaign did not play a role in Goebbels's diaries.

129. Hockerts, *Sittlichkeitsprozesse*, 65, quotes a directive from the Justice Ministry, 13 July 1936.

130. Hockerts, *Sittlichkeitsprozesse*, 66; Besier, *Kirchen*, 3, 739ff.

131. *Goebbels TB*, 21 October 1936.

132. *Akten Bischöfe*, 3, No. 316.

133. Ludwig Volk (ed.), *Akten Kardinal Michael Faulhabers*, 2 (Paderborn, 1978), No. 572. Hess was present at the meeting although he remained silent.

134. These events are extensively documented in Joachim Kuropka (ed.), *Zur Sache – Das Kreuz! Untersuchungen zur Geschichte des Konflikts um Kreuz und Lutherbild in den Schulen Oldenburgs, zur Wirkungsgeschichte eines Massenprotestes und zum Problem nationalsozialistischer Herrschaft in einer agrarisch-katholischen Region* (Vechta, 1987).

135. *RGBl.* 1936 I, 993; for the history and content of the law see Michael Buddrus, *Totale Erziehung für den totalen Krieg. Hitler Jugend und nationalsozialistische Jugendpolitik*, 1 (Munich, 2003), 250ff.

136. *Akten Faulhabers*, No. 592.

137. Ibid., No. 599.

138. On Hitler's response to the meeting with Faulhaber see *Goebbels TB*, 6, 10, and 15 November 1936.

139. Ibid., 5 January 1937.

CONFLICT WITH THE CHURCHES AND CULTURAL POLICY

1. *Goebbels TB*, 31 January 1937; *Regierung Hitler,* 4, No. 23f.

2. *Regierung Hitler*, 3, No. 587. Eltz visited Faulhaber on 13 December 1936 for a discussion about Church policy. Faulhaber gave him a report on the meeting with Hitler on 4 November 1936.

3. *Goebbels TB*, 5 January 1937.

4. BAB, R 43 II/945, Statement by the Minister of Transport. 20 January 1937. Hitler had removed the draft law from the agenda of the next cabinet meeting. See ibid., minute of 26 January 1937.

5. On Kerrl's policy see Meier, *Kirchenkampf,* 2, 78ff.; Besier, *Kirchen,* 3, 631ff.

6. *Goebbels TB*, 14 January 1937. The use of the Goebbels diaries for this topic by Hockerts is of fundamental importance. See Hockerts, 'Die Goebbels-Tagebücher 1932–1941. Eine neue Hauptquelle zur Erforschung der national-sozialistischen Kirchenpolitik', in Dieter Albrecht (ed.), *Politik und Konfession. Festschrift für Konrad Repgen zum 60. Geburtstag* (Berlin, 1983), 371ff.

7. *Goebbels TB*, 16 February 1937.

8. *Dokumente Kirchenpolitik*, 3, No. 149 II.

9. Hockerts, 'Goebbels-Tagebücher', 372f.; *PA* 1937, No. 424; *VB* (B), 'Befriedungswerk des Führers für die evangelische Kirche' (headline).

10. *Goebbels TB*, 23 February 1937; Hockerts, 'Goebbels-Tagebücher', 374 and 379.

11. Ibid., 374; Meier, *Kirchenkampf,* 2, 154.

12. For details see Besier, *Kirchen,* 3, 657ff., and 693 on the Concordat negotiations.

13. Heinz Albert Raem, *Pius XI und der Nationalsozialismus. Die Enzyklika 'Mit brennender Sorge' vom 14. März 1937* (Paderborn, 1979); Besier, *Kirchen,* 3, 777ff.

14. *Goebbels TB*, 23 March 1937; *Dokumente Kirchenpolitik*, 4, No. 10 II.

15. *ADAP* D 1, No. 642, Reference to Hitler's directive of 6 April 1937. On this dating see Hockerts, *Sittlichkeitsprozesse*, 73.

16. *Goebbels TB*, 2 April 1937. Goebbels sent someone to Brussels to report.

17. Ibid., 29 and 30 April 1937; *PA* 1937, No. 985 and No. 991. The *VB* was used as the main newspaper for the campaign. See Hockerts, *Sittlichkeitsprozesse*, 96ff., also 99 on the background to the Belgian murder case.

18. Hockerts, *Sittlichkeitsprozesse*, 48ff.

19. *Goebbels TB*, 12 May 1937.

20. Domarus, 1, 689ff., quote, 690f.

21. On the preparation of the speech see *Goebbels TB*, 25 and 26 May 1937.

22. Ibid., 28 May 1937.

23. *VB*, 29 May 1937. On the speech see *Goebbels TB*, 30 May 1937; on the response ibid., 31 May and 1 June 1937. On the instructions to the press see *PA* 1937, Nos. 1221, 1245, and 1256. See also Hockerts, *Sittlichkeitsprozesse*, 112ff.

24. *ADAP* D 1, No. 658.

25. This was a reply to Pacelli's statement of 21 May in response to the first German complaints about Mundelein, in which Pacelli had asked what the German government was doing about the abuse of Church figures in Germany *ADAP* D 1, No. 655.

26. *ADAP* D 1, No. 705, according to Raem, *Pius XI.*, 159f., on 22 June 1937. *ADAP* D 1, No. 661; Besier, *Kirchen*, 3, 799ff.

27. *ADAP* D 1, No. 681.

28. Barely legible.

29. *Goebbels TB*, 3 June 1937.

30. PA 1937, Nos. 1333, 1371, 1435, 1491, 1518, 1571, and 1600.

31. Domarus, 1, 520, 544, 612, and 614.

32. Excerpts of the speech in Domarus, 1, 702ff., quote 704. He had made similar statements on 6 June 1937 in Regensburg. See ibid., 698ff. (relevant quote on 700).

33. The date of 25 July is clear from *Goebbels TB*, 26 July 1937. Hockerts, *Sittlichkeitsprozesse*, 74, gives 21 July as the date of the decision. For the announcement of a pause in the trials see *PA* 1937, No. 1848.

34. *Goebbels TB*, 5, 7, 8, 10, 11, and 13 August 1937.

35. Rolf Eilers, *Die nationalsozialistische Schulpolitik. Eine Studie zur Funktion der Erziehung im totalitären Staat* (Cologne and Opladen, 1963); Jörg Thierfelder, 'Die Auseinandersetzungen um Schulreform und Religionsunterricht im Dritten Reich zwischen Staat und evangelischer Kirche in Württemberg', in Manfred Heinemann (ed.), *Erziehung und Schulung im Dritten Reich*, 1 (Stuttgart, 1980), 230–50; Agnes Lange-Stuke, *Die Schulpolitik. Im Dritten Reich. Die katholische Bekenntnisschule im Bistum Hildesheim von 1933 bis 1948* (Hildesheim, 1989).

36. BAB, R 43 II/945, Statements by various ministries in summer 1937; Minute of 9 August 1937 on not signing; 10 August 1937, request for it to be presented again on 20 August 1937. The matter was not raised again.

37. *Goebbels TB*, 6 November 1937.

38. Ibid., 7 December 1937.

39. Ibid., 22 December 1937.

40. Domarus, 1, 742.

41. Ibid., 745. Domarus noted here information from one of the propaganda chiefs.

42. Ibid., 761ff., quotes 761f.

43. Edict of the Führer and Reich Chancellor concerning the Creation of a National Prize for Art and Scholarship. See *RGBl.* 1937 I, 305.

44. Hans Kerrl (ed.), *Reichstagung in Nürnberg 1937. Der Parteitag der Arbeit* (Berlin, 1938), 77ff.

45. *VB* (B), 31 January 1938, 'Der Führer empfängt die Träger des Deutschen Nationalpreises für Kunst und Wissenschaft'.

46. *Goebbels TB*, 6 and 7 June 1937.

47. Ibid., 19 June 1937; Hoffmann, *Hitler*, 143ff. See also Karl Heinz Meissner, "'DeutschesVolk, gib uns vier Jahre Zeit...' " Nationalsozialistische Kunstpolitik 1933–37. Große deutsche Kunstausstellung – Ausstellung "Entartete Kunst" München 1937', in Jürgen Harten, Hans-Werner Schmidt, and Marie Luise Syringe (eds), *Die Axt hat geblüht... Europäische Konflikte der 30er Jahre in Erinnerung an die frühe Avantgarde, 11. Oktober bis 6. Dezember 1987* (Düsseldorf, 1987), 368–76; Meissner, 'Große Deutsche Kunstausstellung', in *Stationen der Moderne. Die bedeutenden Kunstausstellungen des 20. Jahrhunderts in Deutschland. Ausstellungskatalog* (Berlin, 1988), 276–84; Ines Schlenker, *Hitler's Salon. The 'Große Deutsche Kunstausstellung' at the Haus der Deutschen Kunst in Munich 1937–1944* (Oxford, 2007).

48. On the preparations for this exhibition see *Goebbels TB*, 5, 12, and 19 June. Mario-Andreas von Lüttichau, "'Deutsche Kunst". Der Katalog', in Peter-Klaus Schuster (ed.), *Die 'Kunststadt' München 1937. Nationalsozialismus und 'Entartete Kunst'* (Munich, 1987), 120–83, provides a reconstruction of the exhibition 'Entartete Kunst'. See also Meissner, "'Volk"'; Katrin Engelhardt, 'Die Ausstellung "Entartete Kunst" in Berlin 1938. Rekonstruktion und Analyse', in Uwe Fleckner, *Angriff auf die Avantgarde. Kunst und Kunstpolitik im Nationalsozialismus* (Berlin, 2007), 89–187; Christoph Zuschlag, *'Entartete Kunst'. Ausstellungsstrategien im Nazi-Deutschland* (Worms, 1995); *Führer durch die Ausstellung*.

49. *Goebbels TB*, 30 June 1937.

50. Ibid., 1 July 1937. The edict of 30 June is published in Engelhardt, 'Ausstellung', 94. On the preparations for the exhibition see, in particular, Zuschlag, *'Kunst'*, 169ff.

51. Engelhardt, 'Ausstellung', 94.

52. On the Goebbels family's itinerary see *Goebbels TB*, 4–10 July. Hitler had already invited Goebbels to the Obersalzberg when the latter asked him for leave.

53. Ibid., 12 July 1937.

54. Zuschlag, *'Kunst'*; *Führer durch die Ausstellung*.

55. When the exhibition was finally shown in Berlin it was not 'educational enough' for Goebbels. He thus had it rearranged. See *Goebbels TB*, 28 February, 1 and 2 March 1938.

56. Ibid., 1 August 1937.

57. Zuschlag, *'Kunst'*, 205ff., on this second wave of confiscations and the subsequent disposal of the works; Law concerning the Confiscation of the Products of Degenerate Art of 31 May 1938 (*RGBl*. 1938 I, 612). See also Longerich, *Goebbels*, 349.

58. *Reichstagung Nürnberg 1934*, speech on culture, 140ff., esp. 157.

59. Domarus, 1, 705ff., quotes 705f. and 708–10.

60. Reports in the *VB* (N), 18 July 1937.

61. Only a few days after this speech the Law concerning the Confiscation of the Products of Degenerate Art of 31 May 1938 was promulgated. See *RGBl*. 1938 I, 612.

62. *Reden des Führers am Parteitag der Arbeit* 1937 (Munich, 1937), speech on culture, 26–50, esp. 34; *Reden des Führers am Parteitag Großdeutschland 1938*, speech on culture 29–46, esp. 33; on the opening of the Greater German Art Exhibition of 1938 see Domarus, 1, 705ff., esp. 708.

63. Domarus, 2, 1218f., quote, 1218.

64. On the nineteenth century as his model see his speech on the opening of the 1938 art exhibition in Domarus, 1, 878.

65. See the seminal study by Schwarz, *Geniewahn*. On Hitler's favourite painters see also the list in Picker, *Tischgespräche*, 687 (Picker's comments).

66. Schwarz, *Geniewahn*, 71.

67. Ibid., 237f.

68. Ibid., 70ff., 180, and 271f. In 1938/39 Hitler ordered the transfer of the Schack-Galerie, which was owned by Prussia, to the Reich and gave instructions that, together with the paintings owned by Bavaria, it should be turned into a gallery for German nineteenth-century artists. He also planned after the war to exhibit his own collection of paintings in the gallery, which had become vacant, until the Führer museum in Linz had been completed.

69. Ibid., 73f.

70. Ibid., 105ff., based on the catalogue of the collection now housed in the Library of Congress.

71. Ibid., 160ff.

72. Ibid., 179ff.

73. Ibid., 133ff.

74. Ibid., 189ff.

75. In 1925 Hitler had already prepared a detailed plan for a German National Museum, in which he intended to reflect through the organization of the space the relative importance of the most important artists. See ibid., 103ff.

76. Ibid., 221ff.

77. Ibid., 232ff.; Schwarz, *Hitlers Museum. Die Fotoalben Gemäldegalerie Linz. Dokumente zum 'Führermuseum'* (Vienna, Cologne, and Weimar, 2002); Günther Haase, *Die Kunstsammlung Adolf Hitler. Eine Dokumentation* (Berlin, 2002).

78. 'Kulturtagung 1935', 38; 'Der Führer auf der Kulturtagung', in *Reden des Führers am Parteitag der Ehre 1936* (Munich, 1936), 41.

79. *Reden des Führers am Parteitag der Arbeit 1937* (Munich, 1937), 26–50, quotes 47f.

80. For instances of this contemporary title, which was often used, see Barbara Miller Lane, *Architektur und Politik in Deutschland 1918–1945* (Brunswick, 1986), 237.

81. Speaking to Goebbels. See *Goebbels TB*, 8 April 1941.

82. On antiquity as a model see, for example, the speech on culture in *Die Reden Adolf Hitlers am Reichsparteitag 1933* (Munich, 1933), 22–31, esp. 27; Domarus, 1, 878; Thomas Mathieu, *Kunstauffassungen und Kulturpolitik im Nationalsozialismus. Studien zu Adolf Hitler, Joseph Goebbels, Alfred Rosenberg, Baldur von Schirach, Heinrich Himmler, Albert Speer, Wihelm Frick* (Saarbrücken, 1997), 28ff.

83. Schwarz, *Geniewahn*, 83ff.

84. Alexander Kropp, *Die politische Bedeutung der NS-Repräsentationsarchitektur. Die Neugestaltungspläne Albert Speers für den Umbau Berlins zur 'Welthauptstadt Germania' 1936–1942/43* (Neuried, 2005), 85f.; Hans J. Reichhardt and Wolfgang Schäche, *Von Berlin nach Germania. Über die Zerstörungen der 'Reichshauptstadt' durch Albert Speers Neugestaltungsplanungen* (Berlin, 1998), 49ff.

85. Domarus, 1, 664ff., 674; Edict concerning the Appointment of a General Buildings Inspector for the Reich Capital. See *RGBl.* 1937 I, 103ff.

86. Law concerning the Redevelopment of German Cities of 4 October 1937. See *RGBl.* 1937 I, 1054; Decrees concerning the Redevelopment of the Reich Capital Berlin, 5 November 1937. See ibid., 1162; Second Edict concerning a General Buildings Inspector for the Reich Capital and the First Decree to Implement the Edict concerning a General Buildings Inspector for the Reich Capital of 20 January 1938. See *RGBl.* 1938 I, 35. See also Jost Dülffer, Jochen Thies, and Josef Henke, *Hitlers Städte. Baupolitik im Dritten Reich. Eine Dokumentation* (Cologne and Vienna, 1978); Thies, *Architekt*; Werner Durth and Winfried Nerdinger (eds), *Architektur und Städtebau der 30er/40er Jahre* (Bonn, 1993); Helmut Weihsmann, *Bauen unterm Hakenkreuz. Architektur des Untergangs* (Vienna, 1998); Dieter Bartetzko, *Illusionen in Stein. Stimmungsarchitektur im Nationalsozialismus* (Berlin, 2012).

87. Press statement of 29 April 1938 (as a facsimile in Dülffer, Thies, and Henke, *Städte*, 168ff.); on Munich see, in particular, Weihsmann, *Bauen*, 650ff.

88. Hermann Giesler, *Ein anderer Hitler. Bericht seines Architekten Hermann Giesler. Erlebnisse, Gespräche, Reflexionen* (Leoni am Starnberger See, 1997), 107ff., 152ff., and 241ff.

89. Edict of the Führer and Reich Chancellor concerning the Redevelopment of the Capital of the Movement, 21 December 1938 (*RGBl.* 1938 I, 1891f.); Certificate of Appointment dated 21 December 1938 in Giesler, *Hitler*, Facsimile, 144.

90. Dülffer, Thies, and Henke, *Städte*, 191.

91. Reichsstatthalter Hamburg to the Reich and Prussian Minister of Transport, 7 September 1936, on Hitler's idea for an Elbe bridge, which he had 'mentioned over a year ago'. See Dülffer, Thies, and Henke, *Städte*, facsimile, 194f.; Edict of the Führer and Reich Chancellor concerning the Construction of the Elbe Bridge in Hamburg, 31 May 1938. See *RGBl.* 1938 I, 611f.; Führer edict concerning Urban Building Projects in the Hansa City of Hamburg, 17 February 1939 (*RGBl.* 1939 I, 265). On the plan to redevelop Hamburg see Weihsmann, *Bauen*, 407ff.

92. Speer to Lammers, 15 February 1939 (Dülffer, Thies, and Henke, *Städte*, facsimile, 257); Giesler, *Hitler*, 213ff.; Weihsmann, *Bauen*, 942ff.

93. Führer edicts, 17 February 1939 (*RGBl.* 1939 I, 363ff.).

94. Speer, *Erinnerungen*, 191.

95. Described in detail for the individual cities in Weihsmann, *Bauen*.

96. Examples in Nerdinger (ed.), *Bauen*, 28ff., for Bavaria.

97. Examples in Weihsmann, *Bauen*, 247 (Augsburg), 267 (Bayreuth), 297 (Bochum), 365 (Dortmund), 840f. (Stuttgart), 912 (Würzburg), and 868ff. (Weimar).

98. Angela Schönberger, *Die Neue Reichskanzlei von Albert Speer. Zum Zusammenhang von nationalsozialistischer Ideologie und Architektur* (Berlin, 1981), 23ff.

99. *Die Kunst im Dritten Reich*, 3 (1939), 279.

100. BAB, R 43 II/1181a, Minutes of the meetings on 29 March and 5 July 1938; Schönberger, *Reichskanzlei*, 38ff.

101. Ibid., 40; the sketch is portrayed there as Plan 24 (Source Archive A. Speer).

102. BAB, R 43 II/1051, 1051a and c, and 1052a. The file 1051 contains Speer's first bill re: Preparations for the Redevelopment of Vossstrasse 2–4 of 25 November 1935. In the files 1051a and c there are letters from Speer to Lammers of 22 and 28 May 1936 concerning Hitler's approval of the plans that had been submitted. See Schönberger, *Reichskanzlei*, 40f.

103. BAB, R 43 II/1052a, Lammers to the Finance Minister Schwerin von Krosigk, 16 October 1936; Schönberger, *Reichskanzlei*, 41.

104. BAB, R 43 II/1052a, Speer to Lammers, 17 May 1937; Schönberger, *Reichskanzlei*, 43f.

105. Published in ibid., 177ff.; *VB* (M), 3 August 1938, 'Der Führer bei den Arbeitern am Neubau der Reichskanzlei'.

106. Schönberger, *Reichskanzlei*, 68f.

107. For a detailed description of the building see ibid., 70ff.

108. See his speeches on the opening of the first and second German Architecture and Art Exhibitions in January and December 1938. See Domarus, 1, 778ff. and 983ff.

109. *PA* 1938, Nos 268 and 282.

110. Lars Olaf Larsson, *Die Neugestaltung der Reichshauptstadt. Albert Speers Generalbebauungsplan für Berlin* (Stuttgart, 1978); Kropp, *Bedeutung*, esp. 115ff.; Reichardt and Schäche, *Berlin*, esp. 80ff.

111. Domarus, 1, 983ff., quote 984.

112. Dülffer, Thies, and Henke, *Städte*, 289ff., quote 297f.

113. Markus Urban, *Die Konsensfabrik. Funktion und Wahrnehmung der NS-Reichsparteitage 1933–1941* (Göttingen, 2007), 379ff.; Sabine Behrenbeck, *Der Kult um die toten Helden* (Vierow bei Greifswald, 1996), 326ff.

114. Urban, *Konsensfabrik*, 382ff.

115. *VB*, 13 September 1936. The rhetorical climax of this section, the 'we are now one', was omitted in later Party publications. See *Reden Parteitag 1936*, 47–50, quote 48. This was pointed out by Hubert Cancik, '"Wir sind jetzt eins". Rhetorik und Mystik in einer Rede Hitlers (Nürnberg 11.9.36)', in Günter Kehrer (ed.), *Zur Religionsgeschichte der Bundesrepublik Deutschland* (Munich, 1980), 24. Cancik provides a comprehensive interpretation of the speech and highlights, expounding, among other things, the use of biblical references.

116. For a description of the sacrificial ceremony on 9 November and its interpretation see Behrenbeck, *Kult*, 299ff.

117. Domarus, 1, 555f.

118. Behrenbeck, *Kult*, 376f, quoted from the original soundtrack of the speech in the film 'Ewige Wache' of 1936.

119. Domarus, 1, 892ff., quotes 893f.

120. Speer, *Tagebücher*, 403. Speer, however, interprets this 'canonization' as if Hitler was wanting to establish a Church, which is contrary to his statements on this issue.

HITLER'S REGIME

1. Huber, *Verfassungsrecht*, 194.

2. Ibid., 230.

3. Ibid., 237; Lothar Gruchmann, 'Die "Reichsregierung" im Führerstaat. Stellung und Funktion des Kabinetts im nationalsozialistischen Herrschaftssystem', in Günter Doeker-Mach (ed.), *Klassenjustiz und Pluralismus. Festschrift für Ernst Fraenkel zum 75. Geburtstag am 26. Dezember 1973* (Hamburg, 1973), 188; Dieter Rebentisch, *Führerstaat und Verwaltung im Zweiten Weltkrieg. Verfassungsentwicklung und Verfassungspolitik 1939–1945* (Stuttgart, 1989), 43f.

4. Gruchmann, '"Reichsregierung"', 193.

5. Rebentisch, *Führerstaat*, 41; for details see BAB, R 43 II/138c and 1386b.

6. Rebentisch, *Führerstaat*, 46ff.

7. Gruchmann, '"Reichsregierung"', 193.

8. Examples in Kershaw, *Hitler*, 1, 675, and, for wartime, in Rebentisch, *Führerstaat*, 380ff.

9. Broszat, *Staat*, 360ff.

10. *Regierung Hitler* 4, No. 21. On the plans see *Goebbels TB*, 7 and 25 August 1935, 27 January 1937, 7 March and 12 May 1938, 3 November 1939, and 2 December 1944.

11. Führer edict concerning the Deputizing for and Succession to the Führer and Reich Chancellor of 7 December 1934 (BAB, R 43 II/1660); Law concerning the Succession to the Führer and Reich Chancellor, 13 December 1934 (IfZ, 1206–NG); after the promulgation of the law he renewed the regulation of the succession in a further Führer edict of 19 December 1934. The procedure is documented in *Regierung Hitler*, 2, Nos 58 and 63.

12. Hitler's directive of 2 June 1933, in Armin Nolzen, 'Die Reichsorganisationsleitung als Verwaltungsbehörde der NSDAP. Kompetenzen, Strukturen und administrative Praktiken nach 1933', in Sven Reichardt und Wolfgang Seibel (eds), *Der prekäre Staat. Herrschen und Verwalten im Nationalsozialismus* (Frankfurt a. M., 2011), 125.

13. Nolzen, 'Reichsorganisationsleitung'.

14. Ulf Lükemann, 'Der Reichsschatzmeister der NSDAP. Ein Beitrag zur inneren Parteistruktur', Dissertation, Berlin, 1963, 50f.

15. Longerich, *Stellvertreter*, 99ff.

16. Ibid., 40ff.

17. Nolzen, 'NSDAP', 101; Michael H. Kater, *The Nazi Party. A Social Profile of Members and Leaders 1919–1945* (Cambridge, MA and Oxford, 1983), 264.

18. *Parteistatistik der NSDAP. Stand 1. Januar 1935*, 4 vols (Munich, 1936), 2, 3.

19. Nolzen, 'NSDAP', 109.

20. *Parteistatistik* 3, 4.

21. *Parteistatistik* 2, 7 (beginning of 1935); this proportion remained the same in the following years. See Nolzen, 'NSDAP', 109.

22. Carl-Wilhelm Reibel, *Das Fundament der Diktatur. Die NSDAP-Ortsgruppe, 1932–1945* (Paderborn, 2002), 49ff.

23. Ibid., 273.

24. Ibid., 111ff. Not every post was always filled in every local branch.

25. Reichsorganisationsleiter der NSDAP (ed.), *Organisationsbuch der NSDAP*, 2nd edn (Munich, 1937), 29.

26. Reibel, *Fundament*, 56ff.

27. Ibid., 271ff.

28. Dieter Rebentisch, 'Die "politische Beurteilung" als Herrschaftsinstrument der NSDAP', in Detlev Peukert and Jürgen Reulecke (eds), *Die Reihen fast geschlossen. Beiträge zur Geschichte des Alltags unterm Nationalsozialismus* (Wuppertal, 1981), 107–25. Political assessments were also required for the appointment of guardians or for permission to appeal against dismissal.

29. Reibel, *Fundament*, 310.

30. Reinhard Mann, *Protest und Kontrolle im Dritten Reich. Nationalsozialistische Herrschaft im Alltag einer rheinischen Großstadt* (Frankfurt a. M. and New York, 1987), 292; Eric A. Johnson, *Der nationalsozialistische Terror. Gestapo, Juden, und gewöhnliche Deutsche* (Berlin, 2001), 364: 6 per cent of each; the numbers increased during the war.

31. Rebentisch, *Führerstaat*, 76.

32. Quoted from Gisela Miller-Kipp, '"Totale Erfassung" – aber wie? Die Hitler-Jugend: Politische Funktion, psychosoziales Funktionieren und Moment des Widerstands', in Stephanie Becker and Christoph Studt (eds), *'Und sie werden nicht mehr frei sein ihr ganzes Leben'. Funktion und Stellenwert der NSDAP, ihrer Gliederungen und angeschlossenen Verbände im 'Dritten Reich'* (Münster, 2012), 89.

33. Führer decree on the Character and Purpose of the DAF, 24 October 1934, discussed in Michael Schneider, *Unterm Hakenkreuz. Arbeiter und Arbeiterbewegung 1933 bis 1939* (Bonn, 1999), 181ff.

34. Ibid., 178ff.

35. Ibid., 195ff.

36. Rüdiger Hachtmann, *Das Wirtschaftsimperium der Deutschen Arbeitsfront 1933–1945* (Göttingen, 2012).

37. Schneider, *Hakenkreuz*, 228ff.

38. For details see Vorländer, *NSV*, 44ff.

39. Ibid., 117.

40. Miller-Kipp, '"Erfassung"'; on the HJ see above all Michael Buddrus, *Totale Erziehung für den totalen Krieg. Hitlerjugend und nationalsozialistische Jugendpolitik*, 2 vols (Munich, 2003); Michael H. Kater, *Hitler-Jugend* (Darmstadt, 2005).

41. Buddrus, *Erziehung* 1, 369ff.

42. Domarus, 1, 533.

43. Miller-Kipp, "'Erfassung'", 98.

44. *Parteistatistik* 3, 112, for 1935; Miller-Kipp, "'Erfassung'", 93f.

45. Law concerning the Hitler Youth (*RGBl.* 1936 I, 993).

46. Second Decree implementing the HJ Law, 25 March 1939 (*RGBl.* 1939 I, 710).

47. Jill Stephenson, *The Nazi Organisation of Women* (London, 1981), 97ff.

48. Domarus, 1, 449ff., quotes 450f.

49. *Parteistatistik* 3, 54f.

50. Stephenson, *Nazi Organisation*, 165. On the activities of the Deutsches Frauenwerk in general see ibid., 156ff. For further literature on the women's organizations see Dorothee Klinksiek, *Die Frau im NS-Staat* (Stuttgart, 1982); Claudia Koonz, *Mütter im Vaterland* (Freiburg i. Br., 1991); Massimiliano Livi, *Getrud Scholtz-Klink. Die Reichsfrauenführerin. Politische Handlungsräume und Identitätsprobleme der Frauen im Nationalsozialismus am Beispiel der 'Führerin aller deutscher Frauen'* (Münster, 2005).

51. Stephenson, *Nazi Organisation*, 163ff.

52. For details see Dorothee Hochstetter, *Motorisierung und Volksgemeinschaft. Das nationalsozialistische Kraftfahrkorps (NSKK) 1931–1945* (Munich, 2005).

53. Willi Feiten, *Der nationalsozialistische Lehrerbund. Entwicklung und Organisation. Ein Beitrag zum Aufbau und Organisationsstruktur des nationalsozialistischen Herrschaftssystems* (Weinheim, 1981); Michael Sunnus, *Der NS-Rechtswahrerbund (1928–1945) Zur Geschichte der nationalsozialistischen Juristenorganisation* (Frankfurt a. M., 1990); Michael Kater, *Ärzte als Hitlers Helfer* (Vienna, 2000); Grüttner, *Studenten*; Anne Christine Nagel "'Er ist der Schrecken überhapt der Hochschule". Der nationalsozialistische Deutsche Dozentenbund in der Wissenschaftspolitik des Dritten Reiches', in Joachim Scholtyseck and Christoph Studt (eds), *Universitäten und Studenten im Dritten Reich* (Berlin, 2008), 115–32.

54. On this scenario see Rüdiger Hachtmann, 'Elastisch, dynamisch und von katastrophaler Effizienz. Zur Struktur der neuen Staatlichkeit des Nationalsozialismus', in Reichardt and Seibel (eds), *Prekärer Staat*, 51.

55. The situation in 1935, according to Peter Hüttenberger, *Die Gauleiter. Studie zum Wandel, des Machtgefüges in der NSDAP* (Stuttgart, 1969), 74ff. In addition to the 30 Gauleiters in the Reich territory there was Forster (Danzig) and Bohle (Foreign Organization). Gauleiter Josef Wagner was responsible for the South Westphalian and Silesian Gaus.

56. Ibid., esp. 79f.

57. *RGBl.* 1939 I, 49ff.

58. Peter Diehl-Thiele, *Partei und Staat im Dritten Reich. Untersuchungen zum Verhältnis von NSDAP und allgemeiner innerer Staatsverwaltung 1933–1945* (Munich, 1971), 3; Hans Mommsen, *Beamtentum im Dritten Reich. Mit ausgewählten Quellen zur nationalsozialistischen Beamtenpolitik* (Stuttgart, 1966), 125.

59. Rebentisch, *Führerstaat*, 70.

60. Mommsen, 'Reichsreform und Regionalgewalten – Das Phantom der Mittelinstanz 1933–1945', in Oliver Janz (ed), *Zentralismus und Föderalismus*

im 19. Und 20. Jahrhundert (Berlin, 2000), 227–38; Walter Baum, 'Die "Reichsreform" im Dritten Reich', in *VfZ* 3 (1955), 36–56; Broszat, *Staat*, 156ff.

61. Ibid., 334ff.

62. Jacobsen, *Außenpolitik*, 252ff.

63. Hierzu Broszat, *Staat*, 332ff.

64. Hachtmann, 'Elastisch', 52ff.; Hachtmann and Winfried Süss (eds), *Hitlers Kommissare. Führerbeauftrage und sektorale Sondergewalten in der nationalsozialistischen Diktatur* (Göttingen, 2006), especially the introduction by the two editors.

65. Kube, *Pour le mérite*.

66. Longerich, *Himmler*, 399ff.

67. Martin Moll was the first to draw attention to the significance of these occasions for the cohesion of the regime. Hitherto they had been downplayed by scholars or regarded as beer evenings; see 'Steuerungsinstrument im Ämterchaos? Die Tagungen der Reichs- und Gauleiter der NSDAP', in *VfZ* 49 (2001), 215–73.

68. *Regierung Hitler* notes Reichsstatthalter conferences on 26 May, 6 July, and 28 September 1933, and on 22 March and 1 November 1934.

69. Hachtmann, 'Elastisch', 60ff.; for Gau Mecklenburg during wartime there are minutes of regular meetings of the Nazi leadership. Such meetings probably took place in the other Gaus. See Michael Buddrus (ed.), *Mecklenburg im Zweiten Weltkrieg. Die Tagungen des Gauleiters Friedrich Hildebrand mit den NS-Führungsgremien des Gaues Mecklenburg 1939–1945* (Bremen, 2009).

70. See, in particular, the memoirs of his two valets, Karl Wilhelm Krause, *Zehn Jahre (Tag und Nacht) Kammerdiener bei Hitler* (Hamburg, 1949), Heinz Linge, *Bis zum Untergang. Als Chef des persönlichen Dienstes bei Hitler*, ed. Werner Maser (Munich, 1982); see also Speer, *Erinnerungen*; Otto Dietrich, *Zwölf Jahre mit Hitler* (Munich, 1955); Wiedemann, *Mann*; *Goebbels TB*; Kershaw, *Hitler*, 1, 669ff.; Ullrich, *Hitler*, 627ff.

71. Huber, *Verfassungsrecht*, 194.

72. Ibid., 194.

73. Ibid., 157.

74. The analysis of quotations by Domarus, shows that during 1933/34 Hitler used the term 'national community' above all to appeal to the workers. After 1933 it appears less and less frequently as a topic in his speeches. In 1938 it appears again in the context of the integration of national comrades living outside the Reich. But during the war it disappeared almost completely from his vocabulary. Mentions in 1933: 18 times, 1934: 12 times, 1935: 11 times, 1936: 5 times, 1937: 13 times, 1938: 38 times.

75. See the account by Hans-Ulrich Wehler, *Deutsche Gesellschaftsgeschichte*, 4 (Munich, 2003), who gives great weight to these factors, especially pp. 771ff.

76. In view of the ambiguity and lack of definition of the concept, it is problematic to attempt to use this highly ideologically charged propaganda slogan as an analytical tool for understanding Nazi politics. For such attempts see Michael Wildt, *Volksgemeinschaft als Selbstermächtigung: Gewalt gegen Juden in der deutschen*

Provinz 1919 bis 1939 (Hamburg, 2007); Frank Bajohr and Michael Wildt (eds), *Volksgemeinschaft. Neue Forschungen zur Gesellschaft des Nationalsozialismus* (Frankfurt a. M., 2009); Martina Steber and Bernhard Gotto (eds), *Visions of Community in Nazi Germany. Social Engineering and Private Lives* (Oxford, 2014); Dietmar von Reeken and Malte Thiessen (eds), '*Volksgemeinschaft' als soziale Praxis. Neue Forschungen zur NS-Gesellschaft vor Ort* (Paderborn, 2013); Detlef Schmiechen-Ackermann (ed.), *'Volksgemeinschaft'. Mythos, wirkungsmächtige Verheißung oder soziale Realität im 'Dritten Reich'? Zwischenbilanz einer kontroversen Debatte* (Paderborn, 2012). For a critique see Ian Kershaw, '"Volksgemeinschaft". Potenzial und Grenzen eines neuen Forschungskonzepts', in *VfZ* 59 (2011), 1–17.

77. That is my fundamental reservation regarding the conclusions of Ian Kershaw's *Führer-Mythos*; see also Ludolf Herbst, *Hitlers Charisma. Die Erfindung eines deutschen Messias* (Frankfurt a. M., 2010), 270f. In 1934 a large number of reports reaching the anti-regime Sopade noted that Hitler was being largely excluded from the general criticism. However, from autumn 1934 onwards this trend was in reverse.

RESETTING FOREIGN POLICY

1. *Goebbels TB*, 23 February and 13 July 1937.
2. For example, on 4 May 1937, when he received Lord Lothian, one of the main British supporters of appeasement and Lloyd George's former secretary, in the Reich Chancellery. See James R. M. Butler, *Lord Lothian (Philip Kerr) 1882–1940* (London, 1960), 337ff. [minutes of the meeting]; Henke, *England*, 81ff. He impressed the Labour Party pacifist, George Lansbury, on 4 February 1937, as being willing to compromise. See Schmidt, *Statist*, 341f. and 349f.; on Lansbury see *Goebbels TB*, 20 April and 12 May 1937. However, General Ironside was disappointed by his visit in September. Hitler's encounter with the Duke of Windsor, recently abdicated as king, in October 1937 left Hitler with the regretful feeling that with the change of monarch the chance of an alliance with Britain had been lost forever. See Schmidt, *Statist*, 383; Henke, *England*, 67f. For an overview see Henke, *England*, 71; Bentley B. Gilbert, *Britain since 1918* (New York, 1967), 102f.
3. *Goebbels TB*, 31 May–2 June 1937, on the 'Leipzig' incident see also 20, 23, 24 June 1937. Hans-Henning Abendroth, *Hitler in der spanischen Arena. Die deutsch–spanischen Beziehungen im Spannungsfeld der europäischen Interessenpolitik vom Ausbruch des Bürgerkrieges bis zum Ausbruch des Weltkrieges 1919–1939* (Paderborn, 1973), 163ff.; Manfred Merkes, *Die deutsche Politik im spanischen Bürgerkrieg* (Bonn, 1969), 276. On the Condor Legion see Stefanie Schüler-Springorum, *Krieg und Fliegen. Die Legion Condor im spanischen Bürgerkrieg* (Paderborn, 2010).
4. *ADAP* D 3, No. 354.
5. *ADAP* C 6, No. 889, editor's note; Henke, *England*, 93ff.; Merkes, *Politik*, 290ff.
6. *Goebbels TB*, 15 March 1937. That contradicts Kershaw, *Hitler*, 2 (Stuttgart, 2000), 85, who deduces from Goebbels's notes that Hitler did not begin to 'focus on Austria and Czechoslovakia' until the summer of 1937.

7. From the end of 1936 onwards Czechoslovakia sought to stop the German press campaign. See *ADAP* C 6, No. 78, No. 153 and No. 239; Goebbels was not unreceptive to the idea of a press truce (*Goebbels TB*, 23 January), but then, at the end of March, concentrated on the Sudeten German question. See ibid., 2 and 3 March 1937. For the fundamental reorientation of German press policy towards Czechoslovakia see *PA* 1937, No. 550.

8. During his Italian visit in meetings on 15 and 23 January (*ADAP* D 1, No. 199 and No. 207f.). See also Schausberger, *Griff*, 377f.; Kube, *Pour le mérite*, 225ff.; Malcolm Muggeridge (ed.), *Ciano's Diplomatic Papers. Being a Record of Nearly 200 Conversations Held during the Years 1936–1942 with Hitler, Mussolini, Franco, Goering, Ribbentrop . . . and Many Other World Diplomatic and Military Figures* (London, 1948), 80ff.

9. On Göring's visit in April see Schmidt, *Statist*, 352f. On Neurath's visit in May see *ADAP* D 6, No. 350.

10. Schausberger, *Griff*, 378f.

11. Ibid., 408ff.; *Goebbels TB*, 13 July 1937. The banned party was given the opportunity, among other things, to appear in public; persecuted Nazis were only to be given a light sentence or amnestied, and *Mein Kampf* was permitted to be sold.

12. Schausberger, *Griff*, 410; the appointment occurred on the occasion of an assessment of the Vienna meetings on the Obersalzberg. See *Goebbels TB*, 13 July 1937; *ADAP* D 1, No. 241; Keppler's formal appointment only occurred in September by Hess.

13. Domarus 1, 711ff., quote, 711; *VB* (B), 2 August 1937, 'Überwältigende Manifestation des deutschen Volkstums' (headline). See also *Goebbels TB*, 1 and 2 August 1937.

14. Ibid., 3 August 1937.

15. Ibid., 14 September 1937.

16. Domarus 1, 726ff., quotes 729.

17. PA 1937, No. 2219. For the published text of the speech see *VB* (B), 10 September 1939, 'Dr. Goebbels enthüllt die dunklen Pläne des Bolschewismus'.

18. *ADAP* D 1, No. 2, and C 6, No. 568.

19. On the course of the visit see *VB* (B), 25–29 September 1937; Domarus 1, 733ff.

20. Schmidt, *Statist*, 375.

21. *VB*, 26 and 29 September 1937, 'Dr. Goebbels meldet den Aufmarsch von drei Millionen Menschen'; *Sopade* 1937, 1219.

22. *ADAP* D 1, No. 10; Galeazzo Ciano, *Ciano's Hidden Diary 1937–1938* (New York, 1953), 20 October 1937. On the additional protocol to the Anti-Comintern pact and other secret agreements see above p. 468.

23. *ADAP* D 1, No. 17.

24. Lipski, *Diplomat*, Doc. 73; *ADAP* D 5, No. 18. On the evening preceding the signing the deputy Polish foreign minister had a conversation with Göring, in which the latter once again emphasized that Germany had no territorial claims on Poland. See Wojciechowski, *Beziehungen*, 333f., on the basis of Polish documents.

25. See below, p. 600f.

26. This applied to the territory of the kingdom of Bohemia. See Günter Wollstein, *Das 'Großdeutschland' der Paulskirche. Nationale Ziele in der bürgerlichen Revolution von 1848/49* (Düsseldorf, 1977) 189ff.

27. Smelser, *Sudetenproblem*, 132ff.

28. *PA* 1937, Nos 2496, 2502, 2506, 2512, 2523, and 2530.

29. *Goebbels TB*, 4 November 1937. On the halt to the campaign see *ADAP* D 2, No. 11; *PA* 1937, Nos 2687 and 2702.

30. Schwarzenbeck, *Pressepolitik*, 247ff.; *ADAP* D 2, Nos 12 and 15–18.

31. Ibid., No. 29; Report of the German ambassador about the success of the Czech measures against the émigré press in ibid., No. 47. On the 'press truce' see Schwarzenbeck, *Pressepolitik*, 247ff.

32. Smelser, *Sudetenproblem*, 178ff.; Rolf Gebel, *'Heim ins Reich!' Konrad Henlein und der Reichsgau Sudetenland (1938–1945)* (Munich, 1999), 55.

33. Recorded as *IMT* 25, 386-PS, 402–13. On the history of its survival see Walter Bussmann, 'Zur Enstehung und Überlieferung der "Hoßbach Niederschrift"', in *VfZ* 16 (1968), 373–84. Bradley F. Smith, 'Die Überlieferung der Hoßbach-Niederschrift im Lichte neuer Quellen', in *VfZ* 38 (1990), 329–36.

34. Thomas Sarholz, 'Die Auswirkungen der Kontingentierung von Eisen und Stahl auf die Aufrüstung der Wehrmacht von 1936 bis 1939', Dissertation, Technical University, Darmstadt, 1983, 249ff. See also BAF, RH 15/149, General Army Office, Fromm's speaker's notes concerning the effects of the shortage of raw materials, to C in C Army 29 October 1937.

35. *Goebbels TB*, 23 February 1937.

36. This context has been overlooked by some authors in their interpretation of the Hossbach memorandum so that, as a result, they reach the erroneous conclusion that, on 5 November, Hitler revealed his plans for the establishment of an empire covering eastern Europe (living space) during the period 1943–45. Hildebrand, *Vergangene Reich*, 741, refers to the years 1943–45 as the deadline he had set for the campaign to conquer eastern Europe. See also Richard Overy, 'Hitler's War Plans and the German Economy', in Robert W. D. Boyce and Esmonde M. Robertson (eds), *Paths to War. New Essays on the Origins of the Second World War* (London, 1989), 107.

37. *IMT* 25, 386-PS, 402–13.

38. BAF, RL 3/201, note; Sarholz, 'Auswirkungen', 255ff.; Hossbach, *Wehrmacht*, 120.

39. *IMT* 34, 175-C, 734ff.

40. *ADAP* D 7, Appendix. III. K. In the appendix of 7 December 1937 to the directive for the uniform preparations for war by the Wehrmacht of 24 June 1937 Blomberg had announced that, if the political situation during 1938 did not change to Germany's disadvantage, he would no longer work on the scenario of a two-front war with the main focus on the West. See *IMT* 34, 175-C, 745ff. On this see Müller, *Heer*, 247ff.

41. Interpreter Schmidt emphasizes in his account (*Statist*, 385) that Hitler had adopted an arrogant tone demonstrating his increased self-confidence vis-à-vis Britain.
42. *ADAP* D 1, No. 31.
43. This is also clear from the assessment of the meeting by foreign minister, Neurath, who was present on 19 November. See ibid., No. 33.
44. Henke, *England*, 67f.; Schmidt, *Statist*, 383.
45. Ribbentrop, *London*, 91ff.
46. *ADAP* D 1, No. 93.
47. Michalka, *Ribbentrop*, 215ff.; Henke, *England*, 69ff.
48. *ADAP* D 5, No. 149. See Jörg K. Hoensch, *Der ungarische Revisionismus und die Zerschlagung der Tschechoslowakei* (Tübingen, 1967), 51. Hoensch assumes that Hitler revealed his plans to his Hungarian guests to a far greater extent than is suggested by the minutes. This is also indicated by the Hungarian note on the meetings between Göring, Darányi, and Kánya on 2 November 1937, which has survived. See Lajos Kerekes (ed.), *Allianz Hitler–Horthy–Mussolini. Dokumente zur ungarischen Außenpolitik* (Budapest, 1966), No. 19. On 31 March 1938, the Hungarian ambassador in Berlin told state secretary von Weizsäcker that Hitler had promised to return to Hungary the territories ceded to Czechoslovakia. See *ADAP* D 2 No. 114.
49. *ADAP* D 5, No. 29; Wojciechowski, *Beziehungen*, 386f.; Hoensch, *Revisionismus*, 58f. and 66f.
50. Ibid., 6of.; Wojciechowski, *Beziehungen*, 404f.
51. *ADAP* D 5, No. 163.

FROM THE BLOMBERG–FRITSCH CRISIS TO THE ANSCHLUSS

1. *Sopade* 1937, 9ff. (Fear of war), 33ff. (Food supplies), 53ff. (Raw materials crisis), 216ff. (Church struggle), 371ff. ((Food supplies), 480ff. (general mood, various factors), 533ff. (Corruption in the Party), 597ff. (Discontent among business-men), 641ff. (Raw materials shortages) and 659ff. (Food shortages). The discontent continued into the second half of the year.
2. Ibid., 763 (Revival of the fear of war), 919. 'People are concerned about the threat of war, partly for fear of it, partly, in the case of young people, in the hope of becoming heroes', 1085ff. (Fear of war, but also hope for war), 1365ff. ('War is increasingly seen as unavoidable, some people are afraid, others are looking forward to it.' This is true both of supporters and of opponents.')
3. Ibid, 1527ff.
4. A 'Schacht crisis' had been rumbling on since March 1937. See *Goebbels TB*, 19 and 21 March, 12 and 14 August, 5, 9, and 10 September, and 27 October 1937; Kopper, *Schacht*, 312ff.
5. *Goebbels TB*, 29 October, 2, 3, 4, and 6 November 1937.
6. Willi A. Boelcke, *Die deutsche Wirtschaft 1930–1945. Interna des Reichswirts-chaftsministeriums* (Düsseldorf, 1983), 178ff.

7. On the Blomberg–Fritsch Crisis see Müller, *Heer*, 255ff.; Karl Heinz Janssen and Fritz Tobias, *Der Sturz der Generäle. Hitler und die Blomberg–Fritsch-Krise* (Munich, 1994); Kirstin A. Schäfer, *Werner von Blomberg. Hitlers Erster Feldmarschall. Eine Biographie* (Paderborn, 2006), 180ff.

8. On the secretiveness surrounding the wedding see Hossbach, *Wehrmacht*, 105f.; *Goebbels TB*, 13 January 1938.

9. *Goebbels TB*, 26 and 27 January 1938.

10. Kube, *Pour le mérite*, 197. However, there is no firm proof of a plot by Göring against Blomberg.

11. Janssen and Tobias, *Sturz*, 86ff.

12. Ibid., 104ff.

13. *Goebbels TB*, 26 January and 1 February 1938; various similar entries between 26 January and 2 February 1938.

14. Wiedemann, *Mann*, 112; Nikolaus von Below, *Als Hitlers Adjutant 1937–1945* (Mainz, 1980), 67.

15. *Goebbels TB*, 1 February 1938; Hossbach, *Wehrmacht*, 111; Wiedemann, *Mann*, 113; Below, *Adjutant*, 67.

16. See the worried entries in *Goebbels TB*, 28 January, 2, 3, and 4 February 1938.

17. Ibid., 2–5 February 1938.

18. Domarus, 1, 781.

19. BAB, R 43 II/1660, Führer edict, 23 April 1938.

20. Edict concerning the Command of the Wehrmacht (*RGBl.* 1938 I, 111); for the announcement of the various appointments see Domarus, 1, 783ff.

21. For the details of the reshuffle see Janssen and Tobias, *Sturz*, 148ff.; *PA* 1938, Nos 359 and 361.

22. As Hitler put it in his article 'Die Reichskanzlei', although in it he maintained that he had assigned the whole project to Speer on 10 January, whereas, in fact, the latter had been working on it for two years. For Hitler's order for the completion of the building dated 27 January 1938 see Schönberger, *Reichskanzlei*, 176, sourced in BAB, R 43 II/1052; see also 46ff. Hitler retrospectively gave as his motive for speeding up the construction his 'decision' to incorporate Austria and establish the 'Greater German Reich'.

23. *Goebbels TB*, 6 February 1938. *Regierung Hitler*, 5, No. 35, notes the address without giving further details. The communiqué about the meeting, which was issued in the evening is in BAB, R 43 II/1477.

24. Janssen and Tobias, *Sturz*, 173ff.

25. Domarus, 1, 842.

26. Ibid., 881.

27. On Göring's initiatives in 1933 see above p. 366. In 1936, he once again made a number of such statements. *ADAP* D 1, No. 169, contains details of the meeting between Göring and Schuschnigg on 10 October. On the following day Göring told the Hungarian foreign minister Austria must sooner or later join up with Germany. See Kerekes (ed.), *Allianz*, No. 14. On 26 October Göring explained his plans for their future relationship to the Austrian ambassador. The latter

concluded that the Germans 'had not yet given up their plans for a Greater Germany'. See *Der Hochverratsprozess gegen Dr. Guido Schmidt vor dem Wiener Volksgericht. Die gerichtlichen Protokolle, mit den Zeugenaussagen, unveröffentlichen Dokumenten, sämtlichen Geheimbriefen und Geheimakten* (Vienna, 1947), 489ff. In January and April 1937 Göring launched initiatives with Mussolini, see above p. 528. See also *Hochverratsprozess*, 299ff., where Göring, during his interrogation by the Austrian judicial authorities in 1946, emphasized that he had always been assertive in his demand for Anschluss with Austria. See also Kube, *Pour le mérite*, 215ff.; Martens, *Göring*, 114ff.

28. *Goebbels TB*, 13 July 1937; *PA* 1937, No. 1729.
29. *ADAP* D 1, Nr. 256.
30. See Göring's statement of 6 July 1946 to the Austrian judge, Sucher, in Nuremberg in *Hochverratsprozess*, 299ff. As a starting point for the conversation he had shown Mussolini a fresco-style map of central Europe in which Austria was already included as part of the Reich.
31. *ADAP* C 6, No. 568.
32. In November 1937 Göring made it very clear to the US ambassador in Paris, William Bullitt, that Austria and the Sudetenland had to be included in the Reich. See *Foreign Relations of the United States* 1937 I, 171ff., and *IMT* 37, 151-L 152ff. During the same month he showed the same map to the Austrian foreign minister, Schmidt, during his visit to Carinhall that he had shown to Mussolini in September. See *Hochverratsprozess*, 300; Kube, *Pour le mérite*, 238f. See also Kerekes (ed.), *Allianz*, No. 19.
33. Weinberg, *Foreign Policy*, 502f.
34. Schausberger, *Griff*; Dokumentationsarchiv des österreichischen Widerstandes (ed.), *'Anschluß' 1938 Eine Dokumentation*, compiled by Heinz Arnberger et al. (Vienna, 1988); *Anschluss 1938. Protokoll des Symposiums in Wien am 14. und 15. März 1978* (Vienna, 1981); Gerhard Botz, *Die Eingliederung Österreichs in das Deutsche Reich. Planung und Verwirklichung des politisch-administrativen Anschlusses (1938–1940)* (Vienna, 1976); Botz, *Nationalsozialismus in Wien. Machtübernahme, Herrschaftssicherung, Radikalisierung 1938/39* (Vienna, 2008); Werner Welzig (ed.), *'Anschluss'. März/April 1938 in Österreich* (Vienna, 2010); Gerhard Stourzh and Brigitta Zaar (eds), *Österreich, Deutschland und die Mächte. Internationale und österreichische Aspekte des 'Anschlusses' vom März 1936* (Vienna, 1990); Weinberg, *Foreign Policy*, 484ff.
35. Schausberger, *Griff*, 496ff.
36. *Goebbels TB*, 15 December 1937.
37. Karl Stuhlpfarrer, 'Der deutsche Plan einer Währungsunion mit Österreich' in *Anschluss 1938*, 290.
38. *ADAP* D 1, No. 80.
39. Ibid., No. 280; Schausberger, *Griff*, 507ff.
40. On Göring's plan for a currency union see Kube, *Pour le mérite*, 238ff.; Stuhlpfarrer, 'Plan'. There is important information in the Reich Finance Ministry file BAB, R 2/14.599, which contains, in particular, the minutes of an

inter-ministerial meeting on 21 February held to discuss this matter. See also the minute of the RFM on this discussion on 23 February 1938: 'President Keppler and his assistant Dr. Wesemaier [Veesenmayer, P.L.] stated that the Führer and Field-Marshal Göring want a complete currency union'. On the same day Göring also advocated the project in a meeting with Hitler (see below p. 547).

41. Schausberger, *Griff*, 498f. and 519ff.; *ADAP* D 1, No. 273; Papen, *Wahrheit*, 458ff.
42. Schausberger, *Griff*, 514f.; *ADAP* D 1, No. 293.
43. Ibid., No. 294f.; Schausberger, *Griff*, 519ff.; Kershaw, *Hitler*, 2, 116ff.; Weinberg, *Foreign Policy*, 506ff.; Kurt Schuschnigg, *Im Kampf gegen Hitler. Die Überwindung der Anschlussidee* (Munich and Vienna, 1969), 233ff., on the encounter. On the presence of the generals see Below, *Adjutant*, 84f.; Werner Maser (ed.), *Wilhelm Keitel, Mein Leben: Pflichterfüllung bis zum Untergang. Hitlers Generalfeldmarschall und Chef des Oberkommandos der Wehrmacht in Selbstzeugnissen* (Berlin, 1998), 217.
44. *Goebbels TB*, 21 February 1938.
45. Ibid., 19 and 20 February 1938; *PA* 1938, No. 444; Ralf Richard Koerner, *So haben sie es damals gemacht. Die Propagandavorbereitungen zum Österreichanschluss durch das Hitlerregime 1933–1938. Die publizistische Behandlung der Österreichfrage und die Anschlussvorbereitungen in der Tagespresse des Dritten Reiches (1933–1938)* (Vienna, 1958), 68ff.
46. *IMT* 28, 1780-PS, 367; Erwin A. Schmidl, *März 38. Der deutsche Einmarsch in Österreich* (Vienna, 1987), 31f.
47. Peter Broucek (ed.), *Ein General im Zwielicht. Die Erinnerungen Edmund Glaises von Horstenau*, 3 vols (Vienna, 1980–88), 2, 238ff.
48. Schausberger, *Griff*, 535ff.
49. Domarus, 1, 792ff., quotes 801 and 803; see Kershaw, *Hitler*, 1, 118f.
50. *ADAP* D 1, No. 318.
51. Schausberger, *Griff*, 542f.; Weinberg, *Foreign Policy*, 510ff.
52. *PA* 1939, Nos 557, 564, and 618: 'Zurückhaltung' und 'Vorsicht'; *Goebbels TB*, 1 March 1938; Koerner, *Propagandavorbereitungen*, 75ff.
53. *ADAP* D 1, No. 328; Schausberger, *Griff*, 543f.; Kershaw, *Hitler*, 1, 118f.
54. BAB, R 2/14.599, Minute, 1 March 1938, on Keppler's statement.
55. *ADAP* D 1, No. 138; Nevile Henderson, *Fehlschlag einer Mission. Berlin 1937–1939* (Zurich, 1940), 129ff.
56. This is the apt summing up of the situation in Schuschnigg, *Kampf*, 295.
57. On Keppler's activities see his reports in *ADAP* D 1, Nos 333–35. See also Schuschnigg, *Kampf*, 289ff.; Schausberger, *Griff*, 549ff.
58. Ibid., 552f.
59. *IMT* 28, 1780-PS, 371.
60. *Goebbels TB*, 10 March 1938.
61. Ibid., 11 March 1938.
62. Schuschnigg too reached this conclusion – retrospectively: 'In fact the events of 10 March were provoked by the planned referendum'. See Schuschnigg, *Kampf*, 296.

63. *Goebbels TB*, 11 March 1938. On the propaganda measures then initiated by Goebbels see *PA* 1938, Nos 724 and 727.

64. See Schmidl, *März 38*; IMT 28, 1780-PS, 371.

65. Domarus, 1, 809f.

66. IMT 31, 2949-PS, 354ff. According to *Goebbels TB,* 12 March 1938, on the afternoon of 11 March the invasion was still 'uncertain'. A few hours later the situation had changed: 'We dictate [*sic!*] a telegram for Seiss-Inquart [*sic!*] in which he requests aid from the German government'. The support by Kube, *Pour le mérite*, 245f., among others, for Göring's claim at the Nuremberg trial (*IMT* 9, 296f.) that he had seized the initiative lacks sufficient evidential proof. In fact, it is clear from the entry in Goebbels' diary for 13 March that the leadership was acting in concert.

67. *Goebbels TB*, 12 March 1938; Schausberger, *Griff*, 556ff.; Below, *Adjutant*, 90.

68. *ADAP* D 1, No. 352.

69. IMT 31, 2949-PS, 369. For the role of Prince Philip in German–Italian relations see Jonathan Petropoulos, *Royals and the Reich. The Princes von Hessen in Nazi Germany* (Oxford and New York, 2006), 177ff.

70. Andreas Nierhaus, 'Der "Anschluss" und seine Bilder – Inszenierung, Ästhetisierung, Historisierung', in Werner Welzig (ed.), *'Anschluss'. März/April 1938 in Österreich* (Vienna, 2010); Gerhard Jagschitz, 'Photographie und "Anschluss" im März 1938', in Oliver Rathkolb et al. (eds), *Die veruntreute Wahrheit. Hitlers Propagandisten in Österreichs Medien* (Salzburg, 1988).

71. *Goebbels TB*, 13 March 1938; on the text see Domarus, 1, 815ff. On the propaganda treatment see *PA* 1938, Nos 728f. and 733.

72. Domarus, 1, 817ff.; Below, *Adjutant*, 91ff.; Keitel, *Leben*, 219f.

73. Domarus, 1, 817f. On his stay in Linz see also Dietrich, *Jahre*, 52f.

74. *RGBl.* 1938 I, 237f. The law was drafted by the head of the department for constitutional and administrative matters in the Reich Interior Ministry, Wilhelm Stuckart, who had been summoned to Linz by Hitler. See Botz, *Eingliederung*, 62.

75. Domarus, 1, 821.

76. According to Goebbels this plan emerged on 11 March. See *TB*, 12 March 1938.

77. *RGBl.* 1938 I, 237f. To reconstruct the decision-making process see Below, *Adjutant*, 92. The improvisation is also clear from an official 'personal report' by the head of the department in the Propaganda ministry. See Alfred Ingemar Berndt, *Meilensteine des Dritten Reiches. Erlebnisschilderungen großer Tage* (Munich, 1938), 214. For the importance of the stopover in Linz for the decision-making process see Botz, 'Hitlers Aufenthalt in Linz im März 1938 und der Anschluss', in *Historisches Jahrbuch der Stadt Linz* 1970, 185–214.

78. Domarus, 1, 821.

79. Dokumentationsarchiv (ed.), 'Anschluß', Doc. 104f.

80. *Goebbels TB*, 14, 15, and 16 March (there still with the title Reichspropagandahauptamt) and 17, 19, and 20 March 1938.

81. Botz, *Nationalsozialismus*, 74f.

82. Ibid., 137ff.; Jonny Moser, 'Die Apokalypse der Wiener Juden', in Historisches Museum der Stadt Wien (ed.), *Wien 1938. 110 Sonderausstellung, 11. März bis 30. Juni 1988* (Vienna, 1988), 286–97; Herbert Rosenkranz, *Verfolgung und Selbstbehauptung. Die Juden in Österreich 1938–1945* (Wien, 1978).

83. Botz, *Nationalsozialismus*, 99ff.

84. Domarus, 1, 824f.

85. Ibid., 825; see also Gerhard Engel, *Heeresadjutant bei Hitler 1938–1943. Aufzeichnungen des Majors Engel*, ed. Hildegard von Kotze (Stuttgart, 1974), 15f., whose entry concerning the constitutional position of the Catholic Church is understandable in the context of Hitler's next encounter on 9 April. See above p. 557. Maximilian Liebmann, *Theodor Innitzer und der Anschluss. Österreichs Kirche 1938* (Graz, 1988), 73.

86. Botz, *Nationalsozialismus*, 157ff.; Liebmann, *Innitzer*, 85ff. On the generally positive attitude to Innitzer of the Nazi leadership see *Goebbels TB*, 2, 3, and 7 April 1938.

87. *VB* (B), 16 March 1938, 'Heute Freudentag in Berlin' (headline) and Goebbels's appeal.

88. *Goebbels TB*, 17 March 1938; Domarus, 1, 825f.; *VB* (B), 17 March 1938, 'Triumphaler Einzug des Führers in die Hauptstadt des Großdeutschen Reiches'.

89. Kershaw, *Hitler-Mythos*, 160ff., quote 161; Hellmuth Auerbach, 'Volksstimmung und veröffentlichte Meinung in Deutschland zwischen März und November 1938', in Franz Knipping and Klaus-Jürgen Müller (eds), *Machtbewusstsein in Deutschland am Vorabend des Zweiten Weltkrieges* (Paderborn, 1984), 273–95.

90. BAF, RW 19/86, Current Economic situation, 1 April 1939; Volkmann, 'NS-Wirtschaft', 381ff.; Sarholz, *Auswirkungen*, 283ff.

THE SUDETEN CRISIS

1. On 11 March, the evening preceding the Anschluss, Jodl noted a remark by Hitler to the effect that after the incorporation of Austria there was no need to hurry to 'deal with the Czech question', but preparations for Case Green should be pushed forward energetically and geared to the new strategic situation. See *IMT* 28, 1780-PS, 372.

2. E.g. *Goebbels TB*, 7 March 1938: 'And one day Czechoslovakia will collapse under our blows...the Führer is glad that Prague is so intransigent because it makes it all the more certain that one day it will be ripped apart'.

3. *Goebbels TB*, 20 March 1938.

4. *ADAP* D 2, No. 107; see Smelser, *Sudetenproblem*, 193f.; Helmuth K. G. Rönnefarth, *Die Sudetenkrise in der internationalen Politik*, 2 parts (Wiesbaden, 1961) 1, 218f. See also the similar watchword 'always demand more than can be granted' in *Goebbels TB*, 15 April 1938.

5. *ADAP* D 2, No. 109.

6. Ibid., No. 135; see Rönnefarth, *Sudetenkrise* 1, 231ff.; Smelser, *Sudetenproblem*, 198.

7. *ADAP* D 2, No. 133.

8. Klaus-Jürgen Müller, *General Ludwig Beck. Studien und Dokumente zur politisch-militärischen Vorstellungswelt und Tätigkeit des Generalstabschefs des deutschen Heeres 1933–1938* (Boppard am Rhein, 1980), No. 45; Klaus-Jürgen Müller, *Generaloberst Ludwig Beck. Eine Biographie* (Paderborn, 2007), 313ff.

9. Domarus 1, 826ff.

10. Heiber (ed.), *Goebbels Reden* 1, No. 33; *VB* (N), 9 and 10 April 1938.

11. *Goebbels TB*, 10 April, and 3 April 1938: Innitzer had been 'very shocked and depressed by the Vatican declaration'.

12. Ibid., 10 April 1938; see also Engel, *Heeresadjutant*, 15f., on Hitler's first meeting with Innitzer on 15 March, according to which Hitler had subsequently said that the Catholic church in Austria was a state church and had a very different attitude to the state from the one in Germany, which, as a result of the need for confessional parity, had always been political. Goebbels's diary entry enables the meeting to appear in a completely different light. According to Liebmann, *Innitzer*, 142f. (which appeared before the publication of the Goebbels diaries) the only thing known about the meeting was that Hitler had told Innitzer coldly that he had been prepared to give a binding declaration concerning the status of the Catholic church in Austria, but now, after Innitzer's recent statements, he was no longer in a position to do so.

13. Domarus 1, 848ff., quote 849.

14. *Sopade* 1938, 419ff., detail on numerous cases in which ballot secrecy had not been preserved and the results had been manipulated. Goebbels admitted there had been irregularities in Munich where Gauleiter Wagner had 'cheated a bit', unfortunately 'very stupidly'. See *Goebbels TB*, 26 April 1938; for the description of a concrete case of ballot manipulation see also Auerbach, 'Volksstimmung', 279. Jung, *Plebiszit*, 109ff.

15. Führer edict., 23 April 1938 (*RGBl.* 1938 I, 407f.).

16. Botz, *Eingliederung*, 86ff.

17. Longerich, *Stellvertreter*, 132ff.; Botz, *Eingliederung*, 108ff.; on the pre-history of this constitutional model see Rebentisch, *Führerstaat*, 231ff. On Hitler's role in the drafting of the Eastern Marches Law see BAB, R 43 II/1353b, Hess to Lammers, 19 February 1939; ibid., R 43 II/1366, Lammers to the Reich ministers, 14 April 1939. Eastern Marches Law (*RGBl.* 1939 I, 777); Sudetengau Law (ibid., 780).

18. On the programme of visits see Domarus, 1, 856ff. On Hitler's stay in Florence see Schwarz, *Geniewahn*, 15ff. On the trip see Wiedemann, *Mann*, 133ff.

19. Ciano, *Diary*, 5 May 1938.

20. *ADAP* D 1, No. 759.

21. Domarus, 1, 861.

22. *ADAP* D 1, No. 761.

23. Ibid., No. 762. See also *Goebbels TB*, 7 May 1938.

24. Ibid., 20 May 1938; *PA* 1938, Nos. 1437 and 1448; on the implementation of these directives see, for example, the *FZ* and *DAZ*, which switched their

coverage to a more aggressive tone on the 19th; see Schwarzenbeck, *Pressepolitik*, 293ff.

25. *ADAP* D 2, No. 175. Repeated in Kershaw, *Hitler*, 2, 149, but with the sense distorted.

26. On the weekend crisis see Rönnefarth, *Sudetenkrise*, 1, 277ff.; Weinberg, *Foreign Policy*, 563ff. See, in particular, the documents in *ADAP* D 2, No. 169ff. France und Czechoslovakia had signed a treaty of alliance and friendship in January 1924.

27. *Goebbels TB*, 22 May 1938; see *DAZ*, *FZ*, and *VB* from 21 May 1938.

28. For the start of the campaign see *DAZ*, 22–25 May 1938; *FZ*, 22–27 May 1938; *VB*, 22–26 May 1938. For the instructions see PA 1938, Nos 1467 and 1504.

29. *IMT* 28, 1780-PS, 372, here also the explicit context for the directive for Case Green.

30. Müller, *Beck/Studien*, No. 45; also Wiedemann, *Mann*, 127f., and IfZ, 3037-PS (affidavit) on the meeting. See Kershaw, *Hitler*, 1, 152.

31. Domarus, 1, 897ff., quote 903.

32. Ibid., 974ff., quote 975.

33. Domarus, 2, 1048f.

34. Ibid., 1153.

35. *ADAP* D 2, No. 221; Rönnefarth, *Sudetenkrise*, 1, 310; Smelser, *Sudetenproblem*, 201.

36. In the old version of the directive for Case Green of December 1937 the commander-in-chief of the Wehrmacht had made a war against Czechoslovakia before Germany was fully ready for war dependent on the unlikelihood of intervention by the western powers; a two-front war had to be avoided (ADAP D 7, Appendix III K, 547ff.).

37. *Beck/Studien*, No. 46f.; Müller, *Beck*, 180 and 324ff. On the conflict between Hitler and Beck see also Kershaw, *Hitler* 2, 153ff.

38. Müller, *Heer*, Doc. 115; Below, *Adjutant*, 103f.; IfZ, ED 1, Liebmann, Personal experiences at the meeting; Müller, *Heer*, 314.

39. Müller, *Beck/Studien*, 298ff.

40. Dieter Bettinger and Martin Büren, *Der Westwall. Die Geschichte der deutschen Westbefestigung im Dritten Reich*, 2 vols (Osnabrück, 1990); Seidler, *Todt*, 163ff.

41. Memorandum on the question of our fortifications in Otto-Wilhelm Förster, *Das Befestigungswesen. Rückblick und Ausschau* (Neckargemünd, 1960), 123–48, quote 123.

42. For Hitler's criticism of the West Wall works see Engel, *Heeresadjutant*, 27f. and 32. Hitler regularly inspected the work on the fortifications (see below p. 670) and emphasized their strategic importance in major speeches. See 12 September 1938 (Final speech at the Party Rally in Domarus, 1, 897ff., 903f.: 'the most gigantic fortification project of all time') and 9 October (ibid., 954ff., quote 955).

43. Michael Geyer, 'Rüstungsbeschleunigung und Inflation. Zur Inflationsdenkschrift des Oberkommandos der Wehrmacht vom November 1938', in *MGM* 30 (1981), 135; Tooze, *Ökonomie*, 273ff.

44. Geyer, 'Rüstungsbeschleunigung', Doc. 3 and p. 129.

45. BAF, RH 15/150, Army General Staff (Hellmann) Note, 2 June 1938: Meeting of Göring with the commander-in-chief of the Army, the Chief of the General Staff, and the inspector of the pioneers and fortfications.

46. Sarholz, *Auswirkungen*, 308f.; BAF, RH 15/150, 14 June 1938, Transcript by an officer from the General Army Office.

47. BAF, RH 15/150, Wa.A. to Wa J Rü, 30 May 1938.

48. The Provisional Aircraft Procurement Programme No. 8 (3rd draft) of 3 June 1938 already envisaged the construction of more than 24,000 aircraft. See BAF, RL 3/55: 23,783 up to 1 April 1942, 3. Draft; Geyer, 'Rüstungsbeschleunigung', 134 and 176; Sarholz, *Auswirkungen*, 334. See also Budrass, *Flugzeugindustrie*, 536ff.; Deist, 'Aufrüstung', 586ff.

49. Ibid, 587f.

50. *IMT* 38, 140-R, 375ff.

51. Dülffer, *Weimar*, 471ff.

52. Petzina, *Autarkiepolitik*, 96ff.; Volkmann, 'NS-Wirtschaft', 358ff.; BAF, R 2501/6581, Reichsbank memorandum: The supply situation in the German economy, 27 June 1938. According to it, domestic supplies, particularly of textile fibres, oil, rubber, iron, non-ferrous metals, and fats were critical.

53. Petzina, *Autarkiepolitik*, 116ff.

54. Tooze, *Ökonomie*, 297ff.; Gottfried Plumpe, *Die I.G. Farbenindustrie AG. Wirtschaft, Technik und Politik 1904–1945* (Berlin, 1990), 722ff., discusses the system using the example of the General Plenipotentiary for Special Questions relating to the Production of Chemicals, Karl Krauch.

55. Gerhard Th. Mollin, *Montankonzerne und 'Drittes Reich'. Der Gegensatz zwischen Monopolindustrie und Befehlswirtschaft in der deutschen Rüstung und Expansion 1936–1944* (Göttingen, 1988), 70ff. and 102ff.; Matthias Riedel, *Eisen und Kohle für das Dritte Reich. Paul Pleigers Stellung in der NS-Wirtschaft* (Göttingen, 1973), 156f.

56. Petzina, *Autarkiepolitik*, 106f.; Riedel, *Eisen*, 233ff.

57. On exploiting the labour market see Tooze, *Ökonomie*, 306ff.; Timothy W. Mason, *Arbeiterklasse und Volksgemeinschaft. Dokumente und Materialien zur deutschen Arbeiterpolitik 1936–1939* (Opladen, 1975), Doc. 144f.

58. Sarholz, *Auswirkungen*, 305.

59. On labour conscription see in particular Mason, *Arbeiterklasse*, 665ff., with the relevant documents. The practice of continually extending conscription required a new version of the decree of 22 June (*RGBl.* 1938 I, 652f.; new version in *RGBl.* 1939 I, 206ff.).

60. Darré gave this figure at the 6th Reich Peasant Congress in Goslar 1938. See Corni/Gies, 'Blut', Doc. 113. The SD's annual report for 1938 stated on the basis of figures from the Reich Food Estate that there was a shortage of 600,000 agricultural workers and of 333,000 marriageable women in agriculture. See Heinz Boberach (ed.), *Meldungen aus dem Reich 1938–1945. Die geheimen Lageberichte des Sicherheitsdienstes der SS*, 17 vols (Herrsching, 1984), 2, 161. On the shortage of agricultural workers see also *Sopade* 1938, 724ff.

61. *Meldungen*, 2, 161; Kershaw, *Opinion*, 55ff.

62. *Meldungen*, 2, 161; on the continuing shortages see *Sopade* 1938, 631ff.

63. Excerpts from Heydrich's express letter of 1 June in Wolfgang Ayass, '"Ein Gebot der nationalen Arbeitsdisziplin". Die Aktion "Arbeitsscheu Reich 1938"'; in Ayass, *Feinderklärung und Prävention. Kriminalbiologie, Zigeunerforschung und Asozialenpolitik* (Berlin, 1988), 54f.; Ayass, *'Asoziale' im Nationalsozialismus* (Stuttgart, 1995), 139ff.

64. Mason, *Arbeiterklasse*, 745ff.; Decree on the Setting of Wages (*RGBl.* 1939 I, 779).

65. BAB, R 2501/6581, Economic and Statistical Department 23 July 1938: Confidential Reich Bank matter. On the Development of the German Prices and Wages Situation since 1933. This picture of only a slight increase in real wages has been confirmed by economic historians. Rüdiger Hachtmann, 'Lebenshaltungskosten und Reallöhne während des "Dritten Reiches"', in *Vierteljahrschrift für Sozial-und Wirtschaftsgeschichte* 75 (1988), 32–73 claims that the net wages of industrial workers increased by 25 per cent between 1932/33–1938, while prices increased by around 15–20 per cent. After discussing maximum and minimum values, André Steiner in 'Zur Neuschätzung der Lebenshaltungskostenindex für die Vorkriegszeit des Nationalsozialismus', in *Jahrbuch für Wirtschaftsgeschichte* (2005/2) 129–52 estimates the increase in the real weekly wages of industrial workers between 1932 and 1938 as probably 1 per cent.

66. Hachtmann, 'Lebenshaltungskosten', 69.

67. Kershaw, *Opinion*, 98ff.; numerous examples in *Sopade* 1938, 713ff.

68. Kershaw, *Opinion*, 105ff.

69. *Meldungen*, 2, 166ff.; *Sopade* 1937 notes as early as September an increasing rejection of the regime among the middle class (1231ff.); Kershaw, *Opinion*, 132ff.

70. Tooze, *Ökonomie*, 303. Private housing construction was also virtually brought to a standstill by the ban on mortgage credit by the Reich Bank. See Tilman Harlander, *Zwischen Heimstätte und Wohnmaschine. Wohnungsbau und Wohnungspolitik in der Zeit des Nationalsozialismus* (Basel, 1995), 139. IfZ, 5328-NG: Göring issued a circular on 18 June banning all public and private building work apart from that which was for the defence of the Reich or the redevelopment of cities. Exceptions were permitted only for projects of special importance such as workers' housing estates and the construction of small flats. Excerpts from Göring's directive were published by the Reich Finance Minister on 5 July (ibid.).

71. Tooze, *Ökonomie*, 304f.; Alfred C. Mierzejewski, *Hitler's Trains. The German National Railway and the Third Reich* (Stroud, 2005); BAB, R 2501/658, Economic and Statistical department of the Reich Bank, 4 August 1938: Table of the length of journeys on some important railway sections. See also *Sopade* 1938, 613ff.

72. BAB, R 2501/6581, German morale, hygiene, and culture statistics of the past 10 years, 15 July 1938. The basic conclusions of this report are confirmed by Jörg Baten and Andrea Wagner, 'Mangelernährung. Krankheit und Sterblichkeit im

NS Wirtschaftsaufschwung (1933–1937)', in *Jahrbuch für Wirtschaftsgeschichte* (2003/1), 99–123.

73. *Meldungen* 2, 157ff., quotes 157f.

74. *Sopade* 1937, see above, p. 1104, note 1; 1938, 67ff and 631ff.; 1939, 624ff. and 859ff.

75. *Sopade* 1938, 684ff.: Little enthusiasm for war (except among young people), similarly 704ff. (Supplement), 913ff. (Fear of war), see also 970ff. (Supplement).

76. *Meldungen*, 2, 72f.; Kershaw, *Hitler-Mythos*, 164f.; Auerbach, 'Volksstimmung', esp. 281f.

77. *Goebbels TB*, 30 May 1938; *VB* (B), 30 May 1938, 'Scharfe Abrechnung mit den Friedensstörern' (about the speech).

78. *Goebbels TB*, 1 and 3 June 1938; *PA* 1938, Nos 1551 and 1565; *VB* (B), 3 June 1938; *MNN*, 2 and 3 June 1938; *DAZ*, 2 June (M und E); Schwarzenbeck, *Pressepolitik*, 313f.

79. Judging by his diary entries (*Goebbels TB*, 4, 5, and 8–12 June), the performance of the press lagged behind the propaganda minister's expectations. See *PA* 1938, Nos 1601 and 1613. On the start of the press campaign see, for example, *FZ*, 3 June 1938 (leader) and 7 June (contributions on 'incidents'). The *DAZ* reported until 11 June regularly on its front page about such incidents; the *VB* (B) carried headlines from 2–9, 11–13, and 18 June 1938.

80. *Goebbels TB*, 17 June 1938.

81. Ibid., 18 June 1938; *FZ,* 19 June 1938, 'Reichsminister Dr. Goebbels in Königsberg'.

82. *Goebbels TB*, 1 and 2 July 1938; *PA* 1938, Nos 1974, 1981, 1988, and 2008. In the second half of the month the German press polemics against Prague died down, which is evident in the pages of the *VB, FZ,* and *DAZ*. See also Schwarzenbeck, *Pressepolitik*, 314ff.

83. *PA* 1938, Nos 1992, 2015, 2056, and 2075; *Goebbels TB*, 23 April 1939: 'On the Führer's orders I invite 20,000 Sudeten Germans to the Breslau Gymnasts' Festival'.

84. Ibid, 17 July 1938: 'Our campaign against Prague is boring the public a bit. One can't keep a crisis going for months on end'.

85. See above p. 529.

86. *Goebbels TB*, 30 November 1937.

87. Adam, *Judenpolitik*, 174ff.

88. For the start of Jewish persecution in annexed Austria see Botz, *Nationalsozialismus*, 126ff.; Longerich, *Politik*, 162ff.; Rosenkranz, *Verfolgung*, 20ff.

89. *Goebbels TB*, 11 April 1938: 'The Führer wants to force all the Jews out of Germany. To Madagascar or somewhere else'.

90. For details on the 'Berlin action' see Longerich, *Politik*, 172ff.; see, in particular, Wolf Gruner, 'Lesen brauchen sie nicht zu können…. Die "Denkschrift über die Behandlung der Juden in der Reichshauptstadt auf allen Gebieten des öffentlichen Lebens" vom Mai 1938', in *Jahrbuch für Antisemitismusforschung* 4 (1995), 305–41.

91. *Goebbels TB*, 23 April 1938.

92. Ibid., 25 April (Meeting with Helldorf), 30 April (Hitler's approval) and 31 May 1938 (Goebbels/Helldorf).

93. Ibid., 2, 3, 4, and 11 June 1938.

94. Longerich, *Politik*, 177; OA Moscow, 500-1-261, Minute. Head of the SD Jewish department 8 June 1938. According to this, it was stated confidentially at a meeting with Heydrich on 1 June that, in order to carry out important earth works, on the 'Führer's' orders asocial and criminal Jews were to be arrested throughout the Reich.

95. Longerich, *Politik*, 179f.; OA Moscow, 500-1-261, SD Jewish department to SD Higher Section South, 29 June 1938: This stopped the action. In the fair copy the words 'on the Führer's orders' were replaced by 'on orders from above'.

96. Longerich, *Politik*, 182f.

97. *Goebbels TB*, 25 July 1938.

98. Longerich, 'Davon', 114; *Goebbels TB*, 9 July 1938 (on Stuttgart).

99. Longerich, 'Davon', 114.

100. Domarus, 1, 880ff.

101. Müller, *Beck*, 339ff.

102. Müller, *Beck/Studien* No. 49 (also the draft, 15 July 1938, No. 48).

103. Ibid., No. 50f.

104. Ibid., No. 52.

105. For this interpretation (summing up) see Müller, 'Struktur und Entwicklung der national-konservativen Opposition', in Thomas Vogel (ed.), *Aufstand des Gewissens. Militärischer Widerstand gegen Hitler und das NS-Regime 1933 bis 1945. Begleitband zur Wanderausstellung des Militärgeschichtlichen Forschungsamtes* (Hamburg, 2001), 334.

106. Müller, *Beck/Studien*, No. 54.

107. Müller, *Beck*, 351ff. (on 4 August).

108. Engel, *Heeresadjutant*, 18 July 1938; Hitler also expressed negative views on the memorandum to Brauchitsch on 24 July (ibid.).

109. Below, *Adjutant*, 112.

110. *IMT* 28, 1780-PS, 373f.; Müller, *Heer*, 338; Müller, *Beck*, 355.

111. Müller, *Heer*, 339, and Müller, *Beck*, 356; Below, *Adjutant*, 115; Anton Hoch and Hermann Weiss, 'Die Erinnerungen des Generalobersten Wilhelm Adam', in Benz (ed.), *Miscelleanea*, 54f.; If Z, ED 109/3, Adam Memoirs (about 15 August), and ED 1, Liebmann, Personal experiences during the years 1938/39; Keitel, *Leben*, 224.

112. Müller, *Beck*, 357. For his farewell address see Hossbach, *Wehrmacht*, 129f.

113. Peter Hoffmann, *Widerstand – Staatsstreich – Attentat. Der Kampf der Opposition gegen Hitler* (Munich and Zurich, 1995), 109ff.; Müller, *Heer*, 345ff.; Müller, 'Struktur', 337ff.; Marion Thielenhaus, *Zwischen Anpassung und Widerstand: deutsche Diplomaten 1938–1941. Die politischen Aktivitäten der Beamtengruppe um Ernst von Weizsäcker im Auswärtigen Amt* (Paderborn, 1984), 48ff.; Rainer A. Blasius, *Für Großdeutschland – gegen den großen Krieg. Staatssekretär Ernst Freiherr von Weizsäcker in den Krisen um die Tschechoslowakei und Polen 1938/39* (Cologne and Vienna, 1981).

114. *ADAP* D 2, Nos 248 and 284. On these initiatives see Hoensch, *Revisionismus*, 71f.

115. *ADAP* D 2, No. 383 (with the quote) and No. 390. See also Helmut Krausnick et al. (eds), *Helmuth Groscurth, Tagebücher eines Abwehroffiziers 1938–1940. Mit weiteren Dokumenten zur Militäropposition gegen Hitler* (Stuttgart, 1970), 108; Hoensch, *Revisionismus*, 76ff.; Weinberg, *Foreign Policy*, 593ff.

116. Schwarzenbeck, *Pressepolitik*, 340ff. On the resumption of the campaign see *PA* 1938, Nos 2353 and 2372; *VB* (B), 26–30 August; *MNN*, 29 and 30 August; *DAZ*, 26–30 August.

117. Paul Vyšný, *The Runciman Mission to Czechoslovakia. Prelude to Munich* (Houndmills, 2003).

118. BAB, NS 10/125, 20 July 1938: 'The Führer has ordered K. Henlein to be in Bayreuth on the 23rd at 17.00'; 23 July 1938: '17.00 K. Hähnlein's [*sic!*] visit'. Goebbels notes Henlein's presence in Breslau on 1 August 1938 (*Goebbels TB*).

119. Groscurth, *Tagebücher*, 112f.; Rönnefarth, *Sudetenkrise* 1, 475; *Goebbels TB*, 2 and 3 September 1938; BAB, NS 10/125, 1 and 2 September 1938.

120. *ADAP* D 2, No. 424. On the worsening of the Sudeten crisis in the late summer see Kershaw, *Hitler*, 2, 162ff.; Weinberg, *Foreign Policy*, 600ff.; Smelser, *Sudetenproblem*, 209ff.; Rönnefarth, *Sudetenkrise* 1, 497ff.

121. Groscurth, *Tagebücher*, 104 and 111.

122. *Goebbels TB*, 9 September 1938.

123. *PA* 1938, Nos 2455–2461, 2465f. and 2468; *Goebbels TB*, 8 and 9 September. See, for example, the reporting of the *VB* (B), 8 September 1939, 'Prager Regierung nicht mehr Herr ihrer Polizei' (headline); 9 September, 'Prag spielt mit dem Feuer'; see also Smelser, *Sudetenproblem*, 210f.; Schwarzenbeck, *Pressepolitik*, 350; Rönnefarth, *Sudetenkrise* 1, 478ff.

124. Keitel, *Leben*, 227.

125. *ADAP* D 2, No. 448.

126. Domarus, 1, 897ff., quotes 901 and 904; *Goebbels TB*, 13 September 1938; Schwarzenbeck, *Pressepolitik*, 354ff.; Rönnefarth, *Sudetenkrise* 1, 497ff.

127. Ibid., 493f.

128. *PA* 1938, Nos 2524 and 2533; *VB* (B), 14 September 1938, 'Feuerüberfälle, Morde, Standrecht' (headline); 15 September 1938, '30 neue Opfer tschechischer Mordschützen'. Goebbels even contributed an aggressive leader to the main Party newspaper under a pseudonym. See *VB* (B), 14 September 1938, 'Wie lange noch?' On this climax of the crisis see *Goebbels TB*, 14 and 15 September 1938.

129. Smelser, *Sudetenproblem*, 212f.

130. *PA* 1938, Nos. 2533, 2549–2553, 2558–2562, 2569–2572, 2574f., and 2580–2584. According to *Goebbels TB*, 17 September 1938, these polemics were intended to continue until the start of the Godesberg meeting. See also Schwarzenbeck, *Pressepolitik*, 359f.

131. Schmidt, *Statist*, 402.

132. *ADAP* D 2, No. 487; Schmidt, *Statist*, 402ff.; *DBFP* 3/2, No. 895; Below, *Adjutant*, 122; Rönnefarth, *Sudetenkrise* 1, 523ff.; Weinberg, *Foreign Policy*, 611ff.; Kershaw, *Hitler*, 2, 165ff.

133. Leonidas E. Hill (ed.), *Die Weizsäcker-Papiere*, Part 2: 1933–1950 (Berlin, 1974), 143.

134. Hitler told Goebbels on 17 September that the plebiscite being sought by Chamberlain 'doesn't quite suit us'. But if this solution was 'being seriously proposed' then 'we can't do much about it at the moment'. See *TB*, 18 September 1938.

135. *ADAP* D 2, No. 532; later the Germans said that they would give the British delegation a copy of Schmidt's transcript of the proceedings from memory. See ibid., No. 544.

136. *Goebbels TB*, 19 September 1938.

137. Rönnefarth, *Sudetenkrise* 1, 540ff.; Weinberg, *Foreign Policy*, 618f.; *ADAP* D 2, No. 523; *Goebbels TB*, 20 September 1938.

138. Ibid., 20 September 1938.

139. *ADAP* D 2, Nos 541 and No. 554; Hoensch, *Revisionismus*, 88ff.

140. Wojciechowski, *Beziehungen*, 472ff., on the meeting, of which there is no German record. According to this, Hitler stated that they could move to recognize frontiers and he also raised the issue of the autobahn, but said it was a project for the future. See Lipski, *Diplomat*, Doc. 99. *ADAP* D 2, No. 553 (Polish notes to the Czech and British governments).

141. Hoensch, *Die Slowakei und Hitlers Ostpolitik. Hlinkas Slowakische Volkspartei zwischen Autonomie und Separation 1938/1939* (Cologne and Graz, 1965), 87ff.

142. *DBFP* 3/2, Doc. 1005; Weinberg, *Foreign Policy*, 623f.

143. *PA* 1938, Nos. 2613–2615, 2623, 2627f., and 2632.

144. Ibid., Nos 2596 and 2606–2608; see also the reporting in the *VB* (B), 20–22. September.

145. Hitler had discussed this line with Goebbels and Ribbentrop the night before. See *Goebbels TB*, 22 and 23 September 1938. *ADAP* D 2, No. 562; Rönnefahrt, *Sudetenkrise*, 1, 581ff.; Kershaw, *Hitler*, 2, 169ff.; Schmidt, *Statist*, 407ff.; Weinberg, *Foreign Policy*, 624ff.

146. On the negotiations see *ADAP* D 2, Nos 572ff.; Rönnefarth, *Sudetenkrise*, 1, 585ff.

147. *ADAP* D 2, No. 583f.

148. *Goebbels TB*, 26 September 1938.

149. See *ADAP* D 2, No. 619.

150. Rönnefarth, *Sudetenkrise* 1, 615; *Goebbels TB*, 27 September 1938.

151. Schmidt, *Statist*, 414ff.

152. *Goebbels TB,* 26 September 1938; *VB* (B), 26 September 1938 on the event.

153. Domarus, 1, 923ff., quotes 924 and 932.

154. *PA* 1938, Nos 2683f. and 2686f.; *DAZ* (E), 27 September 1938, Commentary: 'Der Spieler'; *VB* (B), 27 September 1938, 'Wir sind entschlossen' (headline); Schwarzenbeck, *Pressepolitik*, 380f.

155. *ADAP* D 2, No. 634f.

156. *Goebbels TB*, 28 September 1938; Schmidt, *Statist*, 416; Kershaw, *Hitler* 2, 174; Rönnefarth, Sudetenkrise 1, 618f.

157. *Goebbels TB*, 27 September; Hoensch, *Revisionismus*, 89 and 99f.; Kerekes (ed.), *Allianz*, 37.

158. *IMT* 28, 1780-PS, 388.

159. Ruth Andreas-Friedrich, *Schauplatz Berlin. Ein deutsches Tagebuch* (Munich, 1962), 5f.; Schmidt, *Statist*, 417f.; William L. Shirer, *Berlin Diary. The Journal of a Foreign Correspondent 1934–1941* (New York, 1942), 114f.; on the lack of enthusiasm for war see also *Sopade* 1938, 913ff.; Henderson, *Fehlschlag*, 183; Alfred Ingemar Berndt, *Der Marsch, ins Großdeutsche Reich* (Munich, 1939), 222. Kershaw, *Hitler-Mythos*, 170, claims that after the Sudeten crisis Hitler's popularity was threatened for the first time.

160. Below, *Adjutant*, 127.

161. Hill (ed.), *Weizsäcker-Papiere*, 9 October 1938 and 171. Goebbels noted significantly that the division's march past had 'left behind everywhere a very depressing impression'. See *Goebbels TB* 29 September 1938.

162. *Meldungen* 2, 72; Kershaw, *Hitler-Mythos*, 165ff., with examples from Bavaria; Auerbach, 'Volksstimmung', 282.

163. On Hitler's change of mind see Weinberg, *Foreign Policy*, 628ff.; Kershaw, Hitler, 2, 175f.

164. *Goebbels TB*, 29 September 1938.

165. Ibid.; *PA* 1938, Nos 2704 and 2706. *VB* (B), 28 September 1938, 'Massenkundgebung der NSDAP im Lustgarten' (Announcement); 29 September 1938, 'Millionen-Kundgebungen im ganzen Reich'; *FZ* (M), 29 September 1938, 'Das Treuebekenntnis zum Führer'.

166. On the immediate pre-history see Rönnefarth, *Sudetenkrise* 1, 623ff.; David Faber, *Munich. The 1938 Appeasement Crisis* (London, 2009), 391ff.

167. Schmidt, *Statist*, 425f.; Henderson, *Fehlschlag*, 190.

168. *ADAP* D 2, Nos 670 and 674f. On the Munich conference see Jürgen Zarusky and Martin Zückert (eds), *Das Münchener Abkommen von 1938 in europäischer Perspektive* (Munich, 2013); Weinberg, *Foreign Policy*, 632ff.; Rönnefarth, *Sudetenkrise*, 1, 623ff.; Boris Celovsky, *Das Münchner Abkommen 1938* (Stuttgart, 1958).

169. Sarholz, *Auswirkungen*, 326.

170. Wojciechowski, *Beziehungen*, 502ff.

171. Hoensch, *Revisionismus*, 108f.

172. See below, p. 586.

173. Schmidt, *Statist*, 425.

174. *ADAP* D 5, No. 676.

175. *ADAP* D 4, No. 369; for an assessment see Franz Knipping, Die deutsch–französische Erklärung vom 6. Dezember 1938', in Klaus Hildebrand and Ferdinand Werner (eds), *Deutschland – Frankreich 1936–1939. Deutsch-französisches Historikerkolloquium des Deutschen Historischen Instituts Paris (Bonn 26. bis 29. September 1979)* (Munich, 1981), 523–51.

AFTER MUNICH

1. On the delay or ultimate refusal of Germany to give the guarantee see *ADAP* D 4, Nos 107, 168, 175f., 178, 183, and 370.

2. Hoensch, *Slowakei*, 98ff. and 210ff.

3. On the redefining of Germany's position on the Slovak and Carpatho-Ukraine questions see the note for Hitler of 7 October by the head of the Foreign Ministry's political department, Woermann (ADAP D 4, No. 45). See also ibid., Nos 46 and 50. See Hoensch, *Revisionismus*, 128f.

4. Wojciechowski, *Beziehungen*, 533; Albert S. Kotowski, "'Ukrainisches Piemont'? Die Karpatenukraine am Vorabend des Zweiten Weltkrieges', in *Jahrbücher für die Geschichte Osteuropas*, new series 49 (2001), 78.

5. *ADAP* D 4, No. 61.

6. Ibid., No. 62; on the two meetings see Hoensch, *Revisionismus*, 142ff.

7. On Hitler's dissatisfaction with Hungary's policies see also *ADAP* D 5, Nos 252 and 272f.

8. *ADAP* D 4, No. 72; Hoensch, *Revisionismus*, 155f. Göring had already received the Slovak minister, Ďurčanský. See *ADAP* D 4, No. 68.

9. Ibid., No. 99; on the Vienna conference see also Ciano, *Diary*, 2 and 3 November 1938.

10. *ADAP* D 4, No. 128; Kerekes (ed.), *Allianz*, No. 47; Hoensch, *Revisionismus*, 216ff.

11. Ribbentrop, *London*, 154.

12. *ADAP* D 5, No. 81; Lipski, *Diplomat*, Doc. 124; Wojciechowski, *Beziehungen*, 539ff.

13. *ADAP* D 5, No. 101.

14. Mario Toscano, *The Origins of the Pact of Steel* (Baltimore, 1967), 5ff.

15. Ibid., 52ff.

16. *ADAP* D 4, No. 400.

17. Ibid, No. 542; Toscano, *Origins*, 122ff.

18. Ibid., 153ff. On the background see *ADAP* D 6, 68f. (editor's elucidations) and No. 270.

19. Georg Thomas, *Geschichte der deutschen Wehr- und Rüstungswirtschaft (1918– 1943/45)*, ed. Wolfgang Birkenfeld (Boppard am Rh., 1966), 509. This states that, according to notes by Colonel Jansen, on 29 March 1940 Thomas told the inspectors: 'Then came Munich day. I received instructions over the telephone: "Now, make all the preparations necessary for war against England. Deadline 1942!".' According to this, the source was not, as Tooze puts it in *Ökonomie*, 338, a diary entry by Thomas.

20. *IMT* 27, 1301–PS, 160ff.

21. *PA* 1939, No. 2955; see also Nos 3017 and 3079. From the beginning of November the Wehrmacht propaganda office published its own journal, *Die Wehrmacht* (No. 3095). However, on 1 November, instructions were once again given to be cautious when dealing with military matters (No. 3106), and

Wehrmacht propaganda was only begun again on a large scale in spring 1939, which is not made clear in the account by Sywottek, *Mobilmachung*, 166ff.

22. On three trips in October see Domarus, 1, 949ff., 959, and 961f.

23. *IMT* 34, 136-C, 477ff.

24. Wildt, *Volksgemeinschaft*, 312ff.; Longerich, *Politik*, 190ff.

25. OA Moskau, 500-1-316, SD situation report, Central Department II/1, 1–31 October 1938.

26. Ralph Weingarten, *Die Hilfeleistung der westlichen Welt bei der Endlösung der deutschen Judenfrage. Das 'Intergovernmental Committee on Political Refugees' IGC 1938–1939* (Berne, 1981); Peter Longerich, *Holocaust. The Nazi Persecution and Murder of the Jews* (Oxford, 2010), 125ff.

27. On the background to and establishment of the Central Office see Hans Safrian, *Die Eichmann-Männer* (Vienna, 1993), 23ff.; Herbert Rosenkranz, *Verfolgung und Selbstbehauptung. Die Juden in Österreich 1938–1945* (Vienna, 1978), 120ff.

28. On the November pogrom 1938 see Dieter Obst, *'Reichskristallnacht' Ursachen und Verlauf des antisemitischen Pogroms vom November 1938* (Frankfurt a. M., 1991); Hans-Jürgen Döscher, *'Reichskristallnacht'. Die Novemberpogrome 1938* (Frankfurt a. M., 1988); on the background see in more detail: Longerich, *Politik*, 190ff. Most recently, Alan E. Steinweis, *Kristallnacht 1938. Ein deutscher Pogrom* (Stuttgart, 2011).

29. *PA* 1938, No. 3167 on the assassination, Nos 3176, 3178–3181, and 3184–3186.

30. On the events in Kurhessen see Obst, *'Reichskristallnacht'*, 67ff.; Wolf-Arno Kropat, *Kristallnacht in Hessen. Der Judenpogrom vom November 1938. Eine Dokumentation* (Wiesbaden, 1998), 21ff. On Goebbels's role during the progrom see Longerich, *Goebbels*, 293ff.

31. *Goebbels TB*, 9 November 1938.

32. Kropat, *Kristallnacht*, 66ff. and 79ff.; for further details see Steinweis, *Kristallnacht*, 35ff.

33. According to Below, *Adjutant*, 136, Hitler received the news in the afternoon in his flat. This is confirmed by Dietrich (*Jahre*, 55f.), though he was not present. According to Gauleiter Jordan, *Erlebt*, 180, the Party functionaries were already aware of the news before the event took place. Goebbels (*TB*, 10 November 1938) received the news in the afternoon.

34. Ibid.

35. Obst, 'Reichskristallnacht', 101ff.; Steinweis, *Kristallnacht*, 62ff.

36. *IMT* 25, 374-PS, 376ff.; *Goebbels TB*, 10 November 1938.

37. On these arrests see Harry Stein, 'Das Sonderlager im Konzentrationslager Buchenwald nach den Pogromen 1938', in Monica Kingreen (ed.), *'Nach der Kristallnacht'. Jüdisches leben und anti-Jüdische Politik in Frankfurt am Main 1938–1945* (Frankfurt a. M., 1999), 19–54; Barbara Distel, '"Die letzte ernste Warnung vor der Vernichtung". Zur Verschleppung der "Aktionsjuden" in die Konzentrationslager nach dem 9. November 1938', in *Zeitschrift für Geschichtswissenschaft* 46 (1998), 985–990; Wolfgang Benz, 'Mitglieder der Häftlingsgesellschaft auf Zeit: die "Aktionsjuden" 1938/39', in *Dachauer Hefte* 21 (2005), 179–196.; Heiko Pollmeier,

'Inhaftierung und Lagererfahrung deutscher Juden im November 1938', in *Jahrbuch für Antisemitismusforschung* 8 (1999), 107–30; Obst, *'Reichskristallnacht'*, 279ff.; Steinweis, *Kristallnacht*, 111ff., on the fate of those imprisoned.

38. BAB, NS 36/13, published in Peter Longerich (ed.), *Die Ermordung der europäischen Juden. Eine umfassende Dokumentation des Holocaust 1941–1945* (Munich, 1989), 43ff.

39. In Buchenwald alone 227 of the prisoners died in the first six weeks after their incarceration; in all the camps taken together it is estimated to have been around 400. See Stein, 'Sonderlager', 46f.

40. Angela Hermann, 'Hitler und sein Stoßtrupp in der "Reichskristallnacht"', in *VfZ* 56 (2008), 603–19.

41. *VB* (M), 10 November, 'Der Führer bei seinen SS-Männern'.

42. *VB* (N), 11 November 1938.

43. *Der Angriff*, 12 November 1938, 'Empfang im Führerbau'; *Goebbels TB*, 11 November 1938.

44. Domarus, 1, 973ff., quotes 974.

45. Longerich, *'Davon'*, 129ff.

46. *Goebbels TB*, 17 and 24 November 1938.

47. Longerich, *'Davon'*, 136ff. On the carrying out of the campaigns see among others *Goebbels TB*, 17–25 November 1938; *PA* 1938, No. 3275; *VB* (N), 14 November 1938, a Goebbels leading article, which was recommended to the press for reprinting, and 24 November 1938, 'Keine Kompromisse in der Judenfrage!'. See also Herbert Obenaus, 'The Germans: "An Antisemitic people". The Press Campaign after 9 November 1938', in David Bankier (ed.), *Probing the Depths of German Antisemitism: German Society and the Persecution of the Jews 1933–1941* (New York, 2000), 147–80.

48. *PA* 1938, No. 3310. Goebbels made clear his dissatisfaction with the, in his view, still too moderate tone of the reporting at the press conference on 22 November (No. 3336). See also Nos 3334, 3337, 3378, 3388, 3398, 3418, 3450, 3483, and 3612, also *PA* 1939, No. 68. Sänger, *Politik*, 64.

49. See the internal Party instruction 'For speakers' use only', quoted in Christian T. Barth, *Goebbels und die Juden* (Paderborn, 2003), 267.

50. Decree concerning the Atonement Contribution by Jews of German Nationality (*RGBl.* 1938 I, 1579); First Decree to Exclude Jews from Economic Life (ibid., 1580), and First Implementation Decree of 23 November 1938 (ibid., 1642); Decree concerning the Re-establishment of the Streetscape by Jewish Businesses (ibid., 1581).

51. See in detail Adam, *Judenpolitik*, 212ff.; Joseph Walk (ed.), *Das Sonderrecht für die Juden im NS-Staat. Eine Sammlung der gesetzlichen Massnahmen und Richtlinien* (Heidelberg, 1996), Section III.

52. *IMT* 28, 1816-PS, 499ff.

53. Götz Aly and Susanne Heim, 'Staatliche und organische Lösung. Die Rede Hermann Görings über die Judenfrage vom 6. Dezember 1938', in *Jahrbuch für Antisemitismusforschung* 2 (1993), 378–414.

54. *ADAP* D 4, No. 271.

55. On the Fischböck Plan see *ADAP* C 5, No. 650. The transfer of the assignment to Schacht was announced by Göring at the meeting on 6 December.

56. *ADAP* D 5, No. 659: According to Schacht, on 2 February Hitler had agreed to the discussions in London and instructed him to continue them.

57. BAB, R 2501/6641, Rublee to Schacht, 23 December 1938; *ADAP* C 5, No. 661. On the Schacht–Rublee negotiations see Weingarten, *Hilfeleistung*, 127ff.; Albert Fischer, *Hjalmar Schacht und Deutschlands 'Judenfrage'. Der 'Wirtschaftsdiktator' und die Vertreibung der Juden aus der deutschen Wirtschaft* (Cologne, Weimar, and Vienna, 1995), 216ff.

58. Weingarten, *Hilfeleistung*, 135ff.

59. See Herbert A. Strauss, 'Jewish Emigration from Germany. Nazi Policy and Jewish Responses' in *Leo Baeck Institute Yearbook* 25 (1980), 313–61 (I) and 26 (1981), 343–409.

60. On 14 November, on Heydrich's instructions, department II of the SD Main Office had already prepared four versions of a badge for marking Jews. See OA Moskau, 500-1-659.

61. Aly and Heim, 'Ordnung'. The conference held in the Interior Ministry on 16 December 1938 was important for the further administrative implementation of the anti-Semitic measures. See Susanne Heim and Götz Aly (eds), *Bevölkerungsstruktur und Massenmord. Neue Dokumente zur deutschen Politik der Jahre 1938 bis 1945* (Berlin, 1991), Doc. 1.

62. *IMT* 25, 069-PS, 131ff.

63. Walk (ed.), *Sonderrecht*, Section III, No. 154.

64. Law on Tenancies with Jews, 30 April 1939 (*RGBl.* 1939 I, 864).

65. Circular Decree from the Reich Interior Minister. See *Reichsministerialblatt der inneren Verwaltung (RBliV)* 1939, 1291, 16 June 1939.

66. Walk (ed.), *Sonderrecht*, Section III, 273ff.

67. Thus, at a meeting on 28 February 1939 'the wartime service of Jews' was considered and confinement to barracks was contemplated. See OA Moskau, 504-2-2 [20], Minute of the Chief of the Security Police, 1 March 1939, published in Konrad Kwiet, 'Forced Labour of German Jews in Nazi Germany', in *Leo Baeck Institute Yearbook* 36 (1991), 408ff. See also Gruner, *Der geschlossene Arbeitseinsatz deutscher Juden. Zur Zwangsarbeit als Element der Verfolgung 1938–1943* (Berlin, 1997), 83f.

68. Tooze, *Ökonomie,* 343f.

69. BAF, RM 7/1207.

70. Mason, *Arbeiterklasse*, Doc. 152.

71. See Tooze, *Ökonomie,* 342.

72. Mark Spoerer, *Vom Scheingewinn zum Rüstungsboom. Die Eigenkapitalrentabilität der deutschen Industrieaktiengesellschaften 1925–1941* (Stuttgart, 1996), 90.

73. Peter Kirchberg, 'Typisierung in der deutschen Kraftfahrindustrie und der Generalbevollmächtigte für das Kraftfahrwesen. Ein Beitrag zur Problematik staatsmonopolistischer Kriegsvorbereitung', in *Jahrbuch für Wirtschaftsgeschichte*

(1969/2), 117–42; Decree concerning the Standardization of Types in the German Motor Industry (*RGBl.* 1939 I, 386).

74. IfZ, 1276-NG, Göring to Todt, Appointmnent of a general plenipotentiary for the construction industry, 9 December 1938.

75. BAF, RL 3/2198, Minute of meetings with Göring on 26 October 1938, 7 November 1938, which resulted in the construction programme of 6 December 1938; see Budrass, *Flugzeugindustrie*, 557ff.

76. BAF, RL 3/1011, Aircraft construction programme No. 11, first to third drafts, see Budrass, *Flugzeugindustrie*, 566f.

77. Salewski, *Seekriegsleitung* 3, No. 1; Dülffer, *Weimar*, 488ff.; Salewski, *Seekriegsleitung* 2, 39, and 57; Deist, 'Aufrüstung', 550 and 559.

78. Salewski, *Seekriegsleitung* 1, 59; Dülffer, *Weimar*, 492ff.; Deist, 'Aufrüstung', 562f.

79. BAF, RM 7/1207, Naval Command Office, Plan of the monthly fuel requirement for the navy; see Wilhelm Meier-Dörnberg, *Die Ölversorgung der Kriegsmarine 1935 bis 1945* (Freiburg, 1973).

80. Salewski, *Seekriegsleitung* 1, 60.

81. BAF, RM 7/1207, Raeder memorandum (3 September 1938); Kershaw, *Hitler*, 2, 220.

82. IfZ, Da 03.03, Budget 1939 (Berlin 1941).

83. *IMT* 27, 1301-PS, 166ff.

84. *IMT* 36, 363-EC, 365ff.; Geyer, 'Rüstungsbeschleunigung', 145.

85. *IMT* 27, 1301-PS, 166ff.

86. BAF, RH 15/151, Reports Nos 1 and 2, 10 February 1939, and Brauchitsch to Keitel, 10 December 1938.

87. See the Reich Bank's memorandum concerning inflationary tendencies composed a few days after the Munich agreement in BAB, R 2501/6521; Tooze, *Ökonomie*, 334ff.; *IMT* 36, 611-EC, 582ff.

88. Considered in detail in Tooze, *Ökonomie,* 349f.; *IMT* 36, 369-EC, 365ff., here p. 365.

89. Kopper, *Schacht*, 327ff.

90. The Reich Bank's statutes were altered in June 1939. The money supply could now be increased at will. See Tooze, *Ökonomie*, 351.

91. *ADAP* D 5, No. 119; Schmidt, *Statist*, 433f.

92. Kotowski, 'Piemont'.

93. Ibid., 67. See also *PA* 1938, Nos 3432, 3627, and 3635.

94. *ADAP* D 5, No. 119.

95. Ibid., No. 120.

96. Ibid., No. 126; Schmidt, *Statist*, 434f.

97. In response to a query from King Carol II of Romania as to 'Germany's attitude towards a Ukrainian state that made itself independent of the Bolshevik regime in Moscow', Göring responded on 26 November 1938 significantly 'that we would support a Ukrainian freedom movement in every way'. See *ADAP* D 5, No. 257. Horthy spoke to the German ambassador about the 'anticipated German involvement in the Ukraine, which, together with similar action by

Italy and Japan, must happen at some point in order to resist the Bolshevik threat.' See *ADAP* D 4, No. 118. The fact that the Chief of the General Staff, Halder, had already referred to the impending annexation of the Ukraine in December 1938 is confirmed by the statement of the former US Consul in Berlin, Geist. See *IMT* 28, 1759-PS, 234ff.

98. *Goebbels TB*, 1 February, and 3 February 1939, on Hitler's intense preoccupation with foreign policy issues.

99. *ADAP* D 5, No. 272.

100. Rönnefahrt, *Sudetenkrise* 1, 714; Heinrich Bodensieck, 'Der Plan eines "Freundschaftsvertrages" zwischen dem Reich und der Tschecho-Slovakei im Jahre 1938', in *Zeitschrift für Ostforschung* 10 (1961), 462–76; *ADAP* D 4, 161: the treaty preparations envisaged the draft of a treaty of friendship, an agreement on economic union, and a military pact, and would have placed Czechoslovakia in a similar state of dependence on the Reich as the 'Protectorate' created in 1939.

101. Ibid., No. 158.

102. Ibid., No. 159.

103. *ADAP* D 5, No. 272.

104. *ADAP* D 4, No. 158.

105. At these meetings it was generally agreed to make Schacht's ideas the basis for future emigration policy. See OA Moskau, 500-1-638, Minutes, 19 January 1939.

106. BAB, R 58/276. The compulsory amalgamation in this organization was, however, only ordered on 4 July 1939 by the 10th Decree implementing the Reich Citizenship Law. See *RGBl.* 1939 I, 1097. For details on the background see Wolf Gruner, 'Poverty and Persecution. The Reichsvereinigung, the Jewish Population, and Anti-Jewish Policy in the Nazi State 1939–1945', in *Yad Vashem Studies* 27 (1999), 28ff.; Esriel Hildesheimer, *Jüdische Selbstverwaltung unter dem NS-Regime. Der Existenzkampf der Reichsvertretung und Reichsvereinigung der Juden in Deutschland* (Tübingen, 1994), 79ff.

107. *ADAP* D 5, No. 664.

108. He had not made this demand publicly in 1938, and in 1937 only on 3 October on the Bückeberg in connection with the colonial question, and on 21 November at an anniversary celebration of the Augsburg local branch of the Party. See Domarus, 1, 760. At the beginning of November he told Goebbels they must treat the colonial question in a dilatory fashion. See *TB*, 3 November 1937.

109. See, for example, 'Rede Friedrich Schmidt'; *Der Hoheitsträger*, 11 (November 1938), with relevant Lebensraum quotations from *MK*; see also Groscurth, *Tagebücher*, 166f. referring to a speech by Hitler to troop commanders on 10 February 1939; on this see in detail Sywottek, *Mobilmachung*, 180ff.

110. Ibid., 183. On the further use of the topic in propaganda see below p. 618.

111. Domarus, 2, 1047ff. For the relevant passage see 1055-8; on the dissemination of the speech by propaganda see Longerich, *'Davon'*, 142.

112. Domarus, 2, 1077ff.

113. Kershaw, *Hitler*, 2, 230ff.; Hoensch, *Slowakei*, 210ff.

114. Ibid., 224ff.

115. *ADAP* D 4, No. 168; Hoensch, *Slowakei*, 226ff.

116. Hill (ed.), *Weizsäcker-Papiere*, 13 February 1940.

117. *Goebbels TB*, 11 March 1939.

118. *PA* 1939, Nos 737, 757, 762, 770–772, and 776, see also Nos 781–790.

119. *Goebbels TB*, 11 March 1939; Hoensch, *Slowakei*, 268ff.

120. Ibid., 281ff.

121. Domarus, 2, 1090.

122. Below, *Adjutant*, 151; Keitel, *Leben*, 235.

123. *ADAP* D 4, Nos 198 and 228; see also Hoensch, *Revisionismus*, 259.

124. *ADAP* D 4, No. 210.

125. Ibid., No. 237.

126. Ibid., No. 202; *Goebbels TB*, 14 March 1939.

127. *ADAP* D 4, No. 209; see also Hoensch, *Slowakei*, 290ff.

128. *Goebbels TB*, 15 March 1939.

129. *ADAP* D 6, No. 10.

130. Ibid., No. 40.

131. *ADAP* D 4, No. 228; Schmidt, *Statist*, 435ff.; Below, *Adjutant*, 154; Keitel, *Leben*, 236.

132. *ADAP* D 4, No. 229.

133. Domarus, 2, 1098f.; Below, *Adjutant*, 153f.

134. Edict of the Führer and Reichskanzler concerning the Protectorate of Bohemia and Moravia, 16 March 1939. See *RGBl.* 1939 I, 485ff.

135. Domarus, 2, 1101ff.; Below, *Adjutant*, 154f.

136. *PA* 1939, No. 856.

137. *Goebbels TB*, 20 March 1939; *VB* (B), 20 March 1939, 'Der triumphale Empfang Adolf Hitlers in Berlin – eine stolze Dankes-Kundgebung des ganzen deutschen Volkes'.

138. Kershaw, *Hitler-Mythos*, 172, based on various reports from Bavaria; *Sopade* 1939, 275ff.

139. Below, *Adjutant*, 158.

140. Chamberlain announced his departure from the policy of 'Appeasement' adopted hitherto in his Birmingham speech of 17 March published in Neville Chamberlain, *The Struggle for Peace* (London, 1939), 411ff. For the British cabinet's response to the occupation of Bohemia and Moravia see Weinberg, *Foreign Policy*, 698ff.

141. Protests: *DBFP* 3/4, Nos 308 and 401; *ADAP* D 6, Nos 19f. and 26. For the summoning of the ambassadors see ibid., 308 (Note). See also Martin Broszat, 'Die Reaktion der Mächte auf den 15. März 1938', in *Bohemia* 8 (1967), 253–80.

142. *Goebbels TB*, 20 March 1939.

143. Ernst-Albrecht Plieg, *Das Memelland 1920–1939. Deutsche Autonomiebestrebungen im litauischen Gesamtstaat* (Würzburg, 1962); Joachim Tauber, 'Deutschland,

Litauen, und das Memelgebiet 1938/39', in Jürgen Zarusky and Martin Zuckert (eds), *Das Münchener Abkommen*, 429–440.

144. *IMT* 34, 136-C, 477. Referred to in detail above, p. 589.

145. Plieg, *Memelland*, 193ff. Neumann, the leading figure on the list of Memel Germans, had been receiving instructions from Berlin from summer 1938 onwards. See *ADAP* D 5, Nos 349, 361, 364, 369–372, and 382.

146. Ibid., No. 381.

147. Ibid., Nos 399ff.; for the text of the treaty see ibid., 440f. (note).

148. Domarus, 2, 1112f.

149. *Goebbels TB*, 25 March 1939.

INTO WAR

1. Hermann Graml, *Europas Weg in den Krieg. Hitler und die Mächte* (Munich, 1990), 151ff. and 184ff.; Weinberg, *Foreign Policy*, 695ff.

2. *ADAP* D 6, No. 61.

3. Ibid., Nos 73 and 88.

4. Ibid., Nos 101 and 118; Lipski, *Diplomat*, Doc. 139; *Schulthess' 1939*, 331f. and 335ff. (on the events in London); Kershaw, *Hitler*, 2, 240ff.

5. Through a statement by Daladier on 13 April. See *Schulthess' 1939*, 424f.

6. *ADAP* D 6, No. 99.

7. From the end of February 1939 onwards, Goebbels had published a series of violently anti-British leaders in the *VB*, which were also given prominence in the rest of the press: 'Krieg in Sicht' (25 February), 'Schluß mit der Moral-Heuchelei' (21 March), 'Moral der Reichen' (25 March). On the anti-British *VB* articles see also Helmut Michels, *Ideologie und Propaganda. Die Rolle von Joseph Goebbels in der nationalsozialistischen Außenpolitik bis 1939* (Frankfurt a. M., 1992), 395ff.; Longerich, *Goebbels*, 406f. On the campaign in general see the press instructions for 21 and 29 March 1939 (PA 1939, Nos 885 and 967). It was restarted at the beginning of April in a toned down form. See ibid., Nos 1013, 1019f., 1023, 1031, and 1074.

8. Domarus, 2, 1119, quotes p. 1122f.

9. Ibid., 1127.

10. *IMT* 34, 120-C, 380ff. Hitler's signature was procured on 11 April 1939, in other words after Easter; he signed some parts of the comprehensive directive later. The additional directive to Keitel to complete everything by 1 September was issued before 3 April 1939.

11. See the address to the generals by Halder, Chief of the General Staff, in the second half of April. Halder encouraged them to believe in a triumphal victory against Poland and played down the threat of intervention by the western powers. See Christian Hartmann and Sergej Z. Sluč, 'Franz Halder und die Kriegsvorbereitungen im Frühjahr 1939. Eine Ansprache des Generalstabschefs des Heeres', in *VfZ* 45 (1997), 467–95. The authenticity of the copy has been questioned by Klaus Mayer, 'Eine authentische Halder-Ansprache? Kritische Anmerkungen zu einem Dokumentenfund im früheren Moskauer

Sonderarchiv', in *MGM* 58 (1999), 471–527. The positive response of the military to Hitler's anti-Polish policy is, however, not in dispute. See Müller, *Heer*, 390ff.

12. *ADAP* 6 No. 169; Graml, *Weg*, 20ff.

13. Groscurth, *Tagebücher*, 173; Graml, *Weg*, 200f.

14. On the celebrations see Domarus, 2, 1144ff.; *Goebbels TB*, 20 and 21 April 1939; Peter Bucher, 'Hitlers 50. Geburtstag. Zur Quellenvielfalt im Bundesarchiv', in Heinz Boberach and Hans Bohms (eds), *Aus der Arbeit des Bundesarchivs. Beiträge zum Archivwesen, zur Quellenkunde und Zeitgeschichte* (Boppard am Rhein, 1977), 423–46; Kurt Pätzold, 'Hitlers fünfzigster Geburtstag am 20. April 1939', in Dietrich Eichholtz and Pätzold (eds), *Der Weg in den Krieg. Studien zur Geschichte der Vorkriegsjahre (1935/36 bis 1939)* (Cologne 1989), 309–46.; Kershaw, *Hitler*, 2, 247ff.; Armin Fuhrer, *'Führergeburtstag' Die perfide Propaganda des NS-Regimes mit dem 20. April* (Berlin, 2014), 93ff.; BAB, NS 10/127, Working plan for the Celebration of the Führer's 50th Birthday, 12 April 1939, and Schedule for the Celebration of the Führer's 50th Birthday timed to the Minute, 16 April 1939; *VB* (B), Special supplement for 20 April and the 21 April 1939 issue.

15. Ibid., 19 April 1939.

16. Law concerning Special National Holidays, 17 April 1939, and Decree implementing the Law concerning Special National Holidays. See *RGBl.* 1939 I, 763f.

17. Fritz Terveen, 'Der Filmbericht über Hitlers 50. Geburtstag. Ein Beispiel nationalsozialistischer Selbstdarstellung und Propaganda', in *VjZ* 7 (1959), 75–84.

18. VB (N) Special supplement, 20 April 1939.

19. *DAZ*, 20 April 1939.

20. *Meldungen*, 2, 292ff.

21. *Sopade* 1939, 119ff.

22. Ibid., 9; see also 187ff. (Shortage of agricultural workers), 227ff. (Disappointed hopes of the middle class), 303ff. (Among the bourgeoisie there is an apocalyptic mood), 359ff. (Workers' attitude), 625ff. (Further deterioration in the supply of foodstuffs), 757ff. (Workers' attitude), 859ff. (Food shortages), 868ff. (Decline of the artisan class). Kershaw, *Hitler-Mythos*, 148ff., on the middle class's increasingly critical attitude.

23. On Hitler's birthday see *Sopade* 1939, 435ff.

24. Ibid., 442.

25. On the provisional propaganda treatment of Roosevelt's initiative see PA 1939, Nos 1129 and 1139f.

26. *VB* (B), 22 April 1939, 'Lord Halifax macht Witze' (Leader), and 27 April 1939, 'Ein paar Worte über politischen Takt' (Leader); see also PA 1939, No. 1234.

27. Domarus, 2, 1148ff. On the speech see also: Kershaw, *Hitler*, 2, 254f. On the abrogation of the pacts with Poland and Britain see *ADAP* D 6, No. 276f.

28. This section of the speech alone takes up 12 pages in Domarus's edition (1266ff.). Goebbels had ensured that a few days earlier the *12 Uhr Blatt* had published 'an article attacking Roosevelt' (*TB*, 18 April 1939); *12 Uhr Blatt*, 17 April 1938, 'Was sagen Sie nun, Herr Roosevelt?'.

29. PA 1939, Nos 1275, 1343, and 1383. The campaign reached an initial climax with two Goebbels articles in the *VB* against the allegedly anti-German tendencies in Poland; in a statement aimed at the rest of the press the propaganda ministry referred to a 'warning shot'. See the *VB* [B], 5 May 1939, 'Quo Vadis, Polonia?', and 13 May 1939, 'Bajonette als Wegweiser'; *PA* 1939, No. 1458.

30. *Goebbels TB*, 2 May 1939.

31. *PA* 1939, Nos 1338, 1343, and 1363. On the provisional attitude of reserve see also *Goebbels TB*, 7 May 1939.

32. *PA* 1939, Nos 1362, 1378, 1380, 1566, and 1862; extensive material on the 'attempt to make the Wehrmacht popular' in Sywottek, *Mobilmachung*, 166.

33. Domarus, 2 1189f.; see the continuous reporting in the *VB* from 16 to 19 May 1939, which, as was the case with the rest of the press and despite all its efforts, was criticized as inadequate by the propaganda ministry.

34. *ADAP* D 6, Nos 377 and 385. This was launched by a Goebbels leader in the *VB* (B), 20 May 1939, 'Die Einkreiser'.

35. *ADAP* D 6, Nos 78 and 131.

36. *Schulthess' 1939*, 338f. and 424f.

37. On the Anglo-Turkish solidarity pact see ibid., 353; *DBFP* 3/5, No. 506. See also *ADAP* D 6, No. 413.

38. On German–Italian relations since early 1939 see Graml, *Weg*, 216ff.; Weinberg, *Foreign Policy*, 714ff.

39. Karl Stuhlpfarrer, *Umsiedlung Südtirol 1939–1940*, 2 vols (Vienna, 1985); Leopold Steurer, *Südtirol zwischen Rom und Berlin 1919–1939* (Vienna, Munich, and Zurich, 1980).

40. Toscano, *Origins*, 153ff.; Ciano, *Diary*, 3, 6, and 8 March 1938.

41. *ADAP* D 4, Nos 543, 547, 549, and 555; on the increasingly controversial response to the project in Japan see the reports of the German embassy in Tokyo in April and May 1939 (*ADAP* D 6, Nos 254, 266, 275, 298, 306, 322, 326, 339, 344, and 363); on the decision-making process in the Japanese cabinet see ibid., Nos 400, 410, and 427. In the end the Germans failed to receive any news about a Japanese decision, which Ribbentrop complained about via the German embassy in Tokyo (ibid., No. 447). Toscano, *Origins*, 105.

42. Ibid., 307ff.

43. *ADAP* D 6, Nos 52 and 205.

44. Ibid., No. 341; see also ibid., 367ff. Mussolini had told Ciano before the negotiations that Italy still needed three more years of peace. See Toscano, *Origins*, 289f. On the further course of the negotiations see *ADAP* D 6, Nos 369–71 and 386; Schmidt, *Statist*, 445.

45. *ADAP* D 6, No. 426.

46. Ciano, *Diary*, 21–23 May 1939.

47. *ADAP* D 6, No. 459.

48. See the documents in ibid., Appendix, 929ff., among them, in particular, I, III, VI, IX, und XII.

49. Weinberg, *Foreign Policy*, 738ff.; Graml, *Weg*, 221ff.

50. Peter Klefisch, *Das Dritte Reich und Belgien 1933–1939* (Frankfurt a. M., 1998), 247ff.; *ADAP* D 5, No. 475.

51. *ADAP* D 6, No. 461.

52. Ibid., No. 485; Treaties: *RGBl.* 1939 II, 945f. and 947f.

53. *Schulthess' 1939*, 130.

54. Johann Wuescht, *Jugoslawien und das Dritte Reich. Eine dokumentierte Geschichte der deutsch–jugoslawischen Beziehungen von 1933 bis 1945* (Stuttgart, 1969), 121ff. On the German attempts to persuade Yugoslavia to quit the League of Nations see ADAP D 6, Nos 474, 534, 637, 675, 720, 733, and 745.

55. Ibid., Nos 578 and 712.

56. Ibid., No. 784.

57. Ibid., No. 433; see Kershaw, *Hitler*, 2, 256ff.

58. See above p. 592.

59. Tooze, *Ökonomie,* 363ff.

60. BAF, RH 15/151, 7 February 1939 includes another version from 8 February. According to Bernhard R. Kroener, *Generaloberst Friedrich Fromm. 'Der starke Mann im Heimatkriegsgebiet'. Eine Biographie* (Paderborn, 2005), 318, this report was sent to Hitler on 10 February 1939.

61. BAF, RH 15/151; Kroener, *Fromm*, 319.

62. BAF, RH 15/152.

63. Ibid., Brauchitsch to Keitel, 19 June 1939.

64. *IMT* 36, 28-EC, S. 112ff.; Tooze, *Ökonomie*, 362f., refers to this address, which starkly outlined the weaknesses in German armaments production in 1939.

65. On the military preparations in Britain see Marian Zgórniak, *Europa am Abgrund – 1938* (Münster, Hamburg, and London, 2002), 235ff.

66. Tooze, *Ökonomie*, 365f. (on the basis of German documents in the Imperial War Museum, London).

67. Ibid, 367ff.; Bernd-Jürgen Wendt, 'Durch das "strategische Fenster" in den zweiten Weltkrieg. Die Motive Hitlers', in Uwe Backes, Eckhard Jesse, and Rainer Zitelmann (eds), *Die Schatten der Vergangenheit. Impulse zur Historisierung des Nationalsozialismus* (Frankfurt a. M., 1990), esp. 367f.

68. *PA* 1939, Nos 1819, 1922, 1951, 1960, 1993, and 2015.

69. Domarus, 2, 1204.

70. Ibid., 1205ff., quotes 1207f.; PA 1939, No. 1731.

71. Domarus, 2, 1209ff., quote 1211.

72. Ibid., 1212f.; Below, *Adjutant*, 168f.

73. *DBFP* 3/6, No. 136.

74. Domarus, 2, 1215.

75. *Goebbels TB*, 5 July 1939.

76. Leaders in the *VB*, 20 May 1939, 'Die Einkreiser'; 27 May 1939, 'Nochmals: Die Einkreiser'; 3 June 1939, 'Klassenkampf der Völker?'; 19 June 1939, 'Erkläre mir, Graf Oerindur...'; 24 June 1939, 'Die abgehackten Kinderhände'; 30 June 1939, 'Das schreckliche Wort von der Einkreisung'. Speeches: *VB* (B), 22 June 1939, 'Die Sonnwendfeier des Gaues Berlin' (headline); 24 June 1939, 'Dr. Goebbels

sprach vor Berliner Arbeitern'; on the Goebbels speech at the Essen Gau Day on 25 June see the report in *Der Angriff* of 26 June 1939. The propaganda ministry had instructed the press to give prominence to the Danzig speech. It was a 'sounding balloon intended to test the international atmosphere for the settlement of the Danzig question etc.'. See PA 1939, No. 1890; *VB* (B), 19 June 1939, 'Danzig – Pflegestätte unserer Kultur'.

77. On the campaign see *PA* 1939, Nos 1975, 2060, 2101, 2182, 2200, 2254, and 2379. Sywottek, *Mobilmachung*, 180ff. on the main propaganda topics (Living space) 199ff. (Encirclement) and 186ff. (War guilt).

78. *Goebbels TB*, 5 and 9 July 1939.

79. *VB* (B), 14 July 1939, 'So sieht Englands Propaganda aus'; *Goebbels TB*, 5, 8, 9, and 12–14 July 1939; *PA* 1939, Nos 2237, 2296, 2310, also No. 2346. See *VB* (B), 19 July 1939, 'Neue Enthüllungen über King-Hall' (headline).

80. Domarus, 2, 1219f.

81. *Goebbels TB*, 23 and 25–28 July 1939. See also Speer, *Erinnerungen*, 165, who stated that Hitler sent the Goebbelses back to Berlin.

82. On the customs conflict see Carl J. Burckhardt, *Meine Danziger Mission 1937–1939* (Munich, 1960), 336ff.; Weinberg, *Foreign Policy*, 730.

83. *ADAP* D 6, Nos 774 and 780.

84. *PA* 1939, Nos 2659, 2661, 2681, 2695, and 2707.

85. In its official reply of 10 August 1939 the Polish government pointed out that there was no legal basis whatsoever for Germany's interference in Danzig's affairs. See *ADAP* D 7, No. 10. *ADAP* D 6, No. 785, concerning Forster's stay at the Berghof from 7 to 9 August 1939.

86. Domarus, 2, 1222.

87. *VB*, 11 August 1939, 'Der historische Protest'.

88. Burckhardt, *Mission*, 339ff.

89. This passage is missing from *DFBP* 3/6, No. 669, and is only in Burckhardt's memoirs (*Mission*, 348).

90. *ADAP* D 7, No. 43; see also Schmidt, *Statist*, 447; on Ciano's meeting with Ribbentrop see Ciano, *Diary*, 11 August 1939; Weinberg, *Foreign Policy*, 741ff.

91. *ADAP* D 7, No. 47. Both meetings took place in Ribbentrop's presence. On the stay in Berchtesgaden see also Ciano, *Diary*, 10–13 August 1939.

92. Franz Halder, *Kriegstagebuch. Tägliche Aufzeichnungen des Chefs des Generalstabes des Heeres 1939–1942*, ed. Hans-Adolf Jacobsen, 3 vols (Stuttgart, 1962–64) (KTB), 1, 14 August 1939.

93. See below pp. 664ff.

94. Domarus, 2, 1229.

95. *Goebbels TB*, 12 and 16 August 1939; PA 1939, Nos 2709, 2745, 2757, 2774, 2789, 2794, and 2810.

96. Ibid., Nos 2836 and 2843. See also the reports in the *VB* and the *DAZ* during these days, which, from 16 August onwards, were dominated by propaganda.

97. *Goebbels TB*, 20 August 1939.

98. See *PA* 1939, Nos 2871, 2888, 2921, 2923, 2976, 2986, and 3006.

99. *ADAP* D 7, No. 119, The passing on of a report by Veesenmayer, according to which Forster intended to increase his demands to such an extent that the Poles would be unable to accept them. On the approval of the foreign ministry see ibid., No. 139. On the further course of the negotiations see ibid., Nos 188, 197, and 232.

100. On the appointment see ibid., No. 224.

101. Ibid., Nos 176 and 244. The military plans did not, however, at this stage envisage an attack on the Westerplatte. See Bertil Stjernfelt and Klaus-Richard Böhme, *Westerplatte 1939* (Freiburg i. Breisgau, 1979), 68ff.

102. *ADAP* D 6, No. 1. In a speech on 10 March Stalin had commented on reports in the Western press about alleged German plans to take over the Ukraine and had gone on to attack the western powers; the Soviet Union would be careful not 'to be drawn into conflicts by those who wanted to provoke war and who were used to getting others to pull their chestnuts out of the fire'. After the war Ribbentrop, *London*, 171, maintained that this speech had prompted his change of stance towards the Soviet Union. However, according to Gustav Hilger, a member of the German embassy in Moscow, who was summoned to Hitler on 10 May 1939 to give his views on Soviet policy, at this point neither Hitler nor Ribbentrop were aware of Stalin's speech. See Hilger, *Wir und der Kreml. Deutsch-Sowjetische Beziehungen 1918–1941. Erinnerungen eines deutschen Diplomaten* (Frankfurt a. M. and Berlin, 1955), 280; 274ff. on the rapprochement between the Soviet Union and the Reich in general. Hitler referred later to Stalin's 'chestnuts' comment. See p. 630.

103. On these signals see Graml, *Weg*, 253ff.; Weinberg, *Foreign Policy*, 718ff. This can be followed in detail in the following German documents: *ADAP* D 6, Nos 215, 332, 406, 424, and 478.

104. Weinberg, *Foreign Policy*, 719ff.; Geoffrey Roberts, *The Unholy Alliance. Stalin's Pact with Hitler* (London, 1989), 118ff.

105. *ADAP* D 6, Nos 441f.; Graml, *Weg*, 258ff.

106. *ADAP* D 6, Nos 446 and 451f.; Graml, *Weg*, 261f.

107. For details see ibid., 265ff.

108. *ADAP* D 6, Nos 583, 588, 628, and 700. *Goebbels TB*, 9 July 1939: Hitler 'no longer believes that London and Moscow will reach agreement. Then the path will be clear for us.'

109. *ADAP* D 6, No. 729.

110. Ibid., Nos 758 and 760; Graml, *Weg*, 269ff.

111. *ADAP* D 7,/ No. 50.

112. Ibid., No. 56.

113. Roberts, *Alliance*, 141.

114. *ADAP* D 7, No. 70.

115. Ibid., No. 75.

116. Ibid., No. 105.

117. Ibid., No. 113.

118. Ibid., No. 131.

119. Ibid., Nos 125 and 132.

120. Referred to in ibid., No. 142.

121. Ibid., No. 142.

122. According to Peter Herde, *Italien, Deutschland und der Weg in den Krieg im Pazifik 1941* (Wiesbaden, 1983), 12, in the Japanese view the treaty, a breach of the appendix to the Anti-Comintern Pact, represented the 'nadir' in their mutual relations. Foreign Minister Ciano told the German Finance Minister, Schwerin-Krosigk on 23 August that, unlike Hitler, he did not believe that the pact would prevent the western powers from going to war. See *ADAP* D 7, No. 227.

123. Domarus, 2, 1233; also: PA 1939, Nos 2861ff. and 2870.

124. Winfried Baumgart, 'Zur Ansprache Hitlers vor den Führern der Wehrmacht am 22. August 1939. Eine quellenkritische Untersuchung', in *VfZ* 19 (1971), 120–49.

125. So far the following sources have emerged: 1. Two unsigned transcriptions from the files of the OKW, which Winfried Baumgart with some justification has attributed to Admiral Canaris (798-PS and 1014-PS, both in *IMT* 26, 338ff. and 523ff.); 2. A record by Chief of the General Staff, Halder, in note form that closely matches document 1 (Halder, *KTB*, 1, 22 August 1939); 3. an account by Admiral Boehm, which he placed at the disposal of the defence in the Nuremberg Trial and which does not contain the much tougher statements in documents 1 and 2. At the beginning of the 1970s Boehm disputed the authenticity of the other two documents in these crucial points, *IMT* 41, 16ff.; Hermann Böhm, 'Zur Ansprache Hitlers vor den Führern der Wehrmacht am 22. August 1939', in *VfZ* 19 (1971), 294–300, and Baumgart's 'Zur Ansprache Hitlers vor den Führern der Wehrmacht am 22. August 1939. Erwiderung', in *VfZ* 19 (1971), 301–4; 4. A report by General Liebmann (published in Baumgart, 'Ansprache', 141–8, also IfZ ED 1, Persönliche Erlebnisse); 5. A relatively brief account by Admiral Albrecht (published in Baumgart, 'Ansprache', 148f.); 6. A record by an unknown author that was leaked to Louis Lochner in 1939. This document contains the most aggressive statements, including Hitler's announcement that after Stalin's death he would move against the Soviet Union. In view of the uncertainty of its authorship and provenance this document is problematic (*ADAP* D 7, 171f.); 7. A record by the person who kept the official diary of the OKW, Greiner. It is not however, based on his own notes but essentially on document 1, Percy Ernst Schramm (ed.), *Kriegstagebuch des Oberkommandos der Wehrmacht (Wehrmachtführungsstab)*, 4 vols. (Frankfurt a. M., 1961–65) (*KTB, OKW*, 1, 947); 8. A brief and relatively superficial report by Hitler's Luftwaffe adjutant (Below, *Adjutant*, 180f.); 9. Notes by the Abwehr officer, Groscurth, concerning a conversation with Canaris, in which the latter reported details of the speech (Groscurth, *Tagebücher*, 179f.), a diary entry that supports Baumgart's claim for Canaris's authorship. The following account is

based largely on versions 1 and 2. Important additions from other sources will be duly noted.

126. On his intention to attack Poland see the Liebmann version; on the decision taken early that year see the Albrecht version.

127. Albrecht version: 'Germany's favourable situation, which compels us to embark on this conflict now, since it will happen sooner or later anyway.'

128. Liebmann: 'The German people will have to get used to fighting, and the Polish campaign will be good practice.'

129. On the assumption that the western powers would not intervene see Liebmann (Baumgart, 'Ansprache', 146) and Albrecht (ibid., 148).

130. Liebmann (Baumgart, 'Ansprache', 146) and Albrecht (ibid., 148).

131. *IMT* 26, 798-PS, 338ff.

132. Liebmann: 'that at the last moment some guy will put a spanner in the works by offering to mediate' (Baumgart, 'Ansprache', 146). After the speech Hitler told his Army adjutant, Engel, that the only thing he was afraid of was that 'some bleeding heart could ruin it all by coming up with a whole lot of wimpish proposals'. See Engel, *Heeresadjutant*, 22 August 1939.

133. Halder: 'Goal: Destruction of Poland – Removal of its vital strength' Albrecht only: 'Offensive, ruthless form of attack, Persecution'. Engel, *Heeresadjutant*, 22 August: After the speech Hitler had declared himself convinced 'England and France were only bluffing'. According to the memoirs of Below (A*djutant*, 177f.), the Wehrmacht was already preparing for the start of the war from 12 August onwards.

134. Halder, *KTB*, 1, 23 August, on a meeting with Keitel, the Chief of the General Staff of the Luftwaffe, and the Chief of Staff of the Navy: 'Y=26.8. (Saturday) final decision – No more orders – X-Hour: 4.30 am?? – 4.15 am??.'

135. See Liebmann's report (Baumgart, 'Ansprache', 146).

136. *Hitler-Bild*, 107ff.; Schmidt, *Statist*, 449f.; Below, *Adjutant*, 182ff., on Hitler's response to the signing of the treaty.

137. Ribbentrop, *London*, 178ff.

138. *ADAP* D 7, Nos 205 and 210.

139. Ibid., No. 228f.

140. Ibid., Nos 200f.; *DBFP* 3/7, Nos 178 and 200.

141. Weizsäcker records Hitler's contradictory attitude during these days in his memoirs (*Erinnerungen*, 254).

142. *Goebbels TB*, 24 August 1939.

143. Domarus, 2, 1253.

144. Ribbentrop, *London*, 186.

145. Weizsäcker, *Erinnerungen*, 254; *Hitler-Bild*, 118.

146. *ADAP* D 7, No. 266.

147. Ibid., No. 265; *DBFP* 3/7, No. 283f.; Henderson, *Fehlschlag*, 298ff.; Schmidt, *Statist*, 458f.

148. *Goebbels TB*, 26 August 1939.

149. *ADAP D* 7, 237, Editor's note concerning the meeting on 25 August. See Robert Coulondre, *Von Moskau nach Berlin 1936–1939 Erinnerungen des französischen Botschafters* (Bonn, 1950), 422f.; Schmidt, *Statist*, 459ff.; Weinberg, *Foreign Policy*, 768f.

150. Hill (ed.), *Weizsäcker-Papiere*, 25 August 1939; Halder, *KTB*, 1, 26 August 1939.

151. *ADAP* D 7, Nr. 271; Schmidt, *Statist*, 461f.; Weinberg, *Foreign Policy*, 770ff.

152. Hitler appeared 'very affected' by the bad news (Ribbentrop, *London*, 187), 'extremely disappointed and disgruntled' (Schmidt, *Statist*, 461f), 'rather downcast' (Halder, *KTB*, 1, 26 August 1939). *Goebbels TB*, 26 August 1939: 'The Führer ponders and muses. It's a serious blow for him'. Engel, *Heeresadjutant*, 25 August 1939: 'Führer was at first depressed. One could see that he was rather at a loss'.

153. According to Halder, *KTB*, 1, the treaty was signed at 17.00 (25 August 1939) and was made public at 16.30 (28 August 1939).

154. Ibid., 25 August 1939.

155. For troop reinforcements see Graml, *Weg*, 292; IfZ, F 34/1, Vormann, 11f.; Halder, *KTB*, 1, 27–31 August 1939; Engel, *Heeresadjutant*, 26 August 1939.

156. Halder, *KTB*, 1, 26 August 1939.

157. *ADAP* D 7, No. 277.

158. Ibid., No. 301.

159. Ibid., No. 307; Ciano, *Diary*, 25 August 1939: Ambassador Mackensen had asked him to make the list as comprehensive as possible in order to have a moderating effect on his government. On the formulation of the reply see ibid., 26 August 1939.

160. *ADAP* D 7, Nos 317 and 320.

161. Birger Dahlerus, *Der letzte Versuch London-Berlin, Sommer 1939* (Munich, 1948), 19ff.

162. Ibid., 51ff.

163. Halder, *KTB*, 1, 26 August 1939.

164. *ADAP* D 7, No. 324.

165. *Goebbels TB*, 27 August 1939, also 28 August 1939 concerning the letter.

166. *ADAP* D 7, No. 324, also note on 277 re: confidentiality, and No. 354.

167. Halder, *KTB*, 1, 28 August, notes for Hitler's address to the deputies; the content is consistent with the statements in Groscurth, *Tagebücher*, 190, and Hill, (ed.), *Weizsäcker-Papiere*, 28 August 1939. See Domarus, 2, 1276f.

168. *Goebbels TB*, 28 August 1939.

169. *ADAP* D 7, No. 350; see also Ciano, *Diary*, 27 August 1939. According to Ciano's notes the Italians were surprised to hear from the British about the German proposal of a treaty.

170. *Goebbels TB*, 28 August 1939.

171. Dahlerus, *Versuch*, 75ff.

172. *ADAP* D 7, No. 384; Henderson, *Fehlschlag*, 302f.; Weinberg, *Foreign Policy*, 777.

173. Halder, *KTB*, 1, 28 August 1939; Hill (ed.), *Weizsäcker-Papiere*, 31 August 1939, documents Weizsäcker' continuing irritation at Hitler's policy.

174. *ADAP* D 7, No. 421.

175. *Goebbels TB*, 30 August 1939.

176. Henderson, *Fehlschlag*, 304ff.; Schmidt, *Statist*, 464f.; *DBFP* 3/7, No. 455; Halder, *KTB*, 1, 28 August 1939: 'Account: We demand Danzig, a corridor through the Corridor and a plebiscite on the lines of the Saar one. England may accept. Poland probably not. Split!' See ibid., 29 August 1939, on Poland: 'Führer wants to receive them tomorrow. Basic idea: set out a whole lot of demographic and democratic demands. Plebiscite within 6 months under international guarantee'. Halder noted a further schedule: '30. 8. Poles in Berlin. 31. 8. Break down. 1. 9. Use of force.' See also Weinberg, *Foreign Policy*, 777ff.

177. `ADAP D 7, No. 417f.; Ciano, *Diary*, 29 August 1939; Schmidt, *Statist*, 465.

178. Dahlerus, *Versuch*, 92ff.

179. *RGBl.* 1939 I, 1539f.

180. *ADAP* D 7, No. 450; *DBFP* 3/7, Nos 504, 520, and 570f.

181. *ADAP* D 7, No. 461.

182. Ibid., No. 493; Halder, *KTB*, 1, 30 and 31 August 1939: Preparations for the attack on 1 September.

183. *ADAP* D 7, Nos 476 and 482; *Goebbels TB*, 1 September 1939; Hill (ed.), *Weizsäcker-Papiere*, 31 August 1939; Schmidt, *Statist*, 469.

184. *ADAP* D 7, 390 (note).

185. *Goebbels TB*, 1 September 1939.

186. The argument that Hitler was forced to act was put forward above all by Tim Mason and has been largely rejected by other scholars. The dynamic created by rearmament played a role in 'accelerating his aggressive policy' but it did not by any means compel him to start a world war in summer 1939. See Richard Overy, 'Hitler's War Plans and the German Economy', in Robert W. D. Boyce and Esmonde M. Robertson (eds), *Paths to War. New Essays on the Origins of the Second World War* (Basingstoke and London, 1989), 96–127; for Mason's final position see Timothy W. Mason, 'The Domestic Dynamics of Nazi Conquests. A Response to Critics' in Mason, *Nazism, Fascism and the Working Class*, ed. Jane Caplan (Cambridge and New York), 295–322.

THE OUTBREAK OF WAR

1. Jürgen Runzheimer, 'Die Grenzzwischenfälle am Abend vor dem deutschen Angriff auf Polen', in Wolfgang Benz and Hermann Graml (eds), *Sommer 1939. Die Großmächte und der Europäische Krieg* (Stuttgart, 1979), 107–40; Stjernfelt/ Böhme, *Westerplatte*, 78ff.; Horst Rohde, 'Hitlers erster Blitzkrieg und seine Auswirkungen auf Nordosteuropa', in Klaus A. Maier et al., *Die Errichtung der Hegemonie auf dem europäischen Kontinent* (Stuttgart, 1979), 111ff.

2. Domarus, 2, 1307.

3. Ibid., 1312ff., quotes 1315.

4. Ibid., 1314.

5. Ibid., 1316.

6. Law concerning the Reunification of the City of Danzig with the Reich, 1 September 1939 (*RGBl.* 1939 I, 1547f.).

7. *ADAP* D 7, No. 504.

8. Dahlerus, *Versuch*, 125ff.

9. *ADAP* D 7, Nos 513 and 515.

10. Ibid., Nos 535, 539, 541, 554, and 558. See also *Goebbels TB*, 4 September 1939, on Hitler's reaction. According to Goebbels, on 2 September Hitler would still have been prepared to agree to an international conference (without preconditions), provided that he had the 'security' of a territorial gain (ibid., 3 September 1939).

11. *ADAP* D 7, Nos 560–63.

12. Schmidt, *Statist*, 472f.; Ribbentrop, *London*, 202, on the same situation: 'Hitler didn't say a word, he had reckoned with them declaring war.' See *Goebbels TB*, 4 September 1939.

13. Ibid., 15 September, see also 9 September 1939.

14. Below, *Adjutant*, 208; Jochen von Lang, *Der Adjutant. Karl Wolff: Der Mann zwischen Hitler und Himmler* (Munich, 1985), 133ff.; Otto Dietrich, *Auf den Straßen des Sieges. Erlebnisse mit dem Führer in Polen* (Munich, 1940), 27ff.

15. Keitel, *Leben*, 253f.; Franz W. Seidler and Dieter Zeigert, *Die Führerhauptquartiere. Anlagen und Planungen im Zweiten Weltkrieg* (Munich, 2000), 124f.; BAF, RW 47/4 KTB, Führerhauptquartier. To begin with, the train was in Bad Polzin and Plietznitz stations, then at the army training ground in Groß-Born. On 8 September it travelled to Ilnau, on the 12th to Gogolin (both in Upper Silesia). On the 17th Hitler was in Berlin and then set off for Danzig on the 18th. On the inspection trips he made from his mobile headquarters see Domarus, 2, 1347ff. See also the propaganda publications by Dietrich, *Straßen* (with a map of the 'front trips') and Heinrich Hoffmann (ed.), *Hitler in Polen* (Berlin, 1939), and the daily press reports, for example in the *VB*.

16. See *ADAP* D 7, No. 567.

17. Domarus, 2, 1354ff.

18. Ibid., 1368.

19. Helmut Krausnick, 'Die Einsatzgruppen vom Anschluß Österreichs bis zum Feldzug gegen die Sowjetunion. Entwicklung und Verhältnis zur Wehrmacht', in Krausnick and Hans-Heinrich Wilhelm, *Die Truppe des Weltanschauungskrieges. Die Einsatzgruppen der Sicherheitspolizei und des SD 1938–1942* (Stuttgart, 1981), 33ff. For a detailed account of the leadership cadre see Alexander B. Rossino, *Hitler Strikes Poland. Blitzkrieg, Ideology and Atrocity* (Lawrence, 2003), 29ff. On the German terror in Poland during the war see Czeslaw Madajczyk, *Die Okkupationspolitik Deutschlands in Polen 1939–1945* (Berlin, 1987), 14ff.

20. BAB, R 58/241, Directives for the External Deployment of the Security Police and the SD, 31 July 1939; see Krausnick, 'Einsatzgruppen', 36.

21. Dorothee Weitbrecht, 'Ermächtigung zur Vernichtung. Die Einsatzgruppen in Polen im Herbst 1939', in Backes, Jesse and Zitelmann (eds), *Schatten*, 59ff.

22. Krausnick, 'Einsatzgruppen', 44.

23. BAB, R 58/825, 8 September 1939.

24. Ibid., 14 October 1939.

25. Halder, *KTB* 1, 19 September 1939. Generalquartiermeister Eduard Wagner reports in his diary (Elizabeth Wagner (ed.), *Der Generalquartiermeister. Briefe und Tagebuchaufzeichnungen des Generalquartiermeisters des Heeres. General der Artillerie Eduard Wagner* (Munich and Vienna, 1963)), for 19 September 1939 an 'important, necessary, and forthright conversation' with Heydrich.

26. Krausnick, 'Hitler und die Morde in Polen. Ein Beitrag zum Konflikt zwischen Heer und SS um die Verwaltung der besetzten Gebiete', in *VfZ* 11 (1963), 196–209.

27. Ibid.

28. Christian Jansen and Arno Weckbecker, *Der 'volksdeutsche Selbstschutz' in Polen 1939/40* (Munich, 1992), 27ff.; Wlodzimierz Jastrzębski, *Der Bromberger Blutsonntag. Legende und Wirklichkeit* (Poznan, 1990). In fact, 4,500–5,000 ethnic Germans were killed during the war. See Jansen and Weckbecker, *'Selbstschutz'*, 28; Madajczyk, *Okkupationspolitik*, 13.

29. Jansen and Weckbecker, *'Selbstschutz'*, 82ff.

30. On the role of the uniformed police see Klaus-Michael Mallmann, '"...Mißgeburten, die nicht auf dieser Welt gehören". Die deutsche Ordnungspolizei in Polen 1939–1941', in Mallmann and Bogdan Musial (eds), *Genesis des Genozids. Polen 1939–1941* (Darmstadt, 2004).

31. Martin Cüppers, '"...auf eine so saubere und anständige SS-mäßige Art". Die Waffen SS in Polen 1939–1941', in Mallmann and Musial, *Genesis*, 90–110.

32. Joachim Böhler, *Auftakt zum Vernichtungskrieg. Die Wehrmacht in Polen 1939* (Frankfurt a. M., 2006).

33. Madajczyk, *Okkupationspolitik*, 12.

34. Groscurth, *Tagebücher*, 202 (private diary), on this information from Halder.

35. Krausnick, 'Einsatzgruppen', 49.

36. Groscurth, *Tagebücher*, 357ff.

37. Müller, *Heer*, Appendix, No. 45.

38. Krausnick, 'Einsatzgruppen', 80ff.

39. *RGBl.* 1939 I, 2017f. See in detail Bianca Vieregge, *Die Gerichtsbarkeit einer 'Elite'. Nationalsozialistische Rechtsprechung am Beispiel der SS-und-Polizei-Gerichtsbarkeit* (Baden-Baden, 2002).

40. *Meldungen*, 2, 330f., 347 ('General desire for peace'), 356, 364 ('Confidence'), 372 ('Good mood') and 381 ('Mood calm. Desire for peace'). *Goebbels TB*, 22 and 24 September 1939. *Sopade* 1939, 975ff. (Inconsistent mood) and 980ff. (No enthusiasm for war. People don't believe in war against the western powers).

41. Domarus, 2, 1317.

42. Willi A. Boelcke (ed.), *Kriegspropaganda 1939–1941. Geheime Ministerkonferenzen im Reichspropagandaministerium* (Stuttgart, 1966), 26 October 1939, 2 and 3 November 1939, 7.

43. See below p. 837.

44. Michael Wildt, *Generation der Unbedingten. Das Führungskorps des Reichssicherheitshauptamtes* (Hamburg, 2003), 259ff.

45. Decree concerning Exceptional Radio Measures, 2 September 1939 (*RGBl.* 1939 I, 1683); see Michael P. Hensle, *Rundfunkverbrechen. Das Hören von 'Feindsendern' im Nationalsozialismus* (Berlin, 2003).

46. *RGBl.* 1939 I, 1609ff.

47. Ibid., 1679.

48. Ibid., 2378.

49. Martin Broszat, 'Zur Perversion der Strafjustiz im Dritten Reich', in *VfZ* 6 (1958), 390–443; Hans-Joachim Heuer, *Geheime Staatspolizei. Über das Töten und die Tendenzen der Entzivilisierung* (Berlin, 1995); Longerich, *Himmler*, 489f.

50. Himmler minute, 20 November 1939, quoted in Ulrich Herbert, *Fremdarbeiter. Politik und Praxis des 'Ausländer-Einsatzes' in der Kriegswirtschaft des Dritten Reiches* (Bonn, 1999), 91.

51. The provision and distribution of food supplies was governed by a total of nine decrees issued on 7 September on the basis of the Decree for the Provisional Securing of Supplies Vital for the German People of 27 August 1939 (*RGBl.* 1939 I, 1498ff.; for supplementary decrees see 1705ff.).

52. See Hubert Schmitz, *Die Bewirtschaftung der Nahrungsmittel und Verbrauchsgüter 1939–1950. Dargestellt an dem Beispiel der Stadt Essen* (Essen, 1956).

53. On the population's concern see *Meldungen*, 2, 339ff. (esp. 345f.), 347ff. (esp. 355f.), 364ff. (esp. 368ff.), 381ff. (esp. 387). These reactions prompted the propaganda minister to make objections. See *Goebbels TB*, 13 (plant closures, wages) 19, 20, 21, and 23 September (all entries on wages policy of the Economics Ministry), and 8 ('luxury shoes without coupons') and 10 October 1939 (on the 'awful mistakes of the Economics Ministry').

54. Dietrich Eichholtz, *Geschichte der deutschen Kriegswirtschaft 1939–1945*, 3 vols (Munich, 2003), 1, 70ff.; Rolf-Dieter Müller, 'Die Mobilisierung der deutschen Wirtschaft für Hitlers Kriegführung', in Bernhard R. Kroener, Müller, and Hans Umbreit (eds), *Organisierung und Mobilisierung des deutschen Machtbereichs*, 1 (Stuttgart, 1988), 375ff.; Mason, *Arbeiterklasse*, 1136ff.; Tooze, *Ökonomie*, 410ff.

55. Führer Edict concerning the Creation of a Ministerial Council for the Defence of the Reich (*RGBl.* 1939 I, 1639); Müller, 'Mobilisierung', 366; Rebentisch, *Führerstaat*, 117ff., on the Reich Defence Commissioners, 132ff.

56. On Hitler's exercise of control see Rebentisch, *Führerstaat*, 122f.; according to a post-war statement of Lammers, Hitler generally required the decrees of the Ministerial Council to be submitted to him for approval. See IfZ, MB 26, Fall XI (Wilhelmstrasse trial), Prot., 20034 and 20156. See also *IMT* 31, 2852-PS, 224ff.

57. Petzina, *Autarkiepolitik*, 135; Tooze, *Ökonomie*, 389.

58. *Goebbels TB*, 24 September 1939; see also 27 September 1939.

59. *ADAPD* 8, No. 138. See also Bernd Martin, 'Britisch–Deutsche Friedenskontakte in den ersten Monaten des Zweiten Weltkrieges. Eine Dokumentation über die Vermittlungsversuche von Birger Dahlerus', in *Zeitschrift für Politik*, new series 19 (1972), 206–22.

60. Hans-Adolf Jacobsen, *Fall Gelb. Der Kampf um den deutschen Operationsplan zur Westoffensive 1940* (Wiesbaden, 1957), 7.

61. Halder, *KTB* 1, 27 September 1939; Below, *Adjutant*, 210f.; Walter Warlimont, *Im Hauptquartier der deutschen Wehrmacht 1939–1945. Grundlagen, Formen, Gestalten* (Augsburg, 1990), 51; Jacobsen, *Fall Gelb*, 8f.

62. Halder, *KTB*, 1, 28 September 1939.

63. Müller, *Heer*, 474ff. See also the entries in Halder, *KTB*, 1, 28 September 1939, according to which Halder was collecting relevant material for a fundamental confrontation with Hitler about what was possible; ibid., 4 October 1939, where he noted Göring's opinion that 'we can't mount an offensive now'. Wilhelm von Leeb, *Tagebuchaufzeichnungen* und Lagebeurteilungen *aus zwei Weltkriegen* (Stuttgart, 1976), 3 and 9 October 1939, was also critical of the continuation of the war; according to Fedor von Bock, *Zwischen Pflicht und Verweigerung. Das Kriegstagebuch* (Munich, 1995), 11 October 1939, generals Reichenau and Kluge rejected an offensive 'at this juncture'. In view of these contradictory views Jodl feared a 'very serious crisis' at the beginning of October. See Halder, *KTB*, 1, 4 October 1939.

64. Ibid., 7 September 1939: On 7 September Hitler stated that if Poland indicated it was willing to negotiate, he would be contented with territorial concessions. He would also demand that Warsaw abandoned its treaties with France and Britain and he wanted an independent West Ukraine. However, with the Soviet invasion on 17 September this idea was no longer viable. Five days later, Keitel stated in a meeting that 'an independent rump Poland' was 'the Führer's preferable solution because he could then negotiate peace in the East with a Polish government'. On the same day Hitler expressed to Brauchitsch relatively modest ambitions for annexations in Poland ('eastern Upper Silesia and the Corridor if the West stays out of it'). See Groscurth, *Tagebücher*, 357; Halder, *KTB*, 1, 12 September 1939. In his Artushof speech on 19 September Hitler also left open the future status of Poland. See Domarus, 2, 1354ff. Hitler also referred to the 'creation of a Polish state' in his speech of 6 October, although by then he was already making plans for a German occupation regime in central Poland. See Kershaw, *Hitler*, 2, 331f.

65. *Goebbels TB*, 30 September 1939. Rosenberg's notes from the same day make very similar comments about Hitler's plans for Poland. See Rosenberg, *Tagebücher*, 29 September 1939.

66. See below p. 666.

67. *Goebbels TB*, 1 October 1939.

68. *ADAP* D 8, No. 157.

69. Ibid., Nos 159 and 193.

70. Also ibid., No. 104, on Molotov's indifference to the maintenance of a Polish state.

71. Ibid., No. 158.

72. Ibid., No. 161.

73. Walther Hubatsch (ed.), *Hitlers Weisungen für die Kriegsführung 1939–1945* (Coblenz, 1983).

74. Domarus, 2, 1376; on the visit to the Belvedere see the brief DNB report in ibid.

75. Ibid., 1377ff., quote 1383; Kershaw, *Hitler*, 2, 364f.

76. *Meldungen*, 2, 339f.; *Goebbels TB*, 11–14 October 1939.

77. On the resistance of and protests from the military see in detail Krausnick, 'Einsatzgruppen', 96ff.

78. Martin Broszat, *Nationalsozialistische Polenpolitik 1939–1945* (Stuttgart, 1961), 32f.

79. In directive No. 5 of 30 September Hitler had already instructed that the new eastern border should include, in addition to the old areas of German settlement, 'those territories, which are particularly valuable militarily, economically or in terms of their significance for communications'. See Hubatsch (ed.), *Weisungen*.

80. BAB, R 43 II/646a, Lammers at the top level meeting on 27 October 1939: Hitler 'wants a greater subordination of the judicial and financial authorities to the Reich governors'; see ibid., Hess to Lammers, 25 October 1939; Rebentisch, *Führerstaat*, 172ff.

81. On 5 October 1939 Hitler agreed to Gauleiter Forster's request for the establishment of a civilian administration in Danzig and West Prussia, but on the following day he decided to incorporate the whole of the new Reich territory in one go (BAB, R 43 II/646a und 644a, Reich Chancellery minutes). On 8 October he ordered the creation of the two new Reich Gaus in the Führer Edict concerning the Organization and Administration of the Eastern Territories (*RGBl*. 1939 I, 2042f.). On 9 October he told Goebbels that the Poles were to be 'pressed into their reduced state and be left entirely to themselves' (*Goebbels TB*, 10 October, see also 14 October 1939). On 12 October the Führer Edict concerning the Administration of the Occupied Polish Territories was issued (*RGBl*. 1939 I, 2077f.), creating the General Government and appointing Frank Governor General. The Führer Edict concerning the Transfer of the Administration in the General Government to the Governor General of 19 October fixed the date for the transfer as 25 October, published in *Führer-Erlasse 1939–1945* (Stuttgart, 1997). The publication of the two edicts followed on 18 and 24 October 1939. See Broszat, *Polenpolitik*, 26ff.; Rebentisch, *Führerstaat*, 163ff.

82. *Führer-Erlasse* No. 12; Longerich, *Himmler*, 449f., with an overview of the background.

83. *IMT* 26, 864-PS, 378ff., emphasis in the original; Halder, *KTB*, 1, 18 October 1939; *Goebbels TB*, 1 November 1939, with similar comments by Hitler; Rebentisch, *Führerstaat*, 172f.

84. *Goebbels TB*, 10 October 1939.

85. Rosenberg, *Tagebücher*, 29 September 1939.

86. Jansen and Weckbecker, '*Selbstschutz*', 154ff.

87. Ibid., 96ff. and 154.

88. See in detail Volker Riess, *Die Anfänge der Vernichtung 'lebensunwerten Lebens' in den Reichsgauen Danzig-Westpreußen und Wartheland 1939/40* (Frankfurt a. M., 1995); for the estimate of the number of victims see ibid., 355. On Pomerania see also Heike Bernhardt, *Anstaltspsychiatrie und 'Euthanasie' in Pommern 1933–1945. Die Krankenmorde an Kindern und Erwachsenen am Beispiel der Landesheilanstalt Uekermünde* (Frankfurt a. M., 1994).

89. Riess, *Anfänge*, 290ff.

90. Madajczyk (*Okkupationspolitik*), who has systematically researched the German terror (186ff.), refers to 50,000 deaths in autumn 1939 (15).

91. See Heydrich's remarks at the meetings of the departmental heads of the security police on 14 and 21 September (BAB, R 58/825), and Heydrich's express letter to the Einsatzgruppen, 21 September 1939 (*VEJ*, 4, No. 12). See also Halder, *KTB*, 1, 20 September 1939, on Hitler's remarks to Brauchitsch on the same day ('There is the general idea of a ghetto, but it's not yet clear in detail'). Detailed account in Longerich, *Politik*, 251ff.; Longerich, *Himmler*, 455f.

92. On Hitler's statements (on the basis of Goebbels's and Rosenberg's diary entries) see above p. 660f; on Heydrich see BAB, R 58/825, Departmental chiefs' meeting, 29 September 1939.

93. Andreas Hillgruber (ed.), *Staatsmänner und Diplomaten bei Hitler. Vertrauliche Aufzeichnungen über Unterredungen mit Vertretern des Auslandes* (Frankfurt a. M., 1967), 1, 29f.

94. *ADAP* D 8, No. 176.

95. *Verhandlungen des Reichstages* 460, 51ff.

96. Confidential Information (from the propaganda ministry), 9 October 1939, published in Hagemann, *Presselenkung*, 145; Jonny Moser, 'Nisko: The First Experiment in deportation', in *Simon Wiesenthal Center Annual*, 2/1 (1995), 3, points out that the Belgrade newspaper *Vreme* was already reporting the plans for a reservation on 19 September. The Black Book published by Jacob Apenszlak in 1943 refers to reports about the Nisko project in the *Luxemburger Wort* (21 November 1939), in the Swiss *Neue Zeitung* (1 November 1939), and in the *Spectator* of December 1939 (p. 92). See also *The Times*, 16 December 1939, 'Lublin for the Jews'.

97. YV, 053/87 (Gestapo files from Mährisch-Ostrau), Eichmann note, 6 October 1939, about his mission. On the autumn deportations see Miroslav Kärny, 'Nisko in der Geschichte der Endlösung', in *Judaica Bohemiae* 23 (1987); Seev Goshen, 'Eichmann und die Nisko-Aktion im Oktober 1939. Eine Fallstudie zur NS-Judenpolitik in der letzten Etappe vor der "Endlösung"', in *VfZ* 29 (1981), 74–96.; Goshen, 'Nisko. Ein Ausnahmefall unter den Judenlagern der SS', in *VfZ* 40 (1992), 95–106; Moser, 'Nisko'; H. G. Adler, *Der verwaltete Mensch. Studien zur Deportation der Juden aus Deutschland* (Tübingen, 1974), 125ff.; Christopher Browning, 'Die nationalsozialistische Umsiedlungspolitik und die Suche nach einer "Lösung der Judenfrage" 1939–1942', in Browning, *Der Weg zur 'Endlösung'. Entscheidungen und Täter* (Bonn, 1998), 17ff.; Longerich, *Politik*, 256ff.; Safrian, *Eichmann-Männer*, 68ff.; Ludmila Nesládková (ed.), *The Case Nisko in the History of the Final Solution of the Jewish Problem in Commemoration of the 55th Anniversary of the First Deportation of Jews in Europe 1994* (Ostrava, 1995).

98. See Safrian, *Eichmann-Männer*, 77ff. On the carrying out of the deportations see Goshen, 'Eichmann', 86; Rosenkranz, *Verfolgung* (on Vienna); on the deportation from Mährisch-Ostrau see Kärny, 'Nisko', 96ff., and Lukás Přibyl, 'Das Schicksal des dritten Transports aus dem Protektorat nach Nisko', in *Theresienstädter*

Studien und Dokumente 2000, 297–342. The deportations from the Kattowitz (Katovice) district and from Mährisch-Ostrau had already been initiated or prepared by the Wehrmacht and the Gestapo in the Protectorate in mid-September.

99. On 16 October Eichmann told the head of the Reich Criminal Police Office, Nebe, that the deportations from the old Reich would begin in around two or three weeks. See YV, 053/87, Telegram from SD Danube to SD-Main Office, 16 October 1939.

100. Ibid., Günther note, 11 October 1939, about remarks by Eichmann to the Silesian Gauleiter; Eichmann also made remarks in Vienna about a commission from the Führer (quoted in Gerhard Botz, *Wohnungspolitik und Judendeportation in Wien 1938 bis 1945. Zur Funktion des Antisemitismus als Ersatz nationalsozialistischer Sozialpolitik* (Vienna and Salzburg, 1975), 105).

101. YV, 053/87, Note of 6 October 1939.

102. Ibid., Note by the Mährisch-Ostrau Gestapo office, 21 October 1939. See also letter from Himmler to Bürckel, 9 November 1939 (Botz, *Wohnungspolitik*, 196); *IMT* 32, 3398-PS, 255ff. The last deportation train reached Nisko on 28 October.

103. Götz Aly, *'Endlösung'. Völkerverschiebung und der Mord an den europäischen Juden* (Frankfurt a. M., 1995), 35ff.

104. *IMT* 26, 864-PS, IS. 378f. On the concerns of the military about a further concentration of Jews in the Lublin region see also Krüger, 1 December 1939 (*Das Diensttagebuch des deutschen Generalgouverneurs in Polen 1939–45*, ed. Werner Präg und Wolfgang Jacobmeyer (Stuttgart, 1975), 55f.). On the OKW's negative attitude towards a concentration of Jews near the line of demarcation see BAB, R 69/1146, ca. November 1940, 'Long-term plan of the RSHA'.

105. Since September 1939 the Einsatzgruppen and the Wehrmacht had been forcibly driving tens of thousands of Jews over the line of demarcation into the Soviet occupation zone. See Christopher Browning, *Die Entfesselung der 'Endlösung'. Nationalsozialistische Judenpolitik 1939–1942* (Berlin, 2006), 56f.; Joachim Böhler, '"Tragische Verstrickung" oder Auftakt zum Vernichtungskrieg? Die Wehrmacht in Polen 1939', in Mallmann and Musial (eds), *Genesis*, 45ff.

106. On the Weimar debate see Schmuhl, *Rassenhygiene*, 115ff.; Michael Schwartz, '"Euthanasie"–Debatten in Deutschland (1895–1945)', in *VfZ* 46 (1998), 617–65. On the actual developments in psychiatry between 1914 and 1933 see Heinz Faulstich, *Hungersterben in der Psychiatrie 1914–1949. Mit einer Topographie der NS-Psychiatrie* (Freiburg i. Br., 1998), 25ff.

107. On the 'deplorable state of psychiatry' before the start of the Second World War see Dirk Blasius, *'Einfache Seelenstörung'. Geschichte der deutschen Psychiatrie 1800–1945* (Frankfurt a. M., 1994) in particular 145ff.; Michael Burleigh, *Tod und Erlösung. Euthanasie in Deutschland 1900–1945* (Zurich, 2002), 63ff.; Ludwig Siemen, *Menschen blieben auf der Strecke. Psychiatrie zwischen Reform und Nationalsozialismus* (Gütersloh, 1987); Hans-Walter Schmuhl, 'Kontinuität oder Diskontinuität? Zum epochalen Charakter der Psychiatrie

im Nationalsozialismus', in Franz-Werner Kersting, Karl Teppe, and Bernd Walter (eds), *Nach Hadamar. Zum Verhältnis von Psychiatrie und Gesellschaft im 20. Jahrhundert* (Paderborn, 1993), 112–36; Faulstich, *Hungersterben*, 101ff.

108. Schmuhl, *Rassenhygiene*, 178ff.; Schwartz, '"Euthanasie"-Debatten', 643ff.

109. Hanns Kerrl, *Nationalsozialistisches Strafrecht. Denkschrift des preußischen Justizministers* (Berlin, 1933), 87.

110. *Quellen zur Reform des Straf-und Strafprozessrechts*, Abt. 2/2, 17th Session, 1 March 1934, 425f. (Gürtner), 20th Session, 16 April 1934, 531 (Freisler). See Schmuhl, *Rassenhygiene*, 291ff.; Lothar Gruchmann, 'Euthanasie und Justiz im Dritten Reich', in *VjZ* 12 (1984), 235ff.

111. Schwartz, '"Euthanasie"-Debatten', 647ff.; for the permission to abort for 'genetic reasons' granted by the circular from the Reich Doctors' Leader, Wagner, of 13 September 1934, and the amendment of the law in 1935 see Schmuhl, *Rassenhygiene*, 161ff.

112. *MK*, 447f.

113. Karl Binding and Alfred Hoche, *Die Freigabe der Vernichtung lebensunwerten Lebens. Ihr Maß und ihre Form* (Leipzig, 1920).

114. Quoted from RSA 3, Doc. 64. The term 'weakest', as used in the edition, refers to the children who were to be got rid of. The term 'weakest' as used, for example, in Schmuhl, *Rassenhygiene*, 152, would also include adults. In relation to this number Hitler was not referring to an annual quota but an overall total of victims.

115. See above p. 437.

116. Alexander Mitscherlich and Fred Mielke (eds), *Medizin ohne Menschlichkeit. Dokumente des Nürnberger Ärzteprozesses* (Frankfurt a. M., 1960), 184; IfZ, MB 12, Proceedings of the Doctors' Trial, 2414.

117. Schmuhl, *Rassenhygiene*, 180, concludes, therefore, that it is unclear whether or not Hitler was committed to 'euthanasia' from 1933 onwards. Kershaw's statement (*Hitler*, 2, 353), that we know on the basis of Brandt's post-war testimony that Hitler was advocating 'euthanasia' at the latest from 1933 is incorrect, while the 'well-known views on euthanasia from the 1920s' referred to (p. 350) do not in fact exist.

118. There was some confusion about the identity of the child after the medical historian, Udo Benzenhöfer, who in 1998 believed he had solved the problem, then had to disavow this 'discovery'. In the meantime this false information had been adopted in the literature; see Udo Benzenhöfer, 'Der Fall "Kind Knauer"', in *Deutsches Ärzteblatt* 95 (1998), 954–5; Benzenhöfer, 'Brandt, S. Richtigstellung', in *Deutsches Ärzteblatt* 104 (2007), 3232; Ulf Schmidt, 'Reassessing the Beginning of the "Euthanasia Programme"', in *German History* 17 (1999), 543–57; Schmidt, *Karl Brandt: The Nazi Doctor. Medicine and Power in the Third Reich* (London, 2007), Engl. edn., 117ff. In the German edition, however, the mistake is corrected (Ulf Schmidt, *Hitlers Arzt Karl Brandt. Medizin und Macht im Dritten Reich* (Berlin, 2009), 177ff.).

119. On the children's 'euthanasia' programme see Schmuhl, *Rassenhygiene*, 182ff.; Aly, *Die 'Euthanasie' 1939–1945. Eine Gesellschaftsgeschichte* (Frankfurt a. M.,

2013), 109ff.; Burleigh, *Tod*, 117ff.; Henry Friedlander, *Der Weg zum NS-Genozid. Von der Euthanasie zur Endlösung* (Berlin, 1997), 84ff.; Ernst Klee, *'Euthanasie' im NS-Staat. Die 'Vernichtung lebensunwerten Lebens'* (Frankfurt a. M., 2010), 334ff.

120. On the organizational preparations for the T4 action see Friedlander, *Weg*, 117ff.; Burleigh, *Tod*, 137ff.; Schmuhl, *Rassenhygiene*, 190ff.; Aly, *Belasteten*, 42ff.; Klee, *'Euthanasie'*, 112ff.

121. *IMT* 26, 630-PS, 169; see also Gruchmann, 'Euthanasie', 241.

122. IfZ, MB 12, Fall I (Doctors' Trial), Brandt statement, 2412f.: According to this, in September 1939 a further meeting took place in Zoppot between Conti, Lammers, and Hitler, at which a fruitless discussion was held about the introduction of a 'euthanasia' law.

123. In October 1940 it was intended to murder between 130,000 and 150,000 people. In January a figure of 100,000 was mentioned: *IMT* 35, 906-D, 681ff. ('30,000 dealt with, a further 100,000–120,000 to go'). *Goebbels TB*, 30 January 1941 (about a meeting with Bouhler): '40,000 have gone, 60,000 have still to go'.

124. For example, in the preparatory phase with the number of potential 'euthanasia' victims assumed to be around 60,000, Brandt no longer believed it was necessary to keep it secret, according to a witness statement by an associate of Hefelmann (quoted in Aly, *'Endlösung'*, 54). On the inadequate concealment of the 'euthanasia' programme see Winfried Süss, *Der 'Volkskörper' im Krieg. Gesundheitspolitik, Gesundheitsverhältnisse und Krankenmord im nationalsozialistischen Deutschland 1939–1945* (Munich, 2003), 129f.; Klee, *'Euthanasie'*, 172ff. and 210ff.

125. For examples of 'euthanasia' propaganda see Klee, *'Euthanasie'* [1983], 76f. and 175f.

126. Friedlander, *Weg*, 418ff.

RESISTANCE

1. Halder, *KTB*, 1, 7 October 1939.

2. Hans-Adolf Jacobsen (ed.), *Dokumente zur Vorgeschichte des Westfeldzuges 1939–1940* (Göttingen, Berlin, and Frankfurt a. M., 1956), Nos 3 and 3a; Halder, *KTB*, 1, 10 October 1939; Jacobsen, *Fall Gelb*, 12ff.; Müller, *Heer*, 475f.; Kershaw, *Hitler*, 2, 365; Hubatsch (ed.), *Weisungen*, No. 6.

3. Domarus, 2, 1398.

4. *Goebbels TB*, 14 October 1941.

5. Müller, *Heer*, 471ff.; Hoffmann, *Widerstand*, 165ff.; Erich Kosthorst, *Die deutsche Opposition gegen Hitler zwischen Polen- und Frankreichfeldzug* (Bonn, 1954); Harold C. Deutsch, *Verschwörung gegen den Krieg. Der Widerstand in den Jahren 1939/40* (Munich, 1969), 146ff.

6. Halder, *KTB*, 1, 14 October 1939; the three alternatives are in the minute 'OB'; the further comments reflect the results of the discussion between Halder and Brauchitsch. See also Müller, *Heer*, 480f.

7. Halder, *KTB*, 1, 17 October 1939.

8. Hubatsch (ed.), *Weisungen*, signed 'on behalf of Keitel'.

9. Jacobsen (ed.), *Dokumente*, No. 10.

10. See Groscurth, *Tagebücher*, 385, from a 'reliable source'; Müller, *Heer*, 493; Kershaw, *Hitler*, 2, 365.

11. Halder, *KTB*, 1, 22 October, see also 27 October 1939.

12. Bock, C-in-C of Army Group B, expressed concerns about an attack at this time of year because of doubts about air support. Brauchitsch and Halder were surprised by Hitler's intention to launch the main attack south of the Meuse. See Bock, *Pflicht*, 67ff.

13. On Hitler's directives and their revision see Halder, *KTB*, 1, 25 and 27–29 October 1939; Leeb, *Tagebuchaufzeichnungen*, 31 October 1939 (based on information from Stülpnagel). On the new version of the directive see Jacobsen (ed.), *Dokumente*, Doc. 11. For comment see Jacobsen, *Fall Gelb*, 41ff.

14. *Halder, KTB* 1, 27 October 1939.

15. Leeb, *Tagebuchaufzeichnungen*, 31 October 1939 and Appendix VI; Halder*, KTB* 1, 2 and 3 November 1939; Bock, *Pflicht*, 1 November 1939.

16. Deutsch, *Verschwörung*, 241ff.; Müller, *Heer*, 520ff.; Hoffmann, *Widerstand*, 177; *KTB OKW*, 1, 951f.; Halder, *KTB*, 1, 5 November 1939; Groscurth, *Tagebücher*, 225 and 305; Keitel, *Leben*, 260f.; Below, *Adjutant*, 213; Engel, *Heeresadjutant*, 7 November 1939; Christian Hartmann, *Halder. Generalstabschef Hitlers 1938–1942* (Paderborn, 1991), 159f.

17. Domarus, 2, 1405ff.

18. Lothar Gruchmann (ed.), *Autobiographie eines Attentäters: Johann Georg Elser. Der Anschlag auf Hitler im Bürgerbräu 1939* (Stuttgart, 1989); Anton Hoch and Lothar Gruchmann, *Georg Elser, der Attentäter aus dem Volke. Der Anschlag auf Hitler im Münchner Bürgerbräu 1939* (Frankfurt a. M., 1980); Anton Hoch, 'Das Attentat auf Hitler im Münchner Bürgerbräukeller 1939', in *VfZ* 17 (1969), 383–413; Kershaw, *Hitler*, 2, 371ff.

19. *Goebbels TB*, 9 November 1939.

20. Boelcke (ed.), *Kriegspropaganda*, 11 November 1939, 1 and 13 November 1939, 1; *DAZ*, 10 November 1939 (A), 'Hintergründe und Vorbereitungen'; *Der Angriff*, 11 November 1939, 'Mit Pfund und Höllenmaschine'.

21. *Goebbels TB*, 9–15 November 1939.

22. Ibid., 16 and 17 November 1939.

23. *VB* (B), 22 November 1939, 'Der Attentäter gefaßt' (headline); 23 November 1939, 'Otto Strasser das Werkzeug des englischen Geheimdienstes' (headline); 24 November 1939, 'Captain Stevens sagt aus' (headline); 25 November 1939, 'So wurde Strassers Werkzeug Elser zur Strecke gebracht', similarly *DAZ* and *Angriff* from 22 November 1939.

24. Domarus, 2, 1420ff.; *ADAP* D 8, No. 384. See Kershaw, *Hitler* 2, 377ff.

25. Bock, *Pflicht*, 78f.

26. Halder, *KTB* 1, 23 November 1939; Nuremberg statement by Brauchitsch, *IMT* 20, 628; Müller, *Heer*, 550.

27. The Swedish deliveries of iron ore from north Sweden via Narvik and the North Sea were reduced to a quarter in autumn and winter 1939/40, while the central Swedish ore could continue to be transported via the Baltic without hindrance. During the war Finland delivered the whole of its copper production to Germany. Romanian oil deliveries were interrupted on the outbreak of war, but from December onwards the oil began flowing again. See Berthold Puchert, 'Der deutsche Außenhandel im Zweiten Weltkrieg', in Eichholtz, *Geschichte*, 403ff., 413, 415, and 418f.

28. Tooze, *Ökonomie*, 390f.; Müller, 384.

29. Budra., *Flugzeugindustrie*, 588ff.; BAF, RL 3/874, Hitler Order, 21 August 1939, and Procurement Plan No. 13.

30. Salewski, *Seekriegsleitung* 1, 129–32.

31. Tooze, *Ökonomie*, 396; BAF, RW 19/205, internal monthly reports, November 1939; RW 19/1945, Minute about a meeting with Thomas, 1 December 1939, noting that Hitler was 'not in the least satisfied' with the performance of the munitions sector as planned and carried out hitherto.

32. BAF, RW 19/164 and RH 15/160, 10 January 1940.

33. Tooze, *Ökonomie*, 397.

34. Ibid., 411ff.; the argument, influential in the literature, that the war effort during the first years had hardly affected German living standards has been convincingly disproved, above all by Richard Overy in 'Guns or Butter? Living Standards, Finance, and Labour in Germany 1939–1942', in Overy, *War and Economy in the Third Reich* (Oxford, 1994), 259–314.

35. Ibid., 403ff.; *RGBl.* 1940 I, 513.

36. Tooze, *Ökonomie*, 407ff.

37. Jacobsen, *Fall Gelb*, 93ff.

38. Domarus, 2, 1446.

39. Horst Boog, *Die deutsche Luftwaffenführung 1935–1945. Führungsprobleme, Spitzengliederung, Generalstabsausbildung* (Stuttgart, 1982), 514.

40. *Halder, KTB* 1, 12 January 1940.

41. Ibid., 20 January 1940.

42. Ibid., 21 January 1940.

43. Jacobsen, *Fall Gelb*, 106.

44. Hans Umbreit, 'Der Kampf um die Vormachtstellung in Westeuropa', in Klaus A. Maier et al. (eds), *Die Errichtung der Hegemonie auf dem europäischen Kontinent* (Stuttgart, 1979), 248; Jacobsen (ed.), *Dokumente*, No. 11. Thus Jodl told Halder on 17 November that Hitler feared a German attack could be blocked by the Belgian canal system; the dictator considered that the 'southern flank offered more opportunities' (Halder, *KTB*, 1, 17 November 1939).

45. Umbreit, 'Kampf', 249.

46. Ibid., 252ff.; Jacobsen, *Fall Gelb*, 112ff. On the implementation of the new plan see Halder, *KTB*, 1, 18 February 1940; Jacobsen (ed.), *Dokumente*, Nos 19 and 44; *IMT* 28, 1809-PS, 402; Erich Manstein, *Verlorene Siege* (Bonn, 1955), 91ff. and 118ff.

47. *Goebbels TB*, 22 January 1940.

48. Ibid., 6 February 1940.

49. *ADAP* D 8, No. 504.

50. *Goebbels TB*, 8 and 10 March 1940.

51. *ADAP* D 8, No. 663. On 10 January, however, Ribbentrop had expressed surprise to Attolico at the 'anti-Bolshevik tone' in Mussolini's letter and dismissed the idea of a settlement with the western powers through the creation of a Polish state (ibid., No. 518).

52. *Goebbels TB*, 29 December 1939.

53. Ibid., 12 January, also 25 January 1940.

54. Ibid., 15 March 1940.

55. *ADAP* D 8, Nos 637 and 640–643. The experienced Welles soon realized that the official line had been set for all the discussions with Germans. See Sumner Welles, *The Time for Decision* (New York, 1944), 104; for the meeting with Ribbentrop, 90ff.

56. *ADAP* D 8, No. 649; Welles, *Time*, 101ff.

57. *ADAP* D 8, No. 665.

58. Ibid., Nos 667 and 669f.; see also Schmidt, *Statist*, 48; Ciano, *Diary*, 10 and 11 March 1940.

59. *IMT* 28, 1809-PS, 412.

60. *ADAP* D 9, No. 1; Kershaw, *Hitler*, 2, 396ff.; Schmidt, *Statist*, 488ff.; Ciano, *Diary*, 18 March 1940.

61. Klaus A. Maier and Bernd Stegemann, 'Die Sicherung der europäischen Nordflanke', in Maier et al., *Errichtung.*, 196f. On the background see Robert Bohn, *Reichskommissariat Norwegen. 'Nationalsozialistische Neuordnung' und Kriegswirtschaft* (Munich, 2000), 15ff.; Carl-Axel Gemzell, *Raeder, Hitler und Skandinavien. Der Kampf für einen maritimen Operationsplan* (Lund, 1965); Hans-Dietrich Loock, *Quisling, Rosenberg und Terboven. Zur Vorgeschichte und Geschichte der nationalsozialistischen Revolution in Norwegen* (Stuttgart, 1970), 518ff.; Salewski, *Seekriegsleitung* 1, 175ff.

62. Gerhard Wagner (ed.), *Lagevorträge des Oberbefehlshabers der Kriegsmarine vor Hitler 1939–1945* (Munich, 1972); IfZ, 1811-PS, Jodl Diary, 13 December 1939. *ADAP* D 8, 408, note: there are no documents covering the meetings between Hitler and Quisling on 13 and 18 December.

63. Rohde, '"Blitzkrieg"', 150ff.; Gerd R. Ueberschär, *Hitler und Finnland 1939–1941. Die deutsch–finnischen Beziehungen während des Hitler–Stalin-Paktes* (Wiesbaden, 1978), 92ff.

64. Ibid., 140ff.

65. 'Deutschland und die finnische Frage' (quote); on the assumed authorship see Ueberschär, *Hitler*, 112f.

66. *ADAP* D 8, No. 443; *Lagevorträge*, 12 December 1939.

67. *IMT* 34, 063-C, 269f.

68. Salewski, *Seekriegsleitung* 1, 179f.

69. *IMT* 28, 1809-PS, 406. On the leadership structure for the Weser Exercise, which was totally geared to Hitler, see Warlimont, *Hauptquartier*, 82ff.

70. Hubatsch (ed.), *Weisungen*.

71. *IMT* 28, 1809-PS, 411.

72. Ibid., 412: 'Motivating people for the planned action' will be 'difficult'.

73. Ueberschär, *Hitler*, 134ff.

74. *Goebbels TB*, 9 April 1940.

75. Ibid., 10 April 1940.

76. Ibid., 11 April 1940.

77. *ADAP* D 9, Nos 82 and 92 (Mussolini's reply).

78. Walther Hubatsch, *Weserübung. Die deutsche Besetzung von Dänemark und Norwegen 1940. Nach amtl. Unterlagen dargestellt* (Göttingen, 1960), 110ff.

79. *IMT* 28, 1809-PS, 397ff., quote 422.

80. Maier and Stegemann, 'Sicherung', 219.

WAR IN THE WEST

1. *Halder, KTB*, 1, 6 March 1940; *IMT* 28, 1809-PS, 409f.; Jacobsen, *Fall Gelb*, 137f.

2. *IMT* 28, 1809-PS, 415f.; Jacobsen, *Fall Gelb*, 138.

3. *IMT* 28, 1809-PS, 425–428; Jacobsen, *Fall Gelb*, 137. From November 1939 onwards the date of the attack was postponed a total of 29 times (ibid., 141).

4. *ADAP* D 9, No. 214f.

5. Umbreit, 'Kampf', 285.

6. Seidler and Zeigert, *Führerhauptquartiere*, 163ff.; BAF, RW 47/6, *KTB* Führerhauptquartier, 10 May 1940.

7. This is the conclusion of Warlimont, *Hauptquartier*, 108; Hubatsch (ed.), *Weisungen*, No. 11.

8. Halder, *KTB* 1, 17 (with additional information from Halder for the editor of the KTB) and 18 May 1940. See also *IMT* 28, 1809-PS, 430.

9. Halder, *KTB* 1, 18 May 1940.

10. *IMT* 28, 1809-PS, 433f. See Karl-Heinz Frieser, *Blitzkrieg-Legende. Der Westfeldzug 1940* (Munich, 1993), 363ff.; Kershaw, *Hitler*, 2, 400; Umbreit, 'Kampf', 293f.

11. On 25 May the question of whether they should circumvent Paris to the west was heatedly debated by Hitler, Brauchitsch, and Halder, with Halder taking note of the 'Führer's very vigorously argued ideas'. See Halder, *KTB*, 1, 25 May 1940.

12. Ibid., 23 May 1940. Halder was now critical of this transfer of the 4th Army, which had appeared to him desirable on 17 May.

13. *IMT* 28, 1809-PS, 433, refers to a crisis of confidence.

14. Halder, *KTB*, 1, 26 May 1940.

15. *Goebbels TB*, 5 June 1940.

16. *ADAP* D 9, No. 356; see Ciano, *Diary*, 30 May 1940.

17. *ADAP* D 9, No. 357; see Ciano, *Diary*, 31 May 1940; ADAP D 9, No. 370.

18. Ibid., No. 372; see Malte König, *Kooperation als Machtkampf. Das faschistische Achsenbündnis Berlin–Rom im Krieg 1940/41* (Cologne, 2007), 24.

19. Halder, *KTB*, 1, 5, 6, and 10 June 1940.

20. *Goebbels TB*, 6 June 1940. This meeting took place in the 'Eagle's Nest'; at the beginning of July the headquarters was moved to the south Belgian village of Brûly-de-Pesche (Halder, *KTB*, 1, 3 June 1940); Warlimont, *Hauptquartier*, 116; Christa Schroeder, *Er war mein Chef. Aus dem Nachlaß der Sekretärin von Adolf Hitler* (ed.), Anton Joachimsthaler (Munich, 1985), 102ff. (with varying dates); Seidler and Zeigert, *Führerhauptquartiere*, 173ff. Hitler moved into his new quarters on 6 June (BAF, RW 47/6).

21. Umbreit, 'Kampf', 302ff.

22. *Goebbels TB*, 15 June 1940.

23. On the meetings see Schmidt, *Statist*, 494f.; Ciano, *Diary*, 18/19 June 1940, records very clearly Mussolini's disappointment at his missed opportunity for winning military fame.

24. The idea first emerged on 20 May. See *IMT* 28, 1809-PS, 309ff., Jodl Diary.

25. Schmidt, *Statist*, 498f.; Keitel, *Leben*, 269f.; Eberhard Jäckel, *Frankreich in Hitlers Europa. Die deutsche Frankreichpolitik im Zweiten Weltkrieg* (Stuttgart, 1966), 38ff.

26. Keitel, *Leben*, 269, on Hitler's authorship.

27. Domarus, 2, 1530.

28. Umbreit, 'Kampf', 316ff.

29. This is the convincing interpretation of Frieser, *Blitzkrieg-Legende*, 409ff.

30. For reports by participants see Keitel, *Leben*, 273f.; Arno Breker, *Im Strahlungsfeld der Ereignisse. Leben und Wirken eines Künstlers. Porträts, Begegnungen, Schicksale* (Preußisch Oldendorf, 1972), 151ff.; Engel, *Heeresadjutant*, 26 June 1940; Hermann Giesler, *Ein anderer Hitler. Bericht seines Architekten Hermann Giesler. Erlebnisse, Gespräche, Reflexionen* (Leoni am Starnberger See, 1977), 386ff.; Speer, *Erinnerungen*, 185ff. As a result of erroneous statements by the contemporary witnesses (Speer: 28 June, Engel: 26 June) there has been confusion in the literature about the date of the visit: Kershaw, *Hitler*, 2, for example, gives 28 June, Cédric Gruat, *Hitler in Paris. Juni 1940* (Berlin and Schmalkalden, 2011), discusses whether the visit took place on 23 or 26 June 1940. The puzzle can be solved, however, with the help of the Führer headquarters diary. See BAF, RW 47/6.

31. The *VB* on 30 June 1940, the Berlin *Illustrierte Zeitung* on 4 July 1940.

32. Picker, *Tischgespräche*, 21 July 1941; Hitler, *Monologe*, 25/26 September–11 October and 29 October 1941, 13/14 January 1942, and 13 June 1943.

33. Edict of 25 June 1940. See Speer, *Erinnerungen*, Facsimile on p. 191.

34. On the preparation and implementation see *Goebbels TB*, 3–7 July; BAB, R 55/20007, Working plan for the Führer's return from the battlefield and the Reichstag session on 3 July1940; announcements and reports in the *VB* (B), 6 and 7 July 1940.

35. *ADAP* D 10, No. 129.

36. See, in particular, Kershaw, *Hitler*, 2, 407; Kershaw, *Hitler-Mythos*, 136f.; Thamer, *Verführung*, 648. For a different view see Below, *Adjutant*, 237: 'The response to the western campaign was a mixture of fear, incomprehension and grudging admiration'.

37. *Goebbels TB*, 25 June and 3 July 1940.

38. Ibid., 9 July 1940.

39. Jäckel, *Frankreich*, 55.

40. Hans-Adolf Jacobsen, *1939–1945. Der Zweite Weltkrieg in Chronik und Dokumenten* (Darmstadt, 1961), 149f. For the collection of relevant excerpts from Halder's diary see Karl Klee, *Dokumente zum Unternehmen 'Seelöwe'. Die geplante deutsche Landung in England 1940* (Göttingen, 1959), 136ff.; Karl Klee, *Das Unternehmen 'Seelöwe'. Die geplante deutsche Landung in England 1940* (Göttingen, 1958), 63ff.

41. On 21 May tête-à-tête, on 20 June together with Keitel. See Klee, *Dokumente*, 238f. Below, *Adjutant*, 236 recalls that Hitler hardly discussed the question of an invasion of Britain in the second half of June. See Klee, *'Seelöwe'*, 57ff.

42. Klee, *Dokumente*, 240ff.; on this see Klee, *'Seelöwe'*, 66. At the end of June Jodl described the invasion in a memorandum as 'ultima ratio'. See *IMT* 28, 1776-PS, 301ff., here p. 302; see Klee, *'Seelöwe'*, 61f.

43. Halder, *KTB* 2, 13 July 1940; Klee, *'Seelöwe'*, 71f. The creation of a colonial empire in central Africa, on the other hand, was not one of Hitler's priorities at this time; rather he regarded the African colonies (including Britain's colonial possessions, whose future depended on the development of the war with that country), as bargaining tools in his negotiations with France, Italy, and Spain. His comment during the meeting on 13 July that 'we shall claim the French and Belgian Congo', suggests that this demand was not a high priority and that it was far more modest than that envisaged by the simultaneous plans of the Foreign Ministry and the Navy. See Hildebrand, *Reich*, 653ff.; Gerhard Schreiber, 'Die politische und militärische Entwicklung im Mittelmeerraum 1939/40', in Screiber, Bernd Stegemann and Detlef Vogel, *Der Mittelmeerraum und Südosteuropa. Von der 'non belligeranza' Italiens bis zum Kriegseintritt der Vereinigten Staaten* (Stuttgart, 1984), 250ff.; Karsten Linne, *Deutschland jenseits des Äquators? Die NS-Kolonialplanungen für Afrika* (Berlin, 2008).

44. *ADAP* D 10, No. 166.

45. Sebastian Balta, *Rumänien und die Großmächte in der Ära Antonescu 1940–1944* (Stuttgart, 2005), 71ff.

46. Halder, *KTB*, 1, 22 May 1940, concerning Brauchitsch's presentation to Hitler: 'Führer thinks that Russia will accept his request for it to restrict itself to Bessarabia'.

47. *ADAP* D 10, No. 4: On 23 June Schulenburg was informed by Molotov that a 'solution to the Bessarabian question could no longer be delayed'; they were seeking a peaceful solution but if necessary were prepared to use force.

48. Ibid., No. 56.

49. In the Second Vienna Award, Romania agreed to a partial return of Transylvania to Hungary (see below p. 706). In the Treaty of Craiova it had to give the southern part of the Dobruschda to Bulgaria.

50. Hillgruber, *Strategie*, 178ff.; Ralf-Dieter Müller, *Der Feind steht im Osten. Hitlers geheime Pläne für einen Krieg gegen die Sowjetunion im Jahr 1939* (Berlin, 2011), 184ff.

51. Halder, *KTB*, 1, 30 June 1940; see also Müller, *Feind*, 196, who points out that the remark cannot be simply interpreted as 'Hitler's view', as the editor, Jacobsen, assumed.

52. Halder, *KTB*, 2, 3 July 1940.

53. *Goebbels TB*, 20 July 1940; for Hitler's directive concerning Preparations for an Invasion of England see Hubatsch (ed.), *Weisungen*, No. 16. On Hitler' stay on the Obersalzberg see Kershaw, *Hitler*, 2, 407ff.

54. *VB* (B), 20 July 1940, 'Die monumentale Rede Adolf Hitlers'.

55. Domarus, 2, 1562.

56. That is clear from the introductory sentence: 'It has been reported to the Führer'. See Müller, *Feind*, 211. This was also the interpretation of Hillgruber, *Strategie*, 218, and Heinrich Uhlig, 'Das Einwirken Hitlers auf Planung und Führung des Ostfeldzuges', in *Aus Politik und Zeitgeschichte* 1960, 165.

57. Halder, *KTB*, 2, 22 July 1940; Hillgruber, *Strategie*, 216ff.

58. Domarus, 2, 1562.

59. Bernhard von Lossberg, a former colleague of Jodl's, claimed in a written statement of 7 September 1956, that as early as July 1940 he had on his own initiative produced a 30-page plan and given it to Jodl (IfZ, ZS 97). Warlimont, *Hauptquartier,* 126f., however, describes Jodl's revelation of the plan to the L staff (to which Lossberg also belonged) on the 29th as coming as a complete surprise. This can be seen as a retrospective attempt to cover up the staff's initiative. See IfZ, ZS 678, Manuscript: Hitler, a military leader? Account of conversations with Frigate Captain Meckel, early summer 1946: 'The army [sic!] had already learned of the Führer's intentions when these were still being considered. Thus a plan of operations was drafted even before one had been ordered.' See also Kershaw, *Hitler*, 2, 415; Hillgruber, *Strategie*, 222.

60. Halder, *KTB*, 2, 22, 26, and 27 July 1940. See also 29 July 1941 on the order to the chief of the general staff of the 18th Army, Marx, to prepare a plan of attack. This was already ready on 5 August (Jacobsen, *1939–1945*, 164ff.). Marx had already produced a plan for Halder at the beginning of July for a preventive attack by the 18th Army against the Soviet Union (Halder, *KTB*, 2, 4 July 1941); Müller, *Feind*, 204ff. and 221ff.; Ernst Klink, 'Die Landkriegsführung', in Horst Boog et al., *Der Angriff auf die Sowjetunion* (Frankfurt a. M., 1991), 263 and 271ff.

61. Halder, *KTB*, 2.

62. Ibid.; see Kershaw, *Hitler*, 2, 416f.

63. Halder, *KTB*, 2, 31 July 1940.

64. On the Madagascar project see Adler, *Mensch*, 69ff.; Magnus Brechtken, *'Madagaskar' für die Juden'. Antisemitische Idee und politische Praxis 1885–1945* (Munich, 1997) (contains a comprehensive bibliography of the older literature); Browning, *Die 'Endlösung' und das Auswärtige Amt. Das Referat D III der Abteilung Deutschland 1940–1943* (Darmstadt, 2010), 54ff.; Hans Jansen, *Der Madagaskar-Plan. Die beabsichtigte Deportation der europäischen Juden nach Madagascar* (Munich, 1997), esp. 320ff.; Leni Yahil, 'Madagascar: Phantom of a Solution for the Jewish Question', in Bela Vargo and George L. Mosse (eds),

Jews and Non-Jews in eastern Europe 1918–1945 (New York, 1974), 313–34; Longerich, *Politik*, 273ff.

65. See in detail Brechtken, 'Madagaskar'.

66. Published in *VfZ* 5 (1957), 194–8 (with a brief introduction by Krausnick). Himmler had also recommended in this memorandum the removal of 'racially valuable' children from their Polish parents; while this would be 'cruel and tragic', it would be preferable to 'extermination'.

67. Ibid.; the minute about Hitler's reaction was dated 28 May 1940.

68. Ciano, *Diary*, 18/19 June 1940; Schmidt, *Statist*, 494f.; *Lagevorträge*; *ADAP* D 10, Doc. 345; *Goebbels TB*, 17 August 1940.

69. *ADAP* D 10, No. 101.

70. PAA, Inland II g 177.

71. BAB, R 113/1645, Spatial planning assessment of Madagascar, 21 August 1940.

72. PAA, Inland II g 177, Heydrich letter, 24 June 1940. According to Rademacher, 30 August 1940, in the meantime Ribbentrop had ordered the participation of the RSHA in the planning (ibid.).

73. Ibid.

74. Ibid. Brack is wrongly referred to as Brake, but given his correct title (Oberbefehlsleiter).

75. According to RSHA information for Himmler (Hildebrand, *Reich*, 739).

76. For details see Longerich, *Goebbels*, 459; Main source: *Goebbels TB*, 20, 25, and 26 July.

77. Jäckel, *Frankreich*, 75ff.

78. BAB, R 43 II/1334a. The wording of this quotation by Bormann can be regarded as accurate on the basis of a copy produced by the Reich Interior Ministry. See Rebentisch, *Führerstaat*, 251.

79. Alfred Gottwaldt and Diana Schulle, *Die 'Judendeportationen' aus dem deutschen Reich 1941–1945. Eine kommentierte Chronologie* (Wiesbaden, 2005), 37ff.; Jacob Toury, 'Die Entstehungsgeschichte des Austreibungsbefehls gegen die Juden der Saarpfalz und Badens (20/23 Oktober 1940) – Camp de Gurs', in *Jahrbuch des Instituts für deutsche Geschichte* 15 (1986), 431–64. Toury points out (443) that in the draft of a letter of 7 December 1940 Rademacher corrected the formulation 'deportation ordered by the Führer' to 'deportation approved by the Führer'.

80. Frank, *Diensttagebuch*, 12 July 1940.

81. Biuletyn, Doc. 38.

82. *Goebbels TB*, 25 July 1940.

83. Ibid., 26 July and 1 August 1940.

84. Hubatsch (ed.), *Weisungen*.

85. *Goebbels TB*, 5 and 7 August 1940.

86. Klee, *Dokumente*, 238 (Raeder); *KTB OKW* 1, 32; Bock, *Pflicht*, 165.

87. *Goebbels TB*, 7–10 August 1940.

88. Basil Collier, *The Defence of the United Kingdom* (London, 1957), 163ff., on the preparations.

89. Ibid., 183ff. and 456f.

90. Ibid., 203ff. and 458ff.

91. Kurt Mehner (ed.), *Die geheimen Tagesberichte der deutschen Wehrmachtführung im Zweiten Weltkrieg 1939–1945. Die gegenseitige Lageunterrichtung der Wehrmacht-, Heeres- und Luftwaffenführung über alle Haupt- und Nebenkriegsschauplätze: 'Lage West' (OKW-Kriegsschauplätze Nord, West, Italien, Balkan), 'Lage Ost' (OKH) and 'Luftlage Reich'*, 12 vols (Osnabrück 1984–1995). On the – unauthorized – attack on London see Klaus A. Maier, 'Die Luftschlacht um England', in Maier, *Errichtung*, 386.

92. Mehner (ed.), *Tagesberichte*, 26 August 1940 for Berlin. 29 August–1 September 1940.

93. Domarus, 2, 1575ff., quote p. 1580.

94. On the British attacks see Mehner (ed.), *Tagesberichte*. Führer directive for attacks on the population and air defences of major English cities, including London, 5 September 1940 (quoted in Maier, 'Luftschlacht', 386). See also *Goebbels TB*, 5 and 8 September 1940.

95. BAK, ZSg. 102/27, 10 and 18 September 1940; *VB* (B), 11 September 1940, photo page; 14 September, 'Englands Schuldkonto wächst weiter'.

96. Halder, *KTB*, 2, 14 September 1940.

97. KTB OKW 1, S 82.

98. Halder, *KTB*, 2, 7 October 1940.

DIPLOMATIC SOUNDINGS

1. Kershaw, *Hitler*, 2, 438; Gerhard Weinberg, *Eine Welt in Waffen. Die globale Geschichte des Zweiten Weltkriegs* (Stuttgart, 1995), 188ff.

2. Sommer, *Deutschland*, 349ff.

3. According to ibid., 380ff., Hitler's decision can be dated to the second week in August.

4. Hillgruber, *Strategie*, 203; Sommer, *Deutschland*, 429.

5. See Michalka, *Ribbentrop*, 286ff., who describes Ribbentrop's policy as an 'alternative' to Hitler's programme.

6. *Lagevorträge*, 6 and 26 September 1940; Hillgruber, *Strategie*, 188ff.; Salewski, *Seekriegsleitung* 1, 280ff.

7. On 26 July Hitler met the Romanian prime minister and his foreign minister on the Obersalzberg. Hitler offered the Romanians a guarantee of Romania's territorial integrity, but linked this to the signing of a long-term economic agreement. See *ADAP* D 10, No. 234. On 27 July Hitler received the Bulgarian head of state and offered him support for the transfer of south Dobruschka (ibid., No. 245). On 29 July Ribbentrop instructed the German envoy in Bucharest to recommend to the Romanian government the transfer of south Dobruschka to Bulgaria (ibid., No. 253). The Romanians followed this advice (ibid., Nos 262 and 323). The Germans were prepared to give military support to Hungary's revisionist objectives (ibid., No. 146). However, Hitler requested King Carol to agree to negotiate with both countries about their revisionist

aims (ibid., No. 171). See Hans-Joachim Hoppe, *Bulgarien, Hitlers eigenwilliger Verbündeter. Eine Fallstudie zur nationalsozialistischen Südosteuropapolitik* (Stuttgart, 1979), 82ff.

8. *ADAP* D 10, No. 347.

9. Ibid., Nos 384, 376, and 399f.

10. Ibid., No. 407; Ciano, *Diary*, 28 August 1941.

11. *ADAP* D 10, No. 413, Docs 408–10 on the conference.

12. Friedrich Christof, *Befriedung im Donauraum. Der zweite Wiener Schiedsspruch und die deutsch–ungarischen diplomatischen Beziehungen 1939–1942* (Frankfurt a. M., 1998), esp. 69ff.

13. *ADAP* D 11, Nos. 17, 19, and 21; Balta, *Rumänien*, 77ff.; Andreas Hillgruber, *Hitler, König Carol und Marschall Antonescu. Die deutsch–rumänischen Beziehungen 1938–1944* (Wiesbaden, 1954), 93ff.

14. *ADAP* D 11, No. 75.

15. Ibid., No. 84.

16. Gerd R. Ueberschär, 'Die Einbeziehung Skandinaviens in die Planung "Barbarossa"', in Borg et al., *Angriff*, in particular the concluding assessment on p. 448, which strongly emphasizes Hitler's role. For more detail see Ueberschär, *Hitler und Finnland 1939–1941. Die deutsch–finnischen Beziehungen während des Hitler–Stalin-Paktes* (Wiesbaden, 1978), 196ff.; see also Halder, *KTB*, 2, 22 August 1940.

17. Ibid., 18 August 1940.

18. *ADAP* D 10, No. 330.

19. On the agreement see *ADAP* D 11, No. 86; Ueberschär, *Hitler*, 202ff.

20. Donald S. Detwiler, *Hitler, Franco und Gibraltar. Die Frage des spanischen Eintritts in den Zweiten Weltkrieg* (Wiesbaden, 1962), 30ff.; Charles B. Burdick, *Germany's Military Strategy and Spain in World War II* (Syracuse, 1968), 19ff.; *KTB OKW* 1, 69 and 78.

21. Halder, *KTB*, 2, 14 September 1940.

22. *ADAP* D 11, Nos. 63, 66f., 70, 88, 97, and 117. See Detwiler, *Hitler*, 37ff.; Burdick, *Strategy*, 43ff.

23. Halder, *KTB*, 2, 4 October 1940; on the sources see Hildebrand, *Reich*, 678.

24. *ADAP* D 11, Nos 212 and 227; Schmidt, *Statist*, 514ff. See Jäckel, *Frankreich*, 115ff.; Kershaw, *Hitler*, 2, 441ff.

25. *ADAP* D 11, Nos. 220 and 221; see Detwiler, *Hitler*, 56ff.; Schmidt, *Statist*, 510ff.

26. Detwiler, *Hitler*, documentary appendix, 118f. *ADAP* D 11, 394f.

27. *Goebbels TB*, 31 October 1940.

28. Halder, *KTB*, 2, 1 November 1940.

29. *ADAP* D 11, Nos. 73, 79, and 87.

30. Ibid., No. 87.

31. Ibid., No. 82.

32. Ibid., No. 118.

33. Ibid., No. 149. According to Schmidt, *Statist*, 509, Hitler talked for three hours. On the meeting see also Ciano, *Diary*, 4 October 1940.

34. Ibid., 12 October 1940. On Ciano's irritation see also *ADAP* D 11, No. 192.

35. Schmidt, *Statist*, 516. On the communications problems between the allies see *ADAP* D 11, Nos 383 and 199 with note 10; Erich Kordt, *Wahn und Wirklichkeit* (Stuttgart, 1947), 266; König, *Kooperation*, 34ff.

36. *ADAP* D 11, No. 246.

37. On the background see *Goebbels TB*, 10 and 17 July (first information on the plan to send troops to Romania), 9 October (about troop movements) and 14 October 1940 (military mission). See also König, *Kooperation*, 32.

38. On the preparations for the Balkan war see *KTB OKW* 1, 204 and 224; Hubatsch (ed.), *Weisungen*, Nos 18 and 20; Detlef Vogel, 'Das Eingreifen Deutschlands auf dem Balkan', in Gerhard Schreiber et al., *Mittelmeerraum*, 422ff.

39. *Goebbels TB,* 12 November 1940.

40. Schmidt, *Statist*, 426. The *VB* (M), 13 November 1940, described the reception in Berlin as 'solemn' and 'dignified' and made no mention of the reaction of the population.

41. Halder, *KTB*, 2, 4 November 1940.

42. Hubatsch (ed.), *Weisungen*.

43. *ADAP* D 11, No. 325.

44. Ibid., No. 326.

45. Schmidt, *Statist*, 531.

46. Stalin's instructions for Molotov are published in Lev Bezymenskij, 'Der Berlin-Besuch von V. M. Molotov im November 1940 im Lichte neuer Dokumente aus sowjetischen Geheimarchiven', in *MGM* 57 (1998), 199–215.

47. Domarus, 2, 1613; Schmidt, *Statist*, 532 and 535.

48. Molotov stated that they 'envisaged sorting out the Finnish question in the same way as in the Baltic and in Bessarabia'. See *ADAP* D 11, No. 328.

49. That is clear from Stalin's instructions. See Bezymenskij, 'Berlin-Besuch'.

50. *ADAP* D 11, No. 328.

51. Ibid., No. 329.

52. Ibid., No. 404.

53. *KTB OKW* 1, 179.

54. *ADAP* D 11, No. 369. In reply to an earlier request to join the Tripartite Pact, Boris had replied in a letter to Hitler on 22 October that it would be better if Bulgaria continued with its existing policy for the time being (ibid., No. 217). See Hoppe, *Bulgarien*, 96ff.

55. *ADAP* D 11, No. 378.

56. Ibid., No. 430.

57. Ibid., No. 384.

58. Ibid., No. 438.

59. Ibid., No. 352, also No. 357; see Detwiler, *Hitler*, 71ff.

60. The C-in-C Army assumed that the operation would be wrapped up by the end of February and that the troops would be deployable again from the middle of May. Draft for Directive No. 19 in Hubatsch (ed.), *Weisungen*, 86ff.; *KTB OKW* 1, 203ff. See Detwiler, *Hitler*, 80ff.; Burdick, *Strategy*, 63ff.

61. *ADAP* D 11, No. 414.

62. Ibid., No. 420.

63. Ibid., No. 369.

64. Ibid., No. 353; *Ciano*, Diary, 18/19 November 1940.

65. *ADAP* D 11, No. 383.

66. *Schulthess' 1940*, 227, 232, and 234.

67. *ADAP* D 11, No. 380.

68. Ibid., No. 381. See Schmidt, *Statist*, 523; Antonescu's post-war statement (to the Soviet prosecutors) in *IMT* 7, 338f. See also *ADAP* D 11, Nos 387–9; Balta, *Rumänien*, 105ff.

69. *ADAP* D 11, No. 500; *KTB OKW* 1, 219.

70. *ADAP* D 11, Nos 479 and 497.

71. Hubatsch (ed.), *Weisungen*, No. 19a; see Detwiler, *Hitler*, 84ff.; Burdick, *Strategy*, 103f.

72. *ADAP* D 11, No. 477.

73. Hubatsch (ed.), *Weisungen*.

74. *ADAP* D 11, No. 564; see also Schmidt, *Statist*, 524.

75. Hubatsch (ed.), *Weisungen*.

76. Hillgruber, *Strategie*, 203.

77. Halder, *KTB*, 2, 13 December 1940.

THE EXPANSION OF THE WAR

1. Record in *IMT* 34, 170-C, 696.

2. *KTB OKW* 1, 253ff., esp. 257f.; Halder, KTB, 2, 16 January 1941. See Hillgruber, *Strategie*, 364f.

3. *ADAP* D 11, No. 672. On the preparations and meetings see Ciano, *Diary*, 18–21 January 1941; König, *Kooperation*, 49ff.; Hillgruber, *Strategie*, 347.

4. *IMT* 34, 134-C, 467ff.; *ADAP* D 11, No. 679.

5. Ciano, Diary, 18–21 January 1941.

6. *KTB OKW* 1, 253ff.

7. *ADAP* D 12, No. 22.

8. Ibid., No. 95; Burdick, *Strategy*, 117ff. On 25 March Hitler told Ciano that in doing so Franco had effectively abrogated the agreement of Hendaye. See Hillgruber (ed.), *Staatsmänner* 1, 234ff. and 236. For details see *ADAP* D 11, Nos 677, 682, 692, 695, 702, 707, 718, 725, and 728.

9. Halder, *KTB*, 2, 28 January 1941. According to the editor's note these statements can be attributed to Halder.

10. Bock, *Pflicht*, 173f.

11. *KTB OKW* 1, 297ff.; Halder, *KTB*, 2, 2 and 3 February 1941, on Halder's presentation notes and his summing up of the presentation; see also *IMT* 26, 872-PS, 391ff.; Klink, 'Landkriegsführung', 295f.; see Below, *Adjutant*, 261f.

12. Gruchmann, *Weltkrieg*, 107.

13. *KTB OKW* 1, 253ff. Two days later he confirmed these decisions in his Directive No. 22. See Hubatsch (ed.) *Weisungen*.

14. *KTB OKW* 1, 300ff.; Hubatsch (ed.), *Weisungen*, No. 22d; Halder, *KTB*, 2, 3 February 1941; *ADAP* D 12, No. 17: Hitler informed Mussolini he was sending another Panzer division to North Africa, but made it a condition that the defence should be carried out offensively. See also Stegemann, 'Kriegführung', 600f.

15. Domarus, 2, 1657ff.

16. Halder, *KTB* 2, 4 November 1940

17. In November, by referring to the plans for the military build-up in the East, which was already under way, Frank was able initially to prevent any further deportations from the Warthegau into his territory. See Biuletyn, Doc. 50; Aly, 'Endlösung', 201f.

18. *Goebbels TB*, 5 November 1940, concerning a conversation at which, among others, Gauleiters Koch und Forster, who wanted 'to dump their rubbish in the General Government', were present. In fact, by the end of 1940 more than 48,000 former Polish citizens, Jews and non-Jews, from the district of Zichenau, from Gau Danzig-Westpreußen, and from Upper Silesia had been deported to the General Government. See Madajczyk, *Okkupationspolitik*, 356f.

19. *IMT* 39, 172–USSR, 425ff.

20. Adler, *Mensch*, 147ff.; Gruner, 'Kollektivausweisung'; Gottwaldt/Schulle, *'Judendeportationen'*, 46ff.

21. Longerich, *Politik*, 285ff.

22. *Goebbels TB*, 19 August 1941; see also Longerich, *Holocaust*, 265f.

23. *ADAP* D 11, Nos 295, 345 and 556. See also Hoppe, *Bulgarien*, 108f.

24. The Bulgarian prime minister had expressed these doubts to Hitler once again at a meeting at the beginning of January. See *ADAP* D 11, No. 606. Nevertheless, on Hitler's instructions the military preparations were continued (ibid., No. 644).

25. Ibid., Nos 648f., 658, and 660. See Hoppe, *Bulgarien*, 108ff.; Vogel, 'Eingreifen', 427ff.

26. *ADAP* D 12, No. 51. On Hitler's decision-making see also *ADAP* D 11, Nos 724 and 738. In response to Bulgaria's request the deadlines for the invasion were once again postponed for a few days. See ADAP D 12, Nos 54 and 86.

27. *ADAP* D 11, No. 714; Text of the agreement in *Monatshefte für Auswärtige Politik* 8 (1941), 232; Vogel, 'Eingreifen', 429f.

28. Hoppe, *Bulgarien*, 114ff.; Domarus, 2, 1671.

29. *ADAP* D 12, No. 114.

30. Domarus, 2, 1670.

31. *ADAP* D 12, No. 117.

32. Ibid., Nos 48 and 47; Vogel, 'Eingreifen', 438ff.

33. On the meeting see *ADAP* D 12, No. 130.

34. This was a rhetorical comeback to Paul's statement, that, if he were to follow the Germans' advice, he was afraid that 'in 6 months' time he would no longer be there' (ibid.).

35. Vogel, 'Eingreifen', 439; *ADAP* D 12, Nos 131, 138, 144, 175, and 205.

36. Vogel, 'Eingreifen', 442ff.

37. Domarus, 2, 1671 (according to the DNB).

38. *ADAP* D 12, No. 281.

39. *IMT* 28, 1746-PS, 21ff.; Halder, *KTB* 2, 27 March 1941; Below, *Adjutant*, 264; Klaus Olshausen, *Zwischenspiel auf dem Balkan. Die deutsche Politik gegenüber Jugoslawien und Griechenland von März bis Juli 1941* ((Stuttgart, 1973), 50ff.

40. Klink, 'Landkriegsführung', 296; Halder, *KTB* 2, 17 March 1941; *KTB OKW* 1, 360f.

41. Hubatsch (ed.), *Weisungen*, 106ff.

42. *ADAP* D 12, No. 215.

43. Ibid., No. 215f.; Olshausen, *Zwischenspiel*, 52f.

44. *ADAP* D 12, No. 227f.

45. Ibid., Nos 261, 264, 267, 282, 287, 296, and 307; Olshausen, *Zwischenspiel*, 65ff.

46. Ibid., 74ff.

47. *IMT* 28, 1835-PS, 565ff.

48. *ADAP* D 12, Nos 224, 226, 281, and 289.

49. Hubatsch (ed.), *Weisungen*, No. 26.

50. *ADAP* D 12, Nos 235 and 237.

51. Ibid., No. 265.

52. *Goebbels TB*, 6 April 1941.

53. Ibid., 8, 9, and 30 April 1941.

54. Ibid., 8 April 1941.

55. Martin L. van Creveld, *Hitler's Strategy 1940–1941. The Balkan Clue* (Cambridge, 1973), 154ff.; Vogel, 'Eingreifen', 458ff.; Olshausen, *Zwischenspiel*, 97ff. On the direct involvement of the 'Reich Chancellery' in the bombing of Belgrade see *KTB OKW* 1, 375.

56. Domarus, 2, 1691; Below, *Adjutant* 268f. Seidler and Zeigert, *Führerhauptquartiere*, 130ff.

57. *IMT* 27, 1192-PS, 60ff.

58. Olshausen, *Zwischenspiel*, 162ff.; Hitler's agreement ('Führer directive') is in *ADAP* D 12, No. 319.

59. On the division in detail see Olshausen, *Zwischenspiel*, 174ff. During the meetings between Ribbentrop and Ciano on 21 April 1941 in Vienna, a number of points were still in dispute. See *ADAP* D 12, No 378.

60. Hubatsch (ed.), *Weisungen*.

61. Olshausen, *Zwischenspiel*, 113ff.

62. On Hitler's attitude see in particular Halder, *KTB*, 2, 21 and 22 April 1941. On Italy's discontent see *ADAP* D 12, Nos 379 and 409. See Olshausen, *Zwischenspiel*, 120ff.; König, *Kooperation*, 69ff.

63. Hubatsch (ed.), *Weisungen*, No. 28.

64. Creveld, *Strategy*, 166ff.

65. Stegemann, 'Kriegführung', 615ff.

66. *ADAP* D 12, No. 423.

67. Halder, *KTB* 2, 30 April 1941; Jacobsen, *1939–1945*, No. 61.

68. Domarus, 2, 1703ff., quotes pp. 1704 and 1708.

69. Hillgruber, *Strategie*, 409ff.

70. *ADAP* D 12, Nos 222, also 218, 230, 233, and 278; Schmidt, *Statist*, 536ff.

71. *ADAP* D 12, No. 218, see also Nos 230 and 233, where he once again refers to Singapore.

72. Ibid., No. 230.

73. At the reception for Matsuoka on 28 March 1941 Hitler told Ōshima that if the Soviet Union attacked Japan Germany for its part would not hesitate to attack the Soviet Union. Ribbentrop told Ōshima that this promise was a binding 'commitment' by Hitler. See Andreas Hillgruber, 'Japan und der Fall "Barbarossa". Japanische Dokumente zu den Gesprächen Hitlers und Ribbentrops mit Botschafter Oshima vom Februar bis Juni 1941', in Hillgruber, *Deutsche Großmacht- und Weltpolitik* (Düsseldorf, 1977), Doc. 2.

74. *ADAP* D 12, No. 233.

75. Schmidt, *Statist*, 541.

76. *ADAP* D 12, No. 266; see Schmidt, *Statist*, 548.

77. *VB*, 13 May 1941.

78. *Goebbels TB*, 13 May 1941; the official Party communiqué was, for example, published in *VB* (B), 13 May 1941. On Hess's flight see Rainer F. Schmidt, *Rudolf Heß. 'Botengang eines Toren'? Der Flug nach Großbritannien vom 10. Mai 1941* (Munich, 2000); Pätzold and Weissbecker, *Heß*, 261ff.

79. BAK, ZSg. 102, 13 May 1941 (midday), TP 1.

80. See the correspondence between Bormann and Goebbels in BAB, NS 18/211 and Bormann's circular of 11 June 1941 in NS 18/70. On Hitler's dispute with Hess in February 1940 see Bormann's entries in his office for 24 and 25 February 1940 in NS 26/16. On 7 May, in other words before Hess's flight, Bormann had already warned about these allegedly dangerous teachings in a circular to the Gauleiters, citing Hitler. In other words, he had openly adopted a different standpoint to Hess on this issue (NS 22/29). See Longerich, *Stellvertreter*, 153f.

81. BAB, R 43 II/1213; Führer edict, 29 May 1941 (*RGBl.* 1941 I, 295).

82. BAB, R 43 II/1660, Edict concerning the Führer's Deputy, 29 June 1941. According to the note Lammers added the same day, this meant that the regulation of the succession made on 1 September 1939 was now redundant.

83. Domarus, 2, 1715f.

84. *Goebbels TB*, 16 May 1941, see also 17 and 18 May 1941; Boelcke (ed.), *Kriegspropaganda*, 19 May 1941, 1.

85. On Hess's flight see Longerich, *Stellvertreter*, 146ff.; Martin, *Friedensinitiativen*, 425ff.; Schmidt, *Heß*; David Stafford (ed.), *Flight from Reality. Rudolf Hess and his Mission to Scotland 1941* (London, 2002); Peter Raina, *A Daring Venture. Rudolf Hess and the Ill-fated Peace Mission of 1941* (Oxford, 2014); Hillgruber, *Strategie*, 514, assumes Hess had been given an assignment by Hitler.

86. *KTB OKW* 1, 341.

87. BAF, RW 19/185.

88. Hubatsch (ed.), *Weisungen*, No. 21a.

89. *KTB OKW* 1, 341.

90. Halder, *KTB*, 2.

91. Ibid.

92. Jacobsen, 'Kommissarbefehl', Docs 5a and 8.

93. Ibid, Docs. 6f. and 12.

94. Ibid., Doc. 11.

95. Keitel statement, 4 April 1946, in *IMT* 10, 532; on Hitler's address see briefly Halder, *KTB*, 2, 14 June 1941.

96. Jacobsen, 'Kommissarbefehl und Massenexekutionen sowjetischer Kriegsgefangener', in Buchheim et al., *Anatomie*, Doc. 3; identical draft by the OKH of 26 March 1941 in ibid., Doc. 2.

97. Ibid., Doc. 9.

98. On the details of the orders see Longerich, *Politik*, 315ff.; for the main written orders from Heydrich see BAB, R 70/31 and 32, published in Peter Longerich (ed.), *Die Ermordung der europäischen Juden. Eine umfassende Dokumentation des Holocaust 1941–1945* (Munich, 1989), 116ff.

99. There is evidence that Chief of the General Staff, Halder, was already contemplating the conquest of Gibraltar and Malta, and an attack on Egypt from February 1941 onwards. See Halder, *KTB*, 2, 25 February and 16 March 1941; Schreiber, 'Politik', 573ff.

100. Ibid., 576; Burdick, *Strategy*, 119ff.

101. Jacobsen, *1939–1945*, Nos 62a and b; Hillgruber, *Strategie*, 459f.; Schreiber, 'Politik', 541f.; Burdick, *Strategy*, 133ff.

102. *KTB OKW* 1, 328. Halder, *KTB* 2, 25 February 1941: with Brauchitsch 'operation against Afghanistan', with Heusinger 'Afghanistan – Persia'. On the background see Hillgruber, *Strategie*, 383ff. In 1937 Germany had made a number of secret agreements with Afghanistan concerning infrastructure projects, the Army, police and government services and had excellent relations with the Afghan economics minister, Abdul Majid Khan. On economic relations see, in particular, Inge Kircheisen, 'Afghanistan – umkämpftes Vorfeld Indiens', in Johannes Glasneck and Kircheisen, *Türkei und Afghanistan – Brennpunkte der Orientpolitik im Zweiten Weltkrieg* (Berlin, 1968), 182ff.

103. Halder, *KTB*, 2, 7 April 1941. See also Erhard Moritz, 'Planungen für die Kriegführung des deutschen Heeres in Afrika und Vorderasien', in *Militärgeschichte* 16 (1977), 323–33, with further documents of the OKH from the period April to July 1941 concerning the choice of emphasis and operations after Barbarossa.

104. *ADAP* D 12, Nos 158, 467, and 598. See also the quotes from unpublished Foreign Ministry documents in Hillgruber, *Strategie*, 387; Kircheisen, 'Afghanistan', 224ff.

105. Halder, *KTB* 3, 30 June 1941.

106. Hillgruber, *Strategie*, 481ff.; *ADAP* D 12, Nos 257, 300, 323, 425, and 553; Jan Kuhlmann, *Subhas Chandra Bose und die Indienpolitik der Achsenmächte* (Berlin, 2003), 131ff.; Romain Hayes, *Subhas Chandra Bose in Nazi Germany. Politics, Intelligence and Propaganda* (London, 2011), 29ff. Hitler explained to Bose that

he had withheld permission for the publication of the Indian declaration during a meeting with him on 27 May 1942 (*ADAP* E 2, No. 247); Kuhlmann, *Bose*, 227ff., Hayes, *Bose*, 114ff.

107. *ADAP* D 12, Nos 350 and 427 (Hitler's reply).

108. Ibid., No. 293; *ADAP* D 11, No. 680.

109. Schreiber, 'Politik', 547ff.; Hubatsch (ed.), *Weisungen*, No. 30.

110. Ibid., No. 30. On Irak see Hillgruber, *Strategie*, 473ff.; Schreiber, 'Politik', 546ff.

111. *ADAP* D 12, Nos 417, 421, 459, 462, and 475. On the whole question of Franco–German cooperation in spring 1941 see Jäckel, *Frankreich*, 157ff.; Hillgruber, *Strategie*, 451ff.; Schreiber, 'Politik', 532ff.

112. *ADAP* D 12, No. 490f.

113. Ibid., No. 559.

114. Schreiber, 'Politik', 561ff.

115. *Lagevorträge*, 22 May 1941, and appendix 2. See also Salewski, *Seekriegsleitung* 1, 375ff.

116. Halder, *KTB*, 2, 15 April 1941.

117. *Lagevorträge*, 227ff.

118. *ADAP* D 12, Nos 167 and 210.

119. Hillgruber, *Strategie*, 398ff.; Saul Friedländer, *Auftakt zum Untergang. Hitler und die Vereinigten Staaten von Amerika 1939–1941* (Stuttgart, 1965), 104ff. and 136ff.; *Lagevorträge*, 20 April 1941.

120. *KTB Seekriegsleitung*, 25 April 1941; *ADAP* D 12, No. 608; *Lagevorträge*, 21 June 1941.

121. Salewski, *Seekriegsleitung* 1, 449ff.

122. Although the original draft was not signed by Hitler, it was regarded by the Wehrmacht branches as an instruction and later directives from Hitler referred to it. The draft of 19 June received its final and authoritative form on 30 June (discussed by Hubatsch in Hubatsch (ed.), *Weisungen*, 133f.)

123. Hillgruber, *Strategie*, 378ff.

124. Ciano, *Diary*, 31 May 1941.

125. Schmidt, *Statist*, 550; Ciano, *Diary*, 1 and 2 June 1941; *ADAP* D 12, No. 584.

126. Ibid., No. 603.

127. *Archiv der Gegenwart* 1941, 5063.

128. Report in the *VB*, 8 June 1941. There is no account of the meeting from the German side.

129. Schmidt, *Statist*, 550; *ADAP* D 12, No. 614; Balta, *Rumänien*, 186ff.

130. *ADAP* D 12, No. 644.

131. Below, *Adjutant*, 267f.; Halder, *KTB*, 2, 14 June 1941.

132. *Goebbels TB*, 16 June 1941.

OPERATION BARBAROSSA

1. *Goebbels TB*, 22 June 1941.

2. Finland, Estonia, Latvia, Lithuania, Poland, and Romania.

3. Domarus, 2, 1726ff.

4. *ADAP* D 13, No. 664; for a report on this meeting see Schmidt, *Statist*, 550ff.

5. *ADAP* D 13, No. 659; text of the German note in *Monatshefte für Auswärtige Politik* 1941, 551ff.

6. *ADAP* D 13, No. 662.

7. Ibid., No. 660.

8. Ciano, *Diary*, 22 June 1941.

9. OA Moscow, 1363–3, Conference of ministers, 23 June 1941; see also *Goebbels TB*, 24 June 1941.

10. Decisive for his change of mind was his meeting with Hitler on 8 July (ibid., 9 July); but see also his entry for 3 July 1941.

11. The argument, which keeps appearing in the literature and is in line with contemporary Nazi propaganda, that Hitler was preempting an attack by the Soviet Union cannot be adequately proved on the basis of Soviet documents. Moreover, this line of argument ignores an essential point, namely that, as has been extensively outlined in the previous chapters, Hitler's decision to attack was made not in response to an immediate threat from the Soviet Union, but in the context of an overall strategy. See Gerd R. Ueberschär and Lev A. Bezymenskij (eds), *Der deutsche Angriff auf die Sowjetunion 1941. Die Kontroverse um die Präventivkriegsthese* (Darmstadt, 2011), in particular the contribution from Nicolaj M. Romanicev, 'Militärische Pläne eines Gegenschlags der UdSSR', who shows that the Soviet Union was not planning a preemptive strike; see also Gabriel Gorodetsky, *Die große Täuschung. Hitler, Stalin und das Unternehmen 'Barbarossa'* (Berlin, 2001), 298ff. From the extensive literature see Bianca Pietrow-Ennker (ed.), *Präventivkrieg? Der deutsche Angriff auf die Sowjetunion* (Frankfurt a. M., 2000); Bernd Wegner, 'Präventivkrieg 1941? Zur Kontroverse um ein militärhistorisches Scheinproblem', in Jürgen Elvert and Susanne Krauss (eds), *Historische Debatten und Kontroversen im 19. und 20. Jahrhundwert. Jubiläumstagung der Ranke-Gesellschaft in Essen, 2001* (Stuttgart, 2003), 206–19; Rainer F. Schmidt, 'Appeasement oder Angriff? Eine kritische Bestandsaufnahme der sog. Präventivkriegsdebatte über den 22. Juni 1941', in Elvert and Krauss (eds), *Historische Debatten*, 220–33; Bogdan Musial, *Kampfplatz Deutschland. Stalins Kriegspläne gegen den Westen* (Berlin, 2008) also reject the preventive war thesis. By contrast, the argument is supported by, among others, Joachim Hoffmann, *Stalins Vernichtungskrieg 1941–1945. Planung, Ausführung und Dokumentation* (Munich, 2000).

12. Seidler and Zeigert, *Führerhauptquartiere*, 193ff. On the gloomy atmosphere prevailing there see Schmidt, *Statist*, 555ff.; Picker, *Tischgespräche*, 18ff.; Schroeder, *Chef*, 111ff.; Alfons Schulz, *Drei Jahre in der Nachrichtenzentrale des Führerhauptquartiers* (Stein am Rhein, 1996), 39f.; Below, *Adjutant*, 281; Warlimont, *Hauptquartier*, 188ff.

13. Klink, 'Landkriegsführung', 321; Boog, 'Die Luftwaffe' in Boog et al., *Angriff*, 362.

14. Halder, *KTB*, 2, Appendix 2.

15. Ibid., 26 July and 5 August 1940; on the plan of the Chief of the General Staff of the 18th Army, Marcks, see Ingo Lachnit and Friedhelm Klein, 'Der "Operationsentwurf Ost" des Generalmajors Marcks vom 5. August 1940', in *Wehrforschung* 2 (1972), 114–23; *KTB OKW* 1, 208f.; Ernst Klink, 'Heer und Kriegsmarine' in Boog et al., *Angriff*, 541ff.; Hartmann, *Halder*, 224ff., esp. 237.

16. Klink, 'Heer', 550ff. and 557ff.

17. See Halder, *KTB* 3, 28 June and 2 July 1941; Heinz Guderian, *Erinnerungen eines Soldaten* (Stuttgart, 1996), 143f.; for the advance on Bobrujsk, which was reached on 28 June, see Klink, 'Heer', 543f. The crossing of the Dnieper by Guderian's panzer group east of Bobrujsk did not take place until 10 and 11 July 1941 (Guderian, *Erinnerungen* 154).

18. Halder, *KTB*, 3, 3 July 1941.

19. Hitler emphasized right from the start that he did not want primarily to conquer the enemy's capital city but to destroy their main forces. See *KTB OKW* 1, 1019f.

20. Halder, *KTB*, 3, 30 June 1940, on Hitler's comments.

21. However, because of the changed situation resulting from further directives issued by Hitler in July the memorandum was not sent. See *KTB OKW* 1, 5, 1031ff.

22. *Halder KTB*, 3, 3 July 1941; *KTB OKW* 1, 1020.

23. Ibid., No. 67, 1020.

24. Halder, *KTB*, 3, 8 July 1941. Hitler did not exclude the possibility that Panzer Group 3 might later be deployed to surround Moscow.

25. On 12 July Halder told Brauchitsch, that he was 'by no means committed to the two panzer groups continuing to charge eastwards' and could imagine diverting them to the north and south. On 13 July, at a meeting with Hitler he argued that the two panzer groups should 'decide not to charge ahead...towards Moscow' and first of all surround and destroy the enemy forces in front of Army Group Centre. While Hitler agreed with this view in principle, he proposed that Panzer Group 3 provide support for Army Group North (ibid.). See also Klink, 'Heer', 547ff.

26. *Halder, KTB*, 3.

27. Hubatsch (ed.), *Weisungen*, No. 33. See also comments by Hitler during his visit to Army Group North on 21 July 1941, which were along the same lines, in *KTB OKW* 1, 1029f. See Klink, 'Heer', 576ff.

28. He subordinated Panzer Group 3 temporarily to Army Group North; after the conclusion of the operations there it was 'expected' to return to AG Centre in order to advance towards the Volga. Panzer Group 2, which in the meantime had been attached to the 4th Panzer Army, was meant to advance towards the south-east and, after conquering the industrial area round Kharkov, over the Don towards the Caucasus. See Hubatsch (ed.), *Weisungen*, No. 33a.

29. *KTB OKW* 1, 1030f. and 1034f.; Halder, *KTB*, 3, 23 July 1941, with sceptical comments about Hitler's aims. For the contents of his presentation to Hitler on 23 July see ibid.

30. Klink, 'Heer', 579, discusses the 'working papers' that Halder gave to the Army groups before the meeting. During a meeting with the Army Group chiefs on 25 July he tried to prepare them for dealing with 'spanners in the works from on high' (by which he meant Hitler's interventions): 'Have patience but also resist in time'. They should send suitable front line officers to report to HQ because he 'believes the front more than he does us' (Halder, *KTB*, 3).

31. Ibid., 26 July 1941.

32. Ibid.

33. Bock, commander of AG B, prompted by Brauchitsch, declared that, if Panzer Group 2 were diverted towards Gomel, it would be too weak to mount the decisive attack on Moscow. See Bock, *Pflicht*, 231ff.; Halder, *KTB*, 3, 28 July 1941; Klink, 'Heer', 581. At the end of July Jodl too advocated an advance on Moscow, above all because that was where 'the only forces that the enemy can concentrate are likely to be found'; this action would after all correspond to 'the principle which the Führer has always maintained of first of all destroying the enemy's strength'. See *KTB OKW* 1, 1036f.

34. Ibid., 1040f.

35. Hubatsch (ed.), *Weisungen*, No. 34. Halder saw a 'ray of hope' in the directive (Halder, *KTB*, 3, 30 July 1941). For an assessment see Klink, 'Heer', 583.

36. Field-Marshal Bock strongly supported this proposal because such an advance could prove 'decisive'. See *KTB OKW* 1, 1041ff. 'The Führer has been covertly persuaded, on the basis of his own tactical principles, to move towards our operational goals. For the moment that is a relief' (Halder, *KTB*, 3, 5 August 1941). See also ibid., 6 and 7 August 1941; *KTB OKW* 1, 1043f.; Warlimont, *Hauptquartier*, 201.

37. Hubatsch (ed.), *Weisungen*. Halder's comments, *KTB*, 3, 13 and 14 August 1941.

38. Ibid., 14 August 1941. However, Halder could not get his way (ibid., 15 and 16 August 1941). On the whole issue see Klink, 'Heer', 586ff.

39. *Goebbels TB*, 19 August 1941.

40. *KTB OKW* 1, 1045.

41. Ibid., 1055ff.; Halder, *KTB*, 3, 18 August 1941.

42. *KTB OKW* 1, 1054f.

43. Ibid., 1061ff.

44. Ibid., 1063ff.

45. Halder, *KTB*, 3, 22 August 1941.

46. That was how Halder assessed it. See ibid., 30 August 1941.

47. Ibid., 23 August 1941; Guderian, *Erinnerungen*, 179f.; Bock, *Pflicht*, 256f.

48. Halder, *KTB*, 3, 24 August 1941; Guderian, *Erinnerungen*, 180ff.; Bock, *Pflicht*, 257.

49. *Goebbels TB*, 19 August 1941.

50. Halder, *KTB*, 3, 11 August 1941.

51. Klink, 'Heer', 594.

52. See above p. 738f.

53. Halder, *KTB*, 3, 8 July 1941.

54. Hubatsch (ed.), *Weisungen*, No. 32b.

55. These included the Allied awareness of the provisioning of submarines at sea, the torpedoing of the cruiser 'Lützow' in June, and the stagnation of the U-boat war during the summer. See Salewski, *Seekriegsleitung* 1, 436ff. and 449ff. The naval high command's attempt to re-launch the campaign in the North Atlantic with capital ships failed, in the first instance because of a shortage of oil.

56. *KTB OKW* 1, 1041ff.

57. *ADAP* D 13, No. 265; see Schreiber, *Politik*, 586f. Hitler's approval is clear from Keitel's covering letter of 1 September 1941.

58. OKH reached this conclusion in October 1942: *KTB OKW* 1, 1072f.

59. *Lagevorträge*, 9 July 1941.

60. See above p. 727.

61. *ADAP*, D 13, No. 89; see also Friedländer, *Auftakt*, 156ff. and 183ff.

62. Hillgruber (ed.), *Staatsmänner* 1, 292ff., esp. 299 and 302.

63. Picker, *Tischgespräche*, 10 September 1941: He would no longer be there to see it, but one day Great Britain and Germany would wage war on the USA; *ADAP*, D13, No. 424: 'A later generation would have to get to grips with the problem of Europe-America', Hitler told Ciano on 25 October 1941.

64. *Goebbels TB*, 19 August 1941.

65. *Lagevorträge*, 17 September 1941.

66. *Goebbels TB*, 24 September, 4 October, and 22 November 1941,

67. *ADAP* D 13, Nos 35f., 53, 63–65, 89, 105, 239, and Appendix IV.

68. Japan decided in August not to take part in the war in the East (Hillgruber, 'Japan', 234).

69. *Goebbels TB*, 9 July and 19 August 1941; *Lagevorträge*, 26 August 1941.

70. *ADAP* D 13, No. 291.

71. Halder, *KTB* 3, 10 September 1941; *Goebbels TB*, 24 September and 22 November 1941.

72. Hitler, *Monologe*, 5 July 1941.

73. Werner Koeppen, *Herbst 1941 im 'Führerhauptquartier'. Berichte Werner Koeppens an seinen Minister Alfred Rosenberg*, ed. Martin Voigt (Coblenz, 2002), 24 September 1941.

74. Hitler, *Monologe*, 17 September 1941.

75. Koeppen, *Herbst*, 24 September 1941.

76. Hitler, *Monologe*, 27 July 1941. In fact, the line that was supposed to mark the border with the east was intended to run 200 to 300 kilometres east of the Urals.

77. *Goebbels TB*, 19 August 1941.

78. Koeppen, *Herbst*, 10 September 1941; Hitler, *Monologe*, 25/26 September, 29 October 1941, and 6 August 1942.

79. *Goebbels TB*, 19 August 1941.

80. Ibid., 24 September 1941.

81. Speech of 8 November 1941 in the Munich Löwenbräukeller (Domarus, 2, 1775).

82. *KTB Seekriegsleitung*, 29 September 1941.

83. Hitler, *Monologe*, 5/6 July 1941.

84. Koeppen, *Herbst*, 24 September 1941. On the Urals as the frontier see Hitler, *Monologe*, 5/6 July and 25 September 1941; on the qualification that the actual line of demarcation would have to be a few hundred kilometres east of the mountains see ibid., 27 July 1941.

85. Ibid., 25 September 1941.

86. *Goebbels TB*, 9 July, 19 August, 24 September, and 4 October 1941.

87. Koeppen, *Herbst*, 24 September 1941. The same line of thought appears in Hitler, *Monologe*, 23 September 1941.

88. Ibid., 10 October 1941.

89. Ibid., 17 September 1941.

90. So Koeppen, *Herbst*, 18 October 1941; Hitler, *Monologe*, 17 October 1941.

91. Ibid., 13 October 1941.

92. Eugen Kreidler, *Die Eisenbahnen im Machtbereich der Achsenmächte während des Zweiten Weltkrieges. Einsatz und Leistung für die Wehrmacht und Kriegswirtschaft* (Göttingen, Frankfurt a. M., and Zurich, 1975), 204 and 281; Anton Joachimsthaler, *Die Breitspurbahn Hitlers. Eine Dokumentation über die geplante transkontinentale 3-Meter Breitspureisenbahn der Jahre 1942 bis 1945* (Freiburg i. Br., 1981).

93. Hitler, *Monologe*, 8/9–10/11 August 1941.

94. Ibid., 17 October 1941, evening. On 4 October he spoke of 5 million peasant farms that would have to have been settled there in fifty years' time. See Koeppen, *Herbst*, 5 October 1941.

95. Ibid., 18 October 1941.

96. Hitler, *Monologe*, 5/6 July 1941.

97. Ibid., 27 July 1941; *Goebbels TB*, 30 November and 13 December 1941 (on Hitler's speech to the Gauleiters on 12 December).

98. Hitler, *Monologe*, 27 July 1941 (quote); Koeppen, *Herbst*, 5 October 1941. Hitler also referred to the future role of the defeated in his speech of 12 December. See *Goebbels TB*, 13 December 1941.

99. Hitler, *Monologe*, 27 July 1941.

100. Ibid., 8/9–10/11 August 1941 and 17 September 1941.

101. Ibid., 17 October 1941, evening. See also Koeppen, *Herbst*, 18 October 1941, on this monologue.

102. Hitler, *Monologe*, 1/2 August 1941.

103. Ibid., 8/9–10/11 August 1941.

104. Ibid., 19/20 August 1941.

105. Ibid., 17 September 1941.

106. Ibid., 22/23 September 1941.

107. Ibid., 26/27 October 1941, similarly on 17 September 1941.

108. *IMT* 38, 221-L, S. 86ff. There is another detailed account in the shape of the new edition of the Rosenberg diaries (Rosenberg, *Tagebücher*, 20 July 1941).

109. In mid-July, on Himmler's instructions, his chief settlement planner, Meyer, had produced a 'General Plan for the East', which, in contrast to previous

plans, included not only the annexed Polish territories but also the whole of the General Government and the neighbouring territories to the east. See Madajczyk, *Vom Generalplan Ost zum Generalsiedlungsplan* (Munich, 1994); Isabel Heinemann, *'Rasse, Siedlung, deutsches Blut'. Das Rasse- und Siedlungshauptamt der SS und die rassenpolitische Neuordnung Europas* (Göttingen, 2003), 362f.

110. IfZ, 2718-PS, 2 May 1941. See, in particular, Christian Gerlach, *Kalkulierte Morde. Die deutsche Wirtschafts- und Vernichtungspolitik in Weißrussland 1941 bis 1944* (Hamburg, 1999), 46ff.; Alex J. Kay, '"Germany's Staatssekretäre", Mass Starvation and the Meeting of 2 May 1941', in *Journal of Contemporary History* 41 (2006), 685–700.

111. *'Führer-Erlasse'*, No. 99. At the beginning of April Rosenberg was already envisaged for this role as a result of Hitler's assignment to him to establish an office for 'eastern questions'. See Piper, *Rosenberg*, 509.

112. Rosenberg had at first proposed Lohse for 'Eastland', while Göring had proposed Koch. After lengthy discussion Hitler decided – 'Solomonically' as Rosenberg put it – to appoint Lohse for Eastland and Koch for the Ukraine. See Rosenberg, *Tagebücher*, 20 July 1941.

113. According to his own account, Rosenberg had argued on the 16th that, instead of 'making 120 million people into enemies through indiscriminate, albeit necessary, harsh treatment' it would be better to win over half of them as allies by 'differentiating between them according to their relative value'; 'thus we should confiscate *more* where the people were less valuable as allies and less where they would be more so' (ibid., 20 July 1944, emphasis in the original). On Rosenberg's ideas about occupation see Piper, *Rosenberg*, 509ff.

114. *'Führer-Erlasse'*, No. 100.

115. Himmler to Lammers, 10 June 1941 (BAB, R 6/21). See also IfZ, 3726-NO, Rosenberg statement, 14 June 1941, and memorandum.

116. See Stahlecker (commander of Einsatzgruppe A) to Heydrich, 10 August 1941 (StA Riga, 1026-1-3), in which he points out that 'dealing with the Jewish question is part of the policing of the newly occupied eastern territories, so that, according to paragraphs I and II of the Führer edict concerning the policing of the occupied eastern territories of 18 July 1941, the Reichsführer SS is entitled to give directives to the Reich commissar'.

117. See above pp. 730ff.

118. Longerich, *Holocaust*, 255.

119. See above, p. 753.

120. ZStL, Doc. UdSSR, No. 401.

121. *Meldungen*, 7, 2426f.; *Goebbels TB*, 23 June 1941.

122. *Die Wehrmachtberichte 1939–1945* (Munich, 1985), 1, 23–28 June 1941; *Goebbels TB*, in particular 27 June 1941.

123. *Meldungen*, 7, 2440f.

124. *Goebbels TB*, 29 June 1941.

125. *Wehrmachtberichte*, 1, 29 June 1941.

126. *Meldungen*, 7, 2458f.

127. *Goebbels TB*, 5 July 1941.

128. OA Moscow, 1363–3, Conference of Ministers, 5 July 1941.

129. BAK, ZSg. 102/33, 5 July 1941, The daily instruction supplemented by the *Vertrauliche Information* of 5 July 1941; ZSg. 102/35, 7 July 1941. The *VB* (B) of 6 July 1941 was entirely focused on this propaganda campaign. See also *Der Angriff*, 6 July 1941, 'Viehische Bluttaten der GPU-Kommissare'. Goebbels prescribed the tone of the campaign in an article in the *VB* of 7 July 1941 with the title 'The veil is lifted'.

130. *Goebbels TB*, 9 July 1941.

131. OA Moscow, 1363–3, Conference of Ministers.

132. For details see Longerich, *'Davon'*, 160f.

133. To Goebbels on 18 August (*Goebbels TB*, 19 August 1941).

134. *Meldungen*, 7, 2471f., 2486f., 2502, 2514f., 2545, and 2559f. See also *Goebbels TB*, 10 and 14 July, also 17 and 23 July 1941.

135. *Meldungen*, 7, on food supplies: 2487, 2502f., 2511ff., and 2530; on the air raids: 2502, 2529f., and 2545f.

136. *Goebbels TB*, 3, 6, 7, and 24 July 1941.

137. *Meldungen*, 7, 2578 and 2591f. (concerns that it could turn into a 'lengthy war of position').

138. Ibid., 2608f. ('decline in expectations').

139. *Goebbels TB*, 24 July 1941; on the need for propaganda to 'toughen people up' see also 26 and 28 July 1941; on the deterioration in mood see also 27 and 29 July and 7, 9, and 10 August 1941.

140. *Meldungen*, 7, 2529f., 2545f., and 2590.

141. A reference to this in Lammers to Bormann, 14 April 1942, in which a directive of Hitler's, issued in July, is referred to, which Bormann had been given the responsibility of implementing (BAB, R 43 II/158).

142. See the numerous complaints and objections in the Reich Chancellery files: BAB, R 43 II/159, 1271, 1271a, 1271b, and 1272. On the 'monastery storm' see Ludwig Volk, 'Episkopat und Kirchenkampf im Zweiten Weltkrieg', in Albrecht (ed.), *Katholische Kirche*, 92ff. In mid-July Cardinal Bertram complained in detail to Goebbels in the name of the German Bishops' Conference about the difficulties being made for the Catholic Church. Goebbels did not reply. See *Goebbels TB*, 20 July 1941.

143. See below p. 764.

144. *Wehrmachtberichte*, 1, 6 August 1941. *Meldungen*, 7, 2618, 2631, and 2643 (growing confidence); *Meldungen*, 8, 2659 (once again mixed), 2671 (Confidence but concern because of the length of the war), and 2684 (increasing numbers of rumours; the hopes for a quick end to the war are being 'reluctantly' abandoned).

THE RADICALIZATION OF JEWISH POLICY

1. On 21 April Goebbels had already instructed his state secretary, Gutterer, to prepare for the marking out of Jews. See Boelcke (ed.), *Kriegspropaganda; Akten*

Partei-Kanzlei, Microfiches, vol. 4, 76074, Tiessler submission, 21 July 1941. At the beginning of July Goebbels pressed Bormann to get Hitler to approve the marking out of the Jews (ibid., 74650f., Tiessler minute for the Party Chancellery, 3 July 1941). On the earlier proposals by the security police and the staff of the Deputy Führer see Longerich, *'Davon'*, 165 and 393 (with further bibliographical references). On the re-adoption of the initiative by Goebbels see *Goebbels TB*, 12 August 1941.

2. Lösener, 'Rassereferent'.

3. *Goebbels TB*, 19 August 1941.

4. Ibid., 20 August 1941. Lösener reported to his minister, Frick, on the 15 August meeting in the Propaganda Ministry that, 'on the question of the evacuation of the Jews from the old Reich', Eichmann had said that, in response to a request from Obergruppenführer Heydrich, the 'Führer' 'had rejected evacuations during the war, whereupon the former had worked out a proposal aimed at a partial evacuation of the larger cities.' See Lösener, 'Rassereferent', 303. However, as the entries in the *Goebbels TB* show, the deportation ban had not yet been implemented during the war in the East.

5. See above, p. 762.

6. On the pastoral letter see Nowak, *'Euthanasie' und Sterilisierung im 'Dritten Reich'. Die Konfrontation der evangelischen und katholischen Kirche mit dem Gesetz zur Verhütung erbkranken Nachwuchses und der 'Euthanasie'-Aktion* (Göttingen, 1978), 112.

7. Ibid., 161ff.; Heinrich Portmann, *Der Bischof von Münster* (Münster, 1947), 143ff. Texts of the Galen sermons of 12 and 20 July and 3 August 1941 in Peter Löffler (ed.), *Bischof Clement August Graf von Galen. Akten, Briefe und Predigten 1933–1946*, 2 (Mainz, 1988), Nos 333, 336, and 341. On people's awareness of the 'Euthanasia' programme in the Reich and the protests see Marlis Steinert, *Hitlers Krieg und die Deutschen. Stimmung und Haltung der deutschen Bevölkerung im Zweiten Weltkrieg* (Düsseldorf, 1970), 152ff.; Schmuhl, *Rassenhygiene*, 312ff.; Longerich, *'Davon'*, 162ff.

8. *Goebbels TB*, 11 July 1941.

9. On Bertram's letter see Nowak, *'Euthanasie'*, 160.

10. *Goebbels TB*, 14 and 18 August 1941.

11. *Akten Partei-Kanzlei*, Part II, Microfiche 60.332f. (BA, NS 18/200), Goebbels circular to the Reichsleiters and Gauleiters, 24 August 1941.

12. On the halt to T4 see Klee, 'Euthanasie', 333ff. Four days before his visit to Hitler Goebbels was determined to ask him whether he wanted a public discussion about 'euthanasia' at that time; he advised against. See *Goebbels TB*, 15 August 1941. In his account of the meeting of 18 August the 'euthanasia' question is not explicitly referred to. On 22 August Goebbels was already aware of its impending suspension (ibid., 23 August 1941).

13. The senior Westphalian official, Kolbow, stated in a minute of 31 July 1941, that the action was going ahead briskly in Westphalia and would be finished in around two or three weeks. (Facsimile in Karl Teppe, *Massenmord auf dem*

Dienstweg. Hitlers 'Euthanasie'-Erlaß und seine Durchführung in den westfälischen Provinzialanstalten (Münster, 1989), 21.) For details see Longerich, *'Davon'*, 170.

14. On the (decentralized) continuation of 'euthanasia' see Süss, *'Volkskörper'*, 310ff.; he discusses estimates of the number of victims, which vary between 72,000 and 117,000. See also Schmuhl, *Rassenhygiene*, 220ff.

15. BAB, R 43 II/737b, Brandt to Bormann, 24 August 1941, Bormann to Lammers, 25 August 1941, and a circular from the Reich HQ of the NSDAP (Brandt), 8 October 1941. On the halt to 'euthanasia' and the Brandt action see Faulstich, *Hungersterben*, 271ff.; Süss, *'Volkskörper'*, 127ff. and 281ff.; Schmuhl, *Rassenhygiene*, 210ff.; Aly, 'Endlösung', 312ff.; Schmidt, *Arzt*, 251ff.

16. Walter Ziegler, 'Der Kampf um die Schulkreuze im Dritten Reich', in Hans Maier (ed.), *Das Kreuz im Widerspruch. Der Kruzifix-Beschluss des Bundesverfassungsgerichts in der Kontroverse* (Freiburg, 1996); Wagner's edict dated 23 April 1941. Walter Ziegler (ed.), *Die kirchliche Lage in Bayern nach den Regierungspräsidentenberichten 1933–1945*, 4 (Mainz, 1973), Nos 122–26. See also *Goebbels TB*, 29 August and 4 September 1941.

17. Hitler, *Monologe*, 14 October, 22 and 30 November 1941; *Goebbels TB*, 13 and 14 December 1941.

18. Klink, 'Heer', 595ff.

19. *Meldungen*, 8, 2671, 2684ff., 2712f., 2724 ('signs of a certain trepidation'), 2737f., 2849, and 2760 ('in view of winter coming a certain despondency'). See also the reaction in the *Goebbels TB*, 18, 25, and 28 August and 5 September 1941.

20. *Meldungen* 8, 2771 (mixed picture), 2787 ('improved mood'), 2795 ('more confident' mood) and 2809 ('positive picture'). On the change in the mood see also *Goebbels TB*, 20, 21, and 23 September 1941.

21. Ibid., 27 September 1941; on the very positive mood also 25–28 September 1941.

22. On 17 September C-in-C AG Centre presented Halder with the operational plans for the offensive later named 'Typhoon'. See Klink, 'Heer', 659. The order of 26 September approving it is published in Klaus Reinhardt, *Die Wende vor Moskau. Das Scheitern der Strategie Hitlers im Winter 1941/42* (Stuttgart, 1972), Appendix 1.

23. Klink, 'Heer', 660ff.

24. Domarus, 2, 1758ff., quotes 1761–63.

25. Koeppen, *Herbst*, 55.

26. Ibid., 69.

27. *Wehrmachtberichte*, 1, 8 October 1941.

28. BAK, ZSg. 109/26, *Vertrauliche Information* (Mitteilungsblatt) of 9 October 1941; *Goebbels TB*, 10 October 1941. Manuscript by the head of the historical section of the OKW, Scherff, 13 February 1942, concerning Hitler's statement: 'Dietrich's speech on his orders' (published in Marianne Feuersenger, *Mein Kriegstagebuch. Zwischen Führerhauptquartier und Berliner Wirklichkeit* (Freiburg i. Br., 1982) 90); Pyta, 'Schicksalsgemeinschaft', 40, refers to this; Dietrich, *Jahre*, 101; Stefan Krings, *Hitlers Pressechef. Otto Dietrich (1897–1952). Eine Biographie* (Göttingen, 2010), 413ff., with more evidence.

29. Klink, 'Heer', 66off.; Reinhardt, *Wende*, 63ff.

30. *KTB OKW* 1, 1070f.; Klink, 'Heer', 663.

31. *Goebbels TB*, 11, also 12 October 1941.

32. Goebbels gave the start signal at the propaganda ministry's conference on 21 August 1941. For details see Longerich, *'Davon'*, 169ff.

33. Theodore Kaufman, *Germany Must Perish* (Newark n.d. [Beginning of 1941]); see Wolfgang Benz, 'Judenvernichtung aus Notwehr? Die Legende um Theodore N. Kaufman', in *VfZ* 29 (1981), 615–30.

34. *Goebbels TB*, 19 August 1941. On the production of the pamphlet see ibid., 13, 29, and 30 August 1941.

35. On this campaign see Longerich, *'Davon'*, 168f.

36. BAK, ZSg. 102/34, 12 September, midday; *Goebbels TB*, 13 September 1941.

37. For detailed evidence see Longerich, *'Davon'*, 169.

38. BAB, R 8150/18.

39. On the reactions see Longerich, *'Davon'*, 171ff. On Goebbels's saying quoted in the caption see BAB, NS 18/188, copy by the Reich propaganda headquarters, 25 September 1941.

40. On the announcement see BAK, ZSg. 102/34. Longerich, *'Davon'*, 173ff.

41. Gruner, 'Kollektivausweisung', 48; *Der Dienstkalender Heinrich Himmlers 1941/42*, ed. Peter Witte (Hamburg, 1999), 2 and 4 September 1941; a few days later Eichmann informed Rademacher, who was on the Germany desk in the Foreign Ministry, that at that moment it was impossible to accommodate Jews from Serbia or the Reich in the General Government. See Robert M. Kempner, *Eichmann und Komplizen* (Zurich, 1961), 291. Koppe's letter of 10 September 1941 has not survived, but can be reconstructed from the letter book of the Reichsführer SS's personal staff (editorial note in the *Dienstkalender*, 4 September 1941).

42. Alfred Eisfeld and Victor Herdt (eds), *Deportation, Sondersiedlung, Arbeitsarmee. Deutsche in der Sowjetunion 1941 bis 1956* (Cologne, 1966), 54f. For the views of the German leadership see *Goebbels TB*, 9 September 1941. Rosenberg mentions the Soviet decision in his diary on 12 September 1941, and is extremely upset about it (Rosenberg, *Tagebücher*).

43. Ibid., 12 September 1941. A few days before he had already had a tough statement prepared, which Hitler then 'toughened up still further' (ibid.).

44. *Dienstkalender*, 16 September 1941; Zeitschel to Dannecker, 8 October 1941, on the results of this meeting, published in Serge Klarsfeld (ed.), *Die Endlösung der Judenfrage in Frankreich. Deutsche Dokumente 1941–1944* (Paris, 1977), 23ff.

45. Hillgruber, *Strategie*, 694 on the meeting between Hitler and Ribbentrop; *Dienstkalender*, 17 September 1941; Peter Witte, 'Zwei Entscheidungen in der "Endlösung der Judenfrage". Deportationen nach Lodz und Vernichtung in Chelmno', in *Theresienstädter Studien und Dokumente* 1995, 38ff.

46. Longerich (ed.), *Ermordung*, 157.

47. *Goebbels TB*, 24 September 1941.

48. Koeppen, *Herbst*, 21 September 1941. Koeppen was Rosenberg's liaison officer in Hitler's headquarters. The information for the second part of the quotation

in Koeppen's note comes from Gustav Adolf Steengracht von Moyland on Ribbentrop's personal staff.

49. The fact that in many places the deportations were carried out in public and observed by the population has been documented in numerous local studies. For details see Longerich, *'Davon'*, 194ff. See also the photo album by Klaus Hesse and Philipp Springer, *Vor aller Augen. Fotodokumente des nationalsozialistischen Terrors in der Provinz*, ed. Reinhard Rürup (Essen, 2002), 135ff.

50. The reports in the international press, which since the start of the deportations had reported in detail on these events, fulfilled Hitler's intention of putting pressure on the United States. See, for example, *NZZ*, 20 October 1941 (UPI report, 18 October 1941), about deportations from the Rhineland and Berlin to Poland: 'It is reported that these Jews number almost 20,000. It is reported that yesterday around 5,000 Jews left the capital. They are to be transported first to Litzmannstadt (formerly Lodz) and probably be taken later to the General Government.' The *New York Times* already had this report on 18 October 1941 with further details about the situation of the Berlin Jews. On 22 October, based on a UPI report of 20 October, the *NZZ* announced that the deportations would be continued.

51. Goebbels gave instructions that foreign correspondents asking questions should be told that the Jews were being 'deployed for work in the east'. See BAB, NS 18 alt/622, Minutes of the propaganda conference, 23 October 1941. For details see Longerich, *'Davon'*, 182f.

52. Ibid., 183ff.

53. This is shown by a series of mood reports, which also noted critical comments. See ibid., 194ff.

54. It is clear from the records of the office of the General Inspector for the Reich Capital that, after an initial action at the beginning of January and a second in May, in August 1941 Speer began a 'further action to clear around 5,000 Jewish homes'. See Susanne Willems, *Der entsiedelte Jude. Albert Speer's Wohnungsmarktpolitik für den Berliner Hauptstadtbau* (Berlin, 2002), 27ff., 195ff., and 258ff. In September 1941, on the initiative of the Gau headquarters, the Jews in Hannover were forced at short notice to move in together into sixteen houses. It was planned to rehouse them in a barracks. See Marlis Buchholz, *Die hannoverschen Judenhäuser. Zur Situation der Juden in der Zeit der Ghettoisierung und Verfolgung 1941 bis 1945* (Hildesheim, 1987), 28ff.; see also the report in the *New York Times*, 9 September 1941. In May 1941 the Cologne Jews were ordered at short notice to leave a number of 'Jewish' houses in privileged neighbourhoods; the plan to accommodate them in barracks was not implemented, however. See Horst Matzerath, 'Der Weg der Kölner Juden in den Holocaust. Versuch einer Rekonstruktion', in *Die jüdischen Opfer des Nationalsozialismus aus Köln* (Cologne, 1995), 534. On the deportation of the Breslau Jews to Tomersdorf near Görlitz see Willy Cohn, *Als Jude in Breslau – 1941. Aus den Tagebüchern von Willy Israel Cohn*, ed. Joseph Walk (Jerusalem, 1975), 8, 9, 15, and 23 August, and 11 September 1941.

55. See Witte, 'Entscheidungen', 45, who refers to pressure from the Gauleiter for the deportations from Hamburg. Browning, *Entfesselung*, 468, quotes a statement in a post-war trial in the Cologne regional court, according to which the Cologne Gauleiter sent a delegation to Hitler with the same request.

56. Detlev Brandes, *Die Tschechen unter deutschem Protektorat*, 1 (Munich, 1969), 207ff.; Walter Manoschek, *'Serbien ist judenfrei'. Militärische Besatzungspolitik und Judenvernichtung in Serbien 1941/42* (Munich, 1993), 43ff.; Ahlrich Meyer, '"…dass französische Verhältnisse anders sind als polnische". Die Bekämpfung des Widerstands durch die deutsche Militärverwaltung in Frankreich 1941', in Guus Meershoeck et al., *Repression und Kriegsverbrechen. Die Bekämpfung von Widerstands- und Partisanenbewegungen gegen die deutsche Besatzung in West- und Südosteuropa* (Berlin, 1997), 43–93; Wolfram Weber, *Die innere Sicherheit im besetzten Belgien und Nordfrankreich, 1940–1944. Ein Beitrag zur Geschichte der Besatzungsverwaltungen* (Düsseldorf, 1978), 59ff.; *Die Okkupationspolitik des deutsche Faschismus in Dänemark und Norwegen (1940–1945)*, ed. Fritz Petrick (Berlin and Heidelberg, 1992), 33; Peter Klein, 'Die Rolle der Vernichtungslager Kulmhof (Chelmno), Belzec, (Belzec) und Auschwitz-Birkenau in den frühen Deportationsvorbereitungen', in Dittmar Dahlmann and Gerhard Hirschfeld (eds), *Lager, Zwangsarbeit, Vertreibung und Deportation. Dimensionen der Massenverbrechen in der Sowjetunion und in Deutschland 1933 bis 1945* (Essen, 1999), 473.

57. *Goebbels TB*, 24 September and 4 October 1941.

58. Ibid., 26 and 30 October 1941.

59. On 28 September Keitel modified the order so that hostages from nationalist and bourgeois democratic circles could also be shot. See *KTB OKW* 1, 1068f.; *IMT* 27, 1590-PS, 373f.

60. Manoschek, *'Serbien'*, 55ff.

61. Koeppen, *Herbst*, 7 October 1941, about the previous day.

62. *Dienstkalender*, 20 October 1941. The editors quote from a statement to the Slovak state council by Mach on 26 March 1942, which reveals the German offer.

63. Ulrich Herbert, 'Die deutsche Militärverwaltung in Paris und die Deportation der französischen Juden', in Christian Jansen et al., *Von der Aufgabe der Freiheit. Politische Verantwortung und bürgerliche Gesellschaft im 19. und 20. Jahrhundert. Festschrift für Hans Mommsen zum 5. November 1995* (Berlin, 1995), 437ff.

64. Browning, *Entfesselung*, 471.

65. Hitler, *Monologe*, 25 October 1941.

66. BAB, NS 19/2655, Uebelhör to Himmler, 4 and 9 October 1941, Heydrich to Himmler, 8 October 1941, and Himmler to Uebelhör and Greiser, 10 and 11 October 1941; further material in the same file. Here too a complaint from the head of the Wehrmacht Armaments Office, Thomas, to Himmler, 11 October 1941, and Himmler's reply, 22 October 1941.

67. Ibid., Heydrich to Himmler, 8 October 1941.

68. Eichmann Trial, Doc. 1544; Gottwaldt and Schulle, *'Judendeportationen'*; Adler, *Mensch*; also the contributions by Ino Arndt and Heinz Boberach on the

German Reich, by Ino Arndt on Luxemburg, by Jonny Moser on Austria, and by Eva Schmidt-Hartmann on Czechoslovakia in Wolfgang Benz (ed.), *Dimension*. On the deportation of the Burgenland Gypsies see Michael Zimmermann, *Rassenutopie und Genozid. Die nationalsozialistische 'Lösung der Zigeunerfrage'* (Hamburg, 1996), 223ff.

69. On the deportations to Riga see Wolfgang Scheffler, 'Das Schicksal der in die baltischen Staaten deportierten deutschen, österreichischen und tschechoslovakischen Juden 1941–1943', in Wolfgang Scheffler and Diana Schulle (eds), *Buch der Erinnerung. Die ins Baltikum deportierten deutschen, österreichischen und tschechoslowakischen Juden*, 1 (Munich, 2003), 1–43; Gottwaldt and Schulle, 'Judendeportationen', 110ff.

70. Scheffler, 'Massenmord in Kowno', in Scheffler, and Schulle (eds), *Buch*, 83–7.

71. On the seven deportations to Minsk that took place between 11 November and 5 December 1941 see Gottwaldt and Schulle, '*Judendeportationen*', 84ff.

72. *Goebbels TB*, 17 and 22 November 1941.

73. This is clear from a message from Reich governor Greiser to Himmler of 1 May 1942, in which he refers to the 'special treatment' agreed at the time. See Longerich, *Himmler*, 563f.

74. Peter Klein, *Die 'Ghettoverwaltung Litzmannstadt' 1940–1944. Eine Dienstelle im Spannungsfeld zwischen Kommunalbürokratie und staatlicher Verfolgungspolitik* (Hamburg, 2009), 437ff.; Michael Alberti, *Die Verfolgung und Vernichtung der Juden im Reichsgau Wartheland 1939–1945* (Wiesbaden, 2006), 400ff.

75. Longerich, *Himmler*, 563ff.

76. *Dienstkalender*, 13 October 1941; for details see Longerich, *Himmler*, 565.

77. *Dienstkalender*, 14 December 1941; BAB, NS 19/1583, Brack to Himmler, 23 June 1942; Patricia Heberer, 'Eine Kontinuität der Tötungsoperationen. T4-Täter und die "Aktion Reinhardt"', in Bogdan Musial (ed.), *'Aktion Reinhardt'. Der Völkermord an den Juden im Generalgouvernement 1941–1944* (Osnabrück, 2004), 295.

78. If Z, 365-NO, Wetzel to Lohse, 25 October 1941; see Andrej Angrick and Peter Klein, *Die 'Endlösung' in Riga. Ausbeutung und Vernichtung 1941–1944* (Darmstadt, 2006), 338ff.

79. Christian Gerlach, 'Failure of Plans for an SS Extermination Camp in Mogilev, Belorussia', in *Holocaust and Genocide Studies* 11/1 (1997), 60–78. In November 1941 the SS ordered the construction of a large crematorium, which suggests plans for the construction of a large extermination camp. In fact, the ovens were delivered to Auschwitz in 1942.

80. Dieter Pohl, *Nationalsozialistische Judenverfolgung in Ostgalizien 1941–1944. Organisation und Durchführung eines staatlichen Massenverbrechens* (Munich, 1996), 140ff.

THE WINTER CRISIS OF 1941/42

1. Klink, 'Heer', 663; Reinhardt, *Wende*, 82f.

2. Ibid., 84f.; OKH Directives of 27 and 30 October 1941, Source: BAF, KTB AG Centre C. On 19 October he had advocated the withdrawal of the 2nd Panzer

Army to the south, but had then given way to Bock's concerns (ibid., 85f., see KTB AG Centre, 19 and 28 October 1941).

3. Reinhardt, *Wende*, 82.

4. *ADAP* D 13, Nos 433 and 424.

5. Reinhardt, *Wende*, 73.

6. Wagner, *Generalquartiermeister*, 20 October.

7. Reinhardt, *Wende*, 86.

8. *Meldungen*, 8, 2927f.; see also *Goebbels TB*, 4 November 1941.

9. Ibid., 11 January 1942; see also 24 November and 7 December 1941 and 3 January 1942.

10. Ibid., 7 November 1941.

11. Ibid., 5 January 1942. For the change in the propaganda line see Longerich, *Goebbels*, 495ff.

12. Domarus, 2, 1771ff.; on the speech see Kershaw, *Hitler*, 2, 586f.

13. Domarus, 2, 1771ff., quotes 1773f. and 1778.

14. *Goebbels TB*, 4 November 1941.

15. Ibid., 22 November 1941.

16. The German press was instructed to regard the article as the official propaganda line. See BAK, ZSg. 102/35, 6 November 1941, 13.

17. *VB* (B), 9 November 1941, 'Wann oder Wie'.

18. *Goebbels TB*, 22 November 1941.

19. Kershaw, *Hitler*, 2, 587f.; *Goebbels TB*, 10 November 1941, with detailed comments.

20. See also ibid., 4 November 1941.

21. For details see Longerich, *'Davon'*, 191f.

22. Joseph Goebbels, *Das eherne Herz. Rede vor der Deutschen Akademie, gehalten am 1. Dezember 1941 in der Neuen Aula der Friedrich-Wilhelm Universität zu Berlin* (Munich and Berlin, 1941). The passage concerning the 'annihilation' of the Jews is on p. 35.

23. Engel, *Heeresadjutant*, 2, 16, 22, and 24 November 1941.

24. Halder, *KTB*, 3, 19 November 1941.

25. Reinhardt, *Wende*, 115.

26. Halder, *KTB*, 3, 10 November 1941.

27. *KTB OKW* 1, 1074f.

28. Klink, 'Heer', 677ff.; Reinhardt, *Wende*, 126ff.

29. Ibid., 136f.

30. Ibid., 144ff.

31. Klink, 'Heer', 685ff.

32. Ibid., 615f.

33. Ibid., 622.

34. Koeppen, *Herbst*, 26 October 1941.

35. *Goebbels TB*, 11 and 13 November 1941.

36. Halder, *KTB*, 3, 19 November 1941.

37. *Goebbels TB*, 30 November 1941.

38. Klink, 'Heer', 685ff.
39. Ibid., 618ff.
40. Halder, *KTB*, 3, 30 November and 1 December 1941; on the dismissal see also the euphemistic account in *Goebbels TB*, 17 December 1941.
41. Domarus, 2, 1787f.; Halder, *KTB*, 3, 3 December 1941; Klink, 'Heer', 620.
42. Ibid., 686; Halder, *KTB*, 3, 6 December 1941.
43. Hoffmann, 'Kriegführung', 915f.
44. Ibid., 909ff.; Klink, 'Heer', 689ff.; Reinhardt, *Wende*, 197ff.
45. Halder, *KTB*, 3, 7 December 1941; Engel, *Heeresadjutant*, 6 December 1941: 'Trust between F. and the commanders-in-chief can no longer be repaired'. See Klink, 'Heer', 687.
46. Hubatsch (ed.), *Weisungen*.
47. Halder, *KTB*, 3, 7 December 1941; *Dienstkalender*, 7 December 1941.
48. *ADAP* D 13, Nos 480, 486–488, and 492.
49. Ibid., No. 512. On the extension of the war at the end of 1941 see Friedländer, *Auftakt*; Eberhard Jäckel, 'Die deutsche Kriegserklärung an die Vereinigten Staaten von 1941', in Friedrich J. Kroneck and Thomas Oppermann, *Im Dienste Deutschlands und des Rechts. Festschrift für Wilhelm G. Grewe zum 70. Geburtstag am 16. Oktober 1981* (Baden-Baden, 1981), 117–32; Herde, *Italien*; Weinberg, *Welt*, 274ff.
50. *IMT* 35, 656-D, 320ff.; Jäckel, 'Kriegserklärung', 128, disputes its authenticity.
51. This is the argument in Herde, *Italien*, 77.
52. *ADAP* D 13, No. 537. The demarche to the German government mentioned here has not survived. For the reconstruction of this document, which was given to Ribbentrop on 1 or 2 December 1941, see ibid., 767.
53. Ibid., No. 546.
54. Jäckel, 'Kriegserklärung', 137.
55. There were an increasing number of indications in Berlin before the attack began: Ambassador Ott (Tokyo) informed the Foreign Ministry in Berlin on 5 December that the Japanese foreign ministry was coming to the conclusion that 'for domestic political reasons a declaration of a state of war with, or a declaration of war on, America simultaneously with, or after the start of, hostilities was unavoidable'. See *ADAP* D 13, No. 545, arrival on 6 December, at 12.55.
56. Domarus, 2, 1794ff.; Kershaw, *Hitler*, 2, 599ff.
57. For the text of the agreement see Domarus, 2, 1809f. See also *ADAP* D 13, No. 577.
58. On Goebbels see above, p. 779. On Rosenberg's press conference of 18 November 1941 see Wilhelm, *Rassenpolitik*, 131ff., see PAA, Pol XIII, 25, VAA-Reports; see the report of a press reporter published in Jürgen Hagemann, *Presselenkung im Dritten Reich* (Bonn, 1970), 146.
59. Two days after Hitler's speech Rosenberg discussed with Hitler the text of a speech he wanted to make a few days later in the Sportpalast (IMT 27, 1517-PS, 270ff.). Both concluded that Rosenberg should alter an anti-Semitic passage in

it and no longer – as he had done a few days before – speak of the 'extermination of the Jews'. However, the softening of the language was purely a matter of propaganda, presumably because further anti-Semitic threats to the United States were considered counter-productive so soon after the declaration of war. Hitler emphasized to Rosenberg his basic position that 'they had imposed the war on us and they had brought about all the destruction; it was not surprising if they were the first to feel its consequences'.

60. When, on 18 December 1941, Himmler visited Hitler to agree on what further action he should take on the 'Jewish question', he noted the words: 'exterminate them as partisans' (*Dienstkalender*). This specifically authorized Himmler to carry out and extend the mass murder of the Soviet Jews under the pretext of 'combatting partisans'.

61. In January Hitler appeared to Goebbels as far as the 'Jewish question' was concerned as 'consistent', not 'inhibited by bourgeois sentimentality'. Berlin and then the whole of the Reich territory should be 'cleared as soon as possible'. 'What happens to them then doesn't interest us in the least. They sought this fate; they started the war to achieve it and now they must pay the price'. See *Goebbels TB*, 18 January, and 20 January 1942.

62. I consider Christian Gerlach's claim in 'Die Wannsee-Konferenz, das Schicksal der deutschen Juden und Hitlers politische Grundentscheidung, alle Juden Europas zu ermorden', in *Werkstatt Geschichte* 6/18 (1997), 7–44, that this speech represented Hitler's announcement of his fundamental decision to murder the European Jews is too far-reaching an interpretation, although the speech undoubtedly had an important effect in further radicalizing Jewish persecution.

63. *Goebbels TB*, 13 December 1941.

64. Hillgruber (ed.), *Staatsmänner* 1, 357ff.

65. Reinhardt, *Wende*, 219ff.; *KTB OKW* 1, 1083; Halder, *KTB*, 3, 15 December 1941.

66. *KTB OKW* 1, 1084f.; Klink, 'Heer', 696.

67. *KTB OKW* 1, 1084f.

68. According to an entry in KTB AG Centre, 16 December 1941, according to a statement by Schmundt. See Johannes Hürter, *Hitlers Heerführer. Die deutschen Oberbefehlshaber im Krieg gegen die Sowjetunion 1941/42* (Munich, 2006), 325; this was already the assessment of Reinhardt, *Wende*, 223.

69. Excerpt from KTB AG Centre, 16 December 1941, published in Reinhardt, *Wende*, Appendix IV; Bock, *Pflicht*, 349ff. Bock had already described this problem to Brauchitsch on 13 December 1941 (ibid.). See also Reinhardt, *Wende*, 219ff.; Hürter, *Heerführer*, 318ff.; Klink, 'Heer', 695ff.

70. KTB AG Centre, 16 December 1941, published in Reinhardt, *Wende*, Appendix IV; Bock, *Pflicht*, 354.

71. Halder, *KTB*, 3, 16 December 1941.

72. Klink, 'Heer', 697.

73. See Halder, *KTB*, 3, 10 November and 5 December 1941; Engel, *Heeresadjutant*, 6 and 7 December 1941; Klink, 'Heer', 697f.; on Hitler's announcement of the

change in the high command see Domarus, 2, 1813. During the following months, Hitler referred to Brauchitsch on several occasions in conversation with Goebbels in the most contemptuous terms, accusing him of being mainly to blame for the winter crisis. See *Goebbels TB*, 20 January, 20 March, and 24 August 1942.

74. Ibid., 8 September 1941; on Hitler's increasingly critical attitude to Brauchitsch see also 24 September 1941.

75. On the changes see Hürter, *Heerführer*, 601f.

76. Falkenhorst, Wehrmacht commander in Norway, was effectively replaced as commander of the forces in north Finland and ordered back to Oslo through the creation, on 27 December, of a new Army High Command Lapland under General Dietl. See Ueberschär, 'Kriegführung', 988. Hitler told Goebbels already in mid-November about the impending replacement of Leeb and the dismissal of Brauchitsch. See *Goebbels TB*, 18 December 1941.

77. Engel, *Heeresadjutant*, 22 November and 7 December 1941; according to this, this proposal had originally come from Schmundt.

78. *KTB OKW* 1, 1085; see also Halder, *KTB*, 3, 20 December 1941; similarly, also Hitler's directive to AG Centre, 20 December 1941, in Jacobsen, *Weg*, 134f., quoted extensively in Kershaw, *Hitler*, 2, 608f.

79. Guderian, *Erinnerungen*, 240ff.; Halder, *KTB*, 3, 26 December 1941. Kershaw, *Hitler*, 2, 609f.; Klink, 'Heer', 699 and 702.

80. Hoffman, 'Kriegführung', 916ff.

81. Halder, *KTB*, 3, 29 December 1941

82. Heiner Möllers, 'Sponeck. Hans Emil Otto Graf von', in *Neue Deutsche Biographie* 24 (2010), 736f.

83. Halder, *KTB*, 3, 15 January 1942: 'Strauss can't go on any longer'; Hürter, *Heerführer*, 664f.

84. Klink, 'Heer', 708.

85. According to Heinrich Bücheler, *Hoepner. Ein deutsches Soldatenschicksal des zwanzigsten Jahrhunderts* (Herford, 1980), 166ff.; see Hürter, *Heerführer*, 336f.

86. Halder, *KTB*, 3, 19 January 1942; Hürter, *Heerführer*, 340.

87. Ibid., 327; assessment in Reinhardt, *Wende*, 221: The order to hold the line was 'the only feasible solution' but was 'carried out in a rigid and uncompromising way'. Klink, 'Heer', 703, writes of the end of the mission-type tactics in the German army.

88. *Goebbels TB*, 20 January 1942.

89. Klink, 'Heer', 704ff., on the rearguard actions of AG Centre.

90. See Halder, *KTB*, 3, 30 December 1941–14 January 1942 on the – in some cases – very heated discussions between the c-in-c of the AG, Kluge, and Hitler, who kept insisting on holding the front line.

91. *KTB OKW* 2, 1268f.; Klink, 'Heer', 707; Reinhardt, *Wende*, 246ff.

92. Klink, 'Heer', 712ff., on the rearguard actions of AG North.

93. Ibid., 727ff., on the defensive actions of AG South.

94. At the beginning of December, the Wehrmacht reports were still noting place names, encouraging optimism (*Wehrmachtberichte*, 1, 1 December 1941: 'Rostov

area', ditto 2 and 3 December 1941:'front in front of Moscow'), but were then largely restricted to bland or suggestive statements about 'local clashes' and planned 'shortening of the front' (for example 8 and 17 December 1941). Only from mid-January onwards are there occasional mentions of place names, which were intended to dispel rumours of a much more substantial retreat: 13 January 'east of Kharkov', 3 February, 'north-east of Taganrog'.

95. See, in particular *Meldungen*, 8, 3043, 3059f., and 3069f. After Japan's entry into the war became for a time a talking point, concern about the war came to pre-dominate during December and January, as the SD reports testify. The reports from the Reich propaganda offices quoted by Goebbels are similarly negative. See *Goebbels TB*, 3 and 16 January 1942. See also Kershaw, *Hitler-Mythos*, 216f.

96. *Goebbels TB*, 14 and 19 December 1941.

97. Goebbels, *Herz*, 131–7; on the winter clothes collection see also OA Moscow, 1363–3, Conference of Ministers, 20–22 December 1941.

98. Domarus, 2, 1815.

99. Führer decree for the Protection of the Collection of Winter Clothing for the Front, 23 December 1941 (*RGBl.* 1941 I, 797).

100. *Goebbels TB*, 2 January 1942.

101. *VB* (M), 12 and 15 January 1942.

102. *Meldungen*, 9, 3120 and 3151. For further material on the negative effect of the announcement see Kershaw, *Hitler-Mythos*, 216.

103. See Feuersenger, *Kriegstagebuch*, 90.

104. *Goebbels TB*, 28 December 1941.

105. Ibid., 5, 8, 12, and 15 January 1942.

106. Longerich, *Goebbels*, 502f.

107. Since December the topic of the eastern front was played down significantly in the *VB*; instead, prominence was given to the situation in East Asia. It was only on 23 February 1942 that the *VB* once again had a headline about the eastern front.

108. Werner Rahn, 'Der Krieg im Pazifik', in Horst Boog et al. (eds), *Der globale Krieg. Die Ausweitung zum Weltkrieg und der Wechsel der Initiative 1941–1943* (Stuttgart, 1990), esp. 237ff. On the press reporting see *DAZ* and *VB*, in which, during the first weeks of January, East Asia dominated the headlines.

109. See *Wehrmachtberichte*, 2, 1 and 19 (Feodosia), 7 (Kharkov), and 15 January 1942 (Taganrog).

110. Reinhard Stumpf, 'Der Krieg im Mittelmeerraum 1942/43. Die Operationen in Nord-Afrika und im mittleren Mittelmeer', in Boog et al. (eds), *Krieg*, 573ff., on the military situation. For propaganda directives on the offensive see BAK, ZSg. 102/36, 24 January 1942, TP 1. The *VB* (B) made a big thing of Rommel's successes on 25, 26, and 30 January; the *DAZ* on 26 January; *Das Reich* had a double-page spread on 25 January 1942 ('Rommels klassisches Beispiel'). On the Rommel propaganda see Maurice Philip Remy, *Mythos Rommel* (Munich, 2002), 85ff.; Ralf Georg Reuth, *Rommel. Das Ende einer Legende* (Zurich and Munich, 2004), 150ff.

111. *Goebbels TB*, 24 and 25 January 1942; OA Moscow, 1363–3, Conference of Ministers, 26, 27, and 30 January, and 4 February 1942.

112. *Meldungen*, 9, 3233ff. and 3262f.

113. On the speech see Domarus, 2, 1826ff., quotes 1827, 1829, 1832, and 1834, emphases in the original.

114. *Meldungen*, 9, 3235.

115. This interpretation of the Wannsee conference follows the account in Longerich, *Politik*, 466ff. (updated in the revised English version, *Holocaust*, 305ff.). See also Norbert Kampe and Peter Klein (eds), *Die Wannsee-Konferenz am 20. Januar 1942. Dokumente, Forschungsstand, Kontroversen*, (Cologne, Weimar, and Vienna, 2013).

116. *Goebbels TB*, 15 February 1942.

117. Domarus, 2, 1843ff.

THE PINNACLE OF POWER

1. *Goebbels TB*, 13, similarly 15 February 1942.

2. Ibid., 14 and 15 February 1942.

3. Salewski, *Seekriegsleitung*, 2, 1ff.

4. For the gradual improvement in the situation on the eastern front from the German perspective see Klink, 'Heer', 685ff.

5. Halder, *KTB*, 3, 18 February 1942; Klink, 'Heer', 720.

6. BAK, ZSg. 102/36, 22 February 1942; see press reports, for example, *VB* (B), 23 February 1942, 'Zur Lage im Osten'.

7. *Meldungen*, 9, 3233ff., 3262ff., 3273f., 3294f., 3314f., 3336ff., 3349f., 3365f., 3392ff., and 3408ff. During the following period, concern about the eastern front was replaced with worries about food supplies. The Goebbels diaries convey a similar picture based on the reports of the Reich propaganda offices (20 and 26 February, 12 and 19 March 1942).

8. On 6 April the meat ration was cut from 1,600 to 1,200 grams per day. See Schmitz, *Bewirtschaftung*, 466, Table.

9. *Meldungen*, 10, 3566ff. (mixed picture), 3595ff. (gradually increasing confidence), 3613ff. (relatively confident), 3626ff. (mixed mood), 3638ff. (winter's wait-and-see attitude overcome) and 3659ff. (mixed).

10. Domarus, 2, 1848ff., quote 1850.

11. See Hitler's speech on Ganzenmüller's appointment as state secretary in the Transport Ministry, 24 May 1942: Willi A. Boelcke (ed.), *Deutschlands Rüstung im Zweiten Weltkrieg. Hitlers Konferenzen mit Albert Speer 1942–1945* (Frankfurt a. M., 1969), 126ff. See also Picker, *Tischgespräche*, 21 May 1942; Ciano, *Diary*, 29 April–2 May 1942; Hillgruber (ed.), *Staatsmänner*, 2, esp. 44.

12. *Goebbels TB*, 20 March 1942.

13. Reinhardt, *Wende*, 107ff.; Müller, 'Mobilisierung', 567ff.; Eichholtz, *Geschichte*, 2, 11ff.

14. 'Führer-Erlasse', No. 124.

15. BAB, R 43 II/670a, Bormann to Lammers, 15 October 1941; IfZ, 194-EC, Keitel directive, 31 October 1941. The conditions for the 'labour deployment' of the POWs and the 'voluntary' workers from the Soviet Union were regulated by Göring's guidelines of 7 November (*IMT* 27, 1193-PS, 56ff.).

16. Herbert, *Fremdarbeiter*, 163ff.; Christian Streit, *Keine Kameraden. Die Wehrmacht und die sowjetischen Kriegsgefangenen* (Stuttgart, 1978) 244ff.

17. Führer order re: Armaments, 10 January 1942 (Thomas, *Geschichte*, Appendix No. 16). On the reforms introduced by Todt see Eichholtz, *Geschichte*, 2, 49ff.; Müller, 'Mobilisierung', 664ff. There is no reliable evidence for speculation that Hitler or Himmler murdered Todt. See Kershaw, *Hitler*, 2, 663f.

18. On his appointment and the start of his work see Rolf-Dieter Müller, 'Albert Speer und die Rüstungspolitik im Totalen Krieg', in Bernhard Kroener (ed.), *Das Deutsche Reich und der Zweite Weltkrieg. Kriegsverwaltung, Wirtschaft und personelle Ressourcen* (Stuttgart, 1999), 275ff.; Joachim Fest, *Speer. Eine Biographie* (Berlin, 1999), 175ff.; Eichholtz, *Geschichte*, 2, 55ff.; Gregor Janssen, *Das Ministerium Speer. Deutschlands Rüstung im Krieg* (Berlin, 1969), 33ff.; Tooze, *Ökonomie*, 634ff.

19. Eichholtz points this out in *Geschichte*, 2, 57f.

20. On Speer as a 'propaganda genius' see important points in Tooze, *Ökonomie* 636ff. with numerous examples.

21. For criticism of the 'miracle man Speer', see Tooze, *Ökonomie*, 634ff.; Jonas Scherner and Jochen Streb, 'Das Ende eines Mythos? Albert Speer und das sogenannte Rüstungswunder', in *Vierteljahrsschrift für Sozial-und Wirtschaftsgeschichte* 93 (2006), 172–96.

22. *RGBl.* 1942 I, 179. On the appointment see Bernhard R. Kroener, '"Menschenbewirtschaftung", Bevölkerungsverteilung und personelle Rüstung in der zweiten Kriegshälfte (1942–1944)' in Kroener et al., *Organisation und Mobilmachung des deutschen Machtbereichs* (Stuttgart, 1999), 779ff.; Eichholtz, *Geschichte*, 2, 74ff.; Rebentisch, *Führerstaat*, 355ff.

23. Speer, *Erinnerungen*, 215ff.; Eichholtz, *Geschichte*, 2, 59ff.

24. After his meeting at headquarters on 19 February Speer noted Hitler's explicit approval of the system of 'self-responsibility in industry' as point 5. See Boelcke (ed.), 'Rüstung', 64f.

25. Müller, 'Speer', 312ff. On the establishment of the armaments organization see Budrass, *Flugzeugindustrie*, 741ff.; on the main committee, Naval Construction, see Boelcke (ed.), *Rüstung*, 77; Eichholtz, *Geschichte*, 2, 66; on the main committee, Rail Vehicles, see Boelcke (ed.), *Rüstung*, 123 and 126ff.; Eichholtz, *Geschichte*, 2, 66.

26. *RGBl.* 1942 I, 165; Boelcke (ed.), *Rüstung*, 64.

27. Edict concerning the Uniform Coordination of the Armaments Economy, 7 May 1942 ('Führer-Erlasse', No. 157). His gradual process of clearing people out is described in detail in Thomas, *Geschichte*, 307ff. Since summer 1943, with Hitler's support, Speer had been gradually taking over the military armaments organizations in France, Belgium, the Netherlands, and Denmark. See Janssen, *Speer*, 53f.; Müller, 'Speer', 289ff. and 365ff.

28. Ibid., 303ff.; Eichholtz, *Geschichte*, 2, 79ff.; BAB, R 3/1562, Göring edict concerning a 'Central Planning Office', 22 April 1942 (copy).

29. Müller, 'Speer', 307ff.; Eichholtz, *Geschichte*, 2, 94ff.; Thomas, *Geschichte*, 313ff.; Decree concerning the Reich Defence Commissioners and the Unification of the Economic Administration, 16 November 1942 (*RGBl.* 1942 I, 649ff.).

30. Boelcke (ed.), *Rüstung*, 135.

31. According to Boelcke in his introduction (ibid., 4).

32. Eichholtz, *Geschichte*, 2, 73; Müller, 'Speer', 546ff.

33. Tooze, *Ökonomie*, 652ff.; see above, p. 799 with note 17.

34. Boelcke (ed.), *Rüstung*, 143f.

35. Ibid., 126. Röchling visited Hitler in his headquarters a month later. See ibid., 122; Picker, *Tischgespräche*, 18 May 1942.

36. Boelcke (ed.), *Rüstung*, 170ff.

37. Hans Kehrl, *Krisenmanager im Dritten Reich. 6 Jahre Frieden, 6 Jahre Krieg. Erinnerungen* (Düsseldorf, 1973), 278.

38. BAB, R 3/1692, Meeting of the Central Planning Office, 23 October 1942: according to Speer, Pleiger had sent a letter effectively forecasting the collapse of coal supplies during the coming winter. See also the quote in R 2/1694, meeting of 28 October 1942: Household supplies were cut from 1,270 to 1,100 tons. See Tooze, *Ökonomie*, 656ff. On the creation of the RVE see Eichholtz, *Geschichte*, 2, 84ff.

39. Rolf Wagenführ, *Die deutsche Industrie im Kriege 1939–1945* (Berlin, 1963), 69 (figures in percentages of total value).

40. Overview in Spoerer, *Zwangsarbeit*, 37ff.

41. *Der Arbeitseinsatz im Großdeutschen Reich*, 20 February and 30 April 1943; the calculation in Herbert, *Fremdarbeiter*, 210, is incorrect. On the Soviet POWs see Streit, *Kameraden*, 274. At the end of 1942, Sauckel maintained that, since 1 April, his organization had recruited around 2.8 million extra workers, among them over 400,000 POWs. However, this appears to apply to those recruited rather than those actually deployed. See Herbert, *Fremdarbeiter*, 209.

42. Streit, *Kameraden*, 244ff.

43. Herbert, *Fremdarbeiter*, 178ff. This is based on the 'eastern edicts' of the RSHA of 20 February 1942: BAB, RD 19/3, Section 2 A IIIf, 15ff., quote p. 25.

44. Boelcke (ed.), *Rüstung*, 86.

45. See Dieter Pohl, *Von der "Judenpolitik" zum Judenmord. Der Distrikt Lublin des Generalgouvernements 1939–1944* (Frankfurt a. M., 1993), 113ff.; David Silberklang, 'Die Juden und die ersten Deportationen aus dem Distrikt Lublin', in *'Aktion Reinhardt'*, 141–64; Dieter Pohl, *Nationalsozialistische Judenverfolgung in Ostgalizien 1941–1944. Organisation und Durchführung eines staatlichen Massenverbrechens* (Munich, 1996), 179ff.

46. Adler, *Theresienstadt*, 50f.

47. Gottwaldt and Schulle, 'Judendeportationen', 182ff.

48. Pohl, 'Judenpolitik', 116ff.

49. *Dienstkalender*, 20 October 1941.

50. Ladislav Lipscher, *Die Juden im slowakischen Staat 1939–1945* (Munich and Vienna, 1980), 99ff.; Büchler, 'Deportation'.

51. Klarsfeld (ed.), *Vichy*, 34ff.; Herbert, 'Militärverwaltung'.

52. This is how Heydrich put it during a visit to Bratislawa on 10 April 1942. See Longerich, *Politik*, 492.

53. *Goebbels TB*, 20 March 1942.

54. Ibid., 27 March 1942.

55. Ibid., 27 April 1942.

56. Sybille Steinbacher, '*Musterstadt' Auschwitz. Germanisierungspolitik und Judenmord in Oberschlesien* (Munich, 2000), 285ff.; Danuta Czech, *Kalendarium der Ereignisse im Konzentrationslager Auschwitz-Birkenau 1939–1945* (Reinbek b. Hamburg, 1989), 20 March and 12 May 1942.

57. On the judicial crisis see Rebentisch, *Führerstaat*, 399; Kershaw, *Hitler*, 2, 370f.; Gruchmann, '"Generalangriff gegen die Justiz"? Der Reichstagsbeschluß vom 26. April 1942 und seine Bedeutung für die Maßregelung der deutschen Richter durch Hitler', in *VfZ* 51 (2003), 509–20.

58. Picker, *Tischgespräche*, 8 February 1942.

59. *RGBl.* 1942 I, 139f.

60. Dieter Kolbe, *Reichsgerichtspräsident Dr. Erwin Bumke. Studien zum Niedergang des Reichsgerichts und der deutschen Rechtspflege* (Karlsruhe, 1975), 337ff.; Jens Luge, *Die Rechtsstaatlichkeit der Strafrechtspflege im Oldenburger Land 1932–1945* (Hanover, 1993), 181ff.

61. This became clear in 1937/38 in the so-called Fabig case. See Gruchmann, *Justiz*, 192ff.

62. See also the report by Hitler's pilot, Bauer, concerning the dictator's irritated comments about the verdict in Picker, *Tischgespräche*, 22 March 1942.

63. The legal basis for the reconsideration of a case that had been legally completed had been created in September 1939. See *RGBl.* 1939 I, 184, Law concerning the Alteration of Regulations governing Criminal Proceedings etc.

64. BAB, R 43 II/1560, Letter of 24 March 1942, and Reich Chancellery minute, 1 April 1942, concerning Schlegelberger's note.

65. Picker, *Tischgespräche*, 29 March 1942.

66. 'Führer-Erlasse', No. 153.

67. Domarus, 2, 1868.

68. Ibid., 1874.

69. *RGBl.* 1942 I, 247.

70. In fact the ministerial bureaucracy took over responsibility for the 'conscientious review', which, according to the Reichstag resolution, was envisaged for every individual case and, as a result, neutralized the threat of Hitler intervening. Individual judges were dismissed, but in a legal fashion that preserved their rights as civil servants. See Gruchmann '"Generalangriff"'.

71. *Meldungen*, 10, 3671ff., 3685, 3696, and 3708 (about the continuing discontent); *Goebbels TB*, 27, 28, and 30 April 1942. See also ibid., 6, 8, and 13 May 1942 about the impact of Hitler's speech, above all among jurists.

72. Ibid., 13 April 1942.
73. *VB* (B), 20 April 1942, 'In Dankbarkeit und Treue'.
74. Hubatsch (ed.), *Weisungen*, No. 41; the directive was preceded by a meeting with Hitler on 28 March. See Halder, *KTB*, 3, 28 March 1942. Bernd Wegner, 'Der Krieg gegen die Sowjetunion 1942/43', in Boog et al., *Globaler Krieg*, 761ff.
75. Ibid., 774ff.; Hartmann, *Halder*, 311ff.
76. Halder, *KTB*, 3, 21 April 1942. On the situation regarding the troops and the matériel of the army in the east in spring 1942 see Wegner, 'Krieg', 778ff.
77. Ibid., 791ff.
78. For details see ibid., 816ff. Also see Hans Wimpffen, 'Die zweite ungarische Armee im Feldzug gegen die Sowjetunion. Ein Beitrag zur Koalitions-kriegsführung im Zweiten Weltkrieg', Dissertation. Würzburg, 1968; Thomas Schlemmer (ed.), *Die Italiener an der Ostfront 1942/43. Dokumente zu Mussolinis Krieg gegen die Sowjetunion* (Munich, 2005), esp. 23ff. (reinforcement of Italian forces in 1942) and 58ff. (deployment during the summer offensive); on the negotiations with Romania see *ADAP* E I, No. 244; Hillgruber (ed.), *Staatsmänner*, 2, Doc. 2.
79. Wegner, 'Krieg', 762ff.; Situation reports 13 February 1942, and situation assessment of the 20th according to Wegner, 'Krieg'; Salewski, *Seekriegsleitung*, 3, No. 12.
80. Wegner, 'Krieg', 767.
81. Halder, *KTB*, 3, 8 May 1942.
82. Wegner, 'Krieg', 841ff.
83. Ibid., 852ff.
84. *Meldungen*, 10, 3696f., 3708, 3718, 3729, 3746f., 3752f., 3787ff., 3802ff., 3823f., 3836ff., 3852, and 3872f. The positive news from North Africa is already reflected in the last two reports.
85. Röver died on 15 May in the Berlin Charité hospital. Repeated rumours that he had been killed because of his growing criticism of the regime cannot be proved. See Carl Röver, *Der Bericht des Reichsstatthalters von Oldenburg und Bremen und Gauleiters des Gaues Weser-Ems über die Lage der NSDAP aus dem Jahre 1942*, ed. Michael Rademacher (Vechta, 2000), Introduction.
86. *Goebbels TB*, 23 May 1942.
87. On the bombing of Lübeck see Olaf Gröhler, *Bombenkrieg gegen Deutschland* (Berlin, 1990), 36ff. and 48ff.
88. On these raids see Collier, *Defence*, 303ff. and 514f. (table); Horst Boog, 'Strategischer Luftkrieg in Europa und Reichsluftverteidigung 1943–1944', in Boog et al., *Das Deutsche Reich in der Defensive. Strategischer Luftkrieg im Westen und in Ostasien 1943–1944/45* (Stuttgart and Munich, 2011), 560.
89. On the motives for this raid see, in particular, his comments to Goebbels (*TB*, 27 April and 30 May 1942).
90. For an overview see Gröhler, *Bombenkrieg*, 76f.
91. See Heinz Dieter Hölsken, *Die V-Waffen. Entstehung – Propaganda – Kriegseinsatz* (Stuttgart, 1984), 85.

92. See below, p. 874.

93. However, Himmler's office diary contains a possible insight into the decision-making process, as it refers to seven meetings between Himmler and Heydrich between the end of April and the beginning of May in three different places (Berlin, Munich, and Prague) and two meetings of Himmler with Hitler on 23 April and 3 May 1942. See Longerich, *Holocaust*, 359.

94. From 11 May 1942 onwards almost all the Jews from the Reich were either shot or gassed in gas vans on their arrival at Maly Trostenez, a train station near Minsk. See activity report, 17 May 1942, in *Unsere Ehre heißt Treue. Kriegstagebuch des Kommandostabes Reichsführer SS. Tätigkeitsberichte der 1. und 2. SS-Inf. Brigade, der 1. SS-Kavallerie-Brigade und von Sonderkommandos der SS*, ed. Fritz Baade (Vienna, 1985), 236ff.; Gottwaldt and Schulle, 'Judendeportationen', 237ff.; Peter Junge-Wentrup (ed.), *Das Vernichtungslager Trostenez in der europäischen Erinnerung. Materialien zur Internationalen Konferenz vom 21. bis 24 März 2013 in Minsk* (Dortmund, 2013); Paul Kohl (ed.), *Das Vernichtungslager Trostenez. Augenzeugenberichte und Dokumente* (Dortmund, 2003). Between 4 and 15 May, the Jews who had been transported from the Reich to Lodz in autumn 1941 – more than 10,000 people – were already being murdered in gas vans in Chelmno. See Lucjan Dobroszycki (ed.), *The Chronicle of the Łódź Ghetto 1941–1944* (New Haven, CT and London, 1984), 159ff. From mid-May onwards Jews from the Reich who had been taken from the 'Theresienstadt old people's ghetto', were murdered in the Sobibor extermination camp. See Gottwaldt and Schulle, *'Judendeportationen'*, 206. From the beginning of April, and increasingly from the middle of June, the same thing happened to Jews who were transported directly from the Reich to Sobibor (ibid., 211ff.). From the beginning to the middle of June, transports from Slovakia were also murdered in Sobibor. See Yehoshua Büchler, 'The Deportation of Slovakian Jews to the Lublin District of Poland in 1942', in *Holocaust and Genocide Studies* 6 (1991), 153 and 166. See also Jules Schelvis, *Vernichtungslager Sobibór* (Berlin, 1998).

95. Führer edict concerning the Establishment of a State Secretary for Security Affairs in the General Government 7 May 1942 (*RGBl.* 1942 I, 293); Edict concerning the Transfer of Responsibilities to the State Secretary for Security Affairs (*Verordnungsblatt des Generalgouvernements* 1942, 321ff.); see Longerich, *Himmler*, 583f.

96. Longerich, *Holocaust*, 332ff.; Bogdan Musial, *Deutsche Zivilverwaltung und Judenverfolgung im Generalgouvernement. Eine Fallstudie zum Distrikt Lublin 1939–1944* (Wiesbaden, 1999), 242ff.; Pohl, *Judenverfolgung*, 203ff.; Robert Seidel, *Deutsche Besatzungspolitik in Polen. Der Distrikt Radom 1939–1945* (Paderborn, 2006), 289ff.; Steinbacher, *'Musterstadt'*, 273ff.

97. On the Reich Commissariats in Eastland and Ukraine see Yitzhak Arad, *The Holocaust in the Soviet Union* (Lincoln, NE 2009), 251ff. and 263ff.; Longerich, *Holocaust*, 345ff.

98. Wolfgang Scheffler, 'Der Brandanschlag im Berliner Lustgarten im Mai 1942 und seine Folgen. Eine quellenkritische Betrachtung', in *Berlin in Geschichte und*

Gegenwart (1984), 111. However, it is not clear whether these measures occurred on Goebbels's initiative, as he claims in *Goebbels TB*, 25 May 1942, or whether Hitler passed on the order directly to Himmler, or rather Heydrich. (Scheffler, 'Brandanschlag', 106.)

99. Brandes, *Tschechen*, 1, 251ff.; Guenter Deschner, *Reinhard Heydrich. Statthalter der totalen Macht* (Esslingen, 1977), 273ff.; Helmut G. Haasis, *Tod in Prag. Das Attentat auf Reinhard Heydrich* (Reinbek b. Hamburg, 2002); Eduard Calic, *Reinhard Heydrich, Schlüsselfigur des Dritten Reiches* (Düsseldorf, 1982), 476ff.

100. Frank's minute of 28 May 1942, quoted in Václav Král (ed.), *Die Deutschen in der Tschechoslowakei. Dokumentensammlung* (Prague, 1964), 474ff.

101. *Goebbels TB*, 30 May 1942.

102. See above p. 825.

103. In the conversation that he had tête-à-tête with Hitler Goebbels evidently used remarks that the dictator had made at his daily lunch party.

104. In Hitler's terminology, in so far as it is recorded in Goebbels's diary, he makes a definite distinction between west and central Europe, which would support this interpretation.

105. *VB* (N), 10 June 1942, 'Der Führer am Sarge Heydrichs'.

106. Text of the speech in BAB, NS 19/4009.

107. Domarus, 2, 1891.

108. Frank's notes in Kràl (ed.), *Deutschen*, 474ff.; Brandes, *Tschechen* 1, 260f.

109. Ibid., 262ff.; Heinemann, *'Rasse'*, 515ff.

110. Picker, *Tischgespräche*, 22 June 1942.

111. Gottwaldt and Schulle, *'Judendeportationen'*, 213.

112. Ibid., 260ff.

113. Czech, *Kalendarium*.

114. Klarsfeld (ed.), *Vichy*, 379f. and 390. On 21 July 1942, for the first time, Jews 'incapable of work' from France like those from Slovakia were selected out and murdered. See ibid., 412.

115. Gottwaldt and Schulle, *'Judendeportationen'*, 242ff.

116. Raul Hilberg, *Die Vernichtung der europäischen Juden. Die Gesamtgeschichte des Holocaust* (Frankfurt a. M., 1990), 761ff.; Sundhaussen, 'Jugoslawien', 323; Alexander Korb, *Im Schatten des Weltkriegs. Massengewalt der Ustaša gegen Serbien. Juden und Roma in Kroatien 1941–1945* (Hamburg, 2013); Czech, *Kalendarium*, 18, 22, 26, and 30 August 1942.

117. PAA, Inland II g 200, Killinger to FM, 12 August 1942, and to Himmler, 26 July 1942; Browning, *'Endlösung'*, 162ff.

118. Hannu Rautkallio, *Finland and the Holocaust. The Rescue of Finland's Jews* (New York, 1987), 163ff.; however, shortly afterwards Finland did deliver up some Jewish refugees. See Antero Holmila, 'Finland and the Holocaust. A Reassessment', in *Holocaust and Genocide Studies* 13 (2009), 413–40.

119. Yitzhak Arad, *Belzec, Sobibor, Treblinka. The Operation Reinhard Death Camps* (Bloomington IN, 1987), 381ff. (overview of figures in tables); Steinbacher, 'Musterstadt', 278ff.

120. *Dienstkalender*, the state secretary in the transport ministry, Ganzenmüller, responded to Wolff's query on 29 July 1942 (BAB, NS 19/2655). See also Rudolf Höss, *Kommandant in Auschwitz. Autobiographische Aufzeichnungen* (Stuttgart, 1958), 157ff. and 176ff.; Longerich (ed.), *Ermordung*, 201.

121. IfZ, 626–NO.

122. See above p. 786. Hitler's decision cannot be dated; Keitel, however, referred to it in an order of 23 July 1942. See BAB, NS 19/1671. Himmler announced the new task on 31 July. See Reinhard Rürup (ed.), *Der Krieg gegen die Sowjetunion. Eine Dokumentation* (Berlin, 1991), 132. On Himmler's appointment see Longerich, *Himmler*, 646f.

123. Hubatsch (ed.), *Weisungen*, No. 46.

124. IfZ, 3392–NO, published in the illustrations section of Gerald Fleming, *Hitler and the Final Solution* (Berkeley et al., 1984).

125. Stumpf, 'Krieg', 594ff.

126. Domarus, 2, 1893.

127. Stumpf, 'Krieg', 594ff.

128. Ibid., 648ff.

129. Wegner, 'Krieg.' 868ff.

130. Bock, *Pflicht*, 457ff., 3–13 July 1941; Below, *Adjutant*, 313, refers to a 'bitter row between Hitler and Halder and Bock'; Halder, *KTB* 3, 5 (lively debate during the Führer presentation) and 6 July 1942: Bock was unable to take a uniform line in his leadership of his armies. On Bock's dismissal see Wegner, 'Krieg', 884f.; Hürter, *Heerführer*, 602f.

131. On the special atmosphere in Winniza see Schroeder, *Chef*, 138ff. and 142ff.; Felix Hartlaub, *Im Sperrkreis. Aufzeichnungen aus dem Zweiten Weltkrieg*, ed. Geno Hartlaub (Frankfurt a. M., 1984), 117ff.; Below, *Adjutant, 313*. On the lay-out see Seidler and Zeigert, *Führerhauptquartiere*, 221ff.

132. Hubatsch (ed.), *Weisungen*, No. 44; Halder, *KTB*, 3, 23 July 1942; *KTB OKW* 2, 1284; Wegner, 'Krieg', 888ff.

133. Halder, *KTB*, 3, 6, 12, and 30 July 1942; Below, *Adjutant,* 313; Wegner, 'Krieg', 893f.; Hartmann, *Halder*, 325.

134. Hubatsch (ed.), *Weisungen*, No. 45.

135. Wegner, 'Krieg', 892f.

136. Halder, *KTB*, 3, 23 July 1942.

137. *Goebbels TB*, 20 March 1942.

138. Rothenberger had made a name for himself with a memorandum (IfZ, 75-NG, Thoughts about a National Socialist Judicial Reform, Hamburg, 31 March 1942) in which he had demanded the 'creation of a National Socialist type of judge'. See Sarah Schädler, *'Justizkrise' und 'Justizreform' im Nationalsozialismus. Das Reichsjustizministerium unter Reichsjustizminister Thierack (1942–1945)* (Tübingen, 2009), 107f.

139. Christoph Klessmann, 'Der Generalgouverneur Hans Frank', in *VfZ* 19 (1971), esp. 258.

140. Führer edict concerning Special Powers for the Reich Minister of Justice, 20 August 1942 (*RGBl.* 1942 I, 535).

141. Gruchmann, 'Hitler.' Schädler, *'Justizkrise'*, 112ff.

142. Hitler, *Monologe*, 20 August 1942, midday.

143. Gruchmann, 'Hitler', 91.

144. *IMT* 26, 654-PS, 200ff.; Nikolaus Wachsmann, *Gefangen unter Hitler. Justizterror und Strafvollzug im NS-Staat* (Munich, 2006), 310ff.

145. Boelcke (ed.), *Rüstung*, 189; see also *Goebbels TB*, 30 September 1942.

HITLER'S EMPIRE

1. For the August speech see NS 19/1704, Berger minute; *Dienstkalender*, 527; for the speech on 16 September see BAB, NS 19/4009.

2. Robert Bohn, *Reichskommissariat Norwegen. 'Nationalsozialistische Neuordnung' und Kriegswirtschaft* (Munich, 2000), 48ff.; *ADAP* E 1, Nos 248 and 262; E 3, Nos 182 and 293; E 5, No. 310; E 6, No. 353.

3. Konrad Kwiet, *Reichskommissariat Niederlande. Versuch und Scheitern nationalsozialistischer Neuordnung* (Stuttgart, 1968) 133ff.; *ADAP* E 4, No. 284.

4. Wilfried Wagner, 'Belgien in der deutschen Politik während des Zweiten Weltkrieges', Dissertation, Frankfurt a. M., 1974, 143ff., 205ff., and 255ff.; Benoît Majerus, 'Von Falkenhausen zu Falkenhausen. Die deutsche Verwaltung Belgiens in den zwei Weltkriegen', in Günther Kronenbitter et al., *Besatzung, Funktion und Gestalt militärischer Fremdherrschaft von der Antike bis zum 20. Jahrhundert* (Paderborn, 2006), 137.

5. *ADAP* D 13, Nos 498 and 507–511.

6. Peter Longerich, *Propagandisten im Krieg. Die Presseabteilung des Auswärtigen Amtes unter Ribbentrop* (Munich, 1987), 87ff.

7. *ADAP* E 4, No. 124.

8. Christopher Browning, 'Unterstaatssekretär Martin Luther and the Ribbentrop Foreign Office', in *Journal of Contemporary History* 12 (1977), 333.

9. *Goebbels TB*, 23 January, 9 March, and 4 June 1943.

10. Longerich, *Propagandisten*, 40; *ADAP* E 5, No. 229.

11. Jäckel, *Frankreich*, esp. 59f., 116f., and 165ff.; *ADAP* D 13, No. 327; Picker, *Tischgespräche*, 1 April 1942.

12. Longerich, *Himmler*, 629ff. and 693ff.

13. Hans Umbreit, 'Die deutsche Herrschaft in den besetzten Gebieten 1942–1945', in Kroener et al. (eds), *Organisation*, 183; on the economic exploitation of the occupied territories in general see ibid, 183ff.

14. Eichholtz, *Geschichte*, 2, 492ff.

15. Ibid., 499ff.

16. Umbreit, 'Herrschaft', 218.

17. *Der Arbeitseinsatz im Großdeutschen Reich*, 31 January 1944.

18. Eichholtz, *Geschichte* 2, estimates the total sum derived from the occupied territories up until September 1944 as almost 84 billion RM, the clearing debts (i.e. the debts left over from the operation of the clearing system) at 31.5 billion RM; Boelcke estimates a total of 90. 3 billion and estimates the clearing

debt up until the end of 1944 as over 20 billion RM. This should be set against expenditure for the Wehrmacht of 414 billion RM (Boelcke, *Die Kosten von Hitlers Krieg. Kriegsfinanzierung und finanzielles Kriegserbe in Deutschland 1933–1948* (Paderborn, 1985), 98 and 108ff.).

19. Eichholtz, *Geschichte*, 2, 505ff., estimates that in 1943 only 9.3 per cent of German armaments production was based in the occupied territories.

20. See the overview in Mark Mazower, Hitlers *Imperium. Europa unter der Herrschaft des Nationalsozialismus* (Munich, 2009), 247ff.

21. On resistance in Europe and how it was combatted see Jürgen Haestrup, *European Resistance Movements 1939–1945. A Complete History* (Westport, CT and London, 1981); Jacques Semelin, *Unarmed against Hitler. Civilian Resistance in Europe* (Westport, CT and London, 1993); Mazower, *Hitlers Imperium*, 430ff.; Longerich, *Himmler*, 646ff. and 672ff.

22. See above, p. 658f.

23. He also declined to grant Lammers greater powers to adjudicate significant disputes over spheres of responsibility. See Rebentisch, *Führerstaat,* 372f.; BAB, R 43 II/958.

24. Rebentisch, *Führerstaat*, 375. Hitler's view was communicated to the government departments through an Interior Ministry circular dated 21 April 1939.

25. The regulation, which was initially intended to apply for six months, became a permanent arrangement. See Rebentisch, *Führerstaat*, 373.

26. Ibid., 374.

27. Ibid., 384ff.; BAB, R 43 II/695, Reich Chancellery circular, 17 September 1939; R 43 II/694, Lammers to Hierl, 20 July 1941, according to which Hitler had forbidden orders requiring his signature to be presented through the so-called 'ambush method'.

28. Rebentisch, *Führerstaat*, 393ff.

29. Kube, *Pour le mérite*, 324ff.; Martens, *Göring*, 173ff.

30. See in detail Longerich, *Himmler*.

31. For details see Longerich, *Goebbels*.

32. Müller, 'Speer'; Fest, *Speer*; Werner Durth, *Deutsche Architekten. Biographische Verflechtungen 1900–1970* (Munich, 1992), 237ff.

33. Smelser, *Ley*, 257ff.

34. On Sauckel see above, p. 799; Führer edict concerning Medical and Health Services 28 July 1942 (*RGBl.* 1942 I, 515); Schmidt, *Arzt*; Führer edict concerning the Appointment of a Reich Commissar for Shipping, 30 May 1942 (*'Führer-Erlasse'*, No. 163).

35. Michael Bloch, *Ribbentrop* (London, 1992).

36. Günter Neliba, *Wihelm Frick. Der Legalist des Unrechtsstaates. Eine Biographie* (Paderborn, 1992), 324ff.

37. Lehmann, 'Backe'.

38. Alfred Gottwaldt, *Dorpmüllers Reichsbahn. Die Ära des Reichsverkehrsministers Julius Dorpmüller 1920–1945* (Freiburg i. Br., 2009), 192ff.

39. See above, p. 823f.

40. Longerich, *Stellvertreter*, 150ff.; Rebentisch, *Führerstaat*, 376 and 441ff. Participation in legislation was extended as a result of the implementation decree of 16 January 1942. See *RGBl.* 1942 I, 35.

41. Longerich, *Stellvertreter*, 204ff.

42. Rebentisch, *Führerstaat*, 245ff.

43. Picker, *Tischgespräche*, 24 June 1942; see also the survey, which Lammers launched among the Reich governors, following an instruction by Hitler of March 1941, with the aim of giving these officials more autonomy and freedom of action. See BAB, R 43 II/1394. In Hitler's view the boundaries of the Party's Gaus and those of the state's administrative districts should coincide in future. Circular R 114/42, 31 July 1942, published in *Verfügungen* 1, 242ff. See also Rebentisch, *Führerstaat*, 251, 259, and 279.

44. Decree concerning the Reich Defence Commissioners and the Unification of the Economic Administration, 16 November 1942 (*RGBl.* 1942 I, 649ff.).

45. Rebentisch, *Führerstaat*, 132.

46. Ibid., 273ff.; Karl Teppe, 'Der Reichsverteidigungskommissar. Organisation und Praxis in Westfalen', in Dieter Rebentisch and Teppe, *Verwaltung contra Menschenführung im Staat Hitlers. Studien zum politisch-administrativen System* (Göttingen, 1986); as a case study see Ralf Blank, 'Albert Hoffmann als Reichsverteidigungskommissar im Gau Westfalen-Süd 1943–1945. Eine biografische Skizze', in Wolf Gruner and Armin Nolzen (eds), *'Bürokratien'. Initiative und Effizienz* (Berlin, 2001), 189–210.

47. Hüttenberger, *Gauleiter*, 213ff.

48. On the development of the NSDAP during the war see Armin Nolzen, 'Die NSDAP, der Krieg und die deutsche Gesellschaft', in Jörg Echternkamp (ed.), *Die deutsche Kriegsgesellschaft 1939–1945* (Munich, 2004), 99–193; Reibel, *Fundament*.

49. Nolzen, 'NSDAP', 101.

50. Rebentisch, *Führerstaat*, 400f.

51. See above, p. 516.

THE TURNING POINT IN THE WAR AND RADICALIZATION

1. Wegner, 'Krieg', 962ff.; Manfred Kehrig, *Stalingrad. Analyse und Dokumentation einer Schlacht* (Stuttgart, 1974), 28.

2. *KTB OKW* 2, 669; also Halder, *KTB*, 3, 31 August 1942; see also Kershaw, *Hitler*, 2, 701.

3. Halder, *KTB*, 3, from 12 August 1942; Wegner, 'Krieg', 927ff.

4. Ibid., 942ff.

5. Warlimont, *Hauptquartier*, 262f.; Halder, *KTB*, 3, 7 August 1942; Wegner, 'Krieg', 906ff.; Kershaw, *Hitler*, 2, 697f.

6. *Goebbels TB*, 20 August 1942.

7. Ibid., 15 August 1942.

8. *KTB OKW* 2, 704.

9. There are various versions of how the confrontation developed, possibly over several days. See Warlimont, *Hauptquartier*, 263; Adolf Heusinger, *Befehl im*

Widerstreit. Schicksalsstunden der deutschen Armee 1923–1945 (Tübingen and Stuttgart, 1950), 201f.; Engel, *Heeresadjutant*, 4 September 1942; Halder, *KTB*, 3, 24 August 1942.

10. Ibid., 27 and 28 August 1942; Wegner, 'Krieg', 898ff.

11. *KTB OKW* 2, 658; Halder, *KTB*, 3, 21 and 30 August 1942, concerning Hitler's serious reproaches directed at the generals; Engel, *Heeresadjutant*, 16 August 1942; Kershaw, *Hitler* 2, 699f.

12. Wegner, 'Krieg', 940ff.; *KTB OKW* 2, 662; Engel, *Heeresadjutant*, 31 August 1942.

13. *KTB OKW* 2, 674f.

14. Keitel, *Leben*, 369.

15. Halder, *KTB*, 3, 9 September 1942.

16. *KTB OKW* 2, 695ff. See also Engel, *Heeresadjutant*, 7 September 1942; Halder, *KTB*, 3, 8, and 9 September 1942.

17. Engel, *Heeresadjutant*, 14 September 1942; on this crisis see Wegner, 'Krieg', 951ff.

18. Keitel, *Leben*, 370.

19. Franz Halder, *Hitler als Feldherr* (Munich, 1949), 52, concerning other serious confrontations with Hitler.

20. Wegner, 'Krieg', 951f.; Below, *Adjutant*, 315; Warlimont, *Hauptquartier*, 268; Halder, KTB, 3, 11 September. According to Heiber (*Lagebesprechungen*, 14) Hitler had already had the idea of establishing a stenography department from July 1942 onwards.

21. Engel, *Heeresadjutant*, 18 September 1942; Warlimont, *Hauptquartier*, 268f.; Heusinger, *Befehl*, 205ff.; Kershaw, *Hitler*, 2, 698ff.

22. Engel, *Heeresadjutant*, 24 September 1942; Warlimont, *Hauptquartier*, 263; see also Hartmann, *Halder*, 329ff.

23. Halder, *KTB*, 3, 24 September 1942.

24. Hartmann, *Halder*, 337ff.; Friedrich-Christian Stahl, 'Generaloberst Kurt Zeitzler', in Gerd R. Überschär (ed.), *Hitlers militärische Elite. Vom Kriegsbeginn bis zum Weltkriegsende*, 2 (Darmstadt, 1998), 283–92.

25. Domarus, 2, 1912.

26. BAK, ZSg. 109/37, Press directives, 15 September 1942, TP 1. The premature announcement that the city had fallen provoked a quarrel with Goebbels. For details see Longerich, *Goebbels*, 535f.

27. Domarus, 2, 1916.

28. Stumpf, 'Die alliierte Landung in Nordwestafrika und der Rückzug der deutsch–italienischen Panzerarmee nach Tunesien', in Horst Boog (ed.), *Krieg*, 702ff.

29. BAK, ZSg. 102/40, Press directives, 3 October 1930 (M), TP 1. See also *VB* (B), 1 October 1942, 'Der Führer: Niemand kann uns den Sieg entreißen!', and 3 October 1942, 'Generalfeldmarschall beim Führer'; Remy, *Mythos*, 111; Reuth, *Rommel*, 98ff.

30. Stumpf, 'Landung', 704.

31. *Goebbels TB*, 8 November 1942; Stumpf, 'Landung', 710ff.

32. Domarus, 2, 1933ff.; Kershaw, *Hitler*, 2, 708f.

33. For the speech see Domarus, 2, 1933f., quotes 1937f. He had made similar statements in his speech opening the Winter Aid programme; see ibid., 1920.

34. *ADAP* E 4, No. 151.

35. *Goebbels TB*, 10 and 11 November 1942.

36. Stumpf, 'Landung', 743ff.; *Goebbels TB*, 11, 12 and 13 November 1942.

37. Stumpf, 'Landung', 721.

38. Ibid., 725ff.; *Goebbels TB*, 14–19 November 1942.

39. Engel, *Heeresadjutant*, 2 October 1942.

40. Wegner, 'Krieg', 994ff.; Kehrig, *Stalingrad*, 36ff.

41. Below, *Adjutant*, 323f.; Wegner, 'Krieg', 997ff.; Kehrig, *Stalingrad*, 131ff.

42. Wegner, 'Krieg', 1024; Kehrig, *Stalingrad*, 168f.

43. Wegner, 'Krieg', 1024ff.; Engel, *Heeresadjutant*, 24, 25, and 26 November 1942; Kehrig, *Stalingrad*, 218ff.

44. Wegner, 'Krieg', 1031ff.

45. Zeitzler to Manstein, 26 November 1942, published in Kehrig, *Stalingrad*, Doc. 18.

46. Below, *Adjutant*, 325f.; see also Kershaw, *Hitler*, 2, 719.

47. Kehrig, *Stalingrad*, Doc. 35. See also Engel, *Adjutant*, 18 and 19 December 1942; Manstein, *Siege*, 351ff.; Kehrig, *Stalingrad*, 307ff.; Wegner, 'Krieg', 1035ff.

48. *KTB OKW* 2, 1318f.; Wegner, 'Krieg', 1064f.

49. Hillgruber (ed.), *Staatsmänner*, 2, No. 22. Assessments of these meetings in Schmidt, *Statist*, 577f.; Ciano, *Diary*, 18 December 1942.

50. *Das Reich*, 8 November 1942, 'Vor die Probe gestellt'; see also *Goebbels TB*, 26 October 1942.

51. BAB, NS 18/200, minute, 25 December 1942.

52. BAB, NS 26/12, Bormann's appointments diary, 27 December 1942; *Goebbels TB*, 29 December 1942.

53. BAB, R 43 II/655, Ministerial submission from state secretary Naumann.

54. Ibid., Bormann to Lammers, 1 January 1943.

55. Ibid., Invitation; on this and the following measures see Rebentisch, *Führerstaat*, 474ff.; Herbst, *Krieg*, 199ff.; Longerich, *Stellvertreter*, 187ff.; Kroener, '"Menschenbewirtschaftung"', 847ff.

56. 'Führer-Erlasse', No. 222; labour conscription was envisaged as being from 17 to 65 for men and for women from 17 to 50. See also *Goebbels TB*, 15 January 1943.

57. BAB, R 43 II/655, Lammers's minute on the interview on 13 January 1943.

58. BAB, R 43 II/654, Lammers's minute, 24 January 1943. This decision was reflected in the published version of the draft of the Decree for the Conscription of Men and Women for Tasks of National Importance of 27 January 1943 proposed by Sauckel on 1 January 1943. See *RGBl.* 1943 I, 67f.

59. *Goebbels TB*, 23 January 1943.

60. BAB, R 43 II/654a, Minutes. There were eleven meetings between January and the end of August 1943. See Rebentisch, *Führerstaat*, 479.

61. See *Das Reich*, 17 and 24 January 1943, 'Der totale Krieg' und 'Die Optik des Krieges'. See also already on 3 January 1943, 'Die Heimat im Kriege'.

62. Kehrig, *Stalingrad*, 477ff.

63. *Wehrmachtberichte*, 16 and 22 January 1943.

64. Ibid., 27 December 1942. For example, during the last week of January the *VB* contained daily headlines about the heroic resistance in Stalingrad. In his speech of 30 January Göring tried to compare it with the self-sacrifice of the 300 Spartans defending the Thermopylae pass against the attacking Persians in 480 BC. See Domarus, 2, 1975f.

65. Kehrig, *Stalingrad*, 523.

66. Wegner, 'Krieg', 1059f.; Kehrig, *Stalingrad*, 531ff.

67. Wegner, 'Krieg', 1057f.; Manstein, *Siege*, 390f. For Hitler's response see Paulus's statement *IMT* 7, 320.

68. *Goebbels TB*, 30 January 1943 for the preparations.

69. Wegner, 'Krieg', 1060.

70. Heiber (ed.), *Lagebesprechungen*, 120ff., esp. 124ff.

71. For the figures see Kehrig, *Stalingrad*, 670ff.

72. BAK, ZSg. 109/4.2.43, TP 1, for the announcement of the defeat see *Meldungen*, 12, 4750f.

73. *Goebbels TB*, 6 February 1943, also 7 February 1943. Goebbels, Speer, Ganzenmüller, Funk, Backe, General von Unruh, and Sauckel all spoke at the meeting. Sauckel's contribution is in IMT 27, 1739-PS, 584ff. On the meeting see Moll, 'Steuerungsinstrument', 249ff.

74. The content of the speech is in *Goebbels TB*, 8 February 1943, and has already been discussed in Kershaw, *Hitler*, 2, 726ff.

75. As, for example, in his leading articles in *Das Reich*, 31 January 1943, 'Der Blick nach vorne', and 7 February 1943, 'Die harte Lehre'.

76. *VB* (N), 31 January 1943, 'Die Proklamation des Führers am 30. Januar 1943' (headline). The text of Goebbels's speech was published on the following day: 'Reichsminister Dr. Goebbels in the Berlin Sportpalast'.

77. *Goebbels TB*, 31 January, 4 and 5 February 1943. The assessment of the reception of the speech in the SD reports (*Meldungen*, 12, 4732f.) was positive, but not nearly as euphoric as Goebbels claimed.

78. *Goebbels TB*, 26 January, 2 and 5 February 1943.

79. In the 28 January 1943 meeting of the Committee of Three, Lammers and Bormann could refer to a decision by Hitler that, in relation to the dispute over business closures, unnecessary unemployment should be avoided, an attitude which inevitably had a negative impact on the whole programme. See the note in BAB, R 43II/662. This meeting decided on the final version of the Decree for the Freeing-Up of Labour for Deployment on Tasks Vital for the War Effort. See *RGBl.* 1943 I, 75f., which was implemented through three circular decrees of 30 January; these allowed plenty of room for manoeuvre to enable the supply needs of the population to be generously accommodated. See BAB, R 43 II/662. The final report of the Committee of Three of summer 1944 estimated the number of workers freed up by the closure programme as 150,000 (R 43 II/664a). See Herbst, *Krieg*, 212ff.; Rebentisch, *Führerstaat*, 488ff.

80. *Goebbels TB*, 8 February 1943.

81. Ibid., 9 February 1943.

82. *Das Reich*, 14 February 1943, 'Unser Wille und Weg'; *Goebbels TB*, 4 February 1943. Goebbels kept referring to the 'real mood of the population' (ibid., 12, 15, and 18 February 1943), which is not confirmed by the SD reports (*Meldungen*). See ibid., 12, 4783, 4799ff., and 4821ff.

83. The text of the speech is in *VB* (N), 20 February 1943 (also published in Heiber (ed.), *Goebbels Reden*, 2, No. 17). On the Sportpalast demonstration see *Goebbels TB*, 15 February 1943, also 16 and 18 February 1943; Iring Fetscher, *Joseph Goebbels im Berliner Sportpalast 1943: 'Wollt Ihr den totalen Krieg?'* (Hamburg, 1998); Jens Kegel, *'Wollt Ihr den totalen Krieg'. Eine semiotische und linguistische Gesamtanalyse der Rede Goebbels' im Berliner Sportpalast am 18. Februar 1943* (Tübingen, 2006); Willi A. Boelcke, 'Goebbels und die Kundgebung im Berliner Sportpalast vom 18. Februar 1943', in *Jahrbuch für die Geschichte Mittel- und Ostdeutschlands* 19 (1970), 234–55; Günter Moltmann, 'Goebbels' Rede zum totalen Krieg am 18. Februar 1943' in *VfZ* 12 (1964), 13–43.

84. *Goebbels TB*, 19 February 1943.

85. Ibid.

86. Ibid., 21, 22, 25–27 February 1943, criticism of the SD report already also on 12 December 1942. *Meldungen*, 12, 4831f.; BAB, R 55/603, 27 February 1943, Circulars to the Reich propaganda offices with the warning that it would be better to deal with the negative, 'but in no way typical, views expressed in their area by using the methods employed in the time of struggle'. Referred to already in Steinert, *Krieg*, 43.

87. *VB* (B), 25 February 1943, 'Unser Glaube und Fanatismus stärker denn je!' (headline). On the failure to develop a European propaganda campaign see above, p. 826.

88. On this visit see Manstein, *Siege*, 467 and 482.

89. Wegner, 'Krieg', 1078ff.

90. For quote see Domarus, 2, 1996f.

91. For the discussion between Rommel and Hitler on 10 and 11 March 1943 see Erwin Rommel, *Krieg ohne Hass (Afrikanische Memoiren)*, ed. Lucie Marie Rommel and Fritz Bayerlein (Heidenheim and Brenz, 1950), 372ff. After personal visits, both Warlimont (in February) and Below (in March 1943) had reached the conclusion that Germany's position in Africa was no longer tenable. See Warlimont, *Hauptquartier*, 326; Below, *Adjutant*, 333f.

92. See below, p. 915.

93. Wegner, 'Krieg', 1080.

94. *Meldungen*, 13, 4869f. (improvement), 4887f. (in general the situation on the eastern front was regarded as secure), 4902f. (cautious attitude towards the military situation), 4923f. (concern about air raids), 4943f. (cautious attitude towards the situation on the eastern front), 4966f. (re-conquest of Kharkov a 'turning point') and 4981f. (overall a positive reaction to Hitler's Heroes' Memorial Day speech).

95. *Das Reich*, 11 April 1943, 'Stimmung und Haltung'.

96. See *Goebbels TB*, 2, 4, 11, and 17 April 1943; on the attitude of the SD reports see *Meldungen*, 1, 36.

97. *Goebbels TB*, 22 March 1943.

98. According to information Goebbels received two months later, between 22 June 1941 and the end of April 1942, the Wehrmacht had a total of 459,750 soldiers killed in action (ibid., 14 May 1942).

99. Ibid., 26 March 1943, see also 27 March 1943.

100. Domarus, 2, 1999ff.

101. However, the story is based entirely on Gersdorff's own memoirs, Rudolph Christoph von Gersdorff, *Soldat im Untergang* (Frankfurt a. M., 1979), 128ff.

102. *Goebbels TB*, 20 May 1943, also 11 May 1943.

103. Ibid., 27 January 1943.

104. Ibid., 22 March, also 10 May 1943.

105. Lothar Gruchmann, 'Korruption im Dritten Reich. Zur Lebensmittelversorgung der NS-Führerschaft', in *VfZ* 42 (1994), 509–20.

106. *Goebbels TB*, 22 March 1943.

107. On Goebbels's retreat from total war see Longerich, *Goebbels*, 569f.

108. Longerich, *Goebbels*, 558f. Apart from the evidence in the Goebbels diaries see also Speer, *Erinnerungen*, 271ff.

109. *Goebbels TB*, 22 March 1943.

110. Adler, *Mensch*, 224ff. The Berlin action was linked to a resettlement programme in Zamość in the district of Lublin. See Bruno Wasser, *Himmlers Raumplanung im Osten. Der Generalplan Ost in Polen 1940–1944* (Basel, 1993), 135ff. In Berlin there occurred the so-called Rosenstrasse protests by partners of Jews who had been arrested and who were in so-called 'mixed marriages'. See Wolf Gruner, *Widerstand in der Rosenstraße. Die Fabrik-Aktion und die Verfolgung der 'Mischehen' 1943* (Frankfurt a. M., 2005), who corrects Nathan Stolzfus, *Resistance of the Heart. Intermarriage and the Rosenstrasse Protest in Nazi Germany* (New York, 1996). On the deportations that followed the 'factory action' see Gottwaldt and Schulle, 'Judendeportationen', 400ff.

111. Adler, *Mensch*, 201.

112. Gottwaldt and Schulle, 'Judendeportationen', 419ff.

113. *Goebbels TB*, 9 March 1943.

114. See above, p. 827.

115. *Goebbels TB*, 11 February, 9 and 21 March 1943. See also the extensive material in BAB, R 55/799 and 1435.

116. Gerd Kaiser, *Katyn. Das Staatsverbrechen – das Staatsgeheimnis* (Berlin, 2002).

117. *Goebbels TB*, 14, 15, and 17 April 1943.

118. Fleming, *Hitler*, 152.

119. *Goebbels TB*, 25, 29, and 30 April 1943.

120. BAK, NL 1118/138, Ministerial conferences, 17–28 April 1943; details in Longerich, *'Davon'*, 268ff.

121. *Goebbels TB*, 27, 28, and 29 April 1943.

122. 'Der Krieg und die Juden'.

123. On this series of meetings see Kershaw, *Hitler*, 2, 756ff.

124. *ADAP* E 5, No. 273.

125. Frederic B. Chary, *The History of Bulgaria* (Santa Barbara, CA, 2011), 101ff. and 129ff.

126. Nir Baruch, *Der Freikauf. Zar Boris und das Schicksal der Bulgarischen Juden* (Sofia, 1996), 137ff.

127. See above, p. 851.

128. There are no minutes of the meeting between Mussolini and Hitler in the ADAP. But see Schmidt, *Statist*, 563; Eugen Dollmann, *Dolmetscher der Diktatoren* (Bayreuth, 1963), 35ff.; see also *ADAP* E 5, Nos 286 and 291 (Ribbentrop and Bastiani).

129. This is, at any rate, what Ribbentrop told the Hungarian ambassador. See Sztojay to Horthy, 28 April 1943, published in Jenő Lévai (ed.), *Eichmann in Ungarn. Dokumente* (Budapest, 1961), 61ff. On Mussolini's attitude see Longerich, *Politik*, 553f.

130. Hillgruber (ed.), *Staatsmänner*, 2, No. 29f.

131. Longerich, *Holocaust*, 370.

132. Hillgruber (ed.), *Staatsmänner*, 2, No. 32.

133. Ibid., No. 32; Continuation of the conversation in No. 33.

134. Ibid., No. 34.

135. *ADAP* E 5, No. 347; Hillgruber (ed.), *Staatsmänner*, 2, No. 35; on the comments made at table see Peter Broucek (ed.), *Ein General im Zwielicht. Die Erinnerungen Edmund Glaises von Horstenau*, 3 (Vienna, 1988), 208; on the deportations from Croatia see above, p. 819.

136. Hillgruber (ed.), *Staatsmänner*, 2, No. 36; Communiqué in Domarus, 2, 2008; *ADAP* E 5, Nos 193, 277, and 353. See Jäckel, *Frankreich*, 273ff.

137. *Goebbels TB*, 8 May 1943.

138. Ibid., 13 May 1943.

139. Hillgruber (ed.), *Staatsmänner*, 2, No. 30.

140. *Goebbels TB*, 13 May 1943.

141. Longerich, *'Davon'*, 271ff.; *Goebbels TB*, 10 May 1943.

142. Ibid., 20 May 1943.

143. The press announced on 18 and 19 May 1943 that the bombing of the dams had been proposed by a Jewish scientist (see, for example, *DAZ* and *VB*). On the bombing see Gröhler, *Bombenkrieg*, 151ff.

144. *VB* (B), 13 May 1943, 'Judas Lieblingsplan: Die Hungerpeitsche für Europa' (Comment).

145. On the details see Longerich, *'Davon'*, 277.

146. See, in particular, *Meldungen*, 13, 5144ff. and 5290f., and numerous other reports on mood referred to in Longerich, *'Davon'*, 281ff.,

147. BAB, NS 18/225. In the draft of the circular, which Tiessler, Goebbels's liaison with Bormann, had prepared, the propaganda minister referred to a 'Führer assignment', but in the published circular this was not mentioned. See ibid., Tiessler note to Goebbels, 19 May 1943.

148. BAB, NS 6/344, R 33/43g.

149. On Jewish persecution in France following the occupation of the southern zone see Klarsfeld (ed.), *Vichy*, 193ff.; Susan Zuccotti, *The Holocaust, the French, and the Jews* (New York, 1993), 166ff.; Renée Poznanski, *Jews in France during World War II* (Hanover, NH, 2001), 356ff.

150. Danuta Czech, 'Deportation und Vernichtung der griechischen Juden im KL. Auschwitz' in *Hefte von Auschwitz* II (1970), 5–37; Hagen Fleischer, 'Griechenland' in Benz (ed.), *Dimension*; Steven B. Bowman, *The Agony of Greek Jews 1940–1945* (Stanford, 2009).

151. Chary, *Bulgaria*, 178ff. and 101ff.

152. Longerich, *Holocaust*, 378ff. (Poland), 382ff. (Soviet Union), 387ff. (Netherlands, Belgium, and Croatia), 395 (France), and 404 (Slovakia).

153. Gerhard Schreiber, 'Das Ende des nordafrikanischen Feldzugs und der Krieg in Italien', in Karl-Heinz Frieser (ed.), *Die Ostfront 1943/44. Der Krieg im Osten und an den Nebenfronten* (Munich, 2007), 1108.

154. *Goebbels TB*, 14 May 1943; Text in Domarus, 2, 2015.

155. On the guidelines for dealing with the African defeat see BAK, ZSg. 109/42, 13 May 1943, II. Erläuterungen zur TP.

156. *DAZ*, 12 May (M); *VB* (N), 13 May 1943.

157. *Meldungen*, 11, 4258ff. and 4279f.; *Goebbels TB*, 2 October 1942.

158. Heiber (ed.), *Lagebesprechungen*, 205ff.; *Weisungen* Nos 48a and b from the same day, 19 May 1943, concerning the defence of Italy with the use solely of German troops and of the Balkans 'with the use solely of German and Bulgarian troops' (Hubatsch (ed.), *Weisungen*, No. 48b). Hitler declined to sign these directives for security reasons but the planning continued (*KTB OKW* 3, 781ff.); Heiber (ed.), *Lagebesprechungen*, 220ff., for Hitler's very evident doubts about Italy's loyalty, which he expressed on 20 May. See also Warlimont, *Hauptquartier*, 335f.; Josef Schröder, *Italiens Kriegsaustritt 1943. Die deutschen Gegenmaßnahmen im italienischen Raum: Fall 'Alarich' und 'Achse'* (Göttingen, 1969), 176ff.

159. Domarus, 2, 1999ff.; *Goebbels TB*, 21–23 May 1943.

160. Heiber (ed.), *Lagebesprechungen*, 507ff.; Rahn, 'Seekrieg', 347ff.

161. BAK, ZSg. 109/42, 10 May 1943, TP 2; *VB* (B), 11 May 1943, 'Veränderung der Lebensmittelrationen'.

162. *Goebbels TB*, 20, 21, and 25 March 1943.

163. Christoph Buchheim, 'Der Mythos vom "Wohlleben". Der Lebensstandard der deutschen Bevölkerung im Zweiten Weltkrieg', in *VfZ* 58 (2010), 299–328, esp. 311f.

164. Ralf Blank, '"Battle of the Ruhr". Luftangriffe auf das Ruhrgebiet 1943', in *Westfälische Forschungen* 63 (2013), 319–41.

165. *Goebbels TB*, 25 June 1943; to Speer at the end of June: Janssen, *Ministerium*, 147, based on BAB R 3/1507; Boelcke (ed.), *Rüstung*, 28 June 1943, 7.

166. *Meldungen*, 13, 5272ff. (cut in meat rations) and 5277ff. (air war, North Africa, food supply situation).

167. Ibid., 5285f. and 5311. This picture corresponds to the impressions Goebbels was getting from the reports of the Reich propaganda offices and the Gau headquarters. See *Goebbels TB*, 14, 25, and 28 May, and 5 June 1943.

168. BAB, R3/1738, Speer–Chronik, 13 May 1943; Rolf–Dieter Müller, 'Albert Speer und die Rüstungspolitik im totalen Krieg', in Kroener et al. (eds), *Organisation*, 332.

169. On the event see *VB* (B), 7 June 1943, 'Bezwingender Eindruck der Kundgebung im Sportpalast'.

170. *Goebbels TB*, 4 June 1943; Speer, *Erinnerungen*, 280f.

171. *Meldungen*, 14, 5341ff. Speer, *Erinnerungen*, 281 on the 'lack of success' of his speech.

172. *Meldungen*, 14, 5357ff. and 5398ff.

173. *Goebbels TB*, 25 June 1943.

174. *KTB OKW* 3, 1420ff.

175. Thus, looking back at the situation conference on 26 July 1943 (Heiber (ed.), *Lagebesprechungen*, 369). On 15 May he was planning, if necessary, to transfer twelve divisions from the eastern front to Italy. See Frieser, 'Die Schlacht am Kursker Bogen', in Frieser, *Ostfront.*, 140.

176. Warlimont, *Hauptquartier*, 347f.

177. On the Battle of Kursk see Manstein, *Siege*, 497ff.; Guderian, *Erinnerungen*, 282ff.; Frieser, 'Schlacht'; Alfred Philippi and Ferdinand Heim, *Der Feldzug gegen Sowjetrußland 1941–1945. Ein operativer Überblick* (Stuttgart, 1962), 211ff.; Kershaw, *Hitler*, 2, 770ff.

178. According to Manstein, *Siege*, 495f.

179. Schröder, *Kriegsaustritt*, 158ff.; Schreiber, 'Ende', 1109ff.

180. Frieser 'Schlacht', 174ff.

181. Ibid., 139ff. In fact, the corps was not transferred to Italy in the originally envisaged strength.

182. Ibid., 190ff.

183. Schmidt, *Statist*, 580.

184. *Goebbels TB*, 30 November 1942.

185. *ADAP* E 6, No. 166. This information had also reached Goebbels by the 24th. See *TB*, 25 June 1943.

186. On the meeting of the Grand Council see Hans Woller, *Die Abrechnung mit dem Faschismus in Italien 1943 bis 1948* (Munich, 1996), 9ff.; Richard J. B. Bosworth, *Mussolini* (London, 2002), 400f.

187. Heiber (ed.), *Lagebesprechungen*, 316.

188. Ibid., 329.

189. Ibid., 312ff.; Summary of the measures taken in Warlimont, *Hauptquartier*, 381; Schröder, *Kriegsaustritt*, 216ff.

190. *Goebbels TB*, 27 July 1943.

191. Heiber (ed.), *Lagebesprechungen*, 353ff.; Schröder, *Kriegsaustritt*, 245ff.

192. *Goebbels TB*, 27 July 1943.

193. *ADAP* E 6, No. 217.

194. *Goebbels TB*, 23 September 1943.

195. Schreiber, 'Ende', 1114.

196. Hitler told Goebbels he was convinced that the Italians would leave the alliance with Germany if they 'can get reasonable conditions from the Allies'; indeed, he assumed that Mussolini's overthrow had already been discussed with the enemy. See *Goebbels TB*, 10 August 1943 and 23 August 1943.

197. Helmut Heiber, 'Der Tod des Zaren Boris', in *VfZ* 9 (1961), 384–416; Hoppe, *Bulgarien*, 141ff.

198. Gröhler, *Bombenkrieg*, 106ff.; Hans Brunswig, *Feuersturm über Hamburg. Die Luftangriffe auf Hamburg im 2. Weltkrieg und ihre Folgen* (Stuttgart, 1978); Martin Middlebrook, *Hamburg. Juli 1943. Alliierte Luftstreitkräfte gegen eine deutsche Stadt* (Berlin and Frankfurt a. M., 1983).

199. Gröhler, *Bombenkrieg*, 178.

200. *Goebbels TB*, 25 June 1943.

201. Walter Dornberger, *Peenemünde. Die Geschichte der V-Waffen* (Esslingen, 1981), 77ff.

202. Michael J. Neufeld, *Die Rakete und das Reich. Werner von Braun, Peenemünde und der Beginn des Raketenzeitalters* (Berlin, 1997), 167.

203. Boelcke (ed.), *Rüstung*, 23 June 1942, 21.

204. Heinz-Dieter Hölsken, *Die V-Waffen. Enstehung – Propaganda – Kriegseinsatz* (Stuttgart, 1984), 14ff.; Müller, 'Speer', 575ff.; Boog, 'Reichsluftverteidigung', 380ff.; Neufeld, *Rakete*, 204f.

205. Hölsken, *V-Waffen*, 33ff.; Horst Boog, 'Strategischer Luftkrieg in Europa und Reichsluftverteidigung 1943–1944', in Borg, et al. (eds), *Das Deutsche Reich*, 381f.

206. Dornberger, *Peenemünde*, 107ff.; Hölsken, *V-Waffen*, 44.

207. Janssen, *Ministerium*, 195. On the preparations see Boelcke (ed.), *Rüstung*, 17/18 July 1943, 19. See also Hölsken, *V-Waffen*, 33ff., 46, and 89f.; Boog, 'Reichsluft-verteidigung', 381f.; Albert Speer, *Der Sklavenstaat. Meine Auseinandersetzungen mit der SS* (Stuttgart, 1981), 288; Speer, *Erinnerungen*, 377f.; Dornberger, *Peenemünde*, 114ff.; Neufeld, *Rakete*, 232ff.

208. Hölsken, *V-Waffen*, 47ff.; Müller, 'Speer', 584ff.; Boelcke (ed.), *Rüstung*, 28 June 1943, 9.

209. Hölsken, *V-Waffen*, 50ff.; Neufeld, *Rakete*, 238ff.; Boelcke (ed.), *Rüstung*, 19–22 August 1943, 24.

210. *Goebbels TB*, 25 June, 21 August, 10 and 24 September, 27 October, and 20 December 1943.

211. Hölsken, *V-Waffen*, 43f., 52, 56, 64, 71f., 74, and 90; Boog, 'Reichsluftverteidigung', 382f.; Karl-Heinz Ludwig, 'Die "Hochdruckpumpe", ein Beispiel technischer Fehleinschätzung im 2. Weltkrieg', in *Technikgeschichte* 38 (1971), 142–55.

212. Boelcke (ed.), *Rüstung*, 19–22 August 1943, 23; 30 September/October 1943, 7; 14/15 October 1943, 16; 25–28 January 1944, 7.

213. Hölsken, *V-Waffen*, 68ff.; Boelcke (ed.), *Rüstung*, 6/7 April 1944, 19.

214. Hölsken, *V-Waffen*, 74.

215. According to Horst Hano, *Die Taktik der Pressepropaganda des Hitlerregimes 1943–1945. Eine Untersuchung auf Grund unveröffentlichter Dokumente des Sicherheitsdienstes*

und des Reichsministeriums für Volksaufklärung und Propaganda (Munich, 1963), 69f.; see also *Goebbels TB*, 2 July 1943.

216. *Meldungen*, 14, 5413ff., concerning widespread rumours in the Reich about retaliation.

217. Domarus, 2, 2035ff., quote 2038.

218. *Meldungen* 15, 5753f. (after Hitler's announcement of retaliation people were now 'really believing in it', but immediately there were doubts about when it would happen), 5833f. (more rumours about retaliation) and 5885ff., quote 5886.

219. Schreiber, 'Ende', 1127 and 1118.

220. *Goebbels TB*, 8 September 1943.

221. Schröder, *Kriegsaustritt*, 281ff.; *ADAP* E 6, No. 291.

222. *Goebbels TB*, 10 September 1943. On 9 August Hitler was already determined to 'use the favourable opportunity to bring South Tyrol back to the Reich' (ibid., 10 August 1943).

223. Ibid., 10 and 21 August 1943.

224. Domarus, 2, 2035ff., quotes 2036 and 2038.

225. Schröder, *Kriegsaustritt*, 283ff.; Schreiber, 'Ende', 1119ff.

226. *ADAP* E 6, No. 314.

227. Gerhard Schreiber, *Die italienischen Militärinternierten im deutschen Machtbereich 1943–1945. Verraten – Verachtet – Vergessen* (Munich, 1990).

228. Schreiber, 'Ende', 1126ff.; Schröder, *Kriegsaustritt*, 293ff.

229. Ibid., 320ff.

230. *Goebbels TB*, 15–19 September 1943.

231. Domarus, 2, 2041.

232. Schröder, *Kriegsaustritt*, 325.

233. On its formation see Dianella Gagliani, 'Diktat oder Konsens? Die Republik von Salò und das Dritte Reich', in Lutz Klinkhammer et al., *Die 'Achse' im Krieg. Politik, Ideologie und Kriegführung 1939–1945* (Paderborn, 2010), 436–71.

234. *Goebbels TB*, 23 September 1943.

235. Karl-Heinz Frieser, 'Die Rückzugsoperationen der Heeresgruppe Süd in der Ukraine', in Frieser (ed.), *Ostfront*, 357ff. and 362ff.

236. Frieser, 'Der Rückzug der Heeresgruppe Mitte nach Weißrußland', in Frieser (ed.), *Ostfront*, 301ff.

WITH HIS BACK TO THE WALL

1. Warlimont, *Hauptquartier*, 427.

2. In the case of Bulgaria the western powers made their agreement to an armistice in September 1944 specifically dependent on the suspension of its anti-Semitic laws (Baruch, *Freikauf*, 159ff.). See also ibid., 148f., according to which there are indications that, during their first attempts to lure Bulgaria away from the Axis, the Americans raised the issue of its Jewish policy.

3. *ADAP* E 6, No. 311.

4. *Die Okkupationspolitik des deutschen Faschismus in Dänemark und Norwegen (1940–1945)*, ed. Fritz Petrick (Berlin and Heidelberg, 1992), No. 240.

5. Lutz Klinkhammer, 'Polizeiliche Kooperation unter deutscher Besatzung. Mechanismen der Repression in der "Repubblica Sociale Italiana"', in Klinkhammer et al., *Die 'Achse'*, 487.

6. Klinkhammer, *Bündnis*; Carlo Gentile, *Wehrmacht, Waffen-SS und Polizei im Kampf gegen Partisanen und Zivilbevölkerung in Italien 1939–1945* (Paderborn and Munich, 2012).

7. On Jewish persecution in Italy after September 1943 see Liliana Picciotto Fargion, 'Italian', in Benz (ed.), *Dimension*, 199–227; Meir Michaelis, *Mussolini and the Jews. German–Italian Relations and the Jewish Question in Italy 1922–1945* (Oxford, 1978), 342ff.; Klinkhammer, *Bündnis*, 530ff.

8. Ibid., 535.

9. On the deportations see Errikos Sevillias, *Athens–Auschwitz* (Athens, 1983) (from the former Italian zone of occupation); Gerhard Grimm, 'Albanien', in Benz, (ed.), *Dimension*, 227; Hagen Fleischer, 'Griechenland', in Benz (ed.), *Dimension*, 265ff. (Greek islands); Sundhaussen, 'Jugoslawien', in Benz (ed.), *Dimension*, 325.

10. On German Jewish policy in France after the collapse of Italy see Klarsfeld, *Vichy*, 276ff.; Jonathan Steinberg, *Deutsche, Italiener und Juden. Der italienische Widerstand gegen den Holocaust* (Göttingen, 1992), 120ff.; Zuccotti, *Holocaust*, 180ff.; Poznanski, *Jews*, 390ff.

11. Klarsfeld, *Vichy*, 278ff.; Zuccotti, *Holocaust*, 181ff.

12. Klarsfeld, *Vichy*, 289.

13. Walter Stucki, *Von Petain zur Vierten Republik. Vichy 1944* (Berne, 1947), 160ff. On the reshuffle of the French government see Jäckel, *Frankreich*, 283ff.

14. Ibid., 293ff.

15. Klarsfeld, *Vichy*, 298ff.; Zuccotti, *Holocaust*, 190ff.; Bernd Kasten, 'Gute Franzosen'. *Die französische Polizei und die deutsche Besatzungsmacht im besetzten Frankreich, 1940–1945* (Sigmaringen, 1993), 120ff.

16. Klarsfeld, *Vichy*, 574ff.; Zuccotti, *Holocaust*, 197ff.

17. BAB, NS 19/3302, Best to Himmler, 22 August 1943; see Herbert, *Best*, 351; see also *ADAP* E 6, No. 259.

18. Ibid., No. 268.

19. In January 1943 Best had already pointed out to Berlin that an increase in Jewish persecution in Denmark would mean the end of his policy of cooperation with the Danish government (*ADAP* E 5, Nos 39 and 344). Luther, Ribbentrop, and Himmler had agreed with this view (PAA, Inland II g 184, Luther to Ribbentrop, 28 January 1943, and Ribbentrop's marginalia on this document of 1 February 1943). In June Himmler decided that no further measures involving Jewish policy in Denmark should be taken until he issued a new order (ibid., Wagner to Kaltenbrunner, 30 June 1943). On these events see Herbert, *Best*, 361f.

20. *ADAP*, E 6, No. 287. On the interpretation of this telegram see, in particular, Herbert, *Best*, 362ff. Best also wanted to secure the command over all police

troops deployed in Denmark and to establish a special court under his chairmanship. See *ADAP* E 6, No. 271.

21. Ibid., No. 332.

22. Ibid., No. 344.

23. Gunnar S. Paulsson, '"The Bridge over Oeresund". The Historiography on the Expulsion of the Jews from Nazi-occupied Denmark', in *Journal of Contemporary History* 30 (1995), 437.

24. For details see Yahil, *Rescue*, 223ff. On the rescue operation and its background see also Paulsson, '"Bridge"', a reply from Hans Kirchhoff, 'Denmark. A Light in the Darkness of the Holocaust? A Reply to Gunnar S. Paulsson', in *Journal of Contemporary History* 30 (1995), 465–79, and Kirchhoff, 'The Rescue of the Danish Jews in October 1943', in David Bankier and Israel Gutman (eds), *New Europe and the Final Solution* (Jerusalem, 2003), 539–55.

25. PAA, Inland II g 184, Telegram, 5 October 1943.

26. Führer edict 20 August 1943 (*RGBl.* 1943 I, 527).

27. Lammers explained it in this way in a circular of 8 May in BAB, R 43 II/1512. On Bormann's appointment see Longerich, *Stellvertreter*, 167ff.

28. Rebentisch, *Führerstaat*, 401.

29. See Speer, *Erinnerungen*, 326f.

30. Eichholtz, *Geschichte* 2, 146ff.; Boelcke (ed.), *Rüstung*, 28 June 1943, 28.

31. Führer edict concerning Concentration in the War Economy (*RGBl.* 1943 I, 529); Müller, 'Speer', 337f.; Speer, *Erinnerungen*, 287ff.

32. Eichholtz, *Geschichte* 2, 148ff.; Müller, 'Speer', 343f.; BAB, R 3/1562, Göring edict, 4 September 1943.

33. Müller, 'Speer', 341f.; Eichholtz, *Geschichte*, 2, 162ff.; BAB, R 3/306, Speer edict, 29 October 1943, concerning the Distribution of Responsibilities in the War Economy.

34. *Goebbels TB*, 25 June 1943; on positive assessments see also 20 May, 8 June, 10 and 28 August, 29 September, and 3 October 1943.

35. Speer, *Erinnerungen*, 325.

36. Ibid., 325ff.; Müller, 'Speer', 339f. Speer's Posen speech is in BAB, R 3/1548.

37. Heinrich Himmler, *Geheimreden 1933 bis 1945 und andere Ansprachen*, ed. Bradley F. Smith and Agnes Peterson (Frankfurt a. M., 1974), 162ff.

38. *Goebbels TB*, 7 October 1943.

39. Edict concerning the Preparations for the Reconstruction of Bomb-damaged Cities, 11 October 1943 (*RGBl.* 1943 I, 575f.); Speer, *Erinnerungen*, 327f.

40. Müller 'Speer', 378.

41. On the meeting see *IMT* 27, 1292-PS, 104ff.; Kroener, '"Menschenbewirtschaftung"', 901ff.; Eichholtz, *Geschichte*, 2, 225ff.; Speer, *Erinnerungen*, 333f.: Hitler's behaviour towards him was 'cold and impolite'.

42. Boelcke (ed.), *Rüstung*, 30 September 1943, 22; Speer, *Erinnerungen*, 322ff.; for the literature see Kroener, '"Menschenbewirtschaftung"', 899ff.

43. Herbst, *Krieg*, 267ff.; Eichholtz, *Geschichte*, 2, 164ff.; Müller, 'Speer', 348ff.

44. *Goebbels TB*, 7 and 20 October 1943, 6 and 12 January 1944.

45. See above, p. 729.

46. On his illness and his estrangement from Hitler see Speer, *Erinnerungen*, 339ff.; Fest, *Speer*, 268ff.

47. Speer, *Erinnerungen*, 339ff.; Müller, 'Speer', 382ff. The events are principally covered in the files BAB, R 3/1572, 1573, 1575, 1588, 1590, and 1605. On the tense relationship with Bormann see *Goebbels TB*, 6 February 1944.

48. BAB, R 3/1515, Memoranda, 25 January 1944; Speer, *Erinnerungen*, 340f.; Eichholtz, *Geschichte* 3, 11ff.; Müller, 'Speer', 380f.

49. *Goebbels TB*, 10 September and 28 October 1943.

50. Bernd Martin, 'Deutsch-sowjetische Sondierungen über einen separaten Friedensschluß im Zweiten Weltkrieg. Bericht und Dokumentation', in Inge Auerbach (ed.), *Felder und Vorfelder russischer Geschichte. Studien zu Ehren von Peter Scheibert* (Freiburg i. Br., 1985), 286.

51. These considerations are above all reflected in his directive No. 51, 3 November 1943, and the supplementary directive 51a (Hubatsch (ed.), *Weisungen*).

52. See the contributions by Frieser, 'Rückzug', esp. 301ff., 'Rückzugsoperationen', esp. 362ff., and 'Das Ausweichen der Heeresgruppe Nord von Leningrad ins Baltikum', in Frieser, *Ostfront* esp. 282f.

53. Frieser, 'Rückzugsoperationen', 367ff.

54. Manstein, *Siege*, 554.

55. *Goebbels TB*, 9 November 1943.

56. Heiber (ed.), *Lagebesprechungen,* 486ff.: Hitler claimed that for Army Group South counter operations were 'the equivalent of bolting' (p. 493). Frieser, 'Rückzugsoperationen', 387ff.

57. On this conversation see Manstein, *Siege*, 569ff. Detailed account in Kershaw, *Hitler* 2, 800ff.; Frieser, 'Rückzugsoperationen', 391.

58. Guderian, *Erinnerungen*, 294ff.

59. BAB, NS 18/189, Bormann to Rosenberg, 13 December 1943 (Akten Partei-Kanzlei, Teil I, Regest 21943).

60. Bormann to Rosenberg, 30 November 1943, further elucidation to Rosenberg on 12 and 29 December 1943, and further groundwork by Bormann in Akten Partei-Kanzlei, Teil I, Regest 27691. The introduction of the term NS Leadership Officer occurred through the OKH edict of 28 November 1943. See Volker Berghahn, 'NSDAP und "geistige Führung" der Wehrmacht 1939–1943', in *VfZ* 17 (1969), 51ff.; Arne W. G. Zoepf, *Wehrmacht zwischen Tradition und Ideologie. Der NS-Führungsoffizier im Zweiten Weltkrieg* (Frankfurt a. M., 1988), 65ff. Hitler had already outlined the basic idea of a politically indoctrinated officer in October 1943 in an address to officers in Bad Schachen. See Berghahn, 'NSDAP', 51.

61. According to Bormann's explanation to Rosenberg in his letter of 30 November 1943; Hitler's agreement is clear from statements during the meeting of 7 January 1944 (BAB, NS 8/174, 189, and 190).

62. Waldemar Besson, 'Zur Geschichte des nationalsozialistischen Führungs-Offiziers (NSFO)', in *VfZ* 9 (1961), Doc. 5. The wording and style indicate Bormann's authorship.

63. Ibid., Doc. 7, where the 'sole responsibility of the commanding officer for the political-ideological leadership and training' is established; this source contains further basic documents concerning the NS-Leadership Officer.

64. Documented in Weinberg, 'Adolf Hitler und der NS-Führungsoffizier (NSFO)', in *VfZ* 12 (1964), 443–58.

65. On the annoyance this propaganda caused Hitler and his entourage see Rudolf Schmundt, *Tätigkeitsbericht des Chefs des Heerespersonalamtes General der Infanterie Rudolf Schmundt, fortgef. von Wilhelm Burgdorf*, ed. Dermot Bradley and Richard Schulze-Kossens (Osnabrück, 1984), 12 September 1943; Wegner, Die 'Aporie des Krieges', in Frieser, *Ostfront*, 225f.

66. Complete text in IfZ, F 19/3.

67. Zoepf, *Wehrmacht*, 247ff.: 1. Conference in Posen, 24–26 January 1944 for over a hundred generals and admirals, with a subsequent address by Hitler in the Führer headquarters; 2. conference in Sonthofen, April 1944; 3. Conference in Sonthofen 5–7 May 1944; 4. Conference in Sonthofen, 23–26 May 1944; 5. Conference in Sonthofen, 19–22 June 1944, with a concluding speech by Hitler in the Plattlerhof. Hans-Heinrich Wilhelm, 'Hitlers Ansprache vor Generalen und Offizieren am 26. Mai 1944', in *MGM* 20 (1976), 134, mentions conferences on 27 January, 26 April, 26 May, 22 June, and 13 July 1944; Text of the speech on 22 June 1944 in Hans-Adolf Jacobsen and Werner Jochmann (eds), *Ausgewählte Dokumente zur Geschichte des Nationalsozialismus 1933–1945* (no page numbers).

68. Manstein, *Siege*, 579ff. Manstein's quotation of the speech and his interjection is a reproduction of the content and not the actual wording of the original (IfZ, F 19/3). The quarrel intensified when Hitler claimed that a personal letter from the field-marshal dealing with the situation of his army group was an attempt to protect his back.

69. Schmundt, *Tätigkeitsbericht*, 27 January 1944. Hitler had contemplated dismissing Manstein the previous autumn. See ibid., 25 October 1943.

70. Frieser, 'Rückzugsoperationen', 393ff.

71. Ibid., 392ff., Manstein, *Siege*, 576f.

72. Frieser, 'Rückzugsoperationen', 394ff.

73. Frieser, 'Rückzug', 312ff.

74. Frieser, 'Rückzugsoperationen', 420ff.

75. Klaus Schönherr, 'Der Rückzug der Heeresgruppe A über die Krim bis Rumänien', in Frieser (ed.), *Ostfront.*, 469ff.

76. Frieser, 'Ausweichen', 284ff.

77. Schreiber, 'Ende', 145ff.

78. *Goebbels TB*, 4 March 1944.

79. This is emphasized by Michael Salewski in 'Die Abwehr der Invasion als Schlüssel zum "Endsieg"?', in Rolf-Dieter Müller and Hans-Erich Volkmann (eds), *Wehrmacht. Mythos und Realität* (Munich, 1999), 210–23.

80. Evening situation conference on 20 December 1943. See Heiber (ed.), *Lagebesprechungen*, 440ff.; *Goebbels TB*, 4 March 1944.

81. *KTB OKW* 4, 270.

82. Kehrl, *Krisenmanager*, 362f., according to statements by Keitel.

83. Detlef Vogel, 'Deutsche und alliierte Kriegführung im Westen', in Horst Boog et al. (eds), *Das Deutsche Reich in der Defensive. Strategischer Luftkrieg in Europa, Krieg im Westen, und in Ostasien 1943–1944/45* (Stuttgart and Munich, 2001), 478.

84. Ibid., 463ff.

85. Gröhler, *Bombenkrieg*, 188.

86. *Goebbels TB*, 20 December 1943.

87. Ibid., 21 December 1943; 'Führer-Erlasse', No. 288.

88. Longerich, *Goebbels*, 605ff.

89. On the condition of German society at the end of the war see Sven Keller, *Volksgemeinschaft am Ende. Gesellschaft und Gewalt 1944/45* (Munich, 2013); Bernd Rusinek, *Gesellschaft in der Katastrophe. Terror, Illegalität, Widerstand – Köln 1944/45* (Essen, 1989).

90. *Goebbels TB*, 10 February 1944. In the SD reports (Berichte zu Inlandsfragen) the speech was not mentioned at all, a remarkable contrast to earlier Führer speeches, which were normally followed by reports of a substantial increase in confidence in the leadership.

91. Ibid., 28 February 1944.

92. Ibid., 18 April 1944.

93. Ibid., 16 and 17 February, 4, 11, 14, and 15 March 1944.

94. Ellen Gibbels, *Hitlers Parkinson-Krankheit. Zur Frage eines hirnorganischen Psychosyndroms* (Berlin, 1990); Gibbels, 'Hitlers Nervenkrankheit. Eine neurologisch-psychiatrische Studie', in *VfZ* 41 (1994), 155–200; Hans-Joachim Neumann and Henrik Eberle, *War Hitler krank? Ein abschließender Befund* (Bergisch-Gladbach, 2009); Ernst-Georg Schenck, *Patient Hitler. Eine medizinische Biographie* (Düsseldorf, 1989).

95. Kershaw, *Hitler*, 2, S. 797.

96. Medical historians are largely in agreement that Hitler's illnesses and his consumption of medicines did not significantly impair his abilities as a politician. For example, right up until the end he could sustain his concentration during lengthy meetings, make detailed statements, and compose substantial texts. See Neumann and Eberle, *Hitler*, 290ff (summing up). Gibbels assumes a 'slight organic change in Hitler's personality as a result of his Parkinson's disease', but it is unlikely to have influenced his political or military decisions (Gibbels, 'Nervenkrankheit', 214). However, these diagnoses are to be understood more in terms of a certification of competence: Hitler should not be regarded primarily as a 'sick person' and – crucially – should be considered fully responsible for his actions. However, in the case of such an extreme personality, the link between his physical condition and his political actions is much more complex. It cannot be proved that Hitler was dependent on drugs, as is claimed in the volume by Ohler that appeared shortly before the publication of this book (Norman Ohler, *Der totale Rausch. Drogen im Dritten Reich* (Cologne, 2015), 141ff.). The only written evidence for the assertion that he was dependent on cocaine as a result of his medical treatment the 20 July is the statement of Erwin

Giesing, the doctor treating him; but this cannot be regarded as a reliable source. The injection of the stimulant, Eudokal, by Morell is confirmed only for certain phases (in summer 1943 and from September to December 1944), which argues against drug dependency. Ohler himself concedes that certain striking features of Hitler's behaviour, which he attributes to the consumption of drugs (in particular excessive activity, a torrent of words, a complete lack of empathy, illusory states of euphoria), were part of his personality.

97. *Goebbels TB*, 18 January 1944; during Speer's stay in the sanatorium he gave his state secretary, Naumann, the task of maintaining direct contact. See ibid., 6 February and 9 March 1944.

98. Ibid., 29 February 1944.

99. Ibid., 15 March 1944.

100. Ibid., 25 January, also 15 March and 18 April 1944.

101. Kerekes (ed.), *Allianz*, No. 122.

102. See *Goebbels TB*, 22 January, 22 March, and 7 May 1943.

103. *ADAP* E 7, No. 236–238.

104. *Goebbels TB*, 15 March 1944 on the preparations for the action.

105. On the meeting between Hitler and Horthy see Schmidt, *Statist*, 587f.; Nikolaus von Horthy, *Ein Leben für Ungarn* (Bonn, 1953), 253ff.

106. Warlimont, *Hauptquartier*, 442f.

107. Igor Philip Matić, *Edmund Veesenmayer. Agent und Diplomat der nationalsozialistischen Expansionspolitik* (Munich, 2002); Krisztián Ungváry, 'Kriegsschauplatz Ungarn', in Frieser (ed.), *Ostfront.*, 857ff.

108. Frieser, 'Rückzugsoperationen', 419ff. and 432ff.

109. Hubatsch (ed.), *Weisungen*, No. 53, which also includes the text of the attachments to this directive.

110. Frieser, 'Rückzugsoperationen', 424ff.

111. *Goebbels TB*, 3 and 11 March, 14 April 1944.

112. Ibid., 22 and 29 February, 11 and 14 March 1944.

113. See also Manstein, *Siege*, 602f.

114. *Goebbels TB*, 20 March 1944, who may, however, have overestimated the success of the event as he wanted to claim responsibility for it. Schmundt, *Tätigkeitsbericht*, 3 and 19 March 1944.

115. Ibid., 16 April 1944.

116. Manstein, *Siege*, 610ff.; Frieser, 'Rückzugsoperationen', 438f.

117. Ibid., 440ff.

118. Ibid., 448.

119. Manstein, *Siege*, 615f.

120. Klaus Schönherr, 'Ferdinand Schörner – der idealtypische Nazigeneral', in Ronald Smelser and Enrico Syring (eds), *Die Militärelite des Dritten Reiches – 27 biographische Skizzen* (Berlin and Frankfurt a. M., 1995).

121. *Wehrmachtberichte* 3.

122. On the persecution and deportation of the Hungarian Jews see Randolph L. Braham, *The Politics of Genocide. The Holocaust in Hungary*, 2 vols (New York,

1994); Christian Gerlach and Götz Aly, *Das letzte Kapitel. Realpolitik, Ideologie und der Mord an den ungarischen Juden 1944/1945* (Stuttgart and Zurich, 2002).

123. *Goebbels TB*, 27 April 1944.

124. PAA, Inland II g 210, published in Braham, *Destruction*, 700f. On this set of issues see also Braham, Politics, S. 884f.

125. *ADAP* E 8, No. 22f.

126. *Goebbels TB*, 27 April 1944.

127. For details see Longerich, *'Davon'*, 298ff.

128. Wilhelm, 'Ansprache'.

DEFEAT LOOMS

1. Wolfgang Schumann (ed.), *Deutschland im Zweiten Weltkrieg*, 5 (Berlin, 1984), 354; Gröhler, *Bombenkrieg*, 213f.; Eichholtz, Geschichte, 3, 14ff.; Müller, 'Speer', 390ff.; Speer, *Erinnerungen*, 343f. According to *Goebbels TB*, 3 April 1944, Bormann objected to Hanke's appointment.

2. Eichholtz, *Geschichte*, 3, 19.

3. Boelcke (ed.), *Rüstung*, 3–5 June 1944, 20. See also Müller, 'Speer', 396f.

4. Boelcke (ed.), *Rüstung*, 6–7 April 1944, 16. In April 1943, at an armaments meeting with Speer, Hitler had demanded that particularly vulnerable production processes should take place in plants that were fully protected by concrete. See ibid., 11 April 1943, 4; Frederic Gümmer, *Die Rolle der Untertageverlagerung in der deutschen Rüstungsproduktion 1943–1945* (Munich, 2007).

5. On the conflict between Speer and Dorsch see Janssen, *Ministerium*, 158ff.

6. Ibid., 162 (based on BAB, R 3/1576).

7. Speer, *Erinnerungen*, 348f.

8. Janssen, *Ministerium*, 160f.; Speer, *Erinnerungen*, 352ff.

9. Eichholtz, *Geschichte* 3, 228f.; Kroener, '"Menschenbewirtschaftung"', 906ff.; Kehrl, *Krisenmanager*, 344 and 346ff. BAB, R 43 II/651, Minutes of the meetings on 25 and 27 April 1944.

10. Speer, *Erinnerungen*, 359.

11. There were attacks on Cologne (Mehner (ed.), *Tagesberichte*, 20 and 22 April 1944), Munich on 24 April (Hans-Günter Richardi, *Bomber über München. Der Luftkrieg von 1939 bis 1945, dargestellt am Beispiel der 'Hauptstadt der Bewegung'* (Munich, 1992), 238ff.; Irmtraud Permooser, *Der Luftkrieg über München 1942–1945. Bomben auf die Hauptstadt der Bewegung* (Oberhaching, 1996), 198f.) and on Berlin at the end of April and in May (Mehner (ed.), *Tagesberichte*, 29 April, 7, 8, 19, and 24 May as well as a continuation on 25 May 1944).

12. Boelcke (ed.), *Rüstung*, 22–23 May 1944; Gröhler, *Bombenkrieg*, 222ff.; Eichholtz, *Geschichte*, 3, 32ff.

13. Ibid., 35; see also Birkenfeld, *Treibstoff*, 189f. and 238ff.

14. Boog, 'Reichsluftverteidigung', 126ff.

15. In autumn 1943 Hitler had decided to deploy the Me 262 above all as a bomber, and Göring had promised him that the bomber would be ready for action by

May 1944. On Hitler's decision of 26 November 1943 see Ralf Schabel, *Die Illusion der Wunderwaffen. Die Rolle der Düsenflugzeuge und Flugabwehrraketen in der Rüstungspolitik des Dritten Reiches* (Munich, 1994), 190; Adolf Galland, *Die Ersten und die Letzten. Die Jagdflieger im Zweiten Weltkrieg* (Darmstadt, 1953), 353; Below, *Adjutant*, 354f. According to Schabel, *Illusion*, 180, the demand for a fast bomber was not at all naïve or unreasonable and would have served to fill the gap before the jet bomber Ar 234 could be introduced. See ibid., 240f. At a meeting with Speer and Milch in January 1944 Hitler once again advocated the deployment of the Me 262 as a bomber. See Kershaw, *Hitler*, 2, 839f.; Speer, *Erinnerungen*, 372f.

16. Schabel, *Illusion*, 226ff.; Galland, *Ersten*, 355; BAB, NS 6/152, Bormann note of 21 May 1944; Below, *Adjutant*, 370f.

17. Boelcke (ed.), *Rüstung*, 3–5 June 1944, 19.

18. Ibid., Points 21–23.

19. *Wehrmachtberichte* 3, 5 June 1944.

20. *Goebbels TB*, 6 June 1944.

21. See the reflections in Frieser, 'Der Zusammenbruch der Heeresgruppe Mitte im Sommer 1944', in Frieser (ed.), *Ostfront*, 496ff.

22. Hans Speidel, *Aus unserer Zeit. Erinnerungen* (Berlin, 1977), 178ff.; Below, *Adjutant*, 375.

23. On 16 May Hitler ordered the 'long-range attack' on Britain to start in June. See Hubatsch (ed.), *Weisungen*, No. 55. The attack should actually have begun a few days earlier than 15 June, but had to be postponed for technical reasons. See Boog, 'Reichsluftverteidigung', 391.

24. Heiber (ed.), *Goebbels Reden*, 2, No. 26, esp. 335. For further hints see Hölsken, *V-Waffen*, 100ff.; *Goebbels TB*, 15 and 17 January, 19 February, 9 April, and 3 June 1944; Steinert, *Krieg*, 433f.

25. *Goebbels TB*, 18 June 1944.

26. BAK, ZSg. 109/50, 17 June 1944, TP 1, and 20 June 1944, TP 1.

27. Ibid., 24 June 1944, TP 1, Introduction of the term V1; Hölsken, *V-Waffen*, 106. Goebbels claimed to have been responsible for the term (*TB*, 22 June 1944).

28. Ibid. For the statistics on successful hits see Boog, 'Reichsluftverteidigung', 397.

29. *Goebbels TB*, 18 June 1944. This is clear, first, from the reports of the Reich propaganda offices (ibid., 30 June, also 1 and 7 July 1944), and, secondly, from the reports from the SD regions (*Meldungen*, 17, 6595ff. and 6613ff.). See also Hölsken, *V-Waffen*, 197.

30. *Goebbels TB*, 6 June 1944 (concerning the meeting on the previous day).

31. Ibid., 22 June 1944.

32. Ibid.

33. Thus, at the beginning of July, Goebbels instructed the media 'to emphasize even more than before the retributive character of our weapon' (ibid., 2 July 1944). See also his article in *Das Reich*, 23 July 1944, on the 'Issue of Retribution'. He tried to sustain the hope that the new technology would produce a decisive change in the war by announcing further V weapons in his radio address of 26

July. See Heiber (ed.), *Goebbels Reden*, 2, No. 27, 356f. A few days later he published another article in *Das Reich* on the theme of 'Catching Up and Overtaking'. On the V weapons propaganda in July see also Hölsken, *V-Waffen*, 107f.

34. *Goebbels TB*, 22 June 1944.
35. Frieser, 'Zusammenbruch', esp. 537ff.
36. Guderian, *Erinnerungen*, 302f.
37. Detlef Vogel, 'Deutsche und alliierte Kriegführung im Westen', in Boog et al. (eds), *Das Deutsche Reich*, 549.
38. Ibid., 479; Hendrik Thoss, 'Sperrle, Hugo Wilhelm', in *Neue Deutsche Biographie*, 24 (2010), 671f.
39. Below, *Adjutant*, 378; Guderian, *Erinnerungen*, 318ff.; on the reshuffle in July see Kershaw, *Hitler*, 2, 857f.
40. On 27–28 June 1944. See Wolf Keilig, *Die Generale des Heeres* (Friedberg, 1983), 57 and 228.
41. *KTB OKW* 4, 1572f. The letter is a reconstruction produced by Speidel (*Zeit*, 187). The telex was sent by the c-in-c West, Kluge, who supported Rommel's initiative (*KTB OKW* 4, 1574ff.).
42. Führer edict concerning the Establishment of Civil Administration in the Occupied Territories of Belgium and Northern France (*'Führer-Erlasse'*, No. 338).
43. Hubatsch (ed.), *Weisungen*, No. 57.
44. Below, *Adjutant*, 380.
45. BAB, R 3/1551; Speer, *Erinnerungen*, 359f.
46. Müller, 'Speer', 399ff., Eichholtz, *Geschichte* 3, 38ff. (text of edict, 39).
47. Edict concerning the Intermediate Level Authorities (Mittelinstanz), 22 June 1944, and supplementary edict, 14 July 1944 (Nachrichten des Reichsministeriums für Bewaffnung und Kriegsproduktion, 21 July 1944).
48. According to Speer, *Erinnerungen*, 369ff., the speech was 'proof of his shocking state of exhaustion'; Kehrl, *Krisenmanager*, 395ff., claims that the audience had generally gained the impression that Hitler was no longer capable of governing.
49. Speech of 26 June at the Plattlerhof, published in *'Es spricht'*, 335ff. (dated there as 4 July 1944). On the meetings in Essen and Linz see Eichholtz, *Geschichte*, 3, 42ff.; on Hitler's speech in detail see Herbst, *Krieg*, 333ff.
50. Boelcke (ed.), *Rüstung,* 3–5 June 1944, 23.
51. *IMT* 34, 4006-PS, 44f.; on Sauckel's subordination to Speer see Eichholtz, *Geschichte*, 3, 231ff.
52. BAB, R 43 II/651, Sauckel to Hitler.
53. *IMT* 33, 3819-PS, 186ff.; BAB, R 43 II/651, Sauckel report, 17 July 1944, and minutes; Kroener, '"Menschenbewirtschaftung"', 913f.
54. Müller, 'Speer', 399.
55. *Das Reich*, 2 July 1944, 'Führen wir einen Totalen Krieg?'.
56. *VB* (B), 9 July 1944, 'Mit allen Mitteln gegen den Feind' (headline); *Goebbels TB*, 8 July 1944; on total war, in particular his comments on the reports on the content of letters, see also 15 July 1944.

57. Boelcke (ed.), *Rüstung*, 6–8. July 1944, 2.

58. *Goebbels TB*, 11 July 1944. On the following day Speer gave him the memorandum to read, in which, on 30 July, he had drawn Hitler's attention to the catastrophic effect of the air raids on the hydrogenation plants. See Birkenfeld, *Treibstoff*, 238ff. His increasing closeness to Speer is evident in his diaries: 11 May, 6, 27, 29, and 30 June 1944.

59. Both published in Wolfgang Bleyer, 'Pläne der faschistischen Führung zum totalen Krieg im Sommer 1944', in *Zeitschrift für Geschichtswissenschaft* 17 (1969), 1317ff. and 1320ff.

60. Longerich, 'Joseph Goebbels und der Totale Krieg. Eine unbekannte Denkschrift des Propagandaministers vom 18. Juli 1944', in *VfZ* 35 (1987), 289–314.

20 JULY 1944

1. In explaining the remarkable ability of the regime to sustain itself primarily in terms of the 'structures of National Socialist rule', Ian Kershaw (in *Das Ende. Kampf bis in den Untergang. NS-Deutschland 1944/45* (Munich, 2011), 541) in my view underestimates Hitler's independent role. This example shows the inadequacy of an explanation that sees Hitler's personality and structure as antipodes.

2. For the resistance to Hitler (a selection) see Jürgen Schmädeke and Peter Steinbach (eds), *Der Widerstand gegen den Nationalsozialismus. Die deutsche Gesellschaft und der Widerstand gegen Hitler* (Munich, 1994); Hoffmann, *Widerstand*; Joachim Fest, *Staatsstreich. Der lange Weg zum 20. Juli* (Berlin, 1994); Peter Steinbach and Johannes Tuchel (eds), *Widerstand gegen die nationalsozialistische Diktatur 1933–1945* (Bonn, 2004); Ger van Roon, *Widerstand im Dritten Reich. Ein Überblick* (Munich, 1990); Hans-Adolf Jacobsen (ed.), *'Spiegelbild einer Verschwörung'. Die Opposition gegen Hitler und der Staatsstreich vom 20. Juli 1944 in der SD-Berichterstattung. Geheime Dokumente aus dem ehemaligen Reichssicherheitshauptamt*, 2 vols (Stuttgart, 1984); Eberhard Zeller, *Geist der Freiheit. Der zwanzigste Juli* (Berlin, 2004).

3. Hoffmann, *Widerstand*, 329ff. Among the sympathizers were von Kleist, von Gersdorff, von Hardenberg, von Lehndorff, and von Schlabrendorff.

4. Parssinen, *Oster*.

5. Helena P. Page, *Friedrich Olbricht. Ein Mann des 20. Juli* (Bonn, 1992).

6. Günter Brakelmann, *Der Kreisauer Kreis. Chronologie, Kurzbiographien, und Texte aus dem Widerstand* (Münster, 2003).

7. Hoffmann, *Widerstand*, 337f.; Fabian von Schlabrendorff, *Offiziere gegen Hitler* (Berlin, 1994), 56ff. and 61.

8. Hoffmann, *Widerstand*, 343, 350, and 374ff.

9. See Hoffmann's reconstruction in ibid., 348f.

10. Ibid., 350f.; Schlabrendorff, *Offiziere*, 66ff.

11. Hoffmann, *Widerstand*, 360ff.

12. Ibid., 396. On Stauffenberg see Hoffmann, *Claus Schenk Graf von Stauffenberg. Die Biographie* (Munich, 2007)

13. Hoffmann, *Widerstand*, 429ff. and 439ff.

14. Ibid., 396ff.
15. Ibid., 469; Zeller, *Geist*, 367.
16. Hoffmann, *Widerstand*, 469; Jacobsen (ed.), 'Spiegelbild', 121 and 130; Schlabrendorff, *Offiziere*, 118f.
17. Hoffmann, *Widerstand*, 471ff.; Schlabrendorff, *Offiziere*, 119.
18. On the assassination attempt see Hoffmann, *Widerstand*, 486ff.; Fest, *Staatsstreich*, 258ff.; Kershaw, *Hitler*, 2, 882ff.; Below, *Adjutant*, 381ff.; Schroeder, *Chef*, 147f.
19. Domarus, 2, 2127.
20. On the events in Berlin see Hoffmann, *Widerstand*, 506ff.; Kershaw, *Hitler*, 2, 885ff.; Fest, *Staatsstreich*, 262ff.; Zeller, *Geist*, 397f.; Speer, *Erinnerungen*, 381ff.
21. Hoffmann, *Widerstand*, 540ff.
22. Hans W. Hagen, 'Bericht über meine Tätigkeit als Verbindungsoffizier des Wachbataillons "Großdeutschland" zum Reichsministerium für Volksaufklärung und Propaganda am 20. Juli 1944', in Jacobsen, 'Spiegelbild', 12–15; Otto-Ernst Remer, 'Der Ablauf der Ereignisse am 20. 7. 1944, wie ich sie als Kommandeur des Wachbataillons "Großdeutschland" erlebte', in Jacobsen, 'Spiegelbild', 633–645. See Hoffmann, *Widerstand*, 528ff. and 592ff.
23. Kroener, *Fromm,* 679ff.; Hoffmann, *Widerstand*, 620ff.
24. Domarus, 2, 2127ff.
25. Ibid., 2129.
26. *Goebbels TB*, 3 and 24 August 1944.

TOTAL WAR

1. *'Führer-Erlasse'*, No. 340f.
2. *Goebbels TB*, 23 July 1944; BAB, R 43 II/664a, Minutes of the Chefbesprechung of 22 July 1944.
3. *RGBl.* 1944 I, 161f.; BAB, R 43 II/664a, Lammers's note about the address on 25 July 1944, and Goebbels's certificate of appointment, 25 July 1944; on the Führer edict see Rebentisch, *Führerstaat*, 516f.
4. An appeal process was envisaged against his 'directives'; the issuing of 'legal provisions and basic administrative regulations' in the sphere of total war was a matter for the highest Reich authorities. The sentence stating that Bormann would support these measures 'by deploying the Party' underlined the fact that Goebbels's powers did not cover the Party. Moreover, Lammers produced a list of central Reich agencies to which the plenipotentiary's orders did not apply. See BAB, R 43 II/664a, Lammers to Goebbels, 26 July 1944.
5. Eichholtz, *Geschichte*, 3, 51.
6. Frieser, 'Zusammenbruch', 572ff.
7. Klaus Schönherr, 'Die Kämpfe um Galizien und die Beskiden', in Frieser, *Ostfront*, 712ff.
8. Vogel, 'Kriegführung', 556ff.
9. Speer: BAB R 3/1553, Transcript IfZ, Fa 35/2, and final version of the manuscript; Speer, *Erinnerungen*, 402; Himmler, 'Rede Himmlers'; Goebbels: Heiber

(ed.), *Goebbels Reden*, 2, No. 28; *Goebbels TB*, 4 August 1944; on the meeting see Moll, 'Steuerungsinstrument', 265ff.

10. Domarus, 2, 2138f.
11. *Goebbels TB*, 23 July 1944.
12. BAB, R 55/614, Circulars from the propaganda headquarters concerning these demonstrations, 23 July 1944, and directives for the events.
13. *Meldungen*, 17, 6684ff.
14. *Goebbels TB*, 23 July 1944.
15. Ibid., 3 August 1944.
16. Armin Ramm, *Der 20. Juli vor dem Volksgerichtshof* (Berlin, 2007), 69ff.; Guderian, *Erinnerungen*, 313ff.
17. Remy, *Rommel*, 304ff.; Reuth, *Rommel*, 225ff.
18. *Goebbels TB*, 3 August 1944.
19. *VB* (B), 9 August 1944, 'Acht Verbrecher vom 20. Juli traf die verdiente Strafe' (headline).
20. Ramm, *20. Juli*, 342f.
21. *Goebbels TB*, 16 August 1944.
22. Ramm, *20. Juli*, 449ff., with an overview of the trials.
23. Vogel, 'Kriegführung', 581ff.
24. On Kluge's dismissal and suicide see Guderian, *Erinnerungen*, 335; Gersdorff, *Soldat*, 156f.; Hitler's comments in Heiber (ed.), *Lagebesprechungen*, 610ff.; Schmundt, *Tätigkeitsbericht*, 19, 20, 22, and 28 August on the investigation into the cause of death. See also Kershaw, *Hitler*, 2, 938f.
25. Vogel, 'Kriegführung', 556ff.
26. Domarus, 2, 2142; Schumann (ed.), *Deutschland*, 5, 665.
27. Vogel, 'Kriegführung', 560ff.
28. Hubatsch (ed.), *Weisungen*, Nos 61–63. At the end of July he had issued similar orders for northern Italy. See ibid., Nos 60, 60a, and 60b.
29. Ibid., Nos 64a and 64b.
30. Leitz, *Nazi Germany*, 107.
31. Klaus Schönherr, 'Die Rückzugskämpfe in Rumänien und Siebenbürgen', in Frieser (ed.), *Ostfront.*, 546ff. and 773ff.
32. Guderian, *Erinnerungen*, 329f.
33. Schönherr, 'Rückzugskämpfe', 773ff.
34. Ibid., 816ff.; Hoppe, *Bulgarien*, 180ff.
35. Schönherr, 'Der Rückzug aus Griechenland' in Frieser (ed.), *Ostfront*, 1089–99.
36. Bernd Wegner, 'Das Kriegsende in Skandinavien' in Frieser (ed.), *Ostfront*, 979f. and 991ff.
37. Speer, *Erinnerungen*, 405ff.; *Goebbels TB*, 3 and 20 September 1944.
38. Longerich, *Goebbels*, 633ff.
39. BAB, R 43 II/666b, Führerinformation, 11 August 1944. Goebbels succeeded in removing his doubts and so theatres, orchestral, and variety performances and the like were closed, 'initially' for six months (*Goebbels TB*, 24 August 1944).
40. Ibid., 5 October 1944, also 24 August 1944.

41. BAB, R 43 II/665, Bormann to Goebbels, 14 August 1944; R 43 II/666b, Führerinformation, 17 August 1944.

42. *Goebbels TB*, 24 August 1944.

43. Ibid., 17, and 20 September 1944.

44. Ibid., 24 August 1944.

45. BAB, R 43 II/1363, Minute, 20 September 1943, and further correspondence.

46. *Goebbels TB*, 10 August 1944; on the economics ministry see Herbst, *Krieg*, 344.

47. *Goebbels TB*, 24 October 1944.

48. Schmundt, *Tagesbericht*, 6, 11, 14, 23, 30 October, 15 and 24 November, and 5 December 1944.

49. Gröhler, *Bombenkrieg*, 371, 374, and 489.

50. Vogel, 'Kriegführung', 606ff. and 615.

51. *Goebbels TB*, 23 and 25 September 1944.

52. Longerich, *Goebbels*, 644; Kershaw, *Hitler*, 2, 948ff.

53. Frieser, 'Rückzugskämpfe', 642ff.

54. *Goebbels TB*, 24 October 1944; Kershaw, *Hitler*, 2, 959.

55. Karl-Heinz Frieser, 'Die erfolgreichen Abwehrkämpfe der Heeresgruppe Mitte im Herbst 1944', in Frieser, *Ostfront.*, 612ff.

56. *Goebbels TB*, 9, 11, 17, 20–22, and 29 November 1944 for particularly worried entries. On military developments see Vogel, 'Kriegführung', 614ff.

57. *Wehrmachtberichte* 3, 8 November 1944; Hölsken, *V-Waffen*, 137ff.

58. *Goebbels TB*, 13 November 1944.

59. Domarus, 2, 2160ff.

60. Below, *Adjutant*, 395.

61. Kershaw, *Hitler*, 2, 962; *Goebbels TB*, 24 November 1944.

62. For the complaints about the lack of a public statement from Hitler see ibid., 11, 12, 14, 16–18, and 30 September, 4, 9, 10, and 13 November, and 3 December 1944.

63. Ibid., 30 September and 6 (quote), 8, 9, and 30 October 1944; Kershaw, *Hitler*, 2, 945.

64. *Goebbels TB*, 3 December 1944.

65. Ibid.

66. Reproduced in Heiber (ed.), *Lagebesprechungen*, 713ff.; see also Below, *Adjutant*, 397f. He had also outlined the aims of the offensive to Goebbels in detail on 1 December (*Goebbels TB*, 2 December 1945).

67. Vogel, 'Kriegführung', 625ff.

68. Below, *Adjutant*, 398.

THE END

1. Richard Lakowski, 'Der Zusammenbruch der deutschen Verteidigung zwischen Ostsee und Karpaten', in Müller, *Das Deutsche Reich*, 516ff.; Guderian, *Erinnerungen*, 345ff.

2. Lakowski, 'Zusammenbruch', 524; Guderian, *Erinnerungen*, 357.

3. Lakowski, 'Zusammenbruch', 524; Longerich, *Himmler*, 737ff.

4. Frieser, 'Rückzugskämpfe'.
5. Wegner, 'Kriegsende'; *Lagevorträge*, 10 March 1945.
6. Guderian, *Erinnerungen*, 374f.; Gerhard Boldt, *Die letzten Tage der Reichskanzlei* (Hamburg and Stuttgart, 1947), 20. Gerhard Boldt, a cavalry captain on the general staff, accompanied Guderian.
7. Detailed evidence in Wegner, 'Deutschland'.
8. *MK*, 250; on the trope of a heroic downfall see Wegner, 'Deutschland'.
9. *Goebbels TB*, 6 February 1945.
10. Kershaw, *Hitler*, 2, 1002ff.
11. *Goebbels TB*, 1 (Eva Braun) and 6 February 1945. On 11 February Hitler reaffirmed his decision to remain in Berlin (ibid., 12 February 1945). See also Heike B. Görtemaker, *Eva Braun. Leben mit Hitler* (Munich, 2010), 263f.
12. *Goebbels TB*, 1 February 1945.
13. Ibid., 4 April 1945.
14. Guderian, *Erinnerungen*, 375f.
15. Lakowski, 'Zusammenbruch', 552ff., 556ff., and 575ff.
16. John Zimmermann, 'Die deutsche militärische Kriegsführung im Westen 1944/45', in Müller, *Das Deutsche Reich*, 411ff.
17. Ibid., 422ff.
18. Andreas Kunz, *Wehrmacht und Niederlage. Die bewaffnete Macht in der Endphase der nationalsozialistischen Herrschaft 1944 bis 1945* (Munich, 2005), 278; Guderian, *Erinnerungen*, 380.
19. Zimmermann, 'Kriegsführung', 430ff.
20. Ungváry, 'Kriegsschauplatz', 926ff.
21. Ibid., 944ff.
22. Guderian, *Erinnerungen*, 387 and 389.
23. *Goebbels TB*, 5 March 1943.
24. Ibid., 23 March 1945.
25. Ibid., 8 March 1945.
26. Ibid., 12 March 1945.
27. Ibid., 8 April 1945.
28. For details see Longerich, *Goebbels*, 667f.
29. *UF* 22, No. 3607f.; see also Fest, *Speer*, 336ff.
30. '*Führer-Erlasse*', No. 394.
31. Speer told the Nuremberg military tribunal that, on 29 March, he had sent Hitler a note containing these comments made by the dictator on 18 March. See *IMT* 16, 547f.; *IMT* 41, Speer-24, 426ff.
32. *Goebbels TB*, 31 March 1945; *UF*, No. 3604c.
33. Ibid., No. 3604d; Klaus-Dietmar Henke, *Die amerikanische Besetzung Deutschlands* (Munich, 1995), 561ff.
34. Domarus, 2, 2211.
35. *Goebbels TB*, 27 and 28 March 1945.
36. Ibid., 31 March 1945.
37. Zimmermann, 'Kriegsführung', 435ff.

38. Hubatsch (ed.), *Weisungen*, No. 73a.

39. Speer, *Erinnerungen*, 467; Below, *Adjutant*, 408, reports, however, that Hitler responded relatively calmly to this news.

40. For the text see Hubatsch (ed.), *Weisungen*, No. 74.

41. See ibid., No. 75; *VB*, 17 April 1945.

42. Lakowski, 'Zusammenbruch', 588ff.

43. Ibid., 633ff.

44. Ibid., 435ff.

45. Domarus, 2, 1228.

46. Ibid., 1223.

47. Kershaw, *Hitler*, 2, 1027ff.

48. Speer, *Erinnerungen*, 476ff.; Below, *Adjutant*, 410f.; Heinz Linge, *Bis zum Untergang. Als Chef des persönlichen Dienstes bei Hitler*, ed. Werner Maser (Munich, 1982), 270ff.; Artur Axmann, *'Das kann doch nicht das Ende sein'. Hitlers letzter Reichsjugendführer erinnert sich* (Coblenz, 1995), 418; Keitel, *Leben*, 378ff.; Kershaw, *Hitler*, 2, 1027ff.; Anton Joachimsthaler, *Hitlers Ende. Legende und Dokumente* (Munich, 2004), 138ff.

49. Ibid., 143.

50. Karl Koller, *Der letzte Monat, 14. April bis 27. Mai 1945. Tagebuchaufzeichnungen des ehemaligen Chefs des Generalstabs der deutschen Luftwaffe. Mit dem Urteil der Spruchkammer im Entnazifierungsverfahren* (Munich, 1985); Wilfred von Oven, *Mit Goebbels bis zum Ende*, 2 vols (Buenos Aires, 1949/50), 2, 22 April 1945, 310f.; LA Berlin, Rep. 058, No. 6012, Statement by Günther Schwägermann, Hanover, 16 February 1948; Kershaw, *Hitler*, 2, 1034ff.; Joachimsthaler, *Ende*, 145ff.; on the Battle of Berlin see Lakowski, 'Zusammenbruch', 656ff.

51. Koller, *Monat*, 54f. and 58f.; Joachimsthaler, *Ende*, 147ff.; Keitel, *Leben*, 382ff.; Below, *Adjutant*, 411.

52. Ibid.; Joachimsthaler, *Ende*, 157.

53. Oven, *Goebbels* 2, 22 April 1945, 310f.; LA Berlin, Rep. 058, No. 6012, Statement by Günther Schwägermann, Hanover, 16 February 1948.

54. In his radio address of 28 February (Heiber (ed.), *Goebbels Reden*, 2, No. 30) and in *Das Reich*, 15 April 1945, 'Der Einsatz des eigenen Lebens' (Leader).

55. *Goebbels TB*, 5 March 1945.

56. *KTB OKW* 4, 1262.

57. *Der Spiegel* 3/1966, *Lagebesprechungen*, 23 April 1945.

58. Speer, *Erinnerungen*, 482ff.

59. Domarus, 2, 2228; on Hitler's response see Speer, *Erinnerungen*, 485f.

60. Lakowski, 'Zusammenbruch', 668ff.

61. Koller, *Monat*, 100.

62. *Der Spiegel*, 3/1966, *Lagebesprechungen*, 25 April 1945. Hitler repeated these ideas in the situation conference on the evening of 25 April.

63. Ibid.

64. Longerich, *Himmler*, 751.

65. Joachimsthaler, *Ende*, 185; Registry Office certificate published in Domarus, 2, 2234.

Bibliography

ARCHIVES

Bayerisches Hauptstaatsarchiv, Munich (BHStA)
MA Ministerium des Äußeren
MI Ministerium des Inneren
NL Ehard
Slg P Sammlung Personen
Varia

Bundesarchiv, Abt. Berlin (BAB)
BDC Oberstes Parteigericht
NS 1 Reichsschatzmeister der NSDAP
NS 6 Partei-Kanzlei der NSDAP
NS 8 Kanzlei Rosenberg
NS 10 Adjutantur des Führers
NS 18 Reichspropagandaleitung
NS 19 Persönlicher Stab Reichsführer-SS
NS 22 Reichsorganisationsleiter der NSDAP
NS 23 Sturmabteilung der NSDAP
NS 26 Hauptarchiv der NDSAP
NS 36 Oberstes Parteigericht der NSDAP
NS 51 Kanzlei des Führers
R 2 Reichsministerium für Finanzen
R 3 Reichsministerium für Rüstung und Kriegsproduktion
R 6 Reichsministerium für die besetzten Ostgebiete
R 18 Reichsministerium des Inneren
R 43 II Neue Reichskanzlei
R 55 Reichsministerium für Volksaufklärung und Propaganda
R 58 Reichssicherheitshauptamt
R 69 Reichskommissar für die Festigung Deutschen Volkstums
R 70 Besetzte Gebiete
R 72 Stahlhelm, Bund der Frontsoldaten
R 113 Reichsstelle für Raumordnung
R 1501 Reichsministerium des Inneren

R 2501 Deutsche Reichsbank
R 8005 Deutschnationale Volkspartei
R 8048 Alldeutscher Verband
R 8150 Reichsvereinigung der Juden in Deutschland
RD 19 Drucksachen

Bundesarchiv, Abt. Koblenz (BAK)

NL 1231 Hugenberg
NL 1118 Goebbels
ZSg 102 Sammlung Sänger zur Pressepolitik des NS-Staats
ZSg 109 Sammlung Oberweitmann zur Pressepolitik des NS-Staats

Bundesarchiv Militärarchiv, Freiburg (BAF)

RH 15 OKH/Allgemeines Heeresamt
RL 3 Luftwaffenrüstung
RM 7 Seekriegsleitung
RW 19 OKW/Wehrwirtschafts- und Rüstungsamt
RW 47 Führerhauptquartier

Institut für Zeitgeschichte, Munich (IfZ)

Da Drucksachen
ED Nachlässe
F Manuskripte
Fb Gerichtsakten
Gm Gerichtsakten
MA, MB Mikrofilme
Nürnberger Dokumente aus den Serien EC, NG, NI, NO, PS
ZS Zeugenschrifttum

Kriegsarchiv, Munich (KAM, Bayerisches Hauptstaatsarchiv)

RD 6
RIB 12
RIR 16
RIR 17
2. Inf.Rgt.
Gruppenkdo. 4
Höherer Auflösungsstab 102
Kriegsstammrollen
Offizierspersonalakten
SchützenRgt. 41

Landesarchiv Berlin (LA Berlin)

Rep 58

Landeshauptarchiv Linz (LHA)

NL Jetzinger

National Archives and Records Administration, College Park (NARA)
T 581

Osobyi Archiv, Moscow (OA Moskau)
Collection 500
Collection 504
Collection 1363

Österreichisches Staatsarchiv, Wien (ÖStA)
Archiv der Republik/Bundeskanzleramt

Politisches Archiv des Auswärtigen Amtes, Berlin (PAA)
Inland II g
Pol XIII

Staatsarchiv Munich (SAM)
Polizeidirektion
Spruchkammerakten
Staatsanwaltschaften

Staatsarchiv Riga (StA Riga)
Collection 1026

Yad Vashem
O 53 Gestapo Mährisch-Ostrau

Zentrale Stelle, Ludwigsburg (ZStL)
Dokumentation UdSSR

PERIODICALS

Der Angriff
Der Arbeitseinsatz im Großdeutschen Reich
Archiv der Gegenwart
Auf gut deutsch
Bayerischer Kurier
Berliner Tageblatt
Biuletyn Zydowskiego Instytutu Historycznego 12 (1960)
Börsenblatt des deutschen Buchhandels
Deutsche Allgemeine Zeitung
Deutscher Reichsanzeiger und Preußischer Staatsanzeiger
Frankfurter Zeitung
Geisteschristentum
Der Hoheitsträger
Kölnische Volkszeitung
Linzer Tagespost

Monatshefte für Auswärtige Politik

Münchener Beobachter

Münchner Neueste Nachrichten

Münchener Post

Münchner Zeitung

Nachrichten des Reichsministeriums für Bewaffnung und Kriegsproduktion

Nationalsozialistische Briefe

Neue Zürcher Zeitung

New Republic

Preußische Gesetzsammlung

Das Reich

Reichsgesetzblatt

Reichsmarine. Zeitschrift für deutsche Seegeltung und Seefahrt

Schulthess' Europäischer Geschichtskalender

Statistisches Jahrbuch für das Deutsche Reich

Unser Wille und Weg

Verordnungsblatt des Generalgouvernements 1942

Völkischer Beobachter

Völkischer Kurier

Vossische Zeitung

12 Uhr Blatt

CONTEMPORARY PUBLICATIONS

Agricola, Germanus [i.e. Johannes Dingfelder], *Geldwahn und Rettung. Sammlung der in der Zeit vom 7. 9. 1919 bis 31. 1. 1920 im Münchner Beobachter erschienenen Aufsätze* (Munich, 1920).

Apenszlak, Jacob (ed.), *The Black Book of Polish Jewry. An Account of the Martyrdom of Polish Jewry under the Nazi Occupation* (New York, 1943).

Baligand, Maximilian von, 'Ende wie Anfang', in Fridolin Solleder (ed.), *Vier Jahre Westfront. Die Geschichte des Regiments List. Reserve-Infanterie-Regiment 16* (Munich, 1932), 328–36.

Beckmann, Walther, *Bayerisches Reserve-Infanterie-Regiment Nr. 16 »Regiment List«* (Berlin 1939).

Beiträge zur Vorgeschichte und Geschichte der Julirevolte, hg. auf Grund amtlicher Quellen (Vienna, 1934).

Berber, Friedrich (ed.), *Locarno. Eine Dokumentensammlung* (Berlin, 1936).

Berndt, Alfred Ingemar, *Meilensteine des Dritten Reiches. Erlebnisschilderungen großer Tage* (Munich, 1938).

Berndt, Alfred Ingemar, *Der Marsch ins Großdeutsche Reich* (Munich, 1939).

Binding, Karl and Hoche, Alfred, *Die Freigabe der Vernichtung lebensunwerten Lebens. Ihr Maß und ihre Form* (Leipzig, 1920).

Bouhler, Philipp, *Kampf um Deutschland. Ein Lesebuch für die deutsche Jugend* (Munich, 1938).

Brandmayer, Balthasar, *Zwei Meldegänger* (Überlingen am Bodensee, 1932).

Buttmann, Rudolf, *Bayerische Politik 1924–1928* (Munich, 1928).

Chamberlain, Neville, *The Struggle for Peace* (London, 1939).

Czech-Jochberg, Erich, *Adolf Hitler und sein Stab* (Oldenburg i. O., 1933).

Dietrich, Otto, *Mit Hitler in die Macht. Persönliche Erlebnisse mit meinem Führer* (Munich, 1934).

Dietrich, Otto, *Auf den Straßen des Sieges. Erlebnisse mit dem Führer in Polen* (Munich, 1940).

Dohrmann, Franz, *Predigt zum Feldgottesdienst am 2. Oktober 1935 bei der Weihe der Hindenburggruft im Reichsehrenmal Tannenberg* (Wuppertal-Barmen, 1935).

Drexler, Anton, *Mein politisches Erwachen. Aus dem Tagebuch eines deutschen sozialistischen Arbeiters* (Munich, 1919).

Eichelsdörfer, Georg, 'Das Gefecht bei Fromelles, 9. und 10. Mai 1915', in Fridolin Solleder (ed.), *Vier Jahre Westfront. Die Geschichte des Regiments List. Reserve-Infanterie-Regiment 16* (Munich, 1932), 130–41.

Eichelsdörfer, Georg, 'Die Schlacht bei Neuve Chapelle', in Fridolin Solleder (ed.), *Vier Jahre Westfront. Die Geschichte des Regiments List. Reserve-Infanterie-Regiment 16* (Munich, 1932), 106–12.

Eichelsdörfer, Georg, 'Sturm auf das beilförmige Waldstück', in Fridolin Solleder (ed.), *Vier Jahre Westfront. Die Geschichte des Regiments List. Reserve-Infanterie-Regiment 16* (Munich, 1932), 73–8.

Engelbrechten, Julius K. von, 'Erinnerungen ans List-Regiment (Bayr. Reserve-Infanterie-Regiment 16) 1914–1918', in *Das Bayernland* 32 (1920), 49–65.

Engelbrechten, Julius K. von, *Eine braune Armee entsteht. Die Geschichte der Berlin-Brandenburger SA* (Munich, 1937).

Engelbrechten, Julius K. von, with Volz, Hans, *Wir wandern durch das nationalsozialistische Berlin* (Munich, 1937).

Feder, Gottfried, 'Das Radikalmittel', in *Süddeutsche Monatshefte* 16 (1919), 307–20.

Feder, Gottfried, *Das Manifest zur Brechung der Zinsknechtschaft des Geldes* [1919] (Munich, 1932).

Foreign Relations of the United States. Diplomatic Papers, 1937, vol. 1: *General*, ed. The United States Department of State (Washington, 1937).

Führer durch die Ausstellung Entartete Kunst (Berlin, 1935).

'Der Führer auf der Kulturtagung', in *Reden des Führers am Parteitag der Ehre 1936* (Munich, 1936), 27–46.

Gauger, Joseph (ed.), *Chronik der Kirchenwirren*, Part 2 (Wuppertal-Elberfeld, 1935).

Gehring, Egid, 'Am Schicksalsstrom Deutschlands. Stimmungsbilder aus der zweiten Marneschlacht im Juli 1918', in Fridolin Solleder (ed.), *Vier Jahre Westfront. Die Geschichte des Regiments List. Reserve-Infanterie-Regiment 16* (Munich, 1932), 316–24.

Goebbels, Joseph, *'Der Nazi-Sozi'. Fragen und Antworten für den Nationalsozialisten* (Munich 1930), 2nd edn, (Munich, 1931).

Goebbels, Joseph, *Das eherne Herz. Rede vor der Deutschen Akademie, gehalten am 1. Dezember 1941 in der Neuen Aula der Friedrich-Wilhelm-Universität zu Berlin* (Munich/Berlin, 1941).

Hadamovsky, Eugen, 'Großkampftage der Rundfunkpropaganda. Vom 30. Januar bis zum "Tag der erwachenden Nation"', in Hadamovsky, *Dein Rundfunk. Das Rundfunkbuch für alle Volksgenossen* (Munich, 1934), 82–90.

Heidegger, Martin, *Die Selbstbehauptung der deutschen Universität. Rede, gehalten bei der feierlichen Übernahme des Rektorats der Universität Freiburg i. Br. am 27. Mai 1933* (Breslau, 1933).

Heiden, Konrad, *Adolf Hitler. Eine Biographie*, vol. 1 (Zurich, 1936).

Heinz, Heinz A., *Germany's Hitler* (London, 1934).

Henderson, Nevile, *Fehlschlag einer Mission: Berlin 1937 bis 1939* (Zurich, 1940).

Heydrich, Reinhard, 'Die Bekämpfung der Staatsfeinde', in *Deutsches Recht*, 15 April 1936, 121–3.

Hitler, Adolf, *Mein Kampf*, 286–90 edn (Munich, 1938).

Hitler, Adolf, 'Die Reichskanzlei', in *Die Kunst im Dritten Reich* 3 (1939), 279.

Hoegner, Wilhelm, *Hitler und Kahr. Die bayerischen Napoleonsgrößen von 1923. Ein im Untersuchungsausschuß des Bayerischen Landtages aufgedeckter Justizskandal*, 2 vols (Munich, 1928).

Hoffmann, Heinrich (ed.) *Deutschlands Erwachen in Bild und Wort. Photographische Zeitdokumente*, Text by Marc Sesselmann (Munich, 1924).

Hoffmann, Heinrich (ed.), *Hitler in Polen* (Berlin, 1939).

Huber, Ernst Rudolf, *Verfassungsrecht des Großdeutschen Reiches*, 2nd enlarged edn (Hamburg, 1941).

'Industrie und Reichstagswahlen', in *Geschäftliche Mitteilungen für die Mitglieder des Reichsverbandes der Deutschen Industrie*, 25 August 1930.

Kallenbach, Hans, *Mit Adolf Hitler auf Festung Landsberg. Nach Aufzeichnungen des Mitgefangenen Oberleutnant a. D. Hans Kallenbach*, ed. Ulf Uweson, (Munich, 1933).

Kasper, Gerhard et al. (eds) *Die deutsche Hochschulverwaltung. Sammlung der das Hochschulwesen betreffenden Gesetze, Verordnungen und Erlasse*, 2 vols (Berlin 1942/43).

Kaufman, Theodore N., *Germany Must Perish*, Newark, no date [Beginning of 1941].

Kerrl, Hanns, *Nationalsozialistisches Strafrecht. Denkschrift des preußischen Justizministers* (Berlin, 1933).

Kerrl, Hanns (ed.), *Reichstagung in Nürnberg 1937. Der Parteitag der Arbeit* (Berlin 1938).

'Bei der Kulturtagung des Reichsparteitages 1935', in *Die Reden Adolf Hitlers am Parteitag der Freiheit 1935* (Munich, 1935), 28–42.

Le Bon, Gustave, *Die Psychologie der Massen* (Leipzig, 1908).

Lenz, F., 'Die Stellung des Nationalsozialismus zur Rassenhygiene', in *Archiv für Rassen- und Gesellschafts-Biologie einschließlich Rassen- und Gesellschafts-Hygiene* 25 (1931), 300–8.

List-Regiment, no editor, no place of publication [c. 1915].

Lüdecke, Kurt G. W., *I Knew Hitler. The Story of a Nazi Who Escaped the Blood Purge* (London, 1938).

Ludendorff, Erich, *Vom Feldherrn zum Weltrevolutionär und Wegbereiter deutscher Volksschöpfung* vol. 1 (Munich, 1934).

Mayr, Karl, 'I was Hitler's Boss', in *Current History* 4 (November 1941), 193–9.

Mend, Hans, *Adolf Hitler im Felde 1914–1918* (Diessen near Munich), 1931.

Organisationsbuch der NSDAP, ed. the NSDAP Reichsorganisationsleiter, 2nd edn (Munich, 1937).

Österreichisches statistisches Handbuch 1900, (Vienna, 1901) and *1910* (Vienna, 1911).

Paquin, E., *Der Vereinsführer im neuen Reich. Praktischer Wegweiser für Führer von Vereinen, Verbänden, Innungen, Genossenschaften und sonstigen Organisationen* (Hösel, 1934).

Parteistatistik der NSDAP. Stand: 1. Januar 1935, 4 vols (Munich, 1935/36).

Parteitag der Freiheit vom 10.–16. September 1935. Offizieller Bericht über den Verlauf des Reichsparteitages mit sämtlichen Kongreßreden (Munich, 1935).

Pudor, Heinrich, 'Kultur-Antisemitismus oder Pogrom-Antisemitismus?' in *Deutscher Volksrat*, 8 August 1919.

Das Recht der Reichskulturkammer. Sammlung der für den Kulturstand geltenden Gesetze und Verordnungen, der amtlichen Anordnungen und Bekanntmachungen der Reichskulturkammer und ihrer Einzelkammern ed. Karl–Dietrich Schrieber, Alfred Metten, and Herbert Collatz and authorized by the senior management of the Reichskulturkammer, 2 vols (Berlin, 1943).

'Rede des Leiters des Hauptschulungsamtes der NSDAP, Friedrich Schmidt, Oktober 1938', in *Reden und Vorträge anläßlich der Tagung der Gau- und Kreisschulungsleiter auf der Ordensburg Krössinsee (Pommern) vom 16.–24. 10. 1938* (Munich, 1938).

Die Reden Adolf Hitlers am Parteitag der Freiheit 1935 (Munich, 1935).

Die Reden Adolf Hitlers am Reichsparteitag 1933 (Munich, 1934).

Reden des Führers am Parteitag der Arbeit 1937 (Munich, 1937).

Reden des Führers am Parteitag Großdeutschland 1938 (Munich, 1938).

Reden des Führers auf dem Parteitag der Ehre 1936 (Munich, 1936).

Reichstagung in Nürnberg 1934, hg. im Auftrage des Frankenführers Julius Streicher (Berlin, 1934).

Röhm, Ernst, *Die Geschichte eines Hochverräters*, 6th edn (Munich, 1934).

Röhm, Ernst, *Die nationalsozialistische Revolution und die SA. Rede vor dem Diplomatischen Korps und der Auslandspresse in Berlin am 18. April 1934* (Berlin, 1934).

Rossbach, Julius R., *Die Massenseele. Psychologische Betrachtungen über die Entstehung von Volks- (Massen-)Bewegungen (Revolutionen)* (Munich, 1919).

Rubenbaucr, Franz, 'Der Sturm auf Ypern. Freiwillige vor!', in Fridolin Solleder (ed.), *Vier Jahre Westfront. Die Geschichte des Regiments List. Reserve-Infanterie-Regiment 16* (Munich 1932), 3–47.

Rubenbauer, Franz, 'Im Schützengraben vor Messines', in Fridolin Solleder (ed.), *Vier Jahre Westfront. Die Geschichte des Regiments List. Reserve-Infanterie-Regiment 16* (Munich, 1932), 65f.

Rubenbauer, Franz, 'Oostaverne-Wytschaete', in Fridolin Solleder (ed.), *Vier Jahre Westfront. Die Geschichte des Regiments List. Reserve-Infanterie-Regiment 16* (Munich, 1932), 66–7.

Rubenbauer, Franz, 'Tage der Ruhe in Werwick-Comines', in Fridolin Solleder (ed.), *Vier Jahre Westfront. Die Geschichte des Regiments List. Reserve-Infanterie-Regiment 16* (Munich, 1932), 59–64.

Schilling, Alexander, *Dr. Walter Riehl und die Geschichte des Nationalsozialismus* (Leipzig, 1933).

Schott, Georg, *Das Volksbuch vom Hitler* (Munich, 1924).

Schröder, Georg, 'Das nationalsozialistische Wirtschaftsprogramm', in *Der Arbeitgeber*, 15 July 1930.

Schwendemann, Karl, *Abrüstung und Sicherheit. Handbuch der Sicherheitsfrage und der Abrüstungskonferenz. Mit einer Sammlung der wichtigsten Dokumente*, 2 vols (Leipzig, 1932/1933).

Sebottendorf, Rudolf von, *Bevor Hitler kam. Urkundliches aus der Frühzeit der nationalsozialistischen Bewegung*, Munich, 1933, and 2nd edn (Munich, 1934).

Shirer, William L., *Berlin Diary. The Journal of a Foreign Correspondent 1934–1941* (New York, 1942).

Solleder, Fridolin, 'Das neue Jahr', in Fridolin Solleder (ed.), *Vier Jahre Westfront. Die Geschichte des Regiments List. Reserve-Infanterie-Regiment 16* (Munich, 1932), 97–105.

Solleder, Fridolin, 'Zwischen zwei Gefechten. Die neue Stellung bei Fromelles', in Fridolin Solleder (ed.), *Vier Jahre Westfront. Die Geschichte des Regiments List. Reserve-Infanterie-Regiment 16* (Munich, 1932), 120–9.

Strasser, Gregor, *Arbeit und Brot! Reichstagsrede am 10. Mai 1932* (Munich, 1932).

Strasser, Otto, *Ministersessel oder Revolution? Eine wahrheitsgemäße Darstellung meiner Trennung von der NSDAP* (Berlin, 1933).

Stresemann, Gustav, Die Entwicklung des Berliner Flaschenbiergeschäfts. Eine wirtschaftliche Studie, Dissertation (Leipzig, 1900).

Tafel, Paul, *Das neue Deutschland. Ein Rätestaat auf nationaler Grundlage* (Munich, 1920).

Tafel, Paul, *Die Teuerung. Ihre Ursachen und ihre Überwindung* (Leipzig, 1922).

Tafel, Paul, *Parlamentarismus und Volksvertretung* (Munich, 1922).

Tubeuf, Freiherr von, 'Das Regiment hört auf den Namen Tubeuf', in Fridolin Solleder (ed.), *Vier Jahre Westfront. Die Geschichte des Regiments List. Reserve-Infanterie-Regiment 16* (Munich, 1932), 275–310.

Verfügungen, Anordnungen, Bekanntgaben, ed. by the Partei-Kanzlei, 7 vols (Munich, 1942–1944).

W., v., 'Osttaverne-Wytschaete', in *ListRegiment, 1915* (stops at the end of 1915), 31–8.

Wiedemann, Friedrich, 'Das Gefecht bei Fromelles am 19. und 20. Juli 1916', in Fridolin Solleder (ed.), *Vier Jahre Westfront. Die Geschichte des Regiments List. Reserve-Infanterie-Regiment 16* (Munich, 1932), 214–27.

Wiedemann, Friedrich, 'Der zweite Kriegswinter bei Fromelles', in Fridolin Solleder (ed.), *Vier Jahre Westfront. Die Geschichte des Regiments List. Reserve-Infanterie-Regiment 16* (Munich, 1932), 189–207.

Wiedemann, Friedrich, 'Die Sommeschlacht', in Fridolin Solleder (ed.), *Vier Jahre Westfront. Die Geschichte des Regiments List. Reserve-Infanterie-Regiment 16* (Munich, 1932), 237–60.

Wilamowitz-Moellendorff, Fanny Gräfin von, *Carin Göring* (Berlin, 1934).

DOCUMENTS, MEMOIRS, AND COLLECTIONS OF SOURCES AFTER 1945

Akten deutscher Bischöfe über die Lage der Kirche 1933–1945, eds Bernhard Stasiewski and Ludwig Volk, 5 vols (Mainz, 1968–1983).

Akten Kardinal Michael von Faulhabers, vol. 2, ed. Ludwig Volk (Paderborn, 1978).

Akten der Partei-Kanzlei der NSDAP. Rekonstruktion eines verlorengegangenen Bestandes. Sammlung der in anderen Provenienzen überlieferten Korrespondenzen, Niederschriften von Besprechungen usw. mit dem Stellvertreter des Führers und seinem Stab bzw. der Partei-Kanzlei, ihren Ämtern, Referaten und Unterabteilungen sowie mit Hess und Bormann persönlich, ed. the Institut für Zeitgeschichte, Part 1 ed. Helmut Heiber, Part 2 ed. Peter Longerich (Munich, 1983/1992).

Akten zur deutschen auswärtigen Politik 1918–1945. Aus dem Archiv des Auswärtigen Amtes, Series C: 1933–1937, Series D: 1937–1941, and Series E: 1941–1945 (Göttingen, 1950–1981).

Album Rubonorum 1875–1972 ed. Woldemar Helb, 4th edn (Neustadt a. d. Aisch, 1972).

Andreas-Friedrich, Ruth, *Schauplatz Berlin. Ein deutsches Tagebuch* (Munich, 1962).

Axmann, Artur, *'Das kann doch nicht das Ende sein'. Hitlers letzter Reichsjugendführer erinnert sich* (Coblenz, 1995).

Banken, Ralf, '"An der Spitze aller Künste steht die Staatskunst". Das Protokoll der NSDAP Wirtschaftsbesprechungen Februar/März 1931', in Johannes Bähr and Ralf Banken (eds), *Wirtschaftssteuerung durch Recht im Nationalsozialismus. Studien zur Entwicklung des Wirtschaftsrechts im Interventionsstaat des 'Dritten Reichs'* (Frankfurt a. M., 2006), 511–88.

Barkai, Avraham, 'Wirtschaftliche Grundanschauungen und Ziele der N.S.D.A.P. Ein unveröffentlichtes Dokument aus dem Jahre 1931' in *Jahrbuch des Instituts für Deutsche Geschichte* 7 (1978), 355–85.

Baur, Hans, *Ich flog Mächtige der Erde* (Kempten, 1956).

Becker, Winfried, 'Die nationalsozialistische Machtergreifung in Bayern. Ein Dokumentarbericht Heinrich Helds aus dem Jahre 1933' in *Historisches Jahrbuch* 112 (1992), 412–35.

Below, Nicolaus von, *Als Hitlers Adjutant, 1937–45* (Mainz, 1980).

Berichte des SD und der Gestapo über Kirchen und Kirchenvolk in Deutschland 1934–1944, ed. Heinz Boberach (Mainz, 1971).

Bevölkerungsstruktur und Massenmord. Neue Dokumente zur deutschen Politik der Jahre 1938 bis 1945, edited with a commentary by Susanne Heim and Götz Aly (Berlin, 1991).

Bock, Fedor von, *Zwischen Pflicht und Verweigerung. Das Kriegstagebuch*, ed. Klaus Gerbet (Munich, 1995).

Boelcke, Willi A. (ed.) *Kriegspropaganda 1939–1941. Geheime Ministerkonferenzen im Reichspropagandaministerium* (Stuttgart, 1966).

Boelcke, Willi A. (ed.), *Deutschlands Rüstung im Zweiten Weltkrieg. Hitlers Konferenzen mit Albert Speer 1942–1945* (Frankfurt a. M., 1969).

Boldt, Gerhard, *Die letzten Tage der Reichskanzlei* (Hamburg and Stuttgart, 1947).

Braham, Randolph L., *The Destruction of Hungarian Jewry. A Documentary Account* (New York, 1963).

Breker, Arno, *Im Strahlungsfeld der Ereignisse. Leben und Wirken eines Künstlers. Porträts, Begegnungen, Schicksale* (Preussisch Oldendorf, 1972).

British and Foreign State Papers 139 (1935) Microfiche (Washington, DC, 1969).

Broucek, Peter (ed.), *Ein General im Zwielicht. Die Erinnerungen Edmund Glaises von Horstenau*, 3 vols (Vienna, 1980–1988).

Brüning, Heinrich, *Memoiren 1918–1934* (Stuttgart 1970).

Buddrus, Michael (ed.), *Mecklenburg im Zweiten Weltkrieg. Die Tagungen des Gauleiters Friedrich Hildebrand mit den NS-Führungsgremien des Gaues Mecklenburg 1939–1945* (Bremen, 2009).

Burckhardt, Carl J., *Meine Danziger Mission 1937–1939* (Munich, 1960).

Ciano, Galeazzo, *Ciano's Diplomatic Papers. Being a Record of Nearly 200 Conversations Held during the Years 1936–1942 with Hitler, Mussolini, Franco, Goering, Ribbentrop . . . and Many Other World Diplomatic and Political Figures*, ed. Malcolm Muggeridge (London, 1948).

Ciano, Galeazzo, *Ciano's Hidden Diary 1937–1938* (New York, 1953).

Cohn, Willy, *Als Jude in Breslau – 1941. Aus den Tagebüchern von Willy Israel Cohn*, ed. Joseph Walk (Jerusalem, 1975).

Conrad, Walter, *Der Kampf um die Kanzeln. Erinnerungen und Dokumente aus der Hitlerzeit* (Berlin, 1957).

Coulondre, Robert, *Von Moskau nach Berlin 1936–1939. Erinnerungen des französischen Botschafters* (Bonn, 1950).

Czech, Danuta, *Kalendarium der Ereignisse im Konzentrationslager Auschwitz-Birkenau. 1939–1945* (Reinbek bei Hamburg, 1989).

Dahlerus, Birger, *Der letzte Versuch. London–Berlin, Sommer 1939* (Munich, 1948).

Delmer, Sefton, *Die Deutschen und ich* (Hamburg, 1962).

Deuerlein, Ernst (ed.), *Der Hitler-Putsch: bayerische Dokumente zum 8./9. November 1923* (Stuttgart, 1962)

Deuerlein, Ernst, *Der Aufstieg der NSDAP in Augenzeugenberichten* (Munich, 1974).

Deutschland-Berichte der Sozialdemokratischen Partei Deutschlands. Sopade 1934–1940, reprint (Salzhausen, 1980).

Diels, Rudolf, *Lucifer ante portas. Zwischen Severing und Heydrich* (Stuttgart, 1950).

Der Dienstkalender Heinrich Himmlers 1941/42, edited with an introduction and commentary by Peter Witte et al. for the Forschungsstelle für Zeitgeschichte in Hamburg (Hamburg, 1999).

Das Diensttagebuch des deutschen Generalgouverneurs in Polen 1939–1945, ed. Werner Präg and Wolfgang Jacobmeyer (Stuttgart, 1975).

Dietrich, Otto, *Zwölf Jahre mit Hitler* (Munich, 1955).

Dirksen, Herbert von, *Moskau, Tokio, London. Erinnerungen und Betrachtungen zu 20 Jahren deutscher Außenpolitik 1919–1939* (Stuttgart, 1949).

Dobroszycki, Lucjan (ed.), *The Chronicle of the Łódź Ghetto 1941–1944* (New Haven, CT and London, 1984).

I Documenti Diplomatici Italiani, Series 8: *1935–1939,* vol. 5 (Rome, 1994).

Documents on British Foreign Policy, Series 2: *1929–1938* (London, 1947–1984), Series 3: *1938/39* (London, 1949–1955).

Dokumentationsarchiv des österreichischen Widerstandes (ed.), *'Anschluß' 1938. Eine Dokumentation*, compiled by Heinz Arnberger et al. (Vienna, 1988).

Dokumente der deutschen Politik und Geschichte von 1848 bis zur Gegenwart. Ein Quellenwerk für die politische Bildung und staatsbürgerliche Erziehung, ed. Johannes Hohlfeld, 9 vols (Berlin, 1951–1956).

Dokumente über die Verfolgung der jüdischen Bürger in Baden-Württemberg durch das Nationalsozialistische Regime 1933–1945 ed. Paul Sauer for the Stuttgart Archives, 2 vols (Stuttgart, 1966).

Dokumente zur Kirchenpolitik des Dritten Reiches, 5 vols, eds Gertraud Grünzinger (vol. 3 onwards) and Carsten Nicolaisen (Gütersloh and Munich, 1971–2008).

Dollmann, Eugen, *Dolmetscher der Diktatoren* (Bayreuth, 1963).

Eden, Anthony, *Angesichts der Diktatoren. Memoiren 1923–1938* (Cologne and Berlin, 1964).

Engel, Gerhard, *Heeresadjutant bei Hitler 1938–1943. Aufzeichnungen des Majors Engel*, ed. Hildegard von Kotze (Stuttgart, 1974).

'Es spricht der Führer'. 7 exemplarische Hitler-Reden ed. and with notes by Hildegard von Kotze, Helmut Krausnick, and F. A. Krummacher (Gütersloh, 1966).

Falter, Jürgen, Thomas Lindenberger, and Siegfried Schumann, *Wahlen und Abstimmungen in der Weimarer Republik. Materialien zum Wahlverhalten 1919–1933* (Munich, 1986).

Feuersenger, Marianne, *Mein Kriegstagebuch. Zwischen Führerhauptquartier und Berliner Wirklichkeit* with a preface by Kurt Sontheimer (Freiburg i. Br., Basel, and Vienna, 1982).

Frank, Hans, *Im Angesicht des Galgens. Deutung Hitlers und seiner Zeit auf Grund eigener Erlebnisse und Erkenntnisse. Geschrieben im Nürnberger Justizgefängnis* (Munich-Gräfelfing, 1953).

Frauenfeld, Alfred, *Und trage keine Reu'. Vom Wiener Gauleiter zum Generalkommissar der Krim. Erinnerungen und Aufzeichnungen* (Leoni am Starnberger See, 1978).

'Führer-Erlasse' 1939–1945. Edition sämtlicher überlieferter, nicht im Reichsgesetzblatt abgedruckter, von Hitler während des Zweiten Weltkrieges schriftlich erteilter Direktiven aus den Bereichen Staat, Partei, Wirtschaft, Besatzungspolitik und Militärverwaltung, compiled and with an introduction by Martin Moll (Stuttgart, 1997).

Galland, Adolf, *Die Ersten und die Letzten. Die Jagdflieger im Zweiten Weltkrieg* (Darmstadt, 1953).

Gersdorff, Rudolf-Christoph von, *Soldat im Untergang* (Frankfurt a. M., Berlin, and Vienna, 1979).

Giesler, Hermann, *Ein anderer Hitler. Bericht seines Architekten Hermann Giesler. Erlebnisse, Gespräche, Reflexionen* (Leoni am Starnberger See, 1977).

Goerdeler, Carl Friedrich, *Politische Schriften und Briefe Carl Friedrich Goerdelers*, eds Sabine Gillmann und Hans Mommsen, vol. 1 (Munich, 2003).

Groscurth, Helmuth, *Tagebücher eines Abwehroffiziers 1938–1940. Mit weiteren Dokumenten zur Militäropposition gegen Hitler*, eds, Helmut Krausnick, Harold C. Deutsch, and Hildegard von Kotze (Stuttgart, 1970).

Gruchmann, Lothar, 'Hitlers Denkschrift an die bayerische Justiz vom 16. Mai 1923. Ein verloren geglaubtes Dokument', in *VfZ* 39 (1991), 305–38.

Guderian, Heinz, *Erinnerungen eines Soldaten* (Stuttgart, 1996).

Haase, Günther, *Die Kunstsammlung Adolf Hitler. Eine Dokumentation* (Berlin, 2002).

Hagen, 'Bericht über meine Tätigkeit als Verbindungsoffizier des Wachbataillons "Großdeutschland" zum Reichsministerium für Volksaufklärung und Propaganda am 20. Juli 1944', in Hans-Adolf Jacobsen (ed.), *'Spiegelbild einer Verschwörung'. Die Opposition gegen Hitler und der Staatsstreich vom 20. Juli 1944 in der SD-Berichterstattung. Geheime Dokumente aus dem ehemaligen Reichssicherheitshauptamt*, 2 vols (Stuttgart, 1984), 12–15.

Halder, Franz, *Hitler als Feldherr* (Munich, 1949).

Halder, Franz, *Kriegstagebuch. Tägliche Aufzeichnungen des Chefs des Generalstabes des Heeres 1939–1942*, ed. Hans-Adolf Jacobsen with Alfred Philippi, 3 vols (Stuttgart, 1962–1964).

Hanfstaengl, Ernst, *Zwischen Weißem und Braunem Haus. Memoiren eines politischen Außenseiters* (Munich, 1970).

Hartlaub, Felix, *Im Sperrkreis. Aufzeichnungen aus dem Zweiten Weltkrieg*, ed. Geno Hartlaub (Frankfurt a. M., 1984).

Hassell, Ulrich von, *Die Hassell-Tagebücher 1938–1944. Aufzeichnungen vom Andern Deutschland*, revised and extended edn based on the manuscript by Friedrich Freiherr Hiller von Gaertringen (Berlin, 1994).

Heiber, Helmut (ed.), *Hitlers Lagebesprechungen. Die Protokollfragmente seiner militärischen Konferenzen 1942–1945* (Stuttgart, 1962).

Heiber, Helmut (ed.), *Goebbels Reden 1932–1945*, authorized edn (Bindlach, 1991).

Helfferich, Emil, *1932–1946. Tatsachen. Ein Beitrag zur Wahrheitsfindung* (Jever, 1969).

Hess, Rudolf, *Briefe 1908–1933*, ed. Wolf Rüdiger Heß (Munich, 1987).

Heusinger, Adolf, *Befehl im Widerstreit. Schicksalsstunden der deutschen Armee 1923–1945* (Tübingen and Stuttgart, 1950).

Hilger, Gustav, *Wir und der Kreml. Deutsch-sowjetische Beziehungen 1918–1941. Erinnerungen eines deutschen Diplomaten* (Frankfurt a. M. and Berlin, 1955).

Hill, Leonidas E. (ed.), *Die Weizsäcker-Papiere*, Part 2: *1933–1950* (Berlin, 1974).

Hillgruber, Andreas (ed.), *Staatsmänner und Diplomaten bei Hitler. Vertrauliche Aufzeichnungen über Unterredungen mit Vertretern des Auslandes*, 2 vols (Frankfurt a. M., 1967/1970).

Hillgruber, Andreas, 'Japan und der Fall "Barbarossa". Japanische Dokumente zu den Gesprächen Hitlers und Ribbentrops mit Botschafter Oshima vom Februar bis Juni 1941', in Hillgruber, *Deutsche Großmacht- und Weltpolitik* (Düsseldorf, 1977), 223–52.

Himmler, Heinrich, *Geheimreden 1933 bis 1945 und andere Ansprachen*, ed. Bradley F. Smith and Agnes Peterson (Frankfurt a. M., 1974).

Hitler, Adolf, *Reden und Proklamationen 1932–1945. Kommentiert von einem deutschen Zeitgenossen*, 2 vols, ed. Max Domarus (Neustadt a. d. Aisch, 1963).

Hitler, Adolf, *Monologe im Führerhauptquartier 1941–1944*, recorded by Heinrich Heim, ed. and with a commentary by Werner Jochmann (Hamburg, 1980).

Hitler, Adolf, *Reden, Schriften, Anordnungen: Februar 1925 bis Januar 1933*, ed. by the Institut für Zeitgeschichte, 17 vols (Munich, 1992–2003).

Das Hitler-Bild. Die Erinnerungen des Fotografen Heinrich Hoffmann, recorded by and published from the private papers of Joe J. Heydecker (St. Pölten, 2008).

Der Hitler-Prozeß 1924. Wortlaut der Hauptverhandlung vor dem Volksgericht München I, ed. with a commentary by Lothar Gruchmann, Reinhard Weber, and Otto Gritschneder, 4 vols (Munich, 1997–1999).

'Hitlers Brief an Reichenau vom 4. Dezember 1932', ed. Thilo Vogelsang, in *VfZ* 7 (1959), 429–437.

Der Hochverratsprozess gegen Dr. Guido Schmidt vor dem Wiener Volksgericht. Die gerichtlichen Protokolle, mit den Zeugenaussagen, unveröffentlichten Dokumenten, sämtlichen Geheimbriefen und Geheimakten (Vienna, 1947).

Hofer, Walther, *Der Nationalsozialismus – Dokumente 1933 bis 1945* (Frankfurt a. M., 1957).

Hofer et al., *Der Reichstagsbrand – Eine wissenschaftliche Dokumentation* (Freiburg i. Br., 1992).

Hoffmann, Heinrich, *Hitler, wie ich ihn sah. Aufzeichnungen seines Leibphotographen* (Munich, 1974).

Horthy, Nikolaus von, *Ein Leben für Ungarn* (Bonn, 1953).

Höss, Rudolf, *Kommandant in Auschwitz. Autobiographische Aufzeichnungen* (Stuttgart, 1958).

Hossbach, Friedrich, *Zwischen Wehrmacht und Hitler 1934–1938*, 2nd edn (Göttingen 1965).

Hubatsch, Walther, *Hindenburg und der Staat. Aus den Papieren des Generalfeldmarschalls und Reichspräsidenten von 1878 bis 1934* (Göttingen, 1966).

Hubatsch, Walther, (ed.), *Hitlers Weisungen für die Kriegsführung 1939–1945*, 2nd edn (Coblenz, 1983).

International Military Tribunal: Der Prozess gegen die Hauptkriegsverbrecher vor dem Internationalen Militärgerichtshof, 14. Oktober 1945 bis 1. Oktober 1946, 42 vols (Nuremberg, 1947–1949).

Jacobsen, Hans-Adolf (ed.), *Dokumente zur Vorgeschichte des Westfeldzuges 1939–1940* (Göttingen, Berlin, and Frankfurt a. M., 1956).

Jacobsen, Hans-Adolf, *1939–1945. Der Zweite Weltkrieg in Chronik und Dokumenten, Percy Ernst Schramm zum 65. Geburtstag*, 5th edn (Darmstadt, 1961).

Jacobsen, Hans-Adolf (ed.), *'Spiegelbild einer Verschwörung'. Die Opposition gegen Hitler und der Staatsstreich vom 20. Juli 1944 in der SD-Berichterstattung. Geheime Dokumente aus dem ehemaligen Reichssicherheitshauptamt*, 2 vols (Stuttgart, 1984).

Jacobsen, Hans-Adolf and Werner Jochmann (eds), *Ausgewählte Dokumente zur Geschichte des Nationalsozialismus 1933–1945*, 3 vols (Bielefeld, 1961–1966).

Jochmann, Werner, *Nationalsozialismus und Revolution. Ursprung und Geschichte der NSDAP in Hamburg 1922–1933. Dokumente* (Frankfurt a. M., 1963).

Das Kabinett von Papen (1932). Akten der Reichskanzlei ed. Karl-Heinz Minuth, 2 vols (Munich, 1989).

Das Kabinett von Schleicher 1932/3. Akten der Reichskanzlei, ed. Anton Golecki (Munich, 1986).

Die Kabinette Brüning I und II. Akten der Reichskanzlei, 3 vols, ed. Tilman Koops (Boppard am Rhein, 1982–1990).

Kehrl, Hans, *Krisenmanager im Dritten Reich. 6 Jahre Frieden, 6 Jahre Krieg. Erinnerungen* (Düsseldorf, 1973).

Keitel, Wilhelm, *Mein Leben: Pflichterfüllung bis zum Untergang. Hitlers Generalfeldmarschall und Chef des Oberkommandos der Wehrmacht in Selbstzeugnissen*, ed. Werner Maser (Berlin, 1998).

Kerekes, Lajos (ed.), *Allianz Hitler–Horthy–Mussolini. Dokumente zur ungarischen Außenpolitik* (Budapest, 1966).

Kirchliches Jahrbuch für die Evangelische Kirche in Deutschland 1933–1944, founded by Johannes Schneider, ed. Joachim Beckmann (Gütersloh, 1948).

Klarsfeld, Serge (ed.), *Die Endlösung der Judenfrage in Frankreich. Deutsche Dokumente 1941–1944* (Paris, 1977).

Kleist-Schmenzin, Ewald von, 'Die letzte Möglichkeit', in *Politische Studien* 10 (1959), 89–92.

Koeppen, Werner, *Herbst 1941 im 'Führerhauptquartier'. Berichte Werner Koeppens an seinen Minister Alfred Rosenberg*, ed. with a commentary by Martin Vogt (Coblenz, 2002).

Kohl, Paul (ed.), *Das Vernichtungslager Trostenez. Augenzeugenberichte und Dokumente* (Dortmund, 2003).

Koller, Karl, *Der letzte Monat, 14. April bis 27. Mai 1945. Tagebuchaufzeichnung des ehemaligen Chefs des Generalstabs der deutschen Luftwaffe. Mit dem Urteil der Spruchkammer im Entnazifizierungsverfahren* (Munich, 1985).

Kordt, Erich, *Wahn und Wirklichkeit*, ed. Karl Heinz Abshagen (Stuttgart, 1947).

Král, Václav (ed.), *Die Deutschen in der Tschechoslowakei. Dokumentensammlung* (Prague, 1964).

Krause, Karl Wilhelm, *Zehn Jahre [Tag und Nacht] Kammerdiener bei Hitler* (Hamburg, [1949]).

Krebs, Albert, *Tendenzen und Gestalten der NSDAP. Erinnerungen an die Frühzeit der Partei* (Stuttgart, 1959).

Das Kriegstagebuch der Seekriegsleitung, Teil A, eds. Werner Rahm and Gerhard Schreiber, 78 vols (Herford, 1988–1997).

Kriegstagebuch des Oberkommandos der Wehrmacht (Wehrmachtführungsstab), ed. Percy Ernst Schramm, 4 vols (Frankfurt a. M., 1961–1965).

Krogmann, Carl Vincent, *Es ging um Deutschlands Zukunft: 1932–1939. Erlebtes diktiert von dem früheren Regierenden Bürgermeister von Hamburg* (Leoni am Starnberger See, 1976).

Kropat, Wolf-Arno, *Kristallnacht in Hessen. Der Judenpogrom vom November 1938. Eine Dokumentation* (Wiesbaden, 1988).

Kübel, Johannes, *Erinnerungen. Mensch und Christ, Theologe, Pfarrer und Kirchenmann, zum 100. Geburtstag*, ed. Martha Frommer (Villingen-Schwenningen, 1972).

Kubizek, August, *Adolf Hitler, mein Jugendfreund* (Graz, 1995).

Kulka, Otto Dov and Eberhard Jäckel (eds), *Die Juden in den geheimen NS-Stimmungsberichten 1933–1945* (Düsseldorf, 2004).

Kursell, Otto von, *Erinnerungen an Dr. Max von Scheubner-Richter*, ed. Henrik Fischer (Munich, 1969).

Lagevorträge des Oberbefehlshabers der Kriegsmarine vor Hitler 1939–1945, ed. Gerhard Wagner (Munich, 1972).

Leeb, Wilhelm von, *Tagebuchaufzeichnungen und Lagebeurteilungen aus zwei Weltkriegen*, ed. from his private papers and with a short account of his life by Georg Meyer (Stuttgart, 1976).

Lévai, Jenő (ed.), *Eichmann in Ungarn. Dokumente* (Budapest, 1961).

Linge, Heinz, *Bis zum Untergang. Als Chef des persönlichen Dienstes bei Hitler*, ed. Werner Maser (Munich, 1982).

Lipski, Józef, *Diplomat in Berlin, 1933–1939. Papers and Memoirs of Józef Lipski, Ambassador of Poland* (New York and London, 1968).

Löffler, Peter (ed.), *Bischof Clement August Graf von Galen. Akten, Briefe und Predigten 1933–1946*, vol. 2 (Mainz, 1988).

Lösener, Bernhard, 'Als Rassereferent im Reichsministerium des Innern', ed. by Walter Strauss, in *VfZ* 9 (1961), 262–313.

Luther, Hans, *Vor dem Abgrund: 1930–1933. Reichsbankpräsident in Krisenzeiten*, with an introduction by Edgar Salin (Berlin, 1964).

Manstein, Erich von, *Verlorene Siege* (Bonn, 1955).

Marckhgott, Gerhart, '"…Von der Hohlheit des gemächlichen Lebens". Neues Material über die Familie Hitler in Linz', in *Jahrbuch des Oberösterreichischen Muselvereins* 138/1 (Linz, 1993), 267–77.

Maser, Werner (ed.), *Paul Devrient: mein Schüler Adolf Hitler. Das Tagebuch seines Lehrers* (Munich, 2003).

Mason, Timothy W., *Arbeiterklasse und Volksgemeinschaft. Dokumente und Materialien zur deutschen Arbeiterpolitik 1936–1939* (Opladen, 1975).

Medizin ohne Menschlichkeit. Dokumente des Nürnberger Ärzteprozesses, ed. and with a commentary by Alexander Mitscherlich and Fred Mielke (Frankfurt a. M., 1960).

Mehner, Kurt (ed.), *Die geheimen Tagesberichte der Deutschen Wehrmachtführung im Zweiten Weltkrieg 1939–1945. Die gegenseitige Lageunterrichtung der Wehrmacht-, Heeres- und Luftwaffenführung über alle Haupt- und Nebenkriegsschauplätze: 'Lage*

West' (OKW-Kriegsschauplätze Nord, West, Italien, Balkan), 'Lage Ost' (OKH) und 'Luftlage Reich', 12 vols (Osnabrück, 1984–1995).

Meissner, Otto, *Staatssekretär unter Ebert, Hindenburg, Hitler. Der Schicksalsweg des deutschen Volkes von 1918 bis 1945, wie ich ihn erlebte* (Hamburg, 1950).

Meldungen aus dem Reich 1938–1945. Die geheimen Lageberichte des Sicherheitsdienstes der SS, ed. and with an introduction by Heinz Boberach, 17 vols (Herrsching, 1984).

Morsey, Rudolf (ed.), *Die Protokolle der Reichstagsfraktion und des Fraktionsvorstands der deutschen Zentrumspartei 1926–1933* (Mainz, 1969).

Morsey, Rudolf (ed.), *Fritz Gerlich – ein Publizist gegen Hitler. Briefe und Akten 1930–1934* (Paderborn, 2010).

Müller, Karl Alexander von, *Mars und Venus. Erinnerungen 1914–1919* (Munich, 1954).

Müller, Karl Alexander von, *Im Wandel einer Welt. Erinnerungen*, vol. 3, ed. Otto Alexander Müller (Munich, 1966).

Müller, Klaus-Jürgen, 'Reichswehr und "Röhm-Affäre". Aus den Akten des Wehrkreiskommandos (Bayer.) VII [Dokumentation]', in *MGM* 1 (1968), 107–44.

Nadolny, Rudolf, *Mein Beitrag. Erinnerungen eines Botschafters des Deutschen Reiches*, ed. Günter Wollstein (Cologne, 1985).

NS-Presseanweisungen der Vorkriegszeit. Edition und Dokumentation, ed. Hans Bohrmann and Gabriele Toepser-Ziegert, 7 vols (Munich, 1984–2001).

Official Documents Concerning Polish-German and Polish Soviet Relations 1933–1939 (New York, no date).

Die Okkupationspolitik des deutschen Faschismus in Dänemark und Norwegen (1940–1945), documents selected and introduced by Fritz Petrick (Berlin and Heidelberg, 1992).

Oven, Wilfred von, *Mit Goebbels bis zum Ende*, 2 vols (Buenos Aires, 1949/50).

Papen, Franz von, *Der Wahrheit eine Gasse* (Innsbruck, 1952).

Petzold, Joachim, 'Wirtschaftsbesprechungen der NSDAP in den Jahren 1930 und 1931', in *Jahrbuch für Wirtschaftsgeschichte* (1982), 189–223.

Picker, Henry, *Hitlers Tischgespräche im Führerhauptquartier. Entstehung, Struktur und Folgen des Nationalsozialismus* (Berlin, 1997).

Politik und Wirtschaft in der Krise, 1930–1932. Quellen zur Ära Brüning, ed. by Ilse Maurer and Udo Wengst, 2 parts (Düsseldorf, 1980).

Pünder, Hermann, *Politik in der Reichskanzlei. Aufzeichnungen aus den Jahren 1929–1932*, ed. Thilo Vogelsang (Stuttgart, 1961).

Quellen zur Reform des Straf- und Strafprozessrechts, 2. Abt.: NS-Zeit (1933–1939) – Strafgesetzbuch, vol. 2, eds Jürgen Regge and Werner Schubert (Berlin, 1994).

Rautenberg, Hans-Jürgen, 'Drei Dokumente zur Planung eines 300,000 Mann-Friedensheeres aus dem Dezember 1933', in *MGM* 22 (1977), 103–39.

Reck-Malleczewen, Friedrich Percyval, *Tagebuch eines Verzweifelten*, new edn (Stuttgart, 1966).

Regierung Hitler 1933–1945. Akten der Reichskanzlei, ed. Friedrich Hartmannsgruber, 7 vols (Berlin and Munich, 1983–2015).

Remer, Otto Ernst, 'Der Ablauf der Ereignisse am 20. 7. 1944, wie ich sie als Kommandeur des Wachbataillons Großdeutschland erlebte' in Hans-Adolf Jacobsen (ed.), *'Spiegelbild einer Verschwörung'. Die Opposition gegen Hitler und der Staatsstreich vom 20. Juli 1944 in der SD-Berichterstattung. Geheime Dokumente aus dem ehemaligen Reichssicherheitshauptamt*, 2 vols (Stuttgart 1984), 633–45.

Ribbentrop, Joachim von, *Zwischen London und Moskau. Erinnerungen und letzte Aufzeichnungen*, ed. by Annelies von Ribbentrop from private papers (Leoni am Starnberger See, 1953).

Ritter, Ernst (ed.), *Reichskommissar für Überwachung der Öffentlichen Ordnung und Nachrichtensammelstelle im Reichsministerium des Innern. Lageberichte (1920–1929) und Meldungen (1929–1933)*, microfiche, 1979.

Rommel, Erwin, *Krieg ohne Hass [Afrikanische Memoiren]*, eds Lucie-Marie Rommel and Fritz Bayerlein (Heidenheim and Brenz, 1950).

Rosenberg, Alfred, *Letzte Aufzeichnungen. Ideale und Idole der nationalsozialistischen Revolution* (Göttingen, 1955).

Rosenberg, Alfred, *Das politische Tagebuch Alfred Rosenbergs aus den Jahren 1934/1935 und 1939/1940*, ed. and with notes by Hans-Günther Seraphim on the basis of a photographic reproduction of the MS from the Nuremberg files (Göttingen, 1956).

Rosenberg, Alfred, *Die Tagebücher von 1934 bis 1944*, ed. and with a commentary by Jürgen Matthäus and Frank Bajohr (Frankfurt a. M., 2015).

Röver, Carl, *Der Bericht des Reichsstatthalters von Oldenburg und Bremen und Gauleiters des Gaues Weser-Ems über die Lage der NSDAP aus dem Jahre 1942*, ed. with an introduction by Michael Rademacher (Vechta, 2000).

Rürup, Reinhard (ed.), *Der Krieg gegen die Sowjetunion 1941–1945. Eine Dokumentation* (Berlin, 1991).

Rürup, Reinhard (ed.), *1936. Die Olympischen Spiele und der Nationalsozialismus. Eine Dokumentation* (Berlin, 1996).

Sänger, Fritz, *Politik der Täuschungen. Missbrauch der Presse im Dritten Reich. Weisungen, Informationen, Notizen, 1933–1939* (Vienna, 1975).

Schlabrendorff, Fabian von, *Offiziere gegen Hitler*, new, revised, and extended edn. by Walter Bussmann based on the edn by Gero von Gaevernitz (Berlin, 1994).

Schlemmer, Thomas (ed.), *Die Italiener an der Ostfront 1942/43. Dokumente zu Mussolinis Krieg gegen die Sowjetunion* (Munich, 2005).

Schmidt, Paul, *Statist auf diplomatischer Bühne 1923–45. Erlebnisse des Chefdolmetschers im Auswärtigen Amt mit den Staatsmännern Europas* (Bonn, 1949).

Schmidt-Hannover, Otto, *Umdenken oder Anarchie. Männer – Schicksale – Lehren* (Göttingen, 1959).

Schmundt, Rudolf, *Tätigkeitsbericht des Chefs des Heerespersonalamtes General der Infanterie Rudolf Schmundt*, continued by Wilhelm Burgdorf, eds Dermot Bradley and Richard Schulze-Kossens (Osnabrück, 1984).

Schroeder, Christa, *Er war mein Chef. Aus dem Nachlaß der Sekretärin von Adolf Hitler*, ed. Anton Joachimsthaler (Munich, 1985).

Schuschnigg, Kurt, *Im Kampf gegen Hitler. Die Überwindung der Anschlußidee* (Munich and Vienna, 1969).

Schwarz, Birgit, *Hitlers Museum. Die Fotoalben Gemäldegalerie Linz. Dokumente zum 'Führermuseum'* (Vienna, Cologne, and Weimar, 2002).

Speer, Albert, *Erinnerungen* (Berlin, 1969).

Speer, Albert, *Spandauer Tagebücher* (Berlin, 1975).

Speer, Albert, *Der Sklavenstaat. Meine Auseinandersetzungen mit der SS* (Stuttgart, 1981).

Staatliche Akten über die Reichskonkordatsverhandlungen 1933, ed. Alfons Kupper (Mainz, 1969).

Stampfer, Friedrich, *Erfahrungen und Erkenntnisse. Aufzeichnungen aus meinem Leben* (Cologne, 1957).

Strasser, Otto, *Mein Kampf. [Eine politische Autobiographie]*, with a foreword by Gerhard Zwerenz (Frankfurt a. M., 1969).

Die Tagebücher von Joseph Goebbels, 2 parts, 9 und 15 vols, ed. by Elke Fröhlich et al. for the Institut für Zeitgeschichte and with support from the Russian State Archives (Munich, 1993–2006).

Thomas, Georg, *Geschichte der deutschen Wehr- und Rüstungswirtschaft [1918–1943/1945]*, ed. Wolfgang Birkenfeld (Boppard am Rhein, 1966).

Timpke, Henning (ed.), *Dokumente zur Gleichschaltung des Landes Hamburg 1933* (Frankfurt a. M., 1964).

Treue, Wilhelm, 'Hitlers Denkschrift zum Vierjahresplan 1936', in *VfZ* 3 (1955), 184–210.

The Trial of Adolf Eichmann. Record of Proceedings in the District Court of Jerusalem, 9 vols (Jerusalem, 1992–1995).

Trials of War Criminals before the Nuernberg Military Tribunals under Control Council Law No. 10, Nuernberg October 1946–April 1949, 15 vols (Washington, 1949–1953).

Tschirschky, Fritz Günther von, *Erinnerungen eines Hochverräters* (Stuttgart, 1972).

Tyrell, Albrecht (ed.), *Führer befiehl . . . Selbstzeugnisse aus der »Kampfzeit« der NSDAP. Dokumentation und Analyse* (Düsseldorf, 1969).

Unsere Ehre heißt Treue. Kriegstagebuch des Kommandostabes Reichsführer SS: Tätigkeitsberichte der 1. und 2. SS-Inf. Brigade, der 1. SS-Kavallerie-Brigade und von Sonderkommandos der SS, ed. Fritz Baade (Vienna, 1965).

Ursachen und Folgen. Vom deutschen Zusammenbruch 1918 und 1945 bis zur staatlichen Neuordnung Deutschlands in der Gegenwart. Eine Urkunden- und Dokumentensammlung zur Zeitgeschichte eds, Herbert Michaelis and Ernst Schraepler, 27 vols (Berlin, 1958–1979).

Die Verfolgung und Ermordung der europäischen Juden durch das nationalsozialistische Deutschland 1933–1945 vol. 4, ed. Klaus-Peter Friedrich (Munich, 2011).

Vogelsang, Thilo, 'Neue Dokumente zur Geschichte der Reichswehr 1930–1933', in *VfZ* 2 (1954), 397–436.

Wagener, Otto, *Hitler aus nächster Nähe. Aufzeichnungen eines Vertrauten 1929–1932*, ed. Henry Ashby Turner (Frankfurt a. M., 1978).

Wagenführ, Rolf, *Die deutsche Industrie im Kriege 1939–1945* (Berlin, 1963).

Wagner, Eduard, *Der Generalquartiermeister. Briefe und Tagebuchaufzeichnungen des Generalquartiermeisters des Heeres, General der Artillerie Eduard Wagner*, ed. Elisabeth Wagner (Munich and Vienna, 1963).

Walk, Joseph (ed.), *Das Sonderrecht für die Juden im NS-Staat. Eine Sammlung der gesetzlichen Maßnahmen und Richtlinien* (Heidelberg, 1996).

Warlimont, Walter, *Im Hauptquartier der deutschen Wehrmacht, 1939–1945. Grundlagen, Formen, Gestalten* (Augsburg, 1990).

Die Wehrmachtberichte 1939–1945, 3 vols (Munich, 1985).

Weiss, Hermann and Paul Hoser eds, *Reinhold G. Quaatz. Die Deutschnationalen und die Zerstörung der Weimarer Republik. Aus dem Tagebuch von Reinhold Quaatz* (Munich, 1989).

Weizsäcker, Ernst von, *Erinnerungen*, ed. Richard von Weizsäcker (Munich, 1950).

Welles, Sumner, *The Time for Decision* (New York, 1944).

Wiedemann, Fritz, *Der Mann, der Feldherr werden wollte. Erlebnisse und Erfahrungen des Vorgesetzten Hitlers im 1. Weltkrieg und seines späteren Persönlichen Adjutanten* (Velbert and Kettwig, 1964).

Winzer, Otto, *Zwölf Jahre Kampf gegen Faschismus und Krieg. Ein Beitrag zur Geschichte der Kommunistischen Partei Deutschlands 1933 bis 1945* (Berlin, 1955).

Wirsching, Andreas, '"Man kann nur Boden germanisieren". Eine neue Quelle zu Hitlers Rede vor den Spitzen der Reichswehr am 3. Februar 1933', in *VfZ* 49 (2001), 517–51.

Wulf, Joseph, *Musik im Dritten Reich. Eine Dokumentation* (Gütersloh, 1963).

POST-1945 SECONDARY LITERATURE

Abel, Karl-Dietrich, *Presselenkung im NS-Staat. Eine Studie zur Geschichte der Publizistik in der nationalsozialistischen Zeit* (Berlin, 1968).

Abendroth, Hans-Henning, *Hitler in der spanischen Arena. Die deutsch-spanischen Beziehungen im Spannungsfeld der europäischen Interessenpolitik vom Ausbruch des Bürgerkrieges bis zum Ausbruch des Weltkrieges 1919–1939* (Paderborn, 1973).

Adam, Uwe Dietrich, *Judenpolitik im Dritten Reich* (Düsseldorf, 1972).

Adler, H. G., *Theresienstadt 1941–1945. Das Antlitz einer Zwangsgemeinschaft. Geschichte, Soziologie, Psychologie*, 2nd revised and expanded edn (Tübingen, 1960).

Adler, H. G., *Der verwaltete Mensch. Studien zur Deportation der Juden aus Deutschland* (Tübingen, 1974).

Ahlheim, Hannah, *Deutsche, kauft nicht bei Juden! Antisemitismus und politischer Boykott in Deutschland 1924 bis 1935* (Göttingen, 2011).

Alberti, Michael, *Die Verfolgung und Vernichtung der Juden im Reichsgau Wartheland 1939–1945* (Wiesbaden, 2006).

Albrecht, Gerd, *Nationalsozialistische Filmpolitik. Eine soziologische Untersuchung über die Spielfilme des Dritten Reiches* (Stuttgart, 1969).

Albrecht, Joachim, *Die Avantgarde des 'Dritten Reiches'. Die Coburger NSDAP während der Weimarer Republik 1922–1933* (Frankfurt a. M., 2005).

Albrecht, Kai-Britt, 'Renn, Ludwig', in *Neue Deutsche Biographie* 21 (2003), 426–7.

Allen, William Sheridan, *'Das haben wir nicht gewollt!'. Die nationalsozialistische Machtergreifung in einer Kleinstadt 1930–1935* (Gütersloh, 1966).

Aly, Götz, *'Endlösung'. Völkerverschiebung und der Mord an den europäischen Juden* (Frankfurt a. M., 1995).

Aly, Götz, *Die Belasteten. 'Euthanasie' 1939–1945. Eine Gesellschaftsgeschichte* (Frankfurt a. M., 2013).

Aly, Götz and Susanne Heim, 'Staatliche Ordnung und organische Lösung. Die Rede Hermann Görings "über die Judenfrage" vom 6. Dezember 1938', in *Jahrbuch für Antisemitismusforschung* 2 (1993), 378–414.

Angrick, Andrej and Peter Klein, *Die 'Endlösung' in Riga. Ausbeutung und Vernichtung 1941–1944* (Darmstadt, 2006).

Anschluß 1938. Protokoll des Symposiums in Wien am 14. und 15. März 1978 (Vienna, 1981).

Arad, Yitzhak, *Belzec, Sobibor, Treblinka. The Operation Reinhard Death Camps* (Bloomington and Indianapolis, Ind., 1987).

Arad, Yitzhak, *The Holocaust in the Soviet Union* (Lincoln, NE, 2009).

Armbruster, Jan, 'Die Behandlung Adolf Hitlers im Lazarett Pasewalk 1918. Historische Mythenbildung durch einseitige bzw. spekulative Pathographie', in *Journal für Neurologie, Neurochirurgie und Psychiatrie* 10/4 (2009), 18–23.

Auerbach, Hellmuth, 'Volksstimmung und veröffentlichte Meinung in Deutschland zwischen März und November 1938', in Franz Knipping und Klaus-Jürgen Müller (eds), *Machtbewußtsein in Deutschland am Vorabend des Zweiten Weltkrieges* (Paderborn, 1984), 273–95.

Ay, Karl-Ludwig, 'Von der Räterepublik zur Ordnungszelle Bayern. Die politischen Rahmenbedingungen für den Aufstieg Hitlers in München', in Björn Mensing and Friedrich Prinz (eds), *Irrlicht im leuchtenden München? Der Nationalsozialismus in der 'Hauptstadt der Bewegung'* (Regensburg, 1991), 9–26.

Ayass, Wolfgang, '"Ein Gebot der nationalen Arbeitsdisziplin": Die Aktion "Arbeitsscheu Reich" 1938', in Ayaß, *Feindererklärung und Prävention. Kriminalbiologie, Zigeunerforschung und Asozialenpolitik* (Berlin, 1988), 43–74.

Ayass, Wolfgang, *'Asoziale' im Nationalsozialismus* (Stuttgart, 1995).

Bach, Steven, *Leni. The Life and Work of Leni Riefenstahl* (New York, 2007).

Backes, Uwe et al., *Reichstagsbrand – Aufklärung einer historischen Legende* (Munich and Zurich, 1986).

Bahne, Siegfried, 'Die Kommunistische Partei Deutschlands', in Erich Matthias and Rudolf Morsey (eds), *Das Ende der Parteien 1933* (Düsseldorf, 1960), 655–739.

Bajohr, Frank and Michael Wildt, *Volksgemeinschaft. Neue Forschungen zur Gesellschaft des Nationalsozialismus* (Frankfurt a. M., 2009).

Balderston, Theo, *The Origins and Course of the German Economic Crisis, November 1923 to May 1932* (Berlin, 1993).

Balta, Sebastian, *Rumänien und die Großmächte in der Ära Antonescu (1940–1944)* (Stuttgart, 2005).

Banken, Ralf, 'Das nationalsozialistische Devisenrecht als Steuerungs- und Diskriminierungsinstrument 1933–1945', in Johannes Bähr and Ralf Banken (eds), *Wirtschaftssteuerung durch Recht im Nationalsozialismus. Studien zur Entwicklung des Wirtschaftsrechts im Interventionsstaat des 'Dritten Reichs'* (Frankfurt a. M., 2006), 121–236.

Bankier, David, *Die öffentliche Meinung im Hitler-Staat. Die 'Endlösung' und die Deutschen. Eine Berichtigung* (Berlin, 1995).

Banuls, André, 'Das völkische Blatt *Der Scherer*. Ein Beitrag zu Hitlers Schulzeit', in *VfZ* 18 (1970), 196–203.

Baranowski, Shelley, *Strength through Joy: Consumerism and Mass Tourism in the Third Reich* (Cambridge, 2004).

Barbian, Jan-Pieter, *Literaturpolitik im 'Dritten Reich'. Institutionen, Kompetenzen, Betätigungsfelder* (Frankfurt a. M., 1993).

Barkai, Avraham, *Das Wirtschaftssystem des Nationalsozialismus. Der historische und ideologische Hintergrund, 1933–1936* (Cologne, 1977).

Barkai, Avraham, *Vom Boykott zur 'Entjudung'. Der wirtschaftliche Existenzkampf der Juden im Dritten Reich 1933–1943* (Frankfurt a. M., 1988).

Bartetzko, Dieter, *Illusionen in Stein. Stimmungsarchitektur im Nationalsozialismus*, revised and expanded authorized edn (Berlin, 2012).

Barth, Boris, *Dolchstoßlegenden und politische Desintegration. Das Trauma der deutschen Niederlage im Ersten Weltkrieg 1914–1933* (Düsseldorf, 2003).

Barth, Christian T., *Goebbels und die Juden* (Paderborn, 2003).

Barthel, Rolf, 'Rüstungswirtschaftliche Forderungen der Reichswehrführung im Juni 1934', in *Zeitschrift für Militärgeschichte* 9 (1970), 83–92.

Baruch, Nir, *Der Freikauf. Zar Boris und das Schicksal der bulgarischen Juden* (Sofia, 1996).

Baten, Jörg and Andrea Wagner, 'Mangelernährung, Krankheit und Sterblichkeit im NSWirtschaftsaufschwung (1933–1937)', in *Jahrbuch für Wirtschaftsgeschichte* (2003), No. 1, 99–123.

Bauer, Kurt, *Elementar-Ereignis. Die österreichischen Nationalsozialisten und der Juliputsch 1934* (Vienna, 2003).

Baum, Walter, 'Die "Reichsreform" im Dritten Reich', in *VfZ* 3 (1955), 36–56.

Baumgart, Winfried, 'Zur Ansprache Hitlers vor den Führern der Wehrmacht am 22. August 1939. Eine quellenkritische Untersuchung', in *VfZ* 16 (1968), 120–49.

Baumgart, Winfried, 'Zur Ansprache Hitlers vor den Führern der Wehrmacht am 22. August 1939. Erwiderung', in *VfZ* 19 (1971), 301–4.

Baur, Johannes, *Die russische Kolonie in München 1900–1945. Deutsch–russische Beziehungen im 20. Jahrhundert* (Wiesbaden, 1998).

Bavendamm, Dirk, *Der junge Hitler. Korrekturen einer Biographie 1889–1914* (Graz, 2009).

Becker, Franz, 'Schneller, lauter, schöner? Die Olympischen Spiele von 1936 in Berlin als Medienspektakel', in Friedrich Lenger and Ansgar Nünning (eds), *Medienereignisse der Moderne* (Darmstadt, 2008), 95–113.

Beduhn, Ralf, 'Berlin 1936: Olympia im Potemkinschen Dorf', in Jürgen Bellers (ed.), *Die Olympiade Berlin 1936 im Spiegel der ausländischen Presse* (Münster, 1986), 250–66.

Behrenbeck, Sabine, *Der Kult um die toten Helden* (Vierow b. Greifswald, 1996).

Behrens, Beate, *Mit Hitler zur Macht. Aufstieg des Nationalsozialismus in Mecklenburg und Lübeck 1922–1933* (Rostock, 1998).

Bellers, Jürgen (ed.), *Die Olympiade Berlin 1936 im Spiegel der ausländischen Presse* (Münster, 1986).

Benz, Wolfgang, 'Judenvernichtung aus Notwehr? Die Legende um Theodore N. Kaufman', in *VfZ* 29 (1981), 615–30.

Benz, Wolfgang, (ed.), *Dimension des Völkermords. Die Zahl der jüdischen Opfer des Nationalsozialismus* (Munich, 1991).

Benz, Wolfgang, 'Mitglieder der Häftlingsgesellschaft auf Zeit: "Die Aktionsjuden" 1938/39', in *Dachauer Hefte* 21 (2005), 179–96.

Benzenhöfer, Udo, 'Der Fall "Kind Knauer"', in *Deutsches Ärzteblatt* 95 (1998), 954–5.

Benzenhöfer, Udo, 'Brandt, S. Richtigstellung', in *Deutsches Ärzteblatt* 104 (2007), 3232.

Berg, Thomas von, *Korruption und Bereicherung. Politische Biographie des Münchner NSDAP-Fraktionsvorsitzenden Christian Weber (1883–1945)* (Munich, 2003).

Bergbauer, Knut, Sabine Fröhlich, and Stefanie Schüler-Springorum, *Denkmalsfigur. Biographische Annäherung an Hans Litten (1903–1938)* (Göttingen, 2008).

Berghahn, Volker, 'Das Ende des Stahlhelm', in *VfZ* 13 (1965), 446–51.

Berghahn, Volker, *Der Stahlhelm. Bund der Frontsoldaten 1918–1935* (Düsseldorf, 1966).

Berghahn, Volker, 'NSDAP und "geistige Führung" der Wehrmacht 1939–1943', in *VfZ* 17 (1969), 17–72.

Berghoff, Hartmut and Cornelia Rauh-Kühne, *Fritz K. Ein deutsches Leben im zwanzigsten Jahrhundert* (Stuttgart, 2000).

Bernett, Hajo, *Sportpolitik im Dritten Reich. Aus den Akten der Reichskanzlei* (Stuttgart, 1971).

Bernett, Hajo, 'Der deutsche Sport im Jahre 1933', in *Stadion. Internationale Zeitschrift für Geschichte des Sports und der Körperkultur* VII/2 (1981), 225–83.

Bernett, Hajo, *Der Weg des Sports in die nationalsozialistische Diktatur. Die Entstehung des Deutschen (Nationalsozialistischen) Reichsbundes für Leibesübungen* (Schorndorf, 1983).

Bernhardt, Heike, *Anstaltspsychiatrie und 'Euthanasie' in Pommern 1933–1945. Die Krankenmorde an Kindern und Erwachsenen am Beispiel der Landesheilanstalt Ueckermünde* (Frankfurt a. M., 1994).

Besier, Gerhard, *Die Kirchen und das Dritte Reich*, vol. 3 (Berlin, 2001).

Bessel, Richard, 'The Potempa Murder', in *Central European History* 10 (1977), 241–54.

Besson, Waldemar, 'Zur Geschichte des nationalsozialistischen Führungs-Offiziers (NSFO)', in *VfZ* 9 (1961), 76–83.

Bettinger, Dieter and Martin Büren, *Der Westwall. Die Geschichte der deutschen Westbefestigung im Dritten Reich*, 2 vols (Osnabrück, 1990).

Bezymenskij, Lev A., 'Der Berlin-Besuch von V.M. Molotov im November 1940 im Lichte neuer Dokumente aus sowjetischen Geheimarchiven', in *MGM* 57 (1998), 199–215.

Biesemann, Jörg, *Das Ermächtigungsgesetz als Grundlage der Gesetzgebung im national-sozialistischen Staat. Ein Beitrag zur Stellung des Gesetzes in der Verfassungsgeschichte 1919–1945* (Münster, 1985).

Binion, Rudolph, *'...daß ihr mich gefunden habt'. Hitler und die Deutschen. Eine Psychohistorie* (Stuttgart, 1978).

Birkenfeld, Wolfgang, *Der synthetische Treibstoff 1933–1945. Ein Beitrag zur nationalsozi-alistischen Wirtschafts- und Rüstungspolitik* (Göttingen, Berlin, and Frankfurt a. M., 1964).

Blank, Ralf, 'Albert Hoffmann als Reichsverteidigungskommissar im Gau Westfalen-Süd 1943–1945. Eine biografische Skizze', in Wolf Gruner and Armin Nolzen (eds), *'Bürokratien'. Initiative und Effizienz* (Berlin, 2001), 189–210.

Blank, Ralf, '"Battle of the Ruhr". Luftangriffe auf das Ruhrgebiet 1943', in *Westfälische Forschungen* 63 (2013), 319–41.

Blasius, Dirk, *'Einfache Seelenstörung'. Geschichte der deutschen Psychiatrie 1800–1945* (Frankfurt a. M., 1994).

Blasius, Rainer A., *Für Großdeutschland – gegen den großen Krieg. Staatssekretär Ernst Freiherr von Weizsäcker in den Krisen um die Tschechoslowakei und Polen 1938/39* (Cologne and Vienna, 1981).

Bleyer, Wolfgang, 'Pläne der faschistischen Führung zum totalen Krieg im Sommer 1944', in *Zeitschrift für Geschichtswissenschaft* 17 (1969), 1313–29.

Bloch, Michael, *Ribbentrop* (London, 1992).

Boch, Volker, *Die Olympischen Spiele unter Berücksichtigung des jüdischen Sports* (Konstanz, 2002).

Bock, Gisela, *Zwangssterilisation im Nationalsozialismus. Studien zur Rassenpolitik und Frauenpolitik* (Opladen, 1986).

Bodensieck, Heinrich, 'Der Plan eines "Freundschaftsvertrages" zwischen dem Reich und der Tschecho-Slowakei im Jahre 1938', in *Zeitschrift für Ostforschung* 10 (1961), 462–76.

Boelcke, Willi A., 'Goebbels und die Kundgebung im Berliner Sportpalast vom 18. Februar 1943', in *Jahrbuch für die Geschichte Mittel- und Ostdeutschlands* 19 (1970), 234–55.

Boelcke, Willi A., *Die deutsche Wirtschaft 1930–1945. Interna des Reichswirtschaftsmin-isteriums* (Düsseldorf, 1983).

Boelcke, Willi A., *Die Kosten von Hitlers Krieg. Kriegsfinanzierung und finanzielles Kriegserbe in Deutschland 1933–1948* (Paderborn, 1985).

Böhler, Joachim, '"Tragische Verstrickung" oder Auftakt zum Vernichtungkrieg? Die Wehrmacht in Polen 1939', in Klaus-Michael Mallmann and Bogdan Musial (eds), *Genesis des Genozids. Polen 1939–1941* (Darmstadt, 2004), 36–57.

Böhler, Joachim, *Auftakt zum Vernichtungkrieg. Die Wehrmacht in Polen 1939* (Frankfurt a. M., 2006).

Böhm, Herrmann, 'Zur Ansprache Hitlers vor den Führern der Wehrmacht am 22. August 1939', in *VfZ* 19 (1971), 294–300.

Bohn, Robert, *Reichskommissariat Norwegen. »Nationalsozialistische Neuordnung« und Kriegswirtschaft* (Munich, 2000).

Boog, Horst, *Die deutsche Luftwaffenführung 1935–1945. Führungsprobleme, Spitzengliederung, Generalstabsausbildung* (Stuttgart, 1982).

Boog, Horst, 'Der anglo-amerikanische strategische Luftkrieg über Europa und die deutsche Luftverteidigung', in Boog et al., *Der globale Krieg. Die Ausweitung zum Weltkrieg und der Wechsel der Initiative 1941–1943* (Stuttgart, 1990), 429–565.

Boog, Horst, 'Die Luftwaffe', in Boog et al., *Der Angriff auf die Sowjetunion*, updated edn (Frankfurt a. M., 1991), 328–62.

Boog, Horst, 'Strategischer Luftkrieg in Europa und Reichsluftverteidigung 1943–1944', in Boog, Gerhard Krebs, and Detlef Vogel (eds), *Das Deutsche Reich in der Defensive. Strategischer Luftkrieg im Westen und in Ostasien 1943–1944/45* (Stuttgart and Munich. 2011), 1–415.

Borchmeyer, Walter, *Hugenbergs Ringen in deutschen Schicksalsstunden. Tatsachen und Entscheidungen in den Verfahren zu Detmold und Düsseldorf 1949/50* (Detmold, 1951).

Borggräfe, Henning, *Schützenvereine im Nationalsozialismus. Pflege der 'Volksgemeinschaft' und Vorbereitung auf den Krieg (1933–1945)* (Münster, 2010).

Borrmann, Norbert, *Paul Schultze-Naumburg 1869–1949. Maler, Publizist, Architekt. Vom Kulturreformer der Jahrhundertwende zum Kulturpolitiker im Dritten Reich. Ein Lebens- und Zeitdokument* (Essen, 1989).

Bösch, Frank, *Das konservative Milieu. Vereinskultur und lokale Sammlungspolitik in ost- und westdeutschen Regionen (1900–1960)* (Göttingen, 2002).

Bosl, Karl (ed.), *Bayern im Umbruch. Die Revolution von 1918, ihre Voraussetzungen, ihr Verlauf und ihre Folgen* (Munich and Vienna), 1969.

Bosworth, Richard J. B., *Mussolini* (London, 2002).

Botz, Gerhard, 'Hitlers Aufenthalt in Linz im März 1938 und der Anschluß', in *Historisches Jahrbuch der Stadt Linz 1970*, 185–214.

Botz, Gerhard, *Wohnungspolitik und Judendeportation in Wien, 1938 bis 1945. Zur Funktion des Antisemitismus als Ersatz nationalsozialistischer Sozialpolitik* (Vienna and Salzburg, 1975).

Botz, Gerhard, *Die Eingliederung Österreichs in das Deutsche Reich. Planung und Verwirklichung des politisch-administrativen Anschlusses (1938–1940)*, 2nd expanded edn (Vienna, 1976).

Botz, Gerhard, *Nationalsozialismus in Wien. Machtübernahme, Herrschaftssicherung, Radikalisierung 1938/39*, revised and expanded edn (Vienna, 2008).

Bowman, Steven B., *The Agony of Greek Jews, 1040–1945* (Stanford, 2009).

Boyer, John W., *Karl Lueger (1844–1910). Christlichsoziale Politik als Beruf* (Vienna, Cologne, and Weimar, 2010).

Bracher, Karl Dietrich, *Die Auflösung der Weimarer Republik. Eine Studie zum Problem des Machtverfalls in der Demokratie* (Königstein i. Ts., 1978).

Bracher, Karl Dietrich, *Stufen der Machtergreifung* (Frankfurt a. M., 1983).

Braham, Randolph L., *The Politics of Genocide. The Holocaust in Hungary*, 2 vols (New York, 1994).

Brakelmann, Günter, *Der Kreisauer Kreis. Chronologie, Kurzbiographien und Texte aus dem Widerstand* (Münster, 2003).

Brandes, Detlev, *Die Tschechen unter deutschem Protektorat*, vol. 1 (Munich, 1969).

Braubach, Max, *Der Einmarsch deutscher Truppen in die entmilitarisierte Zone am Rhein im März 1936. Ein Beitrag zur Vorgeschichte des Zweiten Weltkrieges* (Cologne, 1956).

Brechenmacher, Thomas (ed.), *Das Reichskonkordat 1933. Forschungsstand, Kontroversen, Dokumente* (Paderborn, 2007).

Brechtken, Magnus, *'Madagaskar für die Juden'. Antisemitische Idee und politische Praxis 1885–1945* (Munich, 1997).

Brenner, Hildegard, *Die Kunstpolitik des Nationalsozialismus* (Reinbek b. Hamburg, 1963).

Brenner, Hildegard, *Ende einer bürgerlichen Kunstinstitution. Die politische Formierung der Preußischen Akademie der Künste 1933* (Stuttgart, 1972).

Broszat, Martin, 'Zur Perversion der Strafjustiz im Dritten Reich', in *VfZ* 6 (1958), 390–443.

Broszat, Martin, *Nationalsozialistische Polenpolitik. 1939–1945* (Stuttgart, 1961).

Broszat, Martin, 'Nationalsozialistische Konzentrationslager 1933–1945', in Hans Buchheim et al., *Anatomie des SS-Staates*, vol. 2 (Olten and Freiburg, 1965), 9–162.

Broszat, Martin, 'Die Reaktion der Mächte auf den 15. März 1938', in *Bohemia* 8 (1967), 253–80.

Broszat, Martin, *Der Staat Hitlers. Grundlegung und Entwicklung seiner inneren Verfassung* (Munich, 1969).

Broszat, Martin, 'Der Zweite Weltkrieg: Ein Krieg der "alten" Eliten, der Nationalsozialisten oder der Krieg Hitlers?', in Broszat and Klaus Schwabe (eds), *Die deutschen Eliten und der Weg in den Zweiten Weltkrieg* (Munich, 1989), 25–71.

Broszat, Martin and Klaus Schwabe (eds), *Die deutschen Eliten und der Weg in den Zweiten Weltkrieg* (Munich, 1989).

Browning, Christopher R., 'Unterstaatssekretär Martin Luther and the Ribbentrop Foreign Office', in *Journal of Contemporary History* 12 (1977), 313–44.

Browning, Christopher R., 'Die nationalsozialistische Umsiedlungspolitik und die Suche nach einer "Lösung der Judenfrage" 1939–1942', in Browning, *Der Weg zur 'Endlösung'. Entscheidungen und Täter* (Bonn, 1998), 13–36.

Browning, Christopher R., *Die Entfesselung der 'Endlösung'. Nationalsozialistische Judenpolitik 1939–1942* (Berlin, 2006).

Browning, Christopher R., *Die 'Endlösung' und das Auswärtige Amt. Das Referat D III der Abteilung Deutschland 1940–1943* (Darmstadt, 2010).

Brucker-Boroujerdi, Ute and Wolfgang Wippermann, 'Das "Zigeunerlager" Marzahn', in Wolfgang Ribbe (ed.), *Berlin-Forschungen II* (Berlin, 1987), 189–201.

Brüggemann, Karsten, 'Max Erwin von Scheubner-Richter (1884–1923) – der Führer des "Führers"?', in Michael Gerleff (ed.), *Deutschbalten, Weimarer Republik und Drittes Reich*, vol. 1 (Cologne, 2001), 119–45.

Brunner, Claudia, *Arbeitslosigkeit im NS-Staat. Das Beispiel München* (Pfaffenweiler, 1997).

Brunswig, Hans, *Feuersturm über Hamburg. Die Luftangriffe auf Hamburg im 2. Weltkrieg und ihre Folgen* (Stuttgart, 1978).

Bücheler, Heinrich, *Hoepner, Ein deutsches Soldatenschicksal des zwanzigsten Jahrhunderts* (Herford, 1980).

Bucher, Peter, 'Hitlers 50. Geburtstag. Zur Quellenvielfalt im Bundesarchiv', in Heinz Boberach and Hans Bohms (eds), *Aus der Arbeit des Bundesarchivs. Beiträge zum Archivwesen, zur Quellenkunde und Zeitgeschichte* (Boppard am Rhein, 1977), 423–46.

Buchheim, Christoph, 'Das NS-Regime und die Überwindung der Weltwirtschaftskrise in Deutschland', in *VfZ* 56 (2008), 381–414.

Buchheim, Christoph, 'Der Mythos vom "Wohlleben". Der Lebensstandard der deutschen Bevölkerung im Zweiten Weltkrieg', in *VfZ* 58 (2010), 299–328.

Buchheim, Hans, 'Die Eingliederung des "Stahlhelm" in die SA', in *Gutachten des Instituts für Zeitgeschichte*, Munich, 1958, vol. 1, 370–7.

Buchheim, Hans, 'Die organisatorische Entwicklung der Politischen Polizei in Deutschland in den Jahren 1933 und 1934', in *Gutachten des Instituts für Zeitgeschichte*, vol. 1 (Munich, 1958), 294–307.

Buchheim, Hans, 'Die staatsrechtliche Bedeutung des Eides auf Hitler als Führer der nationalsozialistischen Bewegung', in *Gutachten des Instituts für Zeitgeschichte*, vol. 1 (Munich, 1958), 328–30.

Buchholz, Marlis, *Die hannoverschen Judenhäuser. Zur Situation der Juden in der Zeit der Ghettoisierung und Verfolgung 1941 bis 1945* (Hildesheim, 1987).

Buchholz, Wolfhard, *Die nationalsozialistische Gemeinschaft 'Kraft durch Freude': Freizeitgestaltung und Arbeiterschaft im Dritten Reich*, Dissertation, Munich, 1976.

Büchler, Yehoshua, 'The Deportation of Slovakian Jews to the Lublin District of Poland in 1942', in *Holocaust and Genocide Studies* 6 (1991), 151–66.

Buddrus, Michael, *Totale Erziehung für den totalen Krieg. Hitlerjugend und nationalsozialistische Jugendpolitik*, 2 vols (Munich, 2003).

Budra, Lutz, *Flugzeugindustrie und Luftrüstung in Deutschland 1918–1945* (Düsseldorf, 1998).

Bukey, Evan Burr, *'Patenstadt des Führers'. Eine Politik- und Sozialgeschichte von Linz 1908–1945* (Frankfurt a. M. and New York, 1993).

Bullock, Alan, *Hitler. Eine Studie über Tyrannei*, revised edn (Düsseldorf, 1971).

Burdick, Charles B., *Germany's Military Strategy and Spain in World War II* (Syracuse, 1968).

Burleigh, Michael, *Tod und Erlösung. Euthanasie in Deutschland 1900–1945* (Zurich, 2002).

Bußmann, Walter, 'Zur Entstehung und Überlieferung der "Hoßbach-Niederschrift"', in *VfZ* 16 (1968), 373–84.

Butler, James R. M., *Lord Lothian (Philip Kerr) 1882–1940* (London, 1960).

Büttner, Ursula and Werner Jochmann, *Hamburg auf dem Weg ins Dritte Reich. Entwicklungsjahre 1931–1933* (Hamburg, 1983).

Calic, Eduard, *Reinhard Heydrich. Schlüsselfigur des Dritten Reiches* (Düsseldorf, 1982).

Cancik, Hubert, '"Wir sind jetzt eins". Rhetorik und Mystik in einer Rede Hitlers (Nürnberg, 11.9.36)', in Günter Kehrer (ed.), *Zur Religionsgeschichte der Bundesrepublik Deutschland*, (Munich, 1980), 13–48.

Cary, Noel D., 'The Making of the Reich President, 1925. German Conservatism and the Nomination of Paul von Hindenburg', in *Central European History* 23 (1990), 179–204.

Cebulla, Florian, *Rundfunk und ländliche Gesellschaft 1924–1941* (Göttingen, 2004).

Celovsky, Boris, *Das Münchner Abkommen 1938* (Stuttgart, 1958).

Chary, Frederick B., *The History of Bulgaria* (Santa Barbara, CA, 2011).

Chaussy, Ulrich, *Nachbar Hitler. Führerkult und Heimatzerstörung am Obersalzberg* (Berlin, 1995).

Christof, Friedrich, *Befriedung im Donauraum. Der zweite Wiener Schiedsspruch und die deutsch-ungarischen diplomatischen Beziehungen 1939–1942* (Frankfurt a. M., 1998).

Ciolek-Kümper, Jutta, *Wahlkampf in Lippe. Die Wahlkampfpropaganda der NSDAP zur Landtagswahl am 15. Januar 1933* (Munich, 1976).

Collier, Basil, *The Defence of the United Kingdom* (London, 1957).

Corni, Gustavo, *Hitler and the Peasants. Agrarian Policy of the Third Reich, 1930–1939* (New York, Oxford, and Munich, 1990).

Corni, Gustavo and Horst Gies, *'Blut und Boden'. Rassenideologie und Agrarpolitik im Staat Hitlers* (Idstein, 1994).

Corni, Gustavo and Horst Gies, *Brot, Butter, Kanonen. Die Ernährungswirtschaft in Deutschland unter der Diktatur Hitlers* (Berlin, 1997).

Creveld, Martin L. van, *Hitler's Strategy 1940–1941. The Balkan Clue* (Cambridge, 1973).

Cüppers, Martin, '"...auf eine so saubere und anständige SS-mäßige Art". Die Waffen-SS in Polen 1939–1941', in Klaus-Michael Mallmann and Bogdan Musial (eds), *Genesis des Genozids. Polen 1939–1941* (Darmstadt, 2004), 90–110.

Czech, Danuta, 'Deportation und Vernichtung der griechischen Juden im KL Auschwitz', in *Hefte von Auschwitz* 11 (1970), 5–37.

Dahm, Volker, 'Anfänge und Ideologie der Reichskulturkammer. Die "Berufsgemeinschaft" als Instrument kulturpolitischer Steuerung und sozialer Reglementierung', in *VfZ* 34 (1986), 53–84.

Deiseroth, Dieter (ed.), *Der Reichstagsbrand und der Prozess vor dem Reichsgericht* (Berlin, 2006).

Deist, Wilhelm, 'Die Aufrüstung der Wehrmacht', in Deist et al. (eds), *Ursachen und Voraussetzungen des Zweiten Weltkrieges* (Frankfurt a. M., 1991), 439–637.

Dengg, Sören, *Deutschlands Austritt aus dem Völkerbund und Schachts 'Neuer Plan'. Zum Verhältnis von Außenpolitik und Außenwirtschaftspolitik in der Übergangsphase von der Weimarer Republik zum Dritten Reich (1929–1934)* (Frankfurt a. M., 1986).

Deschner, Guenter, *Reinhard Heydrich. Statthalter der totalen Macht* (Esslingen, 1977).

Detwiler, Donald S., *Hitler, Franco und Gibraltar. Die Frage des spanischen Eintritts in den Zweiten Weltkrieg* (Wiesbaden, 1962).

Deutsch, Harold C., *Verschwörung gegen den Krieg. Der Widerstand in den Jahren 1939/40* (Munich, 1969).

Diehl, James M., *Paramilitary Politics in Weimar Germany* (Bloomington and London, 1977).

Diehl-Thiele, Peter, *Partei und Staat im Dritten Reich. Untersuchungen zum Verhältnis von NSDAP und allgemeiner innerer Staatsverwaltung 1933–1945* (Munich, 1971).

Diem, Veronika, 'Friedrich Beck (1889–1934) und die Gründungsgeschichte des Münchner Studentenwerks', in Elisabeth Kraus (ed.), *Die Universität München im Dritten Reich. Aufsätze. Teil 1* (Munich, 2006), 43–71.

Diller, Ansgar, *Rundfunkpolitik im Dritten Reich* (Munich, 1980).

Distel, Barbara, '"Die letzte ernste Warnung vor der Vernichtung". Zur Verschleppung der "Aktionsjuden" in die Konzentrationslager nach dem 9. November 1938', in *Zeitschrift für Geschichtswissenschaft* 46 (1998), 985–90.

Domröse, Ortwin, *Der NS-Staat in Bayern von der Machtergreifung bis zum Röhm-Putsch* (Munich, 1974).

Dornberger, Walter, *Peenemünde. Die Geschichte der V-Waffen* (Esslingen, 1981).

Döscher, Hans-Jürgen, *'Reichskristallnacht'. Die Novemberpogrome 1938* (Frankfurt a. M., 1988).

Douglas, Donald Morse, *The Early Ortsgruppen. The Development of National Socialist Local Groups, 1919–1923*, Dissertation, Lawrence/Kan. 1968.

Drobisch, Klaus and Günther Wieland, *System der Konzentrationslager 1933–1939* (Berlin, 1993).

Duesterberg, Theodor, *Der Stahlhelm und Hitler*, 2nd edn (Hamelin, 1950).

Duhnke, Horst, *Die KPD von 1933 bis 1945* (Cologne, 1972).

Dülffer, Jost, *Weimar, Hitler und die Marine. Reichspolitik und Flottenbau 1920–1939*, with a postscript by Jürgen Rohwer (Düsseldorf, 1973).

Dülffer, Jost, Jochen Thies, and Josef Henke, *Hitlers Städte. Baupolitik im Dritten Reich. Eine Dokumentation* (Cologne and Vienna, 1978).

Durth, Werner, *Deutsche Architekten. Biographische Verflechtungen 1900–1970* (Munich, 1992).

Durth, Werner and Winfried Nerdinger eds, *Architektur und Städtebau der 30er/40er Jahre* (Bonn, 1993).

Eberle, Henrik, *Die Martin-Luther-Universität in der Zeit des Nationalsozialismus 1933–1945* (Halle, 2002).

Ebi, Michael, *Export um jeden Preis. Die deutsche Exportförderung von 1932–1938* (Stuttgart, 2004).

Edelmann, Heidrun, *Vom Luxusgut zum Gebrauchsgegenstand. Die Geschichte der Verbreitung von Personenkraftwagen in Deutschland* (Frankfurt a. M., 1989).

Ehni, Hans-Peter, *Bollwerk Preußen? Preußen-Regierung, Reich-Länder-Problem und Sozialdemokratie 1928–1932* (Bonn-Bad Godesberg, 1975).

Eicher, Thomas, 'Spielplanstrukturen 1929–1944', in Eicher, Barbara Panse and Henning Rischbieter, *Theater im »Dritten Reich«. Theaterpolitik, Spielplanstruktur, NS-Dramatik*, (Seelze and Velbert, 2000), 279–486.

Eichholtz, Dietrich, *Geschichte der deutschen Kriegswirtschaft 1939–1945*, 3 vols (Munich, 2003).

Eilers, Rolf, *Die nationalsozialistische Schulpolitik. Eine Studie zur Funktion der Erziehung im totalitären Staat* (Cologne and Opladen, 1963).

Eisfeld, Alfred and Victor Herdt (eds), *Deportation, Sondersiedlung, Arbeitsarmee. Deutsche in der Sowjetunion 1941 bis 1956* (Cologne, 1996).

Embacher, Helga, 'Von liberal zu national: Das Linzer Vereinswesen 1848–1938', in *Historisches Jahrbuch der Stadt Linz* 1991, 41–110.

Emmerson, James Thomas, *The Rhineland Crisis, 7 March 1936: A Study in Multilateral Diplomacy* (London, 1977).

Engelbrecht, Helmut, *Geschichte des österreichischen Bildungswesens. Erziehung und Unterricht auf dem Boden Österreichs*, vol. 4 (Vienna, 1986).

Engelhardt, Katrin, 'Die Ausstellung "Entartete Kunst" in Berlin 1938. Rekonstruktion und Analyse', in Uwe Fleckner (ed.), *Angriff auf die Avantgarde. Kunst und Kunstpolitik im Nationalsozialismus* (Berlin, 2007), 89–187.

Engelman, Max, *Dietrich Eckart and the Genesis of Nazism*, Ph.D. Washington University, Saint Louis, MO, 1971.

Epping-Jäger, Cornelia, 'Lautsprecher Hitler. Über eine Form der Massenkommunikation im Nationalsozialismus', in Gerhard Paul and Ralph Schock (eds), *Sound des Jahrhunderts. Geräusche, Töne, Stimmen 1889 bis heute* (Bonn, 2013), 180–5.

Erger, Johannes, *Der Kapp-Lüttwitz-Putsch. Ein Beitrag zur deutschen Innenpolitik 1919/1920* (Düsseldorf, 1967).

Essner, Cornelia, *Die 'Nürnberger Gesetze' oder die Verwaltung des Rassenwahns 1933–1945* (Paderborn, 2002).

Evans, Richard J. and Dick Geary (eds), *The German Unemployed: Experiences and Consequences of Mass Unemployment from the Weimar Republic to the Third Reich* (London, 1987).

Faber, David, *Munich. The 1938 Appeasement Crisis* (London, 2009).

Falter, Jürgen W., *Hitlers Wähler* (Munich, 1991).

Falter, Jürgen W., 'Die "Märzgefallenen" von 1933. Neue Forschungsergebnisse zum sozialen Wandel innerhalb der NSDAP-Mitgliedschaft während der Machtergreifungsphase', in *Geschichte und Gesellschaft* 1998, 595–616.

Fargion, Liliana Picciotto, 'Italien', in Wolfgang Benz (ed.), *Dimension des Völkermords. Die Zahl der jüdischen Opfer des Nationalsozialismus* (Munich, 1991), 199–227.

Faulstich, Heinz, *Hungersterben in der Psychiatrie 1914–1949. Mit einer Topographie der NS-Psychiatrie* (Freiburg i. Br., 1998).

Faust, Anselm, *Der Nationalsozialistische Deutsche Studentenbund. Studenten und Nationalsozialismus in der Weimarer Republik*, 2 vols (Düsseldorf, 1973).

Faustmann, Uwe Julius, *Die Reichskulturkammer. Aufbau, Funktion und Grundlagen einer Körperschaft des öffentlichen Rechts im nationalsozialistischen Regime* (Aachen, 1995).

Feiten, Willi, *Der nationalsozialistische Lehrerbund. Entwicklung und Organisation. Ein Beitrag zum Aufbau und zur Organisationsstruktur des nationalsozialistischen Herrschaftssystems* (Weinheim, 1981).

Feldbauer, Gerhard and Joachim Petzold, 'Deutscher Herrenklub', in Dieter Fricke, *Lexikon zur Parteiengeschichte. Die bürgerlichen und kleinbürgerlichen Parteien und Verbände in Deutschland (1789–1945)*, vol. 2 (Leipzig, 1984), 107–15.

Fenske, Hans, *Konservatismus und Rechtsradikalismus in Bayern nach 1918* (Bad Homburg, 1969).

Fest, Joachim, *Hitler. Eine Biographie* (Frankfurt a. M., 1970).

Fest, Joachim, *Staatsstreich. Der lange Weg zum 20. Juli* (Berlin, 1994).

Fest, Joachim, *Speer. Eine Biographie* (Berlin, 1999).

Fest, Joachim, *Die unbeantwortbaren Fragen. Notizen über Gespräche mit Albert Speer zwischen Ende 1966 und 1981* (Reinbek b. Hamburg, 2005).

Fetscher, Iring, *Joseph Goebbels im Berliner Sportpalast 1943: 'Wollt ihr den totalen Krieg?'* (Hamburg, 1998).

Fiederlein, Friedrich Martin, *Der deutsche Osten und die Regierungen Brüning, Papen, Schleicher* (Würzburg, 1967).

Fischer, Albert, *Hjalmar Schacht und Deutschlands 'Judenfrage'. Der 'Wirtschaftsdiktator' und die Vertreibung der Juden aus der deutschen Wirtschaft* (Cologne, Weimar, and Vienna, 1995).

Flechtmann, Frank, 'Casanova, Vidoq, Toifl, Mauss. Ein Beitrag zur Kulturgeschichte des Spitzels', in *Geschichte, Politik und ihre Didaktik* 26 (1998), 281–6.

Fleischer, Hagen, 'Griechenland', in Wolfgang Benz (ed.), *Dimension des Völkermords. Die Zahl der jüdischen Opfer des Nationalsozialismus* (Munich, 1991), 241–74.

Fleming, Gerald, *Hitler and the Final Solution* (Berkeley, Los Angeles, and London, 1984).

Förster, Otto-Wilhelm, *Das Befestigungswesen. Rückblick und Ausschau* (Neckargemünd, 1960).

Frank, Claudia, *Der 'Reichsnährstand' und seine Ursprünge. Struktur, Funktion und ideologische Konzeption* (Hamburg, 1988).

Franz-Willing, *Ursprung der Hitlerbewegung. 1919–1922* (Preussisch Oldendorf, 1974).

Franz-Willing, Georg, *Putsch und Verbotszeit der Hitlerbewegung. November 1923– Februar 1925* (Preussisch Oldendorf, 1997).

Frei, Bruno, *Carl von Ossietzky: eine politische Biographie* (Berlin, 1978).

Freudenthal, Herbert, *Vereine in Hamburg. Ein Beitrag zur Geschichte und Volkskunde der Geselligkeit* (Hamburg, 1968).

Friedlander, Henry, *Der Weg zum NS-Genozid. Von der Euthanasie zur Endlösung* (Berlin, 1997).

Friedländer, Saul, *Auftakt zum Untergang. Hitler und die Vereinigten Staaten von Amerika 1939–1941* (Stuttgart, 1965).

Friedländer, Saul, *Das Dritte Reich und die Juden*, vol. 1 (Munich, 2000).

Frieser, Karl-Heinz, *Blitzkrieg-Legende. Der Westfeldzug 1940* (Munich, 1995).

Frieser, Karl-Heinz, 'Das Ausweichen der Heeresgruppe Nord von Leningrad ins Baltikum', in Frieser (ed.), *Die Ostfront 1943/44. Der Krieg im Osten und an den Nebenfronten* (Munich, 2007), 278–96.

Frieser, Karl-Heinz, 'Der Rückzug der Heeresgruppe Mitte nach Weißrußland', in Frieser (ed.), *Die Ostfront 1943/44. Der Krieg im Osten und an den Nebenfronten* (Munich, 2007), 297–338.

Frieser, Karl-Heinz, 'Der Zusammenbruch der Heeresgruppe Mitte im Sommer 1944', in Frieser (ed.), *Die Ostfront 1943/44. Der Krieg im Osten und an den Nebenfronten* (Munich, 2007), 526–603.

Frieser, Karl-Heinz, 'Die erfolgreichen Abwehrkämpfe der Heeresgruppe Mitte im Herbst 1944', in Frieser (ed.), *Die Ostfront 1943/44. Der Krieg im Osten und an den Nebenfronten* (Munich, 2007), 604–22.

Frieser, Karl-Heinz, 'Die Rückzugskämpfe der Heeresgruppe Nord bis Kurland', in Frieser (ed.), *Die Ostfront 1943/44. Der Krieg im Osten und an den Nebenfronten*, (Munich, 2007), 623–78.

Frieser, Karl-Heinz, 'Die Rückzugsoperationen der Heeresgruppe Süd in der Ukraine', in Frieser (ed.), *Die Ostfront 1943/44. Der Krieg im Osten und an den Nebenfronten* (Munich, 2007), 339–450.

Frieser, Karl-Heinz, 'Die Schlacht am Kursker Bogen', in Frieser (ed.), *Die Ostfront 1943/44. Der Krieg im Osten und an den Nebenfronten*, (Munich, 2007), 83–208.

Frommelt, Reinhard, *Paneuropa oder Mitteleuropa. Einigungsbestrebungen im Kalkül deutscher Wirtschaft und Politik 1918–1933* (Stuttgart, 1977).

Fuchs, Friedrich, *Die Beziehungen zwischen der Freien Stadt Danzig und dem Deutschen Reich in der Zeit von 1920 bis 1939. Unter besonderer Berücksichtigung der Judenfrage in beiden Staaten* (Freiburg i. Br., 1999).

Fuhrer, Armin, *Hitlers Spiele. Olympia 1936 in Berlin* (Berlin, 2011).

Fuhrer, Armin, *'Führergeburtstag'. Die perfide Propaganda des NS-Regimes mit dem 20. April* (Berlin, 2014).

Funke, Manfred, '7. März 1936. Fallstudie zum außenpolitischen Führungsstil Hitlers', in Wolfgang Michalka (ed.), *Nationalsozialistische Außenpolitik* (Darmstadt, 1978), 277–324.

Gaertringen, Friedrich Frhr. Hiller von, 'Die Deutschnationale Volkspartei', in Erich Matthias and Rudolf Morsey (eds), *Das Ende der Parteien 1933* (Düsseldorf, 1960), 543–652.

Gagliani, Dianella, 'Diktat oder Konsens? Die Republik von Salò und das Dritte Reich', in Lutz Klinkhammer, Amedeo Osti Guerazzi, and Thomas Schlemmer (eds), *Die »Achse« im Krieg. Politik, Ideologie und Kriegführung. 1939–1945* (Paderborn, 2010,), 456–71.

Gebel, Ralf, *'Heim ins Reich!' Konrad Henlein und der Reichsgau Sudetenland (1938–1945)* (Munich, 1999).

Gelderblom, Bernhard, 'Die Reichserntedankfeste auf dem Bückeberg 1933–1937. Ein Volk dankt seinem Verführer', in Gerd Biegel and Wulf Otte (eds), *Ein Volk dankt seinem (Ver)führer: Die Reichserntedankfeste auf dem Bückeberg 1933–1937. Vorträge zur Ausstellung* (Brunswick, 2002), 19–62.

Gelhaus, Hubert, *1933. 365 ganz normale Tage. Beobachtungen zum nationalsozialistischen Alltag in Cloppenburg und Umgebung (Südoldenburg)* (Oldenburg, 1988).

Gemzell, Carl-Axel, *Raeder, Hitler und Skandinavien. Der Kampf für einen maritimen Operationsplan* (Lund, 1965).

Genschel, Helmut, *Die Verdrängung der Juden aus der Wirtschaft im Dritten Reich* (Göttingen, 1966).

Gentile, Carlo, *Wehrmacht, Waffen-SS und Polizei im Kampf gegen Partisanen und Zivilbevölkerung in Italien 1943–1945* (Paderborn and Munich, 2012).

Gerlach, Christian, 'Die Wannsee-Konferenz, das Schicksal der deutschen Juden und Hitlers politische Grundentscheidung, alle Juden Europas zu ermorden', in *WerkstattGeschichte* 6/18 (1997), 7–44.

Gerlach, Christian, 'Failure of Plans for an SS Extermination Camp in Mogilev, Belorussia', in *Holocaust and Genocide Studies* 11/1 (1997), 60–78.

Gerlach, Christian and Götz Aly, *Das letzte Kapitel. Realpolitik, Ideologie und der Mord an den ungarischen Juden 1944/1945* (Stuttgart and Zurich, 2002).

Geschichtswerkstatt Neuhausen e.V. (ed.), *Zum Beispiel Neuhausen 1918–1933. Die nationalsozialistische 'Kampfzeit' in einem Stadtteil der ehemaligen 'Hauptstadt der Bewegung'* (Munich, 1993).

Geyer, Martin H., *Verkehrte Welt. Revolution, Inflation und Moderne, München, 1914– 1924* (Göttingen, 1998).

Geyer, Michael, 'Das zweite Rüstungsprogramm (1930 bis 1934)', in *MGM* 17 (1975), 125–172.

Geyer, Michael, *Aufrüstung oder Sicherheit. Die Reichswehr in der Krise der Machtpolitik, 1924–1936* (Wiesbaden, 1980).

Geyer, Michael, 'Rüstungsbeschleunigung und Inflation. Zur Inflationsdenkschrift des Oberkommandos der Wehrmacht vom November 1938', in *MGM* 30 (1981), 121–86.

Gibbels, Ellen, *Hitlers Parkinson-Krankheit. Zur Frage eines hirnorganischen Psychosyndroms* (Berlin, 1990).

Gibbels, Ellen, 'Hitlers Nervenkrankheit. Eine neurologisch-psychiatrische Studie', in *VfZ* 41 (1994), 155–200.

Gies, Horst, R., *Walther Darré und die nationalsozialistische Bauernpolitik in den Jahren 1930 bis 1933* (Frankfurt a. M., 1966).

Gilbert, Bentley B., *Britain since 1918* (New York, 1967).

Gilbhard, Hermann, *Die Thule-Gesellschaft. Vom okkulten Mummenschanz zum Hakenkreuz* (Munich, 1994).

Giro, Helmut-Dieter, *Frankreich und die Remilitarisierung des Rheinlandes. Hitlers Weg in den Krieg?* (Essen, 2006).

Glenthøj, Jørgen, 'Hindenburg, Göring und die evangelischen Kirchenführer. Ein Beitrag zur Beleuchtung des staatspolitischen Hintergrundes der Kanzleraudienz am 25. Januar 1934', in *Zur Geschichte des Kirchenkampfes. Gesammelte Aufsätze*, ed. Heinz Brunotte and Ernst Wolff, vol. 1 (Göttingen 1965), 45–91.

Golczewski, Frank, *Deutsche und Ukrainer 1914–1939* (Paderborn, 2010).

Göppinger, Horst, *Die Verfolgung der Juristen jüdischer Abstammung durch den Nationalsozialismus* (Villingen (Schwarzwald), 1963).

Gordon, Harold J., *Hitlerputsch 1923. Machtkampf in Bayern 1923–1924* (Munich, 1978).

Gorodetsky, Gabriel, *Die große Täuschung. Hitler, Stalin und das Unternehmen 'Barbarossa'* (Berlin, 2001).

Görtemaker, Heike B., *Eva Braun. Leben mit Hitler* (Munich, 2010).

Goshen, Seev, 'Eichmann und die Nisko-Aktion im Oktober 1939. Eine Fallstudie zur NS-Judenpolitik in der letzten Etappe vor der "Endlösung"', in *VfZ* 29 (1981), 74–96.

Goshen, Seev, 'Nisko. Ein Ausnahmefall unter den Judenlagern der SS', in *VfZ* 40 (1992), 95–106.

Gossweiler, Kurt, *Kapital, Reichswehr und NSDAP. Zur Frühgeschichte des deutschen Faschismus 1919–1924* (Cologne, 1982).

Gottwaldt, Alfred, *Dorpmüllers Reichsbahn. Die Ära des Reichsverkehrsministers Julius Dorpmüller, 1920–1945* (Freiburg i. Br., 2009).

Gottwaldt, Alfred and Diana Schulle, *Die 'Judendeportationen' aus dem Deutschen Reich 1941–1945. Eine kommentierte Chronologie* (Wiesbaden, 2005).

Graham, Cooper C., *Leni Riefenstahl and Olympia* (Metuchen, NJ, 1986).

Graml, Hermann, *Europas Weg in den Krieg. Hitler und die Mächte 1939* (Munich, 1990).

Granier, Gerhard, *Magnus von Levetzow: Seeoffizier, Monarchist und Wegbereiter Hitlers. Lebensweg und ausgewählte Dokumente* (Boppard am Rhein, 1982).

Grass, Karl Martin, *Edgar Jung, Papenkreis und Röhmkrise 1933/34*, Dissertation, Heidelberg, 1966.

Grau, Bernhard, *Kurt Eisner 1867–1919. Eine Biographie* (Munich, 2001).

Greiner, Josef, *Das Ende des Hitler-Mythos* (Zurich, Leipzig, and Vienna, 1947).

Grimm, Gerhard, 'Albanien', in Wolfgang Benz (ed.), *Dimension des Völkermords. Die Zahl der jüdischen Opfer des Nationalsozialismus* (Munich, 1991), 229–40.

Gritschneder, Otto, *Bewährungsfrist für den Terroristen Adolf H. Der Hitler-Putsch und die bayerische Justiz* (Munich, 1990).

Gröhler, Olaf, *Bombenkrieg gegen Deutschland* (Berlin, 1990).

Grothe, Ewald, 'Die Olympischen Spiele von 1936. Höhepunkt der NS-Propaganda?', in *GWU* 59 (2008), 291–307.

Gruat, Cédric, *Hitler in Paris. Juni 1940* (Berlin and Schmalkalden, 2011).

Gruchmann, Lothar, 'Hitler über die Justiz. Das Tischgespräch vom 20. August 1942', in *VfZ* 12 (1964), 86–101.

Gruchmann, Lothar, *Der Zweite Weltkrieg. Kriegführung und Politik* (Munich, 1967).

Gruchmann, Lothar, 'Euthanasie und Justiz im Dritten Reich', in *VfZ* 20 (1972), 235–79.

Gruchmann, Lothar, 'Die "Reichsregierung" im Führerstaat. Stellung und Funktion des Kabinetts im nationalsozialistischen Herrschaftssystem', in Günther Doeker-Mach (ed.), *Klassenjustiz und Pluralismus. Festschrift für Ernst Fraenkel zum 75. Geburtstag am 26. Dezember 1973* (Hamburg 1973), 187–223.

Gruchmann, Lothar, *Justiz im Dritten Reich 1933–1940. Anpassung und Unterwerfung in der Ära Gürtner* (Munich, 1988).

Gruchmann, Lothar (ed.), *Autobiographie eines Attentäters: Johann Georg Elser. Der Anschlag auf Hitler im Bürgerbräu 1939* (Stuttgart, 1989).

Gruchmann, Lothar, 'Korruption im Dritten Reich. Zur Lebensmittelversorgung der NS-Führerschaft', in *VfZ* 42 (1994), 571–93.

Gruchmann, Lothar, 'Generalangriff gegen die Justiz? Der Reichstagsbeschluß vom 26. April 1942 und seine Bedeutung für die Maßregelung der deutschen Richter durch Hitler', in *VfZ* 51 (2003), 509–20.

Gruner, Wolf, 'Lesen brauchen sie nicht zu können…Die "Denkschrift über die Behandlung der Juden in der Reichshauptstadt auf allen Gebieten des öffentlichen Lebens" vom Mai 1938', in *Jahrbuch für Antisemitismusforschung* 4 (1995), 305–41.

Gruner, Wolf, *Der geschlossene Arbeitseinsatz deutscher Juden. Zur Zwangsarbeit als Element der Verfolgung 1938–1943* (Berlin, 1997).

Gruner, Wolf, 'Poverty and Persecution. The Reichsvereinigung, the Jewish Population, and Anti-Jewish Policy in the Nazi State, 1939–1945', in *Yad Vashem Studies* 27 (1999), 23–60.

Gruner, Wolf, 'Von der Kollektivausweisung zur Deportation der Juden aus Deutschland (1938–1945). Neue Perspektiven und Dokumente', in Birthe Kundus und Beate Meyer (eds), *Die Deportation der Juden aus Deutschland. Pläne – Praxis – Reaktionen 1938–1945* (Göttingen, 2004), 21–62.

Gruner, Wolf, *Widerstand in der Rosenstraße. Die Fabrik-Aktion und die Verfolgung der 'Mischehen' 1943* (Frankfurt a. M., 2005).

Grüttner, Michael, *Studenten im Dritten Reich* (Paderborn and Munich, 1995).

Grüttner, Michael and Sven Kinas, 'Die Vertreibung von Wissenschaftlern aus den deutschen Universitäten 1933–1945', in *VfZ* 55 (2007), 123–86.

Gümmer, Frederic, *Die Rolle der Untertageverlagerung in der deutschen Rüstungsproduktion 1943–1945* (Munich, 2007).

Gun, Erin E., *Eva Braun-Hitler. Leben und Schicksal*, unaltered new edn (Kiel, 1994).

Haasis, Hellmut G., *Tod in Prag. Das Attentat auf Reinhard Heydrich* (Reinbek b. Hamburg, 2002).

Hachtmann, Rüdiger, 'Lebenshaltungskosten und Reallöhne während des "Dritten Reiches"', in *Vierteljahrschrift für Sozial- und Wirtschaftsgeschichte* 75 (1988), 32–73.

Hachtmann, Rüdiger, 'Elastisch, dynamisch und von katastrophaler Effizienz. Zur Struktur der neuen Staatlichkeit des Nationalsozialismus', in Sven Reichardt und Wolfgang Seibel (eds), *Der prekäre Staat. Herrschen und Verwalten im Nationalsozialismus* (Frankfurt a. M., 2011), 29–73.

Hachtmann, Rüdiger, *Das Wirtschaftsimperium der Deutschen Arbeitsfront 1933–1945* (Göttingen, 2012).

Hachtmann, Rüdiger and Winfried Süss (eds), *Hitlers Kommissare. Führerbeauftragte und sektorale Sondergewalten in der nationalsozialistischen Diktatur* (Göttingen, 2006).

Hacket, David Andrew, *The Nazi Party in the Reichstag Election of 1930*, Dissertation, University of Wisconsin, 1971.

Haestrup, Jürgen, *European Resistance Movements, 1939–1945. A Complete History* (Westport, CT and London, 1981).

Hagemann, Jürgen, *Die Presselenkung im Dritten Reich* (Bonn, 1970).

Hahn, Judith, 'Erwin Villain und Leonardo Conti: Scharmützel unter NS-Kameraden', in *Deutsches Ärzteblatt* 104/42 (2007), A2862–A4.

Hale, Oron James, 'Adolf Hitler: Taxpayer', in *American Historical Review* 60 (1955), 830–42.

Hamann, Brigitte, *Hitlers Wien. Lehrjahre eines Diktators* (Munich, 1996).

Hamann, Brigitte, *Winifred Wagner oder Hitlers Bayreuth* (Munich and Zurich, 2006).

Hamann, Brigitte, *Hitlers Edeljude. Das Leben des Armenarztes Eduard Bloch* (Munich, 2008).

Hambrecht, Rainer, *Der Aufstieg der NSDAP in Mittel- und Oberfranken 1925–1933*, (Nuremberg, 1976).

Hancock, Eleanor, *Ernst Röhm. Hitler's SA Chief of Staff* (New York, 2008).

Hano, Horst, *Die Taktik der Pressepropaganda des Hitlerregimes 1943–1945. Eine Untersuchung auf Grund unveröffentlichter Dokumente des Sicherheitsdienstes und des Reichsministeriums für Volksaufklärung und Propaganda* (Munich, 1963).

Harlander, Tilman, *Zwischen Heimstätte und Wohnmaschine. Wohnungsbau und Wohnungspolitik in der Zeit des Nationalsozialismus* (Basel, Berlin, and Boston, 1995).

Hartmann, Christian, *Halder. Generalstabschef Hitlers 1938–1942* (Paderborn, 1991).

Hartmann, Christian, and Sergej Z. Sluč, 'Franz Halder und die Kriegsvorbereitungen im Frühjahr 1939. Eine Ansprache des Generalstabschefs des Heeres', in *VfZ* 45 (1997), 467–95.

Haselbeck, Franz, 'Das Gefangenenlager Traunstein-Au', in *Jahrbuch des Historischen Vereins für den Chiemgau zu Traunstein* 7 (1995), 241–90.

Haupt, Klaus, *Egon Erwin Kisch (1885–1948). Der Rasende Reporter aus dem Prager 'Haus zu den zwei goldenen Bären'* (Teetz and Berlin, 2008).

Hauss, Hanns-Jochen, *Die erste Volkswahl des deutschen Reichspräsidenten. Eine Untersuchung ihrer verfassungspolitischen Grundlagen, ihrer Vorgeschichte und ihres Verlaufs unter besonderer Berücksichtigung des Anteils Bayerns und der Bayerischen Volkspartei* (Lassleben and Kallmünz, 1965).

Hausser, Paul, *Soldaten wie andere auch. Der Weg der Waffen-SS* (Osnabrück, 1966).

Hayes, Romain, *Subhas Chandra Bose in Nazi Germany. Politics, Intelligence and Propaganda 1941–43* (London, 2011).

Heberer, Patricia, 'Eine Kontinuität der Tötungsoperationen. T4-Täter und die "Aktion Reinhardt"', in Bogdan Musial (ed.), *'Aktion Reinhardt'. Der Völkermord an den Juden im Generalgouvernement 1941–1944* (Osnabrück, 2004), 285–308.

Hehl, Ulrich von, 'Die Kontroverse um den Reichstagsbrand', in *VfZ* 36 (1988), 259–80.

Heiber, Helmut, 'Der Tod des Zaren Boris', in *VfZ* 9 (1961), 384–416.

Heilbronner, Oded, *Die Achillesferse des deutschen Katholizismus* (Gerlingen 1998).

Heinemann, Isabel, *'Rasse, Siedlung, deutsches Blut'. Das Rasse- und Siedlungshauptamt der SS und die rassenpolitische Neuordnung Europas* (Göttingen, 2003).

Heinemann, Winfried, *Des 'Führers' General Eduard Dietl* (Paderborn, 2004).

Henke, Josef, *England in Hitlers politischem Kalkül 1935–1939* (Boppard am Rhein, 1973).

Henke, Klaus-Dietmar, *Die amerikanische Besetzung Deutschlands* (Munich, 1995).

Henning, Hansjoachim, 'Kraftfahrzeugindustrie und Autobahnbau in der Wirtschaftspolitik des Nationalsozialismus 1933–1936', in *Vierteljahrschrift für Sozial- und Wirtschaftsgeschichte* 65 (1978), 217–42.

Hensle, Michael P., *Rundfunkverbrechen. Das Hören von 'Feindsendern' im Nationalsozialismus* (Berlin, 2003).

Hepp, Michael (ed.), *Die Ausbürgerung deutscher Staatsangehöriger 1933–45 nach den im Reichsanzeiger veröffentlichten Listen*, 3 vols (Munich, 1985).

Herbert, Ulrich, 'Die deutsche Militärverwaltung in Paris und die Deportation der französischen Juden', in Christian Jansen, Lutz Niethammer, and Bernd Weisbrod (eds), *Von der Aufgabe der Freiheit. Politische Verantwortung und bürgerliche Gesellschaft im 19. und 20. Jahrhundert. Festschrift für Hans Mommsen zum 5. November 1995,* (Berlin, 1995), 427–50.

Herbert, Ulrich, *Best. Biographische Studien über Radikalismus, Weltanschauung und Vernunft 1903–1989* (Bonn, 1996).

Herbert, Ulrich, *Fremdarbeiter. Politik und Praxis des 'Ausländer-Einsatzes' in der Kriegswirtschaft des Dritten Reiches* (Bonn, 1999).

Herbst, Ludolf, *Der Totale Krieg und die Ordnung der Wirtschaft. Die Kriegswirtschaft im Spannungsfeld zwischen Ideologie und Propaganda 1939–1945* (Stuttgart, 1982).

Herbst, Ludolf, *Hitlers Charisma. Die Erfindung eines deutschen Messias* (Frankfurt a. M., 2010).

Herde, Peter, *Italien, Deutschland und der Weg in den Krieg im Pazifik 1941* (Wiesbaden, 1983).

Hering, Rainer, *Konstruierte Nation. Der Alldeutsche Verband 1890 bis 1939* (Hamburg, 2003).

Hermann, Angela, 'Hitler und sein Stoßtrupp in der "Reichskristallnacht"', in *VfZ* 56 (2008), 603–19.

Herrmann, Volker, *Vom Arbeitsmarkt zum Arbeitseinsatz. Zur Geschichte der Reichsanstalt für Arbeitsvermittlung und Arbeitslosenversicherung 1929–1939* (Frankfurt a. M., 1993).

Hertzman, Lewis, *DNVP: Right-Wing Opposition in the Weimar Republic 1918–1924* (Lincoln, NE, 1963).

Herz, Rudolf, *Hoffmann & Hitler. Fotografie als Medium des Führer-Mythos* (Munich, 1994).

Hesse, Klaus and Philipp Springer, *Vor aller Augen. Fotodokumente des nationalsozialistischen Terrors in der Provinz,* ed. Reinhard Rürup for the Topography of Terror Foundation (Essen, 2002).

Hetzer, Gerhard, 'Die Industriestadt Augsburg. Eine Sozialgeschichte der Arbeiteropposition', in Martin Broszat (ed.), *Bayern in der NS-Zeit*, vol. 3, Part B (Munich, 1981), 1–234.

Heuer, Hans-Joachim, *Geheime Staatspolizei. Über das Töten und die Tendenzen der Entzivilisierung* (Berlin, 1995).

Hilberg, Raul, *Die Vernichtung der europäischen Juden. Die Gesamtgeschichte des Holocaust,* 3 vols, revised and expanded edn (Frankfurt a. M., 1990).

Hildebrand, Klaus, *Vom Reich zum Weltreich. Hitler, NSDAP und koloniale Frage 1919–1945* (Munich, 1969).

Hildebrand, Klaus, *Deutsche Außenpolitik 1933–1945. Kalkül oder Dogma?* (Stuttgart, Berlin, and Cologne, 1990).

Hildebrand, Klaus, *Das vergangene Reich. Deutsche Außenpoltiik von Bismarck bis Hitler* (Berlin, 1999).

Hildesheimer, Esriel, *Jüdische Selbstverwaltung unter dem NS-Regime. Der Existenzkampf der Reichsvertretung und Reichsvereinigung der Juden in Deutschland* (Tübingen, 1994).

Hillgruber, Andreas, *Hitler, König Carol und Marschall Antonescu. Die deutsch-rumänischen Beziehungen 1938–1944* (Wiesbaden, 1954).

Hillgruber, Andreas, *Hitlers Strategie. Politik und Kriegführung 1940/1941* (Frankfurt a. M., 1965).

Hillgruber, Andreas, *Kontinuität und Diskontinuität in der deutschen Außenpolitik von Bismarck bis Hitler* (Düsseldorf, 1969).

Hillgruber, Andreas, 'Die "Endlösung" und das deutsche Ostimperium als Kernstück des rassenideologischen Programms des Nationalsozialismus', in Wolfgang Wippermann (ed.), *Kontroversen um Hitler* (Frankfurt a. M., 1986), 219–47.

Hillmayr, Heinrich, *Roter und Weißer Terror in Bayern nach 1918. Ursachen, Erscheinungsformen und Folgen der Gewalttätigkeiten im Verlauf der revolutionären Ereignisse nach dem Ende des Ersten Weltkrieges* (Munich, 1974).

Hilton, Christopher, *Hitler's Olympics: The 1936 Berlin Olympic Games* (Stroud, 2006).

Hirte, Chris, *Erich Mühsam. Eine Biographie* (Freiburg i. Br., 2009).

Höbelt, Lothar, *Kornblume und Kaiseradler. Die deutschfreiheitlichen Parteien Altösterreichs 1882–1918* (Vienna and Munich, 1993).

Hoch, Anton, 'Das Attentat auf Hitler im Münchner Bürgerbräukeller 1939', in *VfZ* 17 (1969), 383–413.

Hoch, Anton, and Lothar Gruchmann, *Georg Elser: Der Attentäter aus dem Volke. Der Anschlag auf Hitler im Münchner Bürgerbräu 1939* (Frankfurt a. M., 1980).

Hoch, Anton, and Hermann Weiss, 'Die Erinnerungen des Generalobersten Wilhelm Adam', in Wolfgang Benz (ed.), *Miscelleanea. Festschrift für Helmut Krausnick zum 75. Geburtstag* (Stuttgart, 1980), 32–62.

Hochstetter, Dorothee, *Motorisierung und 'Volksgemeinschaft'. Das Nationalsozialistische Kraftfahrkorps (NSKK) 1931–1945* (Munich, 2005).

Hockerts, Hans-Günther, *Die Sittlichkeitsprozesse gegen katholische Ordensangehörige und Priester 1936/1937. Eine Studie zur nationalsozialistischen Herrschaftstechnik und zum Kirchenkampf* (Mainz, 1971).

Hockerts, Hans-Günther, 'Die Goebbels-Tagebücher 1932–1941. Eine neue Hauptquelle zur Erforschung der nationalsozialistischen Kirchenpolitik', in Dieter Albrecht (ed.), *Politik und Konfession. Festschrift für Konrad Repgen zum 60. Geburtstag* (Berlin, 1983), 359–92.

Hoensch, Jörg K., *Die Slowakei und Hitlers Ostpolitik. Hlinkas Slowakische Volkspartei zwischen Autonomie und Separation 1938/1939* (Cologne and Graz, 1965).

Hoensch, Jörg K., *Der ungarische Revisionismus und die Zerschlagung der Tschechoslowakei* (Tübingen, 1967).

Hofer, Andreas, *Kapitänleutnant Hellmuth von Mücke. Marineoffizier – Politiker – Widerstandskämpfer. Ein Leben zwischen den Fronten* (Marburg, 2003).

Hoffmann, Hilmar, *Mythos Olympia – Autonomie und Unterwerfung von Sport und Kultur. Hitlers Olympiade, olympische Kultur und Riefenstahls Olympia-Film* (Berlin, 1993).

Hoffmann, Joachim, 'Die Kriegführung aus der Sicht der Sowjetunion', in Horst Boog et al., *Der Angriff auf die Sowjetunion*, updated edn (Frankfurt a. M., 1991), 848–964.

Hoffmann, Joachim, *Stalins Vernichtungskrieg 1941–1945. Planung, Ausführung und Dokumentation*, 6th edn (Munich, 2000).

Hoffmann, Peter, *Widerstand – Staatsstreich – Attentat. Der Kampf der Opposition gegen Hitler* (Munich and Zurich, 1995).

Hoffmann, Peter, *Claus Schenk Graf von Stauffenberg. Die Biographie* (Munich, 2007).

Höhne, Heinz, *Mordsache Röhm. Hitlers Durchbruch zur Alleinherrschaft 1933–1934* (Reinbek b. Hamburg, 1984).

Holmila, Antero, 'Finland and the Holocaust. A Reassessment', in *Holocaust and Genocide Studies* 23 (2009), 413–40.

Hölsken, Heinz Dieter, *Die V-Waffen. Entstehung – Propaganda – Kriegseinsatz* (Stuttgart, 1984).

Hömig, Herbert, *Das preußische Zentrum in der Weimarer Republik* (Mainz, 1979).

Höner, Sabine, *Der nationalsozialistische Zugriff auf Preußen. Preußischer Staat und nationalsozialistische Machteroberungsstrategie 1928–1934* (Bochum, 1984).

Hoppe, Hans-Joachim, *Bulgarien, Hitlers eigenwilliger Verbündeter. Eine Fallstudie zur nationalsozialistischen Südosteuropapolitik* (Stuttgart, 1979).

Horn, Wolfgang, *Der Marsch zur Machtergreifung. Die NSDAP bis 1933* (Königstein i. Ts. and Düsseldorf, 1980).

Hörster-Philipps, Ulrike, *Konservative Politik in der Endphase der Weimarer Republik. Die Regierung Franz von Papen* (Cologne, 1982).

Horstmann, Bernhard, *Hitler in Pasewalk. Die Hypnose und ihre Folgen* (Düsseldorf, 2004).

Hoser, Paul, 'Hitler und die Katholische Kirche. Zwei Briefe aus dem Jahr 1927', in *VfZ* 42 (1994), 473–92.

Hubatsch, Walther, *Weserübung. Die deutsche Besetzung von Dänemark und Norwegen 1940. Nach amtl. Unterlagen dargestellt* (Göttingen, 1960).

Huber, Bernhard, 'Georg Neithardt – nur ein unpolitischer Richter?', in Marita Krauss (ed.), *Rechte Karrieren in München. Von der Weimarer Zeit bis in die Nachkriegsjahre* (Munich, 2010), 95–113.

Huber, Ernst Rudolf, *Deutsche Verfassungsgeschichte seit 1789*, vol. 7 (Stuttgart, 1984).

Humann, Detlev, *'Arbeitsschlacht'. Arbeitsbeschaffung und Propaganda in der NS-Zeit 1933–1939* (Göttingen, 2011).

Hürter, Johannes, *Wilhelm Groener. Reichswehrminister am Ende der Weimarer Republik (1928–1932)* (Munich, 1993).

Hürter, Johannes, *Hitlers Heerführer. Die deutschen Oberbefehlshaber im Krieg gegen die Sowjetunion 1941/42* (Munich, 2006).

Hüttenberger, Peter, *Die Gauleiter. Studie zum Wandel des Machtgefüges in der NSDAP* (Stuttgart, 1969).

Jablonsky, David, *The Nazi Party in Dissolution. Hitler and the Verbotzeit 1923–1925* (London and Totowa, NJ, 1989).

Jäckel, Eberhard, *Frankreich in Hitlers Europa. Die deutsche Frankreichpolitik im Zweiten Weltkrieg* (Stuttgart, 1966).

Jäckel, Eberhard, 'Die deutsche Kriegserklärung an die Vereinigten Staaten von 1941', in Friedrich J. Kroneck and Thomas Oppermann (eds), *Im Dienste Deutschlands und des Rechts, Festschrift für Wilhelm G. Grewe zum 70. Geburtstag am 16. Oktober 1981* (Baden–Baden, 1981), 117–37.

Jäckel, Eberhard, *Hitlers Weltanschauung. Entwurf einer Herrschaft* (Stuttgart, 1991).

Jacobsen, Hans-Adolf, *Fall Gelb. Der Kampf um den deutschen Operationsplan zur Westoffensive 1940* (Wiesbaden, 1957).

Jacobsen, Hans-Adolf, *Nationalsozialistische Außenpolitik 1933–1938* (Frankfurt a. M. and Berlin, 1968).

Jacobsen, Hans-Adolf, *Der Weg zur Teilung der Welt. Politik und Strategie 1939–1945* (Koblenz and Bonn, 1977).

Jacobsen, Hans-Adolf, (ed.) *Karl Haushofer. Leben und Werk*, vol. 1 (Boppard am Rhein, 1979).

Jacobsen, Hans-Adolf, 'Kommissarbefehl und Massenexekutionen sowjetischer Kriegsgefangener', in Hans Buchheim et al., *Anatomie des SS-Staates*, vol. 2, 4th edn (Munich, 1984), 137–233.

Jäger, Wolfgang, *Es begann am 30. Januar* (Munich, 1958).

Jagschitz, Gerhard, *Der Putsch. Die Nationalsozialisten 1934 in Österreich* (Graz, 1976).

Jagschitz, Gerhard, 'Photographie und "Anschluß" im März 1938', in Oliver Rathkolb, Wolfgang Duchkowitsch, and Fritz Hausjell (eds, *Die veruntreute Wahrheit. Hitlers Propagandisten in Österreichs Medien* (Salzburg, 1988), 52–81.

Jahr, Christian, 'Die nationalsozialistische Machtübernahme und ihre Folgen', in Michael Grüttner (ed.), *Geschichte der Universität unter den Linden. Biographie einer Institution*, vol. 2 (Berlin, 2012), 295–324.

James, Harold, *Deutschland in der Weltwirtschaftskrise 1924–1936* (Stuttgart, 1988).

Jansen, Christian and Arno Weckbecker, *Der 'Volksdeutsche Selbstschutz' in Polen 1939/40* (Munich, 1992).

Jansen, Hans, *Der Madagaskar-Plan. Die beabsichtigte Deportation der europäischen Juden nach Madagaskar* (Munich, 1997).

Janssen, Gregor, *Das Ministerium Speer. Deutschlands Rüstung im Krieg*, 2nd edn (Berlin, 1969).

Janssen, Karl Heinz and Fritz Tobias, *Der Sturz der Generäle. Hitler und die Blomberg-Fritsch-Krise* (Munich, 1994).

Jasch, Hans Christian, *Staatssekretär Wilhelm Stuckart und die Judenpolitik. Der Mythos von der sauberen Verwaltung* (Munich, 2012).

Jastrzębski, Włodzimierz, *Der Bromberger Blutsonntag. Legende und Wirklichkeit* (Poznan, 1990).

Jetzinger, Franz, *Hitlers Jugend. Phantasie, Lügen – und die Wahrheit* (Vienna, 1956).

Joachimsthaler, Anton, *Die Breitspurbahn Hitlers. Eine Dokumentation über die geplante transkontinentale 3-Meter-Breitspureisenbahn der Jahre 1942 bis 1945* (Freiburg i. Br., 1981).

Joachimsthaler, Anton, *Hitlers Weg begann in München. 1913–1923*, with a preface by Ian Kershaw (Munich, 2000).

Joachimsthaler, Anton, *Hitlers Liste. Ein Dokument persönlicher Beziehungen* (Munich, 2003).

Joachimsthaler, Anton, *Hitlers Ende. Legende und Dokumente*, 2nd edn (Munich, 2004).

Johnson, Eric A., *Der nationalsozialistische Terror. Gestapo, Juden und gewöhnliche Deutsche* (Berlin, 2001).

Jones, Larry Eugene, 'Nationalists, Nazis, and the Assault against Weimar. Revisiting the Harzburg Rally of October 1931', in *German Studies Review* 29 (2006), 483–94.

Jones, Sidney J., *Hitlers Weg begann in Wien. 1907–1913* (Munich, 1999).

Jordan, Rudolf, *Erlebt und erlitten. Weg eines Gauleiters von München bis Moskau* (Leoni am Starnberger See, 1971).

Das Juliabkommen von 1936. Vorgeschichte, Hintergründe und Folgen. Protokoll des Symposiums in Wien am 10. und 11. Juni 1976 (Munich, 1977).

Jung, Otmar, *Direkte Demokratie in der Weimarer Republik. Die Fälle 'Aufwertung', 'Fürstenenteignung', 'Panzerkreuzerverbot' und 'Youngplan'* (Frankfurt a. M., 1989).

Jung, Otmar, *Plebiszit und Diktatur. Die Volksabstimmungen der Nationalsozialisten: die Fälle 'Austritt aus dem Völkerbund' (1933), 'Staatsoberhaupt' (1934) und 'Anschluss Österreichs' (1938)* (Tübingen, 1995).

Junge-Wentrup, Peter (ed.), *Das Vernichtungslager Trostenez in der europäischen Erinnerung. Materialien zur Internationalen Konferenz vom 21. bis 24. März 2013 in Minsk* (Dortmund, 2013).

Junker, Detlef, *Die Deutsche Zentrumspartei und Hitler 1932–1933. Ein Beitrag zur Problematik des politischen Katholizismus in Deutschland* (Stuttgart, 1969).

Kahl, Wolfgang, 'Die Geschichte der Bayerischen Hochschulen', in Max-Emanuel Geis (ed.), *Hochschulrecht im Freistaat Bayern. Handbuch für Wissenschaft und Praxis* (Heidelberg, 2009), 1–26.

Kaiser, Gerd, *Katyn. Das Staatsverbrechen – das Staatsgeheimnis* (Berlin, 2002).

Kampe, Norbert and Peter Klein (eds), *Die Wannsee-Konferenz am 20. Januar 1942. Dokumente, Forschungsstand, Kontroversen* (Cologne, Weimar, and Vienna, 2013).

Kandl, Eleonore, 'Hitlers Österreichbild', MS, Vienna, 1963.

Karnick, Hannes and Wolfgang Richter, *Niemöller. Was würde Jesus dazu sagen? Eine Reise durch ein protestantisches Leben* (Frankfurt a. M., 1986).

Kárny, Miroslav, 'Nisko in der Geschichte der Endlösung', in *Judaica Bohemiae* 23 (1987), 69–84.

Kasten, Bernd, *'Gute Franzosen'. Die französische Polizei und die deutsche Besatzungsmacht im besetzten Frankreich, 1940–1944* (Sigmaringen, 1993).

Kater, Michael H., 'Zur Soziographie der frühen NSDAP', in *VfZ* 19 (1971), 124–59.

Kater, Michael H., *The Nazi Party. A Social Profile of Members and Leaders. 1919–1945* (Cambridge, MA and Oxford, 1983).

Kater, Michael H., *Ärzte als Hitlers Helfer* (Vienna, 2000).

Kater, Michael H., *Hitler-Jugend* (Darmstadt, 2005).

Kay, Alex J., 'Germany's Staatssekretäre, Mass Starvation and the Meeting of 2 May 1941', in *Journal of Contemporary History* 41 (2006), 685–700.

Kegel, Jens, *'Wollt Ihr den totalen Krieg?' Eine semiotische und linguistische Gesamtanalyse der Rede Goebbels' im Berliner Sportpalast am 18. Februar 1943* (Tübingen, 2006).

Kehrig, Manfred, *Stalingrad. Analyse und Dokumentation einer Schlacht* (Stuttgart, 1974).

Keilig, Wolf, *Die Generale des Heeres* (Friedberg, 1983).

Keller, Sven, *Volksgemeinschaft am Ende. Gesellschaft und Gewalt 1944/45* (Munich, 2013).

Kellerhoff, Sven Felix, *Der Reichstagsbrand. Die Karriere eines Kriminalfalls* (Berlin, 2008).

Kellogg, Michael, *The Russian Roots of Nazism. White Émigrés and the Making of National Socialism, 1917–1945* (Cambridge, 2005).

Kempner, Robert M. W., *Eichmann und Komplizen*, Zurich (Stuttgart, and Vienna, 1961).

Kershaw, Ian, *Hitler*, 2 vols, Stuttgart 1998/2000.

Kershaw, Ian, *Der Hitler-Mythos. Führerkultur und Volksmeinung* (Stuttgart, 1999).

Kershaw, Ian, *Popular Opinion and Political Dissent in the Third Reich: Bavaria 1933–1945* (Oxford, 2002).

Kershaw, Ian, *Hitlers Freunde in England. Lord Londonderry und der Weg in den Krieg* (Munich, 2005).

Kershaw, Ian, *Das Ende. Kampf bis in den Untergang: NS-Deutschland 1944/45* (Munich, 2011).

Kershaw, Ian, '"Volksgemeinschaft". Potenzial und Grenzen eines neuen Forschungskonzepts', in *VfZ* 59 (2011), 1–17.

Kiiskinen, Elina, *Die Deutschnationale Volkspartei in Bayern (Bayerische Mittelpartei) in der Regierungspolitik des Freistaats während der Weimarer Zeit. Von nationaler Erneuerung zu nationalem Untergang* (Munich, 2005).

Kimmel, Günther, 'Das Konzentrationslager Dachau. Eine Studie zu den national-sozialistischen Gewaltverbrechen', in Martin Broszat and Elke Fröhlich (eds), *Bayern in der NS-Zeit*, vol. 2, Part A (Munich, 1979), 349–413.

Kindermann, Gottfried-Karl, *Hitlers Niederlage in Österreich. Bewaffneter NS-Putsch, Kanzler-Mord und Österreichs Abwehrsieg 1934* (Hamburg, 1984).

Kindleberger, Charles P., *Die Weltwirtschaftskrise 1929–1939* (Munich, 1973).

Kirchberg, Peter, 'Typisierung in der deutschen Kraftfahrindustrie und der General-albevollmächtigte für das Kraftfahrwesen. Ein Beitrag zur Problematik staatsmo-nopolistischer Kriegsvorbereitung', in *Jahrbuch für Wirtschaftsgeschichte* (1969), vol. 2, 117–42.

Kircheisen, Inge, 'Afghanistan – umkämpftes Vorfeld Indiens', in Johannes Glasneck and Inge Kircheisen, *Türkei und Afghanistan – Brennpunkte der Orientpolitik im Zweiten Weltkrieg* (Berlin, 1968), 159–274.

Kirchhoff, Hans, 'Denmark: A Light in the Darkness of the Holocaust? A Reply to Gunnar S. Paulsson', in *Journal of Contemporary History* 30 (1995), 465–79.

Kirchhoff, Hans, 'The Rescue of the Danish Jews in October 1943', in David Bankier and Israel Gutman (eds), *Nazi Europe and the Final Solution*, (Jerusalem, 2003), 539–55.

Kissener, Michael (ed.), *Der Weg in den Nationalsozialismus 1933/34* (Darmstadt, 2009).

Kissenkoetter, Udo, *Gregor Straßer und die NSDAP* (Stuttgart, 1978).

Klarsfeld, Serge, *Vichy – Auschwitz. Die Zusammenarbeit der deutschen und französischen Behörden bei der 'Endlösung der Judenfrage' in Frankreich* (Nördlingen, 1989).

Klee, Ernst, 'Euthanasie' im NS-Staat. Die 'Vernichtung lebensunwerten Lebens', new, revised edn (Frankfurt a. M., 2010) (1st edn, 1983).

Klee, Karl, Das Unternehmen »Seelöwe«. Die geplante deutsche Landung in England 1940 (Göttingen, Berlin, and Frankfurt a. M., 1958).

Klee, Karl, Dokumente zum Unternehmen 'Seelöwe'. Die geplante deutsche Landung in England 1940 (Göttingen, Berlin, and Frankfurt a. M., 1959).

Klefisch, Peter, Das Dritte Reich und Belgien 1933–1939 (Frankfurt a. M., 1998).

Klein, Peter, 'Die Rolle der Vernichtungslager Kulmhof (Chełmno), Belzec (Bełżec) und Auschwitz-Birkenau in den frühen Deportationsvorbereitungen', in Dittmar Dahlmann and Gerhard Hirschfeld (eds), Lager, Zwangsarbeit, Vertreibung und Deportation. Dimensionen der Massenverbrechen in der Sowjetunion und in Deutschland 1933 bis 1945 (Essen, 1999), 459–84.

Klein, Peter, Die 'Ghettoverwaltung Litzmannstadt' 1940–1944. Eine Dienststelle im Spannungsfeld von Kommunalbürokratie und staatlicher Verfolgungspolitik (Hamburg, 2009).

Klessmann, Christoph, 'Der Generalgouverneur Hans Frank', in VfZ 19 (1971), 245–60.

Klink, Ernst, 'Die Landkriegsführung', in Horst Boog et al., Der Angriff auf die Sowjetunion, updated edn (Frankfurt a. M., 1991), 246–328.

Klink, Ernst, 'Heer und Kriegsmarine', in Horst Boog et al., Der Angriff auf die Sowjetunion, updated edn (Frankfurt a. M., 1991), 541–735.

Klinkhammer, Lutz, Zwischen Bündnis und Besatzung. Das nationalsozialistische Deutschland und die Republik von Saló 1943–1945 (Tübingen, 1993).

Klinkhammer, Lutz, 'Polizeiliche Kooperation unter deutscher Besatzung. Mechanismen der Repression in der "Repubblica Sociale Italiana"', in Klinkhammer, Amedeo Osti Guerazzi, und Thomas Schlemmer (eds), Die 'Achse' im Krieg. Politik, Ideologie und Kriegführung 1939–1945 (Paderborn, 2010), 472–91.

Klinksiek, Dorothee, Die Frau im NS-Staat (Stuttgart, 1982).

Klönne, Arno, Jugend im Dritten Reich. Die Hitler-Jugend und ihre Gegner (Cologne, 2003).

Kluke, Paul, 'Der Fall Potempa', in VfZ 5 (1957), 279–97.

Knipping, Franz, 'Die deutsch-französische Erklärung vom 6. Dezember 1938', in Klaus Hildebrand and Karl Ferdinand Werner (eds), Deutschland – Frankreich 1936–1939. Deutsch-französisches Historikerkolloquium des Deutschen Historischen Instituts Paris (Bonn, 26. bis 29. September 1979) (Munich, 1981), 523–51.

Koerner, Ralf Richard, So haben sie es damals gemacht. Die Propagandavorbereitungen zum Österreichanschluß durch das Hitlerregime 1933–1938. Die publizistische Behandlung der Österreichfrage und die Anschlußvorbereitungen in der Tagespresse des Dritten Reiches (1933–1938) (Vienna, 1958).

Köglmeier, Georg, Die zentralen Rätegremien in Bayern 1918/19. Legitimation – Organisation – Funktion (Munich, 2001).

Köhn, Michael, Zahnärzte 1933–1945. Berufsverbot, Emigration, Verfolgung (Berlin, 1994).

Kolbe, Dieter, Reichsgerichtspräsident Dr. Erwin Bumke. Studien zum Niedergang des Reichsgerichts und der deutschen Rechtspflege (Karlsruhe, 1975).

König, Malte, *Kooperation als Machtkampf. Das faschistische Achsenbündnis Berlin–Rom im Krieg 1940/41* (Cologne, 2007).

König, Wolfgang, *Volkswagen, Volksempfänger, Volksgemeinschaft. 'Volksprodukte' im Dritten Reich. Vom Scheitern einer nationalsozialistischen Konsumgesellschaft* (Paderborn, 2004).

Koonz, Claudia, *Mütter im Vaterland* (Freiburg i. Br., 1991).

Köpf, Gerhard, 'Hitlers psychogene Erblindung. Geschichte einer Krankenakte', in *Nervenheilkunde* 24 (2005), 783–90.

Kopper, Christoph, *Hjalmar Schacht. Aufstieg und Fall von Hitlers mächtigstem Bankier* (Munich, 2006).

Korb, Alexander, *Im Schatten des Weltkriegs. Massengewalt der Ustaša gegen Serben, Juden und Roma in Kroatien 1941–1945* (Hamburg, 2013).

Kornrumpf, Martin, *Hafraba e. V. Deutsche Autobahn-Planung 1926–1934* (Bonn, 1990).

Kosthorst, Erich, *Die deutsche Opposition gegen Hitler zwischen Polen- und Frankreichfeldzug* (Bonn, 1954).

Koszyk, Kurt, *Zwischen Kaiserreich und Diktatur. Die sozialdemokratische Presse von 1914 bis 1933* (Heidelberg, 1958).

Koszyk, Kurt, *Deutsche Presse 1914–1945* (Berlin, 1972).

Koszyk, Kurt, 'Paul Reusch und die *Münchner Neuesten Nachrichten*. Zum Problem von Industrie und Presse in der Endphase der Weimarer Republik', in *VfZ* 20 (1972), 75–103.

Kotowski, Albert S., '"Ukrainisches Piemont"? Die Karpatenukraine am Vorabend des Zweiten Weltkrieges', in *Jahrbücher für Geschichte Osteuropas* New Series 49 (2001), 67–95.

Krach, Tillmann, *Jüdische Rechtsanwälte in Preußen. Über die Bedeutung der freien Advokatur und ihre Zerstörung durch den Nationalsozialismus* (Munich, 1991).

Krausnick, Helmut, 'Vorgeschichte und Beginn des militärischen Widerstandes gegen Hitler', in Krausnick, *Vollmacht des Gewissens* (Frankfurt a. M., 1960), 177–532.

Krausnick, Helmut, 'Hitler und die Morde in Polen. Ein Beitrag zum Konflikt zwischen Heer und SS um die Verwaltung der besetzten Gebiete', in *VfZ* 11 (1963), 196–209.

Krausnick, Helmut, 'Die Einsatzgruppen vom Anschluß Österreichs bis zum Feldzug gegen die Sowjetunion. Entwicklung und Verhältnis zur Wehrmacht', in Krausnick and Hans-Heinrich Wilhelm, *Die Truppe des Weltanschauungskrieges. Die Einsatzgruppen der Sicherheitspolizei und des SD 1938–1942* (Stuttgart, 1981), 13–278.

Krebs, Gerhard, 'Von Hitlers Machtübernahme zum Pazifischen Krieg (1933–1941)', in Krebs and Bernd Marin (eds), *Formierung und Fall der Achse Berlin-Tokyo* (Munich, 1994), 11–26.

Kreidler, Eugen, *Die Eisenbahnen im Machtbereich der Achsenmächte während des Zweiten Weltkrieges. Einsatz und Leistung für die Wehrmacht und Kriegswirtschaft* (Göttingen, Frankfurt a. M., and Zurich, 1975).

Krings, Stefan, *Hitlers Pressechef. Otto Dietrich (1897–1952). Eine Biographie* (Göttingen, 2010).

Kroener, Bernhard R., '"Menschenbewirtschaftung", Bevölkerungsverteilung und personelle Rüstung in der zweiten Kriegshälfte (1942–1944)', in Kroener,

Rolf-Dieter Müller, and Hans Umbreit, *Organisation und Mobilmachung des deutschen Machtbereichs*, 2nd half volume (Stuttgart, 1999), 777–1001.

Kroener, Bernhard R., *Generaloberst Friedrich Fromm. 'Der starke Mann im Heimatkriegsgebiet'. Eine Biographie*, (Paderborn, 2005).

Krohn, Claus-Dieter, et al. (eds), *Handbuch der deutschsprachigen Emigration 1933–1945* (Darmstadt, 1998).

Kropp, Alexander, *Die politische Bedeutung der NS-Repräsentationsarchitektur. Die Neugestaltungspläne Albert Speers für den Umbau Berlins zur 'Welthauptstadt Germania' 1936–1942/43* (Neuried, 2005).

Krüger, Arnd, *Die Olympischen Spiele 1936 und die Weltmeinung. Ihre außenpolitische Bedeutung unter besonderer Berücksichtigung der USA* (Berlin and Munich, 1972).

Krüger, Arnd, *Theodor Lewald. Sportführer ins Dritte Reich*, (Berlin, Munich, and Frankfurt a. M., 1975).

Krüger, Arnd, (ed.), *The Nazi Olympics: Sport, Politics, and Appeasement in the 1930s* (Urbana and Chicago, IL, 2003).

Kube, Alfred, *Pour le mérite und Hakenkreuz. Hermann Göring im Dritten Reich* (Munich, 1986).

Kuhlmann, Jan, *Subhas Chandra Bose und die Indienpolitik der Achsenmächte* (Berlin, 2003).

Kuhn, Axel, *Hitlers außenpolitisches Programm. Entstehung und Entwicklung 1919–1939* (Stuttgart, 1970).

Kühnl, Reinhard, *Die nationalsozialistische Linke 1925–1930* (Meisenheim a. Glan, 1966).

Kühnl, Reinhard, 'Zur Programmatik der nationalsozialistischen Linken: Das Strasser-Programm von 1925/26', in *VfZ* 14 (1966), 317–33.

Kunz, Andreas, *Wehrmacht und Niederlage. Die bewaffnete Macht in der Endphase der nationalsozialistischen Herrschaft 1944 bis 1945*, (Munich, 2005).

Kuropka, Joachim (ed.) *Zur Sache – Das Kreuz! Untersuchungen zur Geschichte des Konflikts um Kreuz und Lutherbild in den Schulen Oldenburgs, zur Wirkungsgeschichte eines Massenprotestes und zum Problem nationalsozialistischer Herrschaft in einer agrarisch-katholischen Region* (Vechta, 1987).

Kuropka, Joachim (ed.), *Grenzen des katholischen Milieus. Stabilität und Gefährdung katholischer Milieus in der Endphase der Weimarer Republik und in der NS-Zeit* (Münster, 2013).

Kwiet, Konrad, *Reichskommissariat Niederlande. Versuch und Scheitern nationalsozialistischer Neuordnung* (Stuttgart, 1968).

Kwiet, Konrad, 'Forced Labour of German Jews in Nazi Germany', in *Leo Baeck Institute Year Book* 36 (1991), 389–410.

Lachnit, Ingo and Friedhelm Klein, 'Der "Operationsentwurf Ost" des Generalmajors Marcks vom 5. August 1940', in *Wehrforschung* 2 (1972), 114–23.

Lakowski, Richard, 'Der Zusammenbruch der deutschen Verteidigung zwischen Ostsee und Karpaten', in Rolf-Dieter Müller (ed.), *Das Deutsche Reich und der Zweite Weltkrieg. Die militärische Niederwerfung der Wehrmacht* (Munich, 2008), 491–679.

Lang, Jochen von, *Der Adjutant. Karl Wolff: Der Mann zwischen Hitler und Himmler* (Munich, 1985).

Lange-Stuke, Agnes, *Die Schulpolitik im Dritten Reich. Die katholische Bekenntnisschule im Bistum Hildesheim von 1933 bis 1948* (Hildesheim, 1989).

Large, David Clay, *Nazi Games. The Olympics of 1936* (London and New York, 2007).

Larsson, Lars Olof, *Die Neugestaltung der Reichshauptstadt. Albert Speers Generalbebauungsplan für Berlin* (Stuttgart, 1978).

Lau, Dirk, 'Wahlkämpfe der Weimarer Republik. Propaganda und Programme der politischen Parteien bei den Wahlen zum Deutschen Reichstag von 1924 bis 1930', unpublished dissertation, University of Mainz, 1995.

Lehmann, Joachim, 'Herbert Backe – Technokrat und Agrarideologe', in Ronald Smelser, Enrico Syring, and Rainer Zitelmann (eds), *Die braune Elite II* (Darmstadt, 1993), 1–12.

Leicht, Johannes, *Heinrich Claß 1868–1953. Die politische Biographie eines Alldeutschen* (Paderborn, 2012).

Leitz, Christian, *Economic Relations between Nazi Germany and Franco's Spain, 1936–1945* (Oxford, 1996).

Leitz, Christian, *Nazi Germany and Neutral Europe during the Second World War* (Manchester, 2000).

Leni, Yahil, *The Rescue of Danish Jewry. Test of a Democracy* (Philadelphia, PA, 1969).

Liebmann, Maximilian, *Theodor Innitzer und der Anschluss. Österreichs Kirche 1938* (Graz, 1988).

Linne, Karsten, *Deutschland jenseits des Äquators? Die NS-Kolonialplanungen für Afrika* (Berlin, 2008).

Lipscher, Ladislav, *Die Juden im slowakischen Staat 1939–1945* (Munich and Vienna, 1980).

Livi, Massimiliano, *Gertrud Scholtz-Klink. Die Reichsfrauenführerin. Politische Handlungsräume und Identitätsprobleme der Frauen im Nationalsozialismus am Beispiel der 'Führerin aller deutschen Frauen'* (Münster, 2005).

Lohalm, Uwe, *Völkischer Radikalismus. Die Geschichte des Deutschvölkischen Schutz- und Trutz-Bundes 1919–1923* (Hamburg, 1970).

Longerich, Peter, 'Joseph Goebbels und der Totale Krieg. Eine unbekannte Denkschrift des Propagandaministers vom 18. Juli 1944', in *VfZ* 35 (1987), 289–314.

Longerich, Peter, *Propagandisten im Krieg. Die Presseabteilung des Auswärtigen Amtes unter Ribbentrop* (Munich, 1987).

Longerich, Peter, (ed. with Dieter Pohl), *Die Ermordung der europäischen Juden. Eine umfassende Dokumentation des Holocaust 1941–1945* (Munich, 1989).

Longerich, Peter, *Hitlers Stellvertreter. Führung der Partei und Kontrolle des Staatsapparates durch den Stab Heß und die Partei-Kanzlei Bormann* (Munich, 1992).

Longerich, Peter, *Politik der Vernichtung. Die Verfolgung und Ermordung der europäischen Juden 1933–1945* (Munich and Zurich, 1998).

Longerich, Peter, *Geschichte der SA* (Munich, 2003).

Longerich, Peter, *'Davon haben wir nichts gewusst!' Die Deutschen und die Judenverfolgung 1933–1945* (Munich, 2006).

Longerich, Peter, *Heinrich Himmler. Biographie* (Munich, 2008).

Longerich, Peter, *Holocaust. The Nazi Persecution and Murder of the Jews* (Oxford, 2010).

Longerich, Peter, *Joseph Goebbels. Biographie* (Munich, 2010).

Loock, Hans-Dietrich, *Quisling, Rosenberg und Terboven. Zur Vorgeschichte und Geschichte der nationalsozialistischen Revolution in Norwegen* (Stuttgart, 1970).

Ludwig, Karl-Heinz, 'Die "Hochdruckpumpe", ein Beispiel technischer Fehleinschätzung im 2. Weltkrieg', in *Technikgeschichte* 38 (1971), 142–55.

Ludwig, Karl-Heinz, *Technik und Ingenieure im Dritten Reich* (Düsseldorf, 1974).

Luge, Jens, *Die Rechtsstaatlichkeit der Strafrechtspflege im Oldenburger Land 1932–1945* (Hanover, 1993).

Lükemann, Ulf, *Der Reichsschatzmeister der NSDAP. Ein Beitrag zur inneren Parteistruktur*, Dissertation, Berlin, 1963.

Lüttichau, Mario-Andreas von, '"Deutsche Kunst". Der Katalog', in Peter-Klaus Schuster (ed.), *Die 'Kunststadt' München 1937. Nationalsozialismus und 'Entartete Kunst'* (Munich, 1987), 120–83.

Machtan, Lothar, *Hitlers Geheimnis. Das Doppelleben eines Diktators* (Berlin, 2001).

Madajczyk, Czesław, *Die Okkupationspolitik Deutschlands in Polen 1939–1945* (Berlin, 1987).

Madajczyk, Czesław, (ed.), *Vom Generalplan Ost zum Generalsiedlungsplan* (Munich, 1994).

Madden, J. Paul, *The Social Composition of the Nazi Party 1919–1930*, Dissertation University of Oklahoma, 1976.

Maier, Klaus A., 'Die Luftschlacht um England', in Maier et al., *Die Errichtung der Hegemonie auf dem europäischen Kontinent* (Stuttgart, 1979), 375–408.

Maier, Klaus A. and Bernd Stegemann, 'Die Sicherung der europäischen Nordflanke', in Maier et al., *Die Errichtung der Hegemonie auf dem europäischen Kontinent* (Stuttgart, 1979), 189–231.

Majer, Diemut, *'Fremdvölkische' im Dritten Reich. Ein Beitrag zur nationalsozialistischen Rechtssetzung und Rechtspraxis in Verwaltung und Justiz unter besonderer Berücksichtigung der eingegliederten Ostgebiete und des Generalgouvernements* (Boppard am Rhein, 1993).

Majerus, Benoît, 'Von Falkenhausen zu Falkenhausen. Die deutsche Verwaltung Belgiens in den zwei Weltkriegen', in Günther Kronenbitter, Markus Pöhlmann, and Dierk Walter (eds), *Besatzung. Funktion und Gestalt militärischer Fremdherrschaft von der Antike bis zum 20. Jahrhundert* (Paderborn, 2006), 131–46.

Mallmann, Klaus-Michael, '"…Mißgeburten, die nicht auf diese Welt gehören". Die deutsche Ordnungspolizei in Polen 1939–1941', in Mallmann und Bogdan Musial (eds), *Genesis des Genozids. Polen 1939–1941* (Darmstadt, 2004), 71–89.

Mandell, Richard, *Hitlers Olympiade. Berlin 1936* (Munich, 1980).

Mann, Reinhard, *Protest und Kontrolle im Dritten Reich. Nationalsozialistische Herrschaft im Alltag einer rheinischen Großstadt* (Frankfurt a. M. and New York, 1987).

Manoschek, Walter, *'Serbien ist judenfrei'. Militärische Besatzungspolitik und Judenvernichtung in Serbien 1941/42* (Munich, 1993).

Martens, Stefan, *Hermann Göring. 'Erster Paladin des Führers' und 'Zweiter Mann im Reich'* (Paderborn, 1985).

Martin, Bernd, 'Britisch-deutsche Friedenskontakte in den ersten Monaten des Zweiten Weltkrieges. Eine Dokumentation über die Vermittlungsversuche von Birger Dahlerus', in *Zeitschrift für Politik*, New Series 19 (1972), 206–22.

Martin, Bernd, *Friedensinitiativen und Machtpolitik im Zweiten Weltkrieg 1939–1942* (Düsseldorf, 1974).

Martin, Bernd, 'Die deutsch-japanischen Beziehungen während des Dritten Reiches', in Manfred Funke (ed.), *Hitler und die Mächte. Materialien zur Außenpolitik des Dritten Reiches* (Düsseldorf, 1976), 454–70.

Martin, Bernd, 'Deutsch-sowjetische Sondierungen über einen separaten Friedensschluß im Zweiten Weltkrieg. Bericht und Dokumentation', in Inge Auerbach (ed.), *Felder und Vorfelder russischer Geschichte. Studien zu Ehren von Peter Scheibert* (Freiburg i. Br., 1985), 280–308.

Martynkewicz, Wolfgang, *Salon Deutschland. Geist und Macht* (Berlin, 2009).

März, Markus, *Nationale Sozialisten in der NSDAP. Strukturen, Ideologie, Publizistik und Biographien des national-sozialistischen Straßer-Kreises von der AG Nordwest bis zum Kampf-Verlag 1925–1930*, (Graz, 2010).

Maser, Werner, *Der Sturm auf die Republik. Frühgeschichte der NSDAP* (Frankfurt a. M., 1981).

Mason, Timothy W., 'The Domestic Dynamics of Nazi Conquests. A Response to Critics', in Mason, *Nazism, Fascism and the Working Class*, ed. Jane Caplan (Cambridge and New York, 1995), 295–322.

Mathieu, Thomas, *Kunstauffassungen und Kulturpolitik im Nationalsozialismus. Studien zu Adolf Hitler, Joseph Goebbels, Alfred Rosenberg, Baldur von Schirach, Heinrich Himmler, Albert Speer, Wilhelm Frick* (Saarbrücken, 1997).

Matić, Igor-Philip, *Edmund Veesenmayer. Agent und Diplomat der nationalsozialistischen Expansionspolitik* (Munich, 2002).

Matthias, Erich, 'Die Sozialdemokratische Partei Deutschlands', in Matthias and Rudolf Morsey (eds), *Das Ende der Parteien 1933* (Düsseldorf, 1960), 101–278.

Matthiesen, Helge, *Bürgertum und Nationalsozialismus in Thüringen. Das bürgerliche Gotha von 1918 bis 1930* (Jena, 1994).

Matthiesen, Helge, *Greifswald in Vorpommern. Konservatives Milieu im Kaiserreich, in Demokratie und Diktatur 1900–1990* (Düsseldorf, 2000).

Mattioli, Aram, *Experimentierfeld der Gewalt. Der Abessinienkrieg und seine internationale Bedeutung 1935–1941* (Zurich, 2005).

Matussek, Paul, Peter Matussek, and Jan Marbach, *Hitler – Karriere eines Wahns* (Munich, 2000).

Matzerath, Horst, *Nationalsozialismus und kommunale Selbstverwaltung* (Stuttgart, 1970).

Matzerath, Horst, 'Der Weg der Kölner Juden in den Holocaust. Versuch einer Rekonstruktion', in *Die jüdischen Opfer des Nationalsozialismus aus Köln* (Cologne, 1995), 530–53.

Mayer, Klaus, 'Eine authentische Halder-Ansprache? Kritische Anmerkungen zu einem Dokumentenfund im früheren Moskauer Sonderarchiv', in *MGM* 58 (1999), 471–527.

Mazower, Mark, *Hitlers Imperium. Europa unter der Herrschaft des Nationalsozialismus* (Munich, 2009).

McGuiness, Brian, *Wittgensteins frühe Jahre* (Frankfurt a. M., 1988).

Meier, Kurt, *Der evangelische Kirchenkampf*, 3 vols (Göttingen, 1976–84).

Meier-Dörnberg, Wilhelm, *Die Ölversorgung der Kriegsmarine 1935 bis 1945* (Freiburg, 1973).

Meier-Welcker, Hans, 'Aus dem Briefwechsel zweier junger Offiziere des Reichsheeres 1930–1938', in *MGM* 14 (1973), 57–100.

Meining, Stefan, 'Ein erster Ansturm der Antisemiten: 1919–1923', in Douglas Bokovoy and Stefan Meining (eds), *Versagte Heimat. Jüdisches Leben in Münchens Isarvorstadt 1914–1945* (Munich, 1994), 53–74.

Meissner, Karl-Heinz, '"Deutsches Volk, gib uns vier Jahre Zeit..." Nationalsozialistische Kunstpolitik 1933–37. Große Deutsche Kunstausstellung – Ausstellung "Entartete Kunst" München 1937', in Jürgen Harten, Hans-Werner Schmidt, and Marie Luise Syring (eds), *'Die Axt hat geblüht...'. Europäische Konflikte der 30er Jahre in Erinnerung an die frühe Avantgarde, 11. Oktober bis 6. Dezember 1987* (Düsseldorf, 1987), 368–76.

Meissner, Karl-Heinz, 'Große Deutsche Kunstausstellung', in *Stationen der Moderne. Die bedeutenden Kunstausstellungen des 20. Jahrhunderts in Deutschland, Ausstellungskatalog* (Berlin, 1988), 276–84.

Meister, Rainer, *Die große Depression. Zwangslagen und Handlungsspielräume der Wirtschafts- und Finanzpolitik in Deutschland 1929–1932* (Regensburg, 1991).

Menges, Franz, *Hans Schmelzle. Bayerischer Staatsrat im Ministerium des Äußeren und Finanzminister. Eine politische Biographie mit Quellenanhang* (Munich, 1972).

Merkenich, Stephanie, *Grüne Front gegen Weimar. Reichs-Landbund und agrarischer Lobbyismus 1918–1933* (Düsseldorf, 1998).

Merkes, Manfred, *Die deutsche Politik im spanischen Bürgerkrieg 1936–1939*, 2nd revised and expanded edn (Bonn, 1969).

Merson, Allan, *Kommunistischer Widerstand in Nazideutschland* (Bonn, 1999).

Merz, Johannes, 'Auf dem Weg zur Räterepublik. Staatskrise und Regierungsbildung in Bayern nach dem Tode Eisners (Februar/März 1919)', in *Zeitschrift für bayerische Landesgeschichte* 66 (2003), 541–64.

Meyer, Ahlrich, '"...dass französische Verhältnisse anders sind als polnische". Die Bekämpfung des Widerstands durch die deutsche Militärverwaltung in Frankreich 1941', in Guus Meershoeck et al., *Repression und Kriegsverbrechen. Die Bekämpfung von Widerstands- und Partisanenbewegungen gegen die deutsche Besatzung in West- und Südosteuropa* (Berlin, 1997), 43–93.

Michaelis, Meir, *Mussolini and the Jews. German–Italian Relations and the Jewish Question in Italy, 1922–1945* (Oxford, 1978).

Michalka, Wolfgang, *Ribbentrop und die deutsche Weltpolitik 1933–1940. Außenpolitische Konzeptionen und Entscheidungsprozesse im Dritten Reich* (Munich, 1980).

Michels, Helmut, *Ideologie und Propaganda. Die Rolle von Joseph Goebbels in der nationalsozialistischen Außenpolitik bis 1939* (Frankfurt a. M., 1992).

Middlebrook, Martin, *Hamburg Juli 43. Alliierte Luftstreitkräfte gegen eine deutsche Stadt* (Berlin and Frankfurt a. M., 1983).

Mierzejewski, Alfred C., *Hitler's Trains. The German National Railway and the Third Reich* (Stroud, 2005).

Miller, Alice, *Am Anfang war Erziehung* (Frankfurt a. M., 1980).

Miller-Kipp, Gisela, '"Totale Erfassung" – aber wie? Die Hitler-Jugend: Politische Funktion, psychosoziales Funktionieren und Moment des Widerstands', in Stephanie Becker and Christoph Studt (eds), *'Und sie werden nicht mehr frei sein ihr ganzes Leben'. Funktion und Stellenwert der NSDAP, ihrer Gliederungen und angeschlossenen Verbände im 'Dritten Reich'* (Münster, 2012), 87–104.

Miller Lane, Barbara, *Architektur und Politik in Deutschland 1918–1945* (Braunschweig, 1986).

Mitchell, Allan, *Revolution in Bayern 1918/1919. Die Eisner-Regierung und die Räterepublik* (Munich, 1967).

Moll, Martin, 'Steuerungsinstrument im "Ämterchaos"? Die Tagungen der Reichs- und Gauleiter der NSDAP', in *VfZ* 49 (2001), 215–73.

Möllers, Heiner, 'Sponeck, Hans Emil Otto Graf von', in *Neue Deutsche Biographie* 24 (2010), 736f.

Mollin, Gerhard Th., *Montankonzerne und 'Drittes Reich'. Der Gegensatz zwischen Monopolindustrie und Befehlswirtschaft in der deutschen Rüstung und Expansion 1936–1944* (Göttingen, 1988).

Moltmann, Günter, 'Goebbels' Rede zum totalen Krieg am 18. Februar 1943', in *VfZ* 12 (1964), 13–43.

Mommsen, Hans, *Beamtentum im Dritten Reich. Mit ausgewählten Quellen zur nationalsozialistischen Beamtenpolitik* (Stuttgart, 1966).

Mommsen, Hans, 'Nationalsozialismus', in *Sowjetsystem und demokratische Gesellschaft. Eine vergleichende Enzyklopädie*, vol. 4 (Freiburg, 1971), columns 695–713.

Mommsen, Hans, 'Reichsreform und Regionalgewalten – Das Phantom der Mittelinstanz 1933–1945', in Oliver Janz (ed.), *Zentralismus und Föderalismus im 19. und 20. Jahrhundert* (Berlin 2000), 227–38.

Mommsen, Hans and Manfred Grieger, *Das Volkswagenwerk und seine Arbeiter im Dritten Reich* (Düsseldorf, 1996).

Moreau, Patrick, *Nationalsozialismus von links. Die 'Kampfgemeinschaft Revolutionärer Nationalsozialisten' und die 'Schwarze Front' Otto Strassers 1930–1935* (Stuttgart, 1985).

Moritz, Erhard, 'Planungen für die Kriegführung des deutschen Heeres in Afrika und Vorderasien', in *Militärgeschichte* 16 (1977), 323–33.

Morsch, Günter, *Arbeit und Brot. Studien zu Lage, Stimmung, Einstellung und Verhalten der deutschen Arbeiterschaft 1933–1936/37* (Frankfurt a. M., 1993).

Morsey, Rudolf, 'Die Deutsche Zentrumspartei', in Erich Matthias and Morsey (eds), *Das Ende der Parteien 1933* (Düsseldorf, 1960), 281–453.

Morsey, Rudolf, 'Hitlers Verhandlungen mit der Zentrumsführung am 31. Januar 1933', in *VfZ* 9 (1961), 182–94.

Morsey, Rudolf, *Der Untergang des politischen Katholizismus. Die Zentrumspartei zwischen christlichem Selbstverständnis und 'nationaler Erhebung' 1932/33* (Stuttgart and Zurich, 1977).

Moser, Jonny, 'Die Apokalypse der Wiener Juden', in Historisches Museum der Stadt Wien (ed.), *Wien 1938. 110. Sonderausstellung, 11. März bis 30. Juni 1988* (Vienna, 1988), 286–97.

Moser, Jonny, 'Nisko: The First Experiment in Deportation', in *Simon Wiesenthal Center Annual* 2/1 (1995), 1–30.

Mühl-Benninghaus, Sigrun, *Das Beamtentum in der NS-Diktatur bis zum Ausbruch des Zweiten Weltkrieges. Zu Enstehen, Inhalt und Durchführung der einschlägigen Beamtengesetze* (Düsseldorf, 1996).

Mühle, Robert W., *Frankreich und Hitler. Die französische Deutschland- und Außenpolitik 1933–1935* (Paderborn, 1995).

Mühlen, Patrick von zur, *'Schlagt Hitler an der Saar!' Abstimmungskampf, Emigration und Widerstand im Saargebiet 1933–1935* (Bonn, 1979).

Mühlenfeld, Daniel, 'Zur Bedeutung der NS-Propaganda für die Eroberung staatlicher Macht und die Sicherung politischer Loyalität', in Christian A. Braun, Michael Mayer, and Sebastian Weitkamp (eds), *Deformation der Gesellschaft? Neue Forschungen zum Nationalsozialismus* (Berlin, 2008), 93–117.

Mulders, Jean Paul, *Auf der Suche nach Hitlers Sohn. Eine Beweisaufnahme* (Munich, 2009).

Müller, Klaus-Jürgen, *Das Heer und Hitler. Armee und nationalsozialistisches Regime 1933–1940*, (Stuttgart, 1969).

Müller, Klaus-Jürgen, *General Ludwig Beck. Studien und Dokumente zur politisch-militärischen Vorstellungswelt und Tätigkeit des Generalstabschefs des deutschen Heeres 1933–1938* (Boppard am Rhein, 1980).

Müller, Klaus-Jürgen, 'Struktur und Entwicklung der national-konservativen Opposition', in *Aufstand des Gewissens. Militärischer Widerstand gegen Hitler und das NS-Regime 1933 bis 1945. Begleitband zur Wanderausstellung des Militärgeschichtlichen Forschungsamtes*, ed. Thomas Vogel, 6th edn (Hamburg, 2001), 89–135.

Müller, Klaus-Jürgen, *Generaloberst Ludwig Beck. Eine Biographie* (Paderborn, 2007).

Müller, Rolf-Dieter, 'Die Mobilisierung der deutschen Wirtschaft für Hitlers Kriegführung', in Bernhard R. Kroener, Müller, and Hans Umbreit, *Organisierung und Mobilisierung des deutschen Machtbereichs*, vol. 1 (Stuttgart, 1988), 349–689.

Müller, Rolf-Dieter, 'Albert Speer und die Rüstungspolitik im totalen Krieg', in Bernhard R. Kroener (ed.), *Das Deutsche Reich und der Zweite Weltkrieg. Kriegsverwaltung, Wirtschaft und personelle Ressourcen* (Stuttgart, 1999), 275–773.

Müller, Rolf-Dieter, *Der Feind steht im Osten. Hitlers geheime Pläne für einen Krieg gegen die Sowjetunion im Jahr 1939* (Berlin, 2011).

Müller-Rytlewski, Marlene, *Der verlängerte Krieg. Hitlers propagandistisches Wirken in einer historisch desorientierten und sozial fragmentierten Gesellschaft* (Munich, 1989).

Musial, Bogdan, *Deutsche Zivilverwaltung und Judenverfolgung im Generalgouvernement. Eine Fallstudie zum Distrikt Lublin 1939–1944* (Wiesbaden, 1999).

Musial, Bogdan, *Kampfplatz Deutschland. Stalins Kriegspläne gegen den Westen* (Berlin, 2008).

Muth, Heinrich, 'Das "Kölner Gespräch" am 4. Januar 1933', in *GWU* 37 (1986), 463–80 and 529–41.

Nagel, Anne Christine, '"Er ist der Schrecken überhaupt der Hochschule." Der Nationalsozialistische Deutsche Dozentenbund in der Wissenschaftspolitik des Dritten Reiches', in Joachim Scholtyseck and Christoph Studt (eds), *Universitäten und Studenten im Dritten Reich* (Berlin, 2008), 115–32.

Neebe, Reinhard, *Großindustrie, Staat und NSDAP 1930–1933. Paul Silverberg und der Reichsverband der Deutschen Industrie in der Krise der Weimarer Republik* (Göttingen, 1981).

Neliba, Günter, 'Wilhelm Frick und Thüringen als Experimentierfeld für die nationalsozialistische Machtergreifung', in Detlev Heiden and Günther Mai (eds), *Thüringen auf dem Weg ins 'Dritte Reich'* (Erfurt, 1996), 95–118.

Nerdinger, Winfried (ed.), *Bauen im Nationalsozialismus. Bayern 1933–1945, Ausstellung des Architekturmuseums der Technischen Universität München und des Münchner Stadtmuseum* (Munich, 1993).

Nesládková, Ludmila (ed.), *The Case Nisko in the History of the Final Solution of the Jewish Problem in Commemoration of the 55th Anniversary of the First Deportation of Jews in Europe 1994* (Ostrava, 1995).

Neufeld, Michael J., *Die Rakete und das Reich. Wernher von Braun, Peenemünde und der Beginn des Raketenzeitalters* (Berlin, 1997).

Neumann, Hans-Joachim and Henrik Eberle, *War Hitler krank? Ein abschließender Befund* (Bergisch-Gladbach, 2009).

Nierhaus, Andreas, 'Der "Anschluss" und seine Bilder – Inszenierung, Ästhetisierung, Historisierung', in Werner Welzig (ed.) in collaboration with Hanno Biber and Claudia Resch, *'Anschluss'. März/April 1938 in Österreich* (Vienna, 2010), 89–110.

Nolzen, Armin, 'Die NSDAP, der Krieg und die deutsche Gesellschaft', in Jörg Echternkamp (ed.), *Die deutsche Kriegsgesellschaft 1939–1945* (Munich, 2004), 99–193.

Nolzen, Armin, 'Die Reichsorganisationsleitung als Verwaltungsbehörde der NSDAP. Kompetenzen, Strukturen und administrative Praktiken nach 1933', in Sven Reichardt and Wolfgang Seibel (eds), *Der prekäre Staat. Herrschen und Verwalten im Nationalsozialismus* (Frankfurt a. M., 2011), 121–66.

North, Stephen Graeme, *Rudolf Heß. A Political Biography* (Saarbrücken, 2010).

Nowak, Kurt, *'Euthanasie' und Sterilisierung im 'Dritten Reich'. Die Konfrontation der evangelischen und katholischen Kirche mit dem Gesetz zur Verhütung erbkranken Nachwuchses und der 'Euthanasie'-Aktion* (Göttingen, 1978).

Nusser, Horst G. W., *Konservative Wehrverbände in Bayern, Preußen und Österreich 1918–1933* (Munich, 1973).

Nüsslein, Timo, *Paul Ludwig Troost (1878–1934)* (Vienna, Cologne, and Weimar, 2012).

Obenaus, Herbert, 'The Germans: "An Antisemitic People". The Press Campaign after 9 November 1938', in David Bankier (ed.), *Probing the Depths of German*

Antisemitism: German Society and the Persecution of the Jews, 1933–1941 (New York, 2000), 147–80.

Obst, Dieter, *'Reichskristallnacht'. Ursachen und Verlauf des antisemitischen Pogroms vom November 1938* (Frankfurt a. M., 1991).

Odenwald, Florian, *Der nazistische Kampf gegen das 'Undeutsche' in Theater und Film 1920–1945* (Munich, 2006).

Ohler, Norman, *Der totale Rausch. Drogen im Dritten Reich* (Cologne, 2015).

Olshausen, Klaus, *Zwischenspiel auf dem Balkan. Die deutsche Politik gegenüber Jugoslawien und Griechenland von März bis Juli 1941* (Stuttgart, 1973).

Orlow, Dietrich, *The History of the Nazi Party*, vol. 1 (Newton Abbot, 1971).

Orth, Karin, *Das System der nationalsozialistischen Konzentrationslager. Eine politische Organisationsgeschichte* (Hamburg, 1999).

Orth, Rainer, *Der SD-Mann Johannes Schmidt. Der Mörder des Reichskanzlers Kurt von Schleicher?* (Marburg, 2012).

Overy, Richard, 'Hitler's War Plans and the German Economy', in Robert W. D. Boyce and Esmonde M. Robertson (eds), *Paths to War. New Essays on the Origins of the Second World War* (Basingstoke and London, 1989), 96–127.

Overy, Richard, 'Guns or Butter? Living Standards, Finance, and Labour in Germany, 1939–1942', in Overy, *War and Economy in the Third Reich* (Oxford, 1994), 259–314.

Page, Helena P., *Friedrich Olbricht. Ein Mann des 20. Juli* (Bonn, 1992).

Parssinen, Terry, *The Oster Conspiracy of 1938. The Unknown Story of the Military Plot to Kill Hitler and Avert World War II* (London, 2004).

Pätzold, Kurt, *Faschismus, Rassenwahn, Judenverfolgung. Eine Studie zur politischen Strategie und Taktik des faschistischen deutschen Imperialismus (1933–1945)* (Berlin, 1975).

Pätzold, Kurt, 'Hitlers fünfzigster Geburtstag am 20. April 1939', in Dietrich Eichholtz and Pätzold (eds), *Der Weg in den Krieg. Studien zur Geschichte der Vorkriegsjahre (1935/36 bis 1939)* (Cologne, 1989), 309–46.

Pätzold, Kurt and Manfred Weissbecker, *Rudolf Heß. Der Mann an Hitlers Seite* (Leipzig, 1999).

Pätzold, Kurt and Manfred Weissbecker, *Geschichte der NSDAP 1920–1945* (Cologne, 2009).

Paul, Gerhard, *'Deutsche Mutter – heim zu Dir!' Warum es mißlang, Hitler an der Saar zu schlagen. Der Saarkampf 1933–1935* (Cologne, 1984).

Paul, Gerhard, *Aufstand der Bilder. Die NS-Propaganda vor 1933* (Bonn, 1990).

Pauley, Bruce F., *Der Weg in den Nationalsozialismus. Ursprünge und Entwicklung in Österreich* (Vienna, 1988).

Paulsson, Gunnar S., '"The Bridge over Oeresund". The Historiography on the Expulsion of the Jews from Nazi-Occupied Denmark', in *Journal of Contemporary History* 30 (1995), 431–64.

Permooser, Irmtraud, *Der Luftkrieg über München 1942–1945. Bomben auf die Hauptstadt der Bewegung* (Oberhaching, 1996).

Petersen, Jens, *Hitler – Mussolini. Die Entstehung der Achse Berlin-Rom 1933–1936* (Tübingen, 1973).

Petropoulos, Jonathan, *Royals and the Reich. The Princes von Hessen in Nazi Germany* (Oxford and New York, 2006).

Petzina, Dietmar, *Autarkiepolitik im Dritten Reich. Der nationalsozialistische Vierjahresplan* (Stuttgart, 1968).

Petzold, Joachim, 'Claß und Hitler. Über die Förderung der frühen Nazibewegung durch den Alldeutschen Verband und dessen Einfluß auf die nazistische Ideologie', in *Jahrbuch für Geschichte* 21 (1980), 247–88.

Petzold, Joachim, *Franz von Papen. Ein deutsches Verhängnis* (Munich and Berlin, 1995).

Pfeiffer, Lorenz, '"…Unser Verein ist judenfrei" – Die Rolle der deutschen Turn- und Sportbewegung in dem politischen und gesellschaftlichen Wandlungsprozess nach dem 30. Januar 1933', in *Historical Social Research* 32 (2007), 92–109.

Phelps, Reginald H., '"Before Hitler Came". Thule Society and Germanen Orden', in *The Journal of Modern History* 35 (1963), 245–61.

Phelps, Reginald H., 'Hitler als Parteiredner im Jahre 1920', in *VfZ* 11 (1963), 274–330.

Philippi, Alfred and Ferdinand Heim, *Der Feldzug gegen Sowjetrußland 1941–1945. Ein operativer Überblick* (Stuttgart, 1962).

Pietrow-Ennker, Bianka (ed.), *Präventivkrieg? Der deutsche Angriff auf die Sowjetunion* (Frankfurt a. M., 2000).

Piper, Ernst, *Alfred Rosenberg. Hitlers Chefideologe* (Munich, 2005).

Plehwe, Friedrich-Karl von, *Reichskanzler Kurt von Schleicher. Weimars letzte Chance gegen Hitler* (Frankfurt a. M. and Berlin, 1990).

Plewnia, Margarete, *Auf dem Weg zu Hitler. Der völkische Publizist Dietrich Eckart* (Bremen, 1970).

Plieg, Ernst-Albrecht, *Das Memelland 1920–1939. Deutsche Autonomiebestrebungen im Litauischen Gesamtstaat* (Würzburg, 1962).

Plöckinger, Othmar, *Geschichte eines Buches: Adolf Hitlers 'Mein Kampf', 1922–1945,* (Munich, 2006).

Plöckinger, Othmar, 'Adolf Hitler als Hörer an der Universität München im Jahre 1919. Zum Verhältnis zwischen Reichswehr und Universität', in Elisabeth Kraus (ed.), *Die Universität München im Dritten Reich. Aufsätze*, Part 2 (Munich, 2008), 13–47.

Plöckinger, Othmar, *Unter Soldaten und Agitatoren. Hitlers prägende Jahre im deutschen Militär 1918–1920* (Paderborn, 1920).

Plumpe, Gottfried, *Die I.G. Farbenindustrie AG. Wirtschaft, Technik und Politik 1904–1945* (Berlin, 1990).

Pohl, Dieter, *Von der »Judenpolitik« zum Judenmord. Der Distrikt Lublin des Generalgouvernements 1939–1944* (Frankfurt a. M., 1993).

Pohl, Dieter, *Nationalsozialistische Judenverfolgung in Ostgalizien 1941–1944. Organisation und Durchführung eines staatlichen Massenverbrechens* (Munich, 1996).

Pollmeier, Heiko, 'Inhaftierung und Lagererfahrung deutscher Juden im November 1938', in *Jahrbuch für Antisemitismusforschung* 8 (1999), 107–30.

Portmann, Heinrich, *Der Bischof von Münster* (Münster, 1947).

Poznanski, Renée, *Jews in France during World War II* (Hanover, NH, 2001).

Přibyl, Lukáš, 'Das Schicksal des dritten Transports aus dem Protektorat nach Nisko', in *Theresienstädter Studien und Dokumente 2000*, 297–342.

Prieberg, Fred K., *Musik im NS-Staat* (Frankfurt a. M., 1982).

Prieberg, Fred K., *Kraftprobe. Wilhelm Furtwängler im Dritten Reich* (Wiesbaden, 1986).

Puchert, Berthold, 'Der deutsche Außenhandel im Zweiten Weltkrieg', in Dietrich Eichholtz, *Geschichte der deutschen Kriegswirtschaft 1939–1945*, 3 vols (Munich, 2003), 393–508.

Pyta, Wolfram, *Dorfgemeinschaft und Parteipolitik 1918–1933. Die Verschränkung von Milieu und Parteien in den protestantischen Landgebieten Deutschlands in der Weimarer Republik* (Düsseldorf, 1996).

Pyta, Wolfram, *Hindenburg. Herrschaft zwischen Hohenzollern und Hitler* (Munich, 2007).

Pyta, Wolfram, 'Weltanschauliche und strategische Schicksalsgemeinschaft. Die Bedeutung Japans für das weltpolitische Kalkül Hitlers', in Martin Cüppers, Jürgen Matthäus, and Andrej Angrick (eds), *Naziverbrechen. Täter, Taten, Bewältigungsversuche* (Darmstadt, 2013), 21–44.

Pyta, Wolfram, *Hitler. Der Künstler als Politiker und Feldherr. Eine Herrschaftsanalyse* (Munich, 2015).

Quint, Herbert A., *Porsche. Der Weg eines Zeitalters* (Stuttgart, 1951).

Radetz, Walter, *Der Stärkere. Ein Buch über Werner Seelenbinder* (Berlin, 1982).

Raem, Heinz-Albert, *Pius XI. und der Nationalsozialismus. Die Enzyklika 'Mit brennender Sorge' vom 14. März 1937* (Paderborn, 1979).

Rahn, Werner, 'Der Krieg im Pazifik', in Horst Boog et al., *Der globale Krieg. Die Ausweitung zum Weltkrieg und der Wechsel der Initiative 1941–1943* (Stuttgart, 1990), 171–271.

Rahn, Werner, 'Der Seekrieg im Atlantik und Nordmeer', in Horst Boog et al., *Der globale Krieg. Die Ausweitung zum Weltkrieg und der Wechsel der Initiative 1941–1943* (Stuttgart, 1990), 275–425.

Raina, Peter, *A Daring Venture. Rudolf Hess and the Ill-Fated Peace Mission of 1941* (Oxford, 2014).

Ramm, Arnim, *Der 20. Juli 1944 vor dem Volksgerichtshof* (Berlin, 2007).

Rapp, Petra Madeleine, *Die Devisenprozesse gegen katholische Ordensangehörige und Geistliche im Dritten Reich. Eine Untersuchung zum Konflikt deutscher Orden und Klöster in wirtschaftlicher Notlage, totalitärer Machtausübung des nationalsozialistischen Regimes und im Kirchenkampf 1935/36*, Dissertation, Bonn, 1981.

Rauh-Kühne, Cornelia, *Katholisches Milieu und Kleinstadtgesellschaft. Ettlingen 1918–1939* (Sigmaringen, 1991).

Rautenberg, Hans-Jürgen, *Deutsche Rüstungspolitik vom Beginn der Genfer Abrüstungskonferenz bis zur Wiedereinführung der Allgemeinen Wehrpflicht 1932–1935* (Bonn, 1973).

Rautkallio, Hannu, *Finland and the Holocaust. The Rescue of Finland's Jews* (New York, 1987).

Rebentisch, Dieter, 'Die "politische Beurteilung" als Herrschaftsinstrument der NSDAP', in Detlev Peukert and Jürgen Reulecke (eds), *Die Reihen fast geschlossen. Beiträge zur Geschichte des Alltags unterm Nationalsozialismus* (Wuppertal, 1981), 107–25.

Rebentisch, Dieter, *Führerstaat und Verwaltung im Zweiten Weltkrieg. Verfassungsentwicklung und Verfassungspolitik 1939–1945* (Stuttgart, 1989).

Reeken, Dietmar von and Malte Thiessen (eds), *'Volksgemeinschaft' als soziale Praxis. Neue Forschungen zur NS-Gesellschaft vor Ort* (Paderborn, 2013).

Reibel, Carl-Wilhelm, *Das Fundament der Diktatur. Die NSDAP-Ortsgruppe. 1932–1945* (Paderborn, 2002).

Reich, Ines, *Carl Friedrich Goerdeler. Ein Oberbürgermeister gegen den NS-Staat*, Cologne (Weimar, and Vienna, 1997).

Reichhardt, Hans J. and Wolfgang Schäche, *Von Berlin nach Germania. Über die Zerstörungen der 'Reichshauptstadt' durch Albert Speers Neugestaltungsplanungen* (Berlin, 1998).

Reinhardt, Klaus, *Die Wende vor Moskau. Das Scheitern der Strategie Hitlers im Winter 1941/42* (Stuttgart, 1972).

Remy, Maurice Philip, *Mythos Rommel* (Munich, 2002).

Repgen, Konrad, 'Über die Entstehung der Reichskonkordats-Offerte im Frühjahr 1933 und die Bedeutung des Reichskonkordats. Kritische Bemerkungen zu einem neuen Buch', in *VfZ* 26 (1978), 499–534.

Reupke, Hans, *Der Nationalsozialismus und die Wirtschaft* (Berlin, 1931).

Reuth, Ralf Georg, *Rommel. Das Ende einer Legende* (Zurich and Munich, 2004).

Reuth, Ralf Georg, *Hitlers Judenhass. Klischee und Wirklichkeit* (Munich and Zurich, 2009).

Richardi, Hans-Günter, *Bomber über München. Der Luftkrieg von 1939 bis 1945, dargestellt am Beispiel der 'Hauptstadt der Bewegung'* (Munich, 1992).

Richardi, Hans-Günter and Klaus Schumann, *Geheimakte Gerlich/Bell. Röhms Pläne für ein Reich ohne Hitler* (Munich, 1993).

Riedel, Matthias, *Eisen und Kohle für das Dritte Reich. Paul Pleigers Stellung in der NS-Wirtschaft* (Göttingen, 1973).

Riess, Volker, *Die Anfänge der Vernichtung 'lebensunwerten Lebens' in den Reichsgauen Danzig-Westpreußen und Wartheland 1939/40* (Frankfurt a. M., 1995).

Rischbieter, Henning, 'NS-Theaterpolitik', in Thomas Eicher, Barbara Panse, and Rischbieter, *Theater im 'Dritten Reich'. Theaterpolitik, Spielplanstruktur, NS-Dramatik* (Seelze and Velbert, 2000), 11–277.

Ritschl, Albert, *Deutschlands Krise und Konjunktur 1924–1934. Binnenkonjunktur, Auslandsverschuldung und Reparationsproblem zwischen Dawes-Plan und Transfersperre* (Berlin, 2002).

Ritthaler, Anton, 'Eine Etappe auf Hitlers Weg zur ungeteilten Macht. Hugenbergs Rücktritt als Reichsminister', in *VfZ* 8 (1960), 193–219.

Roberts, Geoffrey, *The Unholy Alliance. Stalin's Pact with Hitler* (London, 1989).

Robertson, Esmonde M., 'Zur Wiederbesetzung des Rheinlands 1936', in *VfZ* 10 (1962), 178–205.

Rohde, Horst, 'Hitlers erster "Blitzkrieg" und seine Auswirkungen auf Nordosteuropa', in Klaus A. Maier et al., *Die Errichtung der Hegemonie auf dem europäischen Kontinent* (Stuttgart, 1979), 79–156.

Röhl, Klaus Rainer, *Nähe zum Gegner. Kommunisten und Nationalsozialisten im Berliner BVG-Streik von 1932* (Frankfurt a. M. and New York, 1994).

Romanicev, Nicolaj M., 'Militärische Pläne eines Gegenschlags der UdSSR', in Gerd R. Ueberschär and Lev A. Bezymenskij (eds), *Der deutsche Angriff auf die Sowjetunion 1941. Die Kontroverse um die Präventivkriegsthese*, 2nd edn (Darmstadt, 2011), 90–102.

Rönnefarth, Helmuth K. G., *Die Sudetenkrise in der internationalen Politik*, 2 parts (Wiesbaden, 1961).

Roon, Ger van, *Widerstand im Dritten Reich. Ein Überblick*, 5th revised edn (Munich, 1990).

Rösch, Mathias, *Die Münchner NSDAP 1925–1933. Eine Untersuchung zur inneren Struktur der NSDAP in der Weimarer Republik* (Munich, 2002).

Rosenkranz, Herbert, *Verfolgung und Selbstbehauptung. Die Juden in Österreich 1938–1945* (Vienna, 1978).

Ross, Dieter, *Hitler und Dollfuß. Die deutsche Österreich-Politik 1933–1934* (Hamburg, 1966).

Rossino, Alexander B., *Hitler Strikes Poland. Blitzkrieg, Ideology, and Atrocity* (Lawrence, 2003).

Rother, Rainer, *Leni Riefenstahl. Die Verführung des Talents* (Berlin, 2000).

Runzheimer, Jürgen, 'Die Grenzzwischenfälle am Abend vor dem deutschen Angriff auf Polen', in Wolfgang Benz and Hermann Graml (eds), *Sommer 1939. Die Großmächte und der Europäische Krieg* (Stuttgart, 1979), 107–40.

Rusinek, Bernd, *Gesellschaft in der Katastrophe. Terror, Illegalität, Widerstand – Köln 1944/45* (Essen, 1989).

Ryback, Timothy W., *Hitlers Bücher. Seine Bibliothek – sein Denken*, (Cologne, 2010).

Sabrow, Martin, 'Der "Tag von Potsdam". Zur doppelten Karriere eines politischen Mythos', in Christoph Kopke (ed.), *Der Tag von Potsdam. Der 21. März 1933 und die Errichtung der nationalsozialistischen Diktatur* (Berlin, 2013), 47–86.

Sachsse, Christoph and Florian Tennstedt, *Der Wohlfahrtsstaat im Nationalsozialismus* (Stuttgart, 1992).

Safrian, Hans, *Die Eichmann-Männer* (Vienna, 1993).

Salewski, Michael, *Die deutsche Seekriegsleitung 1935–1945*, 3 vols (Frankfurt a. M. and Munich, 1970–75).

Salewski, Michael, 'Marineleitung und politische Führung 1931–1935', in *MGM* (1971/2), 113–58.

Salewski, Michael, 'Die Abwehr der Invasion als Schlüssel zum "Endsieg"?', in Rolf-Dieter Müller and Hans-Erich Volkmann (eds), *Wehrmacht. Mythos und Realität* (Munich, 1999), 210–23.

Sammet, Rainer, *'Dolchstoß'. Deutschland und die Auseinandersetzung mit der Niederlage im Ersten Weltkrieg (1918–1933)* (Berlin, 2003).

Sarholz, Thomas, *Die Auswirkungen der Kontingentierung von Eisen und Stahl auf die Aufrüstung der Wehrmacht von 1936 bis 1939*, Dissertation, Technical University of Darmstadt, 1983.

Sauer, Wolfgang, *Die Mobilmachung der Gewalt* (Frankfurt a. M., Berlin and Vienna, 1974).

Schabel, Ralf, *Die Illusion der Wunderwaffen. Die Rolle der Düsenflugzeuge und Flugabwehrraketen in der Rüstungspolitik des Dritten Reiches* (Munich, 1994).

Schäche, Wolfgang, *Architektur und Städtebau in Berlin zwischen 1933 und 1945. Planen und Bauen unter der Ägide der Stadtverwaltung* (Berlin, 1991).

Schacht, Hjalmar, *76 Jahre meines Lebens* (Bad Wörishofen, 1953).

Schädler, Sarah, *'Justizkrise' und 'Justizreform' im Nationalsozialismus. Das Reichsjustizministerium unter Reichsjustizminister Thierack (1942–1945)* (Tübingen, 2009).

Schäfer, Gerhard, *Der Einbruch des Reichsbischofs in die württembergische Landeskirche 1934* (Stuttgart, 1974).

Schäfer, Kirstin A., *Werner von Blomberg. Hitlers erster Feldmarschall. Eine Biographie* (Paderborn, 2006).

Schafranek, Hans, *Sommerfest und Preisschießen. Die unbekannte Geschichte des NS-Putsches im Jahre 1934* (Vienna, 2006).

Schausberger, Norbert, *Der Griff nach Österreich. Der Anschluß* (Vienna and Munich, 1978).

Scheffler, Wolfgang, 'Der Brandanschlag im Berliner Lustgarten im Mai 1942 und seine Folgen. Einequellenkritische Betrachtung', in *Berlin in Geschichte und Gegenwart* (1984), 91–118.

Scheffler, Wolfgang, 'Das Schicksal der in die baltischen Staaten deportierten deutschen, österreichischen und tschechoslowakischen Juden 1941–1945', in Wolfgang Scheffler and Diana Schulle (eds), *Buch der Erinnerung. Die ins Baltikum deportierten deutschen, österreichischen und tschechoslowakischen Juden* vol. 1 (Munich, 2003), 1–43.

Scheffler, Wolfgang, 'Massenmord in Kowno', in Wolfgang Scheffler and Diana Schulle (ed.), *Buch der Erinnerung. Die ins Baltikum deportierten deutschen, österreichischen und tschechoslowakischen Juden* vol. 1 (Munich, 2003), 83–7.

Scheibe, Dietrich and Margit Wiegold-Bovermann, *'Morgen werden wir die Gewerkschaftshäuser besetzen'. Die Zerschlagung der Gewerkschaften in Rheinland-Westfalen-Lippe am 2. Mai 1933* (Essen, 2003).

Schellenberger, Barbara, 'Adalbert Probst (1900–1934), Katholischer Jugendführer – Opfer des Nationalsozialismus', in *Düsseldorfer Jahrbuch. Beiträge zur Geschichte des Niederrheins* 69, S. 279–86.

Schelvis, Jules, *Vernichtungslager Sobibór* (Berlin, 1998).

Schepua, Michael, '"Machtergreifung" und Etablierung des NS-Systems in einem Industriezentrum: Ludwigshafen und Oppau 1933–1938', in Hans-Georg Meyer und Hans Berkessel (eds), *Die Zeit des Nationalsozialismus in Rheinland-Pfalz*, vol. 1 (Mainz, 2000), 82–97.

Scherner, Jonas and Jochen Streb, 'Das Ende eines Mythos? Albert Speer und das sogenannte Rüstungswunder', in *Vierteljahrschrift für Sozial- und Wirtschaftsgeschichte* 93 (2006), 172–96.

Schieder, Wolfgang, 'Spanischer Bürgerkrieg und Vierjahresplan. Zur Struktur nationalsozialistischer Außenpolitik', in Wolfgang Michalka (ed.), *Nationalsozialistische Außenpolitik* (Darmstadt, 1978), 325–59.

Schieder, Wolfgang, 'Faschismus im politischen Transfer. Giuseppe Renzetti als faschistischer Propagandist und Geheimagent in Berlin 1922–1941', in Sven Reichardt und Armin Nolzen (eds), *Faschismus in Italien und Deutschland, Studien zu Transfer und Vergleich* (Göttingen, 2005), 28–58.

Schiefer, Markus, 'Vom "Blauen Bock" in die Residenz', in Marita Krauss (ed.), *Rechte Karrieren in München. Von der Weimarer Zeit bis in die Nachkriegsjahre* (Munich, 2010), 152–65.

Schildt, Gerhard, *Die Arbeitsgemeinschaft Nord-West. Untersuchungen zur Geschichte der NSDAP 1925/26* (Freiburg i. Br., 1964).

Schindler, Margot, *Wegmüssen. Die Entsiedlung des Raumes Döllersheim (Niederösterreich) 1938–1942. Volkskundliche Aspekte* (Vienna, 1988).

Schirmann, Léon, *Altonaer Blutsonntag, 17. Juli 1932. Dichtungen und Wahrheit* (Hamburg, 1994).

Schlenker, Ines, *Hitler's Salon. The 'Große Deutsche Kunstausstellung' at the Haus der Deutschen Kunst in Munich 1937–1944* (Oxford, 2007).

Schmädeke, Jürgen and Peter Steinbach (eds), *Der Widerstand gegen den Nationalsozialismus. Die deutsche Gesellschaft und der Widerstand gegen Hitler*, 3rd and new edn (Munich, 1994).

Schmidl, Erwin A., *März 38. Der deutsche Einmarsch in Österreich* (Vienna, 1987).

Schmidt, Daniel, 'Der SA-Führer Hans Ramshorn. Ein Leben zwischen Gewalt und Gemeinschaft (1892–1934)', in *VfZ* 60 (2012), 201–35.

Schmidt, Jochen, *Geschichte des Genie-Gedankens*, vol. 2 (Darmstadt, 1985).

Schmidt, Rainer F., *Rudolf Heß. 'Botengang eines Toren?'. Der Flug nach Großbritannien vom 10. Mai 1941*, 2nd edn (Munich, 2000).

Schmidt, Rainer F., 'Appeasement oder Angriff? Eine kritische Bestandsaufnahme der sog. "Präventivkriegsdebatte" über den 22. Juni 1941', in Jürgen Elvert and Susanne Krauss (eds), *Historische Debatten und Kontroversen im 19. und 20. Jahrhundert. Jubiläumstagung der Ranke-Gesellschaft in Essen, 2001* (Stuttgart, 2003), 220–33.

Schmidt, Ulf, 'Reassessing the Beginning of the "Euthanasia" Programme', in *German History* 17 (1999), 543–57.

Schmidt, Ulf, *Karl Brandt: The Nazi Doctor. Medicine and Power in the Third Reich* (London, 2007).

Schmidt, Ulf, *Hitlers Arzt Karl Brandt. Medizin und Macht im Dritten Reich* (Berlin, 2009).

Schmiechen-Ackermann, Detlef (ed.), *'Volksgemeinschaft'. Mythos, wirkungsmächtige Verheißung oder soziale Realität im 'Dritten Reich'? Zwischenbilanz einer kontroversen Debatte* (Paderborn, 2012).

Schmitz, Hubert, *Die Bewirtschaftung der Nahrungsmittel und Verbrauchsgüter 1939–1950. Dargestellt an dem Beispiel der Stadt Essen* (Essen, 1956).

Schmuhl, Hans-Walter, *Rassenhygiene, Nationalsozialismus, Euthanasie. Von der Verhütung zur Vernichtung 'lebensunwerten Lebens' 1890–1945*, 2nd edn (Göttingen, 1992).

Schmuhl, Hans-Walter, 'Kontinuität oder Diskontinuität? Zum epochalen Charakter der Psychiatrie im Nationalsozialismus', in Franz-Werner Kersting, Karl Teppe, and Bernd Walter (eds), *Nach Hadamar. Zum Verhältnis von Psychiatrie und Gesellschaft im 20. Jahrhundert* (Paderborn, 1993), 112–36.

Schneider, Hans, *Neues vom Reichstagsbrand? Eine Dokumentation. Ein Versäumnis der deutschen Geschichtsschreibung*, with a preface by Iring Fetscher and essays by Dieter Deiseroth, Hersch Fischler, Wolf-Dieter Narr (Berlin, 2004).

Schneider, Michael, *Unterm Hakenkreuz. Arbeiter und Arbeiterbewegung 1933 bis 1939* (Bonn, 1999).

Schoeps, Julius H. and Werner Tress (eds), *Orte der Bücherverbrennungen in Deutschland 1933* (Hildesheim, Zurich, and New York, 2008).

Schoeps, Julius H. and Werner Tress (eds), *Verfemt und Verboten. Vorgeschichte und Folgen der Bücherverbrennungen 1933* (Hildesheim, 2010).

Scholder, Klaus, *Die Kirchen und das Dritte Reich*, 2 vols (Berlin, 1977/1985).

Scholder, Klaus, 'Altes und Neues zur Vorgeschichte des Reichskonkordats. Erwiderung auf Konrad Repgen', in *VfZ* 26 (1978), 535–70.

Schönberger, Angela, *Die Neue Reichskanzlei von Albert Speer. Zum Zusammenhang von nationalsozialistischer Ideologie und Architektur* (Berlin, 1981).

Schönherr, Klaus, 'Ferdinand Schörner – Der idealtypische Nazigeneral', in Roland Smelser und Enrico Syring (eds), *Die Militärelite des Dritten Reiches – 27 biographische Skizzen* (Berlin and Frankfurt a. M., 1995), 497–509.

Schönherr, Klaus, 'Der Rückzug aus Griechenland', in Karl-Heinz Frieser (ed.), *Die Ostfront 1943/44. Der Krieg im Osten und an den Nebenfronten* (Munich, 2007), 1089–99.

Schönherr, Klaus, 'Der Rückzug der Heeresgruppe A über die Krim bis Rumänien', in Karl-Heinz Frieser (ed.), *Die Ostfront 1943/44. Der Krieg im Osten und an den Nebenfronten* (Munich, 2007), 451–90.

Schönherr, Klaus, 'Die Kämpfe um Galizien und die Beskiden', in Karl-Heinz Frieser (ed.), *Die Ostfront 1943/44. Der Krieg im Osten und an den Nebenfronten* (Munich, 2007), 679–730.

Schönherr, Klaus, 'Die Rückzugskämpfe in Rumänien und Siebenbürgen', in Karl-Heinz Frieser (ed.), *Die Ostfront 1943/44. Der Krieg im Osten und an den Nebenfronten* (Munich, 2007), 731–848.

Schreiber, Gerhard, 'Die politische und militärische Entwicklung im Mittelmeerraum 1939/40', in Schreiber, Bernd Stegemann, and Detlef Vogel, *Der Mittelmeerraum und Südosteuropa. Von der »non belligeranza« Italiens bis zum Kriegseintritt der Vereinigten Staaten* (Stuttgart, 1984), 4–271.

Schreiber, Gerhard, 'Politik und Kriegführung 1941', in Schreiber, Bernd Stegemann, and Detlef Vogel, *Der Mittelmeerraum und Südosteuropa. Von der »non belligeranza« Italiens bis zum Kriegseintritt der Vereinigten Staaten* (Stuttgart, 1984), 514–87.

Schreiber, Gerhard, *Die italienischen Militärinternierten im deutschen Machtbereich 1943–1945. Verraten – verachtet – vergessen* (Munich, 1990).

Schreiber, Gerhard, 'Das Ende des nordafrikanischen Feldzugs und der Krieg in Italien', in Karl-Heinz Frieser (ed.), *Die Ostfront 1943/44. Der Krieg im Osten und an den Nebenfronten* (Munich, 2007), 1101–62.

Schreiner, Klaus, '"Wann kommt der Retter Deutschlands?" Formen und Funktionen von politischem Messianismus in der Weimarer Republik', in *Saeculum* 49 (1998), 107–60.

Schröder, Josef, *Italiens Kriegsaustritt 1943. Die deutschen Gegenmaßnahmen im italienischen Raum: Fall 'Alarich' und 'Achse'* (Göttingen, 1969).

Schuhladen-Krämer, Jürgen, 'Die Exekutoren des Terrors: Hermann Mattheiß, Walter Stahlecker, Friedrich Mußgay. Leiter der Geheimen Staatspolizeileitstelle Stuttgart', in Michael Kissener and Joachim Scholtyseck (eds), *Die Führer der Provinz. NS-Biographien aus Baden und Württemberg* (Constance, 1999), 405–43.

Schüler-Springorum, Stefanie, *Krieg und Fliegen. Die Legion Condor im Spanischen Bürgerkrieg* (Paderborn, 2010).

Schulz, Alfons, *Drei Jahre in der Nachrichtenzentrale des Führerhauptquartiers* (Stein am Rhein, 1996).

Schulz, Gerhard, *Die Anfänge des totalitären Maßnahmenstaates*, (Frankfurt a. M., 1974).

Schulz, Gerhard, *Die Periode der Konsolidierung und Revision des Bismarckschen Reichsaufbaus 1919–1930*, 2nd edn (Berlin and New York, 1987).

Schulz, Gerhard, *Von Brüning zu Hitler. Der Wandel des politischen Systems in Deutschland 1930–1933* (Berlin and New York, 1992).

Schulze, Dietmar, 'Der "Röhm-Putsch" in der Provinz Sachsen', in *Hallische Beiträge zur Zeitgeschichte* 15 (2005), 9–34.

Schulze, Hagen, *Otto Braun oder Preußens demokratische Sendung. Eine Biographie* (Berlin, 1977).

Schulze, Hagen, *Weimar. Deutschland 1917–1933* (Berlin, 1982).

Schumacher, Martin, *Mittelstandsfront und Republik. Die Wirtschaftspartei – Reichspartei des deutschen Mittelstandes, 1919–1933*, ed. Kommission für Geschichte des Parlamentarismus und der politischen Parteien (Düsseldorf, 1972).

Schumann, Wolfgang (ed.), *Deutschland im Zweiten Weltkrieg*, vol. 5 (Berlin, 1984).

Schüren, Ulrich, *Der Volksentscheid zur Fürstenenteignung 1926. Die Vermögensauseinandersetzung mit den depossedierten Landesherren als Problem der deutschen Innenpolitik unter besonderer Berücksichtigung der Verhältnisse in Preußen* (Düsseldorf, 1978).

Schütz, Erhard and Eckhard Gruber, *Mythos Reichsautobahn. Bau und Inszenierung der 'Straßen des Führers' 1933–1941* (Berlin, 1996).

Schwaab, Edleff H., *Hitler's Mind. A Plunge into Madness* (New York and Westport, CT, 1992).

Schwartz, Michael, '"Euthanasie"-Debatten in Deutschland (1895–1945)', in *VfZ* 46 (1998), 617–65.

Schwarz, Birgit, *Geniewahn. Hitler und die Kunst* (Vienna, 2009).

Schwarzenbeck, Engelbert, *Nationalsozialistische Pressepolitik und die Sudetenkrise 1938* (Munich, 1979).

Schwarzwäller, Wulf, *Rudolf Heß. Der Stellvertreter* (Munich, 1987).

Schweitzer, Arthur, *Die Nazifizierung des Mittelstandes*, with a foreword by G. Eisermann (Stuttgart, 1970).

Schwend, Karl, 'Die Bayerische Volkspartei', in Erich Matthias und Rudolf Morsey (eds), *Das Ende der Parteien 1933* (Düsseldorf, 1960), 457–519.

Seidel, Robert, *Deutsche Besatzungspolitik in Polen. Der Distrikt Radom 1939–1945* (Paderborn, 2006).

Seidler, Franz W., *Fritz Todt. Baumeister des Dritten Reiches* (Frankfurt a. M. and Berlin, 1988).

Seidler, Franz W. and Dieter Zeigert, *Die Führerhauptquartiere. Anlagen und Planungen im Zweiten Weltkrieg* (Munich, 2000).

Seier, Hellmut, 'Der Rektor als Führer. Zur Hochschulpolitik des Reichserziehungsministeriums 1934–1945', in *VfZ* 12 (1964), 105–46.

Selig, Wolfram, 'Die Opfer des Röhm-Putsches in München', in Winfried Becker and Werner Chrobak (eds), *Staat, Kultur, Politik. Beiträge zur Geschichte Bayerns und des Katholizismus. Festschrift zum 65. Geburtstag von Dieter Albrecht* (Lassleben, 1992), 341–56.

Seligmann, Michael, *Aufstand der Räte. Die erste bayerische Räterepublik vom 7. April 1919* (Grafenau-Döffingen, 1989).

Semelin, Jacques, *Unarmed against Hitler. Civilian Resistance in Europe* (Westport, CT and London, 1993).

Sereny, Gitta, *Das Ringen mit der Wahrheit. Albert Speer und das deutsche Trauma* (Frankfurt a. M., 1996).

Sevillias, Errikos, *Athens – Auschwitz* (Athens, 1983).

Siemen, Ludwig, *Menschen blieben auf der Strecke. Psychiatrie zwischen Reform und Nationalsozialismus* (Gütersloh, 1987).

Sigmund, Anna Maria, *Des Führers bester Freund. Adolf Hitler, seine Nichte Geli Raubal und der 'Ehrenarier' Emil Maurice – eine Dreiecksbeziehung* (Munich, 2003).

Silberklang, David, 'Die Juden und die ersten Deportationen aus dem Distrikt Lublin', in *'Aktion Reinhardt'. Der Völkermord an den Juden im Generalgouvernement 1941–1944* (Osnabrück, 2004), 141–64.

Silverman, Dan P., *Hitler's Economy. Nazi Work Creation Programs 1933–1936* (Cambridge, MA and London, 1998).

Slapnicka, Harry, 'Linz, Oberösterreich und die "Tschechische Frage"', in *Historisches Jahrbuch der Stadt Linz 1977*, 209–32.

Slapnicka, Harry, *Oberösterreich unter Kaiser Franz Joseph (1861 bis 1918)* (Linz, 1982).

Smelser, Ronald, *Das Sudetenproblem und das Dritte Reich 1933–1938. Von der Volkstumspolitik zur nationalsozialistischen Außenpolitik* (Munich, 1980).

Smelser, Ronald *Robert Ley. Hitlers Mann an der 'Arbeitsfront'. Eine Biographie* (Paderborn, 1989).

Smith, Arthur L., 'Kurt Lüdecke: "The Man Who Knew Hitler"', in *German Studies Review* 26/3 (2003), 597–606.

Smith, Bradley F., *Alfred Hitler. His Family, Childhood and Youth* (Stanford, 1967).

Smith, Bradley F., 'Die Überlieferung der Hoßbach-Niederschrift im Lichte neuer Quellen', in *VfZ* 38 (1990), 329–36.

Sodeikat, Ernst, 'Der Nationalsozialismus und die Danziger Opposition', in *VfZ* 14 (1966), 139–74.

Söhngen, Oskar, 'Hindenburgs Eingreifen in den Kirchenkampf 1933. Heinrich Bornkamm zum 60. Geburtstag', in Heinz Brunotte and Ernst Wolf (eds), *Zur Geschichte des Kirchenkampfs. Gesammelte Aufsätze* (Göttingen, 1965), 30–44.

Sommer, Theo, *Deutschland und Japan zwischen den Mächten 1935–1940. Vom Antikominternpakt zum Dreimächtepakt. Eine Studie zur diplomatischen Vorgeschichte des Zweiten Weltkrieges* (Tübingen, 1962).

Sontheimer, Kurt, *Antidemokratisches Denken in der Weimarer Republik. Die politischen Ideen des deutschen Nationalismus zwischen 1918 und 1933* (Munich, 1968).

Speckner, Herbert, *Die Ordnungszelle Bayern. Studien zur Politik des bayerischen Bürgertums, insbesondere der Bayerischen Volkspartei, von der Revolution bis zum Ende des Kabinetts Dr. von Kahr*, Dissertation, Erlangen, 1955.

Spoerer, Mark, *Vom Scheingewinn zum Rüstungsboom. Die Eigenkapitalrentabilität der deutschen Industrieaktiengesellschaften 1925–1941* (Stuttgart, 1996).

Spoerer, Mark, *Zwangsarbeit unter dem Hackenkreuz. Ausländische Zivilarbeiter, Kriegsgefangene und Häftlinge im deutschen Reich und im besetzten Europa 1939–1945* (Stuttgart, 2001).

Stachura, Peter D., '"Der Fall Strasser". Gregor Strasser, Hitler and National Socialism, 1930–1932', in Stachura (ed.), *The Shaping of the Nazi State* (London, 1978), 88–130.

Stachura, Peter D., 'Der kritische Wendepunkt? Die NSDAP und die Reichstagswahlen vom 28. Mai 1928', in *VfZ* 26 (1978), 66–99.

Stachura, Peter D. (ed.), *Unemployment and the Great Depression in Weimar Germany* (New York, 1986).

Stafford, David (ed.), *Flight from Reality. Rudolf Hess and his Mission to Scotland, 1941* (London, 2002).

Stahl, Friedrich-Christian, 'Generaloberst Kurt Zeitzler', in Gerd R. Ueberschär (ed.), *Hitlers militärische Elite. Vom Kriegsbeginn bis zum Weltkriegsende*, vol. 2 (Darmstadt, 1998), 283–92.

Steber, Martina and Bernhard Gotto, *Visions of Community in Nazi Germany. Social Engineering and Private Lives* (Oxford, 2014).

Stegemann, Bernd, 'Die italienisch-deutsche Kriegführung im Mittelmeer und in Afrika', in Gerhard Schreiber, Stegemann, and Detlef Vogel, *Der Mittelmeerraum und Südosteuropa. Von der 'non belligeranza' Italiens bis zum Kriegseintritt der Vereinigten Staaten* (Stuttgart, 1984), 591–682.

Stein, Alfred, 'Adolf Hitler und Gustav Le Bon. Der Meister der Massenbewegung und sein Lehrer', in *GWU* 6 (1955), 362–68.

Stein, Harry, 'Das Sonderlager im Konzentrationslager Buchenwald nach den Pogromen 1938', in Monica Kingreen (ed.), *'Nach der Kristallnacht'. Jüdisches Leben und antijüdische Politik in Frankfurt am Main 1938–1945* (Frankfurt a. M., 1999), 19–54.

Steinbach, Peter and Johannes Tuchel (eds), *Widerstand gegen die nationalsozialistische Diktatur 1933–1945* (Bonn, 2004).

Steinbacher, Sybille, *'Musterstadt' Auschwitz. Germanisierungspolitik und Judenmord in Oberschlesien* (Munich, 2000).

Steinberg, Jonathan, *Deutsche, Italiener und Juden. Der italienische Widerstand gegen den Holocaust* (Göttingen, 1992).

Steinberg, Rolf (ed.), *Nazi Kitsch. Mit einem dokumentarischen Anhang über den Kleinkitsch von 1933* (Darmstadt, 1975).

Steiner, André, 'Zur Neuschätzung des Lebenshaltungskostenindex für die Vorkriegszeit des Nationalsozialismus', in *Jahrbuch für Wirtschaftsgeschichte* (2005), Nr. 2, 129–52.

Steinert, Marlis, *Hitlers Krieg und die Deutschen. Stimmung und Haltung der deutschen Bevölkerung im Zweiten Weltkrieg* (Düsseldorf, 1970).

Steininger, Benjamin, *Raum-Maschine Reichsautobahn. Zur Dynamik eines bekannt/ unbekannten Bauwerks* (Berlin, 2005).

Steinweis, Alan E., *Kristallnacht 1938. Ein deutscher Pogrom* (Stuttgart, 2011).

Stelzner, Jürgen, *Arbeitsbeschaffung und Wiederaufrüstung 1933–1936. Nationalsozialistische Beschäftigungspolitik und Aufbau der Wehr- und Rüstungswirtschaft* (Bamberg, 1976).

Stephenson, Jill, *The Nazi Organisation of Women* (London, 1981).

Steurer, Leopold, *Südtirol zwischen Rom und Berlin 1919–1939* (Vienna, Munich, and Zurich, 1980).

Stierlin, Helmut, *Adolf Hitler. Familienperspektiven* (Frankfurt a. M., 1975).

Stjernfelt, Bertil and Klaus-Richard Böhme, *Westerplatte 1939* (Freiburg i. Br., 1979).

Stöckel, Karin, *Berlin im olympischen Rausch. Die Organisation der Olympischen Spiele 1936* (Hamburg, 2009).

Stöckel, Sigrid (ed.), *Die 'rechte Nation' und ihr Verleger. Politik und Popularisierung im J. F. Lehmanns Verlag 1890–1979* (Berlin, 2002).

Stoltenberg, Gerhard, *Politische Strömungen im schleswig-holsteinischen Landvolk 1918– 1933. Ein Beitrag zur politischen Meinungsbildung in der Weimarer Republik* (Düsseldorf, 1962).

Stolzfus, Nathan, *Resistance of the Heart. Intermarriage and the Rosenstrasse Protest in Nazi Germany* (New York, 1996).

Stourzh, Gerhard and Brigitta Zaar (eds), *Österreich, Deutschland und die Mächte. Internationale und österreichische Aspekte des 'Anschlusses' vom März 1936* (Vienna, 1990).

Strauss, Herbert A., 'Jewish Emigration from Germany. Nazi Policies and Jewish Responses', in *Leo Baeck Institute Year Book* 25 (1980), 313–61 (I), and 26 (1981), 343–409.

Streit, Christian, *Keine Kameraden. Die Wehrmacht und die sowjetischen Kriegsgefangenen 1941–1945* (Stuttgart, 1978).

Strenge, Irene, *Machtübernahme 1933 – alles auf legalem Weg?* (Berlin, 2002).

Strenge, Irene, *Kurt von Schleicher. Politik im Reichswehrministerium am Ende der Weimarer Republik* (Berlin, 2006).

Stroech, Jürgen, 'Zur Herstellung und Verbreitung der illegalen "Roten Fahne" 1933–1938', in *Beiträge zur Geschichte der Arbeiterbewegung* 19 (1977), 81–91.

Stucki, Walter, *Von Petain zur Vierten Republik. Vichy 1944* (Berne, 1947).

Stuhlpfarrer, Karl, 'Der deutsche Plan einer Währungsunion mit Österreich', in *Anschluß 1938. Protokoll des Symposiums in Wien am 14. und 15. März 1978* (Vienna, 1981), 271–94.

Stuhlpfarrer, Karl, *Umsiedlung Südtirol 1939–1940*, 2 vols (Vienna, 1985).

Stumpf, Reinhard, 'Der Krieg im Mittelmeerraum 1942/43: Die Operationen in Nordafrika und im mittleren Mittelmeer', in Horst Boog et al., *Der globale Krieg. Die Ausweitung zum Weltkrieg und der Wechsel der Initiative 1941–1943* (Stuttgart, 1990), 567–757.

Stumpf, Reinhard, 'Die alliierte Landung in Nordwestafrika und der Rückzug der deutsch-italienischen Panzerarmee nach Tunesien', in Horst Boog et al., *Der globale Krieg. Die Ausweitung zum Weltkrieg und der Wechsel der Initiative 1941–1943* (Stuttgart, 1990), 710–757.

Sundhaussen, Holm, 'Jugoslawien', in Wolfgang Benz (ed.), *Dimension des Völkermords. Die Zahl der jüdischen Opfer des Nationalsozialismus* (Munich, 1991), 311–30.

Sunnus, Michael, *Der NS-Rechtswahrerbund (1928–1945). Zur Geschichte der nationalsozialistischen Juristenorganisation* (Frankfurt a. M., 1990).

Süss, Winfried, *Der 'Volkskörper' im Krieg. Gesundheitspolitik, Gesundheitsverhältnisse und Krankenmord im nationalsozialistischen Deutschland 1939–1945* (Munich, 2003).

Sywottek, Jutta, *Mobilmachung für den totalen Krieg. Die propagandistische Vorbereitung der deutschen Bevölkerung auf den Zweiten Weltkrieg* (Opladen, 1976).

Tauber, Joachim, 'Deutschland, Litauen und das Memelgebiet 1938/39', in Jürgen Zarusky and Martin Zückert (eds), *Das Münchener Abkommen von 1938 in europäischer Perspektive* (Munich, 2013), 429–40.

Teppe, Karl, 'Der Reichsverteidigungskommissar. Organisation und Praxis in Westfalen', in Dieter Rebentisch and Teppe (eds), *Verwaltung contra Menschenführung im Staat Hitlers. Studien zum politisch-administrativen System* (Göttingen, 1986), 278–301.

Teppe, Karl, *Massenmord auf dem Dienstweg. Hitlers 'Euthanasie'-Erlaß und seine Durchführung in den Westfälischen Provinzialanstalten* (Münster, 1989).

Terhalle, Maximilian, *Otto Schmidt (1888–1971). Gegner Hitlers und Intimus Hugenbergs*, Dissertation, Bonn, 2006.

Terhalle, Maximilian, *Deutschnational in Weimar. Die politische Biographie des Reichstagsabgeordneten Otto Schmidt(-Hannover) 1888–1971* (Cologne, 2009).

Terveen, Fritz, 'Der Filmbericht über Hitlers 50. Geburtstag. Ein Beispiel nationalsozialistischer Selbstdarstellung und Propaganda', in *VfZ* 7 (1959), 75–84.

Thamer, Hans-Ulrich, *Verführung und Gewalt. Deutschland 1933–1945* (Berlin, 1986).

Thielenhaus, Marion, *Zwischen Anpassung und Widerstand: deutsche Diplomaten 1938– 1941. Die politischen Aktivitäten der Beamtengruppe um Ernst von Weizsäcker im Auswärtigen Amt* (Paderborn, 1984).

Thierfelder, Jörg, 'Die Auseinandersetzungen um Schulform und Religionsunterricht im Dritten Reich zwischen Staat und evangelischer Kirche in Württemberg', in Manfred Heinemann (ed.), *Erziehung und Schulung im Dritten Reich*, vol. 1 (Stuttgart, 1980), 230–50.

Thies, Jochen, *Architekt der Weltherrschaft. Die 'Endziele' Hitlers* (Königstein i. Ts., 1980).

Thoss, Bruno, *Der Ludendorff-Kreis 1919–1923. München als Zentrum der mitteleuropäischen Gegenrevolution zwischen Revolution und Hitler-Putsch* (Munich, 1978).

Thoss, Hendrik, 'Sperrle, Hugo Wilhelm', in *Neue Deutsche Biographie* 24 (2010), 671–2.

Tobias, Fritz, *Der Reichstagsbrand – Legende und Wirklichkeit* (Rastatt, 1962).

Tooze, Adam J., *Ökonomie der Zerstörung. Die Geschichte der Wirtschaft im Nationalsozialismus* (Munich, 2007).

Toscano, Mario, *The Origins of the Pact of Steel* (Baltimore, 1967).

Toury, Jacob, 'Die Entstehungsgeschichte des Austreibungsbefehls gegen die Juden der Saarpfalz und Badens (22./23. Oktober 1940 – Camp de Gurs)', in *Jahrbuch des Instituts für Deutsche Geschichte* 15 (1986), 431–64.

Tracey, Donald R., 'Der Aufstieg der NSDAP bis 1930', in Detlev Heiden and Günther Mai (eds), *Thüringen auf dem Weg ins 'Dritte Reich'* (Erfurt, 1996), 65–93.

Tress, Werner, 'Phasen und Akteure der Bücherverbrennungen in Deutschland 1933', in Julius H. Schoeps and Tress (eds), *Orte der Bücherverbrennungen in Deutschland 1933*, (Hildesheim, Zurich, and New York, 2008), 9–28.

Treviranus, Gottfried Reinhold, *Das Ende von Weimar. Heinrich Brüning und seine Zeit* (Düsseldorf and Vienna, 1968).

Trimborn, Jürgen, *Riefenstahl. Eine deutsche Karriere. Biographie* (Berlin, 2002).

Tuchel, Johannes, *Konzentrationslager. Organisationsgeschichte und Funktion der 'Inspektion der Konzentrationslager' 1934–1938* (Boppard am Rhein, 1991).

Turner, Henry Ashby, *Die Großunternehmer und der Aufstieg Hitlers* (Berlin, 1985).

Turner, Henry Ashby, *Hitlers Weg zur Macht. Der Januar 1933* (Munich, 1997).

Turner, Henry Ashby and Horst Matzerath, 'Die Selbstfinanzierung der NSDAP', in *Geschichte und Gesellschaft* 1 (1977), 59–92.

Tweraser, Kurt, 'Dr. Carl Beuerle – Schönerers Apostel in Linz', in *Historisches Jahrbuch der Stadt Linz 1989*, 67–84.

Tweraser, Kurt, 'Das politische Parteiensystem im Linzer Gemeinderat', in Fritz Mayhofer und Walter Schuster (eds), *Linz im 20. Jahrhundert* 2 vols (Linz, 2010), vol. 1, 93–210.

Tyrell, Albrecht, 'Führergedanke und Gauleiterwechsel. Die Teilung des Gaues Rheinland der NSDAP 1931', in *VfZ* 23 (1975), 341–74.

Tyrell, Albrecht, *Vom Trommler zum Führer. Der Wandel von Hitlers Selbstverständnis zwischen 1919 und 1924 und die Entwicklung der NSDAP* (Munich, 1975).

Tyrell, Albrecht, 'Gottfried Feder and the NSDAP', in Peter D. Stachura (ed.), *The Shaping of the Nazi State* (London, 1978), 48–87.

Ueberschär, Gerd R., *Hitler und Finnland 1939–1941. Die deutsch-finnischen Beziehungen während des Hitler-Stalin-Paktes* (Wiesbaden, 1978).

Ueberschär, Gerd R., 'Die Einbeziehung Skandinaviens in die Planung "Barbarossa"', in Horst Boog et al., *Der Angriff auf die Sowjetunion*, updated edn (Frankfurt a. M., 1991), 442–97.

Ueberschär, Gerd R., 'Kriegführung und Politik in Nordeuropa', in Horst Boog et al., *Der Angriff auf die Sowjetunion*, updated edn (Frankfurt a. M., 1991), 965–1050.

Ueberschär, Gerd R. and Lev. A. Bezymenskij (eds), *Der deutsche Angriff auf die Sowjetunion 1941. Die Kontroverse um die Präventivkriegsthese*, 2nd edn (Darmstadt, 2011).

Uhlig, Heinrich, *Die Warenhäuser im Dritten Reich* (Cologne, 1956).

Uhlig, Heinrich, 'Das Einwirken Hitlers auf Planung und Führung des Ostfeldzuges', in *Aus Politik und Zeitgeschichte* 1960, 161–98.

Ullrich, Volker, *Adolf Hitler. Die Jahre des Aufstiegs. Biographie* (Frankfurt a. M., 2013).

Umbreit, Hans, 'Der Kampf um die Vormachtstellung in Westeuropa', in Klaus A. Maier et al., *Die Errichtung der Hegemonie auf dem europäischen Kontinent* (Stuttgart, 1979), 235–327.

Umbreit, Hans, 'Die deutsche Herrschaft in den besetzten Gebieten 1942–1945', in Bernhard R. Kroener, Rolf-Dieter Müller, and Umbreit, *Organisation und Mobilmachung des deutschen Machtbereichs*, 2nd half volume (Stuttgart, 1999), 3–260.

Ungváry, Krisztián, 'Kriegsschauplatz Ungarn', in Karl-Heinz Frieser (ed.), *Die Ostfront 1943/44. Der Krieg im Osten und an den Nebenfronten* (Munich, 2007), 849–958.

Unruh, Karl, *Langemarck. Legende und Wirklichkeit* (Koblenz, 1986).

Urban, Markus, *Die Konsensfabrik. Funktion und Wahrnehmung der NS-Reichsparteitage 1933–1941* (Göttingen, 2007).

Vezina, Birgit, *Die 'Gleichschaltung' der Universität Heidelberg im Zuge der nationalsozialistischen Machtergreifung* (Heidelberg, 1982).

Vieregge, Bianca, *Die Gerichtsbarkeit einer 'Elite'. Nationalsozialistische Rechtsprechung am Beispiel der SS- und-Polizei-Gerichtsbarkeit* (Baden-Baden, 2002).

Vinnai, Gerhard, *Hitler – Scheitern und Vernichtungswut. Zur Genese des faschistischen Täters* (Gießen, 2004).

Vogel, Detlef, 'Das Eingreifen Deutschlands auf dem Balkan', in Gerhard Schreiber, Bernd Stegemann, and Vogel, *Der Mittelmeerraum und Südosteuropa. Von der 'non belligeranza' Italiens bis zum Kriegseintritt der Vereinigten Staaten* (Stuttgart, 1984), 417–511.

Vogel, Detlef, 'Deutsche und alliierte Kriegführung im Westen', in Horst Boog, Gerhard Krebs, and Vogel, *Das Deutsche Reich in der Defensive. Strategischer Luftkrieg in Europa, Krieg im Westen und in Ostasien 1943–1944/45* (Stuttgart and München, 2001), 419–639.

Vogelsang, Thilo, *Reichswehr, Staat und NSDAP. Beiträge zur deutschen Geschichte 1930–1932* (Stuttgart, 1962).

Volk, Ludwig, *Der bayerische Episkopat und der Nationalsozialismus 1930–1934* (Mainz, 1965).

Volk, Ludwig, *Das Reichskonkordat vom 20. Juli 1933. Von den Ansätzen in der Weimarer Republik bis zur Ratifizierung am 10. September 1933* (Mainz, 1972).

Volk, Ludwig, 'Episkopat und Kirchenkampf im Zweiten Weltkrieg', in Dieter Albrecht (ed.), *Katholische Kirche und Nationalsozialismus. Ausgewählte Aufsätze von Ludwig Volk* (Mainz, 1987), 83–97.

Völker, Karl-Heinz, *Die deutsche Luftwaffe 1933–1939. Aufbau, Führung und Rüstung der Luftwaffe sowie die Entwicklung der deutschen Luftkriegstheorie* (Stuttgart, 1967).

Völker, Karl-Heinz, 'Die NS-Wirtschaft in Vorbereitung des Krieges' in Wilhelm Deist et al. (eds), *Ursachen und Voraussetzungen des Zweiten Weltkrieges* (Frankfurt a. M., 1991), 211–435.

Volkmann, Hans-Erich, 'Aspekte der nationalsozialistischen "Wehrwirtschaft" 1933–1936', in *Francia* 5 (1977), 513–38.

Volsansky, Gabriele, *Pakt auf Zeit. Das Deutsch-Österreichische Juli-Abkommen 1936* (Vienna, Cologne, and Weimar, 2001).

Vorländer, Herwart, *Die NSV. Darstellung und Dokumentation einer nationalsozialistischen Organisation* (Boppard am Rhein, 1988).

Vyšný, Paul, *The Runciman Mission to Czechoslovakia. Prelude to Munich* (Houndmills, 2003).

Wachsmann, Nikolaus, *Gefangen unter Hitler. Justizterror und Strafvollzug im NS-Staat* (Munich, 2006).

Wachtler, Johann, *Zwischen Revolutionserwartung und Untergang. Die Vorbereitung der KPD auf die Illegalität in den Jahren 1929–1933* (Frankfurt a. M., Berne, and New York, 1983).

Wagner, Andreas, *'Machtergreifung' in Sachsen. NSDAP und staatliche Verwaltung 1930–1935* (Cologne, 2004).

Wagner, Patrick, *Volksgemeinschaft ohne Verbrecher. Konzeptionen und Praxis der Kriminalpolizei in der Zeit der Weimarer Republik und des Nationalsozialismus* (Hamburg, 1996).

Wagner, Wilfried, *Belgien in der deutschen Politik während des zweiten Weltkrieges*, Dissertation, Frankfurt a. M., 1974.

Walter, Dirk, *Antisemitische Kriminalität und Gewalt. Judenfeindschaft in der Weimarer Republik* (Bonn, 1999).

Wasser, Bruno, *Himmlers Raumplanung im Osten. Der Generalplan Ost in Polen 1940–1944* (Basel, 1993).

Watt, Donald Cameron, 'Die bayerischen Bemühungen um Ausweisung Hitlers 1924', in *VfZ* 6 (1958), 270–80.

Weber, Thomas, *Hitlers erster Krieg. Der Gefreite Hitler im Weltkrieg – Mythos und Wahrheit* (Berlin, 2011).

Weber, Wolfram, *Die Innere Sicherheit im besetzten Belgien und Nordfrankreich, 1940–1944. Ein Beitrag zur Geschichte der Besatzungsverwaltungen* (Düsseldorf, 1978).

Wegner, Bernd, 'Der Krieg gegen die Sowjetunion 1942/43', in Horst Boog et al., *Der globale Krieg. Die Ausweitung zum Weltkrieg und der Wechsel der Initiative 1941–1943* (Stuttgart, 1990), 759–1093.

Wegner, Bernd, *Hitlers politische Soldaten. Die Waffen-SS 1933–1945. Leitbild, Struktur und Funktion einer nationalsozialistischen Elite*, 6th edn (Paderborn, 1999).

Wegner, Bernd, 'Präventivkrieg 1941? Zur Kontroverse um ein militärhistorisches Scheinproblem', in Jürgen Elvert und Susanne Krauss (eds), *Historische Debatten und Kontroversen im 19. und 20. Jahrhundert. Jubiläumstagung der Ranke-Gesellschaft in Essen, 2001* (Stuttgart, 2003), 206–19.

Wegner, Bernd, 'Das Kriegsende in Skandinavien', in Karl-Heinz Frieser (ed.), *Die Ostfront 1943/44. Der Krieg im Osten und an den Nebenfronten* (Munich), 2007, 961–1008.

Wegner, Bernd, 'Deutschland am Abgrund', in Karl-Heinz Frieser (ed.), *Die Ostfront 1943/44. Der Krieg im Osten und an den Nebenfronten* (Munich, 2007), 1165–224.

Wegner, Bernd, 'Die Aporie des Krieges', in Karl-Heinz Frieser (ed.), *Die Ostfront 1943/44. Der Krieg im Osten und an den Nebenfronten* (Munich, 2007), 211–76.

Wehler, Hans-Ulrich, *Deutsche Gesellschaftsgeschichte*, vol. 4, 2nd edn (Munich, 2003).

Weichlein, Siegfried, *Sozialmilieus und politische Kultur in der Weimarer Republik. Lebenswelt, Vereinskultur, Politik in Hessen* (Göttingen, 1996).

Weigel, Björn, '"Märzgefallene" und Aufnahmestopp im Frühjahr 1933. Eine Studie über den Opportunismus', in Wolfgang Benz (ed.), *Wie wurde man Parteigenosse? Die NSDAP und ihre Mitglieder* (Frankfurt a. M., 2009), 91–110.

Weihsmann, Helmut, *Bauen unterm Hakenkreuz. Architektur des Untergangs* (Vienna, 1998).

Weimer, Wolfgang, 'Der Philosoph und der Diktator. Arthur Schopenhauer und Adolf Hitler', in *Schopenhauer Jahrbuch* 84 (2003), 157–67.

Weinberg, Gerhard L., 'Die geheimen Abkommen zum Antikominternpakt', in *VfZ* 2 (1954), 193–201.

Weinberg, Gerhard L., 'Secret Hitler-Beneš Negotiations in 1936–37', in *Journal of Central European Affairs* 19 (1959/60), 366–74.

Weinberg, Gerhard L., 'Adolf Hitler und der NS-Führungsoffizier (NSFO)'. in *VfZ* 12 (1964), 443–58.

Weinberg, Gerhard L., 'Die deutsche Außenpolitik und Österreich 1937/38', in Gerald Stourzh and Brigitta Zaar (eds), *Österreich, Deutschland und die Mächte. Internationale und österreichische Aspekte des 'Anschlusses' vom März 1938* (Vienna, 1990), 61–74.

Weinberg, Gerhard L., *Eine Welt in Waffen. Die globale Geschichte des Zweiten Weltkriegs* (Stuttgart, 1995).

Weinberg, Gerhard L., *Hitler's Foreign Policy 1933–1939. The Road to World War II* (New York, 2010).

Weingarten, Ralph, *Die Hilfeleistung der westlichen Welt bei der Endlösung der deutschen Judenfrage. Das 'Intergovernmental Committee on Political Refugees' IGC 1938–1939* (Berne, 1981).

Weiss, Ernst, *Der Augenzeuge* (Icking bei München, 1963).

Weissbecker, Manfred, 'Die Deutschsozialistische Partei 1919–1922', in Dieter Fricke (ed.), *Lexikon zur Parteiengeschichte*, vol. 2 (Leipzig, 1984), 547–49.

Weitbrecht, Dorothee, 'Ermächtigung zur Vernichtung. Die Einsatzgruppen in Polen im Herbst 1939', in Klaus-Michael Mallmann and Bogdan Musial (eds), *Genesis des Genozids. Polen 1939–1941* (Darmstadt, 2004), 57–70.

Welzig, Werner (ed.), *'Anschluss'. März/April 1938 in Österreich* (Vienna, 2010).

Wendt, Bernd-Jürgen, 'Durch das "strategische Fenster" in den Zweiten Weltkrieg. Die Motive Hitlers', in Uwe Backes, Eckhard Jesse, and Rainer Zitelmann (eds), *Die Schatten der Vergangenheit. Impulse zur Historisierung des Nationalsozialismus* (Frankfurt a. M., 1990), 344–74.

Wengst, Udo, 'Der Reichsverband der Deutschen Industrie in den ersten Monaten des Dritten Reiches', in *VfZ* 28 (1980), 94–110.

Werner, Andreas, *SA und NSDAP. SA: »Wehrverband«, »Parteitruppe« oder »Revolutionsarmee«? Studien zur Geschichte der SA und der NSDAP 1920–1933*, Dissertation, Erlangen-Nuremberg, 1965.

Whiteside, Andrew G., *The Socialism of Fools: Georg Ritter von Schönerer and Austrian Pan-Germanism* (Berkeley, CA and Los Angeles, 1975).

Wiesemann, Falk, *Die Vorgeschichte der nationalsozialistischen Machtübernahme in Bayern 1932/1933* (Berlin, 1975).

Wiggershaus, Norbert Theodor, *Der deutsch-englische Flottenvertrag vom 18. Juni 1935. England und die geheime deutsche Aufrüstung 1933–1935* (Bonn, 1972).

Wildt, Michael, *Generation des Unbedingten. Das Führungskorps des Reichssicherheitshauptamtes* (Hamburg, 2003).

Wildt, Michael, *Volksgemeinschaft als Selbstermächtigung. Gewalt gegen Juden in der deutschen Provinz 1919 bis 1939* (Hamburg, 2007).

Wilhelm, Friedrich, *Die Polizei im NS-Staat. Die Geschichte ihrer Organisation im Überblick* (Paderborn, 1997).

Wilhelm, Hans-Heinrich, 'Hitlers Ansprache vor Generalen und Offizieren am 26. Mai 1944', in *MGM* 20 (1976), 123–70.

Wilhelm, Hans-Heinrich, *Rassenpolitik und Kriegführung. Sicherheitspolizei und Wehrmacht in Polen und in der Sowjetunion 1939–1942* (Passau, 1991).

Willems, Susanne, *Der entsiedelte Jude. Albert Speers Wohnungsmarktpolitik für den Berliner Hauptstadtbau* (Berlin, 2002).

Wimpffen, Hans, 'Die zweite ungarische Armee im Feldzug gegen die Sowjetunion. Ein Beitrag zur Koalitionskriegsführung im Zweiten Weltkrieg', Dissertation, Würzburg, 1968.

Winkler, Heinrich August, *Mittelstand, Demokratie und Nationalsozialismus. Die politische Entwicklung von Handwerk und Kleinhandel in der Weimarer Republik* (Cologne, 1972).

Winkler, Heinrich August, *Von der Revolution zur Stabilisierung. Arbeiter und Arbeiterbewegung in der Weimarer Republik 1918 bis 1924* (Berlin, 1984).

Winkler, Heinrich August, *Der Weg in die Katastrophe. Arbeiter und Arbeiterbewegung in der Weimarer Republik 1930 bis 1933* (Berlin and Bonn, 1987).

Winkler, Heinrich August, *Weimar 1918–1933. Die Geschichte der ersten deutschen Demokratie* (Munich, 1993).

Wippermann, Klaus W., *Politische Propaganda und staatsbürgerliche Bildung. Die Reichszentrale für Heimatdienst in der Weimarer Republik* (Bonn, 1976).

Wirsching, Andreas (ed.), *Das Jahr 1933. Die nationalsozialistische Machteroberung und die deutsche Gesellschaft* (Göttingen, 2009).

Witte, Peter, 'Zwei Entscheidungen in der "Endlösung der Judenfrage". Deportationen nach Lodz und Vernichtung in Chelmno', in *Theresienstädter Studien und Dokumente* 1995, 38–68.

Wojciechowski, Marian, *Die polnisch-deutschen Beziehungen 1933–1938* (Leiden, 1971).

Woller, Hans, *Die Abrechnung mit dem Faschismus in Italien 1943 bis 1948* (Munich, 1996).

Wollstein, Günter, 'Eine Denkschrift des Staatssekretärs Bernhard von Bülow vom März 1933. Wilhelminische Konzeption der Außenpolitik zu Beginn der nationalsozialistischen Herrschaft', in *MGM* 13 (1973), 77–94.

Wollstein, Günter, *Vom Weimarer Revisionismus zu Hitler. Das Deutsche Reich und die Großmächte in der Anfangsphase der nationalsozialistischen Herrschaft in Deutschland* (Bonn, 1973).

Wollstein, Günter, *Das 'Großdeutschland' der Paulskirche. Nationale Ziele in der bürgerlichen Revolution 1848/49* (Düsseldorf, 1977).

Wörtz, Ulrich, *Programmatik und Führerprinzip. Das Problem des Straßer-Kreises in der NSDAP. Eine historisch-politische Studie zum Verhältnis von sachlichem Programm und persönlicher Führung in einer totalitären Bewegung* (Erlangen, 1966).

Wuescht, Johann, *Jugoslawien und das Dritte Reich. Eine dokumentierte Geschichte der deutsch-jugoslawischen Beziehungen von 1933 bis 1945* (Stuttgart, 1969).

Yahil, Leni, 'Madagascar: Phantom of a Solution for the Jewish Question', in Bela Vago and George L. Mosse (eds), *Jews and Non-Jews in Eastern Europe 1918–1945* (New York, 1974), 315–34.

Zarusky, Jürgen and Martin Zückert (eds), *Das Münchener Abkommen von 1938 in europäischer Perspektive* (Munich, 2013).

Zdral, Wolfgang, *Die Hitlers. Die unbekannte Familie des Führers* (Bergisch-Gladbach, 2008).

Zeller, Eberhard, *Geist der Freiheit. Der zwanzigste Juli*, new edn (Berlin, 2004).

Zelnhefer, Siegfried, *Die Reichsparteitage der NSDAP. Geschichte, Struktur und Bedeutung der größten Propagandafeste im nationalsozialistischen Feierjahr* (Nuremberg, 1991).

Zgórniak, Marian, *Europa am Abgrund – 1938* (Münster, Hamburg, and London, 2002).

Ziegler, Walter, (ed.) *Die kirchliche Lage in Bayern nach den Regierungspräsidentenberichten 1933–1943*, vol. 4 (Mainz, 1973).

Ziegler, Walter, 'Der Kampf um die Schulkreuze im Dritten Reich', in Hans Maier (ed.), *Das Kreuz im Widerspruch. Der Kruzifix-Beschluss des Bundesverfassungsgerichts in der Kontroverse* (Freiburg, Basel, and Vienna, 1996), 40–51.

Zimmermann, John, 'Die deutsche militärische Kriegsführung im Westen 1944/45', in Rolf-Dieter Müller (ed.), *Das Deutsche Reich und der Zweite Weltkrieg. Die militärische Niederwerfung der Wehrmacht* (Munich, 2008), 277–468.

Zimmermann, Michael, *Rassenutopie und Genozid. Die nationalsozialistische 'Lösung der Zigeunerfrage'* (Hamburg, 1996).

Zoepf, Arne W. G., *Wehrmacht zwischen Tradition und Ideologie. Der NS-Führungsoffizier im Zweiten Weltkrieg* (Frankfurt a. M., 1988).

Zofka, Zdenek, *Die Ausbreitung des Nationalsozialismus auf dem Lande. Eine regionale Fallstudie zur politischen Einstellung der Landbevölkerung in der Zeit des Aufstiegs und der Machtergreifung der NSDAP 1928–1936* (Munich, 1979).

Zollitsch, Wolfgang, *Arbeiter zwischen Weltwirtschaftskrise und Nationalsozialismus. Ein Beitrag zur Sozialgeschichte der Jahre 1928 bis 1936* (Göttingen, 1990).

Zuccotti, Susan, *The Holocaust, the French, and the Jews* (New York, 1993).

Zuckmayer, Carl, *Als wär's ein Stück von mir. Horen der Freundschaft* (Frankfurt a. M., 1971).

Zuschlag, Christoph, *'Entartete Kunst'. Ausstellungsstrategien im Nazi-Deutschland* (Worms, 1995).

List of Illustrations

Index